D1287569

Anthropology Today

The Inventory Papers

International Symposium on Anthropology

Wenner-Gren Foundation for Anthropological Research, Incorporated

Contributors:

ERWIN H. ACKERKNECHT

MARSTON BATES

RALPH BEALS

WENDELL C. BENNETT

DAVID BIDNEY

WILLIAM C. BOYD

G. S. CARTER

ALFONSO CASO

WILLIAM CAUDILL

ELIOT D. CHAPPLE

PIERRE TEILHARD DE CHARDIN

V. GORDON CHILDE

J. GRAHAME D. CLARK

DARYLL FORDE

JOSEPH H. GREENBERG

MARY R. HAAS

A. IRVING HALLOWELL

ROBERT F. HEIZER

G. JAN HELD

JULES HENRY

HARRY HOIJER

EDWARD A. KENNARD

CLYDE KLUCKHOHN

ALEX D. KRIEGER

CLAUDE LÉVI-STRAUSS

OSCAR LEWIS

FLOYD G. LOUNSBURY

GORDON MACGREGOR

ANDRÉ MARTINET

MARGARET MEAD

ALFRED MÉTRAUX

CARLOS MONGE

HALLAM L. MOVIUS, JR.

GEORGE P. MURDOCK

RUSSELL W. NEWMAN

F. S. C. NORTHROP

KENNETH P. OAKLEY

BENJAMIN D. PAUL

ROBERT REDFIELD

IRVING ROUSE

JOHN HOWLAND ROWE

MEYER SCHAPIRO

MELFORD E. SPIRO

JULIAN H. STEWARD

WILLIAM L. STRAUS, JR.

WM. DUNCAN STRONG

J. M. TANNER

STITH THOMPSON

HENRI V. VALLOIS

S. L. WASHBURN

HANS WEINERT

GORDON R. WILLEY

With a Preface by Paul Fejos
and an Introduction by A. L. Kroeber

International Symposium on anthropology, = New York, 1952.

GN 4
.I 52
1970

Anthropology Today

An Encyclopedic Inventory

Prepared under the Chairmanship of

A. L. KROEBER

THE ·UNIVERSITY OF CHICAGO PRESS

CHICAGO & LONDON

The INTERNATIONAL SYMPOSIUM ON ANTHROPOLOGY and the publication of the Inventory Papers were made possible by funds granted by the Wenner-Gren Foundation for Anthropological Research, Incorporated, a foundation endowed for scientific, educational, and charitable purposes. The Wenner-Gren Foundation is not, however, the author or publisher of this volume, and is not to be understood as endorsing, by virtue of its grant, any of the statements made, or views expressed, herein.

INDIANA
PURDUE
LIBRARY
APR 1976
FORT WAYNE

WITHDRAWN

International Standard Book Number: 0-226-45420-7

THE UNIVERSITY OF CHICAGO PRESS, CHICAGO 60637
The University of Chicago Press, Ltd., London

Copyright 1953 by The University of Chicago. All rights reserved. Protected by the International Copyright Union. Published 1953. Eighth Impression 1970.
Printed in the United States of America

Preface

Dur**ing** 1951, the Viking Fund, Incorporated, observed both its tenth anniversary and a change of name to the Wenner-Gren Foundation for Anthropological Research, Incorporated. The occasion seemed fitting for an appraisal of the significance of the Foundation's concentration of effort, during the first decade of its existence, in furthering research and education in anthropology. A volume, entitled *The First Ten Years*, resulted from this retrospective survey.

Throughout the preparation of this volume, one was impressed by the increase in rate and amount of change in anthropological thought during the period under review. Since 1941, the anthropological discipline has experienced a world at war and has witnessed growing public awareness of other lands and peoples throughout all parts of the world. A sense of the interrelatedness of all things emerged in a trend toward scientific "team-research," co-ordinated investigations, and the introduction into academic curriculums of interdisciplinary area-study programs and field schools. Research in other disciplines has made such contributions to anthropology as carbon 14 dating, from nuclear physics, and blood grouping, from genetics. Anthropologists have given increased attention to the interrelation of the study of culture and that of personality psychology; more anthropologists have concerned themselves with social anthropology, with contemporary cultures, and with problems of applied anthropology and action research. It has been the Foundation's privilege and pleasure both to be of service to and to follow the scholars along the advancing edge of the conceptual frontier.

The Wenner-Gren Foundation International Symposium on Anthropology had its origin in the idea for a world conference of anthropologists presented in a letter from the director of research to the members of the Board of Directors of the Wenner-Gren Foundation for Anthropological Research on September 18, 1951. That letter proposed a symposium to which scholars from nearly all major regions of the world would be invited, in order to assess the accomplishments of anthropological science to date and to solicit answers on what direction future research would be likely to take, so that the Wenner-Gren Foundation might be provided with a concrete basis on which to erect its future policies.

Dr. Alfred L. Kroeber agreed to act as president of the symposium. At his suggestion, the following anthropologists were invited to act as members of a planning group: Dr. Wendell C. Bennett, chairman of the Department of Anthropology at Yale University and president for 1952 of the American Anthropological Association; Dr. Harry Hoijer, of the University of California at Los Angeles, *Memoirs* editor, American Anthropological Association; Dr. Clyde Kluckhohn, director of the Russian Research Center at Harvard University and former president of the American Anthropological Association; Dr. Ralph Linton, Sterling Professor of Anthropology at Yale University and former president of the American Anthropological Association; Dr. David G. Mandelbaum, of the University of California; Dr. William Duncan Strong, of Columbia University, former president of the American Ethnological Society; and Dr. S. L. Washburn, of the University of Chicago, president for 1952 of the American Association of Physical Anthropologists. These scholars, except Dr. Linton, who was then confined in a hospital, met for the first time as a planning group at the home of the Foundation on November 9–10, 1951.

At this meeting the scholars were presented with copies of "A Tentative Proposal for an International Symposium on Anthropology," setting forth the results of informal preliminary conversations by the director of research with Drs. Kroeber and Washburn. This paper established "A World Survey of the Status of Anthropology" as the theme for a symposium to be held in late spring of 1952 and suggested that the symposium participants be selected not merely as outstanding specialists but for their ability to synthesize the views of others and their broad grasp of anthropology in its totality. It further suggested that planning for the symposium, as well as for the publications likely to result therefrom, be in terms of three categories: (1) an inventory of modern anthropology, (2) an appraisal of modern anthropology, and (3) a handbook of world resources for research and education in anthropology.

The planning group first selected forty-eight topics for inventory papers most needed as a basis for discussion; second, they suggested the names of scholars best qualified to deal with these topics. It was recommended that all authors of inventory papers be invited to attend the international symposium. Many of the suggestions made at this meeting were incorporated into a preliminary "Announcement of an International Symposium on Anthropology," copies of which were later sent to members of the planning group for comment.

The director of research, with Professor Meyer Fortes from England, met again with Drs. Mandelbaum, Strong, and Washburn at the annual meeting of the American Anthropological Association at Chicago during November 15–17, 1951. The members of the planning group suggested issues which might be treated in specific inventory papers, as aids in the preparation of invitations.

On December 1, 1951, Drs. Kroeber, Kluckhohn, and Bennett met again at the home of the Foundation, and the following recommendations were formulated: (1) that the international symposium should be held June 9–20, 1952; (2) that the tentative program for the international symposium be adopted; and (3) that Drs. Fred Eggan, Alexander Spoehr, Irving Rouse, Carl F. Voegelin, and W. W. Howells be invited to act as editors for the second volume, stemming from the symposium discussion.

By December 18, 1951, all invitations to attend the symposium had been dispatched to thirty-one foreign scholars and, by December 21, to fifty-eight United States scholars. By January 10, 1952, sixty-five replies had been received; of these, six indicated regrets that previous commitments prevented their attendance. A meeting was held with Dr. Kroeber on January 15 to select substitutes for these scholars.

On February 2, members of the planning group met with the United States scholars invited to act as co-chairmen for the various sessions of the international symposium and with the editors of the appraisal volume. The purpose of the meeting was to brief each chairman on the relation of his session of the symposium to all other sessions, so that discussion might be organized to provide maximum continuity. The final program, including the names of principal discussants, was formulated, session by session, at that time, with full responsibility for organization and presentation at each half-day session transmitted to its respective co-chairmen— one American, one from overseas.

The editorial team for the appraisal volume eventually came to consist of Drs. Loren Eiseley, Irving Rouse, Sol Tax, and Carl F. Voegelin. They met on March 8 with Dr. Kroeber, to define their task and determine on a division of labor among themselves.

The concept of an "inventory paper," the interrelation of the full range of topics covered, and the function of the inventory papers in the International Symposium on Anthropology are discussed by Dr. Kroeber in his Introduction, which follows.

On behalf of the Board of Directors of the Wenner-Gren Foundation, I wish publicly to extend grateful thanks to all who have participated so generously in the realization of this volume. Truly, the extent of co-operation has been great. Scarcely a year will elapse between the origin of the idea and the distribution of the published work, and thus one of the prime requirements of an "inventory" or "stock-taking"—that of being "up-to-date"—is fulfilled. This volume is a testimonial to Dr. Kroeber and the members of the planning group, who gave to it organization and selected its contributors; to the authors of the papers, who, on very short notice, so readily participated in the common effort.

Especial praise must be given to all members of the Wenner-Gren Foundation staff, who participated directly or indirectly in the preparation of this work, particularly to the Executive Secretary, Mrs. G. W. O'Brian. Warmest personal thanks are extended to the Foundation's Assistant Director, Mr. William L. Thomas, Jr., and to Miss Anna Pikelis, whose combined task principally has been to close the gap between the dream and the reality of the Wenner-Gren Foundation International Symposium on Anthropology.

PAUL FEJOS

NEW YORK CITY
June 29, 1952

Table of Contents

Theory

PROBLEMS OF PROCESS

Method

Results

Table of Contents

PROBLEMS OF APPLICATION

INDEX

Introduction

By A. L. KROEBER

DR. FEJOS has told in the Preface how the tenth anniversary of the Wenner-Gren Foundation, and the resulting review and appraisal of its efforts, led to the concept of an international symposium in the science of anthropology to which the Foundation is dedicated.

This idea fell within the limits of realization because, as compared with most other sciences, the profession of anthropology had remained fairly limited in the number of participants. The American Anthropological Association numbers about six hundred Fellows or working anthropologists. The *International Directory of Anthropologists,* issued in 1950 with the aid of the National Research Council, lists about twenty-five hundred names from all countries. While here and there a pertinent figure may have failed to be listed, the total includes many others who are primarily anatomists, linguists, sociologists, curators, administrators, or lecturers and to whom participation in anthropology is marginal. The number of active professional anthropologists in the world is probably under rather than above two thousand.

This is a modest number compared with the tens of thousands of, say, chemists or economists in the world or the several thousand historians or psychologists in the United States alone. It means that a far greater proportion of anthropologists than members of the other sciences have met face to face, know one another as personalities in the flesh. This condition, in turn, tends to strip meetings and conferences of formality: freely spoken interchange of opinion is an accustomed habit and breeds more fruitful exchange even in newcomers. A certain intimacy of climate which pervades anthropological interrelations held out for a symposium a promise of stimulus and advance in thinking. After all, about 4 per cent of the world's anthropologists were represented by the eighty members who sat down together in one room.

But, if the profession is small, the subject matter of anthropology is enormous, as well as unusually varied. There was therefore every prospect of advantage to be gained from a gathering that would envisage the field as a whole with the intent of pulling together what belongs together.

After all, the subject of anthropology is limited only by man. It is not restricted by time—it goes back into geology as far as man can be traced. It is not restricted by region but is world-wide in scope. It has specialized on the primitives because no other science would deal seriously with them, but it has never renounced its intent to understand the high civilizations also. Anthropology is interested in what is most exotic in mankind but equally in ourselves, here, now, at home. It concerns itself with men's physiques, with their societies, with the communications and products—the languages and cultures—of these societies. It wants to know about particular languages and particular cultures in order to appraise the range and variety of human speech and civilization. Still more does it want to understand speech and civilization in general, in the abstract: the nature and process of language and culture. Sociology, economics, government, and jurisprudence investigate social, economic, political, and legal functionings, particularly in our own or other advance civilizations. Anthropology tries to formulate the interactions of these more special activities within the total culture of which they form a part, and equally so, whether the culture be high or low, present or past.

It is evident that anthropology—however specific it may often be in dealing with data—aims at being ultimately a co-ordinating science, somewhat as a legitimate holding corporation co-ordinates constituent companies. We anthropologists will never know China as intensively as a Sinologist does, or prices, credit, and banking as well as an economist, or heredity with the fulness of the genetic biologist. But we face what these more intensive scholars only glance at intermittently and tangentially, if at all: to try to understand in some measure how Chinese civilization and economics and human heredity, and some dozens of other highly developed special bodies of knowledge, do indeed interrelate in being all parts of "man"—flowing out of man, centered in him, products of him.

It may sound like a pipe dream—to forge together this vast array of knowledge, to hammer it into a set of coherent interpretations. Perhaps it is a dream; but some dreams come true. Leonardo da Vinci's sketched-out dreams of flying machines came true, when physics and engineering had developed sufficiently.

And there is one principle that anthropology already has in hand to serve toward a larger synthesis of understanding: the concept of culture.

This is the idea of culture—of human civilizations, whether rudimentary or advanced—as something entirely a part of nature, wholly an evolutionary development within nature, and therefore to be investigated by the methods of fundamental natural science, but an unprecedented, unique, and richly ramifying development of nature. It is culture that is at once the precondition of all human history and its abiding and growing precipitate. It is the hereditary faculty for culture that is the most distinctive feature of man as an animal. It is that part of the larger whole of culture which we ordinarily call "speech" that makes the accumulation of the remaining part of culture possible; and it is this remainder—culture in the more specific sense—that gives speech most of its content, gives us human beings something to talk about. Social behavior extends far back in the history of life on earth—certain insect families are much more effectively socialized than we are. But culture is a peculiarly human "invention"—or windfall; and in man culture, though secondary in origin, overshadows society, to the extent that human society is more affected and molded by culture than culture can be derived from society. Even the individual viewed as abstracted from his society is culturally influenced to a degree that makes it an unending task of the individualizing psychologist to hold his "cultural variable constant" before he can hope to make "pure" psychological findings. It is even possible to consider rat and other animal psychology an attempt to sidestep this perennial bothersome variable of culture. In spite of which, personality-in-culture, or culture-and-personality, has crept back into both psychology and anthropology as a frankly avowed and increasingly practiced field of study.

So the principle of culture already gives anthropology a viewpoint of enormous range, a center for co-ordination of most phenomena that relate to man. And we anthropologists feel that this is only a beginning.

The basic procedure of the Wenner-Gren Foundation International Symposium on Anthropology comprised four steps. The first was planning: this has been described by Dr. Fejos in the Preface. The second was the preparation by fifty authors of fifty "background" or "inventory" papers—forming this volume and to be discussed in a moment. The third step was the Symposium itself, the gathering of eighty scholars to discuss for a fortnight the problems raised in the fifty inventory papers. The record of this discussion will appear within a few months in a second volume, which will signalize completion of the fourth step, namely, the editing of the proceedings or transcript of the Symposium.

What is an inventory or background paper?

It is a systematic overview of the methods deployed and substantive results obtained by research along a particular front—a subject or field or segment of anthropology—as this has developed, particularly in recent years. Each inventory paper takes stock of the methods gradually defined and refined in this subject or field and the principal findings made. At the edge of these findings, just beyond, loom the unresolved problems whose solution will bring the advances of the coming years. The discussion of these problems constitutes the Symposium; its record goes into a second volume; the basis of the discussion is given in the present book. Thus, in short, this volume is a summary of what we know in and around anthropology in 1952; the volume to come is a synthesis of what we expect to find out more about soon.

Each of the fifty inventory papers deals with a topic, an area of interest, as it has more or less naturally and spontaneously emerged through the prosecution of research. Together, the fifty papers constitute fifty chapters, each a résumé of thinking and inquiry on an important problem center in the science of anthropology.

A. L. KROEBER

BERKELEY, CALIFORNIA
July 22, 1952

Problems of the Historical Approach

Long-Range Dating in Archeology[1]

By ROBERT F. HEIZER

INTRODUCTION

BEYOND THE points in time where precise dates for archeological materials derived from dendrochronology (tree-rings) and ancient calendar systems or dynastic lists, such as those of the Near East and Middle America, can tell us the age of archeological remains, there lies the long past for which only relative and approximate chronologies are now available. This paper is concerned with the methods and results of prehistoric time-reckoning as they are or may be applied to archeological remains. By one means or another, almost any find can be dated, provided only that the necessary minimum required observations on its occurrence be performed. But since the usefulness of an archeological date is directly proportional to its precision, merely to determine, for example, that an archeological object dates from the second interglacial stage of the Pleistocene cannot tell us much about the relational position of the cultural materials, since that phase of the Pleistocene had a probable duration of about 200,000 years.

The primary aim of the prehistorian

is cultural interpretation, and, because he is fundamentally a specialist in the art of excavation, he rarely controls the requisite training to make all the necessary chemical, physical, or geological observations and reach the conclusions which lead to the dating of the materials which he has excavated. In short, no one individual can hope to be sufficiently expert in such varied fields as nuclear physics, paleobotany, geology, and paleontology to make the studies so often required for the temporal placement of an archeological find. The interdisciplinary approach is necessary, and this is made possible by securing the assistance of specialists in those fields which are directly concerned with the particular situation. Johnson and Raup (1947, p. 63) observe: "In order to arrive at a full understanding of human history archaeologists must be prepared to devote an increasing amount of time to the study of factors by which dates can be established. This involves, eventually, extensive collaboration among a number of scientific fields."

Because the physical and cultural record of man is largely restricted to the Pleistocene epoch, it will be this terminal segment of the geological past which concerns us here. Three chief factors—(1) the gradual increase in numbers of the Hominidae during the Pleistocene period; (2) the gradual quantitative acceleration of culture; and (3) the destructive forces of nature,

1. This paper amounts to little more than a catalogue of methods for deriving long-range chronology. For what merit it may have, some credit is due the following persons who have contributed information and assistance: E. Antevs, J. G. D. Clark, E. S. Deevey, Jr., H. P. Hansen, T. D. McCown, H. Movius, Jr., K. P. Oakley, J. H. Rowe, Howel Williams, and R. J. Squier.

3

such as glacial processes, erosion, and deposition—all contribute to explain the undoubted fact that the evidence of human activity is inversely correlated with past time, so that in the most remote ranges of the Pleistocene only few evidences of man's actions are to be found, while in the postglacial period of the last 10,000 years or so remains are much more common. It is not that the evidence of the earliest tools or bones of man is unimportant, but they and their makers are anonymous and only imperfectly known at best. With the later prehistoric cultures some identification of peoples and some embodiment of cultural remains is to be felt. Compare here the richness of detail of the accounts of Movius (1949a) on the Lower Paleolithic cultures of southern and eastern Asia to that of Childe (1950) on prehistoric European migrations. In the later Pleistocene we begin to be able to see ourselves, to speak concretely of racial and cultural entities, and to tie these to the proto-historic and historic present. For these reasons, among others, the chronology of man since he became an abundant form and began to leave appreciable quantities of diverse artifacts behind is of particular concern. This special concern, happily, coincides with the fact that, as we approach the present, an increasingly larger amount of physical evidence of past environment has been spared destruction or alteration and is thus available for observation with reference to chronology.

It is customary in archeological chronology to distinguish two orders of datings: (1) *direct* or absolute, where the date is expressed in actual years, and (2) *indirect* or relative, where the date of the evidence of man's activity is determined by association with some *tertium quid,* for example, a geologic feature, whose approximate age is known. In a strict sense, direct dating may be interpreted as the assignment of age in years to an object *per se,* and only objects such as coins with an impressed mint date or a wooden roof beam whose exact cutting date can be determined by tree-ring count, or organic material which can be precisely dated by the radiocarbon method, would fall into this category.[2] Other age determinations for individual prehistoric objects or culture deposits are, with very few exceptions, dated as having been deposited not earlier than a certain date (*terminus a quo*), or not later than a certain date (*terminus ad quem*). Reflection on this matter leads to the conclusion that it is not the method which is really significant but its degree of reliability and precision.

It may be observed that the extent of the applicability of a dating technique has a bearing upon its importance, for if the method is too limited in application, either because the requirements of the material or situation are so specific as to be rarely encountered or because of the extreme technicalities of the laboratory processes, it will be of limited value. The nearer the method approaches the condition of being of world-wide or universal application, the more important it becomes.

CLASSIFICATION OF TIME-RECKONING METHODS

Except in those rare instances in which it is possible to determine the antiquity of an object from the piece itself, all dates are derived through the intermediacy of observation or experiment in one or more of the physical or natural sciences. For this reason I have chosen to classify, with reference to the

2. Both tree-ring dates and radiocarbon age determinations are subject to errors as regards inferring the precise point in past time to which the samples presumably refer. Wooden beams may be reused, and radiocarbon materials are subject to contamination. For these and other reasons, we can only say that tree-ring and C^{14} dates are potentially, not automatically, absolute dating means.

scientific field primarily concerned, the various methods of determining chronology.

Since dating of archeologic materials is usually done with reference to the chronology of some series of events or processes in the natural or physical sciences,[3] it follows that any chronological sequence within the Pleistocene period may aid, in some fashion, in determining the age of those cultural materials. This is what Oakley, in the following paper, refers to as "R. dates." Therefore, our review of dating methods must include a description and evaluation of the means of the temporal ordering of Pleistocene events and processes.

I. METHODS IN THE PHYSICAL SCIENCES

1. ASTRONOMICAL

The results of the most ambitious and inclusive effort to devise an exact chronology for the Pleistocene period have been presented by the British geochronologist, Frederick E. Zeuner, in his two books, *The Pleistocene Period* (1945) and *Dating the Past* (1950). The basis of the scheme is changes in the astronomical elements of the inclination of the earth's axis (obliquity of the ecliptic, with a mean length of periodicity of 42,000 years), the eccentricity of the earth's orbit (mean length of periodicity 92,000 years), and the longitude of the perihelion (precession of the equinoxes, with a mean length of

3. Specifically excepted here as a chronological method is that one sometimes used by archeologists or geologists who date geological events on the basis of the types of artifacts occurring in the deposits. Although this is doubtless in some situations an acceptable method, there are strong objections to it, as pointed out by Movius (1949b, p. 1447) and Zeuner (1950, p. 47). Examples of dating geological strata by contained or associated artifacts occur in the papers of Högbom (1923), Buchner and Buchner (1940), Antevs (in Harrington, 1948, p. 120), and Bryan (1950, p. 119).

periodicity 21,000 years). J. N. Stockwell, an American astronomic mathematician, devised the formulas for calculating the secular changes of these elements, and the necessary calculations were performed by the German, Ludwig Pilgrim, in 1904. In 1920 the Serbian physicist and mathematician, Milutin Milankovitch, determined the fluctuations of solar radiation received by the earth's atmosphere and, shortly after, calculated, at the request of the German climatologist, W. Köppen, the radiation changes on latitudes 55°, 60°, and 65° for the last 650,000 years. Köppen then interpreted Milankovitch's radiation graph as representing the Pleistocene glacial and interglacial alternations. A number of other workers, of whom Soergel and F. E. Zeuner are perhaps best known, have been concerned with the development of the astronomical chronology of the Pleistocene, and there is by no means uniform agreement in this matter either upon causes of glaciation or upon the absolute chronology. For a review of the divergent views of R. Spitaler, W. Wundt, and others see Blanchard (1941), Flint (1945, pp. 27–29), Zeuner (1945, 1950), Braidwood (1946), Landsberg (1949), and Zeuner (1950, pp. 393–95) notes that a number of geologists find their data agreeable with the astronomical absolute chronology, and he is at some pains to answer a series of objections which have been raised against the "astronomical theory." Zeuner (1950, pp. 44–45) views, as "valuable evidence confirming the correctness of the astronomical chronology of the Pleistocene Ice Age and its human industries," the findings of W. H. Bradley, H. Korn, and G. K. Gilbert with regard to Eocene, Carboniferous, and Cretaceous banded sediments as showing evidence of the 21,000-year periodicity ascribable to the precession of the equinoxes.

The great significance to prehisto-

rians of the astronomical chronology of
the Pleistocene is that it has been taken
up by Zeuner, who has attempted to
give, in most detailed fashion, the chronology of man and culture for the last
600,000 years. Unfortunately, the correctness of the astronomical chronology
does not now seem sufficiently agreed
upon for prehistorians to accept it un-
qualifiedly; and, where some archeologists employ it as a "working theory"
(Braidwood, 1946; Childe, 1950), others (e.g., Movius) reject it because its
precision may be spurious. Speaking
generally, prehistorians are much
interested in the Milankovitch-Zeuner
scheme but prefer to wait until it is
proved before recasting the Paleolithic
culture sequence in terms of absolute
dates. This caution is well advised, for
there can be nothing gained by archeologists in risking the hard-won results
of the relative geological chronology
against a method of absolute chronology
which, though attractive, may turn out
to be an illusion.

2. GEOLOGICAL

Of all the techniques for achieving
chronology, those in the geological field
are most numerous. Of the several
American workers who have labored in
the difficult field of dating older archeological remains by geological methods,
the names of Ernst Antevs and Kirk
Bryan stand out above all others. The
real accomplishments in this direction
have largely been due to their efforts.
Geological dating serves two primary
purposes: (1) establishing of time relations and (2) allowing certain inferences to be drawn regarding the biogeographical or ecological conditions of
the past.

Movius (1949*b*, pp. 1448–49) says:

Prehistoric archaeology is a social science, a specialized subdivision of cultural
anthropology, and the objects with which
it deals must always be regarded as the imperishable products of man's manufacture

. . . . The soundest approach to the study
of a series of tools from a given horizon
seems to be through the natural sciences
which are concerned with the sequence
and correlation of events during the Pleistocene—geologic, climatic, and biologic.
Since they alone are capable of introducing
the all important and closely interwoven
time and environmental factors, the essential interest of prehistoric archaeologists in
them may be summarized as follows: (1)
for the establishment of a relative time
scale by which the fossil remains of early
man and his cultural relics may be placed
in their proper sequence; (2) for the study
of developing technology and material culture, as well as the survival(s) of ancient
tool-making habits or traditions; and (3)
for the reconstruction of the changing environmental (biogeographical *or* ecological) conditions which confronted man during the Pleistocene in his effort to gain
dominance over the forces supplied by nature.

a) Stratigraphic-geomorphic method.
—The stratigraphic-geomorphic method
rests, as the term implies, upon geological stratification, whose sequence can
be determined, and upon geomorpho-
logical features, such as terraces and
other depositional or erosional physiographic features. The dating of human
evidences associated with such features
may derive from identifying the stratum
or geomorphic feature as having been
formed under certain specific climatic
conditions whose approximate position
in time is already known. The archeologic finds must be made in strata
whose stratigraphic relationship to adjacent deposits can be established, or
the particular stratum must be related
to some local geologic event, such as
terrace formations, lake strands, glacial
deposits, etc. The local sequence must
then be referable to some wider chronology, such as that of Pleistocene glaciation, or to postglacial climatic history. Open sites are usually more easily
dated by this method than cave sites,
which, because of the depositional his-

tory in a closed area, may not exhibit a stratification which is directly referable to geological strata outside the cave.

The history of postglacial climates in the Old and New Worlds is now reasonably accurately known through paleontological and palynological studies. Antevs (1948, 1952) has summarized the basis for our knowledge of and chronology for postglacial climates and suggests the term "Neothermal" for the period when primary reference is to temperature. In the postglacial period he distinguishes the "Anathermal" age, which begins about 7000 B.C., "when the temperature in the southern parts of the previously glaciated areas had risen to equal that of present," and ends about 5000 B.C. The second postglacial temperature age, called "Altithermal," ranges from 5000 to 2500 B.C. and was an arid period. From about 2000 or 2500 B.C. and extending to the present is the "Medithermal" age, beginning as a relatively cool and moist period, becoming somewhat warmer. It is this frame of reference into which so many stratigraphic and positional archeological sequences can be placed in western North America. The levels of the Great Basin lakes fluctuated in concert with these climatic alternations, and detailed studies of strand lines by Gilbert (1890), Antevs (1925, 1945, 1948), and Jones (1925) have led to a quite precise reconstruction of the history of the "pluvial" lakes. The American postglacial dates rest ultimately upon the European chronology, which is founded upon the glacial and postglacial varve sequence, which, in turn, is correlated with the American varve chronology. This matter is detailed by Antevs in numerous papers cited here. The beginning date of the Medithermal age, however, has been independently determined by calculating the time required for the present concentration of salts in the Great Basin lakes, which were dry during the

middle postglacial (Altithermal) age. Studies by Van Winkle (1914, pp. 117–23) and Gale (1915, pp. 259, 263–64), of the salines in Owens Lake, California, and Abert and Summer lakes, Oregon, show that about 4,000 years are required to account for the concentration of salt in these lakes (Antevs, 1938b). This time datum at *ca.* 2000 B.C. is a useful one in postglacial chronological studies, since it marks the end of the middle postglacial climatic optimum.

The development in the American Southwest of what Bryan has aptly called the method of "alluvial chronology" has covered a period of the last twenty-five years. Throughout the area three alluvial formations may be identified, and the very considerable amount of investigation of these horizons has been well summarized by Bryan (1950). Bryan's colleague, J. T. Hack (1942, 1945) has published two classic studies of this type. Other illustrations of the method are on the relationship of archeological materials with geological deposits in western Texas (Kelley, Campbell, and Lehmer, 1940); the careful studies by Antevs (1941, 1949a) on the age of the Cochise culture sites; the investigations by Bryan (1938) and Antevs (1949b) of the Clovis sites; the work on alluvial and dune deposits in New Mexico by Bryan and McCann (1943); Judson's (1949) review of the Pleistocene stratigraphy of Boston and its relation to the Boylston Street Fishweir; the monumental study of Pleistocene deposits in India and their relationship to Paleolithic cultures by De Terra and Paterson (1939); and De Terra's work (1946; De Terra, Romero, and Stewart, 1949) on the stratigraphy, climate, and cultures of the valley of Mexico.

Interpretation of the stratigraphic levels of rock-shelters or caves through correlation with geological horizons outside the cave or with periods of climatic history has been successfully accomplished by Antevs at Bat Cave, New Mexico (Mangelsdorf and Smith, 1949, p. 217), where a climatic sequence was apparent; by Heizer and Antevs at Leonard Rockshelter, Nevada (Heizer, 1951); by Bryan (1950) at Ventana Cave, Arizona, where inferences on climatic changes of the past whose approximate dates are known permitted assigning the age of the various layers; by Bryan (1941) at Sandia Cave, New Mexico, where the deposits were correlated with the glacial chronology; and by Bryan at the site of La Colombière, France (Movius, 1950). Laïs (1941) discusses the climatic interpretation of cave strata, and Bryan (in Moss, 1951, p. 3) and Bryan and Ray (1940, pp. 45–46) discuss the interpretation of problems of cave stratigraphy.

b) Association with glacial deposits. —The history of the Pleistocene Ice Age as recorded in the sequential series of glacial and interglacial deposits has been the subject of uncounted investigations. A review of recent trends in Pleistocene research has been published by the members of the Committee on Interrelations of Pleistocene Research of the National Research Council in the *Bulletin of the Geological Society of America*, Vol. LX, No. 9 (September, 1949). The exact chronology of the Pleistocene, in both the Old World and the New World, is uncertain, though it is generally assumed that the history of major glacial advance and retreat with correlated elevation and lowering of the sea-levels (eustatic changes) has been due to factors which have exercised a similar and synchronous effect in both hemispheres. Ray (1949, p. 1471) says: "Ultimately this [i.e., the Pleistocene] chronology will rest on the series of world-wide climatic fluctuations, of which, unfortunately, neither the cause nor the detailed story is now known." The assumption is generally made that the glacial stages of Europe and North America were synchronous, as indicated

by the correlation tables presented in Bryan and Ray (1940, Table 1), Bryan (1941, Table 1; 1950, Tables 5–7), Flint (1947), and Deevey (1949, Table 6). Confirmation or denial of absolute correlations of this sort may result from analysis of a larger body of radiocarbon dates for late glacial and postglacial events.

As examples of successful attempts to date archeological deposits in caves and open sites through correlation with deposits ascribable to mountain glaciation and whose position is known in the Pleistocene glacial sequence, there may be cited the reports of Kimball and Zeuner (1947) concerning the age of the Magdalenian in relation to the terraces of the upper Rhine; of Breuil and Koslowski (1931–32), who correlated the Paleolithic culture succession with the Somme Valley Pleistocene terraces; of Bryan and Ray (1940), who fixed the age of the Lindenmeier site in Colorado as equivalent to that of the third advance of the Wisconsin ice sheet in the Rocky Mountains; of Bryan (1941), who correlated the deposits of Sandia Cave, New Mexico, with the glacial chronology; of Schultz and Eiseley (1936), who concluded that the Scottsbluff bison quarry in Nebraska was occupied at the same time as the Lindenmeier site; of De Terra and Paterson (1939), who assigned the artifact complexes of India to stages of Himalayan glaciation; of Bryan (Movius, 1950), who succeeded in dating the rock-shelter of La Colombière, France, with glacial deposits; of Hack (1943) and Moss (1951), who assign the age of the Finley site, Wyoming, to the fourth Wisconsin (W4) ice advance; and of Schultz and Frankforter (1948), who identify the Lime Creek site, Ft-41, as situated at the base of Terrace 2 of late Pleistocene date.

Until the absolute chronology of the Pleistocene is better understood, such "datings" as are given archeological sites in terms of Pleistocene ice advance or retreat are only guesses based upon assumed correlation between independent stratigraphic columns. Thus the Mankato ice advance is variously dated by the radiocarbon method (to be explained below) at *ca.* 11,000 years ago; by Antevs on the basis of varve counts at *ca.* 20,000 years ago (Antevs, 1948, p. 2); by Schultz, Lueninghoener, and Frankforter (1951, p. 35), on the basis of Nebraska terrace studies, at 7,000 to 8,000 years ago; and by Bryan and Ray (1940, p. 68) at about 25,000 years ago.

c) Glacial varve sequence. — The Swedish word *varve* was proposed by Baron Gerard de Geer in 1912 as an international term for the annual deposit of any sediment, regardless of its origin. With the last northward retreat of the Würm ice in Europe and the Wisconsin ice in North America, there were deposited in the meltwater lakes in front of the ice thin layers of finely divided material (silt and clay). Each year two "members," which together form one varve, are deposited, a thin, finely divided winter layer and a thicker summer layer. Credit for first appreciating the geochronologic possibilities of postglacial varves is properly granted to De Geer, and the development of the method and the results obtained have been largely by him and his several students. The work of Sauramo in Finland, Antevs in North America, and Lidén in Sweden is of fundamental importance to the development of the late glacial and postglacial chronology.

As the ice retreated and meltwater varves were laid down, the annual deposits of one lake would be in part earlier than in another lake a little farther north. This circumstance of overlap permits the sequential geographical tracking of the varve series. The field and laboratory methods of counting, recording, and correlating varve series are complex, and the reader is referred to discussions by Antevs (1922; 1925,

chap. iii; 1928), Sauramo (1923), De Geer (1929, 1937, 1940), and Zeuner (1950, pp. 23–26). All these papers contain extensive bibliographies.

The Swedish varve chronology dates from the time of ice recession from the extreme south to the high mountains where the ice sheet divided. At Lake Ragunda some 3,000 varves were added to the time scale, and among them was a distinctively thick varve which De Geer took to date the ice bipartition. Since this prominent varve could be recognized widely, De Geer took this as the beginning of the postglacial and denoted it the "zero-varve," all superjacent varves being prefixed with a plus sign, and all subjacent and earlier varves being indicated by a minus sign (De Geer, 1940). In north-central Sweden, R. Lidén (1913, 1938) found postglacial varves which gave the tie-in with the present, and from these De Geer was able to date his "zero-varve" as having been deposited in 6839 B.C. In Finland M. Sauramo has conducted varve investigations whose counts have been correlated with the Swedish series (De Geer, 1943; Zeuner, 1950, p. 32) to produce the combined Finno-Swedish varve chronology. M. Vierke (1937) has reviewed the important matter of moraines and limits of the last glaciation in northern Europe. There is no widespread agreement on the beginning date of the accurate or proved varve series. De Geer suggests 18,000 years; Antevs believes 13,500 years B.P. (before present) is its maximum accuracy; and Zeuner (1950, p. 45) suggests 10,000 years.

Late glacial varves have been counted by Antevs in North America between New York and northern Ontario. Here, unfortunately, not only are there some lacunae in the series, which must be filled by estimating and extrapolation, but also the terminal or historic anchor is not determinable, so that the North American varve chronology still floats in time. Antevs, who is fully cognizant of the difficulties, has proposed a correlation of the Finno-Swedish and North American varve series through what are taken to be synchronous events of major ice-retreat oscillation (Antevs, 1947, 1948). Bryan and Ray (1940, pp. 52–69) have reviewed the North American varve data and suggest a reduction of dates.

It will by now, in the light of the statements made above, be apparent that, if the Atlantic can be chronologically spanned by means of the varve chronology, a time-reckoning method of great utility is at hand. Antevs' correlation of general European-American events, such as halting of ice retreat with notable moraine deposition, suggests certain major time blocs for varves on both sides of the Atlantic; and this seems reasonable. But much doubt is entertained over De Geer's claim that *annual* variations in varve series as widely separated as Iceland, India, Chile, New Zealand, and East Africa can be dated *directly* on the Finno-Swedish time scale (De Geer, 1921, 1929, 1934; Reeds, 1929; Zeuner, 1950, pp. 38–43). De Geer applies the term "teleconnexion" to this method of world-wide correlation. Mrs. E. H. de Geer (1942) in a review of late glacial and postglacial varved clay and tree-ring datings has suggested the possibility of applying this combined method on a world-wide scale.

In summary, the late Pleistocene and postglacial varve chronology is apparently fairly reliable for the last 10,000 years or so (Antevs says the last 11,400 years) in the Baltic region, though Lidén's critical data which prove the historic tie-in have not been adequately published (Childe, 1950, p. 4). Uncertainty also obtains with regard to the annual character of all varves which have been counted (Flint, 1945, pp. 12–21; Zeuner, 1950, pp. 35–36); and Goldthwait (1938) believes that, since ice

retreat was irregular, the varve record may not be so accurate a time-reckoning method as is generally believed.

Although glacial varve dating is commonly believed to represent a *direct* dating method, the fact that there is no instance of cultural materials imbedded in varve deposits (the Minnesota skeleton is not here admitted as such—see Antevs, 1938) illustrates the point that, although the chronology *per se* may be an annual one covering the last 10,000 or more years, it is, when applied to archeology, *indirect*. What may be associated with varves is a former strand line or a pollen zone or climatic (temperature) age which can thus be varve-dated, and the association of these elsewhere with archeological remains will yield an approximate date for the artifacts. Childe (1950, p. 4) and Zeuner (1950, p. 46) make this point clear, and the latter's statement is worth quoting:

Generally speaking, two ways are available for linking up prehistoric finds and varve-countings. The first applies to finds made in Fennoscandia on raised beaches which represent certain phases in the evolution of the Baltic Sea which, in turn can be correlated with varve-sections. The other relies on finds made in peat or other organic or semi-organic sediments. The climatic phase during which these layers were formed is often determinable by means of botanical investigation, and since the climatic development of the late Glacial and Postglacial depended on the recession of the ice, connexions with the phases of the Baltic, with certain moraines, or even with sections of varved clay, may be established. It is evident that, in this manner, varve dates can be linked up with certain events in climatic history, and therefore with certain archaeological horizons, but owing to the several intermediaries the dating work is bound to progress slowly, and the results are usually reliable within certain limits only.

d) Changes in shore-line level.—Evidences of ancient human occupation can sometimes be dated with reference to their location on, or in immediate proximity to, strand lines which mark the former levels of lakes or seas and which have, either through sinking or elevation of the land (isostatic changes of level) or through the world-wide changes in sea-level (eustatic changes in level), been altered. Thus Mathiessen (1927, Part 1, pp. 6–10, 129–30) was able to point to shore elevation in the amount of 5–15 meters in the central Eskimo region since occupation there by the Thule culture group, and by this to explain the abandonment of the area by these people because of shallowing of the sea. Since the rate of shore elevation was not known, no calculation of the time required could be made. A similar situation observed by J. Bird with reference to prehistoric midden locations on Beagle Channel, south of Tierra del Fuego, led to important chronological conclusions. By determining the minimum uplift rate at 0.75 meters per 300 years, he calculated that the age of the sites was not less than 1,800 years (Bird, 1938, pp. 262–64; 1946, p. 21). In southern New England the Grassy Island site has been studied by Johnson and Raup (1947) and Deevey (1948), with the result that evidence is deduced for the rate of postglacial rise of sea-level of about 1 foot per century, and by this means an approximate date for the site has been calculated. Rouse (1951, pp. 21–34) has ingeniously inferred Florida archeological chronology by correlation of his stratigraphy with eustatic sea-level. Greenman and Stanley (1940; also Greenman, 1943) have ingeniously dated several sites in Ontario by calculating the rate of the lowering of water from the Nipissing stage level and the rate of isostatic postglacial tilting of the Great Lakes region. The matter of coastal stability with reference to shell heaps has been discussed by Goldthwait (1935) for New England, and Greengo (1951) has summarized the in-

formation relative to California. A very extensive literature exists on the matter of eustatic fluctuations in sea-level (cf. Blanc, 1937; Zeuner, 1945, chap. ix; Flint, 1947; Zeuner, 1950, pp. 127–29) and correlated beaches and thalassostatic terraces. Bradley (1938) shows how archeology could profit from the study of deep-sea sediment cores (to be discussed below) through demonstrating climatic change and correlation with Pleistocene sea-levels.

In the Baltic region isostatic changes in land-level resulting in the elevation of shore lines may have important implications for archeology. Thus the sites of the Ertebölle ("Kitchen-midden") culture are correlated with the Littorina Sea beach line in southern Finland (summary in Zeuner, 1950, Fig. 20; Clark, 1936; Movius, 1942). Many phases of the postglacial history of the Baltic are directly associated with varved clay deposits, and changes in the salinity of the Baltic (e.g., between the Ice Lake and Yoldia Sea phases) have left their traces in the varves. Thus the Littorina Sea has been correlated with varves and dated in years so that the Ertebölle and other Scandinavian cultures are indirectly, but more or less precisely, dated (cf. Nilsson, 1935). Raised strand lines, moraines, and varved clay deposits may rarely have deposited upon them peat layers whose analysis permits assigning the particular floral assemblage an approximate or maximum date in terms of varve counts.

In the arid Great Basin region of far-western North America there is preserved abundant evidence of ancient fresh-water pluvial lakes in the form of old beach lines and sedimentary deposits on which there may occur artifacts (Antevs, 1925; Jones, 1925; Blackwelder and Ellsworth, 1936; Hubbs and Miller, 1948). An important precaution must be observed in associating surficial artifact remains with ancient beach lines and from this inferring that the culture was contemporaneous with the water-level at the time the beach was formed. In order for such correlation to be proved, it must be established that the remains of the culture phase do not occur at elevations lower than the strand line, for such occurrences negate the specific temporal community of the strand line and the culture phase. In the southern California desert region, where there is abundant evidence of Pleistocene and postglacial lakes, archeologists and geologists have worked together in presenting a detailed picture of the association of culture materials with certain strand lines, and thus dating the cultures through analysis of lake history (Campbell *et al.*, 1937; Antevs, 1937). However, this neat picture is hardly as convincing as it appears, for the culture–shoreline correlation is challenged by the finding of similar stone implements at *lower* elevations, which would have been submerged at the time the culture was supposed to have been in operation (Rogers, 1939, p. 43). The fact that none of the stone implements found on the old beaches are water-worn also demonstrates that the presumption of exact contemporaneousness of the beach and tools is untenable. The relation of Fayum lake-levels to Paleolithic sites is discussed by Zeuner (1950, p. 232).

e) Rate of stream-channel meandering. — With the publication by Fisk (1944) on the geology of the lower alluvial valley of the Mississippi River (see also Matthes, 1951), archeologists were presented with a ready-made, though rough, chronology for those sites which occupy positions on former channels. The potentialities of the method were noted earlier by Chawner (1936, pp. 44–45), Ford (1936, p. 238), Kniffen (1936, p. 417), and Osborne (1943).

Fisk determined from aerial photographs the sequence of river courses and carefully mapped these. The estimate of rate of meander progression derives from observations made since 1765, and the location of the main stream is identified at 100-year intervals for the last 2,000 years (meander stages Nos. 1–20). Archeologists may plot the location of prehistoric sites on the meander map and thus determine the minimum date or *terminus ad quem* for the site. Details of the method and its practical application are contained in the recent reports by Ford (1951, 1952) and Phillips, Ford, and Griffin (1951, esp. pp. 295–306).

The value of the method lies in its yielding dates which may be accurate within a century but in many cases it can only yield a meander date which is minimal, and which may actually be rather older. Thus Ford (1951, p. 19) concludes that the Marksville site was occupied some time after A.D. 300 and the neighboring Greenhouse site was abandoned before A.D. 1500 and says: "This is a long time interval that leaves plenty of leeway for guessing the actual period of occupation." The absolute dating of the meander chronology through stages 1–20 may be actually as proposed by Fisk (1944), but this matter will be susceptible to checking by the tree-ring (cf. Hawley, 1941; Bell, 1951) or carbon 14 methods. Krieger's (1946) extension of the Southwestern dendrochronology by means of trade sherds found in lower Mississippi Valley sites is checked by Phillips, Ford, and Griffin (1951, Fig. 60) with their tentative site—meander-channel stage correlation, with the result that a fair correspondence is found. The stream-meander method is important in that it shows real promise of ultimately being of primary assistance in setting the prehistory of the United States in a precise chronological frame; and, when this is realized, it will probably be possible to extend the horizon dates into periph-eral areas which demand chronological ordering.

f) Rate of dune migration.—Strong (1935, pp. 236–39) discusses the rela-tion of dunes in the vicinity of Signal Butte, Nebraska, and concludes that "the estimated time of dune movement . . . should roughly correspond to the minimum age of the aeolian deposit on top of Signal Butte." The detailed ob-servations and data upon which his estimates rest have not been published, but Strong was sufficiently confident of the method at the time to propose a date of from 8,000 to 10,000 years for the Level I deposits at Signal Butte. Recent reinvestigation of the same site leads Bliss (1950) to suggest a reduced date of 3,000 years for the Signal Butte I stratum.

g) Rate of travertine deposition.—The problem of the rate of growth of stalagmites and stalactites has ac-cumulated a large bibliography (e.g., Farrington, 1901). Much of this litera-ture has little or no possible bearing upon archeology, but V. C. Allison, after making a general study of the subject (Allison, 1923), proceeded to apply the data to the solution of the problem of the antiquity of the de-posits in Jacob's Cavern, Missouri (Al-lison, 1926). His conclusions on the chronology of the site are perhaps the most remarkable ever offered for any prehistoric site as regards precision in absolute dates. Allison's paper, though striking for its ingenuity, does not seem convincing in view of the numerous assumptions which are involved. Con-tributions by Starmans (1947) on solu-tion deposits of layered cave strata with a method for calculating the rate of accumulation and by Swinnerton (1925) on estimating the time since the Tazewell deglaciation in Ohio based upon the precipitation of traver-tine at springs by estimating the an-nual rate of accumulation and taking

into account known variables are of interest and possible application to archeology.

Calcareous tufa deposits which can be correlated or are associated with archeological materials may contribute to the solution of the problem of de-termining rates of deposition of geolog-ical formations (Clark, 1938; Rieth, 1938). Climatic phases may be indicat-ed by stalagmite layers in caves (Zeu-ner, 1945, pp. 20, 176) and may thus contribute to the relative dating of archeological materials found above or below the lime stratum, as in Sandia Cave, New Mexico (Bryan, 1941, pp. 49, 52); in the Grotte de l'Observatoire, Monaco (Boule and Villeneuve, 1927); in Pin Hole cave, England (Armstrong, 1939); in Castillo cave, Spain (Ober-maier, 1924); in the Ehringsdorf traver-tine deposits of Germany (Soergel, 1926); and in a number of the Italo-French Riviera caves (Zeuner, 1945, pp. 179–82).

h) Various Pleistocene geological processes with determinable rates.—The following summary concerns a number of different methods for estimating Pleistocene and postglacial chronology by means of extrapolation of rates of processes. Most of these are summa-rized by R. F. Flint (1945).

The rate of retreat of Niagara and St. Anthony Falls has been variously used in estimating the duration of post-glacial time (Flint, 1945, pp. 3–7), but too many variables enter for the figures to be considered reliable. Part of the gorge has been re-exhumed, and the estimates therefore do not apply to all of post-Mankato time. Armstrong (1936) has estimated the antiquity of man in Africa from the amount of channel erosion at Victoria Falls.

The rate of retreat of the wave-cut cliffs at Lake Ontario was estimated by Coleman (1914) in an effort to deter-mine the amount of time since ice retreat. The method and results were critically reviewed by Spencer (1917).

Wright (1912) attempted to determine the amount of postglacial time in an Ohio locality by extrapolating backward from a short, known rate datum of creek erosion, to determine the time required for the erosion of the entire stream valley. The figure arrived at is certainly too small. Sayles (1937) suggests a method of checking other estimates of postglacial time by studying the erosion of postglacial consequent streams.

The rate of river delta-building to gain time estimates has been applied to the Bear River, British Columbia (Hansen, 1934); the Fraser River, British Columbia (Johnston, 1921); the Nile River, Egypt (Ball, 1939); and the Muota River, Switzerland (Heim, 1894; Collet, 1925).

The depth of the leached and oxidized zone in glacial deposits (till, gravel, or loess) in Iowa was studied by Kay (1931) and his estimates for the duration of the Pleistocene (700,000 years) and of the Mankato advance (25,000 years ago) have been widely used. Kay's 25,000-year estimate was derived from the Niagara Falls recession estimate and is therefore questionable. However, the *relative* durations of the Pleistocene based on post-Mankato leaching are still accepted. Thornbury (1940) made similar studies of the glacial drifts in Indiana, using Kay's figure of 25,000 years for post-Mankato time; and, by measuring the depth of leaching and calculating the rate of formation of gumbotil, he arrived at slightly different time estimates for the duration of the Pleistocene.

The stratigraphy of Bermuda, consisting essentially of calcareous aeolianite alternating with red and brown clays which are the product of decomposition of the underlying aeolianite, was studied by Sayles (1931). The clay soils are believed to have formed during interglacial periods of high sea-level and less strong winds than during the glacial periods. Employing the post-Mankato measure of Kay (25,000 years) the values of the Pleistocene time units were calculated.

The degree of erosional loss of the several glacial drift sheets in the Mississippi Basin was studied by Leverett (1930), the measure of rate being again that of the post-Mankato period of 25,000 years, as proposed by Kay. The results are somewhat, but not violently, different from those of Kay and Thornbury. Holmes (1935) made a similar study of the erosion of an interglacial valley in central New York, using an estimate of the postglacial unit of 20,000 years.

3. RADIOACTIVITY METHODS

The determination of the duration of geological time by measurement of the disintegration products of radioactive elements has long been used, and the methods and results can be easily located (Holmes, 1931; Goodman, 1942). Of primary interest to archeologists are two methods of time-reckoning by radioactivity, since they will yield dates within the recent past. These are the radiocarbon (carbon 14) technique for calculating the age of organic materials and the radium ratio method for calculating the age of certain stratified sediments, such as glacial varved clays and ocean-floor deposits.

a) *Radioactive carbon* (C^{14}) *method.*—The development of this technique dates to 1931, when, at the University of Chicago, an unknown radioactivity was detected. In the following decade this was identified as that of carbon 14 whose source lay in the high atmosphere, where cosmic radiation produces neutrons which are converted to radiocarbon by reaction with nitrogen according to the formula: neutron $+$ $N^{14} =$ proton $+$ C^{14}. These carbon atoms unite with oxygen in the atmosphere to form carbon dioxide in the same manner as does ordinary carbon (C^{12}), and as such are circulated through the biosphere. An extended technical account of the principles has been recently published by W. F. Libby (1952), Institute for Nuclear Studies, University of Chicago, who has been largely responsible for the development and application of the method (see also Merrill, 1948; Deevey, 1951a).

The C^{14} atoms have a half-life of 5,568 ± 30 years. In the life-process of oxygen exchange in plants and animals, the amount of radiocarbon uptake is sufficient to effect a level of equilibrium with that in the atmosphere. Thus organisms during life possess a specific activity of 15.6 disintegrations per minute per gram of carbon in their bodies. After life and C^{14} intake cease and the equilibrium is halted, radioactive disintegration of the C^{14} occurs, and after 5,568 years this activity will have decreased to 7.8 disintegrations per minute per gram of carbon. Once these facts were established, some very extensive laboratory testing of organic samples of living material from various latitudes, altitudes, and geographical situations was performed, with the result that the C^{14} value for living matter was confirmed (Libby, Anderson, and Arnold, 1949). The next step was to assay ancient samples whose age was already known, in order to assess the assumption that the radiocarbon level in the recent past has been the same as at present. These tests confirmed this assumption, in that the amount of radioactive carbon present was equal to that predicted (Arnold and Libby, 1949). The final phase of the research by Libby has been to determine the age of numerous samples of unknown age, and as of mid-1951 some 300 samples had been dated. The age of these samples ranged from a few hundred years to over 20,000 years. The list of materials and their radiocarbon dates have been published on several occasions (Arnold and Libby, 1950; Arnold and Libby, 1951; Flint and Deevey, 1951; Johnson, 1951; Libby, 1951). Expert critical assessment of the radiocarbon date series has been performed in a series of articles (Flint and Deevey, 1951; Godwin, 1951; Johnson, 1951). The majority opinion is that the method is sound, provided that the proper precautions are observed in selecting samples which have not been contaminated by the addition of radiocarbon from more recent materials (see discussions by Bartlett, 1951; Flint and Deevey, 1951, pp. 259–60; Bliss, 1952; Libby, 1952, pp. 42–43).

Libby (1952, p. 43; see also Collier, 1951, p. 6) recommends the following amounts and materials as most desirable (in the order given) for age determination: charcoal (1 ounce) or charred organic material such as heavily burned bone (2 pounds); well-preserved wood (2 ounces); grasses, cloth, and peat (2 ounces); well-preserved antler and similar horny substances (2 or 3 pounds); well-preserved, unaltered shell (4 ounces).

The dates derived through measurement of the level of radioactivity of C^{14} are not precise and absolute dates but are in each instance accompanied by a ± error of 100 to 1,200 years, the magnitude of the error being in part a function of the age of the material. This error is assumed not to exceed the sampling error in counting in runs of 48 hours. If the counting period were extended, the error could be reduced in the direction of greater accuracy. On the other hand, the assumption that nothing but random events is responsible for the errors may easily be erroneous. The significance of this error has been commented on by Collier (in Johnson, 1951, p. 47) as follows:

The error figure given represents the standard deviation of the mean (one sigma). This means that there is one chance in three that the true date will fall outside of one sigma and one chance in twenty that it will fall outside of two sigma. To use sample 75 (2665 ± 200) as an example, there is one chance in three that the true date of the sample is outside the range 2465–2865, and one in twenty that it is outside the range 2265–3065.

With the establishment of C^{14} laboratories at Columbia University, the University of Michigan, the University of Pennsylvania, and Yale University, further refinements of the method may be expected. Although the utility of the radiocarbon dating method is restricted, owing to the limitations imposed by the length of half-life and low specific activity of C^{14}, nevertheless some important conclusions have been reached on the basis of age determinations of a large series of organic samples whose character is primarily geological. Thus Flint and Deevey (1951) point out that the dates of certain events occurring at the end of the last glacial age appear to be much earlier than heretofore supposed; that radiocarbon dates for specific climatic and glaciologic effects in northern and western Europe and central and northern North America prove to be closely equivalent, so that the possibility of intercontinental correlation of such events is thereby much strengthened; and that, if time rates for geologic, botanic, or pedologic processes such as retreat of glacial ice, postglacial plant succession, or calcium carbonate leaching of soils can be determined within the effective range of the radiocarbon method (i.e., 20,000–30,000 years), it may be possible to use these figures to assign rates or elapsed time by extrapolation to predate horizons which might theoretically include the whole span of the Pleistocene. Of primary concern is the dating of the Mankato

glacial subage of the Wisconsin glaciation; for all the North American Pleistocene dating is based upon the assumed date of 25,000 years (Kay, 1931) since the Mankato maximum, and this figure has been long used, as detailed in another section of this paper, for computing the age of the Pleistocene and its subdivisions. Flint and Deevey accept the C^{14} date of 11,000 years for the Mankato glacial maximum, though Antevs does not, and Moss (1951, pp. 79, 81) and Schultz, Lueninghoener, and Frankforter (1951, pp. 35–37) treat the Mankato date tentatively in attempting a geological fit.

Although the dating limit of 20,000–30,000 years imposed by the radiocarbon method is likely to include most of the period of man's presence in the New World, the real limitation in archeological dating is the requirement that unaltered organic materials be used, and in many instances these will not be available.

b) Radium method.—The radium activity dating method is briefly discussed by Merrill (1948). This cannot be applied directly to archeological specimens but rather to determining the age of sediments in which archeological remains may occur, or with which the deposits in which man's activity is present may be correlated and thus, indirectly, yield an archeological date.

Piggot and Urry (1942) determined the radioactivity of deep-sea core samples at a number of points along the cores. This activity, it is assumed, is caused by a constant amount of uranium and an additional amount of ionium and radium. The latter two elements are reduced in time from their initial ratio to the amounts that are in radioactive equilibrium with the available uranium. Mathematical analysis of the variation of radioactivity with distance from the surface in the core sample leads to a dating of each point analyzed along the core. The younger parts can be dated to within 100–200 years, and the maximum age determination is about 300,000 years. In two cores at the precise point where a distinctive volcanic ash layer was identified, ages of 13,300 and 13,100 years were determined.

The ocean bottom beyond the continental shelves is covered with sediments which accumulate at an exceedingly slow rate. A few feet of these sediments may provide a continuous record of the history of terrestrial events for the previous million years. Urry (1948a) concludes that the preliminary studies thus far made indicate that "the effects of glaciation over widely separated areas of the northern hemisphere are roughly contemporaneous," an observation which will be of the utmost significance in archeological dating, since it may be the means of dating and correlating glacial phenomena on both sides of the Atlantic (Bramlette and Bradley, 1940; Flint, 1945, p. 29; Kuenen, 1946; Pettersson, 1950; Zeuner, 1950, pp. 334–37, 401; Ovey, 1951).

Urry (1948b) has studied the radium content of varved clays and has indicated a method by which individual varves can be dated by their radium activity much in the same manner as deep-sea sediments are dated. A possible check of the annual varve-count dating method of Antevs and De Geer and a means of determining the exact temporal hiatus of the several lacunae in the North American varve series counted by Antevs is thus indicated. The radium contents of summer and winter portions of the Hartford varves vary rhythmically. When the radium contents of summer and winter varves are plotted against time (as measured by the standard varve-counting method), they exhibit slopes of opposite sign. This variability permits Urry to calculate the age of individual varves,

and he gives the example of varve No. 3700, which is 18,000 years old on the basis of the winter curve and 17,700 years old on the basis of the summer curve.

Schlundt and Moore (1909) considered the radium dating method for the travertine deposited by thermal waters in Yellowstone Park. The travertine is overlaid by detritus deposited by the latest glacial action at the Mammoth Hot Springs locality. Finding that the early travertine contained about 1 per cent of the amount of radium in travertine now being deposited and assuming that both deposits originally contained the same radium level, a figure of about 11,200 years (almost exactly that of the Mankato maximum on the basis of recent radiocarbon dates) can be calculated by using the figure of 1,690 years for the radium half-life.

In each of the investigations described above, no direct dating of implements or human bones has been, or can be, made, but the methods are nevertheless important from the standpoint of aiding in the erection of a world-wide Pleistocene and postglacial chronology which will enable archeologists to date those finds which occur in certain geologic contexts.

4. PEDOLOGICAL METHODS

The extraction of relative chronology may be accomplished from the study of soils either by computing the rate of soil formation and development or weathering or by inferring from the position and nature of the soil the climatic conditions under which it was formed and, through this, arriving at a date by correlation with the otherwise established climatic sequence (Thorp, 1949).

Although Nikiforoff (1942, p. 850) says, "we do not know the velocity of soil development," some progress on the problem of rate of soil development in specific situations has been made, as the data cited by Zeuner (1950, pp. 342–43), Li (1943), and Hunt and Sokoloff (1950, p. 110) attest. The method outlined by Siniaguin (1943) for determining the absolute age of soils by measuring the stratigraphic concentration and migration of phosphates has not, so far as I can determine, been checked by other workers. Although it be freely admitted that the specific stratigraphic conditions may vary, it would seem that there is a sufficient number of chronological methods which could be brought to bear upon the problem of dating a large enough number of particular instances of soil profiles so that some rather specific ideas of the time factor involved in their formation would result. One suspects that the reason we know so little about soil development rates is that pedologists in general are not historically minded.

The importance of soils in interpreting archeological situations may be appreciated by referring to the papers of Louis (1945), Leighton (1934, 1936, 1937), Piggott (1949), Storie and Harradine (1950), Bourdier (1947), Guillien (1950), Alimen (1950), Alimen and David (1949), Clark (1936), Bryan and Albritton (1943), Bryan (1948), and Moss (1951, p. 40). Hayden (1945) shows how the concentration of salt in adobe wall footings due to evaporation of the ground water varies and can be used to differentiate time relations of different sections of a site in Arizona. Cook (1949, *passim*, esp. pp. 23–24) has published an excellent study of soil deposition in Mexico and has made some observations on the rate of soil weathering. The methods of the sedimentary petrologist can be an aid in understanding pedologic situations, as illustrated by the work of Krynine (1939), Cailleux (1946), and De Heinzelin (1946); and the chemical analysis of deposits may also be enlightening in pointing out

processes of deposition and postdepositional alteration (Allison, 1926, p. 318; Buehrer, 1950). Arrhenius (1931) in a study of the phosphoric acid content of Swedish sites found that it was not possible to use quantitative phosphoric acid measurements to determine the age of sites, but he points out that one can readily identify the location of sites by the soil chemistry.

V. P. Sokoloff (1952) has proposed a chronologic method which depends upon the determination of the distribution patterns and magnitudes of the trace minerals and metals (zinc, copper, tin, lead, gold, manganese, phosphorus, nitrogen, etc.) in archeological sites and, by comparison of these data with control series from site layers of known age, permits him to infer the age of the undated level by calculating the rate of dissipation of the trace elements. The original amounts of the trace elements which are chemical relics of the by-products of habitation can scarcely be inferred with precision, although the detailed study of refuse midden components (cf. Cook and Heizer, 1951) may give some insight into the variety and quantity of food resources exploited by the original inhabitants. Sokoloff (1952, p. 281) says the Chinchifoonie midden in Georgia "may well be 100,000 years old or so," but one might wish to check this age assignment with other methods before accepting it.

5. CHEMICAL METHODS

a) Chemical analysis of bone.—The gross differences in the weight, color, and density of human and animal bones found under different conditions are readily apparent. Although there are well-documented instances of heavily mineralized bones which are, as a result of being subject to solutions in a specific situation, not more than a few hundred years old (Vinton, 1951), nevertheless it is generally true that the degree of fossilization is a rough measure of age (Rogers, 1924; Paine, 1937; Barber, 1939). Bone, however, is an intricate complex of organic and inorganic compounds whose exact nature is as yet only imperfectly understood (Jaffe and Sherwood, 1951), and the qualitative alterations which result in bone in its long sojourn in the ground are likewise complex and only vaguely known. It is clear that any attempt to trace the progressive alteration of bone constituents through time in the hope of assigning some rate to the process and thereby derive chronology must come through investigation of the degree of permanence or amount of alteration of those constituents which give promise of behaving in an orderly, rather than a random, fashion.

Gangl (1936) studied the fat content of a series of European bones, and his findings indicate that this substance persisted for several thousand years after burial, being subject to gradual decrease. Gangl's data suggest a means of deriving age in years within a ± 500-year range, though it should be noted that in open sites in California no traces of fat remain in human bones after being buried 100 years (Cook and Heizer, 1947, p. 207). Thunberg (1947) studied the citric acid content of medieval and prehistoric bone material, with results which indicate a progressive alteration of this component and which may be used as a rough measure of age. F. E. Koby determined that the ossein of bones from the St. Brais caverns in the Jura Mountains contained 0.0213 per cent of nitrogen compared to 0.055 per cent in fresh bone, 0.022–0.023 per cent in bones 2,000 years old, and 0.015 per cent in bones of the Aurignacian period of the Upper Paleolithic (Vaufrey, 1949, p. 161). Tanabe (1944) reported on the calcium and phosphorus content of human bones from a Japanese shell mound, and Watanabe (1950) discusses the relation of midden soils to bone mineralization in Japanese sites. In addition, his paper includes a valuable summary of earlier work of this sort.

The affinity of free fluorine ions present in the ground water with the hydroxyapatite in bone leads to the formation of fluorapatite, an extremely stable mineral which is notably resistant to leaching, weathering, or other alteration. With the passage of time, the fluorapatite undergoes gradual and progressive quantitative increase. Since the fluorine level of ground waters will vary, there may exist no direct comparability in the fluorine content of bones of the same antiquity from different regions. The primary value of the fluorine content of bone for chronology, therefore, lies in distinguishing the *relative* ages of different bones which come from the same deposit. The fluorine method of relative dating has a long history (Oakley, 1950) but may be said to have begun with the work of Middleton (1844) and was brought to practical completion by the French mineralogist, A. Carnot (1893). A recent revival of interest in the fluorine dating method, primarily by K. P. Oakley (1950), has re-established its value as a means of distinguishing the relative ages of certain human skeletal materials which have been claimed to be very ancient. As Oakley (1950, p. 45) points out, the fluorine method "is not applicable in regions where fluorine is excessively abundant, or in tropical regions of tropical weathering where mineralization can occur rapidly and in haphazard fashion."

For the last five years a program of investigation into the nature and extent of chemical alteration of the constituents of archeological human bone has been carried out at the University of California. For prehistoric sites in central California, it appears that general agreement obtains between the degree of mineralization of human bones and their antiquity and that, specifically, the contained water and organic matter in human bones tend to decrease in a relatively orderly manner with the passage of time (Cook and Heizer, 1947; Heizer and Cook, 1949, 1952; Heizer, 1950; Cook, 1951a, 1951b). As of this moment, a chronological method based upon bone mineralization has not yet been developed, but there is good evidence to indicate that such a method is possible, and the investigation is continuing with this goal in mind.

b) Rock weathering and flint patination.—The calculation by Matthes (1930, pp. 70–72) of the time elapsed since the Illinoian glaciation on the basis of the degree of weathering of an aplite dike in Yosemite National Park illustrates the method of rock weathering to infer geological time. In archeology an example of the same technique has been presented by Schofield (1932), who estimated the time involved in the weathering of granite to derive the age of some Bushman rock paintings in South Africa. Such estimates can, at best, give only the relative magnitude of time involved, and no precise time estimates are possible.

The patination (i.e., surface oxidation) of stone tools depends upon several factors: the material itself, the conditions to which the tools have been subjected since they were fashioned, and the length of time to which the tools have been subject to alteration on or under the ground surface. Service (1941) has argued that lithic patina is so variable that it is not useful as an age criterion; but Rogers (1939, pp. 19–20) has been able to assign *relative* ages of stone tools on the basis of their type and degree of patination in southern California (cf. Laudermilk, 1931), as have Kelly (1938, pp. 3–6) in Georgia and De Terra and Paterson (1939, pp. 328, 333–34) in India. Renaud (1936, pp. 5–7) discusses differences in patination of petroglyphs as a means of distinguishing the relative sequence of styles. Hue (1929) reports on the results of laboratory experiments covering a 20-year period on the patination of French flints, and Gehrcke (1933) discusses the dating of flints by measuring the thickness and type of patina. He points out that the alkalinity of the soil is decisive in this respect; and he performed a laboratory experiment of subjecting flint to a 10 per cent NaOH solution for six months, with the result that a patina 0.3 mm. thick was formed. From this he calculated that in alkaline soils a patina 1.0 mm. thick would be formed in 8,000 years and derives the formula $t = 8,000 \times d$, where t is time in years and d is the thickness in millimeters of the white patina resulting from burial in alkaline soils. Gehrcke calculates that the flint tools from La Micoque are 24,000 years old, but archeological opinion is that the age is closer to 100,000 years. The inaccuracy of Gehrcke's method lies, at least in part, in the short period of his controlled observations (six months), a time range which seems rather short to extrapolate back to 24,000 or more years.

Thus far, we may conclude, flint patination is primarily useful as a means of distinguishing relative ages of different lots of implements from the same region, and the use of the method for calculating absolute age from thickness of patination by Gehrcke is inaccurate and unreliable.

6. GEOPHYSICAL METHODS

a) Paleomagnetism.—According to Folgheraiter (1896), Robert Boyle knew by the end of the seventeenth century that permanent magnetic orientation of magnetic particles in fired bricks occurred and that this orientation coincided with the direction of the earth's magnetic field. This was confirmed by two Italian workers, S. Gherardi and

M. Melloni, in 1853. In the past century a very large amount of experimentation and observation has been conducted with reference to the direction of the earth's magnetic field in the past. Favorite laboratory material has been ancient pottery of known date within whose walls the magnetic particles become oriented and locked upon firing and which still retain their original orientation. The remanent magnetism of ceramics is treated by Folgheraiter (1896, 1897a, b, 1899a–d), Carlheim-Gyllenskiöld (1897), Mercanton (1902a, b, 1907, 1910a, b, 1918, 1923), Raymond (1904, 1910), Guebhard (1909, 1910), Vire (1909), Koenigsberger (1933), and Thellier (1951). Although this documentation may appear extensive, it is but a fraction of the total bibliography on the subject. From time to time archeologists have seen the possibility of dating ceramic specimens by determining the orientation of the magnetic particles in the pottery and identifying the date with reference to the graph of the periodic curve of the inclination of the earth's magnetic field. Unfortunately, the method is not so simple, largely because the direction of the magnetic field in the past is only incompletely understood. In addition, there are complicating factors, such as the requirement that the position of the pottery vessel when it was fired must be known, because, if the vessel has been reheated (as in the case of a cooking pot), the original magnetic orientation is altered. It would seem, however, that, if a specific program of securing pottery specimens which could be precisely dated by some *tertium quid*, such as tree-rings or radiocarbon, the secular variation of magnetic declination could be adequately graphed against time and thus yield a calendar to which the magnetic orientation of pottery of unknown date could be referred (cf. Jones, 1928). Gehrcke (1933, p. 149)

appreciated this possibility when he stated: "Man wird nun, vorausgesetzt dass man eine genügende Menge empirischen Materials hat, umgekehrt aus der grösse des remanenten Magnetismus von Gesteinen das absolute Alter derselben zu bestimmen vermögen, und man kann auch aus den Verhältniszahlen der Grössen der Remanenz die relativen Zeiten bestimmen." Even though a method of general chronology based upon the dated fluctuations in magnetic orientation is not developed, the method will still have a limited utility in enabling archeologists to distinguish relatively fine time distinctions between different sets of pottery vessels within a site or between sites within an area.

Since the foregoing remarks are intended to represent the briefest possible statement, further reference is made to the summaries of the subject by Manley (1949) and Hopwood (1913, pp. 21–22). Contemporary experts in terrestrial magnetism, among whom are Louis Neel and Émile Thellier in France and E. A. Johnson and A. G. McNish in the United States, will be the persons to whom to look for assistance in any attempt to develop a chronological method based on remanent magnetism in bricks or pottery.

Geologists are conscious of paleomagnetism, and a number of studies of the magnetic orientation of grains in varved glacial clays and drill cores have been performed. Reference is made to the papers by Johnson and McNish (1939), Fleming, Johnson, and McNish (1940), McNish and Johnson (1940), McNish (1941), Ising (1942), Hoylman and Durbin (1944), and Benedikt (1943). Johnson and McNish (1939) examined Antevs' 500-year varve series at West Hartford, Connecticut, and his 200-year series at New Haven and conclude: "The direction of polarization in the varve is interpreted as a direct measure of the direction of the magnetic compass at the time the deposits were laid down," and "the rate of secular variation in this prehistoric period did not differ appreciably from the rates observed in historic times" (see also McNish, 1941). McNish and Johnson (1940, p. 347) say: "In view of the foregoing results [of studies of the secular variation in declination in New England from magnetic polarization of glacial varves] it seems likely that this method of investigation will supply reliable knowledge of variations in the Earth's magnetic field in past ages," a statement of interest to archeologists, who could use such knowledge. The magnetic orientation of deep-sea sediments has also been studied by McNish and Johnson (1938*a*, *b*), who conclude that this may "furnish a means of dating sediments by their magnetic orientation." Ising (1942, 1943), in studying the magnetic properties of varved clay, noted that the magnetic susceptibility shows a variation which follows the varve pattern. Lynton (1937), in a laboratory study of the orientation of deep-well cores by their magnetic polarity, suggested that the rate of deposition could be determined, provided that it could be established that the polarity had a definite periodicity (cf. Mercanton, 1926). That periodicity of secular variation of magnetic declination may occur and be demonstrable is shown by the results of studies by Chevallier (1925) of magnetic declination in Sicily from A.D. 1000 to the present where the material used was dated lava flows in the Mount Etna region. He found that the magnetic declination of lavas *in situ* had varied in this period from 18° W. through north to 18° E. for different dates, and back again. He concluded that the change is periodic and repeats itself in about 720 years (cf. Manley, 1949).

As anticipated by the last statement, lavas evince remanent magnetism, and many studies of this phenomenon have been made. Thellier (1940), at the request of Paul Rivet, investigated the pedregal of San Angel, Mexico, but the computed date was *ca.* A.D. 1500, which was obviously too late, and nothing further seems to have been done with it (see also Chevallier, 1939). A series of obviously late lava flows at Lassen Volcanic National Park, California, were studied by A. Jones (1928), who was able to map the flows and seriate them according to their remanent magnetism. He dates the eruptions as occurring in A.D. 1846, 1800, 1300–1350, 1130–1200, 1120–50, 650, 500 (see also Finch and Anderson, 1930, p. 253). Finch (1937) subsequently worked out a tree-ring calendar for dating recent volcanic events at Mount Lassen and was able to point to eruptions in A.D. 1785, 1720, 1666, 1567, and 1485–1680.

The reader will probably by now have wondered what particular relevance remanent magnetism in bricks, pottery, glacial varves, and lava flows may have to long-range archeological chronology. The relevance is simply that what appears to be a *potential* method for both direct and indirect archeological chronology and long-range geological dating is available but that the necessary attention by prehistorians to the subject has not yet been given.

b) Vulcanology.—A volcanic eruption may deposit lava or pumice over archeological deposits. The date of the eruption may be known historically, as in the case of Pompeii, which was covered by ash from the eruption of Vesuvius in A.D. 79, or the instance of the eruption of Sunset Crater, Arizona, which forced the Puebloan abandonment of the immediate region and which has been dated by the tree-ring method (Colton, 1932, 1945; McGregor, 1936*a*, *b*). Other eruptions whose lava flows or pumice ejecta covered village sites in prehistoric times may also be assigned in some cases a guess date, as in the instance of the eruption of Mount Mazama, Oregon (in whose caldera now lies Crater Lake), which was dated as occurring from 4,000 to 7,000 years ago by Williams (1942, pp. 212–14). That Williams' methods were sound is indicated by the radiocarbon check date of 6,453 ± 250 years. It may be noted in passing that other pre-C[14] guess dates for the Mazama eruption run from 8,000 to 14,000 years (Allison, 1946; Hansen, 1946, 1947).[4] The covering of pyramids and occupation sites of the Archaic (= Middle Cultures) of the valley of Mexico by the pedregal of San Angel is well known (Gamio, 1920), and the radiocarbon date corresponds well with the guess date suggested by several geologists (Vaillant, 1935, p. 165). The developmental history of Mount Vesuvius has been carefully worked out by Rittmann (1933), and he dates the several explosive maxima by the process of association with "dated" archeological materials.

Since lavas and pumice from different eruptions usually vary sufficiently in their lithologic character to be readily recognized, a pumice layer which was widely distributed by the winds may serve as a useful stratigraphic horizon marker. If the particular pumice deposit is datable (e.g., those from Mount Mazama or Sunset Crater), a chronological-stratigraphic datum of great importance is available in determining the time order of subsequent pre- or posteruptive discoveries. This technique is neatly illustrated by the work of Thorarinsson (1944), who determined the dates and lithologic character of the volcanic ash from the several eruptions of Mount Hecla in

4. Antevs (letter, May, 1952) says that the Mazama eruption antedated the Altithermal (dry) age of the Middle Postglacial, the implication being that the C[14] date is not old enough.

Iceland, and thereby found the key to the regional stratigraphic chronology through identification of the ash strata. Horberg (1952), in identifying and describing a volcanic ash deposit in Canada, points out that, since it is of Mankato or early postglacial date and is situated in southern Alberta on what is presumed to be the route of entry of ancient man into mid–North America, this ash may prove of use in dating local archeological deposits if and when they are found. The great value of volcanic ash layers for purposes of stratigraphic correlation is illustrated in the papers of Bramlette and Bradley (1940, pp. vii, 2–3, 5), Hansen (1947), Leonard (1947), and Frye, Swineford, and Leonard (1948). Auer (1950) has compared and correlated the pollen profiles in bogs of Patagonia and Tierra del Fuego through the use of volcanic ash layers and has then cross-correlated the Fuego-Patagonian data with those from Europe, where the plant succession is dated, in order to derive the southern South American postglacial dates (see review of Auer by Freile, 1952). As discussed above with reference to varves, such long-distance teleconnections may be inaccurate, since a similar series of events need not necessarily prove that they occurred simultaneously. The postglacial chronology of Patagonia and Tierra del Fuego has also been studied by Salmi (1941), who believed that he was able to arrange a sequential stratigraphic series of overlapping postglacial pumice layers extending from Lake Lacar in the north to Tierra del Fuego in the south (*ibid.*, Figs. 17, 18). He proposes that in the postglacial period the ice caps diminished during climatic optima and that, when the ice pressure on the magma chambers diminished from lightening of the ice load, a stage of increased explosive activity was instituted. He interprets the sequence of pumice layers which are correlated with pollen profiles as indicating correlated periodicity of explosive maxima and climatic optima.

c) *Seismology.*—Even earthquakes, it seems, have been appealed to in the attempt to determine the chronological ordering of archeological data. The best-known instance is by Schaeffer (1948, pp. 1–5, 255–56, 560), who proposes that throughout the Near East between 2400 B.C. and 1225 B.C. there occurred a series of major seismic disturbances whose destructive effects may be detected in the major sites. Two major quakes, one between 2200 and 2100 B.C., occurring at the terminus of Troy III period, and one in 1365 B.C., equated with the end of Troy VI period, are pointed out. There are a number of other earthquakes which enter into Schaeffer's "stratigraphie sismologique." The method has been criticized by Hanfmann (1951), who shows that historical records of earthquakes from Sumerian times on indicate none of such magnitude as those postulated by Schaeffer and that Schaeffer does not support his thesis by considering dated earthquakes. The seismologists themselves are of the opinion that the highly destructive effects proposed by Schaeffer are too widespread and that there is no evidence that the seismic intensity has altered in the Near East in the time period treated by him (cf. Daniel, 1950, p. 255).

7. RATE OF ACCUMULATION OF CULTURAL OR NATURAL DEPOSITS

A widely used method for estimating the time required for a given amount of occupation refuse to accumulate will give, at best, only an approximation. When this method is the only one available, these estimates are better than nothing. For all such rate-of-increment calculations some unit must be determined to use as a multiplicative or extrapolative factor. Even when the unit measure is available, other factors which may have affected the constancy of the rate must be considered. In short, the compounding of variables of different ranks of probability can never result in answers which have reliability.

Pumpelly (1908, pp. 54–57) calculated that the culture strata at Anau accumulated at the rate of 2.5 feet per century and made observations in Egypt, where he found the rate of refuse accumulation to range between 1.43 and 1.9 feet per century and to average 1.6 feet. His Anau dates (*ibid.*, p. 57) seem rather old (Daniel, 1950, p. 212, calls them "inflated"). H. Schmidt, Pumpelly's archeologist, came to quite different conclusions on chronology on the basis of cross-dating with other archeological areas (Schmidt, 1909, pp. 179–86). Ghirshman (1938–39) made similar calculations to derive the age of the site of Sialk, but the general opinion is that his estimates are too small.

Nelson (1909, pp. 345–46), Cook (1946), Schenck (1926, pp. 205–12), and Gifford (1916) have made calculations of the antiquity of certain San Francisco Bay shell mounds by estimating the rate of refuse accumulation (see also Heizer and Mills, 1952, p. 8). On the basis of their conclusions, a chronology of the culture horizons of the adjacent lower Sacramento Valley was suggested (Heizer, 1949, pp. 37–40), which has been checked at one point with radiocarbon dates with good results, so that on the basis of this limited evidence the earlier shell-mound age calculations do appear reliable. Lothrop (1928, p. 197) estimated the total population and volume of middens and computed, through the rate of accumulation, the antiquity of refuse deposits in Tierra del Fuego sites. His estimates may be compared with those of Bird (1938), which are based on different data. Vaillant (1935, pp. 166–67, 257–58) compared the known rate of accumulation at Pecos with the thickness of refuse deposits in some valley of Mexico sites and arrived at some tentative conclusions on the time required for the Mexican middens to develop. Cosgrove and Cosgrove (1932, pp. 100–103) attempted to gain some idea of the time required for the Swarts Ruin deposits to accumulate by estimating the rate of accumulation of refuse strata.

Cave deposits, which are usually difficult to interpret, may be given approximate age dates by estimating the rate of filling, as illustrated by Loud and Harrington's (1929, pp. 120–23) estimate of the age of the culture deposits in Lovelock Cave, Nevada, and Harrington's (1933, p. 171) estimate of the time required for the accumulation of the fill in Gypsum Cave, Nevada. In the case of Lovelock Cave, there are radiocarbon dates for the earliest refuse deposits which agree fairly closely with the earlier estimative date, and the same is true with regard to Gypsum Cave. Curiously enough, the premises upon which the age estimates by Loud and Harrington rest are now known to be incorrect; yet chance or coincidence produced dates which agree comfortably with those derived by a reliable and objective method (radiocarbon) (Kroeber, 1948, p. 681). Statements urging caution in the use of the rate-of-increment method of age determination occur in Schenck (1926, pp. 208–12), Clark (1947, p. 139), and Woolley (1947, p. 79).

The steady accretion of overburden of materials deposited by natural means lying upon culture strata may yield approximate dates for the cultural material, provided that the rate of accumulation can be determined. Dates for prehistoric Peruvian artifacts imbedded in the guano stacks have been ingeniously calculated by Kubler (1948) on the basis of counting the annual guano varves, which are of sufficiently uniform thickness that depth measurements of artifacts can be dated by extrapolating the number of annual guano varves which must have been deposited above them (cf. Hutchinson, 1951, pp. 65–71). Bird (1948, pp. 21, 27–28) estimates the time involved in the building of an artifact-bearing soil profile in the Viru Valley, Peru. In lower Mesopotamia the known rate of alluvial filling of the head of the Persian Gulf and the advance of the coast line at a rate of 1.5 miles per century have aided in establishing the relative time of the founding of certain sites, with the later ones following the seaward advance of the shore (Childe, 1934, p. 132; Lloyd, 1949, pp. 17–18, end-leaf map). The rate of peat accumulation may assist in deriving an estimate of the total age of subjacent materials (Hansen, 1947, pp. 36–38; Hansen and Packard, 1949, pp. 466–67). Champe (1946, pp. 32–33) neatly combines dendrochronologically dated strata with undated layers whose period can be estimated on the basis of the time required for the dated levels to accumulate, and he achieves a total chronology for Ash Hollow Cave, Nebraska. A similar technique for filling the gaps in the pollen profile at Faulensee, Switzerland, by determining the rate of accumulation through varve counts and extrapolating to derive the period of nonvarved layers was applied by Welten (1944) and in another instance by Fromm (1938) in Angermanland, Sweden.

Although tree-ring dating (dendrochronology) is specifically omitted from consideration here, nevertheless the method may be used indirectly to derive more extended chronologies by its application in determining the rates of certain processes, such as glacial ice advance and recession (Capps, 1931, p. 6; Lawrence, 1946, 1950).

1. PALEONTOLOGY

a) Vertebrate paleontology.—The association of archeological cultural or skeletal remains with the bones of extinct animals or living vertebrates no longer resident in the region because of climatic changes usually leads to the presumption that the cultural materials are ancient. The succession of vertebrate forms in the North American Pleistocene is, at best, only generally known (cf. Romer, 1933; Stock, 1936; Scott, 1937; Colbert, 1942; Flint, 1947, pp. 521–45; Hibbard, 1949), while the faunal shifts during cold glacial and warm interglacial stages of the Pleistocene in Europe are well known, and these alternations are correlated with the succession of Paleolithic cultures (Zeuner, 1945, chap. x; 1950). The remains of animal forms may serve as stratigraphic evidence "indicating by the presence or absence of certain now extinct species the relative age of the deposits within the stratigraphical scale" (Zeuner, 1945, p. 27) and, as ecological evidence, "indicating the environment in which they lived and, therefore, the climate" (*ibid.*).

In the New World the occurrence of cultural remains with the bones of extinct animals is documented for North America (Sellards, 1940, 1947), for South America (Bird, 1938), and Mesoamerica (Arellano, 1946). Such evidence, besides indicating the time of the archeological manifestation in the broad sense (e.g., late Pleistocene, post-Pleistocene), may give leads to the climatic situation in which the earliest American Indians lived. Until more is known of the succession of types and the time and reasons for extinction of late Pleistocene forms, such as the large bison, camel, horse, and elephant (Eiseley, 1943), archeologists cannot hope to find paleontology of much assistance in dating cultural manifestations.

b) Micropaleontology. – Under certain conditions sedimentary deposits may contain microfossils which, when studied, will give an excellent idea of the climatic conditions under which the alluvial material was laid down, and, by reference to the already known climatic succession, an approximate date may be assigned to the deposits which may contain archeological remains (Deevey, 1949, p. 1364). In this way, leads as to the placement in the postglacial chronology of cultural materials from Lower Klamath Lake, California, have been made by Conger (1942) through a study of the diatoms. Patrick (1938) studied the diatoms from the Clovis site, and Conger (1949) and Linder (1942) studied the deposits at the Boylston Street Fishweir site in Massachusetts with good results.

Foraminiferal remains may also reflect former climatic conditions, as illustrated by the analyses of sediments at the Boylston Street Fishweir (Stetson and Parker, 1942; Phleger, 1949*a*). Phleger (1948) reports on a submarine core 15.4 meters long from the Caribbean Sea which contained eleven warm–cold-water shifts, interpreted as probably covering the climatic fluctuations of the entire span of the Pleistocene. Such studies (see also Cushman and Henbest, 1940; Phleger and Pettersson, 1947; Pettersson, 1950, p. 44) furnish one means by which the excellent submarine sediment record can be linked with the record of terrestrial Pleistocene glaciation.

c) Conchology.—The shells of mollusks, which may occur either as components of archeological deposits or in naturally deposited strata which can be stratigraphically correlated or associated with cultural deposits, may constitute evidence of former ecological conditions and thus furnish the means of assigning an age to the associated artifacts by reference to the "climatic chronology." The principles of the method of paleoecology through analysis of molluscan remains are presented by Baker (1920, 1930, 1937), Eiseley (1937), and Richards (1937). Examples of the usefulness of the method are the reports of W. T. Clark (1938) on the Pleistocene mollusks from the Clovis site; of Baker (1942) on molluscan remains in late Pleistocene deposits of Lower Klamath Lake; of Clench (1942) on mollusks in the alluvial deposits of the Boylston Street Fishweir; and of Richards (1936) concerning the mollusk remains from the Clovis and Lindenmeier sites.

With the passage of time, not only may there occur structural changes (gross size, measurement of the opening) in the shells, apparently as a result of temperature changes (Morse, 1925), but also there may be evidenced in shell middens a succession of species which reflects different shore or climatic conditions (Byers and Johnson, 1940, pp. 91–92; Morrison, 1942; Goggin, 1948, pp. 228–31; Griffin, 1948; Greengo, 1951).

The measurement of paleotemperatures by the oxygen 18 method (Epstein *et al.*, 1951; Urey *et al.*, 1951) will give precise data on ocean temperatures of the past. If radiocarbon dates for mollusk shells from occupation middens and late Pleistocene deposits could be secured, it seems probable that the temperature component of paleoecology might be rather precisely determined, and such findings would have significance for archeological dating.

2. PALEOBOTANY

Research in the botanical field has been notably oriented along historical lines, with the result that there exists a very considerable published literature detailing important conclusions on the chronology of the past from the standpoint of such approaches as tree-ring counting (dendrochronology) and pollen analysis. To illustrate the diversity of application of the methods of paleobotany, one may cite the conclusion of Chaney that charcoal from Cochise culture sites in Arizona is identifiable as hickory and cottonwood, which indicates a moister climate than now prevails in that region; the inferences on postglacial changes in sea-level derived from a study of the peat deposits of Bermuda (Knox, 1940); and Phleger's (1949*b*, p. 1459) proposal that a direct correlation of North American and European Pleistocene events and sequences can be made by using pollen analysis as a tie-in from terrestrial to submarine profiles in those places where submarine Pleistocene Foraminifera have been deposited near the continental margins.

Pollen analysis, or the microscopic study of pollen grains which have been preserved, has as one of its principal aims the determination of changes in composition of local floristic assemblages. Flowering plants usually produce large quantities of pollen, and under favorable conditions of deposition (usually in lakes or ponds or bogs) there may gradually accumulate on the bottom inorganic and organic sediments, such as peat or pollen. The lakes and bogs formed in the wake of the northward retreat of the last ice sheet furnish ideal situations for pollen preservation; and from these have come the data for the reconstruction of postglacial vegetational history. Specialized techniques for securing core samples of such deposits and of studying the pollen in the laboratory have been developed, and the reader is referred for details to the works of Cain (1939), Erdtman (1943), Hansen (1947, pp. 5–8, 38–40), Godwin (1948), and Faegri and Iversen (1950).

In Europe, regional pollen studies

of postglacial deposits (e.g., Nilsson, 1935, 1948*a, b;* Firbas, 1939; Godwin, 1942) have shown that there obtained here a generally similar sequence of postglacial floral succession, whose course was: (1) late glacial deposits; (2) late glacial treeless tundra; (3) pine and birch forest; (4) hazel and mixed oak forest (transitional); (5) beech forest (Deevey, 1951*c*). A single postglacial chronological system applicable over the whole of Europe, with primary reference to pollen analysis, is not possible to erect because of local climatic changes during the postglacial period, with increasingly colder temperatures from south to north as the ice front was approached, increasing continentality from west to east, and lack of precise knowledge of the rate of forest species migration. A single chronological datum or time marker whose cause was due to a simultaneous event over the whole area and which can be recognized in all or most pollen sequences is therefore essential in order that the several regional sequences can be correlated. Of the various possibilities, the Littorina Sea transgression, the Fennoscandian moraines deposited by the halt of the retreating ice in central Sweden, the Postglacial Climatic Optimum, and the Subboreal Dry Phase have all been tested for use as horizon markers; and, though no common agreement has been reached, it is generally admitted that the second event listed is of particular significance (Zeuner, 1950, **pp.** 105–9). The dates for the European postglacial pollen chronology rest in part upon the glacial varve chronology and in part upon archeological cross-dating. In North America the dating of postglacial vegetational phases, as inferred from pollen analysis, through the varve chronology has not been possible; but radiocarbon dates for vegetal material in peat-bog sequences show promise of solving this difficulty (see especially,

Deevey, 1951*b;* Flint and Deevey, 1951, pp. 269 ff.). In northwestern United States H. P. Hansen's extensive investigations have led him to utilize certain volcanic ash or pumice layers as horizon markers for correlating different pollen profiles (e.g., Hansen, 1946, Figs. 1, 2; Hansen and Packard, 1949, Fig. 3); but Deevey (1949, pp. 1363–64; Flint and Deevey, 1951, pp. 279–80) is not convinced that the pumice layers are being properly interpreted. The postglacial forest sequence and pollen chronology for eastern North America is summarized by Deevey (1949, pp. 1355–64, Table 7) and Sears (1948); for northwestern North America by Hansen (1947); and for Europe by Deevey (1949, Tables 2, 3).

The application of pollen analysis to archeological chronology is discussed by Sears (1937), Eiseley (1939), Godwin (1942, 1946), and Deevey (1944*a*). Examples of the results of the application of the method are presented by Dubois and Dubois (1938), Mitchell (1945), Härri (1940), Firbas (1939), Knox (1942), Benninghoff (1942), Wilson (1949), Hansen (1942; 1946; 1947, pp. 121–22; 1951). Two particular European studies are worth summarizing. Bertsch (1935) studied the extensive peats of the Federsee bog in southwestern Germany, which contain cultural materials ranging from Magdalenian to the historic period. The pollen and archeological sequence was dated in the absence of varves by interpolation from three time datum points: (1) climax of the final glacial phase at 18,000–20,000 B.C.; (2) the maximum of postglacial solar radiation at 8,000–9,000 B.C. (the so-called "Climatic Optimum"); and (3) the historic dates of the Metal Ages chronology. Welten (1944) in a well-known paper (extensively summarized by Deevey, 1946; Godwin, 1945; and Zeuner, 1950, pp. 89–91) presents the results of the pollen analysis of the deposits in a Swiss bog. While pollen boring, Welten detected thin annual sedimentary layers. These were counted, and a rate-of-increment figure was derived which could be applied to those sections of the profile which lacked the annual layers. The result was that Welten could construct a continuous pollen sequence from 7550 B.C. to A.D. 1920, the terminal date being marked by the drainage of the bog. The only other similar instance is the work of Fromm (1938). Schneider (1945) and Flint and Deevey (1951, p. 276) have expressed some doubts as to the absolute accuracy of Welten's chronology, Schneider on the grounds that the sedimentary layers may not be annual, and Flint and Deevey because the extrapolation and interpolation for the missing sedimentary layers may not be accurate.

The correlation of local European pollen profiles is made difficult through the absence of a generally accepted datum marker, as explained above. In spite of this, Deevey (1943a, 1944b, 1951c) and Sears (1942) attempt to correlate the pollen sequences in eastern North America through the equation of climatic stages with those of Sweden (see review and critique in Hansen, 1947, pp. 111–12). It is further suggested that the pollen sequence of

Mexico can be dated and correlated with that of eastern North America (Deevey, 1943b, 1944b; Sears, 1950). The main point with reference to such correlations is that they are still tentative; for, even though it be admitted that the correlation of the North American and European pollen sequences is valid, the very basis of the dated European sequences rests ultimately upon the critical varve data of Lidén (1938), which involves an interpolation of 380 years (A.D. 920–1300) in order to connect it with the present day (cf. Flint and Deevey, 1951, p. 276).

In summary, it is only in Europe that dates may be validly assigned to archeological remains through association with pollen-bearing deposits. In North America the regional pollen sequences, though intensively worked out, still are not dated by anything better than guess correlations with the European sequence. Pollen analysis in connection with archeological remains does furnish a means of accurate correlation with other archeological materials found at different places in the same deposit or in different deposits in the same region, but it must be emphasized that the method can give, generally speaking, only relative chronology.

REFERENCES

ALIMEN, H. 1950. "Indications climatiques dans les couches archéologiques d'un abri (sol polygonal de Mouthiers, Charente)" *Bulletin de la Société préhistorique de France*, XLVII, 286–88.

ALIMEN, H., and DAVID, P. 1949. "Cryoturbations dans des couches archéologiques de la Charente et du Périgord," *Compt. rend. Acad. Sci.*, CCXXIX, 1246.

ALLISON, I. S. 1946. "Early Man in Oregon: Pluvial Lakes and Pumice," *Scientific Monthly*, LXII, 63–65.

ALLISON, V. C. 1923. The Growth of Stalagmites and Stalactites, *Journal of Geology*, XXXI, 106–25.

———. 1926. *The Antiquity of the Deposits in Jacob's Cavern*, Part VI. ("American Museum of Natural History Anthropological Papers," Vol. XIX.)

ANTEVS, E. 1922. *The Recession of the Last Ice Sheet in New England*. ("American Geographical Society Research Series," No. 11.)

———. 1925. *On the Pleistocene History of the Great Basin*, pp. 53–116. ("Carnegie Institution of Washington Publications," No. 352.)

———. 1928. *The Last Glaciation*. ("American Geographical Society Research Series," No. 17.)

———. 1937. "Age of the Lake Mohave

Culture." In CAMPBELL, E. W. C., *et al.*, 1937, pp. 45–49.

——. 1938a. "Was 'Minnesota Girl' Buried in a Gully?" *Journal of Geology*, XLVI, 293–95.

——. 1938b. "Postpluvial Climatic Variations in the Southwest," *Bulletin of the American Meteorological Society*, XIX, 190–93.

——. 1941. *Age of the Cochise Culture Stages*, pp. 31–55. ("Gila Pueblo Medallion Papers," No. 29.)

——. 1945. "Correlation of Wisconsin Glacial Maxima," *American Journal of Science*, CCXLIII-A, 1–39.

——. 1947. Review of F. E. ZEUNER, "Dating the Past," *Journal of Geology*, LV, 527–30.

——. 1948. "Climatic Changes and Prewhite Man," *Bulletin of the University of Utah* ("Biol. Series," Vol. X, No. 7), XXXVIII, No. 20, 168–91.

——. 1949a. *Age of Cochise Artifacts on the Wet Leggett.* ("Fieldiana, Anthropology, Chicago Natural History Museum," Vol. XXXVIII, No. 1.)

——. 1949b. "Geology of the Clovis Sites." In WORMINGTON, H. M., *Ancient Man in North America*," pp. 185–92. ("Denver Museum of Natural History, Popular Series," No. 4.) 3d ed.

[ANTEVS, E.] 1952. "Cenozoic Climates of the Great Basin," *Geologische Rundschau*, XL, 94–108.

ARELLANO, A. R. 1946. "El Elefante fosil de Tepexpan y el hombre primitivo," *Revista mexicana de estudios antropologicos*, VIII, 89–94.

ARMSTRONG, A. L. 1936. "The Antiquity of Man in Africa as Demonstrated at the Victoria Falls," *Reports of the British Association for the Advancement of Science*, pp. 386–87.

——. 1939. "Paleolithic Man in the North Midlands," *Memoirs and Proceedings of the Manchester Literary and Philosophical Society*, LXXXIII, 87–116.

ARNOLD, J. R., and LIBBY, W. F. 1949. "Age Determinations by Radiocarbon Content: Checks with Samples of Known Age," *Science*, CX, 678–80.

——. 1950. *Radiocarbon Dates*. Chicago: Institute for Nuclear Studies, University of Chicago.

——. 1951. "Radiocarbon Dates," *Science*, CXIII, 111–20.

ARRHENIUS, O. 1931. "Markanalysen i arkéologiens tjanst," *Geol. Fören. i Stockholm Förh.*, LIII, 47–59.

AUER, V. 1950. Las Capas volcanicas como base de la cronologia postglacial de Fuegopatagonia," *Revista de investigaciones agricolas*, III, Bull. 2, 49–208.

BAKER, F. C. 1920. "The Life of the Pleistocene or Glacial Period," *Bulletin of the University of Illinois*, XVII, 195–370.

——. 1930. "Influence of the Glacial Period in Changing the Character of the Molluscan Fauna of North America," *Ecology*, XI, 469–80.

——. 1937. "Pleistocene Land and Fresh-Water Mollusca as Indicators of Time and Ecological Conditions." In MACCURDY, G. G. *Early Man*, pp. 67–74. Philadelphia, 1937.

——. 1942. *Mollusca Contained in the Test Pit Deposits*, pp. 117–19. ("Carnegie Institution of Washington Publications," No. 538.)

BALL, J. 1939. *Contributions to the Geography of Egypt.* Cairo.

BARBER, H. 1939. "Untersuchungen über die chemische Veränderung von Knochen bei der Fossilization," *Palaeobiologie*, VII, 217–35.

BARTLETT, H. H. 1951. "Radiocarbon Datability of Peat, Marl, *Caliche* and Archaeological Materials," *Science*, CXIV, 55–56.

BELL, R. E. 1951. "Dendrochronology at the Kincaid Site." In COLE, F.-C., *Kincaid*, Appendix 1, pp. 233–92. Chicago: University of Chicago Press.

BENEDIKT, E. T. 1943. "A Method of Determination of the Direction of the Magnetic Field of the Earth in Geological Epochs," *American Journal of Science*, CCXLI, 124–29.

BENNINGHOFF, W. S. 1942. "The Pollen Analysis of the Lower Peat." In JOHNSON, F. (ed.), 1942, pp. 96–104.

BERTSCH, K. 1935. *Die deutsche Wald im Wechsel der Zeiten*. Tübingen.

BIRD, J. B. 1938. "Antiquity and Migrations of the Early Inhabitants of Patagonia," *Geographical Review*, XXVIII, 250–75.

——. 1946. "The Archeology of Patagonia." In *Handbook of South American Indians*, I, 17–24. (Bureau of American Ethnology Bull. 143.)

———. 1948. "Preceramic Cultures in Chicàma and Virú," *Memoirs of the Society for American Archeology*, IV, 21–28.

BLACKWELDER, E., and ELLSWORTH, E. W. 1936. "Pleistocene Lakes of the Afton Basin, California," *American Journal of Science*, CCXXXI, 453–63.

BLANC, A. C. 1937. "Low Levels of the Mediterranean Sea during the Pleistocene Glaciation," *Quarterly Journal of the Geological Society of London*, XCIII, 643–46.

BLANCHARD, J. 1941. "Chronologie absolue du quaternaire donnée par la théorie du déplacement des pôles," *Bulletin de la Société préhistorique de France*, XXXVIII, 193–201.

BLISS, W. L. 1950. "Early and Late Lithic Horizons in the Plains," *Proceedings of the Sixth Plains Archaeological Conference*, 1948, pp. 108–14. ("University of Utah Anthropological Papers," No. 11.)

———. 1952. "Radiocarbon Contamination," *American Antiquity*, XVII, 250–51.

BOULE, M., and VILLENEUVE, L. 1927. "La Grotte de l'Observatoire à Monaco," *Arch. Inst. paléont. hum., Paris*. (Mém. 1.)

BOURDIER, F. 1947. "Correlations, par la pédologie, entre les glaciations alpines et quelques faunes et industries préhistoriques du Quaternaire européen," *Compt. rend. Acad. Sci.*, CCXXIV, 50.

BRADLEY, W. H. 1938. "Mediterranean Sediments and Pleistocene Sea Levels," *Science*, LXXXVIII, 376–79.

BRAIDWOOD, R. J. 1946. "Geochronology, and Geological Factors Relative to Man's Past." In *Human Origins*, pp. 43–56. 2d ed. Chicago: University of Chicago.

BRAMLETTE, M. N., and BRADLEY, W. H. 1940. *Geology and Biology of North Atlantic Deep-Sea Cores between Newfoundland and Ireland*. (U.S. Geological Survey Prof. Paper 196-A.)

BREUIL, H., and KOSLOWSKI, L. 1931–32. "Étude de stratigraphie paléolithique dans le nord de la France, la Belgique et l'Angleterre," *Anthropologie*, XLI, 449–88; XLII, 42–47, 29–314.

BRYAN, K. 1938. Review of the Geology of the Clovis Finds Reported by Howard and Cotter, *American Antiquity*, IV, 113–30.

———. 1941. *Correlation of the Deposits of Sandia Cave, New Mexico, with the Glacial Chronology*, pp. 45–64. ("Smithsonian Institution, Miscellaneous Collections," Vol. XCIX, No. 23.)

———. 1948. "Los Suelos complejos y fósiles de la altiplanicie de México, en relación a los cambios climaticos," *Bol. Soc. Geol. Mejicana*, XIII, 1–20.

———. 1950. "Geologic Interpretation of the Deposits." In HAURY, E. W., *Ventana Cave*, pp. 75–126. Albuquerque.

BRYAN, K., and ALBRITTON, C. C. 1943. "Soil Phenomena as Evidence of Climatic Change," *American Journal of Science*, CCXLI, 469–90.

BRYAN, K., and McCANN, F. T. 1943. "Sand Dunes and Alluvium near Grants, New Mexico," *American Antiquity*, VIII, 281–90.

BRYAN, K., and RAY, L. R. 1940. *Geologic Antiquity of the Lindenmeier Site in Colorado*. ("Smithsonian Institution, Miscellaneous Collections," Vol. XCIX, No. 2.)

BUCHNER, P., and BUCHNER, G. 1940. "Die Datierung der vorgeschictlichen und geschichtlichen Aüsbruche auf der Insel Ischia," *Naturwissenschaften*, XXVIII, 553–64.

BUEHRER, T. F. 1950. "Chemical Study of the Material from Several Horizons of the Ventana Profile." In HAURY, E. W., *Ventana Cave*, pp. 549–63. Albuquerque.

BYERS, D. S., and JOHNSON, F. 1940. *Two Sites on Martha's Vineyard*. ("Papers of the R. S. Peabody Foundation for Archaeology," Vol. I, No. 1.)

CAILLEUX, A. 1946. "Application de la pétrographie sédimentaire aux recherches préhistoriques," *Bulletin de la Société préhistorique de France*, XLIII, 182–91.

CAIN, S. A. 1939. "Pollen Analysis as a Paleo-ecological Research Method," *Botanical Review*, V, 627–54.

CAMPBELL, E. W. C., *et al.* 1937. *The*

Archeology of Pleistocene Lake Mohave. ("Southwest Museum Papers," No. 11.)

CAPPS, S. R. 1931. *Glaciation in Alaska.* (U.S. Geological Survey Prof. Paper No. 170-A.)

CARLHEIM-GYLLENSKIÖLD, V. 1897. "Sur l'inclinaison de l'aiguille aimantée à l'époque étrusque," *Terrestrial Magnetism,* II, 117–18.

CARNOT, A. 1893. "Recherches sur la composition générale et la teneur en fluor des os modernes et des os fossiles de différents âges," *Annales des mines, Mémoires,* Ser. 9, III, 155–95.

CHAMPE, J. L. 1946. *Ash Hollow Cave.* ("University of Nebraska Studies," n.s., No. 1.)

CHAWNER, W. D. 1936. *Geology of Catahoula and Concordia Parishes, Louisiana.* (Department of Conservation, Louisiana Geological Survey Bull. 9.)

CHEVALLIER, R. 1925. "L'Aimantation des laves de l'Etna et l'orientation du champ terrestre en Sicile du XIIᵉ au XVIIᵉ siècle," *Annales de physique,* Ser. 10, IV, 5–162.

———. 1939. "Mesure de l'aimantation naturelle d'une lave mexicaine," *Journal de physique et de radium,* Ser. 7, X, 115–25.

CHILDE, V. G. 1934. *New Light on the Most Ancient East.* New York.

———. 1950. *Prehistoric Migrations in Europe.* (Inst. Sammenlignende Kulturforskning, Ser. A, "Forelesninger," Vol. XX.)

CLARK, J. G. D. 1936. *The Mesolithic Settlement of Northern Europe.* Cambridge: At the University Press.

———. 1938. "Microlithic Industries from Tufa Deposits at Prestatya, Flintshire, and Blashenwell, Dorset," *Proceedings of the Prehistorical Society,* IV, 330–34.

———. 1947. *Archaeology and Society.* 2d ed. rev. London.

CLARK, W. T., JR. 1938. "Pleistocene Mollusks from the Clovis Gravel Pit and Vicinity," *Proceedings of the Philadelphia Academy of Natural Science,* XC, 119–21.

CLENCH, W. J. 1942. "The Mollusks [from the Boylston Street Fishweir Site]." In JOHNSON, F., 1942, pp. 45–66.

COLBERT, E. H. 1942. "The Association of

Man with Extinct Mammals in the Western Hemisphere," *Proceedings of the Eighth American Scientific Congress,* II, 117–29.

COLEMAN, A. P. 1914. "An Estimate of Post-glacial and Interglacial Time in North America," *Report of the 12th International Geological Congress, 1913, Toronto,* pp. 435–49.

COLLET, L. W. 1925. *Les Lacs.* Paris: O. Doin.

COLLIER, D. 1951. "New Radiocarbon Method for Dating the Past," *Chicago Natural History Museum Bull.* 22, pp. 6–7.

COLTON, H. S. 1932. "Sunset Crater: The Effect of a Volcanic Eruption on an Ancient Pueblo People," *Geographical Review,* XXII, 582–90.

———. 1945. "A Revision of the Date of the Eruption of Sunset Crater," *Southwestern Journal of Anthropology,* I, 345–55.

CONGER, P. S. 1942. *Diatoms from Lower Klamath Lake,* pp. 115–16. ("Carnegie Institution of Washington Publications," No. 538.)

———. 1949. "The Diatoms." In JOHNSON, F., *et al.* (eds.), 1949, pp. 109–23.

COOK, S. F. 1946. "A Reconsideration of Shellmounds with Respect to Population and Nutrition," *American Antiquity,* XII, 51–53.

———. 1949. "Soil Erosion and Population in Central Mexico," *Ibero-Americana,* No. 34.

———. 1951a. *The Fossilization of Human Bone: Calcium, Phosphate, and Carbonate,* pp. 263–80. ("University of California Publications in American Archaeology and Ethnology," Vol. XL.)

———. 1951b. *Chemical Analysis of Fossil Bone,* pp. 73–84. ("University of Michigan Anthropological Papers," No. 8.)

COOK, S. F., and HEIZER, R. F. 1947. "The Quantitative Investigation of Aboriginal Sites: Analysis of Human Bone," *American Journal of Physical Anthropology,* n.s., V, 201–20.

———. 1951. *The Physical Analysis of Nine Indian Mounds of the Lower Sacramento Valley,* pp. 281–312. ("University of California Publications in American Archaeology and Ethnology," Vol. XL.)

COSGROVE, H. S. and C. B. 1932. *The*

Swarts Ruin. ("Peabody Museum Papers," Vol. XV, No. 1.)

CUSHMAN, J. A. and HENBEST, L. G. 1940. "Foraminifera." In BRAMLETTE, M. N., and BRADLEY, W. H., 1940, pp. 35–50.

DANIEL, G. E. 1950. *A Hundred Years of Archaeology.* London.

DEEVEY, E. S., JR. 1943a. "Additional Pollen Analyses from Southern New England," *American Journal of Science,* CCXLI, 717–52.

———. 1943b. "Intento para datar las culturas medias del Valle de México mediánte analisis de polen," *Ciencia México,* IV, 97–105.

———. 1944a. "Pollen Analysis and History," *American Scientist,* XXXII, 39–53.

———. 1944b. "Pollen Analysis and Mexican Archaeology: An Attempt To Apply the Method," *American Antiquity,* X, 135–49.

———. 1946. "An Absolute Pollen Chronology in Switzerland," *American Journal of Science,* CCXLIV, 442–47.

———. 1948. "On the Date of the Last Rise of Sea Level in Southern New England, with Remarks on the Grassy Island Site," *ibid.,* CCXLVI, 329–52.

———. 1949. "Biogeography of the Pleistocene," *Bulletin of the Geological Society of America,* LX, 1315–1416.

———. 1951a. "Radiocarbon Dating," *Scientific American,* CLXXXVI, 24–28.

———. 1951b. "Peat Samples for Radiocarbon Analysis: Problems in Pollen Statistics," *American Journal of Science,* CCXLIX, 473–511.

———. 1951c. "Late Glacial and Postglacial Pollen Diagrams from Maine," *ibid.,* CCXLIX, 177–207.

DUBOIS, G. and C. 1938. "Analyses polliniques de tourbe submergée au Moulin de Luc (Calvados)," *Bulletin de la Société préhistorique de France,* XXXV, 133–35.

EISELEY, L. C. 1937. "Index Mollusca and Their Bearing on Certain Problems of Prehistory: A Critique." In *Twenty-fifth Anniversary Studies, Philadelphia Anthropological Society,* pp. 77–93.

———. 1939. "Pollen Analysis and Its Bearing upon American Prehistory: A Critique," *American Antiquity,* V, 115–39.

———. 1943. "Archaeological Observations on the Problem of Post-glacial Extinction," *ibid.,* VIII, 209–17.

EPSTEIN, S.; BUCHSBAUM, R.; LOWENSTAM, H.; and UREY, H. C. 1951. "Carbonate-Water Isotopic Temperature Scale," *Bulletin of the Geological Society of America,* LXII, 417–26.

ERDTMAN, G. 1943. *An Introduction to Pollen Analysis.* Waltham, Mass.

FAEGRI, K., and IVERSEN, J. 1950. *Text-Book of Modern Pollen Analysis.* Copenhagen: E. Munksgaard.

FARRINGTON, O. C. 1901. *Observations on Indiana Caves.* ("Field Columbian Museum Publications," No. 53; "Geological Series," Vol. I, No. 8.)

FINCH, R. H. 1937. "A Tree Ring Calendar for Dating Volcanic Events at Cinder Cone, Lassen National Park, California," *American Journal of Science,* CCXXXIII, 140–46.

FINCH, R. H., and ANDERSON, C. A. 1930. *The Quartz Basalt Eruptions of Cinder Cone, Lassen Volcanic National Park, California,* pp. 245–73. ("University of California Publications," Bulletin of the Department of Geological Sciences, 19.)

FIRBAS, F. 1939. "Vegetationsentwicklung und Klimawandel in der mitteleuropäischen Spät- und Nacheiszeit," *Naturwissenschaften,* XXVII, 81–89.

FISK, H. N. 1944. *Summary of the Geology of the Lower Alluvial Valley of the Mississippi River.* (War Department, Corps of Engineers, U.S. Army, Mississippi River Commission, Vicksburg, Miss.)

FLEMING, J. A.; JOHNSON, E. A.; and MCNISH, A. G. 1940. "Paleomagnetic Investigations," *International Union of Geodesy, Geophysics, Association of Terrestrial Magnetism and Electricity, Transactions of the Washington Meeting, 1939,* p. 535.

FLINT, R. F. 1945. "Chronology of the Pleistocene Epoch," *Quarterly Journal of the Florida Academy of Science,* VIII, 1–34.

———. 1947. *Glacial Geology and the Pleistocene Epoch.* New York: John Wiley & Sons.

FLINT, R. F., and DEEVEY, E. S., JR. 1951. "Radiocarbon Dating of Late Pleistocene Events," *American Journal of Science*, CCXLIX, 257–300.

FOLGHERAITER, G. 1896. "Ricerche sull' inclinazione magnetica all' epoca etrusca," *Rend. R. Accad. Lincei*, V, 293–300.

——. 1897a. "Sulla forza coercitiva dei vasi etruschi," *ibid.*, VI, 64–70.

——. 1897b. "La Magnetizzazione dell' argilla colla cottura in relazione colle ipotesi sulla fabbricazione del vasellamenero etrusco," *ibid.*, pp. 368–76.

——. 1899a. "Ricerche sull' inclinazione magnetica col mezzo della distribuzione del magnetismo libero nei vasi fittili antichi," *ibid.*, VIII, 69–76.

——. 1899b. "Ricerche sull' inclinazione magnetica nel I secolo a Cr. e nel I secolo dell' era volgare, calcolata da vasi fittili di Arezzo e Pompei," *ibid.*, pp. 121–29.

——. 1899c. "Ricerche sull' inclinazione magnetica durante il periodo di fabbricazione dei vasi fittili greci," *ibid.*, pp. 176–83, 269–75.

——. 1899d. "Sur les variations séculaires de l'inclinaison magnétique dans l'antiquité," *Journal de physique théorique et appliquée*, Ser. 3, VIII, 660–67.

FORD, J. A. 1936. *Analysis of Indian Village Site Collections from Louisiana and Mississippi*. ("Department of Conservation, Louisiana Geological Survey Anthropological Studies," No. 2.)

——. 1951. *Greenhouse: A Troyville-Coles Creek Period Site in Avoyelles Parish, Louisiana*. ("American Museum of Natural History Anthropological Papers," Vol. XLIV, Part I.)

——. 1952. "Mound Builders of the Mississippi," *Scientific American*, CLXXXVI, 23–27.

FREILE, A. J. 1952. Review of V. AUER, "Las Capas volcanicos...," *Geographical Review*, XLII, 327–29.

FROMM, E. 1938. "Geochronologisch datierte Pollendiagramme und Diatoméenanalysen aus Angermland," *Geol. Fören. i Stockholm Förh.*, LX, 365–81.

FRYE, J. C.; SWINEFORD, A.; and LEONARD, A. B., 1948. "Correlation of Pleistocene Deposits of the Central Great Plains with the Glacial Section," *Journal of Geology*, LVI, 501–25.

GALE, H. S. 1915. *Salines in the Owens, Searles, and Panamint Basins, Southeastern California*, pp. 251–323. (U.S. Geological Survey Bull. 580.)

GAMIO, M. 1920. "Las Excavaciones del Pedregal de San Angel y la cultura arcaica del Valle de México," *American Anthropologist*, XXII, 127–43.

GANGL, I. 1936. "Alterbestimmung fossiler Knochenfunde auf chemischen Weg," *Oesterreichische chemische Zeitschrift*, XXXIX, 79–82.

GEER, E. H. DE. 1942. "Planetary Chronology by Varves and (Tree) Rings," *Geol. Fören. i Stockholm Förh.*, LXIV, 185–204.

——. 1943. "Exact Geochronologic Connections: Sweden-Finland," *ibid.*, pp. 225–40.

GEER, G. DE. 1921. "Correlation of Late Glacial Clay Varves in North America with the Swedish Time Scale," *ibid.*, XLIII, 70–73.

——. 1929. *Geochronology, as Based on Solar Radiation, and in Relation to Archeology*, pp. 687–96. ("Smithsonian Institution of Washington Annual Reports," 1928.)

——. 1934. "Equatorial Paleolithic Varves in East Africa," *Geographical Annals*, XVI, 76–96.

——. 1937. "Early Man and Geochronology." In MACCURDY, G. G. (ed.), *Early Man*, pp. 323–26. Philadelphia.

——. 1940. *Geochronologia Suecica Principles*. ("Kon. Svensk. Vet. Akad. Handl.," No. 18.) Stockholm.

GEHRCKE, E. 1933. "Ueber Zeitbestimmungen an Gesteinen jüngerer geologischer Epochen," *Gerlands Beiträge zur Geophysik*, XXXVIII, 147–66.

GHIRSHMAN, R. 1938–39. *Fouilles de Sialk, près de Kashan, 1933, 1934, 1937*. ("Musée du Louvre, Dépt. des antiquités orientales, Sér. Archéologique," Vols. IV–V.)

GIFFORD, E. W. 1916. *Composition of California Shellmounds*. ("University of California Publications in American Archaeology and Ethnology," Vol. XII, No. 1.)

GILBERT, G. K. 1890. *Lake Bonneville*.

("U.S. Geological Survey Monographs," No. 1.)

GODWIN, H. 1942. "Pollen-Analysis and Quaternary Geology," *Proceedings of the Geological Association*, LII, 328–61.

——. 1945. "Archives of the Lakes," *Nature*, CLVI, 383.

——. 1946. "The Relationship of Bog Stratigraphy to Climatic Change and Archaeology," *Proceedings of the Prehistoric Society*, n.s., XII, 1–11.

——. 1948. "The Principles and Practice of Pollen Analysis." In *The Advancement of Science*, IV, 337–38.

——. 1951. "Comments on Radiocarbon Dating for Samples from the British Isles," *American Journal of Science*, CCXLIX, 301–7.

GOGGIN, J. M. 1948. "Florida Archaeology and Recent Ecological Changes," *Journal of the Washington Academy of Science*, XXXVIII, 225–33.

GOLDTHWAIT, J. W. 1938. "The Uncovering of New Hampshire by the Last Ice Sheet," *American Journal of Science*, Ser. 5, XXXVI, 345–72.

GOLDTHWAIT, R. P. 1935. "The Damariscotta Shell Heaps and Coastal Stability," *American Journal of Science*, XXX, 1–13.

GOODMAN, C. 1942. "Geological Applications of Nuclear Physics," *Journal of Applied Physics*, XIII, 276–89.

GREENGO, R. E. 1951. *Molluscan Species in California Shell Middens*. ("University of California Archaeological Survey Reports," No. 13.)

GREENMAN, E. F. 1943. "The Archaeology and Geology of Two Early Sites near Killarney, Ontario," *Papers of the Michigan Academy of Science, Abstracts, and Letters*, XXVIII, 505–30.

GREENMAN, E. F., and STANLEY, G. M. 1940. "A Geologically Dated Camp Site, Georgian Bay, Ontario," *American Antiquity*, V, 194–99.

GRIFFIN, J. W. 1948. "Green Mound: A Chronological Yardstick," *Florida Naturalist*, XXII, 1–8.

GUÉBHARD, A. 1909. "À propos de la polarité magnétique des poteries préhistoriques," *Bulletin de la Société préhistorique de France*, VI, 186.

——. 1910. "La Préhistoire au dehors," *ibid.*, VII, 502–6.

GUILLIEN, Y. 1950. De la climatologie de l'âge du Renne. *Bulletin de la Société préhistorique de France*, XLVII, 162–65.

HACK, J. T. 1942. *The Changing Physical Environment of the Hopi Indians of Arizona*. ("Peabody Museum Papers," Vol. XXXV, No. 1.)

——. 1943. "Antiquity of the Finley Site," *American Antiquity*, VIII, 235–41.

——. 1945. *Recent Geology of the Tsegi Canyon*, pp. 151–58. ("University of California Publications in American Archaeology and Ethnology," Vol. XLIV.)

HANFMANN, G. M. A. 1951. "The Bronze Age in the Near East: A Review Article," *American Journal of Archaeology*, LV, 355–65.

HANSEN, G. 1934. "The Bear River Delta, British Columbia, and Its Significance regarding Pleistocene and Recent Glaciation," *Transactions of the Royal Society of Canada*, Sec. 4, XXVIII, 179–85.

HANSEN, H. P. 1942. *A Pollen Study of Peat Profiles from Lower Klamath Lake of Oregon and California*, pp. 103–14. ("Carnegie Institution of Washington Publications," No. 538.)

——. 1946. "Pollen Analysis and Postglacial Climate and Chronology," *Scientific Monthly*, LXII, 52–62.

——. 1947. "Postglacial Forest Succession, Climate and Chronology in the Pacific Northwest," *Transactions of the American Philosophical Society*, n.s., Vol. XXXVII, Part I.

——. 1951. "Pollen Analysis of Peat Sections from near the Finley Site, Wyoming." In Moss, J. H., 1951, pp. 111–18.

HANSEN, H. P., and PACKARD, E. L. 1949. "Pollen Analysis and the Age of Proboscidian Bones near Silverton, Oregon," *Ecology*, XXX, 461–68.

HÄRRI, H. 1940. *Stratigraphische und Waldgeschichte des Wauwilermooses und ihre Verknüpfung mit den Vorgeschichtlichen Siedlungen*. Zurich: Geobot. Instituts Rübel.

HARRINGTON, M. R. 1933. *Gypsum Cave*,

Nevada. ("Southwest Museum Papers," No. 8.)

———. 1948. *An Ancient Site at Borax Lake, California.* ("Southwest Museum Papers," No. 16.)

HAWLEY, F. M. 1941. *Tree-Ring Analysis and Dating in the Mississippi Drainage.* Chicago: University of Chicago Press.

HAYDEN, J. D. 1945. "Salt Erosion," *American Antiquity,* X, 373–78.

HEIM, A. 1894. "Uber das absolute Alter des Eiszeit," *Naturforsch Gesellsch. Zurkh, Vierteljahrschr.,* Vol. XXXIX.

HEINZELIN, M. J. DE. 1946. Revue des techniques d'étude des sédiments et leur intérêt pour la géologie du Quaternaire," *Bull. Soc. roy. belge d'anthrop. et de préhist.,* LVII, 52–83.

HEIZER, R. F. 1949. "The Archaeology of Central California. I. The Early Horizon." *University of California Anthropological Records,* XII, 1.

———. 1950. *On the Methods of Chemical Analysis of Bone as an Aid to Prehistoric Culture Chronology,* pp. 10–14. ("University of California Archaeological Survey Reports," No. 7, Paper No. 3.)

———. 1951. "Preliminary Report on the Leonard Rockshelter Site, Pershing County, Nevada," *American Antiquity,* XVII, 89–98.

HEIZER, R. F., and COOK, S. F. 1949. "The Archaeology of Central California: A Comparative Analysis of Human Bone from Nine Sites," *University of California Anthropological Reports,* XII, 85–112.

———. 1952. "Fluorine and Other Chemical Tests of Some North American Human and Animal Bones," *American Journal of Physical Anthropology,* n.s., Vol. X (in press).

HEIZER, R. F., and MILLS, J. E. 1952. *The Four Ages of Tsurai.* Berkeley: University of California Press.

HIBBARD, C. W. 1949. "Pleistocene Vertebrate Paleontology in North America," *Bulletin of the Geological Society of America,* LX, 1417–28.

HÖGBOM, I. 1923. "Ancient Inland Dunes of Northern and Middle Europe," *Geog. Annaler,* V, 113–242

HOLMES, A. 1931. "Radioactivity and Geo-

logical Time," *Bulletin of the National Resources Council,* LXXX, 124–459.

HOLMES, C. D. 1935. "Glacial and Interglacial Development of Chittenango Falls State Park in Central New York," *American Journal of Science,* XXIX, 41–47.

HOPWOOD, A. 1913. "The Magnetic Materials in Claywares," *Proceedings of the Royal Society of London,* Ser. A, LXXXIX, 21–30.

HORBERG, L. 1952. "Quaternary Volcanic Ash in Southern Alberta, Canada," *Science,* CXV, 140–41.

HOYLMAN, H. W., and DURBIN, H. A. 1944. "A Study of the [Magnetic] Susceptibility of Sediments," *Transactions of the American Geophysical Union for 1944,* pp. 543–55.

HUBBS, C. L., and MILLER, R. R. 1948. "Correlation between Fish Distribution and Hydrographic History in the Desert Basins of Western United States," *Bulletin of the University of Utah, Biol. Ser.,* X, 18–166.

HUE, E. 1929. "Recherches sur la patine des silex," *Bulletin de la Société préhistorique de France,* XXVI, 461.

HUNT, C. B., and SOKOLOFF, V. P. 1950. *Pre-Wisconsin Soil in the Rocky Mountain Region.* (U.S. Geological Survey Prof. Paper No. 221-G.)

HUTCHINSON, G. E. 1951. "Survey of Contemporary Knowledge of Biogeochemistry. 3. The Biogeochemistry of Vertebrate Excretion," *American Museum of Natural History Bulletin,* Vol. XCVI.

ISING, G. 1942. "Den varviga lerans magnetiska egenskaper," *Geol. Fören. i Stockholm Förh.,* LXIV, 126–42.

———. 1943. "On the Magnetic Properties of Varved Clay," *Arkiv för Matematik, Astronomi och Fysik, utgivet av K. Svenska Vetensk.,* XXIX A, 1–37.

JAFFE, E. B., and SHERWOOD, A. M. 1951. *Physical and Chemical Comparison of Modern and Fossil Tooth and Bone Material.* (U.S. Geological Survey, TEM-149.) Oak Ridge, Tenn.

JOHNSON, E. A., and McNISH, A. G. 1939. "Secular Changes in Magnetic Declination as Deduced from Polarized Varve-Sediments," *Transactions of the Ameri-*

can *Geophysical Union for 1939*, Part 3, p. 358.

JOHNSON, F. (ed.). 1951. *Radiocarbon Dating*. ("Memoirs of the Society for American Archaeology," No. 8.)

JOHNSON, F., *et al.* 1942. *The Boylston Street Fishweir*. ("Papers of the R. S. Peabody Foundation for Archaeology," Vol. II.)

——. (eds.) 1949. *The Boylston Street Fishweir. II.* ("Papers of the R. S. Peabody Foundation for Archaeology," Vol. IV, No. 1.)

JOHNSON, F., and RAUP, H. M. 1947. *Grassy Island.* ("Papers of the R. S. Peabody Foundation for Archaeology," Vol. I, No. 2.)

JOHNSTON, W. A. 1921. *Sedimentation of the Fraser River Delta.* ("Memoirs of the Geological Survey of Canada," No. 125.)

JONES, A. E. 1928. "Magnetism of Cinder Cone Lava Flows, Lassen Volcanic National Park," *Bulletin of the Hawaiian Volcano Observatory*, XVI, 61–63.

JONES, J. C. 1925. *Geologic History of Lake Lahontan*, pp. 3–52. ("Carnegie Institution of Washington Publications," No. 352.)

JUDSON, S. 1949. "Pleistocene Stratigraphy of Boston, Mass., and Its Relation to Boylston Street Fishweir." In JOHNSON, F., *et al.* (eds.), 1949, pp. 7–48.

KAY, G. F. 1931. "Classification and Duration of the Pleistocene Period," *Bulletin of the Geological Society of America*, XLVIII, 425–66.

KELLEY, J. C.; CAMPBELL, T. N.; and LEHMER, D. J. 1940. *The Association of Archaeological Materials with Geological Deposits in the Big Bend Region of Texas.* (Sul Ross State Teachers College Bull. 21, No. 3.)

KELLY, A. R. 1938. *A Preliminary Report on Archaeological explorations at Macon, Georgia*, pp. 1–68. (Bureau of American Ethnology Bull. 119, "Anthropological Papers," No. 1.)

KIMBALL, D., and ZEUNER, F. E. 1947. *The Terraces of the Upper Rhine and the Age of the Magdalenian.* (Institute of Archaeology, University of London, "Occasional Papers," No. 7.)

KNIFFEN, F. B. 1936. *A Preliminary Report of the Mounds and Middens of Plaquemines and St. Bernard Parishes, Lower Mississippi River Delta*, pp. 407–22. (Louisiana Department of Conservation Geological Bull. 8.)

KNOX, A. S. 1940. "The Peat Deposits of Bermuda and Evidences of Postglacial Changes in Sea-Level," *Journal of Geology*, XLVIII, 767–80.

——. 1942. "The Pollen Analysis of the Silt and the Tentative Dating of the [Boylston Street Fishweir] Deposits." In JOHNSON, F., *et al.*, 1942, pp. 96–129.

KOENIGSBERGER, J. 1933. "Zu der Bestimmung des magnetischen Erdfeldes in früherer Zeit aus der Magnetisierung von gebrannten Tongegenständen und von Gesteinen," *Gerlands Beiträge zur Geophysik*, XXXVIII, 47–52.

KRIEGER, A. D. 1946. *Culture Complexes and Chronology in Northern Texas with Extension of Puebloan Datings to the Mississippi Valley.* ("University of Texas Publications," No. 4640.)

KROEBER, A. L. 1948. *Anthropology.* Rev. ed. New York: Harcourt, Brace & Co.

KRYNINE, P. D. 1939. "Petrology of the Karewa Lake Beds." In TERRA, H. DE, and PATERSON, T. T. 1939, pp. 235–51.

KUBLER, G. 1948. *Towards Absolute Time: Guano Archaeology*, pp. 29–50. ("Memoirs of the Society for American Archaeology," No. 4.)

KUENEN, P. H. 1946. "Rate and Mass of Deep-Sea Sedimentation," *American Journal of Science*, CCXLIV, 563–72.

LAÏS, R. 1941. "Ueber Hohlensedimente," *Quartär*, III, 56–108.

LANDSBERG, H. 1949. "Climatology of the Pleistocene," *Bulletin of the Geological Society of America*, LX, 1437–42.

LAUDERMILK, J. D. 1931. "On the Origin of Desert Varnish," *American Journal of Science*, CCXXI, 51–66.

LAWRENCE, D. B. 1946. "The Technique of Dating Recent Prehistoric Glacial Fluctuations from Tree Data," *Mazama*, XXVIII, 57–59.

——. 1950. "Estimating Dates of Recent Glacier Advances and Recession Rates by Studying Tree Growth Layers," *Transactions of the American Geophysical Union*, XXXI, 243–48.

LEIGHTON, M. M. 1934. "Some Observations on the Antiquity of Man in Illinois," *Transactions of the Illinois Academy of Science,* XXV, 83.

——. 1936. *Geological Aspects of the Findings of Primitive Man, near Abilene, Texas.* ("Gila Pueblo Medallion Papers," No. 24.)

——. 1937. "The Significance of Profiles of Weathering in Stratigraphic Archaeology." In MacCurdy, G. G. (ed.), *Early Man,* pp. 163–72.

Leonard, A. B. 1947. "Yarmouthian Molluscan Fauna of the Great Plains and the Missouri Valley Pleistocene," *Bulletin of the Geological Society of America,* LVIII, 1202.

Leverett, F. 1930. "Relative Length of Pleistocene Glacial and Interglacial Stages," *Science,* LXXII, 193–95.

Li, Lien-Chieh. 1943. "Rate of Soil Development as Indicated by Profile Studies in Indian Mounds. Thesis abstract, University of Illinois.

Libby, W. F. 1951. "Radiocarbon Dates. II," *Science,* CXIV, 291–96.

——. 1952. *Radiocarbon Dating.* Chicago: University of Chicago Press.

Libby, W. F.; Anderson, E. C.; and Arnold, J. R. 1949. "Age Determinations by Radiocarbon Content: World-wide Assay of Natural Radiocarbon," *Science,* CIX, 227–28.

Lidén, R. 1913. "Geokronologiska Studier öfver det Finiglaciala Skedet i Angermland," *Sver. geol. unders. Stockholm,* IX, 1–39.

——. 1938. "The Late Quaternary Strandline Changes and Chronology in Angermanland." *Geol. Fören. i Stockholm Förh.,* LX, 397–404.

Linder, D. H. 1942. "The Diatoms [from the Boylston Street Fishweir Deposits]." In Johnson, F., *et al.,* 1942, pp. 67–81.

Lloyd, S. 1949. *Foundations in the Dust.* London: Oxford University Press.

Lothrop, S. K. 1928. *The Indians of Tierra del Fuego.* ("Contributions of the Heye Foundation, Museum of the American Indian," No. 10.)

Loud, L. L., and Harrington, M. R. 1929. *Lovelock Cave,* pp. 1–183. ("University of California Publications in American Anthropology and Ethnology," Vol. XXV.)

Louis, M. 1945. "Pédologie et préhistoire," *Bulletin de la Société préhistorique de France,* XLII, 213–16.

Lynton, E. D. 1937. "Laboratory Orientation of Drill Cores by Their Magnetic Polarity," *Bulletin of the American Association of Petroleum Geologists,* XXI, 580–615.

McGregor, J. C. 1936a. "Dating the Eruption of Sunset Crater, Arizona," *American Antiquity,* II, 15–26.

——. 1936b. *Culture of Sites Which Were Occupied Shortly before the Eruption of Sunset Crater.* (Museum of Northern Arizona Bull. 9.)

McNish, A. G. 1941. "The Significance of Fossil Magnetization," *Proceedings of the American Philosophical Society,* LXXXIV, 225–37.

McNish, A. G., and Johnson, E. A. 1938a. "Preliminary Report on Measurement of Magnetization of Oceanic Sediments," *Transactions of the American Geophysical Union,* p. 206.

——. 1938b. "Magnetization of Sediments from the Bottom of the Atlantic Ocean," *ibid.,* pp. 204–5.

——. 1940. *Determination of the Secular Variation in Declination in New England from Magnetic Polarization of Glacial Varves,* pp. 339–47. (International Union of Geodesy and Geophysics, Association of Terrestrial Magnetism and Electricity, Bull. 11.)

Mangelsdorf, P. C., and Smith, C. E., Jr. 1949. "New Archaeological Evidence on Evolution in Maize," *Botanical Museum Leaflets, Harvard University,* XIII, 213–47.

Manley, H. 1949. "Palaeomagnetism," *Science News,* XII, 44–64.

Mathiessen, T. 1927. "Archaeology of the Central Eskimos," *Report of the Fifth Thule Expedition, 1921–24,* Vol. IV, Part I.

Matthes, F. E. 1930. *Geologic History of the Yosemite Valley.* (U. S. Geological Survey Prof. Paper No. 160.)

Matthes, G. H. 1951. "Paradoxes of the Mississippi," *Scientific American,* CLXXXIV, 19–23.

Mercanton, P. L. 1902a. "Aimantation des poteries lacustres," *Archives des sci-*

ences physiques et naturelles, Per. 4, XIV, 84–85.

———. 1902b. "Étude des propriétés magnétiques des poteries lacustres," *Bull. Soc. sci. nat.*, XXXVIII, 346–55.

———. 1907. "La Méthode de Folgheraiter et son rôle en géophysique," *Archives des sciences physiques et naturelles*, Per. 4, XXIII, 467–82.

———. 1910a. "Stabilité d'aimantation des poteries lacustres," *Bull. Soc. Vaudoise Sci. Nat.*, Ser. 5, XLVI, lxx.

———. 1910b. "Aimantation des poteries lacustres," *ibid.*, pp. xiv–xv.

———. 1918. "État magnétique de terres cuites préhistoriques," *ibid.*, LII, 9–15.

———. 1923. "Encore l'aimantation des terres cuites et la méthode de Folgheraiter," *Archives des sciences physiques et naturelles*, Per. 5, V, 438–41.

———. 1926. "Inversion de l'inclinaison magnétique terrestre aux âges géologiques," *ibid.*, VIII, 345–49.

MERRILL, R. S. 1948. "A Progress Report on the Dating of Archaeological Sites by Means of Radioactive Elements," *American Antiquity*, XIII, 281–86.

MIDDLETON, J. 1844. "On Fluorine in Bones, Its Source and Its Application to the Determination of the Geological Age of Fossil Bones," *Proceedings of the Geological Society of London*, IV, 431–33.

MITCHELL, G. F. 1945. "The Relative Ages of Archaeological Objects Recently Found in Bogs in Ireland," *Proceedings of the Royal Irish Academy*, Vol. L, Sec. C, No. 1, pp. 1–19.

MORRISON, J. P. E. 1942. *Preliminary Report on Mollusks Found in the Shell Mounds of the Pickwick Landing Basin in the Tennessee River Valley*, pp. 341–92. (Bureau of American Ethnology Bull. 129.)

MORSE, E. S. 1925. "Shell-Mounds and Changes in the Shells Composing Them," *Scientific Monthly*, XXI, 429–40.

MOSS, J. H. 1951. *Early Man in the Eden Valley*. ("University of Pennsylvania Museum, Museum Monographs.")

MOVIUS, H. L., JR. 1942. *The Irish Stone Age*. Cambridge: At the University Press.

———. 1949a. "The Lower Paleolithic Cultures of Southern and Eastern Asia." *Transactions of the American Philosophical Society*, n.s., Vol. XXXVIII, Part IV.

———. 1949b. "Old World Paleolithic Archaeology," *Bulletin of the Geological Society of America*, LX, 1443–56.

———. 1950. *Excavations at the Prehistoric Rock-Shelter of La Colombière*, pp. 359–68. ("Smithsonian Institution of Washington Annual Reports," 1949.)

NELSON, N. C. 1909. *Shellmounds of the San Francisco Bay Region*, pp. 309–48. ("University of California Publications in American Anthropology and Ethnology," Vol. VII.)

NIKIFOROFF, C. C. 1942. "Fundamental Formula of Soil Formation," *American Journal of Science*, CCXL, 847–66.

NILSSON, T. 1935. "Die pollenanalytische Zonengliederung der spät- und postglazialen Bildungen Schonens," *Geol. Fören. i Stockholm Förh.*, LVII, 385–562.

———. 1948a. *On the Application of the Scanian Post-glacial Zone System to Danish Pollen-Diagrams*. ("K. Danske Vid. Selsk., Copenhagen, Biol.," Vol. V, No. 5.)

———. 1948b. *Versuch einer Anknüpfung der postglazialen Entwicklung des nordwestdeutschen Flachlandes an die pollenfloristiche Zonengliederung Südskandinaviens*. ("K. Fysiogr. Sällsk. Handl.," Vol. LIX, No. 7.)

OAKLEY, K. P. 1950. "The Fluorine-dating Method," *Yearbook of Physical Anthropology*, V (1949), 44–52. New York: Viking Fund.

OBERMAIER, H. 1924. *Fossil Man in Spain*. London.

OSBORNE, D. 1943. "Physiography and Some Archaeologic Implications in the Kentucky Basin," *American Antiquity*, IX, 180–89.

OVEY, D. D. 1951. "Preliminary Results from the Study of an Ocean Core Obtained by the Swedish Deep Sea Expedition, 1947–48," *Journal of Glaciology*, I, 370–73.

PAINE, G. 1937. "Fossilization of Bone, *American Journal of Science*, CCXXXIV, 148–57.

PATRICK, R. 1938. "Diatom Evidence from the Mammoth Pit (Clovis)," *Proceed-*

ings of the Philadelphia Academy of Natural Science, XC, 15–24.

PETTERSSON, H. 1950. "Exploring the Ocean Floor," *Scientific American*, CLXXXIII, 42–44.

PHILLIPS, P.; FORD, J. A.; and GRIFFIN, J. B. 1951. *Archaeological Survey in the Lower Mississippi Alluvial Valley, 1940–1947.* ("Papers of the Peabody Museum," Vol. XXV.)

PHLEGER, F. B., JR. 1948. *Foraminifera of a Submarine Core from the Caribbean Sea*, pp. 1–9. ("Oceanogr. Institutet i Göteborg, Med.," No. 16.)

———. 1949a. "The Foraminifera." In JOHNSON, F., *et al.* (eds.), 1949, pp. 99–108.

———. 1949b. "Submarine Geology and Pleistocene Research." *Bulletin of the Geological Society of America*, LX, 1457–62.

PHLEGER, F. B., JR., and PETTERSSON, H. 1947. *Foraminifera of Three Submarine Cores from the Tyrrhenian Sea.* (Göteborgs Kungl. Vetensk. ock Vitterhets-Samhälles Handl., Sjätte Folden, Ser. B, Vol. V, No. 5.)

PIGGOT, C. S., and URRY, W. D. 1942. "Time Relations in Ocean Sediments," *Bulletin of the Geological Society of America*, LIII, 1187–1210.

PIGGOTT, S. 1949. "Archaeology and Pedology in Holland," *Archaeology News Letter*, II, No. 6, 94–95.

PUMPELLY, R. 1908. *Explorations in Turkestan.* 2 vols. ("Carnegie Institution of Washington Publications," No. 73.)

RAY, L. R. 1949. "Problems of Pleistocene Stratigraphy," *Bulletin of the Geological Society of America*, LX, 1463–74.

RAYMOND, P. 1904. "La Poterie néolithique et les déviations de l'aiguille aimantée," *Bulletin de la Société préhistorique de France*, I, 204–6.

———. 1910. "La Poterie préhistorique et les déviations de l'aiguille aimantée," *ibid.*, VII, 565–66.

REEDS, C. A. 1929. "Weather and Glaciation," *Bulletin of the Geological Society of America*, XL, 597–630.

RENAUD, E. B. 1936. *The Archaeological Survey of the High Western Plains, Eighth Report.* University of Denver.

RICHARDS, H. G. 1936. "Mollusks Associated with Early Man in the Southwest," *American Naturalist*, LXX, 369–71.

———. 1937. "Marine Pleistocene Mollusks as Indicators of Time and Ecological Conditions." In MACCURDY, G. G. (ed.), *Early Man*, pp. 75–84.

RIETH, A. 1938. "Vorgeschichtliche Funde aus dem Kalktuff der schwäbischen Alb und des württembergischen Muschelkalkgebiets," *Mannus*, II, 562–84.

RITTMANN, A. 1933. Die geologisch bedingte Evolution und Differentiation des Somma-Vesuvmagmas," *Zeitschrift für Vulkanologie*, XV, 8–94.

ROGERS, A. F. 1924. "Mineralogy and Petrology of Fossil Bone," *Bulletin of the Geological Society of America*, XXXV, 535–56.

ROGERS, M. J. 1939. *Early Lithic Industries of the Lower Basin of the Colorado River and Adjacent Desert Areas.* ("San Diego Museum Papers," No. 3.)

ROMER, A. S. 1933. "Pleistocene Vertebrates and Their Bearing on the Problem of the Antiquity of Man in North America." In JENNESS, D., (ed.), *The American Aborigines*, pp. 49–81. Toronto.

ROUSE, I. 1951. *A Survey of Indian River Archaeology, Florida.* ("Yale University Publications in Anthropology," No. 44.)

SALMI, M. 1941. "Die Postglazialen Eruptionsschichten Patagoniens und Feuerlands," *Ann. Acad. Sci. Fennicae*, Ser. A., No. 3. Helsinki.

SAURAMO, M. 1923. "Studies on the Quaternary Varve Sediments in Southern Finland," *Bull. comm. géol. Finlande*, Vol. LX. Helsinki.

SAYLES, R. W. 1931. "Bermuda during the Ice Age," *Proceedings of the American Academy of Arts and Sciences*, LXVI, 382–467.

———. 1937. Post-glacial Consequent Streams in Maine," *Science*, LXXXVII 189.

SCHAEFFER, C. F. A. 1948. *Stratigraphie comparée et chronologie de l'Asie Occidentale.* London: Oxford University Press.

SCHENCK, W. E. 1926. *The Emeryville Shellmound: Final Report*, pp. 147–282. ("University of California Publications in American Archaeology and Ethnology," Vol. XXIII.)

SCHLUNDT, H., and MOORE, R. B. 1909. "Radioactivity of the Thermal Waters of Yellowstone National Park." (U. S. Geological Survey Bull. 395.)

SCHMIDT, H. 1909. "The Archaeological Excavations in Anau and Old Merv." In PUMPELLY, R., 1908, I, 83–212.

SCHNEIDER, J. M. 1945. "Meterologisches zu Weltens Faulenseesediment und swedisch-finnischen Warwen," *Verhandl. Schweiz. Naturforsch. Gesellsch.,* CXV, 125–26.

SCHOFIELD, J. F. 1932. "Weathering of Granite in Relation to the Age of the Bushman Paintings," *South African Journal of Science,* XIX, 770–71.

SCHULTZ, C. B., and EISELEY, L. C. 1936. "An Added Note on the Scottsbluff Quarry," *American Anthropologist,* XXVIII, 321–24.

SCHULTZ, C. B., and FRANKFORTER, W. D. 1948. *Preliminary Report on the Lime Creek Sites.* (Bulletin of the University of Nebraska State Museum, Vol. III, No. 4, Part 2.)

SCHULTZ, C. B.; LUENINGHOENER, G. C.; and FRANKFORTER, W. D. 1951. *A Graphic Résumé of the Pleistocene of Nebraska.* (Bulletin of the University of Nebraska State Museum, Vol. III, No. 6.)

SCOTT, W. B. 1937. *A History of Land Mammals in the Western Hemisphere.* Rev. ed. New York.

SEARS, P. B. 1937. "Pollen Analysis as an Aid in Dating Cultural Deposits in the United States." In MACCURDY, G. G. (ed.), *Early Man,* pp. 61–66.

———. 1942. "Xerothermic Theory," *Botanical Review,* VI, 708–36.

———. 1948. "Forest Sequence and Climatic Change in Northeastern North America since Early Wisconsin Time," *Ecology,* XXIX, 326–34.

———. 1950. "Pollen Analyses in Old and New Mexico," *Bulletin of the Geological Society of America,* LXI, 1171.

SELLARDS, E. H. 1940. "Early Man in America: Index to Localities and Selected Bibliography," *Bulletin of the Geological Society of America,* LI, 373–432.

———. 1947. "Early Man in America: Index to Localities and Selected Bibliography," *ibid.,* LVIII, 955–77.

SERVICE, E. 1941. *Lithic Patina as an Age Criterion,* pp. 553–57. ("Papers of the Michigan Academy of Science," Vol. XXVII, Part 4.)

SINIAGUIN, I. I. 1943. "A Method for Determining the Absolute Age of Soils," *Compt. rend. Acad. Sci. U.S.S.R.,* XL, 335–36.

SOERGEL, W. 1926. "Excursion ins Travertingebiet von Ehringsdorf," *Palaeontologische Zeitschrift,* VIII, 7–33.

SOKOLOFF, V. P. 1952. "Geochemical Dating," *American Antiquity,* XVII, 280–81.

SPENCER, J. W. 1917. "Origin and Age of the Ontario Shoreline," *American Journal of Science,* XLIII, 351–62.

STARMANS, G. A. N. 1947. "A Possible Method of Time Determination," *South African Science,* I, 100–103.

STETSON, H. C., and PARKER, F. L. 1942. "Mechanical Analysis of the Sediments and the Identification of the Foraminifera from the Building Excavation." In JOHNSON, F., *et al.,* 1942, pp. 41–44.

STOCK, C. 1936. "The Succession of Mammalian Forms within the Period in Which Human Remains Are Known to Occur in America," *American Naturalist,* LXX, 324–31.

STORIE, R. E., and HARRADINE, F. 1950. *An Age Estimate of the Burials Unearthed near Concord, California, Based on Pedologic Observations,* pp. 15–19. ("University of California Archaeological Survey Reports," No. 9; Paper No. 7, App. 1.)

STRONG, W. D. 1935. *An Introduction to Nebraska Archaeology.* ("Smithsonian Institution Miscellaneous Collections," Vol. XCIII, No. 10.)

SWINNERTON, A. C. 1925. "A Method of Estimating Postglacial Time," *Science,* LXII, 566.

TERRA, H. DE. 1946. "New Evidence for the Antiquity of Early Man in Mexico," *Revista mexicana de estudios antropologicos,* VIII, 69–88.

TERRA, H. DE, and PATERSON, T. T. 1939. *Studies on the Ice Age in India and*

Associated Human Cultures. ("Carnegie Institution of Washington Publications," No. 493.)

TERRA, H. DE; ROMERO, J.; and STEWART, T. D. 1949. *Tepexpan Man.* ("Viking Fund Publications in Anthropology," No. 11.)

THELLIER, E. 1940. "Sur l'aimantation permanente de quelques échantillons de laves mexicaines," *Compt. rend. Acad. Sci.,* CCXI, 110–12.

———. 1951. "Sur la direction du champ magnétique terrestre, retrouvée sur des parois de fours des époques punique et romaine, à Carthage," *ibid.,* CCXXXIII, 1476–78.

THORARINSSON, S. 1944. "Tefrokronologiska studier på Island," *Medd. f. Stockholms Högskol. Geol. Inst.,* No. 62.

THORNBURY, W. D. 1940. "Weathered Zones and Glacial Chronology in Southern Indiana," *Journal of Geology,* XLVIII, 449–75.

THORP, J. 1949. "Interrelations of Pleistocene Geology and Soil Science," *Bulletin of the Geological Society of America,* LX, 1517–26.

THUNBERG, T. 1947. "The Citric Acid Content of Older, Especially Medieval and Prehistoric Bone Material," *Acta physiol. Scandinav.,* Vol. XIV, Fasc. 3.

UREY, H. C.; LOWENSTAM, H. A.; EPSTEIN, S.; and McKINNEY, C. R. 1951. "Measurement of Paleotemperatures and Temperatures of the Upper Cretaceous of England, Denmark, and the Southeastern United States," *Bulletin of the Geological Society of America,* LXII, 399–416.

URRY, W. D. 1948a. "Marine Sediments and Pleistocene Chronology," *Transactions of the New York Academy of Science,* X, 63–67.

———. 1948b. "The Radium Content of Varved Clay and a Possible Age of the Hartford, Connecticut, Deposits," *American Journal of Science,* CCXLVI, 689–700.

VAILLANT, G. C. 1935. *Excavations at El Arbolillo.* ("American Museum of Natural History Anthropological Papers," No. 35, Part 2.)

VAN WINKLE, W. 1914. *Quality of the surface waters of Oregon.* (U.S. Geological Survey Water Supply Paper No. 363.)

VAUFREY, R. 1949. "L'Étude des sédiments des grottes," *Anthropologie,* LIII, 159–67.

VIERKE, M. 1937. "Die Ostpommerschen Bändertone als Zeitmarken und Klimazeugen," *Abhandl. Geol.-palaeont. Inst. Greifswald,* Vol. XVIII.

VINTON, K. W. 1951. "Unusual Petrification in Tropical Panama," *Scientific Monthly,* LXXII, 397–400.

VIRÉ, A. 1909. "Notes sur la poterie larnaudienne de Baume-les-Messieurs (Jura)," *Bulletin de la Société préhistorique de France,* VI, 145–51.

WELTEN, M. 1944. *Pollenanalytische stratigraphische und geochronologische Untersuchungen aus dem Faulenseemoos bei Spiez.* ("Veröffentl. d. Geobot. Inst. Rübel in Zürich," Vol. XXI.)

WILLIAMS, H. 1942. *Geology of Crater Lake National Park, Oregon,* pp. 1–157. ("Carnegie Institution of Washington Publications," No. 540.)

WILSON, L. R. 1949. "A Microfossil Analysis of the Lower Peat and Associated Sediments at the John Hancock Fishweir Site." In JOHNSON, F., *et al.* (eds.), 1949, pp. 84–98.

WOOLLEY, L. 1947. *Digging Up the Past.* ("Pelican Books.")

WRIGHT, G. F. 1912. "Postglacial Erosion and Oxidation," *Bulletin of the Geological Society of America,* XXIII, 277–96.

ZEUNER, F. E. 1945. "The Pleistocene Period: Its Climate, Chronology and Faunal Successions," *Proceedings of the Royal Society of London.*

———. 1950. *Dating the Past: An Introduction to Geochronology.* Rev. ed. London: Methuen.

Dating Fossil Human Remains

By KENNETH P. OAKLEY

THE PLACING of fossil human remains in their correct time relations is fundamental to an understanding of their significance. In order to clarify the problems involved, it seems desirable to distinguish between the various types of dating. To recognize only two categories, "relative" and "absolute," is to obscure certain important issues. One may take as an illustration of the complexity of a dating problem the question of the antiquity of the Keilor skull, which was found in a river-terrace deposit at Melbourne, Australia. Its age has been provisionally estimated by Zeuner as 150,000 years. It is worth while to consider the assumptions that this estimate involves. First and foremost, it assumes that the skull is contemporary with the containing deposit; further, that there has been no post-Pleistocene warping of the coastal zone of southeastern Australia; and that it is therefore legitimate to correlate the Keilor terrace, on the basis of altitude alone, with the Main Monastirian beach of the Mediterranean: that this marks the high sea-level of the third interglacial; and, finally, that the astronomical theory of glacial oscillations (and, in particular, the Milankovitch curve) is correct. In fact, each of these assumptions is regarded as questionable by one authority or another.

It is suggested that the following types of dating should be distinguished:

RELATIVE DATINGS

R.1.—The age relation between the specimen and its containing deposit or associated fossils.

R.2.—The stage in the local or regional stratigraphical sequence to which the containing deposit (or fauna or culture undoubtedly contemporary with the specimen) can be referred.

R.3.—The inferred position of that stage in terms of world stratigraphy.

R.4.—The geological or archeological age of a specimen inferred from its morphology in the absence of reliable evidence of its association.

ABSOLUTE DATINGS

A.1.—Direct determination of the age of a specimen itself from internal evidence (e.g., C^{14} radioactivity of charred bone).

A.2.—Direct determination of the age of the source deposit from internal evidence (e.g., C^{14} radioactivity of charcoal or shells in the bed).

A.3.—Age in years inferred by correlation of the source bed (or its "horizon") with a deposit whose actual age is known.

A.4.—Age in years inferred from theoretical considerations (e.g., dates obtained by matching the geological record of glacial fluctuations with the curve of past insolation as calculated by Milankovitch or Spitaler).

It is perhaps useful to consider some examples of these various types of dating, and the methods by which they are established.

43

DATINGS OF FOSSIL MEN

The establishment of the "R.1 age" of a specimen, particularly part of a human skeleton (for there is always the possibility of its having been interred), is fundamental to consideration of its R.2, and therefore indirectly its R.3, A.2, A.3, or A.4 age. When the R.1 age of a bone or tooth is in doubt, it can sometimes be determined by the "fluorine test," as in the case of the Galley Hill, Swanscombe, and Piltdown specimens.

Comparison of its fluorine content with that of nearly associated fossil animal bones showed that the Galley Hill skeleton was not contemporary with the Middle Pleistocene gravel terrace in which it lay but was an interment of considerably later date (for details see below, under "Methods of Relative Dating"). Applying the suggested terminology, the "R.1 age" of the skeleton proved to be "post–Middle Pleistocene." To obtain some idea of how much later it was than the containing deposit, its fluorine content was compared with that of specimens from later deposits in the same region whose R.2 or R.3 ages were already known. This comparison made it possible to assess the R.3 age of the Galley Hill skeleton as "late Pleistocene to mid-Holocene." If specimens with well-established R.2 dates within this time range had been available in the same locality for comparison, the R.2 (or R.3) age of the skeleton could have been refined sufficiently to enable one to ascribe an A.3 date to it.

The same test applied to the Swanscombe skull confirmed its R.1 age. It is beyond all doubt contemporary with the Middle Gravel of the Thames 100-foot terrace in which it lay and therefore with the associated Acheulean hand-ax industry and Middle Pleistocene fauna. Recent studies of the small mammals represented in the Swanscombe Middle Gravels suggest that this deposit could be equivalent to the Early or Middle Drenthian stage of the Netherlands sequence. The Upper Drenthian stage is equivalent to the maximum Riss, or Riss II glaciation. However, in general terms, the Swanscombe skull certainly belongs to the end of the Great Interglacial period (i.e., this is its R.3 age). The bulk of the associated fauna, which includes *Elephas antiquus, Elephas* cf. *primigenius, Dama clactoniana, Rhinoceros merckii (megarhinus), Bison,* and *Equus,* indicates that woodlands and grasslands bordered the Thames during the time that Swanscombe man was living there and that conditions were temperate. But the presence in these gravels also of lemming (unknown in earlier fully interglacial beds) suggests that there may already have been some recrudescence of glacial conditions elsewhere and that this was causing a southward spread of animals adapted to cold. It has to be borne in mind, however, that the present restriction of genera such as *Lemmus* to a narrow biota may have been the outcome of competition in late Pleistocene or postglacial times and that in Middle Pleistocene times their range of tolerance may have been considerably wider. Nevertheless, the possibility remains that, in terms of the Alpine chronology, the R.3 age of the Swanscombe skull is closer to Riss I than has generally been assumed. Owing to its position, Britain may have been dominated by Atlantic weather during the weak Riss I glaciation, in which event the great interglacial would not have been effectively terminated until the Riss II glaciation.

A.1 and A.2 dates are unobtainable in the case of specimens whose age is at present beyond the range of the radiocarbon method (35,000 years). According to Zeuner's application of the Milankovitch curve to the glacial succession, the antiquity of the Swanscombe skull is about 250,000 years. This date is arrived at on the assumption that the skull antedates the Riss I phase. If it is contemporary with the Riss I phase, its A.4 age would be reduced on Zeuner's reading to about 200,000 years. This type of A.4 dating is not very satisfying, because the astronomical data can be interpreted in more than one way. Thus, if Spitaler's insolation curve of 1939 is substituted for that of Milankovitch, the A.4 age of the Swanscombe skull would be increased to 600,000 years. It is, however, highly significant that none of the estimates of the time that has elapsed since the maximum Riss glaciation is less than 100,000, and, until an A.3 date can be quoted, it seems best to state the A.4 age of the Swanscombe skull as "more than 100,000 years."

The value of the "fluorine test" for the establishment of the R.1 age of fossil human remains and the relative values of faunal and archeological evidence for establishing their R.1–R.2 dating are well illustrated by recent work on the material from Fontéchevade. At this site in the Charente, western France, two calottes indistinguishable in form from the corresponding parts of skulls of *Homo sapiens* were found in a deposit containing an interglacial fauna and a Clacton-like industry, underlying a complex of cave-earths with Mousterian and Upper Paleolithic occupation layers. The fluorine content of the skull fragments agreed with that of the associated interglacial mammalian bones and was appreciably higher than that of any of the bones which were tested from the overlying deposits. Thus the R.1 age of the skulls is assured. They are contemporary with a Clactonoid industry and an interglacial fauna. The question of their R.2 and R.3 dating is still under consideration.

The Fontéchevade industry has been described as Clactonian passing into Tayacian, and, in the opinion of Breuil (1932), the beginning of the Tayacian at the type site at La Micoque possibly dates from the end of the second interglacial period. Moreover, the greater part of the Fontéchevade industry (including the Levalloisoid cores in the upper, or skull, level) can be matched in the industry of the Clacton Elephant Bed, which, mainly on the evidence of the pollen diagram, can be confidently referred to the middle of the second interglacial period (the Needian stage of the Dutch sequence).

If one relies on the cultural evidence alone in determining their R.3 dating, one might reasonably conclude that the Fontéchevade skulls are of that age. The evidence of the associated larger vertebrates is ambiguous. The fauna includes *Rhinoceros merckii, Dama, Hyena, Cuon, Ursus, Castor,* and *Emys,* all of which have been found in second and third interglacial deposits. The fact that the Fontéchevade fauna is different from that associated with the Mousterian of Acheulean tradition in the Dordogne, assuredly third interglacial in age, has been advanced by Wiegers as an argument in favor of regarding it as second interglacial. But it is probable that the third interglacial period was long enough to have witnessed many shifts in the distribution of species; in any case, the composition of the mammalian fauna would have varied from place to place in accordance with the vegetational environment. Much more significant is the fact that in a fairly large collection of voles from the horizon of the Fontéchevade skulls the late Dr. A. Schreuder was unable to find any extinct species (in a letter to Miss D. M. A. Bate, of March 12, 1950), which one may judge to be a clear indication that the deposit is Upper Pleistocene rather than Middle Pleistocene. Dr. Schreuder pointed out that the Microtinae in the Swanscombe Middle

Gravel were in marked contrast; all those which she had examined from that site proved to be extinct species. It appears that the voles, which were abundant in older Pleistocene times, became extinct during the Riss glaciation, during or after which the modern species multiplied and spread widely. Thus on the evidence of the voles it appears difficult to avoid the conclusion that the Tayacian layer at Fontéchevade belongs to the third interglacial (Eemian stage of the Dutch sequence).

With the R.3 date of the Fontéchevade skulls reasonably assured, it should be possible to express their approximate antiquity in years as soon as the main climatic oscillations of the Pleistocene period have been dated through research which is now in progress (see below, under "Methods of Absolute Dating"). They are considerably pre-Würmian, and, since all estimates of the time which has elapsed since the Würm I glaciation exceed 25,000 years, it is reasonable to express the A.4 age of Fontéchevade man as "probably at least 50,000 years."

The hominoid material from Piltdown is still an enigma from the anatomical point of view and will probably remain so until another mandible of the same type is found in association with its cranium; but the application of the "fluorine test" (for details see below, under "Methods of Relative Dating") has led indirectly to a drastic reduction in the estimated antiquity of *Eoanthropus*, which is now considered to be comparable in age with the Fontéchevade skulls, whereas until recently it was generally considered to date from the beginning of the Pleistocene period.

It is a mistake to suppose that the fluorine content of a fossil bone provides a direct indication of its geological, or R.3, age. In the case of the Piltdown material, fluorine analysis simply showed that, in regard to their R.1 dating, the mandible and cranial fragments could not be separated; they are considerably younger than the Villafranchian (represented by derived fossils in the same bed) and are contemporaneous with the latest fossils in the gravel. That is to say, they date approximately from the time of the final settlement of the gravel bed in which they lay. Their R.2 dating can be obtained only by considering the character and situation of the deposit. It is a seam of river gravel, and from its height above the river at present it is judged to belong to the 50-foot terrace of the Sussex Ouse (Edmunds, 1950). Its R.3 dating is less certain. From the contemporaneous fossils, there is little doubt that it is interglacial; but the 50-foot terraces in the river valleys of southern Britain include deposits of second as well as third interglacial age. For example, the gravel at Grays, Essex, which yielded a tooth of *Macacus* (Montagu, 1951), is almost certainly of Great Interglacial age. However, when one considers the extremely small fluorine content of the contemporaneous fossils in the Piltdown gravel and remembers that most of the 50-foot terrace deposits were formed during the third interglacial, it appears reasonable to conclude that the *Eoanthropus* gravel was probably laid down during that period rather than during the Swanscombe interglacial.

It may well be of considerable significance that Piltdown man and Fontéchevade man appear to be approximately of the same age. This is not the place to discuss the possible significance; but it is worth noting that the only unquestionable paleolithic flint artifacts found at Piltdown may well be Tayacian. Unfortunately, none was found *in situ* with the remains of *Eoanthropus*. At Piltdown, as at Fontéchevade, there is evidence of fire in the gravel, whereas there is no such evidence in the Clacton Elephant Bed.

The revised dating of the Piltdown remains is an interesting reflection on the unreliability of subjective R.1 and R.4 dating. On the basis of their color and physical condition, Hopwood concluded that the specimens of *Eoanthropus* were contemporaneous with the derived Villafranchian fossils. On the basis of the simian morphology of the mandible, *Eoanthropus* has been regarded as Lower Pleistocene by almost all authorities who have attempted to place it stratigraphically.

Before the fluorine test had been applied, some authors felt free to place the mandible with the Villafranchian group of fossils and to regard the cranial bones as Upper Pleistocene or even postglacial. After the publication of the results of the fluorine test, Marston suggested that, if the findings were interpreted on the basis of the data obtained at Swanscombe (more than 30 miles to the north), one might conclude that "*Eoanthropus*" was no older than the Galley Hill skeleton. But this is to misunderstand the method. To assess the R.2 age of a specimen, one first makes a comparison between its fluorine content and that of specimens in the same bed or at the same locality whose R.2–R.3 ages are known. When this was done for the Piltdown material, it was found that the specimens of *Eoanthropus* were certainly not Villafranchian but that, judging on this basis alone, they could belong either to the youngest group of Pleistocene fossils in the bed or to the Holocene group. Since the mandible, canine, and part of the occiput were found *in situ* at the base of the gravel in association with remains of beaver, which showed the same low fluorine content, there can be no reason to doubt that *Eoanthropus* is Pleistocene. The presence of beaver in the gravel is proof that it was laid down by the river. The Ouse has not flowed at this level, 50 feet above its present bed, since early Upper Pleisto-cene times; so that the minimum age of *Eoanthropus* is assured on that score alone. Fluorine has evidently been less abundant in the ground water at Piltdown than at Swanscombe, or at any rate it has been less available (perhaps through an inhibiting action of peat or iron) since Lower Pleistocene, possibly since Middle Pleistocene times. This fact, however, does not invalidate the primary interpretation of the uniformly low fluorine content of all the widely scattered fragments of *Eoanthropus*. It merely makes it difficult to be sure on this evidence alone whether *Eoanthropus* is Middle Pleistocene or early Upper Pleistocene. The balance of the evidence indicates the latter age (the Upper Pleistocene is now generally taken as beginning with the third interglacial).

The A.4 dating of "Piltdown man" has always had a strong popular appeal. Before the application of the fluorine test, estimates varied from 200,000 (Keith, 1925) to 1 million years (Osborn, 1928); subsequently they have varied from 10,000 (Anon., 1951, p. 90) to 100,000 years (Oakley, 1949). It would be wiser to refrain altogether from such estimates in view of the uncertainties involved; but, if a figure must be quoted, it might well take the form of the provisional A.4 dating of Fontéchevade man: "probably at least 50,000 years."

Morphological or R.4 dating is usually quite untrustworthy in the case of Hominoidea, but there are a few examples of almost unquestionable validity. For example, no one would seriously doubt the "Mousterian age" of the Neanderthal skull found at Gibraltar in 1848, although its stratigraphic position and associations are unknown. Whether it is Lower or Upper Mousterian is less certain.

At one time it was believed that taurodontism was confined to the Neanderthal species. Thus two taurodont molars were found in the Ghar Dalam Cave in Malta in 1917 and were regarded by Keith as indicative of *Homo neanderthalensis*. This identification is now considered doubtful. No trace of paleolithic culture has ever been found in Malta. Moreover, according to the published record of the discovery, one of the teeth was associated with Neolithic artifacts. In view of the fact that taurodontism has recently been found in predynastic Egyptians and in the Chalcolithic and later inhabitants of Anatolia (Senyürek, 1949), it appears possible that the Ghar Dalam teeth are post-Pleistocene. An attempt is at present being made to establish their R.1 dating by means of fluorine analysis.

R.1 dating is, of course, of paramount importance where human remains indistinguishable from *Homo sapiens* are found in deposits of early paleolithic age. Among Dr. Leakey's discoveries in East Africa, the Kanam mandible, found with Oldowan pebble tools in a Lower Pleistocene (Kageran) lake bed, and the Kanjera skulls, found with Chelleo-Acheulean tools in a Middle Pleistocene (Kamasian) deposit in the same region, are outstanding examples of such specimens, whose importance depends almost entirely on the confirmation of the R.1 dating which has been claimed for them. Unfortunately, the fluorine test proved to be inapplicable in these particular cases, owing to the extensive alteration which bones at these sites have undergone. In tropical weathering conditions, particularly in volcanic soils, bones are liable to rapid and somewhat random mineralization, with the result sometimes that so much of the original calcium phosphate is replaced by calcium carbonate or silica that the fluorine content bears little or no relation to their antiquity. The following is a partial analysis of the Kanam mandible: $CaCO_3$, 84 per cent; P_2O_5, 4.6 per cent;

F, 1.4 per cent; SiO_2, 2.4 per cent. The percentage fluorine/phosphate ratio (30) is higher than in any other fossil bone which has been analyzed. The composition of an Upper Pleistocene bone from the same region is in striking contrast: $CaCO_3 < 20$ per cent; P_2O_5, 30.5 per cent; F, 5.5 per cent; SiO_2, 0.3 per cent. The excessively high fluorine content of the last specimen shows that in a tropical volcanic environment it is possible for bones to become saturated with fluorine in a comparatively short time.

When the circumstances in which the Kanam jaw was found are considered in detail and in the light of an examination of the beds in the field, it is difficult to believe that the specimen was not contemporaneous with the layer from which it was obtained. The Kanam beds are horizontal and (unlike the Kanjera beds) undisturbed. It is true that there are fissures extending from the present surface almost to the level at which the jaw fragment occurred; but the specimen was not found loose in the section, it was found in an excavated mass of concretionary nodule bed; moreover, it shows a type of mineralization which is apparently peculiar to fossils from this horizon. Boswell found reason to doubt the validity of Leakey's published evidence for the Chelleo-Acheulean age of the Kanjera skulls, and, in consequence, perhaps an undue amount of doubt has fallen on the Kanam jaw. The detailed correlation of the Pleistocene sequences in East Africa and Europe is also a matter of uncertainty; but, assuming that Leakey's R.1–R.2 dating of *Homo "kanamensis"* is correct, it would be approximately contemporary with *Homo heidelbergensis*.

Spectrographic analysis of a series of fossil bones from the region of Kanam and Kanjera was recently undertaken by Dr. H. J. Walls, in the hope of finding that certain elements would prove to be characteristic of the various ages of mineralization; but the results were quite inconclusive. X-ray diffraction sometimes reveals a progressive change in the mineral composition of bones; and it is possible that this may prove a helpful means of distinguishing younger bones from older bones in the Kanam-Kanjera deposits.

It is certainly to be hoped that the R.1 dating of the Kanjera skulls will eventually be placed beyond doubt. Now that precursors of *Homo sapiens* are known from Fontéchevade and Swanscombe, there is no inherent improbability in the Kanjera skulls' being Chelleo-Acheulean. Morphologically, they are much as one might expect in that context: they are thick-walled and could well represent a prototype of the Bushmanoids. They are reminiscent of the skull found in 1863 in interglacial deposits at Olmo in Italy. Fluorine analysis has recently confirmed that the Olmo skull is contemporaneous with horse and ox found in the same layer of clay; but its R.2–R.3 dating unfortunately remains uncertain. The R.1–R.2 dating of the Quinzano skull is at present under investigation.

The fluorine test has also been applied in England to the Bury St. Edmunds, Dartford, Baker's Hole, and London (Lloyds) skulls, all of which have been claimed as early examples of *Homo sapiens.* In none of these cases, however, did the results of the test provide any support for the antiquity claimed.

Confirmation of the R.1 dating of specimens is particularly important where there is a possibility that remains of hominids of two ages have been mixed. Several fossil human femora of modern morphology have been found at the Trinil locality in Java, where the famous skullcap of *Pithecanthropus* was found in 1891. It has been suggested that, since Middle and Upper Pleistocene layers both occur at this locality,

fossils of the two ages may have become confused, and that the femora may not belong to *Pithecanthropus* (Middle Pleistocene) but to an Upper Pleistocene species of *Homo.* Bergman and Karsten have recently shown by means of the fluorine test that these specimens are all contemporary with the Middle Pleistocene fauna. Nevertheless, as at Piltdown, it would not be justifiable to assume that merely because they are of the same age they must necessarily represent a single hominid. In this case they probably do, but it appears, for instance, that two hominids were living contemporaneously at Sangiran in Lower Pleistocene times (*Meganthropus* and *Pithecanthropus robustus*). It is hoped that the relative datings of the various Java hominids and of *Gigantopithecus* will be established by fluorine analysis.

Fluorine analysis has provided support for the presumed contemporaneousness of *Telanthropus* and *Paranthropus* at Swartkrans in the Transvaal; but the use of the fluorine dating method in deposits indurated by travertine requires further investigation. It has been found that bones in calcreted layers contain considerably less fluorine than those in the uncemented deposits of the same age.

Although it is the R.1 dating of human remains that is most often in doubt, there are few cases where the R.1 dating is undoubted, while the R.2 or the R.3 dating is uncertain. The most noteworthy example is the skull represented by a mandible and maxillary fragment found in consolidated dune sand at Rabat in Morocco. In view of its Neanderthaloid character and fossilized condition, there is no reason to doubt its contemporaneousness with the deposit in which it lay; but geologists differ in their opinion as to whether the dune sand in which it occurred was accumulated during the recession of the Milazzian sea, in which case

Rabat man would be approximately contemporary with Heidelberg man, or during the recession of the Tyrrhenian Sea, in which case he would have been more nearly contemporary with Steinheim man. Comparison of the fluorine content of the Rabat jaw with that of fossil bones from the various groups of dune deposits in Morocco might help to throw light on this problem.

In concluding this review of the datings of fossil men, it cannot be emphasized too strongly that, although the fluorine method is valuable for establishing the R.1 dates of specimens found in the Pleistocene, particularly in the older Pleistocene, and occasionally in helping to decide their R.2 dating, it should never be regarded as a direct means of determining R.3 dates. That is to say, the fluorine content of a fossil bone is not *in itself* a reliable indication of its antiquity. The fluorine content of Wadjak skull No. 2 was recently measured, and Bergman and Karsten noted that it was the same as that of some Upper Pleistocene bones in England. But this fact is not very significant, because in fluorine-deficient regions bones of, for example, Pliocene age might have the same fluorine content as bones of, say, the Iron Age in regions where this element was abundant in the soil. The fluorine content of the Wadjak skulls will become significant only when the range of fluorine in the local Pleistocene and post-Pleistocene bones has been established.

METHODS OF RELATIVE DATING

The importance of developing objective methods of R.1 dating in the Pleistocene is well illustrated by the following record of an experience which Brome had while he was excavating at Gibraltar during the last century:

In the excavation of the east fissure the entire skeleton of a horse was met with, at a few feet only below the surface. In general condition the bones presented very much the same character as many of the fossil bones from a greater depth, and had been deprived of the greater part of the animal matter. At first Captain Brome thought he had come upon the remains of a fossil horse; but, to his surprise, when the foot-bones were exhumed, the shoes with which the animal had been shod were found *in situ;* and it was ascertained that the bones, much altered as they were, had belonged to a favourite Arab charger, which had been buried at the spot about twenty-five years before. The instance is a very striking one, in showing the fallacious nature of evidence derived merely from the mineral condition of buried bones when exposed to free percolation of water in a calcareous bed [George Busk, *Trans. Zoöl. Soc. London,* X (1879), 90].

Fortunately, fluorine fixation provides an objective criterion for the relative antiquity of bones in Pleistocene deposits. It has been found that buried bones and teeth absorb fluorine from the ground and that this element is fixed in their substance. Except under some extreme tropical conditions of weathering, the increase of fluorine in bones (and teeth) is gradual. Consequently, when bones of different ages occur under similar conditions at the same site, comparison of their fluorine content provides a useful means of distinguishing them and of estimating their relative antiquity. The explanation of the process of fluorine fixation generally given is as follows. Bones and teeth consist mainly of hydroxyapatite $Ca_{10}(PO_4)_2 \cdot (OH_2)$. This mineral has a strong affinity for fluorine, which in the form of fluorides occurs as a trace in the ground water of sedimentary formations and soils, usually in the proportion of about one part in a million. When fluorine ions come into contact with the mineral matter of bones and teeth, they are absorbed and locked in. In fact, they displace the hydroxyl ions in the ultra-microscopic meshwork of the component hydroxyapatite, which is thus converted, particle by particle, into fluorapatite, $Ca_{10}(PO_4)_2 \cdot F_2$. This form of apatite is more stable and is not readily dissolved; so that, unless conditions in the soil or subsoil become so acid that the whole bone or tooth is destroyed, fluorine ions which have entered their structure are not removed. Owing to the ease with which fluorine ions diffuse and owing to the porosity of bony material, the fixation is not confined to the surface of a bone but takes place uniformly throughout its substance. All types of bone, antler, and dentine are nearly equal in their capacity for absorbing fluorine, but enamel is relatively resistant to the penetration of these ions, particularly in the early stages of fossilization. The theoretical maximum fluorine content of fossil bones is 3.8 per cent. Where the element is excessively abundant, it continues to be absorbed by bones after the whole of their material has been converted into fluorapatite, probably through the partial replacement of fluorapatite by fluorite and the formation of clathrate crystals.

The fluorine-dating method has had a long history. In 1806 the French chemists Fourcroy and Vauquelin had reached the conclusion that buried ivory absorbs fluorine from the soil. In 1844 the English chemist James Middleton claimed that fossil bones contained fluorine precisely in proportion to their antiquity. However, it was obvious to geologists that this was not so, because of the large number of variables involved. But, in rejecting this as a method of absolute dating, they neglected to see its possible value in relative dating. The principle that buried bones accumulate fluorine in course of time appears to have been forgotten until it was rediscovered by the French mining engineer, Adolphe Carnot, in 1892. He showed that it was useful in establishing the relative antiquity of bones. Anthropologists were slow to appreciate

the fact, made so clear by Carnot's research, that fluorine analysis provided a valuable means, for instance, of determining whether a skull or skeleton had been intrusively buried into a Pleistocene deposit or whether it had lain there since the deposit was formed.

Only a few of Carnot's contemporaries realized the potentialities of the method. One of the few was Thomas Wilson, curator of prehistoric archeology in the United States National Museum, who had the "fluorine test" applied to the pelvic bone of the Natchez skeleton, proving that it was substantially of the same antiquity as an associated bone of the extinct *Mylodon*. The method then appears to have been forgotten until the 1940's, when an investigation of the geological factors in endemic fluorosis in England led indirectly to its rediscovery. Its application to the Galley Hill skeleton in 1948 settled half a century of controversy. It may be useful to recapitulate this particular problem and to recall in some detail how the fluorine method solved it.

In 1888 parts of a human skeleton, including a skull (indistinguishable from modern *Homo sapiens*), were found 8 feet below the surface in Middle Pleistocene gravels containing Acheulean hand-axes at Galley Hill near Swanscombe in Kent. The original excavators claimed that there was no evidence of a grave, and they concluded that the skeleton was contemporary with the gravel which contained it. This conclusion has repeatedly been disputed, but it became widely accepted after the discovery of the *sapiens*-like Swanscombe skull in 1935–36. In 1948 we decided to test it by the fluorine dating method. Five samples of the skeleton, together with more than twenty samples of bones from deposits of known ages in the Swanscombe region, were analyzed in the Department of the Government Chemist in London. The results are summarized in Table 1. It is worth emphasizing that the samples from the Middle Pleistocene gravels were chosen to represent a wide range of porosity and types of preservation. An essential basis of the method is to determine the probable range of fluctuation of fluorine content in bones of the age groups to which the doubtful specimen might belong.

TABLE 1

SERIES OF "BONE" SAMPLES FROM MIDDLE PLEISTOCENE GRAVELS AT SWANSCOMBE, KENT*

PER CENT FLUORINE	COMPARE	Per Cent Fluorine
2.0		
2.8		1.9
2.1	Swanscombe skull.........	2.0
		0.2
1.7		0.4
	Galley Hill skeleton........	0.4
1.7		0.4
2.3		0.3
2.0		
1.7	Upper Pleistocene bones (10) >0.8 Post-Pleistocene bones (5) ... <0.4	
2.2†		
2.2†		
2.3†		
2.6†		
2.3		

* *Note.*—It is now a routine procedure in fluorine dating to check the phosphate content of each sample analyzed and to use the percentage fluorine/phosphate ratio as one basis of comparison, particularly where there has been alteration or mineral contamination of the bone.

† Portions of antler, selected for variety in texture.

The application of the fluorine test to the Galley Hill skeleton illustrates the most valid use of this method: to establish the R.1 dating of a specimen which is suspected of being an intrusive burial. The results in this case left the R.2–R.3 dating uncertain. It so happened that all the "Upper Pleistocene" specimens in the control series were Middle Paleolithic, that is to say, early Upper Pleistocene. If a series of bones of *Upper* Paleolithic age had been available in this region for comparison, it might well have served to show that the Galley Hill skeleton is end-Pleistocene rather than postglacial.

The fluorine method is sometimes useful for R.1 dating of another type, where it is a question of distinguishing between fossil bones and teeth of more than one geological age which have become mixed together through natural rearrangement of the deposits, as, for example, in the fluviatile mélange at Piltdown. The Piltdown gravel contains animal remains of at least two ages: an early group, including teeth of *Elephas planifrons* and *Mastodon arvernensis* (Lower Pleistocene), and a later group, including remains of *Castor* and *Cervus elaphus,* post-Villafranchian and probably Middle or Upper Pleistocene. The question to decide was whether the bones and teeth referred to *"Eoanthropus"* belonged to the earlier or the later group. The fluorine content of all the specimens of undoubted Villafranchian age ranged from 1.9 to 3.1 per cent, whereas in the undoubtedly later specimens (representing more than one stage?) it ranged from 0.1 to 1.5 per cent. Seventeen samples of *Eoanthropus* were analyzed and showed 0.1–0.4 per cent fluorine (average, 0.2 per cent). The general significance of these results has been discussed above, but the point to emphasize here is that the test has simply succeeded in establishing the R.1 dating: *Eoanthropus* is not contemporaneous with the associated Villafranchian specimens; it is considerably later. But, as soon as an attempt is made to exact the R.2–R.3 dating of *Eoanthropus* from these results alone, the validity of any conclusion would be much more open to question. The R.2–R.3 dating has to be decided on the basis of other evidence, considered in the light of the fluorine data.

There probably are circumstances in which fluorine analysis could serve in establishing R.3 dating. Where there are several groups of bone-bearing deposits in a region, it may be possible to use it to detect and to assess the magnitude of time gaps which separate them. It is hoped that the R.3 dating of the Rabat jaw and of the Australopithecines may be established in some such way.

Owing to the variation in the abundance of this element in different environments, it is not possible to regard fluorine content as a guide to the R.3 ages of bones found at sites where there are no specimens of known ages for comparison, as the following determinations well illustrate:

	Per Cent Fluorine
Tooth, Villafranchian, Italy	1.6
Bone, *Sinanthropus* deposit, China	1.1
Bone, Eemian, Kent	1.9
Bone, Bronze Age, Essex	1.6

Nevertheless, it appears that the *average* fluorine content of Lower Pleistocene bones is *ca.* 2.0 per cent; of Middle Pleistocene bones, *ca.* 1.5 per cent; and of Upper Pleistocene bones, *ca.* 0.5 per cent.

It is not often possible to use the fluorine method for R.1 dating unless the age difference between the bones which are being differentiated is of the magnitude of a geological stage or substage (depending on the abundance of fluorine in the environment). At localities where fluorine is of only average abundance it is difficult to distinguish clearly between Neolithic and Upper Paleolithic bones because the range of fluorine in the two groups is likely to overlap. The R.1 dating of late Pleistocene and early Holocene bones is best accomplished by combining fluorine analysis with organic analysis. With experiences in mind such as Brome had at Gibraltar, archeologists have become skeptical about the validity of regarding organic content as a guide to the relative antiquity of bones; but the researches of Cook, Heizer, and Olsen are tending to show that in some circum-stances the decline of the organic fraction of bone is more regular than had been supposed. It appears that the C, H, N, and S components are lost at different rates. Van der Vlerk has shown that X-ray diffraction can also be used as a means of differentiating fossil bones of different ages and serves usefully in some cases to supplement the fluorine dating method.

The R.2 and R.3 dating of specimens is usually accomplished by correlation of the containing deposit on the evidence of associated fossils or artifacts. Paleontological and archeological methods of correlating Pleistocene deposits are considered by other authors in this Symposium (Heizer, Movius) (see above, under "Datings of Fossil Men").

METHODS OF ABSOLUTE DATING

The only known means of determining the absolute age of skeletal material from internal evidence (A.1 dating) is by measuring the radioactivity of its organic fraction. At present this is possible only in the case of charred bones, where the organic fraction is relatively large, owing to the adherent films of carbonized fat or "animal charcoal," and in any case is limited to the time range of the radiocarbon method (about 35,000 years).

The fluorine method, as we have seen, is designed for R-dating; but the question of whether it might not be used eventually for A-dating is continually being asked. Middleton in 1844 attempted to calculate the ages of various fossil bones on the basis of their fluorine content; but he made two unjustified assumptions: that the abundance of fluorine in the environment is of the same order of magnitude at all the localities from which his specimens were obtained and that the increase in fluorine content of a bone is a simple linear function of time.

The factors which determine the rate

of fluorination of bone are evidently complex and require experimental investigation. It appears that unit increases of fluorine content represent progressively longer time intervals as the saturation limit is approached. X-ray diffraction studies have indicated that in course of time the component mineral matter undergoes various progressive changes, and these almost certainly affect the rate of fluorination.

Where a sufficient number of bones from successive horizons covering an extensive part of the Pleistocene at one locality have been analyzed, it might be possible with a radiocarbon control point to convert the average fluorine percentages at each horizon into a rough time scale, but probably only after the ideal fluorination curve has been established experimentally.

It is interesting to note that in the Swanscombe region the bones from the Acheulean (Middle Pleistocene) gravels contain, on an average, twice as much fluorine as do the bones in the Upper Pleistocene group. The latter were from the Baker's Hole or Ebbsfleet series, which is certainly at least 25,000 years old, probably more than 50,000. Bearing in mind the probably diminishing rate of fluorination, one may at least conclude from these figures that the provisional A.4 dating of the Swanscombe skull as "more than 100,-000 years" is consistent with the fluorine data.

Beyond the present limits of radiocarbon there are no known radioactivity methods which provide A.1 or A.2 dating of terrestrial specimens. Only one sedimentary rock, of a very rare type, has been dated directly by the radiogenic lead method (i.e., the uranium-rich marine oil shale known as "kolm" in the Upper Cambrian of Sweden).

Igneous rocks containing uranium minerals can be dated directly by determining their content of radiogenic lead or helium. The duration of the geological periods has been estimated by plotting the ages of the few dated igneous rocks as abscissae, and the maximum world thicknesses of the sedimentary strata of each period as ordinates, and drawing a curve through the control points. The most reliable control points are based on determinations of uranium-lead, but the youngest available rocks containing adequate quantities of it are early Tertiary. Supplementary control points are provided by the igneous rocks whose ages have been calculated from radiogenic helium in their component minerals. The youngest of these are Lower Miocene magnetites in Utah (*ca.* 30 million years) and Pliocene basalts in Oregon (*ca.* 13 million years). It should be remembered that the commonly accepted durations of the Miocene, Pliocene, and Pleistocene periods (20, 15, and 1 million years, respectively) have been estimated mainly on the basis of relative maximum thicknesses of the strata.

The length of the Pleistocene has been estimated in many different ways. Most of the estimates fall between 1 million and ½ million years. Now that the Villafranchian stage has been included in the Pleistocene by international agreement, it is important to bear in mind that, judging by the thicknesses of sediment of the various stages in the Java geosyncline, for example, the Lower Pleistocene represents considerably more than half the period.

Kay and Thornbury have attempted to estimate the lengths of the interglacial phases of the Pleistocene period in North America by considering the depths to which the several boulder clays have been leached. This "leaching chronology" has been reviewed by Flint; it is now generally regarded as giving at best only a rough indication that the interglacials were of the order of tens of thousands of years.

A more reliable chronology of the Pleistocene will probably emerge during the next few years from research now being carried out on cores of sediment from the ocean floors. Wiseman and Ovey have shown recently that cores from the middle of the equatorial part of the Atlantic Ocean contain a useful record of climatic oscillations in the form of varying carbonate and foraminiferal content, reflecting changes in the temperature of the surface water. As there is evidence suggesting that the rate of sedimentation of clay in this part of the ocean is constant, there is good hope that, when satisfactory control points have been established, a graph of the variations in carbonate content will provide an absolute chronology applicable to the glacial sequence on the continents.

Urry has introduced a method of estimating directly the age of sediment in deep-sea cores, but it makes a number of assumptions. The elements ionium and uranium are continually precipitated from sea water and accumulate in the sediment, where they disintegrate radioactively in the sequence uranium 238→ionium→radium. After about ½ million years the three elements reach equilibrium. However, up to this limit, assuming that the rate of precipitation of uranium and ionium has been constant, it is possible, by determining the proportion of radium at successive levels in a core of sediment, to assess the dates of past climatic oscillations indicated in it. Thus cores collected by Piggot in the North Atlantic, from the western side of the mid-Atlantic ridge, showed four zones of glacial detritus which were dated by the Urry technique as approximately 20,000, 43,000, 50,000, and 60,000 years old. These are presumed to correspond to the four stages of the last glaciation. The same method has been applied to cores from the floor of the Ross Sea in the Antarctic. Bands of coarse glacial sediment which appeared to correspond to the third glaciation were estimated by Urry to be between 200,000 and 350,000 years old.

These methods are still in their infancy, but within the next decade we may expect to be able to give fairly reliable A.3 dates to any fossil human remains whose R.3 dates are well established.

REFERENCES AND SELECTED LITERATURE

ANON. 1951. In *Cavalcade*, Vol. XIV, No. 4.

BERGMAN, R. A. M., and KARSTEN, P. 1952. *The Fluorine Content of Pithecanthropus and Other Specimens from the Trinil Fauna.* ("Proc. Kon. Ned. Akad. Wetensch.," Ser. B., Vol. LV, No. 2.)

BREUIL, H. 1932. "Le Clactonien," *Préhistoire*, I, Fasc. 2, 125–90.

EDMUNDS, F. H. 1950. "Note on the Gravel Deposit from Which the Piltdown Skull Was Obtained," *Quarterly Journal of the Geological Society*, CVI, 133–34.

FLINT, R. F. 1947. *Glacial Geology and the Pleistocene Epoch.* New York: John Wiley & Sons, Inc.

HEIZER, R. F. 1950. *On the Methods of Chemical Analysis of Bone as an Aid to Prehistoric Culture Chronology*, pp. 10–14. ("Reports of the University of California Archaeological Survey," No. 7.)

HEIZER, R. F., and COOK, S. F. 1952. "Fluorine and Other Chemical Tests for Some North American Human and Fossil Bones," *American Journal of Physical Anthropology.* (Forthcoming.)

HOLMES, A. 1947. "The Construction of a Geological Time-Scale," *Transactions of the Geological Society of Glasgow*, XXI, Part I, 117–52.

HOOIJER, D. A. 1952. "The Geological Age of *Pithecanthropus, Meganthropus,* and *Gigantopithecus*," *American Journal of Physical Anthropology*, n.s., IX, No. 3, 265–81.

KAY, G. F. 1931. "Classification and Duration of the Pleistocene Period," *Bulletin of the Geological Society of America,* XLII, 425–66.

KEITH, A. 1925. *The Antiquity of Man.* Vol. II. 2d ed. London: Williams & Norgate, Ltd.

LEAKEY, L. S. B. 1935. *The Stone Age Races of Kenya,* esp. pp. 9–24. London: Oxford University Press.

MONTAGU, M. F. A. 1951. "The Piltdown Mandible and Cranium," *American Journal of Physical Anthropology,* n.s., IX, No. 4, 464–70.

OAKLEY, K. P. 1949. "Some Applications of the Fluorine Test," *Archaeological News Letter,* II, No. 7, 101–3.

——. 1951. "The Fluorine-dating Method," *Yearbook of Physical Anthropology* (for 1949), V, 44–52.

OAKLEY, K. P., and HOSKINS, C. R. 1950. "New Evidence on the Antiquity of Piltdown Man," *Native,* CLXV, 379–82.

——. 1951. "Application du test de la fluorine aux crânes de Fontéchevade," *Anthropologie,* LV, 239–42.

OAKLEY, K. P., and MONTAGU, M. F. A. 1949. *A Reconsideration of the Galley Hill Skeleton.* (Bulletin of the British Museum [Natural History], "Geological Series," Vol. I, No. 2.)

OLSEN, R. 1950. "The Fluorine Content of Some Miocene Horse Bones," *Science,* CXII, 620–21.

OSBORN, H. F. 1928. *Man Rises to Parnassus,* esp. p. 24. Princeton: Princeton University Press.

OVEY, C. D. 1951. "Preliminary Results from the Study of an Ocean Cave Obtained during the Swedish Deep Sea Expedition, 1947–48," *Journal of Glaciology,* I, 370–73.

SENYÜREK, M. 1949. "The Occurrence of Taurodontism in the Ancient Inhabitants of Anatolia," *Bulletin of Turk Tarih Kuruma,* No. 50, 222–27.

STEWART, T. D. 1951. "The Problem of the Earliest Claimed Representatives of *Homo sapiens,*" *Cold Spring Harbour Symposia on Quantitative Biology,* XV, 97–106.

VLERK, I. M. VAN DER. 1951. "Zeeland in het Ijstijdvak," *Kon. Ned. Akad. Wetensch.,* pp. 110–24.

WIEGERS, F. 1952. "Das geologische Alter des Schädels von Fontéchevade (Charente), *Naturwissenschaftliche Rundschau,* No. 2, pp. 61–64.

WISEMAN, J. D. H. 1950. "Dating the Changing Climate of the Past," *Times* (London), September 22, 1950. (And forthcoming scientific reports on cores obtained during the Swedish Deep Sea Expedition, 1947–48.)

ZEUNER, F. E. 1944. "*Homo sapiens* in Australia Contemporary with *Homo neanderthalensis* in Europe," *Nature,* CLIII, 622.

——. 1950. *Dating the Past.* 2d ed. London: Methuen & Co., Ltd.

The Strategy of Culture History

By IRVING ROUSE

PIONEER RESEARCH in a science like anthropology is perhaps inevitably haphazard. Subsequently, as problems are defined and techniques developed, a more rational approach becomes possible. The investigator learns to define the objectives of his research and to select the techniques which best enable him to attain those objectives. We in anthropology appear to have reached this stage of research planning with respect to the study of culture history, and therefore a review of the objectives of culture-historical research would seem to be in order.

In the Americas, at least, archeologists are coming to recognize that their studies of culture history must take into consideration the pertinent ethnological data, and vice versa. Some have argued that archeology deserves to be regarded as the central discipline for culture-historical research, since it deals with a much longer time perspective than ethnology and has developed sounder techniques for establishing chronology. However, its descriptive data are so fragmentary that it must yield to ethnology with respect to matters of content, particularly of nonmaterial culture. A co-operative approach, utilizing the special advantages of both archeology and ethnology, should yield the best results.

Linguistics and physical anthropology might also have been brought into the discussion. However, these two disciplines require somewhat different approaches—linguistics, because it concentrates upon one aspect of culture, and physical anthropology, because its subject matter is primarily noncultural. Only the archeologist and the ethnologist purport to study culture as a whole, and it is for this reason that their objectives can conveniently be discussed together.

NATURE OF OBJECTIVES

The term "objective" is used in this article to refer to the end-product of any particular segment in the procedure of culture-historical research. For example, if one makes an archeological survey of a region, locates a series of sites, and plots them on a map, then that map is the objective of the research. It is entirely possible, of course, that the research will not end with the production of the map; that, for example, the map will be used as the basis for selecting sites to excavate. Such a use, however, is considered a separate segment in the procedure, having a different objective than the original, purely geographic one.

For the sake of clarity, we assume a one-to-one relationship between any given segment of a procedure and its result or objective. This means that no segment can have more than one objective or vice versa. Classification, for example, cannot be considered an objective, because there are several different

ways of producing a classification of
such cultural phenomena as sites or
communities: by grouping them according to areas, periods, cultural characteristics, tribal organization, or genetic relationships. We regard the end-result
of each of these procedures as a separate objective.

While one may define the goal of any
particular research project in terms of
its objectives, they cannot be considered
the ultimate aim of the research. One
accomplishes a series of objectives, in
order eventually to build up a picture
of the nature and history of the culture
under study. It is this picture, or synthesis of the objectives, which is the
ultimate goal of the research.

CHOICE OF OBJECTIVES

The quality of a synthesis depends in
part upon what objectives are included.
It is therefore important for the investigator to make a good choice of objectives before he begins his research. Two
alternative approaches to this problem
have been proposed. One is to devise
a rigid, all-inclusive program of research, in which one objective follows
logically upon the previous one until
the ultimate, most important objective
is reached. The other alternative is to
consider each objective independently,
bearing in mind that some objectives
must necessarily precede others—that
pottery, for example, must be classified
before a ceramic sequence can be set
up—but nevertheless treating each objective as if it were of equal importance
for building up the culture-historical
picture. Taylor (1948, p. 153) has recently applied the first alternative to
archeology, and his "conjunctive approach" could easily be expanded to
include ethnological studies of culture
history. By contrast, Clark (1947) seems
to favor the other alternative. His is the
one adopted here. It is felt that a rigid,
all-inclusive program of the first type
would require too much time and mon-

ey to be practicable under normal circumstances. Moreover, such a program
involves questions of value—of the importance of one objective relative to the
others—on which it would be difficult,
if not impossible, to reach agreement.
Finally, the second alternative seems to
be more in accord with present and
past practices in anthropology.

In teaching a survey course on world
archeology, the writer has been impressed with the fact that the archeology of each part of the world is characterized by a different series of objectives and that the techniques used to
reach these objectives vary similarly
from area to area. In large part this is
probably due to differences in the nature of the archeological material available in the various areas. One quickly
develops an interest in chronology, for
example, when one excavates in the tells
of the Near East, with their elaborate
stratigraphy (Clark, 1947, pp. 103–5).
On the other hand, chronology assumes
less importance in an area like Polynesia, where the sites are shallow, refuse is sparse, and there seems to have
been relatively little change in culture
through time (Emory, 1943, p. 9).

Once a certain type of approach becomes established in an area, subsequent archeologists tend to adopt it
more or less automatically. It then becomes traditional, and there is resistance to the introduction of new objectives and techniques.

A third factor causing variations in
objectives and techniques is the interests of the people doing the research.
Regions like Middle America, for example, have attracted people interested
in the history of art because the remains
are aesthetically pleasing. Such people
often do not pay so much attention to
the ordinary implements found in the
sites as do, for example, Eskimo archeologists, who are largely recruited from
the ranks of ethnologists and therefore
often use ethnological techniques of

culture-historical study (cf. Morley, 1946; Birket-Smith, 1947).

Finally, archeologists are subject to the pressures of popular interest and of government policy in planning their research. The popular interest in the "Mound Builders" of midwestern United States, for example, is probably responsible for the fact that many more mounds than habitation sites have been dug in that area, if only because it has been easier to raise the money to excavate mounds (Shetrone, 1941). In Europe and Asia, where governments take more interest in archeology, research has often been planned in terms of consideration of national pride or, in the case of the dictatorships, with the purpose of demonstrating official dogma, as Clark (1947, pp. 189–214) has pointed out.

It is probable that all these factors operate to some extent in the field of ethnology as well as archeology. The writer doubts that they can ever be completely eliminated in either field. Nevertheless, one may hope that surveys like the present one will stimulate some workers to introduce into their respective areas objectives which have not yet been applied there but which appear compatible with the nature of the local data and the interests of the anthropologists concerned.

DESCRIPTIVE OBJECTIVES

It is not proposed to enter intensively into a discussion of the objectives of compiling data, since many of these are more pertinent to studies of process and to applied anthropology. Besides, the subject has received little attention in the literature, so far as the writer is aware. We shall therefore only be able to illustrate the variety of kinds of collections, records, and inferences which have been produced during the course of culture-historical research.

COLLECTIONS

Collections of artifacts are more important to the archeologist than to the ethnologist, both because more specimens can usually be obtained in sites than in modern communities (although not always in so great a variety) and because few other data are available to the archeologist. It is therefore better to discuss the kinds of collections in terms of archeology rather than of ethnology. The following five examples will give some idea of the range of variation.

1. American archeologists have developed to a high degree the technique of collecting potsherds from the surfaces of sites, in order to provide a basis for seriating the sites in chronological order. The collections obtained in this fashion not only are limited to pottery but also are made large enough to comprise a considerably larger number of sherds than would be necessary simply to illustrate the ceramic types. This is because the chronology, or subsequent objective, is not based upon the nature of the typology but rather upon the relative frequency, or popularity, of a given type at any point in time and space (see Phillips, Ford, and Griffin, 1951, pp. 219–36, for an illustration of the method and a discussion of the principles involved).

2. A sharply different form of collection is that obtained by excavating stratigraphically in Paleolithic and Paleo-Indian sites, e.g., at Mount Carmel in Palestine (Garrod and Bate, 1937). Such collections are not limited to any particular variety of artifact, such as pottery, but include all the types found. They are segregated by layers of refuse and subdivisions thereof, in order that the succession of occupations may be determined. The number of specimens is relatively large, since it is customary to excavate large areas.

3. United States archeologists have developed the technique of excavating

by arbitrary 10-inch or 25-cm. levels rather than by layers of refuse, in order to obtain better indications of chronology under the conditions of short-term occupancy which prevail in this country (e.g., Phillips, Ford, and Griffin, 1951, pp. 239–306). Again, all types of artifacts found are collected, but the emphasis is upon pottery. Since the area excavated is generally small, the collections are limited in size. They often lack the rarer types of artifacts but are adequate for ceramic seriation of the kind discussed in paragraph 1 above.

4. Another way of limiting one's collection is in terms of the function of the artifacts. Prehistoric archeologists working in Egypt and on the coast of Peru, for example, have often concentrated upon grave objects, either because of the aesthetic quality of these artifacts or because they lend themselves to seriation. On the north coast of Peru, where Mochica pottery portrays scenes from the life of the people, collections from graves have the further advantage that they permit one to reconstruct the life of the people in some detail (Larco Hoyle, 1945).

5. If one chooses to excavate ruins rather than refuse or graves, it is the practice to segregate the collections obtained by construction units, e.g., according to rooms in the pueblos of the American Southwest. Again all types of artifacts are collected and usually in large numbers, since the excavations tend to be extensive. Collections obtained in this manner are used to determine the sequence of construction of rooms, i.e., the growth pattern of the pueblo under investigation, or to work out the way of life of the inhabitants (Taylor, 1948, pp. 175–80).

The foregoing examples illustrate some of the ways in which archeological collections vary in composition, depending upon how they have been obtained and the uses to which they are to be put. It will be noted that the different types of collection lead to different means of establishing chronology or, in paragraphs 4 and 5, of obtaining art objects or reconstructing the life of the people. By carefully selecting from among alternatives like these, both archeologists and ethnologists should be able to increase the efficiency of their research, i.e., to collect the types of artifacts which are best suited to their subsequent objectives.

RECORDS

For the archeologist, the process of recording data consists of taking down information about the details of the environment which are pertinent to his study and about the strata and structures which he encounters and cannot remove to the laboratory. This is ordinarily not a lengthy process, unless one is excavating elaborate ruins or is fortunate enough to be dealing with a civilization, like that of the Maya, which produced carvings and inscriptions (e.g., Morley, 1946). By contrast, most of the ethnologist's information is obtained in the form of records, and therefore it will be advisable to discuss this kind of objective in terms of ethnology rather than of archeology. Again, five examples are given to illustrate the range of variation.

1. Some ethnologists have chosen to collect information concerning a single aspect of culture from a series of tribes, much as the archeologist does when he makes a ceramic survey. An outstanding example is the American Museum of Natural History's program for the study of the Plains Indian sun dance, in which various researchers recorded data on the sun dance among a large number of Plains tribes and Leslie Spier used their data to reconstruct the development and diffusion of the dance (Wissler, 1915–21).

2. Another type of approach has been to collect data from a number of tribes

by means of a questionnaire which covers as many aspects of culture as possible. This is the approach of the Culture Element Distribution Survey of the University of California, which was designed to provide series of trait lists for use in determining the degree of similarity and differences in the cultures of the tribes studied (Kroeber, 1939*b*).

3. The more familiar ethnographic record, which consists of intensive information concerning a single tribe at a given point in its history, should also be mentioned. Malinowski's studies of Trobriand culture is an example (e.g., Malinowski, 1922). These correspond to archeological collections and records made by excavating extensively in a single site or series of related sites.

4. While most ethnological descriptions of culture are restricted to a single period of time, as in paragraph 3, there have also been attempts to record the nature of the culture during successive periods by combined use of historical documents, recollections of informants, and participant observation. This was Malinowski's objective in the study of Oaxaca markets which he was making at the time of his death. His results may be compared with those obtained in archeology by excavation of a stratified site, again with the proviso that they are expressed primarily in terms of records rather than of collections.

5. In all the foregoing examples, the emphasis is upon the customs of a tribe or community as such. The records obtained tell us little, if anything, about the number of people who conform to any particular custom or about the social groups to which these individuals belong. A few recent studies have been directed toward obtaining this kind of data (e.g., Roberts, 1951), which corresponds to that obtained in archeological investigations into the popularity of ceramic types.

The foregoing examples indicate that ethnological records vary in much the same way as do archeological collections and that, in both cases, different kinds of data lend themselves to different methods of interpretation. In other words, the same considerations are involved in the taking of records as in the collection of artifacts.

INFERENCES

Archeologists are accustomed to make inferences concerning nonmaterial culture in an attempt to compensate for their lack of records, basing these partially upon their collections, partially upon conditions in the sites, and partially upon whatever ethnological or historical information may be applicable. Ethnologists do not ordinarily need to have recourse to such inferences, except when the people studied are secretive or have become acculturated and it is desired to reconstruct the aboriginal form of culture. Three examples from archeology will illustrate this kind of objective.

1. Larco Hoyle's reconstruction of Mochica culture in Peru on the basis of scenes portrayed on grave pottery has already been mentioned. This is in the form of a standard ethnographic description. Indeed, some such descriptions have been termed "prehistoric ethnology" (Smith, 1910).

2. Clark (1952) has just published an unusually rich account of economic life in Europe from Mesolithic to Iron times, which is based upon inferences from a wide variety of sources. Although larger in scope than the Plains Indian sun-dance study mentioned above, this would seem to be comparable, to the extent that it is concerned with a restricted aspect of culture but applies to a large number of groups of people.

3. It is common practice among archeologists working in the midwestern and southeastern United States to compile lists of the traits which character-

ize their cultures. While these lists are often based almost entirely on the collections excavated, there is a growing tendency to include inferences concerning nonmaterial culture. For example, the trait list presented for the University of Chicago's excavation at Kincaid in southern Illinois is organized according to the activities of the occupants of the site (Cole *et al.*, 1951, pp. 360–65). There is a close similarity here to the trait lists of the University of California's Culture Element Distribution Survey, which has been described above. As is noted below, both kinds of trait list are designed to be used for the further objective of determining the degree of relationship among the tribes or cultures studied.

CLASSIFICATORY OBJECTIVES

While most cultural information is presented in the form of a simple description, there also exists the possibility of presentation in terms of a classification. This is a common practice in archeology when large numbers of specimens have been collected and it is not feasible to describe each one of them individually. Instead, the investigator groups them into classes and presents the characteristics of the classes.

In this section we will consider only those kinds of classification which are purely factual, i.e., in which the specimens or other materials are grouped solely in terms of their own attributes. Classifications which involve factors of space, time, or genetic relationship will be considered subsequently under separate headings. Since classification is primarily an archeological procedure, our examples will be taken mainly from that field.

It will be convenient to distinguish between two products of classification: the *class*, or series of objects which are grouped together, and the *type*, or series of attributes which are shared by such a group of artifacts and which dis-

tinguish them as a class (Rouse, 1952, pp. 324–30). If one's principal objective in classifying is to produce a description of artifacts, as assumed at the beginning of this section, one is likely to concentrate on the class and to present its characteristics in some detail. If, on the other hand, one is primarily interested in defining units of culture for use in distribution studies or for some other interpretative purpose, then one will probably emphasize the type at the expense of the class.

Some classifiers (e.g., Phillips, Ford, and Griffin, 1951, pp. 61–64) have attempted to strike a compromise between description of the class and definition of the type. However, the attributes which are significant for the first purpose do not necessarily correspond to those which are pertinent to the second, since the first is an empirical approach and the second involves questions of cultural significance (Taylor, 1948, pp. 113–51). Moreover, a thorough description of a class will probably involve many more attributes than will a definition of the type. In the Midwestern Taxonomic System, which is discussed below, for example, only a few of the traits listed for the class are considered "diagnostic" of the type. For these reasons, it will probably be best to regard description of the class and definition of the type as separate objectives.

With this general background, we may turn to a discussion of specific kinds of classificatory objectives. We shall first consider those in which the primary aim is to form classes of artifacts and then those which emphasize types.

CLASSES OF ARTIFACTS

A standard procedure when the objective is to form classes consists of (1) grouping the artifacts according to their material and (2) subdividing the groups in terms of techniques of manufacture, shape, decoration, and function. The result is a hierarchical series of classes, subclasses, and sometimes sub-subclasses, each of the last consisting of all artifacts which are essentially similar in material, technique, and decoration or whatever other criteria may have been used. The archeologist describes these classes by presenting the distinguishing characteristics of their constituent artifact and illustrating representative examples (Osgood, 1942, pp. 22–25).

An alternative procedure, which has recently become widespread in Paleolithic archeology, is to base the classification almost entirely upon techniques of manufacture, i.e., to group the artifacts in terms of the manner in which they were made (Oakley, 1949, pp. 23–33, 40–68). The procedure is well suited to Paleolithic implements for two reasons: first, because these implements are largely made of flint, which retains the scars of manufacture, and, second, because the Paleolithic artisans themselves seem to have been relatively little concerned with the other criteria which might be used for classification, such as shape and decoration.

In the United States there has recently been some tendency to emphasize function as a criterion for classifying nonceramic artifacts (e.g., Taylor, 1948, pp. 170–71). In this procedure, for example, a series of stone implements is sorted into groups of hoes and axes because they appear to be suited to those respective purposes and there is reason to believe that hoes and axes were useful in the culture—an approach which is reminiscent of the ethnological practice of identifying artifacts by inquiring about their use. Classifications of both the technological and the functional kinds are generally nonhierarchical; i.e., each class is considered an independent entity.

TYPES OF ARTIFACTS

American archeologists have been particularly concerned with establishing types of pottery and, more recently, of projectile points for use in seriating sites and in studying stratigraphy, as noted above. They customarily use a binomial nomenclature, with the first term referring to a representative site and the second to one of the attributes diagnostic of the type. Often they group the various types into larger units, called "series" or "wares," although this is not a necessary part of the procedure (see Phillips, Ford, and Griffin, 1951, pp. 61–69, for a more detailed discussion).

Ceramic typology is sometimes applied to complete vessels, but more often to potsherds. Several archeologists (e.g., Krieger, in Newell and Krieger, 1949, pp. 71–80) have questioned the validity of the latter procedure, pointing out that it sometimes results in assigning sherds from the same vessel to different classes and, therefore, in treating them as examples of different types.

TYPES OF PARTS OF ARTIFACTS

Another possibility in studying ceramic typology or in typing any other kind of artifact or structure is to classify in terms of constituent parts of the vessels. In such cases the objective is to establish types of temper, of rim profile, or of design, to give several examples. The writer has applied the rather inappropriate term "mode" to this kind of type in order to distinguish it from types of whole artifacts, whether complete or fragmentary. In this usage a mode may be defined as a series of attributes which are shared by the corresponding parts of a series of artifacts and which distinguish them as a class (Rouse, 1952, pp. 325–26).

Classification to form modes rather than types is advantageous when one is dealing with potsherds, since it side-steps the question of whether to classify them in terms of whole or fragmentary specimens. It has also been applied to objects of art, where there is likewise reason to believe that individual elements of shape and decoration have had different histories and therefore can profitably be studied as separate entities. Proskouriakoff (1950), for example, has applied this approach to Maya sculpture; she establishes a series of types of designs by classifying separately the individual figures sculptured on Maya stelae, without attempting to make an over-all classification of the stelae as such.

TYPES OF CULTURE

Another kind of type is obtained by classifying sites instead of artifacts, structures, or parts thereof. In so doing, one must be careful to deal only with culturally homogeneous sites or else to divide the sites into culturally homogeneous parts, i.e., into units of occupation characterized by different cultural material. One groups the sites and occupation units into classes on the basis of the similarities and differences in their cultural material, notes the elements of culture which are shared by each class, and uses these elements to define the type of culture represented by the class.

This approach has reached its greatest elaboration in the Midwestern Taxonomic System, which, as the name implies, was originally developed by archeologists working in the central part of the United States. In this system the term "component" is applied to the sites and occupation units which are classified, and the term "focus" to the types of culture formed by classifying components. The system also provides for the foci to be grouped into an ascending series of larger units, called "aspects," "phases," and "patterns," much as the

ceramic types discussed above are grouped into wares or series. The procedure is to list the traits of each component as fully as possible, to classify the components in terms of these traits, and to define the resultant foci, aspects, phases, and patterns by noting the traits which are diagnostic of each (McKern, 1939).

Because of the hierarchical arrangement of aspects, phases, and patterns, some commentators have assumed that the Midwestern System is a genetic classification. However, the originators of the system were careful to point out that the only fundamental parts of the classification are the components and foci. They have always regarded the aspects, phases, and patterns merely as arbitrary groupings, designed to provide a means of arranging the foci until a chronology could be developed to take their place. Now that such a chronology is available, there is a tendency to disregard the larger units or, in the case of the Woodland and Mississippi patterns, to reformulate them as time periods (e.g., Phillips, Ford, and Griffin, 1951, pp. 445–51).

Although concerned with archeology rather than with ethnology, the Midwestern Taxonomic System bears a close resemblance to the Culture Element Distribution Survey of the University of California, in its emphasis upon traits and in its use of those traits as a means of expressing similarities and differences in culture. The components of the Midwestern system correspond to the communities studied in the Cultural Element Survey, and, theoretically at least, the foci, aspects, etc., are comparable to the tribes and groupings of tribes with which the Culture Element Survey is concerned. Indeed, as is noted below, one objective which the originators of the Midwestern System had in mind was to try to trace the history of the modern Indian tribes back into the past in terms of the foci and aspects, viewed as prehistoric tribal units (Griffin, 1943, pp. 327–41).

In conclusion, we will note two variations on the kind of cultural units produced by the Midwestern Taxonomic System. Instead of classifying the components in terms of traits, one may do so in terms of types or modes, i.e., in terms of prior classification of the artifacts or parts thereof. An example of classification according to types is the "industries" of French and British prehistorians (e.g., Breuil, 1949, p. 96), and of classification according to modes, the "styles" established by the writer in the West Indies (Rouse, 1952, p. 327). In the former case the scarcity of material other than stone implements has prevented a more detailed classification in terms of culture traits. In the latter the writer has set up both styles and cultures, the styles defined in terms of ceramic modes and the cultures in terms of traits, as in the case of the Midwestern System.

GEOGRAPHICAL OBJECTIVES

One of the simplest things which either the archeologist or the ethnologist can do—although it is sometimes overlooked by amateurs—is to determine the geographical provenience of one's data —whether the latter consist of sites, specimens, records, inferences, and/or one or more of the variety of classes and types which has just been discussed. This is, of course, an objective of most archeological and ethnological surveys. It can be accomplished in a number of different ways, as the following paragraphs will illustrate.

MAPS AND AERIAL PHOTOGRAPHS

The data may be plotted on maps or aerial photographs. By so doing, for example, one can pinpoint the positions of sites or settlements with relatively great accuracy and also determine their relationships to the features of the landscape. British archeology leads the way in both respects, with its Ordnance Survey, which has produced a series of excellent maps showing the positions of the principal sites as well as modern settlements, and with its pioneer work in aerial photography (Atkinson, 1946, pp. 21–31).

Both archeologists and ethnologists have used maps of sites or settlements to study the distribution of population, though this is feasible in archeology only when a chronology is available. For example, the writer recently plotted the distribution of sites by period for the Indian River area of the state of Florida and was thereby able to show that, whereas the center of population had been inland on the St. Johns River during the earlier periods, it later shifted to the coast (Rouse, 1951b, pp. 237–57).

Maps, of course, may also be used to plot the distribution of specimens or of various kinds of culture traits. This is perhaps best illustrated by the work of Swedish anthropologists. In discussing the techniques of South American ceramics, for example, Linné (1925) presents a series of maps which show the occurrences of the techniques in both archeological sites and ethnological communities.

Several American archeologists have studied the distribution of ceramic types in terms of frequencies, or relative popularity, rather than simply by presence or absence. For example, Ford (in Phillips, Ford, and Griffin, 1951, pp. 223–24) has published a series of maps bearing isobar-like lines—Ford refrains from calling these "iso-ceramic lines"— which show the frequencies of occurrence of ceramic types in the lower Mississippi Valley. This kind of approach has not been attempted in ethnology, so far as the writer is aware, but it might well prove fruitful there too.

NATURAL AND CULTURAL AREAS

As an alternative to locating one's data on a map or aerial photograph, one may decide to refer them to natural or cultural areas. In either case the effect is to produce a classification of sites, settlements, or units of culture which is based primarily on geographical factors rather than on cultural criteria, as in the examples previously discussed.

Natural areas are those which have been defined in terms of details of the environment. Such areas figure quite widely in both archeological and ethnological literature (e.g., Fox, 1947; Kroeber, 1939a). One reason is that they have the advantage of remaining relatively constant through time, so that they provide an efficient basis for classifying cultural material of different ages —an important consideration in the field of archeology. They are also useful in examining the relationships between environment and culture, as in the two examples cited.

Culture areas are defined in terms of the distribution of cultural material. Such areas have sometimes been used as a means of establishing a chronology —an approach termed the "age-area concept"—but we shall here consider only their uses as descriptive and classificatory devices, since chronology is discussed in another section. From these points of view, one's objective in establishing culture areas may be simply to delimit the distribution of culture, or else, once such areas have been established, one may use them as a device for classifying cultural material, as in the case of natural areas.

On the whole, the concept of culture areas seems to be more applicable to ethnology than to archeology, for the reason that culture areas are not so likely as natural areas to remain constant through time and therefore cannot be so easily projected back from ethnology into prehistory. For example,

Strong (1933) has shown that the Plains Indian culture area of the western United States, as established ethnologically, does not apply to the archeology, since settled agricultural Indians lived much farther out on the plains in prehistoric than in historic times. Similarly, several attempts to establish archeological culture areas in the midwestern and southeastern United States (e.g., Shetrone, 1941) have failed, apparently because peoples and cultures shifted frequently from one part of that region to another before the arrival of Europeans. Indeed, it was this failure of the attempts to establish culture areas which led to the development of the Midwestern Taxonomic System. The originators of the system decided that, since geography had proved to be a poor criterion for classification, they would try a scheme which did not involve the factor of space (McKern, 1939, pp. 302-3).

On the other hand, Bennett (1948) has recently come to the conclusion that there is a central Andean culture area in South America—he calls it an "area co-tradition"—which has retained its identity throughout the neo-Indian period. He suggests that it may be possible to define similar area co-traditions in other parts of the New World, including the southeastern United States, where, as noted above, experience has proved otherwise. It may be suggested that the concept of area co-tradition—although not necessarily the co-tradition defined without reference to area—will work best in a region where the natives had a settled mode of life, as they did in the central Andes.

In places where area co-traditions cannot be set up, it is still possible to establish archeological culture areas by limiting them to restricted periods of time. The writer has been able to proceed in this manner in the Greater Antilles, for example. There we had to distinguish two series of culture areas, one organized around the islands themselves and the other around the passages between the islands, the former referring to Period I in our chronology and the latter to Period III (Rouse, 1951a).

CULTURE CENTERS

Instead of establishing culture areas having definite geographic bounds, one may choose to set up a series of culture centers (Wissler, 1923, pp. 61–63, 203–5). One's data can then be referred to the center which it most closely resembles, if it seems desirable to do so. This is particularly useful in a region like the American Southwest, where several tribes with different cultures live side by side and it is therefore impossible to define a single, culturally homogeneous area.

POLITICAL AND CARTOGRAPHIC AREAS

Tribal territories, modern political divisions, or cartographic units may also be used as devices for classifying cultural material. The first is standard ethnological practice (e.g., Kroeber, 1939a, pp. 8–12), while the other two have been used as substitutes in archeological research. For example, the Gladwins (1930) have calculated the frequencies of culture phases in the southwestern United States by map quadrangles and have plotted these in the form of pie diagrams, in order to present graphically the range of distribution of each phase.

CHRONOLOGICAL OBJECTIVES

In the foregoing discussion of geographical objectives, we have had occasion to refer several times to the necessity for also taking chronology into consideration. The reason for this is that space and time are complementary. If space may be considered two-dimensional (as expressed in the co-ordinates of a map), then time represents the third dimension (perpendicular to the

map). Archeologists, of course, implicitly recognize this when they prepare charts of culture sequence in which the dimensions of space are portrayed horizontally and the dimension of time vertically (e.g., Heizer, 1949, p. 59). In other words, space and time perspectives are but two aspects of the same problem.

It follows from this that the objectives of chronological research should correspond to those already discussed in connection with geography. There is one practical difference, however. Whereas geographical provenience can be accurately measured, one cannot always determine the exact age of cultural material, particularly in archeology, where records are lacking. For this reason, archeologists are accustomed to distinguish between *absolute time,* which is accurately measured, and *relative time,* in which the age of one's material can only be determined relative to other material or in terms of a system of chronology which expresses sequence rather than duration of time.

As in the case of geographical research, the material dated varies from sites, communities, artifacts, records, and inferences to types, modes, industries, styles, or whatever other unit of culture is pertinent to one's study. It is even advisable in some cases to determine the age of culture areas, as noted above. We have attempted in the following discussion to choose examples which illustrate the dating of as many of these kinds of material as possible.

SEQUENCES

The simplest method of dating is to arrange one's material in chronological order without reference to a separate time scale or series of periods. This is the procedure used in the University of Chicago studies of Illinois archeology, where the objective seems to be merely to determine the succession of cultural foci (Cole *et al.*, 1951, pp. 226–31). Sequences of occupations in stratified sites are also commonly presented in this fashion (e.g., Garrod and Bate, 1937). The procedure appears to be most useful in pioneer studies and in those which are restricted to a small area. It is generally replaced by one or more of the following approaches when the situation becomes complex, since it is not the most efficient way of distinguishing overlaps of cultural material in time or differences in sequence among a large number of areas.

TIME SCALES

We have seen that the most common means of expressing geographical perspective is to locate one's material on maps. The comparable procedure in the dimension of time is to establish a time scale and to determine the chronological position of one's material with reference to this scale. By the term "time scale" is meant a continuous measure of time, resembling a rule. It may be either absolute or relative; in the former case, the divisions of the scale represent fixed intervals of time, while in the latter they are variable and hence do not indicate duration.

The most practical absolute time scale is our Christian calendar. Ethnologists are able to use this at will, except when projecting their data back into prehistoric time, but it is seldom available to archeologists, unless they are fortunate enough to encounter written records which contain dates, either in our own calendar or in a native calendar which can be correlated with ours. The date-bearing stelae of classic Maya sites, for example, provide a means of determining the age of those sites and of their periods of occupation, but it is first necessary to correlate the Maya calendar with our own (Morley, 1946, pp. 459–62).

In the absence of a calendar, archeologists are able to fall back upon a series of techniques, such as radiocarbon dating, dendrochronology, varve analysis, synchronization of one's material with the written history of another area, and calculations based upon the rate of accumulation of refuse, to produce absolute dates expressed in terms of the Christian calendar (Clark, 1947, pp. 136–50). These, however, are only approximations and vary greatly in accuracy. As Johnson has pointed out (in Libby, 1952, p. 101), even dates based upon radiocarbon analysis are best used only in conjunction with one or more of the types of relative chronology discussed below.

Some archeologists who lack any form of absolute dating have substituted relative time scales of their own making. Sir Flinders Petrie's system of sequence dating is perhaps the best example; this scholar set up an arbitrary series of dates, numbered from 1 to 80 (although the first thirty numbers have never been used) and assigned his grave lots to these dates (Petrie, 1899). Recently, Ford has developed a number of comparable time scales for use in seriating surface collections; he presents these graphically, marking off the principal division points with letters rather than numbers (e.g., Phillips, Ford, and Griffin, 1951, Figs. 17–21). Such artificial time scales may lead to problems of correlation with the Christian calendar, as in dealing with native calendars (Childe, 1934, pp. 12–13).

In discussing geographical objectives, we noted that maps have been used to trace the distribution of elements of culture in terms not only of simple occurrence but also of relative frequency or popularity. This is likewise true of time scales. Petrie (1899), for example, only attempted to point out the dates when traits occurred, whereas Ford (Phillips, Ford, and Griffin, 1951) employs his time scales as measures against which to plot the changing frequencies of ceramic types.

PERIODS

We have seen that a time scale is the temporal unit which corresponds to a map in the dimensions of space. There is a similar correspondence between a period in time and an area in space. Like an area, a period delimits the boundaries of cultural distribution and can also be considered a device for classifying cultural material, although with reference to time rather than to space.

In a recent publication (Rouse, 1951b, p. 235), the writer was able to distinguish three kinds of periods, which will here be called "historic," "natural," and "cultural." It is not often that enough data are available to work with all three of these, and, when there are, it may be more practicable to fuse them into a single series of periods. Nevertheless, we shall discuss them separately.

"Historic" periods are those which have been defined in terms of written records. They can usually be dated and are therefore absolute, corresponding in this respect to the absolute time scales discussed above. As an example, we may cite the earliest Chinese dynasties, which, although named and dated by means of the traditional records, are also known through archeological excavation (Creel, 1937, pp. xvi–xxii).

"Natural" periods, like natural areas, are based upon variations in the nature of the environment. They are relative rather than absolute, unless it has been possible to date them by one of the methods of measuring time mentioned above. The criteria used in setting them up vary from sea-level changes, river-terrace sequences, and studies of the meander patterns of rivers to changes in the nature of the soil, in the climate, and in flora and fauna (Clark, 1947, pp. 121–31). When more than one of these criteria are available, it may be necessary to set up a separate series of periods for each (Movius, 1942, Table 1).

Just as natural areas tend to remain relatively constant through time, so natural periods can often be traced with some regularity through space and therefore provide a relatively convenient means of synchronizing cultural material over a large area. They have also proved useful in studies of the relationship between culture and the environment, particularly when considered in connection with natural areas (e.g., Movius, 1942, pp. 257–62).

Natural periods figure most prominently in research on Pleistocene archeology because of the marked changes in environment which took place at that time (Zeuner, 1950). They also play an important role in studies of post-Pleistocene environmentally marginal regions, such as northern Europe, which is on the border line between a temperate and an arctic climate (Movius, 1942), and Florida, which is poorly drained and therefore easily flooded (Rouse, 1951b). Regions like these offer the best opportunity for establishing natural periods, because they are relatively sensitive to changes in the environment.

"Cultural" periods, like cultural areas, are defined in terms of the distribution of culture. If established by use of a calendar or one of the substitute techniques mentioned above, they will represent absolute time. More commonly, however, the periods are based upon seriation, stratigraphy, synchronization, correlation with natural periods, the age-area concept, or some other technique for establishing relative chronology. The criteria used vary greatly, depending upon what kinds of data are available. Paleolithic and Paleo-Indian periods, for example, are defined almost entirely in terms of chipped-stone artifacts (Haury, 1950, pp. 170–75). Neolithic and later periods in the Old World are usually based upon a variety of traits (e.g., Frankfort, 1951, pp. 32–48), while in this country many archeologists define their periods solely in terms of ceramics (e.g., Rouse, 1951*b*, pp. 69–70).

Archeologists have found by experience that cultural periods have a relatively restricted distribution in space. It is therefore common practice to establish a separate set of periods for each area studied. As already noted, these are often presented in the form of charts, with the areas shown across the tops and the periods beneath them (Goggin, 1952, Fig. 2).

Historical, natural, and cultural areas are sometimes considered the end-points of chronological research, as in the example just given. Alternatively, they may be used as the basis for tracing chronological distributions. Hawkes (1940, Tables I–II), for example, presents a pair of charts on which the temporal distribution of the various Paleolithic and Mesolithic cultures in western Europe is shown relative to the natural periods (glacial and climatic) in that area. He also presents maps which complement the charts by portraying the geographical distributions of the cultures. The writer (Rouse, 1939, Chart 6) has charted the frequency distributions of a series of ceramic modes relative to the cultural periods established for northern Haiti. As a final example, we may note that the current charts of California prehistory show culture periods (called "horizons") down the left side and, contrary to the previous examples, culture areas across the top, with cultures (called "facies") in the bodies of the charts (Heizer, 1949, p. 59).

CULTURE CLIMAXES

The concept of "culture center," which was discussed above in the geographical section, has its temporal counterpart in the concept of "climax." Kroeber (1939*a*, pp. 222–28) defines

such a climax as the point at which the culture of a given area reaches its greatest intensity. He notes, for example, that classic Greek civilization culminated in such a climax between 500 and 200 B.C., after which a decline set in. Similarly, Phillips, Ford, and Griffin (1951, p. 453) distinguish two climaxes in the prehistory of the eastern United States, one during the burial mound period about A.D. 500–700 and the other in temple mound times about A.D. 1500–1600.

HORIZONS AND TRADITIONS

While cultural periods and climaxes have a relatively restricted geographical distribution, it often happens that one or more of their traits extend from area to area through a series of contemporaneous periods. Kroeber (1944, pp. 108–11) has applied the term "horizon style" to this phenomenon, as it occurs in Peruvian archeology, where the traits involved are largely ceramic and consist of both techniques of decoration and attributes of design. Such horizon styles are very useful in establishing chronology, because they provide a starting point for seriation, as well as a basis for synchronizing periods over a large region.

It is not uncommon for one or more culture traits to survive from period to period within a single geographic area. Willey (1945) has applied the term "tradition" to this phenomenon, again in connection with Peruvian archeology. He regards a tradition as the counterpart of a horizon style and applies both concepts to the study of ceramic distributions.

STAGES

A final approach to chronology consists of setting up a series of stages reflecting the development of culture instead of simply distribution, as in the case of the periods and horizons just discussed. Morgan and the other evolutionary ethnologists of the last century used this approach, and it is also exemplified by the Stone-Bronze-Iron classification of European prehistory, which originated in the same intellectual climate (Lowie, 1937, pp. 19-29).

While these early evolutionary schemes are still useful as an expression of the degree of cultural development, they have largely been abandoned as a means of presenting chronology because they do not conform to the facts of cultural distribution as now known (Childe, 1951, pp. 161–79). The Stone-Bronze-Iron classification, for example, is homotaxial; i.e., its three stages, as well as their subdivisions, have occurred at different times in different places (Daniel, 1943, pp. 39–43). For this reason, they are rarely employed any more as temporal units in the Western world, although Soviet archeologists still follow this usage (Golomshtok, 1938, p. 445).

On the other hand, the evolutionary approach to chronology has recently been revived in the New World in the form of "developmental classifications." Strong (in Bennett, 1948, p. 98), for example, has set up a series of "cultural epochs," or stages of cultural development, in Virú Valley, Peru, which he believes are applicable to the rest of the central Andes and to Mesoamerica, if not to other parts of the world. His formulation would seem to have two advantages over previous studies of the same kind: (1) in so far as possible, it is based upon observed distributions rather than on conjecture, and (2) for the most part it is defined in terms of degree of development rather than of specific cultural content. It therefore provides a means of expressing the broad sweep of chronology over a whole series of areas without bringing in the differences in detail from area to area.

HISTORIC OBJECTIVES

The foregoing objectives all have a factual orientation, in that they are concerned solely with the nature and distribution of culture. There remains the problem of determining how one's cultural material happened to take on its peculiar characteristics and to occur when and where it did. This is a historical problem and is usually solved by invoking one or more of the following processes of culture history.

It is not within the scope of this paper to discuss the validity of the processes, since to do so would involve questions of theory which are considered in another part of the program. We shall merely consider a representative series of processes as examples of the manner in which archeologists have attempted to explain the character and distribution of cultural material in historical terms.

DIFFUSION AND PERSISTENCE

If geographical study has shown that a type, industry, or other kind of cultural unit has a widespread and continuous distribution in space, it is customary to conclude that the unit has diffused from one point in its distribution to the others—usually from the point where it occurs earliest or in greatest complexity (e.g., Childe, 1950, pp. 9–10). Similarly, if the cultural unit has a continuous distribution through time, it may be said to have persisted from the date of its earliest to the date of its latest occurrence (Rouse, 1939, pp. 14–15).

INDEPENDENT INVENTION

If, on the other hand, the material under study has a discontinuous distribution in either space or time, one may invoke the theory of independent invention or parallel development. Opinion differs as to how great the discontinuity should be before one does this or, indeed, whether independent invention ever takes place at all (Lowie, 1937, p. 158).

MIGRATION AND OTHER MECHANISMS OF SPREAD

After reaching the conclusion that diffusion has taken place, one may proceed to theorize about the manner in which it happened. If a diffused unit is complex, as in the case of a *Kulturkreis*, its spread may be attributed to migration (Schmidt, 1939). If, on the other hand, the unit is relatively simple, anthropologists are more likely to assume that the peoples involved have borrowed the idea from one another (Linton, 1936, pp. 324–46). Alternatively, specimens which appear to be intrusive into a site or community and which occur in such small numbers as to suggest that they have been carried there are best regarded as the result of trade (e.g., Cole *et al.*, 1951, pp. 148–54).

PARTICIPATION IN CULTURE

We have seen that some archeologists trace the geographical and/or temporal distributions of traits in terms of relative frequencies of occurrence. The purpose of so doing is to obtain a measure of the popularity of the traits. It is assumed that these traits are alternatives, to use a term of Linton's (1936, pp. 271–87), and that the individuals participating in the culture have been able to choose from among them. Observations of our own culture have shown that such choices tend to follow the dictates of popularity, and it is believed that this is also true of prehistoric cultures (Phillips, Ford, and Griffin, 1951, pp. 219–23).

The theory of participation in culture is also invoked to explain occurrences of atypical material, such as residues of artifacts left after classification. These residues may be attributed to the individual peculiarities of the artisans (Linton, 1936), unless they prove to be trade objects.

ACCULTURATION

Another way of explaining the nature and distribution of one's cultural material is in terms of contacts between two or more groups of people having different cultures. In ethnology this approach is used mainly in studies of what happens when our civilization comes into contact with "primitive" cultures (Linton, 1940). Archeologists and students of history, on the other hand, deal more often with the mutual interplay of cultures on a more equal basis. Ortiz (1947, pp. 97–103) has suggested substituting the term "transculturation" in such cases, in order to avoid any implication that one of the participating groups is superior to the rest.

ECOLOGICAL ADAPTATION

Both ethnologists and archeologists have frequently had recourse to biological and ecological factors in explaining the facts of culture history. This is well illustrated for ethnology by Kroeber's study of the interrelationships between cultural and natural areas in North America and for archeology by Clark's analysis of the manner in which the economies of prehistoric Europe were adapted to their corresponding biological and physical environments (Kroeber, 1939a; Clark, 1952, pp. 7–21). As both Kroeber and Clark point out, the distribution of cultures and elements of culture sometimes coincides nicely with that of particular biotas and habitats.

PHYLOGENY

A number of archeologists working in the southwestern United States have attempted to explain the particular geographic and temporal distributions of cultures in that area by invoking the biological theory of phylogeny. They have postulated the existence at an early date of a small number of Indian groups, each with its own "basic" culture, and have assumed that these groups, as well as their cultures, gradually split up by a process of fission into the present variety of tribes and cultures. Gladwin and Gladwin (1934) present this reconstruction graphically in the form of a series of diagrams, in which the basic cultures appear at the bottom and lines branch out from them to indicate the presumed lines of descent. Time periods are shown along the sides of the diagrams, but the factor of space is ignored. This type of approach, which amounts to a genetic classification of Southwestern cultures, has been criticized for its failure to take into consideration such historical processes as diffusion and transculturation (Brew, 1946, pp. 44–66).

PARALLEL DEVELOPMENT

An alternate and less rigid genetic approach consists of attributing two or more sequences of types or cultures, such as the traditions discussed above, to parallel development from a single ancestor. The assumption here is that the traits shared by such traditions are the result of common cultural heritage (as in Sapir, 1916, p. 43), but it does not follow that the traditions themselves have to be arranged phylogenetically. Instead, the investigator determines the extension of each tradition in space and time by plotting the distributions of its constituent types or cultures (Goggin, 1952, Fig. 3).

One way of getting at traditions is to start with historic tribes and to work back from them to the prehistoric cultural units which seem to be ancestral. This is known in American archeology as the "direct historical approach" (Strong, 1933, pp. 275–76).

EVOLUTION

The emergence of developmental classifications in American archeology

has already been noted. As Steward (1949) has pointed out, these classifications require the assumption that some elements of culture are more basic than others, with the result that, given the same environmental setting, their appearance in a culture will touch off a series of related changes, which may lift the culture from one stage in the classification to another. Steward has attempted to validate this assumption by comparing the sequences of cultural development in the various arid and semiarid centers of ancient civilization. Regardless of the success of this particular study, it points up the possibility of interpreting the facts of cultural distribution in terms of evolutionary process.

OTHER PROCESSES

Since cultural processes are discussed more fully in another part of this program, it is not considered necessary to give a complete inventory here. We may note in passing, however, that one may also interpret cultural distributions in terms of human physiology or psychology, of art appreciation, or of differences in the physical capabilities of various forms of early man. In any particular instance it is probably best to consider all possible explanations for the facts of culture history (cf. the geological principle of multiple working hypotheses; Chamberlin, 1944).

CONCLUSIONS

An attempt has been made to survey some of the more important objectives of culture-historical research in archeology and ethnology. In conclusion, we would suggest that careful choice among these objectives will improve the efficiency of one's study or program of studies. It is advisable, for example, to avoid duplicating objectives already accomplished as the result of previous research and to select only those objectives which are best suited to the nature of the available data and most compatible with one another, in the sense that they form a logically consistent series, leading to the solution of specific problems. In many cases the success or failure of one's research may depend to a considerable extent upon one's choice of objectives.

REFERENCES

ATKINSON, R. J. C. 1946. *Field Archeology.* London: Methuen & Co., Ltd.

BENNETT, W. C. (ed.). 1948. *A Reappraisal of Peruvian Archaeology.* ("Memoirs of the Society for American Archaeology," No. 4.) Menasha, Wisconsin.

BIRKET-SMITH, K. "Recent Achievements in Eskimo Research," *Journal of the Royal Anthropological Institute,* LXXVII, 145–57. London.

BREUIL, H. 1949. *Beyond the Bounds of History: Scenes from the Old Stone Age.* London: P. R. Gawthorn.

BREW, J. O. 1946. *Archaeology of Alkali Ridge, Southeastern Utah. . . .* ("Papers of the Peabody Museum of American Archaeology and Ethnology, Harvard University," Vol. XXI.) **Cambridge.**

CHAMBERLIN, T. D. 1944. "The Method of Multiple Working Hypotheses," *Scientific Monthly,* LIX, 357–62.

CHILDE, V. GORDON. 1934. *New Light on the Most Ancient East.* New York: D. Appleton–Century Co.

———. 1950. *Prehistoric Migrations in Europe.* Oslo: Instituttet for Sammenlignende Kulturforskning.

———. 1951. *Social Evolution.* New York: Henry Schuman, Inc.

CLARK, G. 1947. *Archaeology and Society.* 2d ed. London: Methuen & Co., Ltd.

CLARK, J. G. D. 1952. *Prehistoric Europe: The Economic Basis.* London: Methuen & Co., Ltd.

COLE, F. C., et al. 1951. *Kincaid: A Prehistoric Illinois Metropolis.* Chicago: University of Chicago Press.

CREEL, H. G. 1937. *Studies in Early Chinese Culture.* Baltimore: Waverly Press, Inc.

DANIEL, G. E. 1943. *The Three Ages: An Essay on Archaeological Method.* Cambridge, England: At the University Press.

EMORY, K. P. 1943. *Polynesian Stone Remains,* pp. 9–21. ("Papers of the Peabody Museum of American Archaeology and Ethnology, Harvard University," Vol. XX.) Cambridge.

FOX, SIR C. 1947. *The Personality of Britain.* 4th ed. Cardiff: National Museum of Wales.

FRANKFORT, H. 1951. *The Birth of Civilization in the Near East.* London: Williams & Norgate.

GARROD, D. A. E., and BATE, D. M. A. 1937. *The Stone Age of Mount Carmel: Excavations at the Wady El-Mughara.* Vol. I. Oxford: Clarendon Press.

GLADWIN, W. and H. S. 1930. *The Western Range of the Red-on-Buff Culture.* ("Gila Pueblo Medallion Papers," No. 5.) Globe, Ariz.: Gila Pueblo.

———. 1934. *A Method for the Designation of Cultures and Their Variations.* ("Gila Pueblo Medallion Papers," No. 15.) Globe, Ariz.: Gila Pueblo.

GOGGIN, J. M. 1952. *Space and Time Perspective in Northern St. Johns Archeology, Florida.* ("Yale University Publications in Anthropology," No. 47.) New Haven.

GOLOMSHTOK, E. A. 1938. "The Old Stone Age in European Russia," *Transactions of the American Philosophical Society,* n.s., XXIX, 191–468. Philadelphia.

GRIFFIN, J. B. 1943. *The Fort Ancient Aspect: Its Cultural and Chronological Position in Mississippi Valley Archaeology.* Ann Arbor: University of Michigan Press.

HAURY, E. W. 1950. *The Stratigraphy and Archaeology of Ventana Cave, Arizona.* Albuquerque, N.M.: University of New Mexico Press.

HAWKES, C. F. C. 1940. *The Prehistoric Foundations of Europe: To the Mycenean Age.* London: Methuen & Co., Ltd.

HEIZER, R. F. (ed.). 1949. *A Manual of Archaeological Field Methods.* Millbrae, Calif.: National Press.

KROEBER, A. L. 1939a. *Cultural and Natural Areas of Native North America.* ("University of California Publications in American Archaeology and Ethnology," Vol. XXXVIII.) Berkeley.

———. 1939b. "Culture Element Distributions. XI. Tribes Surveyed," *Anthropological Records*, Vol. I, No. 7. Berkeley.

———. 1944. *Peruvian Archeology in 1942.* ("Viking Fund Publications in Anthropology," No. 4.) New York.

LARCO HOYLE, R. 1945. *Los Mochicas.* Trujillo, Peru: Museo R. Larco Herrera.

LIBBY, W. F. 1952. *Radiocarbon Dating.* Chicago: University of Chicago Press.

LINNÉ, S. 1925. "The Technique of South American Ceramics," *Göt Kungl. Vetenskaps-och Vitterhets—Samhälles Handlingar*, Vol. XXIX, No. 5, Göteborg.

LINTON, R. 1936. *The Study of Man.* New York: D. Appleton–Century Co.

———. (ed.). 1940. *Acculturation in Seven American Indian Tribes.* New York: D. Appleton–Century Co.

LOWIE, R. H. 1937. *The History of Ethnological Theory.* New York: Farrar & Rinehart, Inc.

McKERN, W. C. 1939. "The Midwestern Taxonomic Method as an Aid to Archaeological Culture Study," *American Anthropologist*, IV, 301–13.

MALINOWSKI, B. 1922. *Argonauts of the Western Pacific.* London: George Routledge & Sons, Ltd.

MORLEY, S. G. 1946. *The Ancient Maya.* Stanford: Stanford University Press.

MOVIUS, H. L., JR. 1942. *The Irish Stone Age: Its Chronology, Development, and Relationships.* Cambridge: At the University Press.

NEWELL, H. P., and KRIEGER, A. D. 1949. *The George C. Davis Site, Cherokee County, Texas.* ("Memoirs of the Society for American Archaeology," No. 5.) Menasha, Wis.

OAKLEY, K. P. 1949. *Man the Tool-Maker.* London: British Museum.

ORTIZ, F. 1947. *Cuban Counterpoint: Tobacco and Sugar.* New York: A. A. Knopf.

OSGOOD, C. 1942. *The Ciboney Culture of Cayo Redondo, Cuba.* ("Yale University Publications in Anthropology," No. 25.) New Haven.

PETRIE, W. M. F. 1899. "Sequence in Prehistoric Remains," *Journal of the Royal Anthropological Institute*, XXIX, 295–301. London.

PHILLIPS, R.; FORD, J. A.; and GRIFFIN, J. B. 1951. *Archaeological Survey in the Lower Mississippi Alluvial Valley, 1940–1947.* ("Papers of the Peabody Museum of American Archaeology and Ethnology, Harvard University," Vol. XXV.) Cambridge.

PROSKOURIAKOFF, T. 1950. *A Study of Classic Maya Sculpture.* ("Carnegie Institution of Washington Publications," No. 593.) Washington, D.C.

ROBERTS, J. M. 1951. *Three Navaho Households: A Comparative Study in Small Group Culture.* ("Papers of the Peabody Museum of American Archaeology and Ethnology, Harvard University," Vol. XL, No. 3.) Cambridge.

ROUSE, I. 1939. *Prehistory in Haiti: A Study in Method.* ("Yale University Publications in Anthropology," No. 21.) New Haven.

———. 1951a. "Areas and Periods of Culture in the Greater Antilles," *Southwestern Journal of Anthropology*, VII, 248–65.

———. 1951b. *A Survey of Indian River Archeology, Florida.* ("Yale University Publications in Anthropology," No. 44.) New Haven.

———. 1952. *Porto Rican Prehistory.* ("Scientific Survey of Porto Rico and the Virgin Islands," Vol. XVIII, Part III.) New York: New York Academy of Sciences.

SAPIR, E. 1916. *Time Perspective in Aboriginal American Culture: A Study in Method.* (Canadian Department of Mines, Geological Survey, Mem. 90; "Anthropological Series," No. 13.) Ottawa.

SCHMIDT, W. 1939. *The Culture Historical Method of Ethnology.* New York: Fortuny's.

SMITH, H. I. 1910. *The Prehistoric Ethnology of a Kentucky Site.* ("Anthropological Papers of the American Museum of Natural History," Vol. VI, No. 1.) New York.

SHETRONE, H. C. 1941. *The Mound-Builders.* New York: D. Appleton–Century Co.

STEWARD, J. H. 1949. "Cultural Causality and Law: A Trial Formulation of the Development of Early Civilizations," *American Anthropologist*, n.s., LI, 1–27.

STRONG, W. D. 1933. "Plains Culture in the Light of Archeology," *American Anthropologist*, n.s., XXXV, 271–87.

TAYLOR, W. W. 1948. *A Study of Archeology*. ("Memoirs of the American Anthropological Association," No. 69.) Menasha, Wis.

WILLEY, G. R. 1945. "Horizon Styles and Pottery Traditions in Peruvian Archaeology," *American Antiquity*, XI, 49–56.

WISSLER, C. (ed.). 1915–21. *Sun Dance of the Plains Indian*. ("Anthropological Papers of the American Museum of Natural History," Vol. XVI, Nos. 1–7.) New York.

———. 1923. *Man and Culture*. New York: Thomas Y. Crowell Co.

ZEUNER, F. E. 1950. *Dating the Past: An Introduction to Geochronology*. 2d ed. London: Methuen & Co., Ltd.

Primates[1]

By WILLIAM L. STRAUS, JR.

SINCE TYSON (1699) described the anatomy of a young chimpanzee and thus founded the science of Primatology, knowledge of the living primates has greatly increased. Yet, despite this, our knowledge of these animals is woefully incomplete, and numerous important areas of investigation remain unexplored.

The study of living non-human primates has two aspects for the anthropologist: first, to throw light upon the physical, psychological, and social nature of man by studying those animals of the zoological group to which he belongs, and, second, to gain, through study of these animals (especially, although not exclusively, of their skeletons), comparative data which are necessary in any attempt to reconstruct primate, and particularly human, phylogeny (especially, although again not exclusively, as an aid in evaluating and interpreting fossil remains). These two aspects, although in some degree differing in purpose and approach, are so closely related and overlap to such an extent that they actually cannot be considered separately.

ANATOMY

SOMATOMETRY

The bodily dimensions and proportions of most living primates are well

known, thanks largely to the pioneer investigations of Mollison (1910) and the later, more extensive studies of Schultz (1926, 1927, 1933, et seq.). For several genera (particularly the anthropoid apes, and also a few of the monkeys) there exists adequate knowledge of the range of variability; for many others, however, measurement has been confined to only a few specimens. Detailed studies of growth changes in the anthropoids and some monkeys, notably the rhesus and proboscis monkeys, have been made by Schultz (1924, 1926, 1927, et seq.); but for many genera information is completely lacking.

In general, however, the gaps in this field of study are relatively minor ones, except for the all-important aspect of growth, particularly prenatal growth. It is largely the lack of material that hinders this latter phase of study, for such material can best be secured from animals collected in their native habitats.

GROSS ANATOMY

Most of our knowledge of non-human primates lies in this field. Yet even here the gaps are little short of appalling. All the anthropoid apes, except the siamang, have received more or less systematic study. Among all the other primates, however, only three Old World monkeys (the rhesus monkey, *Macaca*

---

1. Statements of fact, where not specifically documented, are based upon the texts and bibliographies of publications listed at the end of this paper. Ruch's *Bibliographia primato-* *logica* is to be especially noted; this includes exhaustive bibliographies of the anatomy, physiology, biochemistry, and psychobiology of Primates, up to the year 1941.

77

mulatta; the guereza, *Colobus;* and the langur, *Semnopithecus entellus*), one New World monkey (the common marmoset, *Hapale jacchus*), the tarsier (*Tarsius*), a few lemurs, and, if it be included in the order Primates, the pentailed tree shrew (*Ptilocercus*), have been so treated.

Yet for none of these has such study been other than narrowly basic, resting upon a few specimens. Quantitative studies—excepting only certain parts of the skeleton (notably the skull), particularly of the anthropoids (the monograph on the gibbons by Schultz, 1944, is an outstanding contribution)—have been very few, and in most of these there has been no real attempt at statistical analysis. The mean and the range of variation have too often represented the primatologist's concept of ultimate biometrical study. The variance itself has been neglected. The difficulties, temporal and otherwise, of dissecting and studying the soft parts of large series of animals, even on the rare occasions when such series are available, are too obvious to require comment. The literature, of course, contains a number of descriptions of individual specimens, particularly of anthropoid apes, that can be brought together for analysis; but, aside from the difficulties of gaining access to many of these publications, the accounts are of unequal value and often are difficult to assess. Perhaps of greater value are the special studies that deal with specific organs, organ systems, and regions, often embracing many genera, yet again usually only single specimens. The teeth and the skull have received the greatest attention, the muscles and the thoracic and abdominal viscera have had fairly adequate treatment, but the vascular system and the peripheral nerves have fared relatively poorly. Almost nothing is known about the joints.

Another important factor is that of age. For many reasons, fully mature specimens often are not available. Comparisons have frequently been made of animals of different ages. This has sometimes led, as Osman Hill (1950) has recently pointed out, to erroneous concepts, particularly respecting the anthropoid apes. It may be noted, parenthetically, that this sort of error is not confined to a study of living primates, as witness the sanguine comparisons that have been made of juvenile specimens of *Australopithecus* with adult material of other primates, including man.

Even the teeth, which have always assumed a very great importance in both taxonomic and phylogenetic studies, have rarely received quantitative treatment. Aside from the investigations of Remane (1921) and Ashton and Zuckerman (1950) on the anthropoids, and those of the latter authors on the green monkey (1950–51), there has been little work along this line. Indeed, it is not improbable that undue emphasis has often been placed upon slight differences in dental morphology, with consequent taxonomic or phylogenetic interpretations that would not have been drawn had more information regarding the dental variability of the involved form or forms been available.

In short, except for a small number of studies that deal with the skeleton and the dentition, gross-anatomical studies of non-human primates have largely been confined, frequently of necessity, to single or a few specimens. From this there has arisen the concept of the "type" when thinking of animals of different species or even genera—an unfortunate taxonomic concept that has too often plagued anthropology. It is to be admitted that such "type" study is often imposed by paucity of material and, as such, is but a necessary first step in the knowledge of an animal. It will continue to exist respecting many primates until such time as specimens become available in quantity. But, even with due cognizance of its widely distributed nature and hence of its relative inaccessibility, such material does exist for a number of genera or even species. It is to be expected, for at least some of these forms, that future research will gradually substitute a knowledge of population for that of "type."

A great deal of "hole-filling" is needed in straight morphology, particularly in that of the soft parts. But, again, study of practically untouched animals such as *Aotus*, *Callimico*, *Cacajao*, *Theropithecus*, and *Erythrocebus* will depend upon the availability of material, heretofore lacking. To this group may be added the siamang, *Symphalangus*, which has been but little studied, save for the skeleton. There is even a scarcity in museum collections of postcranial skeletal material of this interesting and important anthropoid ape.

Even many of the better-known forms —indeed, practically all of them—need much more study. The recent Raven memorial volume, *The Anatomy of the Gorilla* (Gregory, 1950), is a case in point. Granting its great merits, this volume cannot be said to be either systematic or comprehensive. Yet we have nothing even comparable to this for any of the other anthropoid apes. And the non-hominoid primates are, as noted above, not much better off.

It is possible that interest in straight, descriptive anatomy of primates has passed its peak. Students have become interested in definite problems, and many of the anatomical gaps will probably be bridged incidentally to the solution of such problems. Thus the anatomy of *Callimico* (hapalid in its limb skeleton and cebid in its skull and teeth) will probably become known when someone becomes deeply interested in the exact zoological status of the Hapalidae and makes a real effort to secure embalmed specimens of that rare genus. Erikson (1952) has demonstrated how interest in a specific prob-

lem—in this instance the locomotor patterns of the platyrrhines—can be a stimulus for the gathering of material.

HISTOLOGY

Histology has been one of the most neglected fields. Whatever little is known of non-human primates has largely been incidental to other investigations, chiefly in the medical sciences. Hence scattered data exist for only a few forms, such as the rhesus monkey, that have been used as laboratory animals. Even the anthropoid apes have not found their way under the microscope, except on relatively rare occasions. Yerkes (1951) has recently pointed out that histological knowledge of the gorilla is almost nonexistent; and the other anthropoids are scarcely better off in this respect.

Even so obvious an organ as the skin has barely been examined histologically, although its importance is not merely morphological but involves physiological and ecological considerations of the greatest interest. Many, if not most, of the few existing observations have been made on young animals, and animals of different ages have sometimes been compared, with undoubtedly misleading conclusions. For the skin is a structure that assuredly undergoes significant age changes (see Straus, 1950).

Comparative studies of the histology of bone fall into the same category. Indeed, it can hardly be said that even a modest beginning has been made in this field. Such studies would be of great value for eventual correlation with comparative studies of the physical and physiological properties of bone and of bones. It may be that the natural reluctance of museums and other repositories of skeletal material to permit mutilation of bones has been the chief deterrent to such investigations.

The list of comparative-histological hiatuses could be extended almost indefinitely. There is little or no knowl-

edge of the endocrine glands, despite
indications of their generic and even
specific physiological variability. Even
such a tissue as skeletal muscle offers
a fruitful field for comparative-histological study.

It is to be doubted whether qualified
workers will be sufficiently interested
—or, in fact, whether they will find it
particularly profitable—to systematically describe conditions over a range of
species. Past attempts at broad comparative-histological studies have not
gone very far. Probably our histological
knowledge will continue to accrue as
an accompaniment of other investigations—ecological, physiological, and
medical—that embrace microscopic
studies. The field is a rich one, however, for anyone with imagination and
proper training. The skin, the endocrine
glands, the digestive system, to mention
only the more obvious, should be fig-
urative gold mines. The nervous system surely needs no comment.

NEUROANATOMY

Discussion of the anatomy of the
nervous system as a separate item is
justified by the fact that the only feature at all peculiar to the Primates as a
zoological order is the unique tendency
toward high development of the central
nervous system, especially the brain,
within a relatively unspecialized body.

A great deal has been done with the
brains of primates other than man,
largely relative to the fissural patterns
of the cerebral cortex (see Connolly,
1950). Indeed, a rather large body of
data has been recorded. Cortical cyto-
architecture has also received considerable attention, but the gaps here are
very great; for such studies are not only
extremely laborious but require properly preserved material, which has been
available for only a few forms. Hence,
despite the classic studies of Brodmann
(1905 *et seq.*), the Vogts (1906 *et seq.*),
Mott and his co-workers (1908 *et seq.*),
and Campbell (1916 *et seq.*), and those
of more recent workers, the number of
genera that have been investigated is
not large. Moreover, knowledge of this
important field necessarily revolves
around the "type," since little is known
of individual variability. Inasmuch as
cortical expansion and differentiation is
certainly one of the most distinctive
features of primate evolution and radiation, and since it reflects so much in
the way of the adaptation and the potentialities of the total organism, the
desirability of filling in the major existing gaps in our knowledge can scarcely
be overemphasized.

In view of the admittedly predominant role of vision in primate evolution,
it is gratifying that we now possess a
considerable amount of data relating
to the visual apparatus (including the
eye, the visual pathways, and the receptive centers; there is a good deal of
information about the retina, the lateral
geniculate body, and even the visual
cortex of a number of genera). Yet conditions are poorly known or even unknown in some of the more important
genera. The necessity of a sound morphological background for physiological
and psychological studies of vision is
too evident to need any special comment.

The cerebellum has fared better than
most of the other parts of the brain,
due largely to the researches of Bolk
(1906). Both the spinal cord and, except for the thalamus, the brain stem
(despite the work of Tilney) represent
almost untapped sources, however, particularly with respect to internal, microscopic anatomy and projection systems.
The little work that has been carried
out on these structures leaves no doubt
that they would yield much to comparative study.

Despite the considerable neuroana-
tomical information that has been gathered, it must be noted that an undue
proportion of it relates to only a few

forms, particularly the more common laboratory types like the macaque and the chimpanzee.

DEVELOPMENT AND GROWTH

As pointed out above, the amount of existing information pertaining to the later, fetal stages of development, although incomplete, is nevertheless large, due chiefly to the continued, systematic investigations of Schultz. Much less is known about the early, embryonic stages that are even more difficult to procure. This is to be greatly regretted, for there is every reason to believe than an understanding of early development, including implantation and membrane formation, is a valuable aid in assessing the phylogenetic relationships of extant forms. Not a little is known about the early stages of development in *Tarsius*, a number of lemurs, platyrrhine and catarrhine monkeys, and the Hylobatinae. Of these, however, the rhesus monkey alone has been intensively studied (see Corner *et al.*, 1941); in fact, in some respects it is better known than man. Very little, however (indeed, almost nothing), is known about the early embryology of the great anthropoid apes. The problem does not appear to be insurmountable, although it is probable that, for some time to come at least, embryologists will have to rely upon the occasional, chance material recovered from animals collected in the wild. Information about the later stages of membrane formation is more plentiful and diverse, and existing studies on placentation embrace a large variety and number of primate genera.

Problems of growth and development in non-human primates will undoubtedly receive much attention, if for no other reason than their obvious bearing upon man. The analysis of primate growth has recently taken on a distinctly experimental tinge. The value of carefully devised experiments in studying growth (e.g., feeding madder or alizarin to study bone growth; cutting muscles to determine their influence upon the developing skeleton) has long been recognized by anatomists, and Washburn (1943 *et seq.*) has recently demonstrated their importance for physical anthropology. Thus it has become apparent that in some instances classical measurement is insufficient by itself and that only properly planned experiments upon growing animals can determine the factors involved in the correlative growth and development of complex mosaics like the skull. Use of experimental methods has hitherto been limited, of necessity, to animals other than primates. The direct application of such methods to primates merely awaits an adequate supply of material.

PHYSIOLOGY

As regards the non-human primates, physiology is largely unexplored territory. What little has been accomplished deals chiefly with one primate, the macaque, particularly the rhesus monkey. The relatively meager existing knowledge of the physiology of the circulatory, respiratory, and digestive systems is almost entirely limited to that animal. This is likewise true of endocrine physiology, which is to be greatly deplored; for studies on the thyroid gland suggest that there can be striking differences in the role of this gland among even closely related species (Fleischmann, Shumacker, and Straus, 1943), and the same is to be suspected of other endocrine organs.

Much more is known about the physiology of reproduction and the physiology of the nervous system. Knowledge of the reproductive physiology of the rhesus monkey rivals that of man. Other macaques and the baboons are rather well understood, but the remaining Cercopithecinae and the Semnopithecinae have had little study. Information about the anthropoid apes is almost entirely restricted to the chimpanzee. The New World monkeys, *Tarsius*, and especially the lemurs, are but poorly known. (See Asdell, 1946.)

There is a large body of literature dealing with the physiology of the nervous system of non-human primates. Most of this concerns the cerebral cortex (chiefly the motor functions), whereas less is known about the brain stem and the cerebellum, little about the spinal cord and the peripheral nerves, and virtually nothing about the autonomic nervous system. Again, however, except for the cerebral cortex (where a wide variety of primates has been investigated), existing knowledge is almost entirely limited to the ubiquitous rhesus monkey. There are a few data relative to the physiology of the eye and the ear in several genera. The physiological maturation of the nervous system has received scant attention; Hines's (1942) careful and thorough study of the development of reflex patterns, posture, and progression in the rhesus monkey is outstanding.

The study of primate muscle physiology has been greatly neglected. When one recalls the striking, unexplained differences in strength between primates of approximately the same weight (as between chimpanzee and man)—differences that cannot be explained on the basis of leverages—the need for such studies is evident.

There are many physiological problems that are particularly pertinent to ecology and psychobiology. Some beginning studies, again largely on the macaque, have been made in the all-important related fields of basal metabolism and temperature regulation. This brings to mind the problem of climatic adaptation. Even excluding man, primates live in very different sorts of climates. This is true not only of different genera and species, but even of members of one and the same species. The

rhesus monkeys offer a challenging problem here. These animals constitute a single species, *Macaca mulatta*, with six recognizable geographical races, that attains a wider distribution in geography and altitude than any other species of monkey—from North India through Burma, Siam, and French Indo-China, well into China (Miller, 1933). It is found from or near sea-level up to 5,000 or 6,000 feet in the Himalayas. And these adaptations to various types of climate have been made without benefit of a culture. Another related case concerns the gorillas, which may constitute two species or only one, depending upon one's taxonomic outlook. The lowland gorilla inhabits the hot, damp, coastal forests of West Africa, whereas the mountain gorilla lives in the mixed bamboo forest of the eastern Congo, ranging in altitude from 7,500 to 12,000 feet (Hooton, 1942). Study of animals from different climatic zones would probably yield rich dividends, particularly if metabolic and other physiological studies were correlated with such anatomical features, for example, as the density of the hair, the character and density of the glands of the skin, and the blood picture. In this connection, the endocrine glands cannot be ignored. The probability of their functional variability in different species has already been mentioned (see also Fleischmann, 1947). Such variability may well have prime adaptive, evolutionary significance.

Modern physiological techniques, however, especially those of neurophysiology, are such that they can be properly used only by those who have special training. To attack many of the problems noted above, the cooperation of primatologists and physiologists is necessary.

Problems of posture and locomotion may be considered here, inasmuch as they are essentially physiological in nature. These problems may be expected to receive a great deal of attention in the future. They can be attacked in two ways: by observation of living animals supplemented by gross-anatomical and metrical studies, and by experimentation in the laboratory. The studies of Pratt (1943) and others on experimentally produced bipedal rats indicate what might be done with primates. The different quadrupedal, pronograde modes of primate locomotion are ripe for analysis. It is clear that to speak of quadrupedal posture and locomotion as if this were a unity, even among primates, is an extreme oversimplification. The same is true of the various types of bimanual locomotion or brachiation. There is ample evidence that the brachiation of *Colobus*, that of the Hylobatinae, that of the great apes, and that of *Ateles* represent different types of adaptations that express themselves in various degrees and kinds of anatomical specializations. Yet these have never been clearly described or properly analyzed. This problem has a great bearing upon that of human evolution. It is probable that at least some of the disagreement about the occurrence or non-occurrence of a brachiating stage in human phylogeny is due to a lack of clarity about what such a stage would involve, and hence is to a large degree semantic in nature.

Any future studies of posture and locomotion—whether bipedal, bimanual, or quadrupedal—must necessarily be physiological as well as anatomical. Too often have posture and locomotion been thought of in terms of skeleton and muscles alone. Yet these are essentially effector organs, for it has been clearly demonstrated that the central nervous system is the prime controlling agent. Any comparative study of posture and locomotion must consider differences in the latter, as well as differences in the vascular mechanisms that also are largely under neural control. Other experimental techniques are ready to be utilized for dynamic analyses of functional problems. The recent development of the "stresscoat" deformation method and of the use of strain gauges, for example, opens up new avenues of attack upon various problems related to the primate skeleton.

BIOCHEMISTRY

Biochemical studies of non-human primates have been largely serological in character. The corpus of knowledge regarding both precipitins and blood groups is by no means inconsiderable and includes numerous genera. But even more extensive studies are needed in this important field. It is to be expected that the recent wide recognition of the great importance of blood-group studies in the anthropology of human racial groups and of their aid in assessing group relationships will provide a stimulus for such studies among non-human primates as well. Cooperation not only between the primatologist and the biochemist but also between interested investigators and zoological parks could be very productive.

The rhesus monkey has been employed rather extensively in various vitamin studies, but virtually nothing is known about the vitamin requirements of other non-human primates. A comparative viewpoint is badly needed here and might produce much of interest, for it may well be that there is variability in the vitamin requirements of primates.

A bare start, although embracing a fair number of genera, chiefly catarrhine, has been made in the field of carbohydrate, fat, and protein metabolism. Studies of the various nitrogenous excretory products of primate urine (see Rheinberger, 1936) have yielded such suggestive results that the fertility of this and related fields for systematic exploration is clearly indicated. The probable ecological, taxonomic, and phylogenetic significance is apparent.

Biochemical studies require special techniques, but some of these are relatively simple and can be mastered without too much difficulty by those who possess fundamental chemical training.

PSYCHOBIOLOGY

The literature in the field of psychobiology is truly extensive. A great deal has been done on the experimental side, and a number of non-human primate genera have received at least some study. But, again, as in so many other areas of investigation, the macaque and the chimpanzee—chiefly because they have been easiest to procure —have received the major share of attention. Thanks largely to the extensive, intensive, and continuing studies of the Yale–Harvard–Orange Park group of investigators, our knowledge of the chimpanzee is very considerable.

Less progress has been made in observational psychobiology, and especially in the very difficult and highly important field of observation of primates in their native habitats. Much, however, has been written, but chiefly by unqualified observers. The careful studies of Carpenter on howling monkeys in Central America (1934) and on gibbons in Siam (1940), and those of Nissen (1931–32) on chimpanzees in French Guinea, are outstanding exceptions. To these must be added the classic pioneer investigations of Zuckerman (1932) on baboons, both in their natural environment and in a colony of animals transplanted from their native habitat. More investigations of animals in their native environments are badly needed. Such studies of the gorilla and the orang-utan are particularly desirable; but political considerations will probably be a barrier to any serious study of the latter for some time to come.

GENETICS

Anthropologists have found genetics to be a valuable tool in the study and analysis of human populations, not only in regard to blood groups but also in regard to gross-morphological and even physiological characters. It is to be expected, therefore, that the methods of population genetics, giving due attention to mutation, selection, migration, and genetic drift, will eventually be applied to other primates and that they will produce important information. The application of such methods, however, has distinct limitations at the present time. Investigations of series of living animals from one area, or even of comparable series of embalmed cadavers, is well-nigh out of the question. But something might be done with skeletal material. The museums of America and Europe possess series of skeletons of single species of primates collected at one locality. Such series, it is true, are not too numerous, and they usually consist largely, if not entirely, of skulls, but some of them are of sufficient size to warrant this sort of studies. One major handicap is that but little or nothing is known about the sizes of the populations (not to mention the sizes of the breeding populations) from which such series have been taken. Yet, despite this, some problems could be attacked successfully. The recent illuminating analysis of samples of two geographically isolated populations of the green monkey (*Cercopithecus aethiops sabaeus*), representing the parent-stock from West Africa and the descendants of animals transplanted to the West Indies, by Ashton and Zuckerman (1950–51), is the sole study of this kind for primates.

Experimental hybridization has been carried out in a number of zoological gardens, but the results of such hybridizations of primates have rarely or never been adequately analyzed from the genetic viewpoint (see Zuckerman,

1933). It is important, for example, not only to know whether a certain interspecific or intergeneric cross is possible, yielding viable hybrids, but especially to know whether or not the F_1 hybrids themselves are fertile. If the latter be true, it would follow that the barriers between the crossable forms must have been entirely geographical down to the present date, and it would indicate, moreover, that genetic barriers such as exist in many groups of animals are slow to form in the primates. Especially illuminating would be the genetic analysis of the backcrosses between the F_1 hybrids and the parent-species. In the hybrid only those dominant traits present in either species, plus such characters as give blending or intermediate effects, would show up. But in the backcrosses it would be possible to determine whether particular traits are due to single gene differences or to multiple factors; whether traits are linked or segregate freely; whether the gene interactions are in all cases harmonious or in some combinations produce disharmonies of structure or physiology; etc. A study of the blood antigens like that carried out by Irwin and his colleagues in crosses between different species of doves and pigeons (1947) could scarcely fail to clarify greatly the problem of the closeness of relationship between species, races, and populations of primates. Some of these problems might be successfully attacked by cooperation between primatologists, geneticists, and zoological gardens.

PALEONTOLOGY

Recent years have witnessed numerous and important discoveries of the fossil remains of various primates. Chief interest has naturally centered upon such forms as the Australopithecinae, with their promise of elucidating the later stages of hominid evolution. Other less dramatic but also highly significant material, however, has been brought to light.

The Primates probably arose from some primitive insectivore-like stock, but whether this was proto-erinaceoid or proto-tupaioid remains a question. Prosimians, both lemuroid and tarsioid, were already differentiated in the Paleocene, so that it may be concluded that the divergence of lemuroids and tarsioids occurred before that date. Barth (1950), however, thinks that a strict separation of lemuroids and tarsioids was not present in the Eocene and hence groups all these early prosimian forms together; he cites the great number of unplaceable genera in support of his contention.

The lemuriform lemurs were present in numbers from the Paleocene through the Eocene. They are represented by the Plesiadapidae (Paleocene-Eocene) and the more generalized Adapidae (Eocene). After the Eocene there is a complete break in their fossil record until they reappear in profusion in the Pleistocene.

The precise relationship of the Lorisiformes to other prosimians is unknown; for their paleontological record has been a blank except for a single genus from the Pliocene of India. The recently unearthed remains of galagine lemurs (as yet undescribed) from Lower Miocene deposits in East Africa (Clark and Leakey, 1951) may throw some light on the history of this group.

The history of the Tupaioidea and their relationships to the undoubted primates remains obscure. Whether they are the most primitive of lemuriform lemurs, as claimed by Le Gros Clark (1934) and Simpson (1945), or whether they are to be regarded as primates at all, are questions that await the discovery of additional paleontological material. The gap between *Anagale* of the Lower Oligocene of Mongolia, described by Simpson over twenty years ago, and the living tupaioids is a great one. *Anagale* appears in some ways to be more lemur-like than are the extant tupaioids, and this is the chief reason (although not the only one) for regarding the latter as true lemuriforms; but this important matter is far from being settled.

Numerous Tarsioidea have been found in the Paleocene and Eocene of North America and in the Eocene of Europe. But they disappear from the fossil record in the Lower Oligocene and are represented in Recent times by only a single genus, *Tarsius,* that ranges from the East Indies to the Philippines. No new fossil material has appeared in recent years to elucidate their phylogenetic relationships to the lemuriform and lorisiform lemurs, on the one hand, and to the simian primates (Anthropoidea or Pithecoidea), on the other hand. Their probable origin from a more generalized, more lemur-like stock which also gave rise to the Lemuriformes and the Lorisiformes is indicated, as has been ably discussed by Simpson. Some workers, such as Le Gros Clark, however, believe that the lemurs and the tarsiers originated independently from the basal primate stock and that the latter did not pass through a lemuroid stage in their evolution.

Many students derive the simian primates from essentially generalized tarsioids; but the evidence for this is derived chiefly from the comparative study of living forms rather than from the fossil record. The presence of certain tarsioid-like characters in the mandible of *Parapithecus,* a catarrhine primate from the Lower Oligocene of Egypt, has been advanced in support of this view. *Pondaungia* and *Amphipithecus,* from the Upper Eocene of Burma, each represented by a single mandibular fragment containing teeth, have been regarded by some investigators as representing a transitional stage from a tarsioid to a simian phase (Pilgrim, 1927; Clark,

1950). Indeed, these specimens have even been advanced as evidence of the origin of the anthropoid ape line of evolution directly from tarsioids without the intervention of a monkey-like phase; and Le Gros Clark thinks it probable that both the cercopithecoid and hominoid sequences may have separated at a stage of evolution represented by *Amphipithecus.* Beyond this, the supposed tarsioid ancestry of the simian primates remains unsupported by concrete evidence. It has been suggested that the simian characters of fossil and living Tarsioidea may well have arisen as parallel developments independently of their counterparts in the Anthropoidea. Indeed, the possible derivation of the latter from a more generalized, more lemur-like prosimian stock, such as the Adapidae, rather than from true tarsioids, certainly cannot be excluded (see Simpson, 1945). In this connection, it may be recalled that *Notharctus,* an adapid of the North American Eocene, has been regarded by some workers as ancestral to the New World monkeys.

The phylogenetic history of the New World monkeys or platyrrhines is quite unknown. Save for a single Miocene genus, *Homunculus,* the fossil record of this group does not extend back beyond the Pleistocene. Not only are these Pleistocene forms similar to extant platyrrhines of the same areas, but even *Homunculus* resembles the living subfamily Aotinae. It is still an open question whether the platyrrhine and catarrhine simians were derived from a single or from separate ancestral prosimian stocks. Nor is there any fossil evidence bearing on the moot question of the exact zoological status of the Hapalidae (marmosets and tamarins)— whether they are truly the most primitive of all living platyrrhines or whether much of their apparent primitiveness represents a specialized retrogression from more generalized cebid ancestors.

The origins of the catarrhine or Old World Anthropoidea are not much clearer. As noted above, Le Gros Clark thinks that the catarrhines may have arisen from tarsioids via a transitional stage resembling *Amphipithecus*. The latter, however, is so fragmentary that it is open to diverse interpretations. It has even been classified (together with the equally obscure *Pondaungia*) as a possible pongid of uncertain affinities (Simpson, 1945). *Parapithecus*, a Lower Oligocene genus represented by a single lower jaw with teeth, has been variously regarded as a primitive Old World monkey, as a primitive anthropoid ape, and as a proto-catarrhine from which all existing catarrhine primates (monkey, apes, man) could have been derived (see Gregory, 1922). Obviously, more material belonging to this highly important genus is badly needed.

The matter of a possible tarsioid origin for the catarrhines has already been discussed. Granting its probability, it remains a question whether any or all of the Anthropoidea of the Old World arose as such directly from prosimian ancestors or whether they first passed through a "platyrrhine" stage more or less resembling the more generalized of the living New World monkeys. Each of these suppositions has its advocates. The many remarkable morphological resemblances between the more advanced platyrrhines and some of the catarrhines bear upon this question. It remains to be determined whether these are merely evolutionary parallelisms or are evidences of an even closer relationship. At the moment, the former interpretation appears to be the more reasonable one.

The history of the Old World monkeys is fragmentary. A number of remains of undoubted cercopithecoids (both cercopithecine and semnopithecine) have been found in Pliocene deposits of the Old World, including Europe; and they have recently been reported, with the characteristic cercopithecoid dental specializations, as occurring in the Lower Miocene of East Africa. If *Moeripithecus* and *Apidium*, both from the Lower Oligocene of Egypt, are accepted as true cercopithecoids, the Old World monkeys had already begun their separate course of evolution at this early date, and the contemporary *Parapithecus* could be regarded as a primitive anthropoid ape. But, as Simpson (1945) has pointed out, the allocation of these two fragments to the Cercopithecidae is dubious. The better-known *Oreopithecus* of the Lower Pliocene, however, is generally regarded as a cercopithecoid, although of uncertain position, for its teeth exhibit peculiarities not found in undoubted Cercopithecidae. All three of these forms (*Moeripithecus, Apidium, Oreopithecus*) are known only from fragments of jaws and teeth, and none of them exhibits the distinct bilophodontism of the molars that is characteristic of the Cercopithecidae. This specialized tendency toward extreme bilophodontism, it must be noted, seems to be the chief taxonomic criterion of a cercopithecoid. It is a criterion that stems from paleontological necessity, since usually only jaws and teeth are preserved as fossils. The question arises as to whether a catarrhine primate can be regarded as a cercopithecoid in the absence of bilophodont molars, even if the rest of its body is truly cercopithecoid. The same sort of problem arises in dealing with the fossils of other catarrhine primates. However, as noted above, the paleontological record has granted the dentition priority in assessing relationships. Hence it is well to recognize that the vertical taxonomy of mammals, and thus of primates, is primarily based upon the teeth and, it may be added, is likely to remain so, at least for a long time. Nevertheless, it should also be recognized that such a taxonomy is inevitably prone to a certain despotism and artificiality, for it tends to ignore the fact that the dentition does not always completely characterize the total animal (a notable example of this among living primates is the lemuriform lemur, *Daubentonia*) and that teeth, moreover, are subject to the same biological variability as other parts of the body.

Recent years have brought highly significant additions to our knowledge of the history of the Hominoidea (anthropoid apes, man). The important group of Lower Miocene apes collected in East Africa by Leakey and the remarkable and rich discoveries of the Australopithecinae in South Africa by Dart and Broom, particularly by the latter, are bringing about a rewriting of the phylogenetic history of the hominoids.

Leaving aside not only ambiguous *Amphipithecus* and *Pondaungia* but also *Parapithecus,* a line of evolution for the Hylobatinae (gibbons, siamang) may now be reasonably postulated on the basis of existing evidence. This would run from *Propliopithecus* of the Lower Oligocene of Egypt to *Limnopithecus* of the Lower Miocene of East Africa, and, from some of the less specialized representatives of the latter genus, to the modern gibbon and siamang. Le Gros Clark also regards *Pliopithecus* of the European Miocene and Lower Pliocene as an offshoot of the *Limnopithecus* stock; but whether *Pliopithecus* is to be viewed as directly ancestral to the modern Hylobatinae or as an independent collateral branch of hylobatine evolution is by no means clear.

This current appraisal of hylobatine phylogeny is founded primarily on characters of the jaws and teeth. Fortunately, recent discoveries of limb-bone material, by no means inconsiderable in nature, of both *Limnopithecus* and *Pliopithecus*, are of great value in helping to elucidate one of the more vexed problems of hominoid evolution. The known limb bones of *Limnopithecus*, although they possess certain hylobatine features, also exhibit definite monkey-like characters and are distinctly cercopithecoid in their proportions (Clark and Thomas, 1951). Much the same is true of *Pliopithecus* (Zapfe, 1952). The hindlimb of *Pliopithecus* is essentially gibbon-like, but some parts of the forelimb skeleton exhibit characters that must be regarded as primitive and which find their counterparts in lemurs. Furthermore, the forelimb is not lengthened as in modern Hylobatinae, the intermembral index being similar to those found among living baboons. Available evidence thus suggests that the precursors of the extant Hylobatinae, at least as late as the Miocene, and perhaps the Pliocene, may well have been quadrupedal animals, and that the striking brachiating specializations so characteristic of the modern gibbons and siamang appeared late in their evolutionary history.

The other known representatives of the East African Lower Miocene Hominoidea belong to two genera, *Proconsul* and *Sivapithecus*, both assigned to that far-flung and heterogeneous group, the Dryopithecinae, hitherto found only in Europe (Middle Miocene through Pliocene) and India (Pliocene) and hitherto known almost entirely from teeth and jaws. *Proconsul*, which is of especial interest, has been described in detail by Le Gros Clark and Leakey (1951), who would derive it from some advanced, *Limnopithecus*-like hylobatine type.

The genus *Proconsul* is represented not only by jaws and teeth, described as three species that exhibit a most remarkable range in size, but also by an invaluable, uniquely preserved skull of the smallest species, *P. africanus*, and by a number of limb bones assigned to the intermediate-sized species, *P. nyanzae*. These present an exceptionally significant combination of characters. In brief, the teeth of *Proconsul* are distinctly of an anthropoid ape type and even show certain specializations in the direction of the living African great apes. The skull, however, definitely approximates those of the smaller cercopithecoid monkeys in its general morphology; and it has a number of primitive features not found in existing great apes. Its endocranial cast, moreover, indicates a brain that was cercopithecoid, rather than anthropoid, in pattern. The limb bones parallel the skull in their many cercopithecoid, non-anthropoid characters. In fact, they strongly suggest that these early Miocene dryopithecines were cursorial quadrupeds, and they provide no indications of a brachiating mode of locomotion as found in the living anthropoids. On the evidence of the teeth —and despite the rest of the skeleton— these creatures have been classified as anthropoid apes, although of a very primitive type. This would seem to be an almost inevitable procedure in view of the dental nature of current primate taxonomy, as already noted above. Save for those who are imbued with awe for the canons of taxonomy, however, it is not of paramount importance whether we regard *Proconsul* as a generalized anthropoid ape or as a somewhat advanced monkey. Of much greater importance is the fact that from animals possessing extremities of this type (but not necessarily from animals of the *Proconsul* group itself, with their distinct dental specializations), as Le Gros Clark and Leakey have pointed out, there could have developed, in one direction, the modern anthropoid apes with their highly specialized limbs adapted to brachiation and, in another direction, the immediate forerunners of the Hominidae. The implication here is that the line leading directly to man never passed through a brachiating phase. This is in accord with other recent assessments of evidence bearing upon this problem (see Straus, 1949).

It should also be noted that the recently unearthed fossil evidence suggests that the gibbons developed their characteristic brachiating specializations independently of the great apes. This finds support from studies of living hylobatines and pongines. For comparisons of the skeleton and muscles of the upper extremities of gibbons and great apes, and of their modes of locomotion, make it evident that the adaptations to a bimanual, brachiating mode of locomotion are different in these two groups of hominoids (Straus, 1940, 1941, 1942). However, as pointed out earlier, the several types of primate brachiation constitute a subject in need of further investigation.

The Australopithecinae will not be discussed at any length here. It is sufficient to note that it is generally recognized that, whatever their precise zoological affinities, they are of the greatest importance for the light that they throw, directly or indirectly, upon certain critical phases in the evolution of the Hominidae. The several different views respecting their exact phylogenetic status and relationships cannot be considered here. But it may be pointed out that these divergent views are possible because certain important problems remain unsettled (see, e.g., Zuckerman, 1950). Their geological age is highly uncertain. The exact character of their habitat has not been established. To some students their posture remains a reasonable point of doubt. The phylogenetic significance of some of their morphological characters is open to different interpretations. The view has been expressed that much of the material needs to be more thoroughly studied and evaluated, particularly by comparison with statistically significant series of other primates. The meaning of the curious giant forms is quite obscure. The enthusiastic attempts to reconstruct the social life of the Australopithecinae have not been calculated to inspire confidence. In short, many important questions remain to be answered. The great quantity of Australopithecine material thus far uncovered, and the prospect of still more to come, betokens years of careful study. The discoverers of this material have accomplished an amazing and highly praiseworthy job under great difficulties. But the lack of adequate comparative material is often all too evident. It would be a great aid in the solution of at least some of the problems relating to the Australopithecinae if casts could be made available to workers in other countries after the original descriptions and analyses of the specimens have been published.

LIST OF REFERENCES

ASDELL, S. A. 1946. *Patterns of Mammalian Reproduction*. Ithaca, N.Y.: Comstock Publishing Co.

ASHTON, E. H., and ZUCKERMAN, S. 1950. "Some Quantitative Dental Characteristics of the Chimpanzee, Gorilla and Orang-outang," *Philosophical Transactions of the Royal Society of London*, ser. B, CCXXXIV, 471–84.

———. 1950–51. "The Influence of Geographic Isolation on the Skull of the Green Monkey (*Cercopithecus aethiops sabaeus*), I–IV," *ibid.*, CXXXVII, 212–38; CXXXVIII, 204–13, 213–18, 354–74.

BARTH, F. 1950. "On the Relationships of Early Primates," *American Journal of Physical Anthropology*, n.s., VIII, 139–49.

BOLK, L. 1906. *Das Cerebellum der Säugetiere*. Jena: Gustav Fischer.

BRODMANN, K. 1905. "Beiträge zur histologischen Lokalisation der Grosshirnrinde. Dritte Mitteilung. Die Rindenfelder der niederen Affen," *Zeitschrift für Psychologie und Neurologie*, IV, 177–226.

CAMPBELL, A. W. 1906. *Histological Studies on the Localisation of Cerebral Function*. Cambridge: At the University Press.

CARPENTER, C. R. 1934. *A Field Study of the Behavior and Social Relations of Howling Monkeys (Alouatta palliata)*. ("Comparative Psychology Monographs," No. 48.)

———. 1940. *A Field Study in Siam of the Behavior and Social Relations of the Gibbon (Hylobates lar)*. ("Comparative Psychology Monographs," No. 84.)

CLARK, W. E. LE GROS. 1934. *Early Fore-runners of Man*. London: Ballière, Tindall & Cox.

———. 1950. "New Palaeontological Evidence Bearing on the Evolution of the Hominoidea," *Quarterly Journal of the Geological Society of London*, CV, 225–64.

CLARK, W. E. LE GROS, and LEAKEY, L. S. B. 1951. *The Miocene Hominoidea of East Africa*. ("Fossil Mammals of Africa," No. 1.) London: British Museum of Natural History.

CLARK, W. E. LE GROS, and THOMAS, D. P. 1951. *Associated Jaws and Limb Bones of Limnopithecus macinnesi*. ("Fossil Mammals of Africa," No. 3.) London: British Museum of Natural History.

CONNOLLY, C. J. 1950. *External Morphology of the Primate Brain*. Springfield, Ill.: Charles C. Thomas.

CORNER, G. W., *et al.* 1941. *Embryology of the Rhesus Monkey (Macaca mulatta)*. ("Carnegie Institution of Washington Publications," No. 538.) Washington, D.C.

ERIKSON, G. E. 1952. "Locomotor Types and Body Proportions in the New World Primates," *Anatomical Records*, CXII, 24. (65th Annual Session of the American Association of Anatomists.) (Abstract.)

FLEISCHMANN, W. 1947. "Comparative Physiology of the Thyroid Hormone," *Quarterly Review of Biology*, XXII, 119–40.

FLEISCHMANN, W.; SHUMACKER, H. B., JR.; and STRAUS, W. L., JR. 1943. "Influence of Age on the Effect of Thyroidectomy in the Rhesus Monkey," *Endocrinology*, XXXII, 238–46.

GREGORY, W. K. 1922. *The Origin and Evolution of the Human Dentition.* Baltimore: Williams & Wilkins Co.

—— (ed.). 1950. *The Anatomy of the Gorilla* (The Henry Cushier Raven Memorial Volume). New York: Columbia University Press.

HILL, W. C. OSMAN. 1950. "Man's Relation to the Apes," *Man,* No. 257.

HINES, MARION. 1942. "The Development and Regression of Reflexes, Postures, and Progression in the Young Macaque." In *Contributions to Embryology,* No. 30, pp. 153–209. ("Carnegie Institution of Washington Publications," No. 196.)

HOOTON, E. 1942. *Man's Poor Relations.* Garden City, N.Y.: Doubleday, Doran & Co.

IRWIN, M. R. 1947. "Immunogenetics," *Advances in Genetics,* I, 133–59. New York: Academic Press.

MILLER, G. S., JR. 1933. "The Groups and Names of Macaques." In HARTMAN, C. G., and STRAUS, W. L., JR. (eds.), *The Anatomy of the Rhesus Monkey,* chap. i, pp. 1–9. Baltimore: Williams & Wilkins Co.

MOLLISON, T. 1910. "Die Körperproportionen der Primaten," *Morphologisches Jahrbuch,* XLII, 79–304.

MOTT, F. W., and KELLEY, AGNES M. 1908. "Complete Survey of the Cell Lamination of the Cerebral Cortex of the Lemur," *Proceedings of the Royal Society of London,* ser. B, LXXX, 488–506.

NISSEN, H. W. 1931–32. *A Field Study of the Chimpanzee.* ("Comparative Psychology Monographs," No. 36.)

PILGRIM, G. E. 1927. "A Sivapithecus Palate and Other Primate Fossils from India," *Palaeontologica Indica,* XIV, 1 ff.

PRATT, L. W. 1943. "Behavior of Bipedal Rats," *Bulletin of the Johns Hopkins Hospital,* LXXII, 265–73.

REMANE, A. 1921. "Beiträge zur Morphologie des Anthropoidengebisses," *Archiv für Naturgeschichte,* LXXXVII A, 1–179.

RHEINBERGER, MARGARET B. 1936. "The Nitrogen Partition in the Urine of Various Primates," *Journal of Biological Chemistry,* CXV, 343–60.

RUCH, T. C. 1941. *Bibliographia primato-logica.* Springfield, Ill., and Baltimore: Charles C. Thomas.

SCHULTZ, A. H. 1924. "Growth Studies on Primates Bearing upon Man's Evolution," *American Journal of Physical Anthropology,* VII, 149–64.

——. 1926. "Fetal Growth of Man and Other Primates," *Quarterly Review of Biology,* I, 465–521.

——. 1927. "Studies on the Growth of Gorilla and of Other Higher Primates," *Memoirs of the Carnegie Museum, Pittsburgh,* XI, 1–87.

——. 1933. "Die Körperproportionen der erwachsenen catarrhinen Primaten, mit spezieller Berücksichtigung der Menschenaffen," *Anthropologischer Anzeiger,* X, 154–85.

——. 1933. "Observations on the Growth, Classification and Evolutionary Specialization of Gibbons and Siamangs," *Human Biology,* V, 212–55, 385–428.

——. 1944. "Age Changes and Variability in Gibbons: A Morphological Study on a Population Sample of a Man-like Ape," *American Journal of Physical Anthropology,* n.s., II, 1–129.

SIMPSON, G. G. 1945. "The Principles of Classification and a Classification of Mammals," *Bulletin of the American Museum of Natural History,* LXXXV, 1–350.

STRAUS, W. L., JR. 1940. "The Posture of the Great Ape Hand in Locomotion and Its Phylogenetic Implications," *American Journal of Physical Anthropology,* XXVII, 199–207.

——. 1941. "The Phylogeny of the Human Forearm Extensors," *Human Biology,* XIII, 23–50, 203–38.

——. 1942. "Rudimentary Digits in Primates," *Quarterly Review of Biology,* XVII, 228–43.

——. 1949. "The Riddle of Man's Ancestry," *ibid.,* XXIV, 200–223.

——. 1950. "The Microscopic Anatomy of the Skin of the Gorilla." In GREGORY, W. K. (ed.), *The Anatomy of the Gorilla,* Part IV, pp. 213–26. New York: Columbia University Press.

TILNEY, F. 1928. *The Brain from Ape to Man: A Contribution to the Study of the Evolution and Development of the Hu* man Brain. 2 vols. New York: Paul B. Hoeber.

TYSON, E. 1699. *Orang-utang, sive Homo sylvestris: or, the Anatomy of a Pygmie Compared with that of a Monkey, an Ape, and a Man. To which is Added, a Philological Essay Concerning the Pygmies, the Cynocephali, the Satyrs, and Sphinges of the Ancients. Wherein it will Appear that they are all either Apes or Monkeys, and not Men, as Formerly Pretended.* London: Thomas Bennet.

VOGT, O. 1906. "Ueber strukturelle Hirncentra, mit besonderer Berücksichtigung der strukturellen Felder des Cortex pallii," *Anatomischer Anzeiger,* XXIX, Erg. H, 74–114.

WASHBURN, S. L. 1951. "The New Physical Anthropology," *Transactions of the New York Academy of Sciences,* ser. II, XIII, 298–304.

WASHBURN, S. L., and DETWILER, S. R. 1943. "An Experiment Bearing on the Problems of Physical Anthropology," *American Journal of Physical Anthropology,* n.s., I, 171–90.

YERKES, R. M. "Gorilla Census and Study," *Journal of Mammology,* XXXII, 429–36.

ZAPFE, H. 1952. *Die Pliopithecus-Funde aus der Spaltenfüllung von Neudorf an der March (CSR),* pp. 1–5. ("Verhandlungen der Geologisches Bundesanstalt 1952," Sonderheft C.)

ZUCKERMAN, S. 1932. *The Social Life of Monkeys and Apes.* London: Kegan Paul, Trench, Trubner & Co.

———. 1933. *Functional Affinities of Man, Monkeys, and Apes.* New York: Harcourt, Brace & Co.

———. 1950. "Taxonomy and Human Evolution," *Biological Reviews,* XXV, 435–85.

The Idea of Fossil Man

By PIERRE TEILHARD DE CHARDIN

I. BIRTH

THE IDEA of the existence of a man who[1] can be regarded as the precursor, both chronologically and morphologically, of the builder of historical civilization— this idea, I submit, represents a surprisingly recent conquest of the modern mind. Today no one any longer questions it or even wonders at it. And yet only a little more than a century ago it would have been as impossible and as shocking for the serious scientist to speak (or even think!) in terms of "fossil man" as it still was, fifty years ago, for official science to suggest the mutability of the atom.

In his classic *Les Hommes fossiles*,[2] Professor M. Boule vividly pictured prehistory's heroic days (in and around 1850), when the best brains of France and England fought hard to break the philosophico-scientific spell which made it almost impossible for the ordinary mind of that time (and this in spite of Buffon, Cuvier, and Lamarck) to conceive of man (or even of apes) as a part of the so-called "extinct world."

Nowadays everyone has heard of the bitter discussions provoked by the first Chelleo-Acheulean hand-axes collected by Boucher de Perthes (1846) in the Pleistocene gravel of the Somme River, a find which coincided with Lartet's discovery of the Miocene *Pliopithecus* and *Dryopithecus* in southern France. Today we smile as we think of the thrills and triumphs experienced by our great predecessors[3] when in 1864 they first observed, on a fragment of mammoth tusk,[4] the carved outline of the mammoth itself—definite testimony, over man's own signature, that man (at that time still believed to have been "created" in 4000 B.C.) had known and hunted the fabulous and (to the scientist of the period) fabulously ancient animal.

These are well-known facts. But they must be remembered and borne in mind if we are to understand fully the many painstaking efforts, both of excavation and of discussion, which the idea of fossil man was destined to undergo before it reached the modern (and probably still immature) version that is commonly accepted today.

II. GROWTH

The fact that they had established beyond doubt man's contemporaneous existence with an extinct Pleistocene fauna did not lead the paleontologists of the 1860's to conclude that man, even at that early stage, could have differed appreciably, either anatomically or mentally, from what we ourselves are at the present day.

1. Judging from the anatomical characteristics, geological horizon, chemical transformation, and faunistic association of his bones.

2. Paris: Masson, 1923.

3. A triumph which resulted in occasional outbursts of an excessive belief in the existence of a "Tertiary man."

4. Unearthed in the Upper Paleolithic cave of La Madeleine, France.

But after overcoming the initial difficulty of visualizing man's high antiquity, the early prehistorians still had to surmount another mental hurdle, namely, a reluctance even to imagine a representative of the human race who would exhibit, osteologically, any prehuman features. Long after Boucher de Perthe's victory, the belief that early man was nothing but a particularly ancient *Homo sapiens* was still widely accepted, a view that was supported by such incidents as the discovery, in the gravel of the Somme (1863), of the perfectly modern-looking[5] lower jaw of Moulin-Quignon and (in 1868) of the more important find of Cro-Magnon man (a typical "white man") in the Upper Pleistocene deposits of Perigord.

Two major and purely accidental events were in great part responsible for the cracking of this narrow frame, each of them initiating and characterizing a particular and transitional stage in the development of human paleontology: first, the discovery of the Neanderthal man, leading to a "Europeo-Neanderthal" conception of fossil man; and, subsequently, the discovery of the Pithecanthropines, which fostered an "Asiatico-prehominian" theory of the origin of man.

Let us consider these two stages, traversed successively in the course of the last fifty years by the science of man, before we attempt, in the third and last part of this paper, to characterize the main conceptions and tendencies which currently prevail among scientists interested today in the problem of fossil man.

A. THE "EUROPEO-NEANDERTHAL" PHASE
OF DEVELOPMENT IN THE SCIENTIFIC
CONCEPTION OF FOSSIL MAN

As early as 1856, the first and most famous Neanderthal calvarium was found in the Rhine Valley. But, strangely enough, owing both to the unsatisfactory state of the fossil's preservation and to the unprepared condition of the scientific minds at the time,[6] the true significance of the specimen was not realized or accepted before the much later discoveries of similar relics, first at Spy (Belgium) in 1887 and soon afterward in southwestern France (Le Moustier, La Chapelle-aux-Saints, La Feyrassie, La Quina, etc.), all the French finds dating from the years 1908–11.

Confronted with such a harvest of remarkably preserved and extremely "primitive" human remains, the anthropologists no longer questioned the existence of some *prae-sapiens*, extinct types of man. But, in an eagerness which is not difficult to understand, they now leaped to the explicit or implicit assumption that the Spy Neanderthal man was the single and unique root from which modern man, as a whole, had grown into existence. This was, of course, an oversimplified view, which induced the bulk of the anthropologists of that time (*a*) to locate the main center of early hominization in the much too small continental corner of western Europe, and (*b*) to assume, for the final development of *Homo sapiens*, the impossibly short span of time separating the deposition of the Mousterian and the Aurignacian cultural layers in the Perigord caves.

Clear traces of this junior period in prehistory, when Neanderthal man was *the* fossil man (or, in reverse, when any true fossil man *had to be* a Neanderthal man) can be found in all the classic scientific books written in the 1920's by such eminent paleontologists as Boule, Keith, Osborn, and others. And even at a later date (that

---

5. That the mandible really belonged to a recently buried modern man was established shortly afterward by John Evans.

6. Cf. the epic discussion between Huxley and Virchow, the latter holding, in opposition to the former, to the theory that the Neanderthal calvarium belonged to a malformed idiot.

is, as late as 1937) I myself can remember the great Hrdlička dismissing *Sinanthropus* as merely one more specimen in the long list of the already known remains of Neanderthal man.

And yet, in the 1920's (that is, at the very time that Boule was writing his *Hommes fossiles*), this oversimplified conception was already difficult to reconcile with such a paleontological reality as the Piltdown man.[7] Obviously, some fossil older than "l'homme de la Chapelle-aux-Saints" and some cradle bigger than the Perigord were needed to explain the origins of man. Why, then, should this "something" else not be represented by the so-called "Prehominians" of Asia?

B. THE "ASIATICO-PREHOMINIAN" PHASE OF DEVELOPMENT IN THE SCIENTIFIC CONCEPTION OF FOSSIL MAN

The *Pithecanthropus* calvarium of Java (1894), just like the Neanderthal calvarium of Germany, was too fragmentary a fossil and came too early to be properly understood at the time of its discovery. And it is, indeed, a most significant fact that, as late as 1923, Boule could still have held it to be his definite scientific opinion that the Trinil skull, found by Dubois, was not human but belonged to some large extinct type of gibbon.

However, a few years later, in the Far East came a sequence of important events: first, in North China, the excavation of a whole series of *Sinanthropus* skulls, associated with ashes and a rich, lithic industry; then, in Java (Oppenhoort, 1931, and Von Koenigswald, 1935), the find of the Solo man and of a harvest of well-preserved, decidedly human, remains of Pithecanthropines; while farther to the west, in

pre-Mousterian horizons, discoveries were made of clearly sub-*sapiens* types of man, both in Germany (Steinheim, 1933) and in Palestine (D. Garrod and McCown, 1932).

The "pan-Neanderthal" theory of human origins had to be abandoned, gradually to be replaced by a complex of new theories which had in common two trends or even assumptions: (*a*) that man originated in central Asia and (*b*) that he was born there of some Pithecanthropine ancestor.

As an extreme example of the first tendency I should like to cite the interesting paper[8] published in Peking (as early as 1925) in which Davidson Black, basing his argument on the stimulating views advanced by W. D. Matthew, who favored the idea of a northern Asiatic center of mammal dispersion, as well as on the bold (but very questionable) theories of Dr. A. Grabau concerning the relationship between the origins of man and the Tertiary uplift of the Himalaya,[9] came to the definite conclusion that high central Asia must be regarded as the cradle of mankind.

A good instance of the second trend of thought is the surprising suggestion made by Weidenreich, on several occasions, that the modern Mongoloids are the direct descendants of *Sinanthropus*.

In his exhaustive book on races Von Eickstedt[10] quotes a long series of authors, all of whom, like himself, favor the hypothesis of an Asiatic origin for man: Abel, Deperet, Gregory, Koppers,

---

7. For the most recent discussion of the possible phylogenic relationship between *Homo sapiens* and Neanderthal man, see F. Clark Howell in *American Journal of Physical Anthropology*, IX (1951), 379–415.

8. Davidson Black, "Asia and the Dispersal of Primates," *Bulletin of the Geological Society of China*, IV (1925), 133–83.

9. Man having supposedly originated from a group of higher apes who had been cut off from the southern forests and isolated in Tibet by the folding of the Himalayan geosyncline.

10. E. von Eickstedt, *Rassenkunde und Rassengeschichte der Menschheit* (Stuttgart: F. Enke, 1934), p. 101.

Mendes-Corrêa, Menghin, Obermaier, Osborn, etc.

But here again, after a while, a weakness developed at the heart of the system. In spite of protracted research, conducted over a period of years in Mongolia, western China, and Chinese Turkestan by American (Roy Chapman Andrews), Chinese (Geological Survey), French (Haardt-Citroën), and Swedish (Sven Hedin) expeditions, absolutely no evidence whatsoever was uncovered which suggested in any way that these areas could ever have played a part in the evolution of the higher Primates, or even in the earlier development of man. In the critical test of actual experience, central Asia, far from being a hot spot and a primordial reservoir, was, on the contrary, found to have been a negative pole, a void area, as far as early hominization is concerned.

Under such conditions, nothing was ultimately left to the prehistorians in their quest for "primordial" man but to turn to the still mysterious depths of continental Africa, whence, at precisely this time, strange reports were forcing their way into scientific circles: an ape-man in the Transvaal (Dart's first *Australopithecus,* 1925) and a puzzling association of human implements and Pliocene-looking fauna in Kenya (Leakey). And, essentially, that is where we still stand today.

III. THE PRESENT STATUS OF THE QUESTION OF FOSSIL MAN

It is almost impossible to describe in a satisfactory way the present stage reached by any current of thought, distorted as the picture is bound to be by lack of perspective and by individual preference. If, however, I reduce my personal angle of estimation as far as I am able to do so, I honestly believe that, considered in its most advanced form, the idea of fossil man can be characterized today as being controlled

in its development by a small group of outstanding views, which are summarized below.

A. THE RISING IMPORTANCE OF CONTINENTAL AFRICA IN THE BIRTH AND EARLY DEVELOPMENT OF MAN

Since the time when Schlosser, in 1911, described the small mandible of *Propliothecus* collected in the Oligocene fresh-water beds of Fayum (Egypt), Africa has gradually taken first place as a purveyor not only of diamonds but of the higher types of fossil Primates. On the one hand, there are the Miocene *Proconsul*-bearing beds of Tanganyika and the harvest of Australopithecines in the prehuman fissure-deposits of the Transvaal. And, on the other, there is the astonishing wealth of older Paleolithic industries distributed widely over Kenya, the Belgian Congo, Rhodesia, and South Africa. As far as fossil apes and fossil man are concerned, between Nairobi and Capetown the more one searches, the more one finds a striking reversal of the conditions encountered in central Asia.

Under the pressure of so much evidence, it becomes both difficult and unscientific not to accept the idea that the Dark Continent (the last to have been opened to scientific investigation) is precisely the one which, during the Upper Cenozoic period, acted as the main laboratory for the zoölogical development and the earliest establishment of man on this planet.

It is apparently in the depths of Africa (and not on the shores of the Mediterranean Sea or on the Asiatic plateau), therefore, that the primeval center of human expansion and dispersion must have been located, long before this center shifted, in much later times, toward (or even split between) Eurasia and America.

Around this fundamental proposition, taken as an explicit or implicit basis, the whole of our perspectives concerning the biological and historical processes of hominization (and also the plans for further research in the field for fossil man) is actually in the course of being broadened and readjusted.

B. THE INITIAL RADIUS AND COMPLEXITY OF THE HUMAN PHYLUM

Almost from birth, the idea of fossil man has aroused an endless and especially bitter controversy among scientists (not to mention the philosophers). Speaking zoölogically, did man develop from a *single* line of descent? Or is he (as a result of some convergency) a product of the coalescence of *several* different types of phyla?

On the one hand, there are the "monophyletists," by far the more numerous fraction among the paleo-anthropologists, who hold that man, if traced back to some pre-Neanderthal or Pithecanthropoid ancestor, would emerge as some well-defined and restricted branch of the higher Primates.

And, on the other hand, there is the whole gamut of the "polyphyletists." Some of these (like Klaatsch)[11] contend that the so-called "human species" is a mixture of chimpanzee, gorilla, and orang strains. Others (with Wood-Jones and Osborn) suggest a quite independent origin ("Tarsioid") for man, with the result that the higher Primates (Simpson's "Hominoidea") should no longer be regarded as a natural but rather as a composite group.[12] And still others (Rosa, Montandon)[13] propound the almost inconceivable theory of a "hologenesis," according to which no "human cradle" must be expected anywhere, since zoölogical speciation (so they claim) never operates locally but takes place only by means of a slow condensation of a cloud of individuals who appear sporadically (and simultaneously) over the whole surface of the earth.

Today we are beginning to understand that between these two conflicting theories of, on the one hand, a narrow, *linear* monophyletism and, on the other hand, a confusing polyphyletism *through convergency* there is room for a third and much more satisfactory hypothesis, well supported experimentally by modern genetics, for a speciation which acts simultaneously on a large population of closely related individuals spread over a limited but sufficiently broad "surface of evolution."[14] For if (and as soon as) such a wide and complex cross-section is assumed to exist at the base of any major animal phylum, and more especially at the base of the human stem, then it becomes quite easy to understand the "bushy" structure, more and more in evidence, in the composition of humanity as observed in its fossil stages.

In our new conception of "natural" zoölogical groups and of broad "monophyletic" structures, in which an ever larger place is given to marginal and *divergent* types at the expense of truly ancestral forms: (*a*) the evolutive roots of Hominidae fit perfectly into a Tertiary cluster of "Pongidoid" Primates; (*b*)

11. Cf., in a less crude way: M. Sera, "I Caratteri della facie e il polifiletismo dei Primati," *Giornale per la morfologia dell'uomo e dei primati*, II (1918); G. Sergi, *Le Origini umane* (Torino: Fratelli Bocca, 1913); Ruggieri V. Giuffrida, *Su l'origine dell'uomo* (Bologna: Nicola Zanichelli, 1921); A. Mendes-Corrêa, *Homo* (Coimbra: "Atlantida," 1926).

12. The theory still finds some supporters. Cf. W. C. Osman Hill, "Man's Relation to the Apes," *Man*, 1950, p. 257. See also *Yearbook of Physical Anthropology* (New York: Wenner-Gren Foundation for Anthropological Research, 1951).

13. D. Rosa, *Ologenesi* (Firenze: A. Bemporad e Figlio, 1918); G. Montandon, *L'Ologénèse humaine* (Paris: F. Alcan, 1928).

14. The idea (formulated under the hypothesis of a "zone of hominization" extending, supposedly, subtropically between the forest and the grassland) was already clearly expressed by E. von Eickstedt in 1925 ("Gedanken über Entwicklung und Gliederung der Menschheit," *Mitteilungen der Anthropologischen Gesellschaft in Wien*, IV, 231–54).

within the Hominidae themselves, such aberrant types as the Pithecanthropines or the Neanderthal man, if compared with the modern living types of man, deserve, most accurately, the name of "Para-hominians" (rather than of Pre-hominians); and (*c*), as a consequence of this clarification, we are in a much better position to appreciate and to handle the major biological problem posed to anthropology by the unquestionable dominance, the subtle complexity, and the progressive unification of *Homo sapiens*.

C. THE PHYLOGENETIC MAKEUP OF *Homo sapiens*

The first, but oversimplified, idea of the early human paleontologists, as I mentioned above, was to connect *Homo sapiens* genetically, and in a direct line, with each newly discovered fossil man, either with the Neanderthal man or with *Pithecanthropus* and *Sinanthropus*.

Today, as a result of a franker recognition and a better understanding of such pre-Neanderthal, "sapientoid" forms as the men of Palestine, the Swanscombe man, the Steinheim man, and the Piltdown man, we are beginning to realize (1) that the formation and rise of *Homo sapiens* has apparently been a long and complicated process, requiring for its achievement (*a*) a complex core of particularly progressive human subforms and (*b*) considerable amounts of both land and time to allow those adaptive elements to react on each other in a biologically constructive manner; and (2) that the process of "sapientization," which the most central portion of the primordial human stock had to undergo in order to become fully hominized, is itself controlled by two main types of antagonistic morphogenetic forces: (*a*) the divergent forces of speciation,[15] which work continu-

ously to produce human subspecific types, and (*b*) the convergent forces of aggregation ("totalization"), which (through interbreeding and socialization) continually compel the newborn types of man into a most remarkable and, so far badly understood, single superarrangement of a *biological nature* —man as a planetary unit.

Here again, judging by the impressive and constantly increasing mass of old Paleolithic industries which is being continuously unearthed in central and South Africa, it appears very possible that the Dark Continent[16] will be recognized "tomorrow" as the main laboratory in which man, after having been first formed as *Homo*, finally succeeded in reaching the level of *Homo sapiens* just before the dawn of the Upper Paleolithic times.

But we can come to no definite conclusion along this line until we first answer the puzzling and still unsolved question which from the outset presented itself to the prehistorians of the Somme Valley: "What kind of man (or, more probably, what kinds of *men*) is to be held responsible for the hand-ax industries that are so characteristic of the oldest and most central culture deposits of the ancient world?"

D. THE NEED AND THE OPPORTUNITIES FOR BETTER-PLANNED EXCAVATIONS

We cannot hope to have a better understanding of fossil man until we know him by better-preserved and more numerous specimens. And we cannot hope to have such specimens until we have more numerous and more efficiently conducted excavations.

In the early days of prehistory, finds of fossil human remains (with the exception of those dug out in Upper Pleistocene open caves) were, perforce, a matter of luck and random research.

15. Or of "lyse"—to use the term created by Dr. C. Blanc, *Sviluppo per lisi delle forme distinte* ("Quaderni di sintesi," No. 2 [Rome: "Partenia," 1946]).

16. That is to say, the same continent which, in much later times, was to act as a blind corner or a "refuge" for human migrations.

Today we know better. And it is therefore surprising that in the case of paleo-anthropology (just as in so many other branches of science) so much effort should still be dispersed among secondary objectives, while so many first-class sites are as yet insufficiently surveyed.

In short, after a century of research, the essence of what experience has taught us concerning the hunt for fossil human bones can be reduced to the following points: (*a*) As far as that most difficult of quests is concerned, the hunt for a "precultural man" (if he existed at all), apparently the only promising fields are the Villafranchian lake or cave deposits of the Old World, south of the Himalayan-Alpine ranges. (*b*) In the easier case of the *old Paleolithic* "cultural man"[17] there is one main, simple, and practical rule for prospecting and excavating: "Still remaining, for the most part,[18] south of the Himalayan-Alpine divide, consider only those deposits, as suitable for survey or research, *in which some animal bones occur in association with human implements.*"[19]

This second directive may, at first glance, seem absurdly "naïve." And yet, aside from a few exceptional places, like northeastern China or Kenya, where fossiliferous Lower Pleistocene soils or lake deposits cover really big areas, it is surprising to observe, if we apply this rule, how little there is left to paleo-anthropological research, even in some of the largest and most promising countries of the world. In India, for instance, where old hand-axes occur "en masse" all the way from the Indus Valley to Madras, I have convinced myself that (with the possible exception of some as yet unexplored caves) the *only area*, so far spotted as being promising for the discovery of fossil man's skeletal remains, is the Narbada basin (in central India). Outside the Narbada lake deposits, no animal bones have ever been found (and consequently no human bones can be expected) in association with stone implements, either because they have been crushed by the gravel or because they have dissolved in the porous loess of the north or in the corrosive laterites of the south.

An urgent and relatively easy task, therefore, and one which I should like to propose to the anthropological organizations of the world, is the making of a *world-map* which would show: (*a*) in what parts of the world we might (or might not) expect to find traces of either precultural or cultural man (early Paleolithic man, or Middle Paleolithic man, or Upper Paleolithic man);[20] (*b*) at what localities, in each of these zones, the "hot spots" (fossiliferous fissures and fresh-water sediments) in which there is a reasonable expectancy of discovering human fossil bones are located.

A basic plan of this kind (by concentrating the work of temporary excavation and permanent collecting on the most strategic sites) would, I believe, immeasurably increase the efficiency of paleo-anthropological research.

17. And if one excepts, of course, the case of wild and unpredictable chance.
18. The western expansion of older Paleolithic man as far north as southern England and the eastern marginal advance of the Pithecanthropines as far as Peking may be regarded as local exceptions to this rule.
19. A fact which simply proves that the sediments were not physically or chemically destructive to the bones.

20. According to the present stage of our knowledge, it would seem that man's expansion has proceeded in three major laps: (*a*) Birth and early development—confined to Africa and southern Asia—culminating in the birth of *Homo sapiens*. (*b*) Expansion of *Homo sapiens* (Middle and Upper Paleolithic) —the slow conquest of northern Eurasia—first appearance in America? (*c*) The final expansion and advanced socialization of *Homo sapiens* (Meso- and Neolithic)—the appearance of new centers of hominization outside continental Africa.

E. FOSSIL MAN AND FUTURE MAN

On the whole, during the course of a century, our knowledge of early man has greatly improved and accelerated. Not only has the idea of the existence of fossil man been so universally accepted that it approaches the "banal," but we have now reached a point from which the main phases of man's descent (or ascent) from his most ancient forerunners can be outlined with safety.

In many of its modalities, of course, the process of man's formation still remains scientifically obscure (through lack of fossil evidence). And yet, even if we cannot pretend to have actually reached a complete solution of that question which Darwin propounded so vividly in 1872 in his *Descent of Man*, the problem has been circumscribed and may be regarded as virtually settled, with the result that the subject of the origin of man is bound (and, as a matter of fact, has already begun) gradually to lose for our minds that prime fascination which it held for our predecessors in its early days.[21]

One century more, perhaps. Then, in accordance with the fate which is common to all types of purely descriptive knowledge (like geography or Linnean systematics), paleo-anthropology, as such, will most probably have become a stabilized branch of science. But then, as compensation, it will also, probably, have become evident to our "descendants" that, by supplying modern society with a historical basis for its belief in some ultra-humanized form of life (and also with a set of biological patterns for its achievement), the study of fossil man, as it was accomplished in the nineteenth and twentieth centuries, was, in retrospect, the condition *sine qua non* for a scientific conception (and a scientific development) of future man.

21. For the modern mind, the problem of origins has been superseded by the question of patterns and processes.

Der fossile Mensch

By HANS WEINERT

Es IST SICHER nicht die Aufgabe eines grundlegenden Diskussionsberichtes, hier noch enimal alle fossilen Menschenfunde einzeln aufzuzählen. Wir werden diese Tatsachen als bekannt voraussetzen dürfen. Mein Bericht soll vielmehr die wichtigsten Probleme aus dem ganzen Gebiet herausgreifen, die man z.T. verschieden beurteilt und sicher auch weiterhin in der Paläanthropologie diskutiert. Wenn wir uns dabei auch auf das Wesentlichste beschränken, so sind heute besonders vier Themen zu nennen. Das sind:

I. Die phyletische Einordnung der Proconsuliden

II. Die phyletische Einordnung der Australopithecinen

III. Die phyletische Einordnung der Neandertaler

IV. Die Vorfahren heutiger Menschenrassen

I. DIE PHYLETISCHE EINORDNUNG DER PROCONSULIDEN

Diese erste Frage kann nur kurz behandelt werden, da sie in Wirklichkeit das Thema "Fossil Man" gar nicht direkt berührt. Es gibt zwei Gründe, dass ich selbst dieses Problem nur kurz an den Anfang stellen will. Zunächst einmal liegt ein umfassendes Werk darüber von Le Gros Clark und Leakey vor mit dem Titel "The miocene Hominoidea of East Africa." Es wäre also überflüssig, darüber noch weiter zu berichten, zumal den Verfassern die Originale und mir nur die von ihnen freundlichst überlassenen Abgüsse vorliegen.

Der zweite Grund ist der, dass meiner Ansicht nach diese Proconsuliden noch keine Möglichkeit bieten, ihnen eine sichere Stellung in der Stammesentwicklung der Menschheit zuzuordnen—und zwar so, dass man auf Grund dieser Proconsulfunde behaupten kann, dass sich im unteren Miocän die Stammeslinien der Anthropoiden (oder Pongiden) von der der Hominiden endgültig getrennt hätten. Gerade der letzte Proconsulfund vom Rusinga Island hat die Meinung aufkommen lassen, dass man diesen zerdrückten Schädel als speziellen Vorläufer der Menschheit anzusehen hätte. Man weiss, dass viele unsachliche Presseberichte sogar sich daran anknüpfen, dass das Fossil im Flugzeug zu Professor Le Gros Clark nach England gebracht wurde. Den Anlass zu solcher Einstellung gab vor allen Dingen die Form des Stirnbeins. Die Supra-Glabellar-Region erscheint bei diesem Stück bekanntlich glatt gerundet und nicht eingebuchtet wie bei allen Anthropoiden. Es ist zu bedenken, dass solche einzelnen Phänotypen keineswegs immer eine Begründung dafür sind, dass auch der Genotypus der wirklichen Stammeslinie ebenso gewesen ist. Wir können in fast allen Stammesreihen Merkmale finden, die Ähnlichkeit mit der Ausbildung eines viel späteren Typus haben. Amerikanische Krallenäffchen, z.B., lassen überraschende Parallelen zu Homo sapiens-Formen erkennen, wenn man sowohl auf die Organisation wie auch auf die Grösse nicht achtet.

Der Proconsul von Rusinga Island war uns durch Bilder längst bekannt. Aber wir waren überrascht über die Kleinheit des ganzen Stückes, als wir den Abguss in natürlicher Grösse erhielten. Von diesem aus bis zum Homo ist doch allein durch die Grösse ein so weiter Abstand gegeben, dass man unmöglich an direkte Verwandtschaft denken darf. Es ist doch eine bekannte Tatsache, dass wohl alle Entwicklungsreihen nicht in gerader Linie, sondern auf Zickzackwegen verlaufen. So kann einmal bei einem einzelnen Merkmal eine äussere Ähnlichkeit mit einem viel späteren oder gar heutigen Typus entstehen, die phylogenetisch nichts zu bedeuten hat.

Der Proconsul von Rusinga Island ist zwar stark zerdrückt und deformiert, aber das Stirnbein scheint wirklich diese gewölbte Form an der Glabella gehabt zu haben.

Wie sieht das Os frontale aber innen aus? Hat der Proconsul Sinus frontales? Und damit kommen wir zu einem allgemein gültigen Problem: In meinem Menschheitsstammbaum habe ich als Erbgruppe die "Summo-Primaten" eingetragen. Das war kein neuer Name für alte Formen. Es ist wohl angebracht, dass wir jetzt den Begriff der "Hominoidea" verwenden, wenn wir Anthropoiden und Hominiden mit einem Wort umfassen wollen. Aber "Summo-Primates" ist das Ergebnis einer Erbforschung und bedeutet, dass die heutigen Formen Gorilla, Schimpanse, Mensch als eine Erbgemeinschaft zusammengehören, zu der Orang-Utan und Gibbon nicht mehr zu rechnen sind. Die Merkmale, die heute die Summo-Primaten verbinden und kennzeichnen, darf ich als bekannt voraussetzen. Es gibt heute keine Art, bei der man im Zweifel sein könnte, ob sie zu den Summo-

Primaten gehört. Aber ebenso sicher wissen wir, dass alle Merkmale, die zur Kennzeichnung der Summo-Primaten nötig sind (wie z.B. Sinus frontales, Interorbitalbreite, Os centrale der Handwurzel, Intermaxillarnaht, Aortenverzweigung, Spermien und Blutserum u.a.) nicht zur gleichen Zeit aufgetreten sind. Wir können wohl nach Erbmerkmalen einen ideellen Stammbaum aufzeichnen, in dem Gorilla, Schimpanse und Mensch und besonders die letzten beiden miteinander verbunden sind; aber deshalb ist es nicht möglich, jedem Fossilfund einen bestimmten Platz in einem solchen Stammbaum zuzuweisen. Das kann gar nicht anders sein, und es ist kein Beweis gegen die Stammesgeschichte.

Im vorliegenden Falle wäre also die Frage, ob diese Proconsuliden Summo-Primaten sind oder nicht. Ich selbst glaube, dass die Gruppe Proconsul nicht sicher eine einheitliche Gruppe (oder Gattung) gewesen ist. Alle Funde zeigen uns morphologisch eine schöne Weiterentwicklung vom primitiven Gibbon- bis zum höheren Schimpansen-Typus. Das genannte Problem ist hier besonders dringend, da die moderne Phylogenie schon lange die Gibboniden von den eigentlichen Anthropoiden abgesondert hat. Wir würden bei den einzelnen Fossilfunden aus dem Miocän Ost-Afrikas also noch nicht einmal sehen können, ob das einzelne Stück in die gibbonide oder anthropoide Gruppe gehört.

Es ist eigentlich selbstverständlich, dass die Stammesentwicklung immer auf solche Schwierigkeiten stösst. Es war deshalb von jeher ein bequemer Ausweg, jedes gefundene Fossil als Spitze eines ausgestorbenen Seitenzweiges anzusehen. Und es ist der gesamten Paläontologie oft verdacht worden, dass sie an die Abzweigungsstellen keine Fossilfunde, sondern ein X setzen muss. Aber es ist leicht erklärlich und oft genug gesagt worden, dass es immer ein grosser Zufall sein würde, eine wirkliche Ahnform, deren Nachkommen bis zum heutigen Tag weiterleben, gefunden zu haben. Aber sicher sind unter unseren Funden auch in der Hominidenreihe solche wirklichen Ahnen gegeben.

Wenn ich also eingangs meinte, dass man z.B. den Proconsul von Rusinga nicht als den Markstein für die Trennung des Anthropoiden- und Hominiden-Weges oder gar für den Beginn der Hominidenreihe setzen darf, dann ist damit nicht gesagt, dass dieser Proconsul nicht in unsere Ahnenreihe gehört, wenn man den Begriff nur weit genug fasst. Wir wollen uns nur bescheiden mit dem Eingeständnis, dass man darüber nichts behaupten darf. Einzelne Merkmale, die wie Kennzeichen eines Hominidenzustandes aussehen, sind noch kein Grund, dem betreffenden Fossilstück eine Sonderstellung einzuräumen, welche die längst erkannte spätere Stufenfolge umwirft. Es wird—wie gesagt—nur in den wenigsten Fällen möglich sein nachzuweisen, dass dem erkennbaren Phänotypus auch der phylogenetisch wichtigere Genotypus entspricht.

II. DIE PHYLOGENETISCHE EINORDNUNG DER AUSTRALOPITHECINEN

Die nächste Frage, die nun wirklich fossile Menschen betrifft, ist die jetzt viel diskutierte Stellung der Australopithecinen Süd-Afrikas. Kennzeichen für das ganze Problem sind allein schon die verschiedenen Namen, die die Entdecker diesen wichtigen Funden gaben. Dart begann mit "Australopithecus" und bleibt auch heute bei diesem Gattungsnamen. Broom sah sich genötigt, später daraus "Plesianthropus" und "Paranthropus" zu machen. Zu einem ganz sicheren Urteil ist wohl nur der berechtigt, der die Fossilien selbst in der Hand hat; aber nach dem Studium der Bilder und Abgüsse—für die ich auch hier noch einmal zu danken habe—komme ich doch zu einem Ergebnis, das wohl jeder anerkennen muss. Eigentlich ist es gar kein Ergebnis; denn es besagt nur, dass niemand imstande ist, mit hinreichender Begründung den Namen "Pithecus" = Menschenaffe oder "Anthropus" = Affenmensch zu vergeben. Beim Studium der Einzelheiten wird jeder zu dem Schluss kommen, dass die Hominidenkennzeichen so stark überwiegen, dass Brooms Namengebung die richtige ist—auch wenn wir davon absehen, die Berechtigung der Einteilung in "Paranthropus" oder "Plesianthropus" oder "Telanthropus" zu prüfen. Hat man aber einen ganzen Schädel, Original oder Abguss, in der Hand, dann wird man zunächst nur auf den Gedanken kommen, in dem Stück einen Anthropoiden zu sehen, der nach dem allgemeinen Eindruck einem Schimpansen noch am nächsten kommt. Aber wir wissen, dass nicht einmal alle Stücke Schimpansengrösse im Schädel besitzen und weiterhin, dass der ganze Körperbau keineswegs einem schimpansoiden Anthropoiden entspricht. Es sind ja auch Schädel gefunden, welche die Schimpansengrösse übertreffen und mit ihren Ausmassen in die frühe Menschheitsstufe des Pithecanthropus hineinreichen.

Wenn wir nun über Afrika hinausgehen, dann haben wir auf Java und in China Gross- und Riesenformen, die hominid sind und doch über alle bekannten Hominidenformen an Grösse weit hinausgehen. Mag man sich darüber streiten, ob die Chansi-Zähne einem Gigantopithecus oder einem Giganthropus gehört haben, die Grösse des "Meganthropus II" von Java zeigt mit seinem massigen Kieferstück, dass er auf die Hominidenseite gehört und den Namen "Meganthropus" zu recht führt.

Damit zeigt sich sogleich ein weiteres Problem: Broom hatte Grund, einzelne Funde aus Transvaal als "Paranthropus crassidens" zu bezeichnen. Die Zahnkronen dieser Stücke sind in ihren Längen- und Breitenmassen ebenso gross wie die Zähne der Meganthropus-Funde. Aber in der Kronen- und Wurzelhöhe sind sie bedeutend kleiner und können deshalb in Kiefern stecken, die nicht durch ihre Übermasse besonders auffallen, wenn sie auch natürlich gross und massig sein müssen.

Wohl in Zusammenhang mit dieser Grosszähnigkeit steht die überraschende Tatsache, dass einzelne Schädel gefunden wurden, deren Temporallinien in der Mitte des Schädels zu einem Knochenkamm zusammenstossen, wie wir ihn in seltenen Fällen auch einmal bei rezenten Schimpansen antreffen. Es ist notwendig, darauf hinzuweisen, dass auch Schimpansenschädel eine solche Median-sagittal-Crista besitzen können. Die übergrosse Crista vom männlichen Gorilla und Orang-Utan ist bei den Australopithecinen noch nicht angetroffen worden.

Aber alle diese Dinge dürfen als bekannt angenommen werden. Man kann das Ergebnis aller Untersuchungen mit den Worten zusammenfassen, die ich meinen Arbeiten über das Thema vorangestellt habe: "Die Vielgestaltigkeit der Summo-Primaten vor der Menschwerdung"; denn dass wir jetzt auf der Seite der Summo-Primaten stehen, dürfte wohl als zweifellos angenommen werden, ohne dass bisher von einem Fund eine sichere Diagnose dafür anzugeben ist.

Es ist folgendes dazu bekannt geworden, was wahrscheinlich gleich hier von Diskussionsteilnehmern ergänzt werden kann. Die vorliegenden Angaben beziehen sich hauptsächlich auf Sinus frontales und Intermaxillarnaht, das sind ja auch die Schädelmerkmale, die für die Summo-Primaten besonders kennzeichnend sind. Andere Kriterien (Foramina, Cristen u.a.) sind variabeler. Schon die Zwischenkieferknochen bilden durch ihr Fehlen wohl ein

Merkmal für Schimpanse und Mensch; aber das Verschwinden der Nähte vollzieht sich bei den anderen Anthropoiden nur zu verschiedenen Alterszeiten. Weist ja auch ein erwachsener Pongidenschädel fast gar keine Suteren mehr auf. Es kommt hinzu, dass man am Fossil auch manchmal nicht genau sehen kann, ob wirklich ein Nahtrest oder nur eine Zersplitterung des versteinerten Knochens vorliegt.

Am sichersten wird die Intermaxillarnaht für den Proconsul angegeben, wo wir sie ja auch nach der ganzen Organisationshöhe am ehesten zu erwarten haben. Bei Australopithecus Africanus soll die Naht im oberen Teil offen sein. Nach Dart ist sie deutlich sichtbar am Palatinum, sei aber auch in der Frontalansicht noch deutlich nachzuweisen. Damit steht der Taungsschädel in diesem Merkmal phylogenetisch tiefer als der Schimpanse, da ein Schimpansenkiefer gleichen Alters meistens keine Zwischenkiefernähte mehr besitzen würde. Die Feststellung der Intermaxillarnaht kann aber nur derjenige machen, der das Fossil selbst untersucht—auch der beste Abguss ist mehrdeutig.

Auch Australopithecus prometheus hat an einem Oberkieferstück die Naht im oberen Teil noch offen. Bei Plesianthropus S2 wird sie an der äusseren Nasalgrenze als ganz verstrichen angegeben. Bei Plesianthropus S1 dagegen sei sie (nach Broom) auch in der Vorderansicht noch deutlich zu sehen. Da es sich hierbei z.T. um erwachsene Individuen handelt, sieht man, wie schwer es ist, für Rezente passende Einteilungen auf Fossilien anzuwenden. Die genannten Schädel würden danach eigentlich eher zum Gorilla oder Orang-Utan passen, obwohl sie i.a. doch am besten Schimpansen entsprechen. Da beim Gorilla die Ossa intermaxillaria noch lange Zeit sichtbar sind, wird der genannte Befund auch Plesianthropus nicht von den Summo-Primaten ausschliessen.

Viel sicherer ist die Feststellung der Sinus frontales; bei Plesianthropus S1, S5 und S7 gibt Broom ihr Vorhandensein an. Es sei nochmals darauf hingewiesen, wie wichtig diese Feststellung für den Proconsul wäre.

Nicht beachtet ist bisher die Interorbitalbreite und ihr Index zur Biorbitalbreite. Mehrere Funde lassen doch Annäherungswerte darüber aufstellen. Es sei daran erinnert, dass der Interorbitalindex 20 eine Trennungslinie zwischen den Summo-Primaten einerseits und dem Orang-Utan und den niederen Katarrhinen andererseits darstellt. Nur Gorilla, Schimpanse und Mensch haben einen so weiten Augenabstand, dass bei adulten Schädeln der Interorbitalindex 25 bis 33 ist, d.h. der innere Augenwinkelabstand beträgt 1/4 bis 1/3 von der Biorbitalbreite, den äusseren Augenrändern. Bei niederen Affen und dem Menschenaffen Orang-Utan bleibt der Index deutlich unter 20; die Interorbitalbreite beträgt noch nicht einmal 1/5 der Biorbitalbreite. Es fehlen diesen Formen ja noch die Ethmoidzellen.

Beim Proconsul-Schädel von Rusinga Island erhält man nach Rekonstruktion der Deformierung einen Interorbitalindex von 17 bis 18; also ein Wert, der noch nicht zu den Summo-Primaten passt. Aber er entspricht meiner Ansicht vom Proconsul.

Dagegen haben die Australopithecinen Indices wie die Summo-Primaten. Schon das Australopithecus-Kind von Taungs hat den Index 20. Bei Plesianthropus S5 und S7 erhält man nach Rekonstruktion die Werte 21,5 und 20,5—der Plesianthropus S7 ist stark verdrückt und am Original würde man genauer messen können. Aber schon äusserlich erscheinen uns die Schädel als "normal" hinsichtlich ihres Augenabstandes. Der grosse Schädel vom Paranthropus crassidens (1949—mit Sagittalcrista) hat einen Interorbitalindex von ca 27.

Es liegen jedenfalls genügend Schädel vor, von denen man den Index bestimmen kann; vielleicht gibt diese Mitteilung Anlass, dass die Bearbeiter der Original-Fossilien die Messungen nachholen. Mit der Ausbildung der Ethmoidzellen ist ja auch die der Sinus frontales verbunden.

In Am. J. Phys. Anthrop., n.s.v. 8, no. 1, March, stellt Broom eine genaue systematische Einordnung auf, die die Einstufung der Australopithecinen darlegt. Ich selbst bin noch nicht davon überzeugt, dass diese Systematik als gesichert gelten kann. Ich glaube, auch Dart nach brieflicher Mitteilung ebenso verstanden zu haben. Die Vielgestaltigkeit ist — wie gesagt — so gross, dass fast jeder neue Fund für unsere Erkenntnis auch wieder Neues bringt. Es ist dabei wohl verständlich, dass Fossilien aus derselben Gegend ähnlicher sein können, weil ja bei ihnen die Möglichkeit näherer Verwandtschaft gegeben ist. Aber es kommen immer wieder Kriterien vor, die jede systematische Einteilung als gewaltsam erscheinen lassen. Broom gab zuerst die Artnamen "robustus" und "crassidens." Ich selbst nannte ein Oberkieferstück aus Ost-Afrika (gefunden von Kohl-Larsen) in Vereinbarung mit Remane "Meganthropus africanus," da sich die Ausmasse ganz in die Variationsbreite der beiden Meganthropus-Mandibeln von Java (von v. Koenigswald) stellten. Dart bleibt bei dem erstgegebenen Namen "Australopithecus" und bezeichnet eine besondere Fundgruppe als "prometheus." Sieht man sich aber die Zähne des Oberkiefers, besonders aber die des Unterkiefers an, so trifft auf sie der Name "crassidens" noch viel eher zu wie für die Paranthropus-Stücke von Swartkrans.

Ein riesiger Unterkiefer, 1949 bei Swartkrans von Robinson gefunden und von Broom und Robinson beschrieben, steht seinen absoluten Ausmassen nach ganz beim Meganthropus von Java. Seine Zähne sind gross, so dass "crassidens" eine richtige Bezeichnung ist—aber viel grösser noch ist der Unterkieferkörper. Er überschreitet das Mass, das für den Kiefer lediglich als Träger der Zähne notwendig gewesen wäre. Die Entdeckung des Mandibulare ist für mich persönlich besonders wichtig, da ich lange vor seiner Entdeckung und vor allen Dingen vier Jahre vor seiner Bekanntgabe (Januar 1952) nach den Unterkieferresten und Zähnen Meganthropus- und Giganthropus-Kiefer ergänzt habe. Eine schönere Bestätigung einer solchen mutmasslich vorhergesagten Rekonstruktion konnte man sich kaum wünschen. Und doch passt dieser Swartkrans-Kiefer wieder zum Thema "Vielgestaltigkeit." Meine Ergänzungen von Plesianthropus-, Paranthropus- und Telanthropus-Mandibeln ergaben nämlich immer ein überraschendes Resultat: trotz ihrer hominiden Bezahnung haben die Unterkiefer eine so lang gestreckte Form, dass ihr Breiten-Längen-Index etwa 110 und darüber beträgt. Sonst haben alle Hominiden—auch die primitivsten—Indices unter 90, d.h. die Breite ihres Condylenabstandes ist grösser als die Länge vom Condylus zum Prosthion (projiziert). Dieser riesige Swartkrans-Kiefer bringt nun wieder Überraschungen. Zunächst einmal ist das von den Australopithecinen her bekannte Missverhältnis zwischen Prämolar-Molar-Reihe und der Ausdehnung der Canini und Incisivi hier so übertrieben, dass bestimmt niemand eine Rekonstruktion gewagt hätte, die bei so grossem Kiefer und grossen Backenzähnen bei einem erwachsenen Individuum so winzige Eck- und Schneidezähne aufweist. Die Vorderzähne nehmen ja kaum mehr Länge ein als die beiden Prämolaren; und dazu dieser massige Unterkieferkörper! Völlig neu ist aber, dass dieser Paranthropus-Kie-

fer viel breiter als lang ist. Da der rechte Condylus fehlt, ist die Rekonstruktion nicht ganz sicher, aber der Breiten-Längen-Index muss zwischen 85 und 80 gelegen haben — bei modernen Menschen kann man ungefähr 83 als Mittelwert angeben. Der grosse Paranthropus wäre also in dieser Hinsicht "übermenschlich." Jedenfalls gleicht er keinem einzigen der heutigen Anthropoiden.

Ob der Telanthropus nicht zu den Australopithecinen, sondern zur Pithecanthropus-Gruppe gehört, ist nach den Bildern allein schwer zu entscheiden; möglich wäre es. Der lange Unterkieferkörper bei niedrigen senkrechten Asten sprechen dafür; aber der Breiten-Längen-Index der Mandibula ist etwa 110 wie bei den Australopithecinen und nicht 87 wie bei der Pithecanthropus-Gruppe.

Der Laie mag vielleicht bei allen Plesianthropus-Schädeln, zu denen man auch Unterkiefer hinzufügen kann, nichts besonderes am Gesichtsskelett entdecken. Aber wenn auch der Plesianthropus im ganzen schimpansoid ist, so sind seine Unterkieferäste und damit auch die Gesichtshöhe viel eher gorilloid. Zuerst mussten wir das ganze Gesicht nach Fossilresten ergänzen, bis wir später auch genügend Unterkiefer mit Ästen bekamen, welche unsere zwangsweise Rekonstruktion bestätigten. Denn vor der Plesianthropus-Entdeckung hatten wir eine gute morphologische und wahrscheinlich auch phylogenetische Reihe vom Schimpansen über die Pithecanthropus-Gruppe zum Homo: die Unterkieferkörper waren lang gestreckt; aber die Unterkieferäste niedrig, breit und senkrecht gestellt, meist mit flacher Incisur. Jetzt bringen die Australopithecinen Unterkiefer, deren Äste ebenso lang und z.T. noch länger sind als die Körper, mit einem spitzen Processus coronoideus und tiefer Incisur, wie wir sie vom Gorilla kennen.

Man könnte noch viele derartige Merkmale anführen, aber ich müsste nur das wiederholen, was die Bearbeiter der Fundstücke (u.a. Dart, Broom, Robinson, Le Gros Clark) aufgezählt haben. Das Ergebnis ist doch das, dass diese endpliocänen Primatenformen sich nicht zwanglos der heutigensystematik einordnen. "Summo-Primaten" dürfen wir sie nennen, weil die Orangiden bestimmt nichts mit ihnen zu tun haben. Aber für jeden der heutigen drei Summo-Primaten: Gorilla, Schimpanse, Mensch haben wir Ähnlichkeiten oder Beziehungen. Bei so naher Verwandtschaft kann man schwer darüber urteilen, ob erblicher Zusammenhang oder Konvergenz vorliegt.

Die Form des Unterkieferastes kann noch am leichtesten als Konvergenzerscheinung gedeutet werden, da auch bei den heutigen Arten die verschiedensten Formen vorkommen. Aber sonst müssen wir uns damit abfinden, dass diese Australopithecinen — um *einen* Namen für sie zu gebrauchen — sowohl Abweichungen wie Übereinstimmungen mit heutigen Summo-Primaten aufweisen, und kein Autor ist berechtigt, daraufhin ihre Stellung im Stammbaum zu begründen oder festzulegen. Es war gesagt, dass wir uns daran gewöhnen müssen, eine Stammesentwicklung nicht geradlinig, sondern auf Zickzackwegen anzunehmen. Da sicher in der Frühzeit Bastardierungsmöglichkeit gegeben war, so wird man heute nicht behaupten dürfen, dass ein einzelnes Stück innerhalb der breiten Entwicklungslinie stand oder einen ausgestorbenen Seitenzweig darstellt.

Die Fossilien brauchen ja zu keiner der drei heutigen Arten zu gehören, sondern können "Australopithecinen" sein, d.h. also ihre eigene Gruppe bilden. Aber auch dabei tritt das Problem auf, ob wir wirklich von *einer* Gruppe sprechen können. Es gibt allein am Schädel auffällig verbindende Merkmale, die eigentlich nur "süd-afrikanisch" sind, dazu gehören die hoch geschwungenen Jochbögen, ferner die lange Backenzahnreihe gegenüber den kleinen Vorderzähnen. Es ist darauf hinzuweisen, dass dadurch das ganze Gebiss auch nicht einfach "hominid" genannt werden kann; wenn auch die Rundung des Zahnbogens, das Fehlen der Diastemata, die kleinen Canini usw. auf den ersten Blick einen menschlichen Eindruck machen.

Als trennend innerhalb der Süd-Afrika-Funde hat Broom schon immer den Unterschied der absoluten Schädelgrösse genannt. Aber ob man wirklich daraufhin "Plesianthropus" und "Paranthropus" systematisch unterscheiden kann? Überraschend waren die beiden Schädel mit der Sagittalcrista. Nach Bild und Abguss scheinen sie aber doch auch wichtige Unterschiede zu haben. Der erste Crista-Schädel hat wohl eine normale Form mit verhältnismässig hoher Crista. Der zweite, der mir im Abguss vorliegt, fällt durch seine grosse Breite und das sehr flache Gesicht auf. Die Crista selbst ist klein. Zu dieser Gesichtsbreite passt andererseits die Swartkrans-Mandibula von 1949, obwohl sie einen noch grösseren Oberschädel voraussetzt. Robinson berechnet bei einem Condylenabstand von 135 mm eine Gehirnschädelbreite von 130 mm und dazu eine Länge von mindestens 180 mm. Wenn man sich die Schädel in vollständiger Form vorstellt, so ergeben sich doch wohl Differenzen, die die systematische Zuordnung erschweren.

Es wäre interessant festzustellen, wie andere Fachleute die Süd-Afrikaner in den menschlichen Stammbaum einordnen wollen. Wäre also der Name "Australopithecus" richtig, oder hätte Broom recht, als er "Plesianthropus" oder "Paranthropus" daraus machte. Begründungen lassen sich für beide Benennungen geben.

Wenn wir die als sicher erkannten

geistigen Fähigkeiten mit hinzurechnen, müssen wir wohl zugeben, dass keiner der heutigen Anthropoiden so hominid ist, wie es diese Süd-Afrikaner am Ausgang der Tertiärzeit bereits gewesen sind.

III. DIE PHYLOGENETISCHE EINORDNUNG DER NEANDERTALER

Das Problem der phyletischen Einordnung ist durch sein Bestehen auch wichtig bei den widerspruchsvollen Ansichten über die Stellung späterer Eiszeitmenschen. Bei der Pithecanthropus-Stufe wird wohl allgemein Zustimmung darüber herrschen, dass die bei ihr, ebenso wie bei den Australopithecinen, schon erkannten Gross- und Riesenformen noch am leichtesten als Seitenzweige aufgefasst werden können, die immer einmal entstehen. Weidenreichs Ansicht, dass die Chansi-Riesen (Gigantopithecus oder Giganthropus) die Ursprungsformen der Menschheit wären, wird wohl nirgends anerkannt worden sein; denn auch bei anderen Tiergruppen sind Riesen doch immer als Endprodukte anzusehen. Süd-Afrika hat uns ferner gezeigt, dass wir immer noch mit Überraschungen rechnen müssen. Es war eher ein Zufall, dass sich vorher die ganze Entwicklungslinie der Menschheit, wenigstens am Anfang, als ziemlich einheitlich darstellte.

Das am meisten umstrittene Problem bei der Weiterentwicklung ist wohl die Stellung des Neandertalers. Ich selbst werde vielfach als der Vertreter der "rückständigen" Meinung hingestellt, der auch den europäischen Neandertaler noch in unserer Vorfahrenreihe belässt—obwohl ich immer betone, dass ich das auch nicht behaupten kann. Aber Süd-Afrika zeigt uns, das wir uns damit abfinden müssen, Verzweigungen oder Zickzackwege im Stammbaum wenigstens als möglich anzuerkennen; denn sonst würde fast kein Fossilfund mehr übrigbleiben, den man als Ahnform anerkennen dürfte. Beim Neandertaler ist allerdings die Annahme dieser Möglichkeit schwieriger als bei den Australopithecinen, da er viel näher an unsere heutige Zeit heranreicht. Aber wenn wir nach den geologischen Datierungen gehen, dann müssen wir den Beginn der Neandertalerzeit doch wohl auf 200 000 Jahre vor uns ansetzen. Für die letzten Neandertalerformen mag das Ende 75 000 Jahre oder noch weniger vor unserer Zeit gelegen haben. Im ganzen liegen darin noch genügend Menschengenerationen, die zu Mutationen Anlass geben konnten.

Einigkeit herrscht wohl in der Auffassung, dass für die Neandertaler-Stufe zwei geologische Perioden in Frage kommen: das letzte Interglacial (Riss-Würm) und die erste Hälfte der letzten Vereisung (Würm). Damit wären für eine Menschheitsstufe zwei unterschiedliche Faunengebeite gegeben: eine Warmzeit mit ihrer entsprechenden Tierwelt und als Abschluss eine Glacialzeit. Es ist deshalb verständlich, wenn man auch beim Menschen zwei unterschiedliche Formengruppen sehen möchte. Aber ich glaube nicht, dass es möglich ist, Neandertaler-Funde nach anatomischen Gesichtspunkten in das Interglacial oder das Glacial einzuordnen. Bei manchen Fossilien ist die Zuordnung durch Beigaben und Umgebung möglich, bei anderen muss sie offen bleiben. Eine wirkliche Unterscheidung der Menschenformen ist aber nicht angängig. Bei allen zugestandenen Unterschieden haben wir für Europa doch eine Menschenform, die man als den Neandertaler bezeichnen kann. Aber man is manchmal überrascht, wenn man nachzählt, wie viele Fundstücke uns eine als "allgemein gültig" geltende Form repräsentieren. So heisst es z.B., dass der Neandertaler kurze, plumpe und nach vorn durchgebogene Femora gehabt hätte; aber nur von vier Individuen ist uns diese typische "Neandertaler-Form" bekannt (es ist: Neandertal, Spy, La Chapelle und La Ferrassie I). Schon ein anderer Oberschenkel aus der La Ferrassie-Gruppe sieht bedeutend "menschlicher" aus. Viele andere Merkmale sind aber wirklich so durchgängig vertreten, dass man von dem Neandertaler sprechen darf. Es ist z.B. überraschend, die äussere Ähnlichkeit des Schädels von La Chapelle mit La Ferrassie I und dem von Cap Circeo (Italien) zu sehen; denn hier kommt auch noch die zufällig gleiche Färbung der Knochen hinzu. Die Argumente, warum viele Autoren den europäischen Neandertaler als ausgestorbenen Seitenzweig betrachten wollen, sind bekannt. Es handelt sich dabei meistens um anatomische Eigenschaften, die einer geraden Entwicklungslinie widersprechen sollen.

Sergi spricht deshalb nur eine sinngemässe Ansicht aus, dass der Neandertaler des älteren Interglacialzeitalters noch in unsere Vorfahrenreihe gehört, der der späteren Glacialperiode jedoch nicht. Das wird man bei vielen Formen als gegeben annehmen dürfen; denn jede Tierart wird zu Beginn ihrer Entwicklung eher sich in eine Entwicklungsrichtung einfügen als am Ende ihrer Periode. Aber für den Neandertaler reichen die Beweise nicht aus; denn Sergis Vertreter der "älteren, entwicklungsfähigen" Stufe sind weibliche und jugendliche Individuen, z.B. Saccopastore I, Gibraltar, Le Moustier. Bei den abseitsstehenden Formen handelt es sich um die bekannten erwachsenen Männer. Das erkennt man an den beiden Saccopastore-Schädeln, die sicher zu einer Gruppe gehörten, eventuell sogar familienverwandt gewesen sein können. Sergis genaue Untersuchungen zeigten ja auch mehrfach Übereinstimmungen dieser beiden römischen Funde. Aber Saccopastore II ist ein männlicher Schädel, der, wenn die fehlende Calotte ergänzt wird, nicht anders aussieht als der von Cap Circeo, wenn auch an der erhaltenen Schädelbasis die Übereinstimmungen mit Saccopastore I deutlich sind. Dabei ist die Geschlechtsdiagnose für diesen ersten Fund wohl ganz einwandfrei: es ist der kleinste und zierlichste Neandertaler-Schädel, den wir besitzen, und da er einem Erwachsenen gehört, so ist er sicher weiblich. Bei dieser Betrachtung zeigen uns gerade die beiden römischen Schädel, dass trotz der gleichen Zeitansetzung, die Geschlechtsmerkmale dieselben sind, die Sergi für die verschiedenen Zeitperioden ansetzt. Natürlich ist die Möglichkeit, dass ein Fossilstück nicht mehr in die Stammeslinie gehört, sondern als Seitenzweig danebensteht um so grösser, je näher seine Zeit an die unsrige heranreicht. Aber man muss bedenken, dass—wie in einem menschlichen Familienstammbaum—nicht nur die Urgrossväter, sondern auch die Uronkel zur Ahnenreihe gehören. Wenn wir also auch zugeben, dass die Neandertalergestalt oder -form mit dem Höhepunkt der letzten Vereisung verschwindet, dann braucht das nicht zu bedeuten, dass die Individuen selbst nachkommenlos ausgestorben sind. Es kann sehr wohl sein, das die Ausbildung einseitiger Merkmale auf immer spätere Lebensjahre verschoben wird und dass bei mutierenden polymeren Genreihen immer weniger Personen zu dieser einseitigen Ausbildung kommen.

Es sind aber nicht nur die Einseitigkeiten beim Neandertaler, die an das Aussterben dieser Menschengruppe denken lassen, sondern wir haben ja auch Fossilfunde, die mehr dem rezenten Homo sapiens gleichen und zeitlich doch älter als der Neandertaler sind oder doch sein sollen. Wenn wir sichere Fundgruppen hätten, bei denen dieses Verhalten nachgewiesen werden kann, dann würde die genannte These sehr gestützt werden. Aber als wirklich einwandfrei kann nur der Schädel von Steinheim dafür herangezogen werden, weil er in der Gesichtsbildung rezenter erscheint als die spitzgesichtigen Neandertaler. Es ist aber zu bemerken, dass ich der einzige Autor bin, der den Steinheim-Schädel genau bearbeitet und—was hier besonders wichtig ist—in seiner ursprünglichen Form rekonstruiert hat. Der Schädel ist viel stärker verdrückt und verbogen, als man nach dem allgemeinen Eindruck annehmen sollte. Dass trotzdem schon bei einem älteren Fund Kennzeichen gefunden werden, die erst viel später als Merkmal der Gesamtstufe allgemeingültig werden, finden wir aber bei allen Entwicklungsreihen. Das bedeutet noch nicht, dass deshalb die ganze ältere Gruppe als "rezent" angesehen werden muss. Der Steinheim-Schädel hat dagegen viel wichtigere Merkmale, die ihn primitiver als den Neandertaler erscheinen lassen. Die Stirn mit der Glabellarausbildung entspricht bei Steinheim mehr der Pithecanthropus-Stufe. Es kommt hinzu, das der ganze Schädel zierlich ist und dass trotz der scharfkantigen Stirn die Geschlechtsdiagnose sehr wohl weiblich sein kann. Auch der rückgebildete Weisheitzahn oder M_3 ist kein modernes Zeichen, wenn man beachtet, das wir bei weiblichen Schimpansen oft genau dieselbe Erscheinung antreffen. So kann Steinheim nur das aussagen, dass einzelne Merkmale, die wir als typisch für den modernen Menschen ansehen, schon bei ihm auftreten.

Eine weitere Auswirkung dieses Fundes ergibt sich bei einem englischen Fossil, nämlich dem Schädelbruchstück von Swanscombe. Ich kann hierzu wohl erst recht darauf hinweisen, dass kein Anderer den Steinheim-Schädel genauer kannte und auch bei Swanscombe selbst gegraben hat. Es wurde gesagt, dass beide Fundstücke sehr genau übereinstimmten und dass auf diese Weise sich die Kulturstufen, die wir für den Steinheimer nicht kennen, beweisen würden. Die Themseschotter von Swanscombe enthalten bekanntlich wunderschöne Acheuléen-Faustkeile; aber nach meinen Empfinden gibt es dort keinen sicheren Beweis, dass Artefakte und Fossilfunde gleichaltrig sein müssen. Wir fanden z.B. 1932 bei Swanscombe Reste aus den verschiedensten Perioden in gleicher Schotterlage.

Die Übereinstimmung der Schädel selbst beruht aber nur auf einer Ähnlichkeit der Parietal- und Occipital-Region und kann nicht viel besagen. Wenn wir das Stirnbein und die scharfkantige Glabellar-Region beim Swanscombe-Fund hätten, dann könnten wir wirklich von Übereinstimmung mit Steinheim sprechen. Aber das erhaltene Bruchstück von Swanscombe kann m.E. keinen sicheren Beweis ergeben. So fehlt also bei dem Themse-Fund beides: die Klarheit über den anatomischen Bau und die Sicherheit der zeitlichen Einordnung. Es wäre wichtig, wenn hiergegen etwas Entscheidendes gesagt werden könnte. Aber selbst dann wäre Swanscombe noch kein Beweis für das Aussterben der Neandertaler-Gruppe. Wir hätten nur noch einmal die Tatsache, dass bei einem älteren Schädel Formenmerkmale auftreten, die besser zur späteren Menschheit als zum Neandertaler passen. Dieser Beweis ist aber in Wirklichkeit gar nicht so wichtig; denn wir brauchen nicht anzunehmen, dass der Steinheim-Schädel ein "Unicum" ist. Es ist erstaunlich, dass wir aus der langandauernden Zeitspanne zwischen dem Ausgang der Pithecanthropus-Stufe und dem Beginn der Neandertaler-Stufe so wenig gesicherte Fossilfunde haben. Eigentlich ist Steinheim der einzige Schädelfund. Es ist deshalb nicht schwierig, ihn als Präneandertaler sowohl nach seiner Form, wie auch nach seiner geologischen Zeitansetzung zu bezeichnen.

Noch ein anderer Fund aus England ist in diesem Zusammenhang zu nennen: der "Eoanthropus dawsoni" von Piltdown. Aber m.E. sind hier alle Fragen gelöst, so weit es möglich ist, und der ungelöste Teil ist durch Diskussion nicht zu klären. Durch die Liebenswürdigkeit des Erstbearbeiters, Sir Arthur Smith-Woodward, mit Unterstützung von Dr. Hopwood konnte ich 1932 sowohl die Originalfossilien wie auch die Fundstätte eingehend studieren und bearbeiten. Fest steht danach folgendes:

1. Es gibt nur einen Piltdown-Fund, nämlich den von Fundplatz I.

2. Von Piltdown II stammt nur ein bedeutungsloses Stück vom Occipitale, das stark abgeschabt, dünn und sehr leicht ist—ganz anders als das Stirnbein und der untere Molar.

3. Dieses Frontale und der Molar sind von Dawson irrtümlich als bei Piltdown II gefunden bezeichnet worden; sie gehören zweifellos zum Schädel I.

4. Ebenso zweifellos gehören Oberschädel und Unterkiefer zusammen. Nur Autoren, die die Funde nicht kennen, konnten behaupten, das Mandibulare stamme von einem tertiären Schimpansen oder gar (nach Weidenreich) von einem Orang-Utan. Der Unterkiefer ist sicher hominid, er muss nur richtig eingestellt und ergänzt werden.

5. Die Zusammensetzung ergibt einen Schädel, der kein Neandertaler und auch kein Pithecanthropus oder Eoanthropus ist; es ist eine primitive Homo sapiens-Form.

6. Ungelöst bleibt die zeitliche Einordnung. Im Piltdown-gravel liegen Reste aller Zeiten nebeneinander. Die rot-braune Färbung kann kein Zeitmass sein. Der Schädel is zeitlich alt oder fossil. Aber auch die Fluor-Apatit-Methode von Oakley hat in Wirklichkeit nur ergeben, dass der Piltdown-Schädel zu den jungen Stücken der dortigen Funde gehört, also anscheinend jungpaläolithisch sein wird.

Mehr getraue ich mir nach allen Untersuchungen und Beweisen nicht zu sagen.

Dann kommt ein Fund, über den ich selbst noch nichts aussagen darf, da ich nur aus den Berichten, besonders aus den Arbeiten und einigen Bildern von Vallois, Paris, das Fossilstück kenne. Es ist das erst 1950 bei Fontéchevade (Dep. Charente) aufgefundene Schädelbruchstück. Es ist geradezu verhängnisvoll, dass hier wieder die wichtigsten Schädelteile, also vor allem die Stirnregion fehlen. Scheitelbeine sind für eine Diagnose sehr ungeeignet, auch wenn noch einige Teile des Frontale oder Occipitale dransitzen. Natürlich besteht kein Zweifel, dass dieses Stück von Fontéchevade eher einem Homo sapiens als einem Neandertaler entspricht, wenn die Fachleute, die es in der Hand haben, dieses Urteil angeben. Aber ich frage mich, zu welchen Schlussfolgerungen der Steinheim-Schädel Anlass gegeben hätte, wenn von ihm auch nur die Scheitelbeine vorhanden wären. Nun kommt bei Fontéchevade hinzu, dass das Fossil erst nach Durchstossung einer zum Moustérien gehörigen Bodenschicht gehoben wurde. Dass man bei "ungestörten" Schichten die grössten Uberraschungen erleben kann, dürfte allgemein bekannt sein; für diese Frage wird aber Vallois der gegebene Berichterstatter sein.

Dabei kommen wir aber zu dem gleichen Schluss wie bei Swanscombe. Sollte nämlich wirklich diese Form sapiensartig und die Schicht prämoustérien sein, so hätten wir wieder ein Fossil, das als einzelnes "rezente" Merkmale vorwegnimmt. Aber es muss immer wieder betont werden, dass weder Swanscombe noch Fontéchevade so sicher in der Aussage sein können wie Steinheim.

Ich glaube, das wir andere Fossilfunde, von denen gelegentlich ihre Sapienszugehörigkeit und ihre zeitliche Einordnung vor der Neandertaler-Periode behauptet wird, ruhig fortlassen können; denn sie haben doch niemals einen so berechtigten Verdacht erregt wie die beiden Stücke von der Themse und aus der Charente. Aber der jetzige Kongress wäre geeignet auch andere Meinungen vorzubringen—auf äussereuropäische Funde soll später eingegangen werden.

Wenn wir mit unseren Schlussfolgerungen bei Europa bleiben und wirklich die drei genannten Stücke Präneandertaler wären, dann ändert das nichts an der Tatsache, dass mindestens 100 000 Jahre lang in Europe eine Menschenform gelebt hat, neben der wir bisher noch nichts anderes oder höher entwickeltes gefunden haben. Überall, wo im letzten Interglacial das Moustérien I und im letzten Glacial das Moustérien II vorliegt, haben wir den "Neandertaler." Soll man glauben, dass sich nur wenige Individuen neben dieser Hauptbevölkerung aufgehalten haben, aus denen die heutigen Menschen hervorgingen, während die Moustérien-Menschen nachkommenlos ausstarben? Das wäre nur möglich, wenn aus einem anderen Gebiet—und dafür könnte wohl nur das westliche Asien infragekommen—ein neuer Menschenstrom nach Europa einbrach. Diese Möglichkeit ist natürlich durchaus gegeben. Aber unmöglich erscheint es fast, dass bei einer solchen Minderheit keine Vermischung mit der bodenständigen Neandertaler-Bevölkerung eingetreten sein soll. Und wenn wirklich nur die Neandertaler-Frau bei der Vermischung ihr Erbgut weitergegeben haben sollte, dann wäre ja auch damit der Neandertaler nicht ganz ohne Nachkommen ausgestorben.

Es genügt wohl der eine Satz, dass die Funde von Krapina (Kroatien) kein Beweis sind für ein Zusammentreffen von Neandertalern und Aurignacien-Menschen, wie Klaatsch es einmal annehmen wollte. Wir sind heute überzeugt, dass wir bei Krapina die Reste einer Kannibalenmahlzeit vor uns haben, deren Opfer lediglich aus Neandertalern bestehen und deren Überwältiger ebenfalls nur Neandertaler waren. Es mag dabei offenbleiben, wie weit es sich hier lediglich um Menschenfresserei handelt, oder ob schon irgendwelche rituellen Vorstellungen dabei vorherrschten. Krapina ist ja nicht der einzige Ort, von dem wir die Urmenschenfunde dem Kannibalismus verdanken.

Wir werden später auch auf Entdeckungen eiszeitlicher Menschen aus Böhmen, Mähren und Süd-Russland zurückkommen müssen. Die erste Fundgegend, die wirklich eine Einwanderung höher organisierter Menschen nach Südost-Europa annehmen lässt, ist Palästina mit der Ausgrabung am Mount Carmel, wo die Orte Tabun und Sukhul und vorher schon Tabgha am See Genezareth zu nennen sind.

Seit langem war den Prähistorikern bekannt, dass hier in Palästina Moustérienkultur vorlag, bis dann nach dem ersten Stirnbein von Tabgha die grossen Gräberfunde von Tabun und Sukhul gemacht wurden. Die ersten Entdeckungen konnte ich selbst noch in London besichtigen; ich habe aber nicht gehört, was aus den weiteren Skeletten geworden ist. Es sollten mindestens neun Bestattungen vorliegen, die als ganze Blöcke nach London gebracht und dort bearbeitet werden sollten. Vielleicht gibt diese Zusammenkunft wieder Gelegenheit, auf diese Frage eine Antwort zu erhalten. Aber das Ergebnis ist auch hier so schon klar. Wir haben in Palästina anscheinend eine sehr unterschiedliche Formengruppe vor uns. Eine Frau von Tabun hat einen so primitiv gebildeten Schädel, wie man ihn noch nicht einmal beim Neandertaler zu erwarten braucht. Andere Männerschädel von Sukhul sehen dagegen viel fortgeschrittener aus, wenn sie auch noch als Neandertaler gelten müssen. Ihre Stirnen sind höher gewölbt und die Unterkiefer nicht einfach fliehend. Ich selbst habe mir schon immer die Frage vorgelegt, wie weit diese Palästina-Funde untereinander als gleichzeitig anzusprechen sind, und ob das Moustérien aus dieser Gegend der Zeit nach der gleichen Kulturperiode Europas wirklich entspricht. Es erscheint mir durchaus möglich, dass wir uns, absolut gerechnet, hier in einer jüngeren Zeit befinden.

Überraschend waren bei den Entdeckungen damals die geraden und schlanken Oberschenkel, die nicht zu dem plumpen und kurzen Femur westeuropäischer Neandertaler passen. Heute ist das keine Überraschung mehr, da wir schon aus der Pithecanthropus-Stufe "menschlicher" geformte Femora besitzen. Danach wäre umgekehrt zu erklären, wie mancher Neandertaler-Mann—es sind ja nicht alle!—zu seinem "Neandertaler Femur" gekommen ist.

Dass also von Palästina und Vorderasien her, etwa gegen Ende der Neandertalerperiode, ein Zustrom nach Europa einsetzte, muss als Möglichkeit durchaus angenommen werden. Wirklich nachweisen können wir solche alten Wanderstrassen natürlich nicht.

Ehe wir an die Frage aussereuropäischer Neandertaler herangehen —Palästina gehört als Mittelmeergebiet zwar nicht zu Europa, aber doch zum europiden Kreis—sind noch Funde aus dem Jungpaläolithicum, aus der Tschechoslowakei und aus Süd-Russland zu beachten.

Es besteht natürlich die verständliche Forderung, dass—wenn der Neandertaler nicht ausstarb—im frühesten Aurignacien Übergangsformen gefunden werden müssen. Man hört manchmal, dass solche Übergänge fehlen; das ist aber nicht der Fall. Vor allen Dingen haben wir zu bedenken, dass von allen Lebewesen aus den Zeiten der Übergänge, in denen viele Mutationen auftraten, nicht allzu viele

Individuen auf unsere Zeit überkommen sind; denn sie sind sicher nicht so zahlreich gewesen wie die neuen Formen, die sich erst wieder ihrer Umgebung anpassten und zur grösseren Ausbreitung kamen. Aber fast alle Funde aus den genannten Gebieten Europas zeigen schon durch die Unsicherheit ihrer Bestimmung, dass ihre Form auch nicht klar unserer Einteilung einzufügen ist. Als wirkliche Neandertaler aus der Tschechoslowakei kennen wir eigentlich nur den Unterkiefer von Ochos. (Das Kieferstück aus der Szipka-Höhle ist zu unsicher.) Auch dieses Fossil habe ich selbst bearbeitet, da es mir einmal zum Ankauf angeboten wurde. Der Unterrand des Kieferkörpers fehlt. Vielleicht war dort der Ansatz einer Kinnbildung vorhanden, die eigentlich über die Neandertaler-Form hinausgeht. Die innere Kinnplatte ist zwar sehr breit und vorgeneigt, aber rein gefühlsmässig hatte ich immer den Eindruck, dass dieses Mandibulare einer späteren Zeit angehören könnte. Ein 1925 gefundener Gehirnschädel von Ganovce, Slowakei, ist jetzt durch Vlcek veröffentlicht worden; er ist später noch eingehender zu behandeln.

Dieses Fossil, das in der Hauptsache aus dem Gehirnausguss des Schädels besteht, scheint zweifellos in die Neandertaler Gruppe zu gehören. Alle anderen Funde aus Böhmen und Mähren werden dem älteren Jungpaläolithicum zugerechnet. Aber das Gehirnschädelstück von Podbaba ist nach neueren Untersuchungen als Neandertaler erklärt worden. Die Stirn ist sehr fliehend und die Stirnhöhlen sind ausserordentlich weit und tief. Es interessiert hier weniger, wohin dieser fossile Vorder-Gehirnschädel wirklich gehört, als die Tatsache, dass man an seiner Anordnung zweifelt.

Dann kamen die grossartigen Entdeckungen von Predmost, die bereits 1894 gefunden wurden. Zuerst wurde ein männlicher und ein weiblicher

Schädel bearbeitet und Bilder und Abgüsse davon veröffentlicht. Als später, 1934, Matiegka die ganze Fundserie beschrieb, erkannte man, warum gerade die genannten Schädel III und IV vorweggenommen wurden: sie imponieren durch ihr neandertalerähnliches Aussehen. Der Mann hat Supraorbitalwülste mit einer Stirneinsenkung über der Glabella, wie wir sie selten beim Homo sapiens finden. Sieht man sich jetzt aber die ganze Serie der reichhaltigen Funde an, dann erkennt man, dass es sich im ganzen doch um Crô-Magnon-Gestalten handelt. Diese haben natürlich ihre Variationsbreite und einige davon sind besonders neandertalerähnlich.

Es wären weiter zu nennen die Calotten von Brünn und Brüx. Hier haben wir, z.T. Stirnbeine, die—aus dem Verband der anderen Knochen gelöst—wahrscheinlich von ihren Entdeckern als Neandertaler angesprochen worden wären. (Man muss bedenken, dass Entdecker es häufig gerne sehen, wenn ihrem Fund ein hohes Alter zugesprochen werden kann.)

Umgekehrt wie beim Podbaba-Schädels ist die Beurteilung des Schädels von Podkumok im Kaukasus. Er ist zuerst als Neandertaler erklärt und später dem Jungpaläolithicum zugeordnet worden. Auch dabei interessiert hier nicht so sehr die wirkliche Einstufung, als die Zweifel daran. Mir sind häufig Schädel oder Schädelstücke zur Bestimmung übergeben worden, weil der Entdecker meinte, "Neandertaler" gefunden zu haben. Wirklich zu nennen ist hierunter das Stirnbein von der unteren Weser (überreicht von v. Buttel-Reepen). Die dicken Überaugenwülste und die scheinbar niedrige Stirn, dazu die absolute Dicke des Knochens und die harte Versteinerung rechtfertigten die Annahme eines Urmenschen-Schädels. Nur der Fachmann konnte nachweisen, dass das Stirnbein am Schädel steiler gestanden hatte, als es isoliert den Anschein hatte. Aber man kann sich nicht vorstellen, dass man eine solche Bildung ohne einen neandertalartigen Vorfahrenzustand annehmen könnte. Ferner sandte mir früher einmal aus Chwalynsk an der Wolga H. Gross verschiedene Schädel, die auch den Eindruck einer Neandertaler-Beziehung machten. Man konnte aber nachweisen, dass diese Wolgastücke wohl als Crô-Magnons in das Magdalénien einzureihen wären.

Auf jeden Fall sehen wir, dass man doch nicht behaupten darf, es gäbe keinerlei Übergangsformen zwischen Neandertaler und Crô-Magnon.

Hiernach stelle ich meine Ansicht über die Frage zur Diskussion: ich kann nicht behaupten, dass die Neandertaler-Menschheit geschlossen in unserer Vorfahrenreihe steht. Aber m.E. ist man auch nicht berechtigt, den Neandertaler als "nachkommenlos ausgestorben" zu bezeichnen. Einzelne anatomische Sonderbildungen genügen dazu nicht—dasselbe gilt auch für andere Urmenschenformen. Die weite Verbreitung über lange Zeitperioden spricht gegen die Ausschaltung. Dabei ist es durchaus möglich, dass von den Nachkommen der als Fossilien in unsere Hände gekommenen Personen der Neandertaler-Stufe heute keiner mehr lebt; denn der bekannte "Ahnenverlust" zeigt uns, dass nur sehr dünne Stammeslinien bis in die Urzeit zurückgehen. Dass es keine "Übergangsformen" gäbe, konnte widerlegt werden, und es ist natürlich, dass aus Übergangsperioden nur wenig Reste wiedergefunden werden. Um nicht zu viel zu behaupten, habe ich ja schon immer von den Menschheits-Stufen und nicht etwa von Menschenrassen gesprochen. In einer "Stufe" kann beides enthalten sein: Ahnen und Nachkommenlosausgestorbene.

IV. DIE VORFAHREN HEUTIGER MENSCHENRASSEN

Wie spärlich die aussereuropäischen Neandertaler-Funde sind, ist bekannt. Es ist natürlich ein Zufall; denn wir haben ja von der ganzen Balkanhalbinsel auch nicht *einen* eiszeitlichen Menschenfund, obwohl diese ganze Halbinsel mit allen heutigen Inseln im Ägäischen Meer bestimmt nicht währen der Eiszeit unbewohnt gewesen ist. Als einwandfreier Neandertalerfund ist wohl nur der Schädel eines Jugendlichen aus Uzbekistan (Samarkand) anzusehen. Nach Weidenreichs bebilderten Beschreibungen gleicht er so sehr dem Jungendlichen von Le Moustier, dass eine Erörterung darüber unnötig ist.

Sonst liefert uns der grosse asiatische Kontinent nichts. Unter den Funden von Chou-Kou-Tien, Peking, beschreibt uns Weidenreich aus späterer Zeit einzelne Stücke, die wohl dem Jungpaläolithicum angehören und Neandertaler-Ähnlichkeit zeigen sollen; gesehen habe ich davon nichts.

So bleiben als einzige Fundstücke die Ngandong-Schädel von Java; sicher stammen sie aus einer Zeit, wo Java noch mit dem Festland verbunden war. Der Entdecker Oppenoorth beschrieb diese elf Calvarien zuerst als Neandertaler unter dem entsprechenden Namen "Homo soloensis." Später vertrat er die Meinung, dass die Stücke aus späterer Zeit stammten und den primitivsten Homo sapiens-Typ vertraten. M.E. ist zu dieser Meinung keine Veranlassung. Es bleibt nur die Frage übrig, ob wir in den Ngandong-Schädeln, die wahrscheinlich auch Mahlzeitüberreste sind, den Neandertaler Asiens vor uns haben. Sicher wäre das zu viel gesagt; denn in der Südost-Ecke des grossen Kontinents konnte sich sehr wohl eine Sonderform entwickeln. Die Eigentümlichkeit der Ngandong-Schädel besteht ja darin, dass ihr Supra-Orbital-Torus einen dikken, aber geraden Balken über den Augenhöhlen bildet—im Gegensatz zu den zwar einheitlichen, aber geschwungenen Überaugenwülsten europäischer Neandertaler. Die Supraglabellar-Einwölbung ist beim Ngandong-Schädel

sehr gering oder fehlt ganz, so dass das Stirnbein flach und fliehend nach hinten verläuft. Diese Eigentümlichkeit gab Veranlassung, die Ngandong-Schädel vielleicht als Vorfahrenformen der ältesten Schädelfunde in Australien anzusehen. Es wäre demnach nicht unmöglich, für die Eingeborenen Australiens eine Ahnenreihe anzunehmen, die vom Pithecanthropus über Ngandong und Wadjak auf Java sich in Australien über Cohuna, Talgai und Jervois bis zu den Heutigen erstreckt.

Bis vor kurzem waren die Ngandong-Schädel in ihrer beschriebenen Stirnform einzigartig—dass sie teilweise sehr gross sind, ist eine Feststellung, die wir nicht zum ersten Male machen. Jetzt zeight aber der Fund von Ganovce-Hradok in der Slowakei, dass diese Ngandong-Stirnform auch in Europa vorkommt. Der slowakische Schädel ist zwar in der Hauptsache Kalkausguss des Gehirnschädels, an dem nur einzelne Deckknochen erhalten sind; aber dieser Ausguss ist ebenso wie beim Taungskind, anscheinend so genau, dass über die Stirnbildung kein Zweifel bestehen kann. Ganovce unterscheidet sich dadurch von allen bekannten europäischen Neandertalern, bei denen, trotz ihrer Niedrigkeit, die Stirn in der Mitte vorgewölbt ist. Das ist ja auch das wesentlichste Unterscheidungsmerkmal zwischen dem Sinanthropus von Peking und dem Pithecanthropus von Java. Es ist natürlich kein Grund, wegen des slowakischen Schädels den Gedanken an die Stammeslinie der Australier aufzugeben; denn wenn irgendwo ein Calvarium gefunden wird, das denen von Ngandong ähnlich sieht, dann bleibt die vermutete Beziehung von Java nach Australien doch bestehen. Ausserdem sind ja sicher verschiedene Menschenwellen in den weddiden Kreis Südost-Asiens eingedrungen. Sie können also nichts daran ändern, dass die eingeborenen Australier lange Zeit mit dem mitgebrachten Dingohund das einzige höhere Säugetier auf Australien geblieben sind; denn die kleinen Nagetiere und Insektenfresser, die mit Tanginseln angetrieben wurden, ändern nichts an dem Gesamtbild der australischen Fauna. Das ist alles, was wir über Asien und Australien heute aussagen können.

Verwickelter ist das Problem für Afrika, weil wir dort zahlreiche Funde zu berücksichtigen haben. Die Australopithecinen wurden genügend besprochen; ihre Vielgestaltigkeit ist so gross, dass sie sowohl eine im frühen Diluvium erloschene Sondergruppe der Primaten vorstellen können, als das sie auch zu den Vorläufern späterer Hominiden hinleiten können.

Der Form nach kommt nun ein Fund aus Ost-Afrika, dessen Altersansetzung umstritten ist. Es sind die von Kohl-Larsen gefundenen Schädelreste vom Njarasa-See oder Leak Easy in Ost-Afrika. Schon der erste Autor, der diese Bruchstücke oberflächlich zusammenfügte (Leakey), erhielt eine Form, die sich vollständig dem Pithecanthropus-Typ anschloss. Bei der genaueren eigenen Bearbeitung mussten wir aber doch noch mehr Schädelstücke in die Gesamtform einfügen, so dass der Schädel im ganzen grösser wurde. Seine Gestalt blieb aber im Pithecanthropus-Kreis und passt am besten zu dem grossen Schädel von Chou-Kou-Tien. Selbstverständlich bringen die vielen kleinen Bruchstücke Gefahr, dass die Zusammensetzung und Rekonstruktion von mir selbst nicht ganz eindeutig ist. Aber es waren doch so viele spiegelbildliche Ergänzungen möglich, dass wir mit hinreichender Sicherheit die erhaltene Form als zutreffend ansehen müssen. Später ist dann von Geologen und Paläontologen, die das Original-Fossil vom Njarasasee nicht gesehen haben, die Zeitansetzung bis ins Jungpaläolithicum hinauf verschoben worden; sogar unter der etwas gewaltsamen Annahme, dass das dreizehige Hipparion in Afrika so lange überlebt haben **könnte**.

Als Bearbeiter und Rekonstrukteur des Africanthropus muss ich aber folgendes dazu sagen: ich habe bis 1942 fast alle wichtigen Menschheits-Fossilien selbst in der Hand gehabt und zum grossen Teil selber bearbeitet. Ich weiss sehr wohl, dass der Versteinerungszustand eines Fossilstückes keinen absoluten Zeitmasstab geben kann. Aber es ist doch auffällig, dass ich noch niemals Knochen in der Hand gehabt habe, die so wenig "Knochen" waren wie die Africanthropus-Reste. Als ich die Stücke beim Internationalen Kongress 1938 in Kopenhagen vorlegte und erklärte, sie seien "mehr Stein als Knochen," wurde mir sehr richtig zugerufen, ich könnte ruhig sagen: "mehr Metall." Dazu mag natürlich der dunkelgrüne Farbton patinierter Bronze (durch Manganerze hervorgerufen) äusseren Anlass geben, aber die Schwere und der Härtegrad bestärken die Tatsache: eher Metall als Stein. Es ist jedenfalls völlig ausgeschlossen, dass Fossilfunde aus dem Magdalenien (wie auch behauptet wurde) ein derartiges Aussehen und eine derartige Konsistenz in so kurzer Zeit bekommen haben sollten.

Da bei der Zusammensetzung keinerlei Absicht vorlag, einen bestimmten Typus zu erreichen, passte hier Form und Erhaltungszustand durchaus zusammen. So kann der Africanthropus also eine weitergebildete Form des Pithecanthropus in Afrika sein und damit ein Nachkomme irgendwelcher Australopithecinen.

Damit steht er ja nicht isoliert da: wir können uns diesen Schädel sehr wohl als Vorläufer des "Homo rhodesiensis" von Broken Hill vorstellen. Mit diesem Fund tritt nun dieselbe Frage auf, die wir für Ngandong (Java) stellten: Ist der Rhodesia-Mensch der Neandertaler Afrikas? oder gehört er wenigstens in seinen Formenkreis? M.E. ist der später gegebene Name "Cyphanthropus" nicht nur nach den Gesetzen der Nomenklatur, sondern auch nach den Ergebnissen der Untersuchung abzulehnen. Der Rhodesia-Schädel gehört unbedingt in die Homo-Gruppe und sein Name "Homo rhodesiensis" mag eine Parallelbezeichnung zum Homo neandertalensis sein.

Jedem Kenner wird aufgefallen sein, dass der Rhodesia-Schädel viel eher zum Ngandong-Menschen als zum europäischen Neandertaler passt. Jedoch ist es selbstverständlich, dass auch er seine Eigenheiten hat. Die beigefundenen Gliedmassenknochen mögen sehr wohl zum Schädel gehören und einen grossen aufrecht gehenden Menschen bezeugen. Ich glaube, dass auch hier keine Diskussion zu der Klärung der Frage weiterhilft. Eines bleibt nur sicher, dass der Broken Hill-Schädel in keiner Weise als Vorläufer der Neger Afrikas erklärt werden kann; es müssten dann die Negerrassen sehr jung sein, so dass der Rhodesia-Mann ein sehr alter Vorläufer mit noch allgemein-urmenschlicher Form ist.

Alles am Rhodesier widerspricht sonst der Ausbildung eines Negerschädels. Man kann natürlich über den Schädel einen Kopf mit dicken Lippen und gekräuselten Haaren rekonstruieren und damit das Äussere eines Negers andeuten; wirklich aussagen können wir darüber nichts.

Aus dem Jungpaläolithicum liegen in Afrika viele Funde vor, die schon immer mit Buschmannformen verglichen wurden. Die ersten wirklichen Negeranzeichen finden wir m.E. bei den Elmenteita-Schädeln aus Ostafrika.

Eine Erschwerung der Diagnose kommt in Afrika dadurch zustande, dass wir mit einer Durchdringung nordafrikanischer Crô-Magnon-Formen entlang der Ostküste des Erdteils bis zum Cap hin rechnen müssen. Man wird nicht unterscheiden können, ob Formen wie die Elmenteita-Schädel uns eine Umwandlung vom intermediären Urmenschen zum Neger darstellen, oder uns etwa Vermischung von Crô-Magnon mit bereits bestehenden Urnegern zeigen.

Ein viel besprochenes Skelett, das ich auch selbst untersuchte, muss aus der ihm zugedachten Einstufung gestrichen werden. Der Oldoway-Fund (von H. Reck) ist ganz bestimmt kein Urmensch und wahrscheinlich auch kein Jungpaläolithiker. Er lag nicht *in* der Schicht II im Oldoway-Graben, so dass die Schicht III, IV und V intakt darüber lagen; sondern es war ein Oberflächenfund auf der zweiten Terrasse. Wir haben noch nie einen zusammengeschnürten Hocker mit angefeilten Schneidezähnen im Paläolithicum festgestellt. Ich glaube, es passt alles dazu, dass das Oldoway-Skelett neolithisch ist; dem entspricht auch die Konsistenz seiner Knochen. Kohl-Larsen lieferte mehrere Knochenstücke, die so sehr von dem umgebenden Stein verbacken waren, dass man sie auf den ersten Blick als "alt" ansehen möchte. Sie gehören aber trotzdem einer Homo sapiens-Form an. Dasselbe gilt m.E. auch von den Bruchstücken, die Leakey bei Kanam und Kanjera fand.

So haben wir für den grossen Erdteil Afrika noch nicht den sicheren Beweis, dass Neandertaler auf ihm lebten, falls nicht der Rhodesia-Mann in diese Stufe gehört. Es ist wieder seltsam, dass der ganze Westen Afrikas, vom Cap bis nach Marokko, keine Fossilien bisher geliefert hat. Die Funde aus Nordafrika und der Sahara entsprechen den europäischen Jungpaläolithikern und brauchen hier nicht als problematisch behandelt zu werden.

Eine Fehlanzeige für den Urmenschen wollen wir jedoch hier noch anbringen. Auf den beiden Kontinenten Amerikas haben wir keine Urmenschen zu erwarten. Es hat sich wohl die Meinung durchgesetzt, dass erst gegen Ende der Eiszeit der Homo sapiens über die Behringstrasse nach Alaska als erster Katarrhine amerikanischen Boden betrat. Ob seitdem 10 000 oder 20 000 Jahre vergangen sind, ist für unsere Diskussion nicht so wichtig.

Wenn wir unsere Problemstellung auf

die wichtigsten Fragen aus der Zeit des "Fossil Man" beschränken wollen, so ist durch die vorhergehenden Äusserungen genügend Stoff zur Besprechung gegeben. Es mag deshalb zunächst einmal gesagt sein, dass alle etwaigen Meinungsverschiedenheiten über die angeschnittenen Fragen, besonders in der Öffentlichkeit, nicht den Eindruck hervorrufen dürfen, als sei für die Wissenschaft der Werdegang der Menschheit noch eine strittige Frage. Wir sind uns vielmehr alle über das Prinzipielle des Entwicklungsganges völlig einig, und es besagt gar nichts, wenn der eine von uns diesem oder jenem Fossilfund eine andere Stellung in der Stammesentwicklung zuweisen möchte als ein anderer. Das sind Einzelheiten, die auch den interessierten Laien eigentlich weniger angehen. Wenn wir bei der Menschheitsentwicklung von "Stufen" sprechen, so ist damit nicht zu viel behauptet. Wir müssen heute wohl folgende Stufen als gegeben anerkennen:

1. die Stufe des Propithecanthropus (Australopithecinen)
2. die Stufe des Pithecanthropus
3. die Stufe des Neandertalers
4. die Stufe des Homo sapiens diluvialis
5. die Stufe des Homo sapiens alluvialis od. rezens.

Ich breche hier bewusst mit dem Beginn der Homo sapiens-Stufe ab. Auch jungpaläolithische Funde gehören natürlich mit unter den Begriff "Fossil Man," aber ausser den Fossilien, die hier genannt wurden, erscheinen mir heute keine mehr so wichtig, dass sie bei einer internationalen Diskussion behandelt werden müssten. Ich nehme dabei z.B. an, dass aus der ältesten Homo sapiens-Zeit die beiden Skelette aus der Doppelbestattung der "Grotte des enfants"—(Grimaldi) heute von keinem Autor mehr als Angehörige einer Negerrasse angesehen werden.

Der Erstbearbeiter dieser Stücke, (Verneau) hat ja auch niemals diese Skelette negrid, sondern nur negroid genannt und schon seit 1874 darauf hingewiesen, dass auch heute noch solche Formen in Italien vorkommen können.

Für die Frage der Mongolen-Entstehung wird ebenfalls ein jungpaläolithischer Fund aus Europa genannt, nämlich der Chancelade-Schädel aus der Dordogne. Man hat zeitweise auch diesen Schädel als speziellen Vorläufer der eigentlichen Nordischen Rasse in Anspruch genommen und zwar wegen seiner "hohen" Augenhöhlen. Es existiert von dem Fund nur ein alter Holzschnitt aus der Arbeit Testuts von 1888. 1937 konnte ich das Fossil untersuchen. Es handelt sich um einen klobigen Crô-Magnon-Schädel, bei dem die Augenhöhlen nur etwas höher sind als bei den "typischen" Crô-Magnons. Aber die Orbitae sind zerbrochen und verdrückt, der Orbital-Index links und rechts ist verschieden. Ein Jahr später konnte Vallois das durch eine Nachuntersuchung bestätigen.

Der Chancelade-Mensch ist durch ein Relief am L'Institut du Paleontologie humaine" (Vallois) als Urmongole (Tungide) verewigt worden. Möglich ist diese Ahnenschaft sehr wohl, aber dann betrifft sie nicht nur den Jungpaläolithiker von Chancelade, sondern auch viele andere seiner Zeitgenossen. Auch der Mann von Combe Capelle passt—wie ich selbst nachwies—zum heutigen Eskimo, ohne dass die europäischen Aurignac- oder Crô-Magnon-Menschen Eskimos gewesen wären. Aber vielleicht zogen sie gegen Ende der Eiszeit doch den nach Nordosten ausweichenden Rentierherden nach und kamen so nach Nordost-Sibirien und dann weiter über das nördlichste Amerika nach Grönland. Auch kulturell gibt es für eine solche Annahme Belege, die aber auch von der Renkultur abhängig sind.

Die Gesamtfrage der Mongolen lässt sich damit aber nicht lösen; denn sicher kommt noch ein südliches Element hinzu. Nur die ureuropäischen Ainus wurden als Abgesprengte nach Ost-Ostasien und weiter auf die japanischen Inseln verdrängt.

Durch die Mannigfaltigkeit der jetzt vorliegenden Funde sehen wir, dass—ähnich wie im Moustérien die Neandertaler-Form—im Jungpaläolithicum die Crô-Magnon-Form als "Zeitsignatur" angesprochen werden kann.

Alle anderen Fragen, die bei den verschiedensten jungpaläolithischen Funden auftreten, sind untergeordneter Natur.

Wir können den Bericht also mit der Feststellung schliessen, dass die Wissenschaft noch manche Frage über die fossilen Menschen zu klären hat, dass aber kein Grund vorliegt, an der längst erkannten Entwicklungslinie des heutigen Menschen zu zweifeln.

V. ZUSAMMENFASSUNG

Aus dem grossen Gebiet "Fossil Man" werden vier Probleme herausgegriffen, die z.T. schon lange von den Fachleuten diskutiert werden. Auch neue Funde haben zu den verschiedensten Deutungen Anlass gegeben. Es handelt sich um folgende Fragen:

I. Die phyletische Einordnung der Proconsuliden

II. Die phyletische Einordnung der Australopithecinen

III. Die phyletische Einordnung der Neandertaler

IV. Die Vorfahren heutiger Menschenrassen.

I. Bei den Proconsuliden (Hopwood) herrscht noch Uneinigkeit darüber, ob diese Primaten bereits den Beginn der Hominiden einleiten oder noch unter den höheren Anthropoiden stehen und gleichsam einen Übergang von den Gibboniden zu den Anthropoiden bilden.

II. Die Australopithecinen Südafrikas werden durch die verschiedenen Namen: Australopithecus, Plesianthropus, Paranthropus und Telanthropus schon als fraglich in ihrer phyletischen Stellung gekennzeichnet. Sie haben sowohl Merkmale, die sie als "pithecus" = Menschenaffe wie auch als "anthropus" also als Affenmensch kennzeichnen.

III. Bei der Neandertaler-Stufe bleibt immer noch Problem, ob der Neandertaler oder wenigstens sein europäischer Zweig nachkommenlos ausgestorben ist. Schon früher wurde die Ansicht vertreten, dass bestimmte anatomische Merkmale am Schädel oder Skelett nicht in die Vorfahrenreihe des Homo sapiens passen. Dann werden einzelne Funde genannt, die älter als der Neandertaler und doch mehr Homo sapiens-ähnlich sein sollen. Zu nennen sind besonders Eoanthropus von Piltdown, Steinheim, Swanscombe und Frontéchevade.

IV. Ungelöst ist schliesslich noch die Frage über die Entstehung der Hauptrassen der heutigen Menschheit. Haben wir "Neandertaler" in Asien und in Afrika? Wann treffen wir unter den fossilen Menschenfunden zum ersten Male die Kennzeichen mongolischer und negrischer Rassenmerkmale? und wo entstand der heutige Europäer, wenn der Neandertaler aus seiner Vorfahrenreihe zu streichen wäre?

Beim Symposium werden sicher Fachleute anwesend sein, die so viele fossile Menschen-Funde selbst bearbeitet haben, dass über diese Fragen authentisch Auskunft gegeben werden kann.

Paleopathology

By ERWIN H. ACKERKNECHT

PALEOPATHOLOGY DEALS with the pathology of prehistoric animals and of man in prehistoric and nonliterate societies. The only documents at its disposal for reconstructing the pathological picture are bones, and sometimes works of art and mummies. The methods of paleopathology have been also occasionally applied with success to "historical" periods where insufficient written documents exist.

The first observations on a pathological fossil bone were published by Esper in 1774 ("sarcoma"—actually healed fracture—in the cave bear, that Job of Paleopathology). Slowly material accumulated first on animals, then on man. These studies gained great impetus in the second half of the nineteenth century, the period of Broca and Virchow. The field became a special discipline during the first thirty years of the twentieth century through the accomplishments of Sir Armand Ruffer (who introduced the name "paleopathology"), Grafton Elliot Smith, Wood Jones, H. U. Williams, Roy L. Moodie, L. Pales, and others. The latter two published treatises on paleopathology (1923 and 1930) with extensive bibliographies. The bibliography after 1930 is given by H. E. Sigerist in Appendix IV of the first volume of his *History of Medicine* (New York, 1951). This period is characterized by the successful use of such technological aids as the X-ray machine and the microscope.

The last twenty years have brought important new detailed knowledge on tumors, prehistoric tuberculosis, etc., although the work has, regrettably enough, not been carried on with the same intensity as before. The main progress during this period lies in the increasing realization that paleopathology gives more than important medical data. *The pathology of a society reflects its general conditions and growth and offers, therefore, valuable clues to an understanding of the total society.* Pioneer work in this direction has been done by Todd, Hooton, Vallois, Ad. Schultz, L. Angel, and others. We have witnessed the first steps from a paleopathology of individuals to a paleopathology of groups and societies. It is to be hoped that, when this point of view is fully assimilated, increased activity in the field will result. In the following survey of the results of this young science, emphasis will be laid on human material. Animal material will be mentioned only occasionally.

THE BONE RECORD

TRAUMATISM

The first healed fractures of animals as evidenced by callus are found in Permian reptiles. A healed fracture was also found in the Neanderthal man. The evidence of healed fractures becomes very extensive in the European Neolithic and in early Egypt. That well-healed fractures alone are no proof for fracture treatment was already maintained by Baudouin and was definitely shown by Ad. Schultz's work on gibbons.

Head injuries are found in *Sinanthropus,* Neanderthal men, Cro-Magnon men, the European Neolithic, and the American pre-Columbian, especially in Peru. The latter prevalence might be due to the use of special weapons like maces. A certain number of the Neolithic and old Peruvian trephinings were apparently provoked by skull fractures. Whether this was the sole reason for trephining is doubtful. Trephining itself is part of paleomedicine, not paleopathology, and therefore is not discussed further here.

Numerous arrowheads have been found in the European Neolithic and in pre-Columbian America, imbedded especially in vertebrae and extremities.

The famous exostosis of Dubois's *Pithecanthropus* might be of traumatic origin.

MALFORMATION

Evidence of dwarfism, achondroplastic and cretinistic, has been found in Egypt, in skeletons and statues. Also an anencephalic mummy has been described. The congenital perforated sternum has been observed in material stemming from Neolithic Europe and from Peru. In the same places evidence of spina bifida was discovered. Other congenital anomalies of the vertebral column have been reported from Peru. Congenital hip luxation was diagnosed in skeletons from Neolithic Europe, pre-Columbian North America, and Peru.

Congenital clubfoot (talipes equinovarus) has been found repeatedly in Egyptian mummies and works of art. G. E. Smith regarded the clubfoot of King Siptah (Nineteenth Dynasty, around 1225 B.C.) as a congenital clubfoot. Slomann interpreted it rather as an aftereffect of *poliomyelitis.* The same interpretation was given by J. K. Mitchell to the shortened femur of a mummy dated about 3700 B.C.; the deformation on the stele of the priest Ruma (Copenhagen) offers itself to the same interpretation. Rolleston diagnosed a Neolithic skeleton from Cissbury as postpoliomyelitic.

Hydrocephalus has been reported from Roman Egypt as well as copperage Turkey, Peru, and ninth-century Germany.

INFLAMMATION (NONSPECIFIC)

If we are to believe the bone record, bacterial infection was a rather early event, and the multicellular organism reacted to this as to other irritations by inflammation that is a combination of necrosis and formation of new tissue.

Periostitis ossificans was first described in Permian reptiles, later in early mammals (especially the cave bear), and eventually in Neolithic man. Osteitis is particularly often represented in the form of *sinusitis* (pre-Columbian North American, Peru, Neolithic France) and mastoiditis (pre-Columbian North American, Peru, Egypt).

The first known cases of osteomyelitis in Permian reptiles were apparently sequels to infected fractures; osteomyelitis again was very prevalent in cave bears. It is found in European Neolithic and ancient Peruvian bones.

Myositis ossificans was found to be common in fossil animals but rare in human remains.

SPECIFIC INFLAMMATION (SYPHILIS, TUBERCULOSIS)

The pre-Columbian existence of syphilis in either hemisphere has been debated heatedly for about four hundred years. It was hoped that paleopathology would eventually decide the question. Starting with Parrot in France in 1877 and with Joseph Jones in North America in 1876, numerous prehistoric bone lesions have been described as syphilitic. Many of these interpretations have been discarded. New suspect specimens have appeared.

There are always two great difficulties to overcome in making a definite diagnosis of pre-Columbian syphilis in a bone: (*a*) Is the bone actually pre-Columbian? (*b*) Were the bone changes actually produced by the *Spirocheta pallida* or by some other infectious agent?

The latter question seems not answerable unless a positive serological reaction or other proof of specificity can be obtained. Such proof has not been produced so far. It should always be remembered by those deciding the case on mere morphology that Virchow was able to demonstrate in the tibia of a cave bear the same changes that are usually attributed to syphilis in human bones.

H. U. Williams, who surveyed the question last in 1932, came to the conclusion that certain bones from Pecos, Paracas, Tennessee Mounds, etc., are beyond any doubt both pre-Columbian and syphilitic. These bones are morphologically strongly suggestive of syphilis. But hardly more so than, e.g., the Neolithic material from Petit Morin in the Museum of St. Germain, from Iran (Krogman), from eleventh-century Russia, from Japan (Adachi), which Williams, with the characteristic fervor of an "American-origin" partisan, disregarded. The safest conclusion seems still to give to none of these inflammatory bone changes the definite label of syphilis.

Some of these bones have meanwhile been claimed as specimens of Paget's disease (osteitis deformans).

The problem is subjectively and objectively somewhat simpler in the case of *tuberculosis*. There is at least one tuberculous affection of the bone, the so-called "Pott's disease," in the vertebral column which it is hard to mistake for any other type of infection. On the basis of numerous cases of Pott's disease

the antiquity of tuberculosis seems now established in both hemispheres. Cases of Pott's disease have been described from predynastic Egypt (3000 B.C.), and from the end of the third millennium in Nubia. A particularly convincing case was described by Smith and Ruffer in the mummy of a priest of Ammon (about 1000 B.C.), where the characteristic psoas abscess also was found. The finding of clay sculptures, picturing the typical hunchback in Pott's disease, reinforce these diagnoses. Tuberculous changes in the hip joints of children (dated 2700 and 1900 B.C.) have also been reported from Egypt.

Only one (controversial) case of Pott's disease has been described from the European Neolithic. Pales feels confident as to the tuberculous nature of a Neolithic hip and an ankylosed foot.

In North America not completely convincing pre-Columbian specimens of Pott's disease have been described by Whitney, Means, and Hrdlička. The findings of Hooton (Pecos) and especially of W. A. Ritchie (New York State) leave little doubt concerning the pre-Columbian existence of tuberculosis in North America. The same can be said for South America after the work of Requena and Garcia Frias. Hunchbacked clay figurines again reinforce the diagnosis in the Western Hemisphere.

A parasitism of a much cruder nature may be mentioned at this point. The hair of Egyptian as well as Peruvian mummies is frequently decorated with the eggs of lice.

OSTEOARTHRITIS AND SPONDYLITIS

Spondylitis is here treated together with osteoarthritis, as it is actually the osteoarthritis of the vertebral column. Osteoarthritis is not subdivided in the following into its rheumatoid and osteoarthritic forms, as this subdivision is at present primarily of clinical interest. Suffice it to say that the material reported below shows both forms of chronic arthritis. If, however, it could be shown that, as suggested by T. D. Stewart, the rheumatoid form is less prevalent in some periods and regions, this would throw an important light on the whole rheumatism problem.

Next to traumatism, arthritis is the oldest and most widespread pathological lesion reported in paleopathology. In the animal kingdom it starts with the dinosaurs of the Comanchian and is continuously found up to the present. In the hominids it has been observed everywhere since Neanderthal man. Egyptian material showing it has existed since 4000 B.C.

Spondylitis, arthritis of the vertebral column, which often transforms the finely structured vertebral column into one solid bony mass, is one of the most frequent and most extensive arthritic lesions. Spondylosis is already present in dinosaurs (*Diplodocus*) of the Secondary. The man of La Chapelle-aux-Saints, a Neanderthal, shows spondylitis of the cervicodorsal and the lumbar parts of the vertebral column. Cro-Magnon men suffered from it. Spondylitis is very frequently seen in European Neolithic, the early Egyptian, and the pre-Columbian American. An interesting feature of spondylitis is the changing seat of the lesion along the vertebral column in animals and men. Different subdivisions of the vertebral column are involved. In early man and primitives, lumbar spondylitis is frequent, while dorsal and cervical are rare (the ancient Egyptians are an exception, with frequent dorsal involvement). In modern man cervical involvement is often found. As similar differences exist between the wild horse and the riding horse (the former shows more dorsal, the latter more lumbar, involvement) or between different species of vertebrates, the conclusions seem legitimate that, *on the one hand, these localizations have something to do with areas of stress and strain and that, on the other hand, conclusions can be drawn from pathological areas as to living conditions and posture of the material under examination.*

Chronic arthritis of the hip joint has so far been observed only in man, not in animals. Here again it begins with the Neanderthalian Homme de la Chapelle, is found in the European Neolithic, frequently in ancient Egypt, and, for unknown reasons, even more frequently in ancient Peru. Pales has suggested that subluxations of the joints form the basis for many of these cases.

Temporo-maxillary arthritis was found in the Neanderthal man of Krapina, but not in other European skeletons. It is rare today in Western countries. It is, on the other hand, fairly frequent among pre-Columbian North and South Americans, and among present-day West Africans and Melanesians, especially in the New Hebrides and in New Caledonia. Pales explains the puzzling fact by the combined action of predisposing racial anatomical structure and particularly coarse food.

Numerous other joints—for instance, of the phalanges—have been found to be affected, e.g., in mosasaurs, cave bears, Neanderthal man, upper Paleolithic men like Cro-Magnon, Neolithic Europeans, ancient Egyptians, Peruvians, and other pre-Columbian Amerindians. The Patagonians show arthritis only in the joints of the upper extremities. Here we again encounter the problem of selective localization, probably connected with zones of particular functional stress.

The universality of arthritis in bones at all periods, climates, and places does not confirm climatic theories of the disease (moist or cold climate). The existence of osteoarthritis in dinosaurs, cave bears, etc., is not in favor of alcohol or tobacco as causative factors.

RICKETS AND SYMMETRICAL
OSTEOPOROSIS

Rickets, an avitaminosis and a bone
disease extremely prevalent during the
last three hundred years, has been
found in a giant Pleistocene wolf and in
a domesticated Egyptian ape, but, in
general, not in early man. No rickets
in the tens of thousands of Egyptian
skeletons examined, none in the extensive pre-Columbian material (this
is consistent with findings in primitives). Only from the Scandinavian
Neolithic and from Indochina (?) has
evidence of rickets been reported. Two
cases of osteomalacia, a disease often
confounded with rickets, have been
seen in Peru.

On the other hand, abundant proof
of a bone disease that is practically
nonexistent among present-day whites
and that might be an avitaminosis—
symmetrical osteoporosis — has been
found in ancient Egypt (Nubia) and
ancient Peru. Pecos also offers several
examples, and it is supposed to have
occurred often among the ancient
Maya. Like rickets, symmetrical osteoporosis, which produces the so-called
"cribra parietalia" and "cribra orbitalia"
—lesions called syphilitic by older authors—is primarily a disease of childhood. Several anemias of childhood and
scurvy produce similar pictures. The
disease is very rare among Neolithic
Europeans and North American pre-
Columbians but is common in many
present-day non-European populations
(African Negroes, Malays, Chinese,
Japanese, etc.). Besides avitaminosis,
mechanical causes (like skull deformation) have been suggested.

TUMORS

Bone tumors in prehistoric men and
animals, especially malignant ones, are
surprisingly rare, as compared to findings in present-day men and animals.
The oldest osteomas are found in
mosasaurs. They occur in the European
Neolithic and rather frequently in ancient Peru, especially as osteomata of
the auditory duct. To differentiate osteomata—true tumors—from exostoses—
mere reactional growth—is not always
simple. Other benign tumors—hemi-
angiomata—have been described in
dinosaurs.

Osteosarcomata have been found in
the cave bear and perhaps the Pleistocene horse. Human osteosarcomata
have been described by Smith and
Dawson from the Fifth Dynasty (*ca.*
2750 B.C.) in Egypt. Recently, sar-
comatous meningiomata have been described in Egyptian skulls of the First
Dynasty (3400 B.C.). Osteosarcomata
occur also in ancient Peruvian skulls.
Moodie has interpreted some of these
Peruvian cranial tumors as residuals of
meningiomata.

Bone defects, especially of the skull
basis and the sacrum, in Neolithic and
ancient Peruvian materials might have
been caused by neighboring cancers of
the soft parts or their metastases. Such
erosions might, of course, also be produced occasionally by aneurysm.

Multiple myeloma has been reported
from Neolithic France and pre-Columbian North America.

DENTAL PATHOLOGY

Pyorrhea appears in the animal series
with the mosasaurs, among hominids
with the Neanderthals. It is found in
ancient Europe, Egypt, Peru, Hawaii,
etc. Abscess resulting from pyorrhea is
described first in an oligocene rhinoceros. In man it starts with the Neanderthal man. Caries, though seen in
mosasaur and cave bear, seems to have
appeared later on a large scale in man.
First clear evidence for it dates from
the Neolithic, especially in Scandinavia.
In ancient Egypt it struck supposedly
only the wealthy. A number of dental
malformations are also on record.

SOFT PARTS

Only a small percentage of diseases leave their marks on the bones. In mummies, fortunately, the soft parts are preserved to a certain extent. Mummification can be spontaneous in very dry climates like that of Arizona. Artificial mummification, supported by a dry climate, was practiced on a large scale in ancient Egypt and Peru. Study of mummies has greatly extended our knowledge of prehistoric disease conditions.

One of the most striking findings in Egyptian mummies (by direct inspection and by X-ray) was that of *arteriosclerosis*. It was first described in the aorta of Merneptah (1225–1215), the Pharaoh of the Exodus. Arteriosclerosis has also been demonstrated in Peruvian mummies.

The *lungs* of mummies have shown the following conditions: silicosis (Basketmaker), anthracosis (Egypt, Basketmaker), pneumonia (Egypt, Basketmaker; one of the Egyptian pneumonias contained bacilli resembling plague bacilli), pleurisy (Egypt).

Kidneys of mummies have presented congenital atrophy (Egypt), multiple abscesses (Egypt), stones (Egypt, Basketmaker). In a mummy of the Twentieth Dynasty (1250–1000) the eggs of *Bilharzia* have been demonstrated. Schistosomiasis, caused by *Bilharzia,* which is still one of the main Egyptian health problems, already existed, apparently, 2000 years ago. Vesicovaginal fistula has been observed in female Egyptian mummies, together with other evidence of difficult birth.

Egyptian mummies have, furthermore, contained gallstones, liver cirrhosis, and chronic appendicitis. Skin changes in one case have strongly suggested smallpox, in another one leprosy. Large spleens have been thought of as possible signs of malaria. Prolapsus of rectum and of female genitalia has been seen.

Ruffer, who did the largest amount of microscopic work in paleopathology and demonstrated a large number of structures, could not find traces of any blood corpuscles. This has unfortunately brought about a somewhat defeatist attitude in the search for the latter, in spite of the fact that G. E. Wilson (1927, Basketmaker) and H. U. Williams (1927, Peruvian mummies) were able to demonstrate red blood corpuscles. Krumbhaar (1936) even found not only erythrocytes but monocytes and polymorphonuclear leukocytes in a pre-Columbian tibia from Peru. Great progress in what we might call "paleophysiology" was achieved when Canela (1936) developed a technique to type blood groups from skeletal material. Wyman and Boyd (1937) followed with important work on blood-grouping in mummies.

ART OBJECTS

Art objects from both hemispheres have already been referred to above in the cases of poliomyelitis, Pott's disease, and dwarfism. In the case of the paleolithic sculptures of obese women it is not clear whether we are dealing with actual representations of the artist's wishful thinking or whether such conditions were spontaneous and pathological or artificially produced. Closer scrutiny of the greatly increased volume of paleolithic art might still yield important discoveries.

Peruvian pottery is particularly rich in pathological representations. The outstanding findings are those of verruga Peruviana (Carrion's disease), uta (leishmaniasis), and sand-flea lesions on the soles of feet.

INTEGRATION

The last twenty years have produced specialized findings of great interest as to the prehistory of, e.g., tuberculosis, tumors, blood corpuscles, etc. Much remains to be done in this field. Important biological hypotheses on the age of infectious diseases like those of the late Charles Nicolle remain still to be integrated with the work of paleopathologists. Certain medical conclusions as to the great age of disease and of certain diseases (tuberculosis, poliomyelitis), the legendary character of ideas of the "healthy wild animal" and the "healthy savage," and the identity of basic disease mechanisms throughout time can be safely made today.

Yet, as mentioned above, another task, even more important than its purely medical implications, faces paleopathology today—the task of integrating its data with other types of information, e.g., from archeology or paleoanthropology, in such a way that it realizes its potentialities for an illumination of human society and its dynamics. On the other hand, all those co-operating in such a synthesis will have to pay more attention to the data of paleopathology than has been done in the past.

Pioneer work in integrating the data of paleopathology was undertaken by Todd (1929), when he reconstructed the duration of life in medieval and in primitive communities from bone material. Vallois did the same for early man (1932).

The most important effort in this direction was made by Hooton in his splendid monograph on Pecos in 1930, when, on the basis of the bone record, he reconstructed the life-history of the settlement, utilizing the archeological findings and his exhaustive study of Pecos paleopathology. Hooton found arthritis, traumatism, sinusitis, mastoiditis, osteomyelitis (syphilis?), osteoporosis, Pott's disease, cancer, etc. That he found so much is probably due less to a particularly high morbidity in Pecos than to

his sustained interest in the problem. Hooton set a shining example, unfortunately isolated so far. If a few more sites had been handled with the same thoroughness, we would probably have achieved far greater progress in our field. Bone material should always be studied beyond the traditional examination for its racial nature and *should receive at least the type of attention that is given to material in legal cases.* Physical anthropology has contributed valuable techniques to legal medicine. It could, in turn, profit from adoption of some techniques of legal medicine and other medical technology.

It is no accident that one of the most significant and brilliant recent contributions in integration has come from a pupil of Hooton, J. L. Angel, in his work on the anthropology of the early Greeks. Angel found the growth of Greek culture between 800 and 500 B.C. connected with such phenomena as an increase in body size, life-span, and population volume and a decrease in arthritis, dental pathology, osteoporosis, and infant mortality. He noticed again a decrease in health after 400 B.C. The fact that the one or the other conclusion of Angel might be based on too small a sample does not detract from the value and interest of his studies as a whole. Sigerist has recently integrated in a similar way cultural and paleopathological data on Egypt in the first volume of his *History of Medicine*.

Another important recent contribution has been the work of Ad. Schultz on Primate pathology. We have already mentioned his work on fractures in gibbons. When, besides the lesions we are familiar with in early man and in mummies, he found a high degree of infestation with plasmodia, filaria, and trypanosoma, the conclusion seems legitimate, in view of biological relationships, that man's ancestors were affected in a similar way.

Biological Basis of Human Behavior

By CARLOS MONGE

I. INTRODUCTION

THE PIONEER research carried out on life in the Andes showed from the beginning that remarkable physiological deviations exist in acclimatized men and that striking changes, such as temporary infertility, as clinical observations pointed out in a few cases, occur in the newcomers. Later on, through biological experimentation, a period of infertility during adaptation to high altitude was found in different animals. Considering these strange facts, the possibility occurred to me of a historical approach to the problem which arose during the conquest of the highlands by the Spaniards, which would be facilitated by the fact that the Crown of Spain fortunately used to send the conquerors accompanied by learned secretaries who recorded the events. Were this guessing to prove useful, we would be able to correlate biological information obtained in the laboratory and social facts gathered from the analysis of the documents of the colonial writers. And, in fact, the truth of this assumption has been confirmed.

In starting the work on man and altitude we had in mind Galen's sentence: "'Man is a whole with his environment," so well pointed out by Hutchins as regards investigation and research in medicine. Man is not an abstraction; he is a part of the environment in which he lives and outside of which he cannot exist. Thus there is "no doubt that physiology lies at the base of behavior," as Coon suggested in regard to anthropology. "As a matter of fact," he says, "very few of the findings of social scientists lend themselves to scientific treatment with the precision which may be accorded to physical aspects of race." It can be added that there is also a lack of interest on the part of biologists in the problem of men and the outside world. Not enough attention has been paid to functional differences among men; it is supposed that they are all physiologically equal. It is not so, indeed! The equation does not hold true, at any rate, for dwellers of the high plateaus. With this idea as a research directive, applied physiology can provide many useful data on biological variations due to environmental changes as they have been found in animals. Research on this subject—heat, cold, and altitude—was started by Dill. Anthropology awaits biological data to further knowledge in this direction.

Correlation between form and function—physical and physiological anthropometry—and comparative physiological research on the so-called "definite" racial groups may prove to be useful by gathering information about respiratory and circulatory functions and other physiological factors. For instance, physical measurements of Andean men allow us to predict a considerable increase over the normal of the "below function" (Peabody) of the thorax, a greater size of the lung, a larger pulmonary blood bed, and consequently a greater quantity of work for the right chambers of the heart. Physiological research has demonstrated this to be the case. The plasticity of bone structure is well adapted to every influence of the external environment. Of course, we have been fortunate enough to work with people adapted to the most extreme limits of altitude environment, and this has permitted us to record extreme deviations.

II. ENVIRONMENT

Three important climatic elements of profound influence can be briefly discussed: altitude, temperature, and atmosphere.

ALTITUDE

According to Bowman, altitudes of 17,000 feet are fit for human living in Peru, as pointed out in his work, *The Andes of Southern Peru*. Places located higher up are inhabited for industrial reasons relating to mining work. Up to 17,000 feet there are ecological conditions to maintain life. There is a diminishing barometric pressure from sea-level to 17,000 feet, at which altitude it is about half the value of that at sea-level, 380 mm. The effect of this general lowering of pressure upon the body is unknown, since the research has been carried out only on diminished oxygen pressure.

TEMPERATURE

Several facts deserve attention. As the land is located in the tropics, the predominant type of climate should be tropical. However, this is not so. Because of the altitude, the weather is, in certain aspects, similar to that found in the arctic regions. The climate is of glacial type, but it is warm during the daytime because of the sun's tropical rays. This makes for a strange combination of climatic factors—heat and cold acting simultaneously—not yet studied in the determination of the resultant weather. It is always cold in the shade, and this is another element to be integrated. There is a marked difference between the extreme day and night temperatures. From approximately 6,000 to 15,000 feet altitude, the climate is cold but has the solar influence we have pointed out. Precipitation is abundant, dryness predominates. At sea-level, tropical or subtropical weather is the rule. The coastal climate is mild, and there is very little rain. Tropical weather and high humidity are notorious in the jungles of central Peru.

ATMOSPHERE

The rarefied atmosphere at high altitude impresses upon the climate a special characteristic of utmost significance in its tremendous influence on the living body. There is a gradual decrease of oxygen pressure from sea-level to the highest altitudes. We will see in the chart the oxygen pressure of the places where our research has been carried out.

At present we will limit ourselves to stating that at sea-level there is an oxygen pressure of 156 mm., one-fifth of the 760-mm. barometric pressure; in Huancayo there is 104 mm. oxygen pressure (518 B.P.); in Morococha there is 89 mm. oxygen pressure (446 B.P.); and in the highest inhabited places there is about 78 mm. oxygen pressure, half the sea-level value (Table 1).

III. MAN UPON THE ANDES

The interplay of the following climatic elements—heat under the tropical sun rays, cold, diminished barometric pressure, diminished pressure of oxygen, increased ultraviolet rays, etc.—has produced a variety of climate where once was developed one of the greatest civilizations of the world. Let us now consider Andean man in his own environment, or, in other words, man as a function of the environment. Who may be called a "high-altitude man"? Does such a man exist as a biological entity? Strictly speaking, we cannot scientifically describe a man at 15,000 feet as a sea-level man has been described, without regard to his highlands environment. If pursuit of knowledge had started in the highlands and a scientist had discovered a sea-level man, how,

in the Andes are rather complex because, with each change in the environment, there occurs a change in the physiology of the body. At sea-level the external milieu is a constant, and physiology expresses itself in only one dimension, horizontally; at high altitudes physiology works out in two dimensions, horizontally and vertically, the outside environment being a variable. The "wisdom of the body" of the acclimatized man is unknown to the sea-level man. While considering man in a static environment, we have gathered

TABLE 1

PLACE	ALTITUDE (FEET)	LONGITUDE	LATITUDE	PRESSURE		TEMPERATURE				PRECIPIT.	RELATIVE HUMIDITY	CLIMATE
				Baromt.	O₂	Max.	Min.	True An. Ave.	Oscil. 24 h.			
Morococha..	14,900	76°08'–	11°37'–	446	89	.....	....	6.25	....	1,189.5	59.60	Puna: cold, high steppe, near glacial
Huancayo...	10,170	71°12'44"	12°04'20"	518	104	30.9	−10.0	12.05	40.9	754.84	77.54	Andean high plateau
Lima.......	500	77°02'14"	12°03'02"	750	156	37.5	9.6	18.40	22.9	39.37	86.80	Dry coast
Iquitos.....	347	75°11'24"	3°45'23"	752	157	37.0	17.8	31.80	13.26	2,878.8	80.10	Humid jungle

then, should he describe him?

In order to discuss the matter and for descriptive reasons, however, we will describe the biological characteristics found in our places of research: Lima, sea-level; Huancayo, 10,170 feet; Oroya, 12,300 feet; and Morococha, 14,900 feet. To do this we have to imagine, for the time being, the outside world as a static environment (Tables 2, 3, 4).

For the sake of brevity, man acclimatized to the high plateaus will be called by us "altitude man." Perhaps there are other reasons, as we will see later on in the course of this discussion.

IV. MAN AND ALTITUDE ENVIRONMENT

At the base of the problem is the necessity of placing Andean men in a dynamic relation with the impact and stress produced by the physiological changes of environment. Life dynamics

some physiological data, but we can only guess the biological responses to the alterations of the environment. This is a promising new field of original research for the development of the science of man.

We have, then, to integrate the biological data supposedly belonging to a fixed milieu with the clinical knowledge of everyday life in the Andes.

Many millions of people have found a permanent residence in the South American high plateaus since prehistoric time. They live, they work, they reproduce. Possibilities of life at high altitude for acclimatized races are exactly the same as for man at sea-level. There is no limit to human development. Some facts need to be emphasized. The vertical geography of the country is the reason for continuous mass movements of population from the highlands to the lowlands and vice versa. Up to the time of the Incas, these migrations occurred chiefly from the high steppes to the coast, always with a return to the place of origin. At present, mass movement operates both ways. However, this form of Andean migration most of the time is only temporary, causing a kind of permanent nomadism either up to the mines or down to the low agricultural lands. As a matter of fact, traveling in Peru is vertical, as it is horizontal in the rest of the world.

This vertical distribution of man in the plateaus of South America has developed in the Andeans special biological devices of adaptative significance which allow them to be in equilibrium with their environment up to 18,000–20,000 feet, as can be seen in altitude flights of Peruvian aviators without oxygen masks. The highest inhabited place in the world was found by Bowman in Peru at 17,400 feet altitude (*op. cit.*). Of course, there is a ceiling of tolerance for any man, above which life is not possible. It is fair to state that human ecology for Andean people may be traced up to 17,400 feet altitude.

Clinical observations show that at these altitudes Andean man is able to perform a most strenuous amount of work in the mines. Indeed, it has been demonstrated (Monge) by clinical tests

TABLE 2*

Hematology	Moroccoсha Natives Altitude 14,900 feet	Oroya Natives Altitude 12,230 feet	Huancayo Natives ‘Altitude 10,170 feet	Morocoсha Men from Huancayo	Lima Men from Huancayo 1st W.	Lima Men from Huancayo 3d W.	Lima Men from Huancayo 8th W	Lima Men from Sea-Level
Red blood cells......... (mill. per cu.mm.)	6.15	5.67	5.65	6.05	5.57	5.37	4.70	5.14
Hemoglobin............ (gr. per 100 ml.)	20.76	18.82	16.85	17.98	16.49	15.95	14.30	16.00
Hematocrit............ (red cells per cent)	59.90	54.10	50.36	54.43	50.67	49.46	43.10	46.80
Reticulocytes.......... (per cent)	1.5	0.8	0.47	1.94	0.77	0.25	0.4	0.5
Total bilirubin........ (mg. per 100 ml.)	1.56	1.47	0.84	0.84	0.91	....	0.83	0.72
Direct bilirubin........ (mg. per 100 ml.)	0.46	....	0.16	0.38	0.26	....	0.33	0.37
Indirect bilirubin....... (mg. per 100 ml.)	1.10	....	0.68	0.46	0.65	....	0.50	0.35
Blood volume.......... (liters)	6.98	6.15	5.36	5.58	5.55	5.49	5.17	5.21
Plasma volume......... (liters)	2.65	2.76	2.55	2.29	2.66	2.67	2.80	2.82
Red cell volume........ (liters)	4.29	3.36	2.79	3.25	2.87	2.79	2.35	2.34
Blood volume.......... (ml. per kg.)	120.8	108.7	87.21	90.64	89.67	88.11	81.70	86.5
Plasma volume......... (ml. per kg.)	46.1	48.9	41.46	38.77	42.83	42.67	44.28	47.1
Red cell volume........ (ml. per kg.)	74.1	59.7	45.45	53.78	46.45	44.75	37.10	38.8
Total hemoglobin....... (gr.)	1,464.00	1,150.00	905.01	1,002.42	894.32	867.26	737.99	788.00
Total hemoglobin....... (gr. per kg.)	25.2	20.7	14.73	16.76	14.80	13.91	11.64	13.2

* Average values of a group of 12 soldiers, born in Huancayo (10,170 ft.), taken up to Morococha (14,900 ft.) and, after a period of 15 days, transferred to sea-level in Lima, where they were followed up for a period of 8 weeks. The other values have been taken from the works of Dr. Hurtado, Dr. Merino, and Dr. Delgado (see Bibliography).

since 1930 that, in general, the work output is higher among the Andeans than that of sea-level people at sea-level.

We have to stress the fact that there are places in the high plateaus or located at higher altitudes unsuitable to

profound differences between the physiology of both groups of dwellers in those localities, a fact which must be borne in mind in anthropology if the problem of life and disease at high altitudes is to be understood. For accuracy, we have stressed that there are

TABLE 3

Relations between Blood Volume, Cell Volume, Plasma Volume, Total Hemoglobin, and O₂ Pressure at Different Altitudes

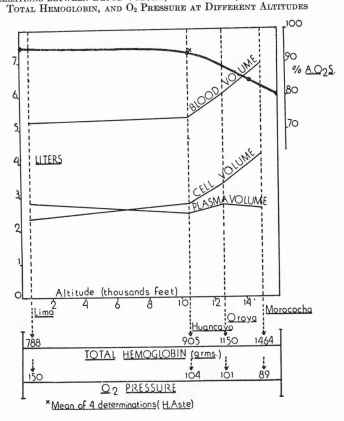

sustain life. This is evident in the mines located at such altitude that labor is possible only for a few hours a day, and the workers are forced to descend to a lower level to spend the night. Since 1928 we have called the places where life develops in every respect "inhabitable localities," to differentiate them from the unnatural localities created for industrial purposes.

We must anticipate that there are

two fundamental aspects in high-altitude research applied to man. Both approaches are necessary: altitude outside the ecological milieu applies to a general knowledge and particularly to aviation physiology; man in his ecological surroundings is primarily a subject for anthropology. Much confusion will be avoided if we have these facts in mind.

As starting points related to life in

a changing-altitude environment, the following can be initially established:

1. The physiological and biochemical systems are different at different altitudes. Their homeostatic integration

state corresponding to the new altitude environment is reached. *Adaptation* leads to *acclimatization*.

3. The new concept of *acclimatization to sea-level* which must take place

TABLE 4*

ACID BASE PATH

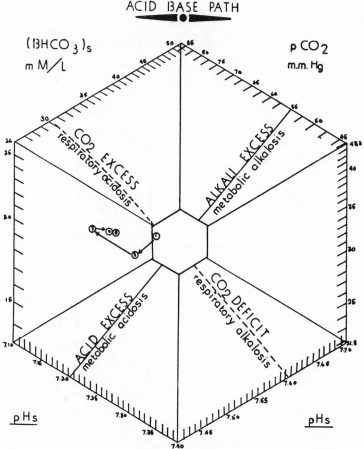

* In Huancayo, the acid-base path is within normal limits; in Morococha (14,900 ft.) pH is shifted to the metabolic acidosis zone; and in Lima (sea-level) pH goes to the respiratory acidosis zone (*follow arrows*). After 2 months, pH has not returned to the normal value.

brings about the "fixity of the internal milieu," which measures the equilibrium of organism and environment present in *congenital acclimatization*.

2. A measurable change of environmental altitude produces a stress, *climatic aggression*, which causes in the organism a succession of adaptive processes, so that a balanced functional

in the organism coming down from the high altitude is now conclusively established. The hyperoxic condition of the lowlands must be balanced by the body. The most obvious phenomenon is destruction of the red blood corpuscles, but there are also readjustments of the other functions occurring until sea-level equilibrium is attained.

4. It is most probable that there might be, for high-altitude men, reversible physiological systems that allow the high-altitude organism to adapt rapidly to the stress represented by the fast change of oxygen pressure. Such adaptability is lost or greatly reduced while approaching sea-level.

5. The inapparent mountain sickness shows two main forms: (*a*) a mild form which allows the individual to live and to reproduce and leads to *acquired acclimatization;* (*b*) a nonreproductive form: the individual lives normally but does not reproduce himself, *individual acclimatization* (such a process is very exceptional).

6. Both congenital and acquired acclimatization to high altitudes can be lost, and then chronic mountain sickness is produced. It is cured by descent to lower or sea-levels.

V. COMPARATIVE ANTHROPOLOGY

If we consider either form or function of man at different altitudes, we find that there is a linear relationship between altitude and the volume of the thorax. There is also a linear relationship between blood volume and altitude. It can be stated, then, that the respiratory activity of the lung and blood is increased. If this is so, the respiratory activity of the circulation is also increased.

Besides, we wanted to find out for an anthropological approach whether in high-altitude man there was a closer relationship between lung volume and total blood volume than in sea-level man, because, according to physical measurements, there is a closer relationship between thorax and height. With the collaboration of Vellard for anthropometry and Monge, Jr., and aided by funds from the Wenner-Gren Foundation, it was possible to plan a program of work which covered these points. The research has been carried out in Peru and Bolivia. It allowed a wider field of people to be studied and permitted a more definite comparative approach. We chose three groups of men:

a) *Lima sea-level group.*—One hundred selected sailors of the Navy School, born on the coast, who had never been in the high plateaus, and who belonged to a typical group of Peruvian sea-coast folk. Average age: twenty to twenty-four years. This group had a variable proportion of mixed blood with Europeans or Indians of the high plateaus.

b) *Bolivia group.*—Fifty young selected soldiers from the indigenous population, born at an altitude of 11,000–15,000 feet, most of them from the Titicaca Lake region. They had never been in the jungle lowlands and belonged to a typical aboriginal people.

c) *Huancayo group.*—One hundred and twenty-five selected soldiers of indigenous extraction, born at about 8,000–12,000 feet altitude, who had never been at sea-level and belonged to a typical group of aboriginal stock. Average age: twenty to twenty-four years. They may be considered as a pure Indian people.

The physical selection of these groups had been very well done, for their admittance and their stay in the armed forces allowed us to obtain the fullest information about them and provided excellent opportunities for physiological work. They all received very good physical training and were submitted to intensive military work. Besides, most of them were trained as athletes, especially the Peruvian sailors, who took part in competitive contests.

It can be seen that the Bolivian highest-altitude group has a thoracic volume 1,506 cc. greater than the thoracic volume of sea-level man and 1,031 cc. greater than the thoracic volume of the Huancayo 10,000-foot man. The Huancayo man's thoracic volume is 475 cc. greater than the sea-level man's. There is thus a linear relationship between altitude and thoracic volume (Table 5).

Of course, we realize that our groups allow only a comparative approach to the problem and are not fitted for general anthropological considerations. Vellard has pointed out that the Lima group includes some men with generations (in some cases very many) of high-altitude ancestors. Those men have shown thoracic anthropometric values rather close to the rest of the subjects. He believes that this has to

volume of blood in the right side of the heart.

The total blood volume and the central (lung) volume are expressed in cubic centimeters per kilogram weight, which facilitates comparative analysis. With the dye dilution method we can obtain the following determinations: blood volume, cardiac output, lung volume, circulation time, blood in right chamber of the heart.

This method has been used by Carlos Monge, Jr. (results to be published) to compare sea-level figures to high-alti-

TABLE 5

VARIATIONS OF THE CHEST MEASUREMENTS AT
DIFFERENT ALTITUDES

Altitude (Feet)	Height (Mm.)	A.P. Diameter (Mm.)	Trans. Diameter (Mm.)	Height of Sternum (Mm.)	Thoracic Volume* (Cc.)
12,000........	1,616	213	283	199	12,150
10,000........	1,603	208	228	185	11,019
Sea-level......	1,653	203	283	183	10,544

* The thoracic volume follows a linear relation with altitude.

be interpreted as their not having been influenced by the upland environment. He is not yet in a position to interpret possible genetic influence concerning shape and form of thorax at different altitudes.

We have found out that there is a close relation between physical and physiological measurements and that this relation applies also to some blood coefficients (Table 6).

We will now refer to Newman's method for thoracic blood measurements, "the dye dilution technique." The charts represent the average figures of nine experiments in Lima (sea-level men) and of eight experiments in Morococha (natives from high altitudes). According to Dr. Newman's work, central volume would represent the pulmonary blood volume. The buildup time would be an index of the

tude coefficients. As predicted from biological considerations, higher blood volume, lung volume, etc., have been found at high altitude. The ratio of lung volume to total blood volume is also higher (Tables 7, 8).

VI. ADAPTATION TO HIGH-ALTITUDE CLIMATE

According to Coon and Birdsell:

One of the major facts in the differentiation of modern racial groups has been natural selection operating in terms of stress and stimuli inherent in the extreme environment. The Mongoloid race was the last of the major groups to differentiate in the fourth glacial period as a result of extreme environmental stressing in the Arctic environment. It has been suggested that adaptation to cold was attained by developing big chests, short extremities and small globular bodies irradiating as little heat as possible. . . . Arctic people present

TABLE 6

COMPARATIVE RELATIONSHIP BETWEEN PHYSICAL AND PHYSIOLOGICAL MEASUREMENTS IN
REGARD TO THE SHAPE OF THE CHEST AND TO SOME BLOOD COEFFICIENTS

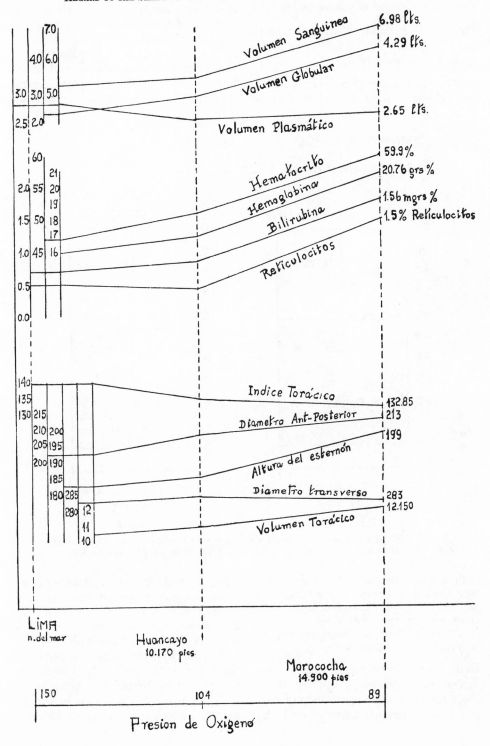

the least possible skin surface to the outside world in proportion to volume and weight.

On the other hand, it would be pertinent to point out the following statement taken from Wulsin:

Mongolia is a dry plateau with an average altitude of about 4,500 feet. Most of

atmosphere, and altitude, which have a strong influence over the climate on account of the latitude. Thus it can be suggested that the Mongolian ancestors in South American high plateaus settled in places where they could maintain their physical traits; physiological adjustments; and resistance to cold,

TABLE 7

LIMA = SEA LEVEL

MOROCOCHA = 15,000 FEET

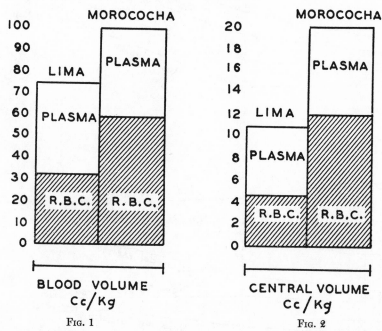

FIG. 1

FIG. 2

FIG. 1.—The values are expressed in cubic centimeters and refer to 1 kilo of body weight
FIG. 2.—The values refer to the lung volume at sea-level as compared to the same at high altitude

the population are pastoral nomads, migratory herders of sheep. The summers are hot and the winters cold with high winds, snow, and temperatures of –40°, –50° F. In their migrations to circumpolar regions they attain 60° latitude north.

Certainly we find here reproduced conditions of environment approximating those found in the upper lands of central South America: extreme cold, dry

hunger, and altitudes. Furthermore, Coon suggests a second effect of cold by its influence on the growing organism through stimulation of adrenals to make people short and globular. This is a mere hypothesis to explain what happened at the end of the fourth glacial period at around 60° latitude.

Today it has been proved in experimental biology that adrenals increase when exposed to cold (Monge, Encina, Caviese). This has been proved in rats brought from lowlands to 15,000 feet altitude. In regard to the explanation

VII. HUMAN BEHAVIOR

In the preceding sections we pointed out the biological basis which builds up the physiological substratum of An-

TABLE 8*

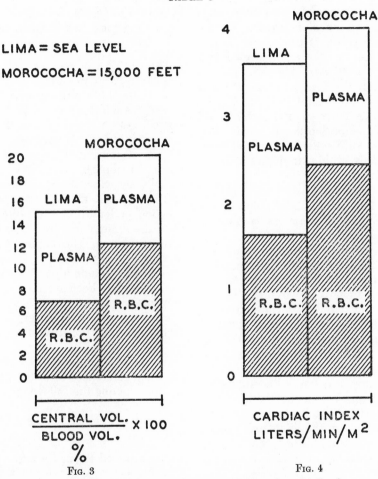

LIMA = SEA LEVEL

MOROCOCHA = 15,000 FEET

Fig. 3

Fig. 4

* The values of Tables 7 and 8 have been taken from the works of Drs. C. Monge, Jr., and A. Cazorla.

Fig. 3.—Relationship between lung volume and total blood volume. It shows a higher blood bed in the chest at high altitudes.

Fig. 4.—No special signification.

that the change in thorax shape is reversible, if a phenotypical change of a temporary nature follows an alteration in environment, it seems to me that the rarefied atmosphere plus cold strongly supports Coon's point of view.

dean man. The stress produced by the high-altitude climate is so striking that it is interesting to recall the reactions of modern philosophers and physiologists about their experiences in the highlands of South America. Keysserling says: "Those altitude men must have a different mineralization. In the high steppes on the Andes there are only two possibilities for a man: to adapt himself or to die." Quite different is the opinion of physiologists tied to the sea-level official knowledge. Barcroft, for instance, impressed by the stress and strain of the anoxia he suffered, wrote in *The Respiratory Function of the Blood:* "The acclimatized man is not the man who has attained to bodily and mental powers as great in Cerro de Pasco (Peru) as he would have in Cambridge. Such a man does not exist. All dwellers at high altitudes are persons of impaired physical and mental powers."

There are two reasons for this misleading interpretation. The first one is that adaptation starts as a malady sometimes unrecognized because of apparent well-being. Barcroft never found high altitudes congenial. Unfortunately, man is prone to hasty generalizations. The second one is that to orthodox sea-level knowledge the deviated physiological findings and abnormal chemical data found at high altitudes appear as facts of pathological significance. Even at present some investigators think that Andean men are borderline to pathological cases. We do not believe this. Our criteria about health and disease and survival in the highlands follow the line of natural history: the "wisdom of the body" to live and reproduce since prehistoric times.

Such a profound influence of the climate up to the point of originating a physiological variety of human people is at the basis of the biological architecture of Andean man and determines his attitudes in every respect—constitution, individual life, migrations, and sociological behavior.

In the following paragraphs we will limit ourselves to presenting some brief references.

INDIVIDUAL BEHAVIOR; ATHLETIC CONSTITUTION OF ANDEAN MAN; PHYSICAL CULTURE AND PHYSICAL EXERTION THE HIGH-ALTITUDE LAW TO MAINTAIN ACCLIMATIZATION; CONTESTS FOR NOBILITY (*huaracu*); NUPTIAL CEREMONIES (*acataymita* AND *paltay*); URGE TO RETURN TO THE SAME CLIMATIC ENVIRONMENT

The native Andean, as well as the conqueror who overcame the aggression of the high altitude and became an acclimated being, developed an adequate constitution. Doubtless the training of athletes at sea-level consists mainly of inuring them to anoxia by means of repeated exercises; such is actually the case, for it is the essence of training that the body is taught to function under extreme conditions beyond the limits normally set by the intake of oxygen. The high-altitude atmosphere being anoxic, it is to be inferred that the individual living at high altitude either becomes an athlete, as it were, or perishes as a victim of fatigue. Logically, then, athleticism must be the norm for the survival of man in the high altitudes.

We find on this subject very enlightened references of historic character, for example the following:

Garcilazo de la Vega, who regards the feast of *huaracu* as equivalent to that of arming knights, assures us that

the boys passed through a most rigorous novitiate, they were chosen from the age of sixteen and they used to go to a house which had been built especially for these procedures in the section of the city called Collcampta, to which I myself walked once and saw a part of these activities. They used to make them fast very strictly for six days. Anyone who seemed thin or weakened by this fast or who asked for more food would be reproached and thrown out of the novitiate. When the fast was over and they had been comforted with a little more food, they examined them for lightness of foot, for which they made them run from the hill called Huanacauri to the very fortress of the city, which must be almost a league and a half, and the first one to arrive was chosen to be captain of the rest [*Comentarios reales* (Lima, 1918), LXXXIII, 194].

CLIMATIC AGGRESSION; ITS EVIDENCE; ANDEAN "AIR-TEMPER" DAMAGING TO COASTAL DWELLERS; COASTAL ATMOS-PHERE DAMAGING TO ANDEANS; ITS UTILIZATION BY THE INCAS

The Viceroy Prince of Esquilache (1621) in the statement which he left for his successor, the Marquis of Guadalcazar, says:

It is to be noted that the Indians are divided into three groups: some are called *yungas* and they are the ones that live on the plains and in the hot valleys, others are the *chaupuyungas* and these are the ones that live in higher regions which correspond to what we in Castilla call foothills, and where air-temper is medium, tending more toward coolness and heat; and the others are the real uplanders, born and raised in these cold lands, and what is done with great care and scruple in the government is not to permit them to change their place of service from one air-temper to another [*Relacióm que el Prícipe de Esquilache hace el Senor Marquez de Guadalcazar sobre el estado en que deja las provincias del Perú* (Madrid: Biblioteca Historia Hispano Americana, 1921), Vol. I].

That the military experience of .the Incas taught them the injury which the coast did to their uplands soldiers may be noted once more during the reign of Hauayna Capac, who, after the conquest of Quito,

went down to the plains, that is the coast, desiring to conquer them.... During this time the Inka has his army renewed three or four times, for as some came, others left, because of the risk to their health which the inlanders run when on the coast, since the latter is a hot region and the other cold [Garcilazo de la Vega, *Comentarios reales*].

BIOLOGICAL BEHAVIOR; RACIAL ACCLIMATIZATION; INTERNAL COLONIZATION (*mitimaes*); BIOCLIMATIC SOCIOLOGY OF INDIANS IN LAND OF INCAS

Much evidence has been found concerning the biological fundamentals of Inca legislation. Some citations are pertinent. We believe that the organization of the *mitmaccuna,* or *mitimaes,* as they are generally called, has a greater importance than that assigned thereto up to the present time. The organization corresponds to what is today known as a policy for interior colonization. One must admit that it fulfilled certain political and economic needs, but it cannot be denied that fundamentally it meant family wandering, by dint of which the adaptation of the Andes people to different climatic environments could be maintained.

HOW THE INKAS DISPOSED OF THEIR NEWLY POSSESSED LANDS, SETTLING STRANGE INDIANS IN THEM WHICH THEY CALLED MITIMAES, AND THE DIFFERENCES THERE WERE IN THEM. The first thing these Kings did upon winning a new province was to take out of it six or seven thousand families and transfer them to other parts in the quiet and pacific provinces, distributing them in different towns; and in exchange for them they put in an equal number of people which they made leave the places where the strangers had been settled, or from wherever they thought best, and among them many nobles of the royal blood.... They took care in this inter-migration that those who were transferred, both the newly conquered and the others, should not move to just any region but more or less to one of the same air-temper and qualities or very similar at least to the region they had left or in which they had grown up.... When some province was sterile as to food such as all the provinces of Collao, because of their great cold, the Inka had indicated lands in the hot valleys of the seacoast on the one hand and on the opposite side of the Andes too, that they sow in those more temperate valleys the things which their people lacked; and since these valleys were twenty, thirty or more leagues away from their own country and they were not able to go and sow the crops there as an enterprise of the entire community as was usually done in the rest of the kingdom, the chiefs were careful to send people in time to do it, who, once they had got their harvest, returned with it to their own towns [Padre B. Cobo, *Historia del Nuevo Mundo* (Seville, 1897), Vol. II].

Even at present this migratory process continues, despite its having gone unnoticed. We once called attention to the nomadism of the workers in the mining regions as well as in the agricultural zones of the lowlands. However, sooner or later he returns to his place of origin, where nature and the accustomed economy of his community furnish him with his ideal life-condition. These cycles are usually annual. No one is surprised any more at the commonplace incident of the workingman who suddenly, when everything seems favorable for him on the coast, leaves for no apparent reason to return to his upland home. Thus he obeys without realizing it an ancestral biological law.

It is not our purpose to derive definite conclusions in this regard. It is up to the sociologists to interpret these phenomena properly. We should rather state that these problems belong to anthropological knowledge and applied anthropology. Biologically we cannot avoid the clear imperative to give them an explanation closely adjusted to the general processes, within which the life of plants, animals, and men develops in the high regions of the Andes.

We have been able to prove that, after a six-month stay at sea-level, young Indians coming from the highlands were not yet equilibrated with the external environment. To attain the fixity of their internal milieu, it was necessary to wait longer. The knowledge of this fact is of the utmost importance for individual health. We do not yet know how long it takes to become acclimatized in the high plateaus in the sense of a perfect equilibrium between internal milieu and environment.

There is a promising field of research concerning the influence of high-altitude climates upon men and their sociological behavior. We are convinced that a systematic research at sea-level carried out along the same lines may prove useful in determining the influence of function upon the body as a biological basis of human behavior.

PERUVIAN BIBLIOGRAPHY CONCERNING BIOLOGICAL AND MEDICAL ASPECTS OF LIFE AT HIGH ALTITUDES

ACCAME, FERRUCCIO. "Efectos de presiones barométricas bajas sobre el semen del carnero," *An. Fac. Med. Lima*, XXVIII (1945), 65–90.

ALHALEL, B. "La Fragilidad capilar en sujetos a nivel del mar, en anoxia crónica y en anoxia aguda, estudio hematológico complementario." Tesis de Bachiller, Facultad de Medicina, Lima, 1949.

ALZAMORA VALDEZ, ELIO. "Aportes para la historia de la neurología en el Perú," *An. Fac. Med. Lima*, XXVII (1944), 96–138.

ARELLANO, ALEJANDRO. "El Líquido céfalo-raquídeo en la altura. Verificación de un caso de enfermedad de Monge," *Rev. Neuropsiq. Lima*, II (1939), 246–53.

ARNÁEZ, ENRIQUE. "Forma de la respiración en la altura," *An. Fac. Med. Lima*, XXV (1942), 2.

ASTE-SALAZAR, J. HUMBERTO. "Exploración funcional del sistema nervioso extra-cardíaco del andino," *An. Fac. Med. Lima*, XIX (1936), 226–309.

ASTE-SALAZAR, J. HUMBERTO, and HURTADO, ALBERTO. "The Affinity of Hemoglobin for Oxygen at Sea Level and High Altitudes," *American Journal of Physiology*, CXLII (1944), 733–43.

BOCANEGRA, RAMÓN. "Duración del sístole

eléctrico (intervalo Q–T) en la anoxia aguda y crónica." Tesis de Bachiller, Facultad de Medicina, Lima, 1949.

CABIESES MOLINA, FERNANDO. "Contribución al estudio del sistema nervioso vegetativo cardiovascular en relación con la vida en las alturas," *An. Fac. Med. Lima,* XXIX (1946), 5–124.

——. "La Acción antifatigante de la cocaina y la habituación a la coca en el Perú," *ibid.,* pp. 316–67.

CASTAÑÓN P., JOSÉ. "Inseminación artificial del ganado lanar en la Sierra del Centro," *Actas de la III Conv. Agronómica* (1944), p. 163.

——. "El Mejoramiento del ganado lanar de la communidad indígena del centro," *ibid.,* p. 196.

CERVELLI, MIGUEL. "La Respuesta cardiovascular al esfuerzo." Tesis de Bachiller, Facultad de Medicina, Lima, 1929.

DELGADO FEBRES, ERNESTO. "La Bilirrubinemia," *An. Fac. Med. Lima,* XXXII (1949), 29–95.

GARCÍA-GODOS, MARIANO. "Influencia de la posición del cuerpo sobre el pulso y la presión arterial. Observaciones hechas a nivel del mar y en la altura," *An. Fac. Med. Lima,* XXVIII (1945), 101–23.

GARCÍA-ROSELL, OVIDIO. "Datos sobre tuberculosis en los Andes." Tesis de Doctor, Facultad de Medicina, Lima, 1936.

GUTIÉRREZ-NORIEGA, C. "El Cocaismo y la alimentación en el Perú," *An. Fac. Med. Lima,* XXXI (1948), 1–90.

GUZMÁN-BARRÓN, A. "El Contenido en vitamina B de algunos alimentos," *Bol. Soc. Quí. Per.,* X (1944), 1.

HAHN, HANS. "Tiempo de reaccion visual y sus variaciones por el factor altura," *An. Fac. Med. Lima,* XXV (1942), 101–15.

HARLAND, S. C. "Estudio del sistema pastoral en alturas superiores a 3,500 metros," (Com. a la III Conv. Agronómica Reg.), *Actas de la III Conv. Agronómica* (1944), p. 175.

HERAUD, CÉSAR. "Enfermedad de los Andes, estudios hematológicos," *An. Fac. Med. Lima,* XI (1928), 261–65.

HURTADO, ALBERTO. "Estudios fisiológicos sobre el hombre de los Andes," *An. Fac. Med. Lima,* XI (1928), 14–75.

——. "Algunas observaciones sobre el volumen del tórax, la capacidad vital y el metabolismo básico en la altura," *ibid.,* pp. 266–305.

——. "Estudios de metabolismo básico en el Perú" (Tesis doctoral), *ibid.*

——. "El Metabolismo básico del soldado Peruano," *Rev. san. militar, Lima,* II (1929), 9–24.

——. "Sobre patología de la altura," *Rev. med. peruana, Lima* (March, 1930), pp. 335–45.

——. "Studies at High Altitude; Blood Observations on the Indian Natives of the Peruvian Andes," *American Journal of Physiology,* C (1932), 487–505.

——. Respiratory Adaptation in the Indian Natives of the Peruvian Andes," *American Journal of Physical Anthropology,* XVII (1932–33), 137–59.

——. *Aspectos fisiologicos y patologicos de la vida en la altura.* Imprenta Rimac, 1937.

——. "Sobre un posible caso de eritremia de la altura," *Actas Acad. cienc. exac., fis. y nat. Lima,* II (1939), 71.

——. "Anoxia crónica" (Com. presentada al VIII Congreso Científico Americano). Washington, 1940.

——. "Chronic Mountain Sickness," *Journal of the American Medical Association,* CXX (1942), 12.

——. "Estimación de la incapacidad causada por la neumoconiosis," *An. Fac. Med. Lima,* XXVII (1944), 1–20.

——. "Aspectos generales de la medicina de aviación" (Conf., Instituto Sanitas, Lima, December, 1948).

——. "El Factor ambiental en química biológica" (Com. presentada al III Congreso Peruano de Química). Lima, 1949.

HURTADO, ALBERTO, and ASTE-SALAZAR, HUMBERTO. "Arterial Blood Gases and Acid-Base Balance at Sea Level and High Altitudes," *Journal of Applied Physiology,* I, No. 4 (1948), 304–25.

HURTADO, ALBERTO; ASTE-SALAZAR, HUMBERTO; MERINO, CÉSAR; VELÁSQUEZ, TULIO; MONGE CASSINELLI, CARLOS; and RÉYNAFARGE, CÉSAR. "Physiological Characteristics of Flight Personnel," *Journal of Aviation Medicine,* XVIII (1947), 406–16.

HURTADO, ALBERTO; DILL, D.; GRAYBIEL, A.; and TAQUINI, A., "Der Gasantasch in den Lungen im Alter," *Zeitschs. f. Altersf.*, II (1940), 20.

HURTADO, ALBERTO, and GUZMÁN-BARRÓN, ALBERTO. "Estudios sobre el indio peruano," *Pub. Fac. Med. Lima* (1930).

HURTADO, ALBERTO, en colaboración con GÚZMAN-BARRÓN; DILL, E.; and EDWARDS, H. "Acute Mountain Sickness: The Effect of Ammonium Chloride," *Journal of Clinical Investigation*, XVI (1937), 541.

HURTADO, ALBERTO; KALTREIDER, NOLAN; and McCANN, WILLIAM S. "Respiratory Adaptation to Anoxemia," *American Journal of Physiology*, CIX (1934), 626–37.

HURTADO, ALBERTO; MERINO, CÉSAR; and DELGADO, F. ERNESTO. "La Influencia de la anoxemia sobre la actividad hematopoyética," *Archives of Internal Medicine*, LXXV (1945), 284; also *An. Fac. Med. Lima*, XXIX (1946), 125–209.

HURTADO, ALBERTO; PONS, JULIO; and MERINO, CÉSAR. "Estudios hematológicos," *An. Fac. Med. Lima*, XIX (1936), 9–48.

HURTADO, ALBERTO, and ROTTA, ANDRÉS. "La Capacidad pulmonar en la altura," *Rev. Soc. biol. Lima*, I (1934), 7.

HURTADO, ALBERTO; ROTTA, ANDRÉS; MERINO, CÉSAR; and PONS, JULIO. "Studies of Myohemoglobin at High Altitude," *American Journal of Medical Science*, CXCIV (1937), 708–13.

LEÓN, ALFREDO. "Algunas consideraciones sobre la capacidad vital en la raza india." Tesis de Bachiller, Facultad de Medicina, Lima, 1928.

MARÍN-ZELADA, J. "La Teoría de Monge en el primer caso de la enfermedad de Vaquez en el Perú." Tesis de Bachiller, Facultad de Medicina, Lima, 1932.

MERINO, CÉSAR. "Pigment Metabolism in the Polycythemia of High Altitudes." (In press.)

MERINO, CÉSAR, and REYNAFARGE, CÉSAR. "Bone Marrow Studies in the Polycythemia of High Altitudes," *Journal of Laboratory and Clinical Medicine*, XXXIV (1949), 2.

MIRANDA, ARTEMIO, and ROTTA, ANDRÉS. "Medidas del corazón en nativos de la altura," *An. Fac. Med. Lima*, XXVII (1944), 49–58.

MONGE C., LUIS; SAN MARTÍN, MAURICIO; CASTAÑÓN, JOSÉ; and ACCAME, FERRUCCIO. "Aspecto zootécnico de la aclimatación y de la adaptación en los Andes (Com. presentada al Primer Congreso Nacional de Ing. Agrónomos, Lima, 1946).

MONGE CASSINELLI, CARLOS. "Glucosa, acido láctico y acido pirúvico a nivel del mar y en la altura," *An. Fac. Med. Lima*, XXXII (1949), 1–28.

MONGE M., CARLOS. "Influencia biológica de los altiplanos en la historia de América," *Buenos Aires, Imp. Penser.*, III (1927), 277.

——. "Sobre un caso de enfermedad de Vaquez," *Crónica médica*, XLV (1928), 3–77.

——. "La Enfermedad de los Andes" (estudios fisiológicos y clínicos), *An. Fac. Med. Lima*, XI (1928), 1–209.

——. "L'Erythrémie des altitudes," *Arch. Mal. cœur*, XXII (1929), 641–51.

——. "L'Erythrémie des altitudes," *Bull. Acad. méd.*, Paris, CI (1929), 562–64.

——. *Les Erythrémies de l'altitude; leurs rapports avec la maladie de Vaquez.* Paris: Masson et Cie, 1929.

——. "La Malattia delle Ande," *Giorn. della Reale Acad. med. Torino*, No. 92 (1929), pp. 143–47.

——. "Eritremia de las alturas o enfermedad de los Andes," *Rev. méd. peruana* (1930).

——. "Les Erythrémies de l'altitude," *Presse méd. Paris* (1930), p. 1767.

——. "La Maladie des Andes," *Rev. Sud-Amér. méd. chir., París*, I (1930), 825–31.

——. "Climatophysiologie des haux plateaux; Climatopathologie des haux plateaux." In *Traité de climatologie biologique et médicale.* Paris: Masson et Cie, 1934.

——. "El Ritmo del pulso en el hombre de los Andes," *Reforma med. Lima* (July, 1934), p. 3; also *An. Fac. Med. Lima*, XVII (1935), 1.

——. "Política sanitaria indiana y colonial en el Tahuantinsuyo" (Com. al X Congreso de Historia de la Medicina de Madrid), *An. Fac. Med. Lima*, XVII (1935), 233–76.

——. "Aclimatación en los Andes. Confirmaciones históricas sobre la 'aggressión climática' en el desenvolvimiento de las sociedades de América," *ibid.,* XIX (1936), 83.

——. "Problemas sanitarios de la vida en las grandes alturas" (Com. al II Conf. Panamer. Buenos Aires, 1935 y III Conf. Direct. Sanidad, Washington, 1936), *Ofic. San. Panamer. Publicación,* No. 121, pp. 290–95.

——. "Sobre algunas manifestaciones congestivas de orden cerebral en las eritremias de la altura," *An. Fac. Med. Lima,* XIX (1936), 83–102.

——. "High Altitude Disease," *Archives of Internal Medicine,* LIX (1937), 32–40.

——. "Perturbaciones psíquicas en la enfermedad de la altura," *Rev. neur. psiq.,* II (1939), 536.

——. "Posibles mecanismos bioquímicos adaptativos a la vida en las alturas," *Actas Acad. cienc. exac., fís. y nat. Lima,* II (1939), 11.

——. "El Sistema nervioso vegetativo del hombre de los Andes," *Jor. neuropsiq. Pan-Amer. Panamá,* II (1939), 56.

——. "Influencia biológica del altiplano en el individuo, la raza, las sociedades y la historia de América" (Discurso de orden en la ceremonia de apertura del Año Académico de la Univ. Mayor de San Marcos), *Rev. Univ.,* I (1940), 10.

——. "Life in the Andes and Chronic Mountain Sickness," *Science Press,* XCV (1942), 79.

——. "La Vida sobre los Andes y el mal de montaña crónico," *An. Fac. Med. Lima,* XXV (1942), 1–16.

——. "Fisiología de la reproducción en la altura. Applicaciones a la industria animal," *ibid.,* pp. 19–33.

——. "El Mal de montaña crónico," *ibid.,* XXVI (1943), 117–48.

——. "Chronic Mountain Sickness," *Physiological Reviews,* XXIII (1943), 166–84.

——. "El Problema de la coca en el Perú," *An. Fac. Med. Lima,* XXIX (1946), 311–15.

——. *Biología andina y de altitud* (informe a la Facultad de Medicina, presentado por el Dr. Carlos Monge, Director del Instituto de Biología y Patología Andina).* Lima, 1947.

——. *Fisiología de la respiración en la altura* (Com. al VII Congreso Panamer. de Tuberculosis, 1947). Lima, 1947.

——. *Acclimatization in the Andes: Historical Confirmations of "Climatic Aggression" in the Development of Andean Man* (Preface of Prof. Isaiah Bowman). Baltimore: Johns Hopkins Press, 1948.

——. *Physiological Adaptation of Dwellers in the Tropic* (Comm. to the IV Congress of Tropical Medicine and Malaria). Washington, 1948.

——. *Physiological Anthropology of the Dwellers in America's High Plateaus* (Comm. to the XXIXth Congress of Americanists). New York, 1949.

MONGE M., CARLOS en colaboracion con el DR. M. RAFAEL ALZAMORA. *Algunas observaciones de la E.C.G. humano consecutivos a los cambios climáticos de altitud* (Com. al III Congreso Interamer. de Cardiología). 1948.

MONGE M., CARLOS; ENCINAS, ENRIQUE; CERVELLI, MIGUEL; PESCE, HUGO; and VILLAGARCÍA, VÍCTOR. "Fisiología andina," *An. Fac. Med. Lima,* XVII (1935), 1–42.

MONGE M., CARLOS; MEJÍA, JORGE; PALTI, VÍCTOR; and SALAS, ARTURO. "Sobre algunos puntos de la bioquimica de la sangre, considera como un sistema fisicoquimico en las alturas habitadas del Perú," *An. Fac. Med. Lima,* XXI (1938), 237–62.

MONGE M., CARLOS, and MORI-CHÁVEZ, PABLO. "Fisiología de la reproducción en la altura," *An. Fac. Med. Lima,* XXV (1942), 34–39.

MONGE M., CARLOS, and PESCE, HUGO. "El Sistema nervioso vegetativo del hombre de los Andes," *An. Fac. Med. Lima,* XVII (1935), 43–59.

MONGE M., CARLOS, and SAN MARTÍN, MAURICIO. "Nota sobre azoospermia de carneros recién llegados a la altura," *An. Fac. Med. Lima,* XXV (1942), 58–61.

——. "Fisiología de la reproducción en el altiplano," *Ann. III Convención Agronómica* (1944), p. 158.

MONGE M., CARLOS, *et al.* "Adaptaciones fisiológicas de los habitantes del trópico en relación con los cambios de altitud,"

An. Fac. Med. Lima, XXXI, No. 4 (1948), 432–52.

MORI-CHÁVEZ, PABLO. "Contribución al estudio del Soroche," *An. Fac. Med. Lima,* XVIII (1935), 126.

——. "Manifestaciones pulmonares del conejo del llano transportado a la altura," *ibid.,* XIX (1936), 137–42.

NICHOLSON, CARLOS. "Historia del relieve del suelo en el Perú," *Rev. Univ. Arequipa,* X (1937), 33.

PALTI, VÍCTOR. "Calcemia y sistema nervioso vegetativo en las altiplanicies andinas," *An. Fac. Med. Lima,* XXII (1939), 75–108.

PEÑALOZA, DANTE. "El Test cardiológico de anoxemia." Tesis de Bachiller, Facultad de Medicina, Lima, 1949.

PERALTA, AURELIO. "Rol de las grandes alturas sobre la evolución de los infartos miocárdicos," *Rev. san policía* (Lima, 1945).

PÉREZ-ARANÍBAR, E. "Contribución al estudio del corazón del hombre en la altura." Tesis Doctoral, Facultad de Medicina, Lima, 1948.

RAVINOVICH, RAFAEL. "Sulfatiazol al nivel del mar y en la altura." Tesis de Bachiller, Facultad de Medicina, Lima, 1946.

REYNAFARGE, CÉSAR. "La Médula ósea en la policitemia del recién nacido," *An. Fac. Med. Lima,* XXX (1947), 217–32.

RÍOS, C. DE LOS. "Contribución al estudio de la electrocardiografía en la altura." Tesis de Bachiller, Facultad de Medicina, Lima, 1948.

RONDÓN, E. "Expedición universitaria al cráter del Misti," *Rev. Univ. Arequipa,* X (1937), 53.

ROSA-MEDINA, E. "Contribución al estudio de la eritremia de las alturas" (Enfermedad de Monge). Tesis de Bachiller, Facultad de Medicina, Lima, 1930.

ROTTA, ANDRÉS. "La Circulación en las grandes alturas," *An. Fac. Med. Lima,* XXI (1938), 285–354.

——. "Physiologic Condition of the Heart in Natives of High Altitudes," *American Heart Journal,* XXXIII (1947), 669–76.

ROTTA, ANDRÉS, and ASCENZO, J. "Registro gráfico de los ruídos cardíacos en sujetos nativos de la altura," *An. Fac. Med. Lima,* XXVII (1944), 147–60.

SÁENZ, RICARDO. "Electrocardiografía en la altura," *An. Fac. Med. Lima,* XXII (1939), 237–59.

SALAS B., ARTURO. "Proteinemia en el hombre de los Andes," *An. Fac. Med. Lima,* XXII (1939), 109–31.

SAN MARTÍN, MAURICIO. "Distribución de la glucosa sanguinea y su variación con el cambio de altitud," *An. Fac. Med. Lima,* XXIII (1940), 312–39.

——. "Problema de los dilutores de semen en la altura," *ibid.,* XXV (1942), 55–57.

SAN MARTÍN, MAURICIO, and ATKINS, JORGE. "Estudios sobre la fertilidad del ganado lanar en la altura," *An. Fac. Med. Lima,* XXV (1942), 41–52.

SAN MARTÍN, MAURICIO; ATKINS, JORGE; and CASTAÑÓN, P. JOSÉ. "Aspectos de la fisiología experimental de la reproducción en la altura," *An. Fac. Med. Lima,* XXVIII (1945), 32–64.

SUMMERS PAGES, PERCY. "La Vitamina C en la alimentación del indígena Huancayo," *An. Fac. Med. Lima,* XXIV (1941), 77–88.

TORRES, HERNÁN. "La Presión arterial en hombres a nivel del Mary y en las altiplanicies andinas," *An. Fac. Med. Lima,* XX (1937), 349–407.

URTEAGA BALLÓN, OSCAR. "Discusión sobre la patogenia de algunos tipos de icteria, con especial referencia a la icteria hemolitica y a la enfermedad de Monge," *An. Fac. Med. Lima,* XXV (1942), 89–99.

——. "Algunas observaciones en el campo de la fisiología, fisiopatología y de la anatomía patológica del hígado en relación con el problema de la icteria," *ibid.,* XXVI (1943), 149–52.

URTEAGA B., OSCAR, and BOISSET, GERARDO. "Sobre la hematología y particularmente la excreción de la bilirrubina en la enfermedad de Monge (Soroche crónico)," *An. Fac. Med. Lima,* XXV (1942), 67–88.

VALDEAVELLANO, JORGE. Comunicación al II Congreso de Oftalmología, Habana, 1947.

VELASQUEZ, Q. TULIO. "El Metabolismo basal en la altura." Tesis de Bachiller, Facultad de Medicina, Lima, 1947.

VILLA-GARCÍA, V. VÍCTOR. "La Carbocidesis en la altura y en la patología funcional del pulmón," *An. Fac. Med. Lima,* XVIII (1935), 181.

Race

By HENRI V. VALLOIS

THE IDEA of "race" originated prior to any scientific definition. The first classifiers acknowledged the existence, among the human species, of distinct groups; but they did not concern themselves with either the nature or the respective positions of such groups. The only problem which occasionally troubled them was that of the plurality of types, a plurality that seemed to contradict the biblical tradition.

Among the naturalists whose works heralded physical anthropology "properly speaking," the discernment of races remained a preconceived one in the sense that it still rested upon conspicuous differences. During a rather long period the identification of new types was not based upon real research but upon the accounts of explorers.

However, yielding now to scientific problems, now to religious scruples, naturalists were gradually induced not only to enumerate "categories" but also to define their nature. This problem was long thought over by anthropologists of the last century; it is still being discussed, and an answer has not yet been unanimously agreed upon.

On the other hand, in reference to the taxonomic status of human races, some evolution of ideas has taken place. Contrary to the opinion formerly held by some authors, anthropologists now more or less agree that all living human populations belong to one and the same species. But dissension has remained as far as the value of subdivisions is concerned, not so much regarding the racial groups or "great races," such as the White or the Black, whose distinctiveness gives rise to little controversy, but as regarding the races properly speaking. The delimitation of these narrower units, existing amid the former, has given rise to many theoretical and practical difficulties. Among the latter, one of the chief difficulties has originated from the long-favored notion of "pure races."

In the last century the idea prevailed that most present-day populations, if not all, were racially mixed. It determined among anthropologists two different attitudes, which have, nevertheless, sometimes coexisted rather contradictorily in the minds of the same authors. On the one hand, these actual populations were thought to be the result of the mixture of primitive pure races, races that anthropological analysis would succeed in separating. On the other hand, the mixture was admitted to be likely to produce new races. Schematically, it should be possible to distinguish a certain number of categories on a theoretical level: first, more or less pure races; then, different series of mixed populations. According to some authors, such mixed populations had the rank of race. For others they were nothing but "ethnic groups" or "peoples" or "tribes," whose racial ingredients the anthropologist was to identify.

Another problem: it was contended for a long time that the "environment" directly transformed living beings. Man should not escape the common law. Therefore, the old naturalists, followed by the anthropologists, often declared that the differentiation of races is due to surroundings, or, in the words of certain others, to "climate." But other anthropologists opposed direct environmental origin for the racial characteristics they considered, on the contrary, as more or less fixed. Once more, what, for some, distinguished races and explained their formation had, for others, neither discriminative nor classificatory value.

Moreover, the situation became further complicated because of the fact that the supporters of the different doctrines had no very fixed ideas about the real nature of racial differences. The old authors often ascribed somatic characters, whose hereditary foundation is now unquestioned, to the immediate influence of external causes. Lawrence attributed the flattening of the nose in black races to the way the women carried their children. Now, as he had adopted a definite position against the inheritance of acquired characteristics, platyrrhiny in his opinion could not be a racial characteristic. Inversely, Buffon seems to have regarded as racial characteristics artificial deformations of whose real origin he was definitely aware!

In short, there prevailed a confused situation, whose many contradictions are not difficult to point out in a retrospective review. On the other hand, it is not easy to restore the historical sequence of notions and ideas, unless one chooses conventionally a certain number of themes. From this point of view, to clear the ground, it is convenient to study different special problems and to retrace rapidly their evolution in time.

RACE AS A MODIFICATION
OF SPECIES DUE TO
EXTERNAL CAUSES

The concept of race as a modification of species due to environment is one of the oldest, but with time it has undergone a profound transformation. In its primitive form it implied the rapid, or even immediate, action of the external factors, so that race appeared as a contingent or transitory phenomenon.

The most simple form of this doctrine is that which postulates the modifying action of mechanical causes. Vesalius attributed the different forms of the cranium to different ways of cradling infants. This idea reappeared from time to time in the literature (Walcher, 1905; Basler, 1927; Ewing, 1950) without any distinction being generally established between possible deformations and more or less constant racial characteristics. J. L. Myres wrote still more recently (1923) that the Mongoloid facial traits are partly attributable to the fact that children were suckled by mares.

Buffon (1749) seems to have admitted the role of mechanical causes, but he attached decisive importance to nutrition and to climate. He was convinced that, in one and the same environment, after some generations, men "would look alike even if they had come from very distant and different countries and if, primitively, they had been very dissimilar."

The same concept, but limited to a determined region of the body, has been found up to the present time. One knows the ideas of Thomson and Buxton (1923) and Davies (1932) on the action of climate upon the shape of the nose. Semenov (1951) and Sergi (1950) in the same way explained the distinctive characteristics of the Mongol and Berber eyes as a defense reaction of the organism against light and the mechanical action of wind.

Originally, this mechanistic point of view reflected the embarrassment of scientists who could not see their way to explaining the existence of a number of different races. Further, it had to be admitted that this plurality of types had been realized in the short space of time, about 6,000 years, between ourselves and the date attributed to the biblical Creation. This raised formidable problems with regard to religion. More than once the tendency to treat racial characteristics as "accidents" or as theoretically transitory fluctuations followed from scruples of this nature. In the past these have been principally theological; in the present, moral.

One must acknowledge, in any case, that the modern concept of the action of external causes on the modification of human types differs profoundly from the former. The naturalists of the last century stuck, above all, to the obvious subdivisions of the human species: varieties or great races. One does not seem to find, in recent anthropological literature, a doctrine that the differences between human varieties are contingent upon and brought about by the rapid action of the environment.

On the contrary, there are, in this modern literature, well-known facts proving the rapid modification of characteristics used to define races properly speaking, that is to say, categories inferior to the great subdivisions. As a matter of fact, when one establishes the increase in stature of a Mongoloid group transplanted into a new geographical setting, compared to the stature of previous generations remaining in the original country, one does not mean that the emigrants have ceased to belong to the Mongoloid family. Shapiro, who made this remarkable discovery (1939), emphasized that, in his opinion, the change could not exceed a certain limit.

Thus restricted, the instability of racial groups is rather generally admitted in recent literature, but it has neither the same sense as it had for former naturalists nor the same sense for all modern authors. For some of these, the more or less rapid modifications explained by environmental causes appear as a phenomenon of secondary importance, although very upsetting for the classifier. Others, having emphasized the extraneous modifications, would rather keep to great subdivisions than to races in the strict sense of the word. Boas had adopted such an attitude. Sarasin thought that usual racial characteristics are of little use when one tries to establish the relationship of groups because of the very fact that these characteristics, in his opinion, are unstable.

It follows that, after having been admitted as a sufficient explanation of racial differences, the variability of the anatomical characteristics finally convinced many anthropologists of the low or nonexistent value of the usual racial descriptions as regards the discrimination of types. Anyway, other arguments followed the simple consideration of instability. Since the beginning of this century, it has more than once been emphasized that characteristics varying under the influence of environment concern the phenotype only: they do not allow the passage from the transitory to the permanent which, by definition, constitutes the very substance of race. With diverse slight alterations and some complementary arguments, this point of view figures often in modern literature.

But all anthropologists do not react in the same way to this problem. Some, as we have said, would rather keep to great subdivisions, such as Blacks and

Whites, which seem to escape controversies. Others try to separate "good" racial characteristics from "bad" ones. Hooton, for some time, wanted to avoid adaptive characteristics (1926). Afterward, he renounced this distinction, which, no doubt, raises other difficult problems. Without introducing such considerations, many anthropologists keep to empirical data; they think, for example, that stature is a bad characteristic, since various observations show that it changes to a considerable extent at very short intervals. Finally, some investigators have shown themselves more exacting and have advocated the exclusive use of characteristics whose genetic foundation is known.

These discussions show that physical anthropology faces an important problem, the co-ordinated and methodical study of which has scarcely been outlined: the problem of the more or less rapid modifications that mankind undergoes at the present time. In this regard the best-known fact is the increase of stature, a phenomenon whose significance is not absolutely clear. Shapiro has collected data (1939) showing that, at least in one particular instance, the real increase of final stature is to all appearances the case. On the other hand, the data of army anthropometry, which attest the universality of this phenomenon, are more delicate to handle. Morant has recently published (1949) a very thorough study wherein he shows that in the English population only the rhythm of growth has changed, the final stature not having undergone an appreciable change. Kil, a short time before (1939), came to a similar conclusion touching the Norwegian population. If this conclusion could be generalized, one should conclude that stature is not such a "bad" characteristic as one thought. Likewise, many statistics have stressed the existence of a gradual increase of the ce-

phalic index in Europe for the last nine or ten centuries, an increase which is now followed in some groups by a diminution (Pittard, 1935; Schlaginhaufen, 1946). One has thus been able to speak (Czekanowski, 1935) of a periodic oscillation of the index. Very recently, Büchi (1950) has shown the existence of "secular" variations in numerous measurements of head and body. But some of these phenomena admit of other explanations, and the controversies they raise are not yet all settled. In any case, all these examples show the uncertainties still besetting the rapid changes of racial characteristics and the pressing necessity of entering upon their exhaustive study.

INSTABILITY OF CHARACTERISTICS DUE TO CROSS-BREEDING; MIXED RACES, INTERMEDIATE TYPES, UNCLASSIFIABLE GROUPS

Among naturalists and anthropologists of the beginning of the last century, human hybridization sometimes appears as a factor of racial differentiation. Nevertheless, this idea has not been indorsed by every author. Broca was one of the first to stress the heterogeneous nature of European populations. Topinard wrote: "We are all half-breeds." For these authors, however, as for many others, mixed populations are not races but complex groups. The anthropologist must submit these to an arduous analysis in order to distinguish their racial components.

During the first decades of this century, a similar concept endeavored to find support in genetics, but this science was very inadequate at the time. Some authors believed that at least some racial characteristics are transmitted in conformity with a very simple Mendelian law and that, in a hybrid population, their segregation should be easy to prove—hence the idea of searching in an ethnic mixture for the elements which have had a share in its formation (Czekanowski, 1928; Davenport, 1929; and others).

Another tendency postulated the appearance, after cross-breeding, of types as characteristic as "pure" races. Meanwhile, the possibility of tracing back their stocks was not excluded: especially in old literature one finds many indications regarding mixed types, the result of a certain race having been crossed with another. But these types are considered stable, more or less homogeneous, and entitled to a taxonomic rank.

Quatrefages was one of the first anthropologists to admit explicitly that cross-breeding begets new races. The exact origin of this notion would be difficult to trace back, and, nearer to our own time, it has found considerable approval. As an example, besides "protomorphic races," which recall primitive mankind, and "archimorphic races," which separated in the process of evolution, Stratz (1903), going back to an already old expression used by Fritsch (1891), distinguished "metamorphic races," born of the mixture of the former. Czekanowski had admitted the existence of hybrid races due to the mixture of primary races; Haddon (1924) expressed the same point of view, his "secondary races" being but the product of two or many primary races, this product then becoming stabilized through geographic isolation.

Contrary to what took place as the century began, the same idea became largely credited in the new anthropological literature inspired by Mendelism. Thus the Negro-American population, notoriously mixed, appears to several recent American authors as a new race, or at least as a race in the making (particularly Coon, Garn, and Birdsell, 1950). Generally speaking, the idea that cross-breeding could produce fixed types, liable to the taxonomic rank of race, is very often admitted nowadays.

Thus the question seems settled on the theoretical plane, but, when it comes to determining the "nature" of some concrete populations, one sees the difficulties reappear. Disagreement may happen regarding those "races" which everyone considers "intermediate." Traditionally, these were classified as "mixed" groups (Biasutti and Giuffrida-Ruggeri's "metamorphic" groups). But in particular cases another point of view has been put forward. The notion of "synthetic types," familiar to paleontologists, has been used to find a place for "intermediate" populations, whose hybrid origin is not obvious. Boule and Vallois (1932) have considered some Ethiopian populations as an undifferentiated form rather than a simple mixture of Whites and Blacks. Fleure (1937) thinks that in the British population there can be found a type prior to the differentiation of tall blond dolichocephals and small brown dolichocephals. Haddon had admitted, on his side, that intermediate types could be undifferentiated types. The elements liable to interpretation vary from one case to another, and, for the time being, genetics affords no help in choosing between these points of view.

After having spoken of races born of cross-breeding and intermediate types, one must recall that most anthropologists, if not all, admit the existence of still other groups which are difficult or impossible to classify. The opinion has sometimes been held that it is wrong to try to fix each group in a precise place in a rigid system of classification. If one reviews the literature, one finds that certain authors have had this ambition but that their attitude has not been shared by most others. Even in the very old classifications, some groups are omitted, not through ignorance, but through caution. Cuvier, for instance, left out of his tripartite plan in an indeterminate position the Amerindians and some other branches of mankind. Perhaps he was only obeying religious scruples. But this factor surely did not intervene with other naturalists and anthropologists. This aspect of the question will be more clearly exposed in the part dealing with classifications. For the time being, it is enough to say that the idea has now largely spread that one cannot strictly classify every human group. In this respect the principal difference is probably the following: for some, there is no chance of reaching a more exhaustive classification; for others, one must distinguish between well-studied populations and those which are, as yet, little known. In this last case the obstacle would be of an accidental nature, even if truly impossible to remove. In any case the idea that every population is practically classifiable in a complete and coherent system is not generally admitted nowadays.

RACE AS A COMBINATION OF CHARACTERISTICS IN INDIVIDUALS

We may now, by successive stages, define more closely the very notion of race. The latter may be understood, first of all, as a combination of characteristics discernible in individuals. Even when not explicitly formulated, this concept seems to have presented itself to the minds of the first naturalists. It held for many anthropologists and was expressed by some, in that in the course of their researches they classified individuals on the basis of random characters rather than working on groups (for example, Von Eickstedt, 1936; Schlaginhaufen, 1946).

The same concept seems to have influenced various definitions of race. Quatrefages (1859): "the totality of similar individuals"; Saller (1931): "a combination of hereditary characteristics of a certain variability ... through which members of one race distinguish themselves from another race"; Martin (1928): "individuals belonging to one race have a certain number of characteristics in common, the combination of which distinguishes them from other groups."

The same idea figures in the first definition of "race" given in 1936 by the Royal Anthropological Institute: the hereditary characteristics which distinguish a race "are held to be such as usually apply to the generality of the individuals studied and not to be pathological characters." But the second definition, following the first, reflects another point of view and considers race as "a biological group or stock possessing in common an undetermined number of associated genetical characteristics by which it can be distinguished from other groups."

This question is linked up with that of the anthropometric "average" man, whose abstract nature seems to have been generally acknowledged. Anyhow, the idea that race is a combination of characteristics repeating itself in each individual case has not been separated from the concept of race as a group, defined by characteristics which do not necessarily combine in the same way in each individual. The difference appears if one compares, for instance, the above-quoted definitions with Broca's or Topinard's, which positively stated that types have no "real existence," or Haddon's point of view, declaring that racial types "exist only in our minds."

RACE AS AN ABSTRACT NOTION

This brings us to a very different idea which has spread more and more, whether linked or not with complementary notions, since the middle of the last century. Broca wrote that "in the experimental sciences, the concept of groups precedes the exact knowledge of every component element." Thus he thought that the physical anthropologist must not try to acknowledge directly every component of one population. The identification of the community is a difficult task, implying long study.

This work must be done in successive stages, and, before acknowledging races, the scientist must describe ethnic types. Topinard (1892) took up this distinction and developed it. The type of a population expresses its more frequent and pronounced characteristics; it is, above all, a "statistical" notion. The type of a race is defined in the same way, with the reservation above, however, that hereditary characteristics are here involved—characteristics which are not attributable to the continuous influence of environment. The determination of races present in a population is a "very laborious operation," for race is not "immediately apparent."

Broca had said that human types "are abstract, ideal concepts." Topinard specifies that race "exists only in a diffused state," for the anthropologist finds himself everywhere in the presence of peoples, not of races. The latter are not "obvious," for the typical individual is rare. "Only chance can give the average cranium or the typical cranium." Broca, after having defined types as abstractions, warned his readers against the tendency of personifying the latter. Topinard illustrates the same thesis with concrete examples but, at the same time, is bent on showing that type, although of an abstract conceptual nature, is a sort of statistical reality.

This way of looking at things had an indisputable effect on later anthropological literature. One finds traces of it in Collignon (1892) and Chantre (1887) and, later, in Deniker (1900), who expressed himself as follows: populations are formed

by the union of individuals belonging usually to two, three, or a greater number of somatological units. These units are theoretical types formed of an aggregation of physical characters combined in a certain way. The separate existence of these units may be established by a minute analysis of the physical characters taken haphazardly in any given ethnic group. Here then are entities, theoretical conceptions exactly like species in zoology; only instead of having within our reach the types of these species as in zoological collections, we are obliged to rest content with approximations thereto, for it is a very rare occurrence to meet with an individual representing the type of the somatological unit to which he belongs.

Among Anglo-American authors who professed similar ideas, one may mention Beddoe (1892–93) and especially Ripley (1899), who expressed himself as follows: "It is not essential to our position, that we should actually be able to isolate any considerable number, nor even a single one, of our perfect racial types in the life." Then he mentions and stresses the following quotation from Topinard:

Race in the present state of things is an abstract conception, a notion of continuity in discontinuity, of unity in diversity. It is the rehabilitation of a real but directly unattainable thing. . . . At the present time rarely, if indeed ever, we discover a single individual corresponding to our racial type in every detail. It exists for us nevertheless.

The idea of "race," an abstract notion, reappears with certain modifications in the works of most Russian physical anthropologists, for example, Vorobieff, as well as in that of Mendes Corrêa (1927), Hooton (1926), and many others. One may say, without risk of committing a grave error, that it is almost a common notion at the present time. Nevertheless, it has not completely supplanted the idea that race manifests itself in the combination of traits in the individual. Sometimes both attitudes coexist in one and the same author. The classifying of individuals by racial categories still exists: Czekanowski even stressed the determination of the systematic status of individuals; he thinks that the consideration of Mendelian laws may make this task easier (1920, 1928).

Developed in the course of the last century, the idea of race as an "abstract notion" precedes, historically speaking, the ideas of the biometrical anthropologists. Apart from a few exceptions, the ideas of the latter were anticipated only from afar. What stands out is the idea that race, at least in the first approximation, is concerned not with individuals but with groups or populations.

BIOMETRICAL ANTHROPOLOGY; THE "STATISTICAL RACE"

Among the physical anthropologists who considered race as an abstract notion, Topinard was probably alone in stressing the fact that racial types are essentially defined by a set of characteristics, such as maximum frequencies, modes, and means. The use of these parameasures became known in anthropology during the last century, but without giving rise to a methodological or doctrinal pronouncement (except for Topinard and, before him, for the Irishman, Grattan, whose article, published in 1858, passed unnoticed).

The essential difference between this tendency and that of the biometrical school consists in the fact that the latter, following Galton's works and Pearson's, use more refined statistical tools and more complex notions than those of mode, means, and dispersion. It consists also in the fact that biometricians were concerned with what Broca or Deniker would have considered types or ethnic groups rather than races. In their studies on European samples, they did not look for racial components, perhaps because, following Pearson, they admitted that the elements amalgamated in these mixtures were nearly impossible to detect. Pearson, indeed, recalled the fact that "we talk as if it was our population which was mixed, and not our germplasm" (1920).

However, the work of the biometrical school—or of the biometrical method—also dealt with widely separated populations or populations belonging to distinct ethnical agglomerations for instance, various tribes of a region; in this case they contributed to the establishment of distinction, sometimes identities, without the admittedly different groups being necessarily racially defined. In opposition to anthropologists who tried to isolate the racial components of populations, biometricians preferred to compare groups which, prior to research, had already been separated according to geographic, ethnographic, or social criteria.

On this level, several attempts have been made to make statistics an instrument of human taxonomy. Pearson (1926) had established the coefficient of racial likeness. Morant and others used it in the comparative study of crania or populations. But the use of this coefficient has not become generalized, and it has been violently criticized on purely mathematical grounds (Fisher, 1936). Czekanowski and his school have also used a statistical process which sometimes causes them to be placed among the representatives of biometry. This method is indeed independent, it does not seem to be comparable to that of Pearson's school, and it has also been criticized for mathematical reasons (Stolyhwo, 1926; Schwidetzki, 1936).

At the present time, two other much more complicated procedures seem highly favored as statistico-taxonomic methods: the discriminant function proposed by Fisher (1940) and the "generalized distance statistic," due to the works of Mahalanobis, Majumdar, and Rao (1941). Stevens (1945) has highly recommended the use of the former in anthropology, but practically speaking, it has hardly begun to spread. As to the "generalized distance," it was used first by the authors of the method, then more recently by Trevor (1947) in his study of certain African populations.

Perfected by distinguished mathematicians, these methods have not been criticized as regards their intrinsic value. But they are too difficult to become widely used. Competent judges have sometimes expressed the opinion that one must have serious reasons to undertake the long and intricate calculations they require. In so far as these two methods are used, they permit one to locate, one with regard to another, several populations simultaneously defined by several characteristics. Besides this, they also enable one to attribute, to one group rather than to another, individuals isolated according to the considered characteristics. The practical difficulties grow with the number of populations and characteristics.

GEOGRAPHICAL OR TERRITORIAL ASPECT OF RACE

We have just seen that the notion of race varies considerably according to epochs, schools, and authors. It is thus interesting to establish that, in the conclusions regarding the identity and number of races, there is often much less disagreement than one could have foretold from the doctrinal or methodological premises. It is probable that some divergences are smoothed out because many physical anthropologists, whether they choose to do so or not, make use of the geographical factor.

On the one hand, it is often admitted that race is "independent" of territory, that its area of dispersion may be discontinuous, and that several races border on the same region. On the other hand, an idea common to authors with different viewpoints consists in the race not being defined by the combination of characteristics one may find in individuals taken one by one, but by a combination of characteristics to be found in a determined geographical setting.

This last idea is implicit in the doctrines of those who, like Agassiz (1853), made the zones occupied by human races correspond to the great subdivisions of animal geography. Although inclosed in a very different context, the same notion is implied in the doctrines which make of race an abstract concept, and sometimes, too, in those of biometricians. Though admitting that a population—at least a European population—is a mixture of races, Broca established maps showing the territorial variations of somatic characteristics and used them to delimit the distribution of racial types. This process has been largely used in anthropology, especially by Ripley, Deniker, Lundborg, and many others. Ehrenreich (1897), Schlaginhaufen (1914), Tchepourkovski (1917), and more recently Bounak (1938) have particularly stressed the importance of the geographical criterion in anthropology. It is probable that the taking into consideration of this principle explains the agreement between classifications which do not make use of exactly the same criteria.

THE CRITERIA OF RACIAL DISTINCTION

Although the choice of different criteria does not in practice involve serious disagreements, it nonetheless creates a serious problem. We have seen, regarding the instability of some somatic descriptions, that anthropologists have sometimes been led to sort out and to choose the "good" racial characteristics, that is to say, those which do not seem to change readily or those which seem, through their nature, to escape natural selection. But the question presents still another aspect.

A type is defined only by a combination of characteristics. Topinard recalled that, if one takes into account only one trait, the type vanishes. How many characteristics must one retain? It is clear that this question has not found a unanimous answer. One can only say that, on the whole, two neighboring tendencies are visible: one prefers to restrict the number of items used in classification, though without limiting the number of studied characteristics. One of the arguments that can be put forward in favor of this restriction is well known: as soon as one multiplies the number of characteristics, that of the classifiable individuals drops sharply. The other tendency, which does not bother with the classification of individuals or at least stresses the study of populations, tends to take a greater number of characteristics into consideration. This second tendency seems to take stock of different considerations: a greater number of racial characteristics will lead to a more complete, more precise, and more "natural" classification. On the contrary, a limited set of traits would risk leaving to one side significant and, from this point of view, important statistical differences.

One cannot say that, during the last decades, the second tendency has taken precedence over the first one. Rather, the two have been combined, and alongside classifications taking into account a limited number of characteristics, more or less sanctioned by custom, one may now find some which also, for instance, take into account the general body configuration. Hooton's (1931–47) represents one of the most conclusive cases.

Thus, by taking into account the general structure of the body, one meanwhile takes the risk of running up against an obstacle. The racial problem is here, in fact, added to that of constitutional types. This superimposition has given rise to the most disparate solutions. For some, constitutions, reduced to morphology only, exist in every race. For others, in two racially distinct populations, one finds different, though perhaps analogous, constitutional types. Yet others envisage constitutional types as mixed with races, notably in European populations, where one has tried to identify leptosomes and Nordics, athletics and Dinarics, pycnics and Alpines.

This last idea seems to have been abandoned. Biometrical research has shown that, in groups definitely distinct from the racial point of view, the same "bipolar deformation" of the mean population type is noticeable, though with some differences, which have been attributed to race (De Sousa, 1934; Schreider, 1951). This suggested the idea that differences in constitutional variations could offer a new criterion of racial distinction (Bean, 1926). But this suggestion has prompted little research.

Another point of view has been put forth regarding the connections between constitution and race. Bounak (1927) has advanced the hypothesis that constitutional types might represent outlines of new races. Weidenreich (1927) professed a similar opinion, when he considered the territorial predominance of some morphological types as otherwise unexplainable. A more moderate hypothesis considers some constitutional characteristics as liable to appear in the formation of races, in so far as these characteristics stand on a genetic basis. But to what extent do they possess such a basis? For lack of direct proofs, constitutionalists so far must be content with favorable presumptive evidence. But these presumptions are few, fewer still than those related to all the racial characteristics whose exact genetic nature is not yet known.

We now come to another aspect of the problem raised by the characteristics used in racial classifications. The idea that race is hereditary is generally admitted. It was certainly familiar to the first naturalists, although they admitted at the same time the rapidly modifying influence of environment and considered racial differences as more or less contingent. All the more reason that this idea of heredity should dominate the recent conceptions of race.

Hrdlička (1941) defined race as "a persistent strain, within any species, or broadly blood-connected individuals carrying steadily, i.e., hereditarily, more or less of well defined physical characteristics which distinguish them fairly from all other strains or races."

Hooton (1931) brings into his definition the idea of "common origin." Boas (1938) uses the same expression and specifies, besides, that race is a "stable type." It would be easy to quote other examples, showing that for anthropologists there is no race without heredity. However, since the earliest stage of its history, physical anthropology has come up, not only against the difficult problem of cross-breedings, but also against that of the modifications due to the continued influence of environment. And one must be careful to emphasize that, in this respect, there was no absolute divergence between partisans and opponents of the theory of acquired characteristics. The first were alone in contending that modifications due to the environment are recorded in the hereditary stock. But both easily acknowledged that certain changes due to external causes are not transmitted to the lineage. The difficulty consisted, therefore, in defining the boundaries of heredity.

Has the situation changed since? Physical anthropology has relied on genetics almost since its origin, and much more so than many branches of zoölogy. Unfortunately, however, genetics has drawn little of its data from man, and, as a result, the anthropologist has been handicapped in making practical use of its findings. Even now, in spite of certain sensational claims, its helpful nature lies almost solely in the study of blood groups. One has thus witnessed the appearance of various conceptions of "serological races" or "physiological races" which have developed progressively from the initial identification of one blood group with a race toward a more elaborated systematics of gene frequencies. These ideas may have satisfied certain anthropologists, but one may say without particular risk that the majority does not seem inclined to accept them as final. One does not feel that they have the right to neglect, for the benefit of serological characteristics alone, the whole body of traits which distinguish the human organism.

It seems that the present situation may be summed up as follows. According to one tendency, it is necessary to base the distinction of human varieties on characteristics whose genetic nature is securely known: therefore, in practice and until we know more, essentially on blood groups. According to the other tendency, physical anthropology must pursue the study of the phenotype. But this second point of view has itself evolved, since several recent anthropologists consider the phenotype as being principally the product of environment: thus implicitly and in spite of genetic premises, their conception of race does not differ practically from that of former naturalists. Buffon and many authors of the last century, whether followers of Lamarck or not, would have indorsed a doctrine explaining a certain number of racial differences environmentally, for instance, through diet (Coon, Garn, and Birdsell, 1950).

It is probable that, being more demanding than their predecessors, the modern neo-Lamarckists would undoubtedly in such a case ask for experimental proofs. In any case, most modern anthropologists interpret the phenotype in a very different manner: though acknowledging its elasticity, they suppose that it reflects, above all, its genotypic background. This justifies the idea of heredity which they maintain in their definitions of race.

For the first tendency, the research upon "good" and "bad" phenotypical characteristics should not be of too great interest. With the second tendency, it keeps all its importance, if by "good" characteristics one understands those which appear as relatively stable. The first tendency may be concerned with the phenotype "as a whole"; the second, hoping that the geneticists will not acknowledge themselves beaten, sometimes tries to establish more or less temporary distinctions and to discern characteristics whose hereditary nature has some chances of being confirmed, even if one cannot make them enter into a precise Mendelian scheme.

THE PROBLEM OF MENTAL CHARACTERISTICS

Yet another aspect worthy of separate consideration is that of the mental characteristics of human races. This question has often been examined in the light of ideas foreign to science. During the last century, some authors kept themselves to physical characteristics only because they felt some repugnance in referring to the "soul" in a matter wherein zoölogy was principally concerned. Very recently, on the contrary, doctrines of political inspiration have proclaimed the intimate liaison between mental characteristics and the variations considered as racial.

If modern anthropologists often take into account physical characteristics only, it is for very different reasons. Some are convinced that mental differences are trivial, except those attributable to the type of culture or to the level of education. Others think that, for lack of precise knowledge, the problem is still too abstruse and the mental characteristics of races too difficult to determine for one to take them into account. Thus, practically, most modern anthropologists consider only the physical differences.

A different attitude is present, however, in a certain number of modern works. Here are some examples. Boas (1931) defined race as "a group of people that have certain bodily and perhaps also mental characteristics in common." Consequently, he adopted a circumspect attitude. Fischer (1933) is more categorical: "Race is a group of men characterized by the common hereditary possession of a physical and mental type distinguishing it from other groups." Czekanowski (1936) attributes to every race a certain number of mental traits: the Nordic race would be full of initiative, disciplined, with a high sense of duty; the Lapponoid race would be intelligent but undisciplined; and so on. Such repertories of mental qualities rarely figure today in the classifications. Czekanowski, besides, endeavored, above all, to acknowledge race according to somatic characteristics. The few anthropologists who take mental characteristics into account seem to add them only when their list of races is established.

One must finally report that the question of mental or cultural characteristics sometimes appears in physical anthropology in a slightly different form and without having repercussions, at least for the time being, on classifications. The notion of "Isolate" seems to act in this way. If the isolation may indeed be geographical, it may also be cultural or social—hence a possible coincidence between physical and mental characteristics. The question is thus raised as to whether it is really a coincidence or a genetically based correlation. Ashley Montagu (1945), for instance, defines race (which he names "ethnic group") as "one of a number of populations comprising the simple species *Homo sapiens* which individually maintain their differences, physical and cultural, by means of isolating mechanisms, such as geographical and social barriers." For certain authors, physical differences determined by cultural isolation, should the occasion arise, may by inverse action lead to hereditary mental differences. Darlington and Mather (1950) go as far as to postulate an accentuation of these differences; they point out "the increasing contrast of genetic capacity for culture between different genetic groups."

The motivation is new, but certain implications of the idea of both biological and social isolation recall a doctrine which formerly met with some success: that connected, among others, with Vacher de Lapouge, which makes races and social classes (1909) "coincide." This doctrine was given up by anthropologists, and we owe its new growth principally to a few geneticists. The problem of cultural differences has been practically left out of the field of anthropology for a long time; in this way, it has some chances of being reinstated. But it is hardly probable that mental and cultural characteristics will ever be used in classifications.

GENERAL RULES OF CLASSIFICATION

After having thus cleared the way, let us investigate the nature of anthropological classifications. Theoretically, a classification may be founded on two distinct criteria: that of likeness (John

Ray was probably the first to follow this principle) and that of kinship (Tournefort). The first classifications of human races, essentially intuitive, were based simultaneously on the idea of likeness and common ancestry, even if these principles were not explicitly formulated. It was only at a later stage, after physical anthropology was born, that the problem was realized to be complex.

Blumenbach was perfectly aware of the relative value of classifications, and he acknowledged that his was arbitrary: the distinction of races, such as he proposed it, was, above all, to be a help to scientists. The idea that the number of races could be nearly unlimited had become familiar to anthropologists from the beginning of the nineteenth century. Hence classification was, above all, for them a means of putting in order a sum of chaotic facts: the number of subdivisions included was largely a question of opportunity or convenience. Naturalists had already proclaimed that classifications had been devised "for the convenience of scientists."

The oldest classifications were the least artificial in reflecting mainly obvious differences, related to the principal varieties or "great races" of recent authors. But the inadequacy of such a scheme whose subdivisions were too large was soon recognized. However, people were not long in acknowledging that a more precise classification was very difficult to accomplish. Moreover, for a long time there was no reliable information regarding many populations. Being doubtful, certain authors preferred to keep to large categories. Others, on the contrary, multiplied races. Because of this, they were more than once reproached for having introduced linguistic or ethnographic groups into classifications which should have taken only somatic characteristics into account.

Toward the end of the last century, however, a considerable effort was made to eliminate in anthropological classification all that was not morphological. Deniker (1889) even tried to establish a "natural" classification, comparable to that of botanists. He systematized several combinations of somatic characteristics and thus defined a large number of races. Others have followed similar methods, but with a more or less different choice of characteristics, so that two classifications inspired by the same "natural" method are not necessarily superimposable. Nor are they necessarily conflicting. A certain number of differences is due only to the number of subdivisions, which vary from one author to another. When the larger categories of one classification agree with categories which another considers as secondary divisions, one may admit that there is no real contradiction. Nor is the disagreement very serious if a group whose existence is acknowledged by two different classifiers is not attached by them to the same category of superior rank (as, for example, the case of Bushmen, Polynesians, etc.). The following case is strange and may seem surprising: one and the same race has been annexed to the blond group by one author, to the brown group by another. Properly speaking, the population which allowed us to acknowledge this "race" numbers, above all, "brunette"-haired individuals.

One must therefore distinguish two distinct aspects in anthropological classifications: that of the identification of types and that of their hierarchical ranking. Regarding the identification, the following factors promote agreement, even if the classifications do not exactly depend on the same criteria: (*a*) The existence of a certain number of categories separated by manifest differences, upon which everyone agrees; on close inspection it is not only the great races one quotes generally in this connection—Yellows, Blacks, Whites, Australoids—but also some other groups, such as the Pygmy races, the Bushman race, the Ainu race. (*b*) The existence, among the great races, of a certain number of types showing a distinctive peculiarity sharp enough to be easily separated within the limits of the White Europeans. Such, for instance, is the case of the fair, blue-eyed element, which is not necessarily dolichocephalic, and even of the brown elements, which are generally distributed among several races; but, as regards the latter, disagreement is greater among the classifiers, sharper distinctions being difficult. In the same way, among the Black great race, the distinction of types, such as the Nilotic race, does not seem to give rise to a discussion. (*c*) A third and last factor is that, as has already been mentioned, all the authors take into account the geographical distribution of the various human groups, even if they do not accept it as a classifying criterion. Bounak (1938) has emphasized that the territorial distribution of the characteristics and of their combinations was neither fortuitous nor completely confused. There is here an element of unification.

One must not conclude from the foregoing, however, that racial classifications are "accidental" and that the basis of all the recent classifications is one and the same. Certain coincidences seem purely fortuitous. Dixon, for instance (1923), based his classification upon three arbitrarily chosen characteristics, more precisely upon three indices, and upon their numerical value. He thus determined a fair number of possible combinations, and it happens that, among the latter, some agree with races known from another source. In this case agreement seems to be due to pure chance. On the contrary, the agreement between Ripley's and Deniker's classifications, as regards the European races, reflects a definite situation, both somatic and geographic. Their differences seem essentially due to the fact that Ripley was satisfied with three principal races, whereas Deniker tried to establish more subtle distinctions.

Finally, one must consider another fact: time affects classifications, and the latest sometimes complement the oldest, without really taking their place. Thus, for Amerindians, Imbelloni's (1938) classification probably may be taken as a development of Eickstedt's (1934).

Although it is fairly easy to acknowledge the agreement between the various classifications regarding the identity or existence of some races, it is with regard to their ranking or reciprocal position that one more easily notices divergences. Must one attribute the Asiatic Negroes to the Black group? Is it correct to unite in one and the same race the various Pygmy types scattered over the world? Are we even right in considering as belonging to the same race human agglomerations which show the same combination of features, though they are separated geographically?

This last question raises the problem in its more general form, and the answer is generally in the affirmative: Two populations showing one combination of characteristics are commonly classified under one racial heading; this is the fundamental principle of racial maps. But this answer again involves the definition or concept of "race," for it is a long time since similarity has been declared not to be proof, but only presumptive evidence, of kinship.

As far back as 1857, Aitken Meigs, after having stressed the gradations linking cranial forms, had expressed the opinion that differences between these did not always imply a diversity of origin and that, inversely, great similarity did not warrant an especially close kinship. The anthropologists of the nineteenth century either invoked the possibility of convergence or recalled that different racial cross-breedings could produce similar types. At the present time, geneticists take over the same concept and recall that one and the same phenotype may suit different genotypes. Here, then, one values the distinction between the classification according to likeness (John Ray) and the classification according to kinship (Tournefort). For some people the fact of race, such as we know it, is nothing but the establishment of a similarity. For others, one must distinguish the particular situations; where similar but geographically separated populations are concerned, one has no right to conclude in favor of their close kinship unless one possesses arguments other than their similarity—archeological, ethnographic, or even historical or linguistic proofs.

In spite of all these reservations, the notion of kinship still remains dominant in the minds of classifiers. Waitz, in one of the best anthropological summaries of the question (1858), declared that, in nearly every classification of mankind, the idea of a common descent of the elements grouped in one and the same race was at least tacitly admitted. The situation does not seem to have changed much since, and the best proof is furnished by the fact that the authors of classifications often publish them with the addition of genealogical trees.

TAXONOMIC POSITION OF RACES

If one admits (Cuénot, 1936, for instance) that the species may be defined by three pairs of criteria: morphology and physiology (M), ecology and distribution (E), internal fecundity and external sterility (S), it appears that the immense majority of men constitutes a group to which the MES triad fully applies. Therefore, they correspond to one and the same species, *Homo sapiens;* and, from the point of view of a general classification, this is a "collective species" (polytypic species, Linnean species).

Being subdivisions of *Homo sapiens,* races are categories inferior to the species. They are, on the other hand, superior to the "elementary species" (biotypes, jordanons) of the geneticists. Obviously, in no human race are the hereditary potentialities homogeneous for all individuals.

Races thus occupy an intermediary place between the collective species and the elementary species. But on such a scale, zoölogists and botanists commonly distinguish two kinds of subdivisions (for certain authors, such as Mayr, 1942, this separation is, for the greater part, artificial): those defined by a precise geographical localization, the *geotypes,* and those defined by life in a given ecological environment, the *ecotypes.* From this point of view, it appears that human races are, above all, geographical units, geotypes. In Europe an extraordinary racial mixture had for centuries created an intermingling which is the despair of physical anthropologists. Even there, one still succeeds, more or less, in placing each race in a limited geographical area. With primitive races (Bushman, African Pygmies, etc.) the localization becomes much more precise, and we have seen that, for some authors, it even becomes the basis of the concept of race. The attribution of a human race to a precise ecological environment is, on the contrary, much more difficult to prove, and most arguments put forward fail in the light of critical investigation. Through selection, certain characteristics undoubtedly have a tendency to be better preserved in certain environments, but one may not say that these environments have really created racial types with all their characteristics. Perhaps the case of various Pyg-

mies is an exception, although one may not positively state that forest is not for them a zone of secondary refuge.

The subdivisions of species do not all have the same value. In the collective species, zoölogists and botanists generally distinguish two degrees: categories of first rank or *subspecies:* they generally have the value of geographic units, of geotypes; and categories of second rank or *varieties,* which also may be geotypes but are often ecotypes, above all, among plants.

For human races, there is also a hierarchy, and people generally agree in recognizing two categories: the *primary races* or *great races* or *racial groups (Rassenkreise)* and the *secondary races* or *second-rank races* (races *sensu stricto* of various authors).

Great races correspond to the fundamental divisions of mankind in our time. Their geographical localization is very marked. They have the value of real subspecies. One may therefore apply to them the trinominal classification: *H. sapiens albus, H. sapiens niger,* and so on.

Various authors (for instance, G. Sergi, 1911; R. Gates, 1948) have likened these categories to species. It is certain that the morphological and probably physiological differences between them may be large. But if one takes into account their unquestionable interfecundity, expressed not only by the production of fruitful hybrids but by that of entire transitional groups, such a notion cannot be defended. The community of structure of all living men, the existence in all of an identical physical background, in spite of a probable diversity in the mental and affective reactions, further add to the former argument. The subspecies of *H. sapiens* are undoubtedly—like every subspecies —new species in the making. They could have reached the superior category, had the isolation which accompanied their birth persisted. Actually, they cannot be considered as having reached this stage. One may even presume, under existing conditions, that they are going to follow an inverse path.

Secondary races are comparable to the "varieties" of botanists and zoölogists, but with this difference, that, as primary races, they are geographical units. They have also been considered by various authors as species, and Giuffrida-Ruggeri (1913) has even pronounced the name of "elementary species." It is only too obvious that such a term cannot be applied to them.

Among the races *sensu stricto,* the existence of third-ranking categories, the *local types,* sometimes also called *subraces* (*Gautypen*), may often be revealed by detailed analysis. The hypothesis has been put forward that these types of third rank would be ecotypes. They are modifications of racial types in a set environment—seaside regions, mountainous regions, desert regions—modifications which one may equate with those of mammals living in the same environment. One should then distinguish among second-ranking races geographical subgroups which one could call "subraces," and ecological subgroups, which could be the real local types. But the exact nature of these local types has not been thoroughly studied. One does not know, in particular, to what extent their characteristics are hereditary.

MISCELLANEOUS

Before finishing this rapid review, one must point out some facts which have not appeared in the previous paragraphs. When anthropology stresses that race is distinguished essentially by physical characteristics, it is sometimes meant that not only anatomy (morphology included) but also physiology is thereby concerned. Actually, physiological anthropology is far behind anatomy, and this not only because of technical difficulties but because functional characteristics are often very unstable, so that differences, if existing, may be established only with great difficulty. No classification as yet takes into account the physiological characteristics; anyhow, such an attempt would be impossible before a sufficient number of comparable data has been collected. (These remarks do not apply to blood groups.)

This does not prevent knowledge of certain differences which are not being used in a general classification. Other important facts have been pointed out regarding pathology: the differences in susceptibility of Blacks and Whites toward certain illnesses is currently admitted. In several cases the hereditary (racial) nature of these differences has been questioned or doubted; but in other cases, regarding, for instance, skin diseases, it does not seem to raise serious objections. Other cases could be quoted, bearing on racially distinct populations: for instance, the very uneven susceptibility to influenza of certain Pacific Islanders compared to that of Chinese workers who have immigrated to their islands (Ednet, Donnelley, Isaacs, and Ingram, 1950).

The racial variations of morbidity have been pointed out for more than a century. Their real scientific study has recently begun. This study, together with its practical importance, must be pointed out without our being able to strike a balance at the present time.

In conclusion, it is advisable to mention that research on subjects of the three main racial groups (Whites, Yellows, and Blacks) agrees on the existence, in each, of twenty-four pairs of chromosomes. The divergences between authors concern the interpretation of male sexual chromosomes, some agreeing on the XO formula, others on the XY, but the partisans of both interpretations use subjects of the same race. Chromosomic racial differences, therefore, do not seem to exist, and there is no reason to speak about cytological races in man.

BRIEF BIBLIOGRAPHY

Count, E. W. 1950. *This Is Race.* New York: Schuman. Contains extracts of the main publications on race for two hundred years.

Bunak, V.; Gremiatzki, M.; *et al.* 1948. "Nauka o racatik i racism." *Nauchnogo Issledovatelskogo Institut antropologii moskovskogo Gosudarstvennogo Universiteta, Trudi,* Vol. IV. Moscow and Leningrad: Academy of Sciences.

Coon, C. S.; Garn, S. M.; and Birdsell, J. B. 1950. *Races: A Study of the Problems of Race Formation in Man.* Springfield, Ill.: Charles C. Thomas.

Eickstedt, E. von. 1938–44. *Rassenkunde und Rassengeschichte der Menschheit.* 2d ed. Stuttgart: Enke.

Hooton, E. A. 1947. *Up from the Ape.* 2d ed. New York: Macmillan Co.

Lundborg, H. 1931. "Die Rassenmischung beim Menschen," *Bibliographia genetica,* Vol. VIII.

Neuville, H. 1933. "L'Espèce, la race et le métissage en anthropologie," *Archives de l'Institut de paléontologie humaine,* Mém. 11. Paris: Masson.

Quatrefages, A. de. 1889. *Introduction à l'étude des races humaines.* Paris: Schleicher.

Topinard, P. 1885. *Anthropologie générale.* Paris: Delahaye.

Old World Prehistory: Paleolithic

By HALLAM L. MOVIUS, JR.

DURING THE last twenty-five years, our knowledge of the Paleolithic period has been greatly extended beyond the confines of western Europe. This has not resulted in the establishment of as coherent a picture of man's early attempts to develop a material culture as was originally expected. For, when we examine the bewildering array of primitive Stone Age assemblages that are constantly being augmented by fresh discoveries, we can hardly compose them into anything even remotely approaching the ordered general scheme conceived by the early workers. This is certainly not due to the fact that, in reaction against the doctrine of direct typological evolution, we have gone too far in the opposite direction but rather because, once De Mortillet's original scheme was rightly abandoned as provincial and inapplicable outside western Europe, no really adequate alternative approach has been proposed. As a matter of fact, most of the original terms developed by De Mortillet for his "classificatory system" are still in use, and they are now employed in several different senses—chronologic, typologic, technologic, and cultural—sometimes in the same breath. Instead of getting bogged down in questions pertaining to terminology at this point, however, I propose to pass on to a brief consideration of some problems of a more fundamental nature. In this paper an attempt has been made to present a synthesis of the various sequences of Paleolithic cultures within the framework of the larger continental areas. Throughout, the major trends as indicated by the most recent results have been stressed.

EUROPE

Paleolithic research, cradled and developed in Europe during the last century, has made many significant contributions during recent years. Only certain of the more important aspects of the field as a whole can be considered here; the selection has been made partly on the basis of new materials and partly on the basis of new methods that have been and are being developed. In view of the overwhelming mass of data, it is very difficult to present a consecutive account covering the region as a whole, although the major trends can be discerned.

LOWER AND MIDDLE PALEOLITHIC

As is well known, the very simple developmental scheme of Abbevillian (formerly Chellian)-Acheulian-Mousterian for the various Lower and Middle Paleolithic assemblages in western Europe was replaced early in the 1930's as the result of Breuil's investigations in the Somme Valley of northern France (Breuil, with Koslowski, 1931, 1932; Breuil, 1939). According to Breuil's so-called "parallel phyla concept," there was a flake-tool tradition (Clactonian-Levalloisian) which developed in a parallel and more or less independent manner to the core-biface tradition (Abbevillian-Acheulian). This has been widely accepted, certain authors even going so far as to conceive of the flake tools as being introduced by a paleo-anthropic stock of fossil man, and the core-biface complex as attributable to men of neanthropic (or *sapiens*) group. Those who implicitly accept the evidence conceive of "mixed" assemblages when hand-axes and flakes occur together, even suggesting that such mixtures resulted from contacts and migrations of different racial elements. Although the parallel phyla concept is not supported by the field evidence, it is still generally accepted by the majority of workers in the field of Paleolithic archeology.

On purely a priori grounds there is something fundamentally unsound with this hypothesis. As early as 1906, Commont described a large series of flake tools from his classic Acheulian locality at St. Acheul, and in 1908 Déchelette clearly stated that flake implements occurred in intimate and direct association with hand-axes at all the main localities in the Somme region. Later, in 1925, the view was further propounded by Obermaier, who remarked that, although the materials from the Somme gravel pits were collected by the workmen and not obtained during the course of controlled excavation, it was impossible to deny the existence of well-made flake tools side by side with hand-axes. This situation was further defined by Kelley in 1937, and the evidence has made some authorities suspicious of the existence of a clear-cut differentiation between the two traditions.

Now the parallel phyla concept has encountered rather considerable difficulties in those parts of the Old World where Lower Paleolithic hand-ax assemblages and advanced flake industries of Levalloisian type have been recognized. As will be discussed pres-

ently, these two traditions constitute inseparable components of one and the same complex throughout Africa, the Middle East, and India. Nowhere in this vast region has a vertical division between the essentially flake and core techniques been reported. On the basis of this overwhelming mass of unanimous evidence, one is perhaps justified in asking whether the concept of a Levalloisian tradition as an entity separate and distinct from an Acheulian tradition has any real validity in western Europe.

Recent investigations in the demonstrably Second Interglacial gravels of the Amiens region (Somme) indicate that the parallel phyla hypothesis is based on an assumption which is not borne out in the field. For three independent investigators, Breuil, Bordes, and Kelley, have described flakes of characteristic Levalloisian type, together with tortoise cores, in direct and indisputable association with Early-Middle Acheulian materials. Therefore, the Lower Paleolithic of western Europe can no longer be considered aberrant with respect to the Great Hand-Axe Complex as a whole in other parts of the Old World. However, the Clactonian flake industry, mainly restricted to England, can be regarded as a separate and distinct entity that has not been defined as yet outside northwestern Europe.

A typological comparison of the various hand-ax assemblages from widely separated areas will reveal that, with the exception of the material from which they are manufactured, the specimens themselves exhibit a striking degree of uniformity. This applies not only to form but also to the technical processes involved in their manufacture, both of which appear to be alarmingly constant. But this observation does not apply to the accompanying flake tools, including the cores from which the latter were struck, which suggests that it is the technique resorted to in the production of flake implements that is of prime importance. In that this is both a manifestation of tradition, on the one hand, and either diffusion of ideas or possible movements of peoples, on the other, it offers a possible solution to the present dilemma. In any event, the application of detailed typology as a means of studying Lower Paleolithic assemblages is getting us absolutely nowhere, and such elaborate sequences as the seven-fold Acheulian succession in northern France is incomprehensible except for the geological basis on which it has been established.

Recently, Van Riet Lowe has convincingly argued that one of the possible lines of escape from the present stalemate of Lower Paleolithic typology is by paying less attention to the form of the finished tools and attempting to reconstruct the process of their manufacture from the very beginning. Other workers are becoming convinced of the validity of this approach. Indeed, as Watson (1950) has observed, it is likely that a Stone Age community quite readily adopted "the shape of a tool it found in use by alien tribes, once its advantages were manifest, but much less likely that it should have the opportunity of learning, or be prepared, to revolutionize its industrial technique in order to reproduce the precise method of manufacture practiced by the original users of the tool." But the real difficulty with this approach is obvious: one should be familiar with the techniques themselves in order to detect them and assess their significance. In order to acquire the requisite insight into working methods, one should actually be able to reproduce them experimentally. Such technical ability is rare, and there are very few Paleolithic archeologists who can lay claim to it. Nevertheless, it is quite likely that when such an analysis of the Lower

Paleolithic hand-ax assemblages can be made, we may discover the existence of just as complex an interplay of techniques as that which exists between the various Middle and Upper Paleolithic traditions of the Old World.

In general, Paleolithic archeologists have not recognized the fact that early men had at their disposal not just one but several different techniques for flaking stone, as Breuil has rightly insisted. In the majority of instances these are common to a whole group of cultural developments at one and the same time, although in different frequencies. But when the finished tools are examined, the degree of typological uniformity within a given complex is indeed astonishing. Apparently this is due in large measure to the fact that approximately 95 per cent of the collections from open sites (i.e., gravel or sand pits) in western Europe have been made by workmen who save only the best hand-axes, flake tools, and nuclei. It is probable that this has given us a completely false picture of many of the assemblages in question. Nevertheless, even in these highly selected series it is possible to recognize the existence of certain specialized techniques which are limited to only one or possibly two kinds of assemblages and hence provide a fairly reliable and distinctive basis for descriptive purposes. These have been intensively studied by François Bordes (1950, 1951), himself an exceedingly skilful artificer of stone artifacts; and the provisional results of his work indicate that a new approach to problems of the Paleolithic is now being developed. Since this is regarded as of fundamental importance, the results of Bordes's investigations will be considered here in some detail.

The evidence of the occurrence of flakes of Levalloisian type in the Second Interglacial gravels of the Somme Valley, previously discussed, demonstrates that in western Europe, as in Africa, the Middle East, and India, the so-called "prepared" striking-platform/tortoise-core technique, or faceted platform technique, first appears in the middle of the Acheulian stage of development, continues during the Upper Acheulian, and reaches its final expression in the Mousterian of Levalloisian facies. In western Europe, however, the situation seems to be somewhat more complicated than elsewhere (South and East Africa, for example), owing to the fact that we also have to consider other traditions, such as the Clactonian and the Tayacian, which are only sporadically found elsewhere. As regards the Clactonian, Hazzledine Warren has recently shown that it is by no means comprised exclusively of flakes. Indeed, many of the pieces described as nuclei are nodules of flint alternately worked on one end to a zig-zag chopping-tool edge. In reality, the developmental pattern of these various assemblages is extremely complex and can be unscrambled only by an intensive investigation of: (a) the flaking techniques employed in the manufacture of the tools, (b) the nature of the raw material available for the production of implements, (c) the typology of the artifacts, and (d) the exact stratigraphic position of each site. The latter problem, of course, belongs in the realm of the natural sciences, and here there is still much basic field work to be done. For our present purposes, however, we can broadly group the localities into the various glacial and interglacial stages, although in many instances it would be very desirable if a more precise relative chronology could be determined.

From a typological point of view, the main criterion for subdividing the Lower and Middle Paleolithic rests on the presence or absence of hand-axes, or *bifaces,* to use a term that does not imply function. Technologically, it is the presence or absence of flakes with faceted striking-platforms and the characteristic Levalloisian preparation of these flakes on the core prior to detachment that are of fundamental importance. But, contrary to generally accepted opinion, these two features are not necessarily related. Therefore, it is necessary to define in a much more precise manner than has previously been attempted exactly what is meant by the "Levalloisian flaking technique," on the one hand, and the discoidal nucleus or "Mousterian flaking technique," on the other. From a historical point of view a Levallois flake is a type of flake first recognized from the gravels at Levallois, a suburb of Paris. Its form has been predetermined on the nucleus by special preparation prior to detachment. For the nucleus an oval-shaped nodule of flint is selected, generally of flattened form, which is roughly flaked along its borders to remove the irregularities. Next the cortex is removed from the upper surface by the detachment of centrally directed flakes, thus forming a surface which recalls the back of a tortoise, the flake scars representing the plates. On one end, perpendicular to the long axis, a striking-platform is prepared by the removal of very small flakes, thereby producing a faceted or scarred surface. A blow delivered by percussion technique (possibly with an intermediate tool) on this surface will yield a flat, oval flake which exhibits on its upper surface the traces of the centrally directed core preparation flakes. These flakes may also be round, triangular, or rectangular, depending on the shape of the nucleus. In the case of the latter, i.e., a rectangular flake, if the length is more than double the width, one has a flake blade, which, if it has been detached from a nucleus that exhibits a series of parallel rather than centrally directed scars, will resemble very closely true blades of the Upper Paleolithic. The

Levalloisian point is a particular type of Levallois flake of elongated triangular form, the shape of which has been predetermined by special preparation of the nucleus.

Now the flakes struck from a certain type of core, known as the "discoidal core" and very typical of Mousterian assemblages, are commonly mistaken for true Levalloisian flakes, as Bordes rightly maintains. The discoidal nucleus also exhibits careful trimming around its edges, as well as the scars of a series of centrally directed flakes. But the objective of the Mousterian knapper was to obtain these centrally directed flakes rather than to prepare the core for the removal of a special type of product. Normally, the discoidal nucleus is more markedly convex (although in certain instances flat or even slightly concave) than the Levalloisian form, and it may be alternately worked on the two faces, giving it a bipyramidal section. In both cases, once the first series of flakes has been removed, the craftsman proceeds by selecting the base of the ridges separating the scars of two previously detached flakes as the striking-platform. According to Bordes, a triangular flake, which resembles a Levalloisian point but with a thick butt and a clumsy appearance, is often produced in this manner. Also in the Mousterian there are flakes with plain, unprepared striking-platforms, frequently inclined toward the lower surface, in which case they are sometimes classed as "Clactonian." But this results from the technique employed—a hammer stone struck on a plain surface—and should not be taken to imply a connection with the true Clactonian assemblages of England. For these pseudo-Clactonian flakes are found in various contexts ranging from the Abbevillian to the Neolithic, including the Upper Paleolithic, and hence the term "Clactonian" should be reserved for the well-known Lower Paleolithic complex in which chopping-tools and choppers constitute the core-tool increment in place of hand-axes. In any case, nothing is yet known to demonstrate a transitional stage between the Clactonian and the typical Mousterian.

After defining the technological processes employed during Middle Paleolithic times in the production of flakes, Bordes applies this to various homogeneous assemblages from different parts of France on a statistical basis. These all come from localities that have produced 100 or more objects that have been selected neither by the workmen nor by collectors for museum display purposes. Of the various indices, four seem to be of fundamental significance, as follows:

1. *Levalloisian index* (*LI*):

$$\frac{\text{Total no. of Levalloisian flakes, points, and blades} \times 100}{\text{Total no. of flakes and blades of all types}}$$

2. *Index of faceting* (*IF*):

$$\frac{\text{Total no. of flakes with faceted butts} \times 100}{\text{Total no. of flakes on which the butt is recognizable}}$$

3. *Index of Levalloisian typology* (*ILty*):

$$\frac{\text{Total no. of Levalloisian flakes, points, and retouched points} \times 100}{\text{Total no. of retouched forms of all types}}$$

4. *Bifacial* (*hand-ax*) *index* (*BI*):

$$\frac{\text{Total no. of bifaces} \times 100}{\text{Total no. of bifacial} + \text{unifacial tools}}$$

The preliminary results of Bordes's study, including those recently published in a joint paper with Bourgon (1951), demonstrate the existence of a broad Mousterian Complex, the fundamental characteristics of which can be expressed statistically for the first time. For all practical purposes, this is comprised of the following two main groups that are further broken down into two categories each of two subdivisions:

Until recently it was maintained that the presence or absence of small, triangular, roughly cordiform or lanceolate hand-axes at sites referable to the Mousterian Complex was of chronological significance. But manifestly this is not true. They may be fairly frequent at one site but completely absent at several others, while the associated flake assemblages remain basically the same. Thus it may well be that, in instances where their occurrence is ex-

Group I: Mousterian with bifaces (hand-axes):

1. Levalloisian technique (LI > 25–30)
    A. With faceted butts (IF > 45)
        a) Micoquian of Levalloisian facies (ILty > 30)
        b) Mousterian of Acheulian tradition: Levalloisian facies (ILty < 30)

2. Non-Levalloisian technique (LI < 25–30)
    A. With faceted butts (IF > 45)
        a) Mousterian of Acheulian tradition: non-Levalloisian facies
    B. With unfaceted butts (IF < 45)
        b) Micoquian of non-Levalloisian facies

Group II: Mousterian without or with very few bifaces (hand-axes):

1. Levalloisian technique (LI > 25–30)
    A. With faceted butts (IF > 45)
        a) Mousterian of Levalloisian facies (ILty > 30)
            (= Levalloisian III, IV, VI, and VII of Breuil's scheme)
        b) Typical Mousterian (ILty < 30)

2. Non-Levalloisian technique (LI < 25–30)
    A. With faceted butts (IF > 45)
        a) Proto-Mousterian and Moustero-Tayacian
    B. With unfaceted butts (IF < 45)
        b) Tayacian and Mousterian of La Quina type (= *Charentian*)

tremely sporadic, we are dealing with intermittent or occasional settlement by hand-ax-using groups rather than with a true component of the technological tradition of the region in question. It is likewise possibly attributable to seasonal factors; for, as is well known, the material traits of one and the same group of hunting peoples may differ very profoundly in different places during different seasons. Furthermore, as McBurney (1950) points out, such a group habitually travels over several hundred miles of territory

during the annual cycle of specialized activities connected with hunting, fishing, and collecting. Certainly in southwestern France hand-axes commonly occur at both Mousterian open-air sites, as well as at the cave and rock-shelter stations, and in both cases the associated flake assemblages are invariably characterized by the faceted striking-platform/disk-shaped core technique. In other words, the presence or absence of these tools has no apparent chronological significance, and may be purely a manifestation of specialized activity.

It is also possible that it is due to geographical factors.

Now the application of the geographical approach to Paleolithic problems was first attempted by Charles McBurney two years ago. But a study of this type can be undertaken only when the data are sufficiently numerous and adequate, a situation that has come about in certain sections of Europe only during the postwar period. Since this approach has been demonstrated to be fundamentally sound, especially for the Mesolithic complexes of northwestern Europe, there is no reason to doubt that it will ultimately prove of great value in interpreting Paleolithic problems. McBurney's preliminary work has a direct bearing on the question of hand-axes at Mousterian localities in western and central Europe as a whole. Thus the sites with hand-axes appear to be mainly confined to the maritime lowlands of western Europe, while in the hilly and mountainous districts of the interior an entirely different tradition is encountered. Although the former region lies in the tundra belt immediately south and west of the margins of the last ice sheets, it nonetheless formed a uniform ecological territory, offering a "maritime forest climate without perennially frozen ground." In the upland regions and in the territory between the limits of the northern and Alpine ice sheets, on the other hand, extreme arctic conditions prevailed, with frozen-soil phenomena; this was the true treeless forest tundra. But the available data are not of a sufficiently precise nature to permit a more detailed consideration of the significance of this observation. Nevertheless, it is important, in that it points the direction that will be followed in the future by research on the Paleolithic cultures of the Old World.

One of the facts that emerged in the late 1920's as the result of Breuil's investigations in the Somme Valley is that the Levalloisian technique is characteristic of sites in the north of France, whereas at contemporary localities of the south (Dordogne region in particular) non-Levalloisian workmanship is more common. Bordes (1951) attributes this in large measure to the nature of the raw material. Certainly, it is a self-evident fact that, in dealing with any Stone Age assemblage, this plays a major role. In any case, the large-sized and more or less flat nodules of flint that occur in the chalk country of northern France lend themselves to the Levalloisian method of preparation of the core, thereby facilitating the detachment of a flake of predetermined form. On the other hand, in the south the majority of the nodules of flint are too small to work in this manner. Furthermore, they are often of globular or irregular outline, and there is nothing to be gained by employing the Levalloisian technique. Here we can only state that we agree completely with Bordes in maintaining that the quality and shape in which the raw material occurs have been factors of prime consideration. But, since the non-Levalloisian facies likewise occurs in regions where large-sized nodules of flint exist, it is certainly not the only one involved.

In order to formulate a possible explanation of this situation, it is necessary to consider such additional matters as: (*a*) the enormous length of time involved, which may well represent several tens of millenniums; (*b*) such geographic (i.e., environmental) conditions as those mentioned above; and (*c*) the type of social unit with which we are dealing. In this connection McBurney (1950) has very aptly stated:

It may be an archaeological truism, but it is nevertheless a point of the utmost practical importance, that assemblages of human artifacts require, as evidence, basically different interpretation to samples of organic fossils such as say, shells or pollen. Whereas the latter may be taken to indicate a semi-permanent biological population, the former, from what we know of modern primitive peoples, may well represent communities who ranged sporadically over wide areas outside their main habitat. An Eskimo tribe, for instance, has been described as making an annual trek of over 200 miles across hostile territory to obtain a much-needed raw material.

This concept is borne out by Bordes's conclusion based on considerations of a purely technological nature, namely, that the only significant difference between the materials from the open-air loess sites of northern France and the cave and rock-shelter stations of the south referable to the Mousterian of Levalloisian facies lies in what he has defined as the "Index of Levalloisian Typology" (ILty). In the case of the former, the percentage of Levalloisian flakes which have remained in mint condition or which have been very little retouched does not fall below 40. On the other hand, the average of the ILty for five typical horizons in the Dordogne which have produced Mousterian of Levalloisian facies is less than 10. Although the significance of this fact is not as yet altogether apparent, the various series under consideration cannot be differentiated on any other basis. Indeed, as Bordes suggests, one wonders if the Dordogne localities should not be regarded as the winter camps of the groups who hunted in the loess regions of the north during the summer season. On this basis the discrepancy in Levalloisian flake utilization may well reflect environmental differences of a seasonal nature but produced in both cases by groups which were basically identical. Surely, even if this interpretation cannot be proved until evidence of a much more refined nature is available, it seems a great deal more plausible than the taxonomic approach that was in vogue until recently; for the latter based its conclusions solely on the form and characteristic re-

touch exhibited by a selected series of the finished pieces.

In their recent joint paper Bordes and Bourgon (1951), employing Bordes's statistical approach, have published a detailed treatise based on their analysis of a large series of sites—caves and rock-shelters, as well as loess stations—referable to the newly defined Mousterian Complex. The graphs indicate that, regardless of the technique(s) employed in the production of flakes, the typology of the fundamental categories of implements is surprisingly constant, with the exception of the recently defined Charentian. This can only mean that the basic way of life during the time span under consideration was broadly similar over very wide areas, but the problem of the particular functions of a given type of scraper or point is just as obscure as ever.

Although still in its infancy, the geographical or environmental approach, as advocated by McBurney and others, will doubtless contribute to an understanding of the range of possibilities concerning what tools were used for. But before it can be tested we urgently need new and reliably documented materials from undisturbed sites. In the meantime, by eliminating the Levalloisian in a cultural sense and defining it as one of two basic flaking techniques in use at one and the same time, Bordes has made a fundamental contribution to the methodology of Paleolithic archeology. It certainly helps materially to clarify the situation with respect to the Lower and Middle Paleolithic succession in western Europe. Furthermore, it removes one very grave difficulty in working in this field, namely, the complete lack of anything approaching truly objective criteria in the study of the materials available from the early hunting and gathering levels. Up to now, much of the work has been completely subjective; therefore, the effect of providing a definitive method for assessing the technological increment in any given assemblage will certainly be far-reaching. It will be interesting to follow the more widespread application of this principle in such areas as the Near East, India, North Africa, Egypt, East and South Africa, for example, where problems of the same kind exist. As the method is more broadly applied, it will inevitably be improved, for it is still somewhat cumbersome. Nonetheless, it offers the only recourse yet devised for analyzing a given assemblage in terms of its several components. When combined with chronological and environmental studies, it is reasonably certain that significant results will accrue.

UPPER PALEOLITHIC

Until the middle 1930's the Upper Paleolithic sequence in western Europe seemed fairly straightforward: Aurignacian, Solutrean, and Magdalenian, just as set forth in all the standard textbooks. According to this concept, the "Aurignacian," as originally defined by Breuil (see Breuil, 1937, for references), could be subdivided into Lower, characterized by large curved points with blunted backs and known as "Châtelperron points"; Middle, with the split-base bone point, the busked graver or burin, and various types of steep scrapers; and Upper, of which a straight point with blunted back, apparently evolved from the Châtelperron type and known as the "Gravette point," was typical. This latter stage immediately preceded the Final Aurignacian with its tanged point, known as the "Font Robert type." However, discoveries of the last fifteen or twenty years have shown that, in reality, the Aurignacian succession is very much more complex than was originally suspected.

Formerly the only Upper Paleolithic complex known outside Europe was the Capsian of North Africa, and, since points with blunted backs are characteristic of the Capsian assemblages, the old Lower and Upper Aurignacian could be conveniently derived from this source. The Middle Aurignacian was supposed to have developed *in situ* during an interval when contact with North Africa was temporarily broken. But recent work has shown that (*a*) from a chronological point of view the Capsian is very late in North Africa; (*b*) it is absent in Spain; (*c*) in North Africa it is essentially an inland development, the coastal region everywhere being an Ibero-Maurusian (Oranian) province; and (*d*) many of the forms most characteristic of the Early Capsian (e.g., microburins and lunates) are completely absent in the Early-Upper Paleolithic assemblages of western Europe. On this basis, the claim of Africa as the homeland of the Lower and Upper Aurignacian has been pretty well ruled out.

But the problems of just what constitutes the Aurignacian and where its various components originated still remain obscure. At the only two really adequately excavated Upper Paleolithic localities in the entire Dordogne region—La Ferrassie and Laugerie-Haute—M. Denis Peyrony has found evidence which seems to suggest that the Aurignacian (as conceived in 1912 by Breuil) is an infinitely more complicated series of assemblages than was originally suspected by the creator of the old threefold scheme. In fact, Peyrony recognizes two separate traditions:

Périgordian = Lower (Châtelperronian) and Upper Aurignacian (Gravette/Font Robert) of the old system
Aurignacian = Middle Aurignacian of the Breuil classification

Peyrony's fundamental thesis is that in its later stages the former coexisted with the latter, a situation which can best be shown in the form of a table (Table 1).

At this juncture the writer does not intend to present a critique of Peyrony's scheme. Suffice it to say, however, that his scheme is in part supported by the stratigraphic evidence, although certain of the substages should doubtless be regarded as local variations. This very fundamental and im-

when we trace these influences back along the main routes of their supposed diffusion that the situation can be in some measure unscrambled. For here we should find definite geographical regions where relatively pure manifestations of given culture complexes can be recognized.

The argument that the very specialized blade technique—the hallmark of

TABLE 1

Breuil's Classification	Garrod's Classification	Peyrony's Classification	
		Périgordian	Aurignacian
Upper Aurignacian	Font Robert stage	5th phase: Tanged points; leaf-like points; Noailles burins	5th phase: Bone points with simple beveled base
	Gravettian stage	4th phase: Gravette points; small-backed blades; female statuettes	4th phase: Bone points with bi-conical section
			3d phase: Bone points with oval section
Middle Aurignacian	Aurignacian	3d phase: Truncated or oblique-ly backed blades; backed blades of misc. types	2d phase: Bone points with dia-mond-shaped section; steep scrapers
		2d phase: Châtelperron points (evolved types); blades with inverse retouch	1st phase: Split-base bone points; steep and carinated scrapers
Lower Aurignacian	Châtelperronian	1st phase: Châtelperron points (basal Périgordian)	

portant problem is urgently in need of further investigation; certainly, it is not possible to interpret the data on the basis of the evidence available at present.

As to Upper Paleolithic origins, Professor Garrod believes that, when sections of Europe other than France are considered, it becomes apparent that the French sequence is the result of successive influences superimposed one on the other. According to this view, on the periphery of its distribution the Upper Paleolithic becomes a more or less heterogeneous mass of successive levels which lack meaning. It is only

the Upper Paleolithic—originated outside western Europe is based on two significant facts: (a) the lack of a developmental sequence between the Mousterian and the earliest phase of the Upper Paleolithic (indeed, no instance of stratigraphic overlap is known in this entire region) and (b) the equally sudden appearance in western Europe at this time of men of developed *sapiens* type. As McBurney (1950) points out, it is considered very unlikely from a biological standpoint that Neanderthal could have evolved into a fully modern form within the time span suggested by the geological evidence, a fact which has convinced most workers that the concept of the rapid immigration into Europe at this time of blade-using modern man should be accepted as a plausible assumption. Nevertheless, it must be frankly admitted at the outset that there is no geological or archeological proof clearly supporting such a postulated earlier occurrence of *Homo sapiens* in association with a blade industry outside the region under consideration.

As to what Garrod has called "Châtelperronian" (= Peyrony's Early Périgordian; Lower Aurignacian of the old scheme), this is claimed to have already had an independent existence in early Upper Pleistocene times in the Near East: Palestine (Mount Carmel Caves) and Syria (Jabrud). Although its precise center is still unknown, it appears in western Europe during the closing stages of the Mousterian as the earliest identifiable blade complex. Possibly it came from central Europe or South Russia, since it is found there at an early date. In any case, nothing has thus far come to light in central Asia to suggest that it originated farther to the east.

The Aurignacian (= Middle Aurignacian of the old system) is also well represented in central Europe, especially in lower Austria and Hungary, as well as through Rumania, the Crimea, and Transcaucasia to the Near East, where it is very widespread and covers a considerably longer time span than in the west. Apparently this manifestation is absent on the South Russian Plain. Although Garrod suggested the Iranian plateau as a possible center where the Aurignacian developed, Coon's recent excavations have certainly contributed nothing to support this hypothesis.

Turning now to Garrod's Gravettian/ Font Robert Complex (= Peyrony's Late Périgordian; Upper Aurignacian of the old scheme), which extends into Spain and Italy, this has a wide distribution in central and eastern Europe and is considered by some authorities to be the classic Upper Paleolithic culture of the South Russian Plain, where true Aurignacian elements seem to be absent. A strong supporting argument for this concept is the fact that in South Russia, central Europe, and the west female statuettes of the Willendorf type are associated with the so-called "Gravettian" complex. Since this stage is absent in the Near East, it is possible that further excavations in the plains region of southern Russia will reveal that the Gravettian was derived from this source. It is also possible, however, that Peyrony is essentially correct in suggesting France for the main center of this development. In any case, on the basis of what we know at present concerning the materials found at stations on the South Russian Plain, this seems to be just as defensible a working hypothesis as any other. Certainly, both Peyrony and Garrod are fully aware that the discoveries of the next generation will, in turn, make further extensive revisions necessary.

In connection with future investigations, it is now generally admitted by Paleolithic archeologists that problems pertaining to the origin and development of the Upper Paleolithic will have to be dealt with on a regional basis. This is certainly a very great step in the right direction. For, in the past, work in this field has been very materially hampered by what may be termed the "index fossil concept"—i.e., approaching central Europe, South Russia, or the Near East (or any other area outside France, for that matter) as if they were some sort of typological appendages of western Europe. In focusing attention on the so-called "pre-Solutrean problem" in central Europe in his recent book, Lothar Zotz, in fact, has advocated this point of view, although the net result is only to complicate further rather than to simplify the problems. For the pre-Solutrean must henceforth be regarded as yet another independent tradition that has to be considered in connection with Early-Upper Paleolithic problems. Zotz notes that bifacial leaf-shaped points, in some instances extremely reminiscent of true Solutrean forms, actually occur sporadically in central Europe in various Late Acheulian, Micoquian, and Mousterian contexts, and he believes that it is from these early developments that the pre-Solutrean is basically derived. The evidence from the most important sites for this development shows that the pre-Solutrean dates from the time of the Würm I/II Interstadial, overlapping and paralleling the Châtelperronian (Early Périgordian). According to Zotz, the pre-Solutrean (also known as the Szeletian or Altmühlian) is a separate cultural manifestation heavily influenced from contemporary Upper Paleolithic sources. In fact, at certain sites it actually underlies Aurignacian horizons. Finally, during Gravettian (Late Périgordian) times, this blossoms out into the true Solutrean of central Europe assigned to the Würm II/III Interstadial on the basis of the evidence from the Czechoslovakian stations of Předmost and Moravany-Dlha.

This evidence certainly opens up a new perspective on Old Stone Age developments in central Europe, made possible only by recognizing and admitting the existence of regional cultural specializations during Middle and Upper Paleolithic times rather than by trying to force the data to fit the strictures of a taxonomic scheme established for an entirely different region over half a century ago. But, at the same time, it makes the problem of where the Solutrean originated even more obscure than ever. Once it was an accepted fact that this complex had reached France

from somewhere to the east, presumably from Hungary. But when the Soviet archeologists failed to find any traces of Solutrean beyond the Dniester, the claim of Hungary began to subside. Then in 1942 Professor Pericot Garcia published the results of his excavations at the Cave of Parpalló near Gandia (south of Valencia in southeastern Spain), where he had discovered a well-developed Solutrean culture with tanged and barbed projectile points, in addition to bifacial leaf-shaped types. The fact that certain of the former were strikingly close to examples known in the Late Aterian of North Africa (Tangier: Mugharet el'Aliya) led many Paleolithic archeologists to suspect that possibly the main focus of the European Solutrean lay in this southwesterly direction. Thus, if Zotz's pre-Solutrean has validity—and there is no reason to suspect otherwise —we now have two centers from which to derive the Solutrean—central Europe and southeastern Spain, where the inspiration apparently came from a Middle Paleolithic derivative known as the Aterian of North Africa. Although in central Europe the pre-Solutrean can also be traced back to Middle Paleolithic sources, this manifestly gets us nowhere with regard to the solution of the problem. In view of the new evidence, however, the development of such a specialized technique as pressure-flaking from complexes on an entirely different technological level from that of the Upper Paleolithic of Europe does not present inherent difficulties of the same magnitude as was true fifteen years ago. Indeed, most workers are quite prepared to accept the Solutrean as due to a diffusion of certain specialized ideas rather than an invasion of new peoples with superior weapons.

By the final stage of the Upper Paleolithic, regional cultural developments can be discerned very clearly. For the Magdalenian, centered in France, is limited in its distribution to western Czechoslovakia, southern Germany, Switzerland, Belgium, and Spain. Elsewhere we have such cultures as the Hamburgian of northwestern Germany, the Creswellian of England, and various evolved Gravettian (in the broad sense) complexes in Italy, parts of central Europe, and South Russia. Because of its truly magnificent naturalistic art, especially that of the Franco-Cantabrian Province, priority here clearly belongs to the Magdalenian, although the discovery of Lascaux some ten years ago has revealed an unexpected richness belonging to an earlier cycle. Now, as is well known, Magdalenian art includes painting in monochrome and polychrome in a wide variety of styles and techniques, engravings on stone, bone, and ivory, and sculptures in both high and low relief. The recent discoveries, especially at Angles-sur-l'Anglin, have emphasized the importance of local centers of artistic development. The real point of issue, however, is whether or not the pictures and drawings were done for purely decorative purposes. It does not seem at all likely that a primitive hunting community, living under the conditions of a rigorous and exacting environment, could have supported a specialized class of professional artists, such as some authorities have suggested. Nevertheless, it is patently clear that certain individuals lived during the Upper Paleolithic who were endowed with a highly developed artistic ability and a true appreciation of aesthetic values. Otherwise, there could not have been such a high development of art. In any case, the whole development clearly owes its existence to the magico-religious idea, especially the custom of hunting magic, as practiced today by living primitive peoples. This is one of the very few problems facing Paleolithic archeologists upon the solution of which ethnological studies would doubtless throw new light.

AFRICA

The Paleolithic of Africa is characterized by a variety of assemblages, some of which are purely local, whereas others are surprisingly similar to, if not identical with, certain of those found in Europe. It is only during recent years that geological investigations on a really adequate basis have been undertaken in this continent, and the results to date indicate that, owing to fluctuations in rainfall, the Pleistocene epoch throughout most of Africa can be subdivided on the basis of a succession of pluvial and interpluvial stages. Perhaps eventually these may be broadly correlated with the successive glacial and interglacial episodes of Europe. The cultural sequences are well established in certain areas, as indicated below, but this does not apply as yet to the continent as a whole.

EGYPT

Even in Paleolithic times Egypt already seems to have been almost as self-sufficient as she was in the dynastic period. Nothing of the rich and complex Upper Paleolithic development of the Near East is found here, but the cause of this cultural isolation from the north and east cannot be explained on the basis of the existing data. The geologic history of the Nile Valley during Late Cenozoic times is well known as the result of the intensive field work done there in the 1920's by Sandford and Arkell for the Oriental Institute of the University of Chicago.

The Abbevillian–Early Acheulian series of the 30-meter terrace calls for no special comment. Some of the very heavily rolled forms may be derived from the 45-meter terrace, although no *in situ* specimens have ever been found there. With the exception of a special form with a triangular section, known as the "Chalossian," these forms are indistinguishable from early Lower Paleolithic materials from western Europe. In association with these early types of hand-axes, very primitive flake tools with plain, high-angled striking-platforms occur. The Late Acheulian of the 15-meter terrace includes pointed hand-axes of Micoquian type, together with developed forms of flake implements; and in the Acheulio-Levalloisian of the 9-meter terrace there are oval or pointed flakes with faceted striking-platforms associated with tortoise-type cores and a few subtriangular hand-axes. In the 3-meter terrace there is a Middle Levalloisian industry in which a reduction in size and an increase in the delicacy of the flakes may be noted. The next series of deposits—the basal aggradational silts—yield an Upper Levalloisian assemblage, including several specialized types of points, as well as a bifacial lanceolate that suggests Aterian examples (Caton-Thompson, 1946*a*, *b*). The associated cores show a wide variety of form; in general, they are narrower than in the preceding stage.

Up to this point the main lines of development in the Kharga oasis and the Fayum follow the same basic pattern as outlined above for the Nile Valley. Subsequent to the time of the deposition of the basal aggradational silts, however, this is no longer true, since in each region there was a gradual industrial differentiation. These are: the Sebilian in Upper Egypt and Nubia; the Epi-Levalloisian in Lower Egypt and the Fayum; and the Khargan and the Aterian in the Kharga oasis. All are basically derived from the Late Levalloisian and perpetuate the same technological tradition. Thus Egypt developed along indigenous lines almost completely undisturbed by contemporary developments from outside the area, except for the appearance of the Aterian in the Kharga oasis, as discussed in the section on North Africa. Here only one of these three specialized complexes—the Sebilian—will be briefly considered.

Typical of the Lower Sebilian are flakes of Levallois type of reduced size, often with steeply retouched edges. One characteristic form exhibits a deliberately shortened striking-platform, giving the flake a squat appearance. In the Middle Sebilian backed lunates made on small flakes rather than on microblades, as well as certain subgeometric forms, appear. True Levalloisian flakes now almost completely disappear, although technologically the industry is clearly in the prepared striking-platform/tortoise-core tradition. The Upper Sebilian, which is probably later in time than the last major pluvial episode, approaches the Lower Natufian of Palestine and the Late Capsian of North Africa—both Mesolithic complexes—in many respects. In fact, at Helwan in Upper Egypt a true microlithic industry occurs, which is very like the Natufian of Palestine. But in the Upper Sebilian the occurrence of highly evolved and much reduced flakes and tortoise cores of basic Levalloisian facies serves to link this mesolithic assemblage with the ancient flaking tradition of the Lower and Middle Paleolithic.

EAST AFRICA

Actually, Paleolithic materials have been reported throughout the entire region intervening between Egypt and British East Africa, including the Anglo-Egyptian Sudan, Ethiopia, and Somaliland, the affinities of which have been assessed on a typological basis. But, since almost none of the horizons can be fitted into any of the established Pleistocene chronologies, there is little to be gained by presenting a regional summary of these materials. Now British East Africa—Kenya, Uganda, and Tanganyika—is bisected by the Great Rift Valley, on the walls of which excellent sections of Pleistocene deposits are exposed. The Paleolithic assemblages from sites to the west of this feature show that in prehistoric times this region belonged in equatorial Africa, just as it does at present. Therefore, it will be considered in a subsequent section; here the materials from the definitely savannah country of most of Kenya and Tanganyika will be described.

The earliest-known and most primitive tools from this area, known as the "Kafuan," consist of pebbles with a single edge, flaked on one side only. The Kafuan implements come from definitely Lower Pleistocene deposits and are regarded as one of the oldest archeological manifestations from anywhere in the world. At the classic Middle Pleistocene locality of Olduvai, in northern Tanganyika, a series of beds covering the range of time represented by the Second (Kamasian) Pluvial, the Second Interpluvial, and the Third (Kanjeran) Pluvial are exposed. During the ensuing interpluvial, severe rifting movements occurred, accompanied by erosion and valley-cutting, which mark the close of the Middle Pleistocene in this area. From the basal beds at Olduvai a pebble-tool industry, more evolved than the Kafuan and known as the "Oldowan," has been described by Leakey (1951). These include true chopping tools with edges alternately flaked in two directions, producing a jagged cutting edge. In the immediately overlying beds, pointed chopping tools appear which are regarded as the forerunners of the true bifacial hand-axes that have been reported from the next series of deposits, in association with various types of massive flake tools. At the horizon of the upper-middle part of Bed II at Olduvai, hand-axes of unmistakably Early Acheulian type appear. In Bed III the pointed hand-axes of Middle Acheulian type are associated with cleavers, made on "side-blow" flakes, and proto-Levalloisian flakes. This developmental sequence culminates in the Late Acheulian of Bed IV, where, in addition to finely made pointed hand-axes, there are

rectangular-shaped cleavers and a fully developed Levalloisian flake industry. No other single locality discovered to date can compare with Olduvai in providing a complete and unbroken record of the entire cycle of Lower Paleolithic cultural development.

Contemporary with the widespread geographical changes marking the close of the Middle Pleistocene in East Africa, two distinct types of tool-making traditions are found: (a) the Early Kenya Stillbay, a Levalloisian derivative in which some surviving Acheulian elements are present, and (b) the Kenya Fauresmith, which is basically of Acheulian inspiration and very similar to the Fauresmith of South Africa. In addition to various types of scrapers and points made on Levalloisian-type flakes, the former is characterized by small- to medium-sized bifacially flaked points that resemble minute hand-axes. This complex is very widespread in South Africa, where it shows a number of regional specializations. The Kenya Fauresmith also extends into Ethiopia; carefully shaped round stone balls constitute part of the assemblage. Since these normally occur in groups of twos or threes at the camp sites, they are regarded as bolas weights for use in hunting.

Following the post-Kanjeran interpluvial, the climate once again became markedly humid, and this interval is known as the "Gamblian Pluvial Period," which is of Upper Pleistocene age. The main cultural development known from deposits of this age is the Kenya Stillbay. Its bifacially flaked points often have secondarily retouched edges; and, in the final stages of the development, leaf-shaped forms appear, apparently worked by the technique of pressure-flaking. In the post-Gamblian dry phase, microlithic tools appear for the first time, and the earliest assemblage in which they are found is known as the "Magosian." From a chronological point of view the Magosian must belong to a fairly late horizon, since certain sites of this complex have yielded pottery. In addition to pottery, a true blade technique now appears in East Africa— called the "Kenya Capsian"—which is the immediate forerunner of the Elmenteitan in many of its most distinctive elements. Apparently contemporary with the latter manifestations there occurs a typical microlithic assemblage, the Kenya Wilton; but, since this has a widespread distribution in South Africa, it will be referred to in the next section.

SOUTH AFRICA

The Pleistocene succession in the basin of the Vaal River from near Johannesburg to the confluence with the Orange River has been worked out in great detail. This is also true of the sequences in northern and southern Rhodesia, but within the compass of the present paper, these latter areas connot be considered. The oldest gravels of the Vaal, probably laid down during basal Pleistocene (Early Kageran) times, have not yielded any artifacts as yet, but in the next younger series of deposits pebble tools occur. These artifacts, which are called "pre-Stellenbosch" and which recall both the Kafuan and the Oldowan of East Africa, are found in a series of gravel terraces that range from 300 to 50 feet above the stream. A lower terrace at +50 feet contains Abbevillian types of hand-axes, in many cases made on pebbles, together with primitive flakes. This assemblage is called "Stellenbosch I." Following the interval of heavy rainfall during which these gravels were accumulated, there was a prolonged dry interval, marked by earth movements, for which there is no record of human occupation in South Africa. This is considered to mark the close of the Lower Pleistocene.

A new series of gravels, aggraded at relatively low elevations, are referable to a sequence of geologic episodes probably related to the Kamasian and Kanjeran pluvial periods of the Middle Pleistocene. Three terraces forming distinct levels at +40 feet, +25 feet, and river-bed level carry deposits which not only yield a very rich fauna, but also five stages representing the entire development of the South African Hand-Axe, or Stellenbosch, Complex. Stage I, in which roughly made Abbevillian-like types and primitive flake artifacts predominate, still contains some pebble tools, but these disappear in Stage II. The hand-axes and cleavers of the latter are now more refined and recall Early Acheulian forms of Europe. Together with the developed hand-axes and cleavers made on "side-blow" flakes of Stage III, the Levalloisian, or prepared striking-platform / tortoise-core technique (also called the "faceted platform technique"), has its inception. Also found in groups of twos and threes are faceted polyhedral stones, regarded by some authorities as bolas stones. The cleavers of Stage IV are characteristic, in that they are now made on end-struck flakes with a trapezoidal- rather than a parallelogram-shaped section. This stage corresponds with the Late Acheulian of East Africa, and during it the prepared striking-platform technique continued to develop. The finely made hand-axes of Stage V are comparable to the Micoquian of Europe; these are associated with cleavers that have flared edges and a variety of tools made for special functions on flakes produced by the Levalloisian technique. The climax of the long, uninterrupted Stellenbosch development was brought to a close by a second interval of earth movements and by a dry climate.

The next series of gravels was laid down during an Upper Pleistocene wet phase, probably corresponding to the Gamblian of East Africa. These sediments contain the Fauresmith assemblage, characterized by a marked refinement in the flake tools of Levalloisian facies and the development of small, relatively slender hand-axes and cleavers. In view of the overwhelming proportion of flake artifacts in the Fauresmith, Van Riet Lowe has suggested the possibility that stabbing and throwing spears, as well as hafted tools and weapons of various sorts, now began to replace the earlier hand implements of the Stellenbosch. Following these aggradations, there was an arid interval when semidesert conditions prevailed. The ensuing wet phase, correlated with the Makalian of East Africa, witnessed the development of a series of assemblages referred to as the Middle Stone Age of South Africa. Hand-axes and cleavers no longer occur, the characteristic tools being made on flakes produced by a developed Levalloisian technique (Stillbay, Pietersburg, Mossel Bay, etc.). These include slender unifacial and bifacial spear and lance points, presumably for stabbing or throwing. In the final stages of the Middle Stone Age, known as the "South African Magosian," microlithic elements appear, just as they do in East Africa.

Wind-blown deposits of the post-Makalian dry interval buried the Middle Stone Age sites. A final minor wet phase, presumably paralleled by the Nakuran of East and equatorial Africa, witnessed the introduction of the so-called "Later Stone Age" cultures—Smithfield and Wilton—which are characterized by (a) small tools, including a large number of microliths, (b) the absence of the old Levalloisian technique, (c) parallel rather than convergent flaking, and (d) the widespread use of indurated shale in the manufacture of tools. Smithfield and Wilton are closely related and reveal varying degrees of influence as the result of contact with the culture introduced by the ancestors of the Bantu-speaking peoples. Since both were still extant at the time the first Europeans arrived in South Africa, the area constitutes one of the few places in the Old World where there exists a direct link between archeology and ethnology.

CENTRAL OR EQUATORIAL AFRICA

A very clear demonstration of response in Paleolithic cultural development to environmental conditions can be seen in the case of central or equatorial Africa, as recently pointed out by Goodwin. Here in what Frobenius has called the "Hylaean Area," or the region of the Selva, a special evolution in material culture took place, which is characterized by the occurrence of (a) the bifacial gouge or chisel, (b) the elongated pick—possibly an adze, (c) the tranchet type of ax, and (d) the elongated lance or spearhead. That this very distinctive assemblage, known as the "Sangoan" (formerly Tumbian) culture, was developed in response to environmental conditions has been established on the basis of distribution studies. These show that everywhere it occurs it is included within the 40-inch isohet, or contour of equivalent rainfall, which roughly delimits the tropical forest or equatorial region of central Africa. In addition to an unusually dense vegetation, typical of this area, are widespread deposits of soft alluvium and humus, the present distribution of which suggests very strongly that during the pluvial periods of the past the 50-inch or even the 60-inch isohet expanded to cover the areas adjacent to this zone. Today these are characterized by parklands and open bush country. With this expansion, the Hylaean area likewise expanded, and with it new types of tools developed to cope with the daily exigencies of life under such conditions. But what the latter actually were cannot as yet be determined.

Now the Lower Paleolithic development of the area is essentially a repetition of what has already been outlined for East and South Africa. From a horizon corresponding with the beginning of Middle Stone Age times in the South African sequence, however, the artifactual development of central Africa contrasts very strikingly with the regional assemblages found to the east and south of it. In the latter regions various types of points, flakes, and blade implements predominate in all the so-called "Middle Stone Age" complexes thus far brought to light. Although certain basic tool types overlap to some extent, it is the environmental background of the Sangoan culture that is of prime importance. Possibly when more is known concerning the scope and limitations imposed on human activities by such environmental conditions, we shall be able better to assess the significance of this and interpret the possible function(s) of the various very specialized types of tools. Since the Sangoan is found in deposits laid down after the Kanjeran pluvial, it is of Upper Pleistocene age. Just as in the case of the Fauresmith of South Africa, this development had its origin in the Great Hand-Axe Complex and carries on the same basic tradition. Indeed, the Sangoan is now generally accepted as a direct derivative of the Acheulian complex, which survived in the Hylaean area well down into Upper Pleistocene times. But in the present state of our knowledge it must be accepted as a fact that the radically different ecological conditions in the "retreat area" resulted in an equally radically different cultural development, since we do not even pretend to understand the dynamics involved.

NORTH AFRICA

North Africa's geographic position places it outside the area of direct contact with glacial and periglacial phenomena, which provide the keystone for chronologic studies in Eurasia. But this is in part offset by the existence of circum-Mediterranean marine phenomena linked with world-wide fluctuations of sea-level during Pleistocene and later time. Also there are indications here of arid and pluvial phases corresponding with interglacial and glacial episodes of the north. The only demonstrably Villafranchian (= basal Pleistocene) locality to yield human artifacts is situated at St. Arnaud, near Setif (Algeria). These consist of very crudely worked pebble tools of roughly spherical form and are the oldest implements ever found in the Old World. Lower Paleolithic hand-axes of both Abbevillian and Acheulian type associated with flake tools have been reported in great numbers throughout the entire area, including the Sahara, which was apparently less arid during Middle Pleistocene times than it is at present. The most important Lower Paleolithic sites are in the vicinity of Casablanca, Palikao (southeast of Mascara), Tabelbala, and Gafsa. Although the relative duration of the Lower Paleolithic is unknown in North Africa, the main developmental sequence seems to coincide broadly with that found elsewhere, and in a few isolated instances geological reference points have been established.

The Middle Paleolithic was very widespread, and it persisted in the North African area at least as late as the time of the Würm I/II Interstadial in terms of the Alpine sequence. A wide range of flake-tool assemblages, the most distinctive feature of which is the prominent role played by the prepared striking-platform/tortoise-core technique, is grouped here. Included in this category is the Mousterian, as well as the Aterian, a specialized Mousterian development characterized by tanged points made on flakes and bifacially worked in some instances. In general, the Mousterian seems to follow the Acheulian and to precede the Aterian, and several regional variations of it are claimed. But at two sites in the western part of the area (Morocco and Tangier) a simplified Mousterian follows the Aterian, while at Sidi-Zin, a recently investigated locality in Tunisia, two Acheulian horizons are separated by one yielding characteristically Mousterian tools. Hence contemporaneousness or noncontemporaneousness of similar morphological assemblages has not been demonstrated for the Middle Paleolithic of North Africa, and the various chronological schemes that have been proposed tend to degenerate into purely typological assessments.

The Capsian and Mouillian (formerly known as the "Oranian" or "Ibero-Maurusian"), both blade-tool complexes distinctive of this area, follow the Mousterian/Aterian development. Both date from the end of Upper Paleolithic times, but their main effervescence was during early postglacial (or postpluvial) times. The Capsian distribution is essentially inland and is centered around Gafsa in southern Tunisia and Tebessa in southeastern Algeria, while the Mouillian occurs everywhere along the coast from southern Tunisia to the Atlantic seaboard of Morocco. The Capsian is characterized by backed blades and points, scrapers, burins, and a very wide range of microlithic forms, the latter occurring almost exclusively at the youngest sites. The Mouillian is likewise a microlithic complex, in which the tools, on the whole, are smaller. Both the Capsian and the Mouillian persisted well after the introduction of Neolithic traits into this area.

ASIA

Recent work on the Paleolithic archeology of Asia indicates that during Middle Pleistocene times this vast region was divided into two major culture provinces, each of which has yielded a distinctive sequence. The first of these, which is in the south and east, includes China, Burma, northwestern India, and Java, where the characteristic implement types consist of choppers and chopping tools that are often made on pebbles. None of the well-known Paleolithic complexes of Europe and western Asia seem to be represented. The second major province includes the Near East, Russian Turkestan, and peninsular India, and here a developmental sequence closely paralleling that of Europe, as well as Africa in its early stages, has been reported. Indeed, during Paleolithic times the entire western portion of Asia apparently was mainly inspired by the same technological innovations that motivated contemporary developments in Europe. In fact, many of the same fundamental techniques and types of tools are common to both regions. On this basis, the region encompassed by the Near Eastern lands may be considered in a sense as a southeasterly extension of a very much larger province. Finally, north-central Asia, which apparently was not occupied until toward the close of the Upper Pleistocene, has produced materials the affinities of which can be traced to both of the major provinces. Although the "Western" increment is dominant, the occurrence of pebble tools at sites in this region attests the extremely late survival of the ancient pebble-tool tradition of the Far East.

THE CHOPPER/CHOPPING-TOOL TRADITION OF SOUTHERN AND EASTERN ASIA

Uninfluenced by contemporary innovations in Africa, Europe, and western Asia, the archaic and very primitive tradition of making implements of the chopper and chopping-tool varieties either on pebbles or roughly tabular blocks persisted in the Far East as long as the practice of making stone tools survived. In Africa, as previously stated, such pebble-tool developments as the Kafuan, the Oldowan, and the pre-Stellenbosch are widespread and first appear in deposits laid down before the close of the Lower Pleistocene. Although human remains from Java show that man was extant at this time in Asia, no artifactual materials older than the Middle Pleistocene have yet come to light. Now the distinguishing feature of the various regional assemblages found in several sections of southern and eastern Asia is not the presence of a limited range of certain very old and fundamental types of tools; rather it is the absence of the two most distinctive features of the various Lower and Middle Paleolithic assemblages of the west. These are (a) the Abbevilleo-Acheulian cycle of hand-ax development and (b) the intimately associated prepared striking-platform/tortoise-core, or Levalloisian, technique. In such intermediate regions as northwestern India a certain degree of overlap and fusion of the two basic technological patterns occurs, since bifacial core implements and Levalloisian-type flakes of Western type are found together with numerous pebble tools reminiscent of those from China and Burma. Below is presented a summary of the sequences in the several regions of southern and eastern Asia under discussion.

BURMA

In the terrace gravels of the Irrawaddy Valley of upper Burma a complex known as the "Anyathian" has been recognized, in which hand-axes are absent. Throughout, the Anyathian is characterized by single-edged core implements made of fossil wood and silicified tuff: choppers, chopping tools, and hand-adzes. In addition, there is a series of large crude flake implements with plain high-angle striking-platforms, comparable with those found in other parts of the world at the same general time horizon, but normally associated with early types of hand-axes. For the Early Anyathian is present in three distinct horizons of the gravels exposed on the two highest terraces of the ancestral Irrawaddy, which are of

Middle Pleistocene age. The Late Anyathian, a direct development from the earlier assemblages, is characterized by smaller and better-made core and flake artifacts, including such specialized types as true scrapers and points. It is found *in situ* in the fourth Irrawaddy terrace and is Upper Pleistocene in date.

CHINA

Current information concerning early man in China during the Middle Pleistocéne is based exclusively on the evidence from the well-known site of Choukoutien, a village at the base of a small limestone hill some 37 miles southwest of Peking. This hill contains an enormously rich series of fissure deposits, three of which were occupied during the interval of time roughly corresponding with the Second Glacial (Mindel), Second Interglacial (Mindel-Riss), and Third Glacial (Riss) stages in terms of the Alpine sequence. These are known as localities 13, 1, and 15. The single artifact from locality 13 is a small pebble tool and is the oldest evidence thus far discovered of human occupation in this part of the world. Associated with the remains of Peking Man (*Sinanthropus*) at the important locality 1 site, a large series of choppers and chopping tools has been described. These are of archaic type and made on river pebbles or other natural pieces of stone; they are associated with a quartz flake industry which includes smaller types of implements, especially scrapers and points. Large hearths occur throughout the deposits, demonstrating that *Sinanthropus* was familiar with the making and use of fire. The third Lower Paleolithic locality, No. 15 of the Choukoutien fissures, has yielded a series of somewhat better-made artifacts than those from locality 1, but nonetheless manufactured by employing the same basic techniques of stone-working which resulted in the production of pebble tools, on the one hand, and quartz flakes, on the other. It is apparent that this complex, known as the "Choukoutienian culture," forms an integral part of the chopper/chopping-tool tradition of eastern Asia.

JAVA

In addition to the famous discoveries of *Pithecanthropus* and other very primitive types of hominids, the former presence of early man on this island is attested by the occurrence of a large number of crude stone artifacts of Lower Paleolithic type from a site just north of Patjitan in south-central Java. Hence this assemblage is known as the "Patjitanian." The main types of implements consist of single-edged choppers, chopping tools, and hand-adzes, manufactured from various silicified rocks, that can scarcely be distinguished from those found in Burma and China. Primitive flakes, with unprepared striking-platforms at a high angle with the long axis of the implement, also occur here. In addition, there is an interesting series of pointed artifacts, including proto-hand-axes and crude hand-axes, the former being unifacial tools (i.e., worked on only one surface), whereas the latter are true bifacial implements. The presence of this hand-ax series in the Patjitanian may be accounted for as either (*a*) the independent development of tools of this type in Java or (*b*) some sort of diffusion or influence from peninsular India, where tools of this type are very common. The absence of hand-axes in Burma and Malaya tends to rule out the latter as a possibility. In defense of the former, all one can say is that a convincing argument can be put forward on typological grounds suggesting that tools of the hand-ax type were independently evolved in Java. But until there is something approaching stratigraphy to go on, it is only possible to speculate. It is a cardinal fact, however, that to date, noth-

ing has been reported from Java attributable to the Levalloisian prepared striking-platform/tortoise-core technique. This evidence shows that the Patjitanian should be included in the larger culture province of southern and eastern Asia which existed during Middle Pleistocene times.

MALAYA

In the Middle Pleistocene tin-gravels of Perak, northern Malaya, a large series of Lower Paleolithic types of implements made of quartzite was discovered in 1938. These occur at a place called Kota Tampan and therefore are referred to as the "Tampanian" culture; they are almost indistinguishable from those found near Patjitan in Java, briefly discussed above.

INDIA

Certain of the Paleolithic assemblages from this vast region demonstrate that during Paleolithic times it was a marginal area intermediate between the two main provinces of western Asia, on the one hand, and southern and eastern Asia, on the other, from the point of view of the fundamental traditions employed in the manufacture of stone tools. In the Punjab Province of northwestern India assemblages of implements characteristic of both the chopper/chopping-tool and the hand-ax/Levalloisian flake complexes are found. In this latter area the earliest tools, which are of Second Glacial age (the so-called "Punjab Flake Industry"), consist of large, crude, heavily worn flakes. This development is followed in the Second Interglacial stage by the Early Soan culture, on the basis of the evidence from a series of sites in the Indus and Soan valleys. Pebble tools, including choppers and chopping tools, as well as flake implements, are characteristic. The latter, massive and crude in the early phases of the Soan, develop into forms described as "proto-Levalloisian." In part contemporary with this fundamentally "Eastern" complex is a series of hand-axes of Abbevillian and Acheulian type that recall not only European and African examples but also those of the Madras region of peninsular India. To date, no clearly stratified site has been found in northwestern India to indicate which of the two basic complexes—the Abbevilleo-Acheulian or the Soan—was the earlier in the Punjab. During Upper Pleistocene time the Late Soan is found. Evolved types of pebble tools and a wide range of flake artifacts produced by the prepared striking-platform/tortoise-core technique are typical. In addition, a few parallel-sided flake blades occur in the Late Soan.

Peninsular India is extremely prolific of Paleolithic localities, and invariably the artifactual materials include hand-axes, cleavers, and flake tools that are very reminiscent of assemblages from South and East Africa. But the actual dating and relative chronology of these sites is very little known; indeed, here Pleistocene geology has lagged far behind archeological discovery. As the result of field investigations undertaken during recent years, reports on collection from some eight or nine main areas are available. Admittedly, this is an impressive beginning, but a very great deal more basic work remains to be done. Since the sequence in the Madras region is reasonably well known, a brief summary of the evidence from Vadamadurai and Attirampakkam—the two richest sites—will be presented.

The oldest material comes from Vadamadurai, where the entire sequence is represented. It includes a series of heavily rolled and patinated flakes and Abbevillian-type hand-axes of crude outline and exhibiting deep, irregular flake scars. These are found in a deposit of boulder conglomerate. On typological grounds the next series may be compared with the Early Acheulian; it

also comes from the boulder conglomerate horizon but is far less patinated than the Abbevillian group. The flakes in this series exhibit less cortex on the upper surface and more primary flaking on the core prior to detachment than is true of the older specimens. From detrital laterites overlying the boulder conglomerate a typical Middle Acheulian assemblage has been described. Some of the associated flakes show definite signs of retouch. The next younger materials are found in the nonlaterized deposits carried on three terraces, which were formed during Upper Pleistocene times but cannot be more precisely dated on the basis of the available evidence. Evolved forms of flat-sectioned hand-axes of Upper Acheulian type with more pronounced secondary working of the edges are found in these terraces at both Vadamadurai and Attirampakkam, together with cleavers, tortoise cores, and flakes with faceted butts. The typical cleavers have parallelogrammic cross-sections produced by the so-called "side-blow" technique; these are practically identical with examples from Stellenbosch V of the Vaal Valley in South Africa and from the site of Tashenghrit in North Africa. Hand-axes with an S-twist also merit special mention. The cores exhibit very regular and even working, while the flake tools have faceted striking-platforms with much primary flaking on the upper surface in the best Levalloisian tradition. Among the types of flake implements, there are some side-scrapers and triangular points definitely retouched for use.

More northerly sites, such as those in the Narbada Valley, in Mayurbhanj, and the Gujarat, have yielded hand-axes associated with cleavers and flakes, similar to the Madras localities. And, together with these characteristic Lower Paleolithic forms, there are pebble tools reminiscent of the Soan complex of the Punjab. In other words, the ancient tool-making tradition of the Far East persisted here, just as it did in northwestern India. On this basis it seems likely that old deposits will ultimately be found in this area containing only choppers and chopping tools made on pebbles.

One problem concerning Old Stone Age developments in India that still remains obscure is what happened here during Upper Paleolithic times. From the Krishna Valley, Kurnool District, Madras, and from Khandivili, near Bombay, true blade industries with burins and other characteristically Upper Paleolithic types have been described. But, as yet, all one can say with regard to dating these assemblages is that they appear to be younger than the last pluvial episode and older than the earliest microlithic assemblages, which have a wide distribution in India in association with deposits of sub-Recent age. In many respects the latter situation is very reminiscent of that found in the Near East, Europe, and Africa; in fact, some of the Indian microlithic assemblages are very suggestive of the Wilton. In any case, before any consecutive picture of Paleolithic developments in India can be presented, much intensive work remains to be done. It is therefore encouraging to note that an active research program has been implemented which will inevitably yield substantial results.

THE NEAR EAST

In the western portion of Asia a Paleolithic succession very closely paralleling that of Europe has been reported, but no synthesis of the materials as a whole has ever appeared. The best stratigraphy thus far reported in detail is that revealed at a series of three caves in the Mount Carmel range, south of Haifa in northern Palestine, excavated in the early 1930's under the direction of Dorothy Garrod in the Wadi el-Mugharet, the Valley of the Caves. Three other very fine stratified sites have been dug subsequently—Ksâr 'Akil (near Beirut, Republic of Lebanon), Jabrud (north of Damascus, Syria) and Umm Qatafa (in the Judaean Desert of southern Palestine), but only the Mount Carmel sites can be considered within the compass of the present paper.

The oldest horizon yields a crude flake industry reminiscent of the Tayacian of western Europe. This, in turn, is overlain by an Upper Acheulian assemblage, including typical pear-shaped hand-axes and a large series of flake tools. A small proportion of these flakes exhibits prepared striking-platforms, just as in the case of the Upper Acheulian of the Nile Valley and the Kharga oasis. The next younger horizon is 7.10 meters thick, and it yielded over 44,500 artifacts of developed Acheulian or Micoquian type, hand-axes comprising 16 per cent of the total. The flake tools consist of a wide range of scraper types, and some of them were struck from tortoise cores with characteristically prepared striking-platforms. A surprising discovery in this horizon is the presence of a small number of blade points of the Châtelperron and Audi types of Europe, together with an increment of other types of true blade tools. The associated fauna indicates that a warm, almost tropical, climate with a heavy rainfall prevailed, which gives way to relatively drier conditions in the following level. The latter contains the Lower Levalloiso–Mousterian, in association with which a series of Neanderthaloid burials was discovered by McCown at the Mugharet es-Skhūl, the smallest of the three Mount Carmel caves. On the basis of the available dating evidence, these can be correlated with the Würm I/II Interstadial in terms of Alpine chronology.

Although a few hand-axes exist in the Lower Levalloiso-Mousterian, the industry is definitely in the prepared striking-platform/tortoise-core tradition. In Europe it would be called Mousterian of Levalloisian facies, on the basis of Bordes's terminology. The overlying Upper Levalloiso-Mousterian yields a somewhat more developed assemblage, but the two subdivisions are basically the same, the leading types being side-scrapers and points. This complex, recently reported by Coon from several localities in Iran, is very widespread throughout the Near East, including Anatolia, Iraq, and Arabia. Furthermore, it presents close analogies with contemporary developments in Egypt.

Next in the Mount Carmel sequence, the next level, called "Lower Aurignacian," yields various types of small, delicate blade tools, including points of Châtelperron type. This is overlain by two horizons of fully developed Middle Aurignacian of classic type. Here steep, keeled, and nose scrapers, small spiky points, end-of-blade scrapers, and a variety of burin types predominate. Comparable industries occur at several sites in the Caucasus and from the middle horizon of Siuren I in the Crimea. At the Mugharet el-Wad the true Middle Aurignacian is overlain by Atlitian, which represents a specialized development based on the Middle Aurignacian tradition. Then there is a break in the sequence, the next occupants of the site being the Natufians, who introduced a microlithic technique, including multi-hafted sickle blades, presumably used for harvesting wild grains.

In addition to Palestine, industries very reminiscent of the Middle Aurignacian of Europe are found in Syria, the Lebanon, and Anatolia. But no true blade complex has yet been identified in Iran, although Coon's material from the Hotu Cave on the southern shore of the Caspian Sea apparently dates from terminal Pleistocene times, and presumably the same is true of Garrod's

"extended Gravettian" from Zarzi in eastern Iraq. In any case the Upper Paleolithic materials thus far brought to light in the Near East give one the impression that at this horizon this region should be regarded as a southerly extension of the Eurasiatic blade-using complex rather than as one of the centers where the latter developed. Indeed, no convincing developmental sequence has been found, and the complex as a whole is entirely lacking in Egypt until Mesolithic times.

CENTRAL ASIA

In central Asia significant Paleolithic discoveries have been made in recent years. In Turkmenia surface finds of Acheulian-type hand-axes have been announced from a site 25 miles east of Krasnovodsk, while in Uzbekistan several Mousterian localities have been excavated, the most important of which is Teshik-Tash. This cave is in the Gissar Mountains, near Baisun, approximately 90 miles south of Samarkand. Here a Neanderthal child's burial was discovered associated with five (possibly six) pairs of horns of the Siberian mountain goat. The occurrence of a fully developed Mousterian assemblage, including a few flakes of classic Levalloisian type, in this remote area demonstrates how very widely this complex was distributed during Upper Pleistocene times. No justification whatsoever, on the basis either of the geological or of the paleontological evidence, can be found to support the claim put forward by the Russians that the Teshik-Tash occupation dates from Middle Pleistocene (Mindel-Riss) times.

SIBERIA

Between the Ob Valley, near Tomsk, on the west and the Baikal region on the east (including Transbaikalia and the upper Lena Valley) over 65 localities of Late Glacial and Early Postglacial age have been investigated. Probably the oldest group of these is later than the maximum of the Würm III (Bühl) substage in terms of the Alpine glacial sequence, and hence roughly corresponds in age with the Magdalenian of western Europe. But the age of the youngest group, classed as Mesolithic by the Russian archeologists, is unknown; very likely they belong to the Boreal or even the Early Atlantic interval of the Baltic succession, since associated with them occurs a modern type of fauna. On the other hand, the wooly rhinoceros and the mammoth are present at the oldest stations, together with other cold forms. The former becomes extinct in the next stage, and the reindeer is very abundant. At the third group of localities the mammoth is extinct, while such tundra forms as the arctic fox and the Saiga antelope have now migrated from the region. Finally, only modern forms are found at the youngest sites, as stated above.

The archeological material from the Siberian loess stations is a curious mixture of (*a*) blade tools, together with antler, bone, and ivory artifacts, of classic Upper Paleolithic type; (*b*) points and scrapers made on flakes of "Mousterian" aspect; and (*c*) pebble tools representing a survival of the ancient chopper/chopping-tool tradition of the Far East. At certain sites the *a* and *b*, or archaic, forms may run as high as 65 per cent of the total series, although found in direct association with such specialized types of bone tools as awls and needles, as well as beads and pendants of bone and ivory. Remains of semisubterranean dwellings with sloping sides and centrally located hearths occur here, just as at Upper Paleolithic sites on the South Russian Plain. Another "western" feature is the female statuary in bone; twenty of these objects were found at one site—Mal'ta (about 54 miles from Irkutsk). At Verkholenskaia Gora (near Irkutsk) several large bifacially flaked laurel-

leaf points were found, together with a typical assemblage of stone, bone, and antler tools, including barbed bone points, in association with an essentially modern type of fauna. Indeed, the most striking feature of this Siberian Paleolithic is the fact of its relatively late survival. In some localities it actually occurs in the uppermost layers of the loess immediately below a horizon of humus containing Neolithic camp sites.

ORDOS REGION OF NORTHERN CHINA

In the very north of Mongolia a few late Upper Paleolithic stations belonging to the Siberian complex have been reported, but from elsewhere in this vast territory there are only sporadic surface finds doubtfully referable to the Paleolithic on a typological basis. Immediately to the south, however, in the great bend of the Yellow River, several very prolific localities were investigated in the 1920's. These materials are associated with demonstrably Upper Pleistocene deposits. Originally classified as "Moustero-Aurignacian," it is now quite apparent that the Paleolithic of the Ordos has much in common with that of the Yenisei-Baikal region of Siberia; for comparable examples of blade implements are found here in direct association with points and scrapers of Mousterian-like appearance and pebble tools of Choukoutienian tradition. But the actual dating and relative chronology of these sites involve many problems, and a great deal more intensive work of a joint archeological-geological nature is needed before it will be possible to reach final conclusions. Also the problem of terminology will have to be considered sooner or later, for the Ordos and Siberian materials simply do not conform with any Upper Paleolithic assemblages thus far described from other regions of the Old World.

GENERAL CONSIDERATIONS

On the basis of the foregoing, one is perhaps justified in asking how the data pertaining to the nature of the relationships between the various tool-making traditions of the Old World Paleolithic can ever be composed into any sort of a rational scheme. It is obvious that this problem is of basic importance, since it strikes at the shackles of several subjective and completely unwarranted assumptions that have been and are being made by workers in the field of Paleolithic archeology. The most fundamental of these concerns the significance of the various complexes with which we are dealing. Are we, in point of fact, actually studying extinct cultures, for is not our material inevitably reduced to the most imperishable vestiges of the material equipment of the different groups of very primitive hunting peoples which occupied various regions of the globe during Pleistocene times? In the light of this approach, one may indeed wonder if we can ever compose our meager data into a pattern which can be dignified by the term "culture." The time has come, however, to recognize the fallacy in the thinking of the school which seeks some sort of biological interpretation for the bewildering new array of primitive Stone Age assemblages of tools that are being constantly augmented by fresh discoveries. Those who champion this approach attribute changes registered in a particular tool-making tradition at a given point in its development or evolution to contact, or even to the actual merging of two or more divergent evolutionary lines. One could even quote instances in which it has been assumed that two totally distinct tool-making traditions have fused in some sort of a matrimonial alliance. The results of these instances of hybridization are, of course, manifest in the literature by various hyphenated terms, some of which have been mentioned in this paper. Although in many instances an extremely plausible case can be made in defense of the latter practice, it is simply begging the issue, for, causally, the arguments may be simply reduced to typological flimflam. Indeed, identification and definition by the typological approach alone ignore every possible cultural interpretation, and we are left with the curious spectacle of tools interacting among themselves. But, in the final analysis, it must be admitted that, except in very broad terms, we know as yet virtually nothing concerning (a) the origin and diffusion of the technological entities with which we are dealing, (b) the kind and degree of interplay that occurs when and if two specific tool-making traditions seem to come into contact with each other in a given region, and (c) the relationships of the main technological processes employed in the manufacture of stone tools and weapons by early men to one another in time and space. In this connection, it is of significance to note that *all* the fundamental processes used by Paleolithic man in Europe to produce tools are being used today, or have been employed during recent times, by the Australian aborigine, although admittedly the forms of the completed artifacts are quite different.

It is clearly apparent that the principles involved in the diffusion and continuity of a certain tool-making tradition cannot be conceived of in terms of the laws of heredity in the genetic sense of the biologist. For they are not passed on from one generation to another by procreation but by instruction and education. Possibly in some instances the intellectual capacity of a given group of Paleolithic hunters may not have been equal to mastering a certain technological development, but this seems very unlikely. In regions where a specific tool-making tradition of an archaic type persisted, such as in the case of the chopper/chopping-tool tradition of southern and eastern Asia, it is very much more likely that this occurred because of a failure of more advanced techniques to diffuse into the area than because the primitive types of mankind who lived there during Middle Pleistocene times were incapable of understanding the new and improved methods that had been and were being developed elsewhere in the Old World. Broadly speaking, Paleolithic archeology is a study of man's progressive ability to utilize and manufacture tools from raw materials supplied by nature, regardless of what tool-making tradition is dominant. Since there is at present no evidence available to indicate that differences in the material culture and behavior of different racial groups is in any sense of biologic origin, it follows that there is no justification for making an exception to this principle in the case of studies relating to fossil man.

A healthy science is one in which there is continuous re-evaluation of the problem in the light of present evidence and application of this re-evaluation to practice and terminology. As humans we think in terms of the labels we put on things. But if the labeling system does not keep up with thought, it is demonstrably a short time before thought ceases. Paleolithic archeologists are neither the only nor the worst offenders in this respect; however, the shortcomings of such fields as mammalogy need not concern us here. Because we deal with concrete physical entities—the stone artifacts made by men who lived many thousands of years ago—there is always a strong temptation to let the objects fascinate us today, just as they did the nineteenth-century collectors. Putting the label on is only half the game; taking it off again is the other half.

Notwithstanding the fact that their field is a humanistic discipline, Paleolithic archeologists must resort to the natural sciences both for chronological

evidence and for indications of past conditions. For during prehistoric times, just as in the historic range, environmental and geographical factors played a dominant role in conditioning the behavior of various early (or primitive) groups of mankind. Indeed, from the point of view of the development of man's material culture in the archeological sense of the term, these factors, including climate, soil, flora, fauna, natural resources, and topography, should be considered as having provided the stage—scenery, backdrops, lighting, etc.—on which the human drama has been played ever since the emergence of the first primitive hominids from the ancestral primate stock. In a sense, therefore, typology is the joint product of cultural tradition and environment, both of which are constantly changing factors. However, the picture is far more complex, since the rate of change and the degree of interplay between man's cultural achievements and the environment to which he was ever struggling to adapt himself and on which he was dependent for his livelihood have been far from constant. The fact that these variables exist only serves as a further reminder that Paleolithic archeology always is to be regarded as a humanistic discipline.

A survey of the available literature from a historical point of view will demonstrate clearly that the reaction of early man to fundamental changes in stage and setting, which repeatedly occurred during Pleistocene time, has not proceeded at a uniform or even predictable rate. The sum total of the data thus far brought to light bearing on the various Middle and Upper Paleolithic complexes of the Old World makes the basis for this observation abundantly clear. Certain significant facts bearing on this problem have been discussed in this paper; here the question of the possible extent of environmental influence on cultural developments during the earlier periods will be briefly considered. In this regard Dixon's (1928) observation that "the dependence of culture on environment and the closeness of correlation between them is greatest in the lower stages of cultural growth" is directly applicable. Indeed, this is the very essence of the problem: Paleolithic archeology cannot be divorced from its background of the natural sciences without denying it the key to the reconstruction and interpretation, in so far as possible, of human activities of the past. Although few Paleolithic archeologists today would disagree with this concept, it was not appreciated by the early workers in the field, who seem to have felt that their job had been completed as soon as they had produced an orderly classification and description of their material and compared it in a superficial and completely subjective manner with analogous collections from elsewhere in the region. Thus the underlying cause of the dilemma in which the subject finds itself at present is the direct result of the shortcomings of the purely formal taxonomic approach. Indeed, many instances could be cited demonstrating how the data have been abstracted from their real context in order to comply with the preconceptions of those who adhere to this system.

In that Paleolithic archeology is dependent on the natural sciences in several fundamental respects, the dividing line between the two fields cannot be clearly defined. Admittedly, man himself is both a natural and a social being. Along with the higher apes, he has inherited certain physical attributes from a common paleo-anthropoidal ancestral stock, but no one can deny that the degree of divergence between man and apes is tremendous. One of the basic reasons for this has been the capacity of the human organism to invent and develop a material culture—to conceive of and manufacture a varied assortment of tools to assist him in his struggle for survival. The archeological record demonstrates that no other single factor has played a comparably fundamental role in the emergence of man as the only mammal which today has become almost entirely liberated from the limiting factors imposed by environmental and geographical conditions. It is therefore the direct result of his ability to apply common sense and reason to the solution of a given problem and, once having arrived at this solution, to be able to impart the knowledge and experience thus obtained to others of his kind which sets the study of early man in a realm apart from the disciplines governing the natural sciences. But, by forming an alliance with the latter, Paleolithic archeologists can relate their materials not only in time but also to the total environmental picture. Ultimately it may even be possible to postulate within certain limits how the objects from the older horizons could have been employed. Certainly, there is much to be found out regarding what they were not used for, especially on the Lower Paleolithic level of development. In any case, owing to the very generalized nature of these earlier assemblages, direct typological comparison for historical purposes seems to be a completely sterile approach.

In addition to environment, there are other basic factors to be considered, three of which have been interacting throughout the entire span of Paleolithic development: (a) the need for a given type of tool, which may have been invented in several places at different times or abandoned if it became useless; (b) the inherent properties of the raw material available for implement manufacture; (c) the extreme degree of conservatism of early man with regard to the technological traditions that he followed in his daily routine, which, in the final analysis, is the sole basis on which the various assemblages in question can be defined objectively, as Bordes has shown. But it is clear that actual cultural connections cannot be studied in a satisfactory manner until the relative dating can be determined through the medium of techniques far more refined than those now available. Since at present it is extremely difficult to establish the relative age of localities only a few miles apart, it is apparent that we are still far from this goal.

Although certain broad-scale chronological tie-ups have been proposed, we are still a very long way from objectivity in any historical reconstruction of the Paleolithic cultures of the Old World. Indeed, those who have attempted such syntheses during recent years must admit that, regardless of the validity of certain basic concepts, the assumptions on which the entire structure is erected are extremely fragile.

REFERENCES AND SELECTED BIBLIOGRAPHY

ALIMEN, HENRIETTE. 1950. *Atlas de Préhistoire*. Vol. I. Paris: N. Boubée et Cie.

BALOUT, LIONEL. 1948. "Quelques Problèmes nord-africains de Chronologie préhistorique," *Revue Africaine*, XCII, 231–62.

———. 1950. "Le Peuplement préhistorique de l'Algérie," *Documents Algériens, Série Culturelle (Préhistoire)*, No. 50.

BORDES, FRANÇOIS. 1950. "Principes d'une Méthode d'Étude des Téchniques de Débitage et de la Typologie du Paléolithique ancien et moyen," *Anthropologie*, LIV, 19–34.

———. 1951. "L'Évolution buissonnante des Industries en Europe occidentale. Considérations théoriques sur le Paléolithique ancien et moyen," *ibid.*, pp. 393–420.

BORDES, FRANÇOIS, and BOURGON, MAURICE. 1951. "Le Complexe Moustérien: Moustériens, Levalloisien et Tayacien," *Anthropologie*, LV, 1–23.

BREUIL, HENRI. 1912. "Les Subdivisions du Paléolithique supérieur et leur Signification," *Compt. rend. du Congrès International d'Anthropologie et d'Archaéologie Préhistorique, 14th Session, Geneva*. 2d ed. Lagny: E. Grevin.

———. 1939. "The Pleistocene Succession in the Somme Valley," *Proceedings of the Prehistoric Society*, n.s., V, 33–38.

BREUIL, HENRI, and KOSLOWSKI, L. 1931. "Études de Stratigraphie Paléolithique dans le Nord de la France, la Belgique et l'Angleterre," *Anthropologie*, XLI, 449–88.

———. 1932. *Ibid.*, XLII, 27–47, 291–314.

———. 1934. *Ibid.*, XLIV, 249–90.

BREUIL, HENRI, and LANTIER, R. 1951. *Les Hommes de la Pierre Ancienne (Paléolithique et Mésolithique)*. Paris: Payot.

CATON-THOMPSON, GERTRUDE. 1946a. "The Aterian: Its Place and Significance in the Palaeolithic World," *Journal of the Royal Anthropological Institute*, LXXVI, 87–130.

———. 1946b. "The Levalloisian Industries of Egypt," *Proceedings of the Prehistoric Society*, XII, No. 4, 57–120.

———. 1952. *Kharga Oasis in Prehistory*. University of London: Athlone Press.

CLARK, J. G. D. 1952. *Prehistoric Europe: The Economic Basis*. New York: Philosophical Library.

COATES, ADRIAN. 1951. *Prelude to History*. London: Methuen & Co.

DIXON, R. B. 1928. *The Building of Cultures*. New York and London: Charles Scribner's Sons.

FURON, RAYMOND. 1951. *Manuel de Préhistoire Générale*. 3d ed. Paris: Payot.

GARROD, D. A. E. 1938. "The Upper Palaeolithic in the Light of Recent Discovery," *Proceedings of the Prehistoric Society*, IV, No. 1, 1–26.

GARROD, D. A. E., and BATE, D. M. A. 1937. *The Stone Age of Mount Carmel: Excavations at the Wady el-Mughara*. Vol. I. Oxford: Clarendon Press.

GOBERT, E. G. 1950. "Le Gisement Paléolithique de Sidi Zin," *Karthago: Revue d'archéologie africaine*, I, 3–51.

GOBERT, E. G., and VAUFREY, R. 1950. *Le Capsien de l'Abri 402 à Moulaires (Tunisie)*. (Direction des Antiquitées et Arts, Tunis, "Notes et Documents," No. 12.)

GOODWIN, A. J. H. 1946. *The Loom of Pre-history: A Commentary and a Select Bibliography of the Prehistory of Southern Africa.* ("South Africa Archaeological Society Handbook Series," No. 2.)

KELLEY, HARPER. 1937. "Acheulian Flake Tools," *Proceedings of the Prehistoric Society,* III, No. 1, 15–28.

KING, W. B. R., and OAKLEY, K. P. 1936. "The Pleistocene Succession in the Lower Parts of the Thames Valley," *Proceedings of the Prehistoric Society,* n.s., II, 52–76.

LEAKEY, L. S. B. 1936. *Stone Age Africa.* London: Oxford University Press.

——. 1951. *Olduvai Gorge: A Report on the Evolution of the Hand-Axe Culture in Beds I–IV.* London and New York: Cambridge University Press.

McBURNEY, C. M. B. 1950. "The Geographical Study of the Older Palaeolithic Stages in Europe," *Proceedings of the Prehistoric Society,* XVI, 163–83.

MOVIUS, H. L., JR. 1948. "The Lower Palaeolithic Cultures of Southern and Eastern Asia," *Transactions of the American Philosophical Society,* XXXVIII, No. 4, 329–420.

——. 1949. "Old World Palaeolithic Archaeology," *Bulletin of the American Geological Society,* LX, 1443–56.

OAKLEY, K. P. 1950. *Man the Tool-Maker.* 2d ed. London: British Museum of Natural History.

PEYRONY, DENIS. 1933. "Les Industries "Aurignaciennes" dans le Bassin de la Vézère: Aurignacien et Périgordien," *Bulletin de la Société préhistorique de France,* XXX, 543–59.

——. 1936. "Le Périgordien et l'Aurignacien (Nouvelles Observations)," *ibid.,* XXXIII, 616–19.

——. 1946. "Une Mise au Point au Sujet de l'Aurignacien et du Périgordien," *ibid.,* XLIII, 232–37.

——. 1948. "Le Périgordien, l'Aurignacien et le Solutréen en Eurasie d'après les dernières Fouilles," *ibid.,* XLV, 305–28.

SAUTER, MARC R. 1948. *Préhistoire de la Méditerranée.* Paris: Payot. Contains bibliography of important works dealing with southern Europe, North Africa, Egypt, Near Eastern lands, and the Balkans.

VAN RIET LOWE, C. 1945. "The Evolution of the Levallois Technique in South Africa," *Man,* Vol. XLV, Art. 37, pp. 49–59.

——. 1948. "The Older Gravels of the Vaal," *Archaeological Survey of the Union of South Africa,* Ser. VI, pp. 19–30. Pretoria: Department of the Interior.

VAUFREY, RAYMOND. 1933. "Notes sur le Capsien," *Anthropologie,* XLIII, 457–83.

——. 1936. "Stratigraphie capsienne," *Swiatowit,* XVI, 15–34.

WATSON, WILLIAM. 1950. Review of *The Lower Palaeolithic Cultures of Southern and Eastern Asia* by H. L. MOVIUS, JR., *Man,* Vol. L, Art. 244, pp. 151–52.

ZOTZ, LOTHAR F. 1951. *Altsteinzeitkunde Mitteleuropas.* Stuttgart: F. Enke.

Old World Prehistory: Neolithic

By V. GORDON CHILDE

DISTINCTION OF NEW STONE AGE FROM OLD

In the Old World "Stone Age," the following criteria have been proposed to distinguish the Neolithic from the preceding stage: (*a*) association with a Recent, as against a Pleistocene, fauna; (*b*) the edging of cutting tools by grinding and polishing instead of mere chipping (hence *âge de la pierre polie*); (*c*) evidences of the domestication of animals and the cultivation of plants. These three criteria have been found not to coincide. Moreover, stone was still extensively used for knives, missile points, agricultural implements, and even axes in the succeeding "Bronze Age." Hence it is proposed to replace the geological and technological criteria *a* and *b* by an economic one, based on *c* but adjusted to preserve a contrast with the next archeological stage. In the following, Neolithic means "a self-sufficing food-producing economy."

CONCRETE EXAMPLE

This definition may appropriately be clarified and given concrete content by a reference to Denmark, where the concept of a "stone age" was first scientifically elaborated. There relics from peat mosses and coastal shell mounds disclose a vigorous, if sparse, population of hunters, fishers, and collectors, while pollen grains preserved in successive layers of the peat illustrate progressive changes in the composition of the forests from which may be deduced consecutive climatic phases—Boreal, At-

lantic, Subboreal, etc. Now at a precise level in several bogs (1) about the end of the Atlantic phase, layers of ashes have been observed, followed by an abrupt decline in the relative frequence of tree pollen and a corresponding rise in the pollen of herbs and grasses. In the sequel tree pollen again increases, but in the exact order—first birch, then hazel, finally mixed oakwood again—that would reflect the natural regeneration of a forest ravaged by fire. But it was no "natural" forest fire. Above the ash layers the bogs show, for the first time, a little cereal pollen and that of *Plantago,* a weed of cultivation. Moreover, from the relevant levels of some bogs and sporadically from certain contemporary shell mounds have been recovered pottery vases, very different in technique and form from those made by the old hunter-fishers, and in these sherds have been observed casts of grains—of barley and of wheat (*Triticum monococcum, T. dicoccum*). A few bones of sheep or goats and of small, and so presumably domesticated, cattle turn up in the same contexts.

So the fires, marked by the ash layers, were lit by farmers carving out for themselves patches of tilth and pasture in the primeval forest. The ashes mark the first colonization of Danish soil by food-producers—the local "Neolithic Revolution." On the other hand, the subsequent regeneration of the forest, wiping out the little clearing, could not have happened, had the colonists possessed substantial flocks and herds to nibble off young trees. It implies rather a simple rural economy like the *jhumming* of the hill tribes in Assam today. By fire, plots are cleared of small trees and scrub. The soil, fertilized by the ashes, is tilled with hoes until exhausted and then abandoned, the whole cycle being repeated elsewhere.

Of course, the new economy thus initiated did not originate in Denmark, since the cereals and animals on which it was based are not native to the zone of temperate forests. The noble grasses from which cereals are sprung probably grew wild in the Mediterranean and subtropical zones, and there, too, wild sheep have existed until the present day. The events in Denmark, just described, are therefore rather distant echoes of a revolution that must have been completed several centuries earlier to the southeast. Nevertheless, we can follow the development of that economy through three periods (termed locally Early, Middle, and Late Neolithic) marked by hundreds of burials richly furnished with weapons and tools of stone, but with none of metal until the beginning of the next archeological period is marked by graves containing daggers and axes and spearheads of bronze.

Still, a couple of gold or bronze trinkets and bone copies of metal pins show that the Danish Late Neolithic overlapped in time with the full Early Bronze Age in Bohemia. Four imported copper axes and a copper dagger were found with Danish pottery belonging to the Middle Neolithic phase. Even from Early Neolithic a few scraps or stray objects of copper survive. How, then, shall we fix the exact upper limit of "Neolithic"? How strictly is "self-sufficing" to be understood?

THE UPPER LIMIT OF NEOLITHIC

No known Neolithic community (save for a couple of exceptionally isolated insular groups) was, in fact, content to rely exclusively on local materials. Indeed, even in the Old Stone Age, communities in the Dordogne used Mediterranean shells as ornaments, and the troglodytes of Grimaldi on the Riviera used the vertebrae of Atlantic fish. Such an occasional employment of exotic imported materials for ornaments was almost universal in the New Stone Age—amazonite at Shaheinab (Khartoum); Red Sea and Mediterranean shells in the Fayum; *Spondylus* shells throughout the Danubian province right up to the Saale and the Middle Rhine. But ornaments are obviously luxuries which, without impairing the economy at all, could be dispensed with. However, tools, too, were often made of exotic materials; thus obsidian knives were used far from any volcano at Sialk I, Hassuna, all over the Aegean throughout the local Neolithic, in Apulia, etc. Middle Neolithic Danubians on the Meuse sometimes used Niedermendig lava from the Moselle for querns. Such materials might, of course, be won and fetched by periodical expeditions sent out by the consuming group, as is done by contemporary Neolithic tribes in Melanesia and even less advanced Australians.

On the other hand, the Neolithic settlers on Lipari (2) must surely have chosen this otherwise uninviting volcanic islet partly at least to satisfy a demand for obsidian by their equally Neolithic cultural kinsmen in Apulia and Sicily. The axes made from Langdale rock (from Cumberland), found in southern England and Scotland, were hardly quarried by expeditions sent from Wiltshire or the Lothians. Rock for axes or querns might indeed be quarried by parties from farming villages, located a few miles away, but their distribution must mean some kind of intertribal barter. And flint was admittedly mined in Neolithic Europe. Even in chalk, the sinking of shafts and the cutting of galleries have inspired pictures of professional miners, encamped permanently round the shafts. Yet, while professional skill must be admitted, there is no need to postulate full-time specialist miners living by bartering their winnings for food produced by the purchasers. Nor were the obsidian knives, Niedermendig lava querns, Langdale`stone axes, or other "imports" mentioned above absolutely indispensable. The Danubian farmers on the Meuse did, in fact, generally grind their grain with grinders of local rock, though doubtless their teeth suffered. Such communities did remain potentially self-sufficient, and flint-miners would not have starved if they could find no market for their products.

The regular use of copper or bronze is taken as marking the end of the Neolithic, because, as soon as anyone had metal weapons, copper was as indispensable for the maintenance of life and independence as U^{236} is today, because full-time specialists were needed to extract and process it and because, unless you lived on a copper lode, you had to import the raw material. For regular supplies you became dependent on technicians outside the local group and must organize your economy to satisfy their demands. Neolithic self-sufficiency is over.

On the other hand, copper objects, as such, no more mark the end of the Neolithic economy than does any other exotic substance. Pins from Dadari and Sialk I, made probably from native copper, mean no more sacrifice of self-sufficiency than do the Red Sea shells and turquoise beads from the same sites. Imported copper objects, as much as imported Mediterranean shells, have been found on European sites that have always, and justly, been regarded as Neolithic. And so, of course, have copper axes and even daggers, as the Middle Neolithic Danish hoard, previously mentioned, shows. But in Denmark,

throughout the Middle and Late Neolithic, the local population was unable to secure regular supplies of metal so continued to manufacture and use stone tools and weapons, sometimes in imitation of metal forms, and made do quite successfully therewith. As a whole, that is, Denmark remained Neolithic.

At the same time, the manufacture and use of quite good stone tools did not end with the Neolithic. Copper and bronze were at first extravagantly costly. Their use was at first restricted to weapons, craft tools, and sacred objects (vessels for use in temples or by a divine king); for agricultural operations, rough work, and for the heads of missiles, stone remained in use far into the "Bronze Age." Even metal weapons, like knight's armor in medieval Europe, might remain the prerogative of a privileged minority, though the equipment would still be essential to the independence of the group as a whole. A "regular use of metal," such as should mark the end of the Neolithic, can be attested only by the findings of metal gear buried in graves or by traces of metalworking (slags, crucibles, etc.) in settlements. The one shows that metal supplies were regular enough to equip at least some members of the community with the indispensable armaments, the other that the village could support and supply a full-time professional smith.

CHALCOLITHIC TO BE INCLUDED UNDER NEOLITHIC

To introduce a special term at the point when stray objects of native, or even smelted, copper make their first appearance in any region would seem illogical. Accordingly, "Neolithic" will include in Egypt not only Merimde and Fayum but also the Badarian and Amratian and in Mesopotamia the whole Hassuna-Halaf range. It should include even Ubaid, if Frankfort's (3) view be correct that the clay axes, knives, and sickles were substitutes for, rather than toy imitations of, the metal ones they copy. It will, however, be more convenient to exclude from the present survey cultures which have once enjoyed a full "Bronze Age" economy but, cut off from sources of metal, have reverted to stone tools and weapons. On the other hand, Susa I, Byblos II, the Alcalà–Los Millares horizon in Iberia, the Kuban and Yamno cultures of South Russia, and the Beaker culture all over Europe can quite logically be ignored as being "'Bronze Age" in the above sense.

VERTICAL DIVISIONS OF THE NEOLITHIC

In so far as the use of metal, while still sporadic, marks a step in the direction of the new Bronze Age economy, it may contribute to a typological division of what was often a long period. The only proper chronological division of the Neolithic in any area must, of course, be based on stratigraphy, and, wherever evidence for such a division is available, we shall use the terms "Lower," "Middle," and "Upper" to denote consecutive divisions in a relative sequence. Where, on the contrary, typological criteria, justified, of course, by stratigraphical observations somewhere, are employed, "Early" and "Late" will replace "Lower" and "Upper." I can thus say that the Lower Neolithic of Thessaly is Late Neolithic. But, once more, even the former divisions refer only to relative chronology. In time Early Neolithic of Denmark would still be Bronze Age in Egypt.

A third vertical division with even less chronological implications will be found useful. While cereals and domestic stock can have been introduced into regions where they are not indigenous only by immigrant cultivators and breeders, once introduced, their use may have been adopted by native mesolithic hunter-fishers. Now the first

Early Neolithic cultures in the British Isles, central, and northern Europe seem to owe nothing to the local mesolithic cultures. They may therefore be termed "primary." In the sequel there emerge, side by side with such primary cultures, others which have adopted much of their economy and equipment but yet exhibit traits of the local mesolithic in a greater emphasis on fishing and the chase, in tools and weapons, and even in burial rites. These—Peterborough, Rinyo, etc., in Britain (4); Hinkelstein, Rössen, etc., in central Europe; the "Dwelling Place culture" of Sweden—will be styled "secondary." Of course, what appear locally "primary" might on a wider view turn out to be themselves "secondary." But in the present state of archeological knowledge most cultures go up to a god in the third generation like Homeric kings.

HORIZONTAL DIVISIONS OF THE NEOLITHIC

In the archeological record the Neolithic appears, from the start, split into an embarrassing multitude of cultures, distinguished most easily by the techniques, forms, and ornamentation of pottery and stone vessels, and into not many fewer by differences in house plans, industrial equipment, armaments, burial rites, fashions in dress, ritual paraphernalia, and art styles. For the self-sufficiency of local groups would of itself facilitate divergent specialization. No enumeration, still less description, of all Neolithic cultures can be here attempted. But it may be useful to indicate the main geographical regions, generally at some time forming cultural provinces, from which material for our synthetic account has been drawn: North Africa; the Nile Valley (Sudan, Upper and Lower Egypt); Palestine; Syria as far as drained into the Mediterranean; Mesopotamia, i.e., the rest of Syria and

Assyria as well as Babylonia; Cilicia; Cyprus; Crete; peninsular Greece; southern Italy (Apulia, Sicily); Malta; Iberia; western Europe (the Iberian peninsula, Switzerland, southern and northern France; Brittany; the British Isles); northern Europe (northern Germany, Denmark, southern Sweden); the Danubian löss-lands from the Meuse to the Vistula, from the Bakony to the Harz; the Ukraine; the Balkans (Save-Danube-Morava-Vardar valleys; Thrace and lower Danube); Iran; China (Kansu, Honan). Some regions, such as India or Anatolia, have been excluded for lack of authenticated relevant material. The whole Boreal zone of Eurasiatic coniferous forests and tundra has been omitted on the pretext that such belated food-producing economies as did arise there are not secondary or even tertiary Neolithic but rather secondary Bronze Age reverted. Southeast Asia is omitted on the same grounds and because no information as to the economy is available until the beginning of written history. Metal was certainly used, at least for ornaments, in the "Brahmigiri stone-axe culture" of peninsular India (5). Even the cultures of Honan and Kansu can be admitted only with reservation, since the available literature mentions hardly any genuine closed finds in which the celebrated pottery is reliably associated with other artifacts, still less with food remains.

PRIMARY ECONOMY

PLANTS CULTIVATED

In all the provinces examined, the Neolithic economy was based on the cultivation of cereals combined with stock-breeding, and, wherever adequate data are available, the only cereals cultivated in the Early Neolithic were wheat and barley (6). Of the wheats, *T. monococcum*, though the least likely to be recognized, has been reported from the Early Neolithic of western and northern Europe, of the Danubian löss lands from the Ukraine, Greece, and Mesopotamia (already at Janmo), and rather unexpectedly from the Middle Neolithic of Lower Egypt (el Omari); *T. dicoccum* (emmer) was probably cultivated equally early all over Europe and even in the Early Neolithic of the Fayum, as in the Late Neolithic (Halafian) of northern Mesopotamia. But wheats of the 42-chromosome groups have not yet been identified with certainty in any pure Neolithic context in Hither Asia, though there seems to be a little mixed with emmer in the Middle Neolithic of el Omari in Egypt, not before Middle Neolithic in Denmark, and only doubtfully in the Early Neolithic of the löss-lands and Switzerland and the Middle Neolithic of Greece. Barleys are as widespread and early as emmer. Millet (*Panicum miliacum*) was cultivated in the Ukraine, in the Lower Neolithic of Thrace (which does not look Early) and in the Late Neolithic of Macedonia, in Switzerland and in Palestine by the beginning of the local Bronze Age. A single grain of rice has been identified in a sherd from Honan of the local "Neolithic" pottery.

In addition to cereals, peas were probably cultivated in Neolithic Europe, vetch in the Middle Neolithic of Lower Egypt. Orchard husbandry is not well attested, but figs may have been cultivated in Middle Neolithic Greece, olives in southern Spain, apples in Switzerland.

DOMESTIC STOCK

All typically Neolithic sites in the Old World have yielded bones of cattle, sheep and/or goats, and pigs, though the latter seem to be missing from the Middle Neolithic Badarian of Egypt, and sheep from Yang-shao-tsun in Kansu, while only sheep and goats are mentioned in the Yamuqian of Palestine and the Khartoum Neolithic. No

economy of proved antiquity was demonstrably based on plant-cultivation
uncombined with stock-breeding. No
doubt the Natufians of Palestine did
reap some kind of grass with specialized reaping knives, and no doubt cereals grew wild around their cave homes.
But there is no evidence that it was
cereals they reaped, still less that they
were cultivated, while only game animals were eaten. So the Natufians must
provisionally rank as still "mesolithic."

Nor is there much better evidence
for stock-breeding uncombined with
cultivation. On the Upper Nile, indeed, at Shaheinab near Khartoum, the
food refuse of a group living mainly
from hunting, fishing, and collecting
included bones of a very small goat
and an equally dwarf sheep, while no
unambiguous agricultural appliances
(sickle teeth or querns) have been reported. Since, however, flint (which, if
used for reaping, acquires a characteristic gloss) was not available and the
excellent pottery has not yet been exhaustively examined for grain impressions, the negative evidence is exceptionally inconclusive. Apart from this
ambiguous Khartoum Neolithic and
still less well-dated assemblages in
North Africa, all Early Neolithic cultures were based on mixed farming.
On the other hand, in the Late Neolithic of the temperate forest zone in
Europe the emphasis shifts toward
stock-breeding and hunting to such an
extent that one might speak of a "separation of pastoral tribes from the mass
of the agricultural barbarians," but
only with the proviso that, wherever
any evidence is available, even the
"pastoral tribes" still cultivated cereals.

For the composition of the livestock,
food refuse (the only available source)
gives unreliable evidence. It is obviously more economical to kill sheep
than cows; on the other hand, in temperate Europe many calves had to be
killed, owing to lack of winter feed.
Still the high proportion of sheep or
goats reported from the earliest sites
in the Near East and the very low proportion of these animals from corresponding sites in the European forest
zone deserve attention.

HUNTING AND GATHERING

Of course, all Neolithic farmers
supplemented their diet with produce
of the chase, fishing, and collecting. In
the Lower Neolithic of the Fayum, indeed, these activities apparently still
played a major role in the economy.
On the contrary, on the Danubian löss-
lands and to a lesser degree in northern and western Europe, bones of
game and hunting equipment are relatively inconspicuous on Early Neolithic
sites; first in Middle and Late Neolithic
is a fuller exploitation of the available
wide food resources archeologically attested.

RURAL ECONOMY

Two systems of cultivation may be
distinguished in advance: (I) dry cultivation, in which the moisture required by the crop is provided by rain,
and (II) wet or irrigation cultivation,
where rivers, torrents, or springs soak
tracts of adjacent land. In a sense intermediate between I and II is the system
reported from central Asia, where
melting snows on the ranges feed seasonal springs that break out on the
lower slopes, forming temporary
marshes on which grain may be sown
to yield a reliable crop (7).

Under dry cultivation any plot will
become exhausted after one or two
croppings. The simplest reaction is to
start again on a fresh plot. The repetition of this process soon uses up all the
land conveniently accessible from a single settlement. Thereupon, the whole
settlement is transferred to a new location and the cycle repeated there. This
is termed "shifting cultivation" (1)
and, though virtually imposed by dry

cultivation, (I, 1) is sometimes today practiced by tribes relying on natural irrigation (II, 1). But even under I the exhaustion is not permanent, and restoration of the soil's fertility can be hastened in various ways, depending on climate and natural vegetation. On prairies and park lands (A) recovery can be accelerated by turning livestock onto exhausted plots (I, A, 2) and, still better, by applying farmyard manure or night soil (I, A, 3). This leads to the familiar rotation between fallow and arable (I, A, 2, or I, A, 3). In woodlands (B) the plot, originally cleared by "slash-and-burn" methods, may be allowed to revert to scrub, which after some years is burned down as at the first clearance. The ashes restore the salts removed from the surface humus by the previous crop. A systematic rotation of scrub and arable is the classical form of *Brandwirtschaft* (I, B, 2), as recently practiced east of the Baltic. Under drier conditions a repetition of slash-and-burn is likely to destroy the humus cover so far that the abandoned clearing no longer reverts to bush but is invaded by grass. The farmer can then apply system I, A, 2.

Throughout the Neolithic in the temperate forest zone of Europe, settlements seem to have been so briefly or intermittently occupied that shifting agriculture (I, B, 1) may be plausibly inferred. And in Upper Egypt the smallness of even the Middle Neolithic Badarian cemeteries suggests shifting agriculture, however the crops were watered. But in Lower Egypt even the Lower Neolithic village of Merimde was occupied, apparently continuously, through several archeological phases, while in Hither Asia tell-formation, beginning even in the Lower Neolithic of Jericho, Mersin, Jarmo, and Sialk, implies continuous habitation based presumably on some form of I, A, 2. So, too, in Crete, Greece, and the Balkans (including the lower Save, the south bank of the middle Danube, and both banks of the lower Danube) most Neolithic settlements take the form of tells, though in Apulia tell-formation has not been observed and shifting agriculture must be assumed for Lower and Middle Neolithic.

METHOD OF CULTIVATION

Since digging-sticks, hoes, and plows can be made entirely of wood, they are not likely to survive in the archeological record. In fact, the earliest actual plows (8) (from upper Italy and Denmark) or representations of plows (from Mesopotamia, Cyprus, and Egypt) belong to the Bronze Age, albeit to its initial phases. Certain heavy stone implements from the Lower Neolithic of Switzerland, Denmark, and the löss-lands have, indeed, been claimed as plow shares on the strength of marks of wear resembling those on wooden plow shares, but this interpretation is even less certain than the treatment of flaked chert and sandstone implements from Neolithic Mesopotamia as hoe blades. On the other hand, undeniable plow furrows have recently been recognized in the soil under Late Neolithic barrows in Denmark and Holland, while the yoking of oxen, presumably to draw plows, is attested in the Upper Neolithic of Switzerland (Vinelz) and in the, probably Middle, Neolithic of the eastern extension of the löss-lands in Poland (9). Hence, while plot cultivation with hoe or digging-stick, appropriate to a I, B, 1 economy, was probably the rule in the temperate forests during the earlier part of the local Neolithic, plow agriculture probably began before the Stone Age ended (at a time when processes considered above combined with climatic factors would have increased the area of grassland). But that was, of course, not before the beginning of the Bronze Age in the Mediterranean area and in Hither Asia and does not help to prove that plow agriculture was Neolithic there.

DWELLINGS

While Neolithic, like Paleolithic, men sheltered or even resided in caves, it is now known that they did not live in holes in the ground ("pit-dwellings") but built quite commodious houses of the most convenient local materials—reeds, pisé, hand-molded bricks, wattle-and-daub, split timbers, or stone (10). On the "Danubian" lösslands the earliest (Lower Neolithic) houses were gabled structures, 6–8 meters wide, but attaining a length of as much as 41 meters, though naturally subdivided like the long houses of the Iroquois or the Kayan. In the same area smaller two-roomed houses, 4.5–6 meters wide and only 6–8 meters long were more normal in the Middle Neolithic and occur also in Switzerland, the Balkans, Greece, the Ukraine, and east of the Baltic. But, in the Late Neolithic, one-roomed huts, only 4–5 meters square, became commoner both in central Europe and in Britain. In Northern Europe a different type of long structure—a row of as many as 26 cabins, each 6 meters long by 3 meters wide, all under one ridgepole—appears from the Early Neolithic.

For the Mediterranean and subtropical zones, where mud was the favorite building material, no generalizations are possible, but even in the Middle Neolithic of Hassuna we have farmhouses composed of several rooms and a courtyard. While circular structures of one kind or another are known from Neolithic Mesopotamia, Cyprus, Thessaly, the Rhineland, etc., their domestic character is in no instance quite beyond question.

FURNITURE

Wooden door frames pivoted on stone sockets in the Neolithic of Hither Asia, on socket holes in the wooden thresholds in temperate Europe. Skara Brae in Orkney shows how Neolithic dwellings, even in the distant Orkney Islands, might be comfortably furnished with fixed beds, wall cupboards, and dresser, and drained by lined channels under the floors, while models of chairs and tables are known from Greece, Thrace, and the Ukraine.

SIZE OF SETTLEMENTS

Even if practicing migratory cultivation, Neolithic farmers lived in regular villages that could be fenced to keep out animals; by Middle Neolithic, these were fortified with ditches and ramparts in western Europe, the lösslands, Greece, Apulia, Palestine, and Cilicia, while around the Alps and in England the houses were built on lake shores or in swamps. If fully explored, such settlements would provide valuable data for estimating the size of the local group and eventually the density of population; but only in temperate Europe have the published excavations been conducted on a large enough scale and with sufficient technical skill to show the number of houses in a single village (see Table 1). Certain areas, though far less reliable, do provide some data for the Near East. In the Lower Neolithic, Jarmo (Kurdistan) (11) covered 3 acres accommodating perhaps 50 houses, while Merimde in Lower Egypt occupied 6 acres. It looks, then, as if Neolithic farming was conducted by groups not exceeding 600 persons.

Long before the attested beginning of "food-production," men had achieved a respectable mastery over nature, and only those techniques will here be mentioned that were developed first or principally after the "Neolithic Revolution."

WOODWORKING TOOLS

"The polished stone celt" was once taken as the hallmark of the New Stone Age but is now known to have been used in the mesolithic of the Baltic and even in the Paleolithic of Russia. It is, however, universal in the Neolithic (save apparently at Sialk in Iran), while the sharpening of flint celts by polishing—attested from the Lower Neolithic in Egypt, Palestine, western and northern Europe—does seem really to be a Neolithic innovation. The edging of flint celts by a transverse blow—the *tranchet technique*—was, however, maintained in northern and western Europe, upper Italy, Palestine, the Kharga

or elbow-shaft (inevitable for adzes) is attested for the Lower Neolithic of Switzerland and the Middle Neolithic of northern Germany. There, mounting with the aid of antler sleeves, known in the mesolithic of western Europe, is attested and also for the löss-lands from the Lower Neolithic; perforated antler sleeves, used in the mesolithic of the Baltic, reappear in the Neolithic of Switzerland, the lower Danubian, the Middle Neolithic of Thessaly, and the Late Neolithic of northern France

TABLE 1

Period	Location	No. of Houses
Lower Neolithic.......	Löss-lands { Köln-Lindental* North Barkaert†	20 long houses 54 one-room huts
Middle Neolithic......	North Dümmer‡ {Löss-lands, Aichbühl Ukraine, Kolomiščina§	?40 one-room huts 22 two-room huts 41 two- to- three-room huts
Late Neolithic........	{Löss-lands, Goldberg Orkney, Skara-Brae	50 one-room huts 6 one-room huts

* Sangmeister, "Zum Charakter der bandkeram. Siedlung," *33 Ber. Römisch-germanisches Kommission* (Berlin, 1943–50).

† *Fra National Muscets Arbejdsmark* (Copenhagen, 1949).

‡ *Germanenerbe*, IV (1939), 230–40.

§ T. Passek, *Periodizatsiya Tripol'skikh Poseleniǐ* (Moskva, 1949).

oasis (12), and Egypt; but in the last-named province it is not certainly attested before the Gerzean "Bronze Age" and is certainly absent from the Fayum, which should be Early Neolithic.

AXES AND ADZES

Celts may be used as axes or adzes (13), and it is noteworthy that woodworkers at first displayed a strong preference for adzes in Cyprus, Greece, the Balkans, the Ukraine, all over the löss-lands, and in the Iberian peninsula, and for axes in Egypt, probably in Crete, in western Europe (north of the Pyrenees), and in the north.

SHAFTING

Besides direct mounting on a straight shaft, the mounting of axes on a knee-

and Orkney. In Early Neolithic perforated ax- or adze-heads are virtually confined to the löss-lands but appear later in Greece, the Balkans, and northwestern Europe (see "stone boring").

TEXTILES

The weaving (14) of flax (or some other vegetable fiber) is attested from Lower Neolithic on, wherever evidence can survive—actual linen from Egypt and western Europe, stone or clay spindle-whorls from Hither Asia, Greece, etc. But such whorls were not used by all Neolithic spinners—not, for instance, in the Swiss Lower Neolithic lake dwellings, which have yielded linen fabric—and perhaps served only for spinning wool. How early the latter material was spun and woven by Neolithic societies is otherwise uncertain. As for textile appliances, a horizontal loom is attested for the Amratian (Middle Neolithic) of Egypt, while there is some evidence for warp-weighted vertical looms in Neolithic Europe.

POTTERY

Pottery, an artificial substance, once regarded as distinctive of Neolithic levels, was, in fact, made by pre-Neolithic societies in Denmark and the Sudan and was, on the other hand, absent from the oldest Neolithic of Mesopotamia (Jarmo), Palestine (Jericho), and Cyprus. All Neolithic pottery was made without the aid of a true (fastspinning) wheel, several methods of freehand building being employed instead. A special kiln has been postulated, but not by all authorities, only for "painted pottery." The earliest pottery of Palestine, Mesopotamia, Iran, Cyprus, Greece, the Ukraine, and possibly Kansu was, in fact, generally fired to give a clear ground surface which might be decorated in darker paints. Such pottery occurs early with other varieties in the Balkans, Dalmatia, and Honan. It appears only in Middle (or Upper) Neolithic strata on the northern Syrian coast, in Cilicia (15) and Apulia, sporadically in Malta and Iberia. Self-colored (black to red) fabrics, on the contrary, characterize the oldest layers in Egypt, northern Syria, Cilicia, Crete, and most of Europe. A coincidence between these two kinds of fabric with arid and moist climatic regimes is obvious, but clearly only partial.

STONE-WORKING

VASES

Vessels more pretentious than mortars were ground out of stone at Jarmo and on Cyprus before vases were molded in clay, and stone vases were also used all over Hither Asia, in Egypt, and in Malta from the beginning of the local Neolithic. A few marble vases in Neolithic horizons in Greece and the Balkans may be merely imports.

BORING AND DRILLING

Stones were perforated for maceheads, etc., in the mesolithic mainly by percussion supplemented by boring; but throughout the Neolithic some sort of drill was regularly used. In the Lower Neolithic of the Danubian lösslands and, perhaps first, in the Middle Neolithic of northern Europe, a hollow drill was certainly employed.

BEADS

From early Neolithic times on in Egypt and the Near East, and in China at some stage (if Chou-chia-chai be Neolithic at all), relatively hard stones were pierced by ingenious drills with string-holes, a centimeter or so long, to form beads. Rather softer stones, like callaïs, Kimmeridge shale, and jet, were likewise drilled in the Middle or Upper Neolithic of Atlantic Europe, including the British Isles, but only amber and shell in northern and central Europe. But the Lower Neolithic Danubians' drill (16) for piercing long beads of shell was essentially the same as the oriental lapidaries' instrument.

WEAPONS

PROJECTILES

The bow as well as the spear-thrower having been widely used even in the Paleolithic, it is not surprising that flint arrowheads are common in the Lower Neolithic of Palestine, Egypt, North Africa, western and northern Europe, as well as in all the secondary Neolithic cultures of Europe. (Stone or bone arrowheads occur in China at Yang-shao-tsun and Chou-chia-chai, but apparently not with the painted Pan-shan pottery.) They are surprisingly absent from the Lower Neolithic of the central European löss-lands, the Balkans, Greece, Mesopotamia, and Iran (13). On the other hand, clay sling-bullets do occur throughout the Neolithic of Mesopotamia, Iran, Greece, and the Balkans and appear with painted pottery in the Middle Neolithic of Syria and Cyprus, in Apulia, and even in China.

MACE-HEADS

Clubs were weighted with pear-shaped or globular stone heads in the Early Neolithic of Lower Egypt, Crete, Mesopotamia, and Iran and in the Middle Neolithic of the löss-lands, western and northern Europe. A flat or disk-shaped type was, however, preferred in the Sudan, in Upper Egypt, in the Lower Neolithic of the löss-lands and in the Middle northern Neolithic, and competed with the piriform in the Late Neolithic (Ghassulian) of Palestine.

Battle-axes of stone, imitating copper versions of perforated antler weapons of mesolithic origin, were popular in northern Europe throughout the Neolithic, but appear on the löss-lands, in northwestern Europe, and in the Balkans mainly in the Late Neolithic. In Greece, Italy, Asia Minor, and Mesopotamia they seem to be "Bronze Age," though in Sumer clay models appear as early as the Ubaid horizon.

BURIAL RITES

Inhumation in a flexed or contracted attitude was almost universal in Neolithic cultures. Extended burial was, however, regularly practiced in northern Europe from the Lower Neolithic, occasionally in northwestern Europe, among some secondary Neolithic groups on the löss-lands, in the Ubaid culture of Mesopotamia, and at Chou-chia-chai in China. Cremation occurs sporadically in the earlier Secondary Neolithic of the löss-lands, in the Mid-

dle and Secondary Neolithic of the British Isles (17) and Brittany, and more widely in Late Neolithic Europe north of the Alps.

Collective burial in natural caves or in built or rock-cut chamber tombs, though practiced by the mesolithic Natufians in Palestine and normally all round the eastern Mediterranean throughout the Bronze Age, is not certainly attested there during the local Neolithic save in some sepulchral caves in Crete (18). It was, however, a general Neolithic—but not certainly "Early"—practice in Sardinia, Malta, and most of western Europe. In northern Europe the earliest dolmens built in the Lower Neolithic were probably not collective tombs (19); but by the Middle Neolithic collective burial in megalithic tombs was general. In Spain and Portugal, as in southern France, the best-known "megalithic tombs" must certainly be classed as Bronze Age, but, despite doubts expressed by Childe and Forde, some such tombs in Portugal and Almeria (20) do seem to illustrate a genuinely Neolithic economy.

The erection of a barrow to mark a single grave hardly began in northwestern Europe and the northern parts of the löss-lands before the Late Neolithic, and most such barrows are actually Bronze Age. But ring ditches, inclosing small cemeteries, have been traced back to the Middle Neolithic in the British Isles (17).

TREPANATION

Three trephined skulls come from Lower Neolithic graves on the löss-lands and two from Denmark (21). In the Late Neolithic the operation was performed with extravagant prodigality in France and surprisingly often in northern Europe and the northwestern part of the löss-lands. While the early Neolithic operations may well have been undertaken for curative purposes, the later cases must be regarded as magical.

FIGURINES

One of the most distinctive and widespread traits of the Neolithic was the manufacture in mud, baked clay, stone, chalk, bone, or ivory of female figurines. While the attitudes and styles vary considerably and their functions were not everywhere necessarily the same, some such figures do occur in the Lower Neolithic of Egypt, Palestine, Syria, Mesopotamia, Iran, Cyprus, Cilicia, Crete, Greece, the western Balkans, the Ukraine, Spain, and, albeit rarely, Britain and France. On the central European löss-lands and in Thrace such figures are exceptional in the Lower Neolithic but very abundant in the Middle ranges. In northern Europe they seem unknown, and also, curiously enough, in southern Italy. In the Late Neolithic, female figurines went out of favor in most of temperate Europe, though they were still made in the Balkans and the Near East.

Male figures, on the other hand, are comparatively rare and mostly Late Neolithic. Phalli occur in Lower Neolithic England and Middle Neolithic Thrace. Models of cattle and other beasts, probably domesticated, and sometimes even of houses, chairs, and tables are often associated with female figurines, save in Egypt and Spain.

AMULETS AND "SEALS"

As magico-religious must rank also beads of stone or ivory carved in the forms of birds, animals, etc., which were early popular in Hither Asia, Egypt, Malta, and Iberia. Ax amulets appear in Neolithic contexts in Crete, Lower Egypt, Malta, northern France, and Brittany, but elsewhere seem rather to be "Bronze Age." On the other hand, button-shaped or other beads, bearing an engraved design and therefore capable of being used as seals, appear

already in the Late Neolithic Halafian culture of Mesopotamia and enjoyed a wide vogue in the immediately succeeding Bronze Age horizons of Iran, Syria, Crete, and Asia Minor. A few in stone go back to the Lower Neolithic in peninsular Greece, while clay copies were current in the Lower Neolithic of the western Balkans and the Ukraine and in the Middle Neolithic of the Danubian löss-lands and Thrace; debased versions reached Apulia and Liguria.

TEMPLES

In the Neolithic levels of Jericho in Palestine and of Eridu and Gawra in Mesopotamia, excavation has exposed buildings which by their position on the site of, and by their resemblance to, historical temples must rank as the dwellings of deities. A trinity of mud effigies was, in fact, found in that at Jericho. Some circular buildings in Neolithic Mesopotamia, Cyprus, and Greece may also have been sacred, while the Neolithic Maltese certainly erected elaborate megalithic temples, but nothing compels us to regard these as residences of deities conceived in human form. Still less can any such inference be drawn from offerings of animals, pots, amber beads, stone implements, etc., deposited in bogs in northern Europe (19) from mesolithic times on or from the more dubious "votives" reported from Cretan caves

CHIEFTAINSHIP

Neither domestic architecture nor funerary practices offer any conclusive evidence for the existence of kings in the Near East during the local Neolithic or in temperate Europe until the late Neolithic. Even Nazi excavators looked in vain for a "Führerhaus" in the Lower Neolithic villages of the löss-lands. In the Late Neolithic, however, on the northern part of the löss-lands and in northern Europe, a few barrows covering mortuary houses do look like tombs of chiefs. In western Europe, too, it has been argued that some "megalithic" tombs were built to contain the bones of members of royal lineages only, and it now seems possible that, in Denmark, only chiefs were buried in the Early Neolithic dolmens. Note in all these cases the prominence of pastoralism in the economy. Of course, the negative evidence is quite insufficient to disprove the existence of chiefs but, as far as it goes, may be used as an argument against concentration of economic power.

ART

The art of Neolithic peasants, in contrast to that of Paleolithic hunters and fishers, was notoriously mainly symbolic. Representations of persons, animals, and things are curiously rare. Most widespread are the clay models (noted above), but these can in no case be called lifelike, and it is often hard to be sure what the artist intended to depict. Badarian and Amratian carvings of beasts and birds, the figures painted on Amratian vases, and the undatable engravings and paintings on rock surfaces in the deserts from the Atlantic to the Red Sea and beyond are indeed perfectly recognizable, but are far less lifelike than the Paleolithic cave drawings of France and Cantabria or the tomb paintings of Old Kingdom Egypt or the proto-historic slate palettes and ivories. Frankfort considers the aim to have been naturalistic, only the execution incompetent. But incompetence alone will not explain the representations of the human figure always less lifelike than those of animals. Even the best statuettes are no more like portraits of actual human beings than are Maori ancestor figures or Haida totem poles. Portraits of real men appear abruptly, at the same moment as writing, on the Narmer palette and the marble head from Uruk-Warka.

ORIGIN OF THE NEOLITHIC REVOLUTION

The conclusions of botanists and zoölogists on the probable habitats of ancestral wheats, barleys, and sheep combine with the scanty direct evidence from the excavations at Jericho, Jarmo, Belt Cave (22), and Hassuna to limit the possible cradles of farming. Most Neolithic grains examined bear witness to a long period of cultivation and selection; only from Jarmo do the wheats approximate to wild forms. The Neolithic economy, based upon a combination of cereal cultivation and stockbreeding, most likely took shape somewhere between the Nile and the Jaxartes. Relying, no doubt, on migratory dry cultivation (I, 1) at first, it could in this ecological zone easily develop a tillage-pasture alternation (I, A, 2), since perennial water supplies are rare enough to discourage nomadism. In Hither Asia this stage had been reached at least by the Middle Neolithic of Hassuna. Theoretically, of course, migratory wet cultivation (II, 1) might be just as old. But sedentary farming settlements based on irrigation (II, 2) are not certainly detectable until the Late Neolithic Halafian (Eridu) and Amratian.

THE "URBAN REVOLUTION"

Theoretically, any Neolithic community must have been able to produce a surplus above the minimum required to enable the group to feed itself and its offspring. In fact, the "imports" already found on Early Neolithic sites do imply such a surplus. But it was irrigation cultivation in the Tigris-Euphrates delta (Sumer) and on the Nile that first yielded a reliable social surplus for "trade" or any other purpose. In Sumer the surplus was concentrated, perhaps from the first colonization of the delta, in the granaries and fields of temples that certainly were founded in the Late Neolithic. In Egypt such concentration

was demonstrably achieved only when
a war chief (who, as such, would concentrate booty in cattle) got himself
identified with the personified symbol
of group solidarity. In each case the
unprecedented accumulation of real
wealth created a new world situation—
a second economic revolution. It created an effective demand, a reliable market, for metals and all sorts of commodities not obtainable in the river
valleys. The satisfying of this demand
offered an assured livelihood to full-
time specialists and gave opportunities
even to distant communities to extract
a slice out of the Sumerian or Egyptian
accumulation. It has even been suggested that the spread of the Neolithic
economy was a by-product of this new
effective demand.

The recent discovery of genuinely
Neolithic cultures in Egypt and Hither
Asia, absolutely prior to the urban revolution and, indeed, to the first indications of the industrial use of metal
anywhere, has today deprived of any
plausibility the theory that all Neolithic
cultures were due to a reversion to the
Stone Age, i.e., to a people who had
once possessed metal tools, the techniques for their production, and the requisite economic organization, but had
for one reason or another lost these.
Some such account, indeed, may still
hold good for the Pacific and even
Southeast Asia; there are some positive
grounds for applying it to some of the
"Neolithic" colonists of Malta and to
those "secondary Neolithic" warrior
groups who seem to have played a
prominent part in spreading the Neolithic economy among the hunter-fishers
of the Boreal zone in Finland, central
Russia, and Siberia. Even in Thrace the
latest reports imply that the "Neolithic"
"Mound Culture" succeeded one of An-
atolian Bronze Age type. But in the rest
of the Old World the well-known Neolithic cultures resemble so closely the
genuinely Neolithic cultures of the

Near East that this reversion theory
may be dismissed.

Nor is it much more likely that trade
to satisfy directly or indirectly the effective demand of the urban civilizations, and to that extent using their
accumulated surplus as trading capital,
played an effective role in the primary
diffusion of the Neolithic economy—i.e.,
of the cereals, sheep, and techniques
on which it was based. Even if the diffusion of megalithic tombs in western
and northern Europe be attributed to
missionaries who were also traders from
the eastern Mediterranean, Early Neolithic farmers had certainly colonized
Denmark, probably also Britain and
France, before any such missionaries
arrived! A strong case can indeed be
made for recognizing "influence" from
the Bronze Age Orient in Late and even
Middle Neolithic cultures in temperate
Europe. (Clay objects from the Middle
Neolithic Danubian II, for instance,
really do look like copies of stone block
vases such as were current in the earliest cities of Egypt and Sumer.) But
the local Neolithic had begun before
such influence is detectable.

THE SPREAD OF THE NEOLITHIC ECONOMY

The first spread of the Neolithic
economy was presumably due to actual
movements of colonization imposed on
Early Neolithic peasants by their migratory rural economy and by their
younger children's need for fresh land.
For it is a truism in demography that
populations quickly respond to such an
enlargement of the food supply as the
Neolithic revolution offered even in its
first stages. Even communities practicing I, 2 or II, 2 must provide for their
younger sons and daughters by planting
colonies on fresh land. Sooner or later
the original bands of migrants or colonists would have been augmented by
secondary Neolithic groups, generated
by the conversion to food-production of

mesolithic hunter-fishers. But the latter would have been likely to modify the original rural economy by altering the balance between stock-breeding and cultivation or otherwise.

The primary spread of Neolithic peasants would have been by land. But, unless we admit independent foci, Cyprus, Crete, Sicily, Malta, and the northern shores of the Mediterranean can have been reached only by sea. In fact, the extensive use of materials like obsidian in Crete, peninsular Greece, Apulia, Sicily, and Malta implies a lot of Neolithic voyaging. There are so many and such close agreements between the Neolithic cultures of Sicily, the Lipari Islands, Apulia, and peninsular Greece that transmarine transmission seems unquestionable. That, too, seems the easiest way of accounting for similar agreements between the Lower Neolithic of Greece and Cyprus and the Middle Neolithic of Cilicia and Syria (Hassuna) (23). Comparable agreements can be observed between the Lower Neolithic in Sicily, Liguria, and the coasts of southern France and eastern Spain (23) and should be explained in the same way.

Were the seed grains and domestic stock conveyed by boatloads of farmers' sons seeking new land across the sea—of course, in the light of information already gathered by fishing expeditions? Or were the voyagers intending merely to camp for a season on the foreign shore in order to obtain by barter from the mesolithic natives obsidian or other commodities for the home market? In the second case the result must be called a "secondary Neolithic" culture, but otherwise the results are essentially the same. Only after the urban revolution, i.e., in the full Bronze Age, would true trading colonies, supplying the reliable civilized market and relying in the last resort on the accumulated social surplus for support, become a significant factor.

A much more formidable obstacle than the sea was presented by the ecological frontier between the Mediterranean and the temperate zones, coinciding largely with the physiographical barrier of the Pyrenees, the Alps, the Balkans, and the Taurus. I, B, 1 and I, A, 1 are different; shifting cultivation is not the same in temperate forests as on grasslands; grazing in woodlands presents problems different from grazing on prairies; houses adapted for mild winters and dry summers are unsuitable where the summers are rainy and the winters snowy. An economy, shaped under the conditions here envisaged would need very drastic adaptation to the temperate European environment. The whole morphology of the Early Neolithic cultures of the löss-lands and western and northern Europe stands in conspicuous contrast to any Greek, Cretan, or Asiatic. (The Neolithic of Honan and Kansu, where the ecological contrast is slight, despite formidable physiographical obstacles, looks, from the very superficial data available, not unlike that familiar in Hither Asia.)

Where, when, and why was the ecological boundary surmounted? The Taurus was never, on the available evidence, crossed by Neolithic peasants; the earliest settlements on the plateau yet known are rightly called "Chalcolithic," since they exhibit an incipient Bronze Age economy. Only one "Neolithic" culture is common to both sides of the Balkan ranges—Childe's Vardar-Morava, Milojčic's Vinča, culture (23) —and it does not initiate either Neolithic series; it is Late (or at least Middle) Neolithic in Thessaly and Macedonia and apparently is preceded by the Starčevo-Körös culture in the middle Danube Basin. In France the impressed cardium-decorated pottery (24), distinctive of the Early Neolithic in southern Italy and all around the western Mediterranean, never penetrates north of the coastal zone. As far as the existing archeological record goes, Mediterranean and temperate cultures are contrasted from the first.

THE NEOLITHIC AS A STAGE

Making due allowance for environmentally controlled divergences, the material classed as "Early Neolithic" from temperate Europe and the Mediterranean at least can legitimately be used to supplement that from Egypt and Hither Asia to document a stage in cultural and economic development intermediate between one characterized by pure food-gathering and one in which the accumulation of a social surplus made possible inter- and intra-communal division of labor and the development of regular trade. Throughout the area here surveyed, the latter developed only out of the Neolithic in Hither Asia directly, in Egypt and the eastern Mediterranean under demonstrable Asiatic influence (seen explicitly in the Gerzean and Early Aegean "Bronze Age" cultures), and elsewhere perhaps always under direct or indirect impulses from literate urban civilizations.

The economic and technological contents of this stage are reasonably definite, their sociological and ideological counterparts less so. It would, for instance, be tempting to treat the widely distributed female figurines as indicative of fertility cults centering round a mother-goddess such as are so widely diffused in the folklore of cereal cultivators. But the very similar Paleolithic figurines, though separated by at least seven millenniums from the earliest Neolithic ones, could just as well be considered indicative of such a cult in the Old Stone Age! And only in Palestine and Mesopotamia did its symbols assume sufficiently human form to need permanent residences during the Neolithic. Again, Neolithic art was highly symbolic, contrasting with the lifelike representations of Paleolithic and civi-lized art. But the Paleolithic carvings from Arudy and Mezin, like those on Australian *churingas,* are just as symbolic and devoid of recognizable representational content as the patterns on any early Neolithic pot! Social institutions, like clans, chiefs, warfare, and suttee, are not much better or worse attested among Early Neolithic than among older or later societies.

THE NEOLITHIC ACHIEVEMENT

The positive achievement of the Neolithic was the elaboration of a rural economy with an appropriate technology—and presumably ideology—adapted to several environments. The adaptation achieved in the Near East during the Neolithic was good enough to survive without any radical modification until the advent of mechanization; but in the zone of temperate forests a durable adjustment was not perfected until the Iron Age. At the same time, a separation of more pastoral tribes from more sedentary farmers began in Europe certainly, and elsewhere probably, in the course of the Neolithic, though the classical forms of pastoral nomadism, based on the horse or the camel, developed only later.

Neolithic farmers discovered and began the exploitation of most of the best agricultural land—but not, for instance, the rich clay soils of England—many sources of natural raw materials, and the main routes for migration and trade both on land and on sea. They devised satisfactory forms of rural dwellings that have persisted in their respective environments until today, modified but little by subsequent urban developments. Finally, Neolithic farmers must have discovered the secrets of metallurgy, and in Hither Asia, initiated organization for the effective application of them. In Europe, however the technical knowledge was acquired, the distributive machinery, equally essential for a Bronze Age economy, was not perfected without further help from the Near East.

KULTURKREISE

The only direct archeological evidence cited by Menghin (25) for the existence of proto-Neolithic *Schweine-züchter* has been invalidated by subsequent botanical and archeological discoveries. The rare bones of pigs—and other domestic animals—from "mesolithic" shell mounds in Denmark prove to be contemporary with, and are therefore derivable from, those Early Neolithic farmers whose spread across Denmark and Sweden was described in the first pages of this article. Pig bones from "Dwelling Places" in eastern Sweden belong to a much later horizon, contemporary with the Middle Neolithic, and illustrate the start of a secondary (or even tertiary) Neolithic culture, the first steps in swine-breeding by autochthonous hunter-fishers, whether the pigs in question were obtained from neighboring farming groups or tamed, in imitation of their practice, from native wild swine. *Reittierzüchter* could hardly be expected to figure directly in the archeological record and certainly cannot be identified in the Neolithic section. For the rest, the present paper deals with facts and not inferences.

BIBLIOGRAPHICAL NOTES

All statements referring to the Near East and Europe are documented in *New Light on the Most Ancient East* (London, 1952) and *The Dawn of European Civilization* (London, 1950), both by V. G. CHILDE. For China have been used "The Prehistory of the Chinese" (*Bulletin of the Museum of Far Eastern Antiquities*, Vol. XV [Stockholm, 1943]), "Chou-chia chai, Kansu" (*ibid.*, Vol. XVII [1945]), and "Prehistoric Sites in Honan" (*ibid.*, Vol. XIX [1947]), all by J. G. ANDERSSON.

1. IVERSEN. "Landnam i Danmarks Stenalder," *Dansk Geol. Undersøgelser,* II Raekke, No. 66 (Copenhagen, 1942).
2. Dr. L. Bernabó Brea has discovered stratified neolithic and later settlements here, but has not yet published on them.
3. FRANKFORT, H. *The Birth of Civilization in the Near East,* London, p. 46, 1951.
4. PIGGOTT, S. *Neolithic Britain.* Oxford, 1952.
5. *Ancient India,* IV (New Delhi, 1948), 202.
6. BERTSCH, K. and F., *Geschichte unserer Kulturpflanzen,* Stuttgart, 1947. JESSEN and HELBAEK, *Biologisk Skrifter,* Vol. III, No. 2, of "Det kog. danske Videnskabs Selskab." Copenhagen, 1942. HATT, G., *Landbrug i Danmarks Forntid.* Copenhagen, 1937. SCHIEMANN, E., *Weizen, Röggen und Gerste.* Jena, 1948. TACKHOLM, V., *Flora of Egypt,* Vol. I. Cairo, 1941.
7. FIELD, H., and PRICE, K. "Early Agriculture in Middle Asia," *Southwestern Journal of Anthropology,* VI (1950), 24.
8. GLOB, P. V., *Ard og Plov.* Aarhus, 1952.
9. NOSEK, S. "Slady kultów religijych wschodniej," *Z Otchłany Wieków,* Vol. XVIII. Warsaw, 1949.
10. CHILDE, V. G. "Neolithic House Types in Temperate Europe," *PPS,* Vol. XV. Cambridge, 1949.
11. *Sumer,* VII, 100. Baghdad, 1951.
12. CATON-THOMPSON, G. *Kharga.* In press.
13. CHILDE, V. G. "Axe and Adze," *JSGU,* Vol. XL. Frauenfeld, 1950.
14. VOGT, E. *Geflechte und Gewebe der Steinzeit.* Basel, 1937.
15. GARSTANG, J. *Mersin.* In press.
16. GLORY, in *Bulletin de la Société préhistorique de France,* XL, 36–40. Paris, 1943.
17. ATKINSON, R. *Excavations at Dorchester, Oxon.* Oxford, 1951.
18. MATZ, F. *Forschungen auf Kreta, 1942.* Berlin, 1951.

19. BECKER, C. J. "Mosefundene Lerkar fra Stenalder," *Aarbøger*. Copenhagen, 1947.

20. LEISNER, G. and V. *Die Megalithgräber der iberischen Halbinsel*. Berlin, 1943.

21. PIGGOTT, S. "A Trepanned Skull of the Beaker Period," *PPS*, VI, 112–31. Cambridge, 1940. MACWHITE, E., in *Quadernos de historia primitiva*, I, 61–69. Madrid, 1946.

22. COON, C. S. *Cave Explorations in Iran, 1949*. Philadelphia, 1951.

23. MILOJČIC, V. *Chronologie der jüngeren Steinzeit Mittel- und Südosteuropas*. Berlin, 1949.

24. BERNABÓ BREA, L. "Le Culture preistoriche della Francia Meridionale," *Rivista di studi Liguri*, XV, 21–45. Bordighera, 1951.

25. MENGHIN, O. *Weltgeschichte der Steinzeit*. Vienna, 1931.

New World Culture History: South America

By WENDELL C. BENNETT

THE PURPOSE of this paper is to present a summary and analysis of the anthropological approaches to the broad subject of culture history as exemplified by studies done on South American materials. The review does not pretend to give proper consideration to the status of field research in South America, since, with the exception of archeological studies directed exclusively at establishing chronology, most field work is not primarily concerned with culture history. In like fashion, many other interesting and significant studies have been eliminated or but briefly mentioned, since they are not directly pertinent to the major topic. In general, all studies of culture history involve reconstruction on a large scale, covering the whole continent or perhaps the whole hemisphere. The significance of these reconstructions and the interpretations based on them depend heavily on the reliability of the available data, whether these be from archeology, ethnology, linguistics, or museum collections. Consequently, a brief review of the general status of anthropological research in South America is basic for the discussion of these approaches.

STATUS

The six volumes of the *Handbook of South American Indians*, published as Bulletin 143 of the Bureau of American Ethnology (1946–50), under the editorship of Julian H. Steward, provides an excellent summary of what is now known about South American Indians. The *Handbook* covers archeology, ethnology, linguistics, cultural geography, and physical anthropology and presents the findings from both a regional and a topical point of view. The *Handbook*, with its accompanying Bibliography, is obviously an excellent source book, but it also includes a great many original studies and new interpretations.

The annual *Handbook of Latin American Studies* (originally published by the Harvard University Press, now by the University of Florida Press) covers both current bibliography and recent field work for South America. Consequently, a combination of the *Handbook of South American Indians* and the *Handbook of Latin American Studies* provides an up-to-date review of the status of anthropological research in South America. The over-all bibliography is enormous, and the quantity of field research is impressive. Nonetheless, considering the size of the South American continent and the cultural complexity presented, it is quite obvious that significant research is still in its infancy. Only a fraction of the field workers have been professionally trained scholars, and many of the pub-

211

lished accounts are little more than casual by-products from travelers and local residents.

The paucity of research in the major brances of anthropology can be briefly illustrated. For example, intensive archeological investigations have been largely limited to certain sections of Peru and northwestern Argentina. Elsewhere, archeological information is spotty and excavation intermittent. In linguistics the situation is far worse. South American Indian languages are noted for their diversity, but, in spite of this, there is as yet no modern, scientific grammar for any language and but few grammars of any kind. The review of physical anthropology, in Volume VI of the *Handbook of South American Indians,* is based on forty-three series for undeformed prehistoric skulls; eighty-eight series for contemporary tribes, with the measurements largely limited to stature and cephalic index; and only forty series for blood typing. The ethnology of southern South America, the Chaco, and East Brazil is reasonably well known, but for the rest of the continent there are only a few full-length monographs. Serious study of the numerous contemporary Indians of the Andes has only been initiated in the past decade. The same is true for other studies in the general field of social anthropology, such as community study, culture and personality, and analysis of non-Indian cultures.

Even this brief review of the status of anthropological research in South America shows clearly that much remains to be done. Here is a vast and complex area awaiting new investigation in every branch of anthropology, and it is encouraging to note that, since the war, renewed efforts are being made by scholars from many parts of the world. The studies of culture history are not limited to field research monographs, but one would feel more confident of reconstruction of history if field data were more adequate.

CULTURE HISTORY

The major approaches developed for the study of culture history are by no means identified with the South American field, and, in fact, many of the ones which are reviewed here could be equally well, if not better, illustrated for other parts of the world. However, there has long been a great interest in the culture history of South America and a considerable body of literature on the subject. This reflects, in part, the scattered nature of the sources, which can best be organized in terms of their distributional patterns. It is perhaps also due to the gross geographical isolation of the South American continent, which makes the study of its cultural growth appear to be comparatively simple. Although no one totally discounts the possibility of trans-Pacific influences, the principal migration route into South America is considered to be through the narrow Isthmus of Panama. Consequently, the reconstructions of South American culture history involve only two basic problems, namely, the relationship with North America through this narrow passage and the independent developments within the continent.

For the purposes of this review, the principal approaches used in the study of South American culture history have been arranged into a few major categories. This is in part artificial, since some approaches fall into more than one category. However, it serves to unite the contributions of the various subdivisions of anthropology, rather than having each discussed separately. Furthermore, it is hoped that this arrangement will allow comparison of the approaches used for South American culture history with work done in other parts of the world and will also permit discussion of the comparative merits of the different approaches.

DISTRIBUTIONAL STUDIES

The tracing and plotting of the distribution of culture elements or patterns, in terms of a large area, is a basic technique in the study of culture history. Distributional studies have been particularly favored for South America, since they can be based on many types of sources, including, naturally, the extensive museum collections. The study of distributions is the principal basis for the following culture-history approaches.

1. CULTURE-AREA APPROACH

The regional distributions of culture features is basic to the establishment of culture areas. Most students recognize several cultural-geographic divisions of the South American continent, based on the major environmental zones, and there has been a number of **detailed classifications** of all tribal cultures into cultural areas. The results range from a simple threefold division (southern hunters, tropical forest agriculturists, sedentary Andean farmers) to the twenty-four culture areas recently proposed by Murdock (1951). The culture-area approach is well known and needs little elaboration here. It is essentially a classificatory device useful in ordering the immense range of ethnographic variations. The resulting classifications vary in terms of the basic criteria utilized. Material culture has frequently been emphasized, since it is so suitable for museum study. Murdock (1951) has established a set of nine basic criteria which he considers to be of the greatest significance. All these are positive, observable features, since he objects to the use of negative criteria, that is, the absence of certain features. The first four volumes of the *Handbook of South American Indians* correspond to four major areas, namely, the marginal tribes, tropical forest tribes, Circum-Caribbean tribes, and the Andean civilizations. This regional arrangement was in part a convenience, although it is defended as a valid classificatory cultural device. In Volume V of the *Handbook,* Julian Steward outlines a new classification of culture areas based on sociopolitical patterns. He insists that this does not correspond at all to one based on culture elements, although the actual rearrangement of allocations of cultures is not great. There have been some attempts to classify archeological materials into culture areas, although without great success. Recently the culture-area approach has been applied to contemporary Brazil and other countries.

Fundamentally, a culture-area classification is horizontal, that is, on one time level, and is not in itself a study of culture history. However, historical interpretations inevitably creep in to explain the formation of culture areas. Likewise, one area, like that of the southern hunters, is likely to be interpreted as representing a cultural manifestation earlier than another—for example, the sedentary Andean farmers. However, while such sequences are tempting, their establishment must depend on other criteria.

2. CO-TRADITION APPROACH

The use of the culture-area classification for the archeological materials of South America would require a well-established relative chronology for the whole continent. In other words, it would be improper to use a horizontal time classification for materials known or suspected to be of different periods. In limited regions like the Central Andes, where chronological sequences are reasonably well established, the culture-area approach can be used for specific time periods. When the archeological cultures of the Central Andes are seen to form culture areas at each successive time period, a new phenomenon is presented, namely, a culture area with time depth. The term "area co-tradition" has been used for this over-all history of an area in which the component cultures have been interrelated over a period of time (Bennett, 1948). The area co-tradition approach assumes cultural continuity within the region and mutual influence of the component cultures both in space and in time. It is felt that the isolation of such cultural time blocks will be useful for comparative purposes. Thus far, only two area co-traditions have been described for South America, namely, for the Central Andes and for northwestern Argentina. Elsewhere, a Mesoamerican co-tradition has been roughly outlined, and Martin and Rinaldo (1951) have described a southwestern United States co-tradition. Thus far, no application has been made of the approach outside the Western Hemisphere.

3. KULTURKREIS APPROACH

The cultural-historical distributional studies, developed originally for Southeast Asia and Oceania, have been extended to the Western Hemisphere and South America. American scholars have generally hesitated to accept interpretation of New World phenomena based on Old World data. However, in spite of their hesitancy, American scholars have made quite similar distributional studies, using their own criteria.

4. AGE-AREA APPROACH

The determination of the age of an element from the extent of its distribution has found frequent application in the South American studies. Some of these have dealt with the whole Western Hemisphere, noting, for example, elements which occur both in southern South America and in northern North America and attributing to them appropriate implications of great antiquity. The pitfalls of interpreting time from distribution of isolated elements have been pointed out many times. Under proper controls, the technique is useful, but the dangers are many. Steward, for example, accepts the merits of age-area interpretation for culture elements and patterns but denies its usefulness for sociopolitical units, since, he argues, these are affected by ecological adaptation to local environments. The same adaptation might well affect all elements.

5. NORDENSKIÖLD APPROACH

The type of distributional study developed by Nordenskiöld and his followers is well known in the South American field. Nordenskiöld (1919) used distributional analysis in order to interpret the culture history of a particular group. For example, he concentrated on two Chaco tribes and made distribution maps of the South American occurrences of the elements of their material culture. In his analysis, he first stripped off those elements which could be attributed to European introduction. He next examined the elements which had an essentially Andean distribution and interpreted these in terms of known Andean sequences. The elements with an Amazonian distribution were then examined. He also noted the characteristic Amazonian traits which were not found in the Chaco. The residue of elements still unaccounted for by the above examination were analyzed as being ancient culture elements, local developments, or from Patagonia to the south. These distributional studies, therefore, did not lead to generalization about the culture history of South America but rather to the analysis of the specific culture history of the two Chaco tribes.

6. COOPER APPROACH

The Cooper distribution studies differ from Nordenskiöld's, in that they are applied to a region rather than to specific tribes and in that time periods are utilized where possible. For example, Cooper (1925) dealt with the whole southern South American area. His analysis covered the material and other cultural elements of every tribe in the region. He examined the evidence for time periods and proposed a modern period; a post-horse period, from accounts following the year 1741; a first contact period, from accounts antedating the year 1670; and an ancient period, based on archeological evidence. Tribe-by-tribe comparisons were made from north to south and east to west for each time period. Those culture traits common to the whole region were generally considered to be ancient. For later periods, historic and archeological drifts were traced. The result is an impressive reconstruction of the culture history of southern South America.

7. LINGUISTIC APPROACH

The known correspondence of language and culture lends considerable support to the reconstruction of culture history on the basis of linguistic relationships and distributions. For the South American field, this approach has thus far had limited significance because of the unbelievable diversity of languages, the unreliability of the data, and the lack of good linguistic classifications. In spite of these handicaps, numerous attempts to interpret the language distribution picture have been made. A common approach is one of establishing the supposed centers of origin of certain of the major linguistic stocks, such as Carib and Arawak, and then tracing the distribution of these languages in migration terms. The cluster of independent language stocks found along the eastern margin of the Andes has frequently led to the hypothesis that this region was a refuge area for earlier peoples. Some detailed studies have been made of the known historic distributions of the Tupi-Guaraní and Quechua languages and their correspondences with political expansion and missionary activity. For the Gê linguistic stock in East Brazil, the close correlation of region, language, and culture has been considered as evidence of long local residence. Some have thought that the great diversity of languages in South America implies great antiquity, although this is based on the unproved assumption that the diversification took place in that continent. Others have thought that South America, because of its geographical position, should preserve languages of the earliest migrants into the Western Hemisphere, but as yet there is no supporting evidence for this thesis. On the contrary, known evidence thus far, for the Chibcha, Arawak, and Carib languages, suggests a south-to-north migration rather than the reverse.

8. PHYSICAL-ANTHROPOLOGICAL APPROACH

The distribution of physical types of man should have historical implications. The summary of physical distributional data in Volume VI of the *Handbook* shows some regional correspondences, but the evidence is too scanty for sound interpretations. The same is true of the studies of blood groups, which suggest several successive migrations of small numbers of persons into South America but without being very specific as yet. There is also a dearth of information on sequences of physical types. In spite of a hundred years of collecting and laboratory research, there is as yet no incontestable evidence of the great antiquity of fossil man in South America, nor are there well-established sequences which can be used for broad historical interpretations.

Most of the distributional studies deal with certain general concepts which need some critical examination. One common and fundamental concept is the influence of environment on distribution. Different scholars illustrate the total range of possibilities from one extreme, which attributes no importance to the environment, to the other, which virtually calls for environmental determinalism. However, the great contrast in the South American environmental zones, from tropics to deserts and from plains to extremely high altitudes, must certainly be considered to some extent in all distributional studies.

In the culture-area classifications, for example, some lump all tropical forest cultures together, largely because the emphasis is placed on the techniques necessary to maintain life in the heavy tropics. On the other hand, Murdock (1951), using his multiple set of positive criteria, subdivides the Amazon region into a dozen culture areas. Few students have failed to be impressed by the striking contrasts between the high-altitude basins of the Andes and the desert Pacific coast of Peru, on the one hand, and the tropical forest plains of Amazonia, on the other. The possibility of distributions from west to east is virtually ignored, not on the basis of known evidence but on the presumption that the contrasting environments would make them illogical. However, one of the most interesting developments in the Central Andean archeological field is the recognition of the close cultural relationships of the highland and coastal areas. In fact, it is now argued that there is closer cultural affiliation between a highland basin and the adjacent Pacific coastal valleys than between two separated highland basins. At the same time, Monge (1948) and his colleagues are studying the biological adaptations which are needed for maintaining life in extremely high altitudes and are implying that these are of a magnitude sufficient to prevent free migration and settlement between coast and highland regions.

It is clear that the environmental factors need more careful consideration in all distribution and migration studies. This is true for the study both of material and of nonmaterial elements and patterns. Steward in Volume V of the *Handbook* argues that his sociopolitical units depend in large part on the population density of a given region, which, in turn, is affected by the success of the subsistence activities in the particular environment. On the other hand, care must be used not to attribute our own reactions to environmental contrast to other people. The Andean mountains present innumerable barriers for modern transportation systems, but for pre-Columbian Indians, who traveled essentially on foot, mountains are of little concern.

Survival and loss of culture elements are two related concepts which are commonly employed in the interpretation of distributions. The comparison of southern South America and northern North America is based on the assumption that elements of an ancient cultural stratum have survived in both these areas (Krickeberg, 1934). For southern Patagonia, stratified archeological deposits show that an essentially similar hunting pattern survived from ancient times up to the historic; but in most parts of the New World survival is an unproved assumption. Likewise, when elements have broken distributions, the concept of loss is frequently invoked as an explanation. Both concepts need more rigorous analysis. As now used, survival and loss are treated as simple factors without any consideration given to the possibility of element substitution, modification, or replacement. Distribution analysis needs refinement in terms of our advanced knowledge of the process of culture change.

Migration and diffusion are generally considered to be the two principal mechanisms of distribution, but there is a definite preference for migration in the South American studies. This is doubtless inspired by the geographical position of the South American continent, with its single land-bridge connection with North America. Since the original population is assumed to have come overland from the north, perforce as migrants, the subsequent movements and distributions are likewise attributed to migration. This, in turn, has fostered the view that mobility is a continuing characteristic of the South American Indians. The *Handbook of South American Indians* illustrates the culture history of South America with maps, on which arrows show significant migrations. In general, people are conceived as moving up and down the Andes, wandering widely on the plains of Patagonia, and utilizing the network of rivers in Amazonia for wide-scale travel. Although it is self-evident that migrations must have taken place in the original populating of the South American continent, the assumption of continuing mobility needs to be examined. A careful review of greater Amazonia does not show wide dispersal of culture types. Instead, the subcultures are well restricted to specific areas. The archeological work on the northern coast of Peru presents convincing evidence of a population continuum over a long period of time. In brief, there is considerable evidence that diffusion is of equal importance with migration as a mechanism of distribution.

The concept of "marginal" is constantly employed in culture-history study based on distributions and is the one which needs the most critical review. The concept of "marginal" is used in numerous different ways. In some cases it is frankly geographic in terms of continental land mass, namely, southern South America as marginal. Again,

cultures are classed as marginal if they are located beyond the limits of native agriculture. In a related sense, marginal cultures are those on the periphery of centers of higher civilization. In a totally different sense, cultures which retain primitive, that is to say, presumably ancient, features are considered to be marginal wherever located, which leads to such terms as "internal marginal" and "submarginal." One of the extreme abuses of the term defines "marginal" in respect to present-day centers. For example, the mouth of the Amazon, today the gateway of water travel to the interior, is likewise considered to have been a focal center in the past, and thus cultures located at the outermost tributaries, along the eastern margin of the Andes, are called "marginal." It is self-evident that such inconsistent applications of the concept of "marginal" lead to equally inconsistent interpretations of the culture history of the continent.

CHRONOLOGICAL STUDIES

The chronological approach to culture history encompasses those studies directed toward the establishment of absolute or relative sequences in specific sites or areas as a basis for extension of these to cover larger regions. Such studies fall rather naturally into two fields, namely, archeology and history.

1. ARCHEOLOGICAL APPROACH

One of the major emphases in the archeological excavations in South America, particularly on the part of the North American and European field workers, has been the establishment of relative chronologies for specific sites and regions. The techniques employed by the archeologists need no particular elaboration here, since they are the standard ones for the field and since they will be discussed in other papers. The principal techniques have been grave isolation (sequence dating), refuse stratigraphy, surface survey, pit sampling, strip matching, and typological analysis. These devices are used first for excavations of specific sites, and the resulting sequences are then matched to set up a relative chronology for larger areas. In spite of the interest and the amount of field work thus far accomplished, there are scarcely a dozen well-established sequences in all South America, and few of these cover any extensive ranges in time. At the present time, it is not possible to set up even a tentative sequence for over-all South America or, for that matter, for , any component country as a whole. Furthermore, the techniques directed toward establishing sequences often provide only limited information on the total cultural content of each period. There is, however, no question that this detailed chronological approach is one of the soundest procedures for establishing a reliable culture history of a region.

The Midwestern Taxonomic System developed by McKern (1939) and others for the numerous unstratified archeological sites in central United States is, like the culture area, primarily a classificatory device rather than a chronological one. To be sure, some students impute a genetic interpretation to the hierarchy of categories which the system employs, but this is unwarranted. Basically, the Midwestern Taxonomic System treats all the material from a given site or level as a component or unit. Components are grouped together as foci on the basis of specific similarities. Larger classificatory compartments, called "aspect," "phase," and "pattern," are based on more limited and more abstract diagnostics. The system can be diagrammed as a series of concentric boxes. Once time sequences can be established with other techniques, the various categories can be rearranged to match. Thus far,

only limited application has been made of this system in South America, specifically in Venezuela and in lowland Argentina. It could profitably be applied to all other regions, since it places the emphasis on the total content of a site, which is parallel to treating cultures as wholes.

2. HISTORICAL APPROACH

In spite of the wealth of historical documents for certain parts of South America, relatively little study has been directed toward the history of Indian culture as opposed to the Spanish. That such studies would be of great importance is amply illustrated by Kubler's article in Volume II of the *Handbook*, which traces the Indian cultures through the colonial and republican periods of Peru. His analysis of the factors which effected changes in the Indian culture during the historical period not only contributes to the process of culture change but also reveals basic trends which can be projected backward to the pre-Spanish periods. The Argentine scholars, among others, have been interested in the identification and location of Indian tribes at the time of first European contact as revealed by historical documents, and this, in turn, has led to an interest in identifying certain archeological sites with historic tribes (Canals Frau, 1940). More work of this kind is needed. It is restricted, unfortunately, because those trained to handle archival records are seldom well versed in archeology, and vice versa. An ideal study, for example, could be made of the Inca period in Peru, based both on the historical accounts and on the archeological remains.

Most reconstructions of culture history proceed from the earliest culture periods to the most recent. The historical materials indicate that the reverse would be important, particularly in areas like the Central Andes, where sizable native populations still exist, historical documents are rich, and archeological remains abundant. For example, the town of Copacabana, on the Bolivian shore of Lake Titicaca, is today an important religious center which attracts Indian pilgrims in great numbers every year. There is historical evidence that such pilgrimage centers were prominent in the days of the Inca empire, at Pachacamac, Peru, and elsewhere. Furthermore, in various periods of the archeological past, large ceremonial sites, like Tiahuanaco in Bolivia and Chavín de Huántar in Peru, seem to have been similar pilgrimage centers. A study of the contemporary compared with the historic would shed considerable light on the interpretation of the past.

BOTANICAL STUDIES

In recent years the interest of the botanists in the domesticated plants of the New World has opened up a new and potentially valuable approach to culture history. The principal findings thus far have been reviewed by Sauer in Volume VI of the *Handbook of South American Indians,* which serves as the source of the comments here presented. The approach might well be called "ethnobotanical culture history," since it involves the technical studies of the botanists, the historical accounts of domesticated plants for different parts of the New World, evidence from archeological sites, study of the importance and integration of domesticated plants in different cultures, and ultimately leads to reconstruction of distributions and migrations.

Much work remains to be done before even a tentatively reliable statement of the results of this approach can be formulated, but some suggestions can be assembled from Sauer's review. Five regional centers of plant domestication loom important in New World prehistory: northern South America (Colombia), Central America (Guate-

mala), the Central Andes (the altiplano), the montaña section on the eastern slopes of the Andes, and tropical Brazil. There is some indication that these centers varied in importance at different time periods, namely, that the northern South American and the Central American centers were the earliest and that the others came into prominence somewhat later. The various suggestions concerning diffusion and perhaps migration, based on the botanical evidence, are listed.

1. An early, trans-Pacific connection is suggested for the introduction to the New World of maize, amaranth, bottle gourd, and cotton.

2. An early south-to-north distribution (Pacific west coast of South America to Central America) is suggested for "pure" and pod corn, cotton, jackbean, and tobacco.

3. A later north-to-south distribution (Guatemala to the Andes and elsewhere) is suggested for dent corn, Inca lima beans, flint corn, the common bean, and one variety of squash.

4. An early northern Andes (Colombia) to Central Andes migration is indicated by the oca, ulluco, mashua, diploid potato, and guayaba.

5. Later, the Central Andes becomes a center for the south and north distribution of quinua, lupine, beans, and potatoes, all types adapted to high-altitude cultivation.

6. A line of distribution from the montaña area, east of the Andes, through the tropics of the Americas is suggested by sweet manioc, peanut, pepper, sweet potato, and one variety of squash.

7. An important interrelationship of the montaña, tropical Brazil, Venezuela, and the West Indies is indicated by bitter manioc, arrowroot, cashew, xanthosoma, and tropical tobacco.

8. A reverse trans-Pacific distribution, from the New World to Oceania,

is suggested by the coconut, sweet potato, jackbean, and cotton.

The above list is compiled from numerous statements in Sauer's article, but it is doubtful that even he would agree to all of it, nor would other botanists and archeologists. The list is intended only to illustrate the possibilities for culture history in this research approach, which demands the co-operation of archeologists and botanists. In future work, advantage should be taken of the exceptional conditions for preservation on the coast of Peru and more systematic collections of plant remains should be made. In the study of plant distributions, environmental and cultural factors are of recognized importance. We need more detailed studies of the economic importance of different domesticated plants to the contemporary and historical peoples. Once again we are faced with the problem of determining whether plant distributions took place by migration, by diffusion, or perhaps by natural means.

INTERPRETATIONAL STUDIES

Obviously, interpretations are basic to every study of culture history. The present section is concerned with a number of particular types of interpretations developed in South American studies, together with some of the specific conclusions arrived at for the southern continent.

1. DEVELOPMENTAL CLASSIFICATION

The archeologists who have concentrated their efforts on establishing regional chronologies have also been concerned with the types of culture change which are revealed by these long time sequences and their developmental implications. Although an interest in archeological trends and their interpretations has been common in other parts of the world, the recent focusing of attention on developmental classification

for Andean South America has been largely inspired by the 1946 Viru Valley Project on the northern coast of Peru, in which a number of North American and Peruvian scholars collaborated. The sequence of cultural periods established for Viru Valley was carefully examined in terms of the economic, technological, political, religious, and artistic achievements. As a result, definite changes in emphasis were noted for successive periods. Later studies (Bennett and Bird, 1949) have examined the changes which took place in all the Central Andes in so far as the cultural sequences could be reconstructed; and the same approach has been applied to other parts of the Americas. The generalized developmental picture for Peru shows a long initial period of technological advancement, in which techniques of cultivation and manufacture were slowly brought under control and which culminated in a period of artistic florescence. Following this, new technological advance is limited, and the emphasis is shifted to sociopolitical controls, which reach their maximum in the formation of the Inca political empire. The Mesoamerican sequence shows certain parallels to the Peruvian. This led Steward (1949) to examine sequences in other parts of the world, on the basis of which he has proposed a hypothetical developmental pattern with implications of cultural causality and law.

2. FORMATIVE PERIOD

Comparison of the developmental sequences established for Mesoamerica and the Central Andes has led to renewed efforts to explain the relationships between these two centers of New World high civilization. Both are conceived to rest on a common cultural basis, previously called the "archaic" but in developmental terms now labeled the "Formative period." The argument runs that an agricultural economy, based on plant domestication presumably in South America, spread throughout the entire area of what is now called "Nuclear America." It is still undetermined whether this complex was spread by migration or by diffusion, or, for that matter, whether it could not have developed independently. In any case, two major centers of advanced civilization grew out of this Formative basis, one in Mesoamerica, one in the Central Andes, in large part independently of each other. These major developments have largely obscured the common Formative pattern, although it is revealed by the archeological findings, but in the intermediate region the Formative complex persisted and spread around the Caribbean area.

3. CIRCUM-CARIBBEAN

This concept of a distinctive and interrelated cultural development around the Caribbean region was advanced by Steward in the course of his work as editor of the *Handbook of South American Indians*. The *Handbook* initially divided the continent into three major regions, namely, southern South America, the Andes, and the tropical forest, and devoted a volume to each. As the material on the tropical forest region grew in magnitude, two volumes were required, one for the tropical forest proper and the other for the northern section, which also included Central America and the Antilles. In summarizing the contents of this additional volume, Steward became convinced that it had considerable cultural unity. With his great interest in developmental classification and his attention to the importance of the Formative period, he conceived of a new interpretation of the Circum-Caribbean cultures which he presented in Volume V of the *Handbook*. The idea is advanced that a separate, distinctive culture pattern, based essentially on the Formative period complex but also incorporating elements from Mesoamerica and the Central Andes, spread throughout Central America, Colombia, Venezuela, and the Antilles. The concept is well presented but needs more thorough examination, particularly since much of the botanical, archeological, and historical evidence indicates a rather sharp division between the Brazilian tropical forest, Venezuela, and the Antilles, on the one hand, and Colombia and Central America, on the other.

Both the Formative period and the Circum-Caribbean, like other large-scale reconstructions, are based on the assumption that an early common, undifferentiated cultural basis existed in the whole area. In the case of the Formative period, some of the cultural content is derived from archeological evidence, but even a greater amount is the result of reconstruction through the least-common-denominator principle. That is, the high civilizations of Mesoamerica and the Central Andes are compared, and the factors which they share in common are attributed to the Formative basis. While it may be logical to assume not only that the simple precedes the complex but that it is also less differentiated, it does need confirmation. It is doubtless true that differences become more pronounced as civilizations become more complex, but it does not follow from this that the simpler earlier cultures are thus more uniform and therefore more closely related.

4. CERAMICS AND CULTURE

The emphasis of archeologists on relative chronology has led to a heavy dependence on ceramics and ceramic fragments as the basic material. Actually, many of the sequences which have been established are essentially for ceramics rather than for total cultures. Considerable advance has been made, however, in defining the relationship of ceramic history to culture history and culture change. Although contributions in this field are by no means restricted to South America, the illustrations in this report are so limited.

Junius Bird in his excavations on the northern coast of Peru encountered a well-defined, pre-ceramic, agricultural horizon. In the past the spread of ceramics and agriculture has often been interpreted as coterminous, but it is now clear that, in coastal Peru, an agriculture economy covers a long time period before the introduction of ceramics. Furthermore, South American distribution studies show that, in Patagonia, ceramics were spread well beyond the limits of agriculture.

Comparisons of ceramic styles and techniques of manufacture are constantly used to match the sequences of two or more regions and to link two or more time periods. In the Central Andes, certain ceramic techniques, styles, and even complexes have widespread distributions which seem to have taken place at approximately the same time periods. These are called "ceramic horizons" and are used to relate the sequences of different regions. Since the rate and extent of trait distribution are commonly considered as factors for judging relative age, the concept of using the spread of a ceramic technique or style as a horizon time marker might be questioned. For Peru it is felt that the spread was too rapid for time differences to be a significant handicap in the matching procedure. Furthermore, it is possible to use fixed sequences of horizon styles. There are, for example, five major horizon styles in prehistoric Peru which occur in the same sequence in a number of different subareas. Thus they serve to match these regions, even though an absolute time scale might show slight differences. For some of the subareas of Peru, some ceramc styles or features are found to persist through several cultural periods. These are called "ceramic traditions" and serve to link periods. A sufficient number of such traditions is thought to indicate regional population and culture continuity.

The classification of ceramics into types and styles is commonly used for most studies of chronology. In a stratigraphic excavation the percentage occurrence of each type or style is plotted and the changes noted for successive levels. For surface or unstratified unit collections, the different patterns of the percentage occurrence of types can be matched as a basis for time reconstruction. While the primary purpose of all these procedures is to establish a relative chronology, analysis of the rate of increase or decrease of a ceramic type throughout time furnishes information about the nature and the rate of cultural change.

Many scholars resist the validity of using material culture alone as a measure of over-all cultural development, and they would doubtless be even more alarmed at the use of one aspect of material culture, namely, ceramics, as an index in itself. Consequently, Willey's article on ceramics in Volume V of the *Handbook of South American Indians* is of considerable interest. In this, Willey presents a technological classification of the ceramics of South America, shows the regional distribution of each category, gives some evidence of sequence occurrences, arranges the categories in a developmental sequence, and attempts to relate this to the over-all culture history of the continent. His arguments merit consideration and again raise the question of using material culture as an index. The archeologists are naturally greatly interested in this, since their findings are dominated by material culture.

Most archeologists agree that ceramics are a reasonably sensitive measure of cultural change. Although ceremonial pottery may change with greater rapidity than the common cooking ware, both present regular modifications when seen through a time framework. The question is often raised as to how long a style can persist with relatively little change. An interesting study in this respect has been published by Tschopik (1950). He has traced contemporary Aymara ceramic styles back to the beginning of the colonial Spanish period and demonstrated that there has been but little change in these four hundred years.

5. ARCHEOLOGICAL SCIENCE

Archeologists have created a specialized terminology for the treatment of their materials. Most of the technical terms refer to categories of artifacts, techniques, classifications of types, and chronological problems and consequently have been little used outside the specialty. No one denies the importance of chronology as a basis for the study of culture history, and certainly more such work is still the most dominant need in South America. Nonetheless, chronology is but a means, not an end in itself. Once sequences, relative or absolute, are established, the archeologists are still faced with the major problem of interpreting these in a significant way for science. One approach to this problem considers the archeological remains as the skeleton of a past culture and attempts to clothe its bare bones in descriptive wrappings borrowed from contemporary ethnography. This has been reasonably successful for a period such as Mochica on the northern coast of Peru, since preservation is good and the ceramic modeling and painting are faithfully realistic. For most periods, however, the limitations of this approach are self-evident, and a forced application often distorts the picture.

In recent years some scholars have been experimenting with new descriptive methods devised to fit the available archeological materials. Habitation patterns are being based on the types and arrangements of house sites. Architectural layouts are being treated as wholes. Analysis is being made of the archeological emphasis of a period, whether on large-scale public building, skilled craftsmanship, or elaboration of grave offerings. The shift in emphasis from one period to another is being studied, even though the functional significance of this cannot be immediately determined. The utilization of an isolated valley is being viewed as a whole and throughout a time period from the earliest remains to the present day.

Such a positive approach to archeological analysis has great promise, since its possibilities are limitless. It will allow the past to be compared with the contemporary on equal terms, unhampered by the limitations which an ethnographic reconstruction approach presents. In time a new and significant vocabulary must be developed to meet the new concepts. The recognition that archeology is a science in its own right is a step forward comparable in magnitude to the distinction between the superorganic and the organic.

6. TECHNICAL ANALYSIS

Ceramics, metals, woven cloth, and other materials have been subjected to technical analysis by the specialists. Such technical studies have the advantage of dealing directly with the materials themselves rather than depending on reconstructions. For example, the basic process used in making a given metal artifact can be analyzed by a metallurgist in terms of the component metals, the heat at which they were fabricated, and the sequence of technical steps employed. For spinning and weaving, graded scales of skills and complexities can be set up to compare the achievements of different past cultures. In South America these technical studies have been largely limited to metals and weaving.

7. ART ANALYSIS

The quantities of materials, particularly archeological finds, which can be properly classified as art objects have attracted the attention of students of art. Once again many of the art studies are not restricted to ethnographic reconstructions. Instead, the scholars can glean a great deal of information about the artistic interests of the peoples of a given period by analysis of the principal media employed, the methods of expression, the iconography, the repetition of design, the interest in realism as against stylization, and the like. Furthermore, broad interpretations can be made of the over-all approach of the artist to his subject. In the chapter on art in Volume V of the *Handbook,* Kroeber characterizes the over-all artistic expression in South American prehistory. He points out that the South American artist, in contrast to those of Mesoamerica, was bound to technology. This is reflected in the limited emphasis placed on sculpture, painting, and architecture in contrast to ceramics, textiles, and metallurgy.

PROBLEM IN CULTURE HISTORY

Up to the present, most students of culture history in South America have directed their efforts to the reconstruction of sequences. Some of the approaches and achievements have been discussed in the previous pages. It is noteworthy that few of the writers reveal any sense of problem, outside the strictly chronological. There are some exceptions, to be sure, such as the cultural-process and functional interests of the students of developmental classification. There is no intent in this discussion to deny the validity and importance of historical approaches and the reconstruction of sequences. However,

chronology must be recognized as merely a setting for scientific study. The ultimate purpose of historical reconstructions is to allow analysis of the process of cultural change, of the study of the relationship of environment to cultural development, and many others.

The present review of anthropological work in South America has been confined to culture history. It is clear, however, that historical study is but one aspect of the total anthropological activity. Many of the field studies, particularly in ethnology, are concerned with South American cultures as illustrations of problems in human behavior and in social science. For example, Holmberg's (1950) study of the Sirionó Indians of Bolivia was directed toward the thesis that perpetual concern about obtaining enough to eat in a nomadic group of this kind would influence many aspects of the cultural behavior. The current series of community studies, principally in Peru and in Brazil, are in no way bound to the subject of culture history. Some are intended to be a sampling of the contemporary cultures of the country. Others are directed toward measuring the impact of modern technology on some of the more backward people of the area. Unfortunately, space does not permit a proper review of these numerous studies.

It is hoped that in the future the students of culture history will devote more attention to the study of problems. For example, the current studies of the Indian cultures in Peru and Bolivia show clearly that the Indians are a social class or caste within a larger system. In other words, one is studying a culture within a culture rather than an independent group. This is often considered to be a modern situation resulting from the European conquest, but there is every reason to believe that similar situations existed in the past, for example, when the Inca absorbed their weaker neighbors into a large political system. The possibility of a culture within a culture is seldom considered by archeologists, even when they encounter markedly different materials in the same period.

The culture historians should devote more attention to recurring historical phenomena in the history of the Western Hemisphere and the possibility of their identification in the more remote past. Two illustrations suffice. One is the introduction of the horse to the plains of Patagonia and to western United States and the similar cultural results in both regions. The other is the phenomenon of revivalism in the Ghost Dance of the Indians of western United States and in the reaction of the Tupi of Brazil following the Portuguese conquest. Such phenomena are useful for historical interpretations but also direct scholarship toward the analysis of possible causal factors. If culture history is to be a part of social science, cause as well as sequence must be included.

REFERENCES

BENNETT, WENDELL C. 1948. *A Reappraisal of Peruvian Archaeology.* ("Memoirs of the Society for American Archaeology," No. 4.) Menasha, Wis.

BENNETT, W. C., and BIRD, JUNIUS. 1949. *Andean Culture History.* ("American Museum of Natural History Handbook Series," No. 15.) New York.

CANALS FRAU, SALVADOR. 1940. "La Distribución geográfica de los aborígenes del Noroeste Argentino en el siglo XVI," *Anales del Instituto de Etnografía Americana,* I, 217–34.

COOPER, JOHN M. 1925. "Culture Diffusion and Culture Areas in Southern South America," *Proceedings of the International Congress of Americanists,* XXI, 406–21.

HOLMBERG, ALLAN R. 1950. *Nomads of the Long Bow.* ("Publications of the Institute of Social Anthropology," No. 10; Smithsonian Institute.) Washington, D.C.: Government Printing Office.

KRICKEBERG, W. 1922. "Die Völker Südamerikas." In BUSCHAN, G. (ed.), *Illustrierte Völkerkunde,* I, 217–423. Stuttgart: Strecker & Schröder.

———. 1934. "Beiträge zur Frage der alten kulturgeschichtlichen Beziehungen zwischen Nord- und Südamerika," *Zeitschrift für Ethnologie,* LXVI, 287–373.

LINNÉ, S. 1925. *The Technique of South American Ceramics.* ("Göt. Kungl. Vetenskaps- och Vitterhets-Samhället Handlingar," Vol. XXIX, No. 5.) Göteborg.

McKERN, W. C. 1939. "The Midwestern Taxonomic Method, as an Aid to Archaeological Culture Study," *American Antiquity,* IV, 301–13.

MARTIN, PAUL S., and RINALDO, J. B. 1951. "The Southwestern Co-tradition," *Southwestern Journal of Anthropology,* VII, 215–29.

MONGE, CARLOS. 1948. *Acclimatization in the Andes.* Baltimore: Johns Hopkins Press.

MURDOCK, GEORGE P. 1951. "South American Culture Areas," *Southwestern Journal of Anthropology,* VII, 415–36.

NORDENSKIÖLD, E. 1919. *An Ethno-geographical Analysis of the Material Culture of Two Indian Tribes in the Gran Chaco.* ("Comparative Ethnographical Studies," No. 1.) Göteborg: Elanders Boktrykeri Aktiebolag.

STEWARD, JULIAN H. 1949. "Cultural Causality and Law: A Trial Formulation of the Development of Early Civilizations," *American Anthropologist,* LI, 1–27.

——— (ed.). 1946–50. *Handbook of South American Indians* (Bureau of American Ethnology Bull. 143.) Vol. I: *The Marginal Tribes* (1946); Vol. II: *The Andean Civilizations* (1946); Vol. III: *The Tropical Forest Tribes* (1948); Vol. IV: *The Circum-Caribbean Tribes* (1948); Vol. V: *The Comparative Ethnology of South American Indians* (1949); Vol. VI: *Physical Anthropology, Linguistics, and Cultural Geography of South American Indians* (1950).

TSCHOPIK, HARRY. 1950. "An Andean Ceramic Tradition in Historical Perspective," *American Antiquity,* XV, 196–218.

New World Culture History: Middle America

By ALFONSO CASO

WHEN WE speak of "cultural horizons in Mesoamerica," we refer to a particular zone of American culture which extends approximately from the southern part of Tamaulipas on the east to the Sinaloa River in western Mexico. This northern boundary follows the western Sierra Madre Mountains to Lake Chapala, then follows the Lerma River and rises again in the east to reach the San Fernando River in Tamaulipas. The southern boundary begins at about the mouth of the Motagua River, continues south almost to Sensenti, Honduras, then turns east, following the present border of El Salvador and Honduras to the big bend of the Lempa River, and follows this stream to the Pacific Ocean.

On the other side of the Lempa River lived Nahuatl-speaking Pipil groups as far south as Ozulután. The Nahuatato lived on the other side of the Gulf of Fonseca, and the end of the gulf was inhabited by Chorotegan peoples. From the Gulf of Fonseca, the line passed through the Estero Real Valley, reaching Managua and Nicaragua lakes, following along the southwestern side of the latter in a line to the Gulf of Nicoya, whose shores were inhabited by Chorotegan groups (Orotiñas and Nicoyas). The area to the west was occupied by small Mesoamerican groups squeezed in among various

peoples down to Panama, where the Ciguas lived around the mouth of the Changuina River and the frontier Island of Tojar.

This delimitation for Mesoamerica is valid only from the sixteenth century. Formerly both northern and southern limits were different, but at the present time insufficient data do not permit an accurate definition of the Mesoamerican frontiers for an earlier date.

Mesoamerica is characterized as a cultural unit not only for the sixteenth century but even much earlier. Through the studies of Mendizábal (1929, n.d.), Wissler (1938), Beals (1932), Sauer (1934, 1935), and Kirchhoff (1943), we have an idea of the cultural elements or traits that can be considered typically Mesoamerican. It would take a long time to enumerate the common elements that make this area a cultural unit and which distinguish it from the Southwest of the United States and the northeastern part of Mexico, on the one hand, and from the Southeast of the United States and the Chibchan, Andean, Amazonian, and so-called "Circum-Caribbean" areas, on the other.

By "cultural horizons in Mesoamerica" we refer to the various periods in Mesoamerican development, each characterized by the presence of one or more very important cultural traits diffused over a wide area. This does not mean that a cultural trait, or traits, was adopted throughout the entire zone at the same time, nor does it necessarily follow that it was taken over by each Mesoamerican group. But undoubtedly the invention or assimilation of these elements must have resulted in a change in the basic pattern. On the other hand, we know far more of the life and culture of Mesoamerican peoples, the closer we approach the time of the Conquest; and the data become scarcer and more vague in proportion as we move backward in time.

The cultural horizons to be discussed here are not time divisions of equal length. On the contrary, the horizons approaching the period of European contact at the time of the Spanish Conquest are shorter. But, as we retreat from this epoch of contact, to which pertain the richer data and the bulk of information, the periods become increasingly longer. For this reason, the dates for the beginning of the historical period and of the Toltec horizon are relatively well established, but the tentative dates of the older periods, being based on today's status of knowledge, are simply those that currently seem most probable to us.

On the other hand, one must take into consideration the fact that the shift from one horizon to another could not possibly have occurred simultaneously throughout all the large area that comprises Mesoamerica. Cultural traits must have diffused more or less rapidly around the immediate area of origin or assimilation; but we can be sure that in the same area, with the exception of cases of conquest, the appearance of these elements and the disappearance of hangovers from former periods must have taken place very gradually.

Having stated these reservations, which one must bear in mind when dealing in general terms with the different horizons, the Mesoamerican area is without a doubt not merely a geographical division but also, as we have seen, a cultural unit. Not only were the diverse cultures that existed in the area related to one another at the time of the Spanish Conquest, but they were themselves the result of still older cultures which also resembled one another or stemmed from a common base. In other words, Mesoamerica not only was a cultural unit at the time of the Conquest but had been so during former epochs. Many traits, some of which are very old, such as writing and the ritual of the calendar, the pyramids and the cult of certain gods, seem to have existed in Mesoamerica even during that horizon which we shall call the "Archaic."

It goes without saying that our knowledge is not sufficient at the present time even to attempt to set up the northern and southern limits of Mesoamerica during each horizon, although, as we have said, we can be sure that such boundaries shifted with time. We also wish to call attention to the fact that the very number of these horizons is, in itself, very arbitrary. By using some other criterion than our own, it would not be difficult to reduce these to half their present number if we were eager to make the system more synthetic, or to double their number by employing more analytical criteria. The presentation of these horizons is no more than a classification, and classifications are not an expression of truth, universally valid, but of criteria that seem useful. With future scientific investigations in the pre-Columbian field —archeological, ethnographic, and historical—it will undoubtedly become necessary one day to rearrange our data.

The following horizons seem significant at the present time. They are listed, beginning with the oldest and ending with the most recent, each accompanied by tentative initial and terminal dates. (1) *Prehistoric horizon.*

This period embraces that span of time from the first settling of the Mesoamerican area to the discovery of agriculture and pottery. 25000 B.C.???–5000 B.C.??? (2) *Primitive horizon.* During this horizon agriculture got under way, being preceded perhaps by horticulture. Another significant achievement was the invention of pottery. Life must have been at least partially sedentary, and people were clustered in small groups, forming tiny farming communities or villages. 5000 B.C.???–1000 B.C.?? (3) *Archaic horizon.* Manifestations of high culture are already evident at this early time. The population must have been concentrated first in large villages and later in cities, which dominated a greater territory. Organized religious cults appear, along with representations of gods, writing, and the calendar system. Pottery, although still simple, is technically very well developed. 1000 B.C.??–200 B.C.?? (4) *Formative horizon.* By now, people are concentrated in large metropolitan centers. Enormous pyramids are constructed, implying an organized priesthood and a fairly sophisticated society. Writing and the calendar ritual take on even greater significance, and the pantheon of gods is richly increased. Pottery, too, becomes more complex, and new forms and techniques of manufacture, color, and decorations appear. Local cultures begin to distinguish themselves. The cult of Tlaloc, the Rain God, appears. 200 B.C.??–A.D. 400? (5) *Classic horizon.* The truly great cultures of Mesoamerica flourish at this time, manifesting characteristic cultures in Teotihuacán, El Tajín, Monte Alban III-A, Tzakol, and what has been called the "Old Empire Maya," and elsewhere. This is a period of intercultural contact and exchange, although local cultures retain their distinct personalities. Perhaps the Quetzalcoatl cult appears at this time. A.D. 400?–A.D. 900? (6) *Toltec*

horizon. The most outstanding characteristic of this period is the appearance of metal and the bow and arrow, new forms of writing, counting and calendrical systems, and new gods. The warrior brotherhoods of the Eagle and Tiger are much in evidence. The influence of Tula is widely felt, and the Mixteca-Puebla culture rises to prominence. We begin to have historical data for this period, transmitted by legend and preserved through manuscripts which can now be interpreted. This is the period of the great historical migrations. A.D. 900??–A.D. 1200? (7) *Historical horizon.* The peoples of this period were probably living much as they had for several centuries when the Spaniards came upon them in the sixteenth century. We have rich and abundant cultural data pertaining to these people. Many old elements were held over, and through the study of these traits, together with those of this period, we can understand how, after the fall of the Toltec empire and the disintegration of the League of Mayapan, new and independent groups gained control. Some of these groups in central Mexico were later concentrated to form the Triple Alliance. A.D. 1200?–A.D. 1521. Let us now pass to a brief discussion of these horizons.

PREHISTORIC HORIZON

Although the story of the settling of Mesoamerica is actually part of a greater problem, that of peopling the continent, we shall limit ourselves here to a discussion of the data that exist concerning the presence of man in Mesoamerica at the end of the Pleistocene and the beginning of the Recent, geologically speaking, and of the evidence for the contemporaneousness of man and extinct fauna. That these data belong to the prehistoric period is unquestionable, since there is no sign of the existence of such fauna along with Mesoamerican peoples.

Only a few years ago, the presence of prehistoric man in Mesoamerica was but a hypothesis, inferred from very scarce and from what seemed to be uncertain data. Recent excavations in the valley of Mexico now leave no room for questioning the fact that man lived here at the same time as the mammoth and actually hunted this beast before the great climatic change which resulted in a hotter and drier climate than we have today and which deposited a thick geological layer known as Caliche III or Barrilaco.

Martínez del Río (1943) and Aveleyra (1950) have studied the older finds in some detail and have made a very careful study of the scientific facts implied, in order to prove concretely that man did exist at this time. Both human remains and artifacts of man's material culture have been taken into consideration.

Listing the discoveries, we find the skeletal remains of the Peñón Man, the Xico lower jaw, and the Tepexpan Man. Prehistoric artifacts include those found by the Comisión Científica de México, those found by Hamy and Engerrand in Campeche, Adan in Mitla, Mülleried in the Petén region and Coahuila, Hughes in Tamaulipas, what De Terra calls artifacts of the San Juan culture at Tepexpan and the Chalco Complex.

However, what really clinches the case for man's existence in the Becerra Formation prior to the Caliche III, or Barrilaco (with an age, according to carbon 14 dating, from 11,000 years ± 500, to 16,000) (1951, p. 8), are the Tepexpan Man (De Terra, Romero, and Stewart, 1949), Arellano's discovery of an articulated mammoth accompanied by an obsidian flake (Arellano, 1946), and especially the recent find, four months ago, in Santa Isabel Iztapan. The latter consists of a young mammoth among whose bones were found six stone implements. All these discoveries belong to the Upper Becerra Formation (Martínez del Río, 1952).

Elsewhere in Mesoamerica, other evidence points to the existence of prehistoric man. We refer now to McNeish's explorations in Tamaulipas (McNeish, 1950), where he stratigraphically distinguished an eight-layer sequence of six cultures, spanning a period from prehistoric times (end of Pleistocene or beginning of Recent) to A.D. 1785, at which date the Pasitas tribe, of the so-called "Los Angeles culture," was wiped out. The Cañón Diablo Complex, that is, McNeish's stratigraphically deepest layer found on the highest river terrace, was not found in assocation with fossils, but he believes it to be of prehistoric date because of its location on the terrace.

We refer now to the human and animal footprints at Lake Managua. These were pressed into soft clay which has since become stone. These footprints were studied by Richardson, Ruppert, and Williams (Richardson, 1940; Richardson and Ruppert, 1941). Recently the latter (Williams, 1950) has again examined them, arriving at the conclusion that they are at least 2,500 years old, but not necessarily more than 5,000. Nevertheless, the presence of bison tracks in the same strata seems to indicate a truly prehistoric age. If the discovery of the Cañón Diablo Complex in the north and the one at Lake Managua in the south should be proved to belong to a really prehistoric horizon, then the evidence for the presence of prehistoric man in Mesoamerica would be strengthened.

In summary, the Mesoamerican finds show that man was inhabiting this part of the continent toward the end of the Pleistocene (Upper Becerra Formation) and at the beginning of the Recent (Totolzingo). This seems logical and is not unexpected, since in both North and South America human and artifact remains point to man's exist-

ence in the two great land masses at
that time. It is therefore quite natural
that, if man passed through the American isthmus region, the only corridor
between North and South America, he
would have lived there a while and left
behind some trace of his existence.

On this first horizon, man must have
had a culture which, in general, resembled the European Paleolithic, as regards the type of life and tools, since
the people lived by hunting the large
game animals which at that time inhabited the valleys and the river basins
of Mesoamerica. In other words, man
lived as a nomad who followed the
herds of elephants, camels, horses, and
bison, making use of the skins for clothing. The *atlatl*, or spear-thrower, must
have been in use and probably the javelin. Other tools included hammer-
stones, knives, beaters, scrapers, and
awls. Sometimes they sharpened bones,
and they knew how to engrave animal
figures on bone as on the specimen
found at Tequisquiac.

It is not known whether at this time
stones were used for grinding seeds
and wild roots or whether they had
baskets or used fruit rinds or husks and
shells for receptacles. During their brief
stopovers they sometimes lived in caves
or rock-shelters, especially on river terraces or lake shores. We do not know
whether they buried their dead and
whether they supplied them with grave
goods. Although Romero (De Terra,
Romero, and Stewart, 1949) is inclined
to think that the Tepexpan Man was
actually buried, because of the resemblance of his posture to that of Archaic
skeletons, this could be simply a coincidence.

If it could be proved that De Terra's
Chalco Complex (De Terra, 1946)
really possesses all the artifacts that he
attributes to it, among which are manos
and metates, it would be one very significant link bridging the gap between
this horizon and the one to follow.

PRIMITIVE HORIZON

The Primitive horizon is one which
we *presume* existed in Mesoamerica,
during which time two very important
features made their appearance: agriculture and pottery. The domesticated
dog and perhaps the turkey were also
known. This period is that era of lithic
tools in which chipped stone gives way
to polished stone.

In general, it may be said that the
cultural traits of this horizon make it
comparable to the Neolithic period of
the Old World. This comparison is to
be taken in a very general way, and we
cannot eliminate the possibility that
men with a late Paleolithic or early
Neolithic European culture might have
kept up a steady stream of migrations,
reaching America by applying their
seafaring knowledge to cross the
rugged Bering Straits. The invention of
agriculture and pottery on this horizon
in Mesoamerica can be postulated; but
up until now, with the exception of
McNeish's La Perra focus in Tamaulipas, of which we shall presently speak,
no evidence of a truly primitive horizon lacking agriculture and pottery has
been revealed within the Mesoamerican limits. Of course, the simple fact
that we have not found it is no sign
that it does not exist. Excavations in
the next few years could uncover just
such a horizon, yielding cultural remains of a truly primitive people.

This is the horizon of which we
know least in Mesoamerica. Remains of
an agricultural and pre-agricultural people have already been discovered in
North and South America. We know
that the Cochise culture of Arizona and
New Mexico already had metates and
manos, which proves the existence of
a people who used this simple device
for grinding seeds and fruit, and they
may well have been the predecessors
of the Mogollon and Hohokam cultures.
The Ventana Cave people of Arizona
were also food-gatherers and used me-

tates and manos (Haury, 1943). Bird (1948) and Strong (1947) found pre-ceramic cultures in the Chicama and Virú valleys dating from 3000 B.C., which preceded the Guanape I people. Other remains of pre-ceramic cultures have been uncovered on the Chilean coast. It would seem hard to believe that, if these primitive cultures existed in both North and South America, they would not also be found in Meso-america.

The La Perra Focus was found by McNeish (1950) underlying material that correlates with Ekholm's Period II of the Panuco region, and this Period II corresponds to the Ticoman-Cuicuilco culture of the valley of Mexico. But the lack of any apparent continuity be-tween the La Perra artifacts and those belonging to the Pueblo I phase of Mc-Neish led him to postulate a great gap between the two cultures. If the La Perra material is earlier than Zacatenco, as the author believes, then 1000 B.C. seems to be the most recent date we can assign to the end of this period. It is very significant that agriculture was already known to the La Perra people; but, on the other hand, they lacked pottery, which led McNeish to suggest that these people were semisedentary, living mainly on the products of agri-culture and food-gathering, and, least of all, by hunting.

Below the La Perra Focus, McNeish found remains of another culture which he calls "Nogales." The latter is distin-guished from the former by the type of lithic instruments present and by the lack of metates, mortars, and manos. According to McNeish, this Nogales culture is pre-agricultural and pre-ceramic and therefore antedates the La Perra Focus.

The Bat Cave discovery reported by Mangelsdorf and Smith (1949) shows that corn was known in New Mexico in very ancient times. According to a com-munication from H. W. Dick to Dr. J. O. Brew, who kindly gave me the data, the earliest maize discovery was in a layer just on the upper gravel, whose carbon 14 date is 3981 B.C. The oldest corn found in the cave is a true pod corn, and, according to Antevs' geological evidence, the layer is dat-able at 2000 B.C. Of even greater sig-nificance, which Mangelsdorf and Smith point out, is the fact that the evolution of the corn observed in a study of the stratified remains of the cave represents a lapse of time of ap-proximately 3,000 years. According to Mangelsdorf, hybridization with *teo-centli*, its introgression, could not have occurred later than 500 B.C. Neverthe-less, he points out, the first and second layers each already yield an ear of corn which shows introgression, al-though these could be intrusive in each case. Mangelsdorf concludes that corn did not originate in New Mexico and therefore must have been imported from some other region, before the evolution began, of course. Now if we accept the fact that corn originated in South America, as several botanists are inclined to believe, or in Chiapas or Guatemala, according to others, con-siderable time would have elapsed be-fore the cultivation of corn could have spread to New Mexico. We can there-fore assume that the Bat Cave dis-covery and the carbon 14 date of the gravel suggest that maize must have been cultivated in Central America at least as early as 3000 B.C. This makes it very improbable, of course, that corn, as a cultivated plant, could have been introduced into the American continent from elsewhere. On the other hand, Mangelsdorf's (Mangelsdorf and Oli-ver, 1951) recent studies deny that maize agriculture existed in Southeast Asia before the discovery of America.

On the basis of our present knowl-edge it would be hard to say which of the plants cultivated in Mesoamerica in the sixteenth century were already being grown during this first agricultural horizon. For the present, it seems best simply to enumerate the most important plants cultivated at that time: corn, bean, *chía* (*Salvia hispanica*), *huauhtli* (*Amaranthus paniculatus*), squash, *chilacayote* (*Cucurbita fixifolia*), sweet potato, yuca or manioc, *jícama* (*Pachyrhizus angulatus*), wild potato, peanut, tomato, *tomate* (*Physalis angulata; coztomatl*), chile pepper, *chayote* (*Sechium edule*), pineapple, avocado, papaya, sweetsop, *chirimoya* (*Annona squamosa; A. reticulata*), soursop, guayaba, *mamey* (*Calocarpum mammosum*), *zapote negro* (*Dyospiros ebenaster*), *zapote blanco* (*Casimiroa edulis*), *zapote amarillo* (*Sargentia gregii*), *chico zapote* (*Achras zapota*), nut, plum, *arrayan* (*Myrtus arrayan*), *tejocote* (*Crataegus mexicana*), *capulin* (*Prunus capuli*), *nanche* (*Byrsonima crassifolia*), cactus, *pitahaya* (*Acanthrocerus pentagonus*), *maguey* (*Agave americana*), *xoconochtli*, *mezquite* (*Prosopis juliflora*), *jinicuil* (*Inga radians*), indigo, *palo de Campeche* (*Hematoxylum campechianum*), tobacco, cotton, rubber, *guayule* (*Parthenium argentatum*), sisal, *zacaton* (*Epicampes macroura*), *ixtle* (*Agave ixtli*), vanilla, coconut, *guamuchil* (*Pithecolobium dulce*), *jocote* (*Spondius lutea*), *achiote* (*Bixa orellana*), *izotl* (*Yucca elephantipes*), *balche* (*Lonchocarpus longistilus*), cacao, *parota* (*Enterolobium cyclocarpum*) (Caso, 1946).

Of course, not every one of these plants listed was grown in all parts of Mesoamerica, not even in the sixteenth century, but they were known at that time throughout the area, owing to trade or tribute, and were taken to all the large economic and political centers. For example, cacao cannot be cultivated in the valley of Mexico, which is at an altitude of more than 7,000 feet, but both as a drink and as a medium of exchange it was a basic element of Aztec economy.

As to whether agriculture was invented in Mesoamerica, in the Amazon Basin, or in Peru, I do not think that at the present time we have sufficient data either to prove its origin in any one of these three regions or to deny independent invention.

As for the origin of pottery, a truly primitive ware has not been found in Mesoamerica. Although baskets covered with clay on the outside have been found in ncrthern Mexico, finds lie outside the boundaries of Mesoamerica (Borbolla, 1946). On the other hand, in the last century and even today in some parts of Chiapas, water has been heated by dropping hot stones into a gourd vessel, called a *huacal*, according to Becerra (1939). It is not unlikely that truly primitive pottery will be found in Mesoamerica in the future, which will help explain the transition which must have taken place between such advanced cultures as the Archaic, and the pre-ceramic and pre-agricultural cultures of the Prehistoric horizon.

Actually, we know very little regarding the Primitive horizon. It is inferred as a step that must have existed between the Prehistoric horizon and that of the Archaic, which follows.

ARCHAIC HORIZON

It may seem strange that I have revived this term which is so out of style in Mesoamerican investigations, but, among the names suggested for early cultures, I have not found one that improves on Spinden's choice for the oldest pottery horizon found in the valley of Mexico (Spinden, 1922).

To me, the Archaic horizon should include only the first part of what has recently been called the "Formative horizon." That is, certain cultures, such as Teotihuacán I and Monte Alban II, seem to be truly formative cultures leading to the great classic cultures;

but I do not see enough traits shared by these phases and the earlier ones to warrant the lumping of all these into what we should call "archaic." The Archaic horizon actually possesses elements that are survivals from the Primitive horizon.

I do not believe that large metropolitan centers existed in any part of Mesoamerica at this time. The people, who depended on agriculture for their living and made pottery technically well-developed, even though still simple in decoration, did not yet have the complex religion, rituals, and social structure that are found on the Formative horizon and which, of course, continue into the later Classic cultures.

Characteristic of this horizon is precisely the fact that the people were sedentary, although they must have depended to a certain extent on hunting, fishing, and gathering. Life rotated around agriculture; the nude, hand-modeled female figurines which are believed to have represented the beginning of a fertility and earth cult had already appeared.

Nevertheless, there are no large representations of gods from this horizon, which we find on later levels. There are no representations of the Rain or Wind God, of the Sun, the Moon or Venus, etc. Even Huehueteotl, the Old God of Fire, does not appear until the Formative horizon. The same holds true for Xipe-Totec, "the Flayed God." This would seem to indicate that, on the Archaic level, Mesoamerican people lived in large villages, where the ceremonial aspects of their society were not yet very developed, rather than in large cities, with ceremonial centers and complex and specialized cults.

Undoubtedly this primitive Archaic horizon must have been very much like those cultures which Vaillant uncovered at El Arbolillo and Zacatenco (Vaillant, 1930), but this would not apply to his upper-level cultures, that is the Tico-man phases (Vaillant, 1931). Ticoman would fall into the true Formative horizon, along with Teotihuacán I and the cultures of Monte Negro, Monte Alban I, Monte Alban II, and Chicanel. On the Formative horizon we will find that the characteristic Mesoamerican ceremonial centers had already become of great significance.

According to carbon 14 dating, which agrees with our guess dates based on archeological analysis, the pottery of Monte Negro has an approximate age of 2,600 years ± 170, which would date it around the sixth century B. C. (Johnson, 1951). Consequently, the Archaic horizon must have developed more or less from 1000 B.C. to 200 B.C. Nevertheless, at the end of this horizon, organized cults, writing, and the calendar system began to appear.

Monte Negro and Monte Alban I in the Oaxaca region mark the end of this horizon or the beginning of the next (Caso, 1939).

FORMATIVE HORIZON

People at this time were already living in large cities. Enormous monuments were constructed, such as the Pyramid of the Sun at Teotihuacán, the pyramid decorated with painted insects in Cholula, the Observatory or Building J in Monte Alban, and Temple E-VII-Sub in Uaxactún. The calendar and writing were already well developed. I believe that it was in this period that the predecessors of the Maya culture discovered the principle of position numerals and the zero. A great number of inventions were made during this period. The pantheon of gods was increased; pottery became more complex, with new forms, techniques, colors, and decorations, one example being an al fresco technique of painting vessels. The Tlaloc "Tiger-Serpent" cult appears, and probably the great culture of La Venta flourished, as well as Monte Alban II and perhaps the oldest phase of Tzakol, which was preceded by such very advanced cultures as Miraflores (Kidder, Jennings, and Shook, 1946). This is the period of San José II, Chamá I and II, and also Holmul I. The horizon is truly formative, because we find the first signs of local variation in cultures, which later becomes so well defined on the Classic horizon. The profile of these local cultures becomes more and more individualized. Nevertheless, the Mesoamerican pantheon of gods has not yet developed to its fullest extent; we do not find the great gods in their characteristic representations, and there is no indication that some of them, such as Quetzalcoatl, were worshiped. On the other hand, the Earth Goddess, the Rain God, the Fire God, and Xipe-Totec are portrayed on various objects of these cultures, already showing the regional styles which were beginning to develop.

In the Huasteca region, Periods I and II of Pavón would fall into the Formative horizon, as would the Prisco level and the lowest strata found at Tancol (Ekholm, 1944).

CLASSIC HORIZON

The Classic horizon includes such manifestations as Teotihuacán II–III, Monte Alban III-A, and Yucuñudahui in Oaxaca; in the Maya area the so-called "Old Empire," Tzakol, San José III, and Chamá III. In the Huasteca region the Classic horizon includes Pavón III and IV and the end of the Prisco phase. El Tajín in the Totonac area is also included here. The corresponding manifestations in western Mexico are Chametla I, Huatabampo, Tuxcacuexco, Los Ortices, and the Delicias and Apatzingán phases in Michoacán (Kelly, 1949). The horizon is characterized by marking the peak of Mesoamerican cultures, that period of greatest achievement in which heights were reached not only in pottery-making but also in art, painting, and sculpture. If we compare what was going on at this time in four places that we are well acquainted with—the Maya area, the valley of Oaxaca, the valley of Mexico, and the central part of Veracruz—we see an extraordinary development of local cultures, with a very distinct personality in the art style, pottery, writing, and calendar of each, although at the same time a free cultural exchange was taking place among these thriving centers. For example, Monte Alban received influences from Teotihuacán and El Tajín; Kaminaljuyú shows ceramic features of El Tajín, Teotihuacán, and Monte Alban; and the influence of Tajín at Teotihuacán is undeniable.

Nevertheless, these relationships should not be interpreted as evidence of conquests or migrations but simply as the result of commercial or cultural contact. Each of these centers mentioned not only was a city but also exercised cultural control over a much greater area. All of which seems to point either to empires subjected to political and military heads or to a confederation of cities that shared a common culture.

The Classic horizon is of great significance to us because at this time the characteristic elements of the historic cultures were already present, and probably a considerable portion of Mesoamerican peoples was already permanently located in the habitat where these Classic cultures developed. Thus, while during former horizons we could not yet speak of a Zapotec culture and we do not even know what to call the predecessors of the Zapotec, from Classic times on, in that area of the Oaxaca Valley which yields remains of Monte Alban III-A, the Zapotec culture was undoubtedly already formed, with its basic elements and characteristics. The same holds true for the Petén Maya and the peoples of highland Guatemala. However, it is improbable that, in the legendary data that have come down to us, we have any true historical facts for this period. This is one reason why it is so urgent that the accurate historical data on the Maya stelae should be interpreted. The earliest data from Mixtec codexes, which I believe date from the end of the seventh century, are so confused with the theogony of that nation that they can hardly be considered historical sources (Caso, 1951). But we can be sure that the Maya stelae will reveal the history of that people, once we are able to translate the inscriptions that are just now beginning to be understood, according to a new interpretation of hieroglyphs (Thompson, 1950).

As regards pottery on this horizon, the discovery of the use of the mold is important; in funerary architecture, the cruciform tomb developed; and in the field of religion, certain deities appear, such as the "Butterfly God." Finally, the appearance of Quetzalcoatl, the "Plumed Serpent," is firmly established, in constant association with the Rain God.

TOLTEC HORIZON

Undoubtedly, a very significant change took place in "Mesoamerican culture during the horizon called the "Toltec." Of course, it is at this time, or possibly at the end of the former horizon, that the use of metal was introduced into Mesoamerica. The knowledge of working gold, silver, and copper probably came from the region of Costa Rica and Panama, penetrated the Maya area, Oaxaca, and then arrived in central Mexico to spread later through the northern part of Mesoamerica. At this time the Aztatlan Complex of Sinaloa was flourishing and, on the northeastern side of Mesoamerica, Pavón V and Las Flores. Clay pipes appear on this horizon.

Another characteristic of the Toltec horizon, aside from the new ceramic features of each zone, is the appearance of the bow and arrow, probably introduced into Mesoamerica by the nomads of northern Mexico, along with the *chita,* or carrying net, and less important features, such as certain feather adornments, etc.

Two significant pottery types appear at this time, Plumbate and Fine Orange.

New forms in sculpture include the so-called *chac-mool,* and other innovations include the formation of societies, such as the Eagle and Tiger Warriors, and architectural features, such as the caryatids which supported tables or thrones, rings for ball courts, the representation of the sun with rays, the *tzompantli* (skull rack), etc. (Caso, 1941). Glyph-writing underwent certain modifications of importance; Aztec gods were represented in sculpture, in painting, and in codexes, with the possible exception of the tribal god, Huitzilopochtli. True historical data for this period are provided through the Mixtec codexes and through legendary narrations which have been preserved through other codexes and legends which the Aztecs and Mayas still remembered.

At the end of this period, the pressure exerted by the nomadic people of the north resulted in large-scale migrations, which spread over central Mexico and whose repercussions were felt to the southern limits of Mesoamerica. Probably toward the end of this period, the Mesoamerican people to the north were overrun, which resulted in the recession of the northern boundary of this culture area.

A new form of writing appears in the codexes and inscriptions, and new ceramic forms also appear. These manifestations are known as the Mixteca-Puebla culture.

Tula, the center of a great empire, exerts an influence felt as far as the southern limits of Mesoamerica, and the influence called "mexicana," which is really Toltec, is apparent in Chichén Itzá, Tulúm, and other Maya cities.

The end of the Toltec horizon marks the beginning of what we call the "Historical."

HISTORICAL HORIZON

The Historical horizon began approximately in the twelfth century A. D., and ended with the arrival of the Spanish Conquistadors in 1519.

Pre-Columbian and post-Columbian codexes and chronicles, together with reports left by the missionaries and Spaniards, provide abundant information regarding the life and culture of Mesoamerican peoples at this time. Other information was kept alive by word of mouth and later, when the Latin way of writing had been learned, was written down either in a native Indian language or in Spanish.

The people who had lived through the upheaval which resulted in the fall of the Toltec empire had settled once more in their own territory, when the Spaniards caught them by surprise. Their cultures were mainly a continuation of those elements which had already existed in Toltec times, with a simple evolution; the calendar, writing, the same way of making numbers, building, pottery-making, and even the same religion were carried over, all of which shows the intimate relationship that existed between this horizon and the former one.

At the time of the arrival of the Spanish Conquistadors, a great seat of power was being created in central Mexico under the Aztecs, while the Maya cities had not yet been able to reorganize themselves after the impact of the fall of Mayapan. The Zapotecs and Mixtecs were fighting each other to gain control of the valley of Oaxaca, and to the south the Maya culture seems to have been set back by the Pipils and Lenca tribes.

REFERENCES

ARELLANO, A. R. V. 1946. "El Elefante fósil de Tepexpan y el hombre primitivo," *Revista mexicana de estudios antropológicos*, VIII, 89–94.

AVELEYRA, LUIS. 1950. *Prehistoria de México.* ("Ediciones mexicanas.") Mexico City.

BEALS, RALPH L. 1932. *The Comparative Ethnology of Northern Mexico before 1750.* ("Ibero Americana," Vol. II.) Berkeley, Calif.

BECERRA, M. E. 1939. "Hervir el agua en *guacal,*" *Revista mexicana de estudios antropológicos*, III, 191–94.

BIRD, J. B. 1948. In BENNETT, WENDELL C. (ed.), *A Reappraisal of Peruvian Archaeology.* ("Memoirs of the Society for American Archaeology," Vol. XIII, No. 4, Part II.)

BORBOLLA, D. F. R. DE LA. 1946. "Arqueología del sur de Durango," *Revista mexicana de estudios antropológicos*, VIII, 111–20.

CASO, A. 1939. "Informe de las exploraciones en Oaxaca, durante la 7a. y la 8a. temporadas," *XXVII Congreso Internacional de Americanistas*, II, 159.

———. 1941. "El complejo arqueológico de Tula y las grandes culturas indígenas de México," *Revista mexicana de estudios antropológicos*, V, 85–95.

———. 1946. "Contribución de las culturas indígenas de México, a la cultura mundial," *México en la cultura*, p. 51. Mexico City.

———. 1951. "Explicación del reverso del Codex Vindobonensis," *Memorias del Colegio Nacional*, V, 9. Mexico City.

EKHOLM, GORDON F. 1944. *Excavations at Tampico and Panuco in the Huasteca, Mexico.* ("Anthropological Papers of the American Museum of Natural History," Vol. XXXVIII, Part V.) New York.

HAURY, EMIL W. 1943. "The Stratigraphy of Ventana Cave, Arizona," *American Antiquity*, VIII, No. 3, 218–23.

JOHNSON, FREDERICK. 1951. "Radiocarbon Dating," *American Antiquity*, XVII, No. 1, Part II, 1–19.

KELLY, ISABEL. 1949. *The Archaeology of the Autlán-Tuxcacuesco Area of Jalisco.* ("Ibero Americana," Vol. XXVII.) Berkeley, Calif.

KIDDER, A. V.; JENNINGS, J. D.; and SHOOK, E. M. 1946. *Excavations at Kaminal Juyu, Guatemala.* ("Publications of the Carnegie Institution of Washington," No. 561.) Washington, D.C.

KIRCHHOFF, PAUL. 1943. "Mesoamérica," *Acta Americana*, I, No. 1, 92–107.

McNEISH, R. S. 1950. "A Synopsis of the Archaeological Sequence in the Sierra de Tamaulipas," *Revista mexicana de estudios antropológicos*, XI, 79–96.

MANGELSDORF, P. C., and OLIVER, DOUGLAS L. 1951. *Whence Came Maize to Asia?* ("Botanical Museum Leaflets, Harvard University," Vol. XIV, No. 10.)

MANGELSDORF, P. C., and SMITH, C. E., JR. 1949. *New Archaeological Evidence on Evolution in Maize.* ("Botanical Museum Leaflets, Harvard University," Vol. XIII, No. 8.)

MARTÍNEZ DEL RÍO, PABLO. 1943. *Los Orígenes americanos.* 2d ed. Mexico City.

———. 1952. *El Mamut de Sta. Isabel Iztapa.* ("Cuadernos americanos," Vol. XI, No. 4.)

MENDIZÁBAL, MIGUEL O. DE. n.d. "Géneros de vida y regímenes alimenticios de los grupos indígenas del territorio mexicano," *Obras completas*, II, 31. Mexico City.

———. 1929. "Influencia de la sal en la distribución geográfica de los grupos indígenas de México," *ibid.*, II, 197. Mexico City.

RICHARDSON, F. B. 1940. *Nicaragua*, pp. 300–301. ("Carnegie Institution of Washington Year Book," No. 40.)

RICHARDSON, F. B., and RUPPERT, K. 1941. *Nicaragua*, pp. 269–71. ("Carnegie Institution of Washington Year Book," No. 41.)

SAUER, CARL. 1934. *The Distribution of Aboriginal Tribes and Languages in N.W. Mexico.* ("Ibero Americana," Vol. V.) Berkeley, Calif.

———. 1935. *Aboriginal Population of N.W. Mexico.* ("Ibero Americana," Vol. X.) Berkeley, Calif.

SPINDEN, H. J. 1922. *Ancient Civilizations of Mexico and Central America*, pp. 43–65. 2d ed. New York.

STRONG, WILLIAM D. 1947. "Finding the Tomb of a Warrior-God," *National Geographic*, XCI, 453–82.

TERRA, HELMUT DE. 1946. "New Evidence for the Antiquity of Early Man in Mexico," *Revista mexicana de estudios antropológicos*, VIII, 69–88.

TERRA, HELMUT DE; ROMERO, JAVIER; and STEWART, T. D., 1949. *Tepexpan Man.* ("Viking Fund Publications in Anthropology," No. 11.) New York.

THOMPSON, J. E. 1950. *Maya Hieroglyphic Writing*, Introd. ("Publications of the Carnegie Institution of Washington," No. 589.) Washington, D.C.

VAILLANT, G. C. 1930. *Excavations at Zacatenco.* ("Anthropological Papers of the American Museum of Natural History," Vol. XXXII, Part I.) New York.

———. 1931. *Excavations at Ticomán* ("Anthropological Papers of the American Museum of Natural History," Vol. XXXII, Part II.) New York.

WILLIAMS, HOWEL. 1950. *Nicaragua*, pp. 198–200. ("Carnegie Institution of Washington Year Book," No. 49.)

WISSLER, CLARK. 1938. *The American Indian.* 3d ed. New York: Oxford University Press.

New World Culture History:
Anglo-America

By ALEX D. KRIEGER

THIS REVIEW will consist of four parts: (1) the degree of success with which archeology has established the initial entrance of man into North America (and therefore the New World); (2) the success with which regional cultural sequences have been established north of Middle America; (3) the principal gaps in knowledge and the reasons therefor; and (4) suggestions for the accomplishment of a fuller, more integrated culture history of Anglo-America (and thus eventually of the New World as a whole).

The treatment of these subjects must necessarily be exceedingly brief. I will not attempt to discuss the stated aims of various members of the profession in North America, or the degree of success with which these aims have been met, for this was done fairly exhaustively by Taylor in *A Study of Archeology* (1948). It will be assumed that the ultimate goal of archeology is the writing of as complete a culture history of native peoples as is possible within the limits of preservation of materials and the sampling of these materials by the most careful field techniques.

There is no need to stress further field work in key areas and on all time levels, for this is obvious and will continue anyway. A much greater need at present is the assimilation and integration of existing data, the creation of interpretative frameworks within which our huge amounts of raw data can be organized clearly and logically for students of history. In this respect we are sadly and inexcusably deficient. In Anglo-America we attack a host of local problems with great vigor, perfect field excavation to a remarkable degree, spend endless hours on the detailed description of objects, burials, buildings, mounds, etc.—but fall down completely in creating the mechanisms necessary for organizing all this information on a continental scale. There is an appalling lack of interest in the solving of interregional problems, a condition long since overcome by every other activity claiming to be a science. Just recently Julian Huxley quite justifiably pointed out that American anthropologists have barely reached the level of organization reached by biologists forty years ago. Until a much more advanced level of organization of data is reached by New World archeologists, it will not be possible to write even a fairly comprehensive culture history of its native peoples.

ENTRANCE OF MAN INTO THE NEW WORLD

Since the Folsom discovery in 1926, students of ancient man in America have taken great delight in destroying over and over the conservative notions of Hrdlička and others that man had occupied America only very recently, perhaps 3,000 years ago. The Folsom discovery made it imperative to raise this estimate to 10,000 or 15,000 years, depending partly upon the date of final retreat of Wisconsin glaciers. Folsom artifacts have now been dated by the radiocarbon method at about 9,900 years, from burned bone of fossil bison at Lubbock, Texas, an excavation conducted by the Texas Memorial Museum. The one date does not, of course, indicate the span of time to be allowed for the manufacture of the specialized Folsom fluted projectile points. There are now many indications that the makers of these artifacts were far from the oldest inhabitants of North America.

Associations of human bones and artifacts with remains of extinct mammals, such as Columbian mammoth, mastodon, horse, camel, musk-ox, sloth, dire wolf, etc., have been reported in various parts of America for more than 100 years. During the last 20–25 years more refined field methods have placed many such associations beyond doubt, so that attention has now shifted toward related problems which have still to be answered. In what order did these large mammals become extinct, and were there time differentials for different parts of the New World? What are the artifact types most consistently associated with different species? Which discoveries provide good evidence that the animals were actually killed and butchered, and which are based on isolated bones which may have entered the archeological sites in some other way? How much time is represented by the total span of cultural evidence associated with extinct fauna? What was the effect of man on the pace of such extinctions as against climatic and biological influences?

In the course of belaboring the former skepticism over the mere idea of contemporaneousness of man and now extinct mammals in the New World, we have, unfortunately, fallen into another dogmatism which is not very different from the old. For the former 3,000 years or so of "allowed antiquity" we have hardly gone further than to substitute another figure of 10,000 or 15,000 years and have proceeded to adjust our thinking around it. Thus countless recent papers insist that it has now been "scientifically proved that man entered the New World at the end of the Pleistocene." The few fluted projectile points found in Alaska (always called "Folsom," but actually much more like Clovis fluted points) are held to constitute proof that Alaska was the steppingstone for the entrance of these ancient points into America from Asia, even though they have not yet been recognized in Asia. The alternative, that fluted points are an American invention, diffused northward into Alaska as game animals moved northward with retreat of the glaciers, has not received due attention.

It has also been taken for granted that whenever artifacts are found in direct association with extinct mammals, these must have been the last survivors of their species. There are now several indications that this was not so. Such late Pleistocene formations as the Becerra of central Mexico; Gamerco and Tsegi in the Southwest; Durst, Neville, and Beaumont in Texas; and undoubtedly others are said by geologists not only to be contemporaneous with the Wisconsin glaciation as a whole but to be of such nature that they cannot yet be subdivided according to Wisconsin climaxes and interstadials. Thus artifacts and fossils found at considerable depths within these formations, as in the Becerra at Tequixquiac, Mexico, may and probably do date far back in Wisconsin time.

Further evidence of this kind is seen in the recovery of a full and flourishing assemblage of late Pleistocene mammals and very crudely chipped flints in the Friesenhahn cavern near San Antonio, Texas, and at Tequixquiac, where the fauna cannot be thought of as on the verge of extinction of any of its species. In the case of Potter Creek Cave in California, excavated in 1904 by paleontologists, some eight or ten bone splinters with bevels and perforations raised heated arguments as to whether they could be man-made, for the associated fauna was considered *Middle* Pleistocene. For this reason, if no other, they were explained away as "water-worn bones." In examining these objects in 1950, the writer became convinced that they are artifacts.

The "rotten flint" artifacts in Georgia raise another problem, that of the time required for the disintegration of flint under certain soil conditions. Chemical analyses of soils inclosing buried archeological zones in Georgia are also receiving attention at present by Sokoloff, with suggestions of much greater antiquity than previously suspected. While it is possible that some of these investigations will meet with disappointment, the writer believes that the next few years will show the presence of man on this continent long before "the end of the Pleistocene." An attitude of skepticism and conservatism is scientifically sound, but it does not necessarily produce correct answers.

All discussions of "early man" in America are complicated by lack of consistent terminology. Some geologists regard the Pleistocene as ended with the last retreat of Wisconsin ice; others regard it as still going on (the present being another interglacial), even though its characteristic large mammalian fauna has disappeared. To get around this difficulty, the term "Holocene" is increasingly used by geologists for the time elapsed since the retreat of Wisconsin glaciers, being preferable to "Recent," "Post-Pleistocene," and "Post-Glacial." Other difficulties are posed by uncertainty over the number of advances of Wisconsin ice: in the Rocky Mountains and eastward the usual

number given is four; in the Great Basin and Sierra Nevada–Cascades the number is usually given as two, with some substages. The problems of correlating terraces with glacial climaxes and interstadials, and with fluctuations in temperature and/or rainfall, are also vastly complicated; undoubtedly, many of the rule-of-thumb simplistic correlations made in the past will have to be re-examined with increasing knowledge of stream hydraulics, gradient, run-off, vegetational changes, and climatic changes in terms of seasonal patterns. The use of artifacts as "index fossils" where organic fossils are rare or missing is beginning to receive some attention, but the archeologist cannot contribute much to geological correlations until he has made much more progress with typological definitions, distributions, and dating.

Another important step is the gradual emergence of the difference between true Folsom points and the much more widely spread, larger, and heavier fluted points, which may temporarily be grouped under the name "Clovis fluted." Recent reports on the Shoop (Pennsylvania), Williamson (Virginia), and Parrish (Kentucky) sites aid in establishing the cultural context of these large fluted points in the Woodlands. East of the Great Plains, however, their approximate age cannot as yet be guessed; they may be coeval with those in the Plains, where they are older than Folsom points, or they may be somewhat later, representing hunters who left the increasingly arid Plains for game in the Eastern forests. At least they must be considerably older than the Archaic cultures.[1]

The Borax Lake discovery in California, widely quoted as a "pre-Fol-

1. The writer prefers to use "Archaic" only for pre-ceramic cultures which contain a polished-stone technology. Manos and milling stones are excluded from this definition because they are smoothed from use only.

som culture" after Harrington, presents a large assemblage of artifact types which do not appear significantly different from what Heizer and his co-workers regard as the Middle Horizon in central California, dating perhaps from 1000 or 500 B.C. to A.D. 500. The seven or eight large fluted points closely resemble Clovis fluted, particularly the specimen associated with mammoth at Dent, Colorado. A logical explanation is that the Borax Lake people found these specimens in the vicinity and reused them, so that their main significance lies in extending the distribution of such points entirely across the continent. They also extend from Alaska to the Texas coast, and one specimen comes from Costa Rica. This enormous distribution throws into relief the comparatively local, central distribution of true Folsom points, confined almost entirely to the Great Plains. The two types do not mix in the same sites where there is good stratigraphic control. At the Clovis site, eastern New Mexico, they come from two very distinct strata, the Folsom points with extinct bison in a diatomaceous lake-bed deposit and the Clovis points from a gray sand below, which has also yielded mammoth remains and bone artifacts.

The diatomaceous clay which contains Folsom fluted points at Lubbock and Clovis suggests a colder and wetter climate than the present. With a radiocarbon date of 9,883 ± 350 years on this deposit at Lubbock, Folsom artifacts seem roughly coeval with the last pluvial and Wisconsin advance (Cochrane), estimated by Antevs to have ended about 7000 B.C.

Although much remains to be learned on this problem—it is barely shaping up at present—this interpretation makes it quite likely that Clovis points are somewhat older than 11,000 years, possibly as much as 15,000 or 18,000 years. The Sandia points should also be of equivalent age, but their relationship to Clovis is still unknown. Sandia points seem to be of very local distribution in New Mexico, contrasting strongly with the immense dispersion of Clovis or Clovis-like fluted points.

Man certainly had some part in the extinction of late Pleistocene mammals, but the primary causes were probably those of diminishing food supply, increased competition, and perhaps some degree of sterility due to diminishing nutrition. The vast expanses of tall, thick, nutritious grasses which are absolutely necessary to account for the great Pleistocene mammals must have been shrinking during early post-glacial time, then disappeared completely during the long dry period (Altithermal) which followed. Man's hunting of the survivors was made easier by their collecting around shrinking water holes.

My conclusions are: in the over-all picture of man in the New World, nothing has been established as to the time of initial entry; that this could have occurred at almost any time during the Wisconsin glaciation if not earlier (suitable game being present at all times and the crossing of the Bering Straits being no problem whenever the sea lowered enough to provide a land bridge or froze over); that cultural material is already on hand which is older than any of the projectile points popularly thought to mark the oldest American occupation; and that, beginning with the oldest known projectile points (Clovis fluted and Sandia), a general cultural sequence can be established. This began at least 12,000 years ago, possibly as much as 18,000. Before long, great improvements will be made over the crude "correlations" of culture and climate which pervade American archeological literature, for only now are the complexities of late-glacial and post-glacial climatic changes beginning to receive proper attention by geologists and archeologists. It is now widely recognized that fluctuations in temperature and precipitation present two different problems, which may cause environmental changes in many different ways. Climates probably change constantly in some degree, as do cultures and the distributions of plants and animals, but we have yet to integrate all these factors.

Finally, let us not imagine that early types of projectile points are a necessary guide to ancient cultures. Some of the amazingly well-preserved cave materials from Nevada, Oregon, and Utah have consistently produced radiocarbon datings ranging up to 11,000 years (possibly more); yet they lack the various projectile points which are such definite guides to early chronology in the Plains and Woodlands. The Great Basin will undoubtedly reveal much older material, as indicated by the obsidian blade found in 1882 by McGee, deeply imbedded in Lake Lahontan gravels. Split and burned bones of horse, camel, and sloth come from several Great Basin sites, but, except for the sloths at Gypsum Cave, these sites with extinct faunal remains have not been even approximately dated.

REGIONAL CULTURE
SEQUENCES

A tracing of the total sequence in each part of Anglo-America would involve much duplication, so I will discuss the earlier remains on a broad, more or less continental, scale and then treat the comparatively late cultures in separate regions. It appears that regional differentiation of economy and artifact types increased steadily with the passage of time.

We have only a few widely scattered clues to the presence of man at all during the most of the Wisconsin glacial stage and are in no position yet to define precise periods or regional specializations. Bones of proboscideans, horse,

camel, sloth, and perhaps other animals with man-made cutting marks on them have been found at two or three dozen points from Manitoba, Canada, to Guatemala, and from Oregon to eastern Florida. Simple bone tools, mainly splinters with beveled edges or smoothed tips, have come from such localities as Potter Creek Cave, California; Tule Springs, Nevada; the lowest cultural levels at Sandia Cave and Clovis, New Mexico; and Tequixquiac and the Texcoco lake bed in Mexico, suggesting a very great distribution of bone implements in glacial times. Long polished and beveled pins of fossil bone and mammoth (?) ivory come from the bed of Lower Klamath Lake near the Oregon-California boundary, the lowest level at Clovis, and near Lake City, Florida, likewise suggesting a former great distribution. Very crudely chipped stone tools in the form of scrapers, choppers, fist axes, and picklike implements come from such widely scattered points as ancient shore lines high above Georgian Bay in Canada, Tule Springs, Nevada, southern Texas, and Campeche; and a crude "scraper" comes from deep within the Becerra formation at Tequixquiac, Mexico.

None of this seemingly very old material has yet been organized into definite complexes. Its variety makes some degree of both temporal and regional differentiation seem likely, but it cannot yet be stated whether an ancient "bone industry" can be distinguished from the oldest stone industries on a time basis, or whether the oldest American cultural remains contained both stone and bone (or ivory) artifacts.

In the interval between the third and fourth Wisconsin advances (assuming that there were four), there is still a lack of regional complexes, except, as we have mentioned, that Sandia points seem to be quite locally distributed in central and eastern New Mexico, while Clovis fluted points must have been used over most of the continent, whether or not they were all on the same general time level. Well-made side and end scrapers accompany both the Clovis and the Sandia types, and the lowest levels of both the Clovis and the Sandia sites include bone artifacts.

On the Folsom time level, roughly 10,000 years ago (and corresponding to Wisconsin 4 or its retreat?), more definite regional differentiation is evident. As mentioned above, cave material from the Great Basin and southeastern Oregon which dates at this approximate time presents a very different array of artifacts from those found in the Great Plains with true Folsom points. Both of these are also distinct from the fluted points, scrapers, lamellar flakes, and blades now known from several sites in the eastern woodlands; and the few artifacts so far found in the uppermost levels of the Becerra formation in central Mexico provide a fourth possible specialization, although this is, of course, highly tentative.

Post-glacial (Holocene) time has been divided by Antevs into three general periods on the basis of temperature changes. The three periods together constitute his "Neothermal age." He estimates that the Anathermal (temperature at first like the present, then growing warmer) lasted from about 7000 to 5000 B.C., the Altithermal (distinctly warmer and drier than the present) from about 5000 to 2500 B.C., and the Medithermal (rebirth of lakes and mountain glaciers) from about 2500 B.C. to the present. Eventually, better datings may alter these limits, and especially is there every probability that these main periods will be subdivided into climatic fluctuations of lesser but nonetheless important magnitudes.

In the Anathermal, regional differentiation at present seems to be not much greater than during the final glaciation. Fluted points seem to have disap-

peared by this time, unless they survived in the Arctic; and instead we have a variety of unfluted points, some of lanceolate form, some with parallel edges, some with broad stems and very shallow incut shoulders, and some with stem notches cut in much more deeply. The chipping on these various forms is sometimes very finely done, with matched pairs of scars or parallel scars crossing the blade diagonally. This so-called "Yuma chipping" is also found on many other projectile points in subsequent cultures. Of the tentative types so far defined, the Plainview and Scottsbluff cover immense areas from Alaska to the Texas coast, and one specimen much like a Scottsbluff was found with a mammoth skeleton in the Texcoco lake bed in March, 1952. The Eden and Long types seem to be primarily Great Plains specializations; and the Browns Valley type seems to belong to Minnesota, so far as known. As most of our knowledge of this stage comes from the Great Plains and the Sulphur Springs stage in southern Arizona, we have yet to draw the contrasts with contemporaneous assemblages in the rest of the continent. The Chalco complex of central Mexico, outlined by De Terra, may belong, at least in part, to this stage, and it seems certain that some of the Great Basin and California discoveries in recent years will also belong to it. Artifact assemblages are, in general, more complicated than before, containing large knife or ax blades, boring or drilling tools, finely made bone needles, stone "gouges," and—most important—the mano and milling stone. The latter indicate man's use of plant foods to supplement the dwindling supply of large Pleistocene mammals, whose extinction was probably complete by the end of this stage.

The Altithermal period corresponds with what has long been termed the "Post-Glacial Climatic Optimum" of Europe and other parts of the Old

World. Since American archeologists are only now beginning to become acquainted with this long era of deficient rainfall and dwindling grasslands, drying of lakes and water courses, wind erosion, etc., we are hardly beyond the point of being able to recognize the geological evidence for such a period, much less of fitting cultural evidence into it. It appears that enormous areas were rendered uninhabitable for game and man alike, but such conditions need not have obtained through 2,500 years. Likely the great drought was broken now and then by better conditions, so that plants, game, and man could have returned to areas temporarily abandoned. In the last three or four years, particularly, simple complexes of knives, scrapers, and projectile points have been discovered in many sites in the arid Southwest and Great Basin which may represent human occupation off and on during the Altithermal. This problem is only beginning to receive attention.

It was during the Altithermal, however, that extremely important new migrations from Asia must have occurred, namely, those that account for the Archaic pattern of culture in the eastern woodlands and near the Pacific Coast. According to the writer's definition (see n. 1), this pattern is defined by the presence of a polished-stone technology and the absence of pottery. It must not be confused with the "Archaic," long used in Middle America for early *ceramic* cultures, a term now being replaced by "Formative" or "pre-Classic." A host of new traits make their appearance in North America, such as a great variety of notched or stemmed projectile points, celts, adzes, grooved axes, polished plummet stones, boatstones and bannerstones (both probably atlatl weights), stone vessels, nut stones, mortar and pestle, tubular pipes, many forms of stone and shell ornaments, burials with offerings and (in some places) considerable amounts of red ochre, the dog (sometimes buried in human cemeteries), and so on. The task of separating what is really new in this period from traits that may have survived from earlier periods remains to be done. Presumably the Arctic as well as the rest of the continent was warmer than at any time since before the Wisconsin glaciations, and Bering Strait probably was crossed by boat; the use of boats and/or dugout canoes must have been spread far and wide over the New World by peoples of this Archaic pattern. Occupation was principally along the sea coasts and major rivers, the great arid regions being still very poor in food resources. Where occupation was possible, man depended upon ever more varied resources, now including fish and shellfish as well as plant food and game. Increasingly sedentary life is shown by the growth of innumerable shell heaps (some of great size) and other refuse middens along the rivers of the eastern woodlands and around the coasts of both North and South America. Population must have increased greatly in these favorable areas over anything previously known in the New World.

Radiocarbon dates so far obtained on Archaic sites in New York and Kentucky range from about 3700 to 2500 B.C., but, of course, their full range has not been determined. In California, Heizer has obtained a date of about 2100 B.C. on the latest of four sites near Sacramento which belong to the Early Horizon and contain a variety of well-made polished stone implements and ornaments. Probably some of the older sites with this industry along the Santa Barbara Channel are of equal age. In the Northwest, Arctic, and most of Canada, the polished-stone technology was present long ago, but no absolute dates comparable to those in the United States have yet been determined. In the Great Basin and Southwest no definite Archaic horizon has been defined, polished-stone artifacts being apparently about as late as the introduction of pottery. Material called "Archaic" is now being described from the Great Plains and Texas; but this term seems to be based on the presence of a considerable variety of chipped-stone artifacts comparable with those of the Archaic in the woodlands, rather than on polished stone; objects of polished stone appear in these central regions, but perhaps only relatively late in the scale.

With this brief background we will turn to a discussion of regional developments. Most of this will be concerned with the Medithermal climatic period, since we have discussed developments up to this point on a very broad basis. Just when the return to cooler and moister conditions began, with consequent rebirth of interior lakes and mountain glaciers and return of grass and game to regions previously made very uninviting to man, is not closely dated as yet; nor is it known whether time differences should be allowed for latitude. Antevs estimates this onset at about 2500 B.C., but other climatologists suggest anywhere from 2500 to 1600 B.C. At any rate, it is fairly certain that all North American ceramic and agricultural horizons fall within the Medithermal.

ARCTIC

As the archeology of the far north can be discussed cogently only by those who have done original work there, I will rely on two recent summaries: Larsen and Rainey, *Ipiutak and the Arctic Whale Hunting Culture* (1948), and Collins, "The Origin and Antiquity of the Eskimo" (1951). The former source gives the chronological scheme in Table 1.

The complexities of tracing individual traits and their supposed direction of diffusion over the vast lands from Bering Straits to Greenland cannot be attempted here. With the exception of Ipiutak and Near Ipiutak, most modern sources support the alignments shown. The Arctic Whale Hunting culture was apparently first established in western Alaska from an Asiatic source and spread eastward eventually to Greenland; the Thule culture was whale-hunting but the older Dorset was not; neither were Ipiutak or Kachemak Bay. In Larsen and Rainey's interpretation, the remarkable culture discovered at Ipiutak, a town of some six hundred houses built on streets along the shore at Point Hope, was considered older than Old Bering Sea but related to it in artistic conceptions. They compared Ipiutak artifacts and burial customs with several cultures in eastern Asia, including an "undeniable resemblance" between masklike carvings on an ivory frame, and ancient Chinese art. The exquisite carvings of this and Old Bering Sea culture were made possible by the use of iron bits in antler and ivory engraving tools. Iron could probably have been obtained by trade from northern China or Korea shortly after the time of Christ. An early position for Ipiutak was also indicated by its lack of pottery, blubber lamps, parts of sleds, boats, and snowshoes and of rubbed-slate artifacts; and by the presence of quantities of finely chipped stone blades, antler and ivory arrowheads, and lances with rows of stone side blades similar to those from early "Neolithic" sites in Siberia.

Most Arctic archeologists have placed the entire span of Eskimo cultures within the Christian Era, and radiocarbon dates, on the whole, support them. The oldest (Okvik) stage of Old Bering Sea has one date of about 300 B.C., but the Ipiutak culture, surprisingly, has two dates of 912 ± 170 and 973 ± 170 years ago, or roughly A.D. 1000. This necessitates a reconsideration of Alaskan chronology and also offers the interesting proposition that the large town of Ipiutak could have existed at the same time as did successful Viking agricultural settlements in southern Greenland. The latter were possible only because of a warm cycle (sometimes termed the "Second Climatic Optimum") which lasted some three centuries before returning cold forced their abandon-

bone and ivory. According to Collins, the investigations by Okladnikov in the Lake Baikal region, and the present conceptions of Eskimo chronology "sustain to a remarkable degree Hatt's views of the origin of Eskimo culture and the development of culture generally in northern Eurasia and America." Perhaps this means that Hatt's older stratum, his "coast culture," largely ac-

TABLE 1

Southeast Alaska	Bering Strait	North Alaska	Arctic Canada	Greenland
Modern	Modern*	Modern*	Central Eskimo	Modern*
				Intermediate*
Kachemak Bay III	Recent Prehistoric*	Tigara*	Eastern Thule*	Inugsik*
				Eastern Thule*
Kachemak Bay II	Punuk*	Western Thule*	Dorset and Western Thule*	Dorset?
	Early Punuk*	Birnirk*		
	Old Bering Sea*	?	Dorset	
Kachemak Bay I	Okvik*	Near Ipiutak		
		Ipiutak		

*Asterisks indicate phases of neo-Eskimo or Arctic Whale Hunting culture.

ment. A temporary warm spell of about the same dates is also indicated by several great droughts and extensive wind erosion in the Southwest.

The old idea of Sollas that Eskimo culture could be traced far back into the Mesolithic period of Europe and western Asia has recently been given new life. Such European Mesolithic traits as pottery lamps, steep-sided, conical-base cooking pots, and barbed bone fish and bird spears occur in prehistoric Eskimo; and geometric designs in European Paleolithic and Mesolithic have been compared with the simpler linear designs of Dorset and Old Bering Sea on

counts for Eskimo origins while his later stratum or "inland culture" accounts for the transfer of snowshoes and other elements typically possessed by Tungusic nomads of Asia to the interior of Alaska and Canada, i.e., to the Athapaskan-speaking peoples, if not the actual migration of these peoples from Asia.

It remains one of our great enigmas that, at the top of the continent, where presumably the ancestors of all American natives crossed from Asia, no real connecting links have been recognized between glacial times and shortly before Christ. Attention has recently been drawn to this gap by recognition of non-Eskimo lithic complexes. The Cape Denbigh Flint Complex, now known from a number of sites in northern Alaska, includes burins which closely resemble those from Mesolithic Europe, small lamellar flakes (knives or scrapers), and polyhedral cores. Such artifacts are, however, found in other Arctic cultures, particularly the Dorset. Dating the Denbigh complex has been obscured by references to its "Folsom and Yuma affinities." A "Folsom point" found with this complex by Giddings is a stubby and perhaps rechipped example of a large fluted point—certainly not a true Folsom in modern terminology. The "Yuma" element consists of parallel flaking scars on some blade fragments, a trait which appears in different chipping industries in North America up to historic times. Even if some affinity with early artifacts in the Great Plains could be demonstrated, the matter of time lag in reaching the Arctic would be like that expressed by Collins for Asiatic derivation of the other elements:

However, unless there is good geological evidence to the contrary, there is no reason to suppose that the Denbigh Flint Complex was particularly ancient. The presence of Paleolithic-Mesolithic burins and other implements is hardly decisive in this regard. The Denbigh people may only have been perpetuating a Paleolithic tradition in the use of these implements long after it had faded away in the Old World, just as much later the Ipiutak Eskimos continued to use side-bladed projectiles of Mesolithic-Neolithic form several thousand years after they had passed out of use in Eurasia.

PACIFIC COAST

We will consider the Pacific Coast to include those parts of California, Oregon, Washington, and British Columbia which lie between the Pacific shores and the crest of the Sierra Ne-vada, Cascades, and northern Coast Ranges, and also the Pacific slope of southern California. A considerable amount of work has been done in scattered parts of this region since the 1870's; but in only two areas has there emerged a chronological framework which has stood the tests of time and criticism. In central California, Heizer, Lillard, Purves, Fenenga, Beardsley, and others have established three sequential "horizons": Early, Middle, and Late. In an excellent paper, Beardsley (1948) graphically summarizes the continuities and changes through these periods in thirty-three sites and discusses important parallels with the eastern United States Archaic pattern. The writer has suggested above that these and other Pacific Coast cultures with a polished-stone industry be considered part of a general North American Archaic. The Early Horizon bears a radiocarbon date of about 2100 B.C. for the latest of four known sites; the Middle dates from perhaps 1000 B.C. to A.D. 500; and the Late continues to historic times. Parallels with the Eastern Archaic are, significantly, strongest in the Early Horizon, after which increasing regional specialization makes them gradually less similar.

Along the Santa Barbara Channel, Rogers and Olson have defined three general periods also: Oak Grove, Hunting, and Canaliño, which should correspond in a broad sense to those of central California. A direct correlation is, however, replete with difficulties and suffers from a lack of dates in the south. Many of these Channel and island sites are enormously large and rich, and, in particular, the Canaliño artifacts present very highly developed crafts for nonagricultural, nonceramic people.

In the San Joaquin Valley, material described by Gifford, Schenck, and Wedel provides further problems in correlation but would not seem to antedate the others. Under the direction of Heizer, the University of California Archaeological Survey has pursued a host of studies in recent years in various parts of California and western Nevada, out of which many new culture complexes should emerge. Pottery is now widely known in the San Joaquin Valley and east of the southern Sierra Nevada, but, instead of being derived from the Southwest, it would appear to be connected with Shoshonian tribes of Nevada and northern Utah. However, a widespread pottery tradition in southern California was probably derived from western Arizona and may be of considerable temporal depth.

The southern coast of British Columbia was long ago investigated by Harlan I. Smith; and in 1938 Drucker and Beardsley conducted an extensive survey in Kwakiutl and Tsimshian territory (1943). Arden King has published on stratified sites on the Puget Sound area; Cressman on a burial site near Gold Hill, Oregon; and Leatherman and the writer on a historic site on Coquille Bay, Oregon. None of these remains appears to represent any considerable antiquity, relating more or less to the immediate ancestors of historic tribes in each case. A polished-stone technology is present along this entire coastal region. There are, however, many indications of older material which has yet to be dated and brought into sequential relationship with the better-known materials; the Malaga Cove, La Jolla, and Tank sites in southern California and Hawver and other caves in the Sierra Nevada come to mind, to mention but a few.

The difficult problem of organizing this Californian material and relating it to culture sequences in the desert areas to the east is receiving the attention of such archeologists as Harrington, Treganza, Brainerd, and Heizer, but it is made doubly difficult because the desert sequence itself is undergoing extensive re-examination.

COLUMBIA RIVER BASIN

Publications on archeological work in central Washington were issued by Harlan I. Smith in 1900 and 1910; by H. W. Krieger in 1928. Collier, Hudson, and Ford (1942) summarize all the work done in this area in connection with their work in the Grand Coulee Dam reservoir, begun by the writer in 1939. Strong, Schenck, and Steward excavated on the Columbia River near The Dalles in 1930. The writer made a survey of the middle reaches of the John Day and Deschutes rivers in 1938, following which Cressman excavated Butte Creek Cave in 1946. Since 1947 the Smithsonian Institution's River Basin Surveys has carried on numerous reconnaissance and excavation projects in the Northwestern reservoir basins. To date, however, no comprehensive over-all interpretations or cultural sequences have been offered. The great bulk of this material would seem to represent historic tribes and their immediate ancestors. Indications of much older occupations are seen in the artifacts found by Cressman under Mount Mazama pumice in the upper Deschutes Valley and in a recently reported "Early Man" site in eastern Washington.

GREAT BASIN

For many years the only archeological reference point in the Great Basin region was the 1929 publication of Loud and Harrington on Lovelock Cave in western Nevada. In 1936 the near-by Humboldt Cave was completely excavated by Heizer, Beardsley, and the writer. From 1934 to 1940 Cressman and several colleagues conducted excavations in southeastern Oregon caves, principally Guano, Catlow, Roaring Springs, Paisley Caves 1, 2, and 3, and Fort Rock. The Paisley and Fort Rock caves produced cultural material both above and below pumice, which fell while hot, firing the dry vegetal refuse below. This situation posed extremely interesting geological problems, for the Paisley pumice came from the explosion of Mount Mazama (the remnants of which now form Crater Lake), while that at Fort Rock came from the later eruption of Newberry Crater. At Paisley the pumice fall occurred when Summer Lake stood some 85 feet higher than at present.

Radiocarbon dates made on a log buried by Mazama pumice give an average of 6,453 ± 250 years on four runs. Previous estimates had ranged from a minimum of 1,000 years to as much as 15,000, with Howel Williams favoring 4,000–7,000 years. Sagebrush fiber sandals from below this pumice in Fort Rock Cave were dated directly by radiocarbon measurement, with the astounding figure of 9,053±350 years, or about 7000 B.C., the beginning of postglacial time. Since then, datings from Nevada and Utah confirm beyond any question that dry vegetal materials may be perfectly preserved this long and even longer. Catlow Cave, too far east to receive these pumice falls, has one date of 959±150 years ago. In spite of these dates, the pumice stratigraphy, and the amount of excavation in southeastern Oregon, there has emerged no interpretation of cultural development or of what changes in culture and environment occurred during the main climatic periods. The evidences of man in association with extinct animals, in Paisley Cave 3 and on Lower Klamath Lake shores, have not been worked out in relation to the other discoveries; they should be older and of Wisconsin age.

Harrington's original estimates on sloth remains and early artifacts from Gypsum Cave in southern Nevada are closely borne out by radiocarbon dates on sloth dung. These are 10,455 ± 350 and 8,527 ± 250 years. It is not abso-lutely certain that any of the artifacts are as old as the higher date, and, since the artifacts are of wood, they could be directly dated.

In west-central Nevada, Heizer and his students in 1950 obtained a long sequence from Leonard Rock Shelter near Lovelock. Utilizing guano and vegetal artifacts from this site, Lovelock Cave, and our excavation in Humboldt Cave in 1936 for obtaining dates, Heizer has worked out the following sequence (see for details 1951*a, b*):

5. Lovelock (cave) culture; dates of 532±300 B.C. from Lovelock Cave and 2 B.C.±175 years from Humboldt Cave; occupation continuing to historic level.
4. Hiatus; no human or bat occupation of caves from about 2500 to 500 B.C.
3. Leonard (cave) culture; dates 4054± 250 and 3786±400 B.C.; terminal date, 2500±250 B.C.
2. Granite Point (lake shore) and Humboldt (cave) cultures; dates 6710±400 and 5088±350 B.C., both in Anathermal age.
1. Bat guano in contact with gravels of Provo Pluvial stage of Lake Lahontan; date 9248±570 B.C.

A cultural hiatus, as well as absence of bat guano, occurs between about 2500 and 500 B.C., when, according to Antevs' estimates of the Altithermal dates, it should occur before 2500 B.C. Heizer suggests that the discrepancy may be due to the rainfall minimum lagging far behind the Altithermal temperature maximum or that still unrecognized surface material may show non-cave occupation during this gap. Beads of *Olivella biplicata* shells in Leonard shelter at a 7,000-year level show that trade was carried on with the Pacific Coast by 5000 B.C., earlier than any direct date in California.

Near Wendover in western Utah, Jennings in 1951 found a long sequence in Danger Cave which promises to match those in Nevada and Oregon.

Dates of 11,453 ± 600 and 11,151 ±
570 years, or about 9500 B.C., were obtained on wood and on sheep dung
just above gravels deposited during a
temporary stand of Lake Bonneville as
it was retreating from its Provo stage.
Hence the final stage of retreat of both
Lake Lahontan and Lake Bonneville
(from their Provo levels) is dated almost exactly the same in two archeological profiles; both agree closely, as
well, with the Armenta Horizon in the
Valley of Mexico, where ancient Lake
Texcoco's retreat occurred 11,003 ± 500
years ago. The Black's Fork lithic complex described by Renaud from western Wyoming, and the Eden Valley site
with its Scottsbluff and Eden type
points, also in western Wyoming, are
other examples of very ancient sites in
the upper Colorado and Green River
country, east of the Great Basin proper.

The southern tip of Nevada and most
of southern Utah have long been considered a periphery of the Southwest
and contain both Basket Maker and
Puebloan-derived remains. Northern
Utah, however, contains several levels
of material, including some pottery,
which do not seem related to the Southwest, as seen in Steward's discussion
of his Promontory Point excavations.
As mentioned previously, this peculiar
(Shoshoni?) pottery occurs over a great
range, from central California perhaps
to Nebraska.

Long regarded as an insignificant
cultural sink into which Basket Maker
and Puebloan elements occasionally
filtered, the Great Basin has come into
its own with a long and fascinating
record of changing culture and environment reflected in the fluctuations of its
great interior lakes. However, the different areal manifestations contrast
strongly with one another, and the task
of integrating them remains to be done.
Steward (1940) has written the only
comprehensive account, now in need
of extensive revisions.

SOUTHWEST

Archeologically, this is the best-
known region north of Middle America,
its spectacular scenery and wonderful
preservation of cave remains and stone
buildings having attracted scholars
from far and wide from the days of
early exploration. A host of excavations
by capable archeologists has built up
a great body of detailed information,
and this region has the added advantage of an accurate system of dating
by tree-rings, instituted by Douglass in
the 1920's. Many geographical and climatic studies by Bryan, Hack, Antevs,
and others have also been conducted
in conjunction with archeology, while
Brew and Kluckhohn have stimulated
thought with theoretical treatises.

Space will permit only the briefest
possible discussion of major changes in
interpretation of cultural data. For
many years, Southwestern prehistory
was considered to revolve around two
major developments in the San Juan
area, a supposed "culture hearth." The
Basket Makers went through two
stages, the first agricultural but nonceramic and the second with both pottery and agriculture; they were then
supposed to have been wiped out by
invasions of a new people, the Pueb-
loans, who built large multi-roomed
structures of stone and carried ceramic
and textile arts to a very high level.
The apex of Puebloan development
occurred in the Classic period, about
A.D. 1000–1200, when they were believed to have spread their influence
over most of the Southwest, then to
have gone into a gradual decline, which
is continuing to the present.

This simplistic picture has now been
altered in every respect. A totally different cultural tradition came to be recognized in southern Arizona, extending over approximately the same time
span as that in the north. The name
"Hohokam" was given this southern
culture by Huntington in 1914, when

he became interested in its irrigation systems and past climatic changes. It was not until 1927, when the Gila Pueblo staff began excavations at Snaketown, that its long life and series of developmental stages became known. In the 1930's a third tradition, called "Mogollon," came to be recognized in west-central New Mexico and eventually from central Arizona to the Pecos River in southern New Mexico. Like the Basket Maker, it was at first believed to have flourished for some centuries after Christ, then been overrun and submerged by expanding Puebloan culture and people. In the course of time, continuing field work showed the distinctive development of all three traditions over a very long time, at least until the fourteenth century. The Basket Maker and northern Pueblo tradition came to be discussed under a single label: "Anasazi"; but in the southern belt Mogollon continued to be used for the earlier manifestations (up to A.D. 800 or 900) and "Pueblo" for the later phases. Difficulties arose over how "Pueblo culture" could be applied outside the Anasazi area (in general, the San Juan River drainage). Meanwhile, Gladwin had recognized a fourth major tradition, which he called the "Yuman root" in far-western Arizona; and from this Colton developed the concept of the Patayan tradition extending down the Colorado River.

A very comprehensive review of all major Southwestern excavations, changing concepts, and the strengths and weaknesses of the various taxonomic systems, has been presented by Brew (1946) in his great volume on Alkali Ridge, Utah. Reed (1946, 1950) proposed new definitions to cut through the masses of accumulated data and conflicting terms and extended the term "Pueblo culture" to cover not only the Anasazi but *also* the Mogollon in its early as well as late ("Puebloan-influenced") phases. In this usage, Mogol-lon is not only an early development paralleling Basket Maker but continues alongside San Juan Puebloan. The northern or Anasazi branch of Pueblo culture survived into historic times, some of its towns still being occupied today, but the southern or Mogollon branch ended probably in the fourteenth century, when it was overrun and destroyed by Apache tribes. The Little Colorado River marks the approximate boundary between these two branches or "complexes" in Arizona, and in New Mexico it is marked by a line running due east through the approximate center of the state.

Present evidence is that Mogollon was the oldest Southwestern tradition, both in agriculture and in pottery-making, although agriculture is of far greater antiquity than the first-known appearance of pottery. The earliest-known pottery in the Southwest is from the Pine Lawn phase of the Mogollon tradition, in Tularosa Cave II, west-central New Mexico. Here Martin obtained two radiocarbon dates of $2,112 \pm 230$ and $2,177 \pm 225$ years, or about 200 ± 160 B.C. On the other hand, the now-famous "primitive corn" from Bat Cave in western New Mexico has a direct date (on cobs) of $2,862 \pm 250$ years, or about 900 ± 250 B.C.; and 1000–1500 B.C. has been postulated for stratigraphically older corn not yet dated. In Tularosa Cave I, Martin found "primitive corn" with a date of about 300 ± 210 B.C. It thus appears certain that a primitive maize was cultivated in this area for at least 1,000 years before pottery and a more advanced type of maize came in around 200 B.C. As most authorities would derive Mogollon pottery in a general way from Formative or Pre-Classic wares in central Mexico, these dates seen in perfect agreement. By contrast, Haury estimates that Hohokam began about A.D. 1; and the oldest-known tree-ring date for agricultural Basket Maker is A.D.

217, from Dupont Cave near Kanab, Utah. The Basket Makers do not seem to have made pottery until A.D. 400 or 500.

With this background, the remarkable sequence in Ventana Cave, southwestern Arizona, can be mentioned for its linking of the known ceramic and pre-ceramic periods in the Southwest. The lowest cultural level in this cave is called by Haury the "Ventana Complex," estimated at 8000 B.C. on the basis of extinct faunal remains and a "Folsom" point (actually, not a Folsom point). The table from Haury's volume (1951, p. 528) (Table 2) on Ventana Cave gives the different interpretations in correlating its pre-ceramic stages with those in the Cochise Basin in southeastern Arizona and with Roger's sequence in the Colorado desert area. After A.D. 1 the Hohokam ceramic levels continue to about A.D. 1400.

In Table 2 the long erosional interval in Hack's and Bryan's columns corresponds to the Altithermal period of

TABLE 2

Time	Antevs	Hack	Bryan	
			Alternative A	Alternative B
A.D. 1	San Pedro	San Pedro	San Pedro	San Pedro
B.C. 1000			Chiricahua–Amargosa II	
2000	San Pedro		*Red sand* Ventana–Amargosa I	Chiricahua–Amargosa II
3000		Chiricahua–Amargosa II	↑	*Red sand* Ventana–Amargosa I
4000			*Erosion*	*Erosion*
5000	Chiricahua–Amargosa II	↑ *Red sand* Ventana–Amargosa I		
6000		*Erosion* ↓		
7000			Unaccounted for	
	———————— *Red sand* Ventana–Amargosa I			
8000			Disconformity ————	

VENTANA COMPLEX
Volcanic debris

Antevs, although Antevs himself places the Chiricahua-Amargosa II cultural material in this gap. There are now several radiocarbon dates which, on the whole, support Bryan's alternative B better than the others. Thus the Benson 5:10 site in the Cochise area has dates of about 500 B.C. and A.D. 200 for the San Pedro stage. Since San Pedro is often termed "Mogollon without pottery," the older date is agreeable. Cochise site 12 and Wet Leggett in New Mexico have dates of about 2050 and 2550 B.C., respectively, for the Chiricahua stage. No dates are available for Ventana-Amargosa I, but, if this belongs after the Altithermal erosional interval, Bryan's estimates again seem closest.

Numerous sites buried in terraces have been found in the Southwest in recent years, and their artifacts likened to those of the Chiricahua and San Pedro stages. The San Jose complex of New Mexico and the Concho of Arizona probably belong in this category, with their various chipped-stone artifacts and milling stones. The better definition of these pre-ceramic stages is now a prime problem in the Southwest, as well as over the rest of the continent.

SOUTHERN TEXAS—NORTHEAST MEXICO

For want of a better label, I will include the area from the northern boundaries of Middle America at the Rio Soto la Marina to the Edwards Plateau of central Texas under this head. In Texas there is evidence for the presence of man back into Wisconsin glacial times, which was touched on in the first section. In postglacial times this region saw developments comparable with the pre-ceramic stages just mentioned for the Southwest. There is as yet no point at which we can say that an Archaic pattern with polished-stone industry began, although my impression is that this occurred later in the central regions than in the eastern United States or the Pacific Coast. Rather, we seem to have hunting, fishing, and gathering peoples of simple material culture living a little-changing pattern of life for many millenniums. The Middle American pattern of intensive agriculture and pottery-making never penetrated it to any extent. If and when migrations occurred from Middle America toward the eastern United States (which I believe did begin sometime between 500 B.C. and A.D. 500, although others would place the time well after A.D. 1000), they left no apparent effect on this intermediate region, passing across it to the more humid forested lands farther east.

So far as evidence goes, this region never became agricultural in pre-European times. Most of it cannot be farmed today without irrigation. About A.D. 1000 or not long after, pottery and a few new traits, such as the bow and arrow, began to filter into it from the Southwest, Middle America, and Caddoan area to the east. Except along the Gulf Coast, pottery is scattered and uncommon, probably all "trade" ware, the natives never making any of their own. Along the central coast of Texas, there is a peculiar ware in some abundance, often decorated with asphaltum, and probably made by Karankawan tribes; so far it has not been related definitely to any specific tradition elsewhere.

GREAT PLAINS

The great region of the Great Plains extends from north of the Edwards Plateau in Texas to southern Alberta and Saskatchewan in Canada. It is almost entirely a vast grassy steppe and probably has been so through most of post-glacial time, supporting great herds of grazing animals. After the extinction of late Pleistocene mammals, which was complete by Altithermal times, if not during the Anathermal, food resources were poor, and man seems to have left the Plains more or less completely. With the return of a favorable climate in the Medithermal age, adequate grass returned and, with it, the incredible herds of modern bison and also pronghorn and deer. Man also occupied the Plains again, but his artifacts were now distinctly different from before, including a much larger range of implements, many of which are comparable to chipped-stone artifacts of the Eastern Archaic pattern. We have mentioned that the Archaic itself must represent some new migrations from Asia, affecting first the eastern woodlands and Pacific Coast, then spreading into the arid interior regions as food was available.

Some time between approximately 2000 and 1000 B.C., the culture represented in Level I of the Signal Butte site in western Nebraska may have become established; undoubtedly, there are contemporaneous complexes yet to be defined. At a time which may be guessed at about 1000 B.C., cordmarked utility pottery of the Woodland tradition began to spread through the Plains, presumably from the Great Lakes area. Eventually it reached as far as central Montana, Yellowstone Park in Wyoming, and the eastern slopes of the Rocky Mountains and as far south as north-central New Mexico, where its typical "amphora" shape and conical bottom are found mixed with Anasazi pottery in some sites. With the passage of time and diffusion among new peoples, some changes must have occurred in the forms and cord-impressed decoration of Woodland pottery; that found in the Canadian River Valley of the Texas Panhandle can easily be distinguished from that in the central Plains, but its northern origin is unmistakable. Its southern limit is the Red River. This continuous distribution of pottery in the Great Plains is not so well known as it should be. Wissler, in his book, *The American Indian*, wrongly shows the Plains as a nonpottery

corridor between the eastern woodlands and the Pueblo area.

Whether agriculture was likewise spread over the Plains in conjunction with pottery is highly dubious, for the Woodland pattern was evidently non-agricultural at first, very similar to the Archaic, except for the addition of pottery. Wedel, in his superb review of culture and climate in the central Plains (1940), states that Woodland remains in eastern Nebraska are found at depths of 6–25 feet in alluvial deposits and that traces of squash and gourds were found in the Walker-Gilmore site, but none of maize or beans. In the Ozark caves, ample evidence for agricultural practices appears long before pottery, but here pottery-making seems to have lagged behind surrounding areas. Assuming that all agriculture in the United States derived originally from Middle America and that the Woodland pottery tradition is Asiatic in origin, these practices must have met and mingled in various ways not yet understood. The old belief that they spread together in the New World is long since dead.

The Hopewellian culture of the Middle West (placed in a Middle Woodland period by Griffin and others) also reached into the Plains in northeastern Oklahoma and eastern Kansas, well after early Woodland. Charred beans and maize were found by Wedel in a site of this culture near Kansas City. Radiocarbon dates between 386 ± 250 B.C. and 1 B.C. ± 200 have been obtained on Hopewell sites in Ohio and Illinois, but they are not accepted everywhere, and there may have been some lag toward the Plains.

Following this phase, the Upper Republican and Nebraska cultures (or "Aspects") developed in the central Plains. They depended upon agriculture and bison-hunting alike, resulting in hundreds of small, but more or less permanent, settlements featured by well-built square houses with four large centerposts and entrance tunnel and a large variety of stone, bone, and antler tools. At this time there was also a thrust of Mississippian culture elements up the Missouri Valley to beyond Omaha. In the sand hills of western Nebraska, the Dismal River culture existed. But in the fifteenth century, approximately, extended droughts and invasions of bison-hunting nomads forced a general withdrawal of agriculturalists from the western and central Plains. About A.D. 1600 radically new cultures appeared, such as protohistoric Pawnee and a westward expansion of "Late Woodland" or "Upper Mississippi" culture, termed "Oneota Aspect." In central Kansas the Paint Creek culture undoubtedly represents the "Quivira" or Wichita people reached by Coronado in 1541. The agricultural and bison-hunting Wichita gradually moved southward until they spread over much of north-central Texas after 1700; they were preceded by an unknown people of similar economy but somewhat different artifact types. Historic archeology in the Plains is receiving much attention, for it involves great complications caused by the shifting westward of many woodland tribes under pressures and conflicts of the French, British, and American colonial expansions; most of these tribes became pure bison hunters. The Mandan and Hidatsa tribes in the Dakotas lived much as the prehistoric Upper Republican people and the historic Pawnee, in earth-covered lodges with tunnel entrance, raising maize, beans, and squashes, making bison-hunting expeditions, and utilizing the skins, bones, and sinews of these animals for all manner of material objects.

MIDDLE WEST

We will consider the Middle West to include the drainages of the upper Mississippi and Ohio rivers with the states of Missouri and Kentucky on the south, and southern Ontario except for its eastern end. Since the issue of Squier and Davis' "Ancient Monuments of the Mississippi Valley" in 1848, a great number of papers has appeared, the majority dealing with "mound builders." It has long been known that there were many different phases of mound-building and associated culture, so that by the 1920's it became evident that some sort of conceptual framework was imperative. We can discuss only these frameworks and datings.

The McKern or "Midwestern Taxonomic System" gained rapid use in the 1930's, classifying cultural material on the ceramic level into three "patterns" —Woodland, Hopewellian, and Mississippian—and subdividing these into phases, aspects, foci, and components, the latter being individual sites or distinct levels in stratified sites. Ford and Willey (1941) presented the first general conceptual scheme for the entire eastern United States, consisting of five stages: Archaic, Burial Mound I and II, and Temple Mound I and II. Unlike the McKern system, these stages are historical-developmental rather than purely classificatory. Within each stage are one or more local sequential complexes; and their traits, continuities, and changes are outlined. The Ford and Willey scheme has enjoyed considerable use in the Southeast, while the McKern system (with variations) has continued to be used in the Middle West. While no one would argue that the Woodland and Mississippi "patterns" (but not the Hopewellian) represent originally totally different traditions, one being largely of northeast Asian origin and the other representing later strong influences from Middle America, many difficult problems arise in trying to classify locally mixed cultures. It certainly is no solution to "assign" a focus or aspect to one or the other pattern on the basis of a majority of traits (which may be as close as 55–45 per cent). The historical processes responsible for the amalgamations should concern us more than the act of classifying.

Griffin (1946) in his "Cultural Change and Continuity in Eastern United States Archaeology" began to use a system of stages somewhat like those of Ford and Willey. These are listed in Table 3.

Whichever system is followed, qualifications are necessary to explain why a given complex should be assigned to a certain stage. While the building of temple mounds occurs most commonly in the Southeast but extends up the Mississippi Valley and lower Ohio Valley into the Middle West, associated artifacts and burial customs diffused farther north and are found in some cases with burial mounds. If the term "Upper Mississippi Phase of the Mississippi Pattern" is used in the Middle West, it must be explained that temple mounds are not present but the material is a fusion of surviving Woodland traits and others of Mississippian derivation. Conversely, if the term "Woodland" is to be used in the Southeast before Mississippian culture becomes dominant, it must be explained that Woodland pottery is not present but

that the southern material is "early Woodland" because it is merely roughly on the same time level. This confusion of culture and time is typical. There is some tendency now to retain McKern's "component," "focus," and "aspect" for organizing blocks of material which contrast with other blocks, then placing them within developmental stages in either Griffin's or Ford and Willey's terminology (or both). Students of Eastern United States archeology are going to have difficulty reconstructing history until they can speak a common language.

Until about 1945, Eastern archeologists strove mightily to compress all their ceramic chronology into 1,000 years or less. Archaic was thought to extend from perhaps 500 B.C. to A.D. 600 or later; Early Woodland or Burial Mound I to A.D. 1000; Middle Woodland (Hopewellian) or Burial Mound II to A.D. 1200 or so; and Late Woodland–Mississippian–Temple Mound I and II from A.D. 1200 to 1700. These guesses were widely accepted as "absolute dates," although slight allowances were made for diffusion of the complexes, highly biased according to which area was favored as "earliest" for each stage. Some felt that this was too constrictive and loosened the scale

TABLE 3

GRIFFIN		FORD AND WILLEY EASTERN UNITED STATES, GENERAL
Middle West	Southeast	
Late Woodland	Late Mississippi Early Mississippi	Temple Mound II Temple Mound I
Middle Woodland (Hopewellian)	Middle Woodland (Marksville)	Burial Mound II
	Early Woodland	Burial Mound I
	Archaic	Archaic
	Paleo-Indian	

here and there, but entirely according to personal inclinations. We now know that pre-ceramic Archaic with polished-stone technology existed as early as 3700 B.C. in Kentucky and 3400 B.C. in New York and that, in New York, Hopewellian-like pottery dates as early as 1000 B.C. in the Middlesex culture. Classic Hopewellian in the Ohio Valley and Illinois now has dates of 386–1 B.C. and may be the culmination of several centuries of development. The early Woodland or Burial Mound I stage must, therefore, have begun sometime between about 2500 and 1000 B.C. in the Middle West; we have mentioned its spread into the central Plains, and such a date would seem agreeable with the deepest buried sites.

Neither the time nor the place of initial Mississippian or Temple Mound I culture in the Eastern states has been established. While one date of A.D. 400 ± 175 has been determined for a temple-mound site in eastern Texas, this has not been generally accepted yet and must be confirmed from related sites. It does not appear out of line with the greater dates for Eastern ceramic cultures generally. In the Middle West, Mississippian culture with temple-mound construction is probably later, owing to its spread up the Mississippi Valley; but an appearance around A.D. 1000 or earlier should not be difficult to believe.

Hopewell itself may well have been influenced to some extent by Pre-Classic Middle American cultures, since maize agriculture was present in New York with the Middlesex culture at 1000 B.C. and could be still older in the Middle West. Hopewell may indeed have resulted from the intrusion of agriculture into this region, meeting peoples of the early Woodland stage. Rocker-stamped pottery also belongs to the Pre-Classic horizon in Middle America and the Chavín horizon in Peru, but it could be argued that this spread south instead of north, for it also occurs in northeastern Asia.

Back of the Archaic are the lithic complexes of the Middle West with fluted points, as exemplified by the Parrish site in Kentucky. Their age and the length of a gap, if any, before Archaic are unknown.

NORTHEAST

The Northeast includes southeastern Ontario and the St. Lawrence Valley of Canada as well as the northeastern United States and Virginia. Primarily in New York but extending into surrounding states and Canada, Ritchie has worked out a long cultural history, successfully combining the McKern taxonomic terminology with Griffin's scheme of period names (see above). Ritchie (1951*a*, *b*) has published two comprehensive summaries. The former lists three subdivisions of the Archaic period, three of the Early Woodland, three Middle Woodland, and five Late Woodland (the last being historic). These sub-periods are broken down into numerous aspects, foci, and components. A simplified chart from the second paper appears below (Table 4).

While Ritchie uses "culture" in this table where "phase" is used in the first paper and Hopewellian is equated to Early Woodland III in the latter, these are minor points, and the sequence provides a very substantial anchor for chronological reckonings all through the Northeast. Ritchie's many other works build up a large body of information showing a continuous cultural history all through the Northeast. A puzzling situation exists in that certain features of the Laurentian culture, particularly ground-slate artifacts, closely resemble those of the Dorset (Eskimo) culture in the eastern Arctic region. With the old estimates for Archaic and Dorset dates (see above), any direct connections between them would be on the order of A.D. 1000. With the Laurentian now going back to about 3000–1000 B.C., new reckonings are in order. Martin, Quimby, and Collier (1947) would place Dorset between A.D. 100 and 1000, but the gap would still be over 1,000 years. There is always the assumption, of course, that the diffusion of such traits was from the Arctic southward to the United States, whereas the possibility of a long-range migration across Canada and then a reversal

There is apparently no evidence for snowshoes, sleds, or toboggans in archeological sites of the Northeast, but their preservation is probably too much to expect. Fortunately for anthropologists, the Northeast has been raised to a level of organization hardly enjoyed by any other North American region by the volume on *Man in Northeastern North America,* edited by F. Johnson (1946). This contains comprehensive discussions on environment, prehistory,

TABLE 4

Historic	Iroquois tribes		Historic Algonkin tribes		A.D. 1609
WOODLAND PERIOD	Late	Iroquois culture	Late Coastal culture		A.D. 1200?
		Owasco culture			A.D. 500?
	Middle Early	Point Peninsula culture Hopewellian culture Middlesex culture		Early Coastal culture	B.C. 998*
ARCHAIC PERIOD		Laurentian culture			B.C. 2980*
		Lamoka culture			B.C. 3433*

*Radiocarbon determination.

toward the north should at least be considered. Whatever develops along this line, Ritchie (1951c) concludes:

There would thus seem to be accumulating from various lines of inquiry, data in support of an early occupation of the coniferous forest zone of North America by nomadic hunting bands from a similar Old World milieu, well adapted to life under boreal conditions by the possession of felling and woodworking tools comprising the adze, gouge, and probably the celt; of tailored skin clothing, as judged by Laurentian eyed bone needles; of numerous varieties of chipped and ground stone knives, lance heads, javelin points, skin and wood scrapers; of barbed bone hunting and fishing points; of combs and probably numerous other traits, including the use of flint and pyrites for fire-making. I can see no reason for denying the probability of Asiatic or Eurasian prototypes for all these traits.

ethnology, physical types, language, and the problems of circumpolar diffusions of culture and peoples.

Johnson (1949) has also been responsible for one of our best examples of co-operative research by archeologists and authorities in sedimentation, paleobotany, peat formation, sea-level changes, climatic change reflected in molluscan species, etc., in the volume on the Boylston Street Fishweir found in the mud of Back Bay in Boston. The date of the great weir (or weirs) has now been placed at between 3767 ± 500 B.C. and 1901 ± 390 B.C. by the radiocarbon method (peat under the weir and wood overlying it, respectively). The associated researches indicated that the weir was made by an Archaic people in a climate warmer than the present, which is agreeable with the dates and the approximate span of the Altithermal age.

Beyond the Archaic we have the usual situation of fluted points and associated artifacts which cannot yet be dated, except that they may fall close to the last glacial phase. Several such complexes are currently being described from Pennsylvania, New York, and Virginia.

SOUTHEAST

Since we have hinted at chronological schemes and dates in the Middle West and Northeast which also affect the southeastern states, these need not be repeated. It may be said, however, that the McKern and Griffin systems have caught on only partially in the Southeast, and discussions are somewhat clearer if the Ford and Willey system is used. The Archaic stage is found throughout this region, from eastern Texas and Oklahoma to the Atlantic Ocean. Three subdivisions have been recognized in the Tennessee River Valley, but their general application has yet to be determined. In Kentucky the Archaic range should be from 4000 or more B.C. to possibly 1000 B.C. The earliest-known pottery of the Southeast should, in general, come after 1000 B.C.; but in southern Georgia and Florida there exists a peculiar fiber-tempered pottery which constitutes a local horizon, called the "Orange period," which is not known in pure form elsewhere. This has a radiocarbon date of about 1600 B.C. and is assigned by some to the end of the Archaic rather than the general Burial Mound I stage. Otherwise, the Tchefuncte of the lower Mississippi Valley and the Deptford farther east constitute a Burial Mound I stage.

Burial Mound II includes the Marksville of the lower Mississippi Valley and Santa Rosa–Swift Creek of southern Georgia and Florida. Again we have a puzzling situation, in that ceramics of Santa Rosa–Swift Creek present a highly developed complex with evidences of trade with the Hopewellian culture; and the following Weeden Island complex, which should logically belong to a Temple Mound I stage on the basis of ceramics, continues the use of burial mounds to a late date. Probably the use of both burial mounds and temple mounds diffused into Florida at a considerably later time than elsewhere in the Southeast and the Middle West.

In 1941, Ford and Willey gave the following estimates for the beginning of these stages in central Louisiana: Burial Mound I, A.D. 750; Burial Mound II, 900; Temple Mound I, 1150; and Temple Mound II from 1550 into historic times after 1700. Radiocarbon datings are, so far, too few and scattered to determine the true dates of these periods, but it is probable that they will have to be loosened all along. Recently, Ford, Griffin, and Phillips reduced these estimates (without considering radiocarbon dates) from one to two centuries each, beginning Temple Mound I (Troyville culture of the lower Mississippi Valley) at A.D. 700. One Marksville date (Burial Mound II) is about A.D. 400, but, since Marksville is related to Hopewellian with dates of 386 to 1 B.C. in the Middle West, it cannot yet be decided whether the radiocarbon dates or the previous estimates are closer to the truth.

Regarding the earliest appearance of a Temple Mound I stage (or the Mississippian pattern in general), it is also best to reserve opinion for the present. A radiocarbon date of A.D. 400 ± 175 has been obtained for a temple-mound site in eastern Texas by the writer, who had previously considered the contemporaneousness of a temple-mound stage in this area and the Burial Mound II stage farther east a distinct possibility. However, this raises still further arguments in regard to absolute chronology versus relative position of Southeastern cultures which cannot be settled yet. I have previously argued, and still do, that chronology in the eastern United States is shot full of preconceptions which are no more than guesses.

The famous situation at Vero and Melbourne in eastern Florida, where a controversy has raged since 1914 over the contemporaneousness of human bones with extinct fauna, has recently been reviewed in its entirety, with many physiographic, climatic, and ar-

PRINCIPAL GAPS IN KNOWLEDGE

Certain unknowns have been pointed out in the sections above and are fairly obvious to regional workers already. Their solution depends upon further field investigations and many more absolute datings. This section, then, will deal with more general aims. In the first section we mentioned the need for a much higher level of organization of data before a cultural history of man in North America can be written as one

TABLE 5

Geological Intervals	Cultural Periods	Dates
Van Valkenburg	Seminole	1750 on
Van Valkenburg	St. Augustine	A.D. 1700–1763
Van Valkenburg	Malabar II	A.D. 1000–1763
Van Valkenburg	Malabar I'	A.D. 1–1000
Melbourne–Van Valkenburg	Malabar I	Time of Christ?
Melbourne–Van Valkenburg	Orange (fiber-tempered pottery)	1000–1 B.C.
Melbourne–Van Valkenburg	Pre-ceramic	2000–1000 B.C., extinct fauna
Melbourne		
Anastasia–Melbourne		
Anastasia		

cheological considerations, by Rouse (1951). He offers the tentative chronology shown in Table 5.

Extensive correspondence with Rouse, however, reveals that he is already dissatisfied with this scale of dates and is preparing a new scale of alternatives. Certainly, the radiocarbon dates in other parts of the eastern United States necessitate a much more liberal scale for the Pre-ceramic (Archaic), and it is quite possible that the Melbourne formation will not be out of line with other formations in North America containing extinct late Pleistocene fauna, with a sea-level here at least 300 feet lower than at present. Lanceolate points have been reported within the last year from the Melbourne formation by Edwards, supporting an earlier position for it.

chapter in the whole history of man. According to Huxley:

Since the mechanism of cultural transformation depends primarily on the accumulation and organization of knowledge and thought, and the transmission of their products, and since man is the only new dominant type which has not broken down into separate species, it seems clear that the enlargement of the common pool of organized knowledge to cover the whole human race is the goal to aim at, and a measure by which human improvement and progress can be gauged.

How close, then, are American anthropologists to achieving an integrated history of man in the New World? It must be admitted that we are still a very long way from such a goal. Archeological work has barely reached a stage of some fairly sound regional sequences; work on the interregional relationships, on temporal alignments, and on the borrowing and modification of cultural ideas is in a state of infancy; translation of archeological data for the use of the ethnologist, and vice versa, is likewise in a state of infancy; physical anthropology remains very largely a discipline of metrical description rather than a determination of populations which can be used by the historians; historical perspective in linguistic taxonomy has so far been predicated mainly on an age-area hypothesis; and no general correlation (positive or negative) of culture, physical type, and language affiliation can be offered. This is doubtless partly inherent in the many difficulties in obtaining the right kind of information in each field and partly due to a commendable unwillingness to make such correlations prematurely; but it is also in great part due to a lack of interest and means. Research workers in each of these fields are nearly all preoccupied with the minutiae of local problems, whether an excavation, laboratory analysis of artifacts, or the structure of a language. Naturally, all these things must be done to increase the body of valid knowledge, but in doing them (I would venture to guess) not one person in twenty ever intends to spend time on a larger synthesis of his own field, not to mention an interdisciplinary synthesis.

While sweeping "correlations" of culture, physical type, and language have been made now and then, they have been torn up pretty drastically as information increases—as they should be. Nonetheless, these efforts fail mainly because they are entirely individual efforts, wherein one person attempts the impossible task of covering all the different branches of anthropology.

In archeology alone, specialization has reached such a degree that we have two or three hundred authorities on lo-

cal problems, but not a single authority on America as a whole; we even have specialists on the different time levels of a single area. Teaching methods may be partly to blame, but principally the fault lies with archeologists themselves: they are individuals working hard on matters that interest them personally, yet are strongly inclined to let someone else worry about the larger syntheses. So far they have shown no inclination to create the mechanisms needed for solving broad problems. Such organization has long been enjoyed by practically every other profession, such as biology, geology, and paleontology, to mention only field sciences. Not that all these have solved their problems, but they have been able to create terminology and frames of reference for effective communication with one another.

Our typological definitions are likewise highly individualistic, determined by inclination or by force of personality in various local situations, without regard to what happens when results must be compared objectively in different areas. It is as though a zoölogist, for example, proceeded to classify animals in one area according to how he felt about it, whether or not it would have any meaning for a colleague in the next area. If they tried to work out relationships and trace sequential evolution, they would have about as much success as American archeologists are having now: some, but not nearly enough. There is a common feeling that archeological ordering into types cannot be compared with biological ordering because the products of man are far more complicated and variable. This I regard as an excuse and not an explanation. The practical motions are, of course, quite different, but ordering is not a goal in itself: it is a tool for understanding and discussing the meaning of accumulated observations. The biologist conducts research for several purposes, such as (1) definition of species or types, (2) taxonomic ordering for convenience in discussing degree of relationship, (3) filling in the known distribution of species or types, (4) taxonomic reordering when necessary, and (5) understanding the mechanisms of change and pattern.

With different terms, typological ordering presents similar problems and aims. Everyone active in the profession is obligated to assist in attaining such goals for the benefit of the profession as a whole.

Finally, in America, almost nothing has been accomplished in integrating cultural changes with changes in climate and environment. On the whole, archeologists refuse to concern themselves with these matters, not reading material already made available by climatologists and being generally suspicious of the whole idea of environmental effects on culture: "Let the climatologists worry about that." This might be harmless, were it not for the fact that, in dealing with the archeological remains of peoples far back in the past, discussions tell how these people were adjusted to the *present* environment. The food resources, population density, degree of mobility, and consequent social structures of these past peoples should also be part and parcel of archeological research—a matter which is beginning to receive attention in some quarters.

SUGGESTIONS FOR FULLER PERSPECTIVES

I will confine my remarks to two main suggestions, both having to do with increasing spatial and temporal perspective in culture histories, whether archeological or ethnological.

The first is that American archeologists create some mechanism for defining types in all aspects of material culture which have demonstrable historical meaning, plotting the distributions of these types on maps, entering time factors where possible, so that eventually the direction of diffusion can be approximated, and then preparing other maps which show how and in what directions trait complexes ("linked traits") were diffused—or modified during diffusion. By "demonstrable historical meaning" I mean types which include ranges of variation in execution but are still entities which can be oriented in time and space. Eventually, a handbook of many hundreds of such types, with condensed descriptions and distribution maps on a continental scale, should be prepared, just as handbooks in many other field sciences have been prepared.

This will, of course, require facilities for a small staff over a period of years. If it took five years, or even ten, to compile such a record, it would still be of enormous practical value. Without it, we are faced with the present incredible situation in which everyone tries to remember the features and distributions of the thousands of "types" and classificatory groups already published. Many new and modified groupings would also emerge from such a study. I do not believe that anyone in this country knows the full distribution of a single type of artifact, burial method, or house construction now. But, in spite of this, we have a steady stream of "historical reconstructions," utilizing highly selective instances of comparable artifacts—often, one may suspect, implying affiliations in certain directions while ignoring others. Such a mapping should also enable us to decide with much greater precision just what traits are valid period "markers" in regional sequences.

The second suggestion comes from my colleague, Charles H. Lange, Jr. He points out that the culture-area concept in general use among American ethnologists has definite advantages for discussion of cultures on the historic level, but he raises the fundamental question of how far back in time such areas have validity. If their boundaries change as we proceed back, how and why do they change? Because of shifts in tribal boundaries due to social factors, because of changes in availability of food resources, or because of increasingly greater uniformity of culture as we proceed backward? As age increases, the chances of preservation decrease, and trait inventories become smaller, generally speaking; but the implements and devices of man also become fewer and cover larger areas with greater uniformity. Some suggestions were made on this for Anglo-America at the beginning of the section on regional sequences.

In place of the culture-area concept, there has recently developed the "co-tradition" of Martin and Rinaldo in the Southwest and Goggin in Florida. The same questions posed above also apply to this concept. Over how much ground does a "co-tradition" have validity at one time, and how much at another

time? Did one of the traditions in a given area once occupy more territory than another, and, if so, did one give way to another? Lange's suggestion is that some agency should ask one or more leading authorities in each general region to prepare an outline of developments through the total known time range to answer the above questions. Such an outline would consist of four parts:

1. Prepare a working hypothesis, discussing the validity of the co-tradition or any other suggested concept and the time over which it is believed valid.
2. Institute a policy of evaluating new data in terms of the trial hypothesis used; state whether alterations are needed and why, preferably by the same person or persons designated under 1.
3. Arrange for reports of this kind to be made at regional conferences.
4. Eventually combine these regional evaluations in a national or continental conference for this express purpose, to see how they can be combined into an effective over-all picture.

REFERENCES

BEARDSLEY, RICHARD K. 1948. "Culture Sequences in Central California Archaeology," *American Antiquity*, XIV, 1–28.

BREW, JOHN OTIS. 1946. *Archaeology of Alkali Ridge, Southeastern Utah.* ("Papers of the Peabody Museum of American Archaeology and Ethnology," Vol. XXI.) Cambridge.

COLLIER, DONALD; HUDSON, ALFRED E.; and FORD, ARLO. 1942. *Archaeology of the Upper Columbia Region.* ("University of Washington Publications in Anthropology," Vol. IX, No. 1.) Seattle.

COLLINS, HENRY B. 1951. "The Origin and Antiquity of the Eskimo," *Smithsonian Institution Report for 1950*, pp. 423–67. Washington, D.C.

DRUCKER, PHILIP, and BEARDSLEY, RICHARD K. 1943. "Archaeological Survey on the Northern Northwest Coast," *Bureau*

of American Ethnology Bull. 133, pp. 17–142. Washington, D.C.

FORD, JAMES A., and WILLEY, GORDON R. 1941. "An Interpretation of the Prehistory of the Eastern United States," *American Anthropologist*, XLIII, 325–63.

GRIFFIN, JAMES B. 1946. "Cultural Change and Continuity in Eastern United States Archaeology." In JOHNSON, F. (ed.), 1946, pp. 37–95.

HAURY, EMIL W., and COLLABORATORS. 1951. *Ventana Cave.* Albuquerque and Tucson: University of New Mexico Press and University of Arizona Press.

HEIZER, ROBERT F. 1951a. "Preliminary Report on Leonard Rock Shelter, Pershing County, Nevada," *American Antiquity*, XVII, 89–98.

———. 1951b. *An Assessment of Certain Radiocarbon Dates from Oregon, Cali-*

fornia, and Nevada, pp. 23–25. ("Memoirs of the Society for American Archaeology," No. 8.) Salt Lake City.

JOHNSON, FREDERICK (ed.). 1946. *Man in Northeastern North America*. ("Papers of the R. S. Peabody Foundation for Archaeology," Vol. III.) Andover.

——. 1949. *The Boylston Street Fishweir*. ("Papers of the R. S. Peabody Foundation for Archaeology," Vol. IV.)

LARSEN, HELGE, and RAINEY, FROELICH. 1948. *Ipiutak and the Arctic Whale Hunting Culture*. ("American Museum of Natural History Anthropological Papers," Vol. XLII.) New York.

MARTIN, PAUL S.; QUIMBY, GEORGE I.; and COLLIER, DONALD. 1947. *Indians before Columbus*. Chicago: University of Chicago Press.

REED, ERIK K. 1946. "The Distinctive Features and Distribution of the San Juan Anasazi Culture," *Southwestern Journal of Anthropology*, II, 295–305.

——. 1950. "Eastern-Central Arizona Archaeology in Relation to the Western Pueblos," *ibid.*, VI, 120–38.

RITCHIE, WILLIAM A. 1951*a*. "A Current Synthesis of New York Prehistory," *American Antiquity*, XVII, 130–36.

——. 1951*b*. "Their Mouths Are Stopped with Dust," *Archaeology*, IV, 136–44.

——. 1951*c*. "Ground Slates: Eskimo or Indian?" *Pennsylvania Archaeologist*, XXI, 46–52.

ROUSE, IRVING. 1951. *A Survey of Indian River Archeology, Florida*. ("Yale University Publications in Anthropology," Vol. XLIV.) New Haven.

STEWARD, JULIAN. 1940. "Native Cultures of the Intermontane (Great Basin) Area," *Smithsonian Miscellaneous Collections*, C, 445–502.

TAYLOR, WALTER W., JR. 1948. *A Study of Archeology*. ("Memoirs of the American Anthropological Association," No. 69.)

WEDEL, WALDO R. 1940. "Culture Sequences in the Central Great Plains," *Smithsonian Miscellaneous Collections*, C, 291–352.

Historical Linguistics and Unwritten Languages

By JOSEPH H. GREENBERG

I. HISTORICAL LINGUISTICS AND DESCRIPTIVE LINGUISTICS

UNLIKE SOME other aspects of anthropology affected by the functionalist attack on history, the validity and fruitfulness of the historic approach in linguistics has never been seriously questioned. The objections which have been raised to certain assumptions of classical Indo-European comparative linguistics, such as the existence of sound laws without exceptions or the overliteral interpretation of the family-tree metaphor of language relationship, have not involved any fundamental doubt as to the legitimacy and value of historical reconstruction as such; at the most, they have, in the case of the Italian group of neo-linguists,[1] suggested specific alternative reconstructions of certain Proto-Indo-European forms.

The possibility of the application of traditional Indo-European methods to "primitive" (i.e., unwritten) languages has been deprecated by some Indo-Europeanists (Vendryes, 1925). It is

evident that, while in principle the same procedures are appropriate, the absence of direct documentation for earlier historic periods is a distinct methodological handicap. The last decades, however, have seen the successful employment of classical reconstruction methods in a number of areas, including Central Algonkian by L. Bloomfield, Bantu by C. Meinhof, and Malayo-Polynesian by O. Dempwolff. It should be borne in mind that in all these cases we have rather closely related forms of speech, so that the task involved is more comparable to the reconstruction of Proto-Germanic or Proto-Slavic than that of Proto-Indo-European. These attempts do furnish an important demonstration of the universal scope of those mechanisms of linguistic change which were already known to function in the more restricted area of the traditionally studied Indo-European, Finno-Ugric, and Semitic stocks (Hockett, 1948).

Much more serious than skepticism regarding the possibility of linguistic reconstruction in the absence of early written records is the widely held opinion, which will be discussed in a later section of this paper, that remote relationships or even those of the order existing within the Indo-European family cannot be established for primitive languages because of the far-reaching

1. The reconstructions of the neo-linguistic school are not generally accepted by other scholars. For an exposition of neo-linguistic method, see G. Bonfante (1945). For a hostile critique see Robert Hall, Jr. (1946). It should perhaps be added that the approach of L. Hjelmsler in Denmark seems to exclude diachronic problems from language in principle but that this remains hardly more than a theoretic model.

influence which one language can exercise on another even in fundamental traits of grammatical structure. It is even claimed that the genetic question here loses its meaning, in that one language can go back to several distinct origins and cannot therefore be said to belong to one family more than to another (Boas, 1920). It is worth observing that even in these cases the value of historic investigation is not denied as providing evidence of specific contacts, even though, it is held, the genetic question cannot be resolved. Thus Uhlenbeck, who, in his later writing, takes the view of genetic connections just mentioned, has lavished much time and effort on an attempt to show resemblances between the Uralic languages and Eskimo which require a historical explanation, while avoiding commitment as to the nature of the historic relationship involved.

While historic linguistics thus continues as a legitimate and major area of linguistic endeavor, it is undeniable that, with the rise of structural schools in European and American linguistics, the center of interest has shifted in the recent period from the historical problems which dominated linguistic science in the nineteenth century to those of synchronic description. The present preoccupation with descriptive formulations, which appears to be the linguistic analogue of the rise of functionalism, can contribute much that is valuable to diachronic studies. Most obviously, perhaps, any advance in descriptive techniques, by improving the quality of the data which constitute the basis of historical investigation, can furnish material for hypotheses of wider historical connections and likewise increase the precision of reconstruction for those already established. Another factor of great significance is the influence of the fundamental approach to language which all structuralists share, whatever their other di-

vergences, namely, the concept of languages as a system of functional units. In its diachronic aspect this provides us with a view of change as related to a system and at least partially explainable in terms of its internal functioning through time. In the realm of sound patterns, some of these implications have been realized for some time. Thus Trubetskoy, as well as others, has distinguished between those sound changes which affect the sound structure of the language and those which leave it unchanged (Jakobson, 1931). This clearly parallels the synchronic distinction between phonetic and phonemic sound differences. Under the influence of this manner of thinking, sound change in language is more and more considered in terms of the shifts and realignment it produces in the sound structure of language rather than as a haphazard set of isolated changes, as in the traditional handbooks of historical linguistics.[2] The more rigorous formulation of alternations in the phonemic shape of morphemes (morphophonemics) has also borne fruit in Hoenigwald's exposition of the bearing of such data on internal reconstruction, that is, the reconstruction of certain aspects of the former states of a given language without resort to either related languages or historical records (Hoenigswald, 1950). Although historical linguists had in effect used this method without formulation, the emphasis on rigorous formulation of assumptions is, on the whole, beneficial in an area, such as historical reconstruction, in which it has so largely been lacking.

Although there is thus no fundamental opposition between the historical and descriptive approaches to language, the focusing of attention on syn-

2. Examples are the recent studies of Grimm's laws and other changes in Germanic by Twaddel and others, and various studies by Martinet of sound shifts (e.g., 1950).

chronic problems in the recent historic period, combined with the traditional concentration of linguistic forces in the areas of a few major Eurasiatic speech families, has led to comparative neglect of the basic problems of historical research in unwritten languages.

II. THE ESTABLISHMENT OF LINGUISTIC RELATIONSHIP

The fundamental achievement of nineteenth-century science in linguistics, as in certain other areas, notably biology, was to replace the traditional static interpretation of similarities in terms of fortuitous coincidence among species as kinds, all of which were created at the same time and could vary only within fixed and narrow limits, with a dynamic historic interpretation of similarities as reflecting specific historical interrelationships of varying degrees of remoteness. Taxonomy, the science of classification, thus was no longer the attempt to find essential features connecting certain things more closely than others as part of a divine plan but rather based itself on the selection of those criteria which reflected actual historic relationships. In the language of biology, it was the search for homologies rather than mere analogies. In spite of the fruitfulness of the Indo-European hypothesis and the further successes of similar hypotheses in establishing the Finno-Ugric, Semitic, and other families, the assumptions on the bases of which these first victories of linguistics as a science were obtained were never clearly formulated, and the extension of these methods to other areas of the world has suffered from the beginning from a lack of clarity regarding the criteria of genetic relationship, resulting, in almost every major area, in a welter of conflicting classifications and even in widespread doubt as to the feasibility of any interpretation of linguistic similarities in terms of historical connections. Yet assumptions which have been the very foundation on which the edifice of modern linguistics has been reared and which have helped give it a rigorousness of method and precision of result which are admittedly superior to those dealing with any other phase of human cultural behavior should not be lightly abandoned unless, of course, the data actually demand it. In what follows, an attempt is made to formulate the principles in accordance with which similarities in language can be given a historical interpretation. It is hoped that this will furnish the guiding principles on the basis of which problems in the subsequent sections referring to specific areas can receive a reasonable solution.

The fundamental assumption concerning language on the basis of which historical interpretation of linguistic similarities becomes possible seems to have been first explicitly formulated by the great Swiss linguist, Ferdinand de Saussure, in his *Cours de linguistique générale*, although its relevance for historical problems is not there stated. According to De Saussure, language is a system of signs having two aspects, the *signifiant* and the *signifié*, equivalent, in the terminology of Bloomfield and of American linguists, to "form" and "meaning," respectively. Moreover, the relationship between these two aspects of the linguistic sign is essentially arbitrary. Given any particular meaning, there is no inherent necessity for any particular set of sounds to designate it in preference to any other. Although first stated in this manner by De Saussure, this assumption actually underlies the nineteenth-century hypotheses of linguistic relationships and represents essentially the solution accepted by all modern linguists of the controversy descending from the Greeks concerning the naturalness versus the conventionality of language.

Given the arbitrariness of the relationship between form and meaning, resemblances between two languages significantly greater than chance must receive a historical explanation, whether of common origin or of borrowing.

This statement regarding the arbitrariness of the sign does need some qualification, in that there is a slight tendency for certain sounds or sound combinations to be connected more frequently with certain meanings than might be expected on a purely chance basis. Conspicuous instances are the nursery words for "mother" and "father" and onomatopoeias for certain species of animals. This is generally recognized as only a slight derogation from the principle of the arbitrariness of the sign, since the sound can never be predicted from the meaning; and, since such instances are relatively a minor factor from the point of view of frequency of occurrence, they will add slightly to the percentage of resemblances to be expected beyond those merely the result of chance between any two unrelated languages; but they are not adequate for the explanation of wholesale resemblances between two particular languages, such as French or Italian. Moreover, the few resemblances which rest on this factor can be allowed for by assigning them less weight in judging instances of possible historical connections between languages. This factor making for specific resemblances between languages will hereafter be called, somewhat inappropriately, "symbolism," in accordance with the terminology employed by psychologists.

Given any specific resemblance both in form and in meaning between two languages, there are four possible classes of explanations. Of these four, two —chance and symbolism—do not involve historic relationship, in contrast to the remaining pair—genetic relationship and borrowing. These four sources of similarity have parallels in nonlinguistic aspects of culture. Genetic relationship corresponds to internal evolution, borrowing to diffusion, chance to convergence through limited possibilities (as in art designs), and symbolism to convergence through similarity of function.

Up to this point resemblances in form between two languages unaccompanied by similarity of meaning and those of meaning not bound to similarity of form have not been considered. I believe that such resemblances must be resolutely excluded as irrelevant for the determination of genetic relationship. They practically always arise through convergence or borrowing. Form without function (e.g., the mere presence of tonal systems or vowel harmony in two languages) or function without form (e.g., the presence of gender morphemes in two languages expressed by different formal means) is often employed as relevant for the determination of relationship, sometimes as the sole criterion, as in Meinhof's definition of Hamitic, or in conjunction with other criteria. The preference for agreements involving meaning without accompanying sound resemblances is sometimes based on metaphysical preconceptions regarding the superiority of form over matter (Kroeber, 1913).

Resemblance in meaning only is frequently the result of convergence through limited possibilities. Important and universal aspects of human experience, such as the category of number or a system of classification based on sex or animation in the noun or one of tense or aspect in the verb, tend to appear independently in the most remote areas of the world and can never be employed as evidence for a historical connection. That the dual number occurs in Yana (California), ancient Greek, and Polynesian is obviously an instance of convergent development. Sometimes semantic similarity without similarity in the formal means of expression is present in contiguous languages of similar or diverse genetic connection. In these cases we have the linguistic analogue of Kroeber's concept of "stimulus diffusion"—indeed, a remarkably clear-cut instance of this process. Languages spoken by people in constant culture contact forming a culture area tend to share many such semantic traits through the mechanism of diffusion. This process may be carried to the point where it is possible to translate almost literally from one language to another. However, since it is precisely the semantic aspect of language which tends to reflect changes in the cultural situation and since such semantic resemblances cover continuous geographical areas, these resemblances are clearly secondary, however far-reaching they may be in extent. Beyond the inherent probabilities, there is much empirical evidence in areas from which documented history exists. Those traits, which various Balkan languages share in common and which are one of the marks of the Balkans as a cultural area, are largely semantic, involving a difference in the phonemic content employed as the mode of expression. Thus Rumanian, Serbian, and Greek express the future by "to wish" followed by an infinitive, but in Rumanian we have (1st person sing.) *voiu* + V, in Serbian *ću* + V, and in Greek *tha* + V. These are all known to be historically relatively recent and not a result of the more remote Indo-European genetic connections which all of them share. Roughly similar arguments hold for resemblances of form without meaning. There are limited possibilities for phonemic systems. For example, such historically unconnected languages as Hausa in West Africa, classical Latin, and the Penutian Yokuts share a five-vowel system with two significant degrees of length (*a, a·, e, e·, i, i·, o, o·, u, u·*). Some resemblances in form without function are the result of the influence of one language on

another, e.g., the clicks of Zulu which have been borrowed from the Khoisan languages. Normally, when related languages have been separated for a fairly long period, we expect, and find, considerable differences both in their sound systems and in their semantic aspects resulting from differential drift and the diversity of the cultural circumstances under which their speakers have lived. Too great similarities in such matters are suspect.

Since, as has been seen, resemblances in form without meaning and meaning without form are normally explainable by hypotheses other than genetic relationship, their presence does not indicate, nor their absence refute, it. Hence they may be left out of consideration as irrelevant for this particular problem.

The evidence relevant to the determination of genetic relationship then becomes the extent and nature of meaning-form resemblances in meaningful elements, normally the minimal element, the morpheme. Lexical resemblance between languages then refers to resemblances in root morphemes, and grammatical resemblances refer to derivational and inflectional morphemes. The two basic methodological problems become the exclusion of convergence and symbolism, on the basis of significantly more than chance resemblance leading to a hypothesis of some kind of historical connection, and among these the segregation of those cases in which borrowing is an adequate explanation of the more-than-chance resemblances from those instances in which this is inadequate and genetic relationship must be posited.

The first approach to the problem of more than chance resemblances is quantitative. We may ask how many resemblances may be expected between any two languages which are not genetically related and have not borrowed from each other or from a mutual source.

Several approaches seem possible. One would involve the calculation for each of the two languages of the expected number of chance resemblances on the basis of its phonemic structure and allowed phonemic sequences arranged in terms of what may be called "resemblance classes," based on a resolution as to what phonemes are to be considered similar to others for the purposes of the comparison. To such a procedure there are several objections. It does not eliminate the factor of symbolism, and it does not take into account the relative frequencies of the phonemes in each language. If, for example, in comparing two particular languages, it were agreed that the labials would all be treated as resembling one another and the dentals likewise and if, in both languages, dentals were five times as frequent as labials, the possibility of chance resemblance would be much greater than if they were equal. This objection could, of course, be met in principle by a weighting in terms of frequency, but in actual practice it would be difficult to carry out.

A more desirable procedure would be the following. Let us suppose that we have a list of one thousand morphemes matched for meaning in the two languages. In language A the first morpheme is *kan*, "one." Instead of calculating the abstract probability of a form resembling *kan* sufficiently to be considered similar, let us actually compare *kan* in form with all the thousand items on the other list. Let us likewise compare the meaning "one" with all the meanings on the other list. The chance probability of the existence of a form resembling *kan*, "one," in both form and meaning in list B will then be the product of form resemblances and meaning resemblances divided by 1,000, the total number of items. We should then do this for each morpheme in list A and total the probabilities. As can be seen, this is a very tedious procedure.

Moreover, it will not include resemblances due to symbolism.

A much more practical method, which takes into account both chance and symbolism, is simply to take a number of languages which are admittedly unrelated and ascertain the number of resemblances actually found. The difficulty here is that results will vary with the phonetic structure of the languages. A number of such counts indicates that approximately 4 per cent is the modal value, employing a very generous interpretation of what constitutes similarity. Where, however, the two languages are similar in the phonemic structure of their morphemes, the degree of resemblance can become significantly larger. For example, between Thai and Jur, a Nilotic language, which have very similar phonemic structures, it reaches 7 per cent. It can be safely asserted that a resemblance of 20 per cent in vocabulary always requires a historical explanation and that, unless similarity of phonetic structure leads to the expectation of a high degree of chance similarity, even 8 per cent is well beyond what can be expected without the intervention of historical factors. This factor of the similarity or difference of the phonemic structure of morphemes is so important that in doubtful cases a simplified version of the second test, that of matching lists, should probably be applied. We might compare a particular form in list B with all those in list A from the phonemic point of view only, allowing merely one meaning, that of its partner in list A, presumably the nearest semantic equivalent. We then compare with the expected frequency of resemblances (which is, of course, smaller than by the first method) only those cases of resemblances on the list in which the two forms are matched as nearest semantic equivalents. Thus, if as our first matching pair we had A *nem*, B *kan*, "one," and later in the list A *ken*, B *sa*, "only," the resemblance between A *ken,* "only," and B *kan,* "one," would be disregarded as not occurring in a matching pair.

In actual fact, however, this test can probably be dispensed with, since the mere quantity of resemblances in the form and meaning of morphemes is not the decisive factor in more doubtful cases. There are additional considerations based on the weightings to be accorded to individual items and the further fact that isolated languages are seldom found. The bringing-in of closely related languages on each side introduces new factors of the highest importance, which should lead to a definite decision.

Other things being equal, the evidential value of a resemblance in form and meaning between elements in two languages is proportional to the length of the item. A comparison such as A, *-k;* B, *-k,* "in," is, from this point of view at least, less significant than such a resemblance as A, *pegadu;* B, *fikato,* "nose." More important is the following consideration. The unit of comparison is the morpheme with its variant allomorphs, if these exist. If the two languages agree in these variations, and particularly if the variants are rather different in phonemic content, we have not only the probability that such-and-such a sequence of phonemes will occur in a particular meaning but the additional factor that it will be accompanied by certain variations in certain combinations. Agreement in such arbitrary morphophonemic variations, **particularly if suppletive, i.e., involving no phonemic resemblance between the** variants, is of a totally different order of probability than the agreement in a nonvarying morpheme or one in which the languages do not exhibit the same variation. Even one instance of this is hardly possible without historical connection of some kind, and, since, moreover, it is hardly likely to be borrowed, it virtually guarantees genetic relation-

ship. We may illustrate from English and German. The morpheme with the main alternant *hæv,* "have," in English resembles the German chief allomorph *ha:b,* "have," both in form and in meaning. In English, *hæv* alternates with *hæ-* before *-z* of the third person singular present (*hæ-z,* "has"). In German, correspondingly, *ha:b* has an alternant *ha-* in a similar environment, before *-t,* indicating third person singular present, to form *ha-t,* "has." Likewise, English *gud,* "good," has the alternant *be-* before *-tər,* "comparative" and *-st,* "superlative." Similarly, German *gu:t,* "good," has the alternant *be-* before *-sər,* "comparative," and *-st,* "superlative." The probability of all this being chance, particularly the latter, which is suppletive, is infinitesimal. Since it is precisely such arbitrary variations, "irregularities" in nontechnical languages, which are subject to analogical pressure, they tend to be erased in one or the other language, even if some instances existed in the parent-languages. Where they exist, however, they are precious indications of a real historical connection.

More generally applicable are considerations arising from the fact that the comparison is only in rare instances between two isolated languages. The problem as to whether the resemblances between two languages are merely the result of chance plus symbolism can then be tested by a number of additional methods. Let us say that, as is frequently the case, one or more other languages or language groups resemble the two languages in question but in the same indecisive way, that is, that this third or fourth language is not conspicuously closer to one than to the other of the two languages with which we have been first concerned. The following fundamental probability consideration applies. The likelihood of finding a resemblance both in form and in meaning simultaneously in three languages is the square of its probability in two languages. In general, the original probability must be raised to the $n-1$-power where a total of n languages is involved, just as the probability of throwing a 6 once on a die is ⅙, but twice is $(⅙)^2$ or $1/36$. Similarly, if each of three languages shows a resemblance of 8 per cent to the other, which might in extreme cases be the result of mere chance, the expectation of the three languages all agreeing in some instance of resemblance in form and meaning will be $(8/100)^2$ or $64/10,000$. In 1,000 comparisons, agreement among all three languages should occur only 6.4 times, that is, it will occur in 0.0064, or less than 1 per cent, of the comparisons. Hence a number of instances of such threefold agreements is highly significant. If four or more languages which are about equally distant from one another agree in a number of instances, a historical connection must be assumed, and if this agreement involves fundamental vocabulary or morphemes with a grammatical function, genetic explanation is the only tenable explanation.

This may be illustrated from the Afroasiatic (Hamito-Semitic) family of languages consisting of five languages or language groups—Egyptian, Berber, Semitic, Chad (Hausa and others), and Cushite. The forms involved are guaranteed as ancestral in each group by the requirement of earliest attestation, as in the requirement for Egyptian that it occur in the Pyramid Texts, our oldest document, or of appearance in at least two genetic subgroups (as in the case of Chad and Cushite), so that, in effect, we are comparing five languages. Allowing again the very high total of 8 per cent of chance resemblance between any two of the languages, the expected number of occurrences of morphemes similar in form and meaning in all five groups simultaneously becomes $(8/100)^4$ or $2,816/100,000,000$. Assuming that about 1,000 forms are

being compared from each language, this leads to the expectation of $2,816/-100,000$ of a morpheme. That is, if one compared a series of five unrelated languages at random, employing 1,000 words in each case, the operation would lead to a single successful case in approximately 35 such sets of comparisons. As a matter of fact, eleven morphemes are found in the case of Hamito-Semitic instead of the expected $1/35$. There is only an infinitesimal probability that this could be the result of pure chance. In this case, the morphemes involved include such examples as *-t*, fem. sing. and *-ka*, second person singular masculine possessive. Genetic relationship, of which there are many other indications, seems the only possible explanation here.

Languages should never be compared in isolation if closer relatives are at hand. For the tendency of those particular forms in a language which resemble another language or group of languages to reappear with considerable frequency in more closely related forms of speech is a valuable index of the existence of a real historical connection. The statistical considerations involved may be illustrated once more from the Hamito-Semitic family. The question whether Hausa is indeed related to Egyptian, Semitic, Berber, and the Chad language has always been treated through isolated comparisons between Hausa and the other groups, while the existence of more than seventy languages of the Chad group which show a close and obvious relation to Hausa has been ignored.

A comparison of basic vocabulary between Hausa and Bedauye, a contemporary language of the Cushite branch of Hamito-Semitic, shows 10 per cent agreement in vocabulary. It is clear that Hausa will have lost certain Proto-Hamito-Semitic words retained by Bedauye, and vice versa. The percentage of retained vocabulary is ex-

pressed by a simple mathematical relation, the square root of the proportion
of resemblances. The proportion of
Hausa vocabulary which is of Proto-
Hamito-Semitic origin should therefore
be $\sqrt{10/100}$, or approximately 32/100.
If we now take another Chad language
belonging to a different subgroup than
Hausa, namely, Musgu, the percentage
of resemblance to Hausa is 20 per cent.
Applying the same reasoning, the percentage of Hausa vocabulary retained
from the time of separation from Musgu, that is, from the Proto-Chad period,
is $\sqrt{20/100}$, or approximately 45/100.
If, then, we take forms found in Hausa
which resemble Egyptian, Berber, Semitic, or Cushite and because of the existence of a true genetic relationship
these forms actually derive from Proto-
Hamito-Semitic, they must also be
Proto-Chad. Since Hausa has lost its
forms since the Proto-Chad period independently of Musgu, which belongs
to another subbranch, a true Proto-
Hamito-Semitic form in Hausa should
reappear by chance in Musgu 32/100 ÷
45/100 of the time, that is, 32/45. On
the other hand, if Hausa is not related
to the other Hamito-Semitic languages,
the apparent resemblances to them are
accidental, and these words should reappear in Musgu no more frequently
than any other, that is, 20 per cent of
the time, 9/45 rather than 32/45. An
actual count shows that, of 30 morphemes in Hausa which resemble those
of branches other than Chad, 22 occur
in Musgu. This is 22/30 or 33/45, remarkably close to the expected 32/45.
On the other hand, of 116 forms which
show no resemblances to those of other
Hamito-Semitic branches, only 14 occur
in Musgu.

Beyond the frequency of resemblances and their distribution in other
languages of the same group, the form
which the resemblances take is likewise
of importance. If the resemblances are

actually the result of historical relationship, even cursory reconstruction should
show greater resemblance in most cases
between the reconstructed forms than
between those of two isolated languages. If the resemblances are all convergences, on the whole, reconstruction
should increase the difference of the
forms. This can be done in a tentative
manner as the comparison proceeds and
without necessarily involving the full
apparatus of formal historical reconstruction, which is often not feasible
with poor material or where the relationship is fairly remote and no written
records are available. If, for example,
we compared present-day Hindustani
and English, we would be struck by a
number of resemblances in basic vocabulary, including numerals, but the
hypothesis of chance convergence
would certainly appear as a plausible
alternative. Even without going beyond
contemporary Germanic languages, on
the one hand, and Indo-Iranian languages, on the other, reconstruction
would show a strong tendency to convergence of forms as we went backward in time, suggesting a real historical connection. Thus English *tuwþ* resembles Hindustani *dā:t* only slightly.
On the Germanic side comparison with
High German *tsa:n* already suggests a
nasal consonant corresponding to the
nasalization of the Hindustani vowel.
Conjecture of a possible *tanþ* or the
like as a source of the English and
German form is confirmed by the Dutch
tand. On the other hand, comparison
of Hindustani with other Aryan languages of India suggests that the Hindustani nasalized and long vowel results from a former short vowel and
nasal consonant, as in Kashmiri and
Sindir *dand*. Reconstruction has thus
brought the forms closer together.

Last, and very important, a degree
of consistency in the sound correspondences is a strong indication of historical connection. Thus, reverting to the

English-Hindustania comparison, the presence of *t* in English *tuw*, "two," *ten*, "ten," and *tuwþ*, "tooth" corresponding to Hindustani *d* in *dō, das*, and *dā:t*, respectively, is a strong indication of real historical relationship.

Assuming that such a relationship has been established, there still remains the problem of whether the resemblances in question can be explained by borrowing. While in particular instances the question of borrowing may be doubtful, I believe it is always possible to tell whether or not a mass of resemblances between two languages is the result of borrowing. The most important consideration is the a priori expectation and historical documentation of the thesis that borrowing in culture words is far more frequent than in fundamental vocabulary and that derivational, inflectional, pronominal morphemes and alternating allomorphs are subject to borrowing least frequently of all.

The oft repeated maxim of the superiority of grammatical over vocabulary evidence for relationship owes what validity it has to this relative impermeability of derivational and inflectional morphemes to borrowing. On the other hand, such elements are shorter, hence more often subject to convergence, and usually few in number, so that in themselves they are sometimes insufficient to lead to a decision. Lexical items are, it is true, more subject to borrowing, but their greater phonemic body and number give them certain compensatory advantages. While it cannot be said, a priori, that any single item might not on occasion be borrowed, fundamental vocabulary seems to be proof against mass borrowing. Swadesh, in a recent discussion of the problem of borrowing versus genetic explanations, presents quantitative evidence for the relative impermeability of fundamental vocabulary in several instances where the history of the language is known (Swadesh, 1951).

The presence of fundamental vocabulary resemblances well beyond chance expectation, not accompanied by resemblances in cultural vocabulary, is thus a sure indication of genetic relationship. This is a frequent, indeed normal, situation where a relationship is of a fairly remote order. Pronoun, body parts, etc., will agree while terms like "pot," "ax," "maize," will disagree. The assumption of borrowing here runs contrary to common sense and documented historic facts. A people so strongly influenced by another that they borrow terms like "I," "one," "head," "blood," will surely have borrowed cultural terms also. Where the mass of resemblances is the result of borrowing, a definite source will appear. The forms will be too similar in view of the historical remoteness of the assumed relationship. Moreover, if, as is usual, the donor language is not isolated, the fact that the resemblances all point to one particular language in the family, usually a geographically adjacent one, will also be diagnostic. Thus the Romance loan words in English are almost all close to French, in addition to hardly penetrating the basic vocabulary of English. If English were really a Romance language, it would show roughly equal similarities to all the Romance languages. The absence of sound correspondences is not a sufficient criterion, since, where loans are numerous, they often show such correspondence. However, the presence of a special set of correspondences will be an important aid in distinguishing loans in doubtful instances. Thus French loan words in English show regular correspondences, such as Fr. *š* = Eng. *č* or Fr. *ā* = Eng. æn (*šās:čæns; šāt: čænt; še:z:čejr*, etc.).

Genetic relationship among languages is, in logical terminology, transitive. By a "transitive" relation is meant a relation such that, if it holds between A and B and between A and C, it must also hold between B and C. If our criteria are correct and languages do have single lines of origin, we should never be led by their application to a situation in which A appears to be related both to B and to C, but B and C themselves cannot be shown to be related. If this were so, A would consist equally of two diverse components, that is, would be a mixed language of elements of B and C. This situation is sometimes said to exist, and even on a mass scale. Africa is perhaps most frequently mentioned in this connection. Thus Boas (1929) writes: ". . . a large number of mixed languages occur in Africa. His [Lepsius'] conclusions are largely corroborated by more recent investigation of the Sudanese languages."

Close investigation shows that, of the hundreds of languages in Africa (800 is the conventional estimate), there is only one language concerning which the problem of genetic affiliation could conceivably lead to two disparate classifications, the Mbugu language of Tanganyika. Even here the answer is clear that, in spite of the borrowing of Bantu prefixes and a large amount of vocabulary, mostly nonfundamental, the language belongs to the Cushite branch of Hamito-Semitic. The pronouns, verb forms, and almost all the fundamental vocabulary are Cushitic. The conventional African classification based on purely formal criteria, such as tone, combined with purely semantic, such as gender, had no connection with historical reality, and the necessarily contradictory results which followed led to the assumption of widespread mixture. If, as was done, we define a Sudanese language as monosyllabic, tonal, and genderless, and a Hamitic language as polysyllabic, toneless, and having sex gender, a polysyllabic, tonal language with sex gender (like Masai) will have to be inter-

preted as the result of a mixture of Sudanic and Hamitic elements.

The last full-scale treatment of this subject is Meillet's, which was followed by the counterarguments of Schuchardt, Boas, and others and a discussion of these objections by Meillet (1914). The present discussion is in fundamental agreement with Meillet in asserting that the genetic question always has a meaning and is susceptible of an unambiguous answer. Meillet differentiates between concrete grammatical resemblances involving both form and meaning and those involving meaning only without form, but only in passing. Similarly, he mentions rather casually the fact that fundamental vocabulary is not commonly borrowed, but does not exploit this insight. The advantages gained by collateral comparison with additional closely related languages, and the statistical significance of coincidences in three or more languages are not considered. The result is an unnecessarily skeptical attitude toward the possibilities of establishing genetic classification where there are no early written documents or where the grammatical apparatus is slight or nonexistent (e.g., Southeast Asia).

The objections of Schuchardt and Boas are in large part taken into account in the present analysis by the distinction between resemblances based on form and meaning which result from contact with other linguistic systems and those involving form only or meaning only. It would perhaps be desirable to distinguish these by the terms "borrowing" and "influence," respectively. Justice is then done to Boas' insistence that diffusion is prominently operative in linguistic as in other cultural phenomena, by setting no limit to influence, which in the case of Creole language reaches its peak, while maintaining, in accordance with all the available evidence, that there are definite bounds to borrowing, since it tends to cluster in nonfundamental vocabulary and makes only rare and sporadic inroads into basic vocabulary and inflectional and derivational morphemes. What is commonly said about the grammatical effects of one language on another refers almost entirely to influence, not borrowing, in the sense of the terms as employed here.

In other words, the effects of one language upon another are extremely widespread, fundamental, and important. What is maintained here is merely that the results are of a kind that can be distinguished from those caused by genetic relationship. Nor is it asserted that the genetic affiliation of a language is the sole important historic fact concerning it. The effects of borrowing and influence, being more recent chronologically and giving specific insights into the nature of the contacts involved, may frequently be of greater significance to the ethnologist and culture historian than the factor of more remote genetic affiliation.

These two types of historical connections between languages are carefully distinguished by Trubetskoy. A group of languages which have affected one another by influence and borrowing and form a group analogous to a culture area is termed a *Sprachbund,* while a group of genetically linked languages is termed a *Sprachfamilie.* They become genera of the larger species, *Sprachgruppe,* taking in all types of historical connections between languages (Trubetskoy, 1928).

The common habit of confusing these two situations by the use of the term "mixed language," as though a language were a mechanical aggregate of a number of components which enter into it the same way but merely in different proportions that English is, say, 48 per cent Germanic, 43 per cent French, 4 per cent Arabic, and 0.03 per cent Aztec (because of "tomato," "metate," etc.) is a gross oversimplification and fails to distinguish the different origin and function of the Germanic as opposed to the Romance-Latin and other components in English.

From what has been said, it should be evident that the establishment of genetic relationships among languages is no mere *jeu d'esprit.* It is the indispensable preliminary to a determination of the causes of resemblances between languages by leaving borrowing as the only remaining source where more than chance resemblance does not lead to a hypothesis of relationship. Where such a relationship is present, it provides the basis for separation of autonomous from foreign elements through reconstruction of the ancestral language. Without such reconstruction, an understanding of the process of change in language undergoes a severe limitation to those few areas of the globe in which documented materials concerning the earlier forms of languages exist.

III. SELECTED REGIONAL SKETCHES

A. AFRICA

The attempt to reduce the number of language families in Africa at all costs, leading to overambitious syntheses combined with a disregard of concrete resemblances in form and meaning between elements of language in favor of typological criteria, such as the presence of tone, noun classes, sex gender, monosyllabic roots, etc., has characterized African linguistic classification from the earliest systematic attempts (Lepsius, F. Müller, etc.) onward.

The dominant classification in England and the United States has been a kind of synthesis, varying in details with different writers, based chiefly on the investigations of Westermann on the Sudanic languages and Meinhof on the Hamitic. Clear statements of the basis of this classification can be found in Werner (1915) and in Tucker (1940), as well as elsewhere. According to this view, there are three great indigenous language families in Africa —Sudanic, Bantu, and Hamitic, with Semitic as a separate but late intrusion and Bushman as possibly related to Sudanic. A disputed point has been the status of Hottentot, which most assign to Hamitic with Meinhof but which some classify with Bushman to form a Khoisan family, while others leave it independent or at any rate unclassified. Each of the three main families has its basic characteristics. Thus Sudanic is monosyllabic, tonal, lacks stress, grammatical gender, and all inflection, and places the genitive before the possessed noun. Hamitic, at the opposite extreme, is defined as polysyllabic, possessing Ablaut variation, having grammatical gender and inflection, lacking tone, and placing the genitive after the noun. In addition, it possesses the characteristic of polarity, which can best be illustrated by an example. The Somali language uses the same affirmative for the singular of the masculine and the plural of the feminine, while another element marks simultaneously the singular of the feminine and the plural of the masculine. Meinhof often expressed the opinion that the Bantu languages, which are assigned characteristics almost midway between the Sudanic and Hamitic families, were the result of a mixture of the two or, as he once expressed it, "had a Hamitic father and Sudanic mother" (Meinhof, 1912).

It is admitted that few languages exhibit the traits of one of these families in full purity. Deviations from the ideal pattern are attributed to influences of one family on the other. It is held that such intimate fusions may result that the choice of the fundamental component can in certain cases be made only by an arbitrary decision. Such mixed groups of languages are the Semi-Bantu, formed from Sudanic and Bantu; Nilo-Hamitic, a fusion of Sudanic with Hamitic; and, in the view of many, Hottentot, with a Sudanic-like Bushman element and a Hamitic element.

It is clear that by applying such criteria, which have no reference to the concrete relations between the form and the meaning of specific linguistic signs, Chinese is a Sudanic language and Old French is Hamitic. The latter, indeed, possesses a very striking bit of polarity in the use of -*s* to indicate the nominative singular and plural accusative of the noun as opposed to a zero suffix indicating the accusative singular and nominative plural (e.g., *murs*: *mur* = *mur*: *murs*). In addition, it possesses gender, Ablaut, and all the other stated characteristics of Hamitic speech. On the other hand, we are led to a crowning absurdity, in that forms of speech that are probably mutually intelligible can be classified as genetically distinct. Thus Meinhof, in classifying the languages of Kordofan, west of the Upper Nile, paid no attention to any other factor than the existence or absence of class prefixes in the noun. Three of these languages—Tegele, Tagoy, and Tumele—are similar, probably to the point of mutual intelligibility. Meinhof (1915–19) states: "A comparison of vocabulary shows that the numerals [*sc.* of Tegele] completely agree with those of Tumele. Moreover they are for the most part identical with the Tagoy numerals. Besides, a number of word stems and some verb forms of Tegele are identical with Tagoy and Tumele. But the grammatical structure of the noun indicates that Tegele is a Sudanic language because noun classification is absent while Tagoy and Tumele have clear noun classes. Apparently there has been a mixture of two diverse elements."

The other classification which has enjoyed currency is that of A. Drexel, adopted with a few modifications by Schmidt and by Kiekers in their respective volumes on the languages of the world. The Drexel classification embodies an attempt to demonstrate *sprachenkreise* in Africa parallel to the *kulturkreise* of the Graebner-Schmidt culture-historical school. This involves such violence to linguistic facts as the separation of the closely knit Mandingo group of languages into two unrelated families and the assumption of special Fulani-Malayo-Polynesian and Kanuri-Sumerian connections. There is no clear statement of the method employed in arriving at such conclusions.

The recent Greenberg (1949–50) classification concentrates on specific criteria which are relevant for actual historical relationship. The large heterogeneous Sudanic group, to which Westermann, in his more recent writings, denied genetic unity is split into a number of major and some minor stocks. The most important of those, Westermann's West Sudanic, shows a genetic relationship to Bantu, as evidenced by a mass of vocabulary resemblances, agreement in noun-class affixes, and phonetic correspondences, including those relating to tone, to which Westermann himself had drawn attention and to which he had even attributed a genetic significance, without, however, modifying his general scheme of language families to take account of it. The Semi-Bantu languages show a special resemblance to the Bantu languages simply because they belong to the same subgroup of languages in the larger family, to which the name "Niger-Congo" is applied. Since these Semi-Bantu languages do not possess common features as against Bantu, the Bantu language must be classified as merely one of over twenty subgroups within that one of the fifteen branches of the vast Niger-Congo family which includes both Bantu and "Semi-Bantu" languages.

Other major independent families formerly classified as Sudanic are Central Saharan, Central Sudanic, and Eastern Sudanic. This latter family includes the so-called "Nilo-Hamitic" languages, along with the closely related Nilotic languages in a single subfamily.

Hottentot is treated along with the central Bushman languages as a single subgroup within the Khoisan languages, the other branches being Northern Bushman and Southern Bushman. The Khoisan languages, in turn, are related to Sandawe and Hatsa in East Africa to form a single Click family. Of Meinhof's various proposed extensions of Hamitic, Fulani is assigned to the westernmost subfamily of Niger-Congo; the "Nilo-Hamitic" languages (Masai, Nandi, etc.) are classed as Eastern Sudanic; and Hottentot belongs to the Click family. Hausa, along with numerous other languages of the Chad family, is put, along with the traditionally Hamitic Berber, Cushite, and Ancient Egyptian and with Semitic, into the Hamito-Semitic family, for which the name "Afroasiatic" is proposed, since there is no linguistic justification for granting Semitic a special status. The term "Hamitic," which has been the basis of much pseudo-historical and pseudo-physical reconstruction in Africa, is thus abandoned as not designating a valid linguistic entity. The Afroasiatic family thus consists of five co-ordinate branches: (1) Berber, (2) Egyptian, (3) Semitic, (4) Cushite, and (5) Chad.

The Greenberg classification assumes a total of sixteen independent families in Africa. There is some possibility of a reduction in this total. The hypotheses of a Kunama–Eastern Sudanic and a Songhai-Niger-Congo relationship, in particular, are worth investigating.

Westermann has indicated his adherence to this new classification in all essentials and is expected to espouse it in a forthcoming article in the journal *Africa*.[3]

There is general agreement on the existence of only two extensive groups of related languages in Oceania—the Malayo-Polynesian and the Australian. The remaining families are the Tasmanian and a whole series of unrelated language families in New Guinea and neighboring islands, to which the cover-name "Papuan" is applied, with the general understanding that there is no proof or even likelihood that these languages form a single stock. Regarding Malayo-Polynesian, there is general consensus concerning which languages are to be included in the family, and the historical work of reconstruction of the ancestral Malayo-Polynesian and other languages will be considered in the following section on "Southeast Asia."

For the other large group, the Australian languages, although the existence of widespread relationships within the continent is asserted by all investigators, there is lack of unanimity regarding the number of families, some maintaining the unity of Australian languages and others denying it.

The linguists of the period before W. Schmidt's important work were acquainted almost exclusively with the languages of the large group which covers all the south and much of the north of the continent and ignored or were unaware of certain languages of the extreme northwestern and north-central parts of Australia which differ considerably from the great mass of Australian languages. These observers, therefore, assumed the unity of all Australian languages and were concerned chiefly with hypotheses of outside connections, with Africa, with India (Dravidian), or, in the case of Trombetti, with an Australian-Papuan-Andama-

3. Personal communication.

nese group. This latter attempt, like all the others, proved abortive in this instance, if for no other reason than that the Papuan member is no linguistic unit of any sort (Ray, 1907).

It was Schmidt (1913, 1914, 1917–18) who laid the foundations of a more careful study of the problem in a series of articles in *Anthropos*, later republished as *Die Gliederung der australischen Sprachen* (1919). Schmidt distinguishes two main families of Australian languages: the southern, which covers approximately the southern two-thirds of the continent, and a northern. He explicitly denies the existence of a genetic relationship between these two groups. Unlike the southern family, which constitutes a true genetic unity, the northern, according to Schmidt, is not a family at all but consists of numerous diverse, unrelated forms of speech. In the light of clear statements to this effect, it is difficult to know what is meant in a historical sense by Schmidt's threefold division of these northern languages into those whose words end in consonants as well as vowels, those whose words end in vowels only, and those whose words end in vowels and liquids but not in other consonants. This last group occupies, according to Schmidt, an intermediate position between the other two, probably through a process of language mixture. This threefold division of the northern languages, as well as the separation into a northern and a southern family, seems strongly motivated by an attempt at correlation with the *kulturkreise* established in this area by the ethnological school of which Schmidt is a leading exponent. Kroeber (1924), in a review of Schmidt's work, criticized this division on the ground of obvious fundamental vocabulary resemblances between the northern and southern languages. He followed this up with a study of the distribution of common vocabulary items, which showed a sublime disregard in their distribution for the fundamental east-west dividing line which Schmidt had drawn across the Australian continent.

In a series of articles in *Oceania* (1939–40, 1941–43), Capell made substantial contributions to our knowledge of the languages of the northwestern and north-central parts of the continent and also revealed the surprising fact that many of these languages had noun-prefix classes resembling those of the Bantu languages in Africa in their general functioning but, one should hasten to add, without specific resemblances to them in form and meaning. Capell asserts the fundamental unity of all Australian languages. He divides them into suffixing languages, roughly equivalent to Schmidt's southern family, and prefixing languages, corresponding to Schmidt's northern division. The criterion employed is existence of verb suffixes or prefixes to form tenses and moods and to indicate pronominal reference. It is admitted that the northern languages are, to some extent, suffixing also. Within the northern group we have, again, a threefold division on principles different from those of Schmidt. Groups with multiple noun classes, two classes, and no classes are distinguished. Capell admits, in effect, that this is not a genetic analysis. It leads, as he himself points out, to an inevitable cul-de-sac similar to that of Meinhof in Africa, cited above. We are confronted with a pair of languages—Nungali and Djämindjung—which are almost identical except that Nungali has noun classes and Djämindjung has none. A similar pair is Maung and Iwaidja. Concerning these latter, Capell observes: "It is safe to say, however, that had Iwaidja multiple classification, it would hardly be more than a dialect of Maung" (Capell, 1939–40, p. 420).

The solution suggested here is a simple one, if one keeps in mind a primary canon of classification, one so obvious that it would hardly seem to need statement, yet is frequently disregarded in practice. Languages should be classified on linguistic evidence alone. Among the irrelevancies to be excluded is the extent of the area in which the language is found and the number of speakers. There is no reason to expect that families of genetically equal rank should necessarily occupy territories approximately equal in extent. Germanic and Tokharian are coordinate branches of Indo-European, but a greater contrast in territory and population could hardly be imagined. Germanic covers substantial portions of four continents and numbers hundreds of millions of speakers. Tokharian has no speakers at all, since it is extinct.

The extent of fundamental vocabulary resemblance, including pronouns, among all languages in Australia and the specific similarities in the noun prefixes which connect many north Australian languages provide sufficient evidence of a single Australian family. This family has numerous subgroups, certainly at least forty, of which the large southern subgroup is just one which has spread over most of the continent (including the Murngin languages in northeast Arnhemland and the languages of the western Torres Straits Islands). The ancestral Australian language had noun classes, and the southern subgroup has, like some of the northern languages (the prefixing, classless language of Capell's classification), lost these classes. It still maintains a survival, however, in the distinction of a masculine and a feminine singular pronoun found in certain southern languages in which the af-formatives employed resemble those of the masculine and feminine singular classes among the class languages.

C. SOUTHEAST ASIA

There are sharp differences of opinion regarding linguistic relationships in this area. The following are the outstanding problems: (1) the validity of Schmidt's hypothesis of an Austroasiatic family consisting of Mon-Khmer, Munda, and other languages; (2) the validity of Schmidt's Austric hypothesis connecting Austroasiatic in turn with Malayo-Polynesian; (3) the affiliations of Thai and Annamite, connected by some with Chinese in one subbranch of the Sino-Tibetan family, while others place Thai with Kadai and Indonesian (Benedict) and Annamite with Austroasiatic (Schmidt and others); (4) the linguistic position of the Man (Miao-Yao) and Min-Hsia dialects spoken by aboriginal populations in China.

Accepting certain earlier suggestions and adding some of his own, Schmidt (1906) has proposed that the following groups of languages are related to one another in his Austroasiatic stock: (1) Mon-Khmer, (2) the Palaung-Wa languages of the middle Salween, (3) Semang-Sakai, (4) Khasi, (5) Nicobarese, (6) the Munda group, (7) Annamite-Muong, (8) the Cham group. If we except Cham, which most writers consider Malayo-Polynesian, a conclusion which can hardly be doubted, then all these languages share numerous resemblances in fundamental vocabulary, extending to pronouns. Moreover, excepting Annamite, which has shed all its morphological processes, there are certain important derivational morphemes whose rather uncommon formal nature (infixes), combined with their basic functions in the grammar, absolutely excludes chance and makes borrowing a completely improbable explanation. I do not see how such coincidences as an infixed -m in the Mon of Burma and the languages of the geographically remote Nicobar Islands, both with agentive meaning, to mention only one of a number of such instances, can be the result of anything but genetic relationship.

Maspero has sought to demonstrate a close connection between Annamite and Thai, which he considers to be Sino-Tibetan. This case rests chiefly on the irrelevant argument from form only —the monosyllabism and tonicity of Annamite, in which it resembles Thai and Chinese. The extensive lexical resemblances to Thai, which hardly touch basic vocabulary, must be looked upon as mostly borrowing with some convergence. On the other hand, the mass of fundamental vocabulary points clearly in the direction of the Austroasiatic languages, and I do not see how any hypothesis of borrowing can explain it. If borrowed, the source is not evident, since Annamite now resembles one, now another, of the Austroasiatic languages. It often shows an independent development from a hypothetical reconstruction which can hardly be the result of anything but internal development from the ancestral Austroasiatic form. Thus Annamite *mōt*, "one," makes sense as an independent contraction from **moyat*, found in this form only in the distant Mundari language of India. The language geographically nearest to Annamite Khmer has *muy*, presumably < *moy* with loss of final *-at*. Santali, the chief Munda language, has *mit* < **miyat* < **moyat*. The absence of the modest morphological apparatus of other Austroasiatic languages in Annamite cannot be used as an argument for any other relationship. The ancient maxim *ex nihilo nihil fit* may be appropriately applied in this instance.

Schmidt's further hypothesis of the relationship of Austroasiatic to the Malayo-Polynesian languages is of a far more doubtful nature. Most of the numerous etymologies proposed by Schmidt are either semantically or phonetically improbable or not attested from a sufficient variety of languages in one family or the other. Even with these eliminated, there remains a considerable number of plausible, or at least possible, etymologies, but very few of these are basic. Both language families employ prefixes and infixes, and the latter mechanism is certainly not very common. However, concrete resemblances in form and meaning of these elements which can reasonably be attributed to the parent-language of both groups are very few. Only *pa-*, causative, seems certain. In view of this, the Austric hypothesis cannot be accepted on present evidence. It needs to be reworked, using Dempwolff and Dyen's reconstructed Malayo-Polynesian forms, as well as taking into account the Thai and Kadai languages, which, as we shall see, are related to Malayo-Polynesian.

The traditional theory regarding Thai is that it forms, along with Chinese, the Sinitic branch of Sino-Tibetan. Benedict has proposed the relationship of Thai to the Kadai group, in which he includes certain languages of northern Indo-China, southern continental China, and the Li dialects of the island of Hainan. He has further posited the relationship of this Thai-Kadai family to Malayo-Polynesian (Benedict, 1942). Of the relation of Thai to the Kadai languages, which in the case of the Li dialects is particularly close, there can be no reasonable doubt. At the least, the traditional theory would have to be revised to include the Kadai languages, along with Thai, in Sinitic. I believe, however, that the connection of Thai with Chinese and Sino-Tibetan must be abandoned altogether and that Benedict's thesis is essentially correct. Thai resemblances to Chinese are clearly borrowings. They include the numerals from 3 on and a number of other words which are certainly the result of cultural contact. Thai is otherwise so aberrant that it must be at least another independent branch of Sino-Tibetan. Yet, when resemblances are found, the forms are always like Chinese—altogether too like Chinese, one should add. Applying a test suggested earlier, it is found that those words in Thai which resemble Malayo-Polynesian tend to reappear in the Kadai languages, while those which are like Chinese do so only rarely. The proportion of fundamental vocabulary resemblances between Thai-Kadai and Malayo-Polynesian runs to quite a high number, far beyond chance and hardly explainable by borrowing, in view of the geographical distances involved.

I believe that Benedict's thesis needs restatement in some details of grouping, where, as so often happens, he has been led astray by nonlinguistic considerations, in this case the importance of Thai as a culture language. Thai shows special resemblance to the Li dialects of such far-reaching importance that Benedict's twofold division of Kadai into Laqua-Li and Lati-Kelao must be emended to put Thai along with Li in the first subgroup. In addition, the language of the Mohammedan population of Hainan does not belong, interestingly enough, with the Li dialects of the rest of the island but forms a third subdivision alongside the continental Lati-Kelao. The emended picture is shown in the accompanying diagram.

The Miao-Yao dialects of China have variously been called "Mon-Khmer" (i.e., Austroasiatic), "Sino-Tibetan," or "independent." There seems no good reason to classify them as other than a separate branch of Sino-Tibetan, no

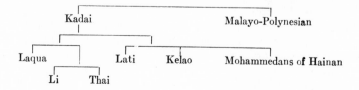

more divergent than, say, the Karen languages of Burma. The evidence cannot be summarized here. The Min-Hsia language has been variously called a "Sino-Tibetan" or "Austroasiatic" language with a Chinese overlay. It likewise seems to be Sino-Tibetan. When the obvious Chinese borrowings are accounted for, the language still appears to show a special affinity to Chinese in fundamentals, so that it should probably be included in the Sinitic subbranch.

The question is here raised concerning the status of the Nehari language of India, classed by Grierson as Munda. It has been strongly influenced by Kurku, a neighboring Munda language; but, when allowance is made for this, the fundamental vocabulary and morphology of the language do not resemble those of any other family in the area. It may therefore be the only language of an independent stock. More material is needed to decide this question.

In summary, the language families of Southeast Asia are probably the following: (1) Sino-Tibetan, (2) Austroasiatic, (3) Kadai-Malayo-Polynesian, (4) Andaman Islands, (5) Nehari(?).

D. AMERICA NORTH OF MEXICO

The present discussion is restricted to a few remarks of somewhat impressionistic character because of my lack of acquaintance with the linguistic data from this area. However, even cursory investigation of the celebrated "disputed" cases, such as Athabaskan-Tlingit-Haida and Algonkin-Wiyot-Yurok, indicate that these relationships are not very distant ones and, indeed, are evident on inspection. Even the much larger Macro-Penutian grouping seems well within the bounds of what can be accepted without more elaborate investigation and marshaling of supporting evidence. The difference between Oregon and California Penu-

tian is comparable to that between any two of the subdivisions of the Eastern Sudanic family in Africa. The status of Algonkin-Mosan and Hokan-Siouan and the position of Zuni (which Sapir himself entered in the Azteco-Tanoan family with a query) strike me as the most doubtful points of Sapir's sixfold classification. The existence of a Gulf group, as set forth recently by Haas, with a membership of Tunican, Natchez, Muskoghean and Timucua appears certain, as does the relationship of the Coahuiltecan languages both to the Gulf group and to the California Hokan in a single complex. Likewise, as Sapir pointed out, Yuki is probably no more than a somewhat divergent California Hokan language. The connection of Siouan-Yuchi and Iroquois-Caddoan with these languages is possible but far from immediately evident. Within Algonkin-Mosan, Salish-Chemakuan-Wakashan seems certain, as does Algonkin-Beothuk-Wiyot-Yurok (Beothuk may well be an Algonkin language). On the other hand, the relation of these two groups to each other and to Kutenai requires further investigation. Within the Azteco-Tanoan group it is clear that Kiowa is close to Tanoan and that Kiowa-Tanoan is related to Uto-Aztecan, as demonstrated by Trager and Whorf. The position of Zuni, as noted above, is very doubtful.

IV. LANGUAGE AND HISTORICAL RECONSTRUCTION

Ethnologists are rightly interested in comparative linguistic work, not so much for its own sake as for the light it sheds on other aspects of culture history. The basis for any discussion of this subject is inevitably the classic treatment of Sapir in his *Time Perspective in Aboriginal American Culture*. In spite of the brevity of this discussion, it is astonishingly complete, and there is little one would want to add to it, in spite of the lapse of time. The single most significant comment that might be made is that it serves as an essentially adequate basis for work in this field but that relatively little has been done toward the actual application of its principles. The problems involved are some of the most difficult in scientific co-operation and not easily solved. On the one hand, linguistic evidence is peculiarly suited to misapplication by ethnologists, who sometimes tend to use it mechanically and without at least an elementary understanding of the linguistic method involved. On the other hand, the linguist is often not greatly interested in problems of culture history, and the recent trend toward concentration in descriptive problems of linguistic structure draws him still further from the ordinary preoccupations of archeologists and historically oriented ethnologists. Perhaps the ultimate solution is an intermediate science, ethnolinguistics, which will treat the very important interstitial problems, both synchronic and historical, which lie between the recognized fields of ethnology and linguistics.

The most important and promising recent development in this area is the possibility of establishing at least an approximate chronology for linguistic events in place of the relative time relations of classical historical linguistics. This method, known as "glottochronology" and developed chiefly by Swadesh and Lees, works on the assumption that rate of change in basic vocabulary is relatively constant. A chronological time scale is provided by comparisons of vocabulary from different time periods of the same languages in areas with recorded history. The results thus far indicate an average of *ca.* 81 per cent retention of basic vocabulary in one millennium. Thus, by comparing two related languages for which no earlier recorded material is available,

the percentage of basic vocabulary differences will allow of an approximation of the date of separation of the two forms of speech.

By combining with this a rigorous application of Sapir's insight regarding the probable center of origin of a linguistic group, on the basis of a center of gravity calculated from the distribution of genetic subgroups, an instrument of historical reconstruction surpassing any previous use of linguistic data for these purposes becomes possible.

The center-of-gravity method may be briefly described as follows: Within each of the genetic subgroups of a linguistic family, the center of distribution is selected. If the subgroup is itself divided into clear dialect areas, the central point of each dialect area is calculated and the position of all is averaged to obtain the probable center of dispersal of the subgroup. The centers of the various subgroups are then averaged to obtain the most probable point of origin for the entire family. A correction in order to minimize the influence of single aberrant groups may be made by calculating a corrected center of gravity from the one reached by the above method. The distance of the center of each subfamily is calculated from the center of gravity of the whole family. Then those subgroups which are most distant are weighted least, by multiplying the center of position of each subgroup by the reciprocal of the ratio of its distance to that of the most distant subgroup, and thus calculating a corrected value. Such results, mechanically arrived at, should, of course, be evaluated in terms of geographical and other collateral knowledge.

V. GOALS, METHODS, AND PROSPECTS

The goals and methods of comparative linguistics, particularly as applied to the field of primitive languages, are clear and generally agreed upon. The aims of this branch of science might be phrased in terms of the establishment of all possible genetic relationships between languages, the detection of all borrowings and the direction they have taken, and the maximal reconstruction of the ancestral languages which have given rise to the present languages. This is of value not only for its own sake and because these results can be employed toward general historical reconstruction but also because it gives us our basic knowledge of historic change in language under diverse circumstances. It is not until considerable data have been amassed in this field and a considerable variety of historical development in different areas has been traced that questions regarding overall change from one morphological or phonological type to another, leading to general laws of linguistic change, can ever be possible.

Problems of method, also, are in the main agreed upon. These resolve themselves into two main types: those pertaining to the determination of relationship and those concerning reconstruction. The latter problems are less controversial, and, in the United States at least, there is general agreement on the employment of what are essentially the procedures of classical Indo-European linguistics. The problems of establishing genetic relationships beyond the most self-evident ones, such as those of Powell in North America, admittedly involve more differences of opinion both in Europe and in America. The abandonment of concrete criteria in favor of meaning without form or form without meaning and the abandonment of the traditional view regarding genetic relationship in some parts of the world in favor of the apparent profundity of analyses in

terms of superposed strata have led only to increasing confusion and conflicting analyses, as they inevitably must. Moreover, only on the basis of clearly defined families established through specific form-meaning resemblances can reconstruction be attempted and with it the possibility of the study of historic process in language.

The greatest single obstacle to the rapid future growth of the field does not lie, however, in any conflict regarding aims or methods. It is rather the lack of trained people in sufficient number to provide the descriptive data for a vast number of languages, some of them near extinction. The topheavy concentration of linguistic scientists in the area of a very small number of language families of Eurasia and the extreme paucity of fully trained workers in such large areas as South America and Oceania are a grave handicap to future development of this field, as well as of linguistics as a whole. At the last meeting of the Linguistic Society of America, approximately 90 per cent of the papers presented on specific languages concerned a single language family, Indo-European.

The absence of effective liaison even between anthropological linguists and other branches of anthropology and its nonexistence in the case of other linguists, while an understandable consequence of the contemporary trend toward specialization, are likewise dangerous. Unless these situations are met and to some degree overcome, comparative linguistics must fall far short of the inherent possibilities afforded by the transparency of its material and the sophistication of its method of making a unique and significant contribution to the science of anthropology as a whole.

LITERATURE CITED

BENEDICT, P. 1942. "Thai, Kadai and Indonesian: A New Alignment in Southwestern Asia," *American Anthropologist,* XLIV, 576–601.

BOAS, F. 1920. "The Classification of American Languages," *American Anthropologist,* XXII, 367–76.

——. 1929. "Classification of American Indian Languages," *Language,* V, 1–7.

BONFANTE, G. 1945. "On Reconstruction and Linguistic Method," *Word,* I, 83–94, 132–61.

CAPELL, A. 1939–40. "The Classification of Languages in North and Northwest Australia," *Oceania,* X, 241–72, 404–33.

——. 1941–43. "Language of Arnhem Land, North Australia," *ibid.,* XII, 364–92; XIII, 24–50.

GREENBERG, J. H. 1949–50. "Studies in African Linguistic Classification," *Southwestern Journal of Anthropology,* V, 79–100, 309–17; VI, 47–63, 143–60, 223–37, 388–98.

HALL, ROBERT, JR. 1946. "Bartoli's 'Neolinguistica,'" *Language,* XXII, 273–83.

HOENIGSWALD, H. 1950. "The Principal Step in Comparative Grammar," *Language,* XXVI, 357–64.

HOCKETT, C. 1948. "Implications of Bloomfield's Algonkin Studies," *Language,* XXIV, 117–31.

JAKOBSON, R. 1931. "Principes de phonologie historique," *TCLP,* IV, 247–67.

KROEBER, A. L. 1913. "The Determination of Linguistic Relationship," *Anthropos,* VIII, 389–401.

——. 1924. "Relationship of the Australian Languages," *Journal and Proceedings of the Royal Society of New South Wales,* pp. 101–17.

MARTINET, A. 1950. "Some Problems of Italic Consonantism," *Word,* VI, 26–41.

MEILLET, A. 1914. "Le Problème de la parenté des langues," *Scientia,* XV, No. XXXV, 3.

MEINHOF, CARL. 1912. *Die Sprachen der Hamiten.* Hamburg: L. Friederichsen.

——. 1915–19. "Sprachstudien im ägyptischen Sudan," *Zeitschrift für Kolonialsprachen,* VI, 161–205; VII, 36–133, 212–50, 326–35; VIII, 46–74, 110–39, 170–96, 257–67; IX, 43–64, 89–117, 167–204, 226–55.

RAY, S. 1907. *Linguistics.* ("Reports of the Cambridge Anthropological Expedition to Torres Straits," Vol. III.) Cambridge: At the University Press.

SCHMIDT, W. 1906. *Die Mon-Khmer Völker.* Braunschweig: F. Vieweg & Sohn.

——. 1913. "Dei Gliederung der australischen Sprachen," *Anthropos,* VIII, 526–54.

——. 1914. *Ibid.,* IX, 980–1018.

——. 1917. *Ibid.,* XII, 437–39.

——. 1918. *Ibid.,* XIII, 747–817.

——. 1919. *Die Gliederung der australischen Sprachen.* Vienna: Mechitharisten-Buchdruckerei.

SWADESH, M. 1951. "Diffusional Cumulation and Archaic Residue as Historical Explanation," *Southwestern Journal of Anthropology,* VII, 1–21.

TRUBETSKOY, N. 1928. *Actes du premier Congrès International de Linguistes à La Haye.* Leiden: Sijthoff.

TUCKER, A. N. 1940. *The Eastern Sudanic Languages.* London: Oxford University Press.

VENDRYES, J. 1925. *Language: A Linguistic Introduction to History.* Translated by PAUL RADIN. New York: A. Knopf.

WERNER, A. 1915. *The Language Families of Africa.* London: Society for Promoting Christian Knowledge.

Style

By MEYER SCHAPIRO

I

By STYLE IS meant the constant form—and sometimes the constant elements, qualities, and expression—in the art of an individual or a group. The term is also applied to the whole activity of an individual or society, as in speaking of a "life-style" or the "style of a civilization."

For the archeologist, style is exemplified in a motive or pattern, or in some directly grasped quality of the work of art, which helps him to localize and date the work and to establish connections between groups of works or between cultures. Style here is a symptomatic trait, like the nonaesthetic features of an artifact. It is studied more often as a diagnostic means than for its own sake as an important constituent of culture. For dealing with style, the archeologist has relatively few aesthetic and physiognomic terms.

To the historian of art, style is an essential object of investigation. He studies its inner correspondences, its life-history, and the problems of its formation and change. He, too, uses style as a criterion of the date and place of origin of works, and as a means of tracing relationships between schools of art. But the style is, above all, a system of forms with a quality and a meaningful expression through which the personality of the artist and the broad outlook of a group are visible. It is also a vehicle of expression within the group, communicating and fixing certain values of religious, social, and moral life through the emotional suggestiveness of forms. It is, besides, a common ground against which innovations and the individuality of particular works may be measured. By considering the succession of works in time and space and by matching the variations of style with historical events and with the varying features of other fields of culture, the historian of art attempts, with the help of common-sense psychology and social theory, to account for the changes of style or specific traits. The historical study of individual and group styles also discloses typical stages and processes in the development of forms.

For the synthesizing historian of culture or the philosopher of history, the style is a manifestation of the culture as a whole, the visible sign of its unity. The style reflects or projects the "inner form" of collective thinking and feeling. What is important here is not the style of an individual or of a single art, but forms and qualities shared by all the arts of a culture during a significant span of time. In this sense one speaks of Classical or Medieval or Renaissance Man with respect to common traits discovered in the art styles of these epochs and documented also in religious and philosophical writings.

The critic, like the artist, tends to conceive of style as a value term; style

287

as such is a quality and the critic can say of a painter that he has "style" or of a writer that he is a "stylist." Although "style" in this normative sense, which is applied mainly to individual artists, seems to be outside the scope of historical and ethnological studies of art, it often occurs here, too, and should be considered seriously. It is a measure of accomplishment and therefore is relevant to understanding of both art and culture as a whole. Even a period style, which for most historians is a collective taste evident in both good and poor works, may be regarded by critics as a great positive achievement. So the Greek classic style was, for Winckelmann and Goethe, not simply a convention of form but a culminating conception with valued qualities not possible in other styles and apparent even in Roman copies of lost Greek originals. Some period styles impress us by their deeply pervasive, complete character, their special adequacy to their content; the collective creation of such a style, like the conscious shaping of a norm of language, is a true achievement. Correspondingly, the presence of the same style in a wide range of arts is often considered a sign of the integration of a culture and the intensity of a high creative moment. Arts that lack a particular distinction or nobility of style are often said to be style-less, and the culture is judged to be weak or decadent. A similar view is held by philosophers of culture and history and by some historians of art.

Common to all these approaches are the assumptions that every style is peculiar to a period of a culture and that, in a given culture or epoch of culture, there is only one style or a limited range of styles. Works in the style of one time could not have been produced in another. These postulates are supported by the fact that the connection between a style and a period, inferred from a few examples, is confirmed by

objects discovered later. Whenever it is possible to locate a work through nonstylistic evidence, this evidence points to the same time and place as do the formal traits, or to a culturally associated region. The unexpected appearance of the style in another region is explained by migration or trade. The style is therefore used with confidence as an independent clue to the time and place of origin of a work of art. Building upon these assumptions, scholars have constructed a systematic, although not complete, picture of the temporal and spatial distribution of styles throughout large regions of the globe. If works of art are grouped in an order corresponding to their original positions in time and space, their styles will show significant relationships which can be co-ordinated with the relationships of the works of art to still other features of the cultural points in time and space.

II

Styles are not usually defined in a strictly logical way. As with languages, the definition indicates the time and place of a style or its author, or the historical relation to other styles, rather than its peculiar features. The characteristics of styles vary continuously and resist a systematic classification into perfectly distinct groups. It is meaningless to ask exactly when ancient art ends and medieval begins. There are, of course, abrupt breaks and reactions in art, but study shows that here, too, there is often anticipation, blending, and continuity. Precise limits are sometimes fixed by convention for simplicity in dealing with historical problems or in isolating a type. In a stream of development the artificial divisions may even be designated by numbers—Styles I, II, III. But the single name given to the style of a period rarely corresponds to a clear and universally accepted characterization of a type. Yet direct acquaintance with an unanalyzed work of art will often permit us to recognize another object of the same origin, just as we recognize a face to be native or foreign. This fact points to a degree of constancy in art that is the basis of all investigation of style. Through careful description and comparison and through formation of a richer, more refined typology adapted to the continuities in development, it has been possible to reduce the areas of vagueness and to advance our knowledge of styles.

Although there is no established system of analysis and writers will stress one or another aspect according to their viewpoint or problem, in general the description of a style refers to three aspects of art: form elements or motives, form relationships, and qualities (including an all-over quality which we may call the "expression").

This conception of style is not arbitrary but has arisen from the experience of investigation. In correlating works of art with an individual or culture, these three aspects provide the broadest, most stable, and therefore most reliable criteria. They are also the most pertinent to modern theory of art, although not in the same degree for all viewpoints. Technique, subject matter, and material may be characteristic of certain groups of works and will sometimes be included in definitions; but more often these features are not so peculiar to the art of a period as the formal and qualitative ones. It is easy to imagine a decided change in material, technique, or subject matter accompanied by little change in the basic form. Or, where these are constant, we often observe that they are less responsive to new artistic aims. A method of stone-cutting will change less rapidly than the sculptor's or architect's forms. Where a technique does coincide with the extension of a style, it is the formal traces of the technique rather than the operations as such that are important

for description of the style. The materials are significant mainly for the textural quality and color, although they may affect the conception of the forms. For the subject matter, we observe that quite different themes—portraits, still lifes, and landscapes—will appear in the same style.

It must be said, too, that form elements or motives, although very striking and essential for the expression, are not sufficient for characterizing a style. The pointed arch is common to Gothic and Islamic architecture, and the round arch to Roman, Byzantine, Romanesque, and Renaissance buildings. In order to distinguish these styles, one must also look for features of another order and, above all, for different ways of combining the elements.

Although some writers conceive of style as a kind of syntax or compositional pattern, which can be analyzed mathematically, in practice one has been unable to do without the vague language of qualities in describing styles. Certain features of light and color in painting are most conveniently specified in qualitative terms and even as tertiary (intersensory) or physiognomic qualities, like cool and warm, gay and sad. The habitual span of light and dark, the intervals between colors in a particular palette—very important for the structure of a work—are distinct relationships between elements, yet are not comprised in a compositional schema of the whole. The complexity of a work of art is such that the description of forms is often incomplete on essential points, limiting itself to a rough account of a few relationships. It is still simpler, as well as more relevant to aesthetic experience, to distinguish lines as hard and soft than to give measurements of their substance. For precision in characterizing a style, these qualities are graded with respect to intensity by comparing different examples directly or by reference to a standard work. Where quantitative measurements have been made, they tend to confirm the conclusions reached through direct qualitative description. Nevertheless, we have no doubt that, in dealing with qualities, much greater precision can be reached.

Analysis applies aesthetic concepts current in the teaching, practice, and criticism of contemporary art; the development of new viewpoints and problems in the latter directs the attention of students to unnoticed features of older styles. But the study of works of other times also influences modern concepts through discovery of aesthetic variants unknown in our own art. As in criticism, so in historical research, the problem of distinguishing or relating two styles discloses unsuspected, subtle characteristics and suggests new concepts of form. The postulate of continuity in culture—a kind of inertia in the physical sense—leads to a search for common features in successive styles that are ordinarily contrasted as opposite poles of form; the resemblances will sometimes be found not so much in obvious aspects as in fairly hidden ones—the line patterns of Renaissance compositions recall features of the older Gothic style, and in contemporary abstract art one observes form relationships like those of Impressionist painting.

The refinement of style analysis has come about in part through problems in which small differences had to be disengaged and described precisely. Examples are the regional variations within the same culture; the process of historical development from year to year; the growth of individual artists and the discrimination of the works of master and pupil, originals and copies. In these studies the criteria for dating and attribution are often physical or external—matters of small symptomatic detail—but here, too, the general trend of research has been to look for fea-

tures that can be formulated in both structural and expressive-physiognomic terms. It is assumed by many students that the expression terms are all translatable into form and quality terms, since the expression depends on particular shapes and colors and will be modified by a small change in the latter The forms are correspondingly regarded as vehicles of a particular affect (apart from the subject matter). But the relationship here is not altogether clear. In general, the study of style tends toward an ever stronger correlation of form and expression. Some descriptions are purely morphological, as of natural objects—indeed, ornament has been characterized, like crystals, in the mathematical language of group theory. But terms like "stylized," "archaistic," "naturalistic," "mannerist," "baroque," are specifically human, referring to artistic processes, and imply some expressive effect. It is only by analogy that mathematical figures have been characterized as "classic" and "romantic."

III

The analysis and characterization of the styles of primitive and early historical cultures have been strongly influenced by the standards of recent Western art. Nevertheless, it may be said that the values of modern art have led to a more sympathetic and objective approach to exotic arts than was possible fifty or a hundred years ago.

In the past, a great deal of primitive work, especially representation, was regarded as artless even by sensitive people; what was valued were mainly the ornamentation and the skills of primitive industry. It was believed that primitive arts were childlike attempts to represent nature—attempts distorted by ignorance and by an irrational content of the monstrous and grotesque. True art was admitted only in the high cultures, where knowledge of natural forms was combined with a rational ideal which brought beauty and decorum to the image of man. Greek art and the art of the Italian High Renaissance were the norms for judging all art, although in time the classic phase of Gothic art was accepted. Ruskin, who admired Byzantine works, could write that in Christian Europe alone "pure and precious ancient art exists, for there is none in America, none in Asia, none in Africa." From such a viewpoint careful discrimination of primitive styles or a penetrating study of their structure and expression was hardly possible.

With the change in Western art during the last seventy years, naturalistic representation has lost its superior status. Basic for contemporary practice and for knowledge of past art is the theoretical view that what counts in all art are the elementary aesthetic components, the qualities and relationships of the fabricated lines, spots, colors, and surfaces. These have two characteristics: they are intrinsically expressive, and they tend to constitute a coherent whole. The same tendencies to coherent and expressive structure are found in the arts of all cultures. There is no privileged content or mode of representation (although the greatest works may, for reasons obscure to us, occur only in certain styles). Perfect art is possible in any subject matter or style. A style is like a language, with an internal order and expressiveness, admitting a varied intensity or delicacy of statement. This approach is a relativism that does not exclude absolute judgments of value; it makes these judgments possible within every framework by abandoning a fixed norm of style. Such ideas are accepted by most students of art today, although not applied with uniform conviction.

As a result of this new approach, all the arts of the world, even the drawings of children and psychotics, have become accessible on a common plane of expressive and form-creating activity. Art is now one of the strongest evidences of the basic unity of mankind.

This radical change in attitude depends partly on the development of modern styles, in which the raw material and distinctive units of operation—the plane of the canvas, the trunk of wood, tool marks, brush strokes, connecting forms, schemas, particles and areas of pure color—are as pronounced as the elements of representation. Even before nonrepresentative styles were created, artists had become more deeply conscious of the aesthetic-constructive components of the work apart from denoted meanings.

Much in the new styles recalls primitive art. Modern artists were, in fact, among the first to appreciate the works of natives as true art. The development of Cubism and Abstraction made the form problem exciting and helped to refine the perception of the creative in primitive work. Expressionism, with its high pathos, disposed our eyes to the simpler, more intense modes of expression, and together with Surrealism, which valued, above all, the irrational and instinctive in the imagination, gave a fresh interest to the products of primitive fantasy. But, with all the obvious resemblances, modern paintings and sculptures differ from the primitive in structure and content. What in primitive art belongs to an established world of collective beliefs and symbols arises in modern art as an individual expression, bearing the marks of a free, experimental attitude to forms. Modern artists feel, nevertheless, a spiritual kinship with the primitive, who is now closer to them than in the past because of their ideal of frankness and intensity of expression and their desire for a simpler life, with more effective participation of the artist in collective occasions than modern society allows.

One result of the modern development has been a tendency to slight the content of past art; the most realistic representations are contemplated as pure constructions of lines and colors. The observer is often indifferent to the original meanings of works, although he may enjoy through them a vague sentiment of the poetic and religious. The form and expressiveness of older works are regarded, then, in isolation, and the history of an art is written as an immanent development of forms. Parallel to this trend, other scholars have carried on fruitful research into the meanings, symbols, and iconographic types of Western art, relying on the literature of mythology and religion; through these studies the knowledge of the content of art has been considerably deepened, and analogies to the character of the styles have been discovered in the content. This has strengthened the view that the development of forms is not autonomous but is connected with changing attitudes and interests that appear more or less clearly in the subject matter of the art.

IV

Students observed early that the traits which make up a style have a quality in common. They all seem to be marked by the expression of the whole, or there is a dominant feature to which the elements have been adapted. The parts of a Greek temple have the air of a family of forms. In Baroque art, a taste for movement determines the loosening of boundaries, the instability of masses, and the multiplication of large contrasts. For many writers a style, whether of an individual or a group, is a pervasive, rigorous unity. Investigation of style is often a search for hidden correspondences explained by an organizing principle which determines both the character of the parts and the patterning of the whole.

This approach is supported by the experience of the student in identifying a style from a small random fragment. A bit of carved stone, the profile of a molding, a few drawn lines, or a single letter from a piece of writing often possesses for the observer the quality of the complete work and can be dated precisely; before these fragments, we have the conviction of insight into the original whole. In a similar way, we recognize by its intrusiveness an added or repaired detail in an old work. The feel of the whole is found in the small parts.

I do not know how far experiments in matching parts from works in different styles would confirm this view. We may be dealing, in some of these observations, with a microstructural level in which similarity of parts only points to the homogeneity of a style or a technique, rather than to a complex unity in the aesthetic sense. Although personal, the painter's touch, described by constants of pressure, rhythm, and size of strokes, may have no obvious relation to other unique characteristics of the larger forms. There are styles in which large parts of a work are conceived and executed differently, without destroying the harmony of the whole. In African sculpture an exceedingly naturalistic, smoothly carved head rises from a rough, almost shapeless body. A normative aesthetic might regard this as imperfect work, but it would be hard to justify this view. In Western paintings of the fifteenth century, realistic figures and landscapes are set against a gold background, which in the Middle Ages had a spiritualistic sense. In Islamic art, as in certain African and Oceanic styles, forms of great clarity and simplicity in three dimensions—metal vessels and animals or the domes of buildings—have surfaces spun with rich mazy patterns; in Gothic and Baroque art, on the contrary, a complex surface treatment is associated with a correspondingly complicated silhouette of the whole. In

Romanesque art the proportions of figures are not submitted to a single canon, as in Greek art, but two or three distinct systems of proportioning exist even within the same sculpture, varying with the size of the figure.

Such variation within a style is also known in literature, sometimes in great works, like Shakespeare's plays, where verse and prose of different texture occur together. French readers of Shakespeare, with the model of their own classical drama before them, were disturbed by the elements of comedy in Shakespeare's tragedies. We understand this contrast as a necessity of the content and the poet's conception of man—the different modes of expression pertain to contrasted types of humanity—but a purist classical taste condemned this as inartistic. In modern literature both kinds of style, the rigorous and the free, coexist and express different viewpoints. It is possible to see the opposed parts as contributing elements in a whole that owes its character to the interplay and balance of contrasted qualities. But the notion of style has lost in that case the crystalline uniformity and simple correspondence of part to whole with which we began. The integation may be of a looser, more complex kind, operating with unlike parts.

Another interesting exception to the homogeneous in style is the difference between the marginal and the dominant fields in certain arts. In early Byzantine works, rulers are represented in statuesque, rigid forms, while the smaller accompanying figures, by the same artist, retain the liveliness of an older episodic, naturalistic style. In Romanesque art this difference can be so marked that scholars have mistakenly supposed that certain Spanish works were done partly by a Christian and partly by a Moslem artist. In some instances the forms in the margin or in the background are more advanced in

style than the central parts, anticipating a later stage of the art. In medieval work the unframed figures on the borders of illuminated manuscripts or on cornices, capitals, and pedestals are often freer and more naturalistic than the main figures. This is surprising, since we would expect to find the most advanced forms in the dominant content. But in medieval art the sculptor or painter is often bolder where he is less bound to an external requirement; he even seeks out and appropriates the regions of freedom. In a similar way an artist's drawings or sketches are more advanced than the finished paintings and suggest another side of his personality. The execution of the landscape backgrounds behind the religious figures in paintings of the fifteenth century is sometimes amazingly modern and in great contrast to the precise forms of the large figures. Such observations teach us the importance of considering in the description and explanation of a style the unhomogeneous, unstable aspect, the obscure tendencies toward new forms.

If in all periods artists strive to create unified works, the strict ideal of consistency is essentially modern. We often observe in civilized as well as primitive art the combination of works of different style into a single whole. Classical gems were frequently incorporated into medieval reliquaries. Few great medieval buildings are homogeneous, since they are the work of many generations of artists. This is widely recognized by historians, although theoreticians of culture have innocently pointed to the conglomerate cathedral of Chartres as a model of stylistic unity, in contrast to the heterogeneous character of stylelessness of the arts of modern society. In the past it was not felt necessary to restore a damaged work or to complete an unfinished one in the style of the original. Hence the strange juxtapositions of styles within some medieval objects. It should be said, however, that some styles, by virtue of their open, irregular forms, can tolerate the unfinished and heterogeneous better than others.

Just as the single work may possess parts that we would judge to belong to different styles, if we found them in separate contexts, so an individual may produce during the same short period works in what are regarded as two styles. An obvious example is the writing of bilingual authors or the work of the same man in different arts or even in different genres of the same art—monumental and easel painting, dramatic and lyric poetry. A large work by an artist who works mainly in the small, or a small work by a master of large forms, can deceive an expert in styles. Not only will the touch change, but also the expression and method of grouping. An artist is not present in the same degree in everything he does, although some traits may be constant. In the twentieth century, some artists have changed their styles so radically during a few years that it would be difficult, if not impossible, to identify these as works of the same hand, should their authorship be forgotten. In the case of Picasso, two styles—Cubism and a kind of classicizing naturalism—were practiced at the same time. One might discover common characters in small features of the two styles—in qualities of the brushstroke, the span of intensity, or in subtle constancies of the spacing and tones—but these are not the elements through which either style would ordinarily be characterized. Even then, as in a statistical account small and large samples of a population give different results, so in works of different scale of parts by one artist the scale may influence the frequency of the tiniest elements or the form of the small units. The modern experience of stylistic variability and of the unhomogeneous within an art style will per-

haps lead to a more refined conception of style. It is evident, at any rate, that the conception of style as a visibly unified constant rests upon a particular norm of stability of style and shifts from the large to the small forms, as the whole becomes more complex.

What has been said here of the limits of uniformity of structure in the single work and in the works of an individual also applies to the style of a group. The group style, like a language, often contains elements that belong to different historical strata. While research looks for criteria permitting one to distinguish accurately the works of different groups and to correlate a style with other characteristics of a group, there are cultures with two or more collective styles of art at the same moment. This phenomenon is often associated with arts of different function or with different classes of artists. The arts practiced by women are of another style than those of the men; religious art differs from profane, and civic from domestic; and in higher cultures the stratification of social classes often entails a variety of styles, not only with respect to the rural and urban, but within the same urban community. This diversity is clear enough today in the coexistence of an official-academic, a mass-commercial, and a freer avant-garde art. But more striking still is the enormous range of styles within the latter—although a common denominator will undoubtedly be found by future historians.

While some critics judge this heterogeneity to be a sign of an unstable, unintegrated culture, it may be regarded as a necessary and valuable consequence of the individual's freedom of choice and of the world scope of modern culture, which permits a greater interaction of styles than was ever possible before. The present diversity continues and intensifies a diversity already noticed in the preceding stages of our culture, including the Middle Ages and the Renaissance, which are held up as models of close integration. The unity of style that is contrasted with the present diversity is one type of style formation, appropriate to particular aims and conditions; to achieve it today would be impossible without destroying the most cherished values of our culture.

If we pass to the relation of group styles of different visual arts in the same period, we observe that, while the Baroque is remarkably similar in architecture, sculpture, and painting, in other periods, e.g., the Carolingian, the early Romanesque, and the modern, these arts differ in essential respects. In England, the drawing and painting of the tenth and eleventh centuries—a time of great accomplishment, when England was a leader in European art—are characterized by an enthusiastic linear style of energetic, ecstatic movement, while the architecture of the same period is inert, massive, and closed and is organized on other principles. Such variety has been explained as a sign of immaturity; but one can point to similar contrasts between two arts in later times, for example, in Holland in the seventeenth century where Rembrandt and his school were contemporary with classicistic Renaissance buildings.

When we compare the styles of arts of the same period in different media—literature, music, painting—the differences are no less striking. But there are epochs with a far-reaching unity, and these have engaged the attention of students more than the examples of diversity. The concept of the Baroque has been applied to architecture, sculpture, painting, music, poetry, drama, gardening, script, and even philosophy and science. The Baroque style has given its name to the entire culture of the seventeenth century, although it does not exclude contrary tendencies

within the same country, as well as a great individuality of national arts. Such styles are the most fascinating to historians and philosophers, who admire in this great spectacle of unity the power of a guiding idea or attitude to impose a common form upon the most varied contexts. The dominant style-giving force is identified by some historians with a world outlook common to the whole society; by others with a particular institution, like the church or the absolute monarchy, which under certain conditions becomes the source of a universal viewpoint and the organizer of all cultural life. This unity is not necessarily organic; it may be likened also, perhaps, to that of a machine with limited freedom of motion; in a complex organism the parts are unlike and the integration is more a matter of functional interdependence than of the repetition of the same pattern in all the organs.

Although so vast a unity of style is an impressive accomplishment and seems to point to a special consciousness of style—the forms of art being felt as a necessary universal language —there are moments of great achievement in a single art with characteristics more or less isolated from those of the other arts. We look in vain in England for a style of painting that corresponds to Elizabethan poetry and drama; just as in Russia in the nineteenth century there was no true parallel in painting to the great movement of literature. In these instances we recognize that the various arts have different roles in the culture and social life of a time and express in their content as well as style different interests and values. The dominant outlook of a time—if it can be isolated—does not affect all the arts in the same degree, nor are all the arts equally capable of expressing the same outlook. Special conditions within an art are often strong enough to determine a deviant expression.

V

The organic conception of style has its counterpart in the search for biological analogies in the growth of forms. One view, patterned on the life-history of the organism, attributes to art a recurrent cycle of childhood, maturity, and old age, which coincides with the rise, maturity, and decline of the culture as a whole. Another view pictures the process as an unfinished evolution from the most primitive to the most advanced forms, in terms of a polarity evident at every step.

In the cyclical process each stage has its characteristic style or series of styles. In an enriched schema, for which the history of Western art is the model, the archaic, classic, baroque, impressionist, and archaistic are types of style that follow in an irreversible course. The classic phase is believed to produce the greatest works; the succeeding ones are a decline. The same series has been observed in the Greek and Roman world and somewhat less clearly in India and the Far East. In other cultures this succession of styles is less evident, although the archaic type is widespread and is sometimes followed by what might be considered a classic phase. It is only by stretching the meaning of the terms that the baroque and impressionist types of style are discovered as tendencies within the simpler developments of primitive arts.

(That the same names, "baroque," "classic," and "impressionist," should be applied both to a unique historical style and to a recurrent type or phase is confusing. We will distinguish the name of the unique style by a capital, e.g., "Baroque." But this will not do away with the awkwardness of speaking of the late phase of the Baroque style of the seventeenth century as "baroque." A similar difficulty exists also with the word "style," which is used for the common forms of a particular period and the common forms of a phase of development found in many periods.)

The cyclical schema of development does not apply smoothly even to the Western world from which it has been abstracted. The classic phase in the Renaissance is preceded by Gothic, Romanesque, and Carolingian styles, which cannot all be fitted into the same category of the archaic. It is possible, however, to break up the Western development into two cycles—the medieval and the modern—and to interpret the late Gothic of northern Europe, which is contemporary with the Italian Renaissance, as a style of the baroque type. But contemporary with the Baroque of the seventeenth century is a classic style which in the late eighteenth century replaces the Baroque.

It has been observed, too, that the late phase of Greco-Roman art, especially in architecture, is no decadent style marking a period of decline, but something new. The archaistic trend is only secondary beside the original achievement of late imperial and early Christian art. In a similar way, the complex art of the twentieth century, whether regarded as the end of an old culture or the beginning of a new, does not correspond to the categories of either a declining or an archaic art.

Because of these and other discrepancies, the long-term cyclical schema, which also measures the duration of a culture, is little used by historians of art. It is only a very rough approximation to the character of several isolated moments in Western art. Yet certain stages and steps of the cycle seem to be frequent enough to warrant further study as typical processes, apart from the theory of a closed cyclical form of development.

Some historians have therefore narrowed the range of the cycles from the long-term development to the history of one or two period styles. In Romanesque art, which belongs to the first stage of the longer Western cycle and shares many features with early Greek and Chinese arts, several phases have been noted within a relatively short period that resemble the archaic, the classic, and the baroque of the cyclical scheme; the same observation has been made about Gothic art. But in Carolingian art the order is different; the more baroque and impressionistic phases are the earlier ones, the classic and archaic come later. This may be due in part to the character of the older works that were copied then; but it shows how difficult it is to systematize the history of art through the cyclical model. In the continuous line of Western art, many new styles have been created without breaks or new beginnings occasioned by the exhaustion or death of a preceding style. In ancient Egypt, on the other hand, the latency of styles is hardly confirmed by the slow course of development; an established style persists here with only slight changes in basic structure for several thousand years, a span of time during which Greek and Western art run twice through the whole cycle of stylistic types.

If the exceptional course of Carolingian art is due to special conditions, perhaps the supposedly autonomous process of development also depends on extra-artistic circumstances. But the theorists of cyclical development have not explored the mechanisms and conditions of growth as the biologists have done. They recognize only a latency that conditions might accelerate or delay but not produce. To account for the individuality of the arts of each cycle, the evident difference between a Greek, a western European, and a Chinese style of the same stage, they generally resort to racial theory, each cycle being carried by a people with unique traits.

In contrast to the cyclical organic pattern of development, a more refined model has been constructed by Heinrich Wölfflin, excluding all value judgment and the vital analogy of birth, maturity, and decay. In a beautiful analysis of the art of the High Renaissance and the seventeenth century, he devised five pairs of polar terms, through which he defined the opposed styles of the two periods. These terms were applied to architecture, sculpture, painting, and the so-called "decorative arts." The linear was contrasted with the picturesque or painterly (*malerisch*), the parallel surface form with the diagonal depth form, the closed (or tectonic) with the open (or a-tectonic), the composite with the fused, the clear with the relatively unclear. The first terms of these pairs characterize the classic Renaissance stage, the second belong to the Baroque. Wölfflin believed that the passage from the first set of qualities to the others was not a peculiarity of the development in this one period, but a necessary process which occurred in most historical epochs. Adama van Scheltema applied these categories to the successive stages of northern European arts from the prehistoric period to the age of the migrations. Wölfflin's model has been used in studies of several other periods as well, and it has served the historians of literature and music and even of economic development. He recognized that the model did not apply uniformly to German and Italian art; and, to explain the deviations, he investigated peculiarities of the two national arts, which he thought were "constants"— the results of native dispositions that modified to some degree the innate normal tendencies of development. The German constant, more dynamic and unstable, favored the second set of qualities, and the Italian, more relaxed and bounded, favored the first. In this way, Wölfflin supposed he could explain the precociously *malerisch* and baroque character of German art in its classic Renaissance phase and the persistent classicism in the Italian Baroque.

The weaknesses of Wölfflin's system have been apparent to most students of art. Not only is it difficult to fit into his scheme the important style called "Mannerism" which comes between the High Renaissance and the Baroque; but the pre-Classic art of the fifteenth century is for him an immature, unintegrated style because of its inaptness for his terms. Modern art, too, cannot be defined through either set of terms, although some modern styles show features from both sets—there are linear compositions which are open and painterly ones which are closed. It is obvious that the linear and painterly are genuine types of style, of which examples occur, with more or less approximation to Wölfflin's model, in other periods. But the particular unity of each set of terms is not a necessary one (although it is possible to argue that the Classic and Baroque of the Renaissance are "pure" styles in which basic processes of art appear in an ideally complete and legible way). We can imagine and discover in history other combinations of five of these ten terms. Mannerism, which had been ignored as a phenomenon of decadence, is now described as a type of art that appears in other periods. Wölfflin cannot be right, then, in supposing that, given the first type of art—the classic phase—the second will follow. That depends perhaps on special circumstances which have been effective in some epochs, but not in all. Wölfflin, however, regards the development as internally determined; outer conditions can only retard or facilitate the process, they are not among its causes. He denied that his terms have any other than artistic meaning; they describe two typical modes of seeing and are independent of an expressive content; although artists may choose themes

more or less in accord with these forms, the latter do not arise as a means of expression. It is remarkable, therefore, that qualities associated with these pure forms should be attributed also to the psychological dispositions of the Italian and German people.

How this process could have been repeated after the seventeenth century in Europe is a mystery, since that required—as in the passage from Neo-Classicism to Romantic painting—a reverse development from the Baroque to the Neo-Classic.

In a later book Wölfflin recanted some of his views, admitting that these pure forms might correspond to a world outlook and that historical circumstances, religion, politics, etc., might influence the development. But he was unable to modify his schemas and interpretations accordingly. In spite of these difficulties, one can only admire Wölfflin for his attempt to rise above the singularities of style to a general construction that simplifies and organizes the field.

To meet the difficulties of Wölfflin's schema, Paul Frankl has conceived a model of development which combines the dual polar structure with a cyclical pattern. He postulates a recurrent movement between two poles of style —a style of Being and a style of Becoming; but within each of these styles are three stages: a preclassic, a classic, and a postclassic; and in the first and third stages he assumes alternative tendencies which correspond to those historical moments, like Mannerism, that would be anomalous in Wölfflin's scheme. What is most original in Frankl's construction—and we cannot begin to indicate its rich nuancing and complex articulation—is that he attempts to deduce this development and its phases (and the many types of style comprehended within his system) from the analysis of elementary forms and the limited number of possible combinations, which he has investigated with great care. His scheme is not designed to describe the actual historical development—a very irregular affair—but to provide a model or ideal plan of the inherent or normal tendencies of development, based on the nature of forms. Numerous factors, social and psychological, constrain or divert the innate tendencies and determine other courses; but the latter are unintelligible, according to Frankl, without reference to his model and his deduction of the formal possibilities.

Frankl's book—a work of over a thousand pages—appeared unfortunately at a moment (1938) when it could not receive the attention it deserved; and since that time it has been practically ignored in the literature, although it is surely the most serious attempt in recent years to create a systematic foundation for the study of art forms. No other writer has analyzed the types of style so thoroughly.

In spite of their insights and ingenuity in constructing models of development, the thoreticians have had relatively little influence on investigation of special problems, perhaps because they have provided no adequate bridge from the model to the unique historical style and its varied developments. The principles by which are explained the broad similarities in development are of a different order from those by which the singular facts are explained. The normal motion and the motion due to supposedly perturbing factors belong to different worlds; the first is inherent in the morphology of styles, the second has a psychological or social origin. It is as if mechanics had two different sets of laws, one for irregular and the other for regular motions; or one for the first and another for the second approximation, in dealing with the same phenomenon. Hence those who are most concerned with a unified approach to the study of art have split the history of style into two aspects which cannot be derived from each other or from some common principle.

Parallel to the theorists of cyclical development, other scholars have approached the development of styles as a continuous, long-term evolutionary process. Here, too, there are poles and stages and some hints of a universal, though not cyclical, process; but the poles are those of the earliest and latest stages and are deduced from a definition of the artist's goal or the nature of art or from a psychological theory.

The first students to investigate the history of primitive art conceived the latter as a development between two poles, the geometrical and the naturalistic. They were supported by observation of the broad growth of art in the historical cultures from geometric or simple, stylized forms to more natural ones; they were sustained also by the idea that the most naturalistic styles of all belonged to the highest type of culture, the most advanced in scientific knowledge, and the most capable of representing the world in accurate images. The process in art agreed with the analogous development in nature from the simple to the complex and was paralleled by the growth of the child's drawings in our own culture from schematic or geometrical forms to naturalistic ones. The origin of certain geometrical forms in primitive industrial techniques also favored this view.

It is challenging and amusing to consider in the light of these arguments the fact that the Paleolithic cave paintings, the oldest known art, are marvels of representation (whatever the elements of schematic form in those works, they are more naturalistic than the succeeding Neolithic and Bronze Age art) and that in the twentieth century naturalistic forms have given way to "abstraction" and so-called "subjective" styles. But, apart from these paradoxical exceptions, one could observe in historical arts—e.g., in the late classic and early Christian periods—how free naturalistic forms are progressively stylized and reduced to ornament. In the late nineteenth century, ornament was often designed by a method of stylization, a geometrizing of natural motives; and those who knew contemporary art were not slow to discern in the geometrical styles of existing primitives the traces of an older more naturalistic model. Study shows that both processes occur in history; there is little reason to regard either one as more typical or more primitive. The geometrical and the naturalistic forms may arise independently in different contexts and coexist within the same culture. The experience of the art of the last fifty years suggests further that the degree of naturalism in art is not a sure indication of the technological or intellectual level of a culture. This does not mean that style is independent of that level but that other concepts than those of the naturalistic and the geometrical must be applied in considering such relationships. The essential opposition is not of the natural and the geometric but of certain modes of composition of natural and geometric motives. From this point of view, modern "abstract" art in its taste for open, asymmetrical, random, tangled, and incomplete forms is much closer to the compositional principles of realistic or Impressionist painting and sculpture than to any primitive art with geometrical elements. Although the character of the themes, whether "abstract" or naturalistic, is important for the concrete aspect of the work of art, historians do not operate so much with categories of the naturalistic and geometrical as with subtler structural concepts, which apply also to architecture, where the problem of representation seems irrelevant. It is with such concepts that Wölfflin and Frankl have constructed their models.

Nevertheless, the representation of natural forms has been a goal in the arts of many cultures. Whether we regard it as a spontaneous common idea or one that has been diffused from a single prehistoric center, the problem of how to represent the human and animal figure has been attacked independently by various cultures. Their solutions present not only similar features in the devices of rendering but also a remarkable parallelism in the successive stages of the solutions. It is fascinating to compare the changing representation of the eyes or of pleated costume in succeeding styles of Greek, Chinese, and medieval European sculpture. The development of such details from a highly schematic to a naturalistic type in the latter two can hardly be referred to a direct influence of Greek models; for the similarities are not only of geographically far separated styles but of distinct series in time. To account for the Chinese and Romanesque forms as copies of the older Greek, we would have to assume that at each stage in the post-Greek styles the artists had recourse to Greek works of the corresponding stage and in the same order. Indeed, some of the cyclical schemas discussed above are, in essence, descriptions of the stages in the development of representation; and it may be asked whether the formal schemas, like Wölfflin's, are not veiled categories of representation, even though they are applied to architecture as well as to sculpture and painting; for the standards of representation in the latter may conceivably determine a general norm of plasticity and structure for all the visual arts.

This aspect of style—the representation of natural forms—has been studied by the classical archeologist, Emanuel Löwy; his little book on *The Rendering of Nature in Early Greek Art,* published in 1900, is still suggestive for modern research and has a wider application than has been recognized.

Löwy has analyzed the general principles of representation in early arts and explained their stages as progressive steps in a steady change from conceptual representation, based on the memory image, to perspective representation, according to direct perception of objects. Since the structure of the memory image is the same in all cultures, the representations based on this psychological process will exhibit common features: (1) The shape and movement of figures and their parts are limited to a few typical forms; (2) the single forms are schematized in regular linear patterns; (3) representation proceeds from the outline, whether the latter is an independent contour or the silhouette of a uniformly colored area; (4) where colors are used, they are without gradation of light and shadow; (5) the parts of a figure are presented to the observer in their broadest aspect; (6) in compositions the figures, with few exceptions, are shown with a minimum of overlapping of their main parts; the real succession of figures in depth is transformed in the image into a juxtaposition on the same plane; (7) the representation of the three-dimensional space in which an action takes place is more or less absent.

Whatever criticisms may be made of Löwy's notion of a memory image as the source of these peculiarities, his account of archaic representation as a universal type, with a characteristic structure, is exceedingly valuable; it has a general application to children's drawings, to the work of modern untrained adults, and to primitives. This analysis does not touch on the individuality of archaic styles, nor does it help us to understand why some cultures develop beyond them and others, like the Egyptian, retain the archaic features for many centuries. Limited by an evolutionary view and a naturalistic value norm, Löwy ignored the perfection and expressiveness of archaic works. Neglecting the specific content of the representations, this approach fails to recognize the role of the content and of emotional factors in the proportioning and accentuation of parts. But these limitations do not lessen the importance of Löwy's book in defining so clearly a widespread type of archaic representation and in tracing the stages of its development into a more naturalistic art.

I may mention here that the reverse process of the conversion of naturalistic to archaic forms, as we see it wherever works of an advanced naturalistic style are copied by primitives, colonials, provincials, and the untrained in the high cultures, can also be formulated through Löwy's principles.

We must mention, finally, as the most constructive and imaginative of the historians who have tried to embrace the whole of artistic development as a single continuous process, Alois Riegl, the author of *Stilfragen* and *Die spätrömische Kunstindustrie*.

Riegl was especially concerned with transitions that mark the beginning of a world-historical epoch (the Old Oriental to the Hellenic, the ancient to the medieval). He gave up not only the normative view that judges the later phases of a cycle as a decline but also the conception of closed cycles. In late Roman art, which was considered decadent in his time, he found a necessary creative link between two great stages of an open development. His account of the process is like Wölfflin's, however, though perhaps independent; he formulates as the poles of the long evolution two types of style, the "haptic" (tactile) and the "optic" (or painterly, impressionistic), which coincide broadly with the poles of Wölfflin's shorter cycles. The process of development from the haptic to the optic is observable in each epoch, but only as part of a longer process, of which the great stages are millennial and correspond to whole cultures. The history of art is, for Riegl, an endless necessary movement from representation based on vision of the object and its parts as proximate, tangible, discrete, and self-sufficient, to the representation of the whole perceptual field as a directly given, but more distant, continuum with merging parts, with an increasing role of the spatial voids, and with a more evident reference to the knowing subject as a constituting factor in perception. This artistic process is also described by Riegl in terms of a faculty psychology; will, feeling, and thought are the successive dominants in shaping our relations to the world; it corresponds in philosophy to the change from a predominantly objective to a subjective outlook.

Riegl does not study this process simply as a development of naturalism from an archaic to an impressionistic stage. Each phase has its special formal and expressive problems, and Riegl has written remarkably penetrating pages on the intimate structure of styles, the principles of composition, and the relations of figure to ground. In his systematic account of ancient art and the art of the early Christian period, he has observed common principles in architecture, sculpture, painting, and ornament, sometimes with surprising acuteness. He has also succeeded in showing unexpected relationships between different aspects of a style. In a work on Dutch group portraiture of the sixteenth and seventeenth centuries, a theme that belongs to art and social history, he has carried through a most delicate analysis of the changing relations between the objective and the subjective elements in portraiture and in the correspondingly variable mode of unifying a represented group which is progressively more attentive to the observer.

His motivation of the process and his explanation of its shifts in time and space are vague and often fantastic. Each great phase corresponds to a racial disposition. The history of Western man from the time of the Old Oriental kingdoms to the present day is divided into three great periods, characterized by the successive predominance of will, feeling, and thought, in Oriental, Classical, and Western Man. Each race plays a prescribed role and retires when its part is done, as if participating in a symphony of world history. The apparent deviations from the expected continuities are saved for the system by a theory of purposive regression which prepares a people for its advanced role. The obvious incidence of social and religious factors in art is judged to be simply a parallel manifestation of a corresponding process in these other fields rather than a possible cause. The basic, immanent development from an objective to a subjective standpoint governs the whole of history, so that all contemporary fields have a deep unity with respect to a common determining process.

This brief summary of Riegl's ideas hardly does justice to the positive features of his work, and especially to his conception of art as an active creative process in which new forms arise from the artist's will to solve specifically artistic problems. Even his racial theories and strange views about the historical situation of an art represent a desire to grasp large relationships, although distorted by an inadequate psychology and social theory; this search for a broad view has become rare in the study of art since his time. And still rarer is its combination with the power of detailed research that Riegl possessed to a high degree.

To summarize the results of modern studies with respect to the cyclical and evolutionary theories:

1. From the viewpoint of historians who have tried to reconstruct the precise order of development, without pre-

suppositions about cycles, there is a continuity in the Near East and Europe from the Neolithic period to the present—perhaps best described as a tree with many branches—in which the most advanced forms of each culture are retained, to some extent, in the early forms of succeeding cultures.

2. On the other hand, there are within that continuity at least two long developments—the ancient Greek and the Western European medieval-modern—which include the broad types of style described in various cyclical theories. But these two cycles are not unconnected; artists in the second cycle often copied surviving works of the first, and it is uncertain whether some of the guiding principles in Western art are not derived from the Greeks.

3. Within these two cycles and in several other cultures (Asiatic and American) occur many examples of similar short developments, especially from an archaic linear type of representation to a more "pictorial" style.

4. Wherever there is a progressive naturalistic art, i.e., one which becomes increasingly naturalistic, we find in the process stages corresponding broadly to the line of archaic, classic, baroque, and impressionist in Western art. Although these styles in the West are not adequately described in terms of their method of representation, they embody specific advances in range or method of representation from a first stage of schematized, so-called "conceptual," representation of isolated objects to a later stage of perspective representation in which continuities of space, movement, light and shadow, and atmosphere have become important.

5. In describing the Western development, which is the model of cyclical theories, historians isolate different aspects of art for the definition of the stylistic types. In several theories the development of representation is the main source of the terms; in others

formal traits, which can be found also in architecture, script, and pottery shapes, are isolated; and, in some accounts, qualities of expression and content are the criteria. It is not always clear which formal traits are really independent of representation. It is possible that a way of seeing objects in nature—the perspective vision as distinguished from the archaic conceptual mode—also affects the design of a column or a pot. But the example of Islamic art, in which representation is secondary, suggests that the development of the period styles in architecture and ornament need not depend on a style of representation. As for expression, there exist in the Baroque art of the seventeenth century intimate works of great tragic sensibility, like Rembrandt's, and monumental works of a profuse splendor; either of these traits can be paralleled in other periods in forms of nonbaroque type. But a true counterpart of Rembrandt's light and shadow will not be found in Greek or Chinese painting, although both are said to have baroque phases.

VI

We shall now consider the explanations of style proposed without reference to cycles and polar developments.

In accounting for the genesis of a style, early investigators gave great weight to the technique, materials, and practical functions of an art. Thus wood-carving favors grooved or wedge-cut relief, the column of the tree trunk gives the statue its cylindrical shape, hard stone yields compact and angular forms, weaving begets stepped and symmetrical patterns, the potter's wheel introduces a perfect roundness, coiling is the source of spirals, etc. This was the approach of Semper and his followers in the last century. Boas, among others, identified style, or at least its formal aspect, with motor habits in the handling of tools. In modern art this viewpoint appears in the program of functionalist architecture and design. It is also behind the older explanation of the Gothic style of architecture as a rational system derived from the rib construction of vaults. Modern sculptors who adhere closely to the block, exploiting the texture and grain of the material and showing the marks of the tool, are supporters of this theory of style. It is related to the immense role of the technological in our own society; modern standards of efficient production have become a norm in art.

There is no doubt that these practical conditions account for some peculiarities of style. They are important also in explaining similarities in primitive and folk arts which appear to be independent of diffusion or imitation of styles. But they are of less interest for highly developed arts. Wood may limit the sculptor's forms, but we know a great variety of styles in wood, some of which even conceal the substance. Riegl observed long ago that the same forms occurred within a culture in works of varied technique, materials, and use; it is this common style that the theory in question has failed to explain. The Gothic style is, broadly speaking, the same in buildings; sculptures of wood, ivory, and stone; panel paintings; stained glass; miniatures; metalwork, enamels, and textiles. It may be that in some instances a style created in one art under the influence of the technique, material, and function of particular objects has been generalized by application to all objects, techniques, and materials. Yet the material is not always prior to the style but may be chosen because of an ideal of expression and artistic quality or for symbolism. The hard substances of old Egyptian art, the use of gold and other precious luminous substances in arts of power, the taste for steel, concrete, and glass in modern design, are not external to the artist's first goal but parts of the original conception. The compactness of the sculpture cut from a tree trunk is a quality that is already present in the artist's idea before he begins to carve. For simple compact forms appear in clay figures and in drawings and paintings where the matter does not limit the design. The compactness may be regarded as a necessary trait of an archaic or a "haptic" style in Löwy's or Riegl's sense.

Turning away from material factors, some historians find in the content of the work of art the source of its style. In the arts of representation, a style is often associated with a distinct body of subject matter, drawn from a single sphere of ideas or experience. Thus in Western art of the fourteenth century, when a new iconography of the life of Christ and of Mary was created in which themes of suffering were favored, we observe new patterns of line and color, which possess a more lyrical, pathetic aspect than did the preceding art. In our own time, a taste for the constructive and rational in industry has led to the use of mechanical motives and a style of forms characterized by coolness, precision, objectivity, and power.

The style in these examples is viewed by many writers as the objective vehicle of the subject matter or of its governing idea. Style, then, is the means of communication, a language not only as a system of devices for conveying a precise message by representing or symbolizing objects and actions but also as a qualitative whole which is capable of suggesting the diffuse connotations as well and intensifying the associated or intrinsic affects. By an effort of imagination based on experience of his medium, the artist discovers the elements and formal relationships which will express the values of the content and look right artistically. Of all the attempts made in this direction, the most successful will be repeated and developed as a norm.

The relationship of content and style is more complex than appears in this theory. There are styles in which the correspondence of the expression and the values of the typical subjects is not at all obvious. If the difference between pagan and Christian art is explained broadly by the difference in religious content, there is nevertheless a long period of time—in fact, many centuries —during which Christian subjects are represented in the style of pagan art. As late as 800, the Libri Carolini speak of the difficulty of distinguishing images of Mary and Venus without the labels. This may be due to the fact that a general outlook of late paganism, more fundamental than the religious doctrines, was still shared by Christians or that the new religion, while important, had not yet transformed the basic attitudes and ways of thinking. Or it may be that the function of art within the religious life was too slight, for not all concepts of the religion find their way into art. But even later, when the Christian style had been established, there were developments in art toward a more naturalistic form and toward imitation of elements of ancient pagan style which were incompatible with the chief ideas of the religion.

A style that arises in connection with a particular content often becomes an accepted mode governing all representations of the period. The Gothic style is applied in religious and secular works alike; and, if it is true that no domestic or civil building in that style has the expressiveness of a cathedral interior, yet in painting and sculpture the religious and secular images are hardly different in form. On the other hand, in periods of a style less pervasive than the Gothic, different idioms or dialects of form are used for different fields of content; this was observed in the discussion of the concept of stylistic unity.

It is such observations that have led students to modify the simple equation of style and the expressive values of a subject matter, according to which the style is the vehicle of the main meanings of the work of art. Instead, the meaning of content has been extended, and attention has been fixed on broader attitudes or on general ways of thinking and feeling, which are believed to shape a style. The style is then viewed as a concrete embodiment or projection of emotional dispositions and habits of thought common to the whole culture. The content as a parallel product of the same viewpoint will therefore often exhibit qualities and structures like those of the style.

These world views or ways of thinking and feeling are usually abstracted by the historian from the philosophical systems and metaphysics of a period or from theology and literature and even from science. Themes like the relation of subject and object, spirit and matter, soul and body, man and nature or God, and conceptions of time and space, self and cosmos are typical fields from which are derived the definitions of the world view (or *Denkweise*) of a period or culture. The latter is then documented by illustrations from many fields, but some writers have attempted to derive it from the works of art themselves. One searches in a style for qualities and structures that can be matched with some aspect of thinking or a world view. Sometimes it is based on a priori deduction of possible world views, given the limited number of solutions of metaphysical problems; or a typology of the possible attitudes of the individual to the world and to his own existence is matched with a typology of styles. We have seen how Riegl apportioned the three faculties of will, feeling, and thought among three races and three major styles.

The attempts to derive style from thought are often too vague to yield more than suggestive *aperçus;* the method breeds analogical speculations which do not hold up under detailed critical study. The history of the analogy drawn between the Gothic cathedral and scholastic theology is an example. The common element in these two contemporary creations has been found in their rationalism and in their irrationality, their idealism and their naturalism, their encyclopedic completeness and their striving for infinity, and recently in their dialectical method. Yet one hesitates to reject such analogies in principle, since the cathedral belongs to the same religious sphere as does contemporary theology.

It is when these ways of thinking and feeling or world views have been formulated as the outlook of a religion or dominant institution or class of which the myths and values are illustrated or symbolized in the work of art that the general intellectual content seems a more promising field for explanation of style. But the content of a work of art often belongs to another region of experience than the one in which both the period style and the dominant mode of thinking have been formed; an example is the secular art of a period in which religious ideas and rituals are primary, and, conversely, the religious art of a secularized culture. In such cases we see how important for a style of art is the character of the dominants in culture, especially of institutions. Not the content as such, but the content as part of a dominant set of beliefs, ideas, and interests, supported by institutions and the forms of everyday life, shapes the common style.

Although the attempts to explain styles as an artistic expression of a world view or mode of thought are often a drastic reduction of the concreteness and richness of art, they have been helpful in revealing unsuspected levels of meaning in art. They have established the practice of interpreting the style itself as an inner content of the art, especially in the nonrepresentational arts. They correspond to the conviction of modern artists that the form elements and structure are a deeply meaningful whole related to metaphysical views.

VII

The theory that the world view or mode of thinking and feeling is the source of long-term constants in style is often formulated as a theory of racial or national character. I have already referred to such concepts in the work of Wölfflin and Riegl. They have been common in European writing on art for over a hundred years and have played a significant role in promoting national consciousness and race feeling; works of art are the chief concrete evidences of the affective world of the ancestors. The persistent teaching that German art is by nature tense and irrational, that its greatness depends on fidelity to the racial character, has helped to produce an acceptance of these traits as a destiny of the people.

The weakness of the racial concept of style is evident from analysis of the history and geography of styles, without reference to biology. The so-called "constant" is less constant than the racially (or nationally) minded historians have assumed. German art includes Classicism and the Biedermeier style, as well as the work of Gruenewald and the modern Expressionists. During the periods of most pronounced Germanic character, the extension of the native style hardly coincides with the boundaries of the preponderant physical type or with the recent national boundaries. This discrepancy holds for the Italian art which is paired with the German as a polar opposite.

Nevertheless, there are striking recurrences in the art of a region or nation which have not been explained. It is astonishing to observe the resemblances between German migrations art and the styles of the Carolingian, Ottonian, and late Gothic periods, then of German rococo architecture, and finally of modern Expressionism. There are great gaps in time between these styles during which the forms can scarcely be described in the traditional German terms. To save the appearance of constancy, German writers have supposed that the intervening phases were dominated by alien influences or were periods of preparation for the ultimate release, or they conceived the deviant qualities as another aspect of German character: the Germans are both irrational and disciplined.

If we restrict ourselves to more modest historical correlations of styles with the dominant personality types of the cultures or groups that have created the styles, we meet several difficulties; some of these have been anticipated in the discussion of the general problem of unity of style.

1. The variation of styles in a culture or group is often considerable within the same period.

2. Until recently, the artists who create the style are generally of another mode of life than those for whom the arts are designed and whose viewpoint, interests, and quality of life are evident in the art. The best examples are the arts of great monarchies, aristocracies, and privileged institutions.

3. What is constant in all the arts of a period (or of several periods) may be less essential for characterizing the style than the variable features; the persistent French quality in the series of styles between 1770 and 1870 is a nuance which is hardly as important for the definition of the period style as the traits that constitute the Rococo, Neo-Classic, Romantic, Realistic, and Impressionist styles.

To explain the changing period styles, historians and critics have felt the need of a theory that relates particular forms to tendencies of character and feeling. Such a theory, concerned with the elements of expression and structure, should tell us what affects and dispositions determine choices of forms. Historians have not waited for experimental psychology to support their physiognomic interpretations of style but, like the thoughtful artists, have resorted to intuitive judgments, relying on direct experience of art. Building up an unsystematic, empirical knowledge of forms, expressions, affects, and qualities, they have tried to control these judgments by constant comparison of works and by reference to contemporary sources of information about the content of the art, assuming that the attitudes which govern the latter must also be projected in the style. The interpretation of Classical style is not founded simply on firsthand experience of Greek buildings and sculptures; it rests also on knowledge of Greek language, literature, religion, mythology, philosophy, and history, which provide an independent picture of the Greek world. But this picture is, in turn, refined and enriched by experience of the visual arts, and our insight is sharpened by knowledge of the very different arts of the neighboring peoples and of the results of attempts to copy the Greek models at later times under other conditions. Today, after the work of nearly two centuries of scholars, a sensitive mind, with relatively little information about Greek culture, can respond directly to the "Greek mind" in those ancient buildings and sculptures.

In physiognomic interpretations of group styles, there is a common assumption that is still problematic: that the psychological explanations of unique features in a modern individual's art can be applied to a whole culture in which the same or similar features are characteristics of a group or period style.

If schizophrenics fill a sheet of paper

with closely crowded elements in repeat patterns, can we explain similar tendencies in the art of a historic or primitive culture by a schizophrenic tendency or dominant schizoid personality type in that culture? We are inclined to doubt such interpretations for two reasons. First, we are not sure that this pattern is uniquely schizoid in modern individuals; it may represent a component of the psychotic personality which also exists in other temperaments as a tendency associated with particular emotional contents or problems. Secondly, this pattern, originating in a single artist of schizoid type, may crystallize as a common convention, accepted by other artists and the public because it satisfies a need and is most adequate to a special problem of decoration or representation, without entailing, however, a notable change in the broad habits and attitudes of the group. This convention may be adopted by artists of varied personality types, who will apply it in distinct ways, filling it with an individual content and expression.

A good instance of this relationship between the psychotic, the normal individual, and the group is the practice of reading object forms in relatively formless spots—as in hallucination and in psychological tests. Leonardo da Vinci proposed this method to artists as a means of invention. It was practiced in China, and later in Western art; today it has become a standard method for artists of different character. In the painter who first introduced the practice and exploited it most fully, it may correspond to a personal disposition; but for many others it is an established technique. What is personally significant is not the practice itself but the kinds of spots chosen and what is seen in them; attention to the latter discloses a great variety of individual reactions.

If art is regarded as a projective technique—and some artists today think of their work in these terms—will interpretation of the work give the same result as a projective test? The tests are so designed as to reduce the number of elements that depend on education, profession, and environment. But the work of art is very much conditioned by these factors. Hence, in discerning the personal expression in a work of art, one must distinguish between those aspects that are conventional and those that are clearly individual. In dealing with the style of a group, however, we consider only such superindividual aspects, abstracting them from the personal variants. How, then, can one apply to the interpretation of the style concepts from individual psychology?

It may be said, of course, that the established norms of a group style are genuine parts of an artist's outlook and response and can be approached as the elements of a modal personality. In the same way the habits and attitudes of scientists that are required by their profession may be an important part of their characters. But do such traits also constitute the typical ones of the culture or the society as a whole? Is an art style that has crystallized as a result of special problems necessarily an expression of the whole group? Or is it only in the special case where the art is open to the common outlook and everyday interests of the entire group that its content and style can be representative of the group?

A common tendency in the physiognomic approach to group style has been to interpret all the elements of representation as expressions. The blank background or negative features like the absence of a horizon and of consistent perspective in paintings are judged to be symptomatic of an attitude to space and time in actual life. The limited space in Greek art is interpreted as a fundamental trait of Greek personality. Yet this blankness of the background, we have seen, is common to many styles; it is found in prehistoric art, in Old Oriental art, in the Far East, in the Middle Ages, and in most primitive painting and relief. The fact that it occurs in modern children's drawings and in the drawings of untrained adults suggests that it belongs to a universal primitive level of representation. But it should be observed that this is also the method of illustration in the most advanced scientific work in the past and today.

This fact does not mean that representation is wholly without expressive personal features. A particular treatment of the "empty" background may become a powerful expressive factor. Careful study of so systematic a method of representation as geometrical perspective shows that within such a scientific system there are many possible choices; the position of the eye-level, the intensity of convergence, the distance of the viewer from the picture plane—all these are expressive choices within the conditions of the system. Moreover, the existence of the system itself presupposes a degree of interest in the environment which is already a cultural trait with a long history.

The fact that an art represents a restricted world does not allow us to infer, however, a corresponding restriction of interests and perceptions in everyday life. We would have to suppose, if this were true, that in Islam people were unconcerned with the human body, and that the present vogue of "abstract" art means a general indifference to the living.

An interesting evidence of the limitations of the assumed identities of the space or time structure of works of art and the space or time experience of individuals is the way in which painters of the thirteenth century represented the new cathedrals. These vast buildings with high vaults and endless vistas in depth are shown as shallow structures, not much larger than the human beings they inclose. The conventions of representation provided no means of re-creating the experience of architectural space, an experience that was surely a factor in the conception of the cathedral and was reported in contemporary descriptions. (It is possible to relate the architectural and pictorial spaces; but the attempt would take us beyond the problems of this paper.) The space of the cathedrals is intensely expressive, but it is a constructed, ideal space, appealing to the imagination, and not an attempt to transpose the space of everyday life. We will understand it better as a creation adequate to a religious conception than as one in which an everyday sentiment of space has been embodied in architecture. It is an ideological space, too, and, if it conveys the feelings of the most inspired religious personalities, it is not a model of an average, collective attitude to space in general, although the cathedral is used by everyone.

The concept of personality in art is most important for the theory that the great artist is the immediate source of the period style. This little-explored view, implicit in much historical research and criticism, regards the group style as an imitation of the style of an original artist. Study of a line of development often leads to the observation that some individual is responsible for the change in the period form. The personality of the great artist and the problems inherited from the preceding generation are the two factors studied. For the personality as a whole is sometimes substituted a weakness or a traumatic experience which activates the individual's will to create. Such a view is little adapted to the understanding of those cultures or historical epochs that have left us no signed works or biographies of artists; but it is the favored view of many students of the art of the last four centuries in Europe. It may be questioned whether it is applicable to cultures in which the individual has less mobility and range of personal action and in which the artist is not a deviant type. The main difficulty, however, arises from the fact that similar stylistic trends often appear independently in different arts at the same time; that great contemporary artists in the same field—Leonardo, Michelangelo, Raphael—show a parallel tendency of style, although each artist has a personal form; and that the new outlook expressed by a single man of genius is anticipated or prepared in preceding works and thought. The great artists of the Gothic period and the Renaissance constitute families with a common heritage and trend. Decisive changes are most often associated with original works of outstanding quality; but the new direction of style and its acceptance are unintelligible without reference to the conditions of the moment and the common ground of the art.

These difficulties and complexities have not led scholars to abandon the psychological approach; long experience with art has established as a plausible principle the notion that an individual style is a personal expression; and continued research has found many confirmations of this, wherever it has been possible to control statements about the personality, built upon the work, by referring to actual information about the artist. Similarly, common traits in the art of a culture or nation can be matched with some features of social life, ideas, customs, general dispositions. But such correlations have been of single elements or aspects of a style with single traits of a people; it is rarely a question of wholes. In our own culture, styles have changed very rapidly, yet the current notions about group traits do not allow sufficiently for corresponding changes in the behavior patterns or provide such a formulation of the group personality that

one can deduce from it how that personality will change under new conditions.

It seems that for explanation of the styles of the higher cultures, with their great variability and intense development, the concepts of group personality current today are too rigid. They underestimate the specialized functions of art which determine characteristics that are superpersonal. But we may ask whether some of the difficulties in applying characterological concepts to national or period styles are not also present in the interpretation of primitive arts. Would a psychological treatment of Sioux art, for example, give us the same picture of Sioux personality as that provided by analysis of Sioux family life, ceremony, and hunting?

VIII

We turn last to explanations of style by the forms of social life. The idea of a connection between these forms and styles is already suggested by the framework of the history of art. Its main divisions, accepted by all students, are also the boundaries of social units—cultures, empires, dynasties, cities, classes, churches, etc.—and periods which mark significant stages in social development. The great historical epochs of art, like antiquity, the Middle Ages, and the modern era, are the same as the epochs of economic history; they correspond to great systems, like feudalism and capitalism. Important economic and political shifts within these systems are often accompanied or followed by shifts in the centers of art and their styles. Religion and major world views are broadly coordinated with these eras in social history.

In many problems the importance of economic, political, and ideological conditions for the creation of a group style (or of a world view that influences a style) is generally admitted.

The distinctiveness of Greek art among the arts of the ancient world can hardly be separated from the forms of Greek society and the city-state. The importance of the burgher class, with its special position in society and its mode of life, for the medieval and early Renaissance art of Florence and for Dutch art of the seventeenth century, is a commonplace. In explaining Baroque art, the Counter-Reformation and the absolute monarchy are constantly cited as the sources of certain features of style. We have interesting studies on a multitude of problems concerning the relationship of particular styles and contents of art to institutions and historical situations. In these studies ideas, traits, and values arising from the conditions of economic, political, and civil life are matched with the new characteristics of an art. Yet, with all this experience, the general principles applied in explanation and the connection of types of art with types of social structure have not been investigated in a systematic way. By the many scholars who adduce piecemeal political or economic facts in order to account for single traits of style or subject matter, little has been done to construct an adequate comprehensive theory. In using such data, scholars will often deny that these "external" relationships can throw any light on the artistic phenomenon as such. They fear "materialism" as a reduction of the spiritual or ideal to sordid practical affairs.

Marxist writers are among the few who have tried to apply a general theory. It is based on Marx's undeveloped view that the higher forms of cultural life correspond to the economic structure of a society, the latter being defined in terms of the relations of classes in the process of production and the technological level. Between the economic relationships and the styles of art intervenes the process of ideological construction, a complex imaginative transposition of class roles and needs, which affects the special field—religion, mythology, or civil life—that provides the chief themes of art.

The great interest of the Marxist approach lies not only in the attempt to interpret the historically changing relations of art and economic life in the light of a general theory of society but also in the weight given to the differences and conflicts within the social group as motors of development, and to the effects of these on outlook, religion, morality, and philosophical ideas.

Only broadly sketched in Marx's works, the theory has rarely been applied systematically in a true spirit of investigation, such as we see in Marx's economic writings. Marxist writing on art has suffered from schematic and premature formulations and from crude judgments imposed by loyalty to a political line.

A theory of style adequate to the psychological and historical problems has still to be created. It waits for a deeper knowledge of the principles of form construction and expression and for a unified theory of the processes of social life in which the practical means of life as well as emotional behavior are comprised.

BIBLIOGRAPHY

Adama van Scheltema, F. 1923. *Die altnordische Kunst.* Berlin: Mauritius-Verlag.

Boas, F. 1927. *Primitive Art.* Cambridge: Harvard University Press.

Coellen, L. 1921. *Der Stil in der bildenden Kunst.* Darmstadt: Arkadenverlag.

Dilthey, W. 1922. *Einleitung in die Geisteswissenschaften* (1883). In: *Gesammelte Schriften,* Vol. I. Leipzig: B. G. Teubner.

Dvořák, M. 1924. *Kunstgeschichte als Geistesgeschichte.* Munich: R. Piper & Co.

Focillon, H. 1934. *La Vie des formes.* Paris: Librairie E. Leroux. English translation: *The Life of Forms in Art.* New York: Wittenborn, Schultz, 1948.

Frankl, P. 1938. *Das System der Kunstwissenschaft.* Brünn and Leipzig: R. M. Rohrer.

Frey, D. 1929. *Gotik und Renaissance als Grundlagen der modernen Weltanschauung.* Augsburg: B. Filser Verlag.

Fry, R. 1920. *Vision and Design.* London: Chatto & Windus.

Hauser, A. 1951. *The Social History of Art.* New York: A. A. Knopf.

Löwy, E. 1900. *Die Naturwiedergabe in der älteren griechischen Kunst.* English translation: *The Rendering of Nature in Early Greek Art.* London: Duckworth & Co., 1907.

Nohl, H. 1920. *Stil und Weltanschauung.* Jena: Diederichs.

Riegl, A. 1893. *Stilfragen: Grundlegungen zu einer Geschichte der Ornamentik.* Berlin: G. Siemens Verlag.

———. 1901. *Die spätrömische Kunstindustrie.* Vienna: Österreichische Staatsdruckerei. 2d ed., 1927.

Schaefer, H. 1922. *Von ägyptischer Kunst.* Leipzig: J. C. Hinrichs.

Semper, G. 1860. *Der Stil in den technischen und tektonischen Künsten.* Munich: F. Bruckmann.

Spengler, O. 1919. *Der Untergang des Abendlandes.* English translation: *The Decline of the West.* New York: A. A. Knopf, 1926–28. Also a French translation.

Weisbach, W. 1921. *Der Barock als Kunst der Gegenreformation.* Berlin: P. Cassirer.

Wölfflin, H. 1915. *Kunstgeschichtliche Grundbegriffe.* Munich: F. Bruckmann. Also an English translation.

———. 1931. *Italien und das deutsche Formgefühl.* Munich: F. Bruckmann.

———. 1940. *Gedanken zur Kunstgeschichte.* Basel: B. Schwabe & Co.

Worringer, W. 1908. *Abstraktion und Einfühlung: Ein Beitrag zur Stilpsychologie.* Munich: R. Piper & Co.

———. 1912. *Formprobleme der Gotik.* Munich: R. Piper & Co. English translation: *Form Problems of the Gothic.* New York: G. E. Stechert & Co., 1920. Also a French translation.

Evolution and Process

By JULIAN H. STEWARD

I. THE MEANING OF EVOLUTION

CULTURAL EVOLUTION, although long an unfashionable concept, has commanded renewed interest in the last two decades. This interest does not indicate any serious reconsideration of the particular historical reconstructions of the nineteenth-century evolutionists, for these were quite thoroughly discredited on empirical grounds. It arises from the potential methodological importance of cultural evolution for contemporary research, from the implications of its scientific objectives, its taxonomic procedures, and its conceptualization of historical change and cultural causality. An appraisal of cultural evolution, therefore, must be concerned with definitions and meanings. But I do not wish to engage in semantics. I shall attempt to show that, if certain distinctions in the concept of evolution are made, we may find certain methodological propositions that find fairly wide acceptance today.

In order to clear the ground, it is necessary first to consider the meaning of cultural evolution in relation to biological evolution; for there is a wide tendency to consider the former as an extension of, and therefore analogous to, the latter. There is, of course, a relationship between biological and cultural evolution, in that a minimal development of the Hominoidae was a precondition of culture. But cultural evolution is an extension of biological evolution only in a chronological sense.[1]

The nature of the evolutionary schemes and of the developmental processes differs profoundly in biology and in culture. In biological evolution it is assumed that all forms are genetically related and that their development is essentially divergent. Parallels, such as the development of flying or warm blood, are superficial and fairly uncommon. The latter, moreover, are generally considered to be instances of convergent evolution rather than true parallels. In cultural evolution, on the other hand, it is assumed that patterns are genetically unrelated and yet pass through parallel and historically independent sequences, while divergent trends, such as those caused by distinctive local environments, are attributed only secondary importance. Such modern-day unilinear evolutionists as Leslie White and V. Gordon Childe evade the awkward facts of cultural divergence and variation by dealing with culture as a whole rather than with particular cultures. But Childe (1951, p. 160) quite explicitly distinguishes biological from cultural evolution by the divergent nature of the former and by the operation of diffusion and the frequency of convergence in the latter. It is interesting that such history as is implied in cultural relativism is rather similar to that of biological evolution; for the variations and unique patterns of the dif-

1. For a discussion of cultural evolution as a continuation of biological evolution see Julian S. Huxley (1952).

313

ferent areas and subareas clearly represent divergent development and presumably an ultimate genetic relationship. It is only the complementary concept of diffusion, a phenomenon unknown in biology, that prevents cultural
relativism from having an exclusively
genetic significance, like that of biological evolution.

Analogies between cultural and biological evolution are also alleged to be
represented by two attributes of each:
first, a tendency toward increasing complexity of forms and, second, the development of superior forms, that is,
improvement or progress. It is, of
course, quite possible to define complexity and progress so as to make
them characteristics of evolution. But
they are not attributes exclusively of
evolution; they may also be considered
characteristics of cultural change or
development as conceived from a nonevolutionary point of view.

The assumption that cultural change
normally involves increasing complexity is found in virtually all historical
interpretations of cultural data. But
complexity in biology and culture differ. As Kroeber (1948, p. 297) states:
"The process of cultural development
is an additive and therefore accumu-
lative one, whereas the process of organic evolution is a substitutive one."
It is on the question not of complexity
but of divergence that the relativists
and evolutionists differ. According to
the former, cumulative change follows
parallel trends, whereas, according to
the latter, it is ordinarily divergent,
though sometimes it is convergent and
occasionally it is parallel.

Although complexity as such is not
distinctive of the evolutionary concept,
an allied concept might be considered
to distinguish both biological and cultural evolution from nonevolutionary
cultural-historical concepts. This is the
concept of organizational types and
levels. Whereas relativism seems to

hold that a rather fixed and qualitatively unique pattern persists in each
cultural tradition, despite cumulative
changes which create quantitative complexity, it is implicit in the evolutionary
view that developmental levels are
marked by the appearance of qualitatively distinctive patterns or types of
organization. Just as simple unicellular
forms of life are succeeded by multicellular and internally specialized
forms which have distinctive kinds of
total organization, so unifamilial and
lineage social forms are succeeded by
multifamilial communities, bands, or
tribes, and these, in turn, by state patterns, each involving not only greater
internal heterogeneity and specialization but wholly new kinds of over-all
integration.[2] Thus evolutionism is distinguished from relativism by the fact
that the former attributes qualitative
distinctiveness to successive stages, regardless of the particular tradition,
whereas the latter attributes it to the
particular tradition rather than to the
development stage.

This brings us to the question of
progress, which is the second characteristic attributed to both biological and
cultural evolution. Progress must be
measured by definable values. Most of
the social sciences are still so ethnocentric, especially in their practical applications, that value judgments are almost inescapable. Even the "Statement
on Human Rights" (1947) offered to
the United Nations by the American
Anthropological Association clearly reflects the American value placed upon
individual rights and political democracy. This or any other criterion of
value, however, certainly does not imply evolution. In fact, the concept of
progress is largely separable from evolution, and it may be approached in
many ways. Kroeber, who is by no
means an evolutionist, suggests three

2. This concept has been developed in
Julian H. Steward (1950, 1951).

criteria for measuring progress: "the atrophy of magic based on psychopathology; the decline of infantile obsession with the outstanding physiological events of human life; and the persistent tendency of technology and science to grow accumulatively" (1948, p. 304). These values are not absolute in a philosophical sense; they are "the ways in which progress may legitimately be considered a property or an attribute of culture." By definition, then, progress may be regarded as a characteristic of any form of cultural change, whether it is considered evolutionary or not.

We must conclude that cultural evolution is not distinguished from cultural relativism or historical particularism by any essential similarity of its developmental scheme with that of biological evolution, by the characteristic of increasing complexity, or by the attribute of progress. This is not to say, however, that evolution lacks distinctive features. The methodology of evolution contains two vitally important assumptions. First, it postulates that genuine parallels of form and function develop in historically independent sequences or cultural traditions. Second, it explains these parallels by the independent operation of identical causality in each case. The methodology is therefore avowedly scientific and generalizing rather than historical and particularizing. It is less concerned with unique and divergent (or convergent) patterns and features of culture—although it does not necessarily deny such divergence—than with parallels and similarities which recur cross-culturally. It endeavors to determine recurrent patterns and processes and to formulate the interrelationships between phenomena in terms of "laws." The nineteenth-century evolutionists are important to contemporary studies more because of their scientific objective and preoccupation with laws than

because of their particular substantive historical reconstructions.

Cultural evolution, then, may be defined broadly as a quest for cultural regularities or laws; but there are three distinctive ways in which evolutionary data may be handled. First, *unilinear evolution,* the classical nineteenth-century formulation, dealt with particular cultures, placing them in stages of a universal sequence. Second, *universal evolution*—a rather arbitrary label to designate the modern revamping of unilinear evolution—is concerned with culture rather than with cultures. Third, *multilinear evolution,* a somewhat less ambitious approach than the other two, is like unilinear evolution in dealing with particular cultures, but it is distinctive in searching for parallels of limited occurrence instead of universals.

The critical differences between these three concepts of evolution have not been recognized, and there is still a general tendency to identify any effort to determine similar form and process in parallel developments with nineteenth-century unilinear evolution and thus categorically to reject it. The Marxist and Communist adoption of nineteenth-century evolutionism, especially of L. H. Morgan's scheme, as official dogma (Tolstoy, 1952) has certainly not favored the acceptability to scientists of the Western nations of anything labeled "evolution."

1. UNILINEAR EVOLUTION

There is no need to discuss the validity of the nineteenth-century evolutionary schemes, for their vulnerability in the face of twentieth-century archeological and ethnographic research has been amply demonstrated. Although no effort has been made to revise these schemes in the light of new empirical data concerning the history of individual cultures—which itself is a somewhat remarkable fact—it does not necessarily follow that L. H. Morgan (1910) and his contemporaries (Tylor, 1865, 1871, 1881, 1899) failed completely to recognize significant patterns and processes of change in particular cases. The inadequacy of unilinear evolution lies largely in the postulated priority of matriarchal patterns over other kinship patterns and in the indiscriminate effort to force the data of all precivilized groups of mankind, which included most of the primitive world, into the categories of "savagery" and "barbarism." The category of "civilization," however, involved a less sweeping generalization for the simple reason that civilization was thought of largely in terms of the Near East, the northern Mediterranean, and northern Europe. Other areas which achieved civilization, particularly the New World, were far less known and have been accorded less attention.

In other words, whereas the historical reconstruction and the deductions derived therefrom were largely wrong as regards early stages of cultural development because they failed to recognize the many varieties of local trends, the analyses of civilization contain many valuable insights because they are based more specifically upon developments which occurred first in Egypt and Mesopotamia and later in Greece, Rome, and northern Europe. Although comparisons with other areas, particularly with the Americas but also with India and China, left much to be desired so far as forms, functions, and developmental processes of civilization in general are concerned, the conclusions may nonetheless be valid under limited circumstances. Thus Henry Maine's insights concerning the processes involved in development from a kin-based society to a territorial, state society undoubtedly throw light on cultural development in many areas, though not necessarily on all. Such categories as "kin-based" and "state"

are too broad; distinctions between particular, though recurrent, types within these categories are needed.

There are probably many developmental forms and processes discussed by the evolutionists which have validity, provided that they are considered qualities of particular cultural traditions rather than universal characteristics of culture. The extremely illuminating analyses that V. Gordon Childe (1934, 1946) and others have given us of cultural development in the eastern Mediterranean and Europe probably would find certain rather precise parallels in other world areas if a truly comparative study were made. Significantly, however, Childe's approach to evolution on a wider scale has entailed a retreat into broad generalizations.

2. UNIVERSAL EVOLUTION

Universal evolution, which is represented today principally by Leslie White and V. Gordon Childe, is the heritage of nineteenth-century unilinear evolution, especially as formulated by L. H. Morgan, in the scope of its generalizations but not in its treatment of particulars. Aware that empirical research of the twentieth century has invalidated the unilinear historical reconstructions of particular cultures, which constituted the essential feature of nineteenth-century schemes, White and Childe endeavor to keep the evolutionary concept of cultural stages alive by relating these stages to the culture of mankind as a whole. The distinctive cultural traditions and the local variations—the culture areas and subareas—which have developed as the result of special historical trends and of cultural ecological adaptations to special environments are excluded as irrelevant. White (1949, pp. 338–39) states: "We may say that culture as a whole serves the need of man as a species. But this does not and cannot help us at all when we try to account for the variations of specific cultures," and "the functioning of any particular culture will of course be conditioned by local environmental conditions. But in a consideration of culture as a whole, we may *average all environments together* to form a constant factor which may be excluded from our formulation of cultural development" (1949, p. 368; italics mine). Childe reconciles the general and particular in much the same way. He writes that "all societies have lived in different historical environments and have passed through different vicissitudes, their traditions have diverged, and so ethnography reveals a multiplicity of cultures, just as does archaeology" (Childe, 1951, p. 32). Childe finds that consideration of the particular is "a serious handicap if our objective is to establish general stages in the evolution of cultures," and, therefore, in order to "discover general laws descriptive of the evolution of all societies, we abstract . . . the peculiarities due to differences of habitat" (1951, p. 35). Diffusion must also be discounted, because any society must be in a position to accept diffused technological and social features. At the same time, while local developments within each general stage are largely divergent, the concept of evolution is salvaged by assuming that diffusion brings technological and social features to all societies, thus convergently recreating the required patterns (Childe, 1951, pp. 160 ff.). This rather involved effort to enlist diffusion in order to offset divergent evolution is based empirically almost exclusively upon Old World data. How Old World and New World parallels would square with such reasoning Childe does not say.

It is interesting that White's theoretical discussions make no reference to his own extensive and detailed studies of the Pueblo Indians and that Childe's superb knowledge of developmental patterns and processes which are dis-closed in the archeology of the Near East and Europe becomes almost an embarrassment in his theoretical discussions. Childe's insights into the cultural development of these two areas are most illuminating, but he merely confuses the two areas when he endeavors to fit them into simplified developmental stages.

It is important to recognize that the evolutionism of White and Childe yields substantive results of a very different order from those of nineteenth-century evolution. The postulated cultural sequences are so general that they are neither very arguable nor very useful. No one disputes that hunting and gathering, which is Childe's diagnostic of "savagery," preceded plant and animal domestication, which is his criterion of "barbarism," and that the latter was a precondition of large populations, cities, internal social differentiation and specialization, and the development of writing and mathematics, which are characteristics of "civilization."

If one examines universal evolution with a view to finding laws or processes of development rather than merely in terms of a sequential reconstruction of culture, it is also difficult to recognize anything strikingly new or controversial. The generalization that culture changes from the simple to the complex and White's "law" that technological development expressed in terms of man's control over energy underlies certain cultural achievements and social changes have long been accepted (White, 1943). Childe's transfer of the Darwinian formula to cultural evolution also will not evoke challenge. Variation is seen as invention, heredity as learning and diffusion, and adaptation and selection as cultural adaptation and choice (Childe, 1951, pp. 175–79). It is certainly a worthy objective to seek universal laws of cultural change. It must be stressed, however, that all universal laws thus far postulated are concerned with the fact that culture changes—that any culture changes—and thus cannot explain particular features of particular cultures. In this respect, the "laws" of cultural and biological evolution are similar. Variation, heredity, and natural selection cannot explain a single life-form, for they do not deal with the characteristics of particular species and do not take into account the incalculable number of particular circumstances and factors that cause biological differentiation in each species. Similarly, White's law of energy levels, for example, can tell us nothing about the development of the characteristics of individual cultures. We may deduce from the data of both biological and cultural evolution that new organization forms will appear in succession, but the specific nature of these forms can be understood only by tracing the history of each in great detail.

The problem and method of universal evolution thus differ from those of unilinear evolution. Right or wrong, the nineteenth-century evolutionists did attempt to explain concretely why a matriarchy should precede other social forms, why animism was the precursor of gods and spirits, why a kin-based society evolved into a territorial-based, state-controlled society, and other specific features of culture.

3. MULTILINEAR EVOLUTION

Multilinear evolution is essentially a methodology based on the assumption that significant regularities in cultural change occur, and it is concerned with the determination of cultural laws. It is inevitably concerned also with historical reconstruction, but it does not expect that historical data can be classified in universal stages. It is interested in particular cultures, but, instead of finding local variations and diversity troublesome facts which force the frame of reference from the partic-

ular to the general, it deals only with those limited parallels of form, function, and sequence which have empirical validity. What is lost in universality will be gained in concreteness and specificity. Multilinear evolution, therefore, has no a priori scheme or laws. It recognizes that the cultural traditions of different areas may be wholly or partly distinctive, and it simply poses the question of whether any genuine or meaningful similarities between certain cultures exist and whether these lend themselves to formulation. These similarities may involve salient features of whole cultures, or they may involve only special features, such as clans, men's societies, social classes of various kinds, priesthoods, military patterns, and the like.

It may be objected that a limited formulation which postulates that some special feature—let us say a clan—has developed in two or more cultures independently for the same reasons cannot be considered evolution. We thus return to definitions. If evolution can be considered an interest in determining recurrent forms, processes, and functions rather than world-embracing schemes and universal laws, then many efforts to make scientific generalizations, whether they deal with synchronic, functional relationships or with diachronic, sequential relationships and whether they embrace few or many cultures, are methodologically akin to evolution. The nineteenth-century evolutionists were deeply interested in making generalizations.

II. THE METHOD OF MULTILINEAR EVOLUTION

1. PARALLELISM AND CAUSALITY

An implicit interest in parallelism and causality has always been present in cultural studies, and it seems to have increased during the last two decades. It would be quite surprising, in fact, if anyone held so tenaciously to the logical implications of the relativist position as to claim that understandings derived from the analysis of one culture did not provide some insights as to form, function, and process in others. The difficulty is in raising these insights from the level of hunches to that of explicit formulations. Postulated parallels and recurrent cause-and-effect relations are regarded with suspicion. They may be questioned on empirical grounds, or the inherent difficulty of deriving cultural laws may be attacked on philosophical grounds. The methodology of cultural studies thus remains predominantly that of historical particularizing rather than of scientific generalizing.

A genuine interest in parallels, however, has been clearly expressed by many scholars who have made outstanding contributions within the framework of the so-called "Boas school." Thus Lowie, who was unsparing of L. H. Morgan's unilinear reconstruction (Lowie, 1920), not only recognizes independent invention and parallel development in many features, such as moieties, a dual system of numbers, messianic cults, and others (Lowie, 1940, pp. 376–77), but he is quite prepared to accept a kind of necessity in cultural development to the extent that certain cultural achievements presuppose others. "If a tribe practices metallurgy it is clearly not on the plane of savagery; only stock-breeders and farmers forge metals" (1940, p. 45). But he denies that cultures can be graded on the basis of metallurgy because the Africans, for example, were metallurgists but lacked other features of more developed civilizations. Although Lowie cannot accept Morgan's unilinear evolution,[3] he

3. Lowie (1946), in a reply to White, stressed the fact that Morgan, Tylor, and others were forcing the historical data of particular cultures into unilinear schemes rather than dealing with the evolution of an abstract or generalized world culture.

is in accord with most of the profession in accepting such generalizations as universal evolution has to offer, and, moreover, he is something of a multilinear evolutionist. Who, then, is more of an evolutionist, Lowie or White?

American anthropologists have traditionally assumed that there were Old World and New World parallels in the invention of farming, stock-breeding, ceramics, metallurgy, states, priests, temples, the zero and mathematics, writing, and other features. It would perhaps be going too far to say that this makes them multilinear evolutionists. When the question of parallel cultural causality arises, these similarities are held to be only superficial or to represent convergent evolution, or else it is said that the historical and functional relationships involved are as yet too imperfectly understood to permit formulation in terms of cross-cultural regularities. Nevertheless, many persons have recognized such a deep significance in these parallels that they believe diffusion must have occurred between the hemispheres, while others have attempted to formulate Old and New World sequences in terms of comparable developmental periods.

Kroeber (1948, p. 241) did not hesitate to conclude from the numerous parallels in different parts of the world that

culture relations or patterns develop spontaneously or from within probably more frequently than as a result of direct taking-over. Also, the types of culture forms being limited in number, the same type is frequently evolved independently. Thus, monarchical and democratic societies, feudal or caste-divided ones, priest-ridden and relatively irreligious ones, expansive and mercantile or self-sufficient and agricultural nations, evolve over and over again.

Elsewhere, I have called attention to statements by Lesser, Boas, Kidder, and others that cross-cultural understandings in terms of laws, regularities, or parallels—those who object to "laws may use some other term—is a major objective of anthropology (Steward, 1949, 1950). The list could be extended to include a substantial portion of the profession.

The determination and analysis of parallels as a methodological objective of multilinear evolution need not be carried out on a purely cultural level. Leslie White (1949, chap. xiv) has argued so cogently in favor of understanding cultural change in strictly culturological terms that the impression may stand that culturology and evolution are synonymous. It is beyond the scope of this paper to argue the matter. But I must insist that White's elimination of both the human and the environmental factors is an aspect of his concern with culture rather than with cultures. I have endeavored in various studies to demonstrate how cultural-ecological adaptations—the adaptive processes through which a historically derived culture is modified in a particular environment—are among the important creative processes in cultural change (Steward, 1938). There are certain problems in which man's rational and emotional potentials are not a zero factor in the equation. Thus Kluckhohn (1949, p. 267) suggests: "If a tribe's customary outlet for aggression in war is blocked, one may predict an increase in intratribal hostility (perhaps in the form of witchcraft) or in pathological states of melancholy resultant upon anger being turned inward against the self." This psychological attribute of human beings which channels aggression in certain ways may be a significant factor in the formulation of certain cultural parallels. For example, among the Iroquois and their neighbors, war captives were adopted as members of the captor's family, then tortured and killed. Raymond Scheele (1947) has suggested that this pattern provides a means of diverting latent hostilities against kin to members of an alien group. A similar pattern is found among the Tupinamba of South America and among tribes in other parts of the world. Although the psychological premises and the cultural manifestations may be open to question, the data suggest a useful cross-cultural formulation of certain modes of behavior.

The kinds of parallels or similarities with which multilinear evolution deals are distinguished by their limited occurrence and their specificity. For this reason, the outstanding methodological problem of multilinear evolution is an appropriate taxonomy of cultural phenomena.

2. CULTURAL TAXONOMY

Any science must have precise means of identifying and classifying the recurrent phenomena with which it deals. It is symptomatic of the historical rather than the scientific orientation of cultural studies that there are few terms designating whole cultures or components of cultures which may be employed cross-culturally. "Plains culture," "East African cattle culture," "Chinese civilization," and the like designate culture areas which are conceived as unique patterns and complexes of elements. A great many sociological terms, such as "band," "tribe," "clan," "class," "state," "priest," and "shaman," are used to describe features which are found repeatedly in generically unrelated cultures, but they are much too general even to suggest parallels of form or process. The most precise terms designate very special technological features, such as "bow," "atlatl," or "ikat weaving." Such features, however, generally imply no large patterns, and the only inference ordinarily drawn from their distributions is that diffusion has taken place.

The present status of cultural taxonomy reveals a preoccupation with relativism, and practically all systems of classification are fundamentally derived from the culture-area concept. Basically, the culture area is characterized by a distinctive element content, which, on a tribal level at least, constitutes the shared behavior of all members of the society. Classification may give equal weight to all elements, as in Klimek's statistical handling of the culture-element lists which were compiled in the University of California survey of western tribes or as in the midwestern or McKern method of classifying archeological complexes. The former yields culture areas and subareas; the latter gives categories of associated elements, which of themselves are placed neither in time nor in space. Following Wissler, culture-area classifications have tended strongly to emphasize economic features, although not all postulate so close a relationship between culture and environment as Wissler, and noneconomic traits receive emphasis which varies with the individual scholar and which may lead to a diversity of classificatory schemes for the same data. Thus South America has been grouped into five areas by Wissler (1938), eleven by Stout (1938), three by Cooper (1942) and by Bennett and Bird (1949), four by the *Handbook of South American Indians* (Steward, 1946–50), and twenty-four by Murdock (1951), each giving primacy to features of interest to the individual. All these classifications are particular to the data of South America. None endeavors to recognize in any of the three to twenty-four areas structural or developmental features which are common to areas outside South America.

Classifications of cultures in terms of value system or ethos has essentially the same basis as that of culture areas. Such classifications all presuppose a common core of shared culture traits which cause all members of the society to have the same outlook and psycho-

logical characteristics. Benedict's concept of pattern, Gorer's and Mead's concept of national character, and Morris Opler's concept of themes derive from a taxonomic approach that is basically like that of Wissler, Kroeber, Murdock, Herskovits, and others.

If a taxonomic system is to be devised for the purpose of determining cross-cultural parallels and regularities rather than of stressing contrasts and differences, there is needed a concept which may be designated "culture type."[4] The difficulty of empirical determination of significant types has constituted the principal obstacle to a systematic search for regularities and parallels. A culture type by the present definition differs from a culture area in several respects. First, it is characterized by selected features rather than by its total element content. Since no two cultures are quite alike in their totality, it is necessary to select special constellations of features which are found among two or more, but not necessarily among all, cultures. Second, the selection of diagnostic features will be determined by the problem and frame of reference. Conceivably, any aspect of culture may be attributed primary taxonomic importance. Third, the selected features will be presumed to have the same functional interrelationship with one another in each case.

Illustrative of cultural types are Wittfogel's oriental absolute society (1938, 1940), which involves regularities between a special kind of sociopolitical structure and an irrigation economy; the present author's patrilineal band, which is characterized by certain relationships between a hunting economy, descent, marriage, and land tenure (Steward, 1936); Redfield's folk soci-

4. Ralph Linton uses the term "culture type" but clearly has in mind the culture-area concept rather than types which are found in different cultural traditions (1936, p. 392).

ety (1941, 1947), which has certain general features common to many, if not most, societies at a simple development or integrational level and which reacts to urban influences—at least to influences of the modern industrial type of urbanism—according to postulated regularities; and a feudal society (Princeton Conference, 1951), which once characterized both Japan and Europe, where it exhibited similarities in social and political structure and economy.

These types are based primarily upon sociological features, because interest happens to center upon such matters and perhaps because sociopolitical structure lends itself to classification and is more readily formulated than are other aspects of culture. Economic patterns are generally ascribed considerable importance, because they are inextricably related to social and political patterns. Certain aspects of religion, however, are also included in Redfield's types. In an elaboration of Wittfogel's irrigation societies, the author has tentatively formulated developmental types which include not only social and political patterns but also technological, intellectual, military, and religious features that mark successive eras in the history of these societies (1949).

A taxonomic scheme designed to facilitate the determination of parallels and regularities in terms of concrete characteristics and developmental processes will have to distinguish innumerable culture types, many of which are not now recognized. A methodology like that of White and of Childe, which ignores local particulars and deals only with world stages, will not serve the purpose we have in mind. A stage of Hunting and Gathering, for example—or of Savagery, to use the evolutionists' term—is far too broad a category. The functional relations and cultural-ecological adaptations which led to a patri-

lineal band, consisting of a localized lineage, were very different from those which produced a nomadic, bilateral band composed of many unrelated families (Steward, 1936). But these are only two of many types of hunting and gathering societies which developed as the result of particular cultural-historical and cultural-ecological circumstances. There are also types characterized by dispersed family groups, such as the Shoshoni and Eskimo, and by cohesive tribelets, such as those of California. Moreover, it does not at all follow that all hunters and gatherers are classifiable into types which have cross-cultural significance. Many may be unique, except as some limited feature of their culture parallels a similar feature of another culture—for instance, the development of clans.

Since hunting and gathering tribes fall into an undetermined number of cultural types, it follows that in any larger developmental scheme we cannot be certain that any type can be taken as representative of an early stage, except in characteristics that are so general as to signify nothing very startling about cultural development. The absence of dense and stable populations; of large permanent towns; of social classes and other kinds of complex internal specialization; of priesthoods, group ceremonialism, money, investment, writing, mathematics, and other characteristics of civilized people is not surprising. The particular forms of marriage, family, social structure, economic co-operation, socioreligious patterns, and other features differ in each type. Consequently, if our search is for the detailed processes by which hunters and gatherers were converted into farmers or herdsmen and these latter into more "civilized" people, it is necessary to deal with particular types.

Among the farming cultures there is also a large variety of cultural types which have not been systematically classified with any problem of cross-cultural parallels in mind. Irrigation civilizations have received considerable attention, but the term "tropical forest agriculture" still refers to farming in the tropical rain forests rather than to specific cultural features. Possibly each of the culture areas of the Old and New World rain forests, including the northern hardwood forests, has or had a unique culture type. But it is also possible that significant parallels would be disclosed if an effort were made to recognize them.

At present, interest in parallels centers in the development of Old and New World civilizations. The parallels are striking and undeniable. They include the independent development—independent, that is, according to most but not all anthropologists—of an impressive list of basic features: domesticated plants and animals, irrigation, large towns and cities, metallurgy, social classes, states and empires, priesthoods, writing, calendars, and mathematics. Although there is still considerable tendency to stress the distinguishing features of each center or tradition and thus to view each as a culture area rather than as a culture type, interest in function and processes is gradually leading toward the use of comparable terminology. Instead of narrow technological terms, like "Old Stone Age," "New Stone Age," and "Bronze Age," such potentially typological terms as "Formative," "Florescent" or "Classical," and "Empire" or "Fusion" are being used for the New World. For Old World development, Childe has introduced partially equivalent terms, such as "urban revolution."[5] I think it is safe to predict that, as interest centers more and more upon the functional interrelationship of cultural features and upon the processes by which cultures are

5. These terms and their significance have been reviewed in Julian H. Steward (1949) and in Wendell C. Bennett (1948).

adapted to a variety of environments, a taxonomy suggesting significant parallels will appear.

The taxonomic basis of an evolutionary approach is no less applicable to contemporary trends of cultural change than to pre-Columbian changes. Today the many varieties of native cultures which characterize the distinctive culture areas are being strongly influenced by industrial patterns which are diffusing primarily from Europe and America. There appear, however, to be rather striking parallels in the consequences of the diffused patterns. These are classifiable in terms of trends toward the production of cash commodities, purchase of manufactured articles, individualization of land tenure, appearance of a cash-based rationale in values and goals, reduction of the kinship group to the nuclear family, emergence of middle classes of business, service, and professional personnel, sharpening of interclass tensions, and rise of nationalistic ideologies. All these are features which also characterize the peoples of Euro-American nations, but it would be too simple an explanation to say that they, too, were merely diffused from Europe. Detailed study of native populations discloses processes which made their development inevitable, even in the absence of sustained, face-to-face contacts between the native populations and Europeans, which might have introduced new practices and a new ethic. There is good reason to believe that the very fundamental changes now occurring in the most remote parts of the world are susceptible to formulation in terms of parallels or regularities, despite various local overtones which derive from the native cultural tradition. Although no very deliberate effort to formulate these regularities has yet been made, considerable contemporary research is directly concerned with modern trends, and the substantive results are probably sufficiently detailed to permit preliminary formulations.

Not all parallels need be based essentially upon a developmental sequence. Thus Redfield's postulated regularities in the changes of a folk society under urbanizing influence can hardly be called "evolution." However, it is our basic premise that the crucial methodological feature of evolution is the determination of recurrent causal relationships in independent cultural traditions. In each of the cultural types mentioned above, certain features are functionally related to others, and a time depth or development is necessarily implied; for, regardless of which features are considered causes and which are considered effects, it is assumed that some must always be accompanied by others under stipulated conditions. Whether it requires ten or twenty years or hundreds of years for the relationship to become established, a development through time must always take place. Therefore, parallel developments which require only a few years and involve only a limited number of features are no less evolution, from a scientific point of view, than sequences involving whole cultures and covering millennia.

III. CONCLUSIONS

Cultural evolution may be regarded either as a special type of historical reconstruction or as a particular methodology or approach. The historical reconstructions of the nineteenth-century unilinear evolutionists are distinctive for the assumption that *all* cultures pass through parallel and genetically unrelated sequences. This assumption is in conflict with the twentieth-century cultural relativists or historical particularists, who regard cultural development as essentially divergent, except as diffusion tends to level differences. This disagreement concerning fundamental historical fact is reflected in cultural taxonomy. The major categories of the unilinear evolutionists are primarily developmental stages applicable to all cultures; those of the relativists and particularists are culture areas or traditions.

Twentieth-century research has accumulated a mass of evidence which overwhelmingly supports the contention that particular cultures diverge significantly from one another and do not pass through unilinear stages. Since this basic fact of cultural history is no longer a matter of major controversy, those who have sought to keep the tradition of nineteenth-century evolution alive have been forced to shift their frame of reference from the particular to the general. They concede that particular cultures have distinguishing features caused by divergent development as well as by the stage of development, but they now profess to be interested in the evolution of culture and not of cultures. Their reconstruction of world culture history, therefore, is made in such general terms as to be quite acceptable to everyone. No one doubts that hunting and gathering preceded farming and herding and that the last two were preconditions of "civilization," which is broadly characterized by dense and stable populations, metallurgy, intellectual achievements, social heterogeneity and internal specialization, and other features.

Because the weight of evidence now seems to support divergent cultural development, the proposition that there are significant parallels in cultural history is regarded with suspicion. Nonetheless, probably most anthropologists recognize some similarities in form, function, and developmental processes in certain cultures of different traditions. If interest in these parallels can be divested of the all-or-none dogma that, because cultural development is now known not to be wholly unilinear, each tradition must be wholly unique, a basis may be laid for historical reconstruction which takes into account cross-cultural similarities as well as differences. The formulation of the similarities in terms of recurrent relationships will require a taxonomy of significant features. The taxonomy may be based upon few or many features and upon a varying number of different cultures. The developmental formulation may involve long or short historical sequences.

For those who are interested in cultural laws, regularities, or formulations, the greatest promise lies in analysis and comparison of limited similarities and parallels, that is, in multilinear evolution rather than in unilinear evolution and universal evolution. Unilinear evolution is discredited, except as it provides limited insights concerning particular types of culture. Universal evolution has yet to provide any very new formulations that will explain any and all cultures. The most fruitful course of investigation would seem to be the search for laws which formulate particular phenomena with reference to particular circumstances.

REFERENCES AND SELECTED BIBLIOGRAPHY

BENNETT, WENDELL C. (ed.). 1948. *A Reappraisal of Peruvian Archaeology.* ("Memoirs of the Society for American Archaeology," Vol. XIII, Part II.) Menasha, Wis.

BENNETT, WENDELL C., and BIRD, JUNIUS B. 1949. *Andean Culture History.* ("American Museum of Natural History Handbook Series," No. 15.) New York.

CHILDE, V. Gordon. 1934. *New Light on the Most Ancient East.* New York: D. Appleton–Century Co.

———. 1946. *What Happened in History.* New York: Pelican Books.

———. 1951. *Social Evolution.* London and New York: H. Schuman.

COOPER, JOHN M. 1942. "Areal and Temporal Aspects of Aboriginal South American Culture," *Primitive Man,* XV, Nos. 1 and 2, 1–38.

HUXLEY, JULIAN S. 1952. "Biological Evolution and Human History" (brief of a paper presented at supper-conference, Wenner-Gren Foundation, June 8, 1951), *American Anthropological Association News Bulletin,* VI, 15–16.

KLUCKHOHN, CLYDE. 1949. *Mirror for Man.* New York: Whittlesey House, McGraw-Hill Book Co., Inc.

KROEBER, ALFRED L. 1948. *Anthropology.* New York: Harcourt, Brace & Co.

LINTON, RALPH. 1936. *The Study of Man.* New York: Appleton-Century-Crofts.

LOWIE, ROBERT H. 1920. *Primitive Society.* New York: Liveright.

———. 1940. *An Introduction to Cultural Anthropology.* New York: Farrar & Rinehart.

———. 1946. "Evolution in Cultural Anthropology: A Reply to Leslie White," *American Anthropologist,* XLVIII, 223–33.

MORGAN, L. H. 1910. *Ancient Society.* Chicago: Charles H. Kerr & Co. (First published in 1877.)

MURDOCK, GEORGE PETER. 1951. "South American Culture Areas," *Southwestern Journal of Anthropology,* VII, 415–36.

PRINCETON CONFERENCE. 1951. Unpublished summary of a conference held at Princeton University in honor of Arnold Toynbee.

REDFIELD, ROBERT. 1941. *The Folk Culture of Yucatan.* Chicago: University of Chicago Press.

———. 1947. "The Folk Society," *American Journal of Sociology,* LII, 293–308.

SCHEELE, RAYMOND. 1947. "Warfare among the Iroquois and Their Neighbors." Thesis submitted in partial fulfilment of the requirements for the Ph.D. degree, Columbia University.

"Statement on Human Rights." 1947. *American Anthropologist,* XLIX, 539–43.

STERN, BERNARD. 1931. *Lewis H. Morgan, Social Evolutionist.* Chicago: University of Chicago Press.

STERN, BERNARD. 1946. "Lewis H. Morgan Today: An Appraisal of His Scientific Contributions," *Science and Society*, X, No. 2, 172–76.

STEWARD, JULIAN H. 1936. "The Economic and Social Basis of Primitive Bands." In *Essays in Honor of Alfred L. Kroeber*. Berkeley: University of California Press.

——. 1938. *Basin-Plateau Aboriginal Socio-political Groups*. (Bureau of American Ethnology Bull. 120.)

——. (ed.). 1946–50. *Handbook of South American Indians*. (Bureau of American Ethnology Bull. 143.) 6 vols. Washington, D.C.

——. 1949. "Cultural Causality and Law: A Trial Formulation of the Development of Early Civilizations," *American Anthropologist*, LI, 1–27.

——. 1950. *Area Research: Theory and Practice*. (Social Science Research Council Bull. 63.) New York.

——. 1951. "Levels of Sociocultural Integration: An Operational Concept," *Southwestern Journal of Anthropology*, VII, 374–90.

STOUT, DAVID. 1938. "Cultural Types and Culture Areas in South America," *Papers of the Michigan Academy of Science, Arts, and Letters*, XXIII, 73–86.

TOLSTOY, P. 1952. "Morgan and Soviet Anthropological Thought," *American Anthropologist*, LIV, 8–17.

TYLOR, E. B. 1865. *Researches into the Early History of Mankind and the Development of Civilization*. London: John Murray.

——. 1871. *Primitive Culture*. London: John Murray.

——. 1881. *Anthropology*. London: Watts & Co.

——. 1899. *Anthropology: An Introduction to the Study of Man and Civilization*. New York: D. Appleton & Co.

WHITE, LESLIE A. 1943. "Energy and the Evolution of Culture," *American Anthropologist*, XLV, 335–56.

——. 1949. *The Science of Culture*. New York: Farrar, Strauss.

WISSLER, CLARK. 1938. *The American Indian*. New York and London: Oxford University Press.

WITTFOGEL, KARL A. 1938. "Die Theorie der orientalischen Gesellschaft," *Zeitschrift für Sozialforschung*, VII, No. 1, 90–122.

——. 1940. "The Society of Prehistoric China," *Studies in Philosophy and Social Science, 1939*, VIII, 138–86.

The Theory of Evolution and the Evolution of Man

By G. S. CARTER

MAN IS AN animal, and, however greatly his present state differs from that of the rest of the animal kingdom, we must accept that he arose from subhuman ancestors by a process of evolution. And, since the life of those ancestors must have been very like that of other animals, the process by which he evolved must have been similar to that which other animals undergo. If so, it is clear that some consideration of the general theory of evolution is required before the special case of the evolution of man can be discussed.

Our views of the general theory of evolution in animals have recently undergone great change. It may therefore be useful to state the theory in a modern form as a basis for discussion of human evolution. I propose first to do this,[1] and then to discuss, in so far as a biologist and not an anthropologist can do so, the evolution of man in the light of the modern theory.

It is nearly a century since the publication in 1859 of *The Origin of Species*, in which Darwin set out the theory of evolution which most biologists accept, in however modified a form, today. Before that date zoölogists had for a century or more considered the possibility that evolution had taken place, and one theory to account for it, that of La-

1. A more detailed account can be found in Carter (1951), which contains a bibliography.

marck, had been put forward in 1809. But before the publication of Darwin's book the majority of zoölogists had not been convinced of the truth of evolution, and no theory had been generally accepted. Darwin succeeded in convincing most zoölogists that the evolution of animals has indeed occurred in nature—by collecting a vast body of evidence and by stating it with great skill—and also in providing a theory to account for evolution that was acceptable to many. We need not, I think, further consider the Lamarckian theory, for in the intervening century no incontrovertible evidence in favor of it has been brought forward, and our present knowledge of genetics makes it very difficult to believe in the inheritance of "acquired characters," which this theory requires. We have no *proof* that Lamarckian inheritance is impossible, and, if it does occur, it will demand modification of our theory, but until its occurrence is shown to be real we should not base our theories upon it.

Since 1859 the Darwinian theory has been continually discussed by zoölogists, and from time to time opinion has veered both for and against it. During the latter part of the nineteenth century the theory was more and more generally accepted, until by 1890 opposition to it was negligible. One can-

327

not read the writings of zoölogists of that time without realizing that almost all of them regarded the truth of the Darwinian theory as an established fact which no reasonable biologist could question. However, their position was open to attack along at least two lines. First, there was hardly any direct evidence that natural selection is effective in nature; and, second, their knowledge of the laws of inheritance was very slight, and Darwin's assumption that small inherited variations are universal among animals had certainly not been proved to be true. But these and other objections were disregarded, and, indeed, hardly appreciated, before the last years of the century.

In 1900 Mendel's work was rediscovered; it was confirmed in the first few years of this century. That heritable variations occur in the form of mutations was established, though many of the differences between individual organisms in nature were found to be due to the action of the environment on the organisms, and not to be inherited (Johannsen, 1903). All the same, mutation, being inherited variation, provided a *possible* basis for the action of selection. But, on further consideration, difficulties very soon arose; it appeared that the mutations with which the geneticists were working were by no means a *suitable* material for the types of change that the paleontologists and morphologists found in evolving animals.

The most direct evidence of the nature of evolutionary change is that which paleontology gives when a sequence of forms, clearly descended from one another, are found in consecutive strata laid down without intermissions. In such sequences the evolutionary changes are not large—on the species level rather than on that of genera or families—for the series of strata are never long by paleontological standards, though they may represent

deposition for many thousands of years. Of these sequences, the Devonian series of the Grand Canyon, investigated by Fenton (1931, p. 1), and that of the Cretaceous in the English Chalk (Rowe, 1899, p. 494) are good examples, and in them we can directly observe at least the smaller evolutionary changes (*micro-evolution*). We find the changes to be *continuous*, *gradual*—sudden and large changes are not, in general, found —*progressive*, and *directional*—continuing in the same directions for long periods. Also, the changes occur simultaneously in many characters of the body of an organism, which thereby becomes altered in its general form. These characters we may take to be generally characteristic of the changes of micro-evolution.

Very similar conclusions were reached in the study of larger evolutionary changes by the methods of both paleontology and comparative morphology. Here also the changes appeared to be gradual, continuous, and directional.

In contrast, the mutations with which the early geneticists were working were large changes, often degenerative—i.e., resulting in loss rather than in elaboration of structure—random in direction, and uncorrelated with one another in their occurrence. It seemed to the paleontologists and morphologists that these mutations were not a suitable material on which could be founded evolutionary changes such as those that are observed in nature. They concluded that mutations had little to do with evolution as they observed it. A clear dilemma was reached between the views of the geneticists, who believed that mutation was the only form of hereditary variation that occurs in animals, and the paleontologists and morphologists, who found that mutation was useless as a basis for evolution. The result was that many biologists came to feel that the nineteenth-century acceptance of the Darwinian theory lacked a logical background, and even to doubt whether the theory was at all generally true. Opinion veered strongly against the theory.

If it were true that mutations of the kind used by the early geneticists are the only type of hereditary change in animals, the dilemma would be inescapable, for the paleontologists and morphologists were undoubtedly right in holding that such mutations could not be the background of the evolution they observed. But the history of evolutionary theory in the last forty years has been a gradual escape from the dilemma by modification of our views of the nature of the genetic material of the animal body—the genotype—and of the changes that occur in this material—the mutations. The escape has also been helped by a great broadening of our study of evolution in many directions. We have, I think, now reached a point at which it is possible to put forward a modified form of the Darwinian theory that is in accord with all the relevant facts not only of genetics but also of all the other branches of biology. The progress toward an accepted theory may not yet be complete, but at least the advance in the last forty years has been remarkable. With this advance has gone revival of interest in evolutionary theory and of belief in the Darwinian theory. Opinion has swung back toward the acceptance of fifty or sixty years ago.

In the following sections I shall give a summary of the results on which our present theory is founded and of the theory to which they lead. I shall start with the two subjects in which nineteenth-century biology was particularly weak, the study of selection and of heredity.

SELECTION IN NATURE

It cannot be said that our *direct* evidence for the effectiveness of selection in nature is much more satisfactory now than it was sixty years ago. We now know of several cases in which a variety has appeared in a species and has spread, sometimes so as largely to replace the original form. Of these cases one of the best known is that of the melanic varieties of moths that have spread in industrial districts of England and other parts of Europe. These varieties are believed, and in one case (Ford, 1940, p. 227) have been shown, to be based on Mendelian mutations. It is believed that the mutations became of selective advantage against the darker color of the background as industrialization increased. If so, this is a clear case of the spread of a mutation under selection.

The effectiveness of selection in nature is a very difficult subject for experimentation. Many experiments have been carried out in which varieties have been found to be selected, but much of this work lacks proper controls and cannot be regarded as conclusive. Some, however, is not open to this criticism (e.g., Popham, 1943, p. 105; 1944, p. 74; 1948, p. 768); and it seems that we may conclude from the whole body of experimental results that advantageous differentiations of the kinds used in the experiments will be selected and will therefore spread through the population. But in all this experimental work large variations that will give large selective differences have been used, necessarily so, because experiments with small differences in selective value would be extremely difficult and, indeed, impossible in practice. We shall, however, find that much the larger part of evolutionary change is based on mutations of small expression in the body of the animal (the phenotype) and of small selective value. We still lack direct evidence of the selection of these small differences.

The belief that these small differentiations (*micromutations*), as well as the larger differentiations, are subject to selection is founded on logical deduction, not on experimental evidence. But of this belief it can be said:

1. That the logical deduction is very direct. If animals reproduce, as they do, at a greater rate than is needed to maintain their numbers and if hereditable variation of any kind occurs, it is very difficult to avoid the conclusion that the selective advantage of the variations will play some part in the choice of the surviving individuals; i.e., that there will be selection.

2. That it is no satisfactory argument against the effectiveness of selection to say that a large proportion of the natural death rate is often controlled by chance and is therefore nonselective. This is undoubtedly true, and it will reduce the selective advantage of any variation, but selection will still be effective if the remaining advantage is large enough to allow the variety to spread. Mathematical study of selection shows that, under the conditions that necessarily follow from the accepted results of genetics, the minimum selective advantage required for spread of a variety through a population may be very small (Fisher, 1930; Wright, 1931, p. 97). The minimum advantage is smaller, the larger the population in which selection is occurring. It may be taken to be roughly equal to $1/N$ in normal circumstances,[2] where N is the effective number of breeding individuals in the population. In large populations of 10^5 or 10^6 individuals, this is clearly a much smaller advantage than could be observed or used in experiments, and even in populations of 1,000 individuals it would not be easy to get reliable experimental results with ad-

2. A selective advantage of $1/N$ implies that $N + 1$ of the selected types survives in each generation for every N of the nonselected type. The "effective numbers of breeding individuals" is not always the same as the actual number of these individuals. In some circumstances it may be considerably smaller (S. Wright, 1931, p. 97).

vantages of the minimum size. But in still smaller populations the selective advantage may need to be considerable if it is to be effective.

3. That in artificial selection variations based on micromutation may certainly be selected, and that much of the variation we find between closely related forms in nature is also based on micromutation. This variation has presumably been selected.

4. That if natural variations of any kind are selected and a significant proportion of them are hereditable, as they are known to be, there is no escape from the conclusion that the selection will be effective in producing modification of the population as a whole and so in controlling its evolution.

We may, I think, certainly conclude that, though the effectiveness of the selection of small variations has not been directly proved, it is very hard to doubt that selection of them, as well as of larger variations, is effective in nature. The burden of proof is on those who question the effectiveness of selection. It seems that we shall not be likely to go astray if we accept its effectiveness as one of the basic postulates of our theory of evolution.

RECENT GENETICS

Recent advances in our knowledge of the genetics of animals date from 1910, when Morgan first used *Drosophila* as an experimental animal. Though most of the work has been done on this genus, the chief results have been confirmed in other animals, and the modern conception of the genotype must be accepted as general to multicellular animals, at least in its broad features. In so far as they are important to our discussion, the results of forty years' work may be very briefly summarized as follows:

1. By linkage analysis, and later by observation of the giant salivary gland chromosomes, the location of the genes

in the chromosomes and their linear arrangement were finally proved.

2. The existence of two different types of mutation was established. Of these, one type (*gene mutation*) is caused by chemical or physical change in the gene; the other by alterations in the arrangement of the genes in the chromosomes (*chromosome mutations*). There is no corresponding difference in the type of phenotypic effect; both produce similar types of change in the body.

3. It was found that there occur mutations of much smaller phenotypic effect than those previously studied (*micromutations*) and that they are so frequent that in many species every individual differs from the rest of the population in the number of mutations of this type that are present in its genotype. These micromutations are responsible for individual variation, so far as it is hereditary, and for much of the rapid response that we observe when animals are exposed to artificial selection. Many of them (*modifiers*) seem to act in the phenotype only by quantitative modification of the action of genes of larger effect, and, in any case, the action of micromutation is, in general, quantitative, altering the extent of the expression of some feature, not controlling its presence or absence. Many micromutations are caused by changes in the position in the chromosome of the gene whose action is modified. This is known as the *position effect*.

4. Genes interact in very many ways. It is found that the action of a gene in any part of the body is altered by changes in many other genes and perhaps potentially by change in any gene of the genotype, though many genes may not recognizably alter the effect. The conclusion thus becomes unavoidable that each organ is controlled not by one or a few genes, which was what the early geneticists thought—the "mo-saic" theory of gene action—but by the whole genotype. This is not surprising, since the whole genotype is contained in each cell of the body. The view to which we have now come is called the "polygenic" theory of gene action.

5. Genes have been shown in all probability to produce their effects in the body by controlling the efficiency of enzymes, each gene possibly controlling a single enzyme. Their action on the enzyme may take place at any point of the life-history and may modify the body or its activities at any time later than the first action.

The result of these developments of genetic theory has been to remove most of the contradictions, so evident forty years ago, between the results of genetics and the conclusions of paleontological and morphological observation. We now see that selection applied to natural genotypes will result first in recombination of the genetic material already present in the genotype—the more favorable combinations of genes will be selected. Second, any new mutations that occur in the genotypes will be accepted or discarded. Since by far the most frequent differences between the genotypes in any population are micromutations, the changes under selection will very largely be based on these small differences. Any larger mutations present or arising in the population will also be subjected to selection, often only after their effects in the phenotype have been altered by selection of modifying micromutations.

Selection of this kind will produce change as gradual, as quantitative, and often as directional as that observed in evolution. The changes will be gradual, for the effects of each micromutation, though itself an all-or-none effect, are small, and many micromutations act on each character of the body; it will be quantitative, for modification is a quantitative alteration in the expression of a gene; it may be directional if the direction of selection is maintained constant. Also, the modifying action of micromutations does not cause destruction of organized structure and is therefore not degenerative.

It seems, then, that we now have a fairly complete genetic background for the interpretation of the minor changes of evolution. Whether we can give a similarly complete interpretation of the larger changes, by which new classes, orders, and families are evolved, is to my mind more doubtful. It is true that all evolutionary change, large or small, must have a background of micro-evolution of the same kind as that we have discussed and that the larger changes differ most obviously from the smaller, in that evolution is continued in them for a longer time. But, in evolution continued through the long periods of paleontological time, types of change different from those that we have so far discussed may arise and may require other principles for explanation of their evolution. For example, directional evolutionary trends often continue unchecked for many millions of years and may not be completely accounted for by directional selection (*orthoselection*). It is possible that mutation itself may be to some extent directional, and it is also possible that other causes may be involved. I think also that we have at present no complete parallel in mutation for some of the changes required in the origin of entirely *new* elements of organization.

Nevertheless, there is no doubt that the solution of the contradictions between the conclusions of genetics and paleontology that seemed, forty years ago, to be unavoidable is a large advance.

ECOLOGY

To understand the genetic background of evolutionary change is not enough. The changes are brought about by selection acting on animals in their natural populations, fixing variations in the genotype of the race so that they are inherited by later generations. Are the conditions in which natural populations live also suitable for production of evolutionary changes of the kinds that we observe? We must now discuss this question.

Study of animals in nature shows that most species live in local, partially isolated populations, within which the individuals are in more or less complete contact with one another and interbreed. Across the boundaries between these groups there is less contact and interbreeding. These partially isolated interbreeding populations may be called "demes." The reason for this type of distribution is that animals choose their habitats in parts of the range of their species where the conditions are most suitable for them and where they have most advantage in competition with other species. Almost all species, except perhaps the most highly locomotory such as some birds, are so distributed, and it is, in general, found that migration between one deme and another is much less than would at first sight be expected. Nevertheless, migration occurs, and the isolation of the deme is not usually complete.

The size of the deme is highly variable both in different species and among the demes of a species. It varies from the few individuals in a pool of water in the axil of a leaf of a plant or in a gutter to the vast numbers of a shoal of herring or of a planktonic species in the waters of a lake. The grade of isolation is also highly variable. It may be slight, as between the populations of a species of bird inhabiting neighboring woods, or almost complete, as in the animals of an island separated from other land by a wide stretch of water or in the inhabitants of small aquatic environments separated from one another by land.

For us the important fact is that distribution in demes is an almost general fact of natural history. We shall see that this distribution implies that differentiation will be independent in each deme so long as the isolation is of sufficient grade[3] and is maintained.

Besides the deme, there is one other category of animal natural history that is observable as a fact of nature. This is the species, if that term is used in the sense which is becoming general among ecologists and is now accepted by many systematists. Differentiation in the deme will start as soon as isolation is set up and will continue as long as the isolation is maintained at a sufficient grade. As time goes on, the deme will differ more and more markedly from other demes of the species. In time two demes so differentiated will no longer interbreed if they are brought together by breakdown of the isolation. It is at this point that the ecologist regards the deme as having attained specific differentiation—a new species has evolved. For a species, whether organized into local demes or not, is to the ecologist a group of animals which is capable, if given the opportunity, of living together a common communal life and of *naturally and normally* breeding together (cf. Mayr, 1942, p. 120). Species may occasionally hybridize, that is to say, they may breed across the specific boundaries; but if they are good species they will not commonly and normally do so. Such a definition is by no means free of all difficulty even from the ecological point of view, but it seems to hold for at least the great majority of bisexual, multicellular animals.

This biological definition is very different from that generally given in the past by the systematists. The systematic definition has varied but has often been

3. For two demes to evolve independently in a character of selective advantage $1/n$, it is necessary that migration between the demes should not be more than $1/n$ of the population in each generation (S. Wright, 1931, p. 97).

that a species is a group of animals which (*a*) does not intergrade with other groups; (*b*) is sufficiently distinct, in the opinion of competent systematists, to deserve a specific name; and (*c*) has a geographical distribution that makes origin from a single ancestral group possible. This definition is very largely morphological, as it must be, since systematists have largely dealt with the bodies and not the natural history of animals. It leaves determination of the extent of the species group, at least very largely, to the judgment of the systematist and is therefore not objective. It is based on very different criteria from the ecological definition, but, nevertheless, the great majority of systematic species are also biological species. Occasionally this agreement breaks down. Sometimes it is found that animal groups will not interbreed with other groups from which they are hardly at all differentiated morphologically. These groups must be recognized as distinct biological species, although they would not normally be called distinct species by the systematist. On the other hand, a few cases are known in which systematic species will interbreed when they come into contact and are therefore not good biological species.

The definition of the species has long been regarded as one of the enigmas of zoölogy. Perhaps this has been due partly to the use of the term in different senses by zoölogists whose main interests lie in different branches of the science; it is impossible to define a term consistently if it is to be used in different senses. Partly, too, it has been due to the fact that the species has not been thought of as an objective reality in natural history but rather as a category set up by the systematist for the convenience of his systematic classification. If we may accept the species as that group of animals which will normally interbreed if the opportunity is present, it is clear that we have a concrete definition of the species. It is also clear that this definition determines a stage of differentiation that is of great importance in the study of evolution, for it is from this point onward that differentiations previously acquired can no longer be lost by interbreeding with related groups. Thereafter, the differentiations can be lost only by extinction of the groups bearing them; they have been added to the capital of evolution.

If it were to be shown that the biological species is not equivalent to the systematic, some other term for it would be needed so that we might avoid using the same term in more than one sense. The term "commixuum" has been suggested. But biological and systematic species so frequently agree that it seems better to assume that biologists and systematists are, in fact, describing the same phenomenon, that the systematist means by his species the same thing as the biologist means by his. At least in discussions of evolution, the biological definition has the greater value, since it defines an important stage of evolutionary differentiation. In such discussions it must surely be accepted as the natural definition.

We find, then, that in nature animals are distributed in species and that each species is in most cases distributed in a large number of partially isolated demes. If the isolation were maintained for a long enough time, each deme would evolve into a new species. But the demes will not normally be permanent. Changes in the environment and evolutionary changes in the demes themselves may cause them to spread into new areas and often to fuse with other demes. Environmental change may also cause the division of a deme. Fusion and division of demes will be frequent in the history of a species, and, indeed, the evolution must be thought of as occurring in a plexus of fusing and subdividing demes. But still —and this is the important point for the interpretation of micro-evolution—it is in the relatively small populations of the demes that the evolution is, in fact, taking place. After each fusion the resulting form will be intermediate between the forms of the fusing demes, the characters of selective value in each being retained. Nonadaptive characters may also be retained if any are present in the fusing demes (see below, under "The Action of Selection"). By these fusions and also by migration between demes across the range of the species, variations between the parts of the species will be kept in check and the whole species gradually evolve.

This will be the course of evolution so long as no part of the species is so completely isolated from the rest that fusion of its demes with those of other parts of the species is prevented. When this happens, the isolated part will evolve to form a distinct subspecies and later a species.

Often, however, environmental change may lead to contact between parts of a species that have become differentiated in isolation from one another. If the differentiation between the forms in contact is slight, it is probable that the interbreeding that must follow contact will result in their fusing; but this will not necessarily occur if they had acquired greater differentiation before contact. Hybrids between considerably differentiated forms are always weak, and in both the forms in contact mutations tending to prevent interbreeding—and so production of hybrids—will be of selective value and will spread through the populations. Thus the result of the contact will not be fusion of the two forms but accelerated differentiation until interbreeding ceases and the forms become distinct species.

So far we have considered only the divergent evolution of differentiated forms that have arisen within a single species. We have reached what seems to be a reasonably clear conception of evolution of this type. But evolution also occurs in a single population without isolation of any of its parts; as time goes on, the structure continually changes. Here also the term "species" is used. This successional differentiation is the evolution most frequently observed in paleontology, and it occurs in every living population of animals. The population evolves continually closer adaptation to its environment when this remains constant and re-adapts in response to any changes in the environment that may take place. It may also evolve nonadaptively if the conditions are suitable (cf. below). We have to ask at what stage of this successional evolution the population may be said to have become specifically distinct from its earlier condition.

This is a question rather for the paleontologist than for the zoölogist, who does not, in general, deal with successions of animal forms in time. But perhaps the following suggestions may be made.

So long as estimation of the correct extent of the specific difference is left to the individual worker, there is bound to be large disagreement in the estimations, as there was when zoölogical systematists regarded the species as a category set up by them for their convenience and not otherwise determined in size. In the biological species the specific level of differentiation is determined in nature and is therefore objective and can be accurately observed. May it not then be suggested that it would make for consistency in the use of the term if the naturally occurring differentiation of the biological species were accepted as the yardstick for all estimations of the correct level of the specific difference? It has been mentioned that, in general, biological species agree closely with those of the zoölogical systematist. Probably, to accept the level of the biological species would necessitate no great change in paleontological practice, any more than it has in zoölogical systematics, though it would exclude usages that give abnormally large or small ranges to the species. It is true that the structural differentiation of nearly related biological species varies very greatly—from almost nothing to the full differentiation of a systematic species—but a reasonably clear mean level of differentiation could probably be found, though this might differ from one large group of animals to another.

There are many other difficulties in the use of the term "species" by the paleontologist. For instance, there is the question whether two or more lines evolving in parallel evolution, often at different times, should, when they result in forms that are very similar in structure, each be given a distinct, specific name or the same name. This raises the important question of what character a natural classification should be; but it and many other questions are clearly for solution by the paleontologist rather than the zoölogist.

THE ACTION OF SELECTION

There is still one more approach to the problems of evolution that we must consider. This is the study of the manner in which selection acts on variations of the kinds that we know, from our knowledge of the genotype, to occur in animals. In the last twenty-five years great advances have been made in interpreting the conditions under which such variations are likely to spread through a population.

First, it must be emphasized that, if the reproduction is bisexual, it is the breeding population as a whole that will evolve; no part of the population can evolve independently, so long as interbreeding is general throughout the population. This is a direct result of the mechanism of bisexual reproduction. It derives from the fact that each individual has $2n$ ancestors of the nth generation and that therefore the genotype becomes mixed throughout the population in a few generations. The only exception to this in bisexual animals is when animals breed only, or very largely, with a small group near to them and the mixture of genes through the population is thereby restricted. When this is so, the individuals are effectively isolated from those at a distance from them ("distance isolation"), and the genotype may differ in the parts of the population. If the range of the interbreeding population is large, the differences in its parts caused by distance isolation may occur, although the range of interbreeding of the individuals is large. In some cases such differences give rise to gradients in characters from one side of the range of a population to the other; such a gradient is known as a "cline." These clines may occur not only in single populations but also in species distributed in demes, the characters of the demes altering continuously across the range of the species.

When a population is subjected to selection, the type of change occurring in it will be different according as the characters selected are each controlled by one or many genes. If the control is a single gene, the change will take the form of an increase or decrease in the proportion of the individuals bearing the character. In the much more frequent case in which numerous genes, often each of small expression, control the character, the change will consist of *gradual* modification of the character as selection proceeds, until a limit is reached when all the genes making for the favored change have been selected. This limit can be passed only by new mutation. If, for instance, selection is toward increase in size, there will be a change toward increased size

in all the individuals of the population, and this will go on until the limit is reached.[4] During the evolution, the individuals of the population will vary in size as in other characters, and the change in the population will show itself in a movement of the mean size of the population. These changes in the mean values of the characters of evolving populations are very characteristic of the changes observed both in paleontology and in living nature.

It has been already noted (see above, under "Selection in Nature") that the minimum selective advantage varies inversely with the size of the interbreeding population and that when the population is small (less than an effective breeding population of about 1,000 individuals) considerable selective advantages are necessary if selection is to be effective. In small populations S. Wright (1931, p. 97) believes that genes that have no selective advantage and are therefore nonadaptive may spread independently of selection. This gives a possible basis for interpretation of the many apparently nonadaptive characters of animals, especially among the minor differentiations of species and varieties. Others, however, deny that there is any real nonadaptive evolution of genes (Fisher and Ford, 1947, p. 143).

The rate of spread of a mutation through a population varies inversely with the selective advantage and also with the characters of the gene. It is much more rapid for dominant than for recessive genes and is also different according as the gene is sex-linked or autosomal. Recessive genes may take tens or even hundreds of thousands of generations to become established in all the individuals of a population. The rate of evolution of a population as a whole is, according to S. Wright (1931, p. 97), greatest for medium-sized pop-

4. Or further enlargement becomes disadvantageous.

ulations—those in which the number of the effective breeding population is about equal to the average selective advantage—and less for larger and smaller populations. The rate is also greater in a species divided into demes than in a single undivided population.

Much discussion has been caused by the contradiction that is found between the recessive character of most naturally occurring mutations and the dominance of most characters in the natural genotypes of animals. Since animal genotypes are mostly dominant, it would, at first sight, seem that only the relatively rare dominant mutations are used in evolution. Another apparent difficulty in attributing evolution to the mutations that we observe is the fact that mutations are recurrent, the same mutation occurring frequently in the history of a species. It would seem that those that now occur will have been previously tested by selection for selective advantage and, if not now in the genotype, must have been rejected. Does this mean that even of the dominant mutations only the presumably very rare, new mutations can be of value? In connection with the last of these points, it should be noted that natural environments are continually changing and that, as they change, the selective advantages of mutations will change with them. A mutation that at one time was disadvantageous may later become of value, and the genotype alter as it spreads. We have an example of this in the spread of melanic moths (see above, under "Selection in Nature"). In connection with the dominance of natural genotypes, we have Fisher's theory of the evolution of dominance (1928, p. 115; 1931, p. 345), which claims that a recessive but advantageous mutation will be altered toward dominance as it is selected and spreads,[5] for its more rapid spread as a dominant will be advantageous. Having become dominant, it

will pass into the genotype. Others (Wright, 1931, p. 97) have questioned whether this evolution of dominance will occur; they believe that there would be no sufficient force of selection toward dominance. Different explanations of the dominance of natural genotypes have been offered (Muller, 1934, p. 407; Plunkett, 1933, p. 84). The problem may be regarded as still open.

When we consider the results of the mathematical study of selection in relation to the ecology of natural populations already discussed, a plexus of frequently fusing and subdividing demes, important conclusions emerge. The evolutionary differentiation of the species will take place in the separate populations of the demes, and in each deme the nature of the evolution will vary with the size of the population. The sizes of the demes composing the species and not the size of the species population as a whole will determine the nature of the evolutionary change. In small demes some nonadaptive evolution is to be expected, though even there much of the evolution will be adaptive. It will be adaptive to the immediate environment of the deme, and the characters of the demes will differ in adaptation to the small variations of their environments. Other conclusions may be drawn, but for our present purpose these seem the most important.

THE LARGER EVOLUTIONARY CHANGES

Man has evolved within a single order of the mammals, the Primates, and, whatever his immediate ancestors among the Primates, within a small part of that order. We need only consider the changes by which his special type of primate organization arose. We

5. It is known that the dominant or recessive character of a gene can be altered by modification caused by micromutations.

can, in fact, neglect changes of higher than specific or generic rank.

Human evolution took place during the adaptive radiation by which all the various types of mammals diverged in Tertiary times. We are therefore concerned with the nature of the evolutionary processes that constitute adaptive radiation.

Adaptive radiation is the splitting of a successful group of animals into a large number of adaptive types, each fitting one of the minor habitats and habits of life that are open within the range of the group as a whole. The radiation starts as soon as the group becomes successful—in mammals it started with the radiation of the mammalian orders at the beginning of the Tertiary—and continues as long as the group is successful. Groups of all sizes become differentiated from the major subdivisions down to species. By far the majority of the radiating lines die out in the later course of the radiation; this appears in any of the phylogenetic trees that have been prepared by the paleontologists. Each radiating line represents a habit of life different in at least some features from the habit of the ancestral group, and the group differentiates in adaptation to these features. Man's forebears were a late-radiating line of the Primates, and they adopted a habit of life which differed in many ways from that of his primate ancestors.

In adaptive radiation by far the greater part of the changes of structure take the form of alterations in the relative sizes of parts of the body ("allometric evolution"). There is comparatively little evolution of *new* structure.

In the normal development of an animal some parts grow more slowly or more quickly than the body as a whole, and the sizes of the organs in the adult are determined by these relative growth rates. Part of the allometric changes of evolution is due to the whole body growing larger or smaller in the descendants, for parts which do not grow at the same rate as the body during development will be altered in relative size if the body becomes larger or smaller. Another part of the changes is due to actual change in the relative growth rates.

Mammals, and man among them, show the effects of this allometric evolution very clearly. Every part of the body of man is present in other mammals, but he differs in the sizes of his organs—for instance, in the overgrowth of his brain—from even his nearest relatives.

Other characters of the evolutionary changes of adaptive radiation are that they are *gradual, co-ordinated* in the various parts of the body throughout their course, and often *directional*. Co-ordination between the changes in the parts of the body is necessary so that the animal may always remain viable, and this alone would make it improbable that large and sudden changes would be advantageous; small and gradual changes are much more likely to be of selective value.

There is clear evidence that the rate of evolutionary change is highly variable. Rapid change will generally follow any alteration of the conditions to which the animal is exposed; it will re-adapt rapidly to its altered needs. Alterations of the environmental conditions must occur frequently in any long course of evolution; they will be caused not only by physical changes in the environment but also by migration and change of habit. In view of this, it is perhaps surprising that adaptive radiation is as directional as it is often found to be; if the needs of the animal are so frequently changing, we might expect the direction of its evolution to be equally inconstant. But, in fact, we find in radiating animals trends of change continuing in the same direction for many millions of years. Among the mammals the evolution of the horses is perhaps better known than that of any other group; they show these trends well. They became continually larger between the Eocene and the Miocene, their brains showed trends toward more complicated structure, and their feet toward the single-digit type of the modern horse. These trends were not universal in all the radiating lines of the horses, but they were general enough to be recognized as trends. Such trends are probably due in part to slow response (slow because of the need for co-ordination) to selection acting for a long time in the same direction ("orthoselection"), and in part they may represent gradual improvement in the general organization of the body, which is likely always to be of selective value. It is very unlikely that there is in evolution any true *orthogenesis*—defined as control of the direction of evolution by factors internal to the animal—except in so far as supply of mutation in some but not all directions may possibly exert some control.

One problem in adaptive radiation (as in all larger evolution) is to explain how an animal that has become specialized in one direction is able on occasion to change its habit of life and specialize in another direction. If an animal attempted a life largely different from that it had previously led, we should expect it to die out in competition with forms already adapted to the new life, rather than to readapt. But such changes of habit certainly occur; they have occurred many times in the history of the vertebrates and must also have occurred in the evolution of man. It has been suggested that correlation between the adaptations acquired before the change and those needed in the new life would make the change much easier and may be necessary for any large change in habit of life. This *preadaptation* of the animal could only

be due to chance correlation between the needs before and after the change and would not often occur. Nevertheless, it may be expected to occur occasionally in the paleontological history of a group, and these large changes of habit are themselves infrequent. Preadaptation may perhaps play an important part in evolution, but it cannot be said that its importance is at present accepted by all biologists.

THE EVOLUTION OF MAN

We must now consider how far man's evolution since he arose from his primate ancestors can be interpreted as governed by the same controls as those we have seen to govern the evolution of other animals. There can be no doubt that his evolution has been in many ways most unusual, and it is to be expected that unusual factors may have taken part in its control. But man is an animal, and he arose from animals much less unusual than he himself is. Also, his genotype is similar in its organization to those of other animals, and there should be no great difference in type between the variations that form the raw material of evolution in him and his animal ancestors. His ecology, at least in the earlier stages of his evolution, must have arisen by modification of that of the Primates from which he arose. Changes in ecology undoubtedly occurred in the course of his evolution and must have largely influenced its course, but he must have arisen from a primate life, probably arboreal, very like that of many of our modern Primates. I shall assume, for the sake of the argument, that he early gave up his arboreal life, coming to live an omnivorous life on the ground; that at first he lived in small groups not much larger than the family; and that the size of his communities was enlarged only later when he began to develop a social life.

Though trends are evident in man's

evolution—very clearly, for instance, in the evolution of his brain—the direction in which selection acted on his various characters must have altered frequently as the conditions of his life changed. But this is true of all adaptive radiation, and the changes in the direction of selection would not alter the fundamental characters of the evolution. Nevertheless, these changes in the direction of selection must have resulted in occasional outbursts of rapid evolution. They may also have been responsible for many of man's peculiar features. His completely upright gait was clearly of advantage when he ceased to be arboreal, since it made running on the ground much more effective; it is by no means so clearly adapted to arboreal life, though it is possible that man's immediate arboreal ancestors were more or less upright. An upright gait also had the effect, probably secondary but very important, of freeing his hands for use as grasping organs and for the making and use of tools, an activity which has so often been thought to be fundamental to his mental evolution.

It will be clear from the discussion of the previous pages that the size of human interbreeding communities must have played a considerable part in controlling the type of his evolution. If it is right to assume that, at the start of his evolution from his predecessors, man lived in small communities of approximately family size, these would almost certainly be largely (but not completely) isolated from similar communities. His species at that stage would then give an excellent example of evolution in a plexus of partially isolated demes, in his case in demes of very small size. Evolution of nonadaptive characters would, according to S. Wright (1931, p. 97), have been possible among the differentiations evolved in the demes, and the general stability

of the genotype of the species would be maintained by migration between the demes and by occasional fusions of them. If in man's later evolution he came to live in larger communities, the chief changes to be expected would be that characters of smaller selective advantage would be established by selection, and there would be less possibility of the evolution of nonadaptive characters. Evolution is rapid in any species distributed in demes, but more rapid in moderate-sized rather than very small demes. As we have seen, any large changes in habit often lead to phases of very rapid evolution in adaptation to the changed needs that follow the change in habit. Such outbursts of rapid evolution must have occurred during the evolution of man.

One of the most striking features that distinguishes man's body from the bodies of other mammals is its extraordinary fetalization. In many characters, such as his lack of a complete clothing of hair, the late closure of the sutures of his skull, the posture of his head, and others, man resembles the fetal rather than the adult mammal (cf., e.g., De Beer, 1940 and 1951). In part these characters may be correlated with the elongation of his development that has accompanied the evolution of his complex behavior. Their persistence in the adult implies that in man some developmental changes have been delayed in the life-history so that they occur at a later stage than in other mammals, or even not at all. Such changes in the time relations of the processes of development are frequent in evolution. They are known as "heterochrony" and may occur in either direction. But this does not explain why, in man, so many characters are retarded in development. Not all man's characters are retarded; in some other characters his development is accelerated, e.g., in the development of his brain. The subject has been considerably discussed. No very clear conclusions have, I think, been reached, but the fact is clear that man is peculiar in retaining so many fetal characters in his adult body.

Bodily evolution along these lines must have proceeded in man so long as he was subjected to the forces of natural selection acting in one direction or another. We know that selection is an essential requisite of the progress of evolution, and we find in animals that, if it is removed or seriously weakened, abnormal and inefficient forms soon appear, so that the species begins to degenerate. What are likely to be the effects of removal of all effective force of selection by social legislation in the most recent stages of man's evolution—or in the future—is discussed by Muller (1950, p. 111), who points out that it must lead to inevitable accumulation of deleterious mutations and to ultimate degeneration.

Man has both a body and a mind, and in his evolution both body and mind have evolved. The maintenance of his bodily health is as important to him as the evolution of his mental powers; but in the recent stages of his evolution the most striking feature has been a gradual replacement of his bodily evolution by his mental evolution in his communities, until at the present time it is doubtful whether any further evolution of his body is proceeding. So long as the health of his body is maintained, that may not be unduly harmful.

The subject of man's social evolution is a very different one from that of the evolution that he has shared with other animals. It is a subject for the anthropologist and psychologist rather than for the biologist and will not be discussed here.

REFERENCES

De Beer, G. R. 1940 and 1951. *Embryos and Ancestors.* London: Oxford University Press.

Carter, G. S. 1951. *Animal Evolution.* London: Sidgwick & Jackson.

Fenton, C. L. 1931. *Studies in the Evolution of the Genus Spirifer.* ("Publications of the Wagner Institute of Science," Vol. II.)

Fisher, R. A. 1928. "The Possible Modification of the Response of the Wild Type to Recurrent Mutations," *American Naturalist,* LXII, 115–26.

———. 1930. *The Genetical Theory of Natural Selection.* Oxford: Clarendon Press.

———. 1931. "The Evolution of Dominance," *Biological Review,* VI, 345–68.

Fisher, R. A., and Ford, E. B. 1947. "The Spread of a Gene in Natural Conditions in a Colony of the Moth *Panaxia Dominula L,*" *Heredity,* I, 143–74.

Ford, E. B. 1940. "Genetic Research in the Lepidoptera," *Annals of Eugenics,* X, 227–52.

Johannsen, W. 1903. *Über Erblichkeit in Populationen und reinen Linien.* Jena: G. Fischer Verlag.

Mayr, E. 1942. *Systematics and the Origin of Species.* New York: Columbia University Press.

Mendel, G. J. 1865. "Versuche über Pflanzen-Hybriden," *Verhandlungen des Naturforschenden Vereines,* Vol. X.

Muller, H. J. 1934. "On the Incomplete Dominance of the Normal Allelomorphs of White in *Drosophila,*" *Journal of Genetics,* XXX, 407–14.

———. 1950. "Our Load of Mutations," *American Journal of Human Genetics,* II, 111–76.

Plunkett, C. R. 1933. "A Contribution to the Theory of Dominance," *American Naturalist,* LXVII, 84–85. (Paper No. 41, read at Atlantic City meeting of the Genetics Society of America.)

POPHAM, E. J. 1943. *Proceedings of the Zoölogical Society, London,* Vol. CXIIA.

———. 1944. *Ibid.,* Vol. CXIVA.

———. 1948. *Ibid.,* Vol. CXVII.

ROWE, A. W. 1899. *Quarterly Journal of the Geological Society, London,* Vol. LV.

WRIGHT, S. 1929. "Fisher's Theory of Dominance,"*American Naturalist,* LXIII, 274–79. "The Evolution of Dominance," *ibid.,* pp. 556–61. (Comment on Dr. Fisher's reply.)

———. 1931. "Evolution in Mendelian Populations," *Genetics,* XVI, 97–159.

Archeological Theories and Interpretation: Old World

By J. GRAHAME D. CLARK

ANTIQUARIAN STUDIES first developed in the Old World during the sixteenth century as an aspect of the rise of national feeling which followed the break-up of medieval Christendom. In so far as the early antiquaries interpreted the past, they did so in terms of their own particular group; their interests were mainly literary, and their chief aim was to extend the history of their native lands. Archeology proper, based on the study of material things, first began to develop rapidly during the latter part of the eighteenth century, and it was not until 1836 that sufficient material had been assembled to prompt a logical system of classification.

In C. J. Thomsen's three-period system (1836, 1838–43; see also Daniel, 1943, 1950), originally devised as an aid to the explanation of the collections in the Danish National Museum at Copenhagen, we can detect for the first time the influence of a theory of more than parochial application. Although Lamarck failed to devise a convincing explanation of biological evolution, his transformist ideas influenced profoundly the climate of thought and opinion. Thomsen's classification of archeological material into the three ages of Stone, Bronze, and Iron carried conviction because it was based on the concept of a progressive evolution from rude and simple to more efficient and complex.

The announcement of Darwin's theory of natural selection in 1858[1] gave an immediate and lasting impetus to prehistoric studies. Until a convincing theory of evolution had been given to the world, the study of man was not appreciated by more than a few individuals. One may illustrate this in two ways. For one thing, it is evident that the propounders of the three-period system had no conception of the antiquity of man. For instance, in his book on *The Primeval Antiquities of Denmark*, J. J. A. Worsaae assigned an antiquity (not even a duration) of "at least three thousand years" to the Danish Stone Age,[2] a chronology fully consistent

1. The "theory of natural selection" was first made public at a meeting of the Linnaean Society on July 1, 1858, when Lyell communicated parallel papers by Darwin and Wallace. Darwin did not publish *The Origin of Species* until the following year.

2. On p. 8 of the English translation (Worsaae [1849]), Worsaae argued that "the stone-period must be of extraordinary antiquity. If the Celts possessed settled abodes in the west of Europe, more than two thousand years ago, how much more ancient must be the population which preceded the arrival of the Celts. A great number of years must pass away before a people, like the Celts, could spread themselves over the west of Europe, and render the land productive; it is therefore no exaggeration if we attribute to the stone-period an antiquity of, at least, three thousand years."

343

with that of Archbishop Ussher. On the other hand, the work of those who were, in fact, exploring traces of Paleolithic man was either ignored or explained away. To Dean Buckland, first Reader in Geology at Oxford University and the leading authority on cave exploration of his day, Pleistocene fauna was so much evidence for the biblical Flood, and the Red Lady of Paviland, now recognized as of Upper Paleolithic age, an inserted burial of the Roman period (1823). McEnery's pioneer excavations at Kent's Hole during 1826–41, where he systematically recovered worked flints in association with Pleistocene fauna, were so little regarded that his notebooks were even mislaid after his death (see Garrod, 1926, p. 27). In France it was the same story: Boucher de Perthe's discoveries in the Somme gravels, like those of Tournal in the Grotte de Bize, were ignored by men of science.

Darwin's announcement of the theory of natural selection brought a rapid change of attitude. McEnery's notes were found, and extracts from his *Cavern Researches* were published (1859). That same year a deputation of eminent scientists left England for the Somme Valley and solemnly attested the discoveries of Boucher.[3] The antiquity of man indeed had ceased to be an anomaly and had become a philosophical necessity. There followed an epoch of intensive archeological activity. Systematic investigation of the Dordogne caves was begun by Lartet and Christy in 1863 (1865–75), and two years later Lubbock gave formal recognition to the separate status of the earlier Stone Age by coining the terms "Paleolithic" and "Neolithic" (1865). By 1881 G. de Mortillet had established the main outlines of the classic Paleolithic sequence of France (1881),

a sequence which, so far as its later phases were concerned, was completed by Breuil in the early years of the twentieth century (1912). Within two generations the prehistorians had succeeded, at least in France, in spanning the great gulf of time opened up by acceptance of the idea of human evolution. Yet they were not able to answer nearly quickly enough the questions which called insistently for answers.

While archeologists sweated at their digging, distinguished ethnologists sat cosily at their desks, defining the stages through which in inferior times the human race had passed. The idea that human culture, like the animal world, had evolved gradually from simple beginnings was, as we have seen, already current before Darwin won acceptance for his theory of biological evolution. Moreover, the Swedish zoölogist, Sven Nilsson (1838–43), had already sought in 1838 to deduce from comparative ethnology the stages through which humanity had passed in the course of its history.

It was not for nothing that Nilsson's book was translated into English in 1866 by Sir John Lubbock himself (1866). The concept of evolutionary stages deducible from a knowledge of existing cultures was exactly what the anthropologists of the Darwinian era needed. Of Nilsson's many followers I shall mention only Lewis H. Morgan, who characteristically entitled his chief book *Ancient Society* (1877), even though its conclusions were mainly based on a study of contemporary societies. Rejecting Nilsson's phase of herding and nomadism, Morgan accepted in substance his first, third, and fourth stages, which he dubbed, respectively, "savagery," "barbarism," and "civilization." By further subdividing the first two of these, he characterized seven phases of development through which he supposed mankind to have passed. I say "supposed" advisedly, because of

3. See *Phil. Trans. Royal Society*, Part II (1860), pp. 277–317; *Archaeologia*, XXXVIII (1860), 1–28.

course, these stages were hypothetical. As Dr. Glyn Daniel has recently expressed it (1950, p. 188), his whole scheme, like that of Nilsson, "was based primarily not on archaeological evidence but on the comparative study of modern primitive peoples, the arrangement of these existing economies and societies into an evolutionary sequence, and the projection of this hypothetical sequence into the prehistoric past." Now it would be ridiculous at this time of day to apportion praise or blame to Morgan, Tylor, and the rest: the mid-Victorian anthropologists were confronted by an immense void, for many of them suddenly apprehended, and they merely did what any other scientists would have done under similar circumstances—they plugged the gap with hypotheses. All I am concerned to emphasize at the moment is the fact that their stages were hypothetical; that they were stopgaps against the time when archeological research should have established on a basis of historical fact the actual course of prehistory.

One may legitimately insist, though, that hypothetical prehistory, useful as it may have been seventy or eighty years ago, has long ceased to be respectable. It is not for me to estimate the contribution to ethnology of the culture-historical school of Graebner and Schmidt. What most prehistorians would reject out of hand, though, is any attempt to use the theories of this or any other school (Marxist included) in place of excavation as a means of finding out about the prehistoric past. In this connection I would cite specifically Oswald Menghin's grandiose *Weltgeschichte der Steinzeit* (1931; Clark, 1931). In his opening presidential address to the newly formed Prehistoric Society, Professor Childe (1935, p. 14) pointed out that (*a*) Menghin's "culture cycles" have not been arrived at as a result of wrestling with the archeological data but are, in fact, no more than

"categories borrowed from ethnography into which the archaeological evidence has been fitted"; (*b*) his "culture cycles" do not even exist today—they are "abstractions obtained by isolating traits common to several peoples and areas"; and (*c*) as a result, his "culture traits" are considered without reference to geographical environment. As Childe puts it: "Menghin insists so strongly on an axe as an expression of a historical tradition that the reader may forget that it is an implement for felling trees."

One need hardly feel surprised that, when Menghin's text is examined in close relation to the archeological material, it is seen to abound in contradictions and even in absurdities. To take only one example, Menghin seized upon an assemblage of objects from Kunda in northern Esthonia as a vehicle for the continuation during the postglacial period of his hypothetical "bone culture," without stopping to consider what, in point of fact, these bone and antler objects really signified. In effect, it was a travesty to accept these pieces, all of them from the bed of an old lake and fairly evidently the losses of fishermen, as constituting a veritable culture. Two years after Menghin's book appeared, the Esthonian archeologist Indreko (1948, see esp. pp. 107 ff.) excavated a settlement on the shore of the Kunda lake. There he recovered the true culture of these fishermen, and it comprised, in addition to objects of antler and bone, a broad range of scrapers, knives, and adzes made from flint, quartz, and greenstone. The "bone culture" of Kunda proved to be quite imaginary. As Childe (1935, p. 3) so appositely said in his presidential address, a culture in the archeological sense of the term "is not an *a priori* category elaborated in the studies of philosophers and then imposed from outside upon working archaeologists. Cultures are observed facts."

The attitude revealed in Menghin's

book was indeed anachronistic. This applies with possibly even greater force to the Marxist school of prehistory, shackled as this is to a dogma announced to the world (Marx, 1904, Preface) in the same year as Darwin published his *The Origin of Species.* The mutual attraction of Marxism and prehistory is not hard to understand. To the prehistorian, Marxism might seem to offer an escape from the limitations of archeological evidence: once accept the dogma that the means of production determine the whole structure of society, and the way is open to reconstructing former states of society on the basis of the economic data commonly afforded by archeological research. On the other hand, Marxists find in archeology a means of recovering what they hold to be tangible evidence for the validity of the dogma of the materialist interpretation of history; the very limitations of archeology are, from this point of view, a positive advantage. By a curious inversion Efimenko and other leading Soviet prehistorians of the 1930's actually rejected the classification of prehistoric cultures in terms of material forms in favor of one based on stages in social development, such as preclan, clan, and class societies (for summary with references, see Childe, 1951, pp. 27–29). The short answer to this has recently been given by Childe in his *Social Evolution*, where he points out that "the Russian scheme of classification assumes in advance precisely what archaeological facts have to prove" (1951, p. 29). In reality, it is exceedingly difficult to reach any certain conclusions by archeological means about nonmaterial aspects of life. What is quite sure is that Marxist dogma is no more valid as a substitute for archeological research than were the speculations of Victorian ethnologists. Both are equally out of date.

To return to archeology, it should be emphasized that the period between *The Origin of Species* and the outbreak of the first World War was one of intense activity. The suggestion sometimes made that the prehistorians of this period were blinded by the biological theory of evolution is to betray a lack of historical understanding. The theorisers of the time were the ethnologists, who, until the turn of the century, hardly stirred from their armchairs. When prehistorians did indulge in theory, by no means all of them came out on the side of the evolutionists. In the discussions which raged about the origins of Mycenaean civilization toward the close of the nineteenth century (Daniel, 1950, p. 180), some looked to the north, others to the east; nobody sought an explanation in independent evolution. One of the leading protagonists of the notion that the later prehistoric cultures of Europe were no more than pale reflections of oriental civilizations was Oscar Montelius, the arch-systematizer in terms of periods of the Neolithic and Bronze ages of northern Europe; not only was he fully aware of the historic role of diffusion, but the absolute chronology of his periods was based precisely on contacts between prehistoric and civilized peoples. Prehistorians at this time were preoccupied with establishing time sequences, for the very practical reason that, without some such chronological framework, it was impossible to organize their material or to learn anything of the course of prehistory.

What in reality limited their work was not theoretical obtuseness but historical circumstances. They were pioneers, and they were carrying out their experiments in a restricted part of Europe; the main outlines of Paleolithic archeology were first worked out, for instance, in France, where the sequence happened to be particularly well marked. The first textbooks of prehistory in reality mirrored local results;

yet for long these were the only ones available, and it is not to be wondered at that they should be accepted by students as though of general application.

The great expansion of the area of prehistoric research in the Old World, so largely inspired by the Abbé Henri Breuil during the years immediately after the first World War, soon showed the situation in its true light. As results began to come in from different parts of Africa and Asia and even from central and eastern Europe, it became obvious that the new material would not fit the classic sequence. One of the first to appreciate the implications of the new discoveries was Miss Dorothy Garrod (1928, esp. p. 261). In an address delivered in 1928 she pointed out:

> The classification of de Mortillet is based on discoveries made in Europe, and more especially in Western Europe. It therefore represents correctly the sequence in time of a certain number of Palaeolithic cultures seen, as it were, in section over a very limited part of the earth's surface. . . .
>
> It is becoming more and more clear that it is not in Europe that we must seek the origins of the various Palaeolithic peoples who successively overran the West. . . . The classification of de Mortillet therefore only records the order of arrival in the West of a series of cultures, each of which has originated and probably passed through the greater part of its existence elsewhere.

In point of fact, the unilinear evolutionary sequence had already begun to break down some years before, even for the Lower Paleolithic period. When, for instance, the Germans began to investigate their Pleistocene deposits for traces of the earliest human cultures, they found that the classical hand-axes of Chelles and St. Acheul were replaced, or at least strongly supplemented, by flint industries based on the production of flakes. In his great book *El Hombre fosil,* published in 1916, Obermaier had already recognized the existence of these two contemporary

traditions in the Lower Paleolithic period of Europe. Again, in publishing the early flake industry from Clacton, England, Hazzledine Warren pointed out that it had "no cultural connection with the Chellian or Acheulian stage. As knowledge of the Palaeolithic period increases we are realising more fully the divergence of races and cultures which were living contemporaneously together."[4] It was, of course, this realization that undermined acceptance of the textbook sequence.

The French Upper Paleolithic sequence was more finely drawn and correspondingly more vulnerable. For instance, the earliest of the first three main stages, the Aurignacian, was itself divided into three; the designation of these as Lower, Middle, and Upper recorded stratigraphic facts observed in the excavation of French caves and rock-shelters, but it encouraged in some minds the idea that they represented stages in the evolution of a single culture. Yet, even in 1928, Miss Garrod (1928, p. 263) was able from her own experience to suggest that the Middle Aurignacian might prove to be a separate culture originating somewhere in the area of Palestine, where it played a dominant role in Upper Paleolithic times. When ten years later she came to make a fresh survey of the Upper Paleolithic world (1938), not only had this suggestion been substantially proved, but research in southern Russia and central Europe had made it evident that the Upper Aurignacian or Gravettian of France was, in reality, no more than a western extension of another quite distinct culture, which originated farther north than the Middle or true Aurignacian and spread in from the east. To illustrate her thesis, Miss Garrod published distribution maps showing the geographical extent of what she had shown to be two distinct cultures rather than stages in the

4. *Proc. Prehist. Soc. East Anglia,* III, 602.

unilinear development in western Europe of a single tradition.

It might be thought that the greater variation, shorter duration, and smaller geographical range of the Neolithic and later prehistoric cultures would have made it easier to recognize them. Yet here again one should remember that the early prehistorians were primarily concerned in establishing the sequence of archeological material in the areas in which they worked; only when this stage had been passed, could one expect appreciation of the significance of cultures as distinct from periods. In this respect the prehistorians were not notably behind the ethnologists of the day. After all, until the Torres Straits Expedition at the turn of the century, ethnology, at least as it was conducted from the Old World, seems to have consisted very largely in hypotheticating history, and it needed still another generation before monographs like Radcliffe-Brown's *Andaman Islanders* (1922) began to give tangible evidence of a more scientific outlook.

Between the two world wars the attention of prehistorians, like that of ethnologists, was focused on the definition and interpretation of cultures. We have seen already how, even in Paleolithic archeology, the aim had shifted from the definition of chronological periods to the tracing of the genesis and spread of cultures in time and space. By a curious irony of history, one of the first impulses in the sphere of later prehistory came from a school of perverted racialists. German antiquaries, perhaps more than those of any other European country, had from the beginning been absorbed in the history of their own land and people, as witnessed, for example, by the number of lovingly annotated editions of the *Germania* which appeared from the fifteenth century onward. By playing on this sentiment and inflaming it with a spurious racialism, Gustaf Kossinna

(1912, 1926, and others) built up a pan-German school of prehistory, the aim of which was not merely to glorify the German-Nordic past but to depreciate that of other peoples. Now, however much we may deplore such an attitude and however irretrievably deflated is the chronology by which alone the cultural priority of the Germans could be maintained, Kossinna performed a real service by his insistence that prehistory was concerned with peoples who lived and struggled; his definition of cultural groups and his use of distribution maps to illustrate their geographical spread were much in advance of their time.

The new approach, free from any taint of racial or nationalist propaganda, is seen at its best in V. Gordon Childe's *Dawn of European Civilization,* first published in 1925. In this pioneer work Childe defined and described the Neolithic and Early Bronze Age cultures of prehistoric Europe and, so far as possible, traced their genesis and history. At the end of his book he printed maps illustrating the geographical extent of the main cultures at each of four chronological stages. In this way he demonstrated for the first time the actual culture history of the different parts of Europe from the introduction of farming down to the fall of Cnossus.

Even in his first edition, Childe had already made sufficiently plain the marginal character of Europe in relation to the originative centers of ancient civilization in the Old World. As it happened, though, he wrote his book at a time when great advances were being made in our knowledge of the prehistoric foundations of the ancient civilizations of the Near East.[5] As knowledge of these became available,

5. Childe was himself one of the first to make available these advances in his books *The Most Ancient East* (1928) and *New Light on the Most Ancient East: The Oriental Prelude to European Prehistory* (1934).

they made clearer than ever the parochial character of later European prehistory. In the third edition of the *Dawn* (1939), Childe was very explicit on this matter:

Our knowledge of the archaeology of Europe and of the Ancient East has enormously strengthened the Orientalists' position. Indeed we can now survey continuously interconnected provinces throughout which cultures are seen to be zoned in regularly descending grades round the centres of urban civilization in the Ancient East. Such zoning is the best possible proof of the Orientalists' postulate of diffusion.

Proceeding outward from the territory of civilized societies to those still occupied by savages, the situation visualized by Childe for his fourth period was somewhat as follows (1939, p. 326):[6] (*a*) "fully literate city-dwellers" in peninsular as well as insular Greece; (*b*) "illiterate townsmen" in Macedonia and Sicily; (*c*) "sedentary villagers with at least a specialised bronze industry and regular commerce to support it" in the Middle Danube Basin, southeastern Spain, and perhaps in the Kuban; (*d*) "less stable . . . less highly differentiated" communities from England across south and central Germany and Switzerland to south Russia; (*e*) self-sufficing Neolithic communities in southern Scandinavia, northern Germany, and Orkney; and (*f*) Arctic hunter-fishers in the forests and on the coasts of the far north. In other words, he viewed the later prehistory of Europe in terms not so much of evolutionary stages as of zones of diffusion and devolution.

During the years immediately before the outbreak of the second World War, therefore, it was possible to view Old World prehistory for the first time as something more than a mere succession of periods. On the one hand, prehistorians could take a bird's-eye view of

the Old Stone Age and form some notion of its main lines of development, not as a unilinear growth, but as the product of a complex history. On the other, they could trace the opening-up of a new and much wider perspective, first in the ancient East and then over progressively wider territories.

It was evident, in the first place, that almost the whole of human history had been passed under conditions approximating that of the state of savagery deduced by Morgan and Tylor from comparative ethnography.[7] Throughout Paleolithic and Mesolithic times, subsistence was based solely on such activities as hunting, fishing, fowling, and gathering. So far as one could tell from the archeological evidence, also, social groups were small, there was a good deal of seasonal movement, and there was little scope for subdivision of labor or rapid technical advance.

Second, it was clear that, over very extensive territories, societies on this level were replaced by others which were based on farming and which corresponded with the hypothetical level of barbarism. Beyond any doubt, it was the adoption of farming which provided a way of escape from the narrow world of savagery and in due course formed a basis for the attainment of literate civilization. The significance of farming, recognized already by Nilsson, led Childe (notably, 1936, 1942) to hail its emergence as constituting a "Neolithic revolution," a phrase, however, which has not everywhere met with full acceptance (see Frankfort, 1951, p. 38, n. 3). The truth is that not nearly

---

6. Childe indicated the major zones on the four end-maps.

7. E. B. Tylor and John Lubbock (1865) had compared Paleolithic implements from Europe with those of modern savages as early as 1865. A more elaborate treatment of this theme was given by W. J. Sollas in lectures on "Ancient Hunters and Their Modern Representatives" given to the Royal Institution in 1906 (1909). The same concept underlay Sollas' popular but influential volume, *Ancient Hunters* (1924).

enough has been discovered yet about the exact circumstances under which farming first developed. The excavation of successive levels in the tells has revealed in some detail the elaboration of culture made possible by the adoption of farming but relatively little about primitive Neolithic cultures. Discriminating excavations like those conducted by Braidwood and McCown in strategic parts of Mesopotamia and Iran, backed up by systematic application of Carbon 14 tests, promise results (see Frankfort, 1951, pp. 55 and 56, n. 1); but the fact remains that we are still ignorant about the history of this crucial development. So far as the spread of Neolithic economy to Europe is concerned, there is no doubt that the manner as well as the implications could commonly be described as revolutionary,[8] though on the outer margins the change was often more gradual and much less sweeping, so that it is sometimes difficult to distinguish between food-gatherers and farmers.[9]

Writers have differed over the traits by which they diagnose the appearance of civilization, but from Nilsson onward all have agreed upon the significance of writing. It is not merely that writing inaugurates recorded history; in Childe's phrase it is "a significant, as well as a convenient, mark of civilization" (see Childe, 1950). Economic and social elaboration may, it would seem, proceed up to a certain point, but for anything beyond this the adoption of some conventional method of record and transmission is necessary. Thanks to the circumstance that the ancient Meso-

potamians wrote on clay, it has been possible to trace fairly certainly the context in which writing appeared in different sequences. Among the chief concomitants of literacy, Childe notes the existence of specialists playing no direct part in the production of food; the maintenance of regular trade in raw materials, notably in metals; and the adoption of urban life. Childe, indeed, sought to characterize the transition as an "urban revolution," though what the archeological records appear to most observers to show is rather a very gradual elaboration of economic life, with writing appearing at a certain critical point (e.g., Frankfort, 1951, pp. 55 and 56, n. 1).

In its broadest terms, therefore, the concept of stages in the evolution of culture may be held to have been justified by the results of excavation in the Old World. Yet the value of this can easily be overrated. Outside the main originative centers, in territories like Europe and northwest Africa, diffusion and devolution have played an immeasurably greater part than evolution in the building of cultures. Moreover, useful though it may be to recognize the limitations imposed by basic economic factors, diversity of cultural expression remains the most striking fact of prehistory, as it is of ethnography. The object of prehistory is not only to portray a foreshortened picture of human progress but to comprehend the life and character of all the manifold and historically unique societies of prehistoric times.

Although much research will still need to be directed to the refinement of chronological systems and to the sharper definition of the cultural groupings of antiquity, contemporary prehistorians are now freer than before, particularly in the more completely explored regions, to devote their energies to interpreting archeological data in

8. It has been shown beyond any doubt that in a country like Denmark the earliest Neolithic farmers were intrusive, e.g., by C. J. Becker (1947).

9. The symbiosis of fishing and farming economies which still exists on the northwest coast of Norway can be traced back to the Stone Age; see Clark (1952b, pp. 51 ff. and 62 ff.).

terms of living societies. The classification of material objects may be essential, but only as a preliminary to the realistic appraisal of societies that were once alive. The whole problem is how to make them live, and it is to this that the energies of contemporary prehistorians are increasingly being directed.

Ecologists have shown that, to understand living things, one has to study them in relation to the other elements in the biome and to the soil and climate of the common habitat (Tansley, 1946). Every organism or community of organisms must needs establish relations with all the other elements of the ecosystem to which it belongs and can be fully understood only in its ecological context. This point of view is fully consistent with, and indeed provides a biological basis for, the historical interpretation of cultural development (Clark, 1952b, chap. i). If each culture be viewed as the product of an equation between social inheritance and the various elements in the biome and habitat of the parent-ecosystem, it is hardly to be wondered at in the face of so many variables that the outcome is in every case unique. Ecologically viewed, the diversity of human culture is not an anomaly but almost a necessity of nature.

The ecological approach has been brilliantly exemplified by modern ethnologists, notably by Evans-Pritchard in his study of the Nuer (1940). The situation is much more complicated for prehistorians, though, since no single element in the ecosystem remains constant over any length of time.[10] Yet it is precisely the dynamic character of the relations between human societies and the ecosystems to which they belong that makes them important. During the Old Stone Age, when men

10. These fluctuations, indeed, form the basis of geochronology; see F. E. Zeuner (1950).

were sparsely distributed, were poorly equipped with tools, and lived exclusively by food-gathering, human societies made but a small impression on their environment. As a matter of fact, pollen analysts have succeeded in detecting indications of hunter-fisher groups during postglacial times in parts of northwestern Europe, but these are of a very minor character, involving, for example, a sudden rise and fall in the Chenopodiaceae (Iversen, 1941, p. 39). On the other hand, though the cultural endowment of the men of the Old Stone Age remained stationary or at least progressed very slowly over immense periods of time, the Pleistocene period was marked by great and often repeated fluctuations of climate, vegetation, and fauna (see n. 10). It is becoming ever clearer that understanding of the distribution and migrations of the various Paleolithic cultures revealed by modern prehistoric archeology can be brought about only by correlating more closely cultural with ecological changes over which early man himself exerted no kind of control (e.g., McBurney, 1950).

The spread and intensification of farming, on the other hand, itself precipitated major ecological changes. Recovery of a complete and detailed record of vegetational history for the period in question should reveal not merely the impact of prehistoric farmers but also many vital aspects of their economy. Over large tracts of barbarian Europe, for example, paleo-ecological research has made it possible to trace the spread, first, of a shifting, extensive form of agriculture, accompanied by cutting and burning of forest trees, and then the rise of a more intensive form based on the use of the plow and involving permanent clearance and the creation of fields and meadows. Statistical analysis of the pollen which rained onto ancient bogs and lakes has yielded information about the spread of the new economy—about the transition, if you like, from savagery to barbarism—in temperate Europe, of a kind which could hardly have been obtained by any other means (see Iversen, 1941; Faegri, 1944; Godwin, 1944).

Information about the soils occupied by different groups in prehistoric times has been obtained by systematic plotting of archeological finds on physical base maps. One of the first correlations between culture and soil types was made before the close of the nineteenth century by Penck and Grahmann, who remarked that the Neolithic settlers of central Europe occupied loess formations (see Grahmann, 1898, 1906; Hoops, 1905, pp. 98–99). A great advance was made by Fox in his study of the Cambridge region (1923 and 1948). By plotting a succession of archeological distributions, ranging in age from Neolithic to Anglo-Saxon, on identical maps showing areas of heavier and lighter soils, Fox brought out the dynamic nature of the relationship between economy and land occupation. Changes in the pattern of distribution relative to the geological basis showed that, whereas the earliest farmers of this region confined themselves to the lighter, more easily worked soils, later settlers began to take up the more difficult, but potentially richer, soils needed to support a denser population. A more elaborate survey of a part of northwestern Jutland organized by the National Museum of Denmark between 1942 and 1945 confirmed and amplified Fox's general conclusions and showed beyond any doubt the value of the geographical approach, more especially when taken in conjunction with the results of ecological research (Mathiassen, 1948).

The ecological approach is, of course, by no means limited to the information it can give about such topics as land occupation, forest clearance, and the like. It is vital to the whole question of prehistoric subsistence, whether relating to hunting, agriculture, or herding activities. It is equally essential for a proper assessment of technology, buildings, and means of transportation. There is, indeed, no aspect of economic life that does not gain from being considered from an ecological point of view.

However important the ecological setting may be, it is with the tangible traces of ancient society in the form of objects or structures that the prehistoric archeologist as such is primarily concerned. Prehistorians of the older school paid attention chiefly to the formal, typological characteristics of such material, concentrating on features of value for classification. The modern school is more realistic; it is concerned less with the ideal categories of modern scholars and more with what really happened in prehistoric times. Much more attention is therefore being paid today to the materials from which things were made and to the skills and techniques whereby they were shaped to the needs of society.

To take, first, the case of objects of worked flint and stone, one can point to the very detailed petrological examination of large numbers of ax- and adze-blades carried out in Britain, Germany, and various parts of Scandinavia.[11] By determining the sources of the various stones employed, it has been possible to demonstrate a widespread trade in blades completed up to the stage of polishing. Examination of the actual quarries and places of manufacture has yielded information about the actual extraction and shaping of the material. Particularly outstanding work has been devoted to the technique of the flint-miners of southern England,

11. The most elaborate work to date has been carried out by a subcommittee of the South-Western Group of Museums and Art Galleries in England (see *Proc. Prehist. Soc.,* XVII [1951], 99–158). For a general account see Clark (1952*b*, pp. 245–50).

northern France, and parts of Belgium and Holland (see Clark and Piggott, 1933; Clark, 1952*b*, pp. 174–83). Some prehistorians have sought to throw light on the techniques employed in the production of such objects as hand-axes, laurel-leaf points, blades, and burins, but, successful as such men as Coutier, Knowles (e.g., 1944), and Leakey (e.g., 1934, pp. 47 ff.) have been in producing the forms of prehistoric flint tools, they have not, in fact, done more than demonstrate possible ways in which the various forms could have been produced, and it is noteworthy that different experimenters have arrived at much the same result by different means. The real value of such tests is that they may lead prehistorians to re-examine tools broken in the course of manufacture, as well as the waste products found on prehistoric knapping-places.

So far as bronze objects are concerned, spectrographic as well as chemical analysis has been applied to a wide range of ingots, tools, slags, and natural ores, and the work of men like Desch (1925–38) and Witter (1938) have thrown much light on the source of prehistoric copper. Particularly fine work, also, has been devoted to the actual processes of mining and smelting, notably by Pittioni and Preuschen in the Austrian Alps (Zschocke and Preuschen, 1932; Preuschen and Pittioni, 1937, 1937–38, 1947). As regards the completed products, these were mere lumps of copper-tin alloy of shapes and finish characteristic of the old art-historical school; from a more realistic angle, though, they are the outcome of a highly complex series of processes and activities, which are themselves a main subject matter of prehistory. Perusal of Ándreas Oldeberg's *Metallteknik under Forhistorisk Tid* (1942–43), with its formidable bibliography, should alone be sufficient to demonstrate how much work has already been devoted

to such things as ingots, molds, and metal-smiths' tools, as well as to the examination of visible traces of smithing on finished products. Important studies have also been devoted, for example, to the sources of iron and to the methods of ironworking (Childe, 1944, pp. 13 ff.; Clark, 1952*b*, pp. 199–204; Hatt, 1936; Hauge, 1946; Nielsen, 1920–25, pp. 337–440; Stieren, 1935; Weiershausen, 1939), as well as to the sources and methods of production of a wide range of substances of industrial or decorative value.[12]

Pottery, the third prop of traditional archeology and the basis of a veritable pseudo-science, has also been studied, albeit tentatively, for what it can tell of prehistoric life and activities. Attempts have been made to determine to what extent pottery was made from local clays (e.g., Buttler and Haberey, 1936, pp. 106–9), and a good deal of desultory work has been devoted to the actual building of prehistoric fabrics and to their decoration and firing. Realistic study of hand-made wares has already given us an insight into quite distinct aspects of prehistoric life. Extremely important information about the proportions in which cereal crops were grown among various groups of prehistoric people has been gained from systematic counts of impressions of grains incorporated in the walls of different kinds of pottery and burned out in the firing (Hatt, 1937, pp. 20–22; Jessen and Helbaek, 1944). Again, biochemical investigation of residues in the bases of pots and other containers has already thrown some light on food and drink.[13]

Much more detailed attention than before is being given to the more perishable aspects of material culture,

12. E.g., amber and faïence; see Clark (1952*b*, pp. 261 ff.).

13. As an example one may quote beer residues; see J. Gruss (1931); C. Umbreit (1937, pp. 49 and 54); W. Unverzagt (1930).

which, though doubtless less useful for purposes of classification because less persistent, are now valued for the light they can throw on aspects of daily life not normally preserved. Indeed, excavators are now directing their labors to sites capable of yielding organic materials, in which the archeological record is at present deficient but which nevertheless played so important a part in the life of most prehistoric peoples.[14] Among the perishable aspects of material culture to receive attention from archeologists during recent years, a high place must be given to textiles. Attention may be drawn in particular to the meticulous investigations made by Emil Vogt (1937) on carbonized linen textiles from Neolithic deposits in the Swiss lakes and by Margarethe Hald on woolens from the Bronze Age oak-coffin burials and from the Iron Age bog-finds of Denmark (Broholm and Hald, 1940; Hald, 1950). Important work has also been devoted to such materials as wood, bark, basketry, and hides (Clark, 1952b, pp. 207 ff.). The point need not be labored, though, that, once it is accepted that the aim of archeological research is the understanding of prehistoric life, it follows that the maximum range of material culture must be subjected to the closest scrutiny.

In conclusion, it remains to consider how far the archeological material itself can legitimately be interpreted in terms of extant societies (Clark, 1951). The mere fact that we set out to resuscitate prehistoric societies only emphasizes that they are, in fact, dead. Moreover, they have been dead so long that the traces they leave behind them are vestigial. In seeking to interpret fossils in terms of living organisms, pre-

14. For instance, the English Mesolithic site Star Carr was excavated for the express purpose of recovering elements of the British Maglemosian culture previously missing or poorly represented; see Clark (1949, 1950; also 1952a).

historians find themselves somewhat in the same position as paleontologists. Yet there is a highly important difference. As Professor Garrod stressed (1946, pp. 8 ff.), the archeologist is necessarily concerned with factors distinct from, and altogether more complex than, those which control the organisms and processes of external nature; whereas the natural sciences deal with phenomena which conform to natural laws, archeology is concerned with the results of human activities and with a multitude of unique events conditioned by cultural and even personal factors—in a word, with the phenomena of history. The task of reconstructing the life of prehistoric communities is inherently more difficult and hazardous than deducing the behavior of Pleistocene glaciers from observation of existing glaciers obedient to immutable laws.

To the old evolutionists it seemed self-evident that the observations of modern field ethnographers could be applied directly to the interpretation of prehistoric data. Even as late as 1906 General Pitt-Rivers (Myres, 1906, p. 53) could write that "the existing races, in their respective stages of progression, may be taken as the bona fide representatives of the races of antiquity. . . . They thus afford us living illustrations of the social customs . . . which belong to the ancient races from which they remotely sprang." In this we recognize the failure to appreciate the unique historical character of cultures which vitiated the notion of hypothetical prehistory put forward by mid-Victorian anthropologists. We cannot sufficiently remind ourselves that prehistoric man lived in the remote past and can be studied only by prehistorians.

From this dilemma there is no easy way of escape. What is nevertheless sure is that, as Mr. H. G. Wells (1934, p. 31) once reminded us, we have no hope of interpreting Paleolithic or even Bronze Age society in terms of twentieth-century civilization. If we are compelled to resort to the comparative method, we can at least aim at comparing like, as far as possible, with like. The problem is most acute for the prehistoric peoples most widely separated from ourselves in time, cultural attainment, and even in some cases perhaps by biological endowment. Yet even here we can restrict the field of analogy to societies at a common level of subsistence. Further, it seems legitimate to attach greater significance to analogies drawn from societies existing under ecological conditions which approximate those reconstructed for the prehistoric culture under investigation than those adapted to markedly different environments. Even so, as we know from our knowledge of living peoples, great diversity of cultural expression may be found among communities subject to the same economic limitations and occupying similar, if not identical, environments. This suggests that, although the comparative method is likely to give useful clues to general conditions, it can be a dangerous guide to the particular manifestations of culture with which, after all, the archeologist is mainly concerned. When all is said, the main use of ethnographic comparisons for the interpretation of Old Stone Age cultures is to spur the prehistorian to further effort and provide him with clues for purposive archeological research. By emphasizing the vestigial character of existing archeological data—for instance, the flint implements which constitute almost the sole documents for Lower Paleolithic culture—such comparisons are stimulating archeologists to pay more attention to objects made from the organic materials chiefly used by peoples of simple culture (see Clark, 1952*b*, chap. viii; cf. also above, n. 14). Further, by suggesting a variety of pos-

sible functions for artifacts, they are constantly directing the search for circumstantial clues that might not otherwise even suggest themselves. In other words, as was emphasized in an earlier section of this survey, comparative ethnography cannot in any sense of the term be regarded as a substitute for archeology as a means of discovering the prehistoric past of humanity. On the contrary, its main function is precisely to stimulate and give direction to prehistoric research.

Yet knowledge of existing societies can often be applied much more directly to the interpretation of archeological data where this relates to later periods of prehistory. This applies particularly to cases where historical continuity, both of settlement and of tradition, can be proved, as they sometimes can be, for instance, in the Near East, the Mediterranean, and even in the more accessible parts of temperate Europe.[15] Yet one has to remember that this continuity exists mainly, if not entirely, in the economically most depressed stratum of the population, and it is in the highest degree unlikely that the peasants, herdsmen, or fishers concerned will have remained uninfluenced by usages and ideas from the economically dominant urban stratum. Critically approached, however, folk usage can prove an invaluable guide to prehistorians in interpreting archeological data; and in this connection some of the most valuable sources are to be found in the works of historians and other observers writing at a time when urban influence was far less pervasive than it has since become.[16]

15. A very good example is the continuity of mud-and-reed architecture in southern Mesopotamia, which helped Sir Leonard Woolley (1935) to interpret the traces of prehistoric architecture in Sumer.

16. E.g., Greek and Latin authors such as Homer, Herodotus, Caesar, and Tacitus; later historical writings like the *Historia de gentibus septentrionalibus*, published at Rome in 1555

The direct application of a knowledge of folk usage has been demonstrated again and again in the case of enigmatic artifacts recovered in the course of excavation. One may cite as an example (Casson, 1927, pp. 119–20) the circular clay disks found on Minoan sites in Crete and classified by academic archeologists with a splendid inconsequence as "tables either sacred or otherwise, or else as the lids of pithoi." When Stephanos Xanthoudides came to enter them in the inventory of the Candia Museum, he recognized them from direct personal knowledge as the upper disks of potters' wheels, made intentionally heavy so as to give momentum, like those still used on the island for making pithoi. How truly and with what relevance to archeology did Stanley Casson once write[17] of the East Mediterranean that "the economic condition of peasant and small-town life . . . particularly among the islands, hardly differs in simplicity or complexity from what it was either in the Bronze Age or in Classical Greek times." Folk usage is particularly illuminating in relation to basic subsistence. For instance, on the northern margins of temperate Europe one can still observe societies with mixed economies of the kind which, it may be suspected, were commoner in prehistoric times than archeologists have always recognized.

In areas such as Scandinavia and the Baltic states the peasants have been obliged for the last 3,000–4,000 years or so to supplement the inadequate returns from farming by practicing various forms of hunting and catching; here the same rhythm of plowing, sowing, and harvesting, interspersed with hunting and catching the same land and sea mammals, the same fowls and fishes, has persisted since prehistoric times (Brøgger, 1940). Locally, even as with the islanders of Kihnu and Ruhnu in the Gulf of Riga, who specialize in seal-hunting and exchange fats and skins for the grain, iron, and salt of the Esthonian mainland, we find still before us conditions like those which obtained on the margins of farming culture during Neolithic times (Leinbock, 1932). The methods of hunting, trapping, fishing, and fowling, being closely adapted to the life-habits of the animals concerned, have survived with little alteration since prehistoric times.

Again, many of the basic processes of early farming, for which we have only slight clues from antiquity, may, or could until very recently, be seen in actual operation.[18] The implements of tillage, notably the plow, which reflect in their development so much of the history of agriculture, have survived as a rule only in fragments or in representations often difficult to decipher. As Paul Leser (1931) and his many successors (Clark, 1952b, pp. 100–106; Glob, 1951) have emphasized, the indications from prehistoric cultures can be understood only in relation to the wooden plows still used in backward parts of Europe and of the ancient world.

Houses are another aspect of material culture likely to persist with little alteration until some drastic or prolonged change in economic or social conditions destroys the relations estab-

---

and illustrated with a wealth of the most revealing woodcuts; and the descriptions of observant travelers to outlying parts, such as Martin Martin's *Description of the Western Isles of Scotland* (1704; and Stirling, 1934).

17. Stanley Casson once wrote (1938, p. 466): "The economic condition of peasant and small-town life . . . particularly among the islands, hardly differs in simplicity or complexity from what it was either in the Bronze Age or in Classical Greek times. The average islander and coast-dweller still lives on the same food, and in similar houses to those of his ancestors."

18. This has been illustrated, for example, in the case of seal-hunting in the Baltic area; see Clark (1946).

lished between human needs and potentialities and such factors as climate, topography, and materials for building. Archeological excavation rarely reveals more than the ground plans of prehistoric buildings, which commonly allow a variety of plausible reconstructions. Unless excavators are familiar with analogous structures in actual use, they are liable to overlook the details needed for a right interpretation. It is a matter of history that Franz Oelmann and his pupils (Oelmann, 1927, 1929; Buttler, 1936; Bersu, 1940, esp. pp. 90 ff.) gained their insight into these matters through their study of peasant dwellings, mainly in central Europe. One could illustrate, by reference to almost any aspect of material culture, how much the prehistorian stands to gain by seeking to interpret what he finds in relation to the activities of living societies. The fact remains, though, that prehistoric research is the only way to discover what happened in the prehistoric past. Comparative ethnography can prompt the right questions; only archeology, in conjunction with the various natural sciences on which prehistorians freely draw, can give the right answers.

So far, only a beginning has been made in unraveling the prehistoric past of the Old World, and the way ahead will surely be a long one. Three themes have emerged from our survey. One is the fact of material progress, measurable in growth of population, in increasing knowledge of control over natural forces, and in elaboration of technology, a progress in which many prehistorians have recognized the attainment of such stages as savagery, barbarism, and civilization. The second is the historical uniqueness of each culture, of each communally shared and regulated mode of life, whether observed by ethnologists or partially reconstituted by prehistorians. If the study of man has any purpose, this is surely not to fortify some all-sufficient and soul-destroying dogma, but rather to refresh the human spirit by displaying the manifold diversity of man's achievement in the past as in the present. The third is that prehistory has meaning for us because prehistoric peoples once lived and our life is but a continuation of theirs. As W. G. Collingwood (1944, p. 67) phrased it, "history is concerned not with 'events' but with 'processes.'" The cultural processes which confront us today as students of man had already begun long before history was first written down. As Robert H. Lowie wrote truly (1937, p. 236): "There is only one natural unit for the ethnologist—the culture of all humanity at all periods and in all places."

REFERENCES

BECKER, C. J. 1947. "Mosefundne Lerkar fra Yngre Stenalder." In *Kongelige nordiske oldskriftselskab Aarbøger, 1947*, pp. 285 ff. Copenhagen.

BERSU, G. 1940. "Excavations at Little Woodbury, Wiltshire," *Proceedings of the Prehistoric Society*, VI, 30–111.

BREUIL, H. 1912. "Les Subdivisions du Paléolithique Supérieur et leur signification," *Comptes rendus du Congrès Internationale d'Anthropologie et d'Archéologie Préhistorique, Geneva, 1912*, pp. 165–238. Rev. ed., separately printed, 1937.

BRØGGER, A. W. 1940. "From the Stone Age to the Motor Age," *Antiquity*, XIV, 163–81.

BROHOLM, H. C., and HALD, M. 1940. *Costumes of the Bronze Age in Denmark*. Copenhagen: Nyt Nordisk Forlag.

BUCKLAND, THE REV. WILLIAM. 1823. *Reliquiae diluvianae; or Observations on the Organic Remains Contained in Caves, Fissures, and Diluvial Gravel*, *and on Other Geological Phenomena, Attesting the Action of an Universal Deluge.* London.

BUTTLER, W. 1936. "Pits and Pit-Dwellings in Southeast Europe," *Antiquity,* X, 25–36.

BUTTLER, W., and HABEREY, W. 1936. *Die Bandkeramische Ansiedlung bei Köln-Lindenthal.* Berlin: W. de Gruyter.

CASSON, STANLEY (ed.). 1927. *Essays in Aegean Archaeology: Presented to Sir Arthur Evans.* Oxford: Clarendon Press.

——. 1938. "The Modern Pottery Trade in the Aegean," *Antiquity,* XII, 464–73.

CHILDE, V. G. 1928. *The Most Ancient East.* London: Kegan Paul, Trench, Trubner & Co.

——. 1934. *New Light on the Most Ancient East: The Oriental Prelude to European Prehistory.* London: Kegan Paul, Trench, Trubner & Co.

——. 1935. Presidential address to the Prehistoric Society, *Proceedings of the Prehistoric Society,* Vol. I.

——. 1936. *Man Makes Himself.* London: A. Watts & Co.

——. 1939. *Dawn of European Civilization.* 3d ed. London: Kegan Paul, Trench, Trubner & Co.

——. 1942. *What Happened in History.* New York and Hammondsworth: Pelican Books.

——. 1944. "Archaeological Ages as Technological Stages," *Journal of the Royal Anthropological Institute,* LXXIV, 7–24.

——. 1950. "The Urban Revolution," *Town Planning Review,* XX, No. 1, 3–17.

——. 1951. *Social Evolution.* London: A. Watts & Co.

CLARK, J. G. D. 1931. Review of MENGHIN'S *Weltgeschichte der Steinzeit, Antiquity,* V, 518–21.

——. 1946. "Seal-hunting in the Stone Age of North-western Europe," *Proceedings of the Prehistoric Society,* XII, 12–48.

——. 1949. "A Preliminary Report on Excavations at Star Carr, Seamer, Scarborough, Yorkshire, 1949," *ibid.,* n.s., XV, 52–69.

——. 1950. *Ibid.,* XVI, 109–29.

——. 1951. "Folk-Culture and the Study of European Prehistory." In *Aspects of Archaeology in Britain and Beyond*

(O. G. S. Crawford volume), pp. 49–65. London.

——. 1952a. "A Stone Age Hunters' Camp," *Scientific American,* CLXXXVI, No. 5, 20–25.

——. 1952b. *Prehistoric Europe.* London: Methuen; New York: Philosophical Library.

CLARK, J. G. D., and PIGGOTT, S. 1933. "The Age of the British Flint Mines," *Antiquity,* VII, 166–83.

COLLINGWOOD, W. G. 1944. *An Autobiography.* Hammondsworth, Middlesex: Penguin Books.

DANIEL, G. E. 1943. *The Three Ages: An Essay in Archaeological Method.* Cambridge: At the University Press.

——. 1950. *A Hundred Years of Archaeology.* London: G. Duckworth & Co.

DESCH, C. H. 1925–38. "Reports on the Metallurgical Examination of Specimens for the Sumerian Committee of the British Association," *Reports of the British Association.*

EVANS-PRITCHARD, E. 1940. *The Nuer.* Oxford: Clarendon Press.

FAEGRI, K. 1944. "Studies on the Pleistocene of Western Norway," *III Bømlo, Bergens Museums Arbok 1943,* pp. 79–81. ("Naturvitens-kapelig," rekke No. 8.) Bergen.

FOX, C. 1923 and 1948. *The Archaeology of the Cambridge Region: A Topographical Study of the Bronze Age, Early Iron Age, Roman and Anglo-Saxon Ages with an Introductory Note on the Neolithic Age.* Cambridge: At the University Press.

FRANKFORT, H. 1951. *The Birth of Civilization in the Near East.* London: Williams & Norgate.

GARROD, D. A. E. 1926. *The Upper Palaeolithic Age in Britain.* Oxford: Clarendon Press.

——. 1928. "Nova et vetera: A Plea for a New Method in Palaeolithic Archaeology," *Proceedings of the Prehistoric Society of East Anglia,* V, 260–67.

——. 1938. "The Upper Palaeolithic in the Light of Recent Discovery," *Proceedings of the Prehistoric Society,* IV, 1–26.

——. 1946. *Environment, Tools, and Man.* Cambridge: At the University Press.

GLOB, P. V. 1951. *Ard og plov i Nordens oltid.* Aarhus.

GODWIN, H. 1944. "Age and Origin of the 'Brechland' Heaths of East Anglia," *Nature*, CLIV, 6 ff.

GRAHMANN, R. 1898. *Das Pflanzenleben der schwäbischen Alb*. 1st ed.

———. 1906. *Geographische Zeitschrift*, XII, 305–25.

GRUSS, J. 1931. "Zwei altgermanische Trinkhörner mit Bier- und Metresten," *Prähistorische Zeitschrift*, XXII, 180–91.

HALD, M. 1950. *Olddanske tekstiler*. Copenhagen: Gyldendalske Boghandel, Nordisk Forlag.

HATT, GUDMUND. 1936. "Nye lagttagelser vedrørende oldtidens jernudvinding i jylland," *Kgl. nordiske oldskriftselskab, Aarbøger for nordisk oldkyndighed og historie*, 1. Halvbind, pp. 19–45. Copenhagen.

———. 1937. *Landbrug i Danmarks oldtid*. Copenhagen.

HAUGE, T. D. 1946. *Blesterbruk og Myrjern*. Oslo.

HOOPS, J. 1905. *Waldbäume und Kulturpflanzen im germanischen Altertum*. Strasbourg.

INDREKO, R. 1948. *Die mittlere Steinzeit in Estland*. Stockholm.

IVERSEN, J. 1941. "Land Occupation in Denmark's Stone Age," *Danmarks geologiske undersøgelser*, II. Raekke, No. 66. Copenhagen.

JESSEN, K., and HELBAEK, H. 1944. *Cereals in Great Britain and Ireland in Prehistoric and Early Historic Times*. ("Der kongelig danske videnskabernes selskab, biologiske skrifter," Vol. III, No. 2.) Copenhagen.

KNOWLES, SIR FRANCIS H. S. 1944. *The Manufacture of a Flint Arrowhead by Quartzite Hammerstone*. ("Occasional Papers on Technology," No. 1.) Oxford: Pitt-Rivers Museum.

KOSSINNA, GUSTAF. 1912. *Die deutsche Vorgeschichte eine hervorragend nationale Wissenschaft*. Leipzig: Kabitzsch.

———. 1926. *Ursprung und Verbreitung der Germanen in vor- und frühgeschichtlicher Zeit*. Leipzig: Kabitzsch.

LARTET, E. A. I. H., and CHRISTY, H. 1865–75. *Reliquiae Aquitanicae*. Edited by T. R. JONES. London.

LEAKEY, L. S. B. 1934. *Adam's Ancestors*. London: Methuen.

LEINBOCK, F. 1932. *Die materielle Kultur der Esten*. Tartu: Akadeemiline Kooperatiiv.

LESER, PAUL. 1931. *Entstehung und Verbreitung des Pfluges*. Münster i.W.: Aschendorff.

LOWIE, ROBERT H. 1937. *A History of Ethnological Theory*. New York: Farrar & Rinehart.

LUBBOCK, SIR JOHN. 1865. *Prehistoric Times*. London: Williams & Norgate.

———. (trans.). 1866. *The Primitive Inhabitants of Scandinavia*. London.

McBURNEY, C. B. 1950. "The Geographical Study of the Older Palaeolithic Stages in Europe," *Proceedings of the Prehistoric Society*, XVI, 163–83.

McENERY, J. 1859. *Cavern Researches*. Edited by E. VIVIAN.

MARX, KARL. 1904. Preface to *A Contribution to the Critique of Political Economy*. Chicago: C. H. Kerr Co.

MATHIASSEN, T. 1948. *Studier over Vestjyllands oldtidsbebyggelse*. ("Nationalmuseets skrifter, arkaeologisk-historisk raekke," No. 2.) Copenhagen: Gyldendal.

MENGHIN, OSWALD. 1931. *Weltgeschichte der Steinzeit*. Vienna: A. Schroll & Co.

MORGAN, LEWIS H. 1877. *Ancient Society: or, Researches in the Lines of Human Progress from Savagery through Barbarism to Civilization*. New York: Henry Holt & Co.

MORTILLET, G. DE. 1881. *La Musée préhistorique*. Paris: C. Reinwald.

MYRES, J. L. (ed.). 1906. *The Evolution of Culture and Other Essays*. Oxford: Clarendon Press.

NIELSEN, N. 1920–25. *Mémoires des antiquités du nord*.

NILSSON, SVEN. 1838–43. *Skandinaviens Nordens Urinvånare*. Lund.

OELMANN, F. 1927. *Haus und Hof im Altertum*. Berlin: W. de Gruyter.

———. 1929. "Hausurnen oder Speicherurnen," *Bonner Jahrbücher*, CXXXIV, 1–39.

OLDEBERG, ANDREAS. 1942–43. *Metallteknik under forhistorisk tid*. Lund and Leipzig: Kommissionsverlag O. Harrassowitz.

PREUSCHEN, E., and PITTIONI, R. 1937. "Untersuchungen im Bergbaugebiete

Kelchalpe bei Kitzbühel, Tirol (1931–36)," *Mitteilungen der Prähistorischen Kommission der Akademie der Wissenschaften, in Wien*, III, 1–159.

PREUSCHEN, E., and PITTIONI, R. 1937–38. *Ibid.*

———. 1947. *Ibid.* V, 37–99.

RADCLIFFE-BROWN, A. R. 1922. *Andaman Islanders*. 1st English ed. Cambridge: At the University Press.

SOLLAS, W. J. 1909. "Ancient Hunters and Their Modern Representatives," *Science Progress*, III, 326–53, 500–533, 667–86.

———. 1924. *Ancient Hunters*. 3d ed. 1st ed., 1911. London: Macmillan & Co.

STIEREN, A. 1935. "Vorgeschichtliche Eisenverhüttung in Südwestfalen," *Germania* (Anzeiger der Römisch-germanischen Kommission des deutschen Archäologischen Instituts), XIX, No. 1 (January), 12–20.

TANSLEY, A. G. 1946. *Introduction to Plant Ecology*. London: G. Allen & Unwin.

THOMSEN, C. J. 1836. *Ledetraad til Nordisk oldkyndighed*. Copenhagen.

———. 1838–43. *Skandinaviska Nordens urinvånare*. Copenhagen.

TYLOR, E. B., and LUBBOCK, JOHN. 1865. *Researches into the Early History of Mankind and the Development of Civilization and Prehistoric Times*. London: John Murray.

UMBREIT, C. 1937. *Neue Forschungen zur ostdeutschen Steinzeit und frühen Bronzezeit*. Leipzig: Kabitzsch.

UNVERZAGT, W. 1930. "Römisches Dolium mit Biermaische aus Alzey," *Schumacher Festschrift*, pp. 314–15. Direktion des Römisch-germanischen Zentralmuseums in Mainz, Wilckens.

VOGT, E. 1937. *Geflechte und Gewebe der Steinzeit*. Basel: E. Birkhäuser & Cie.

WEIERSHAUSEN, P. 1939. *Vorgeschichtliche Eisenhütten Deutschlands*. Leipzig: Kabitzsch.

WELLS, H. G. 1934. *The Work, Wealth, and Happiness of Mankind*. London: William Heinemann, Ltd.

WITTER, W. 1938. *Die älteste Erzgewinnung im nordisch-germanischen Lebenskreis*, Vols. I–II. Leipzig: Kabitzsch.

WOOLLEY, SIR LEONARD. 1935. *Development of Sumerian Art*. London: Faber & Faber, Ltd.

WORSAAE, J. J. A. 1849. *The Primeval Antiquities of Denmark*. London: John Henry Parker.

ZEUNER, F. E. 1950. *Dating the Past*. 2d ed. London: Methuen.

ZSCHOCKE, K., and PREUSCHEN, E. 1932. "Das urzeitliche Bergbaugebiet von Mühlbach-Bischofshofen," *Materialien zur Urgeschichte Österreichs*, No. 6. Wien.

Archeological Theories and Interpretation: New World

By GORDON R. WILLEY

INTRODUCTORY

THIS PAPER is a consideration of some of the principal archeological theories now current in the interpretation of the prehistoric scene in the New World. These theories are intimately involved with both the methods and the results of American archeology. For, as problems are conceived in theory, the attack upon problems is similarly conceived, and methods are selected or forged for this purpose. Likewise, as theory sets up the problem frame of reference, results are inevitably conditioned. For these reasons, in examining Americanist archeological theories, we will turn, first, to methodological structure to see how theory is interwoven with this structure; and, second, we will analyze some of the resultant constructs of American data, relating these to theory. In so doing, there will be overlap with colleagues who are treating, respectively, method and result; nevertheless, theory is the central theme of this presentation.

METHODOLOGICAL STRUCTURE

Archeology is concerned with history both in the broader sense of context and process, as these may be traced through the past, and in the narrower sense of space and time systematization of data. Taylor (1948) has made the useful distinction between the former,

which he refers to as "historiography," and the latter, which he has termed "chronicle." These are, in effect, the two major objectives of modern archeology: (1) processual understanding and (2) skeletal chronology and distribution. Although this concept of the duality of these objectives (history as a chronicle versus history as process) is valid from an analytical standpoint, operationally the archeologist must have both objectives in mind. Even the barest sort of chronological-distributional study of artifact forms is necessarily linked with implicit theory involving cultural process. Similarly, antiquarian or purely "phenomenological" interest in artifacts is not entirely bereft of its functional or processual side, for the mere fact that the object is recognized as something made by man is tied to assumptions about past human conduct.

The objectives of archeology, defined in this way, are approached by the study and manipulation of three basic factors: form, space, and time. The forms are the phenomena themselves, the prehistoric creations or manufactures. These may be dealt with in their individual uniqueness or in their similarity, the latter being the typological approach to the data of form. Space and time are the dimensions of the inquiry. Either or both may be co-ordinated with form to give the historical skeleton or chronicle of the particular datum or data under investigation. Forms may, by themselves, be relevant to function or process (as implied by shape and other inherent qualities), or, taken together with space and time co-ordinates, they may suggest cultural processes such as diffusion or independent development.

The basic factors of form, space, and time are not dealt with in the abstract but within either or both of two systems of contextual reference: the natural and the cultural. The natural context refers to environmental conditions as these may be revealed in landscape and climate or in the past geological records of these conditions. Such contexts have a bearing both on functional interpretation (cultural-environmental adjustments or failures to adjust) and space-time systematics (geological dating, tree-ring dating, etc.). The cultural context derives from our acceptance of artifactual remains as products of man's culture. It is the context that allows for the historical tracing of prehistoric-to-ethnohistoric developments and for the functional interpretation of dead remains in the light of the living or documented situation. It has as its deepest basis the commonalty of all mankind as creators and bearers of culture, but it may also be viewed in limited frames of reference for specific problems.

Archeological studies or approaches to the prehistoric data follow along two fundamental lines. These are the lines set by the major objectives: history (as limited chronicle) and process. As noted, it is virtually impossible to follow one line to the complete exclusion of the other, but there are definite tendencies of emphasis. For example, Americanist studies over the last thirty years have been largely preoccupied with historical rather than processual objectives, and archeological problems have been framed in accordance with this emphasis. But, whatever the tendency,

it is quite clear that there are in both the historical and the processual approaches differing and advancing levels of interpretative complexity. These stages of complexity in interpretation grow out of the varying concordances and correlations of the basic factors of form, space, and time and the contextual systems of natural and cultural reference. Utilization of the basic factors along complementary historical and processual lines may be charted as shown in Table 1.

On the first level of complexity under the historical category, we have two operations: (1) the identification of specific forms or descriptive typology and (2) the identification of cultural assemblages through descriptive typology and association. Paralleling this, in the processual category, we have: (1) functional or use identification of specific forms and (2) functional interpretation of cultural assemblages of forms or features. On this first level the factors of time and space do not enter directly into the interpretations either in the historical or in the processual categories. The initial historical operation—the identification of specific forms and their classification under a purely descriptive typology—could be, in itself, a consideration of phenomena for the sake of phenomena alone. This is rarely the case, and "phenomenology" is not generally regarded as archeology. Usually, the initial identifying or typological step is geared to a space-time problem of the second level, and this problem motivation is reflected in the organization of the particular typology. Archeological typology in the United States has reflected this trend in recent years, especially as it concerns ceramics. There has been a growing conviction that pottery types as descriptive categories are valueless unless the categories or types also serve as exponents of spatial and temporal differentiation in the study of cultural materials (see Ford, 1949, p.

40; Drucker, 1943, p. 35; Krieger, 1944; Willey, 1949, p. 5). This view seems justifiable as long as the problem is essentially one of space and time correlations. It is, of course, conceivable that a quite different typological breakdown of the same material could be set up for the study of problems of use or function of pottery. In either case, however, the problems pitched on the second and third levels of interpretative complexity are the determinants for the typological operation of the first level, and such typology is thereby drawn into line with historical or processual objectives at its instigation.

neither space nor time correlates are overtly expressed in this system of archeological culture classification; yet the concept of the assemblage is implicitly grounded in the historical validity of the artifact-feature complex as a *unit.* Such a unity, by the very nature of its internal associations, bespeaks spatial-temporal correlates. The *com-*

TABLE 1

PROBLEM OBJECTIVES	LEVELS OF INTERPRETATIVE COMPLEXITY		
	First	Second	Third
Historical (Descriptive identification and space-time arrangements of data)	1. Identification of specific forms or descriptive typology 2. Identification of cultural assemblages through descriptive typology	1. Culture continuity and change with reference to specific areas 2. Culture continuity and change with reference to the specific chronology of an archeological site or zone	1. Culture continuity and change in both space and time dimensions
Processual (Functional or use identification and interpretations of data)	1. Functional or use interpretation of specific forms 2. Functional interpretation of cultural assemblages of forms or features	1. Functional interpretations of cultural forms or assemblages with reference to specific areas 2. Functional interpretation of cultural forms or assemblages with reference to the specific chronology of an ·archeological site or zone	1. Functional interpretation of cultural forms or assemblages with reference to both area and chronology (usually on a wide scale)

The identification of cultural assemblages through descriptive typology has been conceived of as a step in archeological analysis and synthesis without reference to space or time factors. This has been the *modus operandi* of the American Midwestern Taxonomic System (McKern, 1939). It is true that

ponent, the classificatory unit of the Midwestern system, is an assemblage with a geographical locus (the site) and has sometimes been defined as a time level (period) represented in the human occupation of a particular geographic site. The *focus,* the first order on the ascending taxonomic scale in the Midwestern system, is an abstraction based upon the close typological similarity of two or more *components.* If typological similarity is any indicator of cultural relatedness (and this is surely axiomatic to archeology), then such relatedness carries with it implications of a common or similar history for the *focus*. The same reasoning applies as foci are classified under *aspects,* as aspects are grouped together into *phases,* and as phases are merged as *patterns.* The degree of trait similarity lessens as one works upward in the Midwestern taxonomic hierarchy, and presumably the closeness of historical ties also lessens; yet historical systematization is still inherent in the classification. That this should be so is not, in itself, a drawback. Perhaps the most serious flaw in the Midwestern system is its historicogenetic rigidity. Certain lines and degrees of relationship are laid down from one classificatory order or level to the next, with the result that the extremely complex interrelationships of cultural descent and diffusion are obscured by the arbitrariness of the system. Eventually, the end-product may become as nearly ahistorical as the original classificatory operations of the system, although in a quite different and unintended way.

As there is covert historical theory in the assemblage concept and in the Midwestern Taxonomic System, so there is comparable hidden functional implication. The unity of the assemblage, if historical unity can be assumed, must lead to the conclusion that we are dealing with the remains of an integrated cultural complex in the case of the *component.* The tool types, weapon forms, and settlement traces reflect ancient patterns of behavior that had been welded, with greater or lesser firmness, into a functioning whole. If the data are sufficient, an interpretation of this kind (i.e., hunting community, sedentary village agriculturists, etc.) is certainly feasible on this level. Such functional interpretation is, of course, possible because of the natural and cultural contextual backgrounds which are available even on this simplest level of interpretative complexity. Site ecology provides one such context, while ethnological or modern analogies to artifacts and architectural features afford another.

The second and third levels of interpretative complexity are, in their historical objectives, concerned with the spatial and temporal arrangement of cultural forms. As stated, this has been the primary usage of artifact typology in American studies over the last three decades. On the second level we have two operations: area distribution studies of forms and chronological distribution studies of forms. These may be carried on independently of each other. Holmes's (1903) great work on the pottery of the eastern United States is an example of the former. In this study, ceramic types were plotted geographically over a wide area, and a number of regional correlations were established. These Holmes designated as "provinces." They were, in effect, areas, established solely upon the trait of pottery, without reference to time depth. The theoretical basis behind Holmes's reconstruction is that of the culture area (Wissler, 1926; Kroeber, 1931), a concept widely used in American ethnology. Each area was assumed to have a generative center which produced the distinctively regional types. At the margins of each area there were blendings with the types radiating from another center or centers. These blendings were assumed to result from diffusions, counterdiffusions, and mergers of ideas or actual products originating in the centers. The culture-area concept is still considered useful by American archeologists and is widely employed, although with reservations. The obvious weakness derives from the attempt to infer the time dimension from the geographic-distributional picture alone. This is inherent in the idea of the generative center and its outlying margins with a time flow from center to margins. It has been demonstrated that neither geographical center nor point of cultural intensity or elaboration can be assumed to be the originative center of a type. In other words, the age-area construct is by no means infallible. For a space-time reconstruction other methods than the geographic-distribution study are necessary.

These methods are the principal ones by which culture continuity and change through time may be demonstrated: stratigraphy and seriation. Prior to 1912, stratigraphic studies on the American scene adhered rather closely to the geologic principles of stratigraphy. Sharp distinctions in physical strata were correlated with changes in cultural types. Sometimes these strata involved natural soil deposition; or in other cases, such as that of Uhle's (1903) stratigraphy at Pachacamac in Peru, artifact types were correlated with major architectural and structural levels in a site. Between 1912 and 1924, Nelson (1916), Kroeber (1918), Spier (1919), and Kidder (1924) introduced a significant modification. This was the principle of the correlation of artifact change with relative depth. The method was applicable to refuse deposits which had grown by occupational accretion. Marked physical stratification of deposits was not necessary. The technique consisted of removing detritus and artifacts from arbitrary depth levels. In studying artifact change by levels, percentage fluctuations of types were noted from level to level, so that rising or declining percentage frequencies of types were correlated with time. Deriving in large part from the mechanical nature of the operation, "continuous stratigraphy" of this kind had important theoretical repercussions on the nature of culture continuity and change. With the continuous depositional record of a site occupation before his eyes, the archeologist could not help being impressed with the evidence for culture dynamics. A number of concepts were formulated to account

for the vertical record in the earth. Types were seen in the refuse history at their inception, were observed approaching and attaining a maximum frequency, and were then traced upward to their "death" or disappearance. One type was seen to "replace" another in this time story. If the stylistic division between an earlier and a later type was sharp, it was hypothesized that new or foreign elements were introduced into the life of the site at a particular point in its history. On the other hand, if the intrinsic qualities of two types showed strong similarity and if their frequency histories allowed it, gradual evolutionary change from one type into another was postulated. These theories, born in the techniques of stratigraphic chronological measurement, served as the basis of functional interpretations with reference to the history of the site. Extended to studies of culture change and continuity over a wide area, the third level of interpretative complexity, they form much of the theoretical underpinning of complex functional interpretation.

J. A. Ford (1949, pp. 44–57; 1951, pp. 91–100) has been one of the chief exponents of time-change and continuity studies in American archeology in recent years. Ford's interest has been concentrated largely upon the dynamics of cultural forms (pottery types) and upon the development of theory in connection with this. His graphic presentations of ceramic stratigraphy emphasize the quality of continuity. Individual types are seen as describing unimodal curves upon vertical scale graphs. These recapitulate "life-histories" of types, their origins, climaxes, and eventual disappearances. That types do behave in this fashion, although with varying rates of speed, seems amply demonstrated by stratigraphic evidences from innumerable archeological sites. That there is also a tendency upon the part of the archeologist occasionally to "force" certain types to conform to an expected unimodal curve seems probable. There are two complicating factors here. One is primarily mechanical. Refuse deposition at any site, or at any one location upon a site, may not give a continuous history of site occupation and artifact usage. In some instances these time gaps may be minor and irrelevant; in others they may be long and crucial. Occupation, desertion, and reoccupation may give an extremely fragmentary picture and one that makes a puzzling frequency graph unless the graph curve is "smoothed" to harmonize with what is conceived of as the normal occurrence pattern. Ford is cognizant of this difficulty but has relied upon large random sampling in site excavations to obviate it, feeling that the hiatus-reoccupation situation is the rare one rather than the rule.

The other complicating factor rises out of the hypothesis that typological change or variability in a site need not always be correlated with chronological change. Instead, it may have its origins in functional differentiation of artifact types. Brainerd (1951, p. 307) has suggested that the irregularities in some of his graphs of Maya ceramics result from this; and he further postulates that graphic regularity may be fairly safely assumed to be an expression of time change, while marked irregularity may result from the sudden introduction of sacred or ceremonial wares into what had heretofore been kitchen dumps. Neither of these complicating factors is sufficient to invalidate the method of plotting continuous stratigraphy or of interpreting cultural continuity, gradual replacement, and evolutionary change from its results. They do, however, indicate that the method is not infallible and that it cannot be consistently employed without careful examination of refuse deposition and

cautious trial and retrial of typological formulations.

Seriation, as it has been developed in American archeology, refers to a "horizontal stratigraphy" of artifact types and their associations rather than to seriation by a priori stylistic or evolutionistic principles. Kroeber (1918) practiced it in its simplest form in the Zuñi region of the southwestern United States when he gathered and pocketed pottery-sherd collections from the surfaces of a number of ruins. These collections showed typological overlap, so that some sites were, for example, represented by types A and B, others by types B and C, and still others by types C and D. Assuming each collection to be a valid historical assemblage, it was evident that a seriation running from type A through type D was present. If, then, time direction could be introduced into the series by relating type D to the historic period at Zuñi, the seriation was transformed into a chronology by which the various sites from which the collections were made could be dated.

Ford has elaborated upon this principle in seriational studies in the Virú Valley of Peru (Ford, 1949) and in the Mississippi Valley (Phillips, Ford, and Griffin, 1951, pp. 213–36). By computing percentage frequencies of pottery types from site surface collections, he has arranged these frequencies and collections into a series. The seriation, however, does not follow along simple lines of typological overlap but is constructed, instead, to reproduce the unimodal curves of pottery-type life-histories comparable to those plotted from vertical refuse stratification. As is seen, this builds directly upon the theories of growth, climax, and decline for cultural forms. In general, it appears to be substantiated, in that the life-history curves of the seriated types tend to duplicate those of the vertical stratigraphy. There are, however, more complications and more possibilities for error with this method than with that of vertical continuous stratigraphy. In the first place, the surface collection is less likely to be a valid historical assemblage than is the subsurface deposit. Opportunities for mixture are, obviously, much greater. Secondly, it has not yet been satisfactorily determined that the surface pottery collection of any site is fully representative of all the types once used at that site. Deep and compact refuse sites may show no types characteristic of their earlier strata on the surface. This does not necessarily confuse the seriation, as such a surface collection would be accurately seriated in accordance with the later strata of occupation at the site. Reliance upon the date for the chronological placement of other features at the site would, though, be questionable. A third complication is the possibility that the surface collections of some sites do show a representative sample of several periods or span a time range three or four times as great as the surface collections of other sites. As all collections are treated as single assemblages, this relativity in the time compression involved is almost certain to produce some peculiar distortions. As with the stratigraphic method, Ford and other practitioners of percentile seriation are aware of these complications. Again, their reliance upon useful results is based upon a large sample and a feeling that the difficulties will tend to cancel out. The method undoubtedly has validity and is supported by other lines of evidence in many instances. My own feeling is that it can be considered as an instrument for gross sorting but not for precision analysis.

While Ford has been essentially interested in the perfection of space-time measurements, W. W. Taylor, Jr., has sounded a counternote in his long critique, "A Study of Archaeology" (1948).

Taylor's interests are with descriptive integration and process rather than with spatial-temporal systematics. His "conjunctive approach," which is the bringing to bear of as many kinds of evidence as practical considerations permit in site excavation and analysis, is most directly concerned with what I have classed as functional interpretation of the second level of complexity. Taylor has made clear that he does not eschew historic chronicle or more sweeping historical and processual reconstructions as legitimate goals of archeology. His attack is, rather, that space-time studies of a limited or broad-scale nature will proceed more soundly and effectively if we are better informed as to the mechanics of cultural process and that an understanding of process must begin with the fullest possible recovery of individual site information. Inasmuch as archeological site excavation is permanently destructive, Taylor's argument is hard to refute. The archeologist most assuredly has an obligation to his data, and it is incumbent upon him to make the fullest possible record. Yet of what should this record consist? It is impossible to gather all pertinent information because data are pertinent only in reference to a problem. This leads us to the question as to whether there are not some problems that can be framed only with reference to landmarks wider than the individual site. If there are—and there seem to be—do we not need the broader historical contexts in which to place them? And is it not essential for this historical orientation to push ahead of the more intensive analyses, particularly those aimed at functional understanding of a particular prehistoric community? This has, in any event, been the course of development in American archeology. Whether it is the purest accident or whether there is inherent logic in what has happened remains a matter of speculation and debate. There is, in my mind, no doubt but that Taylor's critique has had a salutary influence on American archeology. The old problem incentive of chronology and distributions of "cultures" in terms of a few marker "fossils" (usually potsherds) was not sufficient to attract archeologists who were also anthropologists. Taylor's strictures helped crystallize this feeling of discontent.

From this outline of archeological methodology, with particular reference to the Americas, it can be seen that theories of culture change and continuity are fundamental to archeological studies of either a predominantly historical or predominantly functional orientation. At the outset, it must be recognized that certain assumptions concerning culture change and continuity underlie most systematic typology. It has been stated that typology with archeological objectives reflects problem motivations and that these motivations are usually the need for spatial-temporal measuring instruments. This is grounded in the assumption that culture change is reflected in material manufactures and that this change proceeds in both temporal and spatial dimensions. There have been two ways of looking at this. One envisages culture change as a continuous stream, to be segmented into types as this best suits the archeologist's purposes (Ford, 1949). The other view tends to conceive of types as once existent realities in the prehistoric culture under examination (Rouse, 1939). For the former position, the establishment of types is a purely arbitrary procedure, entirely imposed upon the prehistoric phenomena by the classifier. The second opinion sees the typological task more as the recognition of existent entities. The two outlooks are not fully antagonistic, and both seem to arrive at similar results. The concept of the arbitrary segmentation of the stream of culture

change is predisposed to overlook factors of acceleration or deceleration in the speed of change and to minimize the sort of sudden change that would, presumably, result from the impact of influences lying outside the particular culture continuum. There are potential correctives here, such as relative depths of culture refuse or correlations with absolute dating factors, that would serve to check false assumptions about the rate of culture change or the relative time spans that the archeologist might assign to the life-histories of certain types. Yet these are often lacking or poorly controlled, and the impulse to "overregularize," as a result of this typological conception and the cultural theory behind it, is a definite danger. The weaknesses of the concept of the type as a prehistoric reality are of an opposite nature. Certain styles or patterns in the manufacture of artifacts are, perhaps, overemphasized by the archeologist. While others, which impress his consciousness to a lesser degree, may be slighted as "transitional," with the vague implications that they are, somehow, of minor importance in the tracing-out of culture history. It is not an "either-or" choice. Both conceptions have merit. The course of ancient cultures can be plotted as a dynamic flow, and, at the same time, it can be kept in mind that prehistoric artisans were aiming at modalities which to them seemed fixed and which, undoubtedly, did not change at a set rate of speed.

To summarize further, the treatment of archeological assemblages in any historicogenetic system has a basis in theories of continuity and change. Even if space and time factors are not formally observed, principles of continuity and change are expressed in the degrees of trait likeness or unlikeness which are the mechanics for establishing the genetic lines binding the assemblages together. In the overtly historical systems, such as those in vogue in the southwestern United States (Gladwin, 1934; Colton, 1939), lines of relationship and descent are expressed in these terms.

The processes by which, or through which, cultural continuity and change are maintained or accomplished have not received study and reflective thought commensurate with the way these concepts have been invoked by American archeologists. "Evolution" and "diffusion" have been tag names employed, but these are broad categories rather than specific explanations, and there have been few clear theoretical formulations along these lines. For example, the historicogenetic schemes of culture, or culture assemblage, classification in the southwestern United States have a dendritic structure, with "basic" or "root" cultures of the earlier periods diversifying into the various "stems" and "branches" of the later time periods. Obviously, the archeologists who have constructed these classificatory schemes have, as their realities, the cultural assemblages which are represented near the top of the "tree." The monogenic "root" or "trunk" is lost in dim antiquity. But the implications are that the processes of cultural development, or evolution, have been those of monogenesis with "basic" or "mother"-cultures, presumably simple in form and content, diversifying into complex, specialized offspring. Apparently, there is a rather simplistic evolutionary or genetic analogy at work here. To be sure, there is some universal basis for expressing the development of human culture in this fashion. At least the relatively simple, relatively homogeneous, material evidences of the Lower Paleolithic of the Old World give way to growing complexity and diversification. But the question might be asked whether this is in any way recapitulated in Arizona and New Mexico by sedentary pottery-makers during the first millennium of the Christian Era. Such a course of development is a possibility; nevertheless, in this case it appears that evolutionary theory has been very naïvely applied. Monogenesis of southwestern cultures is a postulate to be tested, not an axiomatic explanation.

Diffusionist theory in American archeology has probably received more analysis, or analytical speculation, than has evolutionist theory. It is at the core of most archeological interpretation. Trade, migration, gradual borrowing, and idea or stimulus diffusion have all been advanced in specific instances, both with and without supporting evidence. As with evolutionary hypotheses, theories of diffusion may be legitimately brought forward to explain various patternings in space-time distributions. Adequate support for either class of theory will, however, be more effectively marshaled when greater functional understanding of the data in question is achieved.

SOME PREVAILING AMERICANIST RECONSTRUCTIONS

AMERICAN CULTURAL ORIGINS

If a single dominant motif for Americanist reconstructions of New World aboriginal cultures had to be selected, I think we could safely say that this motif has been "isolationism." This statement is not necessarily critical. The prevailing theories concerning the origins of the early lithic and the later Neolithic cultures of the Americas may be the correct ones. At present, these theories have not been satisfactorily proved, but opposing theory is equally undemonstrated. It is of interest, however, that American opinion is predominantly on the side of the "separateness" of American beginnings and developments.

On the question of the first peopling of the American continents there has been little dispute on the score that these migrants were Asiatics who entered from eastern Siberia. There has, however, been considerable debate as to when they arrived and as to their stage of culture upon arrival. Up to about 1920, prevalent theory, championed by Holmes and Hrdlička, sponsored a relatively late entry for man into the Americas of no more than 2000–3000 B.C. Such a migration was thought to have taken place on a very late Paleolithic or Mesolithic threshold. Following the discovery of Folsom, Yuma, and related lithic finds in the western plains of North America, the earlier theories were drastically revised to allow some 10,000–25,000 years for man's occupancy of the Americas. Such a revision suggested a Paleolithic correlation with the Old World, but this correlation was largely one of time period rather than the diffusion of a specific industry or tool forms. American chronology rested upon geological and faunal associations rather than typology. It was, of course, generally assumed that the old lithic assemblages of the high plains were of Old World derivation; but, for the most part, interest centered in them as isolated entities of the American setting, and there was little systematic effort to link them to specific Asiatic or European complexes.

In spite of the geological-paleontological datings of 10,000-year-old artifacts in the Americas (and this has been recently supported by carbon 14 dates which are almost that old), there is some rather serious contrary evidence which questions the American chronological estimates and tends to minimize the isolation of the North American high plains and early lithic assemblages. Ironically, this evidence is of a strictly archeological rather than a natural science nature. It has been pointed out by both Ward and Movius (personal communications, 1950–51) that the Folsom and Yuma flint types (with the

exception of the fluted point) are found in northeastern Siberia in Neolithic rather than Paleolithic contexts. This eastern Siberian Neolithic follows the period of loess deposition in northern Asia. By 2500 B.C. cord-marked pottery was a part of the Neolithic complex in this part of the world, but chipped stonework of a definite Neolithic kind antedated the pottery. Just how far back these eastern Siberian Neolithic points and scrapers can be dated is the crux of the argument, but both Ward and Movius are of the opinion that 4000 B.C. would be the outside limit. If this is true, there is a glaring chronological discrepancy between these Siberian complexes and the early American lithic. There are three possible interpretations of this dilemma: (1) the American dating of Folsom-Yuma is too early; (2) the Siberian dating of the pre-ceramic Neolithic is too late; or (3) the American Folsom-Yuma complexes were independently invented and bear no historical relationship to the Siberian Neolithic complexes. I believe that we can rule the third explanation out as an extreme "isolationist" point of view. This leaves us with the other two explanations, and these two interpretations of cultural beginnings in the New World remain to be tested. I conclude by pointing out only that the interpretation preferred by most American archeologists relies essentially upon evidence of a nonarcheological nature and that artifact typology and artifact assemblages of northeastern Siberia, that part of the Old World closest to their problem, have not been given full consideration in this theoretical reconstruction.

Although the problem of remote origins is of great importance, perhaps the question of American Neolithic beginnings has been of more dramatic interest. In any event, it has been one of the most bitterly fought—and rightly so. For upon this question hangs much of anthropological thought bearing upon the processes and courses of human development. The empires of the Inca and of Mexico astounded not only the conquistadors of the sixteenth century but also social philosophers ever since. Could such feats of duplication take place guided only by the parallel structure of men's minds and bodies, or was the cultural germ transplanted across the oceans?

Most American prehistorians have been disposed to believe the former: independent development of the New World high civilizations over and above an Upper Paleolithic–Mesolithic base. A number of European scholars have taken issue with this "isolationist" view. Their counterarguments have usually taken the form of trait comparisons between Peru-Mexico, on the one hand, and the Near East–Asia, on the other. In my judgment a demonstration of specific high-level intellectual achievements held in common by both the Old and the New World has never been satisfactorily made. By this I mean that such systems as Middle American writing, enumeration, and astronomy are not duplicated or closely approximated in the Old World. Nor are there duplications or approximations of complex art styles, presumably reflective of religious and intellectual systems, between the two hemispheres. These lacks do not, of course, disprove contact, but they allow for certain eliminations. The absence of complex art styles or complex intellectual attainments makes it almost certain that trans-Pacific diffusions, if they did take place, were not carried out by the mechanisms of organized conquest or religious proselytization. In fact, it is unlikely that such diffusions in any way involved hieratic elements of either Old or New World societies.

It is below this hieratic level of complexity that you find the majority of Old and New World parallels. The most intriguing of these are technological elements or complexes, such as the *cire perdue* method of casting metals, resist-process painting, and bark cloth, to say nothing of agriculture, irrigation, and pottery-making. I believe that it is here, with element complexes of this kind, that the case for contact between the Old and the New World Neolithic will eventually stand or fall. If so, students of this problem should focus their attention upon the formative periods of Middle American and Andean civilizations, for it is at the beginning of and during these formative periods that such element complexes first appear on the American scene. If present American dating estimates are correct, this takes us back a millennium or a millennium and a half before the Christian Era.

Another category of traits, crucial to the rise of the American Neolithic, are the food plants upon which the agriculture was based. A tracing-out of the history of these may be the single most decisive factor in the Asiatic-American diffusion problem. Considerable work has been done along this line, but, as yet, there is strong disagreement among authorities.

There is also a final category of traits, many of which are often adduced in argument, that consists of myths or certain features of primitive social organization. Many of these seem to be nearly world wide. It is unlikely that they offer a very fruitful line of investigation for this particular problem. It may be that some do represent relatively late diffusions, but others could well hark back to the time of the first peopling of the American continents. Significantly, they are not essential parts of a sedentary agriculture-based civilization and thus do not necessarily mark an introduction of possibly foreign ideas instrumental in producing such a civilization.

PREHISTORIC-HISTORIC CONTINUITIES

A full appreciation of the time dimension has been archeology's greatest contribution to American anthropological studies. To European colleagues this may seem a statement of the obvious, but it must be remembered that American anthropology and ethnology of the early twentieth century was not historically minded in the sense of time-depth perspective. This was particularly true of North America, where the absence of native written histories and the fast-disappearing Indian populations centered attention upon the flat-dimensional "present" or late historic period.

One of the most outstanding examples of this was in the Great Plains of the United States. Ethnologists had offered speculative "historical reconstructions" of the Plains Indian past, based upon nineteenth-century records and some knowledge of early European colonial events. The significance of the advent of the horse and its impact upon the native cultures had been correctly appraised in part, but the quality of native Plains culture before that event was largely unknown. The nomadic, or seminomadic, horsemen of the later periods led ethnologists to believe that the earlier inhabitants of the region had also been nomads and that, in consequence, their culture had been a rather simple one. Archeology (Strong, 1935; Wedel, 1936) destroyed this hypothesis by showing clearly that the old Plains life had been intensively horticultural and sedentary. Through a series of successive periods prehistoric cultures were linked to proto-historic, historic, and modern descendants. This type of study, sometimes called the "direct historical approach," has a theoretical basis in cultural continuity. Starting with known, documented habitation sites, certain cultural assemblages were identified and associated with particular tribal groups. Earlier archeological assemblages were then sought which were not too sharply divergent from the known historic ones, and the procedure was followed backward in time.

In tracing prehistoric-historic continuities in this fashion, a number of useful working assumptions are at hand, although all of these must be used with some reservations. Continuity of a culture within the same area is a reasonable expectation, but there is always the possibility of regional shifts through time. The Plains studies showed both a certain amount of regional stability as well as some shifting. Cultural continuity within the same area is reasonably good evidence for linguistic and ethnic continuity, although it is by no means infallible. Thus Pawnee and Lower Loup archeological assemblages are identified as the remains of Pawnee tribesmen, but the culturally similar Upper Republican assemblages, more remote in time, can be associated with the linguistic and biological ancestors of the Pawnee only on the basis of reasonable probability and not certainty.

The establishment of prehistoric-to-historic continuity is of utmost importance as a springboard for further archeological interpretation, and, along with general chronological and distributional studies, it is one of the primary historical problems for the American archeologist. In general, the most successful continuities of this sort have been determined for those regions where there has been relatively little ethnic shifting in aboriginal or proto-historic times and where there still remain native populations with predominantly native cultures. The Eskimo area of the north, the pueblos of the southwestern United States, certain regions of Mexico, the Maya country of Central America, and the Quechua and Aymara areas of the Andes are prime examples. In all of them a certain amount of cultural continuity with the archeological past has been maintained, and this can be correlated with ethnic and linguistic continuities. A general, but not absolute, assumption which Americanists have followed in these reconstructions is that gradual and unbroken continuity of culture also implies continuity of population and that a sudden change or break in continuity is a reasonable indicator of population change.

TRADITIONS AND CO-TRADITIONS

An appreciation of cultural continuities through time has led to the formalization of the tradition. The tradition, as defined, may apply to limited facets of culture, such as the tradition of white-on-red painting of ceramics in Andean South America (Willey, 1945), or to more inclusive and complex cultural patternings. In essence, it is the recognition of a specific line, or lines, of continuity through time, a formal acceptance of the rugged persistence of cultural ideas. These traditions are the means by which prehistoric-to-historic continuities are strung together and by which the archeologist traces culture growth in general.

The tradition cannot be changeless within its continuity, but its internal modifications must lie, or be defined, within certain bounds. Otherwise, it is useless as a device for plotting or demonstrating continuity. An example of a tradition of extremely limited or monotonous inner variability is the cord-marked or fabric-marked pottery of eastern North America. Some years ago American archeologists attempted to visualize the cord-marked wares as basically definitive of an area or a certain chronological period. Subsequent research failed to demonstrate clear-cut regional or temporal stability. In certain periods cord-marked wares were found from southern Canada to Florida and from the Atlantic to the Plains; on other chronological levels the distribution was more restricted. Similarly, in some parts of the eastern United States cord-marking appeared as the earliest-known surface treatment for pottery; but in other sections it was found to persist until the founding of the European colonies. Minor typological distinctions within the cord- and fabric-marked ware were found to have specific, limited spatial and temporal utility; but, as a whole, cord- and fabric-marking was best conceived of as a tradition which had expanded or contracted geographically as it had persisted chronologically with relatively slight internal modifications. In contrast to this is the white-on-red pottery tradition of Peru, where a number of quite elaborate and radically different pottery styles are linked together over several hundred years of prehistory by their common possession of a red-and-white color scheme.

A number of traditions in American archeological data come to mind as examples. Among these was the deep-seated bias of the peoples of the Hohokam region of the southwestern United States area for red-on-buff pottery as opposed to a black-on-white ceramic heritage for the northern Southwest. The broad-lined incised decoration which binds Venezuelan and West Indian pottery styles together is another such tradition, while the shell-tempering of Mississippian wares is still another kind of tradition persistence in the ceramic craft.

The examples I have used have been simple ones and confined to pottery because it is with the pottery medium that American archeologists exercise the greatest control of the time factor. Obviously, however, the concept can apply to other media and other ranges of complexity. Maya calendrical lore would be an example of a highly complex, tightly unified tradition which lasted well over 1,000 years and in which can be recognized stylistic and technical period subdivisions.

The theory underlying the tradition concept is well expressed in the term itself. For "tradition" implies deep-set and channeled activity or patterned ways in which the vitality of a culture expresses itself in strong preference to other possible ways. The conditions surrounding this rigidity of expression which results in the long-time traditional expression are an interesting problem for future investigation. In dealing with such things as pottery decoration, the archeologist is undoubtedly investigating what is relatively trivial in past human events. The failure of polychrome painting to take hold on the northern coast of Peru in the face of the white-on-red tradition, despite several attempts to introduce it, may eventually be revealed as nothing more mysterious than an absence of suitable mineral pigments in that part of the country. On the other hand, the unraveling of seemingly insignificant threads in an attempt to factor out causality may lead us to a greater understanding of "tradition set" and "tradition persistence" in institutions which loom larger in human affairs.

It has been pointed out that cultural traditions do not always adhere firmly to given geographical areas, and this is often true. There do, however, appear to be general regional-traditional correlations. The examination of such correlations has led to a related concept, that of the area co-tradition (Bennett, 1948). The co-tradition, as the name suggests, is based upon the persistence of a number of combined and closely interrelated traditions within a specified area. It is not necessarily the history of any specified ethnic group but the history of cultural continuity within area confines. It affords the archeologist a working device in place of the culture area, for the latter lacked the time dimension and was unsuited to problems of prehistory. The area co-tradition is, in effect, the culture area with time depth. Within its spatial and temporal limits it must have several basic consistencies. These are the warp and weft which hold it together in spite of subregional and period-to-period differences. The Peruvian or central Andean co-tradition is a good example. In this highland and coastal area all cultural phases partake of certain minimum traits and trait-complexes—Andean-type agriculture, certain pottery and weaving traditions, and architectural types. These and others are the common denominators of the Peruvian co-tradition and so define it. The Peruvian co-tradition is limited in time from the advent of maize agriculture (about 1000 B.C.) to the collapse of the Inca empire in A.D. 1532.

Comparable area co-traditions have been formulated elsewhere. One of the most recent applications of the concept has been in the southwestern United States (Martin and Rinaldo, 1951). Somewhat earlier, Kirchhoff (1943) defined Mesoamerica as a culture area, and, although he did not use the term "co-tradition," it is evident that his thinking includes time-depth perspective. In the far north an Arctic or Eskimoan tradition is surely indicated. Here Larsen and Rainey have defined a dual traditional emphasis within the larger framework, suggesting a land-hunting versus a sea-mammal–hunting economic dichotomy as this can be applied to the various Eskimo periods or phases. In eastern North America it seems most useful for the present, at least, to conceive of three co-traditions. These are by no means new constructs, for they follow along the old taxonomic divisions of Archaic, Woodland, and Mississippian.

DIFFUSIONS

In recent years systematic American archeology has tended to be confined to distinct natural and cultural regions. These have been areas in which, from the outset, it has been more or less clear that certain traditions, or co-traditions, were dominant. Each such region has served as a sort of problem framework, and the archeologist has had a tendency to "feel at home" within the bounds of his own particular region but to show no great desire to go out of it. As a result, there has been somewhat less interest in problems of interareal diffusion than there had been in an earlier era. To date, these continental and hemisphere-wide problems of prehistoric contact remain largely unsolved. Various hypotheses have been formulated, but most of these have yet to be substantiated.

One of the most brilliant and far-reaching of these theories concerning American-wide diffusions was propounded by Spinden (1917) over 30 years ago. The nexus of this idea was that the seed of American Neolithic life—agriculture, pottery-making, and other sedentary arts—were invented as an integral complex and spread from a single Middle American center to both the northern and the southern continents. This is the New World "Archaic hypothesis." Subsequent investigations have shown Spinden to be incorrect in his selection of certain Mexican assemblages as being fully representative of this earliest "Archaic." The relationships of valley of Mexico "Archaic" with early southern Mexican and Central American cultures are bewilderingly complex, and Spinden's formulation, taken *in toto*, does not resolve all these complexities. Nevertheless, the idea in the abstract still merits attention. Recent concepts of a "New World Formative" cultural level (Steward, 1948; Willey, 1948; Strong, 1948) are restatements of Spinden's original theme. The chief difference is that the center of origin of this "Formative" is not so confidently designated as it was for Spinden's "Archaic." Most archeologists who are now writing on this

problem see a possibility of a center, or centers, of origin lying anywhere between central Mexico and southern Peru. Yet, aside from this, the "Formative" concept stands upon the same theoretical ground as did the "Archaic" hypothesis. Although the diffusion processes of neither have been fully set forth by their proponents, both theories imply the spread of a functionally related complex: maize horticulture, a sedentary way of life, developed craft specialization, including ceramics, and fundamental socioreligious beliefs tied up with an agricultural economy. Spinden defined specific ceramic (figurine) styles as being associated with this diffusion, and it has been the evidence for these that has failed to appear. The promulgators of the "Formative" admit the lack of a common style for their postulated early level and point, rather, to what seems to be a common ceramic heritage of monochrome wares, certain vessel forms, and decorative techniques.

This difference in the evidence for diffusion—style versus technical elements—leads us to the consideration of another concept: the horizon style. The horizon style was first defined by Kroeber (1944, p. 108) in connection with Peruvian studies. It is the phenomenon of a widespread art style which is registered in a number of local sequences. In accordance with the appearance of the same style from one locality to another, the various sequences are synchronized. The significance of the idea is in the phenomenon of the style as a unique entity. If this uniqueness is accepted, then contemporaneousness or near-contemporaneousness for the several local regional manifestations of the style can be assumed and the "horizon" quality inferred. Establishment of the uniqueness of the style depends upon three factors: its technical quality, its content or representation, and its configuration. The last, the configurational aspect of style, is the crucial factor.

Two specimens might reveal fine-line carving on stone (technical) and a jaguar motif (content), but the delineation of the jaguar (configuration) might be quite different in the two cases. In such an event the archeologist would be dealing with two distinct styles.

This problem of stylistic uniqueness has a bearing on the "Archaic" hypothesis as well as upon most other questions of wide-scale American diffusions. If stylistic identity or close similarity can be established, it can be reasonably assumed that the separate occurrences mark an approximately contemporaneous horizon. For the American "Archaic" or "Formative" there does not appear to be any such style horizon; hence contemporaneousness of the various New World "Formative" cultures is questionable.

The lack of a diffused style is undoubtedly indicative of significant qualities in the processes of diffusion. Or, conversely, stylistic diffusion must presuppose certain conditions which are not necessary for other types of diffusion. The archeologist is not yet in a position to be able to say what these conditions may have been. Speculatively, it seems likely that the diffusion of a complex art style, such as the Chavín or the Maya, implies the diffusion of a social, religious, or political system. The transference of the ideas involved in the duplication of such a style suggests intimate contact and interchange between the localities and regions concerned. In this regard it is probably worthy of note that most of the great American prehistoric styles, such as the classic Maya, the Chavín, the Olmec, or the Mochica, are confined to a single co-traditional area or a fraction thereof. Reliable occurrences outside the recognized geographical limits of these styles are found in such totally different contexts that there has been little difficulty in recognizing them as trade items. An exception is the Inca style, which spread into both north and south Andean areas. Here, of course, we have documentary evidence that such a diffusion was backed by imperialistic expansion.

As with the problem of widespread "Archaic" or "Formative" relationships, the specific problems of interareal relationships in the Americas involve diffusion of a nonstylistic kind. The southwestern United States was almost certainly dependent upon the cultures of Mexico, but there are no horizon style linkages and only scant evidences of trade. The contacts here were almost certainly those which permitted the passage of technological ideas (ceramics, irrigation, casting of metals) but did not encourage the transfer of social, religious, or political idea systems and their associated symbols (art styles). A somewhat similar situation obtains between the southeastern United States and Mexico. Here the two areas are separated by several hundred miles of desolate wastelands, but in the Southeast a rich agricultural civilization flourished. Perhaps more than in the Southwest, the Southeast reflects the religious and sociopolitical systems of Middle America. The temple mound–plaza ceremonial centers imply this. There is also a southeastern cult art which suggests parallels to the south; however, this so-called "Southern Cult" (Waring and Holder, 1945) of the Southeast has its distinct style (Krieger, 1945), and, if it was Middle American-inspired, it has undergone serious local transformation.

The same condition prevails between the southwestern and southeastern United States. These areas, separated by the staked plains of Texas and other semidesert regions, probably maintained intermittent contact. There are possibilities that one race of maize was passed between the two and that certain pottery vessel form ideas were exchanged. Stylistically, the pottery assemblages in question are radically distinct, and the contact must have been on the level of a stimulus or idea diffusion (Kroeber, 1940).

In areas to the south of Middle America the story of relationships is still most feebly comprehended. The "Formative" levels of western Honduras bear a general technical similarity to those of Middle America, and there is even one horizon marker, Usulatan ware, which provides a secure linkage to the north. Usulatan is, however, such a simple decorative type that it is more comparable to a technique than to a stylistic configuration. It undoubtedly has some value as a time marker but is difficult to interpret as an indicator of complex diffusion. In Nicaragua and Costa Rica certain decorative elements in Nicoya pottery may be traced back to later Mexican periods and offer evidence of stylistic diffusion. To the south of these countries there is little in the way of stylistic linkage to Middle America. The whole of the lower Central American, Colombian, and Ecuadorian area is chopped into a great number of small stylistic regions. Their cross-relations, one to the other, have not yet been worked out, but it seems unlikely that any major stylistic horizon markers will emerge. The relationships from region to region, again, are those of similar technologies and techniques, including such features as pottery vessel forms, which have a general traditional but not a stylistic bond.

The Peruvian co-tradition area is well cemented by horizon styles. Two of these, the Incaic and the earlier Tiahuanacan, extend southward into Argentina and Chile, where they have horizontal significance. For the earlier periods, however, the Peruvian styles are contained within the co-traditional area; and the rise of farming and pottery-making in the south, if it can be dated as coeval with the Peruvian Formative, is stylistically apart from anything such as Chavín.

Eastward into lowland South America it is possible that there are horizon style phenomena, although these have not yet been plotted in space or time. Nordenskiöld's (1913) excavations in the Mojos of Bolivia revealed ceramics in his later periods which bear a certain style resemblance to lower Amazonian painted types. Also, within the Venezuelan–West Indian broad-lined incised tradition there seem to be stylistic divisions which may mark wide geographical time periods. As yet, between Andes and lowland there is scant stylistic cross-referencing. Vague connections exist between the earlier period ceramics of the Bolivian Mojos and the Bolivian altiplano (Bennett, 1936). East from the Peruvian and Ecuadorian Andes, Tello has claimed Chavín similarities, but these claims pass far beyond recognized limits of stylistic comparisons. Northward, in the Colombian inter-Andean valleys are the most likely prospects for Andean-Orinocan-Amazonian stylistic diffusions. Such styles as the urn burials of the Mosquito region (Bennett, 1946) have lowland parallels.

To sum up, the tracing of specific art styles from one major area, or area co-tradition, to another has not proved possible in the Americas. The almost unquestionable basic relationships that once existed between Middle and South America or Middle America and the areas of the southwestern and southeastern United States will have to be plotted by other types of diffusionist evidence. Stimulus diffusion, the spread of technologies and of specific techniques and technical treatments, will probably be the basis for such studies. Admittedly, this is more tenuous evidence than the comparisons of styles or the identification of specific trade items; but interareal historical reconstruction will not be advanced without continued application to these problems.

DEVELOPMENTAL LEVELS

In recent years the old idea of developmental parallelism has been seriously re-examined by American archeologists and culture historians. This hypothesis has been applied to central Andean archeological data (Bennett, 1948; Larco Hoyle, 1948; Strong, 1948; Willey, 1948; Bennett and Bird, 1949). Middle American data (Armillas, 1948), interarea New World comparisons (Steward, 1947; Willey, 1950; Strong, 1951), and even world-wide comparative evaluations (Steward, 1949). Interpretations have varied somewhat, both in the selections and alignments of data and in the emphasis given to deductions of causality. All, however, have dealt principally with the rise and growth of sedentary agricultural communities, with the subsequent technological developments within these, and with the religious and sociopolitical developments known or implied from the data.

In both Central Andean and Middle American areas these developmental formulations are based upon an initial formational or "Formative" stage, in which the sedentary arts were promulgated and developed toward specialization. This initial formational stage was succeeded by a stage of relative cultural crystallization and rigor in which diverse regional specializations expressed themselves in well-defined styles. As such, this second stage was a flowering of the technical and inventive potential of the first stage and has been called the "Classic" or "Florescent." The third major stage is more difficult to define than the others, as the common-denominator qualities are more difficult to abstract. There is also an interesting shift in criteria for this final stage. Whereas the criteria for the first two recapitulate technological and artistic trends, the third stage is not essentially characterized by these factors. In some regions there is an apparent aesthetic decline, although this is a subjective impression difficult to measure. Certainly, there is no technical falling-off, and in some places, such as the central Andes, there are continued technological advances. The single unifying characteristic of the final stage is, rather, the evidence for widespread social, political and religious disturbances. Classic styles disappear, great classic sites of presumed politicoreligious importance are abandoned, some being destroyed, and large-scale migrations of people take place. It is, of course, possible that the archeologist has been overinfluenced by a knowledge of history or legendary history for this final stage. In both Peru and Mexico it seems to have been encompassed in the terminal 500 years antedating the Spanish, and various native accounts from both areas tell of wars of conquest and general turmoil. These accounts are, to a large extent, supported by archeological evidences of military establishments, fortified strongholds, and the like, all of which seem to be more common to the later Peruvian and Mexican periods. Terms such as "Expansionist" or "Militaristic" have, accordingly, been applied to the third major stage.

There has been a strong tendency to equate these developmental stages not only functionally but chronologically. This has been evidenced both within a co-traditional area, such as the central Andes, and in extending the stages from one major co-traditional area to another. As a tentative device, this sort of developmental chronological chart (see Willey, 1948, 1950; Bennett and Bird, 1949) is permissible where absolute dating factors give no clues as to synchronization. It is not, however, likely that developmental stage lines will ultimately be demonstrated to be chronological horizon lines. Within the central Andean area, for example, it is most unlikely that the qualities or traits which mark the advent of the Classic or Expansionist stages will be found to have occurred simultaneously throughout all coastal and highland regions. The same is true for Middle America, and that there should have been synchronization, or even near-synchronization, between Middle America and Peru in the attainment of these levels or stages is even more dubious. This kind of synchronization, even though it has been projected on a most schematic and trial basis, has given a sort of spurious uniformity to the developmental levels in American high cultures and has aroused skepticism toward the whole construct.

The problem of chronological equations as it pertains to the theory of developmental levels leads us directly back to the matter of diffusion. Are the stage parallelisms which some of us have seen as existent between Middle and South America the result of diffusion or developmental uniformity? I do not believe that the question can be posed this simply, for it seems evident that both forces have been operative. Within either of these co-traditional areas it appears quite certain that diffusion from region to region has taken place but that such diffusions have by no means been uniform outpourings which have spread in evenly distributed waves over the whole area. For example, in Peru, the Mochica ceramic style embraces five or six north-coast valleys. In contrast, the idea of constructing large pyramids of adobe is found throughout the north coast, is well established on the central coast, and at least makes an appearance on the northern boundary of the south coast. On the basis of present knowledge, these two complexes—Mochica art and adobe pyramid mound-building —probably diffused at about the same time; yet their patterns of dispersal are

quite different. Certain forces which permitted, or encouraged, the spread of one inhibited the other. The nature of these forces leads us into an interpretative functional analysis of prehistoric Peruvian societies and their environments, obviously a complex problem. With reference to the developmental and diffusionist question, the point here is that the potentialities of cultural development in any given region are not only conditioned by but also condition diffusion. These potentialities are a complex of natural, social, and cultural endowments. The understanding of their interaction is the ambitious goal of the functional or processual problems which the archeologist sets for himself. But even at our present stage of understanding it appears quite evident that developmental potentialities and the diffusion of ideas are closely interrelated. Certainly, metallurgical techniques, as known in the Andes and in Middle America, have a related history. Their acceptance, rejection, emphasis, or de-emphasis from region to region or major area to area depended upon the varying complex potentialities of peoples, cultures, and natural environment. In a vastly more intricate manner the development, spread, and success or failure of such institutions as kingship or empire were dependent upon what happened when the receiving base was fertilized or stimulated by the transient idea.

As we have discussed above, there is a far-flung distribution of certain elements and technologies which are formational to the American Neolithic-type cultures. The similarity of these elements and technologies and their geographic occurrences make it most likely that they have a common heritage. These diffused elements provided the base for the American agricultural civilizations and, in so doing, set certain wide limits for later cultural growth. These cultural foci of this

"Formative" stage must have had opened before them a number of possible courses for development. The directions which these foci took in their growth were selected from the potentialities which each possessed and from the ideas which each generated and transmitted to others.

FUNCTIONAL RECONSTRUCTIONS

It was specifically indicated in our discussion of methodology that the functional objectives of archeology cannot be divorced from the historical ones. Further, in our review and commentary on reconstructions in American prehistory it has been implicit that a greater functional appreciation of the phenomena involved would lead to clearer understanding of what are generally considered historical relationships. It is thus difficult to select certain archeological interpretations and label them as "functional" or "processual," as opposed to diffusionist or developmental reconstructions. In reviewing such selections the close integration of chronicle and process must be borne in mind.

In making functional interpretations of archeological data there are several lines of evidence or means of approach. Some of these are listed in the methodological Table 1.

There is, first, the use interpretation of an artifact or feature. In some instances this can be done by way of general analogy. A pointed flint with an obvious haft is interpreted as a projectile. Or, in other cases, a metate and mano are explained as corn-grinding instruments by analogy with modern use within certain ethnic areas. Sometimes historic documentation gives the lead, as with the disklike stones in southeastern archeology and early accounts of their use in the "chunkee" game. The limitations of the approach are clear. Many archeological objects or features will probably never be properly explained from a functional standpoint. Beyond the obvious and beyond the specific ethnic or ethnohistoric analogy, there is only the sheerest speculation.

The archeological assemblage can be functionally explained in a manner similar to that applied to the artifact. With the assemblage, of course, the archeologist begins to bridge over into the complexities of the space and time factors. The dimensions of space and time can be correlated with and used to help explain changes in artifacts, features, and assemblages.

A third approach utilizes quantitative factors. The numbers of archeological remains, such as the numbers and sizes of sites, can be used to estimate populations and the disposition of populations. With such an approach a control of the chronological factor is a necessity.

A fourth line of evidence is the correlation of space and time distributions of remains with natural environmental types. In the American field there are numerous examples of this. Rouse's study of culture units centering upon West Indian sea passages rather than islands comes to mind. Such a correlation was strong testimony for sea transport and a marine rather than a land orientation (Rouse, 1951).

A fifth approach combines two or more of those listed and presents a rising complexity of interrelated interpretations. It is on this basis that most archeological interpretation with a strong functional bias has been carried out. Examples of such interpretations are actually more numerous than American archeologists realize. The majority of them are imbedded in "standard" (i.e., historically oriented) monographs on archeology. Others are parts of general cultural-historical reconstructions. Some few have been presented primarily as attempts at functional analysis.

A brilliant example of functional ex-

planation of archeological data is offered from the North American Plains.
Here the archeologist operated with
artifact types and artifact assemblages
from pre- and post-Columbian times.
With the chronological dimension properly in control, it was obvious that certain profound changes had taken place
in Plains Indian culture between the
pre- and the post-1540 date line. These
changes were seen in material culture,
but the implications in changes in house
and community types as well as artifacts reflected important sociopolitical
changes. Added to this was a fairly
rich documentation from the late historic period which filled out the picture
of Indian life in this area in the late
nineteenth century. From these known
referents—artifact and assemblage types,
chronology, and ethnic documentation
—the archeologists and ethnologists
were able to explain much of what took
place in culture change as the result of
the impact of significant technological
innovations brought by the Europeans
(i.e., horses and guns) (see Wissler,
1914; Strong, 1933, 1940).

In a similar way, but with less specific ethnic documentation, archeologists in the eastern United States have
been able to outline events surrounding the introduction of intensive agriculture into this area. To begin with,
there is some documentation for the
nature of eastern culture in its final
post-Columbian periods. This documentation indicates a rich agricultural
ceremonialism in certain southern regions and also shows this ceremonialism to have been associated with a
mound-plaza, community-center complex. It is further known that the mound-
plaza complex is an integral part of
the ceremonial, social, and political life
of the agricultural civilizations of Middle America. The similarity of this
mound-plaza complex between eastern
North America and Middle America
suggests a historical relationship, and

this relationship is further supported
by other archeological evidence linking
these two major areas. Because of the
great chronological depth and elaboration of the mound-plaza complex in
Middle American cultures, it is assumed that this is the parent-area for
the idea, at least as far as the eastern
United States is concerned. With these
facts and hypotheses in mind, it is
noted that the mound-plaza complex is
not known throughout the full range of
eastern chronology but appears for the
first time somewhere in middle-to-late
sequence. With this appearance there
is a number of significant changes in
eastern society and culture as revealed
by archeology. There is a greater utilization of riverine terrace country, there
are more and much larger archeological
sites, and, finally, there are more frequent finds of maize remains. These
the archeologist relates to a specific
new and important change in food
economy. All these link back with the
assumed correlation of the mound-
plaza complex with intensive agriculture. Corollary evidence for such a
change is seen in a decrease in hunting
fetishes (animal teeth, claws, and representations of these) with the rise of
the mound-plaza complex. Parallel
changes in eastern culture are reflected
in a different burial pattern, new pottery styles, and new house types. The
functional interrelationship of these
with intensive horticulture, if such existed, is obscure; but, like the mound-
plaza complex, they may be part of a
historical association. In this particular
example the archeologist has first established, by ethnic documentation and
comparisons to another area, the firm
association of an archeological feature
(the mound-plaza) with an agricultural way of life. Then, by placing the
introduction of this feature in the
chronological sequence of eastern native cultures, he has been able to support his association by correlative evi-

dence of a functional type (i.e., increased population, large centers, etc.).

One of the most interesting Americanist problems in functional interpretation has revolved around prehistoric
urbanization. Middle American archeologists have posed the question as to
what are the factors leading to or promoting urbanization. In this investigation urbanization has been defined as
the permanent concentration of large
nonfood-producing populations. A review of Middle American data seems
to indicate, at the present state of
knowledge, that such true cities or urban areas were best known from the
late prehistoric periods and from upland country. The valley of Mexico is
offered as a classic example, and Te-
nochtitlan, the Aztec capital, was most
surely such an urbanized city. As opposed to this, the earlier Middle American periods and the lowlands seemingly lack evidence of a comparable
urbanization. The functional explanations offered for this dichotomy and
the important exceptions to it are that
large concentrations of nonfood-pro-
ducers are possible only with intensive
food production by others and with
relatively rapid food transport. The valley of Mexico apparently met both
these conditions. *Chinampa*, or floating-
garden farming, is fabulously productive, and water transportation in the
lakes in which the Chinampas were located afforded rapid dispersal of produce. To substantiate this case, the archeologists favoring this interpretation
point to the multiroomed, closely
packed, compartmented dwelling compounds at Teotihuacan as being indicative of early (*ca.* A.D. 500) beginnings
of urbanism in the favorable Mexican
uplands. The lowland picture seems to
be quite different. In the Maya and Olmec areas impressive ceremonial sites
were constructed, but mass dwelling
concentrations were, presumably, prohibited by the limitations of tropical

forest agriculture and transportation
difficulties. Urbanism in the lowlands,
in the framework of this general interpretation, is looked upon as a very late
and politically forced phenomenon.
Mayapan is the type-site for such a development in the Maya region. Here a
walled, urban concentration is viewed
as the result of Mexican influence and
conquest, together with a period of
local troubles and fighting, leading to
more compact living than the environmental potentialities could sustain.
Late-period urbanization on the lowland Veracruz coast is thought to have
been made possible at Cempoala by
artificial irrigation.

This fascinating hypothesis has not
met with general acceptance. Perhaps
greatest of all difficulties is the lack of
adequate settlement study throughout
most of Middle America, particularly
in the lowlands. Incoming data may require drastic revisions in, or demand
the rejection of, these theories; but it is
most significant, I think, that the problem of urbanization and its causes can
be raised in New World archeology.
That such a problem has been framed
as a research theme marks a great advance in Americanist studies.

A somewhat different approach from
those cited is one which I attempted
with Andean data (Willey, 1948).
Here the problem lead was in the detail of the data. The particular phenomena in question were the horizon styles,
the Peruvian-wide distributions of certain art forms at certain times, and the
complete absence of such horizon styles
at other times. What were the causative factors behind these diffusions or
absences of diffusions? In my attempt
to answer this question I projected the
various horizon styles against the backgrounds of what could be reconstructed
of Peruvian society at the respective
time periods involved. These backgrounds could be developed only in
the most general terms, such as "war-

like," "absence of warfare," "small populations," "expanding populations," etc. Nevertheless, these backgrounds, taken in conjunction with the content of the styles themselves, afforded a basis for a number of reasonable conjectures. Most of these conclusions may never go beyond the conjectural stage because of the limitations of the data. For example, Chavín art is depicted as a horizon style which spread in an era of relative peace. Such a condition immediately sets bounds for the mechanisms by which the style could have spread. For identifying this period as a peaceful one, we have only the absences of fortifications or fortified sites, of abundant weapons, of warlike representations in art, and a knowledge that

population groups were relatively small and isolated from one another. This is not absolute proof of nonmilitaristic society, but, in the absence of evidence to the contrary and until such evidence is forthcoming, I think it justifiable to reconstruct on such a foundation.

The examples I have used are only a few from American archeology, selected largely because they are the ones which I know best. I can only mention the work that has been done on the reconstruction of southwestern social organization from a combination of archeological and ethnological data (Strong, 1927; Steward, 1937; and Martin and Rinaldo, 1950), on Arctic economy (Larsen and Rainey, 1948), and numerous other examples dotted over the American continents.

REFERENCES

ARMILLAS, PEDRO. 1948. "A Sequence of Cultural Development in Meso-America." In BENNETT, WENDELL C. (ed.), *A Reappraisal of Peruvian Archaeology*, pp. 105–11. ("Memoirs of the Society for American Archaeology," Vol. XIII, No. 4.)

BENNETT, WENDELL C. 1936. *Excavations in Bolivia.* ("Anthropological Papers of the American Museum of Natural History," Vol. XXXV, Part IV.)

———. 1946. "The Archaeology of Colombia." In STEWARD, JULIAN (ed.), *Handbook of South American Indians*, II, 823–50. (Bureau of American Ethnology Bull. 143.) Washington, D.C.

———. 1948. "The Peruvian Co-tradition." In BENNETT, WENDELL C. (ed.), *A Reappraisal of Peruvian Archaeology*, pp. 1–7. ("Memoirs of the Society for American Archaeology," Vol. XIII, No. 4.)

BENNETT, W. C., and BIRD, JUNIUS B. 1949. *Andean Culture History.* ("American Museum of Natural History Handbook Series," No. 15.)

BRAINERD, G. W. 1951. "The Place of Chronological Ordering in Archaeological Analysis," *American Antiquity*, XVI, 301–13.

COLTON, H. S. 1939. *Prehistoric Culture Units and Their Relationships in Northern Arizona.* (Museum of Northern Arizona Bull. 17.)

DRUCKER, P. 1943. *Ceramic Sequences at Tres Zapotes, Veracruz, Mexico.* (Bureau of American Ethnology Bull. 140.) Washington, D.C.

FORD, J. A. 1949. *Cultural Dating of Prehistoric Sites in Virú Valley, Peru.* ("Anthropological Papers of the American Museum of Natural History," Vol. XLIII, Part I.)

———. 1951. *Greenhouse: A Troyville–Coles Creek Period Site in Avoyelles Parish, Louisiana.* ("Anthropological Papers of the American Museum of Natural History," Vol. XLIV, Part I.)

GLADWIN, W. and H. S. 1934. *A Method for the Designation of Cultures and Their Variations.* ("Medallion Papers," No. 15.) Globe, Ariz.

HOLMES, W. H. 1903. *Aboriginal Pottery of the Eastern United States.* (20th Annual Report of the Bureau of American Ethnology.) Washington, D.C.

KIDDER, A. V. 1924. *An Introduction to Southwestern Archaeology.* Andover, Mass.: R. S. Peabody Foundation.

KIRCHHOFF, P. 1943. "Mesoamerica," *Acta Americana*, I, No. 1, 92 ff.

KRIEGER, A. D. 1944. "The Typological Concept," *American Antiquity*, IX, 271–88.

———. 1945. "An Inquiry into Supposed Mexican Influences on a Prehistoric 'Cult' in the Southern United States," *American Anthropology*, XLVII, 483–515.

KROEBER, A. L. 1918. *Zuñi Potsherds.* ("Anthropological Papers of the American Museum of Natural History," Vol. XVIII, Part IV.)

———. 1931. "The Culture Area and Age Area Concepts of Clark Wissler." In RICE, S. (ed.), *Methods in Social Science.* Chicago.

———. 1940. "Stimulus Diffusion," *American Anthropology*, XLII, 1–20.

———. 1944. *Peruvian Archaeology in 1942.* ("Viking Fund Publications in Anthropology," No. 4.)

LARCO HOYLE, RAFAEL. 1948. *Cronología arqueológica del norte del Peru.* Buenos Aires.

LARSEN, HELGE, and RAINEY, F. 1948. *Ipiutak and the Arctic Whale Hunting Culture.* ("Anthropological Papers of the American Museum of Natural History," Vol. XLII.)

McKERN, W. C. 1939. "The Midwestern Taxonomic Method as an Aid to Archaeological Culture Study," *American Antiquity*, IV, 301–13.

MARTIN, P. S., and RINALDO, J. B. 1950. *Sites of the Reserve Phase, Pine Lawn Valley, Western New Mexico.* ("Fieldiana: Anthropology," Vol. XXXVIII, No. 3.)

———. 1951. "The Southwestern Co-tradition," *Southwestern Journal of Anthropology*, VII, 215–29.

NELSON, N. C. 1916. "Chronology of the Tano Ruins, New Mexico," *American Anthropology*, XVIII, 159–80.

NORDENSKIÖLD, E. VON. 1913. "Urnengräber und Mounds in bolivianischen Flachlände," *Baessler Archiv*, III, 205–55.

PHILLIPS, P.; FORD, J. A.; and GRIFFIN, J. B. 1951. *Archaeological Survey in the Lower Mississippi Alluvial Valley, 1940–47.* ("Papers of the Peabody Museum, Harvard University," Vol. XXV.)

ROUSE, IRVING. 1939. *Prehistory in Haiti: A Study in Method.* ("Yale University Publications in Anthropology," No. 21.)

———. 1951. "Areas and Periods of Culture in the Greater Antilles," *Southwestern Journal of Anthropology*, VII, 248–65.

SPIER, L. 1919. *An Outline for a Chronology of Zuñi Ruins.* ("Anthropological Papers of the American Museum of Natural History," Vol. XVIII, Part III.)

SPINDEN, H. J. 1917. "The Origin and Distribution of Agriculture in America," *Proceedings of the XIXth International Congress of Americanists, Washington, 1915*, pp. 269–76.

STEWARD, J. H. 1937. "Ecological Aspects of Southwestern Society," *Anthropos*, XXXII, 87–104.

———. 1947. "American Culture History in the Light of South America," *Southwestern Journal of Anthropology*, III, 85–107.

———. 1948. "A Functional-Developmental Classification of American High Cultures," *American Antiquity*, XIII, No. 4, 103–4.

———. 1949. "Cultural Causality and Law: A Trial Formulation of the Development of Early Civilizations," *American Anthropology*, LI, 1–27.

STRONG, W. D. 1927. "An Analysis of Southwestern Society," *American Anthropology*, XXIX, 1 ff.

———. 1933. "Plains Culture Area in the Light of Archaeology," *ibid.*, XXXV, 271–87.

———. 1935. *An Introduction to Nebraska Archaeology.* ("Smithsonian Miscellaneous Collections," Vol. XCIII, No. 10.)

———. 1940. *From History to Prehistory in the Northern Great Plains*, pp. 353–94. ("Smithsonian Miscellaneous Collections," Vol. C.)

———. 1948. "Cultural Epochs and Refuse Heap Stratigraphy in Peruvian Archaeology." In BENNETT, WENDELL C. (ed.), *A Reappraisal of Peruvian Archaeology*, pp. 93–102. ("Memoirs of the Society for American Archaeology," Vol. XIII, Part II.)

———. 1951. "Cultural Resemblances in Nuclear America: Parallelism or Diffusion?" In TAX, SOL (ed.), *Selected Papers of the XXIXth International Con-*

gress of Americanists, pp. 271–79. Chicago: University of Chicago Press.

TAYLOR, W. W., JR. 1948. "A Study of Archaeology," *American Anthropologist*, L, No. 3, 223–56.

UHLE, M. 1903. *Pachacamac*. Philadelphia.

WARING, A. J., JR., and HOLDER, P. 1945. "A Prehistoric Ceremonial Complex in the Southeastern United States," *American Anthropology*, XLVII, 1–34.

WEDEL, W. R. 1936. *An Introduction to Pawnee Archaeology*. (Bureau of American Ethnology Bull. 112.) Washington, D.C.

WILLEY, GORDON R. 1945. "Horizon Styles and Pottery Traditions in Peruvian Archaeology," *American Antiquity*, XI, 49–56.

——. 1948. "Functional Analysis of 'Horizon Styles' in Peruvian Archaeology," *ibid.*, XIII, No. 4, 8–15.

——. 1949. *Archaeology of the Florida Gulf Coast*. ("Smithsonian Miscellaneous Collections," Vol. CXIII.)

——. 1950. "Growth Trends in New World Cultures." In *For the Dean: Anniversary Volume for Byron Cummings*. Santa Fe: Southwestern Monuments Assoc.

WISSLER, C. 1914. "Influence of the Horse in the Development of Plains Culture," *American Anthropology*, XVI, 1–25.

——. 1926. *The Relation of Nature to Man in Aboriginal America*. New York and London: Oxford University Press.

Historical Approach in Anthropology

By WM. DUNCAN STRONG

SINCE I believe that not only ethnological methodology (Lesser, 1933) but also all the other subdisciplines at the moment grouped within the discipline of North American anthropology are fundamentally based "on a metaphysic of history," I find the present title almost as all-inclusive as would be the "Biological Approach in Zoölogy." What follows is, therefore, obviously selective and put forward solely as a partial basis for consideration at the present international conference, where many others with wider knowledge, as well as differing national and cultural backgrounds, may extend, enrich, or correct the particular conceptual approach presented here.

It is here set forward that both the biological and the sociocultural aspects of anthropology are fundamentally conditioned by history, using that term in its broadest, though perhaps not lexical, sense. History, so conceived, may for present purposes be defined as recorded change through time and space. Such a concept implies that all biological and cultural historic process is a dynamic continuum, which man, the *only* appraising and recording organism known, variously defines: in its strictly biological sense as organic evolution; in its broader cultural sense as cultural evolution or culture history; in its more specific, undocumented ethno-archeological sense as prehistory; in its verbal but unwritten form as linguistic or traditional history; in its indirect associa-

tion with written history as proto-history; and in its final and very latest manifestation as written or documentary history. To define semantically each of these interlocking segments of one continuous process of change through time and space is an epistemological exercise which I briefly attempted but soon abandoned as beyond my powers and, most certainly, far beyond my heuristic interests.

The definition of human and, equally, of cosmic history as "recorded change through time and space" requires further comment. It is far removed from strict historicity, which implies written documentation, or from that form of historicism which puts uncompromising insistence on the individual and nonrecurrent nature of historical events. The viewpoint here taken, justifiably or not, is that to man the only known historian of humanity, or to the human historian of the various aspects of the cosmos, light years, glacial striae, geological-fossil associations, archeological stratigraphy, cultural complexes and distributions, as well as tribal or national traditions are all historical records, variable in scope, accuracy, and interpretation though they may be. As will be stressed below, I have the deepest respect and appreciation for written history as the direct approach which most effectively opens the way to the more obscure but equally real aspects of man's so-called "prehistoric" and biological past. However, historicity in its broadest sense cannot be limited to that relatively tiny span of time within which man has recorded in a symbolic, spoken, or written form the facts he wished to have remembered. Language, spoken or written, is, seemingly, man's greatest achievement so far, but historic process is infinitely older than speech or writing.

We will pass on to consider the historical approach as it affects all the biological, linguistic, and sociocultural subdisciplines that today are generally grouped together in American anthropology. That this is an arbitrarily limited view, subject to indefinite expansion, has been stated above.

From the broadest historical point of view I incline to the dualistic evolutionary conclusion expressed by Simpson (1950, pp. 344–45):

Man is the result of a purposeless and materialistic process that did not have him in mind. He was not planned. He is a state of matter, a form of life, a sort of animal, and a species of the Order Primates, akin nearly or remotely to all of life and indeed to all that is material. It is, however, a gross misrepresentation to say that he is *just* an accident or *nothing but* an animal. Among all the myriad forms of matter and of life on the earth, or as far as we know in the universe, man is unique. He happens to represent the highest form of organization of matter and energy that has ever appeared. Recognition of this kinship with the rest of the universe is necessary for understanding him, but his essential nature is defined by qualities found nowhere else, not by those he has in common with apes, fishes, trees, fire, or anything other than himself.

It is part of this unique status that in man a new form of evolution begins, overlying and largely dominating the old, organic evolution which nevertheless continues in him. This new form of evolution works in the social structure, as the old evolution does in the breeding population structure, and it depends on learning, the inheritance of knowledge, as the old does on physical inheritance. Its possibility arises

from man's intelligence and associated flexibility of response. His reactions depend far less than other organisms on physically inherited factors, far more on learning and on perception of immediate and new situations.

This flexibility brings with it the power and the need for constant choice between different courses of action. Man plans and has purposes. Plan, purpose, goal, all absent in evolution to this point, enter with the coming of man and are inherent in the new evolution, which is confined to him. With this comes the need for criteria of choice. Good and evil, right and wrong, concepts largely irrelevant in nature except from the human viewpoint, become real and pressing features of the whole cosmos as viewed by man—the only possible way the cosmos can be viewed morally because morals arise only in man.

To which may be added an earlier but similar statement by one who has been designated as the father of anthropology: "Archbishop Sumner formerly maintained that man alone is capable of progressive improvement. That he is capable of incomparably greater and more rapid improvement than is any other animal, admits of no dispute; and this is mainly due to his power of speaking and handing down his acquired knowledge" (Darwin, 1871).

That the majority of those who record themselves as cultural or social anthropologists today would accept this claim of single paternity for their science put forward by Marett (1912) is doubtful. However, there is no doubt that Darwin's evolutionary hypothesis, as well as his insistence on universal organic and human history, set a large part of the stage which modern anthropology has come to occupy. Certainly, the evolutionary hypothesis and the organized beginnings of cultural anthropology appear together (Darwin, 1859; Waitz, 1858–71). In this regard it may be here pointed out that the new or synthetic evolutionary theory (Simpson, 1950, p. 278) and "the new physical anthropology" with genetic orientation (Washburn, 1951) progress hand in hand. Indeed, so obvious is the evolutionary and human historical bent of that healthy division of our science which is concerned with biological man that there seems no need to labor the fact here. Washburn (*ibid.*) states in this regard: "The interpretation of the genetic situation demands an understanding of history." Howells (1952) adds: "A physical anthropologist, instead of yawning at the preoccupation of archeologists with minutiae which he cannot understand, can only be impressed more and more every year by how necessary to him is the information from archeology which alone can keep him from going completely off the track at certain points dealing with human paleontology, or with early population spreads and movements." Since it is so apparent that the evolutionary and historical aspects of physical anthropology are as basic today as they have always been in the past, we may here leave the biological realm and pass over to that second great realm of anthropological science—the sociocultural.

While Tylor defined culture and made the concept stick, it was the archeologist, Boucher de Perthes, who gave it objective, demonstrable time perspective. After much labor and travail he raised the threshold of cultural time from the 4004 B.C. limit of Bishop Usher up to the 250,000–1,000,000-year estimates which are still not agreed upon by geologists and archeologists. As Darwin, who had been a skeptic, said, "he has done for man something like what Agassiz did for glaciers." According to Lowie (1937, pp. 8–9):

The recognition of Boucher de Perthes' thesis marked a new era because it implies that culture dates back to the Pleistocene: the flints were not only made by man, they were obviously more than random freaks and worked in conformity with a social tradition. What is more, Boucher de Perthes was, in modern parlance, something of a functionalist. That is to say, he understood that the artifacts discovered could not be isolated products of some technological instinct, but fitted into a larger context. He maintained stoutly and convincingly that the ancient stone knappers must have had not merely knives and hatchets, but a language, an art, social customs—in short, an equivalent, however rude, of a complete culture. Now it suddenly dawned upon students of civilization that what they had hitherto known was but the final scene of a lengthy drama, that they had been trying to "reconstruct a book from the last chapter."

We will discuss the continuing historical contributions of archeology in more detail later.

Edward B. Tylor was probably as much the father of cultural anthropology as we know it today as Darwin was the particular progenitor of the biological aspects of anthropology. Tylor recognized and defined the role of culture, and his definition, with unlimited variants and refinements (Kroeber and Kluckhohn, 1952), still holds its ground. He was historically minded, and, in explaining the past, he stressed the "good old rule to work from the known to the unknown," applying this method particularly to the past history of institutions. Moreover, in regard to archeology he states:

When an antiquary examines the objects dug up in any place, he can generally judge in what state of civilization its inhabitants have been. Thus if there are found weapons of bronze or iron, bits of fine pottery, bones of domestic cattle, charred corn and scraps of cloth, this would be proof that people lived there in a civilized, or at least highly barbaric condition. If there are only rude implements of stone and bone, but no metal, no earthenware, no remains to show that the land was tilled or cattle kept, this would be evidence that the country had been inhabited by some savage tribe [1881].

As a cultural evolutionist he was far less schematic than Morgan, although his most extreme statement in this regard is very similar:

The institutions of man are as distinctly stratified as the earth on which he lives. They succeed each other in series substantially uniform over the globe, independent of what seem the comparatively superficial differences of race and language, but shaped by similar human nature acting through successively changing conditions in savage, barbaric and civilized life [1888].

This is not the place to summarize the vast and varied work of Tylor, or of that eminent and varied group often linked together as the British Evolutionary School of the later nineteenth and early twentieth centuries. This has been done by many others (Haddon, Marett, Goldenweiser, Radin, Lowie, Pennyman, etc.). Similarly, we may here only mention the cultural evolutionism of Lewis H. Morgan and his colleagues of the later nineteenth century. Morgan's basic premise in *Ancient Society* (1877), expressed eleven years prior to that of Tylor, just cited, is very similar:

Like the successive geological formations, the tribes of mankind may be arranged, according to their relative conditions, into successive strata. When thus arranged, they reveal with some degree of certainty the entire range of human progress from savagery to civilization. A thorough study of each successive stratum will develop whatever is special in its culture and characteristics and yield a definite conception of the whole, in their difference and their relations.

All that can be said here is that, whereas the cultural evolutionary approach of Tylor and Morgan was broadly historical in orientation, its specific delineations by Morgan have proved unacceptable in twentieth-century anthropological theory, with the exception of Soviet Russia, and even there marked revisions in hierarchy and attitude have

been in order (Tolstoy, 1952). We will speak subsequently of the outstanding archeological syntheses of V. Gordon Childe and the culturological approach of Leslie White, both of which, in considerable part, stem from the cultural evolutionism of Morgan and the culture-historical researches of Tylor.

From the standpoint of the broad historical approach in anthropology, viewed even as undialectically as in the present paper, it is hard to classify briefly the British Diffusionist School of Elliot Smith and others which for a short time in the 1920's seemingly outshone the earlier Evolutionary School so cursorily mentioned above. All that can be said here is that, while its aims and assumptions were broadly historical, its criteria for demonstrating single cultural origins and connections to establish widely discontinuous continental distributions seem vague, and its specific records of such events, whether archeological, ethnographic, or (very rarely) documentary, appear to be lacking or inadequate in specificity. The same strictures seem to me to apply, even more, to the recent extreme diffusionistic position of Gladwin (1947). The diffusionistic viewpoints mentioned above have been fluently and popularly set forth, and, since these theories as well as the voluminous criticism they have evoked are so well known, they will not be treated further here. However, this paucity of treatment, as in all cases in the present paper, is due to lack of space as well as to enormousness of subject. It does not imply a denial of the possibility of cultural contacts between peoples of widely separated areas and by widely various means. Linguistic, archeological, ethnological, and, at times, written historical records demonstrate with tangible or other convincing evidence many such occurrences. That trans-Pacific cultural contacts may have occurred between southern Asia and Middle America shortly after the time of Christ (Heine-Geldern and Ekholm, 1951) may yet be demonstrated to the satisfaction of even the most doubting of modern American cultural isolationists. However, it is here set forward that these proofs will be most convincing if they are either documentary or represent specific Asiatic artifact types scientifically recorded from known American archeological levels, or vice versa. This, of course, does not rule out artistic or ethnographic complexes which are less specific in their nature. However, if trans-Pacific contacts have been significant enough noticeably to mold the patterns of the higher cultures of the native New World, there should be some direct evidence, as well as reasonably continuous horticultural and other cultural distributions and temporal alignments. Such have not, as yet, become obvious.

The *kulturkreislehre* of Graebner, Schmidt, and others represents an important and currently active culture-historical–diffusionist school of anthropology. Centering in Germany and Austria, it also has many advocates in Argentina and other parts of South America. The literature of the *kulturkreis* school is very large, is wide and deep in coverage, and, in its conceptual approach, far more rigid and complex than that of the extreme British diffusionists. From the standpoint of our present subject, the *kulturkreislehre* is certainly strongly culture-historical, with evolutionary undertones (Lowie, 1937, p. 190). One of its more recent exponents (Van Bulck, 1932) makes an urgent plea to anchor the *kulturkreis* in every way to the facts established by stratigraphic archeology, physical anthropology, linguistics, and documentary history. The method and its results have been severely criticized by such North American scholars as Boas, Sapir, Goldenweiser, Dixon, and others. It has been more sympathetical-

ly analyzed by Lowie (1937) and especially, and in considerable detail, by Kluckhohn (1936). Since my own knowledge of both the conceptual approach and the world-wide theoretical hypotheses arrived at by this school is at best superficial and, perhaps, influenced by what Schmidt has called "the ethnological Monroe doctrine" (see Kluckhohn, 1936, pp. 185–88), no further attempt will be made here either to outline or, in any fundamental way, to appraise its historical results. Certainly, there are many important things held in common between the *kulturkreislehre* today and the current, co-ordinated, anthropological approach in the United States. Discussion at this conference may well reveal such common factors as well as any basic difference which may unite or separate these two broadly historical approaches.

Before passing on to consider certain other current aspects of anthropology which are predominantly historical in approach, a very brief word may be said concerning primitive linguistics, which by its very nature seems to be historically oriented. As in the case of physical anthropology, time sequence seems inevitable in its considerations and, while the study of primitive (or other) linguistics includes a vast gamut of analytical, functional, or scientific interests and investigations, its core data would seem to be those concerning linguistic change through time and space. Sapir (1916, p. 52) even compares the role of language in relation to culture history as roughly analogous to that of geology to paleontology. Kroeber (1940) and I (1940) have emphasized a certain lag in past historical linguistics in North America; but Kroeber, like Sapir, emphasizes its basic importance to all cultural-historical studies. Fashions vary in linguistics, as in anthropology and other human fields generally; but, to judge from the recent analyses of Hoijer (1946), Voegelin

(1936), Greenberg (1949–50), and others, it seems unlikely that the historic backbone of linguistic studies is being removed or even weakened—indeed, with further development and corroboration of such specifically long-run temporal approaches as the "lexicostatistic dating" of Swadesh and other linguists, the linguistic-geological analogy of Sapir may become even more specific. These matters, I think, we can safely leave for further discussion at the present conference.

Cultural-evolutionary approaches are usually directly or indirectly based upon, or involved with, archeological research. This seems quite logical, for such hypotheses usually rest on some sort of diachronic cultural stage or epoch formulation. Such formulations gain or lose conviction in terms of the objective archeological record. We can for present purposes skip the details of Hesiod's five ages: (1) that of gold and the immortals (peaceful); (2) age of silver (less noble); (3) bronze (a brazen fighting race); (4) the epic heroes (better than bronze); and (5) age of iron and dread sorrow (crime, violence, and worse to come), although these classical deductions have a strangely contemporary ring more in terms of current literature and journalism than in those of modern archeological research. Concerning the earliest of the postclassic stage formulations, it is of value to note that the famous "three-age system"—stone, bronze, and iron—was established by such northern antiquarians as Nyerup, Thomsen, Worsaae, and Nilsson long before they were implicitly taken over as the materialistic-economic background of the extreme Morgan and more moderate Tylorian schemes of cultural or social evolution (Daniel, 1950). The archeological use of the taxonomic approach of Linnaeus in regard to artifacts also goes back to 1849, indicating that the midwestern taxonomic system, with whose name

McKern (1939) is most often associated, has long roots. Dechelette described the three-stage theory as "the cornerstone of modern archeology." However, these early Scandinavian and other archeologists stressed technical and objective methods of excavation, age determination, and classification. They were also diffusionistic as well as evolutionary in their interpretations (Daniel, 1950, p. 45). Further, Nilsson soon arrived at a classification of prehistoric man based on the mode of subsistence (*ibid.*, p. 49) divided into four stages: (1) the savage—or collector, (2) the herdsman or nomad, (3) the agriculturist, and (4) the final stage, of civilization, marked, particularly, by coined money, writing, and the division of labor (*ibid.*, p. 49). We need not critically evaluate this classification here, but, in historical retrospect, it is interesting to note that this presentation of a synthetic scheme for man's cultural evolution, based largely on archeological data, occurred long before the biological evolutionary hypothesis of Darwin, its biocultural-philosophical formulation by Spencer, or the various cultural-historical adaptations which have been made by Tylor, Morgan, Childe, White, and many others, as well as the somewhat similar archeological formulations more recently arrived at, at the Chiclin Conference in Peru in 1946 and the Viking Fund Peruvian Symposium in 1947 (compare Daniel, 1950, pp. 49 ff., and Strong, 1951). Relatively popular or unpopular, the broad historical approach to an understanding of man's biological and cultural history by means of combined written historical, linguistic, ethnographic, archeological, and physical-anthropological techniques began very early and continues with vigor today.

Two outstanding cultural evolutionists at the present time represent quite different approaches. One is V. Gordon Childe, a field archeologist of vast experience, who has drawn together his many detailed published researches as well as those of other Old World students in such brief but searching, generalizing, and popular books as *Man Makes Himself* (1936) and *What Happened in History* (1946), among others. The other avowed cultural evolutionist, or culturologist, is Leslie White, a descriptive field ethnologist in direct research but, above all, an uncompromising theorist believing in evolutionary cultural forces which tend to reduce the human individual to complete insignificance (*The Science of Culture* [1949]). Whereas Childe is basically and broadly historical in his evolutionary approach as the term is used in this paper, White defines all history as pure historicism, i.e., documentary or other records of nonrecurrent events, and is primarily concerned with the "temporal-formal, non-repetitive (evolutionist)" aspects of culture (1945; compare Kroeber, 1946). Both Childe and White correlate the beginnings of symbolic behavior (language) and culture, and both strongly emphasize the direct correlation between technological control of expanding sources of energy and cultural growth. By White, however, the latter is propounded as the basic law of cultural evolution. Childe uses the older evolutionary culture-stage terms, such as "savage," "barbarian," and "civilized," but is most concerned with delineating the rise and cultural effects of two great revolutions of culture, the Neolithic and the Urban.

A firm believer in cultural evolution, Childe, however, is unable to find definite stages in the evolution of the higher civilizations of Europe and the Near East (1951). This will be referred to below. White has forcibly shown how the antievolutionary fervor of the so-called "Boas School" strongly reacted against any formulation or scheme of cultural stages or consideration of comparative cultural values (1947). How-

ever, in terms of historic or even cultural-evolutionary process, White has not as yet defined any general or localized cultural-historical scheme or terminology. Just as some extreme social anthropologists and sociologists seek social laws primarily upon a synchronic level, so White seems to seek culturological laws within his own definition of a specific cultural-evolutionary process rather than through the establishment and interpretation of such specific culture-historical sequences as those demonstrated by Childe. The two differ also in their attitude toward man's relation to culture; according to Childe, *Man Makes Himself*, although technological progress is often stultified by social lag. According to White, man today, as in the past, is the complete pawn of his own greatest creation, i.e., culture. Simpson (1950, p. 291) takes strong exception to this extreme view, pointing out, quite reasonably it seems to me, that because man does not completely control social evolution, this does not mean that he does not control it at all. It also seems to me that White reifies, and at times almost deifies, culture in somewhat the same way that the older evolutionists reified "nature" or others fall back upon the supernatural. Be this as it may, it is obvious that the cultural compulsive is at present basic in the theoretical approach of White and his disciples, and this fact should not be underemphasized in any consideration of their sometimes fatalistic views which they hold with fervor.

Certainly, both Childe and White, in quite different ways, have gone far toward regaining for the cultural-evolutionary school a vitality which it has not had since the days of Morgan and Tylor. If, like Kroeber (1946), I do not see or semantically accept any clear difference in kind between culture history and cultural evolution other than one of relative abstraction, I still welcome scholars who attempt to put interpretation and synthesis into that vast array of, at times, almost miscellaneous human biological, linguistic, and cultural materials so assiduously gathered by many timely, but often uninterpretative, anthropological fact-finders of the first half of the twentieth century. However, had those materials not been gathered when they were, most of them would have been lost forever.

Other anthropologists, not specifically committed to any rigid evolutionary theory of cultural change, have likewise begun to generalize certain of the findings of cultural-historical anthropology. Particularly, modern archeology, which by its very nature is the most objective, long-term, historical tool in the kit of anthropology, has made vast advances in revealing long and continuous culture sequences in the Near and Middle East, the Far East, Africa, and, recently, the Pacific regions. The importance of European archeological results in fact and theory has already been stressed, and the recent broad-gauge interpretative role of such British archeologists as Childe, Grahame Clark, Casson, and many others in other places must be acknowledged (see Daniels, 1950).

In the New World, the "direct historical approach" in archeology, which is a clear application of Tylor's advice to proceed from the known (documentary-ethnological) to the unknown (prehistoric-archeological) and which also establishes the extremely basic criterion of continuity, has been applied by myself and others to the Great Plains, Central America, Peru, and elsewhere with promising results. This approach is also the stated aim of the more recent German diffusionists and has long been explicit in proto-history in other parts of the world. Combined anthropological research in Peru, sparked by archeology, has recently posited on stratigraphic grounds a sequence of roughly sequential culture

epochs, including, from early to late, (1) the prehorticultural, (2) the incipient horticultural, (3) the formative (of local civilizations), (4) the florescent, (5) the fusional, and (6) the imperial epochs (Strong, 1948). These have been variously defined and named in terms of their changing alignments of economic, artistic, political, and militaristic configuration, within what has been termed the Peru-Bolivian co-tradition (see Bennett, 1948, and others in same volume). This generalized scheme has also been applied to the native culture-historical record in Mexico-Guatemala (see Armillas, also Strong, in Bennett, 1948; and Strong, 1951) with a correspondence in epoch sequence which appears to be so close that indirect diffusion as well as parallel culture-growth process seems to be involved. Steward (1949) has carried this comparative approach still further, suggesting that a similar culture-era formulation may well fit the major archeological and early historical periods of the Near East, Egypt, India, and China, as well as what Kroeber has designated "nuclear native America." This widely distributed series of remarkably similar pre-industrial patterns in recurrent eras or epochs strongly suggests cultural-growth regularities of considerable magnitude extending over wide areas and many millenniums.

Steward makes no claim that such, as yet dimly perceived, eras or epochs of cultural growth represent world-wide evolutionary stages applicable to all environments and to every social tradition. The fact, previously mentioned, that Childe (1951) is unable to define any reasonably clear-cut or consistent stages, or eras, in the cultural evolution of the Near East and Europe is a case in point. The specific relations between these two adjacent regions involve widely different environments, late and rapid diffusion, and the Iron Age, as well as the "fuel," or "machine," or "industrial" revolution with which neither Steward nor Childe is here specifically concerned. These late phenomena must be particularly considered in regard to the European and Euro-American culture climaxes of historic times. However, the culture-growth regularities now becoming apparent that coexist between widely separated pre-industrial civilizations in both the Old and the New World seem highly significant. Further detailed elucidation of their reality and extent will undoubtedly throw much more light upon both their historical and their functional significance in regard to recurrent culture change or parallelism over the millenniums. Certainly, the often assumed basic, or perhaps only incidental, roles of diffusion, internal development, and cultural lag in different times and places can only be understood and evaluated within such a world-wide and objective, functional-historical framework. Finally, all such schemes must be subjected to ever recurrent analysis, synthesis, and reanalysis if they are to retain reality and gain utility in the face of rapidly increasing historical knowledge and techniques. Few cultural or other theorists would have predicted the chronological possibilities that have been opened up by the dendrochronological and carbon 14 techniques. Yet, as Darwin stated many years ago, "it is those who know little, and not those who know much, who positively assert that this or that problem will never be solved by science."

It may seem strange that so far in discussing the historical approach in anthropology only indirect mention had been made of the "Boas" (or) " American Historical School." This is due to the fact that, with others, I do not believe that there ever was such a "school" or that the work of Boas and most of his students or disciples has been primarily historical; vast and important as their work has been in many fact-finding, analytical, critical, and functional approaches. Kroeber (1935) has pointed out that, while Boas gathered masses of historical materials and used all historical safeguards in his work, he very rarely did cultural history. Despite Boas' strong denials in this regard (1936), I must agree with Kroeber. For this reason and for lack of space, as in dealing with other important movements and achievements in anthropology, I can only say that the first quarter of the twentieth century in the United States saw all-important anthropological recovery of vanishing basic data but relatively little historical or functional generalization.

It seems to me that the relative and varying emphasis put upon historical or functional process in anthropology, today as in the past, has little to do with Boas, who was a law unto himself. Its roots lie much farther back in the time when the study of human society and culture became nominally subdivided between sociology, the older, and anthropology, the younger, academic sibling. From the time of Comte to the present these two approaches, the elder largely synchronic, the younger usually dominantly diachronic, have drawn apart or merged according to the varying interests and purposes of their various exponents. This has led to many and, to me, sometimes pointless battles between those who believe anthropology represents history and sociology science, that anthropology is "historical" or that it is "functional," and, *in extremis*, whether anthropology is not really "comparative sociology" (Radcliffe-Brown, 1932) or "culturology" (White, 1949). To those semantically inclined these are fascinating and endless problems varying from decade to decade and from scientific personality to personality. To one who freely admits predominantly heuristic interests, they often seem academic.

That the present skeleton account limits itself almost entirely to the historical process is entirely a matter of assigned subject matter. It has no implication whatsoever that "history" is more important than "function" in anthropology or in any other approach to knowledge. On the contrary, it has always seemed to me that either one of these two major approaches is limited and even meaningless without the other (Strong, 1929, p. 349; 1936, p. 370). Here I deal briefly and inadequately with only one of these scientific Siamese twins; the second will undoubtedly be well cared for by others.

In an earlier paper I stated, concerning anthropology in the United States since the time of Morgan, "that dominant schools have never developed and that there has been no rapid overturn of one method of approach by its direct opposite. The same period in England has seen the vogue of the evolutionary, diffusionist, and functional approaches, each being conceived in the minds of its extreme adherents as exclusive of all the others" (1936, p. 365).

This in a general sense I still believe to be true. However, in the last quarter-century the popular emphasis on certain synchronic social problems in anthropology has tended to stress various prevailingly fashionable subjects, such as "functionalism," "acculturation," "culture and personality," or "national character" studies to such an extent that the predominantly diachronic or historical emphasis of cultural and physical anthropology, linguistics, and archeology is often overlooked. Owing to their intense interest in the functional and synchronic, a very productive and vocal group of anthropologists has thereby merged so closely with social psychology and sociology that the never clear or logical borders between these various approaches have tended to disappear. This cross-fertilization accounts in considerable part for the recent accent on the cultural in sociology and, I hope, psychology, as well as for the fact that certain less historically minded members of our own fraternity prefer to be known as "social anthropologists." With Murdock (1951) I am inclined to regard not only the British but also our own "social" anthropologists as primarily on the sociological side of the fence. Since sociology and anthropology have continued to grow up together in an intimate and, at times, exceedingly productive incestuous relationship, the reason for these periodic interchanges of methodological and conceptual approaches between the two seems obvious. No attempt is here made to untangle these intricately tangled roots and branches, but it does seem reasonable to indicate that, in general, the anthropological approach to organized knowledge has emphasized the biological, cultural, and historical aspects of all men's existence, whereas sociology has generally worked with literate, most often Euro-American, societies or with "society" as a whole, and mainly in terms of function and process rather than human history. Since the most promising approach to the deepest human understanding would seem to be complete synthesis of both the historical and the functional, it is a happy omen that the British social anthropologists today are expressing a growing interest in the former process in addition to their deep absorption and great competency in the latter (Firth, 1951). According to an excerpt in an old natural history notebook of mine, probably from Ernest Thompson Seton (1909), "Man is the only animal who concerns himself with the ideals and events of the past; the rest of the animal world is 'strictly up to date.'" It is good to know that in this regard we can include at least some of the social anthropologists with man.

LITERATURE CITED

BENNETT, WENDELL C. (ed.). 1948. *A Reappraisal of Peruvian Archaeology.* ("Memoirs of the Society for American Archaeology," Vol. IV.) Menasha, Wis.

BOAS, FRANZ. 1936. "History and Science in Anthropology: A Reply," in "Discussion and Correspondence," *American Anthropologist,* n.s., XXXVIII, 137–41.

BULCK, GASTON VAN. 1932. *Beiträge zur Methodik der Völkerkunde.* Vienna: Universitäts Institut für Völkerkunde.

CHILDE, V. G. 1936. *Man Makes Himself.* London: Watts & Co.

———. 1946. *What Happened in History.* New York: Penguin Books, Inc.

———. 1951. *Social Evolution.* New York: Henry Schuman.

DANIEL, GLYN E. 1950. *A Hundred Years of Archaeology.* London: G. Duckworth & Co.

DARWIN, CHARLES. 1859. *On the Origin of Species by Means of Natural Selection.* London: John Murray.

———. 1871. *The Descent of Man, and Selection in Relation to Sex.* New York: D. Appleton & Co.

FIRTH, RAYMOND. 1951. "Contemporary British Social Anthropology," *American Anthropologist,* LIII, 474–89.

GLADWIN, HAROLD STERLING. 1947. *Men Out of Asia.* New York: Whittlesey House, McGraw-Hill Book Co.

GREENBERG, JOSEPH H. 1949–50. "Studies in African Linguistic Classification," *Southwestern Journal of Anthropology,* V, 79–100, 190–98, 309–17; VI, 47–63, 143–60, 223–37, 388–98.

HEINE-GELDERN, ROBERT, and EKHOLM, GORDON F. 1951. "Significant Parallels in the Symbolic Arts of Southern Asia and Middle America." In TAX, SOL (ed.), *The Civilizations of Ancient America: Selected Papers of the XXIXth International Congress of Americanists,* pp. 299–309. Chicago: University of Chicago Press.

HOIJER, HARRY, et al. 1946. *Linguistic Structures of Native America.* ("Viking Fund Publications in Anthropology," No. 6.) New York.

HOWELLS, W. W. 1952. "The Study of Anthropology," *American Anthropologist,* LIV, 1–7.

KLUCKHOHN, CLYDE. 1936. "Some Reflections on the Method and Theory of the *Kulturkreislehre*," *American Anthropologist,* n.s., XXXVIII, 157–96.

KROEBER, A. L. 1935. "History and Science in Anthropology," *American Anthropologist,* n.s., XXXVII, 539–69.

———. 1940. "Conclusions: The Present Status of Americanist Problems." In *The Maya and Their Neighbors,* pp. 460–87. New York and London: D. Appleton–Century Co.

———. 1946. "History and Evolution," *Southwestern Journal of Anthropology,* II, 1–15.

KROEBER, A. L., and KLUCKHOHN, CLYDE. 1952. *Culture.* In press.

LESSER, ALEXANDER. 1933. *The Pawnee Ghost Dance Hand Game: A Study of Cultural Change.* ("Columbia University Contributions to Anthropology," Vol. XVI.) New York.

LOWIE, ROBERT H. 1937. *The History of Ethnological Theory.* New York: Farrar-Rinehart.

McKERN, W. C. 1939. "The Midwestern Taxonomic Method as an Aid to Archaeological Culture Study," *American Antiquity,* IV, 301–13.

MARETT, R. R. 1912. *Anthropology.* New York: Henry Holt & Co.

MORGAN, LEWIS H. 1877. *Ancient Society.* New York: Henry Holt & Co.

MURDOCK, GEORGE PETER. 1951. "British Social Anthropology," *American Anthropologist,* LIII, 465–73.

RADCLIFFE-BROWN, A. R. 1932. "The Present Position of Anthropological Studies" (address as President, Anthropology Section, British Association for the Advancement of Science), *Report of the Centenary Meeting, London, Sept. 23–30,* pp. 141–71. London.

SAPIR, E. 1916. *Time Perspective in Aboriginal American Culture.* (Canada Department of Mines, Geological Survey, Mem. 90, "Anthropological Series," No. 13.) Ottawa.

SETON, ERNEST THOMPSON. 1909. *Life-Histories of Northern Animals: An Account of the Mammals of Manitoba.* New York: Charles Scribner's Sons.

SIMPSON, GEORGE GAYLORD. 1950. *The Meaning of Evolution.* New Haven: Yale University Press.

STEWARD, JULIAN H. 1949. "Cultural Causality and Law: A Trial Formulation of the Development of Early Civilizations," *American Anthropologist,* LI, 1–27.

STRONG, WILLIAM DUNCAN. 1929. *Aboriginal Society in Southern California.* ("University of California Publications in American Archaeology and Ethnology," Vol. XXVI.) Berkeley.

———. 1936. "Anthropological Theory and Archaeological Fact." In *Essays in Anthropology in Honor of Alfred Louis Kroeber,* pp. 359–70. Berkeley: University of California Press.

———. 1940. "Anthropological Problems in Central America." In *The Maya and Their Neighbors,* pp. 377–85. New York and London: D. Appleton–Century Co.

———. 1948. "Cultural Epochs and Refuse Stratigraphy in Peruvian Archaeology." In BENNETT, WENDELL C. (ed.), *A Reappraisal of Peruvian Archaeology,* pp. 93–102. ("Memoirs of the Society for American Archaeology," No. 4.) Menasha, Wis.

———. 1951. "Cultural Resemblances in Nuclear America: Parallelism or Diffusion?" In TAX, SOL (ed.), *Civilizations of Ancient America: Selected Papers of the XXIXth International Congress of Americanists,* pp. 271–79. Chicago: University of Chicago Press.

TOLSTOY, P. 1952. "Morgan and Soviet Anthropological Thought," *American Anthropologist,* LIV, 8–17.

TYLOR, EDWARD BURNETT. 1881. *Anthropology: An Introduction to the Study of Man and Civilization.* New York: D. Appleton & Co.

———. 1888. "On a Method of Investigating the Development of Institutions: Applied to Laws of Marriage and Descent," *Journal of the Anthropological Institute of Great Britain and Ireland,* XVIII, 245–72.

VOEGELIN, C. F. 1936. "On Being Unhistorical," in "Discussion and Correspondence," *American Anthropologist,* n.s., XXXVIII, 344–50.

WAITZ, THEODOR. 1858–71. *Anthropologie der Naturvölker.* 6 vols. Leipzig: F. Fleischer.

WASHBURN, S. L. 1951. "The New Physical Anthropology," *Transactions of the New York Academy of Sciences,* Ser. II, XIII, No. 7, 298–304.

WHITE, LESLIE A. 1945. "History, Evolutionism, and Functionalism: Three Types of Interpretation of Culture," *Southwestern Journal of Anthropology,* I, 221–48.

———. 1947. "Evolutionary Stages, Progress, and the Evolution of Cultures," *ibid.,* III, 165–92.

———. 1949. *The Science of Culture: A Study of Man and Civilization.* New York: Farrar, Straus & Co.

Problems of Process

Field Methods and Techniques
in Linguistics

By FLOYD G. LOUNSBURY

In these days of narrower and narrower specialization in the various fields which make up anthropology, many of us look back wistfully to the great men of a generation or two ago who encompassed the whole range of anthropology, knowing that we can never do this. We, too, would like to be "complete anthropologists," but the field has grown beyond our grasp. Most of us have to content ourselves with being archeologists, linguists, ethnologists, physical anthropologists, or even more narrow specialists; and we feel so conscious of the inadequacy of the little that we might be able to contribute to branches other than our own that we are unwilling even to try.

Yet, speaking now for the linguists among us, we realize the smallness of our contingent and the impossibility of accomplishing, by ourselves, more than the smallest portion of the job which we want to see done before it is too late. Most of us are exceedingly grateful for the current contributions of missionaries to our field. Indeed, if a fair portion of the languages of primitive peoples gets documented before vanishing from the earth, it may be due more to the efforts of today's linguistically trained missionaries than to anthropologists or professional linguists. We wish that we had still more help, especially from other anthropologists.

The burden of this paper is that not all of linguistics is so esoteric as to be beyond the reach of any but the lifetime specialists in the subject. As an inventory paper in this series, the function of this paper is to review the various methods and techniques which have been used to gather linguistic data in the field, starting from the simplest and crudest and proceeding to the most refined and complex. There is a field technique which is appropriate to just about any degree of linguistic proficiency (other than absolute zero) and which is suitable to the varying amounts of time which an anthropologist may be able to devote to collecting linguistic data. The different field techniques produce data of differing kinds and degrees of comprehensiveness, and these various types of data have different uses and are applicable to different types of anthropological and linguistic problems.

Since the close dependence of method upon problem is well recognized in anthropology, it falls within the scope of this inventory paper also to point out the problems to which the various orders of data are relevant. As it happens, new uses are currently being found for even some of the simplest and briefest collections of data, as well as for the most elaborate. Any anthropologist in the field, then, can make some useful contribution in the form of linguistic data.

THE DEVELOPMENT OF LINGUISTIC METHODS

In the days before even anthropology was a special pursuit and it was still possible to be an all-round naturalist, linguistic data from primitive tribes were often collected as a matter of course by the explorers and naturalists of the time, just as they collected data on plant life, insects, topography, watercourses, etc. The data consisted of limited vocabularies of from a dozen to a few hundred words. They were represented, or misrepresented, in makeshift transcriptions based on the conventional orthographies of the collectors' own languages, with their inadequacies and inconsistencies. A bit of this sort of collecting is still being carried on by amateurs in many countries. By today's standards, however, it is woefully inadequate, and its uses are accordingly limited. Nevertheless, for a great many languages of the world this is all we have. And we often have occasion to consider ourselves lucky, when working on classification problems for a given area, if we run onto even so much data. For many tribes we have nothing at all.

Perhaps this method of collecting turned out worst when the collector's native language was English, for our English orthography incorporates about the biggest hodgepodge of conflicting conventions of any alphabetically written language. Even Lewis Henry Morgan, who made such an enormous contribution to systematic ethnography, was exceedingly naïve linguistically. His transcriptions of Seneca words are among the poorest. Some slight improvement, at least in certain cases, was achieved by English-speaking collectors with the once fairly widespread convention of "consonants as in English, vowels as in Italian." This served to ward off carrying over a few of the inconsistencies of English spelling into the representation of native words but was still as inadequate as ever in dealing with languages which had other sounds or in which the relationships between sounds were differently structured. Only rarely do the sounds and the orthography of one language furnish anything approaching an adequate framework in terms of which to represent another language.

PHONETICS

The naïve method of transcription just described should have become obsolete as soon as more versatile systems of phonetic transcription were developed, the first of which were nearly a century ago. Since the earliest of these, there have been many variant phonetic alphabets put forth. The principal usages which are current or have been important in anthropological literature are that of Lepsius, that of the International Phonetic Association (IPA), that recommended by the journal *Anthropos*, the early one of the American Anthropological Association, that of Sapir and a group of his students, and that of Bloch and Trager. None of these is totally different from the others, though they vary considerably in details. They simply represent varying attempts at standardization of practice and are landmarks in the development of what is essentially a single, though not too cohesive, tradition.

The transcription of Lepsius (1855) appears to be one of the earliest to formulate usages which in large part are still current and are retained in one or another of the modern systems. It formed the basis especially for much of the German work on African languages. Further development of the Lepsius system is summarized by Meinhof in a volume edited by Heepe (1928). The recommendations of *Anthropos* retain many features of this system but also make a number of additions and innovations. The first version (Schmidt, 1907) appeared in the second volume of that journal. Its form as of 1924 is given by Father Schmidt in Heepe (1928). The IPA system had taken fairly definite shape by 1888, the date of the first revision (*Le Maître Phonétique*, 1888). There have been periodic revisions since then, as more and more different sound types have been discovered in one language or another—and as their printer could be induced to furnish more and more fanciful pieces of type—the last being that of 1947 (*Le Maître Phonétique*, 1947). This system began under Paul Passy and is today associated with the work and the wide influence of the great English phonetician, Daniel Jones. The system of the American Anthropological Association (Boas *et al.*, 1916) was formulated in 1913–15 by a committee consisting of Boas, Goddard, Kroeber, and Sapir, charged with drawing up a phonetic system for transcribing American Indian languages. Sapir and a group of his students later introduced a number of modifications in usage (Herzog *et al.*, 1934), primarily so as to make possible unitary symbols for phonetic clusters when these clusters were interpreted by them as single phonemes. Some symbols from Slavic phonetic conventions, already utilized in the Lepsius system, were introduced into American usage by them and have become more or less standard today. The system of Bloch and Trager (1942) largely avoids adding further to the proliferation of new devices. Except for two of their vowel symbols (to provide a "mean-mid" height) and one or two diacritics, all their practices derive from previous systems. Their usage represents an attempt to simplify and symmetrize a body of already existing conventions. Other systems which at one time or another have fulfilled an important function, such as that of Powell (1877) or the very early one of Ellis (1848), are now of historical interest only.

These, which are the principal conventions that the anthropologist is likely to encounter, have been reviewed here, with notes to sources, only because their variety sometimes confuses the nonspecialist. They are indispensable tools, but their form, like that of all symbols, is arbitrary. Since the advent of phonemics (see following section) there is not even any pressing need for uniformity in phonetic transcription practices. Much more important is a thorough understanding of the articulatory production and acoustic nature of speech sounds. For, without this, one is not equipped to handle any of the tools of transcription. Both these aspects of phonetic science are still in the process of development. The latter especially, with the recent availability of the sound spectrograph, is undergoing rapid advancement. But the basic principles of both are quite clear and are not difficult to understand. Some convenient sources are the works by Bloch and Trager (1942), Jones (1934), and Jespersen (1913) for articulatory phonetics, and Joos (1948) and Potter, Kopp, and Green (1947) for acoustic phonetics. Skill in phonetic transcription is not difficult to acquire and comes with a modicum of practice, once the basic principles are understood. It should be regarded as the minimum essential in the linguistic training of the field anthropologist.

PHONEMICS

One of the first aims in the development of phonetic notations was to furnish auxiliary transcriptions to serve as pronunciation guides for learners of languages with inconsistent orthographies. This being the case, they tended in the beginning (unconsciously on the part of their inventors) to be more or less phonemic in principle; i.e., they largely ignored phonetic differences between sounds which were nondistinctive in the languages under consideration. But the problems of language teaching, of devising auxiliary notations, and of dealing with an ever wider range of languages prompted a great deal of close phonetic observation and experimentation. As the science of phonetics developed, it became possible to observe and to record ever more precisely a multitude of hitherto unnoticed phonetic features in even the well-known western European languages, and a dichotomy grew up between "narrow" and "broad" phonetic transcriptions. The narrow transcriptions were those of the sophisticated observer, noting as much as possible of the objective facts; the broad ones were those of the subjective observer, pruning the facts in accordance with the bias of the language. The narrow transcriptions included all phonetic features impartially (in so far as the training and techniques of the observer permitted); the broad transcriptions largely ignored nondistinctive features and paid heed only to those which were distinctive (occurring in at least some of the same environments, and here contrasting and differentiating meanings) in the given language.

The science of phonemics was born when the relativity of distinctiveness or contrastive value in phonetic features was discovered and fully appreciated. Two different sound types, such as [d] and [t], for example, which contrast in some languages (e.g., French), may fail to contrast in another language (e.g., Oneida) simply because they never occur in the same phonetic environments. A difference in meaning between two forms in the latter language, then, can never hinge solely upon this phonetic difference. The linguist says that the two sound types are in "complementary distribution," that the phonetic differences between them

(in respect to voice and tenseness, in this case) are "nondistinctive," and that they can be grouped into a single "phoneme" or unit class of noncontrasting sound types. The psychologist, on the other hand, may note that speakers of the latter language are quite unaware of the existence of any phonetic difference between the two sounds, that to them they are not two sounds but one.

Phonemics, then, is concerned with cultural relativity in a certain sphere of activity. Its aim when applied to a given language is to separate out that part of the phonetic behavior which, through the arbitrariness of historical developments, happens to be significant in the language from that portion which for similar reasons is nonsignificant. It separates the nonautomatic and meaningful differences from the automatic and predictable and discards the latter. It isolates the "cues" in speech sounds from the unattended background features.

We know that in any language there are many more objectively different sounds than there are significantly different sounds. But the basis of "significance" cannot be known by an outside observer at the outset of his investigation, for it is a relative matter, different in every language. Nor is it known by the native speaker of the language either, for it is a phenomenon of unconscious behavior. It is the problem of the investigator to discover it. For this there is a standard technique.

The principle of phonemics is simple. To be significantly different, two sounds must occur in at least some of the same phonetic environments (else there would not even be the opportunity for contrast), and in these environments the choice between them must depend upon meanings rather than be random (else there still would be no contrast). Conversely, two sounds which either (*a*) do not occur in any of the same phonetic environments or (*b*), although occurring in some of the same environments, never relate to different meanings are not significantly different. In the first case the sounds are said to be in "complementary distribution." In the latter they are in "free variation." Either of these, or any combination of them, is called "noncontrastive distribution." In such cases the choice between sound types is either undetermined or determined by differences in environment, but not by differences in meaning.

To be in noncontrastive distribution is a necessary condition for membership of two sounds in the same phoneme, but it is generally not regarded as a sufficient condition. (The sounds [ŋ] and [h] are in complementary distribution in English.) In addition, some unifying feature is necessary. This may consist of one or more phonetic components (articulatory or acoustic) present in all the members of the given phoneme and distinguishing them from all nonmembers.

The technique of phonemics is simply one of applying the above principles. The first prerequisite is careful observation of the phonetic facts. A reliable phonemicization cannot be made from inaccurate phonetic data. Given the data, the second prerequisite is a careful ordering of those data so as to bring out the facts of distribution of the sound types. One has to discover in what phonetic environments each of the sound types does and may occur in the language under study. Given the facts of distribution, the rest of the process of phonemicization consists in grouping the sound types, according to the phonemic principle, into contrasting classes, such that each class comprises noncontrasting sound types sharing a distinctive common feature.

Phonemicization is included here as a field technique, even though in the building of theoretical systems it is customary to separate the stages of analysis from the stage of data-collecting, with only the latter being considered a field stage. Purely practical considerations, however, necessitate including phonemic analysis, as well as a certain amount of grammatical analysis, in the field stage. While the separation is sound in theory, it would not be practical for a human worker either to collect a large enough sample of random data in sufficient phonetic detail to be adequate for a trustworthy analysis later or to process a sample of this size to discover the facts of distribution. One shortens the work of phonemicization tremendously by making tentative phonemic hypotheses very early in the field stage, using these as guides in the quest for crucial data, submitting them to tests of validity, and revising them where necessary. And one shortens the work of collecting texts and other grammatical data tremendously by being able very early in the game to slough off nonsignificant phonetic detail. Grammatical and other types of analysis also, from the standpoint of theory and in the presentation of analysis, constitute separate levels of procedure and are consequently sometimes described as separate stages distinct from both the phonetic and the phonemic stages. Yet, from the practical point of view of accomplishing the work, it is necessary to include much of these in the field stage also. For, without them, the would-be phonemicizer is limited by his inability to construct crucial cases as he needs them to test the validity of his tentative phonemic hypotheses, and he must wait for such cases to come up at random. In actual practice the collecting of the various orders of data and the working-out of the various levels of analysis are carried on more or less simultaneously. The work proceeds on all fronts, and a picture of the language gradually unfolds in all its aspects. Separation is achieved only in the final presentation and logical justification of the analysis.

It was mentioned in the preceding section (p. 403) that with the advent of phonemic methods there is no longer any need for stressing uniformity in phonetic conventions. Any convenient set of graphic symbols may be chosen to represent the phonemes of a language, since each represents a class of sounds and since each such class is of necessity defined, and its principal allophones described, in any work on the language. There need be no worry about "right" or "wrong" symbols. A practical result of this, of interest to editors, is the reduction in a formerly felt need for a multitude of special characters. There is not even any real need, as was once felt, for a unitary symbol for each phoneme; digraphs (two-letter sequences) are quite acceptable, so long as they are defined and are unambiguous in their reference. Familiarity, suggestibility, and availability of type are the only factors that need enter into the choice of symbols for phonemic transcriptions. The symbols are arbitrary, and their phonetic values are only temporarily assigned.

Convenient references for practical phonemic procedures are Bloch and Trager (1942), Swadesh (1937), Pike (1947), and Jones (1950).

Although there is general agreement as to the basic principles, the purpose, and the general procedure of phonemics, there is a number of areas of disagreement both in theory and in application. The novice and the nonspecialist should be aware of this, but not bewildered by it. The differences derive in part from different weighting of various desiderata in a phonemic analysis, not all of which are always equally relevant or simultaneously attainable. These further relate to slightly divergent philosophical views as to the nature of speech, the nature and locus of structure in language, etc. Some of the points of difference lie in the manner of

regarding variation in contrastive value of phonetic features, such as is dependent either upon particular phonetic environments or upon particular grammatical environments. Other points of difference have to do with the areas in which relative features are admitted along with absolute phonetic features in defining phonemes, the admission or rejection of phonemic intersection (overlapping of phonemes in the phonetic field), the admission or rejection of pattern symmetry as a relevant consideration, etc. Still other differences relate to theory or to terminology only, without consequences for practical application. The bases for relative evaluation of at least some of the desiderata underlying differences in phonemic theory fall within the fields of sciences other than linguistics and are at present insufficiently understood. Some theoretical works, with different orientations, are those of Bloch (1948), Harris (1951), and Trubetzkoy (1939, 1949). The reader is referred also to the paper entitled "Structural Linguistics," by Martinet, in this volume.

GRAMMATICAL DATA AND TEXTS

A complete grammatical analysis need not be carried out while in the field. In fact, if a large enough collection of texts is available, this can be done without access to a native informant. It seems, however, that there is considerable difference among languages in regard to the amount of text necessary for this manner of analysis. For one thing, languages differ greatly in the amount of morphophonemic irregularity which they manifest. As a result, the problem of segmenting forms into their minimal meaningful constituents and the phonemic identification of morphemes may be simple and obvious (as in a "regular" agglutinating language like Quechua) or extremely complex and difficult (as in an "irregular" and highly fusional language like Seneca). Morphological complexity (i.e., elaboration of word structure) also varies. There are languages, like Chinese, where relatively little grammatical business is done within the bounds of the word (derivation by compounding in the case of Chinese), and languages like Iroquoian or Eskimo, where as much can be said within a single word as can be said in a ten- or fifteen-word sentence in English. Nor does it seem to be true that languages with complex morphologies compensate with simple syntax and vice versa. There are too many cases on record in which, by whatever rough yardsticks we can use to judge complexity, even the opposite seems to be true. Further, it must be noted that languages vary greatly in the amount of obligatory classificatory impedimenta, of the type which Sapir referred to as "concrete relational" (Sapir, 1921, chap. vi), which their forms must carry. These serve to relate lexical elements or whole propositions to various arbitrary and logically unnecessary schemes of classification; and, so doing, they either redundantly specify things obvious from larger linguistic or situational contexts or put on an obligatory basis what might otherwise be left optional. These schemes vary from language to language both in kind and in amount and are sometimes held to reflect, or to have once reflected, some significant features of nonlinguistic cultural behavior (Lee, 1944; Hoijer, 1951) or to influence in some manner the larger thought-processes of a people (Whorf, 1949).

Thus, although a grammatical analysis can be made solely from texts, the amount of text which must be processed for this purpose varies with the type of language. Often it is so great that clerical assistance and mechanical means of reproduction are necessary. In any case, effort and time are saved if the subject is explored in the field.

One of the most effective ways of probing grammatical structure in the field is to take a recorded text and run variations of each word and larger construction in it. One queries his informant, varying a part of the meaning of a given text form while holding another part constant, and notes the correlation in constant and variable parts of the new form thus elicited from the informant. With this procedure, forms are segmented into their minimal meaningful parts, and these parts are seen in relation to other contrasting substitutable parts. Whether the analysis gained from one such set can be generalized to another depends upon the degree of regularity of the language. Predictability comes rapidly in a language like Quechua, but slowly in a language like Seneca. A valuable field technique is to try out predictions. If they hold up, the field worker feels that he is beginning to understand the ways of the language. If they fail, he corrects them, acquires some new data, and modifies his view of the system so as to give the unexpected new form a place and a rationale.

A word needs to be said concerning the development of grammatical theory, for this has bearing upon field procedures as well as upon description. It was once thought that the semantic categories present in the forms of Latin grammar were universal linguistic categories imposed by the very nature of reality and inherent in thought. Not only were modern European languages forced into this classical pattern (after all, not too difficult a feat), but various non-Indo-European languages were forced into this Procrustean bed of parts of speech, genders, cases, numbers, tenses, voices, modes, etc. If the fit was not good, the assumption was naturally that it was because the language at hand was rude, uncultivated, or primitive, and spoken by a people in a lower cultural state. Such an approach, unfortunately, still hangs on in the contemporary works of those who have remained isolated from the development of linguistic thought of the past generation. The significance of Boas' linguistic work lies in his discovery that the categories of classical grammar were not absolutes or universals, that languages had many different inherent structures, and that their differences did not correlate with stages of cultural development. Through his own work and through that of his students, he broke down preconceptions of hoary antiquity. It was one more case in the extension of the concept of cultural relativity. Boas worked out his own methods (inadequate, to be sure, by today's standards, but nonetheless a great advance for the time) for describing a language in terms of its own structural categories, and he taught this principle to his students (Boas, 1911, 1922). This principle is still the linguist's guide, both in field work and in the development of theory. One avoids imposing a pattern from without and seeks, instead, to discover that which is inherent within a language.

The roots of modern linguistic theory are several (see Martinet, *op. cit.*). In both Europe and America a strong stimulus has come from the study of non-Indo-European languages. A goal, partially achieved, has been to develop a conceptual framework and a method of analysis which will be equally applicable to any and all languages. In the process of this development there has evolved an increasingly truer picture of the nature of language, including the discovery of a few universals and of a number of the dimensions and ranges of variability in language. The universals are not so many, nor are they of the same kind as were once assumed, but they are of greater general significance.

Almost every new language which is carefully analyzed turns up some phenomena which cannot be adequately treated in terms of existing concepts and which thus reveal flaws or weak points and prompt further refinements in theory. Not only do exotic languages contribute in this manner to the general science of language, but ever closer and more careful observation and analysis of the facts in even the better-known languages turns up unexpected phenomena and has a similar effect.

One result of this continued development of theory is that analyses made by linguists at one period turn out to be quite inadequate and lacking in desired information some years hence. No analysis, then, is final. One must also furnish, in addition to his analysis, an ample body of raw data which can be utilized for reanalysis as theories, problems, and methods evolve. Adequate data for this purpose do not consist in vocabularies, paradigms, or any other manner of isolated forms—as valuable as these may be for certain other purposes (see section on "Field Techniques"). What is needed is a large body of very carefully recorded texts as delivered by native informants. Often one good text is worth more than a book of hasty generalizations. The first duty of the field worker is to preserve the evidence. This is becoming increasingly difficult today because of costs, so that some form of inexpensive reproduction, allowing a limited distribution, seems called for. Although not of great interest to the general reader—even among linguists—they will have increasing value in the future.

Some important works which deal with grammatical analysis are the following: Sapir (1921), Bloomfield (1933), Bloch and Trager (1942), Harris (1942, 1951), Pike (1943), Whorf (1945), Hockett (1947), Wells (1947), and Nida (1949).

SEMANTIC DATA

Improvement in field methods, as they pertain to the collection of phonological and grammatical data, has been linked directly to the building-up of general knowledge and analytical frameworks in those fields rather than to the introduction of any new field methods as such. The field method is, and always has been, simply the interviewing of informants and noting down what they say. There is another kind of linguistic data, which is equally important but for which there has not yet been a corresponding development of general knowledge or workable theory. This is semantics. As a result of the backwardness in this field, linguists are still nowhere nearly so careful about getting the precise meanings, ranges of application, and appropriate contexts for linguistic forms as they are in getting precise data on the forms themselves. This is partly because they would not know just what to do with it if they had it and because they have tended to restrict their interests to that side of the language phenomenon which yields more readily to treatment in a scientific manner. Yet anthropologists will rush in where linguists fear to tread. And, while the results do not yet promise to be spectacular, neither is there cause for early discouragement. There is a real need for the development of methods for the direct acquisition of semantic data in the field.

A conceptual framework for semantic analysis is, in fact, beginning to take shape at the present time, and from two quite different approaches. The one, being developed by Harris (1948, 1952), rejects semantics as such (i.e., the analysis of nonlinguistic contexts or referents) and concentrates instead on extended linguistic contexts. It is, then, not "semantics," but "linguistics" in the accepted narrow sense. The method appears promising. The other approach is to deal with nonlinguistic referents directly. It would thus be a frankly semantic approach. Linguists are generally skeptical of the possibilities in this direction. Yet in one area of vocabulary this method has been applied with fair

rigor for some time, viz., in kinship analysis by anthropologists (Lévi-Strauss, 1945; Murdock, 1949, chap. vi). It has lent itself, moreover, to treatment by componential analysis in a manner quite analogous to the phonetic componential analysis of phonemic systems (Goodenough, 1951; Lounsbury, MS). The analogy is not fortuitous or forced but relates to one and the same principle of perception and attention, viz., that an organism does not respond equally to all features of a situation, but selectively to those features to which, through the learning process, he has developed a habitual response. This is as true for linguistic responses to nonlinguistic stimuli as it is for the various discriminatory responses to linguistically produced acoustic stimuli. Although other parts of vocabulary seem to offer much greater difficulties than does kinship vocabulary, it is not yet to be concluded that this area of behavior lies wholly beyond the reach of scientific procedures.

MECHANICAL AIDS TO DATA COLLECTION

As noted above, the improvement in field methods in linguistics has derived primarily from the development of linguistic theory, the basic field technique still remaining interview sessions with an informant. Modern electronic apparatus can be used to great advantage in the process, however. Some linguists, with a Goethe-like opposition to intervening gadgetry, have been slow to take advantage of what technology has to offer as aids to observation. For the most part, however, they have been eager to use them when the opportunity permitted. The most useful devices have been wire and tape recorders, automatic repeaters, segment isolators, and the sound spectrograph, all of which depend upon magnetic recording and have become available only since the war.

Tape or wire recorders can be profitably used in a number of ways. They may be used to record ordinary dictation sessions with informants and thus to make possible repeated hearings to check difficult points and questionable transcriptions. They may be used in collecting text, so that an informant can tell his story in one piece without interruption for transcription. Then it may be played back, phrase by phrase, as a guide to prevent confusion and aid his memory while he redictates it piecemeal for transcription in the ordinary method. This prevents the mangling of sentences and the abbreviation of stories, which otherwise are inevitable except with the most skilled and patient of informants. Recorders have been used by students of Voegelin in tests of intelligibility between dialects (Hickerson *et al.*, 1952; Voegelin and Harris, 1951). Two recorders have been used together by the writer to record texts and get interlarded translations when there was not sufficient time in the field for collecting texts in the ordinary manner. This merely delays the transcription and necessitates a repeating mechanism to make possible the later transcription.

There are several kinds of automatic repeating devices. For tape or wire, the most easily rigged up is a continuous loop which passes through the playing head, through or around the propulsion mechanism, and then off to a spool or set of spools that take up the slack. Or it may spiral up two grooved spools, returning from the top of one, through the head, to the bottom of the other. A loop is made long enough to hold a few seconds of speech, three to five seconds being optimum. It repeats this automatically, allowing the listener to transcribe. It is a very effective aid in transcribing recordings, for, after a number of such identical repetitions, the phrase, even when from a completely unknown language, engraves itself in every detail upon one's memory. The chief drawback is that the ear can take

only so much of this before it becomes intolerable. More than an hour of such work at a time is not feasible. Another drawback inherent in the loop type is that one cannot use his original recording directly, but must rerecord each successive few-seconds stretch of it onto the loop before being able to hear it repeat. Commercial repeaters, operating on a back-up-and-go-ahead principle, are available on both wire and tape machines. These have the advantage that they make use of the original recording directly, but the repetitions are not automatic but must be foot-controlled. A rhythm can be set up, however, which allows one to get an identical stretch of more or less constant length to repeat over and over. A design for a repeater operating on a still different principle is in existence, but the machine has not been built. It allows both the use of the original recording and the automatic repetition of the loop type and serves also as a segment isolator.

The sound spectrograph is a machine for analyzing the distribution of acoustic energy in the dimensions of frequency and time. Its uses are manifold in revealing hitherto inaccessible acoustic data on speech sounds. It can be used to determine the exact position of vowels at any instant on the resonance formant chart, which corresponds, with some metrical adjustment, to the tongue-position chart of vowels. It can be used for measuring length of phonetic segments. It can give exact intonation contours. It is not a tool that one would use directly to process all of one's recordings, but it can be used to settle difficult points of phonetics. Further information on the machine and its uses can be found in Joos (1948) and in Potter, Kopp, and Green (1947).

Another machine which might be put to use in aiding observation of phonetic detail is the speech stretcher. It allows the playing of a recording at half-speed, while restoring frequency, and thus both pitch and resonance formants, to those of the original. Successful models were built by Joos (1948, pp. 127–29). A commercial model is less successful.

KINDS OF PROBLEMS

The linguistic problems of relevance to general anthropology are of three main types, characterized broadly as historical, structural, and functional. Historical problems have to do with genetic relations between languages, phylogeny, historical connections between ethnic groups, the chronology of splits in speech communities, and the nature and extent of linguistic diffusion. They are of interest primarily to the historical anthropologist. Structural problems are those which concern the analysis of particular languages and the understanding of the speech activity itself. These are of interest primarily to linguists but have important implications for the student of the theory of culture and for the psychologist as well. Functional problems are concerned with the reciprocal causality relations, or correlations, between aspects of cultural behavior and the semantic structure (both in lexicon and in grammar) of particular languages, and with the relation of the speech and symbol faculty to the phenomenon of culture in general. They are of interest to the ethnologist and to social and perception psychologists.

It should be specially noted that problems of the structural and the functional categories have both synchronic and diachronic aspects. Further, in all of these, there are problems concerned with particular languages and problems concerned with language in general. There is concern, then, both with laws of limited validity, localized in place and time, and with general laws.

The problems themselves need not be reviewed individually here. The above brief sketch of the field will suffice as an over-all framework of orientation in which to locate the ends served by data resulting from each of the special field techniques discussed below.

FIELD TECHNIQUES

We may now review a number of linguistic techniques which may be used by the anthropologist or linguist in the field. For each we shall consider the nature and amount of the data to be collected, the manner of collection, the qualifications of the collector, and the use to which the data can be put. We begin with some of those which make the least demands, in terms of training and time, upon the anthropologist. Some of these, either in use of the data or in method of obtaining it, are of recent development.

COLLECTION OF BASIC VOCABULARY

This is probably the simplest useful linguistic project which can be carried out by an anthropologist otherwise occupied in the field and with but little time to devote to linguistics (or by a linguist, traveling or making a survey, with but little time to devote to a single speech community). It consists in collecting something over two hundred items of vocabulary corresponding to the terms in a list, of which considerable use has been made of late. The necessary minimum qualification on the part of the collector is an understanding of phonetics and the ability to take phonetic dictation accurately. Actually, the work amounts to something more than just jotting down a couple hundred words, for they are most useful and the nature of the data can be best understood if each item is obtained in sentences providing a variety of contexts and showing a variety of constructions. Thus the task amounts to nothing much different from what a linguist embarking on a more extensive study might do during his first day in

the field. The difference, however, and
the reason that this can be isolated as
a useful project in itself lie in the selection of the items contained in the
list and in the special uses which have
been discovered recently for data of
this type.

The concept of "basic" vocabulary is
not new. A difference between this and
"cultural" vocabulary has received at
least implicit acknowledgment by historical and comparative linguists. The
latter has been observed to be especially subject to borrowing, and similarities
in this area are no reliable indication
of genetic affiliations. The former, however, has been observed to be far less
liable to borrowing, and similarities in
this area are of greater significance and
generally point to the same conclusions
with regard to phylogenetic connections
as does evidence from comparative
grammar.

It is only recently, however, that it
has become evident how much this
so-called "basic" vocabulary may be
used for. An attempt to clarify the concept led Swadesh to draw up a list of
some two hundred items which seemed
quite likely to refer to constants in
man's environment, or to the most elementary and seemingly universal concepts of his creation. Most of them
generally find their formal expression
in root lexicon, though some of them
frequently appear as affixes. The list is
not perfect, for no such list could be.
But the probability remains exceedingly
small that a significantly large portion
of it would at any one time, in a given
language, be simultaneously affected by
cultural changes so as to bring about
wide-scale loss and replacement of the
forms.

A corollary of this, if it be true, is
that with such specific identifiable
causes of change minimally at work,
such loss and replacement as do take
place in this area of vocabulary should

in some sense be "random." This led
Swadesh and others to compile data on
rates of change in basic vocabulary in
languages for which history provides
the necessary chronology. In those
cases in which it has been tested, the
rates of loss and replacement have
turned out to be remarkably nearly constant (Swadesh, 1951). Thus, whereas rates of change in other aspects of
language (e.g., in phonology, grammar,
lexicon at large, etc.) are known for
their wide variability and unpredicta-
bility, it seems that in rate of change of
basic vocabulary we have something
approaching predictability.

Basic vocabulary, then, offers a technique for establishing chronology. Just
how precise a technique it may be and
what is its margin of error remain to
be seen. The method requires further
testing and refinement. In particular,
testing might be carried out on the
following problems: (1) empirical determination of a maximally stable list;
(2) quantitative prediction of the
Sprachbund effect as reflected in the
discrepancy between actual common
retention and expected common retention between languages in geographic
and cultural contiguity (Swadesh,
1950); (3) determining the effect, if
any, of size of a speech community
upon rate of retention.

When this method has been further
refined, it will furnish an invaluable
chronological technique for the culture
historian working with primitive peoples. Even now enough is known so that
we can apply it cautiously, realizing,
however, that the results which it gives
are tentative and subject to revision.
Its margin of error probably will not
compare unfavorably with those of
other chronological techniques used by
anthropologists and archeologists.

The basic vocabulary list can be
found in the earlier of the Swadesh
articles (1950).

COLLECTION BY MACHINE

The method described above can be carried out in the field, when necessary, by making use of a tape or wire recorder instead of by transcribing directly. This is to be recommended when a worker untrained in phonetics happens to have the opportunity to collect this kind of data and when a linguist back home is sufficiently interested in the area to be willing to undertake the transcription later. In this way one with no linguistic training whatever can bring in useful data. Recordings are a valuable supplement in any case, even when phonetic transcriptions are made directly in the field.

MEASURING DIALECT DISTANCE

Another project which can be accomplished with the aid of a recording machine is the measurement of the degree of mutual intelligibility between dialects. On this, on the degree of intelligibility or unintelligibility, hangs the distinction between dialect and language.

The method involves making recordings of each of the dialects or languages in question, testing them upon speakers of the other languages, and scoring the responses. A quantitative measure of intelligibility is thus obtained. The possibility of such a technique has been discussed among linguists for a decade or more. Modern magnetic recording equipment and portable power sources now make it feasible. The details of a method of applying it were worked out by Voegelin and Harris (1951), and it has been applied in the field by students of Voegelin (1952). The test can be administered and scored even by those who have no knowledge of the languages involved. One caution must be emphasized. Bilingualism of a speaker has sometimes been mistaken for mutual intelligibility of languages.

The distinction between language and dialect is not mere academic hairsplitting. Mutual unintelligibility acts as an effective barrier to diffusion of many kinds of linguistic traits. Thus, the relations between languages are of a different sort from those between dialects, and a different method of historical analysis and interpretation is necessary. Phylogenetic classification is applicable to languages, as it is to any systems in which there have been effective barriers to mutual influence as they have evolved. In dialect study, however, only the geographical "area" methods and interpretation in terms of diffusion are applicable.

DIALECT GEOGRAPHY

The methods of dialect geography are oriented toward the study of the distribution and diffusion of linguistic variations within a given large speech community.

A speech community is an area of continuous mutual intelligibility. Distant points within a speech community, to be sure, may sometimes have mutually unintelligible speech, but there is no sharp boundary of unintelligibility between them, the transition between them being gradual, with adjacent dialects always mutually intelligible. Such is the German-Dutch area, for example, stretching from Austria and Switzerland through Germany to the Netherlands. Only with the extinction of intervening varieties, and their complete replacement by two or more mutually unintelligible varieties from distant localities within the area, can such a single speech community be converted into two or more separate speech communities. When this happens, an at least partially effective barrier to free diffusion, namely, mutual unintelligibility, is introduced into the area.

Extensive work in dialect geography

has been carried out in Europe, especially in the German area, Italy, France, and England, and also in America, in the eastern section of the United States. Some of the aims, methods, and results of this work are summarized in Dauzat (1922), Gamillscheg (1928), Jaberg and Jud (1928), Bach (1934), Kurath (1949), and Pop (1950).

This type of work has consisted largely in recording a number of specific traits of phonetic and lexical variation within a speech community. The distribution of these traits is plotted, and "isoglosses" are drawn, showing the centers and the frontiers of spreading innovations, the principal lines of diffusion, minor barriers to diffusion, etc. A great deal of historical information concerning the movements of population can be gleaned from such study. It would be profitable to undertake it in other ethnic areas of the world; China, for example, or the Quechua-speaking area. Similarly significant results might be expected in these areas. The principal requirement for the worker in this field is good training and practical experience in phonetics, besides a knowledge of at least one variety of the language of the given area.

The dialect geographer, of all linguistic specialists, has the best opportunity to observe and study the process of linguistic change at work, whereas the comparative linguist, with different problems and different methods, is in a better position to view the nature of the results of long-time accumulation due to these processes. Dialect geographers, in their preoccupation with variations in individual traits, however, have tended to give insufficient attention to the structural consequences of such variations.

STANDARD LINGUISTIC FIELD METHOD

The standard linguistic field method is oriented toward a complete structural analysis of a language. It can be carried out only by a worker who is adequately trained in phonetics, in phonemics, and in the general theory of language structure. The data include accurate phonetic transcriptions and much additional text and grammatical material in phonemic transcription. A project of this nature and scope often requires the better part of a year in the field. A single informant may suffice, if he is bilingual, patient, and has skill at narrating events and reciting tribal lore. More frequently, however, a large number of informants must be employed, each of whom has a particular talent. An analysis can be based solely on the speech of a single individual, or it may be broadened to include the ideolectical and dialectical variation within the community. Recording equipment is of great value in this kind of work, for it permits repeated checking of one's phonetic observations, and it aids the informant by allowing him to give his texts first in uninterrupted form, thus avoiding the confusion otherwise inevitable in slow phrase-by-phrase dictation.

A complete analysis of a language, such as is the goal for this kind of field work, is of much wider value both to historical reconstruction and to the further development of linguistic theory than are any of the more restricted types of materials.

SEMANTIC STUDY

As noted earlier, semantic study is an undeveloped field except for the particular area of kinship vocabulary. It is the experience of a number of field workers, however, that informants—like other nonlinguists—are generally more interested in the meanings of their words than they are in the forms. Often they volunteer more information regarding specific semantic referents and appropriate contexts than the linguist is interested in noting down. Such information, where accurate, would be of considerable value. This is especially true when an informant builds up a hypothetical situation and says, "Now this is when you could use this word." The problem of notation, however, is a serious one in this respect, for the recording of semantic detail consumes far more time than the recording of phonetic detail. Here tape or wire recording equipment can be an invaluable aid.

It would be desirable to explore vocabularies of religious terminology, medicinal practice, technology, emotional states, etc., with the same concern for detail that anthropologists expect (but less often achieve) in dealing with the vocabulary of kinship and social organization.

LITERATURE CITED

BACH, ADOLF. 1934. *Deutsche Mundart-forschung: Ihre Wege, Ergebnisse und Aufgaben.* Heidelberg: C. Winter.

BLOCH, BERNARD. 1948. "A Set of Postulates for Phonemic Analysis," *Language*, XXIV, 3–46.

BLOCH, BERNARD, and TRAGER, GEORGE. 1942. *Outline of Linguistic Analysis.* ("Special Publications of the Linguistic Society of America.") Baltimore: Waverly Press.

BLOOMFIELD, LEONARD. 1933. *Language.* New York: Henry Holt & Co.

BOAS, FRANZ. 1911, 1922. *Handbook of American Indian Languages.* (Bureau of American Ethnology Bull. 40, Vols. I and II.) Washington: Government Printing Office.

BOAS, FRANZ; GODDARD, P. E.; SAPIR, E.; and KROEBER, A. L. 1916. *Phonetic Transcription of Indian Languages: Report of Committee of American Anthropological Association.* ("Smithsonian Miscellaneous Collections," Vol. VI, No. 6.)

DAUZAT, ALBERT. 1922. *La Géographie linguistique.* Paris: E. Flammarion.

ELLIS, A. J. 1848. *The Essentials of Phonetics.* London: F. Pitman.

GAMILLSCHEG, ERNST. 1928. *Die Sprachgeographie und ihre Ergebnisse für die allgemeine Sprachwissenschaft.* Bielefeld and Leipzig: Velhagen & Klasing.

GOODENOUGH, WARD H. 1951. *Property, Kin, and Community on Truk.* ("Yale University Publications in Anthropology," No. 46.) New Haven.

HARRIS, ZELLIG S. 1942. "Morpheme Alternants in Linguistic Analysis," *Language*, XVIII, 169–80.

———. 1948. "Componental Analysis of a Hebrew Paradigm," *ibid.*, XXIV, 87–91.

———. 1951. *Methods in Structural Linguistics.* Chicago: University of Chicago Press.

———. 1952. "Discourse Analysis," *Language*, XXVIII, 1–30.

HEEPE, M. (ed.). 1928. *Lautzeichen und ihre Anwendung in verschiedenen Sprachgebieten.* Berlin: Reichsdruckerei.

HERZOG, G.; NEWMAN, S.; SAPIR, E.; SWADESH, M. HAAS; SWADESH, M.; and VOEGELIN, C. 1934. "Some Orthographic Recommendatons," *American Anthropologist*, XXXVI, 629–31.

HICKERSON, H.; TURNER, G.; and HICKERSON, N. 1952. "Testing Procedures for Estimating Transfer of Information among Iroquois Dialects and Languages," *International Journal of American Linguistics*, XVIII, 1–8.

HOCKETT, CHARLES F. 1947. "Problems of Morphemic Analysis," *Language*, XXIII, 321–43.

HOIJER, HARRY. 1951. "Cultural Implications of Some Navaho Linguistic Categories," *Language*, XXVII, 111–20.

JABERG, K., and JUD, J. 1928. *Der Sprachatlas als Forschungsinstrument: Kritische Grundlegung und Einführung in den Sprach- und Sachatlas Italiens und der Südschweiz.* Halle (Saale): M. Niemeyer.

JESPERSEN, OTTO. 1913. *Lehrbuch der Phonetik.* 2d ed. Leipzig and Berlin: B. G. Teubner.

JONES, DANIEL. 1934. *An Outline of English Phonetics.* 6th ed. New York: E. P. Dutton & Co., Inc.

———. 1950. *The Phoneme: Its Nature and Use.* Cambridge (Eng.): W. Heffner & Sons.

Joos, Martin. 1948. *Acoustic Phonetics.* ("Language Monographs," No. 23.) Baltimore: Waverly Press.

Kurath, Hans. 1949. *A Word Geography of the Eastern United States.* Ann Arbor: University of Michigan Press.

Le Maître Phonétique. 1888. III, Nos. 7–8, 57–60.

———. 1947. Vol. LXII, 3d Ser., No. 88, Supplement.

Lee, Dorothy D. 1944. "Linguistic Reflection of Wintu Thought," *International Journal of American Linguistics,* X, 181–87.

Lepsius, R. 1855. *Das allgemeine linguistische Alphabet: Grundsätze der Übertragung fremder Schriftsysteme und bisher noch ungeschriebener Sprachen in europäische Buchstaben.* Berlin: W. Hertz.

Lévi-Strauss, Claude. 1945. "L'Analyse Structurale en Linguistique et en Anthropologie," *Word,* I, 33–53.

Lounsbury, Floyd G. MS. "Semantic Componential Analysis of a Lexical Set."

Murdock, George P. 1949. *Social Structure.* New York: Macmillan Co.

Nida, Eugene A. 1949. *Morphology: The Descriptive Analysis of Words.* 2d and new ed. ("University of Michigan Publications in Linguistics," Vol. II.) Ann Arbor.

Pike, Kenneth L. 1943. "Taxemes and Immediate Constituents," *Language,* XIX, 65–82.

———. 1947. *Phonemics: A Technique for Reducing Languages to Writing.* ("University of Michigan Publications in Linguistics," Vol. III.) Ann Arbor.

Pop, Sever. 1950. *La Dialectologie: Aperçu historique et Méthodes d'Enquêtes linguistiques.* Part I: *Dialectologie romane.* Part II. *Dialectologie non romane.* ("Université de Louvain, Recueil de Travaux d'Histoire et de Philologie," 3d ser., Fasc. 38–39.) Louvain.

Potter, R. K.; Kopp, G. A.; and Green, H. C. 1947. *Visible Speech.* New York: D. Van Nostrand Co., Inc.

Powell, John Wesley. 1877. *Introduction to the Study of Indian Languages, with Words, Phrases, and Sentences To Be Collected.* Washington: Government Printing Office.

Sapir, Edward. 1921. *Language: An Introduction to the Study of Speech.* New York: Harcourt, Brace & Co.

Schmidt, P. Wilhelm. 1907. "Die Sprachlaute und ihre Darstellung in einem allgemeinen linguistischen Alphabet," *Anthropos,* II, 282–329, 508–87, 822–97, 1058–1105.

Swadesh, Morris. 1937. "A Method for Phonetic Accuracy and Speed," *American Anthropologist,* XXXIX, 728–32.

———. 1950. "Salish Internal Relationships," *International Journal of American Linguistics,* XVI, 157–67.

———. 1951. "Diffusional Cumulation and Archaic Residue," *Southwestern Journal of Anthropology,* VII, 1–21.

Trubetzkoy, N. S. 1939. *Grundzüge der Phonologie.* ("Traveaux du Cercle Linguistique de Prague," Vol. VII.) Prague. French translation: J. Cantineau (trans.), *Principes de Phonologie.* Paris: Klincksieck, 1949.

Voegelin, Carl F., and Harris, Zellig S. 1951. "Methods of Determining Intelligibility among Natural Languages," *Proceedings of the American Philosophical Society,* XCV, No. 3, 322–29.

Wells, Rulon S. 1947. "Immediate Constituents," *Language,* XXIII, 81–117.

Whorf, Benjamin L. 1945. "Grammatical Categories," *Language,* XXI, 1–11.

———. 1949. *Four Articles on Metalinguistics.* (Reprints of articles published elsewhere.) Washington: Foreign Service Institute, Department of State.

Psychological Techniques: Projective Tests in Field Work

By JULES HENRY and MELFORD E. SPIRO

INTRODUCTION

FROM ITS inception, anthropological research has been concerned with the study of groups and their modal characteristics, whether these groups were cultures, societies, races, or species. This group orientation not only served to unite all the subdisciplines of anthropology but was entirely adequate for the earlier aims of anthropological science: sociocultural and biological classification and structural analysis. In cultural anthropology[1] research and writing could operate as if the individual did not exist. Propositions concerning human behavior, culture patterns (in the sense of institutional behavior), and culture norms were, explicitly or implicitly, statistical generalizations. The study of the individual did not begin to assume importance in cultural anthropology until anthropologists became interested in (a) cultural dynamics and (b) cultural integration.[2]

In "cultural dynamics" we include studies both in cultural change and in socialization: that is, studies in how whole societies acquire new culture patterns as well as studies in how unsocialized members of any society acquire the culture of that society. Once these areas assumed importance to anthropology, anthropologists were compelled to turn to the individual as a legitimate research concern. The interest in cultural integration, on the other hand, led not only to an interest in the individual as individual but to an interest in personality; for a number of questions, either implying or assuming some relationship between the unique integration of the culture of a particular society and the integration of the personalities of its individuals, were being posed. Thus arose a new branch of inquiry within anthropology[3] known as "personality and culture studies."

Almost from its beginnings, certain methodological problems which the older branches of anthropology had not had to face confronted the field worker in this new area. Regardless of the particular culture-personality relationships with which the researcher was concerned, it is obvious that one of his tasks was to describe personality, whether it was the personalities of a restricted number of individuals or the group personality.[4] Here arose the ques-

1. By "cultural anthropology" we mean the American usage of that term, as well as the British concept of "social anthropology."

2. In "cultural integration" we include such concepts as "cultural configurations," "cultural patterning," "ethos," etc.

3. More specifically, within *American* anthropology, for the study of personality and culture, with notably few exceptions, has been exclusively an American concern.

4. In "group personality" we include such notions as "modal personality," "basic personality structure," "national character," etc.

tion: What techniques are to be used for this purpose? Now it is evident that the anthropologist engaged in more traditional areas of anthropological research was also confronted with methodological problems. But, whatever his problems, they did not involve the basic question as to how he was to identify and describe the phenomenon he was studying. He was reasonably confident that he would be able, on the basis of tried anthropological techniques, to gather his data and to publish them in such a way as to have them accepted by his colleagues as an objective, scientifically controlled picture of the culture.

These two simple desiderata of any scientific investigation were not (and still are not today) so readily satisfied in personality and culture studies. Specifically, the anthropologist in this area of investigation had to invent, discover, or borrow some technique or techniques which would enable him to make valid personality diagnoses and generalizations, for the usual anthropological techniques would not help him here. Furthermore, the techniques used had to be of such a nature that the results of his investigation would be accepted by fellow-scientists as meeting the usual scientific canons of objectivity, validity, reliability, etc.

In the absence of such precise instruments, personality studies in anthropology were (and are) exposed to the criticism of being vague, impressionistic, subjective, and not amenable to check or transubjective verification. Furthermore, since the bias of the observer is inordinately great here, it is naïve, as critics have observed, to accept the investigator's description of the personality structure of the members of a given society; and to compare his description with that of the description of another society by still another investigator using a similar impressionistic technique would consist in com-

pounding a felony. Thus any attempt to formulate hypotheses for cross-cultural testing seemed to be doomed, as the "confidence level" of conclusions based on impressionistic data could not be too high.

PROBLEMS IN THE SELECTION OF TESTS

In casting about for instruments that they might use to reduce the impressionistic quality of their studies, anthropologists turned to psychology. The type of test that anthropologists needed had, so it seemed, to satisfy the following requirements: (*a*) It must measure the personality "as a whole." This vague expression means that no test that seemed to elicit response from a very limited area of the personality would be useful. Hence, for example, even were a really valid instrument for measuring intelligence available, the anthropologist interested in personality and culture would have little interest in it because such a test would touch only one function of the individual. Hence, also, a test that tapped only the individual's potential for hospitality would have little utility, for, again, only one phase of the total personality would be examined. (*b*) The test must not be "culture-bound." Anthropologists had rightly turned their backs on the usual intelligence tests, for they realized not only that "intelligence" itself is a term of doubtful meaning but also that the tests used to measure intelligence in our culture examined intellectual processes only in terms of the relatively fixed categories of our own culture and in terms of the specific content of our culture. Hence, in the study of the total personality, it was found necessary to use a test that would have about the same meaning and evoke the same kind of responses in any culture. This meant that actual test content would have to be minimal and that categories used for interpretation should be invariant, the latter quality being particularly necessary if cross-cultural comparisons were to be made. (*c*) Since in the past it had seemed relatively difficult for a single anthropologist to obtain adequate personality data in the time allotted to the usual field trip on anything but a very small number of individuals, it was felt that a useful test should enable him to study a much larger number of persons than he ordinarily would be able to. (*d*) The test should be relatively short, relatively easy to administer, and capable of analysis by persons other than the anthropologist. The last requirement seemed to have utility, in that it would make possible the checking of the data by independent analysts and by persons whose judgment was not biased by previous knowledge of the people.

The psychological techniques that have been used by anthropologists to study the mental and emotional functioning of peoples outside occidental culture are numerous, and an exhaustive treatment of the subject would require an outlay of time and assume a dimension quite out of keeping with the situation that confronts the authors of the present paper. Hence in this paper we have limited ourselves almost exclusively to *projective tests,* for it is these that, at the present time, are in widest use by anthropologists interested in the field of personality and culture. And this concentration on projective tests by the anthropologists is no accident. They alone, of all psychological tests, seemed to meet the four requirements of valid tests listed above. Within this area of the projective test we concentrate almost exclusively on tests having a fixed character. For this reason we do not discuss word-association tests, for these must be devised on the spot by the anthropologist to suit the conditions of the particular culture in which he is working.

The expression "projective test" des-ignates those tests whose stimulus value is such that, when presented to a subject with proper (and fixed) instructions, they are believed to elicit from him responses representative of his thoughts and *feelings* about himself and the world around him. He thus, according to the rationale of these tests, reads into the relatively neutral material that is presented to him meanings, in the form of stories, answers to questions, interpretations of relatively formless materials, which represent his own attitudes and emotions. He thus "projects" himself and his own world of thoughts and feelings onto the stimuli presented to him.

DESCRIPTIONS OF TESTS

1. *The Rorschach test.*—This test is named after its inventor, Dr. Hermann Rorschach, a Swiss psychiatrist. It consists of ten inkblots varying in form and color. These inkblots are like those made by children in occidental culture by folding a piece of paper, putting ink in the crease, and then pressing the ink between the folds of the paper. The result is a mass of relatively indefinite shape. The standard Rorschach blots (called "plates") are presented to the subject one at a time, and he is asked to tell the examiner what he sees in the blot.

Depending on how it is used, the Rorschach test elicits material covering a wide range of personality characteristics. Among these are: sensitivity to inner promptings as contrasted with responsiveness to outer stimuli; degree of control over the emotions; capacity to relate affectively to other people; capacity to see total situations as contrasted with absorption in petty details; tendencies to submit as contrasted with tendencies to react vigorously to the environment; various aspects of sexuality; degree of hostility; degree of imagination, conformity, originality; tendencies to psychopathy.

2. *The Thematic Apperception test.*
—Devised by Henry Murray, this test consists of twenty pictures and one blank card. Some of the pictures are for males only, some for females only, and some are for both sexes. The blank card is for either sex. The subject is shown the cards in order and asked to make up stories about each one. The stories that the subjects make up are reputed to reveal their sentiments, needs, and past experiences. Many pictures in the series indicate by their artifacts and composition that they have originated in occidental culture. Hence it has sometimes been necessary to design special pictures to suit the environment of primitive subjects.

3. *Free drawings.*—Here the child is asked to draw pictures of anything he wishes to draw. An analysis of the more formal aspects of the drawings, such as line, form, balance, symmetry, rhythm, etc., reveals some of the more dynamic aspects of the child's personality functioning. Analysis of content reveals such things as the child's self-image, relations to parents and siblings, his conceptions of his society, his fantasy life, etc.

4. *Doll play.*—This technique is similar to that of free drawings, in that the child is presented with dolls, with which he is permitted to do whatever he pleases. Here, too, the rationale is that the way in which the child manipulates the dolls reveals a number of things about the child and his perceptions of his environment, such as his relationship to parents and siblings, his conception of sex and sexual processes, his handling of aggression, etc.

5. *The Bender Gestalt test.*—This test consists of a series of nine cards on each of which is printed a design (*Gestalt*) which the subject is asked to copy. The subject's test performance yields material on such personality phenomena as regression, retardation, and personality deviations.

DISCUSSION

Obviously, an adequate paper on psychological techniques used by anthropologists should, among other things, contain some examination of methodology, of the extent to which the tests show what they are supposed to show, of the degree to which they really fulfil the "anthropological ideal," of the contribution the techniques have made to the understanding of primitive peoples. This, however, would go beyond the specific assignment made by the steering committee of the symposium for which this paper was prepared.[5] Hence we have restricted this paper to a descriptive account of the anthropological research that has employed projective techniques.

But before we turn to this, the requirements for this paper demand a survey of the major ideas found in this field. Actually, there have been few works concerned with the broader, theoretical aspects of the cross-cultural application of projective tests and their implications. With a few exceptions, those who have been concerned with the theoretical problems raised by the Rorschach have come to positive conclusions about its validity as an instrument for cross-cultural testing. There have been some strictures, however, and these, interestingly enough, have come from psychologists and not from anthropologists. After reviewing some of the empirical research undertaken by anthropologists, Lantz (1948, p. 291), for example, concludes:

In general it appears that the findings of Rorschach studies in pre-literate societies tend primarily to be highly general and somewhat vague. . . . Rorschach has been devised for a different and more scientific purpose; namely, to describe the dynamic intellectual-emotional configuration among persons in western society. Using it other-

5. A paper dealing with these problems is now in preparation by Jules Henry and Ivan Mensch.

wise results in much speculation without any real scientific basis.

He does see greater hope for the future, however, when more "meaningful results" may possibly be attained by the training of anthropologists in personality theory and psychometric techniques and of psychologists in ethnological problems.

Cook, also a psychologist, administered a series of Rorschachs in Samoa and, on the basis of his experience, concludes that the traditional interpretation of Rorschach scoring criteria must be highly qualified in cross-cultural use (Cook, 1942). He feels that S, for example, cannot be interpreted as a sign of negativism in Samoa, since white is a favorite color in Samoa. A high *F* column cannot be interpreted as an indication of rigidity or compulsiveness or depression because the Samoans, among other things, place a high value on etiquette and formality. The paucity of texture responses is not diagnostically significant but is a function of the Samoan lack of familiarity with many objects having a texture quality. Finally, their high *CF* and *C* columns are a function of their restricted color vocabulary, which precludes fine discriminations in color perception, their meager art, and the few colors to be found in their tropical natural environment. His general conclusion is that the Rorschach method, potentially, "will make possible a more intensive and deeper study of the dynamics of personality and culture," but, in view of the dependence of Rorschach interpretation on norms derived from Western culture, such interpretation "cannot be expected to be valid unless considerable modification and alteration has been made" (1942, p. 60).

Among anthropologists, Hallowell (1941*a*, 1942) has been the most concerned with the theoretical problems involved in the use of the Rorschach.

Once anthropology began to deal with the "intimate connection" between the personality structure of the individuals of a society and their culture, the question arose, Hallowell points out, as to how to derive this personality structure without representative samples of individual personalities. What was required was a technique that would "(*a*) provide an integral picture of the personality organization of the individual; (*b*) be adaptable to use among non-literate groups; (*c*) elicit data under semi-controlled conditions, so that valid comparisons could be made, and (*d*) that the results would lend themselves to group characterization as well as provide data on intra-group variability in personality structure" (1945*a*, p. 198). The Rorschach, he feels, meets these criteria most adequately, for a number of reasons: (1) the equipment is simple, (2) it involves a minimum of verbal instructions, (3) the subjects need not be literate, (4) since there are no right or wrong answers, the subjects cannot tell their answers to others, (5) interpreters may be used, (6) subjects are under no time pressure, (7) it can be used in all age groups, (8) the administrative standards are not rigid.

Once the group results are obtained, it is possible to make studies of both inter- and intra-cultural variations. With respect to the former, the "group results obtained by the Rorschach techniques can aid us in making more valid and precise comparisons of the communal components of personality in different societies, and thus contribute to our knowledge of the nature and range of such differences within the human species" (Hallowell, 1945*a*, p. 205). At the same time, once such differences are found, "it might then be possible to explain these group responses in terms of the specific culture pattern or conditions of life that prevail in different societies" (Hallowell, 1941*b*, p. 32). The comparison of four Rorschach variables would be illuminating from this point of view: differences in modes of apperception are revealed by comparison of the "manner of approach" in the Rorschach; differences in "quality of apperception," by comparison of the "determinants"; differences in content of apperception, by the "content"; and differences in originality of apperception, by the "originals." The cultural determinants of such differences are potentially numerous. But problems of intra-cultural variations, which have been so difficult to get at in the past, can now be handled also. Such problems are: (1) If it is true that primitive societies are more homogeneous culturally, is it also true that the range of personality variation found in them is

smaller? (2) Are there differences in incidence of neurosis and psychosis? (3) Are there differences in role or status personality, such as would distinguish shamans, conjurers, men, women, favored children, etc.? (4) What are the psychological consequences of acculturation? (Hallowell, 1942, p. 205.)

We may now turn to our summary of the research which involves the use of projective tests (Table 1). As already noted, we have limited this summary to those tests which have been used for personality evaluation and, furthermore, to those studies in which some comparison is possible between the ethnographic material and the test results. We group the studies in Table 1 according to techniques used, size of sample, methods, purpose, and results claimed.

BIBLIOGRAPHY

ABEL, THEODORA M., and HSU, FRANCIS L. K. 1949. "Some Aspects of Personality of Chinese as Revealed by the Rorschach Test," *Journal of Projective Techniques*, XIII, 285–301.

BARNOUW, VICTOR. 1950. *Acculturation and Personality among the Wisconsin Chippewa*. ("Memoirs of the American Anthropological Association," No. 72.)

BENEDICT, RUTH. 1946. *The Chrysanthemum and the Sword*. Boston: Houghton Mifflin Co.

BILLIG, OTTO; GILLIN, JOHN; and DAVIDSON, WILLIAM. 1947–48. "Aspects of Personality and Culture in a Guatemalan Community: Ethnological and Rorschach Approaches," *Journal of Personality*, XVI, 153–87, 326–68.

BLEULER, M. and R. 1935. "Rorschach's Ink-Blot Test and Racial Psychology: Mental Peculiarities of Moroccans," *Character and Personality*, IV, 97–114.

CAUDILL, WILLIAM. 1949. "Psychological Characteristics of Acculturated Wisconsin Ojibwa," *American Anthropologist*, LI, 409–27.

COOK, P. H. 1942. "The Application of the Rorschach Test to a Samoan Group,"

Rorschach Research Exchange, VI, 52–60.

DUBOIS, CORA. 1944. *The People of Alor*. Minneapolis: University of Minnesota Press.

HALLOWELL, A. IRVING. 1941*a*. "The Rorschach Method as an Aid in the Study of Personalities in Primitive Societies," *Character and Personality*, IX, 235–45.

——. 1941*b*. "The Rorschach Test as a Tool for Investigating Cultural Variables and Individual Differences in the Study of Personality in Primitive Societies," *Rorschach Research Exchange*, V, 31–34.

——. 1942. "Acculturation Processes and Personality Changes as Indicated by the Rorschach Technique," *ibid.*, VI, 42–50.

——. 1945*a*. "The Rorschach Technique in the Study of Personality and Culture," *American Anthropologist*, XLVII, 195–210.

——. 1945*b*. " 'Popular' Responses and Cultural Differences: An Analysis Based on Frequencies in a Group of American Indian Subjects," *Rorschach Research Exchange*, IX, 153–68.

——. 1946. "Some Psychological Charac-

TABLE 1

Name of Investigators	Groups Studied	Instruments	Size of Sample*	Method of Selection	Purpose	Methods	Results Claimed
1. Abel and Hsu (1949)	Chinese	Rorschach	27 China-born adults of both sexes; 20 American-born adults; all in U.S.A.	Unknown	To show changes taking place in Chinese under acculturation	Tests administered by H Davidson and L. Steinberg; data on Chinese personality and culture by Hsu; "The material was discussed", with workers on Columbia University project Research in Contemporary Cultures; language: English; no life-history data	Marked differences appear between the four groups, ascribable to differences in cultural and sex-determined experience
2. Barnouw (1950)	Ojibwa	Rorschach	107	Unknown	To illuminate personality adjustment in acculturation	Test administered by author, Ritzenthaler, Fried; group records interpreted by Klopfer; certain individual ones by author and Maude Hallowell. English used; life-history data available on some subjects	"The assessment [by Dr. Klopfer] is essentially in agreement with the personality picture which has been described by the ethnographer"; individual Rorschachs in agreement with life-history
3. Benedict (1946)	Japanese in American relocation centers	Rorschach	Unknown	Unknown	To illuminate the character of the Japanese in Japan	Rorschach tests administered by D. Leighton, analyzed by F, Holter; modes of collaboration between Benedict, Leighton, and Holter unknown; language used unknown; life-history data not given on any of the subjects	Test proves that dualism in Japanese personality creates tension
4. Billig, Gillin, and Davidson (1947–48)	Indians and Ladinos in a Guatemalan village	Rorschach	67 adult males, "about evenly divided between Indians and Ladinos"	According to age	To show the difference between the "folk" and the nonfolk personality	Administrator of test unknown; psychologists did not know the culture or the individuals; test administered in Spanish; life-history data available for all subjects, but not given	Ladinos and Indians have different personalities; the folk-urban construct is validated by personality findings
5. Bleuler and Bleuler (1935)	Arabs and Berbers of Chaouia, West Morocco	Rorschach	29 adults	Unknown	1. To test differences in racial character 2. To test cross-cultural validity of Rorschach	One interpreted the Rorschachs "blind"; the other compared the interpretations with his personal knowledge of the individuals tested; character of "personal knowledge" not known; language unknown	1. Test reveals "the essential characteristics of their nationallife, their literature, their art, and their science," all being a function of their "racial character" (p. 111) 2. The Rorschach test is a valuable tool with which to gauge the character of a foreign people
6. Caudill (1949)	Ojibwa (Lac du Flambeau, Wisconsin)	T.A.T.	88 children, aged 6–16.11	Representative sample, with respect to age and sex, of federal day school	To discover what, if any, personality changes accompany cultural changes in an acculturative situation	Administered and interpreted by author, with assistance of W. Henry, the former knowing the culture	1. Personality picture very similar to that of the relatively unacculturated Canadian Ojibwa and Hallowell's reconstruction of aboriginal Eastern Woodland personality structure; thus "there is a strong persistence of Ojibwa personality over a long span of time, and despite the effects of western influence on Ojibwa culture" (p. 425)

*There are occasional differences between the figures given by the authors of the works cited and ours. This is because in some cases the total number of protocols obtained is not the same as the number that actually entered into the calculations. We have generally chosen the latter figure.

423

TABLE 1—*Continued*

Name of Investigators	Groups Studied	Instruments	Size of Sample	Method of Selection	Purpose	Methods	Results Claimed
7. Cook (1942)	Samoans	Rorschach	50 adult males, aged 16–27	Chosen from mission high school, studying to be pastors; aged 16–27; have been in school since age of 7; all come from the families of chiefs or families of pastors	"To see what deviations . . . from the generally accepted criteria of Rorschach interpretation would be found in a non-European cultural group" (p. 88)	Cook administered the test in the native language through an interpreter; examiner knew enough of the native language to check his interpreters; examiner did the interpretations; life-history and data obtained from Samoan schoolmasters; all these data considered by examiner to be worthless for evaluation of individuals	"The Rorschach test cannot be interpreted for Samoans in terms of criteria established with other cultural groups without qualification and modification" (p. 59)
8. Dubois (1944)	Alor	Rorschach	37 adults	Unknown	To establish the "modal personality" of the Alorese	Tests administered by Dubois, scored and interpreted by E. Oberholzer, who states: "It seems futile to make an attempt of this kind with thirty seven Alorese" (p. 630); Oberholzer states (p. 589) that he checked his preliminary Rorschach impressions "with the ethnographer's statements concerning the psychological background of the individuals"	Results sustain the impressions of the ethnologist about the personality of the Alorese
	Alor	Children's drawings	33 boys, 22 girls	Unknown	To establish the "modal personality" of the Alorese	"Children were given pencil and paper, materials which they had never handled, and were asked to draw whatever they wished. An arbitrary time-span of thirty minutes was set"; Dubois made statistical analysis of drawings and interpretation, Schmidl-Waelner as consultant	Results seem to confirm Dubois's impressions of "ego inadequacies and paucity of relationship expression" in the Alorese; thus the hypothesis of the "modal personality" is confirmed
9. Hallowell (1945b)	Ojibwa	Rorschach	151 adults	Random sample	To investigate the nature of popular (P) responses in the Rorschach, to ascertain to what extent they can be applied cross-culturally	Compared Western populars and Ojibwa populars; native language used with interpreter; no life-history data	For purposes of cross-cultural comparisons, it may be necessary to operate with three kinds of populars: "universal populars" are those which occur in a large number of distinct cultural groups; "common populars" are those that occur in a more restricted number of groups; "unique populars" are those which occur only in one cultural group
10. Hallowell (1946)	Ojibwa	Rorschach	151 adults	Random sample; same subjects as above	To investigate to what extent the relatively unacculturated Canadian Ojibwa are similar psychologically to the aboriginal group (17th and 18th centuries)	Compared descriptions of Indians of the Eastern Woodlands made by 17th- and 18th-century observers (primarily, in the Jesuit "Relations") with observations and Rorschachs of unacculturated Ojibwa	1. The comparison revealed that "the same emotional structure [described in the literature] remains characteristic of some of the Indians of the Eastern Woodlands [Ojibwa] at the present time" (p. 218)

TABLE 1—*Continued*

Name of Investigators	Groups Studied	Instruments	Size of Sample	Method of Selection	Purpose	Methods	Results Claimed
11. Hallowell (1951)	Ojibwa	Rorschach	217 adults, aged 16–80	Random sample from 3 Ojibwa groups representing 3 different positions on scale of acculturation	To discover (1) the differences, if any, in Ojibwa modal personality under aboriginal conditions and under conditions of acculturation and (2) the relative differences in psychological adjustment	1. Reconstruct aboriginal personality picture by use of 17th- and 18th-century documents, and field work and Rorschachs from unacculturated Ojibwa, demonstrating the aboriginal personality; the three types of data are in substantial accord 2. Study changes in personality under acculturation by field work and Rorschachs from 3 Ojibwa communities found on a scale of acculturation 3. Measure the relative adjustment of these communities by the use of "Davidson's signs" of adjustment 4. Administration by Hallowell and students, interpretation by Hallowell, statistical treatment by Bennett and Wesman; no life-history data available; native language with interpreter used in unacculturated groups; English used in acculturated group	1. Despite their differential acculturative status, all the groups are remarkably similar psychologically 2. The least-acculturated group is best adjusted, and the most-acculturated, the least adjusted 3. The women are better adjusted than the men, though there are statistical difficulties here
12. Henry and Henry (1944)	Pilagá Indians	Doll play	24 children, 1½–13 years	Total village population of children at the time	To obtain additional data to document the direct observation of child personality and behavior; to test the utility of doll play as a technique in anthropological field method	"Father," "mother," "self," and sibling dolls were named by examiner after the subject's family; play was voluntary and of the "free-play" type; Z. Henry recorded all movements with dolls as they occurred; verbalizations by children were in native language and were recorded in text; 92 play sessions were recorded; each child had from 1 to 12 sessions; protocols analyzed by coding technique after Levy by J. Henry; results compared with day-to-day observations of each child; life-history available, some in monograph	1. Impressions of ethnologists of child behavior and feeling are confirmed 2. Proof of thesis that "under similar conditions of familial tension, children in distinct cultures will develop the same kind of symptom pattern" 3. Patterns of sibling rivalry found in Pilagá culture vary somewhat from those found in our own 4. Certain endopsychic dynamisms postulated by psychoanalysis as universal are found among the Pilagá
13. Schachtel, Henry, and Henry (1942)		Rorschach	13 children, 4–12 years	Random sample	To test the utility of the Rorschach test in a primitive culture; to obtain additional data on child personality; to control biases present in observer	Protocols administered by Z. Henry, analyzed by A. Hartoch; six interoretations are compared with life-histories of the subjects as collected through day-to-day observation of the children, and with doll-play results; all testing done in native language	The Rorschach test is a useful instrument for field research in personality in primitive cultures: "There is a close correspondence between the Rorschach findings and the ethnological facts" (p. 680)

TABLE 1—*Continued*

Name of Investigators	Groups Studied	Instruments	Size of Sample	Method of Selection	Purpose	Methods	Results Claimed
14. Henry (1947)	Hopi and Navaho	T.A.T. (mod.)	15 Hopi and 15 Navaho children, aged 6–18	Selected by staff of the Research on Indian Education without knowledge of author, so as to reflect "the range of problems and situations that any Hopi or Navaho child might encounter" (p. 12)	To investigate the validity of the T.A.T. in studies of "culture-personality interaction"	Tests administered by Joseph and D. Leighton, interpreted blind by Henry; three validating procedures were used: (a) Three judges were presented with the life-histories, Rorschachs, psychological battery of exams, and T.A.T. (a total of 32 personality analyses) and were asked to match the T.A.T. with the other tests, making a total of 24 matched pairs; Judge 1 knew each child through the life-history and the Rorschach, and was partially familiar with the culture; Judge 2 knew each child through the life-history, and knew the culture well; Judge 3 knew each child through the T.A.T. and did not know the culture. (b) The judges were presented with a detailed outline of personality characteristics and were asked to check the information obtained from the T.A.T. with respect to these characteristics with the information obtained from 9 other tests administered to 16 Navaho children. (c) All the Hopi and all the Navaho T.A.T.'s were matched with the anthropological data	a) In the matching study, in which three correct matchings are expected by chance, the results were: Judge 1: correctly matched 18 pairs; Judge 2: correctly matched 24 pairs (this is the judge who knew the culture well); Judge 3: correctly matched 15 pairs b) In the "agreement analysis," out of a total of 451 ratings: (1) there was "essential agreement" between the T.A.T. and at least one other source of data in 375 ratings, or 83.1 per cent of the total; (2) there was "partial agreement" in 66, or 14.7 per cent; (3) there was disagreement in 10 or 2.2 per cent . . . both the Hopi and the Navaho there was "high agreement" between the ethnographic data and the T.A.T. picture
		T.A.T. (mod.)	102 Hopi and 104 Navaho, aged 6–18	These represent the T.A.T.'s collected in the Hopi and Navaho studies listed above	To investigate the "significance" of the T.A.T. in studies in personality and culture, involving problems: 1. Can the T.A.T. be used in cultures other than the American middle class? 2. Upon what areas of personality does the T.A.T. give data? 3. What does the T.A.T. tell us regarding motives? 4. What does the T.A.T. tell us about the person's life-experiences? 5. What can the T.A.T. tell us about the general psychological characteristics of a society and about the cultural factors that are relevant in personality development?	Tests analyzed blind by Henry, and then compared with data derived from other tests and the ethnographic data, first reconstructing a personality picture on the basis of the T.A.T. alone, and then on the basis of all the data, including the T.A.T.	The five problems raised in the Purpose may be answered, as follows: The T.A.T. provides satisfactory answers to all these questions regarding group attitudes toward the physical world, adult pressures, authority systems, interpersonal relations, sex roles, family roles, spontaneity and restraint, acculturation processes, personality characteristics at different age levels (p. 126)

426

TABLE 1—Continued

Name of Investigators	Groups Studied	Instruments	Size of Sample	Method of Selection	Purpose	Methods	Results Claimed
15. Honigman (1949)	Kaska	Rorschach	19 subjects, age and sex distributions unknown	Unknown	To confirm Kaska ethos, derived by ethnographic analysis; to prove that the Kaska possessed a reasonable degree of homogeneity	Tests administered and analyzed by Honigman; tests given in English; four individual analyses presented with life-history data; in all, nine subjects were interviewed	Rorschach results support Honigman's ethnographic analysis of Kaska ethos: ethnographic and Rorschach analysis both demonstrate the same things about Kaska ethos; the hypothesis of "homogeneity" is not discussed in connection with the Rorschach findings
16. Joseph, Spicer, and Chesky (1949)	Papago	Free drawings; T.A.T. (mod.); Rorschach	200 children, aged 6–18	Samples from eastern and western parts of reservation	Description of personality of Papago children	Tests administered by teachers and by Joseph and interpreted by Eubank, Mordy, W. Henry, Havighurst, and Joseph, some knowing the culture and some not; native language used with interpreter; some life-history data available	1. High consistency among the various tests and the ethnographic data 2. Personality of children established by tests
17. Joseph and Murray (1951)	Chamorros and Carolinians of Saipan	(a) Bender Gestalt; (b) Rorschach	200 children, aged 5–17; 30 adults, aged 16–74	Random sample of children; highly selective (acculturated) adult sample	"A deliberate attempt to find out how much information concerning personality structure in a cultural group can be obtained by a relatively short, standardized method" (pp. vii–viii)	All tests administered by authors; Rorschachs interpreted by authors; Bender Gestalt interpreted blind by Bender; test data compared with impressions, documents, and information concerning behavior obtained from military government officials; native language used with interpreter; life-history data available	These tests do give much information regarding personality processes, even in the absence of detailed ethnographic investigations
18. Kluckhohn and Rosenzweig (1949)	Navaho	Rorschach; T.A.T. (mod.)	2 children, aged 13–14	Unknown	Study of two children over a five-year period (1942–47) to discover what light is shed by projective techniques on personality development	Tests administered by Rosenzweig and interpreted by psychiatrist, clinical psychologist, and anthropologist—in most cases independently and blind; detailed life-history data available	The picture obtained by the various techniques and the different interpreters is "on the whole, remarkably consistent.... The personality diagnoses made on the basis of projective tests also check well with the impressions of another set of field workers who used ordinary interview and observation methods. In short, the present paper constitutes a partial validation of projective tests in another culture, with the caution that significant results are peculiarly dependent upon the relation between tester and subject" (pp. 277–78)
19. Leighton and Kluckhohn (1948)	Navaho	Rorschach; T.A.T. (mod.); free drawings	211 children, aged 6–18	Children from three communities representing different ethnic positions on scale of acculturation	Description of personality of Navaho children	Tests administered and analyzed by teachers and by Leighton; all knew the culture; response in native language; Leighton used interpreter	1. Very few over-all characteristics found in total group, but breakdown into four age groups (5–7, 8–10, 11–13, 14–18) revealed important characteristics which served to identify the group 2. High consistency among results of various tests and ethnographic data

TABLE 1—Continued

Name of Investigators	Groups Studied	Instruments	Size of Sample	Method of Selection	Purpose	Methods	Results Claimed
20. Lewis (1951)	Tepoztecans (Mexican village)	Rorschach	106 subjects, aged 5-74	21 families, representing barrio and socio-economic differences	"As one part of a broad ethnographic and historical study of the village"	The Rorschach tests were given in Spanish by Ruth M. Lewis; interpretations by T. M. Abel and R. A. Calabresi; they had read three articles by Lewis and "an earlier version" of a family study; 7 student assistants lived with the families to be tested; when rapport was thus established, R. Lewis was introduced to the family and gave the tests; parents were tested in the home, the children in school	No claims are made
21. Macgregor (1946)	Dakota Indians	T.A.T. (mod.), Rorschach	166 children, 6-18 years	At random from 3 Indian schools	To illustrate personality pathology as a function of cultural breakdown	Test analysts: R. Hassrick, W. E. Henry, R. Havighurst, I. Schmidt, J. Hall, J. Murstine; test administrators unknown; language, English; life-history data available on all subjects; given for 10 of them	Indian children's anxiety, hostility, withdrawness, and apathy, as expected in terms of their cultural disorganization, are proved by the tests
22. Mead (1949)	Arapesh	Rorschach	1 man	An informant	Probably to show the utility of the Rorschach test in primitive cultures	Rorschach given in pidgin by Mead; Protocols scored as follows: (1) card-by-card interpretation by Klopfer in side-by-side consultation with Mead; (2) rapid assessment from Belo's scoring by Wolfenstein; (3) Harrower and Miale discussed protocols and chart and then discussed their findings with Mead before publication; (4) Abel made an interpretation from Belo's scoring; all interpretations made long after publication of Mead's *Sex and Temperament*; abundant ethnographic material obtained from subject is published along with the Rorschach	1. Rorschach is a valuable aid to field research in personality and culture 2. Rorschach technicians can all agree about the fundamentals of the personality dynamics of a primative person
23. Thompson and Joseph (1944)	Hopi	T.A.T. (mod.), Rorschach, free drawings	190 children, aged 6-18	All children, with few exceptions, living in First Mesa and Oraibi	Description of personality of Hopi children	Tests administered by school principal, schoolteachers, and Thompson and Joseph; interpreted by Havighurst, Mordy, Rannells, W. Henry, and Joseph; all except Henry (T.A.T.) knew the culture or participated in the field work; responses in native language, interpreter used; life-history data available on representative sample of children tested	1. Personality characteristics of children established as basis of tests 2. High consistency among results of various tests and ethnographic data
24. Vogt (1952)	Navaho	(a) Rorschach, (b) T.A.T., (c) Veterans T.A.T.	20 adult males, veterans of World War II	Veterans of World War II	To illuminate psychological factors involved in the change of values in acculturation	Tests administered by author and Bert Kaplan; latter interpreted tests, with some knowledge of culture and conversations with the author	The tests, in conjunction with the life-histories and ethnographic data, help to explain the changing values of these veterans

teristics of Northeastern Woodland Indians." In JOHNSON, FREDERICK (ed.), *Man in Northeastern North America*, pp. 195–225. ("Papers of the R. S. Peabody Foundation for Archaeology," Vol. III.)

————. 1951. "Use of Projective Techniques in the Study of Socio-psychological Aspects of Acculturation," *Journal of Projective Techniques*, XV, 27–44.

HENRY, JULES and ZUNIA. 1944. *Doll Play of Pilagá Indian Children.* ("Research Monographs of the American Orthopsychiatric Association," No. 4.)

HENRY, WILLIAM. 1947. *The Thematic Apperception Technique in the Study of Culture-Personality Relations.* ("Genetic Psychology Monographs," Vol. XXXV, first half.)

HONIGMANN, JOHN J. 1949. *Culture and Ethos of Kaska Society.* ("Yale University Publications in Anthropology," No. 40.) New Haven.

JOSEPH, ALICE; SPICER, ROSAMUND B.; and CHESKY, JANE. 1949. *The Desert People: A Study of the Papago Indians.* Chicago: University of Chicago Press.

JOSEPH, ALICE, and MURRAY, V. F. 1951. *Chamorros and Carolinians of Saipan.* Cambridge: Harvard University Press.

KLUCKHOHN, CLYDE, and ROSENZWEIG, JANINE CHAPPAT. 1949. "Two Navaho Children over a Five Year Period," *American Journal of Orthopsychiatry*, XIX, 266–78.

LANTZ, HERMAN. 1948. "Rorschach Testing in Pre-literate Cultures," *American Journal of Orthopsychiatry*, XVIII, 287–91.

LEIGHTON, D., and KLUCKHOHN, C. 1948. *The Children of the People.* Cambridge: Harvard University Press.

LEWIS, OSCAR. 1951. *Life in a Mexican Village.* Urbana: University of Illinois Press.

MACGREGOR, GORDON. 1946. *Warriors without Weapons.* Chicago: University of Chicago Press.

MEAD, MARGARET. 1949. *The Mountain Arapesh*, Vol. V: *The Record of Unabelin with Rorschach Analysis.* ("Anthropological Papers of the American Museum of Natural History.") New York.

SCHACHTEL, ANNA HARTOCH, and HENRY, JULES and ZUNIA. 1942. "Rorschach Analysis of Pilagá Indian Children," *American Journal of Orthopsychiatry*, XII, 679–712.

THOMPSON, LAURA, and JOSEPH, ALICE. 1944. *The Hopi Way.* Chicago: University of Chicago Press.

VOGT, EVON Z. 1952. *Navaho Veterans: A Study of Changing Values.* ("Papers of the Peabody Museum of American Archaeology and Ethnology, Harvard University," Vol. XLI, No. 1.)

Interview Techniques and Field Relationships

By BENJAMIN D. PAUL

THE KIND of information obtained in field interviews largely depends on three factors: (a) the problem interests of the ethnographer, (b) his interviewing skills, and (c) his relations with informants and the community at large. This essay ignores the first factor, gives some consideration to the second, and concentrates on the third, that of the ethnographer's role—his behavior and its influence on the people and hence on the information they give him. This is an aspect of field method that requires codification. In the interest of directing discussion toward such codification, this paper draws on the published and unpublished experiences of field workers to review the areas and types of activity that define the investigator's position in the society he studies. After discussing problems and practices connected with gaining *entrance* (introductions, establishing a role, ethics of role-playing), it takes up the topic of *participation* (types, avenues, limits, hazards, and costs of involvement in the community). The last section concerns *interviewing* techniques (general procedures, the informant, the interview, language and the interpreter, and note-taking).

I. ENTERING THE COMMUNITY

INTRODUCTIONS

There is no prescription for finding the correct entrée into a new commu- nity. It depends on the sophistication of the community and the amount of advance information the investigator is able to get. Frequently he can count on a chain of introductions which leads at least to the threshold of his group. By the time he reaches a provincial center or trading post near his destina- tion, he is likely to have learned the names of people who have contacts with the natives. Here on the periph- eries he can pick up bits of information which will serve to orient him. The novice who is anxious to obtain the full acceptance of the natives sometimes by-passes regional administrators for fear of prejudicing his reception. But it will do him little good to be well received by the natives, only to be im- peded by higher authorities who make it their business to follow the move- ments of strangers. Apprised of his plans, power figures can come to his aid in case of unexpected trouble; unin- formed, they can cause trouble out of mistaken conceptions as to his inten- tions. Whether he asks them to provide an introduction will depend on his esti- mation of how such auspices will pro- mote or prejudice his standing in the community to be studied.

In carrying out investigations in a modern community or in an industrial organization, it has been found expedi- ent, and sometimes essential, to estab- lish the initial contacts with those people who have controlling voices in the community. These may be men who hold status in the power hierarchy or people in informal positions who command respect. Their indorsement of the project can be critical, and they can serve in a useful liaison capacity. This procedure applies equally in the nonoccidental community. The difference is that the native power and prestige structure is not always apparent on first arrival. If the society is stratified, it is easy to identify the elite group, the only problem being that of locating the proper individuals within the upper stratum. Filtering down from the top presents fewer obstacles than attempting to work upward, whether the strata are castes, informal classes, or nobility and commoners.

In relatively homogeneous communities authority may be vested in a chief, a body of elders, or a formally constituted administrative group holding office by appointment or election. But in some groups the men who mold opinion are not always tagged for all to see. Where this is the case, the anthropologist will proceed cautiously, settling down as inconspicuously as possible and biding his time before plying the natives with questions. In due course, if he manages to appear harmless, he will learn the identity of people in prestige positions—an expert craftsman, a medicine man, a famous hunter, a local sage, or perchance a chief who plays his role unobtrusively. Inquisitiveness may serve only to deflect his attention from the respected leader to the disrespected deviant, perhaps the local "wise guy." The rule of starting slowly has its exceptions, of course. There may be ranking families or church leaders who feel slighted if they are not accorded immediate recognition by the newcomer. Out of malice or misunderstanding, they can exploit their prestige to circulate rumors that undermine the field venture before it gets under way.

The strategic value of beginning with the local leaders need not imply that these are necessarily the best sources of ethnographic data.

ESTABLISHING A ROLE

In part, the field worker defines his own role; in part, it is defined for him by the situation and the outlook of the natives. His is the strategy of a player in a game. He cannot predict the precise plays which the other side will make, but he anticipates them as best he can and makes his moves accordingly. His performance is guided by his own conception of the natives' conception of his role. If new in the field, the anthropologist is faced with something of a dilemma. He assumes a role in order to study the culture; yet he must often know the culture before he can assume a satisfactory role. The dilemma is usually resolved through time, granting a degree of tolerance and plasticity on both sides.

The game of achieving mutual understanding takes place within a field of restricted possibilities. The ethnologist's choices are limited by the range of role adaptations he is willing and able to play, as well as by the range of roles the natives find acceptable. His role must fit into the area where these ranges overlap. The natives can conceive, or be induced to conceive, a certain number of alternatives, and, of these, only some are acceptable. For his part, the ethnologist is limited in the accommodations he can make, by his purpose and his personality. He can adjust his plans and often does so. The extent to which he can alter his problem depends upon his ingenuity and the degree to which he is committed by his program or by his sponsoring organization. Because of the frequent need to improvise, the prudent anthropologist strives to retain independence of decision and be prepared to abandon his best-laid plans in favor of what is feasible in the field. Factors of personality impose severer restrictions. Some investigators find role-playing a challenging game, others find it punishing. Some can tolerate appearing ridiculous in native eyes, others need to preserve their dignity. Some can be indifferent to aloofness, others are discouraged by diffidence.

Seldom does it make sense to say in so many words that one is a cultural anthropologist. It is easier to stress an aspect of the discipline that corresponds to something familiar. Some nonliterate groups enjoy discussing abstract topics or have savants of their own. To such people knowledge for its own sake may not seem too strange a quest. Since nearly all natives are aware of cultural differences, if not always sympathetic to divergent practices, they are often intrigued to hear how folk tales and customs of neighboring peoples compare with their own.

Some field workers begin by stating their desire to learn the native language. This is an unobjectionable interest. It places the native in the happy position of an expert and readily leads to the recording of native texts. Once confidence is gained in this manner, the field worker can usually widen his studies by admitting a wish to learn more about local customs. He may explain, whether or not he begins with the language, that he wants to observe the local way of life in order to portray it correctly to people on the outside. Having learned to look with suspicion on professed errands of benevolence, many natives may respond to this philanthropic explanation with little enthusiasm, if it is offered at the outset. But after establishing friendship on other bases, such a statement will not be amiss and may ease later efforts to examine closely into cultural details. In his eagerness to win co-operation, the anthropologist should not imply that his findings will rectify onerous admin-

istrative policies or that his report will quickly earn for the natives the good will of the outside world. Most natives know that books are printed and sold, but they seldom have sufficient perspective to appreciate the specialized circulation of ethnographic accounts. It is not at all unusual to hear natives surmise that the investigator will become wealthy on the sale of his book.

One way to explain anthropology is to accept the pedagogical aspect. People familiar with the schoolteacher role may find it plausible that an instructor from another country should want to gather material for teaching purposes. In Cottonville, Hortense Powdermaker found that the title of "Visiting Teacher," obtained in advance from the Department of Education at Jackson, Mississippi, permitted easy contact with local white and colored education officials, who agreed to sponsor her plan of study and introduce her to other members of the community (Powdermaker, 1939).

Some workers have used the historian approach. The ethnographer may be genuinely interested in learning the traditions and historical background of the group; but, even if his chief concern is with the present situation, he can often overcome initial suspicion by inquiring into the past. At the opportune time he can point out that the past is carried into the present and thus shift his attention to contemporary history. He may, however, find it difficult to make the shift as illustrated by the experience of a young anthropologist whose first field assignment took him to an old community in the American South. Though his main interest was in the contemporary and sociological, he was anxious not to be identified as an obstreperous "outside reformer." He introduced himself by placing a story in the local newspaper, presenting both the historical and the contemporary aspects of the study. The editors chose only to mention "historical study" in the caption. Cast in the role of historian, he was continually directed to informants who were considered experts on local history, and he was ushered on a tour of ancient homes and historical sites. Wherever he turned, he encountered clippings, genealogies, and relics. While the role of historian made his interest in the community legitimate, in the estimation of the "better people," it restricted the categories of persons with whom he could properly associate. Why should a respectable historian, they wondered, be interested in mill workers, lower-class whites, or Negroes?

If the newcomer fails to take steps to clarify his role, the people will attempt to resolve uncertainty by fitting him into a classification familiar to them. In the absence of convincing indications to the contrary, the stranger in a native area will usually be classed as a government official, missionary, or trader, the three main categories of whites known to natives. Such identification will not necessarily jeopardize his reception, but it cannot fail to color his relationships accordingly. When my wife and I arrived in a Guatemalan Indian village, it was apparent that we were not officials of the government. Nor were we taken for American tourists, since we settled down to live among the Indians. We had been cautioned in advance to take up cigarette smoking in order not to be classified as missionaries. But we were unaware that many of the people, assuming our trunks to be filled with trade goods, expected from day to day that we would set up shop. This impression was perforce dispelled in the course of time. Had we realized that we were thought to be merchants, we would not have wondered at the unexpected reception we received on the day of our arrival. Neighbors crowded the doors and peered in at the window. They admir-

ingly fingered our clothes, asked the price of each item, and inquired whether we would sell them a pair of shoes or trousers or a jacket. We were pleased to attract so many people, many of them children with little else to do, and concluded that Guatemalan Indians matched those of Mitla in their boundless curiosity, for we recalled reading Elsie Clews Parsons' statement that the natives of Mitla were always asking the price of everything they saw or heard of. When she mentioned that one of her relatives had been killed in a motorcycle accident, a listener quickly asked how much the motorcycle had cost (Parsons, 1936). We were not wholly wrong in judging the Indians to be curious about prices—and about distances and sizes of buildings and steamboats—but the avidity with which they crowded around to feel and look at everything made better sense in retrospect when we learned that our private residence was assumed to be a public shop. We had to revise our initial exaggerated estimate of their bold inquisitiveness. Inadvertently, the misconception had solved the problem of making friendly contacts, even before we had time to unpack.

The Kwoma had too little contact with missionaries and traders to think of placing John Whiting in either of these two categories. But they were acquainted with Australian government agents, who were dangerous, and labor recruiters, who were both useful and annoying. Since Whiting arrived with a patrol officer and a company of police boys, he was first classed as "government," even though the officer announced to the assembled tribe that Whiting had come to study their language and customs. The official ordered them to construct a house for the anthropologist and warned that if he were harmed the culprit would be severely punished. In part, Whiting was also classed as a labor recruiter, since he brought many boxes of supplies and trade goods. Like many other tribes, the Kwoma regulate their social relationships in terms of an elaborate and wide-reaching kinship system. In so far as Whiting came to be included in the local social structure, he was assigned on the basis of residence to an appropriate Kwoma lineage and, by equation with a given generation, was called "younger brother" or "father" or "elder uncle," depending on the particular "kinsman" who addressed him. Having found a place for Whiting in their kinship map, the Kwoma could orient their social behavior correspondingly (Whiting, 1941).

One group of Navaho Indians, who could not understand why anthropologists should want to know all the things they did, recently hit upon the happy solution of equating the status of inquisitive whites with that of Navaho diviner or "hand trembler." The native term for this office means "one who asks questions." Finding the right role in the field often requires ingenuity on both sides. The task is like that of a man groping for the light switch in a dark room.

ETHICS OF ROLE-PLAYING

The question may well be raised whether assuming a role which will best promote rapport in the field does not, in fact, amount to deception. Is it dishonest initially to claim an interest in learning the native language when, in fact, this is only part of the investigator's purpose? Is it hypocritical to engage in casual conversation without making it explicit that the information will later be recorded? Obviously, these are questions of conscience and personal values. Each person must answer them according to his own lights. There can be no quarrel with the person who judges these acts of commission and omission to be sins. But the man who takes this stand must ask himself still

other questions: Does he practice deception if he decides to "look his best" and avoid controversial discussion when interviewed for a job? Is a storekeeper dishonest when he acts on the principle that "the customer is always right"? In short, is it deceitful to play a role in conformity with local role expectations? Can the bounds of honesty be delimited without relation to social context and social consequences?

All this does not mean, however, that honesty is a purely relative thing and that one is at liberty to say and do whatever is convenient in the field. Every investigator is governed in some degree by a moral code derived from his culture and incorporated into his personality. Some anthropologists feel little disturbance over the role they have to play in the field, while others are troubled by self-accusations of hypocrisy. Even the most rigidly ethical anthropologists have been compelled to make role adaptations in the field in order to get the most accurate picture of native cultural life. The question of honesty or deception is best directed at the *purposes* of field work. The investigator who distorts his published interpretations or prepares a report for a special interest group without pondering the social consequences of his findings (Mead, Chapple, and Brown, 1949) is fundamentally more dishonest than the worker who finds it necessary to use tact and diplomacy in the field to learn the nature and meaning of local practices and thereby advance scientific understanding of the properties of sociocultural systems.

II. PARTICIPATION

TYPES OF PARTICIPATION

Among the long list of anthropologists who have lived with their subjects of study, the extent of participation has varied widely, some workers keeping their social distance by choice or necessity, others thrusting themselves, like

Malinowski among the Trobriand Islanders, into every native activity. Where the environment is inhospitable, there is little choice. One chooses to stay away or accepts the necessity of living with the natives at close quarters. When Allan Holmberg was on the march for game with the Siriono of Bolivia, he spent the night in rude shelters, went weeks without salt, and once became so exhausted after four days of eating only palm cabbage, cusi nuts, and a variety of fruit that he and his Indian companions lacked the strength to kill more than a fraction of the wild peccary they finally encountered. Like the natives themselves, he ate most of his food during the dead of night to avoid being hounded by perennially hungry adults and children (Holmberg, 1950).

Curt Nimuendajú, originally of Germany, took his name from the Indians of Amazonia with whom he lived for decades and among whom he died. To a degree he "went native," but he shaved every day in the jungle and became an ethnographic authority on the area (Baldus, 1946). The man who goes completely native, granting the possibility, participates fully in native life, to be sure, but, in so doing, he ceases to be an observer and can no longer be counted within the fold of anthropologists. Frank Cushing did not become a Zuni, but he became so emotionally identified with the people that he refused to continue publishing his Zuni data.

AVENUES OF PARTICIPATION

Granting initial acceptance by the group and willingness on the part of the ethnographer, the possible ways and means of participating in local activities are virtually endless in their variety. Some are to be sought out, others are not to be avoided. Available avenues obviously depend on the case,

but it may be well to review some of the more general circumstances that facilitate social interaction.

The first is so commonplace that it may escape awareness. This is the avenue of potential solidarities based on the universal recognition of age and sex distinctions. An important factor supporting the feeling of common sex identification is the ever present awareness of *not* belonging socially to the opposite sex, a kind of solidarity by opposition. The fact that the male ethnographer and the local males share a common counteridentification provides at least a potential social bond between the two as implied in the phrase "we men." The rapport channel provided by sharing a sex role may be illustrated by the "we women" solidarity which animated many conversations between my wife and the women of San Pedro la Laguna. The women confided information they would not dare tell any man and were equally curious about the role of women in the United States. The general topic of the woman's lot and the realization that women in both places share the role of wives, if little else, facilitated good relationships and led to my wife's participation in events which I, as a male, could not well hope to witness. Other women going to the field have had similar experiences.

In like manner, membership in a common generation or age group often provides a bond between the ethnographer and natives of similar age. Mutual inclusions and exclusions supply a common ground for the unmarried, the parents of young children, or the older generation. The fact that the ethnographer has kinsmen and perhaps can open a family album strikes a note of interest and sympathy. Rosamund Spicer found that her best opening among the Papago Indians was through her two-year-old son, "who came to speak more Papago than English and quickly won his way into the hearts of the people" (Spicer and Joseph, 1949).

A second avenue of "participation" is to convey appreciation of native skills by making an effort to learn some of the native arts. Though they may value their own ways, most indigenous peoples realize by now that Europeans or Americans devalue their customs. The ethnographer can dissociate himself from this judgmental standpoint through the gesture of participating in the local foodways or by trying his hand at a technical pursuit, such as spearing fish. A woman investigator can similarly try spinning yarn or grinding grain. Without benefit of prior training, the field worker will prove inept in his performance, but, if the effort is made with good grace and a minimum of condescension, the gesture may promote good feeling. The native observers may be amused or engage in banter, but they will usually be pleased to play the role of mentor rather than mere informant.

On his part, the anthropologist has certain skills and material benefits to offer, and these constitute a third and quite important avenue of participation. He can augment the labor force at critical times of the year, helping out in communal harvesting or house-building. Among forest tribes who hunt with spears or arrows, he can materially increase the food supply by shooting wild game with a gun. Where there are roads, he can provide transportation in his car, at the same time profiting from informal conversation. He can distribute photographs, contribute food or money on festive occasions, and enter into gift-exchange relationships with neighbors. If he is able to play an instrument, he can provide music and even organize a local band. In any event, he can scarcely fail to provide recreation, if only by allowing his residence to be used as a gathering place, where callers can gossip as they leaf through picture magazines or try a round of cards or checkers. The children may be attracted by dolls and toys. Perhaps the two most generally useful services that the ethnographer has to offer are those of scribe and druggist. He will be asked to read correspondence or explain regulations which arrive by mail and to compose letters to absent relatives or complete forms for the government. Frequently his home becomes a clinic for natives who come with aches and bruises or bring their children to be cured of infections or to be rid of intestinal worms.

The field worker, in turn, is usually dependent on the community for routine household services. These needs and opportunities provide a fourth avenue of participation. Renting a house or sharing one with a native family automatically sets up a series of personal relationships. The investigator establishes information pipelines if he has occasion to hire domestic assistants or make arrangements to secure laundry service or have milk delivered or firewood supplied. If there are local shops, his patronage will be appreciated; he will meet others who come to shop and will keep informed of current gossip. Emergencies may force field workers to call in native specialists. When we were working in Guatemala, my wife severely dislocated an ankle. Since there was no doctor in the vicinity, we requested the services of an old and celebrated Indian bonesetter who practiced his calling in fulfilment of a supernatural command. He came with his "power," a small magic bone concealed in a large kerchief. Wrapping the kerchief about the injured ankle, he manipulated the foot with both hands, twisting and pulling as his magic bone directed. Our trust in the sacred bonesetter impressed the natives. It also corrected the ankle.

Ritual relationships and honorary memberships constitute still another avenue of participation. The godparent relationship is an important feature of social organization in many Latin-American communities. Respected outsiders in temporary residence are asked from time to time to sponsor the baptism of a local child. Sponsorship of this kind formally inaugurates a special relationship with the kinsmen of the child, entailing mutual rights and obligations. The Zuni Indians eventually made Cushing a local "bow chief."

These five avenues by no means exhaust the circumstances leading to interaction and rapport. In any particular case the kind and degree of participation will vary with the ethnographer and with the community. On the one hand, different investigators choose to participate in varying degrees within the identical community. Among students of the Navaho, some have remained in their field office and have had native informants brought in at the anthropologist's convenience; others have taken up their residence in a Navaho hogan; still others have done this and eaten the native food as well; and some have demonstrated the ultimate in solidarity by enduring the heat of the crowded sweat bath. On the other hand, identical investigators have been forced to participate in different ways by different cultures. Evans-Pritchard writes: "Azande would not allow me to live as one of themselves; Nuer would not allow me to live otherwise. Among Azande I was compelled to live outside the community; among Nuer I was compelled to be a member of it. Azande treated me as a superior; Nuer as an equal" (1940).

LIMITS OF PARTICIPATION

The varied avenues to participation and the advantages of participation (F. Kluckhohn, 1940) should not obscure the fact that the field worker can achieve only partial penetration into the life of the community, even under fa-vorable conditions. He comes as a stranger, and, although he may gain many confidences, he can scarely hope to become so well accepted that people lose sight of his outsider status. His eagerness to accept the natives on their own terms will never completely overcome a cautious attitude born of long-standing distrust of the outsider. Gregory Bateson observes that two choices of role confront the investigator working in New Guinea. Either choice has its limitations. If he exploits his prestige and is addressed in the tone reserved for Europeans, he will see the natives as jolly, obedient, and garrulous, whereas among themselves they may be suspicious and contra-suggestible. If he chooses instead to discard the prestige role, he will be despised by the returned laborers, who feel that a white man ought to behave as a "master" (Bateson, 1934).

The physical capacity of the investigator imposes limits on the extent of participation. Additional limits are set by the privacy in which some actions take place and by the possible reluctance of the anthropologist to intrude upon especially intimate matters. And if he does manage to attend, he must reckon with the fact that his presence alters the behavior he witnesses. Nadel's work in Africa has led him to conclude that "the anthropologist can only be a freak member of the group, not only because of the conspicuous differences in physical characteristics which often exist but also because of inevitable social incompatibilities" (Nadel, 1939).

But granting even that the anthropologist is able to engage effectively in a great number of activities, he is still severely restricted by the limited time at his disposal. The more involved he becomes in community events, the less time he has left to set down on paper what he has seen and done. More than one anthropologist has found himself so successful at gaining good will by performing various services that he was forced to erect barriers and set limits to his participation in order to accomplish a minimum of his own work. The same factors of sex and age which make for solidarity by counteridentification act as barriers to intimacy between the ethnographer and members of opposite sex and divergent age. In stratified societies the field worker who gains a good entrée into one social stratum often finds it more difficult to participate effectively in the other classes or castes of the society.

The most troublesome social cleavage is that of hostile factions. Communities or tribal groups that are split into antagonistic factions are now so common as nearly to constitute the rule. Even under aboriginal conditions social strains of various kinds have resulted in fissions and cleavages from time to time, but these tendencies have been aggravated by the stresses accompanying detribalization and dependency status. Tension may arise between champions of conservatism and native proponents of a progressive policy, or it may flare up in the form of mutually intolerant religious factions. The investigator who wishes to remain neutral is in danger of being caught in the crossfire. He may have to align himself with one side, in order to participate at all.

Even under ideal circumstances, the field worker who does everything the natives do, conceding the possibility, participates in their culture only in limited degree. He may understand the culture well intellectually, but he cannot so completely free himself from his own cultural values and feeling tones as to share entirely the emotional outlook of the natives, who have grown up under quite dissimilar influences. The question of "going native" has been the subject of debate in the anthropological literature. In part the divergence of opinion stems from differences of personality and from the variability

of the cultures to which the anthropologists have been exposed. But in part the disagreement is more apparent than real. It is generally conceded that the field worker can go halfway toward full participation, and it is equally recognized that he cannot go more than halfway. As the following quotations indicate, some anthropologists stress the wisdom of bending in the direction of the culture being studied, while others stress the folly of trying to bend too far.

Goldenweiser advises the investigator to begin by spending a few weeks "living the life of the natives and participating in their culture. The more successful an anthropologist is in doing this, the better foundation he has laid for his future work . . . the ability to 'go native' on the surface is thus a great boon to the anthropological field student" (1937). In apparent opposition to these views, Radin states: "True participation is simply out of the question and romantic participation obscures the situation completely. For any ethnologist to imagine that anything can be gained by 'going native' is a delusion and a snare" (1933). In similar vein, Herskovits writes: "Much nonsense has been written about the need for the student of customs of a people to become 'participant observer' of those customs by doing what, in common parlance, is termed 'going native.' . . . Let it be stated emphatically that this is neither possible nor desirable among the West African Negroes and their New World descendants" (1948).

HAZARDS OF PARTICIPATION

The kindnesses and courtesies of participation that win good will may unexpectedly arouse enmity as well. Out of sympathy for the plight of a friend or neighbor in the field, the ethnographer may grant a small loan or extend assistance in some other way, only to discover that another native equally in need has taken out his resentment over the display of apparent favoritism in surreptitious gossip or innuendo. The favor may alienate the friend himself. Unable to meet his promise of repayment, he may avoid the ethnographer to spare himself embarrassment. Friendship with some persons inspires jealousy in others; not even a politician can win friends without gaining enemies. Labor relations can lead to discontent. If several neighboring families are anxious to have their daughter hired as a domestic assistant, the problem of making a choice is a delicate one. If the person hired proves unsatisfactory, the problem of replacement is more delicate still.

But the greatest peril of participation arises when misfortune strikes the community. In desperation the stricken natives may direct their hostility against the intruder, reading sinister motives into the most charitable and disinterested acts. Characteristically, he will not be approached directly but will become the subject of a whispering campaign to the effect that he is exerting or provoking baleful supernatural pressures. In a Maya village in western Guatemala, Maud Oakes was called in at the last moment to save the favorite granddaughter of a shaman. The medicine came too late. After the girl died, the angered shaman spread the word that the *gringa* (the American woman) was a sorceress with evil medicines. When a serious epidemic struck the village, her photography was blamed. When she takes pictures of the people, it was said, she carries away their spirits on the film; this is the reason so many people die. It was also said she killed people by summoning evil spirits from the hill. She gives things away, it was recalled. What is her real work? Where does her money come from? She gives people medicine, and they pay her nothing. Where is there nowadays a person who gives away presents for

nothing in return? She carries off dead people. Now that she was typed as a witch, it was noticed through a window that she was "eating wood," actually rye crisp. Who but a witch would do so? Luckily, new villains dispossessed her of the scapegoat role. A rumor spread that two *ladinos* (non-Indian countrymen), reeking of corpses, were overheard one night discussing the hundreds of Indian adults and children they were going to carry away (Oakes, 1951).

Oliver La Farge was about to end his field study of the native religion, compounded of Catholic and indigenous practices, when the Indians of Santa Eulalia, also in the Guatemalan highlands, laid a "great curse" upon him. Someone had to be blamed for the run of bad weather that had interfered with the fiestas and damaged the corn fields. La Farge was accused of having stolen sacred idols from a ruin he had cleared and mapped a few months earlier with the aid of a white companion and two native assistants. A divination had produced the answer that two *ladinos* and two Indians had stolen the idols in the dead of night in order to ruin the village. Thereupon, the Indian officials prayed for the death of the guilty four. This was the great curse which stirred up the village and caused natives to pass La Farge in stony silence. La Farge realized that failure to refute the charge would jeopardize the lives of all the natives who had worked for him. He rejected a suggestion that he confess the theft. He knew that the ceremonial Prayermakers of Santa Eulalia were held responsible for the weather. If it was bad, the blame would ordinarily fall upon the religious officials for performing their rituals incorrectly. Having failed to produce the necessary weather, the Prayermakers were in real danger of being jailed. Since no ordinary Indian would dare to touch the sacred idols, La Farge concluded that during his temporary absence the powerful religious organization had secretly removed them, in order to exculpate themselves and, at the same time, frame the ethnographer. The Indians distrusted any outsider, especially one who gave evidence of supernatural connections by his knowledge of esoteric ritual.

Though La Farge had repeatedly denied previously that he was a born shaman, he now decided to fight fire with fire. Letting it be known that he might indeed have sacred power, he announced that he was going forthwith to the *Principal* of the village and that, if the latter and his staff had, in fact, pronounced the curse, he would force a retraction. This impressed the villagers, for a guilty man would scarcely have the self-assurance to confront the highest authority. It also impressed the *Principal*. Asked point blank about the lies being circulated and emphatically warned that the curse, if not rescinded, would be turned back upon those who had falsely laid it, the *Principal*, fearful of La Farge's special power, vigorously denied that such a curse had been laid, attributing the story to idle gossip. The denial was forced in the presence of other Indians, who quickly spread the news. The natives who had sided with La Farge breathed easier (1947).

Some difficulties require bold action, others subside by themselves. The efficacious solution varies with the situation and the temperament of the field worker. More often than not, the harried worker can count on the aid of divided public opinion. Some faithful informant will warn him of impending trouble. Of course, all crises are grist for the ethnographer's mill—if he himself is not ground in. Occasional field workers have paid with their lives for imprudent sexual involvement or highhanded treatment of natives. The general casualty rate among anthropologists, however, appears to be no higher than for any other academic group.

THE COSTS OF PARTICIPATION

The ethnographer pays a price in personal discomfort for playing the role of the good neighbor. The strains of making constant accommodations, of living in the public spotlight, of denying his own preferences, all deplete his patience. He may be able to conceal his exasperation from the people, but he cannot escape the unpleasant effects of suppressed resentment. The first weeks of field work are often trying. The investigator may want to quit and go home, staying only because he is ashamed to give up. Malinowski describes "the feeling of hopelessness and despair after many obstinate but futile attempts had entirely failed to bring me into real touch with the natives or supply me with any material. I had periods of despondency, when I buried myself in the reading of novels, as a man might take to drink in a fit of tropical depression and boredom" (1932).

A letdown may set in long after the work has gotten well under way. The investigator may school himself to accept physical hardship, he may even gain ascetic satisfaction from enduring deprivation, only to be assailed unexpectedly with a craving for a shower or a soft bed or a home-cooked meal. More insidious than material discomforts are the petty and subtle aggravations of social participation. Like the people he studies, the investigator has psychological needs and emotional expectations that fall short of fulfilment. He may grow weary of being perpetually treated in accord with the status assigned him, longing in vain to be accepted as a human being entitled to indulge his idiosyncrasies. Intellectually he may understand the factors of culture and circumstance that interpose barriers between himself and the people, but emotionally he will smart under the sting of psychological rejection. Of his Guatemalan Indian group, La Farge (1947) writes: "Given as they are to dire suspicion and ready hostility, in these close-knit groups I myself can testify that the general assumption of an unpleasant attitude can take most of the joy out of life, even though it is accompanied by no overt action of any kind, but only by whisperings as one goes by, an unfriendly laugh when one has passed, and a constant turning of suspicious eyes in one's direction as one walks about."

If not politely made an outcast, the worker may grow irritable over mounting demands. At first, he will welcome visitors, only too eager to dispense a favor here, a kindness there. He will even accept the neighborhood bore with indulgence. But eventually the requests reach a peak of annoying frequency. If he accedes, he feels increasingly victimized. If he sets arbitrary limits, he is exposed to endless wheedling and to charges of selfishness. Participation implies emotional involvement; observation requires detachment. It is a strain to try to sympathize with others and at the same time strive for scientific objectivity. A crisis can suddenly upset the balance between these opposing forces. Margaret Mead (1949) describes how she "burst into tears of helpless resentment when after sitting up all night with a very sick Balinese child, I went home for a moment, and came back in the chilly dawn of the mountain morning and was bitten by the family dog."

The best remedy for participation fatigue is a vacation, a change of social scenery and relief from role-playing. Where one goes and what he does depend on the particular situation. One solution is to find a retreat not too far distant, where he can regain his equanimity and at the same time take stock of his notes to guide renewed inquiry. Any tension that may have built up in

the community will subside during the interval of his absence or find outlet in other directions. He may be warmly hailed when he returns and be regarded as a real friend who shows his loyalty by coming back.

III. INTERVIEWING TECHNIQUES

GENERAL PROCEDURE

The ultimate sources of information are objects and events. There are behavioral events, such as an exchange of greetings or taking a sweat bath, and there are "natural" events, such as an eclipse or a drought. The ethnographer can witness the event, as an active participant or inactive participant (onlooker), and thus learn by direct *observation*. Or he can elicit information about an event from a person who observed it, thereby performing a type of vicarious observation called *interviewing*. Objects, like events, can be natural or man-made. As in the case of events, knowledge of objects can be gained by observation or by interviewing someone who has observed them. The ethnologist frequently has an additional means of securing data, that of consulting *existing records*. These may include public and private documents, statistical compilations, administrative records, travelers' accounts, and other types of publications. Archival research has been the special province of historians, who have tended to define anything set down by others as evidence and to regard information they might obtain directly through observation and discourse as somehow less legitimate. Some cultural anthropologists have reversed the scales, relying too exclusively on firsthand material. Historical records may reflect bias, but this is equally true of observation and interview; all types of evidence require critical examination.

Interviewing is an indirect means of observation only with reference to events outside the context of the interviewing situation. To receive a description of a dance is less direct than to see the dance. But, in so far as the subject's feelings and judgments are relevant to the inquiry, interviewing is as direct as any other means. The informant is himself an observable object and interviewing is an ongoing social event, enabling the sensitive investigator to observe as he interviews. To a certain extent interviewing and observation are alternative techniques, one substituting for the other according to the nature of the ethnographer's interests, his access to community life, and the availability of informants. But they are also complementary techniques, their combined use providing better perspective than the use of either technique by itself.

The student is sometimes advised to notice "everything"; but this is manifestly impossible. He cannot be everywhere at the same time, and he can never be sensitive to literally everything that occurs even within his field of view, much less record it in all its manifold complexity, short of capturing the event mechanically with sound and ciné equipment. He notes whatever is important or may turn out to be pertinent, but definition of the important depends on the worker's theoretical orientation, his sense of problem, his personal characteristics, familiarity with the ethnographic literature, prior field experience, and a host of other variables.

In most general terms the field worker aims to gather and relate two sets of data, a description of the situation as he sees it, looking from the outside in, and a description of the situation as the native sees it, looking from the inside out. The first comprises the visible world of objects and actions: the people in their material and environmental setting, their groupings and interactions, their techniques and activities. This objective frame of reference the ethnographer shares with the human geographer, the economist, and the natural historian. The subjective frame of reference embraces the world view of the people, the pattern of assumptions that guides their perceptions, the network of meanings that binds their percepts into the semblance of a system, the hierarchy of values animating their actions. The student of culture cannot ignore the objective situation, but it is the subjective view that constitutes his distinctive concern. He needs to know the what and the how, but he also wants to know the cultural wherefore.

A combination of interview and observation yields the best results, whether attention is directed mainly at depicting the objective situation or at uncovering the cultural definitions of the situation; but the balance of emphasis shifts with the frame of reference. The outside view makes heavy demands upon direct observation, with interviewing a supplementary technique, while the inside view places a premium on interviewing, with observation supplementary. It may be more efficient to watch a funeral than to have its procedure described. Conversely, it may be more revealing to ask why the ceremony is conducted the way it is than to infer the cultural reasons from observations alone.

Watching an activity rather than relying on description alerts the observer to features of style and mood and arrangement that might otherwise go undetected. Against the advantages of the observational method are to be set its quantitative and qualitative limitations. For many areas of behavior, the number of cases that come under the direct observation of the field worker are too few to reveal the constancies and the range of variation. Some important events, such as births or deaths or gross violations of custom, may not occur while he is in the field. Others occur but are not accessible to observation because of their intimate nature or because the anthropologist happens to be elsewhere. The interview device enables him to fill out the series of missing cases.

Interviewing is also a corrective for the qualitative shortcomings of direct observation. The presence of the observer influences the event under observation, less so in the case of public and formal performances, more so in the case of informal and private behavior. Cases of domestic quarrels that are witnessed, for instance, should be compared with reports of quarrels that are not witnessed by the investigator. Some social events appear so complex that the novice is unable to find plot or pattern in the midst of all the distracting detail. An advance briefing session with a good informant will prepare him to identify the direction of movement, the transitions, and the principal participants.

THE INFORMANT

In the strictly literal sense an informant is anyone who provides information. In this sense he may be a man in the street drawn into a casual conversation or a person interviewed in his home for one hour and then not seen again. But these are not informants according to customary anthropological usage. To the anthropologist the informant is an articulate member of the studied culture who enters into a more or less personal relationship with the investigator for a relatively long period of time. The same is true of the psychiatric patient in a permissive therapeutic setting, but the primary object of the psychiatric relationship is to bring about emotional learning on the part of the patient, while the express goal of the informant relationship is to bring about cognitive learning on the part of the anthropologist. Nevertheless, the two situations have much in common and the anthropologist stands to profit by becoming more familiar with the dynamics of the interactive process recognized by the therapist, for the mechanics of transference and countertransference, of identification and defense, are likely to assert themselves in any sustained dyadic relationship.

Ideally, informants should be so selected as to comprise a panel representative of the major social subdivisions and categories recognized within the community. From a practical standpoint the range of choice is restricted to those who are accessible, able, and willing. The anthropologist starts slowly and circumspectly, making friendships and accepting calls, assessing the qualities of prospective informants, appraising their areas of competence, and identifying their location in the social network. Within the range of practical choices the field worker makes his selection in such a way as best to approximate the ideal requirement of representativeness, moving further in the desired direction as his circle of acquaintanceship expands.

The anthropologist may think he is making the choices, but in many instances it is equally true that the informants are choosing the anthropologist. Some thrust themselves upon him, others achieve the same end by indirection. Those who are willing to enter into novel relationships rather than to remain within familiar grooves, to examine culture rather than express it in action, are likely, almost by definition, to diverge from the normal. This applies to anthropologists as well as informants. Standing at the peripheries of their respective cultures, they may be in a better position to get next to each other. Peculiarities of temperament and interests may unite them in a hybrid subculture that mediates between the respective parent-cultures.

Two classes of atypical individuals

should be distinguished, those who depart from the cultural mean but retain
their good standing in society and those
who are stigmatized as misfits, derelicts,
or troublemakers. The first category
may include persons who are more reflective than their fellow-men or more
inclined to court new experiences;
these can be safely accepted as informants, for their presence in the ethnographer's camp is unlikely to alienate
others. But the second group, the recognized deviants, can become a public
relations liability. Yet these are the
ones most likely to offer their services
at the outset. On his arrival the anthropologist responds sympathetically to all
gestures of friendship, but he bides his
time, cocking his ear to public opinion,
before settling down to work systematically with informants. Of course, it
may fall within the field worker's purposes to obtain biographical and personality data on social deviants and
marginal persons; but, unless this is his
exclusive interest and the major outlines of the culture are already known,
he will do well to postpone this task
until his general lines of communication within the community are well secured.

It requires patience and tact to build
good working arrangements with informants. A process of mutual learning
and adjustment is involved, and it is a
waste of human relations capital to initiate so many new informant relationships that one is forced to forego the
qualitative gains of following through
on the well-trained informants. Moreover, it may be neither expedient nor
diplomatic to discard loyal informants
at will. These considerations, taken together with the fact that maintenance
of rapport often involves time-consuming courtesies and social interchanges,
restrict the number of informants that
a single investigator can satisfactorily
manage over any given span of time,
quite apart from possible limits set by
factors of access and suitability.

At the same time, requirements of
adequate sampling may exert pressure
to extend the number of sources beyond these limits. These opposing needs
are frequently reconciled by devising
a system of primary and secondary informants. One, two, or several natives
are allowed to become key informants.
Ideally, these are individuals who have
not only proved themselves well informed and well connected but have
demonstrated a capacity to adopt the
standpoint of the investigator, inform-
ing him of rumors and coming events,
suggesting secondary informants, preparing the way, advising on tactics and
tact, securing additional data on their
own, and assisting the anthropologist
in numerous other ways. Such assistants can be told that, as a matter of
policy, their data will be subjected to
verification by interviewing other informants on the same topic, and they
may even take pride in having their accuracy confirmed. In large communities
socio-economic mapping and use of
random-number tables to select households or subjects may prove desirable
for purposes of statistical control. If
this procedure creates new entrée problems for the investigator, his key informants can be valuable as mediating
agents.

INTERVIEWING

Types of interviews in social research
run a wide gamut, ranging from casual
to formal, directive to nondirective,
structured to unstructured. Any or all
of these grades and combinations have
their place in anthropological field
work. The question is not which, but
for what purpose and under what conditions. The distinctive features of ethnographic interviewing are essentially
three: its integration with observation
and participation; the wide and (initially) undefined scope of the informa-

tion it aims to elicit; the breadth of the communication barrier it must bridge. For all these reasons the method must be kept flexible, particularly during the early stages, when part of the interviewing task is to determine the areas and dimensions along which interviewing is to proceed. The characteristic approach is neither directive nor nondirective but a compromise and shuttle between the two extremes; a question is asked or a topic suggested, and the respondent is allowed to answer as he sees fit. This is sometimes called the "open-ended interview."

One of the purposes of the open-ended interview is to disclose topics, viewpoints, and interconnections that might escape notice under a more mechanical type of interrogation. The object is to give the respondent maximum opportunity to reveal how he structures his world of experience. Moreover, his interest is less likely to flag if he is encouraged to talk about the things he wants to talk about. He may not speak freely until he has become accustomed to the ethnographer and assured himself that the newcomer has no threatening intentions. When exploratory conversation has gone far enough to convince the prospective informant that the ethnographer asks harmless questions and when the ethnographer has a fair indication of the topics his visitor is willing to discuss at greater length, continuation on a more explicit interviewing basis can usually be arranged. Once it becomes known that one or two members of the community have settled into the role of regular informants, other individuals may indicate a wish to do the same.

What induces the informant to cooperate with the interviewer? Advancing the cause of science may not be part of the local value system. Nor is the average researcher able to promise that his study will lead to improved conditions. The two types of induce-

ment that operate generally are psychological gratification and material gain. Tangible benefits range from services the anthropologist can perform to gifts and payments. In some cases money may be of less use than wire, flashlights, or containers; but, where cash is an accepted medium of exchange, it is not only equitable but often necessary to compensate informants for loss of productive time. Some anthropologists do not buy information as such but hire informative houseboys or helpers; others pay informants by the hour; still others pay by quantity rather than by time.

Whether or not payment is necessary, it is seldom a sufficient condition for winning the confidence of the informant. The relationship should prove rewarding in itself and not be just a means of earning money. Interviewing will be most productive if the informant is made to feel that he is valued as a person and not merely as a source of data, that he is not pressed to reveal more than he is ready to disclose, that he is talking to someone who is sympathetic as well as curious. In some cultures, subjects will "open up" only after the interviewer has assumed the initiative by asking a series of questions requiring fairly concrete answers. In others they will not tolerate questions demanding direct answers until they have become well acquainted with the investigator. In the early phases of interviewing, the amount of directing will be attuned to the psychological needs of the informant. In the later phases, after rapport has been established, it can be varied according to the informational needs of the interviewer.

When an informant pauses, it is not always necessary to rush in with a new question. After a few moments of silence he may resume of his own accord. Or his hesitation may be a call for encouragement, in which case the interviewer can indicate his attentiveness by reformulating something the subject has just said—"You say it is dangerous to travel when one is angry" —or inviting him to continue by asking a neutral question—"Then what did you do?" or "Did the same thing ever happen to anyone else?" If the informant has nothing more to say on a given topic, the investigator can refer back to something mentioned earlier in the interview or in a previous session, or initiate a new topic by commenting on things he has heard or seen. Accompanying an informant on a walk through the village or the environs or engaging in a joint enterprise, such as making a household census, will stimulate conversation and provide an abundance of leads for later interviews.

A source of inspiration for the interviewer who feels he needs to be reminded of the "obvious" facets of culture he is overlooking is any of a number of published outlines, notably the *Outline of Cultural Materials* (Murdock *et al.*, 1950) and *Notes and Queries on Anthropology* (1951). Leads and lists on special topics are scattered throughout the literature. To cite two at random, both appearing in the same number of the *American Anthropologist*, Simmons (1945) has drawn up a prospectus for field research on the treatment of the aged, and Ackerknecht (1945) has one on collecting data on primitive medicine. It would be a service to ethnography to assemble a memorandum listing all such existing field guides and outlines with a brief description of their content. Of course, an outline is not ordinarily to be used as an interviewing catechism.

Sometimes informants will be less reluctant to discuss a sensitive topic if the interviewer can manage to indicate in a casual way that he already knows something about that topic or if a hy-

pothetical case is set up for discussion (Herskovits, 1948). The interviewer encourages the informant to describe actual or hypothetical events, but he also welcomes generalizations and evaluations, for he is as much interested in ideal patterns, in moral rules and expectancies, as he is in behavioral patterns. He is also interested in temporal patterns. By observation and interview he will get samples of the woman's daily round and of the man's. He will also try to get the life-stories of several informants, if only to place the ethnographic facts in a more meaningful sequential context. The life-history is an invaluable tool for psychocultural research (Dollard, 1935; Saslow and Chapple, 1945; Leighton and Leighton, 1949).

The difficulty of assessing the reliability of information secured through interviewing is partly a function of the time spent in the field, the magnitude of the problem varying inversely with the length of exposure. There are three means of checking the accuracy of an item of information—by observation, through other informants, and through the self-consistency of the original informant. Rarely can a person be deceitful and yet maintain internal consistency over a long series of interviews. At the start, when he has little trust in the investigator, he may be evasive, concealing his possessions and denying practices that outsiders are known to disparage; he may lie, to express independence or resentment; or boast and exaggerate, to create a favorable impression (Passin, 1942). In due time and with due tolerance on the part of the ethnographer, these defenses are relaxed. There is less need to dissimulate and less chance of successful deception. Given a favorable opportunity, informants may make their own retractions. One of the proud Nuer asked Evans-Pritchard whether he believed what they had told him about their lineages. When he replied that he had believed it, the men laughed, and one of them said: "Listen, what we told you yesterday was all nonsense. Now we will tell you correctly" (Evans-Pritchard, 1940).

Sensitivity to the psychological and social status of the informant, repeated interviews, development of trust and mutual understanding, cross-checking with other informants, and direct observation—these are the requisites for getting reliable ethnographic data, and they require time.

Statements made by an informant—what is expressed and what is suppressed—will differ with the social situation. Alone with the interviewer, an informant will say one thing; in the presence of company he may say something else. In the one case his attention is focused on the anthropologist, in the other his reaction is divided. The nature of his audience and the meaning of the audience to the speaker are always controlling factors in deciding what comes to his mind, what he will choose to say, how he will say it, or whether he speaks at all. An informant interviewed in the presence of a child may become guarded. Out of respect or caution, a young man may become reserved or change his tone when an elder enters the room. A woman who has little to say may grow loquacious when interviewed with a companion. In the field the anthropologist cannot always control the social context in which he conducts his interviews. He may want to vary it to observe the difference. In any event, he must make careful note of the social setting, for it will color the information he receives. On some topics a female informant will not tell a male interviewer the same thing she tells a female interviewer, and vice versa. This is not purely a matter of veracity. Truth is not a thing in itself; it has social and cultural dimensions.

Perhaps the most striking and most interesting contrast in interviewing situations is the difference between interviewing a man alone and interviewing in a group—and the difference between cultures in respect to group behavior. The social climate generated by a group situation and the influence it exerts are illustrated by an experience of Smith and Dale with the Ba-Ila. Sitting in company with a group of men, they asked about a well-known custom and were amazed when the first man addressed denied that there ever was such a custom. The rest all backed him up, even those who had previously discussed it with the interviewers. The investigators were later told: "That is . . . the funny little way of the Ba-Ila. The first man had some reason for denying it and of course the others couldn't give him away. My friend there are ways *and* ways of asking questions." The writers never again put direct questions to a company of men (Smith and Dale, 1920). Smith and Dale's lesson is not to be read as ruling out interviewing in all group situations.

The Navaho are different. One field worker carried out many interviews with large numbers of people present. "The behavior of almost all Navaho in these situations is exemplary; the remainder of those present never attempt to interrupt or give their own views until the man first addressed is completely finished. The group situation often renders others present very eager to tell their own stories, but it unquestionably results in statements of 'public' attitudes and diminution in the freedom of communication of some feelings" (unpublished notes). In Nigeria, Nadel (1939) found it profitable to provoke intense arguments between informants. This "bullying" technique is not recommended for all cultures, nor will it suit the temperament of all field workers.

LANGUAGE AND INTERPRETATION

Time is essential for reducing the inadvertent misunderstandings that occur when people with different patterns of thought and speech attempt to communicate. The "same" utterance, even in the same language, means different things at different times and to different people. In one culture the informant may say "two people were there," having in mind not the great number of actual attendants but their leaders; in another culture the statement that "everybody was at the meeting" may refer only to the select body of elders (everybody that matters) and not the total population. Until one learns the local idiom, hyperbole, understatement, and contraction may be mistaken for literal fact. Since language is not only a means of communication but a way of perceiving and classifying the world of experience, exact translation from one language to another is virtually impossible. The ethnographer who knows the local language enjoys many obvious advantages and can explore areas otherwise inaccessible. But even a modest grasp of the language is a considerable asset, provided that the ethnographer realizes the limitations of his incomplete knowledge (Mead, 1939; Henry, 1940; Lowie, 1940; C. Kluckhohn, 1945). He can use critical native phrases as conversational handles rather than rely on ambiguous equivalents in his own tongue. He can exercise some degree of control over the accuracy of the interpreter. Familiarity with the phonemic method, a basic requirement for work in an alien group, enables him to transcribe terms and texts. Even a little of the language will go a long way in social facilitation.

The use of a well-trained interpreter —and the anthropologist may have to do the training—can be of enormous service, but the anthropologist should realize that it is likely to bring a number of disturbing factors into play and should correct or allow for these as best he can; unintended distortions due to the extra link in the chain of communication, deliberate or unconscious biases introduced by the interpreter, the effect of his social status upon the responses of the subject, and the effect of the diminished privacy inherent in a three-way relationship. The triangular situation can also serve a positive purpose, however. Gorer (1938) writes: "Without the use of an interpreter who, with his repetitions which I hardly listened to, would slow down the pace of a conversation sufficiently for me to take full notes, I could never have taken down the life-histories and elaborate ritual in anything like such full detail. When he was not present I had to ask people to wait or to repeat themselves; the Lepchas disliked this."

Interpreters are likely to occupy a marginal position with respect to the native culture and therefore be in good repute with only a limited sector of the native population, usually the more "progressive" element. Where political or religious factions are present, it may be necessary to use different interpreters for different groups. Otherwise, subjects will be guarded in what they say, and interpreters will be prone to edit the information according to their own biases. Matching subject and interpreter by sex will likewise facilitate communication. A *lingua franca* eliminates some of the disadvantages of using an interpreter, but it may thin down and even deceptively impede communication (Bateson, 1934). One small advantage of a secondary language is that it may permit the informant to talk about topics which would evoke inhibiting affect if couched in the natal tongue.

TAKING NOTES

The three prime requisites of good recording are these: recording promptly, noting the context in which the datum was given, and safeguarding the notes. For greater accuracy, information should be written down as soon as possible. In most cases notes can be taken during the interview in script or directly on the typewriter. If this inhibits conversation, notes should be made immediately after the interview, and the interview should not be too lengthy to allow accuracy of recall. Compared to people in literate communities, nonliterate subjects are likely to be less reticent about having "self-revealing" information written down, although they are sometimes more reluctant about matters of private property, owing to local jealousies or fear of tax collection (in Ecuador, tax officials did, in fact, attempt to get Ralph Beals's data). Assumed objections to direct recording often reflect anxieties projected by the interviewer rather than anxiety on the part of the informant. Depending on the topic and the informant and on the writing speed of the recorder, taking notes during the interview may or may not interrupt the flow of conversation. Trained informants have been known to pause and remark: "Why aren't you writing this down?"

It is well to make notes in duplicate, using carbons or ditto masters so that one copy can be mailed back home periodically as protection against loss.

More than one field worker has lost his manuscripts in a capsized canoe or found them damaged by a tropical rainstorm. A set of notes should be retained for occasional review. Inspection of data obtained in previous sessions is helpful in preparing for further interviews.

To preserve the context of a datum, the record should include not only the time and source but specification of the attending circumstances—whether it was recorded on the spot or how long after it was received; whether the information was offered spontaneously or in response to a question; whether the informant was alone or with others, and if so, with whom; any display of feeling that may illuminate the meaning of his remarks. If at all possible, the field notes should show the questions asked as well as the replies. At the very least, volunteered information should be distinguished from replies; symbols such as V and R can be used for this purpose. Somewhere in his notes the observer should record his subjective reactions to the community and to each of his informants, his initial and subsequent impressions, an estimation of the personal qualities of his subjects and of their conceptions of the observer. Observations of this kind will later help him recapture the tone and vividness of his field experience, supply a surer basis for preparing his report, and enable him to provide the reader with background for assaying his interpretations and descriptive generalizations.

BIBLIOGRAPHY AND REFERENCES

ACKERKNECHT, E. H. 1945. "On the Collection of Data Concerning Primitive Medicine," *American Anthropologist,* XLVII, 427–31.

ANONYMOUS. 1945. *Interviewing for NORC.* Denver: National Opinion Research Center.

———. 1949–52. "Field Methods and Techniques," *Human Organization,* all issues of Vol. VIII.

BALDUS, H. 1946. "Curt Nimuendajú, 1883–1945," *American Anthropologist,* XLVIII, 238–43.

BARTLETT, SIR F. 1937. "Psychological Methods and Anthropological Problems," *Africa,* X, 401–20.

BATESON, GREGORY. 1934. "Field Work in Social Psychology in New Guinea." In *Proceedings of the First International Congress of Anthropological and Ethnological Sciences*, p. 153. London.

———. 1944. "Pidgin English and Cross-cultural Communication," *Transactions of the New York Academy of Sciences*, ser. 2, VI, 137–41.

BENNETT, J. W. 1948. "The Study of Cultures: A Survey of Technique and Methodology in Field Work," *American Sociological Review*, XIII, 672–89.

DOLLARD, J. 1935. *Criteria for the Life History*. New Haven: Yale University Press.

DU BOIS, CORA. 1937. "Some Psychological Objectives and Techniques in Ethnography," *Journal of Social Psychology*, VIII, 285–301.

EVANS-PRITCHARD, E. E. 1940. *The Nuer*. Oxford: Clarendon Press.

GOLDENWEISER, A. 1937. *Anthropology*. New York: Crofts.

GORER, G. 1938. *Himalayan Village*. London: Michael Joseph, Ltd.

HARVEY, S. M. 1938. "A Preliminary Investigation of the Interview," *British Journal of Psychology*, XXVIII, 263–87.

HENRY, JULES. 1940. "A Method for Learning To Talk Primitive Languages," *American Anthropologist*, XLII, 635–41.

HERSKOVITS, MELVILLE J. 1948. *Man and His Works*, "The Ethnographer's Laboratory," pp. 79–93. New York: Alfred A. Knopf.

———. 1950. "The Hypothetical Situation: A Technique of Field Research," *Southwestern Journal of Anthropology*, VI, 32–40.

HOLMBERG, A. R. 1950. *Nomads of the Long Bow: The Siriono of Eastern Bolivia*. ("Publications of the Institute of Social Anthropology," No. 10.) Washington, D.C.: Government Printing Office.

HYMAN, H. 1951. "Interviewing as a Scientific Procedure." In LERNER, D., and LASSWELL, H. D. (eds.), *The Policy Sciences: Recent Developments in Scope and Method*, pp. 203–16. Stanford: Stanford University Press.

KLUCKHOHN, CLYDE. 1945. "The Personal Document in Anthropological Science." In GOTTSCHALK, L.; KLUCKHOHN, C.; and ANGELL, R., *The Use of Personal Documents in History, Anthropology, and Sociology*, pp. 79–173. (Social Science Research Council Bull. 53.) New York.

KLUCKHOHN, FLORENCE. 1940. "The Participant-Observer Technique in Small Communities," *American Journal of Sociology*, XLVI, 331–43.

LA FARGE, O. 1947. *Santa Eulalia: The Religion of a Cuchumatan Indian Town*. Chicago: University of Chicago Press.

LASSWELL, H. D. 1939. "The Contributions of Freud's Insight Interview to the Social Sciences," *American Journal of Sociology*, XLV, 375–90.

LEIGHTON, A. H. and DOROTHEA C. 1949. *Gregorio, the Hand Trembler*. ("Peabody Museum Papers," Vol. XL, No. 1.) Cambridge: Harvard University Press.

LINDGREN, ETHEL J. 1934. "Field Work in Social Psychology in Eastern Asia." In *Proceedings of the First International Congress of Anthropological and Ethnological Sciences*, pp. 152–53. London.

LOWIE, ROBERT H. 1940. "Native Languages as Ethnographic Tools," *American Anthropologist*, XLII, 81–89.

MALINOWSKI, B. 1932. *Argonauts of the Western Pacific*, "Field Method," pp. 5–25. London: Routledge.

MEAD, MARGARET. 1933. "More Comprehensive Field Methods," *American Anthropologist*, XXXV, 1–15.

———. 1939. "Native Languages as Field-Work Tools," *ibid.*, XLI, 189–206.

———. 1940. *The Mountain Arapesh. II. Supernaturalism*, "Field Techniques," pp. 325–38. ("Anthropological Papers of the American Museum of Natural History," Vol. XXXVII, Part 3.)

———. 1949. *Male and Female*. New York: Morrow.

———. 1952. "Anthropological Models for the Study of Culture at a Distance (the Single Informant; the Study of Living Communities)." In MEAD, MARGARET, and MÉTRAUX, RHODA, "Research in Contemporary Cultures: A Manual on Theory and Practice in the Study of Culture at a Distance by Inter-disciplinary Groups." MS.

MEAD, MARGARET; CHAPPLE, E. D.; and BROWN, G. G. 1949. "Report of the

Committee on Ethics," *Human Organization*, VIII, 20–21.

MERTON, R., and KENDALL, PATRICIA. 1946. "The Focused Interview," *American Journal of Sociology*, LI, 541–57.

MURDOCK, GEORGE P., et al. 1950. *Outline of Cultural Materials*. 3d rev. ed. New Haven: Human Relations Area Files, Inc.

NADEL, S. F. 1939. "The Interview Technique in Social Anthropology." In BARTLETT, F. et al. (eds.), *The Study of Society: Methods and Problems*, pp. 317–27. London: Routledge.

———. 1951. *The Foundations of Social Anthropology*, "Field Methods," pp. 35–74. Glencoe, Ill.: Free Press.

Notes and Queries on Anthropology, "Methods and Techniques in Social Anthropology," pp. 36–62. 1951. 6th ed. London: Routledge.

OAKES, MAUD. 1951. *The Two Crosses of Todos Santos: Survivals of Mayan Religious Ritual*. New York: Bollingen Foundation, Inc.

OPLER, M. K. 1942. "Psychoanalytic Techniques in Social Analysis," *Journal of Social Psychology*, XV, 91–127.

PARSONS, ELSIE C. 1936. *Mitla: Town of the Souls*. Chicago: University of Chicago Press.

PASSIN, H. 1942. "Tarahumara Prevarication: A Problem in Field Method," *American Anthropologist*, XLIV, 235–47.

POWDERMAKER, HORTENSE. 1939. *After Freedom*. New York: Viking Press.

RADIN, P. 1933. *The Method and Theory of Ethnology*. New York: McGraw-Hill Book Co., Inc.

RICHARDS, AUDREY I. 1935. "The Village Census in the Study of Culture Contact," *Africa*, VIII, 2–33.

———. 1939. "The Development of Field Work Methods in Social Anthropology." In BARTLETT, F., et al. (eds.), *The Study of Society: Methods and Problems*, pp. 272–316. London: Routledge.

RIVERS, W. H. R. 1910. "The Genealogical Method of Anthropological Inquiry," *Sociological Review*, III, 1–12.

ROETHLISBERGER, F., and DIXON, W. J. 1939. *Management and the Worker*, chaps. xii–xiv. Cambridge: Harvard University Press.

ROGERS, C. 1945. "The Non-directive Method as a Technique for Social Research," *American Journal of Sociology*, L, 279–83.

SASLOW, G., and CHAPPLE, E. D. 1945. "A New Life-History Form with Instructions for Its Use," *Applied Anthropology*, IV, 1–18.

SCHAPERA, I. 1935. "Field Methods in the Study of Modern Culture Contacts," *Africa*, VIII, 315–28.

SHEATSLEY, P. B. 1951. "The Art of Interviewing and a Guide to Interviewer Selection and Training." In JAHODA, M.; DEUTSCH, M.; and COOK, S. W., *Research Methods in Social Relations*, pp. 463–92. New York: Dryden Press.

SIMMONS, L. W. 1945. "A Prospectus for Field-Research in the Position and Treatment of the Aged in Primitive and Other Societies," *American Anthropologist*, XLVII, 433–38.

SMITH, E. W., and DALE, A. M. 1920. *The Ila-speaking Peoples of Northern Rhodesia*. 2 vols. London: Macmillan & Co., Ltd.

SPICER, ROSAMUND, and JOSEPH, ALICE. 1949. *The Desert People*. Chicago: University of Chicago Press.

STEMBER, H., and HYMAN, H. 1949. "How Interviewer Effects Operate through Question Form," *International Journal of Opinion and Attitude Research*, III, 493–512.

WARNER, W. L., and LUNT, P. S. 1941. *The Social Life of a Modern Community*, "Field Methods," pp. 38–75. New Haven: Yale University Press.

WHITING, J. 1941. *Becoming a Kwoma*. New Haven: Yale University Press.

WHYTE, W. F. 1951. "Observational Field-Work Methods." In JAHODA, M.; DEUTSCH, M.; and COOK, S. W., *Research Methods in Social Relations*, pp. 493–514. New York: Dryden Press.

Controls and Experiments
in Field Work

By OSCAR LEWIS

ANTHROPOLOGISTS HAVE for a long time been concerned with problems of method and field techniques.[1] However, the interest in the specific subject of control and experiment in field work is relatively recent, and most of the work in this area remains to be done in the future. The preparation of a "background" paper of this kind therefore presents some difficulty because of the relative scarcity of literature which deals directly and explicitly with this subject. This is not to say that anthropologists have not used controls and even experiments, that is, if we do not define these terms too narrowly. However, there has been little discussion of field work and methodology in just these terms, and the use of controls has not been systematic. In the absence of a clear-cut body of data that might

be summarized, I have had to delve into the ethnographic literature to pick out examples of controls implicit in the work or in the formulation of the problem and to survey some of the work in progress which is oriented in an experimental direction.

Before getting into the details of this paper, I would like to point out that the terms "controls" and "experiments" at once suggest a relationship with the physical and biological sciences and to this extent imply a definite value orientation concerning the nature of anthropology and the usefulness of controls and experiments. That there is some divergence of opinion about this was impressed upon me by the differences in the responses of a number of anthropologists whom I interviewed in the preparation of this paper.[2] Some

1. Many of our leading anthropologists have written on the subject at one time or another. For some examples see Herskovits (1949, chap. vi 1950); Kluckhohn has dealt with the problem of method and field techniques in many articles (see, e.g., 1938, 1939, 1951b; Gottschalk, Kluckhohn, and Angell, 1945, pp. 79–176); F. R. Kluckhohn (1940); Malinowski (1922, see the Introduction); Mead (1933, 1939; also see her rather full discussion of field methods in 1940, pp. 325–38, and 1949, pp. 293–302); S. F. Nadel has an excellent general discussion in his recent book (1951); Weakland (1951). See also the regular feature on "Field Methods and Techniques" in *Human Organization* published by the Society for Applied Anthropology.

2. I want to take this opportunity to thank the following anthropologists for their kindness in discussing this subject with me in interviews or correspondence: Helen Codere, Dorothy and Fred Eggan, Meyer Fortes, Irving A. Hallowell, Melville J. Herskovits, Clyde Kluckhohn, Margaret Mead, George P. Murdock, Ralph Linton, Morris Opler, Hortense Powdermaker, Julian Steward, and Sol Tax. I would recommend the interviewing of anthropologists as a good field technique and would agree with Veblen, who wrote many years ago: "It is no less requisite to come into close personal contact with the men engaged than it is to make first-hand acquaintance with the available materials; for it is a common trait of scientists, particularly when occupied with

thought that the question of controls and experiments was an important subject which should be explored to the full because of its potential contribution toward making anthropology more scientific. Others tended to dismiss the subject as havng little import for cultural studies.

This difference in attitude toward the value and possibilities of controls and experiments reflects a more basic divergence in interests and approaches among anthropologists concerning methodology. On the one hand, there are those who would underscore the kinship of anthropology with the natural sciences, would stress the need for quantification, objective tests, experiments, and a general development and improvement of techniques which might lead to greater precision and objectivity in the gathering, reporting, and interpreting of field data. On the other hand, there are those who, though not denying for a moment the kinship of anthropology with the sciences, believe that what needs to be stressed at this time is the kinship of anthropology with the humanities, and, accordingly, they would emphasize the need for insight, empathy, intuition, and the element of art. Moreover, they are much less sanguine about the contribution to anthropology which can come from quantification, control, and experiment, and they point out that some of our most adequate and insightful anthropological monographs were written by missionaries who had had no technical training.[3]

This difference in emphasis is not limited to anthropology, where it is perhaps the weakest. It cuts across most of the social sciences. In sociology it is represented by the differences between Lundberg and Chapin (or one of the small group experimentalists like Bales), on the one hand, and Znaniecki and Becker, on the other. In psychology it is the difference between Cattel and Thurstone as over against Lewin, Kohler, and Allport. In anthropology it can perhaps best be represented by the differences in approach to culture by the trait-list enthusiasts as over against the configurationalists. However, there is considerably more overlapping in anthropology, and this is one of our strengths. In anthropology our differences in emphases have not yet become institutionalized in terms of different subject matter, as in psychology. We suffer less from hardening of the categories. For example, we have no division as clear-cut as that between experimental and clinical psychology. Moreover, unlike psychology—and, I might add, fortunately so—few of us have devoted our lives to the development and refinement of research techniques to the point where we have lost sight of what it was we were studying.[4]

From a cross-disciplinary point of

3. For examples of these divergent emphases compare the editorials on "Field Methods and Techniques" in *Human Organization* with Benedict (1948) and Redfield (1948). Another aspect of the divergence mentioned above is the often discussed question of whether anthropology is a scientific or a historical discipline. For a brief and convenient summary of the highlights of this controversy see M. J. Herskovits (1949, pp. 608–12).

4. As Dr. Redfield has written: "In places the invention and the teaching of special procedures have gone ahead of the possibility of finding out anything very significant with their aid. It is certainly desirable to be precise, but it is quite as needful to be precise about something worth knowing. It is good to teach men and women who are to be social scientists how to use the instruments of observation and analysis that have been developed in their disciplines. But it is not good to neglect that other equally important side of the social sciences" (Redfield, 1948, pp. 188–89).

matter that is in any degree novel and growing, that they know and are willing to impart many things that are not primarily involved in the direct line of their own inquiry and many things, too, to which they may not be ready to commit themselves in print" (Dorfman, 1933).

view, the refreshing thing about anthropologists is their eclecticism, their readiness to invent, borrow, or steal whatever techniques or concepts are available at a given time and jump in to do
the field job. But it must be admitted
that this basically healthy attitude is
also partly responsible for the paucity
of contributions to methodology and
theory. Kluckhohn's observation that
American anthropologists were "devoting an overwhelming proportion of
their energies to the accumulation of
facts" (1939, p. 329) is certainly much
less true today than it was in 1939, but
it still carries some weight.

It seems to me that there is no necessary contradiction between the two
points of view briefly outlined above.
Each supplements the other, and students should be familiar with both. In
a sense we have here a division of labor. From one we can perhaps expect
broader and more meaningful hypotheses and from the other the development of procedures by which these hypotheses may be checked. Both approaches represent significant contributions to anthropology.

Whether one emphasizes quantitative or qualitative analysis is to some
extent related to individual differences
in temperament and background. But
it may also be a function of the state
of knowledge at a given time, the particular nature of the problem, and the
level of abstraction one is working
with. Indeed, it has been asserted that
quantification and measurement and
the categories of time, space, number,
etc., are categories which have been
derived from and for the study of nature but are not adequate for the interpretation of culture or value systems.
Elija Jordan (see 1952, p. 5), an American philosopher of growing reputation,
has suggested that the job of the philosopher is to develop systematically a
new set of categories with which the
anthropologist and other social scientists can study culture.

A somewhat similar position is taken
by the anthropologist and linguist, B. L.
Whorf, who writes (1940):

Measuring, weighing, and pointer-read-
ing devices are seldom needed in linguistics, for quantity and number play little
part in the realm of patterning, where
there are no variables, but instead, abrupt
alterations from one configuration to another. The mathematical sciences require
exact measurement, but what linguistics
requires is, rather, "patternment"—an exactness of relation irrespective of dimensions. Quantity, dimension, magnitude are
metaphors since they do not properly belong in this spaceless, relational world.

Julian Steward (1950, p. 45) has also
written that "cultural patterns cannot
be described mathematically," and
Ruth Benedict made very much the
same point when she said that just as
soon as you begin to quantify, you are
no longer studying culture.[5]

Despite these reservations, it must be
noted that the increased use of quantification has been one of the most significant developments in anthropological
field work in recent years. This development is closely related to some of the
major trends in anthropology in the last
twenty years. The most important of
these trends are: (1) an increasing emphasis upon the study of range of variation in behavior and custom as over
against the older emphasis upon ideal
patterns;[6] (2) the shift from preoccu-

5. This statement was made in conversation
with me shortly before Dr. Benedict's death.

6. That the traditional derivation of culture
patterns neglects range of variation is made
clear by R. Linton in an excellent statement
on anthropological methodology. Linton explains that, in order to describe and manipulate the variety of behavior found in any society, the anthropologist uses the "culture-
pattern construct," which he defines as "the
mode of the finite series of variations which
are included within each of the real culture
patterns." The following example is given:
"Thus, if the investigator finds that members
of a particular society are in the habit of going

pation with the salvaging and reconstruction of rapidly disappearing cultures to the study of functioning societies; (3) greater awareness of methodological problems resulting in part from closer liaison with other disciplines, particularly with philosophy, sociology, and psychology; (4) the increasing use of anthropological data by other disciplines and, in particular, the pressure from psychologists for more data on individual differences; (5) some modification of our earlier role as a one-man expedition of all the social sciences toward greater specialization and limitation of problem; (6) longitudinal studies in which more time is devoted to the study of a single people, for example, Kluckhohn's intensive work with the Navaho over many years; (7) an increase in co-operative

research, in which specialists study a particular aspect of a culture;[7] (8) the development of the field of applied or action anthropology. The cumulative effect of these broad developments upon field-work techniques will be discussed in more detail later.

Because applied and action anthropology are problem-centered, they would seem to be a "natural" for the increased use of controls and experiments. This is ironical in a sense, for a common charge against applied anthropology has been that it was "unscientific." In working for administrators the question of "How many?" becomes particularly pertinent. How many families own land, how many have adopted new practices, how many need medical care? Applied anthropology literally demands quantification.

Anyone who has read the articles on

---

to bed sometime between eight and ten o'clock but that the mode for his series of cases falls at a quarter past nine, he will say that going to bed at quarter past nine is one of the culture patterns of their culture" (1945, pp. 45–46). It could be argued that Linton has touched upon a fundamental weakness in most anthropological field studies. From Linton's use of the word "mode" the reader might infer that the anthropologist studied quantitatively the range of each or any particular behavior and then arrived at the mode, which he reports as the culture pattern. However, it is well known that anthropologists rarely use statistical procedures systematically and by no means arrive at the mode in the traditional statistical manner. Furthermore, the "series of cases" is very often only a small number of all the cases. When the average monograph reports that children are nursed for about two years, there is a high probability that this conclusion was arrived at after talking with a few mothers and making some casual and uncontrolled observations in the community. It would probably not occur to most anthropologists, *or seem important,* to seek out and observe all the children being weaned at the time of the study and to determine their exact ages. *Thus, by calling the culture pattern the mode, Linton is giving statistical dignity to what in most cases is probably no more than the anthropologist's guess.* When Linton explains that "the total culture pattern construct is developed by combining all the culture con-

struct patterns which have been developed," what he is saying is that we are adding up our guesses and arriving at a total guess, namely, the total culture-pattern construct. That anthropologists sometimes guess brilliantly is to their everlasting credit and is a tribute to the element of art in the social sciences. But this is still a far cry from the more exact methods of the natural sciences. And perhaps this is as it should be.

The limitations in anthropological derivations of systematic or total culture patterns are clearly recognized by Kroeber, who seems to accept these limitations as in the nature of things, hardly to be remedied by more informants or other improved field techniques. He writes: "In proportion as the expression of such a large pattern tends to be abstract it becomes arid and lifeless; in proportion as it remains attached to concrete facts it lacks generalization. Perhaps the most vivid and impressive generalizations have been made by frank intuition deployed on a rich body of knowledge and put into skillful words" (1948, p. 317).

7. The more intensive study which comes with specialization naturally leads to more knowledge of range of variation. One might raise the question to what extent the picture of cultural homogeneity of so-called "primitive" societies is a function of the anthropologist's lack of expertness in different aspects of culture.

field methods and techniques in *Human Organization* (and, incidentally, this journal published by the Society for Applied Anthropology is the only anthropological journal in the United States which regularly devotes a section to methods) cannot but be impressed by the perceptible straining for objectivity. Indeed, it is here that we find suggestions for a radical departure from traditional ethnographic techniques. Not content with the mere incorporation of quantification and added controls within the old framework of observational methods, it is suggested that the process of observation itself be set upon a strict operational basis:

> Throughout the field [these] currents of intuition are still strong today, even when stored up or concealed from superficial view by imposing edifices of statistical ingenuity, made possible, although not valid, by assigning number to the intuitions themselves. Much of the energy that might have been turned profitably to improve the quality of observation, in accordance with procedures used in the biological sciences and in chemistry and physics, has been directed toward the minute taxonomic dissections of verbalized intuition, which can be quantified.[8]

The highest degree of objectivity in observing and recording data is the goal. In the absence of the sound motion picture, which is considered the ideal instrument, the field worker must attain the accuracy of the camera:

> The goal of the well-conducted interview is to secure material similar to what would be obtained if the interviewer had been able to follow his subject about with a notebook, recording everything he did and said as accurately as possible.[9]

There is a strong emphasis upon the problems of semantics and the elimination of all intuitive and subjective statements and interpretative judgments. Statements must be "based upon cultural and physical evidence." Thus: "Membership in a group or occupation should be stated in precise terms: 'He was dressed as a Blackfoot,' not 'He is a Blackfoot.' "[10]

At the basis of their operational approach is the "realization that any given sequence of behavior can be broken up into multitudes of actions that are capable of description and differentiation."[11] The "time when" and "place where," as well as the who, what, and how, in relations between people must be recorded in precise detail. "We would like to know that the particular situation being observed began at 3:05 P.M., March 26, and lasted until 5:17 P.M., and that the two persons involved then went away and were not observed together again until three days later, March 29, at 7:00 P.M."[12]

This type of "value-free," atomistic material readily lends itself to objective, graphic recording. Thus workers in this field have been utilizing all types of mapping, particularly spot mapping, flow charts, recording sheets, contact questionnaires, extensionalized interviews, and recording of movements (such as dancing, facial expressions, gestures). These suggested techniques apparently have been helpful in concrete, narrowly defined problems such as might arise in the study of a shoe factory. Whether they are practicable and useful in the study of larger groups such as communities remains to be seen.

In the discussion that follows we will consider, first, controls in field work and, second, experiments in field work. This separate treatment of controls and experiments will facilitate the organization of materials because controls and experiments have not always gone

8. *Human Organization*, X, No. 3 (fall, 1951), 40.

9. *Ibid.*, IX, No. 1 (spring, 1950), 29.

10. *Ibid.*, No. 3 (fall, 1950), p. 29.

11. *Ibid.*, X, No. 1 (spring, 1951), 36.

12. *Ibid.*, IX, No. 4 (winter, 1950), 30.

hand in hand. Under "Controls" we shall deal with the personal equation, group field work, and field techniques (quantification, sampling, etc.), tape recording, photography, etc. Under "Experiments" we shall consider research designs and research problems and restudies.

CONTROLS

For purposes of this paper the term "control" is defined rather broadly to include any technique or method which decreases the probability of error in the observation, collection, and interpretation of field data. Different methods may therefore offer different degrees of control. In this sense one can have control without the controlled group of the laboratory experiment. Indeed, the laboratory experiment is only one type of control. In short, anything which increases the chances of getting more objective, meaningful, and reliable data is a control.

THE PERSONAL EQUATION

Since most field work is done by a single individual, the first question to consider is the problem of control of the personal equation. Nadel (1951, p. 48) has put the question clearly:

Where the human being is the only instrument of observation, the observer's personal equation must be all pervading; and where the data observed are once more human data, the observer's personality might easily override the best intentions of objectivity. In the final interpretation of the data some such bias is probably inevitable. It might be argued that, as long as interpretative and descriptive statements are kept distinct, no harm is done; on the contrary, the personal viewpoints and the varying philosophies which different students of society may bring to their material would all enrich the science of man. Yet in so far as it is also true that even the observation of facts already entails omission, selection, and emphasis, that is a first, inevitable interpretation, the observer's personality cannot be permitted such latitude.

One of the first steps in the development of some control over the personal equation is the training of students. We assume that, by familiarizing the student with the history of the discipline, with the principles of scientific method, with the broad comparative knowledge of cultures the world over, and with a knowledge of the mistakes which have been made in the past, we automatically reduce the probability of error.

In addition, it has been pointed out that to achieve a high degree of objectivity the student must know himself well, be aware of his biases, his value systems, his weaknesses, and his strengths (Lombard, 1950).[13] Presumably, self-awareness is something which develops in most of us with maturity. However, it has also been recommended in some quarters that field workers be psychoanalyzed before going out to the field, on the assumption that this would lead to greater self-awareness. A number of anthropologists have been analyzed with this in mind (and some perhaps for other reasons), and I have been told by at least two anthropologists that they believed their field work improved considerably thereafter. But this is one of those uncontrolled controls in which it is difficult to measure or evaluate the supposed improvement. Perhaps a more convincing case could be made for analysis if the analysis were published, so that we could read the analysis and the monograph hand in hand!

Nadel's suggestions of how to deal with the subjective factor are to the point. He writes (1951, p. 49):

13. M. Mead writes in this connection: "There is no such thing as an unbiased report on any social situation. . . . All of our recent endeavor in the social sciences have been to remove bias . . . in the matter of ethos, the surest and most perfect instrument of understanding is our own emotional response, provided that we can make a disciplined use of it" (*op. cit.*, pp. 299–300).

If subjectivity is unavoidable, it can at least be brought out into the open . . . the reasoning underlying observation and description must be clearly formulated, its premises exactly stated, and its operations shown step by step. . . . The greatest risk of mishandling scientific problems lies not in the different viewpoints and philosophies or perhaps in the divergent personalities of the scientists, but in the inexplicit statement of the assumptions and concepts with which they operate.

GROUP FIELD PARTIES

So far, we have been discussing the individual field worker. However, an additional measure of control in field work may be obtained, at least theoretically, whenever the field party consists of more than one person. Such types of field parties may range from a husband-wife team, to a teacher-student exped tion, to a co-operative field group with specialists from many disciplines.

The husband-wife field-work team has been a common occurrence. The advantages of a husband-wife team for establishing rapport in the field and in assuring against getting only a male's point of view of a culture have often been noted. Less frequently has it been noted that it also offers us a check on the reliability of reporting. The fact that husbands and wives have sometimes given us different interpretations is in itself a contribution to methodology, in that it raises questions about the factors involved in such differences.[14] I suppose that the usefulness, for methodological purposes, of a husband-wife team is directly proportional to their differences in personality, cultural background, value systems, training, and the quality of their interpersonal relations at the time of the field work or at publication.[15]

The frequent practice in the United States of sending out summer field research groups with students recruited from different departments of anthropology would seem to provide a system of checks and balances of points of view, since each department tends to train its students with some major emphasis. It is, of course, difficult to evaluate the extent of this potential control as it works out in practice, for so much depends upon how the field party is organized. However, it would seem that the element of control might be considerably increased on these field trips if the research were consciously organized around this point.

A field party consisting of professional anthropologists from different national cultures sent out to study a single community might serve as an experiment in checking the role of cultural backgrounds of anthropologists. It would be interesting to know what reports we would get on the Hopi from a field party consisting of an American, English, Mexican, Russian, Chinese, and Panamanian anthropologist. In Mexico, American anthropologists (Beals, Foster, Lewis, Redfield, Tax) have had field parties which included students from various Latin-American countries. However, the leadership of Americans and the teacher-student relationship have reduced the element of control.

Research teams consisting of specialists from more than one discipline also provide some measure of control of the personal equation, in that each specialist brings to the problem a new point of view, a different tradition, and different techniques, all of which, in theory, act as a cross-check upon bias. How much of a control is difficult to say and again depends upon the way in which the research team and the research problem are organized.

There have been numerous examples

14. For a striking example see the differences in interpretation of Arapesh temperament by Mead (1935) and Fortune (1939).

15. For this last item I am indebted to Dr. M. Mead.

of group research in which anthropologists have been represented. In the Bureau of Agricultural Economics, anthropologists, sociologists, and psychologists, under the direction of Dr. Carl C. Taylor, worked together in both the planning and the field-work phases in the study of 71 sample counties in the United States.[16] The avowed purpose of this team approach was to combine the anthropologist's emphasis upon intensive, qualitative analysis with the rural sociologist's reliance upon the quantification of data based largely upon schedules and surveys. It should be noted that the sampling procedures used in this research design, in order to select counties typical of the major types of farming regions and culture regions in rural United States, were of the highest caliber and might well serve as a model for future studies.

The Harvard comparative study of values in five cultures (see Kluckhohn, 1951a) and the earlier studies of the Navaho under Kluckhohn's direction employed many persons from different disciplines and from different institutions. One of the most significant methodological aspects of these projects is that they are longitudinal studies and involve work in the same communities over many years. The value of returning again and again to the same community cannot be overemphasized in any consideration of controls.

The Indian Education Research Project, undertaken jointly by the Committee on Human Development of the University of Chicago and the United

States Bureau of Indian Affairs, was begun in 1941 and has involved cooperation among anthropologists, sociologists, psychologists, psychiatrists, medical doctors, geographers, and others. The project has been quite productive (Thompson and Joseph, 1944; Macgregor, 1945; Leighton and Kluckhohn, 1946, 1947; Joseph, Spicer, and Chesky, 1949; Thompson, 1950, 1951).

Fortes worked in collaboration with an economist and a geographer in his survey of the Ashanti; Foster worked with a geographer (Donald Brand) on some aspects of the Tarascan project; Lewis worked with medical doctors, agronomists, and a psychologist in the study of Tepoztlan. Other interesting examples of multidisciplinary research still in progress can be cited. At the University of Michigan, psychologists, sociologists, and anthropologists are cooperating in a study to discover what social resources and typical role adaptations enable persons to function effectively under the pressure of social stress and cultural conflict. The study of Japanese-Americans in Chicago being conducted by Charlotte Babcock, William Caudill, and others includes scholars from the fields of psychology, sociology, and anthropology. The Columbia University Research in Contemporary Cultures under the direction of Margaret Mead includes anthropologists, clinical psychologists, psychoanalysts, historians, political scientists, sociologists, linguists, specialists in literature and the fine arts, and regional specialists. The University of Michigan Center for Japanese Studies, studying culture change in the inland sea region of Japan, includes representatives from geography, political science, and anthropology.

An evaluation of these group projects in terms of the amount of control which derives from the fact that they are multidisciplinary or interdisciplinary is beyond the scope of this paper

---

16. For a few examples of publications resulting from this project see Miner (1949) and Lewis (1948). For a discussion of an earlier BAE interdisciplinary study of rural communities see Steward (1950), who cites other examples of multidiscipline research: The Carnegie Institution of Washington long-range study of the Maya, begun under Kidder's direction in 1920, and the Virú Valley Project, Peru, under the sponsorship of the Institute of Andean Research.

but is something which deserves attention.[17] As Caudill (Caudill and Roberts, 1951, p. 12) cautions in a recent paper on interdisciplinary research, "there is an increasing realization that mere meetings . . . do not produce a unified product; indeed, the product frequently amounts to little more than a diluted version of one of the components." A maximum control would result from working on a common problem, understanding the technical jargon and the basic theoretical formulations of the other disciplines, and working in an atmosphere of smooth interpersonal relations. Some of the pitfalls noted are the pressure of publicity, the low common denominator of common knowledge, the representatives of each discipline being forced into the role of expert, the increased conservatism of participants as their positions are challenged, and the differential status positions of the participants (Caudill and Roberts, 1951).

FIELD TECHNIQUES AND THE PROBLEM OF CONTROL

The time-honored procedures of anthropological field work—observation, participation, the use of informants, census-taking, mapping, the recording of genealogies, case studies, autobiographies, etc.—all provide a degree of control in the observation of data. The relatively few innovations in field research techniques during the past twenty years is striking. Since 1930 only seven articles dealing directly with field methods have appeared in the *American Anthropologist*, and four of these were concerned with learning native languages.

Perhaps the most significant developments in the last twenty years have been the greater attention paid to sampling, the increased use of schedules and questionnaires, the use of more informants in order to cover the major

17. For a brief evaluation of the Tarascan project see Steward (1950, pp. 57–60).

socio-economic, status, and age groupings, the specialization of research (we now get entire volumes on economics, social organization, magic, and other aspects of culture which were formerly dealt with in a single monograph), the intensive use of photography, tape recording of interviews, and family studies. We shall comment on a few of these trends.

The greatest amount of quantification in ethnographic field work has been in the study of economics. This is particularly evident in the analysis of work patterns. A few scattered examples may be in order. Titiev (1944, p. 196) recorded the daily work schedules of five Hopi men over a period of three months; time devoted to work was recorded by Foster (1948, pp. 153–56) in Tzintzuntzan, by Redfield and Villa (1934, p. 80) in Chan Kom, and by Lewis (1951, pp. 145–46) in the analysis of hoe and plow agriculture in Tepoztlan. Lewis (1951, pp. 62–72) also published a synchronic record of the activities of each member of a Tepoztecan household for a period of four days. The number of occupations and the number of people engaged in each have been reported by several anthropologists. Firth's book, *Malay Fishermen* (1946), includes an extensive use of quantification in his study of occupations, economic activities, and production. Studies of the amount of land under cultivation and the size of yields, as well as budget and dietary studies, have been published by a number of field workers.[18]

A scale for the measurement of the

18. For land and yield studies see Redfield and Villa (1934, p. 53), Wagley and Galvao (1949), Lewis (1951, pp. 143 and 147); for diet and budget studies see Harris (1944, pp. 302–35), Redfield and Villa (1934, p. 57), Richards and Widdowson (1936), Lewis (1951, pp. 191–93), Rosemary Firth (1943); for detailed quantitative data on many aspects of economic life see Tax (1952); for an unusually meticulous study suggestive for its method see Henry (1951, pp. 187–219).

distribution of wealth was devised for use in Tepoztlan (Lewis, 1951a, pp. 173–78). Point values were assigned to the different forms of wealth, and a survey of the property owned by each household head made it possible to give each family in the village a point score. The study revealed a much greater range in distribution of wealth than had been expected in this relatively homogeneous village. Quantified in this way, the real economic status of each family was readily correlated with other economic and cultural phenomena. Application of similar scales in other societies might make cross-cultural comparisons more feasible.

Examples of quantification in studies of social organization are much more scarce in ethnographic literature. Kluckhohn's study in 1938 of the range of variation in ceremonial participation is a landmark. To my knowledge, Kluckhohn's lead has hardly been followed. In general, there have been few, if any, sociometric studies of social participation among pre-literate peoples.

Some examples of rather detailed quantitative studies of certain aspects of social organization are Titiev's study (1944) of Old Oraibi, Fortes' study (1949) of the kinship composition of households in an Ashanti community, Lewis' study (1951a, pp. 77–78) of residence and of barrio intermarriage in Tepoztlan.

Studies of culture and personality have given impetus to the use of controls, primarily in the form of tests, such as the Rorschach, T.A.T., doll play, etc. There is no need for a detailed discussion of these tests here, since they will probably be treated in the background paper on "Psychological Techniques." However, it should be noted that, while the application of a similar instrument produces an element of control, there is nevertheless increasing concern among psychologists themselves as to the validity of some of

these instruments even when used within our own society. In the light of this, one must have some reservations about anthropological field studies which rely heavily upon the Rorschach, or similar tests, to get at the personality picture (Thurstone, 1948; Cronbach, 1949; Scheider, 1950; McFarlane and Tuddenham, 1951; Palmer, 1951; Rabin, 1951).

In most ethnographic monographs, the sections dealing with the life-cycle are still very weak, particularly as regards systematic or controlled observation, quantitative data, and the use of sampling. Most sections on the life-cycle still read as if they were reconstructed from accounts of one or a few informants. This is doubly unfortunate, for in culture and personality studies detail and exactitude may be crucial. If, for example, it is reported that infants are swaddled in a certain tribe and then we go on to suggest some relationship between swaddling and character formation, as some do, it would be good to know at least (1) how many children are not swaddled; (2) the range in swaddling practices and beliefs; (3) the range in duration of swaddling, i.e., how many children were swaddled two months, four months, etc.; and (4) finally, some comparison of two groups of children within the same society which were subject to different degrees and types of swaddling. Only in this way might one test the hypothesis as to the effects of swaddling. In other words, for some problems the range rather than the mode may be the crucial datum.

Of course, there have been exceptions, but these exceptions have generally been special studies of some one problem or stage of the life-cycle rather than a part of a complete life-cycle picture. Kluckhohn's study on "Some Aspects of Navaho Infancy and Early Childhood" (1947) is noteworthy for its relatively controlled observations, its emphasis upon the range of child-training practices, and the use of some sampling procedures.

Another example of a careful study of one aspect of the life-cycle is the Henrys' study (1944) of Pilaga children, in which all the children in the community were studied and systematic, direct observations were recorded. Still another example is *The Hopi Child* by Wayne Dennis (1940).

The description of interpersonal relations is another area of weakness in terms of quantification and controlled observation. Many anthropologists are still seeking to isolate and identify the significant variables in this field and are not yet ready for measurement. Moreover, some variables seem less amenable to quantification than others. We have not yet devised accurate measures of hostility, aggression, dominance, submission, etc., for use even within our own society. How much more difficult must it be to derive measures for these variables for cross-cultural purposes! Then, too, some would argue that the *amount* of aggression or dominance is not nearly so significant as its quality and its context.

The use of photography as a method for the objective recording and portrayal of field data is now widely recognized, but its use is limited and uneven. Most anthropologists still use it in the old-fashioned way to illustrate physical types, landscape, and material culture. A major innovation is Bateson and Mead's photographic study of *Balinese Character* (1942; see also Mead and Macgregor, 1951), or what might be called the "Leica approach" to personality. This is undoubtedly the fullest use to date of the photographic approach. Its major methodological contribution is "objective" data, especially desirable in the description of psychological phenomena because of the absence of a precise scientific vocabulary. Excellent recent examples of ethnographic possibilities of good photog-

raphy are the study of Peguche by Collier and Buitrón (1949) and *Navaho Means People,* by McCombe, Vogt, and Kluckhohn (1951).

Recording of music in field work has a long history and does not concern us here. More recently there have been examples of the recording of interviews and the direct recording of life-stories. I can speak about some of the pros and cons from personal experience with these techniques.

It is difficult to generalize about the effect of the recording machine upon the interview situation. Some informants are very much inhibited by the machine, even after excellent rapport is established. In other cases informants respond positively, and the fact that they are being recorded seems to stimulate and release them. In still other cases the presence of the machine has no apparent effect upon the interview.

The most obvious advantage of recording interviews is the accurate, verbatim record which can be repeated at will for purposes of analysis. The recorded interview also acts as a check upon the role of the anthropologist. A comparative study of the recordings of a number of anthropologists might enable us to develop some criteria for good interviewing. Another advantage in having recorded interview materials is for the training of students. It is almost the equivalent of bringing the informant into the classroom. The usefulness of verbatim records for the linguist is obvious. My own recorded material is now being used by the Spanish Department of the University of Illinois for the study of rural Mexican Spanish.

The drawbacks are the high cost of copying data and the inevitable mechanical troubles, particularly when one is working in villages with no electric power and must depend upon batteries. It seems to me that a more practical alternative (and sometimes more pleasant) is to have a good stenographer as a field assistant.

I have heard anthropologists speculate about the possibility of "planting" secret recording apparatus, but I am unable to report examples of this practice—if it has been used. Similarly, to my knowledge the use of one-way screens has not yet been adopted in anthropological field work.

CONTROLS AND EXPERIMENTS IN RESEARCH DESIGN AND RESEARCH PROBLEMS

The comparative method is the nearest approach we have in cultural anthropology to the experiment. It is significant that Nadel, in his recent book (1951), titled the chapters dealing with the comparative method "Experimental Anthropology."[19] The experiment has been defined by Parsons (1937, p. 743) as "nothing but the comparative method where the cases to be compared are produced to order and under controlled conditions."[20] Since, in the study of culture, we cannot as a rule produce the artificial induction of variations under controlled conditions, we do the next-best thing and study variations as they occur over time and compare and correlate. This is the method of co-variation, sometimes also referred to as the "ex post facto experiment."[21]

The comparative method or the method of co-variation can be applied

19. See chaps. ix and x for a competent and detailed discussion of the comparative method in anthropology.

20. It is, of course, understood that the experiment involves not only controlled comparisons but also a hypothesis which is being tested. Anthropologists often referred to primitive societies and history as their laboratory and have suggested that the mere study of human beings in different societies is an experiment. This loose use of the term "experiment" should be differentiated from that of the experimental method.

21. See Greenwood (1945) for a careful exposition of the ex post facto experiment in sociology.

in many situations and on many levels. For example, we can compare institutions or modes of behavior (1) within a single community at a given time; (2) within different communities of a single culture at the same time; (3) within a single community or single culture at different times; (4) in different cultures; and (5) finally, we can compare entire cultures.

All these applications offer some measure of control. However, for the purposes of our paper we are concerned only with the comparative method as it is used in design of field work and the selection of field-work problems. We must therefore put aside many excellent comparative studies done on the basis of library work with secondary sources—for example, Mishkin's study of the differential effect of the horse upon three Plains Indian societies, Spier's study of the Sun Dance, Benedict's study of the guardian spirit, Parsons' study of Pueblo religion, etc.

It should be noted that by far the greater proportion of anthropological field work has been designed in terms of the study of a single community or a single culture. Research designs for field work on a cross-cultural or even multicommunity, comparative basis are strikingly few. We might also observe that the degree of control over data in ethnographic monographs is also a function of the size of the community or society studied. All other things being equal, one can expect a much greater degree of control and coverage of range of variation in a small community than in a large one. Compare, for example, the quality of coverage of Foster's monograph on Tzintzuntzan, a community of about 1,200, or of Redfield and Villa's *Chan Kom*, a community of about 250, with the Herskovits description of Dahomey, with a population of over 100,000. Moreover, I would hazard the guess that there is a direct relationship between the degree to which a monograph concentrates upon the range of variation of any one or more aspects of the culture and the extent to which it is experimental or useful for comparative purposes.

Much of the research done within single communities, but particularly modern studies, utilizes the comparative method to some extent when the researchers study the interrelationships between different aspects of the culture or when they investigate problems or hypotheses. For example, when one studies the relationship between leadership in political life and leadership in religious and ceremonial life, or the relationship between wealth and standard of living, or wealth and the ages of the heads of households, etc., one is using a comparative method. Generally, these kinds of problems are treated as part of a larger descriptive and interpretative study and are not labeled "experimental" or "comparative."

Instances of field studies within a single community which are explicitly labeled experimental or in which there is a clear experimental design are probably very few.[22] The only examples which occur to me are (1) Brown and Hutt, *Anthropology in Action: An Experiment in the Aringa District of the Aringa Province, Tanganyika Territory* (1935). This was described as an "experiment" to determine how useful an anthropologist and an administrator can be to each other in working on a common problem. Its purpose was "to discover what fields of knowledge were of use to the administrator" and "to evolve a simple method of securing and presenting such knowledge in a way that would serve practical ends." An interesting feature of this report is the inclusion (in the Appendix) of a list of the questions asked by the administrator during the course of the experiment and the answers to some of these questions. (2) Spindler and Goldschmidt, "An Experimental Design in the Study of Culture Change" (1952). This is an attempt to relate changes in individual personality with degree of acculturation in the study of the Menominee Indians of Wisconsin. The research design is basically similar to that of Hallowell's earlier study, except that the different acculturation groups, which also represent different socio-economic levels, live within a single Indian reservation. Also, more refined techniques for measuring the level of acculturation were employed. The introduction of a "control group" of whites living on the reservation was meant to serve as a standard against which the Menominee are measured. As the authors point out, this particular "control group," consisting of twelve men, most of whom were married to Menominee women, has severe limitations. However, it completes the "experimental design" nicely. (3) Adair and Leighton's (and others) study of the factors in the acceptance or rejection of improved farming practices in the Fruitland Navaho community. "Predictions will be made on the basis of present knowledge of community structure as to which farmers will take up some of the practices shown and which will resist." A central hypothesis to be tested here is "that technological change is more readily accepted if the technological assistants can work through informal leaders of the population to be helped."[23]

Multiple, full biographies from the same community, done by the same field worker or by many workers as part of a comparative research design, are very few. Only Barton's (1938) three Ifugao biographies come to mind.

The recent interest in intensive family studies exemplifies the use of the comparative method in the design of field

---

22. Time pressure has prevented a survey of the literature from this point of view.

23. *Clearing House Bulletin,* I, No. 1 (summer, 1951), 11.

research and may in the future lead to experimental studies. Here the problem is to determine how different families in a relatively homogeneous culture react to and reinterpret the local culture and to analyze the variables related to these differences. Roberts' study of *Three Navaho Households* is the first publication in this field. His emphasis was upon a detailed comparison of material culture and "some of the more obvious habit relationships" of the three similar groups. He writes (1951, p. 6): "If, despite this presumption of similarity, the three small group cultures were then found to be significantly different from each other in some respects, the hypothesis that every small group defines an independent and unique group-ordered culture would be supported." His survey demonstrates the feasibility of employing small-group cultures as comparative units.

In a forthcoming study of two Mexican peasant families of different socio-economic levels in Tepoztlan, the emphasis is upon a comparison of the economic, social, and religious life of the families *as a whole* and the quality of interpersonal relations. Whole-family studies are particularly suitable for the study of problems in culture and personality. The anthropological approach to family studies (Lewis, 1950) ties in with the currently popular small-group research movement and may lead to a new field of specialization within anthropology.

There are numerous research designs involving more than a single community or culture and employing some experimental or problem approach. A few examples will suffice. A comparative study of the Blackfoot Indians of Canada and the United States was designed by Ruth Benedict to test the effect of differences in government administration and policy upon a people of a common cultural background. The design was excellent, but unfortunately

the project did not materialize as planned. In the course of this study it became clear that it was very difficult to isolate or weigh in the balance the role of a single variable. It turned out that the tribes were put on reservations at different dates, that the pressure of white settlers against the American Blackfoot began much earlier than against the Canadian group, that the land base on the Canadian side differed, and, finally, that a Blackfoot tribe in Canada had the unusual good fortune of getting about a two million dollar trust fund from the sale of land to a railroad and of discovering a coal mine, which became a new source of income.

A comparison of the Oklahoma and Mexican Kickapoo has often been suggested, again with the idea of testing the role of a single variable, namely, different government administration. Africa would seem to be an ideal locale for comparative studies of the effects of differences in colonial policy (French, British, Belgian) upon peoples of common culture.

Lystad's recent comparative study of the Ahafo-Ashanti, in British territory, and the Indenie-Agni, in French territory, is a case in point. Lystad describes the problem as "a laboratory situation for the analysis of the processes by which a culture originally shared by two populations now exhibits differences in two regions in which it has been in contact with two differing ways of life" (1951, p. 1).

Hallowell's study of the relationship between psychological characteristics and degree of acculturation among the Ojibwa is an example of an "experimental" research design based upon the comparative method. Using the Rorschach test (validated by comparison with T.A.T.'s, drawings, direct observation, life-histories, ethnographic data, and historical information) to get at "a model personality picture," Hallowell studied and tested three different groups of Ojibwa, each representing a different level of acculturation. Hallowell also utilized the technique of historical reconstruction from the accounts of early observers who had had direct contact with the Indian of the Eastern Woodlands in the seventeenth and eighteenth centuries, to arrive at an approximate psychological picture of the aboriginal Ojibwa. He used this as a base line against which to judge the direction of psychological change among contemporary Ojibwa (1951).[24]

The use of history as a control in the design of field research has been used often and to good effect. It has been basic to the work of Herskovits and his students in the Afro-American field. Using West Africa as a base line, Herskovits has traced the degree, direction, and type of culture change in the New World under varying conditions. Some of the questions he asks are: "What differences, for example, are to be found in the linguistic adaptation of the Negroes to English, to French, to Spanish, to Portuguese, to Dutch? What are the similarities and differences to be found between the ways of life of Negroes of the same socio-economic classes in these different settings? How has living under Catholicism influenced the development of present-day religious patterns of these Negro groups as against exposure to Protestant tradition? In which aspects of culture, over the whole New World, have African ways proved to be most tenacious?" (1949, p. 613).

Much of the work so far has been limited to the study of survivals of Africanisms. Perhaps at some time in the future it will be possible to take a single West African culture and see what happened to it in various parts of the New World. The publication of

Bascom's materials on Yoruban cults in Cuba and Herskovits' materials on the Yoruban cults in Brazil will be a step in this direction.[25]

A recent field research design which approaches an experimental control is reported in a paper on "Urbanization without Breakdown: A Case Study" (Lewis, 1952). The problem was to test the hypothesis that disorganization and family breakdown result from urbanization. Using a previous study of Tepoztlan as a base line, approximately 100 Tepoztecan families who had moved to Mexico City between 1900 and 1949 were studied. The data were obtained by a schedule supplemented with interviews, psychological testing, and living with a few selected families. The methodological innovation was the fact that it was a follow-up study of families from a specific community that had been previously studied.

The application of the experimental small-group research techniques developed by Bales and others has not made very much headway in anthropological field work. To my knowledge, it has been used by Strodtbeck (1951) in his comparative study of Navaho, Mormon, and Texan couples in the Southwest and by Roberts in a study of Zuni, Mormon, Navaho, and Spanish-American individuals.[26] These narrow-focus, specialized studies are a far cry from the older ethnographic methods and broad objectives. Just where these newer approaches are going it is still too early to say.

RESTUDIES

It seems to me that one type of control in field work has to do with the broad problem of testing the reliability of anthropological reporting. One way of getting at this difficult problem is by

24. A similar study is now being done by Lewis—a comparison of Mexican Indian personality as described by sixteenth-century chroniclers with that obtained from field data in contemporary Mexico.

25. Personal communication from Dr. Herskovits.

26. Personal communication from J. M. Roberts about unpublished paper.

independent restudies of the same community by different observers, preferably at the same time, but conceivably at different times.

The need for restudies as methodological checks has been felt by many anthropologists and nonanthropologists alike. Of course, there is some difference of opinion here, too. On the whole, the attitude toward the reliability of anthropological data has ranged from that of extreme credulity to that of paranoid suspicion. Moreover, those who would emphasize the subjective element—the element of art in field work—tend to be skeptical about the methodological value of restudies. On the other hand, those who have greater faith in objective methods, in operational procedures for observation, are inclined to be more favorable toward restudies. The former would argue that all human beings make errors, that this can be taken for granted, and that we can learn more by going ahead with new studies than by concerning ourselves with past mistakes. The latter would argue that it is important to learn what kind of errors have been made, particularly if the scientific aspect of anthropology is to grow stronger. The former would argue that we do not need to have a restudy to know that there is something wrong with a report. This can be determined in terms of our wider comparative knowledge, in terms of internal consistency, or in terms of whether it agrees with a particular school of thought. The latter would perhaps agree but would add that this is not enough, that we need empirical evidence as to just what the facts are. Finally, some would suggest that there may be a further dichotomy involved, namely, the difference between those who hold that truth is relative and subjective and that each field worker is probably correct within the limits of the problem set and the materials selected for study, and those who hold

that truth is absolute and objective and can be approximated more nearly by some methods than by others.

It must be emphasized that the objective and value of restudies is not to prove one man right and another wrong. It is not a matter of listing another's errors, in itself a distasteful and painful task, but rather of finding out what kind of errors tend to be made by what kind of people under what kind of conditions. Given a sufficiently large number of restudies, it might be possible to develop a theory of observation which would help to evaluate the role of the personal equation, personality, and ideological or cultural variables. One wonders, for example, to what extent what Li An-Che saw in Zuñi was a function of the fact that he was Chinese and had grown up in a very different cultural milieu from Americans, a milieu with a marked patrilineal emphasis but with much less emphasis upon expressiveness. If we could eventually arrive at generalizations in which we could say, given an anthropologist from such and such a cultural background, we can expect that his account of tribe X will be slanted in such and such a way, then we would have made some progress.

In an earlier publication (1951*a*, p. 428) I have summarized some of the reasons for the paucity of restudies in anthropology:

Perhaps most important have been the limited funds for field research, the time pressure of studying tribes who were rapidly becoming extinct, the shortage of field workers, the greater appeal in studying a community never studied before, and finally, the lack of emphasis upon methodology.

Here it may be useful to distinguish four types of restudies: (1) those restudies in which a second or third investigator goes to a community with the express design of re-evaluating the work of his predecessor; (2) those in which the same or an independent investigator goes to a community studied earlier, to study culture change, utilizing the first report as a base line against which to measure and evaluate change; (3) those in which one returns to study some aspect of the culture not studied earlier; and (4) those in which one studies more intensively and perhaps from a new point of view some aspect of the culture studied earlier. There is, of course, some overlapping between these types. All restudies are additive in a sense. However, it is a matter of emphasis in research design.

From the point of view of testing reliability, the first type would seem to be the most suitable, though not without its methodological difficulties. Communities change, and it is sometimes difficult to know to what extent differences in findings reflect changes in the culture. Much depends upon the area and community which is being restudied. In cases where many years have elapsed between the first and second studies and where change has been rapid and profound, it may well be impossible to reconstruct the earlier condition with sufficient accuracy to make it useful for reliability purposes. On the other hand, there are many areas where change is relatively slow and superficial. Moreover, when too many years have not elapsed, it is possible to use the same informants used in the earlier study. Also, the use of village records and archive records can act as a control. Finally, much depends upon the amount of quantitative data in the first report. Where this is full, restudies have a more solid base for comparisons. Indeed, this is perhaps the major positive function of quantification.[27]

To my knowledge, there is not a single published case of a restudy of the first type, that is, where the express purpose was the interest in methodology, the interest in testing an earlier report.[28] The recent restudy of Tepoztlan perhaps comes closest to this type, but even here it was not originally planned with this as the central purpose. The differences between Redfield's and Lewis' findings ranged from matters of small factual detail to those of broad interpretations and total impressions of village life. Except for a few glaring exceptions, most of Red-

27. See, for example, the study of changes in occupations and the growth in specialization over a seventeen-year period in a Mexican village (Lewis, 1951, pp. 101–8).

28. The only example known to me is the case of San Pedro la Laguna, in Guatemala, which was studied by Juan Rosales and later by Benjamin Paul. This case is particularly interesting because it was consciously planned as a methodological check. The problem was to compare the independent report of a native villager with only a minimum of training with that of a professionally trained anthropologist.

Juan Rosales, a native from the near-by village of Panajachel, had worked for Sol Tax as an assistant in gathering field data, filling out questionnaires, etc. He was a schoolteacher and spoke the native Indian language well. Tax sent him to study the village of San Pedro, and later Benjamin Paul studied the same village without having access to the field data of Rosales. The plan was to publish both reports independently. However, after much patient waiting for Rosales to write up his data, the plan was abandoned, and Dr. Paul was given access to the Rosales materials. However, Paul wrote his paper on "Symbolic Sibling Rivalry in a Guatemalan Village" (1950) before reading the Rosales materials. Dr. Paul tells of how gratifying it was for him to find that Rosales had independently recorded the rather esoteric belief upon which the above article was based.

It should be noted that, although this experimental design was well conceived as a check of the factor of professional training, it might have been a more crucial experiment of reliability if both field workers had not been given the same orientation. Both Tax and Paul were from the same department at the University of Chicago, and Rosales was also brought to Chicago for a while. It should be noted, too, that Julio de la Fuente, who has undertaken the heroic task of writing up the Rosales materials, was also trained at Chicago and uses the folk-urban conception as his major theoretical frame of reference (see, e.g., De la Fuente, 1949, pp. 358–65).

field's descriptive data were confirmed by Lewis. The major divergences resulted from differences in research methodology, in interests, and in theoretical orientation, all of which influenced the selection, coverage, and organization of materials. The Lewis study had the advantage of Redfield's pioneer work to start with, more than twice the amount of time for field work, more field assistance, and the development during a period of almost twenty years of new approaches and methods, especially in the field of culture and personality. Lewis studied intensively many aspects of the culture only touched upon in the earlier work, with much more emphasis upon quantification and the study of range of variation. Finally, a fundamental difference in approach in the restudy was the emphasis upon ethnohistory and the effort to see the village not as an isolated society but as part of a larger regional and national framework.[29]

Restudies of the same community for the purpose of studying social change would seem to be one of the most important functions of a restudy approach. The restudy approach provides us with a partial solution to one of the traditional problems in the study of culture change among nonliterate peoples, namely, the difficulty of establishing an accurate base line from which change can be measured. All of us have struggled to piece together such a base line from historical data or comparative materials and are aware of the very unsatisfactory and unequal coverage on various aspects of the culture. Having a base line established by an anthropological study is a boon, even admitting the limitations which come from changing interests and techniques in anthropology itself.

A restudy of the same community by

the same investigator can also make a contribution to the problem of controls, particularly if the investigator is sufficiently aware of the problem of methodology to make explicit the changes in his outlook and approach which may have occurred in the interval between the two studies.

Examples of full restudies of this type are still relatively few: Lynd's *Middletown in Transition,* Redfield's *A Village That Chose Progress,* Lewis' *Life in a Mexican Village: Tepoztlan Restudied.* Restudies of larger units include, among others: three separate and independent restudies of the Ashanti by M. Fortes (1949), R. A. Lystad (1951), and K. A. Busia (1951), respectively; Mair's (1934) restudy of the Baganda, and Powell's[30] restudy of the Trobrianders. A few restudies are now in progress or are being planned. Firth is restudying Tikopia and Margaret Mead plans to restudy Manus in 1953.

By far the largest number of restudies are of the third and fourth types or the purely additive type. Instances of these types are so numerous it would be impossible to mention them within the confines of a short paper.[31] Some peoples have been visited so frequently, particularly by summer laboratories, that they now have professional informants who depend upon the returning anthropologist for their living and who may be kept busy the rest of the year answering questionnaires.

The striking thing about most of

---

29. For a full discussion of some limitations of the community study approach see Steward (1950).

30. I understand from Dr. Fortes that Mr. H. A. Powell, Department of Anthropology, University College, London, has just returned from a restudy of the Trobrianders.

31. A few examples may be cited. For the Kwakiutl there are Boas, Forde, Codere, and Hawthorne; for the Hopi, Cushing, Fewkes, Stephen, Voth, Parsons, Lowie, the Eggans, Beaglehole, Bunzel, Dennis, Forde, Titiev, Simmons and Thompson; for the Blackfoot, Grinnell, McLean, McClintock, Wissler, Schultz, Michelson, Richardson and Hanks, Benedict, Goldfrank, Maslow and Lewis.

these studies (and this applies to many in the third type) is the failure systematically to evaluate the work of their predecessors and to offer some explanation of differences in findings.[32] Rather, each new worker goes on to study something new with but passing reference to earlier work. Now this may mean many things. It may in itself be a testimonial to the reliability of previous reports, that is, by silent affirmation; it may mean that the later investigators went in with the same biases as the former and the lack of difference merely reflects the absence of a critical or fresh outlook; or it may reflect a lack of sensitivity to methodological questions. I suspect that all these factors have been at work to some extent.

Kroeber's six-day restudy of the Seri (1931, p. 3; McGee, 1895–96) is notable as one of the few instances in which a later investigator has troubled to evaluate the earlier findings in some detail and to attempt to explain the differences. Speaking of McGee's work, he says that "it is easy to read between the lines of this description that McGee leaned toward a romantic and imaginative interpretation of the Seri. Also, his actual contacts with the people themselves were brief, and hampered by imperfect communication" (1931, p. 3). Speaking of how he confined himself to the social and religious sides of Seri life, he states: "There was the more reason for this since it is in dealing with these latter aspects, where verbal communications are as important as observation, that McGee's monograph is most tenuous and dubious" (1931, p. 4). However, his criticism is not completely negative, as we can see when he says, referring to McGee again, that "his work impresses me as that of an extraordinarily good observer, keen in seeing significant evidence, but of uncontrolled imagination and unconscious of his preconceptions. It is only fair to state that where he founds an interpretation on slender or uncertain data, he generally indicates the fact to a careful reader" (1931, p. 18).

Emeneau's eight-month restudy of the Todas was intended primarily for linguistic purposes. Emeneau writes:

I had no intention of reinvestigating W. H. R. Rivers' ethnological account when I went to them. However, I found that field work in linguistics is impossible if one does not understand what people are talking about. It proved necessary to check every item of text material by Rivers' account of the ethnology of the tribe, and in the end I found myself with numerous corrections of Rivers' detail, as well as with a few important corrections of the general outline of Toda institutions.[33]

Emeneau has added much new data on the Todas. His major corrections were his findings on the dual descent system and his reinterpretation of the nature of Toda religion (1935, 1937, 1941).

Mair's restudy of the Baganda provides us with a rather balanced and thorough re-evaluation, which challenges many of the earlier findings. Only a sample of the many divergences in findings can be noted here.

After stating many of the positive aspects of Roscoe's earlier work, she writes (1934, pp. xii–xiv):

Nevertheless, it is not altogether satisfactory to the modern anthropologist, for it does not include many data which are now thought indispensable for a sociological study. It does not envisage Baganda society as a mechanism of co-operation, and the links which should connect the structure of kindred and clan, of political and religious authorities, with the normal

---

32. Sol Tax tells of how difficult it is to get students to check upon the reliability of earlier work. In a study of the Fox, which has been going on for about three years under his direction, he has been unable to have any of the field workers check upon a prediction he made many years ago concerning some development in the kinship system.

33. Personal Communication, February, 1952.

organization of daily life, are missing. It describes, for example, very fully the ceremonial connected with marriage but does not analyze the system of co-operation within the household. It does not connect the kinship terms with the obligations recognized between relatives, nor the technical processes with the organization through which they were carried out. It is most inadequate at those points at which the student of economic contact most requires accurate and detailed information—in such questions as the system of economic co-operation, or of land tenure, or the relations between people and chiefs.

Moreover, the disadvantage of working largely on the basis of native statements detached from their context is apparent in certain serious distortions of fact. The political organization, for example, is represented as no more than a system whereby a few tyrannical chiefs preyed on the common people and were in turn preyed on by the king. The summary nature of justice and the arbitrary exercise of power by the king and the most important chiefs are exclusively emphasized, while their obligations towards their people, their place in the maintenance of order, and the checks upon abuse are overlooked.

Again, a highly sensational colour is given to the description of the indigenous religion by the overemphasis of human sacrifice, which is made to seem its central feature. Not only is the aspect of religion as a means of recourse in times of danger or difficulty barely considered, but offerings of human victims to the gods are confused with murders for magical purposes, with political executions for crime, and with the wanton slaughter which was indulged in by some of the kings, so that their total is made to appear enormous.

For these reasons the attempt to make a new reconstruction of the past of Baganda seemed to me necessary. In the event I felt it to be justified beyond my expectations, for the number of old men who remember the days before the influence of Christianity and British administration had effectively penetrated the country, and whose accounts, given at places many miles apart, corroborate one another, is surprisingly large. I have indicated in the text the points at which my informants

differed positively from Roscoe's, those in which they simply denied knowledge of customs which he describes, and those in which I differ from him for reasons of evidence other than that of native statements which contradict those made in his book. In some cases these differences may be due to the falling into disuse of old customs; in others, for the reasons which I give in each context, I think they cannot be.

Fortes' restudy of the Ashanti points to a few important differences from Rattray, particularly as to the nature of the local matrilineal group and the difference between the part played by matrilineal descent and kinship on the father's side in the total social structure.[34] However, there is no attempt at a systematic re-evaluation.

A recent translation from the Russian of G. F. Debets' study of the Chukchee (1945) and of T. Semushkin's Chukotka provides us with another example of a restudy for the purpose of studying social change. An unexpected and highly interesting aspect of these studies is the fact that the investigators disagree strongly with Bogoras' description of the physical characteristics of the people, such as head and facial measurements, beard developments, and hair texture. Debets concludes: "It is clearly indicated that the existing descriptions of racial characteristics of this people must be basically altered."[35]

Elsie Clews Parsons, with typical historical interest, has given us an incisive characterization of the role of the personal equation in explaining differences in findings on the Zuni. Because her statement (1939, pp. 939–40) illustrates several of the problems discussed in the foregoing pages, I shall quote it by way of conclusion:

34. See Fortes (1949). I am also grateful for a personal communication on this from Dr. Fortes.

35. Sonia Bleeker, "Maritime Chukchee Acculturation" (unpublished essay prepared under the direction of Ruth Benedict).

Some of the interpueblo variation now familiar to us may be put down to differences between observers or historians as well as to unequal opportunities for observation. Observation differs within a single pueblo, take Zuni. Cushing, the poet and craftsman, did not see the same facts at Zuni as the museum collectors who were there at the same time. Thirty years later Kroeber visited Zuni and devoted himself to those aspects of culture which in the interval had become more significant to the trained observer of Indian life, to language and social organization. Cushing, Stevenson, and Kroeber—to these three would any culture look alike! Familiar with the medicine bundle-complex of Plains Indians, Kroeber could see homologues in the cane or corn-ear fetishes of Zuni and appreciate the significance of their ceremonial life.

But the actual use of these fetishistic bundles or of other ritual objects, Kroeber unfortunately had no opportunity to see, as had Stevenson or, among Hopi, Voth and Stephen. These scrupulous observers of Hopi ritual were allowed to be present at kiva altar ritual. . . . Is Zuni ritual less intricate than Hopi, or is it merely that part of its complexity has not been recorded? Matilda Stevenson, who usually failed to distinguish between what she saw and what she heard about, was far from being an accurate recorder, nor did she have any facility for interpretation or evaluation. . . . Fortunately, more comparable reports may be expected of recent students who have had more or less the same training, who go over one another's work, and who are learning the tribal languages.

REFERENCES

BARTON, R. F. 1938. *Philippine Pagans.* London: G. Routledge & Sons, Ltd.

BATESON, G., and MEAD, M. 1942. *Balinese Character: A Photographic Analysis.* ("Special Publications of the New York Academy of Sciences," Vol. II.)

BENEDICT, R. 1948. "Anthropology and the Humanities," *American Anthropologist,* L, No. 4, 585–93.

BROWN, G. G., and HUTT, A. M. B. 1935. *Anthropology in Action.* London: Oxford University Press.

BUSIA, K. A. 1951. *Position of the Chief in the Modern Political System of the Ashanti.* London and New York: Oxford University Press; published for the International African Institute.

CAUDILL, W., and ROBERTS, B. H. 1951. "Pitfalls in the Organization of Interdisciplinary Research," *Human Organization,* X, No. 4, 12–15.

COLLIER, J., JR., and BUITRÓN, A. 1949. *The Awakening Valley.* Chicago: University of Chicago Press.

CRONBACH, L. 1949. "Statistical Methods Applied to Rorschach Scores: A Review," *Psychological Bulletin,* XLVI, No. 5, 393–429.

DENNIS, W. 1940. *The Hopi Child.* ("Monographs of the Virginia University Institute for Research in Social Sciences,"

No. 26.) New York: Appleton-Century Co., Inc.

DORFMAN, J. 1933. "An Unpublished Project by Thorstein Veblen for an Ethnological Inquiry," *American Journal of Sociology,* XXXIX, 237–41.

EMENEAU, M. B. 1935. "Toda Culture Thirty-five Years After: An Acculturation Study," *Annals of the Bhandarkar Oriental Research Institute,* XIX, 101–21.

———. 1937. "Toda Marriage Regulations and Taboos," *American Anthropologist,* XXXIX, 103–12.

———. 1941. "Language and Social Forms: A Study of Toda Kinship Terms and Dual Descent." In HALLOWELL, A. I.; NEWMAN, S. S.; and SPIER, L. (eds.), *Language, Culture, and Personality,* pp. 158–79. Menasha, Wis.: Sapir Memorial Publication Fund.

FIRTH, RAYMOND. 1946. *Malay Fishermen: Their Peasant Economy.* London: Kegan Paul.

FIRTH, ROSEMARY. 1943. *Housekeeping among Malay Peasants.* ("London School of Economics Monographs on Social Anthropology," No. 7.) London.

FORTES, MEYER. 1949. "Time and Social Structure: An Ashanti Case Study." In FORTES, MEYER (ed.), *Studies Presented to A. R. Radcliffe-Brown*, pp. 54–84. Oxford: Clarendon Press.

FORTUNE, R. F. 1939. "Arapesh Warfare," *American Anthropologist*, XLI, No. 1, 22–41.

FOSTER, G. 1948. *Empire's Children: The People of Tzintzuntzan*. ("Publications of the Institute of Social Anthropology, Smithsonian Institution," No. 6.) Washington, D.C.

FUENTE, JULIO DE LA. 1949. *Yalalag, una villa zapoteca serrana*. ("Serie científica, Museo Nacional de Antropologia, Mexico.")

GOTTSCHALK, L.; KLUCKHOHN, C.; and ANGELL, R. 1945. *The Use of Personal Documents in History, Anthropology, and Sociology*. (Social Science Research Council Bull. 53.) New York.

GREENWOOD, E. 1945. *Experimental Sociology: A Study in Method*. New York: King's Crown Press.

HALLOWELL, A. I. 1951. "The Use of Projective Techniques in the Study of the Socio-psychological Aspects of Acculturation," *Journal of Projective Techniques*, XV, No. 1, 27–44.

HARRIS, J. S. 1944. "Some Aspects of the Economics of Sixteen Ibo Individuals," *Africa*, XIV, 302–35.

HENRY, J. 1951. "The Economics of Pilagá Food Distribution," *American Anthropologist*, LIII, No. 2, 187–219.

HENRY, J. and Z. 1944. *Doll-Play of Pilagá Indian Children*. ("American Orthopsychiatric Association Monograph Series," No. 4.) New York.

HERSKOVITS, M. J. 1949. *Man and His Works*. New York: A. A. Knopf.

———. 1950. "The Hypothetical Situation: A Technique of Field Research," *Southwestern Journal of Anthropology*, VI, No. 1, 32–40.

JORDAN, E. 1952. *Essays in Criticism*. Chicago: University of Chicago Press.

JOSEPH, A.; SPICER, R.; and CHESKY, J. 1949. *The Desert People: A Study of the Papago Indians of Southern Arizona*. Chicago: University of Chicago Press.

KLUCKHOHN, C. 1938. "Participation in Ceremonials in a Navaho Community," *American Anthropologist*, XL, 359–69.

———. 1939. "The Place of Theory in Anthropological Studies," *Philosophy of Science*, VI, No. 3, 328–44.

———. 1947. "Some Aspects of Navaho Infancy and Early Childhood." In ROHEIM, G. (ed.), *Psychoanalysis and the Social Sciences*, I, 37–86. New York: International Universities Press.

———. 1951a. "A Comparative Study of Values in Five Cultures." In VOGT, E., *Navaho Veterans: A Study of Changing Values*. ("Papers of the Peabody Museum of American Archaeology and Ethnology, Harvard University," Vol. XLI, No. 1.)

———. 1951b. "The Study of Culture." In LERNER, D., and LASSWELL, H. D. (eds.), *The Policy Sciences: Recent Developments in Scope and Method*, pp. 86–101. Stanford: Stanford University Press.

KLUCKHOHN, F. R. 1940. "The Participant Observer Technique in Small Communities," *American Journal of Sociology*, XLVI, No. 3, 331–43.

KROEBER, A. L. 1931. *Report on the Seri*. ("Los Angeles Southwest Museum Papers," Vol. VI.)

———. 1948. *Anthropology*. New York: Harcourt, Brace & Co.

LEIGHTON, D. C., and KLUCKHOHN, C. 1946. *The Navaho*. Cambridge: Harvard University Press.

———. 1947. *Children of the People*. Cambridge: Harvard University Press.

LEWIS, O. 1948. *On Edge of the Black Waxey: A Cultural Survey of Bell County, Texas*. ("Washington University Studies in Social and Philosophical Sciences," No. 7.) St. Louis.

———. 1950. "Anthropological Approach to Family Studies," *American Journal of Sociology*, LV, No. 5, 468–75.

———. 1951. *Life in a Mexican Village: Tepoztlan Restudied*. Urbana, Ill.: University of Illinois Press.

———. 1952. "Urbanization without Breakdown: A Case Study" (paper read at annual meeting of the American Anthropological Association, Chicago), *Scientific Monthly*, LXXV, No. 1, 31–41.

LINTON, R. 1945. *The Cultural Backgrounds of Personality*. New York: Appleton-Century Co., Inc.

LOMBARD, G. F. F. 1950. "Self-awareness and Scientific Method," *Science*, CXII, 289–93.

LYSTAD, R. A. 1951. "Differential Acculturation of the Ahafo-Ashanti of the Gold Coast and the Indenie-Agni of the Ivory Coast." Doctoral dissertation at Northwestern University, Evanston, Ill.

McCOMBE, L.; VOGT, E.; and KLUCKHOHN, C. 1951. *Navaho Means People.* Cambridge: Harvard University Press.

McFARLANE, JEAN W., and TUDDENHAM, R. D. 1951. "Problems in Validating of Projective Techniques." In ANDERSON, H. H. and G. M. L., *Introduction to Projective Techniques,* chap. ii. New York: Prentice-Hall Book Co.

McGEE, W. S. 1895–96. *The Seri Indians.* ("Publications of the U.S. Bureau of Ethnology," Vol. XVII, Part I.)

MACGREGOR, G. 1945. *Warriors without Weapons: A Study of the Society and Personality Development of the Pine Ridge Sioux.* Chicago: University of Chicago Press.

MAIR, L. P. 1934. *An African People in the Twentieth Century.* London: Routledge & Sons, Ltd.

MALINOWSKI, B. 1922. *The Argonauts of the Western Pacific.* London: Routledge & Sons, Ltd.

MEAD, M. 1933. "More Comprehensive Field Methods," *American Anthropologist,* XXXV, No. 1, 1–15.

———. 1935. *Sex and Temperament in Three Primitive Societies.* New York: William Morrow & Co., Inc.

———. 1939. "Native Languages as Field-Work Tools," *American Anthropologist,* XLI, No. 2, 189–205.

———. 1940. *The Mountain Arapesh. II. Supernaturalism.* ("Anthropological Papers of the American Museum of Natural History," Vol. XXXVII, Part III.)

———. 1949. *The Mountain Arapesh. V. The Record of Unabelin with Rorschach Analysis.* ("Anthropological Papers of the American Museum of Natural History," Vol. XLI, Part III.)

MEAD, M., and MACGREGOR, G. 1951. *Growth and Culture: A Photographic Study of Balinese Childhood.* New York: G. P. Putnam's Sons.

MINER, H. 1949. *Culture and Agriculture: An Anthropological Study of a Corn Belt County.* ("Occasional Contributions from the Museum of Anthropology of the University of Michigan," No. 14.) Ann Arbor: University of Michigan Press.

NADEL, S. F. 1951. *The Foundations of Social Anthropology.* Glencoe, Ill.: Free Press.

PALMER, J. O. 1951. *A Dual Approach to Rorschach Validation: A Methodological Study.* ("Psychological Monographs," ed. HERBERT S. CONRAD, Vol. LXV, No. 8 [whole No. 325].) Washington, D.C.: Psychological Association of America.

PARSONS, E. C. 1939. *Pueblo Indian Religion.* Chicago: University of Chicago Press.

PARSONS, T. 1937. *The Structure of Social Action.* New York: McGraw-Hill Book Co.

PAUL, BENJAMIN. 1950a. "Life in a Guatemala Indian Village." Reprinted from *Patterns for Modern Living.* Chicago: Delphian Society.

———. 1950b. "Symbolic Sibling Rivalry in a Guatemalan Indian Village," *American Anthropologist,* LII, No. 2, 205–18.

RABIN, A. I. 1951. "Validating and Experimental Studies with Rorschach Method." In ANDERSON, H. H. and G. M. L., *Introduction to Projective Techniques,* chap. v. New York: Prentice-Hall Book Co.

RADIN, P. 1933. *The Method and Theory of Ethnology.* New York: McGraw-Hill Book Co.

REDFIELD, R. 1948. "The Art of Social Science," *American Journal of Sociology,* LIV, No. 3, 181–90.

REDFIELD, R., and VILLA, A. 1934. *Chan Kom, a Maya Village.* Washington, D.C.: Carnegie Institution of Washington.

RICHARDS, A., and WIDDOWSON, E. M. 1936. "A Dietary Study in North-eastern Rhodesia," *Africa,* IX, 166–96.

ROBERTS, J. M. 1951. *Three Navaho Households.* ("Papers of the Peabody Museum of American Archaeology and Ethnology, Harvard University," Vol. XI, No. 3.)

SCHNEIDER, L. I. 1950. "Rorschach Validation: Some Methodological Aspects," *Psychological Bulletin,* XLVII, No. 6, 493–508.

SPINDLER, G., and GOLDSCHMIDT, W. 1952. "Experimental Design in the Study of Culture Change," *Southwestern Journal of Anthropology,* VIII, No. 1, 68–83.

STEWARD, J. 1950. *Area Research, Theory and Practice*. (Social Science Research Council Bull. 63.) New York.

STRODTBECK, F. L. 1951. "Husband-Wife Interaction over Revealed Differences," *American Sociological Review*, XVI, No. 4, 468–73.

TAX, S. 1952. *Penny Capitalism: A Guatemalan Indian Economy*. ("Smithsonian Institution Publications in Social Anthropology.")

THOMPSON, L. 1950. *Culture in Crisis: A Study of the Hopi Indians*. New York: Harper & Bros.

——. 1951. *Personality and Government*. Mexico City: Inter-American Indian Institute.

THOMPSON, L., and JOSEPH, A. 1944. *The Hopi Way*. ("Indian Education Research Series," No. 1.) Chicago: University of Chicago Press.

THURSTON, L. L. 1948. "The Rorschach in Psychological Science," *Journal of Abnormal and Social Psychology*, XLIII, 471–75.

TITIEV, G. 1944. *Old Oraibi*. ("Papers of the Peabody Museum of American Archaeology and Ethnology, Harvard University," Vol. XXII, No. 1.)

WAGLEY, C., and GALVAO, E. 1949. *The Tenetehara Indians of Brazil*. New York: Columbia University Press.

WEAKLAND, J. H. 1951. "Method in Cultural Anthropology," *Philosophy of Science*, XVIII, No. 1, 55–69.

WHORF, B. L. 1940. "Linguistics as an Exact Science," *Technology Review*, XLIII, No. 2, 61–63, 80–83.

The Processing of Anthropological Materials

By GEORGE P. MURDOCK

I. INTRODUCTION

As THE NUMBER of anthropologists increases and the range of their interests expands, the problem of keeping abreast of current theoretical advances is beginning to be sensed as serious. It pales into insignificance, however, compared with the problem of mastering the descriptive literature of our subject. Whether we are engaged in teaching or research, we repeatedly have need of acquainting ourselves with the ethnographic data pertaining to an area or a subject, and we are all acutely aware of how laborious and time-consuming this task must be if done well. New textbooks and current articles help to keep us up to date on trends in theory, but the descriptive literature accumulates at a rate far beyond the capacity of even the most industrious of us to keep pace.

In sheer bulk, the mass of descriptive material of interest to the anthropologist probably exceeds by several times that of all the rest of the social sciences put together. Psychologists, sociologists, economists, and geographers depend in the main upon the materials which they themselves have accumulated, but for anthropologists the data assembled by themselves constitute but a small proportion of the descriptive materials upon which they depend and must be augmented by vast quantities of infor-

mation gathered by travelers, missionaries, government officials, artists, natural scientists, and historians, as well as by social scientists of several sister-disciplines.

Other social scientists concern themselves in the main only with the complex societies of the present and the historical past—perhaps a hundred all told. Anthropologists share their interest in these higher civilizations but also have an equal concern with the many simpler societies of the world, which probably number at least three thousand. The descriptive data of no other social science can even remotely compare in quantity with the wealth of ethnographic detail available on these thousands of peoples. For a comparable situation one must turn to such biological sciences as botany and zoölogy —fields with innumerably more practitioners and vastly superior research resources in the form of summary compilations and bibliographic aids.

This paper will deal with various aspects of the problem faced by all anthropologists in coping with the magnitude and diversity of their descriptive materials in teaching and research. It will be based primarily upon the experience of the Human Relations Area Files, its predecessor the Cross-Cultural Survey at Yale University, and such related undertakings as the Plains Indians survey at the University of Nebraska, the Navaho and Values projects at Harvard University, and the research on Mongolia and Tibet at the University of Washington. These various projects have in common not only a special awareness of the problems generally encountered by anthropologists in coping with their voluminous descriptive literature but also the specific objective of overcoming a number of them.

Since the development and methodology of the Human Relations Area Files have been fully described elsewhere (Murdock and others, 1950), it will be necessary here only to state that it is a co-operative enterprise of fifteen American universities (Chicago, Colorado, Cornell, Harvard, Hawaii, Indiana, Iowa, Michigan, North Carolina, Oklahoma, Pennsylvania, Southern California, Utah, Washington, and Yale), operating with the aid of foundation and government grants, for the assembly, translation, and classification of the descriptive materials of anthropology and for their reproduction in readily accessible form in files deposited at each of the member institutions.

II. CLASSIFICATION OF CULTURES

Every anthropologist who undertakes a regional or comparative study, as well as most of those who engage in field research, must make a decision as to the social groups which he will treat as cultural units. Will he, for example, select single communities, clusters of communities with essentially identical cultures, or groups bearing traditional tribal names? If the latter, will he follow native usage in regard to nomenclature or the practice of previous anthropologists, or will he define and name his groups according to criteria of his own? In any event he is likely to become acutely aware of the lack of uniform standards for the classification of cultures and the social groups which

bear them. In this respect anthropology presents a striking contrast to botany and zoölogy, with their widely accepted systems of classification.

The Human Relations Area Files faces this problem whenever it initiates work in a new area. It must, before any processing begins, make a definitive decision as to which groups and cultures are to be segregated in separate files as essentially distinct and which are to be grouped in a single file as essentially only subgroups or variants of the same larger culture. Accumulated experience in making such decisions suggests the possibility, as well as the desirability, of establishing a uniform system for the classification of societies and cultures comparable to the systems used in the biological sciences for the classification of organisms. A tentative proposal to this effect is outlined below.

Two types of social and cultural units which have already attained wide acceptance may be adopted as starting points. The first is the local group or community—a band, village, or neighborhood—which seems to be the smallest social group to carry essentially a total culture and thus to parallel roughly the "subvariety" in biology. The cultural system carried by a community may be tentatively called a "local cultural variant." Its content, unlike the body of traits carried by such smaller social groups as families and voluntary associations, covers nearly the entire range of the existing culture, though it may be deficient in some areas, especially the political and economic, where the interdependence of communities produces phenomena identifiable only with some larger social group.

Also widely accepted is the concept of the culture area, which embraces the related cultures of different peoples inhabiting a defined geographical region. A culture area would appear to correspond in general to a "family" in biological classification. Between the established levels of the community and the region, of the local cultural variant, and of the culture area, it seems possible to set up three intermediate social and cultural levels roughly corresponding to the variety, the species, and the genus in biology, as in Table 1.

Admittedly, the degree of social integration and cultural similarity decreases progressively from the smallest to the largest of the above units, but

TABLE 1

Culture-bearing Social Unit	Corresponding Cultural Unit	Analogous Biological Unit
Community....	Local cultural variant	Subvariety
Subtribe.......	Subculture	Variety
Tribe..........	Culture	Species
Nation........	Culture cluster	Genus
Region........	Culture area	Family

the establishment of typical intermediate units is not necessarily more difficult in anthropology than in biology, especially since an element of arbitrariness is recognized as inevitable in any classificatory system. To avoid mere analogy, of course, the criteria employed must be genuinely appropriate to the processes of cultural change and differentiation.

A cultural species will be called simply a "culture," and the people who bear it a "tribe." Occasionally, as in the case of Zuni pueblo, a culture is confined to a single community, so that tribe and community coincide. Far more commonly, however, numerous communities with only slightly differing local cultural variants are spread over a considerable geographical area. When a biological form similarly varies over geographical space, all its members are classed as a single species, however much they differ at the opposite margins of the area, provided that interbreeding regularly takes place between adjacent forms. Only when there occurs a geographical barrier or other break, separating forms which do not interbreed and thus vary around different modes, does the biologist classify forms into separate species.

In the realm of culture the equivalent of interbreeding is diffusion, and barriers to diffusion may be used to separate cultural species, i.e., distinct cultures. Unlike the situation in biology, to be sure, such barriers are only relative rather than absolute. Nevertheless, they seem to be fairly readily determinable. Mountain ranges and bodies of water across which communication is difficult and diffusion consequently slight or sporadic allow the processes of cultural change to produce variations around gradually diverging modes until the cultures on either side of the barrier assume markedly different forms. A similar result can be produced, in the absence of an actual barrier to communication, when adjacent geographical zones provide markedly different natural resources, so that distinctive modes of economic exploitation come into being and give rise to adaptive variations in technology, social organization, and other aspects of culture in the two zones.

Language differences likewise constitute a significant barrier to diffusion. Even in the same geographical area, a boundary between two mutually unintelligible languages may operate to retard diffusion sufficiently so that the groups on either side of the boundary gradually diverge around different modes until they come to possess genuinely distinct, though related, cultures.

There are, of course, other factors which inhibit cultural borrowing, but those of geography and language have probably been the most universal and important in promoting the differentiation of cultural species. We therefore propose to define a culture as including all local cultural variants exhibited by communities within a particular geographical area which speak mutually intelligible languages and have essentially similar forms of economic adjustment.

This conception of a culture, and of the tribe as its social correlate, coincides very closely with actual anthropological usage as this has developed through general consensus rather than explicit definition. One branch of anthropology, i.e., linguistics, has independently evolved a strictly comparable concept, that of a language, which is defined as the variant forms of speech over a geographical area where adjacent forms are always mutually intelligible although those at a distance may not be. The existence and apparent utility of this concept, based on strictly cultural considerations, in one division of our science suggest both the possibility of extending it to the classification of cultures in general and the probability that such an extension, far from being a mere analogy from biology, may have an inherent validity of its own.

If a culture be accepted as the anthropological equivalent, and a tribe as the sociological equivalent, of a biological species, the terms "subculture" and "subtribe" can be reserved for cultural units and social groupings intermediate, respectively, between a culture and a local cultural variant and between a tribe and a single community. If, for example, the Tsimshian of the Northwest Coast are regarded as a tribe, then the Niska, Gitksan, and Tsimshian proper may be considered as subtribes, each with its own subculture and each comprising a number of communities with local cultural variants representing cultural differences of a still lesser magnitude.

Political integration does not ordinarily complicate the problem of classification as long as it has not advanced beyond the tribal level. In some areas of the primitive world, as among the Plains Indians, political organization normally coincides with the tribe; in other areas, e.g., native Australia and New Guinea, each local community is politically autonomous; in still others, political integration commonly encompasses a number of communities, but only those of a subtribe, not of an entire tribe. Whichever of these situations prevails, the determination of social and cultural varieties and species usually presents no difficulties.

Wherever the accidents of political history have united peoples with different cultures under a single unified government, however, the problem of classification is complicated. Social unity exceeds cultural unity and gives rise to institutions, usually economic and often religious as well as political, which, though cultural, are not truly a part of the component cultures. Such cultural phenomena can be described and understood only from the point of view of a social group which embraces several tribes and for which we propose the term "nation." They form part of a cultural category larger than a single culture but smaller than a culture area —one for which the term "culture cluster" is herewith advanced. Wherever cultures have become interdependent through the political and social integration of the groups which carry them, the Human Relations Area Files has usually found it necessary to use the culture cluster rather than the tribe as the unit for classifying anthropological materials.

Situations of this type are common enough in complex modern societies, e.g., the French Canadians and British Canadians, the Flemings and Walloons in Belgium, and the several "tribes" of the Swiss nation. They also occur not infrequently on the primitive level. Thus the League of the Iroquois united into a single nation five tribes with distinct languages and cultures—the Cayuga, Mohawk, Oneida, Onondaga,

and Seneca—and, in Uganda and Ru-
anda, Hima herders, Iru tillers, and
sometimes also pigmy hunters are politically and socially united in a number of separate instances. A similar
phenomenon is observable in caste societies like India. Even in a state which
originally embraced only a single tribe
and culture, social classes may differentiate with time to the point where class
subcultures have really evolved into
distinct cultures and would have to be
treated as such if their bearers were
not socially and politically integrated.

The standard classification of social groups and cultural systems proposed herewith is not so much an innovation as an effort to make explicit,
with only minor reconciliations, a system of categories which appears to be
implicitly accepted in essence by most
anthropologists who have attempted to
classify peoples and cultures in different parts of the world. It may be useful
to call attention here to some of these
regional classifications. The works cited
below by no means constitute a complete compilation; they include only
sources which the writer has had occasion to consult with profit in his own
researches.

For the North American continent,
the most comprehensive classificatory
attempt is that of Kroeber (1939), to
which Murdock (1941) may be considered a supplement. Useful regional
classifications include Beals (1932),
Johnson (1940), Kroeber (1925), Osgood (1936), Park and others (1938),
Ray and others (1938), Sauer (1934),
Speck (1928), Spier (1936), Steward
(1937, 1938), and Swanton (1946).

For South America, all earlier attempts have been superseded by the
classic work of Steward (1946–50),
which Murdock (1951) has adapted to
the specific use of the Human Relations Area Files. An unpublished map
by John H. Rowe incorporates a number of useful corrections.

For Africa, the volumes of the "Ethnographic Survey of Africa," currently
being issued under the general editorship of Daryll Forde, will, when complete, supersede all earlier work as definitely as does Steward's compilation
for South America. The contributions
which have already appeared include
Forde (1951), Forde and Jones (1950),
McCulloch (1950, 1951), Manoukian
(1950, 1952), Tew (1950), and Whiteley (1950). On areas not yet covered
by the Survey, there are useful classifications of the Khoisan and Southeastern Bantu peoples in Schapera (1930,
1937); of the Congo tribes in Czekanowski (1917–27), Maes and Boone
(1935), and Van der Kerken (1944); of
the tribes of Cameroon and French
Equatorial Africa in Bruel (1935) and
Tessmann (1932); of the Nigerian peoples in Meek (1931) and Talbot
(1926); and of the Nilotes in Köhler
(1950). Special attention should also
be called to the noteworthy linguistic
classification by Greenberg (1949–50).

For Asia, an area on which the writer
has done comparatively little ethnographic research, he can cite as useful
from personal experience only Jochelson (1928) and Embree and Dotson
(1950) on the peoples of Asiatic Russia and Southeast Asia, respectively. In
addition, he may mention Gerland
(1892) as still, despite its age, incomparably the best ethnographic atlas; besides the Eurasiatic continent, it covers
Africa, Oceania, and the New World.

For Oceania there are classifications
of the Indonesian peoples in Kennedy
(1942, 1945) and Van Eerde (1920);
of the Philippine peoples in Beyer
(1917) and Tangco (1951); of the aboriginal tribes of Australia in Tindale
(1940); and of the Micronesian peoples
in Murdock (1948). Polynesia presents
few serious problems, but Melanesia
and particularly New Guinea are still
largely *terra incognita*. Rivers (1914)
is still useful, but detailed analyses of

restricted regions like that of Oliver (1949) on Bougainville in the Solomons are urgently needed.

III. GUIDES TO PUBLISHED SOURCES

Every anthropologist, when he undertakes to acquaint himself with a new culture for any scholarly purpose, faces a problem identical with that encountered by the Human Relations Area Files whenever the decision is reached to process a new body of cultural materials, namely, that of discovering the relevant published sources and of determining which of them are the most comprehensive, reliable, and basic. He may in some cases be fortunate enough to secure a recent book or article with a full and critical bibliography, but in most instances he must depend, first of all, upon general bibliographical compilations and secondarily upon notices and reviews in the anthropological journals to bring him in touch with publications postdating the available bibliographies.

The problem of discovering all the relevant sources and selecting the best ones is peculiarly acute in anthropology, as compared with the natural sciences, for a number of reasons. First of all, we lack almost completely the series of abstracts and periodic summaries that are common in other sciences. The only notable exception is *Social Science Abstracts*, which was published from 1929 to 1933 only. In the second place, general bibliographies, even when regional in scope, are practically useless to us, since they are rarely complete or selective and are seldom critically annotated or topically classified. Such resources as we have, in so far as the writer knows them and has found them genuinely useful, are enumerated below.

There are apparently no comprehensive ethnographic bibliographies covering the entire world, although the *Eth-nologischer Anzeiger* (Köln) went far toward filling this need prior to World War II. In addition, several professional journals make an attempt to keep abreast of current publications on a world-wide scale through reviews, book notices, and lists of publications received. Outstanding among them are *Anthropos* (Fribourg), *Anthropologie* (Paris), and the *Zeitschrift für Ethnologie* (Berlin). The *American Anthropologist* (Menasha, Wis.), which at one time ranked with them, has lost most of its usefulness since it discontinued notices of periodical contributions in the second number of Volume LI in 1949. *Man* (London) and *Ethnos* (Stockholm) carry, in general, only book reviews.

For the New World there are comprehensive ethnographic bibliographies by Murdock (1941) for North America and Steward (1946–50) for Central and South America. Current publications are well covered in several periodicals. The *American Anthropologist* is still occasionally of subordinate use, but Americanists today must depend primarily upon the *BBAA* or *Boletin bibliografico de anthropologia americana* (Mexico), the *Journal de la Société des Américanistes* (Paris), and T. F. McIlwraith's annual lists of publications in ethnology, anthropology, and archeology in the *Canadian Historical Review* (Toronto).

For Africa there is a useful but inadequately organized comprehensive bibliography by Wieschhoff (1948), and the volumes of the previously mentioned "Ethnographic Survey of Africa" include excellent coverage of unpublished as well as published sources. Among regional bibliographies that by Schapera (1934) on South Africa is particularly noteworthy for its selectivity and analytical comments. Current publications are admirably recorded in *Africa* (London), which can be supplemented by consulting such other regional journals as *African Affairs* (London), *African Studies* (Johannesburg), *Bibliographie ethnographique du Congo belge et des regions avoisinantes* (Tervueren), *Congo* (Brussels), and the *Journal de la Société des Africanistes* (Paris). A recent venture of considerable promise is *African Abstracts* (London).

For Eurasia, unlike the continents previously considered, there is apparently no single comprehensive bibliography of anthropological materials. The researcher must depend upon regional compilations, of which that by Embree and Dotson (1950) on Southeast Asia is an outstanding example. As regards sources of information about current publications, the writer has had little recent experience, but journals which he recalls consulting with profit in the past include *Bulletin de l'Ecole française d'Extrême-Orient* (Hanoi), *Far Eastern Quarterly* (Lancaster), *Folk-Lore* (London), *Revue des études islamiques* (Paris), *Sociologus* (Berlin), *Transactions of the Asiatic Society of Japan* (Yokohama), and *Zeitschrift für vergleichende Rechtswissenschaft* (Stuttgart), and this list could certainly be considerably expanded by specialists in Asiatic cultures.

For Oceania, we have a fairly complete ethnographic bibliography by Taylor (1951) and the excellent compilation by Kennedy (1945) on Indonesia. Tindale (1940), though incomplete, is useful on Australia. Duff and Allan (1949) have compiled an invaluable selective bibliography specifically on the New Zealand Maori. Current publications on the Pacific area are most fully reported in the *Journal de la Société des Océanistes* (Paris). Other regional journals like *Oceania* (Sydney) and the *Journal of the Polynesian Society* (Wellington) unfortunately present at best only an occasional book review or bibliographical note.

The foregoing discussion of guides to the published literature of anthropology has concentrated upon the field of ethnography, since the writer is not sufficiently familiar with the aids available to linguists, archeologists, folklorists, and physical anthropologists to deal adequately with them. The subject should not be concluded, however, without mention of two important bibliographical aids which are accessible to American scholars, though not in published form. The Peabody Museum at Harvard University has an extraordinarily complete classified card index of anthropological materials for all areas of the world, the potential value of which is impossible to exaggerate. The Cross-Cultural Survey at Yale University has virtually complete bibliographies on some areas, including Micronesia, Formosa, the Ryukyu Islands, and the Amazonian basin of South America, and useful selective bibliographies on many other regions. Only in a few instances as yet have these been reprocessed for the Human Relations Area Files.

IV. LOCATION OF UNPUBLISHED SOURCE MATERIALS

Difficult as it may be to assemble the published sources on a new culture or area, even when one has access to a good library and is familiar with the bibliographical resources, this problem pales into insignificance compared with that of locating important materials which have not been published. Nearly every professional anthropologist in the world has unpublished field materials, often in usable manuscript form. Every university with an active anthropology department has unpublished doctoral and Master's dissertations with invaluable descriptive data. Every ethnological museum has files of manuscript materials, both old and new, which are often of the utmost importance. Missions in all parts of the world and administrative offices in colonial territories often have extensive archives of reports and ethnographic records assembled only for their own local use, with no thought of even eventual publication. Invaluable reports by early travelers and even full-length records of scientific observations often remain in manuscript form in certain parts of the world, perhaps especially in the literate countries of Asia, and are gradually accumulated in the libraries of private collectors. Unpublished materials in these and comparable forms probably equal in bulk, and perhaps in their potential usefulness to anthropologists, the entire body of published materials available in our best libraries.

Of this enormous body of descriptive data, only an infinitesimal fraction is accessible to any individual scholar, even if he makes every effort and utilizes the most modern of reproducing techniques. Short of a large-scale program for the systematic location, reproduction, and distribution of such materials, anthropologists must continue to work in complete ignorance of half of their actual descriptive resources.

V. UTILIZATION OF MATERIALS IN FOREIGN LANGUAGES

Even if he is able to locate all the published sources that he needs, and perhaps some of the relevant unpublished materials as well, the professional anthropologist is often unable to utilize them because of the diversity of languages in which they are written. As a trained scholar he can be expected to command three languages—usually English, German, and French—but somewhere between 20 and 25 per cent of world ethnography is in languages other than these. Much of the best literature on Central and South America is in Spanish. The principal sources on Siberia are in Russian, and on Indonesia in Dutch. A substantial amount of descriptive information on Brazil and Angola is in Portuguese, on Ethiopia in Italian, on Greenland in Danish, on the Belgian Congo in Flemish, on South Africa in Afrikaans, on the Finno-Ugric peoples in Finnish and Swedish, on the Ainu and Formosan aborigines in Japanese. If a scholar is to encompass the major sources on the Ruthenians he must command Polish, Ukrainian, and Magyar as well as German; for the Mongols he needs Russian, Chinese, Mongol, and Japanese. He may even require Latin to use the primary source on some tribes, e.g., the Mojo of Bolivia. In some instances literature in the vernacular, where missionaries have introduced literacy to an aboriginal people, is of major importance.

Rarely can a single scholar command all the languages needed to control the basic literature for any area. American anthropologists commonly underestimate this problem because of the fortunate accident that for native North America the overwhelming bulk of the ethnographic literature is in English and most of the rest in Spanish. Even German and French are rarely needed —the former for such tribes as the Cora, Quiche, Tlingit, and Totonac; the latter for the Otomi and some northern Algonkians and Athapaskans. With these four languages, plus Russian for the Aleut and Danish for the Greenland Eskimo, the ethnographic literature on the entire continent can be fully covered.

This fortunate situation, however, is duplicated nowhere else in the world. In South America, for example, no one language accounts for as much as one-third of the literature. English, French, German, Spanish, and Portuguese are all indispensable, while the chief Bororo source is in Italian, the major Carib source in Dutch, and the standard Mojo monograph in Latin, not to mention substantial works in Swedish and other languages. The situation is equally complex in Africa and Oceania, vastly more so in Eurasia.

The ideal solution to this problem would be a concerted effort to assure the translation of every important work in other languages into either English, French, or German, which are the three traditional vehicles of scholarship and each of which already has a volume of published ethnographic materials at least double that of any other language. In advance of the attainment of this ideal, the anthropologist has only two alternatives: (1) to acquire new languages as he needs them or (2) to arrange for the translation of needed materials in languages which he does not control. For those who choose the latter solution, the experience of the Human Relations Area Files warrants a word of advice. Since competent translators who are genuinely bilingual are rare, one is usually forced to choose between persons whose native language is that of the original text and native speakers of the language into which the translation is to be made, i.e., English in the present instance. Experience has demonstrated overwhelmingly the superiority of the latter class of translators as compared with the former.

VI. LOCATION OF SPECIFIC ITEMS OF INFORMATION

Many types of anthropological research involve assembling specific items of information on many cultures rather than the intensive study of a few. Among them are most comparative studies, analyses of trait distributions, and investigations of particular instances of diffusion. When other scientists approach anthropologists for information, they commonly seek data of this type. The same is true of government agencies in time of war or of peace; they may, for example, want to know about native reactions to strangers for the guidance of castaways or commandos, or about taboos which occupying troops must respect at their peril, or about native medical customs which

might affect the success of a public health program.

When masses of ethnographic literature must be ransacked for specific items of information, the problem of locating the sources themselves is complicated by that of locating the information desired in the sources after they have been assembled. Indexes and tables of contents are frequently of little use. Often the entire literature must be combed almost page by page to make certain that important bits of data have not been overlooked—an immensely time-consuming task. Unless this were done for the Kwakiutl, to choose but a single example, a researcher interested in child-training techniques would miss essential information buried in the midst of a series of recipes for salmon-head soups, and one interested in kinship terminology would find practically nothing except in a work on the mythology of a neighboring tribe.

An unfortunate consequence of this necessity is that hundreds of anthropologists have laboriously combed the same standard ethnographies for different items of information but that the careful notes they have accumulated are rarely of use to anyone else. Another is that dozens of government agencies, at excessive cost, have excerpted masses of information about foreign countries on subjects of immediate pertinence but are no better off than when they started when it becomes imperative to know in a hurry some vital fact of previously unanticipated significance.

VII. CONCLUSION

The problems considered above, some of them hitherto insoluble and others only partially or inadequately solved, are common to all anthropologists and related social scientists. The Human Relations Area Files has made the basic assumption—possibly a rash one—that none of them is inherently incapable of solution and has sought to come to grips with all of them at the same time. Its program of resolution may be summed up as follows:

1. All the peoples and cultures of the world, historical and contemporary as well as primitive, are gradually being classified, on the basis of the criteria discussed above, into groups with distinctive cultures and culture clusters, for each of which a separate file of descriptive data will ultimately, it is hoped, be assembled and reproduced for all participant institutions. The first of a projected series of areal classifications of cultures, Murdock (1951) on South America, has already appeared.

2. With each completed file is included a full analytical bibliography, embracing sources not processed as well as those actually covered.

3. A special effort is made to locate and process unpublished as well as published materials and thus to make previously inaccessible source materials available.

4. All works in other languages are translated into English, but each file includes a photographic reproduction of the original text of all translated sources, so that scholars may readily make comparisons or, if they prefer, use only the original.

5. All materials are transcribed on cards and filed according to a standard system of topical classification, presented in Murdock and others (1950), so that all information on any desired subject for any particular society can be secured in a few moments. Though classified, data are never wrenched from their written context, for a complete set of notes is retained in page order (essentially an exact copy of the original source) in each file in addition to those distributed by topic. Finally, ex-cerpts are rigorously avoided; when a source is considered worth processing, its content is reproduced in its entirety.

Any research involving the use of cultural or background materials from societies for which complete files have been assembled can be accomplished in an inconsequential fraction of the time required to do the same task by the ordinary methods of library research. Completely eliminated are all the labors of compiling bibliographies, physically assembling the sources, translating from foreign languages, and locating the precise information required. Research time can be concentrated almost exclusively upon productive scholarly operations rather than dissipated in routine "legwork." The potential gains can be illustrated by an actual test performed by the writer two years ago. Asked to prepare a paper on family stability in non-European cultures, he planned the research, examined the data on forty representative societies, and wrote the article (Murdock, 1950), all within a total elapsed time of 25 hours. Without the aid of the Human Relations Area Files he could not have turned out a comparable contribution in 25 full research days.

In addition to the scholarly problems adumbrated above, the Human Relations Area Files has had to cope with a host of technical questions, e.g., quality control in translation and classification, alternative systems of photographic reproduction, methods of duplicating pictorial materials, efficient techniques for sorting and filing, and the adaptability of punch-card systems. Not all the problems, either scholarly or technical, have as yet been satisfactorily solved, and constructive suggestions are welcomed.

BIBLIOGRAPHY

BEALS, R. L. 1932. "The Comparative Ethnology of Northern Mexico before 1750," *Ibero-Americana*, II, 93–225. Berkeley.

BEYER, H. O. 1917. *Population of the Philippine Islands in 1916*. Manila: Philippine Education Co.

BRUEL, G. 1935. *La France équatoriale africaine.* Paris.

CZEKANOWSKI, J. 1917–27. *Forschungen im Nil-Kongo-Zwischengebiet.* 5 vols. Leipzig: Klinkhardt.

DUFF, R. S., and ALLAN, R. S. 1949. *Selected Bibliography of the Anthropology of New Zealand, 1900–1948.* Seventh Pacific Science Congress, New Zealand. (Mimeographed.)

EERDE, J. C. VAN. 1920. *Inleiding tot de volkenkunde van Nederlandsch-Indië.* Haarlem.

EMBREE, J. F., and DOTSON, L. O. 1950. *Bibliography of the Peoples and Cultures of the Mainland of Southeast Asia.* ("Yale University Southeast Asia Studies.") New Haven.

FORDE, D. 1951. *The Yoruba-speaking Peoples of South-western Nigeria.* London: International African Institute.

FORDE, D., and JONES, G. I. 1950. *The Ibo and Ibibio-speaking Peoples of Southeastern Nigeria.* London: International African Institute.

GERLAND, G. 1892. *Atlas der Völkerkunde.* (Berghaus' *Physikalischer Atlas*, Abteilung 7.) Gotha.

GREENBERG, J. H. 1949–50. "Studies in African Linguistic Classification," *Southwestern Journal of Anthropology*, V, 79–100, 190–98, 309–17; VI, 47–63, 143–60, 223–37, 388–98.

JOCHELSON, W. 1928. *Peoples of Asiatic Russia.* New York: American Museum of Natural History.

JOHNSON, F. 1940. "The Linguistic Map of Mexico and Central America." In HAY, C. L., *et al.* (eds.), *The Maya and Their Neighbors*, pp. 88–114. New York: Appleton-Century.

KENNEDY, R. 1942. *The Ageless Indies.* New York: John Day.

———. 1945. *Bibliography of Indonesian Peoples and Cultures.* ("Yale Anthropological Studies," Vol. IV.) New Haven.

KERKEN, G. VAN DER. 1944. *L'Ethnie Mongo.* ("Mémoires de l'Institut royal colonial belge," Vol. III.) Brussels.

KÖHLER, O. 1950. "Die Ausbreitung der Niloten," *Beiträge zur Gesellungs- und Völkerwissenschaft, Professor Dr. Richard Thurnwald zu seinem achtzigsten Geburtstag gewidmet*, pp. 159–94. Berlin: Gebr. Mann.

KROEBER, A. L. 1925. *Handbook of the Indians of California.* (Bureau of American Ethnology Bull. 78.) Washington.

———. 1939. *Cultural and Natural Areas of Native North America.* ("University of California Publications in American Archaeology and Ethnology," Vol. XXX-VIII.) Berkeley.

McCULLOCH, M. 1950. *Peoples of Sierra Leone Protectorate.* London: International African Institute.

———. 1951. *The Southern Lunda and Related Peoples.* London: International African Institute.

MAES, J., and BOON, O. 1935. *Les Peuplades du Congo Belge.* ("Musée du Congo Belge, Publications du Bureau de documentation ethnographique," sér. 2, "Monographies idéologiques," Vol. I.)

MANOUKIAN, M. 1950. *Akan and Ga-Adagme Peoples of the Gold Coast.* London: International African Institute.

———. 1952. *Tribes of the Northern Territories of the Gold Coast.* London: International African Institute.

MEEK, C. K. 1931. *Tribal Studies in Northern Nigeria.* London: Kegan Paul, Trench, Trubner & Co.

MURDOCK, G. P. 1941. *Ethnographic Bibliography of North America.* ("Yale Anthropological Studies," Vol. I.) New Haven. (A revised edition is now in press.)

———. 1948. "Anthropology in Micronesia," *Transactions of the New York Academy of Sciences*, ser. 2, XI, 9–16. New York.

———. 1950. "Family Stability in Non-European Cultures," *Annals of the American Academy of Political and Social Science*, CCLXXII, 195–201.

———. 1951. *Outline of South American Cultures.* ("Behavior Science Outlines," Vol. II.) New Haven: Human Relations Area Files, Inc.

MURDOCK, G. P.; FORD, C. S.; HUDSON, A. E.; KENNEDY, R.; SIMMONS, L. W.; and WHITING, J. W. M. 1950. *Outline of Cultural Materials.* ("Behavior Science Outlines," Vol. I.) 3d rev. ed. New Haven: Human Relations Area Files, Inc.

OLIVER, D. L. 1949. *The Peabody Museum Expedition to Bougainville, Solomon Islands, 1938–39.* ("Papers of the Peabody Museum of American Archaeology and Ethnology, Harvard University," Vol. XXIX, No. 1.) Cambridge.

OSGOOD, C. 1936. *The Distribution of the Northern Athapaskan Indians.* ("Yale University Publications in Anthropology," No. 7.) New Haven.

PARK, W. Z., *et al.* 1938. "Tribal Distribution in the Great Basin," *American Anthropologist,* n.s., XL, 622–38.

RAY, V. F., *et al.* 1938. "Tribal Distribution in Eastern Oregon and Adjacent Regions," *American Anthropologist,* n.s., XL, 384–415.

RIVERS, W. H. R. 1914. *The History of Melanesian Society.* 2 vols. Cambridge: At the University Press.

SAUER, C. O. 1934. "The Distribution of Aboriginal Tribes and Languages in Northwestern Mexico," *Ibero-Americana,* V, 1–90.

SCHAPERA, I. 1930. *The Khoisan Peoples of South Africa.* London: G. Routledge & Sons.

——. 1934. "The Present State and Future Development of Ethnographical Research in South Africa," *Bantu Studies,* VIII, 219–342.

——. 1937. *The Bantu-speaking Tribes of South Africa.* London: G. Routledge & Sons.

SPECK, F. G. 1928. *Territorial Subdivisions and Boundaries of the Wampanoag, Massachusett, and Nauset Indians.* ("Indian Notes and Monographs, Museum of the American Indian, Heye Foundation," ser. 2, Vol. XLIV.) New York.

SPIER, L. 1936. *Tribal Distribution in Washington.* ("General Series in Anthropology," Vol. III.) Menasha: George Banta Publishing Co.

STEWARD, J. H. 1937. "Linguistic Distributions and Political Groups of the Great Basin Shoshoneans," *American Anthropologist,* n.s., XXXIX, 625–34.

——. 1938. *Basin-Plateau Aboriginal Socio-political Groups.* (Bureau of American Ethnology Bull. 120.) Washington.

——. (ed.). 1946–50. *Handbook of South American Indians.* 6 vols. (Bureau of American Ethnology Bull. 143.) Washington.

SWANTON, J. R. 1946. *The Indians of the Southeastern United States.* (Bureau of American Ethnology Bull. 137.) Washington.

TALBOT, P. A. 1926. *The Peoples of Southern Nigeria.* 4 vols. London: Oxford University Press.

TANGCO, M. 1951. *The Christian Peoples of the Philippines.* Quezon City.

TAYLOR, C. R. H. 1951. *A Pacific Bibliography.* ("Memoirs of the Polynesian Society," Vol. XXIV.) Wellington.

TESSMANN, G. 1932. "Die Völker und Sprachen Kameruns," *Petermanns Mitteilungen,* LXXVIII, 132–40, 184–90.

TEW, M. 1950. *Peoples of the Lake Nyasa Region.* London: Oxford University Press.

TINDALE, N. B. 1940. "Distribution of Australian Aboriginal Tribes," *Transactions of the Royal Society of South Australia,* LXIV, 140–231.

WHITELEY, W. 1950. *Bemba and Related Peoples of Northern Rhodesia.* London: International African Institute.

WIESCHHOFF, H. A. 1948. *Anthropological Bibliography of Negro Africa.* ("American Oriental Series," Vol. XXIII.) New Haven: American Oriental Society.

The Contributions of Genetics to Anthropology

By WILLIAM C. BOYD

ONE PURPOSE of physical anthropology, according to Morant,[*] has been "to unravel the course of human evolution, and it may be taken for granted to-day that the proper study of the natural history of man is concerned essentially with the mode and the path of his descent." While it is doubtful whether all physical anthropologists restrict their studies solely to data bearing on the course of human evolution, nevertheless Morant is probably right in implying that such information seems of high importance to most workers in the field.

Another problem, closely connected with the first, has been to classify men into physical races. Various systems of classification have been used, which have changed with the advance of the science; at the present time, one of the most valuable tools of classification is our growing knowledge of human genetics.

In studying human races, we must consider not only the present-day frequencies of human physical characteristics but also the probable mechanisms by which evolution brought them about. The main agencies causing evolution are, without doubt, mutation and selection. Before evolutionists became acquainted with genetics, other more mystical evolutionary mechanisms had been proposed, and their influence still lingers in some of the anthropological thought of today. One of these fossil remnants is the concept of orthogenesis.

Some workers, paleontologists in particular, were impressed by the seemingly unerring way in which an organism marched from an undifferentiated beginning towards a definite goal. They considered that such evolution could not be accounted for by the Darwinian concepts of variation and selection but must have been directed from the beginning towards its ultimate destiny by some sort of force. The term "orthogenesis" was proposed for this mechanism by Haacke, and the idea was popularized by Eimer and others.

The concept of orthogenesis usually seems to involve two suppositions. The first of these asserts that there is to be found in nature a tendency towards evolution in straight or continuing lines, as shown by paleontological material. The second is the assumption of the existence of some sort of mystic, vitalistic force or principle which not only determines the tendency of organisms to evolve but also directs their evolution along certain apparently predetermined lines. Modern believers in ortho-

[*] It was the original plan to have the bibliographies of the inventory papers restricted to a selected list of no more than one page in length. This plan was later changed but notice was not given in time for some of the authors to amplify the bibliography and refer to each item specifically in the text.

genesis sometimes disclaim any belief in the second part of the doctrine, but an examination of their writings generally reveals a tendency to rely either on this or on some similar concept of an inherent tendency towards perfection.

Now, there is no doubt that some rectilinearity can often be observed in evolution. According to Simpson, the best part of the paleontological record is made up of lines that evolve more or less in one direction over long periods of time. Nevertheless, rectilinear evolution is far from universal. The example most often quoted is the evolution of the horse, involving a gradual increase in size, reduction in number of toes, increase in height and complication of teeth, as if evolution proceeded unhesitatingly in a straight line from *Eohippus* to the modern horse. But this is totally at variance with the facts. All sorts of horses evolved during the Miocene and Pliocene, differing radically in regard to teeth, toes, and so on. One Miocene line developed exceptionally high teeth; however, this was not a continuation of an old "orthogenetic" trend but a new tendency.

A study of genetics shows that orthogenesis is quite unnecessary to explain the degree of rectilinearity actually observed in evolution. It is true that we now think of evolution as resulting from the action of selection on genetic mutations. But this does not mean that there are no limits to what this mechanism can accomplish. The genes of any animal which survives and competes successfully with its fellows in the struggle for existence must be reasonably harmonious with one another, for anything else is not compatible with the continued existence and reproduction of the animal. Each creature is like its ancestors in all but a few respects. The differences which have arisen must necessarily coexist in harmony with the more extensive, more complex, elements which are not different. Each character

is dependent on the interaction of many genes, so that it will be easier to continue a line of evolutionary change for which many of the modifiers are already present than to start off on an entirely new line. Species are not constructed *de novo*, but on the basis of genotypes already existing. In most cases no sort of modification which is within the capabilities of the existing genes and possible mutations would be definitely advantageous, and in many other cases only one particular modification would be an advantage. Thus the unidirectional trend of much evolution becomes clear from a genetic point of view.

Another feature of genetic knowledge which helps to account for directional evolution is the observation that mutation seldom occurs entirely at random at a gene locus. Usually, certain mutations are more frequent than others, and evolution in a direction utilizing these mutations would thus be easier. Examples are known from many studies on *Drosophila*.

One argument formerly brought up by the orthogeneticists against the postulated predominant role of mutation and selection in evolution depended on the very slight nature of the early stages of certain evolutionary trends. For example, the horns of the titanotheres arose gradually from mere thickenings of the skull bones, and developed into large, fully developed weapons. It was asserted that the incipient stages of this bone thickening could not have been of any advantage or use to the animals possessing them; the structure, it was said, started first, and its usefulness came later. Simpson thinks it quite likely that even the initial stages were, in fact, useful. The titanotheres had already become stocky, lumbering creatures with stout heads, very likely addicted to butting one another and their enemies, as they had no other means of fighting. Thickening of the bones of the butting region, no matter how slight, would constitute a definite advantage. One of the lessons of the modern work on variation and survival is that slight modifications actually have differential effects on mortality, and the mathematical work of Fisher and others has demonstrated how profound may be the effect of very slight selection pressures. *Evolution is best understood by thinking of it as always adaptive.* Modern genetics has shown clearly how, as small differences due to single genes accumulate in the course of evolution, the small differences gradually become major differences. When enough gene differences and/or chromosome alterations have accumulated, we have a new species.

If evolution, essentially, is nothing but a change in gene frequencies, by what processes of genetic change were certain variations brought about? Over long periods of time, varieties of animals which were originally similar or identical may become extremely different from one another. The number of genes eventually involved is doubtless large, and separate species may ultimately result. Nevertheless, as far as we know at present, leaving aside chromosomal rearrangements, with which we shall not deal in the present discussion, all inherited modification is the result of (a) the production of new genes, (b) the loss of genes, and (c) the accumulation of changes in gene frequencies. Let us consider the frequency of any gene (say the blood-group B gene in human populations), and ask ourselves what evolutionary agencies might possibly operate to alter the frequency of this gene. Whatever mechanisms we find in operation are, so far as we know, the same ones which have operated in the past to alter the frequencies of human genes and are going to alter such frequencies in the future.

SELECTION

If a certain dominant human gene had a selective advantage over its recessive allele of only one part in 1,000 (or 0.1 per cent), its frequency in the population in question would be increased from 5 to 50 per cent in somewhat less than 3,000 generations, a period of about 60,000–70,000 years. With the possible exception of the Rh blood factors, there is no evidence concerning physical characteristics which is exact enough to enable us to estimate whether any of them have a selective advantage as great as, or perhaps greater than, this. It is extremely likely that some or most of them do. In particular, the general relation between pigmentation and warm sunny climates suggests a selective advantage for pigmentation genes in such environments. The frequency of blonds among the Scandinavians might suggest that in regions with deficient sunlight the reverse would also be true. The rather highly pigmented Eskimo seem to constitute an exception, but it is the opinion of some scholars that they have not inhabited their present cold environment for nearly as long as 70,000 years. Also, the frequency of recessive genes —and most genes for light pigmentation seem to be recessive—increases much more slowly than that of dominants, especially when they are rather scarce in the population to begin with.

Even dominants increase rather slowly at first, and a population starting with 0.18 per cent of a new advantageous dominant gene with a selective advantage of 0.1 per cent would require 3,500 generations to build the frequency of the new gene up to 5.62 per cent. If we start with 0.27 per cent of an advantageous recessive gene, it would require 16,000 generations, or about 400,000 years, to increase it to 4.54 per cent. Perhaps the Eskimo started with too low a frequency of recessive genes for pigment, and mutations to genes for low pigmentation have rarely occurred in this stock. In Table 1 are shown the probabilities that a recessive gene will become fixed in the population (that is, will completely replace the alternative gene or genes at the same chromosome locus) in various population sizes, in three dif-

TABLE 1*

CHANCES OF "FIXATION" OF A RECESSIVE GENE, ASSUMING ONE SUCH GENE IN POPULATIONS OF VARIOUS SIZES

Population Size	Advantage of $yy=0.01$	No Advantage ("Neutral" Gene)	Disadvantage of $yy=0.01$ (or Advantage $=-0.01$)
10........	0.05	0.05	0.05
50........	0.013	0.010	0.007
200........	0.0057	0.0025	0.0003
800........	0.0027	0.0006	0.0000

* The symbol y represents the recessive gene, and yy the homozygous recessive type. Table is taken from J. Wright, *Heredity*, XXXIII (1942), 333–34.

ferent cases—a selective advantage of the double recessive of 0.01, a selective disadvantage of 0.01, and neutrality (that is, the case in which the gene is neither harmful nor beneficial).

Even with a relatively high selective advantage, such as 1 per cent, when the frequency of the gene being acted on is very small or very large (near zero or near 100 per cent), evolution due to selection is extremely slow. But evolutionary change due to selection may be fairly rapid if the advantageous gene is moderately frequent (see Table 2).

These facts have a bearing on the proposals of eugenists, but the important thing to notice is the considerable evidence that, in nature, natural selection can operate rather rapidly, in terms of the lengths of time which have elapsed, if an adequate supply of new genes, more suitable to changing environments, is available.

In many cases we have actually been able to observe the process of evolution in lower forms, probably by selection, a privilege which was denied Darwin and other pioneers in this field. One of the best-known examples is the increase in the incidence of melanism in certain moths. There seems to be no doubt that melanism among many species has become much more common in

TABLE 2

TIME REQUIRED FOR A GIVEN CHANGE IN THE PER CENT FREQUENCY OF A GENE HAVING A SELECTIVE ADVANTAGE OF 0.01 (I.E., 1 PER CENT) (MODIFIED FROM PÄTAU)*

DOMINANT GENE		RECESSIVE GENE	
Change in Frequency	No. of Generations	Change in Frequency	No. of Generations
0.01– 0.1...	230	0.01– 0.1...	900,230
0.1 – 1.0...	231	0.1 – 1.0...	90,231
1.0 –50.0...	559	1.0 – 3.0...	6,779
50.0 –97.0...	3,481	3.0 –50.0...	3,481
97.0 –99.0...	6,779	50.0 –99.0...	559
99.0 –99.9...	90,231	99.0 –99.9...	231
99.9 –99.99..	900,230	99.9 –99.99..	230

* Little, Brown & Company has kindly given permission to take this and certain of the following tables, in addition to a certain amount of the textual content of this paper, from W. C. Boyd, *Genetics and the Races of Man* (Boston, 1950).

the last century, and that this change has been in some way connected with the progressive industrialization of the areas where these dark-colored moths are found, for the melanotics occur predominantly in and near large cities and in industrial areas. In some cases the entire population of an area has become melanotic. The history of this process has been described by Harrison, and the phenomenon on the Continent of Europe has been described by Hasebroek. A summary of the genetic findings has been given by Ford.

A probable example of the effect of

selection in man is the gradual brachy-cephalization of central Europe, especially among the Slavs (see Table 3).

It has been mentioned by Schwidetsky that well-documented series of skulls from Bohemia and from Russia show that this change progressed from century to century, so that the average cranial index of 73–75 rose as high as 83 by the nineteenth century. Myslivec

TABLE 3

CHANGE IN CRANIAL INDEX OF "NORDIC" AND EAST EUROPEAN TYPES

DATE	CRANIAL INDEX	
	"Nordic"	East European
1200 B.C.	69.2	76.1
A.D. 300.........	69.6	77.1
A.D. 1200	73.5	78.6
A.D. 1935	ca. 81.0	ca. 86.0

suggests that a possible explanation of this phenomenon may be the dominance of the brachycephalic form of head over the dolichocephalic form. This explanation is probably an unconscious expression of the supposed phenomenon of "genophagy."[1] In view of the rapidity with which gene equilibrium is obtained in the absence of selection and mutation, we may doubt that this is really the explanation, for the brachycephalic genes would already have been in equilibrium with the dolichocephalic genes in the early populations. For example, the blood-group gene B was probably introduced into Europe from Asia in historical times. Gene B is dominant over gene O, but there is no evidence that the group O gene is tending to be swamped by B in western Europe (or anywhere

1. Some earlier writers thought that a dominant gene automatically became more and more frequent in a population simply because it was dominant. Since it would thus "eat up" the recessive gene, Laughlin christened this imaginary phenomenon "genophagy."

else). The most probable cause of recent brachycephalization would therefore seem to be the action of natural selection, which leads us to suppose that the brachycephalic individual has some advantage in the struggle for existence over the dolichocephalic individual. What this advantage is, we do not know. Weidenreich suggests that the head of the brachycephalic is balanced better on the vertebral column.

It has been objected that in cases such as this, where we seem to find a secular change in the morphology of a population, the real process has been one of gradual replacement of a long-headed population (for instance) by a roundheaded one. This is always a possibility because man interbreeds so extensively when given a chance and because we cannot obtain data on any population certainly known to have been isolated absolutely over a long period of time. But the way lower forms (e.g., horses) have undergone morphological change during the course of evolution leaves little doubt that such changes do occur, given sufficient time. It does not seem too much to suppose that similar evolutionary forces may act in similar ways in man.

Twenty years ago it was customary to state that valid racial classifications must be based on nonadaptive characters, that is, characters which do not have any great selective value in evolution. One author stated: "If race implies the possession of certain variations as a result of the same ancestry, significant racial criteria should be based principally upon non-adaptive bodily characters." Another wrote: "If a character has selective value, it will be subject to increase or decrease in frequency in the population by the action of selection, and the rate of selection may be surprisingly great. . . . Such characters can be useful only for determining recent prehistory." This second author was myself.

It was largely the work of the geneticists which rescued us from this untenable position. Dobzhansky, after quoting the opinion of one contemporary that "the great majority of racial features are obviously not adaptational," said: "This amounts to rejection of the simplest hypothesis which can account for the origin of racial differentiation, namely that it is brought about, at least in part, by natural selection of genotypes possessing adaptive values higher than other genotypes in the environments in which the species normally lives."

Professor Hooton, after quoting a statement that nonadaptive characters are to be preferred, states that "this insistence upon the use of 'non-adaptive' characters in human taxonomy now seems to me impractical and erroneous." He points out that natural selection is one of the most potent forces in human differentiation and that the mutations most likely to be perpetuated are those with survival value.

It is apparent now that we were mistaken when we looked for racial characteristics which were completely unaffected by natural selection and when we thought that racial characteristics which were completely nonadaptive could be handed down from generation to generation to mark common descent. Like other taxonomists, we must base our categories on characters which are indeed acted on by selective agencies.

Therefore, although I once believed, because the blood groups had no apparent selective advantage, that they were more useful than other physical characters in racial classification, it now seems to me unlikely that they can be absolutely "neutral" selectively and that it is likely that they are no more useful (but, of course, no less) than other human genes. At the moment they have the temporary advantage that we know the mechanism of their inheritance, which we do not know for most other normal human characteristics.

MIXTURE

If two populations mix, the new gene frequencies will depend on the original gene frequencies and the numbers of the two parent-populations. If the numbers of individuals of breeding age in the two populations are to each other as c is to d, and the gene frequencies are q_c and q_d, the new gene frequency in the mixed population will be

$$\frac{c\,q_c + d\,q_d}{c + d}.$$

MUTATION

Mutations are the raw material of evolution. They may be increased in frequency by selection. In the absence of selection, a mutation occurring in a sizable population does not increase in frequency, and it is incorrect to assume that such a mutated gene would spread. As an example, let us consider a hypothetical mutation from the blood-group gene O to the gene B (similar arguments apply to immigration of a group B individual into a population all of group O).

Since we have no evidence of a selective advantage for B in any environment we know about, we may state that if one group B individual, heterozygous for the blood-group B gene, enters a population of 999 individuals, none of whom belongs to blood group B or AB, there is no reason to suppose that at the end of 10 or 10,000 or 10,000,000 years the *proportion* of group B in the population descended from this mixture would be any greater than it was originally, namely, 0.1 per cent. It is easy to show mathematically that a new gene without selective advantage, once it appeared in a population (whether it was brought there by migration or arose *de novo* as the result of mutation), would not in the course of time spread through the population, becoming more and more frequent, even if it were a dominant.

In the fourth generation the number of descendants of any individual will, in the average case, be greater than the number in the first generation (his immediate children). If an individual rears four children, he may reasonably expect to have considerably more than four great-great-grandchildren. This will be especially true if the population as a whole is on the increase. Even in a strictly static population (one not increasing or decreasing in size) each mating yields, *on the average,* two children who reach the mating age, four grandchildren, eight great-grandchildren, etc. There is a *chance* that any of these descendants of a newly introduced or mutated B individual will inherit the factor B. So one can visualize, in a lazy sort of way, how the B factor might spread throughout the whole population, like the mycelium of a mold spreading through bread. But this lazy picture is wrong. If we analyze the process more carefully, we see that our B individual will probably have, in a static population, just two children who grow to maturity and have offspring of their own. The probability that one of these will have the gene B is ½, the probability that both will have gene B is ½ × ½ = ¼. If only one has it, the chances that his offspring belong to blood group B are computed in the same way. The probability that the four grandchildren of the original group B are also group B is 1/16 × 1/16 = 1/256. The further down the generations we go, the less likely it becomes that all the descendants of our group B individual will also be group B, until, in the end, the chances against it are overwhelming. Further analysis shows that the *proportional* representation of B in the gene population is therefore likely to stay the same as in

the beginning, if no other effects operate.

After gene B has been introduced, there seem to be three factors which might affect the total number of B genes in the population: (*a*) increase in the total size of the population, (*b*) random genetic variation (the Sewall Wright effect), and (*c*) the action of selection, if gene B has any selective value.

A factor which can modify the proportions of different *phenotypes* in man (and other organisms) is inbreeding. In its correct sense, inbreeding means mating between close relatives. Unless this occurs, a population, though it may be cut off from all contact with the outside world, is not inbred; it is merely reproductively isolated.

Inbreeding modifies the proportion of genotypes and phenotypes because close relatives are more likely to be of the same genotype than are unrelated members of the population, and thus inbreeding will mean that matings of dominant with dominant, of recessive with recessive, and of heterozygote with heterozygote, will be relatively more frequent than the other matings (dominant with recessives, etc.).

The result of such matings is that the heterozygotes will continue to produce both dominants and recessives among their offspring, but only half of their offspring are heterozygotes, the remainder being equally divided (on the average) between dominants and recessives. Dominant × dominant matings produce only dominants, and recessive × recessive matings produce only recessives. The range of variability of the population is therefore continually reduced, and the proportion of homozygotes is increased at the expense of the heterozygotes.

A fourth evolutionary mechanism is the Sewall Wright effect, or *random genetic drift,* which depends for its operation on the isolation of one small population from other populations with which it might interbreed. The recognition of the great importance of the mechanism of *random drift* in evolution has been largely due to the mathematical work of Wright.

If we choose a very small group consisting, let us say, of four women and four men, from a larger population which has about the usual European distribution of blood groups, and isolate them on a desert island, it might easily happen by chance that no individual of group B (which usually accounts for only 10–15 per cent of an average European population) would be represented in this particular mating group. Even if one B individual were by chance included, he or she would most likely be a heterozygote, that is of the genotype BO,[2] and any child of his would have a 50-50 chance of not belonging to blood group B (in other words of being A or O). Even if he had a fair number of children, therefore, he might fail to produce any child of group B, and gene B would not be represented in the new generation. The chance of no B in one child is $\frac{1}{2}$, of no B in four children $(\frac{1}{2})^4 = 1/16$, an event not too unlikely to occur occasionally. Given this situation, as soon as this hypothetical original group B individual died or passed the age of reproduction, the B gene would thus be irretrievably lost to the tribe, unless it were introduced again by mutation. And, of course, the group B individual might be killed before he reached the mating age, or might be sterile, or for some other reason might fail to leave any offspring.

GENETIC DEFINITION OF RACE

In differentiating one group of people from another, the anthropologist

2. In the population of the United States, over 90 per cent of all group B individuals are heterozygous for this gene.

has had to face the difficult problem of deciding just what physical characters are "significant" in their variations. All the existing human types are interfertile and constitute a single Linnaean species. Within this species there are various groups which differ from one another to a greater or less degree, and some of these we may, if we choose, define as "races."

Our increasing knowledge of human genetics is making it possible to define races by selecting characters whose variations in frequency in different populations are significant because they are known to be the expression of individual human genes.

A classification of men on the basis of gene frequencies has a number of advantages. (1) It is objective. Gene frequencies are determined by straightforward counting, or relatively simple computation from quantitative observations of clear-cut, all-or-none characters. The subjective element which complicates attempts to compare the skin colors of two peoples, for example, does not appear. (2) It is quantitative. The degree of similarity between two populations is not a matter of guesswork, but can be compared by calculating from the frequencies of the genes considered. (3) It makes it possible to predict the composition of a population resulting from mixture in any assigned proportions of two populations of known gene frequencies. (4) It encourages clearer thinking about human taxonomy and human evolution. Emotional bias is less likely to operate than in the case of physical appearance such as stature or skin color. There are no prejudices against genes. (5) It permits a sharp separation of the effects of heredity and environment. In the case of a character like stature, it is difficult to say whether genes or food and climate have contributed more to making two populations alike. In the case of blood groups no such problem arises.

We do not mean to assert that the geneticist can classify mankind with no regard to his recent geographical distribution, and cultural factors such as language, since it is obvious that race, as we understand the term, involves common descent. An anthropologist who studied the inhabitants of the British Isles and disregarded the linguistic and cultural distinction between the English and the Welsh would indeed be foolish. Our procedure will be one of generalization and abstraction. The value of the abstractions will be shown when we apply them to new examples. Thus any combination of gene frequencies which we abstract as characteristic of Africans must not reveal little islands of "Negroes" in northern Europe or pre-Columbian America.

In order to use genetic methods in physical anthropological classification, we must understand two points: (*a*) inheritance is particulate in character, and (*b*) the units of heredity soon reach an equilibrium distribution in a population.

The evidence for point *a* was found by Mendel in his pioneer experiments. It has been confirmed by hundreds of geneticists since. It means that hereditary characters do not blend in offspring. Instead, each gene from a parent remains unaffected, ready to appear in future generations, unchanged by its temporary association with a different gene. A gene for blue eyes may be submerged for generations by dominant genes for dark eyes, but, when it again is combined with another recessive gene, it produces eyes as light and blue as it ever did. The particles of heredity, the genes, do not change by association. If they do change, it is by mutation.

Point *b* means that, in any large population mating at random, the various gene frequencies no longer change—ex-

cept perhaps slowly by selection or mutation—and consequently the physical types (phenotypes) are also constant. The frequency of blue eyes does not decrease, in spite of the fact that blue eyes are recessive. This is the state known to geneticists as "gene equilibrium." Mathematical proof shows that it prevails in a population after one generation of random mating.

One of the clearest expositions of the elementary mathematics underlying the principle of gene equilibrium has been given by Dobzhansky. He says: Suppose that two varieties of a sexually reproducing organism are brought into contact and allowed to interbreed at random. Let us suppose that one variety is homozygous for the dominant gene Y, while the other variety is homozygous for the recessive gene y. If the two varieties are originally present in equal numbers, one half of the original population will consist of YY and the other half of yy individuals. As a result of the mating between these two varieties, we can easily show by writing down the matings and their outcomes that the next generation will consist of 25 per cent of individuals homozygous for Y, 25 per cent homozygous for y, and 50 per cent which are hybrids, or heterozygotes, Yy. In other words, we have again the familiar Mendelian ratio: YY, $2Yy$, yy.

FALLACY OF TYPES

Starting from the concept of genetically determined characters in a population in genetic equilibrium, we may cast about for a sensible method of race classification. One fallacy may be disposed of here. This is the fallacy of the "type."

Boas pointed out in one of his last papers that, although the logical way to express differences between different human groups was to determine the frequency with which various forms occurred in each group, some anthropologists tend to be impressed by the forms which appear most commonly, and tend to combine these frequent forms in their minds into one imaginary individual which they call "The Type." Sargeant established the ideal type of the Harvard student by having a sculptor make a figure of a youth whose body measurements corresponded to the average of the measurements obtained on a large number of Harvard students from about the year 1892. A knowledge of genetics shows that the type concept has no basis in reality.

Suppose we are liberal, and say that a man is like the ideal in respect to any given measurement if he does not deviate more than do 50 per cent of the total examined; we should nevertheless find, as Boas points out, that the number of measurements is such and the number of their combinations is so great that Sargeant would have found, on the average, among 1,024 individuals taken at random at Harvard, just one who corresponded to his ideal type. Human populations as they actually exist do not produce ideal types. Instead, we must deal with the variations in frequencies of many different genes in different populations.

DEFINITION OF RACE

It would be incorrect and meaningless to define a race as "a group of individuals with identical genetic constitutions," since, as pointed out by Dobzhansky and Epling, groups of identical individuals are simply never found. There is a great deal of genetic variation even within the confines of a race. If we should frame a definition of race along these lines, every single individual would have to belong to a separate race, of which he was the only member, except in the case of identical twins, who might belong to the same race. Dobzhansky and Epling also point out that it would be equally fallacious to define a race as a group of individuals having some single gene in common or some chromosome structure in common. Since so many variable genes and chromosome structures exist, and since these different genes and chromosome structures can form a large variety of combinations, we should be certain to find individuals classified as belonging to one race in so far as some gene, say F, was concerned, but who would belong to a different race in regard to the gene G, and a still different race in regard to the gene H. A race is not an individual, and it is not a single genotype, but it is a group of individuals more or less from the same geographical area (a population), usually with a number of identical genes, but in which many different types may occur.

Dobzhansky and Epling propose to define races as (different) populations which are characterized by different frequencies of variable genes and/or chromosome structures. Dahlberg has proposed a definition of race which amounts to much the same thing. He says: "A race is an isolate or a collection of isolates." By an "isolate" is implied a group of individuals isolated geographically or socially or in some other way who consequently do not freely exchange genes with surrounding peoples. But, within the isolate, mating occurs more or less at random. In the ideal case, one would take account of all the variable genes and chromosome structures in order to describe a given race. At present, we are unable to do this, even in the lower forms such as *Drosophila*, where the genetics are much more thoroughly understood than they are with man. Because our knowledge is incomplete, we have to base our classifications on certain genetic differences that we do know about.

First, we have to decide how much difference there must be in the distribution of the known variable genes and chromosome structures between two populations, before we decide to call them two different races. According to Charles and Goodwin, in some cases the number of genes differentiating two different *species* may be of the order of 40. Statistically significant differences may occur between populations of *Drosophila* in localities only a dozen miles apart, and we could, if we liked, say that these populations are racially distinct. If the concept of race is to be taxonomically useful, however, we should not use the term quite so freely, for otherwise we shall have too many races within each species, and the term will lose much of its value for purposes of classification.

Dobzhansky and Epling show that in *Drosophila,* where far more is known about the genetic structure than in man, it would be useless to delineate a race from the possession of any one gene, or any one particular arrangement of genes in any one particular chromosome. Since genes vary independently, individuals identical in respect to one chromosome would frequently be found to differ profoundly in respect to the arrangement of genes in some other chromosome.

Although the genotype of an individual is derived from the population from which it sprang, it is not absolutely predetermined by the genetic composition of this population (except, of course, in respect to genes for which the population is homozygous). And the extent to which the individual can vary depends, in turn, on the degree of genetic variability which is present in the species in question.

If we make a thorough study of man, genetically and morphologically, we must not expect that the various data collected will all be mutually "consistent." In fact, we must be prepared to find that populations in Greenland and in Australia agree quite well in regard to blood-grouping frequencies (A, B, O, at least) (Table 4), while they markedly disagree in regard to the M and N blood types, in regard to skin color, hair form, and other characteristics. Contemporary physical anthropologists accept this as a necessary and not illogical situation.

As data on the physical characteristics of the human race have accumulated, it has become clear that they usually vary independently of one another, and that whatever races we choose to distinguish will be almost entirely arbitrary, and their distribution will depend on the particular characteristics on which we choose to base them. Dahlberg reminds us that the finding of one "racial" difference does not mean we can forthwith assume that many other differences must exist. The observed difference may be the chief or even the only difference. The only instances in which we may expect a "dividend" of additional similarities will be those in which we are studying populations which have long been isolated genetically and thus have had time to undergo considerable differentiation. The situation is entirely different from the case of the chemical elements, where, when we find one test which clearly differentiates sodium and arsenic, for example, we can safely infer the existence of many other important differences.

We may define a human race as a population which differs significantly from other human populations in regard to the frequency of one or more of the genes it possesses. It is an arbitrary matter which, and how many, gene loci we choose to consider as a significant "constellation"; but it seems better, on the one hand, not to designate a multiplicity of races which differ only in regard to a single pair or a single set of allelic genes and, on the other, not to insist that the races we define must differ from one another with respect to all their genes. To define human races on the basis of genetics, we

TABLE 4*

FREQUENCIES OF BLOOD GROUPS O, A, B, AND AB IN TYPICAL POPULATIONS

POPULATION	PLACE	NUMBER TESTED	O	A	B	AB	p	q	r
			Low A, Virtually No B						
Am. Indians (Utes)	Montana	138	97.4	2.6	0	0	0.013	0.0	0.987
Am. Indians (Toba)	Argentina	194	98.5	1.5	0	0	0.007	0	0.993
Am. Indians (Sioux)	S. Dakota	100	91.0	7.0	2.0	0	0.035	0.010	0.955
Am. Indians (Kwakiutl)	B. Columbia	123	85.4	12.2	2.4	0	0.063	0.013	0.926
			Moderate A, Virtually No B						
Am. Indians (Navaho)	N. Mexico	359	77.7	22.5	0	0	0.125	0	0.875
Am. Indians (Pueblo)	Jemez, etc., N.M.	310	78.4	20.0	1.6	0	0.105	0.007	0.885
			High A, Little B						
Am. Indians (Bloods)	Montana	69	17.4	81.2	0	1.4	0.583	0	0.417
Am. Indians (Blackfeet)	Montana	115	23.5	76.5	0	0	0.515	0	0.485
Australian aborigines	South Australia	54	42.6	57.4	0	0	0.346	0	0.654
Australian aborigines	West Australia	243	48.1	51.9	0	0	0.306	0	0.694
Basques	San Sebastián	91	57.2	41.7	1.1	0	0.239	0.008	0.756
Am. Indians (Shoshone)	Wyoming	60	51.6	45.0	1.6	1.6	0.264	0.011	0.718
Polynesians	Hawaii	413	36.5	60.8	2.2	0.5	0.382	0.018	0.604
Eskimo	Cape Farewell	484	41.1	53.8	3.5	1.4	0.333	0.027	0.642
Australian aborigines	Queensland	447	58.6	37.8	3.6	0	0.216	0.023	0.766
Am. Indians (Flatheads)	Montana	258	51.5	42.2	4.7	1.6	0.250	0.032	0.718
			Fairly High A, and Some B						
W. Georgians	Tiflis	707	59.1	34.4	6.1	0.4	0.198	0.038	0.769
English	London	422	47.9	42.4	8.3	1.4	0.250	0.050	0.692
Belgians	Liége	3,500	46.7	41.9	8.3	3.1	0.257	0.058	0.684
Spanish	Spain	1,172	41.5	46.5	9.2	2.2	0.294	0.068	0.645
Swedes	Stockholm	633	37.9	46.1	9.5	6.5	0.301	0.073	0.616
Icelanders	Iceland	800	55.7	32.1	9.6	2.6	0.190	0.062	0.747
Danes	Copenhagen	1,261	40.7	45.3	10.5	3.5	0.290	0.078	0.638
French	Paris	1,265	39.8	42.3	11.8	6.1	0.276	0.088	0.632
Armenians	fr. Turkey	330	27.3	53.9	12.7	6.1	0.379	0.110	0.523
Irish	Dublin	399	55.2	31.1	12.1	1.7	0.186	0.076	0.744
Lapps	Finland	94	33.0	52.1	12.8	2.1	0.323	0.078	0.574
Melanesians	New Guinea	500	37.6	44.4	13.2	4.8	0.293	0.099	0.613
Micronesians	Saipan	293	50.5	33.8	14.0	1.7	0.207	0.093	0.711
Greeks	Athens	1,200	42.0	39.6	14.2	3.7	0.254	0.102	0.648
Germans	Berlin	39,174	36.5	42.5	14.5	6.5	0.285	0.110	0.604
Turks	Istamboul	500	33.8	42.6	14.8	8.8	0.293	0.116	0.581

* "N." signifies north; "S.," "W.," and "E." south, west, and east, respectively; "fr." signifies from; "n." signifies near. In this table the frequencies of the blood groups O, A, B, and AB are given in per cents, but the gene frequencies are given as straight frequencies, following common practice. The symbol p represents the frequency of the gene A; q the frequency of the gene B; and r the frequency of the gene O.

Apropos of this and succeeding tables in this chapter, we may remark again that no one characteristic is enough to differentiate races satisfactorily.

TABLE 4—*Continued*

POPULATION	PLACE	NUMBER TESTED	O	A	B	AB	*p*	*q*	*r*
			High A and High B						
E. Georgians........	Tiflis	1,274	36.8	42.3	15.0	5.9	0.283	0.113	0.607
Bulgarians.........	Sofia	6,060	32.1	44.4	15.4	8.1	0.308	0.123	0.567
Hungarians........	Budapest	624	36.1	41.8	15.9	6.2	0.282	0.120	0.601
Welsh.............	N. towns	192	47.9	32.8	16.2	3.1	0.206	0.108	0.692
Italians...........	Sicily	540	45.9	33.4	17.3	3.4	0.213	0.118	0.678
Siamese...........	Bangkok	213	37.1	17.8	35.2	9.9	0.148	0.257	0.595
Syrians...........	Meshghara	300	39.3	39.0	17.1	4.6	0.258	0.124	0.628
Finns.............	Häme	972	34.0	42.4	17.1	6.5	0.285	0.126	0.583
"Berbers".........	Algiers	300	39.0	37.6	18.6	4.6	0.251	0.134	0.625
Germans...........	Danzig	1,888	33.1	41.6	18.0	7.3	0.288	0.139	0.575
Ukrainians........	Kharkov	310	36.4	38.4	21.6	3.6	0.261	0.158	0.604
Japanese..........	Tokyo	29,799	30.1	38.4	21.9	9.7	0.279	0.172	0.549
Japanese..........	Kyoto	6,205	29.2	38.0	22.2	10.6	0.279	0.177	0.541
Estonians.........	Estonia	1,844	32.3	36.6	22.4	8.7	0.261	0.170	0.589
Madagascans.......	Madagascar	266	45.5	27.5	22.5	4.5	0.180	0.151	0.674
Russians..........	n. Moscow	489	31.9	34.4	24.9	8.8	0.250	0.189	0.565
Abyssinians.......	Abyssinia	400	42.3	26.5	25.3	5.0	0.178	0.172	0.654
Egyptians.........	Cairo	502	27.3	38.5	25.5	8.8	0.288	0.203	0.523
Bogobos...........	Philippines	302	53.6	16.9	26.5	3.0	0.107	0.163	0.732
Chinese...........	Huang-Ho R.	2,127	34.2	30.8	27.7	7.3	0.220	0.201	0.587
'Iraqis...........	Baghdad	386	33.7	31.4	28.2	6.7	0.226	0.208	0.581
Tatars............	Kazan	500	27.8	30.0	28.8	13.4	0.233	0.225	0.527
Pygmies...........	Belgian Congo	1,032	30.6	30.3	29.1	10.0	0.227	0.219	0.554
Arabs, Bedouin..... (Rwala)	Syrian Desert	208	43.3	22.1	30.3	4.3	0.151	0.200	0.658
Egyptians.........	Assiut	419	24.6	34.4	31.0	10.0	0.272	0.250	0.459
Kirghiz...........	U.S.S.R.	500	31.6	27.4	32.2	8.8	0.206	0.236	0.563
Asiatic Indians......	Goa	400	29.2	26.8	34.0	10.0	0.208	0.254	0.540
Chinese...........	Peking	1,000	30.7	25.1	34.2	10.0	0.193	0.250	0.554
Javanese..........	Ampelgading	450	30.4	24.7	37.3	7.6	0.190	0.271	0.552
Buriats...........	N. Irkutsk	1,320	32.4	20.2	39.2	8.2	0.156	0.277	0.570
Asiatic Indians......	Bengal	160	32.5	20.0	39.4	8.1	0.154	0.278	0.571

should know which genes act to determine physical characters, and which genetically determined characters are most useful as a basis for a physical classification. The inherited characters may be divided into three categories: characters which are fairly common and variable, believed to be inherited, although the mechanism has not yet been worked out; rare pathological conditions whose mechanism of inheritance is known; and normal physiological characters inherited by genetic mechanism which is known exactly.

BLOOD GROUPS

Pathological characters are of little use in classification because of their rarity, and the common characters of uncertain hereditary mechanism are not so useful as characters inherited in a known manner. The ten blood-group systems are the only examples of the third class of characters known at present. In order of discovery, they are: the ABO blood groups, the MNS blood groups, the P blood groups, the secreting factor, the Lewis blood groups, the Rh blood groups, the Lutheran blood groups, the Kell blood groups, the Duffy blood groups, and the Kidd blood groups.

The mechanism of inheritance of the ABO blood groups and the MN blood groups is too well known to require retelling. The anti-S serum, which made a subdivision of the MN groups possible, was first reported from Australia by Walsh and Montgomery. A reasonable interpretation of the data is that there are four alleles at the locus of these genes, namely, Ms, MS, Ns, and NS. If, however, an anti-s serum is found, which Race expects, the interpretation that S and s are a separate pair of alleles, linked to the MN locus, will become more probable.

TABLE 5

FREQUENCY OF S-SUBDIVISIONS OF THE M,N FREQUENCIES IN VARIOUS POPULATIONS

POPULATION	FREQUENCY OF GENE			
	Ms	*MS*	*Ns*	*NS*
Australian aborigines......	0.256	0	0.744	0
New Guinea...	0.04	0.01	0.75	0.28
Maori........	0.500	0.014	0.438	0.048
English.......	0.285	0.255	0.386	0.074

The recently discovered anti-S sera enable the former M,N groups to be subdivided. The S,s gene pair might be another pair of alleles linked to the M,N locus, but it is also possible that the new serum simply enables, instead of the M,N pair, four alleles, *Ms, MS, Ns, NS,* to be distinguished. This greatly increases the anthropological usefulness of this system. It is particularly interesting to note that, although the older M,N results did not particularly distinguish the aborigines of New Guinea from those of Australia (thus not seeming to support the marked differences in frequencies of B), the use of the anti-S serum does. The bloods from Australia never reacted with anti-S, while there is an appreciable amount of S-positive blood in New Guinea (see Table 5).

The distribution of ABO blood groups in various populations is shown in Table 4.

The distribution of the blood groups is shown in Table 6.

The P blood groups were discovered by Landsteiner and Levine, the same year in which they found M and N. The antigen P is inherited as a dominant. Gradations in strength of P are observed, as with other blood-group antigens; it may be that multiple alleles are involved.

The ability to secrete blood-group substances A, B, and H(Q) into the saliva and other body fluids in water-soluble form was shown by Schiff and Sasaki to be inherited as a Mendelian pair, S (secretor) being dominant over s.

The Lewis blood groups were discovered by Mourant, who found a "new" antibody in two samples of serum. Andresen independently discovered an antiserum, which he fortunately called "anti-L," since it proved identical with the anti-Lewis. He observed that the proportion of L-positive infants in his population was higher than the proportion of L-positive adults. He proposed the hypothesis, since confirmed, that L was recessive in adults and dominant in children.

The way in which the frequency of Le^a positive reactions falls off during childhood is shown in Table 7. This was the first example of a recessive agglutinogen in man.

The Lewis blood groups were found to be intimately associated with the secreting factor. All adult individuals reacting with anti-Le^a, and therefore, by hypothesis, Le^a/Le^a genetically, were nonsecretors of A, B, and H. Most Le^a negative persons are secretors, but about 1 per cent secrete neither A, B, H, Le^a, nor Le^b. It is thought that they probably secrete an antigen Le^c, not otherwise yet identified. Thus the genes Le^a, Le^b, Le^c, and S,s would form two series of alleles contiguous to each other.

The Rh blood groups were discovered by Landsteiner and Wiener, although others had probably observed

TABLE 6*

FREQUENCIES OF M,N BLOOD TYPES AND *M* AND *N* GENES IN VARIOUS POPULATIONS

POPULATION	PLACE	NUMBER TESTED	M	MN	N	*m*	*n*
Populations with Low N and Therefore High M							
Eskimo...............	E. Greenland	569	83.5	15.6	0.9	0.913	0.087
Am. Indians............ (Navaho)	New Mexico	361	84.5	14.4	1.1	0.917	0.083
Aleuts.................	Aleutian Islands	132	67.5	29.4	3.2	0.822	0.179
Am. Indians............ (Utes)	Utah	104	58.7	34.6	6.7	0.600	0.240
Arabs, Bedouin......... (Rwala)	n. Damascus	208	57.5	36.7	5.8	0.758	0.241
Am. Indians............ (Pueblo)	New Mexico	140	59.3	32.8	7.9	0.757	0.243
Am. Indians............ (Blackfeet)	Montana	95	54.7	40.0	5.3	0.747	0.253
Arabs (Bedouin)........	n. Damascus	80	51.3	40.0	8.7	0.713	0.287
Populations with Low M (High N)							
Australian aborigines....	N.S. Wales	28	0	32.1	67.9	0.160	0.840
Australian aborigines....	Queensland	372	2.4	30.4	67.2	0.176	0.824
Papuans...............	Papua	200	7.0	24.0	69.0	0.190	0.810
Fijians................	Fiji	200	11.0	44.5	44.5	0.332	0.667
Ainu..................	Shizunai	504	17.9	50.2	31.9	0.430	0.570
Populations with "Normal" M and N Frequencies							
Negroes...............	N.Y.C.	730	......	......	28.1	......	*ca.* 0.530
Basques...............	Spain	91	23.1	51.6	25.3	0.489	0.511
Spanish (m)...........	Spain	134	26.9	55.2	17.9	0.545	0.455
Syrians...............	Boarij	131	24.4	52.7	22.9	0.508	0.492
Filipinos..............	Leyte, Samar, etc.	382	25.9	50.3	23.8	0.510	0.490
Egyptians.............	Cairo	502	27.8	48.9	23.3	0.522	0.477
English...............	London	422	28.7	47.4	23.9	0.524	0.476
Lapps.................	Inari, Finland	56	28.6	48.2	23.2	0.527	0.473
Poles.................	Poland	600	28.2	49.0	22.8	0.527	0.473
Egyptians.............	Assiut	419	26.2	53.1	20.7	0.527	0.472
Indonesians...........	Java, etc.	296	30.4	45.6	24.0	0.532	0.468
Irish.................	Dublin	399	30.0	46.7	23.3	0.533	0.466
Danes.................	Copenhagen	2,023	29.1	49.5	21.4	0.538	0.461
Belgians..............	Liége	3,100	28.9	50.3	20.8	0.540	0.460
Germans..............	Berlin	8,144	29.7	50.7	19.6	0.550	0.449
Japanese..............	Kyoto	430	32.0	46.1	21.9	0.551	0.449
Russians..............	Leningrad	701	32.0	46.7	21.3	0.553	0.446
Yugoslavs.............	Moravska	256	30.5	50.0	19.5	0.555	0.445
Germans..............	Danzig	2,018	30.6	50.4	19.0	0.558	0.442
French................	Paris	400	33.0	45.8	21.2	0.559	0.441
Italians...............	Sicily	300	32.0	48.0	20.0	0.560	0.440
Japanese..............	Tokyo	1,100	32.4	47.2	20.4	0.560	0.440
Syrians...............	Meshghara	306	30.7	52.0	17.3	0.567	0.433
Armenians............	fr. Turkey	339	34.2	45.4	20.4	0.569	0.431
Hungarians...........	Budapest	624	33.5	47.9	18.6	0.574	0.425
Chinese...............	Hong Kong	1,029	33.2	48.6	18.2	0.575	0.425
Ukrainians............	Kharkov	310	36.1	44.3	19.6	0.583	0.417

* "(m)" signifies mixed; "N." signifies north, "E." signifies east, "W." signifies west; "n." signifies near; "ca." signifies approximately; "fr." signifies from. M, MN, and N stand for the percentages of the M, MN, and N blood types; *m* stands for the frequency of the gene for M; *n* for the frequency of the gene for N.

TABLE 6—*Continued*

POPULATION	PLACE	NUMBER TESTED	M	MN	N	*m*	*n*
		Populations with "Normal" M and N Frequencies—*Continued*					
Welsh...............	N. towns	192	30.7	55.3	14.0	0.583	0.416
Scots...............	Glasgow	456	35.0	47.9	17.1	0.589	0.410
Swedes..............	Sweden	1,200	36.1	47.0	16.9	0.596	0.404
Estonians...........	Estonia	310	34.8	49.7	15.5	0.596	0.403
'Iraqis..............	Baghdad	387	37.0	47.0	16.0	0.605	0.395
Finns...............	Uusimaa	1,050	37.1	47.2	15.7	0.607	0.393
Arabs, Bedouin....... (Jabour)	n. Mosul	206	36.9	49.5	13.6	0.616	0.383
Russians............	n. Moscow	489	39.9	44.0	16.1	0.619	0.381
E. Caucasians........	Tiflis	134	38.8	47.8	13.4	0.627	0.373
W. Caucasians........	Tiflis	245	40.0	46.5	13.5	0.632	0.367
Finns...............	Karjala	398	45.7	43.2	11.1	0.673	0.327

TABLE 7

DECREASE WITH AGE IN LEWIS POSITIVES

TYPE	CHILDREN								ADULTS	
	0–3 Months		4–6 Months		7–9 Months		10–12 Months			
	No.	Per Cent	No.	Per Cent	No.	Per Cent	No.	Per Cent	No.	Per Cent
Le(a+)........	78	79	74	73	18	36	19	29	166	21
Le(a−)........	21	21	28	27	32	64	46	71	618	79

agglutination due to this system, as they had in the case of other as yet unnamed systems. According to Fisher's (cited by Race) hypothesis, three closely linked adjacent loci, C, D, and E, are involved. According to Wiener's hypothesis, a series of allelomorphic genes, r, R', R'', R_1, R_2, R_o, r^y, R^z are involved. The two theories lead to identical genetic predictions. Other Rh antigens have been found from time to time, so that the following genes are available for the C, D, and E loci, respectively: C, c, C^w, c^v, C^u; D, d, D^u; E, e, E^u. The various antisera are sometimes available pure, more often as mixtures.

The known data regarding the Rh types in various populations are shown in Table 8. No particular dominance relations are observed among these genes. They usually act more strongly when present in double dose.

The antibody which defines the Lutheran blood groups was found by Callender and Race in the serum of a patient who had been transfused many times. The dominant gene responsible for positive reactions was designated as Lu^a and the still hypothetical recessive gene as Lu^b. About 8 per cent of English subjects are positive for Lu^a.

Coombs, Mourant, and Race described a blood-group antibody which was not connected with any of the known antigens. This antibody, which was of the incomplete or "blocking" type, was found in the serum of a mother whose child was thought to be suffering from hemolytic disease. Various other workers later found similar antibodies. About 10 per cent of Bostonians and Londoners react positively with this serum.

The antigen identified by this antibody was called "Kell" and symbolized by K. The allele was symbolized as k. In 1949 Levine found an antibody which reacted with the predicted k antigen, making it possible to separate the heterozygotes Kk from the homozygotes KK.

Cutbush, Mollison, and Parkin reported another blood-group system, called "Duffy" from the name of the patient, who was suffering from hemophilia and who had had several blood transfusions over the preceding twenty years. The gene giving rise to the antigen recognizable by this serum was

TABLE 8

Rh BLOOD TYPES IN VARIOUS POPULATIONS

POPULATION	No. OF PERSONS TESTED	FREQUENCIES OF Rh TYPES (PER CENT)								
		rh cde	Rh₁ CDe	Rh₂ cDE	Rh₁Rh₂ CDe/ cDE	Rh₀ cDe	rh' Cde	rh'' cdE	rh'rh'' Cde/ cdE	Rh₁Rh₂ CDe/ CDE
Basques	167	28.8	55.1	7.8	6.0	0.6	1.8	......		
"Whites" (France)	501	17.0	51.7	13.6	13.0	3.6	0.4	0.8	0	0
Czechs (Prague)	181	16.0	50.3	11.6	11.6	1.1	0.6	0.6	0	0.6
"Whites" (Hollanders)	200	15.4	51.5	12.3	17.7	1.5	1.5	0	0	0
"Whites" (England)	1,038	15.3	54.8	14.7	11.6	2.3	0.6	0.7	0	......
S. Paulo (Brazil)	138	15.2	55.2	10.1	11.6	5.8	1.4	0.7		
"Whites" (Australia)	350	14.9	54.0	12.6	16.6	0.6	0.9	0.6	0	0
"Whites" (England)	927	14.8	54.9	12.2	13.6	2.5	0.7	1.3	......	0.1
"Whites" (U.S.A.)	7,317	14.7	53.5	15.0	12.9	2.2	1.1	0.6	0.01	......
Spanish (Barcelona)	223	13.0	63.2	13.0	9.4	0.5	0	0.5	0	0.5
"Whites" (U.S.A.)	766	12.5	54.7	14.9	13.9	2.2	0.9	0.5	0	0.1
"Arabs" (Baghdad)	300	10.3	50.3	13.7	15.7	8.3	1.0	0.7	0	0
Porto Ricans	179	10.1	39.1	19.6	14.0	15.1	1.7	0.5	0	
Negroes (U.S.A.)	223	8.1	20.2	22.4	5.4	41.2	2.7	0	0	......
Negroes (U.S.A.)	135	7.4	23.7	16.3	4.4	45.9	1.5	0.7	0	0
Asiatic Indians (Moslems)	156	7.1	70.5	5.1	12.8	1.9	2.6	0	0	
S. African Bantu	300	5.3	27.0	0	2.3	64.3	1.0	0	0	
Chinese	132	1.5	60.6	3.0	34.1	0.9	0	0	0	
Japanese	150	1.3	37.4	13.3	47.3	0	0	0	0	0.7
Japanese	180	0.6	51.7	8.3	39.4	0	0	0	0	......
Am. Indians (Mexico, Tuxpan)	95	0	48.1	9.5	38.1	1.1	0	0	0	3.1
Am. Indians (Ramah, N.M.)	105	0	40.0	17.1	36.2	2.9	0.9	0	0	2.9
Am. Indians (Ramah, N.M.)	305	0	28.5	20.0	41.0	0.7	3.0	0	0.7	6.2
Am. Indians (Utah)	104	0	33.7	28.8	37.5	0	0	0	0	......
Am. Indians (Brazil)	238	0	22.7	19.3	53.2	......				4.8
Indonesians	200	0	74	2.5	22.5	0.5	0	0	0.5	0
Filipinos	100	0	87.0	2.0	11.0	0	0	0	0	......
Australian aborigines	100	0	53.0	21.0	15.0	4.0	1.0	0	0	6.0
Australian aborigines	234	0	58.2	8.5	30.4	1.3	1.7	0	0	......
Papuans	100	0	93.0	0	4.0	0	0	0	0	3.0
Maoris	32	0	25.0	31.0	41.0	3.0	0	0	0	......
Admiralty Islanders	112	0	92.9	0.9	6.2	0	0	0	0	
Fijians	110	0	89.1	1.8	9.1	0	0	0	0	
New Caledonians (N and NW)	248	0	77.4	2.1	20.5	0	0	0	0	......
Loyalty Islanders	103	0	77.7	2.9	19.4	0	0	0	0	......
Siamese (Bangkok)	213	0	74.7	3.3	21.1	0.5	0	0	0	3.3

designated as Fy^a and the hypothetical allelic gene as Fy^b. An agglutinin for Fy^b was found in 1951 by Ikin, Mourant, Pettenkofer, and Blumenthal in the blood of a lady in Berlin after the birth of her second child. The child appeared normal, and the antibody, which had a titer of 16,000, was discovered in the course of routine examination of the sera of all the mothers in the hospital.

About 65 per cent of the English are positive to anti-Fy^a, a frequency which makes this a very useful character for legal medicine and suggests that it will be useful in anthropology.

Race, Diamond, *et al.* reported the mode of inheritance of a new blood-group factor discovered by Diamond, called "Kidd." The gene symbol, from the name of the patient's son, is Jk^a, and the hypothetical alternative gene Jk^b. About 70 per cent of Bostonians and Londoners are positive to anti-Jk^a.

Other rare or incompletely studied blood-group factors have been reported. None have any anthropological usefulness as yet.

Another normal characteristic—the ability to taste phenyl-thio-urea (PTC) —is doubtless inherited, but the exact mechanism is not yet clear (Harris). Its anthropological usefulness is therefore less than that of the blood groups.

As characters for use in anthropological classification, the blood groups offer several advantages: (*a*) They are inherited in a known way according to Mendelian principles. (*b*) They are not altered by differences in climate, food, illness, or medical treatment. (*c*) Their frequency in a population is stable, in so far as our observations extend. (*d*) They probably arose very early in the course of man's evolution. (*e*) There is a considerable correlation between geography and the distribution of the blood groups. (*f*) The blood groups are sharply distinguishable "all-or-none" characters which do not grade into one another.

The present author has suggested the following tentative racial classification based on gene frequencies.

1. Early European group (hypothetical). Possessing the highest incidence (over 30 per cent) of the Rh negative type (gene frequency of *rh* 0.6) and probably no group B. A relatively high incidence of the gene *Rh₁* and A₂. Gene N possibly somewhat higher than in present-day Europeans. Represented today by their modern descendants, the Basques.

2. European (Caucasoid) group. Possessing the next highest incidence of *rh* (the Rh negative gene) and relatively high incidence of the genes *Rh₁* and A₂, with moderate frequencies of other blood-group genes. "Normal" frequencies of M and N, i.e., M = *ca.* 30 per cent, MN = *ca.* 49 per cent, N = *ca.* 21 per cent. (The italicized symbols stand for the genes, as opposed to the groups.)

3. African (Negroid) group. Possessing a tremendously high incidence of the gene *Rhº*, a moderate frequency of *rh*, relatively high incidence of genes A₂ and the rare intermediate A (A₁, A₂, etc.) and Rh genes, rather high incidence of gene B. Probably normal M and N.

4. Asiatic (Mongoloid) group. Possessing high frequencies of genes A₁ and B, and the highest known incidence of the rare gene *Rhᶻ*, but little, if any, of the genes A₂ and *rh* (the Rh negative gene). Normal M and N. (It is possible that the inhabitants of India will prove to belong to an Asiatic sub-race, or even a separate race, serologically, but information is still sadly lacking.)

5. American Indian group. Possessing varying (sometimes high, sometimes zero) incidence of gene A₁, no A₂, and probably no B or *rh;* high incidence of gene N. Possessing *Rhᶻ*.

6. Australoid group. Possessing high incidence of gene A_1, no A_2, no rh, high incidence of gene N (and consequently a low incidence of gene M). Possessing Rh^z.

Table 9 shows the world's distribution of these races.

It is encouraging that this classification corresponds well, on the whole, with the facts of geography. It is, however, hardly more than a suggestion of what will eventually be possible when more human genes are investigated and our knowledge of human gene frequencies is extended.

TABLE 9

APPROXIMATE GENE FREQUENCIES IN SIX GENETICALLY DEFINED RACES

Gene	1 Early European	2 European (Caucasian)	3 African (Negroid)	4 Asiatic (Mongoloid)	5 American	6 Australian
$A(p)(A_2+A_1)$....	*ca.* 0.25	0.2–0.3	0.1–0.2	0.15–0.4	0–0.6	0.1–0.6
Ratio, A_2/A_1*..	>0.5?	0.1–0.3	*ca.* 0.4	0	0	0
$B(q)$...........	<0.01?	0.05–0.20	0.05–0.25	0.1–0.3	0	0
$N(n)$...........	>0.5?	0.3–0.5	*ca.* 0.5	0.4–0.5	0.1–0.2	0.8–1.0
Rh neg. (r).....	>0.5?	0.4	*ca.* 0.25	0	0	0
Rh° (R°)......	<0.1?	*ca.* 0.1	*ca.* 0.6	*ca.* 0.1	*ca.* 0.01	*ca.* 0.01
PTC†..........	*ca.* 0.5	0.55–0.7	*ca.* 0.45	0	0	0
Nonsecreting‡...	?	*ca.* 0.5	> 0.6	0?	0	?
Other genes§....	?	r'	A 1,2	R^z	R^z	R^z

* For convenience in calculation, the ratio of the two subgroups, A_2 and A_1, and not the ratio of the gene frequencies, p_2/p is given.

† The recessive gene for not tasting phenyl-thio-carbamide.

‡ The recessive gene for not secreting water-soluble blood-group substances into the gastric juice, saliva, etc.

§ Other genes the frequency of which seems to be higher in this population than in other races.

BIBLIOGRAPHY

BOYD, W. C. 1950. *Genetics and the Races of Man.* Boston: Little, Brown & Co.

DOBZHANSKY, T. 1941. *Genetics and the Origin of Species.* New York: Columbia University Press.

EAST, E. M., and JONES, D. F. 1919. *Inbreeding and Outbreeding.* Philadelphia: J. B. Lippincott Co.

FISHER, R. A. 1930. *The Genetical Theory of Natural Selection.* Oxford: Clarendon Press.

GLASS, B. 1943. *Genes and the Man.* New York: New York Bureau of Publications, Teachers College, Columbia University.

HOGBEN, L. 1931. *Genetic Principles in Medicine and Social Science.* London: Williams & Norgate, Ltd.

MAYR, E. 1942. *Systematics and the Origin of Species.* New York: Columbia University Press.

RACE, R. R., and SANGER, R. 1950. *Blood Groups in Man.* Oxford: Blackwell Scientific Publications.

SIMPSON, G. G. 1944. *Tempo and Mode in Evolution.* New York: Columbia University Press.

———. 1949. *The Meaning of Evolution.* New Haven: Yale University Press.

STERN, C. 1949. *Principles of Human Genetics.* San Francisco: W. H. Freeman & Co.

Universal Categories of Culture[1]

By CLYDE KLUCKHOHN

THERE ARE two interrelated problems: Are there fairly definite limits within which cultural variation is constrained by panhuman regularities in biology, psychology, and the processes of social interaction? Do these limits and also the accompanying trends toward similarities in form and content make for categories of culture which are universal in the sense of being both invariant points of reference for description and comparison and, perhaps, substantive uniformities or near-uniformities? This paper will move back and forth between these two slightly different, but closely connected, frames of reference. First, various aspects of the two problems and their implications must be stated in slightly more expanded form.

There is a certain paradox in recent and contemporary anthropological thinking. Radcliffe-Brown and other British anthropologists have characterized social anthropology as "comparative sociology." American anthropologists of late have stressed the cross-cultural approach, and some of us have justified our sometimes rather imperialistic claims to being the *scientia scientiarum* of human studies on the grounds that only anthropologists transcend the limitations of the categories of their own cultures. Yet genuine comparison is possible only if nonculture-bound units have been isolated.[2]

In fact, linguistics alone of the branches of anthropology has discovered elemental units (phonemes, morphemes, and the like) which are universal, objective, and theoretically meaningful. Even physical anthropology, which deals with the biological givens in a single order, is just beginning to grope its way beyond common-sense concepts such as "nose," "young," "middle-aged," and "old." The whole history of science shows that advance depends upon going beyond "common sense" to abstractions that reveal unobvious relations and common properties of isolable aspects of phenomena. Anthropologists, above all, should realize this because "sense" becomes "common" only in terms of cultural convention, particularly in terms of the conventions of implicit culture.

Cultural anthropology has followed two paths, neither of which makes possible a true and complete comparison. A few anthropologists have organized their descriptions largely along the dimensions recognized by the culture being described. The categories chosen

1. The research assistance of Nathan Gould is gratefully acknowledged.

2. The broad tripartite classification of "cultural" (relation of man to nature, man to man, and "subjective aspects"), upon which there has been a large measure of convergence, does not help us much for comparative purposes. For a detailed discussion see Kroeber and Kluckhohn (1952). Perhaps the "seven major facets" of culture elements used in the 1950 edition of Murdock *et al.*, *Outline of Cultural Materials*, see pp. xix ff., takes us a bit further.

are those which appear explicitly in the native language. This method, in the favorable case, gives a view of experience as it appears consciously to the people studied and avoids the distortions that inevitably result when a culture is dismembered and reassembled arbitrarily according to the classifications familiar to Western thought. On the other hand, no approach which neglects the tacit premises and crypto-categories of the implicit culture really presents a unique cultural world in its totality. Moreover—and more to the point for the present discussion—this path represents untrammeled cultural relativism at its extreme. Each distinct culture becomes, indeed, a self-contained monad which can in the nature of the case be compared with others only vaguely, "intuitively," "artistically."

The second path is the one followed, with numerous variations and compromises, by the overwhelming majority of ethnographers. The selected categories are the well-known ones of the "standard" monograph, typically: physical environment; techniques, economic and technological, for coping with this environment; social organization; religion; sometimes language; more recently, "life-cycle" or methods of childhood training and the like. In the first instance these were common-sense concepts corresponding to nineteenth-century Western notions of the all-pervasive framework of human life. They have been slightly modified in accord, on the one hand, with the empirical generalizations summed up under Wissler's "universal culture pattern" and, on the other hand, with changing theoretical fashions (for example, recent attention to nursing habits, toilet training, etc.).

On the whole, these categories have been crudely serviceable and have made certain meaningful comparisons possible. In broad form, though not in content, they represent rough empirical universals into which descriptive data can conveniently be grouped. Comparative analysis is aided by more truly scientific concepts, purposefully created by anthropologists: Linton's "item," "trait," and "activity"; his "form," "function," "use," and "meaning"; his "universals," "alternatives," and "specialties"; Kroeber's three types of patterns; Opler's "themes"; and Herskovits' "focus." But the data obtained in the field which must serve as our materials for a comparative science continue to be perverted, slightly or greatly, by the prescientific nature of our basic categories. The technical processes of farming or weaving (though not the symbolic accretions of these activities) can be compared with relatively little distortion because of their objectivity and of the limiting "givens" of nature. Our concepts, however, of "economics," "religion," and "politics" have a large element of cultural arbitrariness. Probably the main reason that anthropologists have written so little about "political behavior" is the circumstance that they have felt intuitively uncomfortable, unable to isolate in many cultures an order of phenomena strictly comparable to our category of "government."

In cultural anthropology we are still too close to the phase in linguistics when non-European languages were being forcibly recast into the categories of Latin grammar. We can discover and recognize similarities due to historical connection, but nonhistorically derived similarities, other than the most gross and obvious ones, elude us because our frame is too culture-bound and so insufficiently abstract that we can compare only in terms of specific content. The Human Relations Area Files are admirable in intent and decidedly useful in many ways as they stand. Yet it is the testimony of many who have worked intensively with these materials that the Files bring together much which is conceptually distinct, and separate much that ought to be together. An altogether adequate organization of comparative data must await a better working-out of the theory of the universal categories of culture,[3] both structural principles and content categories. Present methods obtain, organize, and compare in ways that beg questions which are themselves at issue. This is the contemporary paradox of the so-called "comparative" science of cultures.

The present paper cannot hope to resolve this paradox. It can at best state the problem more clearly, focus the central issues, indicate some clues as to the lines along which resolution may eventually take place. First, the state of affairs in a sample of recent monographs will be briefly summarized. There will follow a short historical sketch of anthropological thinking about universal categories. Finally, some aids from biology, psychology, and sociology will be mobilized.

An examination was made of the tables of contents of ninety ethnographic monographs published in English within the last twenty years. Of these, four were works on the cultures of contemporary industrial societies. Studies limited to or focused upon single topics were not examined. Rather, the sample was restricted to general accounts of a people and their culture.

Findings may be summarized as follows: There is a stereotyped scheme with numerous but comparatively mi-

nor variations upon it; genuine innovation is exceedingly rare; reports in the second decade of our sample tended strongly to show more conscious theoretical orientation. Variations reflect, in part, shifting conceptual fashions, in part the interests and presumably the temperaments of individual workers.[4]

Avoidance of explicit theoretical frames of reference is particularly marked in certain series, such as *Anthropological Records* and the Bishop Museum publications. However, the majority of studies which have appeared since World War II exhibit a striving toward problem-centered research and toward (sometimes strained) theoretical sophistication. There is also a greater awareness of the dangers of imposing the categories of the anthropologist's culture upon cultures outside the Western tradition. Honigmann, for example, uses "ideational culture" and avoids "religion" in his treatment of the Kaska.

Expectably, comparability is best where description treats of the satisfaction of basic physical needs or por-

3. Murdock *et al.* (1950, p. xix), state that "they have attempted to group inherently related categories in the same section and they have arranged the sections in an order that is not wholly without logic. Beyond this, however, they insist that the classification is wholly pragmatic. . . . Through trial and error . . . the categories have come to represent a sort of common denominator of the ways in which anthropologists, geographers, sociologists, historians, and non-professional recorders of cultural data habitually organize their materials."

4. Commenting on the comparability of community studies of contemporary societies, Steward (1950, p. 25) states: "In a *comparative approach* to contemporary communities, the problems which are studied in one community—or at least the cultural perspectives acquired in any study—are utilized in the investigation of other communities. Ideally, there is some comparability of research projects that have common purposes, problems, and methods. The widely differing characteristics of communities naturally dictate some differences in approach; but individual interests, purposes, and methods have produced even greater differences, and community studies have little in common beyond the fact that they purport to use a cultural approach."

Commenting on the "more purely ethnographic studies," Steward (1950, p. 26; see illustrations of this, pp. 26–27) states: "These show considerable disparity of emphasis because of varied individual interests. The general chapter headings may be more or less similar, but there is a great difference in purpose and problem."

trays customs directly related to the life-cycle or departs from other biologically or physically given points of reference. The proportion of space given to various topics reflects, of course, theoretical orientation and personal interests.[5] In general, the distribution of attention appears somewhat more "objective" or better balanced in the monographs of the pre–World War II period when theory was less explicit. Reading of prefaces and introductions makes it clear that exigencies of the field situation were also important in influencing the kind and amount of data collected. Finally, there are the technical problems and limitations which Herskovits has discussed.[6]

In short, careful examination confirms an initial impression that the data recorded in recent anthropological monographs are only roughly, loosely, and for certain purposes comparable. About 1939 Malinowski began to publish what he later called his "universal

institutional types."[7] What is substantially a revision of this has recently been presented by Nadel (1951, pp. 135 ff.). However, no ethnography has yet been published which organizes its materials in accord with this theoretical system. Similarly, Leslie White has discussed universal categories of a Morgan-Engels-Marx sort, but his published studies of cultures follow the traditional pattern. The situation remains as Evans-Pritchard described it (1940, p. 261): "These weighty volumes generally record observations in too haphazard a fashion to be either pleasant or profitable reading. This deficiency is due to absence of a body of scientific theory in Social Anthropology."

---

5. Steward (1950, p. 28), who analyzed the relative amount of space accorded different subjects in community studies to determine differences of emphasis, states in summary: "The amount of space devoted to a subject depends somewhat, of course, upon its functional importance in the community. *Nonetheless, even substantially similar communities are given quite unlike treatment, which reflects individual purposes and methods even more than differences in facts*" (my italics).

Discussing "the more purely ethnographic studies" of community life, Steward states that "even these show considerable disparity of emphasis because of varied individual interests. The general chapter headings may be more or less similar, but there is a great difference in purpose and problem. The Lynds' studies of Middletown [1929, 1937] are concerned with how economic factors and changes affect community life, which is described in most of its aspects. West's *Plainville* [1945], Yang's Chinese Village [1945], and Hsu's study of a Chinese community [1948] are interested in the interrelation of culture and personality, and following the current approach to this problem, they accord considerable space to the 'life cycle'—the development

of the individual in the culture. Parsons' Mexican [1936] and Ecuadorian [1945] studies have the very different purpose of determining the native Indian and Spanish elements in the culture of her communities. Redfield's study of Yucatan [1941], though dealing with folk cultures not unlike those recorded by Parsons, is preoccupied with the transformation of folk societies under urbanizing influences. And Fei's monographs on Chinese peasants [e.g., Fei and Chang, 1945], through reporting on people who are similar to those studied by Yang and Hsu, are concerned with rural economy in its relationship to community types and show no interest in culture and personality."

6. "It is impossible for any study of a culture . . . to describe more than a portion of the aspects of the life of a single people. Even those whose aim is to give the most rounded portrayal possible find certain limits which, for technical reasons of time, space and competence they cannot exceed. In practice, language is left to the specialist, and so is music. If any attempt is made to include expressions of the literary arts, this material must commonly be reserved for separate treatment because of its bulk. Some aspects of culture are rarely studied as such; forms of dramatic expression, for instance, since in non-literate societies drama is customarily a part of ritual. The dance, also, has too rarely been analyzed, because of the technical difficulties it presents in the way of valid recording" (1948, p. 238).

7. For his final version see *A Scientific Theory of Culture* (1944, pp. 62 ff.).

Many of the earlier anthropologists were certain that there were universal categories[8] for culture or universal categories which underlay all cultures. Witness the "stages" of the evolutionists and the "elementary ideas" of Bastian. Boas[9] called chapter VI of the 1911 edition of *The Mind of Primitive Man* "The Universality of Culture Traits" and says:

We may therefore base our further considerations on the theory of the similarity of mental functions in all races. Observation has shown, however, that not only emotions, intellect, and will-power of man are alike everywhere, but that much more detailed similarities in thought and action occur among the most diverse peoples.

But, in general, from about this time on, the attention of anthropologists throughout the world appears to have been directed overwhelmingly to the distinctiveness of each culture and to the differences in human custom as opposed to the similarities. The latter, where recognized, were explained historically rather than in terms of the common nature of man and certain invariant properties of the human situation. In the case of the United States, there was the added factor of the anti-theoretical bias of American anthropologists for at least a generation.

Between roughly 1910 and roughly 1940 the only significant anthropological advance[10] in formulating the basic principles upon which all cultures rest appears to be represented by Wissler's discussion of the universal culture pattern, in 1923.[11] However, workers in other disciplines were attempting to establish regularities in human response which transcended cultural difference. Durkheim, Mauss, and other French sociologists propounded their famous principles of collective representations, reciprocity, and the like. Simmel looked for social regularities of a somewhat different type. Birkhoff in his *Aesthetic Measure* tried to develop panhuman canons of artistic response.[12] Zipf discovered the k-constant, applied the harmonic principle to social behavior, and, a little later, enunciated his so-called "law of least effort." The psychoanalysts tried to show the universality of the Oedipus complex, sibling rivalry, and certain sorts of fantasy and symbolic processes. Human geography, in France and elsewhere, abandoned simplist "environmental determinism" in favor of the view that there was a high correlation between certain aspects of culture, especially types of social organization, and certain ecological situations.

These and other movements had an impact upon anthropology. There was probably also within the profession an increasing skepticism of the tautology that culture alone begets or determines culture and of the proposition that culture is purely and solely the precipitate

8. For brief discussions of the history of theories of the universal culture pattern see Murdock (1945) and Herskovits (1948).

9. In the 1938 edition of the same work Boas (p. 195) says: "There is no reason why we should accept Bastian's renunciation. The dynamic forces that mould social life are the same now as those that moulded life thousands of years ago. We can follow the intellectual and emotional drives that actuate man at present and that shape his actions and thoughts."

10. Linton's *Study of Man* (1936) did significantly advance some theoretical aspects. For example, he discusses "the universal reactions of man," such as the dependence of human beings upon emotional responses from one another—a factor to which William James had directed attention.

11. In a sense, as Mr. Gould has pointed out to me, enumerative definitions of culture, of which Tylor's is the classical illustration, may be viewed as statements of the categories of the universal pattern.

12. Cf. a recent statement by Raymond Firth (1951): "I believe that there are universal standards of aesthetic quality, just as there are universal standards of technical efficiency." Such standards are based on "similar psychological impulses."

of the accidents of history.[13] At all events Radcliffe-Brown led off an anthropological search for "universal social laws" in the English-speaking world. Chapple and Arensberg, stimulated alike by Simmel, Radcliffe-Brown, and Malinowski, attempted to establish quantitatively invariant properties of social interaction. Murdock, departing from the Sumner-Keller sociological tradition and from Wissler and other American anthropologists, likewise initiated quantitative work with the aim of factoring out the specifically historical and establishing cross-cultural trends and tendencies. His founding of the Cross-cultural Survey in the thirties appears to have been largely a means

13. The most impressive theoretical statement by an anthropologist signalizing a return to universal processes and factors is contained in A. V. Kidder's paper "Looking Backward" (1940):

"In both hemispheres man started from cultural scratch, as a nomadic hunter, a user of stone tools, a palaeolithic savage. In both he spread over great continents and shaped his life to cope with every sort of environment. Then, in both hemispheres, wild plants were brought under cultivation; population increased; concentrations of people brought elaboration of social groupings and rapid progress in the arts. Pottery came into use, fibres and wools were woven into cloth, animals were domesticated, metal working began—first in gold and copper, then in the harder alloy, bronze. Systems of writing were evolved.

"Not only in material things do the parallels hold. In the New World as well as in the Old, priesthoods grew and, allying themselves with temporal powers, or becoming rulers in their own right, reared to their gods vast temples adorned with painting and sculpture. The priests and chiefs provided for themselves elaborate tombs richly stocked for the future life. In political history it is the same. In both hemispheres group joined group to form tribes; coalitions and conquests brought preeminence; empires grew and assumed the paraphernalia of glory.

"These are astonishing similarities. And if we believe, as most modern students do, that the Indians' achievement was made independently, and that their progress was not stimulated from overseas, then we reach a very significant

to this end.[14] Roheim and other psychoanalytically oriented anthropologists put Freudian theory to the test of field work. Leighton, an anthropologically experienced psychiatrist, formulated, in *The Governing of Men* and *Human Relations in a Changing World,* some principles about raw or subcultural human nature. Forde, Richards, and others in British anthropology and Steward and others in American anthropology put the search for the environmental determinants of culture upon a new and more sophisticated basis. Steward's 1938 paper, "Ecological Aspects of Southwestern Society," was a particularly notable demonstration of certain relationships between forms of social organization and geographical situation.

Two cross-disciplinary papers in which each team of writers included an anthropologist attempted to sketch out the more abstract foundations for a system of categories that would permit true cross-cultural comparability. A quotation from the first of these is appropriate because the present paper represents essentially a modification and a development of the same point of view:[15]

conclusion. We can infer that human beings possess an innate urge to take certain definite steps toward what we call civilization. And that men also possess the innate ability, given proper environmental conditions, to put that urge into effect. In other words, we must consider that civilization is an inevitable response to laws governing the growth of culture and controlling the man-culture relationship."

14. In "The Cross-cultural Survey" (1940, p. 366), Murdock remarks: "To the extent that culture is ideational, we may conclude all cultures should reveal certain similarities, flowing from the universal laws governing the symbolic, mental processes, *e.g.,* the worldwide parallels in the principles of magic."

15. Lynd (1939, p. 124) provides the same clue: ". . . the error lies in seeking to derive the laws of social science from study of sequences observed in a single set of historically conditioned *institutions, qua institutions,* rather than from study of the *full range of*

The following model is intended to cut across ... specialized and narrow abstractions. It does not rest on ... assumptions about "human nature" but abstracts immediately from the concrete behavior of men in social systems. ... Variations in the patterning of different social systems are indefinitely numerous. The principle on which the present outline has been built up is, however, that these variations are grouped about certain *invariant points of reference*. These are to be found in the nature of social systems, in the biological and psychological nature of the component individuals, in the external situations in which they live and act, in the nature of action itself, in the necessity of its coordination in social systems. In the orientation of individuals these "foci" of structure are never ignored. They must in some way be "adapted to" or "taken account of." The ... three main classes of patterns [situational, instrumental, and integrative] are coherently grouped because of their relation in each case to a related group of these foci of patterning. In the first case it is certain facts about the situation in which men are placed, their biological nature and descent, their psychological nature. In the second it is the content of the differentiated functional roles by virtue of which a system of interdependent units becomes possible. In the third, finally, it is certain necessities of the coordinated functioning of a social system as a whole.[16]

The second paper, "The Functional Prerequisites of a Society" (Aberle *et al.*, 1950), refines and elaborates one aspect of the conceptual scheme just referred to. The theoretical takeoff is as follows:

A comparative social science requires a generalized system of concepts which will enable the scientific observer to compare and contrast large bodies of concretely different social phenomena in consistent terms. A promising social analysis is a tentative formulation of the functional prerequisites of a society. Functional prerequisites refer broadly to the things that must get done in any society if it is to continue as a going concern, *i.e.*, the generalized conditions necessary for the maintenance of the system concerned. The specific structural arrangements for meeting the functional prerequisites differ, of course, from one society to another and, in the course of time, change in any given society. Thus all societies must allocate goods and services somehow. A particular society may change from one method, say business enterprise, to another, say a centrally planned economy, without the destruction of the society as a society but merely with a change in its concrete structures.

Florence Kluckhohn (1950), combining sociological and anthropological thinking and conclusions, has provided a frame for comparing the profiles exhibited by different cultures with respect to their premises, tacit and overt, about five universal human problems: "what are the innate predispositions of man? what is the relation of man to nature? what is the significant time dimension? what is the direction in time of the action process? what type of personality is to be most valued? what is the dominant modality of the relationship of man to other men?" Assuming that "all societies find a phraseology within a range of possible phraseologies of basic human problems," she notes: "The problems as stated are constant; they arise inevitably out of the human situation. The phraseology of them is variable but variable only within limits."

Human biology sets limits, supplies potentialities and drives, provides clues which cultures neglect or elaborate.[17] This is standard anthropological doctrine at present, and it may turn out that this is about all there is to it. Yet

behavior around the functional cores these institutions express."

16. J. F. Dunlop, M. P. Gilmore, C. Kluckhohn, T. Parsons, and O. H. Taylor, "Toward a Common Language for the Area of Social Science" (mimeographed, 1941). The above quotation appears in the portion of the complete memorandum printed in T. Parsons (1949).

17. For a recent review see Bergman (1952).

when one learns that the introduction of an electric needle into a certain cortical area of one species of monkey results in these monkeys thereafter defecating upon their own kind, whereas previously they would defecate only upon strangers, one wonders if, after all, there may not be specific biological bases for certain of our social habits.[18] At all events, there is general recognition of the social and cultural implications of such elementary biological facts as the existence of two sexes, the ordinary human life-span, the dependency of human infants (of which the psychoanalysts have made so much). Those features of human cultures such as family life which have their counterparts in lower primates and other mammals presumably have a rather definite biological base. This assumption has recently been discussed by Marston Bates (1950, p. 162 and *passim*) and by Ford and Beach (1951, pp. 3 ff.). Allee's (1951) studies of patterns of social co-operation among animals are also highly suggestive both for biological and for social determinants of universal categories of culture.

The biological leads easily into the psychological. The ways, for instance, in which biological dependency is transformed into psychological dependency have often been discussed. Dreaming, which has surely given rise to many cultural parallels, is both a biological and a psychological process. And the biological nature of man plus his

18. Current experiments at the Orange Park primate laboratory are also interesting. Give chimpanzees an incomplete circle, and they will fill it in, and they will draw a cross to complete the symmetry of a design. This and Schiller's work on perceptual completion suggest a specific biological basis, shared by humans and other primates, for certain tendencies toward closure manifested in human cultures. The facts are well established that such behavior as nursing and walking are dependent more on the myelination of the relevant nerve tracts and less on sociocultural factors than had previously been thought.

psychological capabilities and predispositions interact with certain universalities in man's social interactions and other features of his environing situation. As Bates and others have shown, the sheer territorial dimension of human existence has its effects upon culture. In various studies Steward has generalized some of these. Given the principle of limitation of possibilities, independent parallel developments have occurred again and again. As Steward (1949) says, for example:

In densely settled areas, internal needs will produce an orderly interrelationship of environment, subsistence patterns, special groupings, occupational specializations, and overall political, religious, and perhaps military integrating factors. These interrelated institutions do not have unlimited variability, for they must be adapted to the requirements of subsistence patterns established in particular environments; they involve a cultural ecology.

In psychological language the generalization is that human beings are so constituted that, particularly under conditions of extreme stress, they will often react in roughly similar ways to the same pressures. Nativistic movements constitute a case much studied of late by anthropologists. Details vary widely in accord with the pre-existing cultures, but the broad patterns are very much alike. Marie Bonaparte (1947) has demonstrated that at the time of the fall of France in 1940 a tale with the same general theme ("the myth of the corpse in the car") was told over widely separated areas within such a brief period that the possibility of diffusion must be ruled out. There is considerable evidence of parallelisms in fantasy productions arising over long periods and under "normal" conditions among peoples who cannot be presumed to have had direct or indirect historical contact within a relevant time range. Rank (1914), for instance, has demonstrated remarkable similarities in widespread myths of heroes. In spite of the fact that many psychoanalytic writers have run Freudian theories of panhuman sexual symbolism into the ground, there remain arresting and irreducible resemblances among such symbolisms in the most historically diverse cultures.

Throughout, one can recognize the empirical convergences without necessarily accepting the psychoanalytic interpretations. Thus one can pay due regard to Bonaparte's data without allegiance to her "human sacrifice" explanation. Nevertheless I should like to repeat what I have recently written about psychoanalysis and anthropology (Kluckhohn and Morgan, 1951):

I still believe that some of the cautions uttered by Boas and others on the possible extravagances of interpretations in terms of universal symbolism, completely or largely divorced from minute examination of cultural context, are sound. But the facts uncovered in my own field work and that of my collaborators have forced me to the conclusion that Freud and other psychoanalysts have depicted with astonishing correctness many central themes in motivational life which are universal. The styles of expression of these themes and much of the manifest content are culturally determined, but the underlying psychologic drama transcends cultural difference.

This should not be too surprising—except to an anthropologist overindoctrinated with the theory of cultural relativism—for many of the inescapable givens of human life are also universal. Human anatomy and human physiology are, in the large, about the same the world over. There are two sexes with palpably visible differences in external genitalia and secondary sexual characteristics. All human infants, regardless of culture, know the psychological experience of helplessness and dependency. Situations making for competition for the affection of one or both parents, for sibling rivalry can be to some extent channeled this way or that way by a culture but they cannot be eliminated, given the universality of family life. The trouble has been —because of a series of accidents of intel-

lectual and political history—that the anthropologist for two generations has been obsessed with the differences between peoples, neglecting the equally real similarities—upon which the "universal culture pattern" as well as the psychological uniformities are clearly built.

A. V. Kidder[19] some time ago put the general case cautiously but wisely:

The question . . . is: does culture, although not biologically transmitted, develop and function in response to tendencies—it is perhaps too connotative to call them law—that are comparable to those controlling biological evolution? There seems to be evidence that, in some degree at least, it does. All over the world and among populations that could apparently not possibly have come into contact with each other, similar inventions have been made and have been made in a seemingly predetermined order. Extraordinary similarities are to be observed in the nature and order of appearance among widely separated peoples of certain social practices and religious observances.

These are likenesses, not identities; history, to reverse the proverb, never repeats itself; different environments and differing opportunities have seen to that. But they do seem to indicate that there are definite tendencies and orderlinesses, both in the growth of this compelling force and in man's responses thereto. It is therefore the task of the disciplines concerned with man and his culture—genetics, history, archaeology, sociology, the humanities—to gather and to correlate information which may enable us more fully to understand these now dimly perceived trends and relationships.

Anthropologists have been rightly criticized by sociologists and certain psychologists for neglecting the universalities in interaction processes, the common elements in the structuring of social action. To some extent, as suggested earlier, this has been corrected in recent years by the work of the Brit-

19. Mimeographed document from the Carnegie Institution, quoted in Steward (1950, p. 118).

ish social anthropologists and such Americans as Chapple and Arensberg. It does appear that groups as such have certain basic properties. One may instance Lewin's concept of quasi-stationary equilibrium (cf. Wilson, 1951). A philosopher (Riezler, 1950) has just published a penetrating study of the constant and the variable in human social life which raises many issues too often overlooked by anthropologists.

My colleague, Professor George Homans, has investigated, with the aid of his seminar, the relations between mother's brother and sister's son, father's sister and her brother's son, and brothers and sisters in a considerable range of nonliterate societies. Homans operates upon the hypothesis that there are discoverable structural laws for social conduct in all human societies, but he informs me that this investigation only partially bore out this hypothesis. For the first two relationships there appeared to be patterns that transcended cultural differences. These relationships evidenced considerable regularity, but the relations between brothers and sisters were irregular in the same societies. In some, stringent avoidance was enjoined; in others, brothers and sisters were permitted to be what Lévi-Strauss has called "chaste companions of the bed." The difference seemed to be traceable not to principles of social structure but rather to cultural values, specifically the varying emphasis upon internal as opposed to external controls for moral behavior. I suspect that this work of Homans[20] may represent a broader paradigm: some aspects of culture take their specific forms solely as a result of historical accidents; others are tailored by forces which can properly be designated as universal.

20. Homans has been strongly influenced by Chapple, Arensberg, and other anthropologists who have tried to limit themselves to observable social interaction analyzed in terms of a few simple concepts (cf. 1950).

It is possible, of course, to follow Kroeber (1949)[21] and regard cross-cultural likenesses as being subcultural—as the limits and conditions of culture:

Such more or less recurrent near-regularities of form or process as have to date been formulated for culture are actually mainly sub-cultural in nature. They are limits set to culture by physical or organic factors. The so-called "cultural constants" of family, religion, war, communication, and the like appear to be biopsychological frames variably filled with cultural content, so far as they are more than categories reflecting the compartments of our own Occidental logico-verbal culture. Of processes, diffusion and socialization are both only psychological learning, imitation, and suggestion under special conditions. Custom is psychobiological habit on a social scale and carrying cultural values.

But the universals are part of cultures in the sense that they are incorporated and socially transmitted. Moreover, the "so-called 'cultural constants'" are not mere empty frames. In the case of language, for instance, there are also striking resemblances within the frame. Every phonology is a system, not a random congeries of sound-classes. The differentiating principles of a phonetic system are applied with some consistency to sounds produced in more than one position. In a study just published Jakobson and others (1952) assert: "The inherent distinctive features which we detect in the languages of the world and which underlie their entire lexical and morphological stock amount to twelve binary oppositions." All languages are made up of "vowels" and "consonants." Meaningful utterances in all languages arise from combining morphemes, and there are certain other generalized properties of morphophonemics. All languages exhibit a high degree of flexibility with

21. For a reply to Kroeber's often expressed view that categories, like "sacrifice," are "fake universals" see Lévi-Strauss, *Twentieth Century Sociology*, pp. 523 ff.

respect to the meanings that can be expressed. The subject-predicate form of expression is universal so far as extended and connected discourse is concerned. Possession or the genitive is expressed in all languages. This list could be considerably extended.[22]

It can be argued that even these congruences in content reflect subcultural "limits." That is, the facts that the range of number of phonemes in human languages is narrow and that all languages appear to embrace between five and ten thousand morphemes can be interpreted as reflecting only certain limits of human anatomy and physiology which, assuming the principle of economy or "least effort," make a language based upon forty thousand combinations of two phonemes most unlikely (since the human nervous system is not equipped to "code" and "decode" that fast). The same argument can be advanced as regards the limited range of variation in number of kinship terms and the fundamental contrasts in principles of kinship systems which Murdock has published. However, it is not important whether these phenomena be regarded as universal categories *of* culture or universal categories *for* the comparison of cultures. They reflect, admittedly, "limits" or "conditions" and are in this sense "subcultural."

But it should be noted in passing that features which no one would dispute as cultural are also limiting conditions to other aspects of culture. Thus Boas (1940) has said: "We may . . . consider exogamy as the condition on which totemism arose." Fortes (1949) and Firth (1951) have asserted:

The hypothesis that all kinship institutions derive from the facts of sex, procreation, and child-rearing is acceptable if the emphasis is laid not on their biological and utilitarian value but on the moral values attached by society to these facts, and perpetuated through the social relationships brought into being by their conjunction. . . . The existence of a social system necessitates, in fact, a moral system for its support.

In any case, the crucial point is this: *biological, psychological, and sociosituational universals afford the possibility of comparison of cultures in terms which are not ethnocentric, which depart from "givens," begging no needless questions.*

Most anthropologists would agree that no constant elemental units like atoms, cells, or genes have as yet been satisfactorily established with culture in general.[23] Many would insist that within one aspect of culture, namely, language, such constant elemental units have been isolated: phonemes[24] and morphemes. It is arguable whether such units are, in principle, discoverable in sectors of culture less automatic than speech and less closely tied (in some ways) to biological fact.[25]

22. While most of the points in this and the following paragraph have been familiar to me and used in my lectures for some years, this statement in its present form owes much to a lecture delivered by Dr. Joseph Greenberg in April, 1952, to the staff of the Laboratory of Social Relations, Harvard University. I am grateful to Dr. Greenberg for this help and stimulation.

23. Much of the remaining portion of this paper is drawn, in slightly modified form, from a monograph (*Culture* ["Papers of the Peabody Museum of Harvard University"], in press) by A. L. Kroeber and C. Kluckhohn. While most of the paragraphs utilized here were originally drafted by Kluckhohn, they have been improved by Dr. Kroeber, to whom gratitude is expressed for permission to reuse in this form.

24. R. Jakobson (1949) remarks: "Linguistic analysis with its concept of ultimate phonemic entities signally converges with modern physics which revealed the granular structure of matter as composed of elementary particles."

25. Wiener (1948) and Lévi-Strauss (1951) also present contrasting views on the possibilities of discovering lawful regularities in anthropological data. Wiener argues (*a*) that the obtainable statistical runs are not long enough and (*b*) that observers modify the

Kroeber feels that it is highly unlikely that any such constant elemental
units will be discovered. Their place is
on lower, more basic levels of organization of phenomena. Here and there suggestions have been ventured that there
are such basic elements: the culture
trait, for instance, or the small community of face-to-face relations. But no
such hints have been systematically developed by their proponents, let alone
accepted by others. Culture traits can
obviously be divided and subdivided
and resubdivided at will, according to
occasion or need. Or, for that matter,
they are often combined into larger
complexes which are still treatable, in
ad hoc situations, as unitary traits and
are, in fact, ordinarily spoken of as
traits in such situations. The face-to-
face community, of course, is not actually a unit of culture but the supposed
unit of *social* reference or frame for
what might be called a "minimal culture." At that, even such a social unit
has in most cases no sharply defined
actual limits.

As for the larger groups of phenomena like religion that make up "the universal pattern"—or even subdivisions of
these such as "crisis rites" or "fasting"
—these are recurrent indeed, but they
are not uniform. Anyone can make a
definition that will separate magic from
religion; but no one has yet found a
definition that all other students ac-

cept: the phenomenal contents of the
concepts of religion and magic simply
intergrade too much. This is true even
though almost everyone would agree
in differentiating large masses of specific phenomena as respectively religious and magical—supplicating a powerful but unseen deity in the heavens,
for instance, as against sticking a pin
into an effigy. In short, concepts like religion and magic have an undoubted
heuristic utility in given situations. But
they are altogether too fluid in conceptual range for use either as strict categories or as units from which larger
concepts can be built up. After all, they
are in origin common-sense concepts,
like "boy," "youth," "man," "old man,"
which neither physiologists nor psychologists will wholly discard but
which they will also not attempt to include among the elementary units and
basic concepts upon which they rear
their sciences.

This conclusion of Kroeber's is akin
to what Boas said about social-science
methodology in 1930: "The analysis of
the phenomena is our prime object.
Generalizations will be more significant
the closer we adhere to definite forms.
The attempts to reduce all social phenomena to a closed system of laws applicable to every society and explaining its structure and history do not
seem a promising undertaking" (Boas,
1930, p. 268). The significance of generalizations is proportional to the def-
initeness of the forms and concepts
analyzed out of phenomena—in this
seems to reside the weakness of the
uniformities in culture heretofore suggested; they are *indefinite*.

A case on the other side is put as
follows by Julian Steward (1949) in
his important paper: "Cultural Causality and Law: A Trial Formulation of
the Development of Early Civilization":

It is not necessary that any formulation
of cultural regularities provide an ultimate

phenomena by their conscious study of them.
Lévi-Strauss replies that linguistics at least
can meet these two objections and suggests
that certain aspects of social organization can
also be studied in ways that obviate the difficulties. It may be added that Wiener has remarked in conversation with one of us that
he is convinced of the practicability of devising new mathematical instruments which
would permit of satisfactory treatment of social-science facts. Finally, note Murdock's
(1949, p. 259) finding: "Cultural forms in
the field of social organization reveal a degree
of regularity and of conformity to scientific
law not significantly inferior to that found in
the so-called natural sciences."

explanation of culture change. In the physical and biological sciences, formulations are merely approximations of observed regularities, and they are valid as working hypotheses despite their failure to deal with ultimate realities. So long as a cultural law formulates recurrences of similar inter-relationships of phenomena, it expresses cause and effect in the same way that the law of gravity formulates but does not ultimately explain the attraction between masses of matter. Moreover, like the law of gravity, which has been greatly modified by the theory of relativity, any formulation of cultural data may be useful as a working hypothesis, even though further research requires that it be qualified or reformulated.

Cultural regularities may be formulated on different levels, each in its own terms. At present, the greatest possibilities lie in the purely cultural or superorganic level, for anthropology's traditional primary concern with culture has provided far more data of this kind. Moreover, the greater part of culture history is susceptible to treatment only in superorganic terms. Both sequential or diachronic formulations and synchronic formulations are superorganic, and they may be functional to the extent that the data permit. Redfield's tentative formulation that urban culture contrasts with folk culture in being more individualized, secularized, heterogeneous, and disorganized is synchronic, superorganic, and functional. Morgan's evolutionary schemes and White's formulation concerning the relationship of energy to cultural development are sequential and somewhat functional. Neither type, however, is wholly one or the other. A time-dimension is implied in Redfield's formulation, and synchronic, functional relationships are implied in White's. . . .

The present statement of scientific purpose and methodology rests on a conception of culture that needs clarification. *If the more important institutions of culture can be isolated from their unique setting so as to be typed, classified, and related to recurring antecedents or functional correlates, it follows that it is possible to consider the institutions in question as the basic or constant ones, whereas the features that lend uniqueness are the second-ary or variable ones.* For example, the American high civilizations had agriculture, social classes, and a priest-temple-idol cult. As types, these institutions are abstractions of what was actually present in each area, and they do not take into account the particular crops grown, the precise patterning of the social classes, or the conceptualization of deities, details of ritual, and other religious features of each culture center.

There are, admittedly, few genuine uniformities in culture content unless one states the content in extremely general form—e.g., clothing, shelter, incest taboos, and the like. There are mainly what Kidder has called "likenesses rather than identities." The seventy-two items listed by Murdock (1949, p. 124) "which occur, so far as the author's knowledge goes, in every culture known to history or ethnography" are mainly blanket categories of the "universal ground plan," though a few, such as "modesty concerning natural functions," approach a certain kind of specificity. This list could doubtless be extended. Hallowell[26] in an unpublished paper has suggested self-concepts. Even the most exhaustive list, however, would have to be purged of culture-bound or partially culture-bound categories before it could serve more than the rough heuristic utility suggested by Herskovits' (1948, p. 239) comment on the organization of a "rounded study of a culture":

The assumptions that underlie the progression of topics in such a presentation is that of most descriptive studies. They derive from a logic that proceeds from the consideration of those aspects that supply the physical wants of man, to those that order social relations, and finally to the aspects which, in giving meaning to the universe, sanction everyday living, and in their aesthetic manifestations afford men

26. "The Self and Its Behavioral Environment." To appear in: Geza Roheim (ed.), *Psychoanalysis and the Social Sciences*, Vol. IV.

some of the deepest satisfactions they experience.

A few rather specific content universals have been mentioned earlier. A few others could also be mustered. As Murdock has shown, the nuclear family is universal either as the sole prevailing form or as the basic unit from which more complex familial forms are compounded. Boas (1911) remarked that "the three personal pronouns—I, thou, and he—occur in all human languages."[27] Unilateral preferential cross-cousin marriage takes rather consistently different forms in matrilateral than in patrilateral societies. Institutionalized female homosexuality appears to be largely, if not completely, absent in matrilateral societies.

But, in general, one, *of course*, expects uniqueness in detail—this follows from the very essence of culture theory. As Steward remarks in the passage just quoted, the secondary or variable features of culture naturally exhibit distinctiveness. After all, the *content* of different atoms and of different cells is by no means identical. These are constant elemental units of *form*. Wissler, Murdock, and others have shown that there are a considerable number of categories and of structural principles found in all cultures. Fortes (1949) speaks of kinship as an "irreducible principle of Tale social organization." It appears to be an irreducible principle of all cultures, however much its elaboration and the emphasis upon it may vary. When Fortes also says that "every social system presupposes such basic axioms," he is likewise pointing to a constant elemental unit of each and every culture.

The inescapable fact of cultural relativism does not justify the conclusion that cultures are in all respects utterly disparate monads and hence strictly noncomparable entities. If this were

27. For a fuller discussion of the implications of this and related facts, see Riezler (1950).

literally true, a comparative science of culture would be *ex hypothesi* impossible. It is, unfortunately, the case that up to this point anthropology has not solved very satisfactorily the problem of describing cultures in such a way that objective comparison is possible. Most cultural monographs organize the data in terms of the categories of our own contemporary Western culture: economics, technology, social organization, and the like. Such an ordering, of course, tears many of the facts from their own actual context and loads the analysis. The implicit assumption is that our categories are "given" by nature—an assumption contradicted most emphatically by these very investigations of different cultures. A smaller number of studies have attempted to present the information consistently in terms of the category system and whole way of thought of the culture being described. This approach obviously excludes the immediate possibility of a complete set of common terms of reference for comparison. Such a system of comparable concepts and terms remains to be worked out and will probably be established only gradually.

In principle, however, there is a generalized framework that underlies the more apparent and striking facts of cultural relativity. All cultures constitute so many somewhat distinct answers to essentially the same questions posed by human biology and by the generalities of the human situation. These are the considerations explored by Wissler under the heading of "the universal culture pattern" and by Murdock under the rubric of "the least common denominators of cultures." Every society's patterns for living must provide approved and sanctioned ways for dealing with such universal circumstances as the existence of two sexes; the helplessness of infants; the need for satisfaction of the elementary biological requirements such as food, warmth, and sex;

the presence of individuals of different ages and of differing physical and other capacities. The basic similarities in human biology the world over are vastly more massive than the variations. Equally, there are certain necessities in social life for this kind of animal, regardless of where that life is carried on or in what culture. Co-operation to obtain subsistence and for other ends requires a certain minimum of reciprocal behavior, of a standard system of communication, and, indeed, of mutually accepted values. The facts of human biology and of human gregariousness supply, therefore, certain invariant points of reference from which cross-cultural comparison can start without begging questions that are themselves at issue. As Wissler pointed out, the broad outlines of the ground plan of all cultures are and have to be about the same because men always and everywhere are faced with certain unavoidable problems which arise out of the situation "given" by nature. Since most of the patterns of all cultures crystallize around the same foci, there are significant respects in which each culture is not wholly isolated, self-contained, disparate but rather related to and comparable with all other cultures.

Valid cross-cultural comparison could best proceed from the invariant points of reference supplied by the biological, psychological, and sociosituational "givens" of human life. These and their interrelations determine the likenesses in the broad categories and general assumptions that pervade all cultures because the "givens" provide foci around which and within which the patterns of every culture crystallize. Hence comparison can escape from the bias of any distinct culture by taking as its frame of reference natural limits, conditions, clues, and pressures. Cultural concepts are human artifacts, but the conceptualization of nature is enough bound by stubborn and irreducible fact so that

organisms having the same kind of nervous system will at the very least understand one another, relatively free from arbitrary convention. Hartmann, Kris, and Lowenstein (1951, pp. 13–14) have well joined the various kinds of determinants in this statement from a (tempered) psychoanalytic viewpoint:

The "ubiquity" of certain symbols, particularly of sexual symbols, seems accountable if we keep in mind how fundamentally similar every human infant's situation in the adult world is; how limited the number of meaningful situations is which the infant invests with affect; how typical and invariant the infant's anxieties are, and finally how uniform some of his basic perceptions and bodily sensations are bound to be. The fact that most sexual symbols are related to parts of the body and their function has repeatedly been pointed out. These functions are familiar from a large number of experiences of the child and these experiences themselves are organized in the image of the body, one of the apparatus of the ego. However far the differentiation of human behavior by environmental influences may go, the basic relationship of precepts to parts of the body, of movements to the impulses to caress or hurt, to eliminate or to include, to receive or to retain—at least to these—not only form the basis for the formation of symbols but are equally the basis for the universality of nonverbal communication . . . not only the body is "human"; the fact that the personality is structured, that verbalization is part of the function of the apparatus of all men, that the transition from primary to secondary processes in the child's development, etc., are universal, is bound to influence the formation of symbols. . . . We expect to find "limits" of ubiquity and cultural variations and superimposed symbolic meanings around an ubiquitous core.

. . . Propositions dealing with the oedipus complex imply similar assumptions: the fetalization of the human and the extraordinary dependence of the infant on adult (maternal) care and protection, the development of impulses of a genital order at a time when the child lives among adults, is attached to them and at the same time still totally dependent on them, is the nucleus of a conflict situation which we believe to be universal.

The next step is to organize data and write an ethnography within the framework of the invariant points of reference. The first serious trial will not be easy, but it should be rewarding.

In conclusion, it should be explicitly recognized that this procedure, like any other scientific method, has its cost as well as its gain. In this case, however, the cost would not be greater than in most current practice. This involves abstraction and relative neglect of how the events or patterns described appear or "feel" from the standpoint of participants (cf. Riezler, 1950). It is a question of what MacLeod (1947)[28] has

28. Quoted in Hallowell, *op. cit.*

called "the sociological bias," analogous to the stimulus-receptor bias in the field of perception:

This bias in its most common form involves the acceptance of the structures and processes of society as defined by the sociologist as the true coordinates for the specification of behavior and experience. From this point of view, *e.g.*, the church or the political party in which the individual possesses membership, is regarded as an institution of society, possessing the manifold properties and functions which a many-sided sociological investigation reveals, rather than as the church or political party as it is apprehended and reacted to by the individual. The process of social adjustment, of socialization or of attitude formation thus becomes defined in terms of a set of norms which have reality for the scientific observer, but not necessarily for the individual concerned.

REFERENCES

ABERLE, D.; COHEN, A.; DAVIS, A.; LEVY, M.; and SUTTON, F. 1950. "The Functional Prerequisites of a Society," *Ethics*, LX, No. 2, 100–111.

ALLEE, W. C. 1951. *Cooperation among Animals: With Human Implications.* New York: Henry Schuman.

BATES, MARSTON. 1950. *The Nature of Natural History.* New York: Charles Scribner's Sons.

BERGMAN, R. A. M. 1952. "The Biological Foundations of Society," *Civilisations*, II, No. 1, 1–15.

BOAS, FRANZ. 1911. *Mind of Primitive Man.* New York: Macmillan Co.

———. 1940. "The Origin of Totemism." In his *Race, Language, and Culture*, pp. 316–23. New York: Macmillan Co.

BONAPARTE, MARIE. 1947. *Myths of War.* London: Imago Publishing Co.

EVANS-PRITCHARD, E. E. 1940. *The Nuer.* Oxford: Clarendon Press.

FEI HSIAO-TUNG and CHANG CHIH-I. 1945. *Earthbound China: A Study of Rural Economy in Yünnan.* Chicago: University of Chicago Press.

FIRTH, RAYMOND. 1951. *Elements of Social Organization.* New York: Philosophical Library.

FORD, CLELLAN S., and BEACH, FRANK A. 1951. *Patterns of Sexual Behavior.* New York: Harper & Bros.

FORTES, MEYER. 1949. *The Web of Kinship among the Tallensi.* London: Oxford University Press, for the International African Institute.

HARTMANN, HEINZ; KRIS, ERNST; and LOWENSTEIN, RUDOLPH M. 1951. "Some Psychoanalytic Comments on 'Culture and Personality.'" In *Psychoanalysis and Culture*, pp. 3–31.

HERSKOVITS, MELVILLE. 1948. *Man and His Works.* New York: A. A. Knopf.

HOMANS, GEORGE. 1950. *The Human Group.* New York: Harcourt, Brace & Co.

HSU, FRANCIS L. K. 1948. *Under the Ancestors' Shadow: Chinese Culture and Personality.* New York: Columbia University Press.

JAKOBSON, R. 1949. "On the Identification of Phonemic Entities," *Travaux du Cercle linguistique de Copenhague*, V, 205–13.

JAKOBSON, R.; FANT, C.; and HALLE, M. 1952. *Preliminaries to Speech Analysis.* ("MIT Acoustics Laboratory Technical Reports," No. 13.)

KIDDER, A. V. 1940. "Looking Backward," *Proceedings of the American Philosophical Society*, LXXXIII, No. 4, 527–37.

KLUCKHOHN, CLYDE, and MORGAN, WILLIAM. 1951. "Some Notes on Navaho Dreams." In *Psychoanalysis and Culture*, pp. 120–31.

KLUCKHOHN, FLORENCE. 1950. "Dominant and Substitute Profiles of Cultural Orientations," *Social Forces*, XXVIII, 376–93.

KROEBER, ALFRED L. 1949. "The Concept of Culture in Science," *Journal of General Education*, III, 182–88.

KROEBER, A. L., and KLUCKHOHN, C. 1952. *Culture*, Part III. ("Papers of the Peabody Museum of Harvard University.")

LÉVI-STRAUSS, C. 1951. "Language and the Analysis of Social Laws," *American Anthropologist*, n.s., LIII, No. 2, 155–63.

LINTON, RALPH. 1936. *The Study of Man.* New York: Appleton-Century-Crofts, Inc.

LYND, R. S. 1939. *Knowledge for What?* Princeton: Princeton University Press.

LYND, ROBERT S. and HELEN M. 1929. *Middletown.* New York: Harcourt, Brace & Co.

———. 1937. *Middletown in Transition: A Study in Cultural Conflicts.* New York: Harcourt, Brace & Co.

MACLEOD, ROBERT B. 1947. "The Phenomenological Approach to Social Psychology," *Psychological Review*, LIV, 193–210.

MALINOWSKI, BRONISLAW. 1944. *A Scientific Theory of Culture.* Chapel Hill: University of North Carolina Press.

MURDOCK, G. P. 1940. "The Cross-cultural Survey," *American Sociological Review*, V, No. 3, 361–70.

———. 1945. "The Common Denominator of Cultures." In LINTON, R. (ed.), *The Science of Man in the World Crisis*, pp. 123–42. New York: Columbia University Press.

———. 1949. *Social Structure.* New York: Macmillan Co.

MURDOCK, G. P., et al. 1950. *Outline of Cultural Materials.* New Haven: Human Relations Area Files, Inc.

NADEL, S. F. 1951. *The Foundations of Social Anthropology.* Glencoe, Ill.: Free Press.

PARSONS, ELSIE C. 1936. *Mitla: Town of the Souls, and Other Zapoteco-speaking Pueblos of Oaxaca, Mexico.* Chicago: University of Chicago Press.

———. 1945. *Peguche, Canton of Otavalo, Province of Imbabura, Ecuador: A Study of Andean Indians.* Chicago: University of Chicago Press.

PARSONS, T. 1949. *Essays in Sociological Theory.* Glencoe, Ill.: Free Press.

RANK, OTTO. 1914. *The Myth of the Birth of the Hero.* New York: Journal of Nervous and Mental Disease Publishing Co.

REDFIELD, ROBERT. 1941. *The Folk Culture of Yucatan.* Chicago: University of Chicago Press.

RIEZLER, K. 1950. *Man Mutable and Immutable: The Fundamental Structure of Social Life.* Chicago: Henry Regnery.

STEWARD, JULIAN. 1949. "Cultural Causality and Law: A Trial Formulation of the Development of Early Civilization," *American Anthropologist*, n.s., LI, No. 1, 1–27.

———. 1950. *Area Research: Theory and Practice.* (Social Science Research Council Bull. 63.)

WEST, JAMES. 1945. *Plainville, U.S.A.* New York: Columbia University Press.

WIENER, N. 1948. *Cybernetics.* New York: Technology Press, John Wiley & Sons.

WILSON, A. T. M. 1951. *Some Aspects of Social Process.* (*Journal of Social Issues*, Supplementary Ser., No. 5.)

YANG, MARTIN C. 1945. *A Chinese Village: Taitou, Shantung Province.* New York: Columbia University Press.

Social Structure

By CLAUDE LÉVI-STRAUSS

THE TERM "social structure" refers to a group of problems the scope of which appears so wide and the definition so imprecise that it is hardly possible for a paper strictly limited in size to meet them fully. This is reflected in the program of this symposium, in which problems closely related to social structure have been allotted to several papers, such as those on "Style," "Universal Categories of Culture," "Structural Linguistics." These should be read in connection with the present paper.

On the other hand, studies in social structure have to do with the formal aspects of social phenomena; therefore, they are difficult to define, and still more to discuss, without overlapping other fields pertaining to the exact and natural sciences, where problems are similarly set in formal terms or, rather, where the formal expression of different problems admits of the same kind of treatment. As a matter of fact, the main interest of social-structure studies seems to be that they give the anthropologist hope that, thanks to the formalization of his problems, he may borrow methods and types of solutions from disciplines which have gone far ahead of his own in that direction.

Such being the case, it is obvious that the term "social structure" needs first to be defined and that some explanation should be given of the difference which helps to distinguish studies in social structure from the unlimited field of descriptions, analyses, and theories dealing with social relations at large, confounding themselves with the whole scope of social anthropology. This is all the more necessary, since some of those who have contributed toward setting apart social structure as a special field of anthropological studies conceived the former in many different manners and even sometimes, so it seems, came to nurture grave doubts as to the validity of their enterprise. For instance, Kroeber writes in the second edition of his *Anthropology*:

"Structure" appears to be just a yielding to a word that has a perfectly good meaning but suddenly becomes fashionably attractive for a decade or so—like "streamlining"—and during its vogue tends to be applied indiscriminately because of the pleasurable connotations of its sound. Of course a typical personality can be viewed as having a structure. But so can a physiology, any organism, all societies and all cultures, crystals, machines—in fact everything which is not wholly amorphous has a structure. So what "structure" adds to the meaning of our phrase seems to be nothing, except to provoke a degree of pleasant puzzlement" [Kroeber, 1948, p. 325].[1]

Although this passage concerns more particularly the notion of "basic personality structure," it has devastating implications as regards the generalized use of the notion of structure in anthropology.

1. Compare with the statement by the same author: ". . . the term 'social structure' which is tending to replace 'social organization' without appearing to add either content or emphasis of meaning" (1943, p. 105).

Another reason makes a definition of social structure compulsory: from the structuralist point of view which one has to adopt if only to give the problem its meaning, it would be hopeless to try to reach a valid definition of social structure on an inductive basis, by abstracting common elements from the uses and definitions current among all the scholars who claim to have made "social structure" the object of their studies. If these concepts have a meaning at all, they mean, first, that the notion of structure has a structure. This we shall try to outline from the beginning as a precaution against letting ourselves be submerged by a tedious inventory of books and papers dealing with social relations, the mere listing of which would more than exhaust the limited space at our disposal. In a further stage we will have to see how far and in what directions the term "social structure," as used by the different authors, departs from our definition. This will be done in the section devoted to kinship, since the notion of structure has found in that field its main applications and since anthropologists have generally chosen to express their theoretical views also in that connection.

I. DEFINITION AND PROBLEMS OF METHOD

Passing now to the task of defining "social structure," there is a point which should be cleared up immediately. The term "social structure" has nothing to do with empirical reality but with models which are built up after it. This should help one to clarify the difference between two concepts which are so close to each other that they have often been confused, namely, those of *social structure* and of *social relations*. It will be enough to state at this time that social relations consist of the raw materials out of which the models making up the social structure are built, while social structure can, by no means, be

reduced to the ensemble of the social relations to be described in a given society.[2] Therefore, social structure cannot claim a field of its own among others in the social studies. It is rather a method to be applied to any kind of social studies, similar to the structural analysis current in other disciplines.

Then the question becomes that of ascertaining what kind of model deserves the name "structure." This is not an anthropological question, but one which belongs to the methodology of science in general. Keeping this in mind, we can say that a structure consists of a model meeting with several requirements.

First, the structure exhibits the characteristics of a system. It is made up of several elements none of which can undergo a change without effecting changes in all the other elements.

In the second place, for any given model there should be a possibility of ordering a series of transformations resulting in a group of models of the same type.

In the third place, the above properties make it possible to predict how the model will react if one or more of its elements are submitted to certain modifications.

And, last, the model should be constituted so as to make immediately intelligible all the observed facts.[3]

2. The same idea appears to underlie E. R. Leach's remarkable study, "Jinghpaw Kinship Terminology" (1945).

3. Compare Von Neumann: "Such models (as games) are theoretical constructs with a precise, exhaustive and not too complicated definition; and they must be similar to reality in those respects which are essential to the investigation at hand. To recapitulate in detail: The definition must be precise and exhaustive in order to make a mathematical treatment possible. The construct must not be unduly complicated so that the mathematical treatment can be brought beyond the mere formalism to the point where it yields complete numerical results. Similarity to reali-

These being the requirements for any model with structural value, several consequences follow. These, however, do not pertain to the definition of structure but have to do with the main properties exhibited by, and problems raised by, structural analysis when contemplated in the social and other fields.

A) OBSERVATION AND EXPERIMENTATION

Great care should be taken to distinguish between the observation and the experiment levels. To observe facts and elaborate methodological devices permitting of constructing models out of these facts is not at all the same thing as to experiment on the models. By "experimenting on models," we mean the set of procedures aiming at ascertaining how a given model will react when submitted to change and at comparing models of the same or different types. This distinction is all the more necessary, since many discussions on social structure revolve around the apparent contradiction between the concreteness and individuality of ethnological data and the abstract and formal character generally exhibited by structural studies. This contradiction disappears as one comes to realize that these features belong to two entirely different planes, or rather two stages of the same process. On the observational level, the main—one could almost say the only—rule is that all the facts should be carefully observed and described, without allowing any theoretical preconception to decide whether some are more important and others less. This rule implies, in turn, that facts should be studied in relation to themselves (by what kind of concrete process did they come into being?) and in relation to

the whole (always aiming to relate each modification which can be observed in a sector to the global situation in which it first appeared).

This rule together with its corollaries has been explicitly formulated by K. Goldstein (1951, pp. 18–25) in relation to psychophysiological studies, and it may be considered valid for any kind of structural analysis. Its immediate consequence is that, far from being contradictory, there is a direct relationship between the detail and concreteness of ethnographical description and the validity and generality of the model which is constructed after it. For, though many models may be used as convenient devices to describe and explain the phenomena, it is obvious that the best model will always be that which is *true*, that is, the simplest possible model which, while being extracted exclusively from the facts under consideration, also makes it possible to account for all of them. Therefore, the first task is to ascertain what those facts are.

B) CONSCIOUSNESS AND UNCONSCIOUSNESS

A second distinction has to do with the conscious or unconscious character of the models. In the history of structural thought, Boas may be credited with having introduced this distinction. He made clear that a category of facts can more easily yield to structural analysis when the social group in which they are manifested has not elaborated a conscious model to interpret or justify them (e.g., 1911, p. 67). Some readers may be surprised to find Boas' name quoted in connection with structural theory, since he was often described as one of the main obstacles in its path. But this writer has tried to demonstrate that Boas' shortcomings in matters of structural studies were not in his failure to understand their importance and significance, which he did, as a matter of fact, in the most prophetic way. They

ty is needed to make the operation significant. And this similarity must usually be restricted to a few traits deemed 'essential' *pro tempore* —since otherwise the above requirements would conflict with each other" (Von Neumann and Morgenstern, 1944).

rather resulted from the fact that he imposed on structural studies conditions of validity, some of which will remain forever part of their methodology, while some others are so exacting and impossible to meet that they would have withered scientific development in any field (Lévi-Strauss, 1949*a*).

A structural model may be conscious or unconscious without this difference affecting its nature. It can only be said that when the structure of a certain type of phenomena does not lie at a great depth, it is more likely that some kind of model, standing as a screen to hide it, will exist in the collective consciousness. For conscious models, which are usually known as "norms," are by definition very poor ones, since they are not intended to explain the phenomena but to perpetuate them. Therefore, structural analysis is confronted with a strange paradox well known to the linguist, that is: the more obvious structural organization is, the more difficult it becomes to reach it because of the inaccurate conscious models lying across the path which leads to it.

From the point of view of the degree of consciousness, the anthropologist is confronted with two kinds of situations. He may have to construct a model from phenomena the systematic character of which has evoked no awareness on the part of the culture; this is the kind of simpler situation referred to by Boas as providing the easiest ground for anthropological research. Or else the anthropologist will be dealing, on the one hand, with raw phenomena and, on the other, with the models already constructed by the culture to interpret the former. Though it is likely that, for the reason stated above, these models will prove unsatisfactory, it is by no means necessary that this should always be the case. As a matter of fact, many "primitive" cultures have built models of their marriage regulations which are much more to the point than models

built by professional anthropologists.[4] Thus one cannot dispense with studying a culture's "home-made" models for two reasons. First, these models might prove to be accurate or, at least, to provide some insight into the structure of the phenomena; after all, each culture has its own theoreticians whose contributions deserve the same attention as that which the anthropologist gives to colleagues. And, second, even if the models are biased or erroneous, the very bias and types of errors are a part of the facts under study and probably rank among the most significant ones. But even when taking into consideration these culturally produced models, the anthropologist does not forget—as he has sometimes been accused of doing (Firth, 1951, pp. 28–31)—that the cultural norms are not of themselves structures. Rather, they furnish an important contribution to an understanding of the structures, either as factual documents or as theoretical contributions similar to those of the anthropologist himself.

This point has been given great attention by the French sociological school. Durkheim and Mauss, for instance, have always taken care to substitute, as a starting point for the survey of native categories of thought, the conscious representations prevailing among the natives themselves for those grown out of the anthropologist's own culture. This was undoubtedly an important step, which, nevertheless, fell short of its goal because these authors were not sufficiently aware that native conscious representations, important as they are, may be just as remote from the unconscious reality as any other (Lévi-Strauss, 1951).

c) Structure and Measure

It is often believed that one of the main interests of the notion of structure is to permit the introduction of meas-

4. For examples and detailed discussion see Lévi-Strauss (1949*b*, pp. 558 ff.).

urement in social anthropology. This
view was favored by the frequent appearance of mathematical or semimath-
ematical aids in books or articles dealing with social structure. It is true that
in some cases structural analysis has
made it possible to attach numerical
values to invariants. This was, for instance, the result of Kroeber's studies
of women's dress fashions, a landmark
in structural research (Richardson and
Kroeber, 1940), as well as of a few
other studies which will be discussed
below.

However, one should keep in mind
that there is no necessary connection
between *measure* and *structure*. Structural studies are, in the social sciences,
the indirect outcome of modern developments in mathematics which have
given increasing importance to the
qualitative point of view in contradistinction to the quantitative point of
view of traditional mathematics. Therefore, it has become possible, in fields
such as mathematical logic, set-theory,
group-theory, and topology, to develop
a rigorous approach to problems which
do not admit of a metrical solution. The
outstanding achievements in this connection—which offer themselves as
springboards not yet utilized by social
scientists—are to be found in J. von
Neumann and O. Morgenstern, *Theory
of Games and Economic Behavior*
(1944); N. Wiener, *Cybernetics* (1948);
and C. Shannon and W. Weaver, *The
Mathematical Theory of Communication* (1950).

D) MECHANICAL MODELS AND
STATISTICAL MODELS

A last distinction refers to the relation between the scale of the model and
that of the phenomena. According to
the nature of these phenomena, it becomes possible or impossible to build
a model, the elements of which are on
the same scale as the phenomena themselves. A model the elements of which

are on the same scale as the phenomena
will be called a "mechanical model";
when the elements of the model are
on a different scale, we will be dealing
with a "statistical model." The laws of
marriage provide the best illustration
of this difference. In primitive societies
these laws can be expressed in models
calling for actual grouping of the individuals according to kin or clan; these
are mechanical models. No such distribution exists in our own society, where
types of marriage are determined by
the size of the primary and secondary
groups to which prospective mates belong, social fluidity, amount of information, and the like. A satisfactory (though
yet untried) attempt to formulate the
invariants of our marriage system would
therefore have to determine average
values—thresholds; it would be a statistical model. There may be intermediate forms between these two. Such
is the case in societies which (as even
our own) have a mechanical model to
determine prohibited marriages and rely on a statistical model for those which
are permissible. It should also be kept
in mind that the same phenomena may
admit of different models, some mechanical and some statistical, according
to the way in which they are grouped
together and with other phenomena. A
society which recommends cross-cousin
marriage but where this ideal marriage
type occurs only with limited frequency
needs, in order that the system may be
properly explained, both a mechanical
and a statistical model, as was well
understood by Forde (1941) and Elwin
(1947).

It should also be kept in mind that
what makes social-structure studies valuable is that structures are models, the
formal properties of which can be compared independently of their elements.
The structuralist's task is thus to recognize and isolate levels of reality
which have strategic value from his
point of view, namely, which admit of

representation as models, whatever their kind. It often happens that the same data may be considered from different perspectives embodying equal strategic values, though the resulting models will be in some cases mechanical and in others statistical. This situation is well known in the exact and natural sciences; for instance, the theory of a small number of physical bodies belongs to classical mechanics, but if the number of bodies becomes greater, then one should rely on the laws of thermodynamics, that is, use a statistical model instead of a mechanical one, though the nature of the data remains the same in both cases.

The same situation prevails in the human and the social sciences. If one takes a phenomenon like, for instance, suicide, it can be studied on two different levels. First, it is possible by studying individual situations to establish what may be called mechanical models of suicide, taking into account in each case the personality of the victim, his or her life-history, the characteristics of the primary and secondary groups in which he or she developed, and the like; or else one can build models of a statistical nature, by recording suicide frequency over a certain period of time in one or more societies and in different types of primary and secondary groups, etc. These would be levels at which the structural study of suicide carries a strategic value, that is, where it becomes possible to build models which may be compared (1) for different types of suicides, (2) for different societies, and (3) for different types of social phenomena. Scientific progress consists not only in discovering new invariants belonging to those levels but also in discovering new levels where the study of the same phenomena offers the same strategical value. Such a result was achieved, for instance, by psychoanalysis, which discovered the means to lay out models in

a new field, that of the psychological life of the patient considered as a whole.

The foregoing should help to make clear the dual (and at first sight almost contradictory) nature of structural studies. On the one hand, they aim at isolating strategic levels, and this can be achieved only by "carving out" a certain family of phenomena. From that point of view, each type of structural study appears autonomous, entirely independent of all the others and even of different methodological approaches to the same field. On the other hand, the essential value of these studies is to construct models the formal properties of which can be compared with, and explained by, the same properties as in models corresponding to other strategic levels. Thus it may be said that their ultimate end is to override traditional boundaries between different disciplines and to promote a true interdisciplinary approach.

An example may be given. A great deal of discussion has taken place lately about the difference between history and anthropology, and Kroeber and others have made clear that the time-dimension has very little importance in this connection. From what has been stated above, one can see exactly where the difference lies, not only between these two disciplines but also between them and others. Ethnography and history differ from social anthropology and sociology, inasmuch as the former two aim at gathering data, while the latter two deal with models constructed from these data. Similarly, ethnography and social anthropology correspond to two different stages in the same research, the ultimate result of which is to construct mechanical models, while history (together with its so-called "auxiliary" disciplines) and sociology end ultimately in statistical models. This is the reason why the social sciences, though having to do—

all of them—with the time-dimension, nevertheless deal with two different categories of time. Anthropology uses a "mechanical" time, reversible and non-cumulative. For instance, the model of, let us say, a patrilineal kinship system does not in itself show whether or not the system has always remained patrilineal, or has been preceded by a matrilineal form, or by any number of shifts from patrilineal to matrilineal and vice versa. On the contrary, historical time is "statistical"; it always appears as an oriented and nonreversible process. An evolution which would take back contemporary Italian society to that of the Roman Republic is as impossible to conceive of as is the reversibility of the processes belonging to the second law of thermodynamics.

This discussion helps to clarify Firth's distinction between social structure, which he conceives as outside the time-dimension, and social organization, where time re-enters (1951, p. 40). Also in this connection, the debate which has been going on for the past few years between followers of the Boasian antievolutionist tradition and of Professor Leslie White (1949) may become better understood. The Boasian school has been mainly concerned with models of a mechanical type, and from this point of view the concept of evolution has no operational value. On the other hand, it is certainly legitimate to speak of evolution in a historical and socio-logical sense, but the elements to be organized into an evolutionary process cannot be borrowed from the level of a cultural typology which consists of mechanical models. They should be sought at a sufficiently deep level to insure that these elements will remain unaffected by different cultural contexts (as, let us say, genes are identical elements combined into different patterns corresponding to the different racial [statistical] models) and can ac-

cordingly permit of drawing long statistical runs.

A great deal of inconvenience springs from a situation which obliges the social scientist to "shift" time, according to the kind of study he is contemplating. Natural scientists, who have got used to this difficulty, are making efforts to overcome it. Very important in this connection is Murdock's contention that while a patrilineal system may replace, or grow out of, a matrilineal system, the opposite process cannot take place (1949, pp. 210–20). If this were true, a vectorial factor would for the first time be introduced on an objective basis into social structure. Murdock's demonstration was, however, challenged by Lowie (1948a, pp. 44 ff.) on methodological grounds, and for the time being it is impossible to do more than to call attention to a moot problem, the solution of which, when generally accepted, will have a tremendous bearing upon structural studies, not only in the field of anthropology but in other fields as well.

The distinction between mechanical and statistical models has also become fundamental in another respect: it makes it possible to clarify the role of the comparative method in structural studies. This method was greatly emphasized by both Radcliffe-Brown and Lowie. The former writes (1952, p. 14):

Theoretical sociology is commonly regarded as an inductive science, induction being the logical method of inference by which we arrive at general propositions from the consideration of particular instances. Although Professor Evans-Pritchard . . . seems to imply in some of his statements that the logical method of induction, using comparison, classification and generalization, is not applicable to the phenomena of human social life . . . I hold that social anthropology must depend on systematic comparative studies of many societies.

Writing about religion, he states (1945, p. 1):

The experimental method of social religion . . . means that we must study in the light of our hypothesis a sufficient number of diverse particular religions or religious cults in relation to the particular societies in which they are found. This is a task not for one person but for a number.

Similarly, Lowie, after pointing out (1948a, p. 38) that "the literature of anthropology is full of alleged correlations which lack empirical support," insists on the need of a "broad inductive basis" for generalization (1948a, p. 68). It is interesting to note that by this claim for inductive support these authors dissent not only from Durkheim (1912, p. 593): "when a law has been proved by a well performed experiment, this law is valid universally," but also from Goldstein, who, as already mentioned, has lucidly expressed what may be called "the rules of structuralist method" in a way general enough to make them valid outside the more limited field in which they were first applied by their author. Goldstein remarks that the need to make a thorough study of each case implies that the amount of cases to be studied should be small; and he proceeds by raising the question whether or not the risk exists that the cases under consideration may be special ones, allowing no general conclusions about the others. He answers (1951, p. 25): "This objection completely misunderstands the real situation . . . an accumulation of facts even numerous is of no help if these facts were imperfectly established; it does not lead to the knowledge of things as they really happen. . . . We must choose only these cases which permit of formulating final judgments. And then, what is true for one case will also be true for any other."

Probably very few anthropologists would be ready to support these bold statements. However, no structuralist study may be undertaken without a clear awareness of Goldstein's dilemma: either to study many cases in a superficial and in the end ineffective way; or to limit one's self to a thorough study of a small number of cases, thus proving that, in the end, one well-done experiment is sufficient to make a demonstration.

Now the reason for so many anthropologists' faithfulness to the comparative method may be sought in some sort of confusion between the procedures used to establish mechanical and statistical models. While Durkheim's and Goldstein's position undoubtedly holds true for the former, it is obvious that no statistical model can be achieved without statistics, i.e., by gathering a large amount of data. But in this case the method is no more comparative than in the other, since the data to be collected will be acceptable only in so far as they are all of the same kind. Therefore, we remain confronted with only one alternative, namely, to make a thorough study of one case. The real difference lies in the selection of the "case," which will be patterned so as to include elements which are either on the same scale as the model to be constructed or on a different scale.

After having thus clarified these basic questions revolving around the nature of studies in social structure, it becomes possible to make an inventory of the main fields of inquiry and to discuss some of the results achieved so far.

II. SOCIAL MORPHOLOGY OR GROUP STRUCTURE

In this section, "group" is not intended to mean the social group but, in a more general sense, the way according to which the phenomena under study are grouped together.

The object of social-structure studies is to understand social relations with the aid of models. Now it is impossible to conceive of social relations outside a common frame. Space and time are the two frames we use to situate social relations, either alone or together. These space- and time-dimensions are not the same as the analogous ones used by other disciplines but consist of a "social" space and of a "social" time, meaning that they have no properties outside those which derive from the properties of the social phenomena which "furnish" them. According to their social structure, human societies have elaborated many types of such "continuums," and there should be no undue concern on the part of the anthropologist that, in the course of his studies, he may temporarily have to borrow types widely different from the existing patterns and eventually to evolve new ones.

We have already noticed that the time-continuum may be reversible or oriented in accordance with the level of reality embodying strategical value from the point of view of the research at hand. Many other possibilities may arise: the time-dimension can be conceived of as independent from the observer and unlimited or as a function of the observer's own (biological) time and limited; it may be considered as consisting of parts which are, or are not, homologous with one another, etc. Evans-Pritchard has shown how such formal properties underlie the qualitative distinctions between the observer's life-span, history, legend, and myth (1939, 1940). And his basic distinctions have been found to be valid for contemporary societies (Bernot and Blancard, MS).

What is true of the time-dimension applies equally well to space. It has been Durkheim's and Mauss's great merit to call attention for the first time to the variable properties of space which should be called upon in order to understand properly the structure of several primitive societies (1901–2). In this undertaking they received their inspiration from the work of Cushing, which it has become fashionable in recent years to belittle. However, Cushing's insight and sociological imagination make him deserving of a seat on Morgan's right, as one of the great forerunners of social-structure studies. The gaps and inaccuracies in his descriptions, less serious than the indictment of having "over-interpreted" some of his material, will be viewed in their true proportions when it is realized that, albeit in an unconscious fashion, Cushing was aiming less at giving an actual description of Zuni society than at elaborating a model (his famous seven fold division) which could explain most of its processes and structure.

Social time and space should also be characterized according to scale. There is in social studies a "macro-time" and a "micro-time"; the same distinction applies also to space. This explains how social structure may have to do with prehistory, archeology, and diffusion processes as well as with psychological topology, such as that initiated by Lewin or by Moreno's sociometry. As a matter of fact, structures of the same type may exist on quite different time and space levels, and it is far from inconceivable that, for instance, a statistical model resulting from sociometrical studies might be of greater help in building a similar model in the field of the history of cultures than an apparently more direct approach would have permitted.

Therefore, historicogeographical concerns should not be excluded from the field of structural studies, as was generally implied by the widely accepted opposition between "diffusionism" and "functionalism."[5] A functionalist may be far from a structuralist, as is clearly

5. Never accepted by Lowie; see the Preface in Lowie (1920).

shown by the example of Malinowski. On the other hand, undertakings such as those of G. Dumézil,[6] as well as A. L. Kroeber's personal case of a highly structure-minded scholar devoting most of his time to distribution studies, are proofs that even history can be approached in a structural way.

Since synchronic studies raise fewer problems than diachronic ones (the data being more homogeneous in the first case), the simplest morphological studies are those having to do with the qualitative, nonmeasurable properties of social space, that is, the way according to which social phenomena can be situated on a map and the regularities exhibited in their configurations. Much might have been expected from the researches of the so-called "Chicago school" dealing with urban ecology, and the reasons for the gradual loss of interest along this line of research are not altogether clear. It has to do mostly with ecology, which was made the subject of another paper in this symposium. However, it is not inappropriate to state at this point what kind of relationship prevails between ecology, on the one hand, and social structure, on the other. Both have to do with the spatial distribution of phenomena. But social structure deals exclusively with those "spaces" the determinations of which are of a purely sociological nature, that is, not affected by natural determinants, such as geology, climatology, physiography, and the like. This is the reason why so-called "urban ecology" should have held great interest for the social anthropologist; the urban space is small enough and homogeneous enough (from every point of view except the social one) for all its differential qualitative aspects to be assigned mostly to the action of internal forces accessible to structural sociology.

It would perhaps have been wiser, instead of starting with complex communities hard to isolate from external influences, to approach first—as suggested by Marcel Mauss (1924–25)—those small and relatively isolated communities with which the anthropologist usually deals. A few such studies may be found (e.g., Firth, 1936; Steward, 1938; Nadel, 1947; Forde, 1950), but they rarely and then reluctantly go beyond the descriptive stage. There have been practically no attempts to correlate the spatial configurations with the formal properties of the other aspects of social life.

This is much to be regretted, since in many parts of the world there is an obvious relationship between the social structure and the spatial structure of settlements, villages, or camps. To limit ourselves to America, the camp shapes of Plains Indians have for long demanded attention by virtue of regular variations connected with the social organization of each tribe; and the same holds true for the circular disposition of huts in Gé villages of eastern and central Brazil. In both cases we are dealing with relatively homogeneous cultural areas where important series of concomitant variations may be observed. Another kind of problem results from the comparison of areas where different types of village structures may be compared to different types of social relations, e.g., the circular village structure of the Gé and the parallel-layers structure of the Pueblo. The latter could even be studied diachronically with the archeologist's help, which would raise questions such as the eventual linkage of the transition from semicircular structures to parallel ones, with the shift of village sites from valley to mesa top, of structural distribution of clan houses suggested by many myths to the present-day statistical one, etc.

These few examples are not intended to prove that spatial configuration is the mirror-image of social organization but to call attention to the fact that,

---

6. These researches were summarized by their author in Dumézil (1949).

while among numerous peoples it would be extremely difficult to discover any such relation, among others (who must accordingly have something in common) the existence of a relation is evident, though unclear, and in a third group spatial configuration seems to be almost a projective representation of the social structure. But even the most striking cases call for a critical study; for example, this writer has attempted to demonstrate that, among the Bororo, spatial configuration reflects not the true, unconscious social organization but a model existing consciously in the native mind, though its nature is entirely illusory and even contradictory to reality.[7] Problems of this kind (which are raised not only by the consideration of relatively durable spatial configurations but also in regard to recurrent temporary ones, such as those shown in dance, ritual, etc.) offer an opportunity to study social and mental processes through objective and crystallized external projections of them.

Another approach which may lead more directly to a mathematical expression of social phenomena starts with the numerical properties of human groups. This has traditionally been the field of demography, but it is only recently that a few scholars coming from different horizons—demography, sociology, anthropology—have begun to elaborate a kind of qualitative demography, that is, dealing no longer with continuous variations within human groups selected for empirical reasons but with significant discontinuities evidenced in the behavior of groups considered as wholes and chosen on the basis of these discontinuities. This "socio-demography," as it was called by one of its proponents (De Lestrange, 1951), is

7. C. Lévi-Strauss, "Les Structures sociales dans le Brésil central et oriental," in Sol Tax (ed.), *Indian Tribes of Aboriginal America: Selected Papers of the XXIXth Congress of Americanists* (Chicago: University of Chicago Press, 1952).

"on a level" with social anthropology, and it is not difficult to foresee that in the very near future it will be called upon to provide firm grounds for any kind of anthropological research. Therefore, it is surprising that so little attention was paid in anthropological circles to the study by a demographer, L. Livi, of the formal properties characteristic of the smallest possible size of a group compatible with its existence as a group (1940–41, 1949). His researches, closely connected with G. Dahlberg's, are all the more important for anthropologists, in that the latter usually deal with populations very near Livi's minimum. There is an obvious relation between the functioning and even the durability of the social structure and the actual size of the population (Wagley, 1940). It is thus becoming increasingly evident that formal properties exist which are immediately and directly attached to the absolute size of the population, whatever the group under consideration. These should be the first to be assessed and taken into account in an interpretation of other properties.

Next come numerical properties expressing not the group size taken globally but the size and interaction of subsets of the group which can be defined by significant discontinuities. Two lines of inquiry should be mentioned in this connection.

There is, first, the vast body of researches deriving from the famous "rank-size rule" for cities, which has proved to be applicable in many other social fields, though the original rule remains somewhat controversial (see Davis, 1947; Stewart, 1947; Zipf, 1949).

Of a much more direct bearing on current anthropological research is the recent work of two French demographers, who, by using Dahlberg's demonstration that the size of an isolate (i.e., a group of intermarrying people) can be computed from the frequency of marriages between cross-cousins (Dahlberg, 1948), have succeeded in computing the average size of isolates in all French *departements,* thus throwing open to anthropological investigation the marriage system of a complex modern society (Sutter and Tabah, 1951). The average size of the French isolate varies from less than 1,000 to over 2,800 individuals. This numerical evaluation shows that, even in a modern society, the network of people united by kinship ties is much smaller than might be expected, of about the same size as in primitive groups. The inference is that, while the absolute size of the intermarrying group remains approximately on the same scale in all human societies (the proportion of the French types in relation to the average primitive types being about 10 to 1), a complex society becomes such not so much because of an expansion of the isolate itself as on account of an expansion of other types of social links (economic, political, intellectual); and these are used to connect a great number of isolates which, by themselves, remain relatively static.

But the most striking result of this research is the discovery that the smallest isolates are found not only in mountain areas, as was expected, but also (and even more) in areas including a large urban center; the following *departements:* Rhône (Lyon), Gironde (Bordeaux), and Seine (Paris) are at the bottom of the list, with the size of their isolates respectively 740, 910, and 930. In the Seine *departement,* which is practically reduced to Paris and suburbs, the frequency of consanguineous marriages is higher than in any of the fifteen rural *departements* which surround it (Sutter and Tabah, 1951, p. 489).

It is not necessary to emphasize the bearing of such studies on social structure; the main fact, from the point of view of this paper, is that they at the same time make possible and call for an immediate extension on the anthropological level. An approach has been found which enables one to break down a modern complex society into smaller units which are of the same nature as those commonly studied by anthropologists; on the other hand, this approach remains incomplete, since the absolute size of the isolate is only a part of the phenomenon, the other one, equally important, being the length of the marriage cycles. For a small isolate may admit of long marriage cycles (that is, tending to be of the same size as the isolate itself), while a relatively large isolate can be made up of shorter cycles. This problem, which could be solved only with the help of genealogies, points the way toward close co-operation between the structural demographer and the social anthropologist.

Another contribution, this time on a theoretical level, may be expected from this co-operation. The concept of isolate may help to solve a problem in social structure which has given rise to a controversy between Radcliffe-Brown and Lowie. The former has labeled as "a fantastic reification of abstraction" the suggestion made by some anthropologists, mostly in America, that anthropology should be defined as the study not of society but of culture. To him, "European culture is an abstraction and so is the culture of an African tribe." All that exists is human beings connected by an unlimited series of social relations (Radcliffe-Brown, 1940*b,* pp. 10–11). This, Lowie says, is "a factitious quarrel" (1942, pp. 520–21). However, the misunderstandings which lie at its root appear to be very real, since they were born all over again on the occasion of the publication of a book by White (1949) and its criticism by Bidney (1950, pp. 518–19; see also Radcliffe-Brown, 1949*b*).

It seems that both the reality and the

autonomy of the concept of culture could better be validated if culture were, from an operational point of view, treated in the same way as the geneticist and demographer do for the closely allied concept of "isolate." What is called a "culture" is a fragment of humanity which, from the point of view of the research at hand and of the scale on which it is being carried out, presents, in relation to the rest of humanity, significant discontinuities. If our aim is to ascertain significant discontinuities between, let us say, North America and Europe, then we are dealing with two different cultures; but should we become concerned with significant discontinuities between New York and Chicago, we would be allowed to speak of these two groups as different cultural "units." Since these discontinuities can be reduced to invariants, which is the goal of structural analysis, one sees that culture may, at the same time, correspond to an objective reality and be a function of the kind of research undertaken. Accordingly, the same set of individuals may be considered to be parts of many different cultural contexts: universal, continental, national, provincial, parochial, etc., as well as familial, professional, confessional, political, etc. This is true as a limit; however, anthropologists usually reserve the term "culture" to designate a group of discontinuities which has significance on several of these levels at the same time. That it can never be valid for all levels does not prevent the concept of "culture" from being as fundamental for the anthropologist as that of "isolate" for the demographer. Both belong to the same epistemological family. On a question such as that of the positive character of a concept, the anthropologist can rely on a physicist's judgment; it is Niels Bohr who states (1939, p. 9) that "the traditional differences of [human cultures] in many ways resemble the different equivalent modes in which physical experience can be described."

III. SOCIAL STATICS OR COMMUNICATION STRUCTURES

A society consists of individuals and groups which communicate with one another. The existence of, or lack of, communication can never be defined in an absolute manner. Communication does not cease at society's borders. These borders, rather, constitute thresholds where the rate and forms of communication, without waning altogether, reach a much lower level. This condition is usually meaningful enough for the population, both inside and outside the borders, to become aware of it. This awareness is not, however, a prerequisite for the definition of a given society. It only accompanies the more precise and stable forms.

In any society, communication operates on three different levels: communication of women, communication of goods and services, communication of messages. Therefore, kinship studies, economics, and linguistics approach the same kinds of problems on different strategic levels and really pertain to the same field. Theoretically at least, it might be said that kinship and marriage rules regulate a fourth type of communication, that of genes between phenotypes. Therefore, it should be kept in mind that culture does not consist exclusively of forms of communication of its own, like language, but also (and perhaps mostly) of *rules* stating how the "games of communication" should be played both on the natural and on the cultural level.

The above comparison between the fields of kinship, economics, and linguistics cannot hide the fact that they refer to forms of communication which are on a different scale. Should one try to compute the communication rate involved, on the one hand, in the intermarriages and, on the other, in the exchange of messages going on in a given society, one would probably discover the difference to be of about the same magnitude as, let us say, that between the exchange of heavy molecules of two viscous liquids through a not too permeable film, and radio communication. Thus, from marriage to language one passes from low- to high-speed communication; this comes from the fact that what is communicated in marriage is almost of the same nature as those who communicate (women, on the one hand, men, on the other), while speakers of language are not of the same nature as their utterances. The opposition is thus one of *person* to *symbol*, or of *value* to *sign*. This helps to clarify economics' somewhat intermediate position between these two extremes—goods and services are not persons, but they still are values. And, though neither symbols nor signs, they require symbols or signs to succeed in being exchanged when the exchange system reaches a certain degree of complexity.

From this outline of the structure of social communication derive three important sets of considerations.

First, the position of economics in social structure may be precisely defined. Economics in the past has been suspect among anthropologists. Even in this symposium, no paper was explicitly assigned to economic problems. Yet, whenever this highly important topic has been broached, a close relationship has been shown to prevail between economic pattern and social structure. Since Mauss's pioneer papers (1904–5, 1923–24) and Malinowski's book on the *kula* (1922)—by far his masterpiece—every attempt in this direction has shown that the economic system provides sociological formulations with some of their more fundamental invariants (Speck, 1915; Richards, 1932, 1936, 1939; Steward, 1938;

Evans-Pritchard, 1940; Herskovits, 1940; Wittfogel and Goldfrank, 1943).

The anthropologist's reluctance originated in the condition of economic studies themselves; these were ridden with conflicts between bitterly opposed schools and at the same time bathed in an aura of mystery and conceit. Thus the anthropologist labored under the impression that economics dealt mostly with abstractions and that there was little connection between the actual life of actual groups of people and such notions as value, utility, profit, and the like.

The complete upheaval of economic studies resulting from the publication of Von Neumann and Morgenstern's book (1944) ushers in an era of closer co-operation between the economist and the anthropologist, and for two reasons. First—though economics achieves here a rigorous approach—this book deals not with abstractions such as those just mentioned but with concrete individuals and groups which are represented in their actual and empirical relations of co-operation and competition. Next—and as a consequence—it introduces for the first time mechanical models which are of the same type as, and intermediate between, those used in mathematical physics and in social anthropology—especially in the field of kinship. In this connection it is striking that Von Neumann's models are borrowed from the theory of games, a line of thought which was initiated independently by Kroeber when he compared social institutions "to the play of earnest children" (1942, p. 215). There is, true enough, an important difference between games of entertainment and marriage rules: the former are constructed in such a way as to permit each player to extract from statistical regularities maximal differential values, while marriage rules, acting in the opposite direction, aim at establishing statistical regularities in spite of the differential values existing between individuals and generations. In this sense they constitute a special kind of "upturned game." Nevertheless, they can be treated with the same methods. Besides, such being the rules, each individual and group tries to play it in the "normal" way, that is, by maximizing his own advantages at the expense of the others (i.e., to get more wives or better ones, whether from the aesthetic, erotic, or economic point of view). The theory of courtship is thus a part of formal sociology. To those who are afraid that sociology might in this way get hopelessly involved in individual psychology, it will be enough to recall that Von Neumann has succeeded in giving a mathematical demonstration of the nature and strategy of a psychological technique as sophisticated as bluffing at the game of poker (Von Neumann and Morgenstern, 1944, pp. 186–219).

The next advantage of this increasing consolidation of social anthropology, economics, and linguistics into one great field, that of communication, is to make clear that they consist exclusively of the study of *rules* and have little concern with the nature of the partners (either individuals or groups) whose play is being patterned after these rules. As Von Neumann puts it (*op. cit.*, p. 49): "The game is simply the totality of the rules which describe it." Besides that of game, other operational notions are those of play, move, choice, and strategy. But the nature of the players need not be considered. What is important is to find out when a given player can make a choice and when he cannot.

This outlook should open the study of kinship and marriage to approaches directly derived from the theory of communication. In the terminology of this theory it is possible to speak of the information of a marriage system by the number of choices at the observer's disposal to define the marriage status of an individual. Thus the information

is unity for a dual exogamous system, and, in an Australian kind of kinship typology, it would increase with the logarithm of the number of matrimonial classes. A theoretical system where everybody could marry everybody would be a system with no redundancy, since each marriage choice would not be determined by previous choices, while the positive content of marriage rules constitutes the redundancy of the system under consideration. By studying the percentage of "free" choices in a matrimonial population (not absolutely free, but in relation to certain postulated conditions), it would thus become possible to offer numerical estimates of its entropy, both absolute and relative.

As a consequence, it would become possible to translate statistical models into mechanical ones and vice versa, thus bridging the gap still existing between population studies, on the one hand, and anthropological ones, on the other, thereby laying a foundation for foresight and action. To give an example, in our own society the organization of marriage choices does not go beyond (1) the prohibition of near kin, (2) the size of the isolate, and (3) the accepted standard of behavior, which limits the frequency of certain choices inside the isolate. With these data at hand, one could compute the information of the system, that is, translate our loosely organized and highly statistical marriage system into a mechanical model, thus making possible its comparison with the large series of marriage systems of a "mechanical" type available from simpler societies. Similarly, a great deal of discussion has been carried on recently about the Murngin kinship system, which has been treated by different authors as a 7-class system, or less than 7, or 4, or 32 (Warner, 1930–31; Lévi-Strauss, 1949*b*; Lawrence and Murdock, 1949; Radcliffe-Brown, 1951; Elkin, personal correspondence). By getting a good statistical run of actual marriage choices among other excluded possibilities, one could get at a "true" solution. This conception of a class system as a device to reduce the amount of information required to define several hundred kinship statuses was clearly outlined at first by Professor Lloyd Warner (1937*b*).

In the preceding pages an attempt has been made to assess the bearing of some recent lines of mathematical research upon anthropological studies. We have seen that their main contribution was to provide anthropology with a unifying concept—communication—enabling it to consolidate widely different types of inquiry into one and at the same time providing the theoretical and methodological tools to further knowledge in that direction. The question which should now be raised is: To what extent is social anthropology ready to make use of these tools?

The main feature of the development of social anthropology in the past years has been the increased attention to kinship. This is, indeed, not a new phenomenon, since it can be said that, with his *Systems of Consanguinity and Affinity of the Human Family*, Lewis Morgan's genius at one and the same time founded social anthropology and kinship studies and brought forward the basic reasons for attaching such importance to the latter: permanency, systematic character, continuity of changes (1871). The views outlined in the preceding pages may help to explain this fundamental interest in kinship, since we have considered it as the anthropologist's own and privileged share in the science of communication. But, even if this interpretation were not accepted by all, the fact of the enormous development of kinship studies cannot be denied. It has recently been assessed in various works (Lowie, 1948*a*;

Murdock, 1949; Spoehr, 1950). The latest to appear (Radcliffe-Brown and Forde, 1950) has brought together a tremendous wealth of information. Chapters such as Forde's and Nadel's have added the final stroke to unilineal interpretations. However, one may be permitted to regret that the different outlooks of the contributors, their failure to get together and try to extract from their data a small set of significant variations, might become responsible for discouraging potential field workers instead of clearly showing them the purpose of such studies.

Unfortunately, the amount of usable material in relation to that actually collected remains small. This is clearly reflected in the fact that, in order to undertake his survey, Murdock found it possible to retain information concerning no more than about 250 societies (from our point of view, a still overindulgent estimate) out of the 3,000 to 4,000 distinct societies still in existence (Ford and Beach, 1951, p. 5); an attempt to add material valid on a diachronic level would considerably increase the last number. It is somewhat disheartening that the enormous work devoted in the last fifty years to the gathering of ethnographic material has yielded so little, while kinship has been one of the main concerns of those undertaking them.

However, it should be kept in mind that what has brought about this unhappy result is not a lack of coverage—on the contrary. If the workable material is small, it is rather on account of the inductive illusion: it was believed that as many cultures as possible should be covered, albeit lightly, rather than a few thoroughly enough to yield significant results. Accordingly, there is no lack of consistency in the fact that, following their individual temperaments, anthropologists have preferred one or the other of the alternatives imposed by the situation. While Radcliffe-Brown,

Eggan, Spoehr, Fortes, and this writer have tried to consider limited areas where dense information was available, Murdock has followed the complementary (but not contradictory) path of widening the field even at the expense of the reliability of the data, and Lowie (1948a) has tried to pursue a kind of middle road between the two approaches.

The case of the Pueblo area is especially striking, since for probably no other area in the world is there available such an amount of data and of such controversial quality. It is almost with despair that one comes to realize that the voluminous material accumulated by Voth, Fewkes, Dorsey, Parsons, and, to some extent, Stevenson is practically unworkable, since these authors have been feverishly piling up information without any clear idea of what it meant and, above all, of the hypotheses which it should have helped to check. The situation changed with Lowie's and Kroeber's entering the field, but the lack of statistical data on marriage choices and types of intermarriages, which could have been gathered for more than fifty years, will probably be impossible to overcome. This is much to be regretted, since Eggan's recent book (1950) represents an outstanding example of what can be expected from intensive and thorough study of a limited area. Here we find a new instance of the demonstration made under similar conditions by the same author (1937a, b) and elaborated upon by Spoehr, namely, as the latter puts it, "kinship system does preserve the characteristics of a 'system' despite radical changes in type" (1942, 1947, p. 229). The more recent study of the Pueblo's kinship systems by Eggan confirms the results of these earlier, purely diachronic inquiries. Here we observe closely connected forms, each of which preserves a structural consistency, although they present, in relation to one another, discontinuities which become significant when compared to homologous discontinuities in other fields, such as clan organization, marriage rules, ritual, religious beliefs, etc.

It is by means of such studies, exhibiting a truly "Galilean" outlook,[8] that one may hope to reach a depth where social structure is put on a level with other types of mental structures, particularly the linguistic one, as suggested by this writer (1951). To give an example: it follows from Eggan's survey that the Hopi kinship system requires no less than three different models for the time-dimension: there is, first, an "empty" time, stable and reversible, illustrated by the father's mother's and mother's father's lineage, where the same terms are consistently applied throughout the generations; second, a progressive, nonreversible time, as shown in Ego's (female) lineage with the sequence: grandmother $\rangle$ mother$\rangle$ sister $\rangle$ child $\rangle$ grandchild; and, third, an undulating, cyclical, reversible time, as in Ego's (male) lineage with the indefinite alternation between sister and sister's child. On the other hand, these three "straight" frames are clearly distinct from the "curved" frame of Zuni Ego's (female) lineage, where four terms: mother's mother (or daughter's daughter), mother, daughter, are disposed in a kind of ringlike arrangement, this conceptual grouping being accompanied, as regards the other lineages, by a greater poverty both of terms inside the acknowledged kin and of kin acknowledgment. Since time aspects belong also to linguistic analysis, the questions can be raised whether or not there is a correlation between these fields; if so, at what level; etc. More

8. That is, aiming to determine the law of variation, in contradistinction to the "Aristotelian" outlook mostly concerned with inductive correlations; for this distinction, fundamental to structural analysis, see Lewin (1935).

general problems, though of a similar kind, were raised by L. Thompson (1950) in reference to Whorf's linguistic treatment of Hopi.

Progress in this and other directions would undoubtedly have been more substantial if general agreement had existed among social anthropologists on the definition of social structure, the goals which may be achieved by its study, and the methodological principles to be applied at the different stages of research. Unfortunately, this is not the case, but it may be welcomed as a promising factor that some kind of understanding can be reached, at least on the nature and scope of these differences. This seems an appropriate place to offer a rapid sketch of the attitude of the main contributors to social-structure researches in relation to the working assumptions which were made at the beginning of this paper.

The words "social structure" are in many ways linked with the name of A. R. Radcliffe-Brown. Though his contribution does not limit itself to the study of kinship systems, he has stated the goal of these studies in terms which every scholar in the same field would probably be ready to underwrite: the aim of kinship studies, he says, is (1) to make a systematic classification; (2) to understand particular features of particular systems (*a*) by revealing the particular feature as a part of an organized whole and (*b*) by showing that it is a special example of a recognizable class of phenomena; (3) to arrive at valid generalizations about the nature of human societies. And he concludes: "To reduce this diversity (of 2 or 300 kinship systems) to some sort of order is the task of analysis. . . . We can . . . find . . . beneath the diversities, a limited number of general principles applied and combined in various ways" (1941, p. 17). There is nothing to add to this lucid program besides pointing out that this is precisely what Radcliffe-Brown has done in his study of Australian kinship systems. He brought forth a tremendous amount of material; he introduced some kind of order where there was only chaos; he defined the basic operational terms, such as "cycle," "pair," and "couple." Finally, his discovery of the Kariera system in the region and with the characteristics inferred from the study of the available data and before visiting Australia will forever remain one of the great results of sociostructural studies (1930–31). His masterly Introduction to *African Systems of Kinship and Marriage* may be considered a true treatise on kinship; at the same time it takes a step toward integrating kinship systems of the Western world (which are approached in their early forms) into a world-wide theoretical interpretation. Another capital contribution by the same scholar, about the homologous structure of kinship terminology and behavior, will be dealt with later on.

However, it is obvious that, in many respects, Radcliffe-Brown's conception of social structure differs from the postulates which were set up at the outset of the present paper. In the first place, the notion of structure appears to him as a means to link social anthropology to the biological sciences: "There is a real and significant analogy between organic structure and social structure" (1940*b*, p. 6). Then, instead of "lifting up" kinship studies to put them on the same level as communication theory, as has been suggested by this writer, he has lowered them to the same plane as the phenomena dealt with in descriptive morphology and physiology (1940*b*, p. 10). In that respect, his approach is in line with the naturalistic trend of the British school. In contradistinction to Kroeber (1938, 1942, pp. 205 ff.) and Lowie (1948*a*, chap. iv), who have emphasized the artificiality of kinship, he agrees with Malinowski that biological ties are, at one and the same time, the origin of and the model for every type of kinship tie (Radcliffe-Brown, 1926).

These principles are responsible for two consequences. In the first place, Radcliffe-Brown's empirical approach makes him very reluctant to distinguish between *social structure* and *social relations*. As a matter of fact, social structure appears in his work to be nothing else than the whole network of social relations. It is true that he has sometimes outlined a distinction between *structure* and *structural form*. The latter concept, however, seems to be limited to the diachronic perspective, and its functional role in Radcliffe-Brown's theoretical thought appears quite reduced (1940b, p. 4). This distinction was thoroughly discussed by Fortes, who has contributed a great deal to the distinction, quite foreign to Radcliffe-Brown's outlook, between "model" and "reality" (see above): "structure is not immediately visible in the 'concrete reality.'... When we describe structure ... we are, as it were, in the realm of grammar and syntax, not of the spoken word" (Fortes, 1949, p. 56).

In the second place, this merging of social structure and social relations induces him to break down the former into the simplest forms of the latter, that is, relations between two persons: "The kinship structure of any society consists of a number of ... dyadic relations.... In an Australian tribe, the whole social structure is based on a network of such relations of person to person..." (1940b, p. 3). It may be questioned whether such dyadic relations are the materials out of which social structure is built, or whether they do not themselves result from a pre-existing structure which should be defined in more complex terms. Structural linguistics has a lot to teach in this respect. Examples of the kind of analysis commended by Radcliffe-Brown may be found in the works of

Bateson and Mead. However, in *Naven* (1936), Bateson has gone a step further than Radcliffe-Brown's classification (1941) of dyadic relations according to order: he has attempted to place them in specific categories, an undertaking which implies that there is something more in social structure than the dyadic relations, i.e., the structure itself. This was a significant step toward the communication level (Ruesch and Bateson, 1951). Since it is possible to extend, almost indefinitely, the string of dyadic relations, Radcliffe-Brown has shown some reluctance toward the isolating of social structures conceived as self-sufficient wholes (in this respect he disagrees with Malinowski). His is a philosophy of continuity, not of discontinuity; this accounts for his hostility toward the notion of culture, already alluded to, and his avoiding the teachings of structural linguistics and of modern mathematics.

All these considerations may explain why Radcliffe-Brown, though an incomparable observer, analyst, and classifier, has sometimes proved to be disappointing when he turned to interpretations. These, in his work, often appear vague or circulative. Have marriage prohibitions really no further function than to help perpetuate the kinship system (Radcliffe-Brown, 1949b)? Are all the peculiar features of the Crow-Omaha systems satisfactorily accounted for when it has been said that they emphasize the lineage principle (Radcliffe-Brown, 1941)? These doubts, as well as many others, some of which will find their place later on in this paper, explain why the work of Radcliffe-Brown, to which nobody can deny a central place in social-structure studies, has often given rise to bitter arguments.

For instance, Murdock has called the kind of interpretation to which Radcliffe-Brown seems to be addicted: "mere verbalizations reified into causal forces (1949, p. 121)," and Lowie expressed himself in similar terms (1937, pp. 224–25). As regards Murdock, the lively controversy which has been carried on lately between him and W. H. Lawrence (Lawrence and Murdock, 1949), on the one hand, and Radcliffe-Brown (1951), on the other, may help to clarify the basic differences in their respective positions. This was about the so-called "Murngin type" of kinship system, a focal point in social-structure studies not only because of its many intricacies but because, thanks to Lloyd Warner's book and articles (1930–31, 1937a), we possess a thorough and extensive study of this system. However, Warner's study leaves some basic problems unanswered, especially the way in which marriage takes place on the lateral borders of the system. For Radcliffe-Brown, however, there is no problem involved, since he considers any kind of social organization as a mere conglomerate of simple person-to-person relations and since, in any society, there is always somebody who may be regarded as one's mother's brother's daughter (the preferred spouse among the Murngin) or as standing in an equivalent relation. But the problem is elsewhere: it lies in the fact that the natives have chosen to express these person-to-person relations in a class system, and Warner's description of this system (as acknowledged by himself) makes it impossible in some cases for the same individual to belong simultaneously to the right kind of class and to the right kind of relation. Under these circumstances, Lawrence and Murdock have tried to invent some system which would fit with the requirements of both the marriage rules and a system of the same kind as the one described by Warner. They invented it, however, as a sort of abstract game, the result being that, while their system meets some of the difficulties involved in Warner's account, it also raises many

others. One of the main difficulties implied in Warner's system is that it would require, on the part of the natives, an awareness of relationships too remote to make it believable. Since the new system adds a new line to the seven already assumed by Warner, it goes still further in that direction. Therefore, it seems a good hunch that the "hidden" or "unknown" system underlying the clumsy model which the Murngin borrowed recently from tribes with completely different marriage rules is simpler than the latter and not more complicated.

One sees, then, that Murdock favors a systematic and formal approach, different from Radcliffe-Brown's empirical and naturalistic one. But he remains, at the same time, psychologically and even biologically minded, and he can comply with the resulting requirements only by calling upon other disciplines, such as psychoanalysis and behaviorist psychology. Thus he succeeds in unloading from his interpretations of kinship problems the empiricism which still burdens Radcliffe-Brown's work, though, perhaps, at the risk of leaving them uncompleted or having to be completed on a ground foreign to anthropology, if not contradictory to its goals. Instead of seeing in kinship systems a sociological means to achieve a sociological result, he rather treats them as sociological results deriving from biological and psychological premises (1949, pp. 131–32).

Two parts should be distinguished in Murdock's contribution to the study of social structure. There is, first, a rejuvenation of a statistical method to check assumed correlations between social traits and to establish new ones, a method already tried by Tylor but which Murdock, thanks to the painstaking efforts of his Yale Cross-cultural Survey and the use of a more complex and exacting technique, was able to carry much further than had his predecessor. Everything has been said on the manifold difficulties with which this kind of inquiry is fraught (Lowie, 1948*a*, chap. iii), and, since nobody more than its author is aware of them, it is unnecessary to dwell upon this theme. Let it only be recalled that, while the uncertainty involved in the process of "carving out" the data will always make any alleged correlation dubious, the method is quite efficient in a negative way, that is, to explode false correlations. In this respect Murdock has achieved many results which no social anthropologist can permit himself to ignore.

The second aspect of Murdock's contribution is a scheme of the historical evolution of kinship systems. This suggests a startling conclusion, namely, that the so-called "Hawaiian type" of social organization should be placed at the origin of a much greater number of systems than has generally been admitted since Lowie's criticism of Morgan's similar hypothesis (Lowie, 1920, chap. iii). However, it should be kept in mind that Murdock's scheme is not based upon the consideration of individual societies taken as historicogeographical units or as co-ordinated wholes, but on abstractions and even, if one may say so, on abstractions "twice-removed": in the first place, social organization is isolated from the other aspects of culture (and sometimes even kinship systems from social organization); next, social organization itself is broken up into disconnected elements which are the outcome more of the traditional categories of ethnological thought than of the concrete analysis of each group. This being understood, the method for establishing a historical scheme can only be ideological; it proceeds by extracting common elements belonging to each stage in order to define a previous stage and so on. Therefrom it is obvious that systems placed at the beginning can be

only those which exhibit the more general features, while systems with special features must occupy a more remote rank. In order to clarify this, a comparison may be used, though its oversimplification makes it unfair to Murdock: it is as though the origin of the modern horse were ascribed to the order of vertebrates instead of to *Hipparion.*

Regardless of the difficulties raised by his approach, Murdock's book should be credited with presenting new material and raising fascinating problems, many of which are new to anthropological thought. It is not doing him an injustice, then, to state that his contribution consists more in perfecting a method of discovering new problems than in solving them. Though this method remains "Aristotelian," it is perhaps unavoidable in the development of any science. Murdock has at least been faithful to the best part of the Aristotelian outlook by demonstrating convincingly that "cultural forms in the field of social organization reveal a degree of regularity and of conformity to scientific law not significantly inferior to that found in the so-called natural sciences" (1949, p. 259).

In relation to the distinctions made in the first section of this paper, it can be said that Radcliffe-Brown's work expresses a disregard for the difference between observation and experimentation, while Murdock shows a similar disregard for the difference between mechanical and statistical models (since he tries to construct mechanical models with the help of a statistical method). Conversely, Lowie's work seems to consist entirely in an exacting endeavor to meet the question (which was acknowledged as a prerequisite for any study in social structure): *What are the facts?* When he became active in research as well as in theoretical ethnology, the latter field was fraught with philosophical prejudices and an aura of sociological mysticism; therefore, his paramount contribution toward assessing the subject matter of social anthropology has sometimes been misunderstood and thought of as wholly negative (Kroeber, 1920). But, although this situation made it imperative at that time to state, in the first place, what the facts were *not*, the creative energy liberated by his merciless disintegration of arbitrary systems and alleged correlations has furnished, to a very large extent, the power consumed by his followers. His own positive contributions are not always easy to outline on account of the extreme modesty of his thought and his aversion to any kind of wide-scope theoretical claim. He himself used the words "active skepticism" to outline his position. However, it is Lowie who, as early as 1915, stated in modern terms the role of kinship studies in relation to social behavior and organization: "Sometimes the very essence of social fabric may be demonstrably connected with the mode of classifying kin" (1915, 1929c). In the same paper he was able to reverse the narrow historical trend which, at that time, was blinding anthropological thinking to the universal action of structural forces: exogamy was shown to be a scheme defined by truly genetic characters and, whenever present, determining identical features of social organization, without calling for historicogeographical relations. When, a few years later, he exploded the "matrilineal complex" (1919), he achieved two results which are the fundamentals of social-structure studies. In the first place, by dismissing the notion that every so-called "matrilineal" feature was to be understood as an expression or as a vestige of the complex, he made it possible to break it up into several variables. In the second place, the elements thus liberated could be used for a permutative treatment of the differential features of kinship systems

(Lowie, 1929a). Thus he was laying the foundation for a structural analysis of kinship on two different levels: that of the terminological system, on the one hand, and, on the other, that of the correlation between the system of behavior and terminology, showing the path which, later on, was to be followed by others (Radcliffe-Brown, 1924; Lévi-Strauss, 1945).

Lowie should be credited with many other theoretical contributions: he was probably the first one to demonstrate the true bilateral nature of most of the so-called "unilineal" systems (1920, 1929b). He made clear the impact of residence on filiation (1920). He convincingly dissociated avoidance customs from incest prohibition (1920, pp. 104–5); his care to interpret social organization not only as a set of institutionalized rules but also as the outcome of individual psychological reactions, which sometimes contradicted or inflected the rules, led to the strange result that the same scholar who was so much abused for his famous "shreds and patches" statement on culture was able to offer some of the most thorough and well-balanced pictures we have of cultures treated as wholes (1935, 1948a, chaps. xv, xvi, xvii). Finally, Lowie's role as a promoter and exponent of South American social anthropology is well known; either directly or indirectly through guidance and encouragement, he has contributed toward breaking a new field.

IV. SOCIAL DYNAMICS: SUBORDINATION STRUCTURES

a) ORDER OF ELEMENTS (INDIVIDUALS OR GROUPS) IN THE SOCIAL STRUCTURE

According to this writer's interpretation, which does not need to be expounded systematically, since (in spite of efforts toward objectivity) it probably permeates this paper, kinship systems, marriage rules, and descent groups constitute a co-ordinated ensemble, the function of which is to insure the permanency of the social group by means of intertwining consanguineous and affinal ties. They may be considered as the blueprint of a mechanism which "pumps" women out of their consanguineous families to redistribute them in affinal groups, the result of this process being to create new consanguineous groups and so on. This view results from Linton's classical distinction between "conjugal" and "consanguineous" family (1936, pp. 159–63). If no external factor were affecting this mechanism, it would work indefinitely and the social structure would remain static. This is not the case, however; hence the need to introduce into the theoretical model new elements to account for the diachronic changes of the structure, on the one hand, and, on the other, for the fact that kinship structure does not exhaust social structure. This can be done in three different ways.

As always, the first step consists in ascertaining the facts. Since the time when Lowie expressed regret that so little had been done by anthropologists in the field of political organization (1920, chap. xiii), some progress has been made; in the first place, Lowie himself has clarified the issue by devoting most of his recent book to problems of that sort and by regrouping the facts concerning the American area (1927, 1948a, chaps. vi, vii, xii–xiv, 1948b). A recent work has brought together significant data concerning Africa (Fortes and Evans-Pritchard, 1940). To this day, the best way to organize the still much confused material remains Lowie's basic distinctions (1948a) between social strata, sodalities, and the state.

The second type of approach would be an attempt to correlate the phenomena belonging to the order first studied, i.e., kinship, with phenomena belonging to the new order but showing a direct connection with the former. This approach raises, in turn, two different problems: (1) Can the kinship structure by itself result in structures of a new type (that is, dynamically oriented)? (2) How do *communication structures* and *subordination structures* interact on each other?

The first problem should be related to education, i.e., to the fact that each generation plays alternately a submissive and a dominant part in relation to the preceding and to the following generation. This aspect has been dealt with chiefly by Margaret Mead;[9] its discussion will probably find a more appropriate place in other papers.

Another side of the question lies in the important attempt to correlate a static position in the kinship structure (as defined by terminology) with a dynamic behavior expressed, on the one hand, in rights, duties, obligations, and, on the other, in privileges, avoidance, etc. It is impossible to go into the discussion of these problems to which many writers have contributed. Especially significant is a protracted controversy between Radcliffe-Brown and others (Radcliffe-Brown, 1935, 1940a, 1949a; Opler, 1937, 1947; Brand, 1948) about the kind of correlation which exists, if any, between kin terminology and behavior.

According to Radcliffe-Brown's well-known position, such a correlation exhibits a high degree of accuracy, while his opponents have generally tried to demonstrate that this is neither absolute nor detailed. In contrast to both opinions, this writer has tried to establish that the relation between terminology and behavior is of a dialectical nature. The modalities of behavior between relatives express to some extent

9. In connection with this paper's approach, see particularly Mead (1949).

the terminological classification, and they provide at the same time a means to overcome difficulties and contradictions resulting from this classification. Thus the rules of behavior result from an attempt to overcome contradictions in the field of terminology and marriage rules; the functional unwedging—if one may say so—which is bound to exist between the two orders causes changes in the former, i.e., terminology; and these, in turn, call for new behavior patterns, and so on indefinitely.

The second problem confronts us with the kind of situation arising when the kinship system does not regulate matrimonial exchanges between equals but between members of a hierarchy (either economic or political). Under that heading come the problems of polygamy which, in some cases at least, may be shown to provide a bridge between two different types of guarantees, one collective and political, the other individual and economic (Lévi-Strauss, 1944); and that of hypergamy. This deserves much more attention than it has received so far, since it is the doorway to the study of the caste system (Hocart, 1938; Davis, 1941; Lévi-Strauss, 1949*b*, chaps. xxiv–xxvii) and hence to that of social structures based on race and class distinctions.

The third and last approach to our problem is purely formal. It consists in an a priori deduction of the types of structure likely to result from relations of domination or dependency as they might appear at random. Of a very promising nature for the study of social structure are Rapoport's attempts to make a mathematical theory of the pecking order among hens (1949). It is true that there seems to be a complete opposition between, let us say, the pecking order of hens, which is intransitive and cyclical, and the social order (for instance, the circle of kava in Polynesia), which is transitive and noncyclical (since those who are seated at the far end can never sit at the top). But the study of kinship systems shows precisely that, under given circumstances, an intransitive and cyclical order can result in a transitive and noncyclical one. This happens, for instance, in a hypergamous society where a circulative marriage system with mother's brother's daughter leaves at one end a girl unable to find a husband (since her status is the highest) and at the other end a boy without a wife (since no girl has a lower status than his own). Thus, with the help of such notions as transitivity, order, and cycle, which admit of mathematical treatment, it becomes possible to study, on a purely formal level, generalized types of social structure where both the communication and the subordination aspects become fully integrated. It is also possible to enlarge the field of inquiry and to integrate, for a given society, actual and potential types of order. For instance, in human societies the actual forms of social order are practically always of a transitive and noncyclical type: if A is above B and B above C, then A is above C; and C cannot be above A. But most of the human "potential" or "ideological" forms of social order, as illustrated in politics, myth, and religion, are conceived as intransitive and cyclical; for instance, in tales about kings marrying lasses and in Stendhal's indictment of American democracy as a system where a gentleman takes his orders from his grocer.

b) ORDER OF ORDERS

Thus anthropology considers the whole social fabric as a network of different types of orders. The kinship system provides a way to order individuals according to certain rules; social organization is another way of ordering individuals and groups; social stratifications, whether economic or political, provide us with a third type; and all these orders can themselves be put in order by showing the kind of relationships which exist between them, how they interact on one another on both the synchronic and the diachronic levels. Meyer Fortes has successfully tried to construct models valid not only for one type of order (kinship, social organization, economic relations, etc.) but where numerous models for all types of orders are themselves ordered inside a total model (1949).

When dealing with these orders, however, anthropologists are confronted with a basic problem which was taken up at the beginning of this paper, i.e., to what extent does the manner according to which a society conceives its orders and their ordering correspond to the real situation? It has been shown that this problem can be solved in different ways, depending on the data at hand.

All the models considered so far, however, are "lived-in" orders: they correspond to mechanisms which can be studied from the outside as a part of objective reality. But no systematic studies of these orders can be undertaken without acknowledging the fact that social groups, to achieve their mutual ordering, need to call upon orders of different types, corresponding to a field external to objective reality and which we call the "supernatural." These "thought-of" orders cannot be checked against the experience to which they refer, since they are one and the same thing as this experience. Therefore, we are in the position of studying them only in their relationships with the other types of "lived-in" orders. The "thought-of" orders are those of myth and religion. The question may be raised whether, in our own society, political ideology does not belong to the same category.

After Durkheim, Radcliffe-Brown has contributed greatly to the demonstration that religion is a part of the social structure. The anthropologist's task is to discover correlations between different types of religions and different types of social organization (Radcliffe-Brown, 1945). Radcliffe-Brown failed, however, to achieve significant results for two reasons. In the first place, he tried to link ritual and beliefs directly to sentiments; besides, he was more concerned with giving universal formulation to the kind of correlation prevailing between religion and social structure than in showing the variability of one in relation to the other. It is perhaps as a result of this that the study of religion has fallen into the background, to the extent that the word "religion" does not even appear in the program of this symposium. The field of myth, ritual, and religion seems nevertheless to be one of the more fruitful for the study of social structure; though relatively little has been done in this respect, the results which have been obtained recently are among the most rewarding in our field.

Great strides have been taken toward the study of religious systems as coordinate wholes. Documentary material, such as Radin's *The Road of Life and Death* (1945) or Berndt's *Kunapipi* (1951), should help in undertaking, with respect to several religious cults, the kind of ordering of data so masterfully achieved by Gladys Reichard for the Navaho (1950). This should be completed by small-scale comparative studies on the permanent and nonpermanent elements in religious thought as exemplified by Lowie.

With the help of such well-organized material it becomes possible, as Nadel puts it (1952), to prepare "small-scale models of a comparative analysis ... of an analysis of 'concomitant variations' ... such as any inquiry concerned with the explanation of social facts must employ." The results thus achieved may be small; they are, however, some of the most convincing and rigorous in the entire field of social organization. Nadel himself has proved a correlation be- tween shamanism and some aspects of psychological development (1946); using Indo-European comparative material borrowed from Iceland, Ireland, and the Caucasus, Dumézil has interpreted an enigmatic mythological figure in relation to specific features of social organization (1948); Wittfogel and Goldfrank have shown how significant variations in mythological themes can be related to the socioeconomic background (1943). Monica Hunter has established beyond doubt that the structure of the magical beliefs may vary in correlation with the structure of the society itself (Hunter-Wilson, 1951). These results, together with some others, on which space prevents our commenting, give hope that we may be close to understanding not only what kind of function religious beliefs fulfil in social life (this has been known more or less clearly since Lucretius' time) but how they fulfil this function.

A few words may be added as a conclusion. This paper was started by working out the notion of "model," and the same notion has reappeared at its end. Social anthropology, being in its incipient stage, could only seek, as model for its first models, among those of the simplest kind provided by more advanced sciences, and it was natural enough to seek them in the field of classical mechanics. However, in doing so, anthropology has been working under some sort of illusion since, as Von Neumann puts it (Von Neumann and Morgenstern, 1944, p. 14), "an almost exact theory of a gas, containing about 10^{25} freely moving particles, is incomparably easier than that of the solar system, made up of 9 major bodies." But when it tries to construct its models, anthropology finds itself in a case which is neither the one nor the other: the objects with which we deal—social roles and human beings—are considerably more numerous than those dealt with in Newtonian mechanics and, at the same time, far less numerous than would be required to allow a satisfactory use of the laws of statistics and probability. Thus we found ourselves in an intermediate zone: too complicated for one treatment and not complicated enough for the other.

The tremendous change which was brought about by the theory of communication consists precisely in the discovery of methods to deal with objects—signs—which can be subjected to a rigorous study despite the fact that they are altogether much more numerous than those of classical mechanics and much less than those of thermodynamics. Language consists of morphemes, a few thousand in number; significant regularities in phoneme frequencies can be reached by limited counts. The threshold for the use of statistical laws becomes lower, and that for operating with mechanical models higher, than was the case when operating on other grounds. And, at the same time, the size-order of the phenomena has become significantly closer to that of anthropological data.

Therefore, the present conditions of social-structure studies can be summarized as follows: phenomena were found to be of the same kind as those which, in strategics and communication theory, were made the subject of a rigorous approach. Anthropological facts are on a scale which is sufficiently close to that of these other phenomena as not to preclude their similar treatment. Surprisingly enough, it is at the very moment when anthropology finds itself closer than ever to the long-awaited goal of becoming a true science that the ground seems to fail where it was expected to be the firmest: the facts themselves are lacking, either not numerous' enough or not collected under conditions insuring their comparability.

Though it is not our fault, we have

been behaving like amateur botanists, picking up haphazardly heteroclite specimens, which were further distorted and mutilated by preservation in our herbarium. And we are, all of a sudden, confronted with the need of ordering complete series, ascertaining original shades, and measuring minute parts which have either shrunk or been lost. When we come to realize not only what should be done but also what we should be in a position to do, and when we make at the same time an inventory of our material, we cannot help feeling in a disheartened mood. It looks almost as if cosmic physics was set up to work on Babylonian observations. The celestial bodies are still there, but unfortunately the native cultures where we used to gather our data are disappearing at a fast rate, and what they are being replaced by can only furnish data of a very different type. To adjust our techniques of observation to a theoretical framework which is far more advanced is a paradoxical situation, quite opposite to that which has prevailed in the history of sciences. Nevertheless, such is the challenge to modern anthropology.

REFERENCES

BATESON, G. 1936. *Naven*. Cambridge: At the University Press.

BERNDT, R. A. 1951. *Kunapipi*. New York: International Universities Press.

BERNOT, L., and BLANCARD, R. MS: "Nouville: Un Village français." UNESCO.

BIDNEY, D. 1950. Review of WHITE, L. A. *The Science of Culture*, in *American Anthropologist*, LII, No. 4, Part I, 518–19.

BOAS, F. (ed.). 1911. *Handbook of American Indian Languages*. (Bureau of American Ethnology Bull. 40 [1908], Part I.) Washington, D.C.: Government Printing Office.

BOHR, N. 1939. "Natural Philosophy and Human Culture," *Nature*, CXLIII, 268–72.

BRAND, C. S. 1948. "On Joking Relationships," *American Anthropologist*, L, 160–61.

CUSHING, F. H. 1896. "Outlines of Zuni Creation Myths," *Bureau of American Ethnology, 13th Annual Report, 1891–1892*, pp. 325–447. Washington, D.C.: Government Printing Office.

———. 1920. *Zuni Breadstuff*. ("Indian Notes and Monographs, Museum of the American Indian, Heye Foundation," Vol. VIII.) New York.

DAHLBERG, G. 1948. *Mathematical Methods for Population Genetics*. London and New York: Interscience Publishers.

DAVIS, K. 1941. "Intermarriage in Caste Societies," *American Anthropologist*, XLIII, 376–95.

———. 1947. *The Development of the City in Society: Proceedings of the 1st Conference on Long Term Social Trends, Social Science Research Council*.

DUMÉZIL, G. 1948. *Loki*. Paris: G. P. Maisonneuve.

———. 1949. *L'Heritage indo-européen à Rome*. Paris: Gallimard.

DURKHEIM, E. 1912. *Les Formes élémentaires de la vie religieuse*. ("Bibliothèque de philosophie contemporaine.") Paris: F. Alcan.

DURKHEIM, E., and MAUSS, M. 1901–2 (1903). "De quelques formes primitives de classification: Contribution à l'étude des représentations collectives," *Année sociologique*, VI, 1–72.

EGGAN, F. 1937a. "Historical Changes in the Choctaw Kinship System," *American Anthropologist*, XXXIX, 34–52.

———. (ed.). 1937b. *Social Anthropology of North American Tribes*. Chicago: University of Chicago Press.

———. 1950. *Social Organization of the Western Pueblos*. Chicago: University of Chicago Press.

ELWIN, V. 1947. *The Muria and Their Ghotul*. Oxford: Oxford University Press.

EVANS-PRITCHARD, E. E. 1939. "Nuer Time Reckoning," *Africa*, XII, 189–216.

———. 1940. *The Nuer*. Oxford: Clarendon Press.

FIRTH, R. 1936. *We, the Tikopia*. London and New York: G. Allen & Unwin.

———. 1946. *Malay Fishermen*. London: Kegan Paul, Trench, Trubner & Co.

——. 1951. *Elements of Social Organization*. London: Watts & Co.

FORD, C. S., and BEACH, F. A. 1951. *Patterns of Sexual Behavior*. New York: Harper & Bros.

FORDE, D. 1941. *Marriage and the Family among the Yakö in S.E. Nigeria*. ("Monographs in Social Anthropology," No. 5.) London: London School of Economics and Political Science.

——. 1950. "Double-Descent among the Yakö." In RADCLIFFE-BROWN, A. R., and FORDE, D. (eds.), *African Systems of Kinship and Marriage*. London: Oxford University Press, for the International African Institute.

FORTES, M. (ed.). 1949. *Social Structure: Studies Presented to A. R. Radcliffe-Brown*. Oxford: Clarendon Press.

FORTES, M., and EVANS-PRITCHARD, E. E. 1940. *African Political Systems*. Oxford: Oxford University Press, for the International Institute of African Languages and Cultures.

GOLDSTEIN, K. 1951. *Der Aufbau des Organismus*. French translation. Paris: Gallimard.

HERSKOVITS, M. J. 1940. *The Economic Life of Primitive Peoples*. New York: Alfred A. Knopf.

HOCART, A. M. 1938. *Les Castes*. ("Annales du Musée Guimet bibliothèque du vulganisation," Vol. LIV.) Paris.

HUNTER-WILSON, M. 1951. "Witch Beliefs and Social Structure," *American Journal of Sociology*, LVI, No. 4, 307–13.

KROEBER, A. L. 1920. Review of LOWIE, R. H., *Primitive Society*, in *American Anthropologist*, XXII, No. 4, 377–81.

——. 1938. "Basic and Secondary Patterns of Social Structure," *Journal of the Royal Anthropological Institute*, LXVIII, 299–309.

——. 1942. "The Societies of Primitive Man," *Biological Symposia*, VIII, 205–16.

——. 1943. "Structure, Function, and Pattern in Biology and Anthropology," *Scientific Monthly*, LVI, 105–13.

——. 1948. *Anthropology*. New ed. New York: Harcourt, Brace & Co.

LAWRENCE, W. E., and MURDOCK, G. P. 1949. "Murngin Social Organization," *American Anthropologist*, LI, No. 1, 58–65.

LEACH, E. R. 1945. "Jinghpaw Kinship Terminology," *Journal of the Royal Anthropological Institute*, LXXV, 59–72.

LESTRANGE, M. DE. 1951. "Pour une méthode socio-démographique," *Journal de la Société des Africanistes*, Vol. XXI.

LÉVI-STRAUSS, C. 1944. "The Social and Pyschological Aspects of Chieftainship in a Primitive Tribe: The Nambikuara," *Transactions of the New York Academy of Sciences*, Series II, VII, No. 1, 16–32.

——. 1945. "L'Analyse structurale en linguistique et en anthropologie," *Word*, I, No. 1, 33–53.

——. 1949a. "Histoire et ethnologie," *Revue de métaphysique et de morale*, LIV, Nos. 3–4, 363–91.

——. 1949b. *Les Structures élémentaires de la parenté*. Paris: Presses universitaires de France.

——. 1951. "Language and the Analysis of Social Laws," *American Anthropologist*, LIII, No. 2, 155–63.

LEWIN, K. 1935. *A Dynamic Theory of Personality*. New York: McGraw-Hill Book Co.

LINTON, R. 1936. *The Study of Man*. New York: D. Appleton–Century Co.

LIVI, L. 1940–41. *Trattato di demografia*. Padua: Cedam.

——. 1949. "Considérations théoriques et pratiques sur le concept de 'minimum de population,'" *Population*, IV, No. 4, 754–56.

LOWIE, R. H. 1915. "Exogamy, and the Classificatory Systems of Relationship," *American Anthropologist*, Vol. XVII, No. 2.

——. 1919. "The Matrilineal Complex," *University of California Publications in American Archaeology and Anthropology*, XVI, No. 2, 29–45.

——. 1920. *Primitive Society*. New York: Horace Liveright.

——. 1927. *The Origin of the State*. New York: Harcourt, Brace & Co.

——. 1929a. "Notes on Hopi Clans," pp. 303–60. ("American Museum of Natural History, Anthropological Papers," Vol. XXX, Part VI.)

——. 1929b. "Hopi Kinship," pp. 361–88. ("American Museum of Natural History, Anthropological Papers," Vol. XXX, Part VII.)

——. 1929c. "Relationship Terms." In *Encyclopaedia Britannica*, pp. 84–89. 14th ed. 1948. Chicago, London, and Toronto: Encyclopaedia Britannica, Inc.

——. 1935. *The Crow Indians*. New York: Farrar & Rinehart.

——. 1937. *The History of Ethnological Theory*. New York: Farrar & Rinehart.

——. 1942. "A Marginal Note to Professor Radcliffe-Brown's Paper on 'Social Structure,'" *American Anthropologist*, XLIV, No. 3, 519–21.

——. 1948a. *Social Organization*. New York: Rinehart & Co.

——. 1948b. "Some Aspects of Political Organization among American Aborigines (Huxley Memorial Lecture)," *Journal of the Royal Anthropological Institute*, LXXVIII, 11–24.

MALINOWSKI, B. 1922. *Argonauts of the Western Pacific*. London: George Routledge & Sons, Ltd.

MAUSS, M. 1904–5 (1906). "Essai sur les variations saisonnières dan les sociétés Eskimos: Étude de morphologie sociale." *Année sociologique*, IX, 39–132.

——. 1923–24. "Essai sur le don, forme archaïque de l'échange," *ibid.*, n.s., I, 30–186.

——. 1924–25. "Division et proportion des divisions de la sociologie," *ibid.*, n.s., II, 98 ff.

——. 1950. *Sociologie et anthropologie*. Paris: Presses universitaires de France.

MEAD, M. 1949. "Character Formation and Diachronic Theory." In FORTES, M. (ed.), *Social Structure: Studies Presented to A. R. Radcliffe-Brown*, pp. 18–34. Oxford: Clarendon Press.

MORGAN, L. H. 1871. *Systems of Consanguinity and Affinity of the Human Family*. ("Smithsonian Institution Contributions to Knowledge," Vol. XVII, No. 218.) Washington, D.C.

MURDOCK, G. P. 1949. *Social Structure*. New York: Macmillan Co.

NADEL, S. F. 1946. "Shamanism in the Nuba Mountains," *Journal of the Royal Anthropological Institute*, LXXVI, Part I, 25–38.

——. 1947. *The Nuba*. London and New York: Oxford University Press.

——. 1952. "Witchcraft in Four African Societies: An Essay in Comparison," *American Anthropologist*, LIV, Part I, 18–29.

NEUMANN, J. VON, and MORGENSTERN, O. 1944. *Theory of Games and Economic Behavior*. Princeton, N.J.: Princeton University Press.

OPLER, M. E. 1937. "Apache Data Concerning the Relation of Kinship Terminology to Social Classification," *American Anthropologist*, XXXIX, No. 2, 201–12.

——. 1947. "Rule and Practice in the Behavior Pattern between Jicarilla Apache Affinal Relatives," *American Anthropologist*, XLIX, No. 3, 453–62.

RADCLIFFE-BROWN, A. R. 1924. "The Mother's Brother in South Africa," *South African Journal of Science*, XXI, 542–55.

——. 1926. "Father, Mother, and Child," *Man*, Vol. XXVI, Art. 103, pp. 159–61.

——. 1930–31. "The Social Organization of Australian Tribes," *Oceania*, I, No. 1, 34–63; No. 2, 206–46; No. 3, 322–41; No. 4, 426–56.

——. 1935. "Kinship Terminology in California," *American Anthropologist*, XXXVII, No. 3, 530–35.

——. 1940a. "On Joking Relationships," *Africa*, XIII, No. 3, 195–210.

——. 1940b. "On Social Structure," *Journal of the Royal Anthropological Institute*, LXX, 1–12.

——. 1941. "The Study of Kinship Systems," *ibid.*, LXXI, 1–18.

——. 1945. "Religion and Society (Henry Meyers Lecture)," *ibid.*, LXXV, 33–43.

——. 1949a. "A Further Note on Joking Relationships," *Africa*, XIX, No. 2, 133–40.

——. 1949b. "White's View of a Science of Culture," *American Anthropologist*, LI, No. 3, 503–12.

——. 1951. "Murngin Social Organization," *ibid.*, LIII, No. 1, 37–55.

——. 1952. "Social Anthropology, Past and Present," *Man*, Vol. LII, Art. 14.

RADCLIFFE-BROWN, A. R., and FORDE, D. (eds.). 1950. *African Systems of Kinship and Marriage*. Oxford: Oxford University Press, for the International African Institute.

RADIN, P. 1945. *The Road of Life and Death*. New York: Pantheon Books, Inc.

RAPOPORT, A. 1949. "Outline of Probabilistic Approach to Animal Sociology," *Bulletin of Mathematical Biophysics,* XI, 183–96, 273–81.

REICHARD, G. A. 1950. *Navaho Religion: A Study in Symbolism.* 2 vols. ("Bollingen Series," No. XVIII.) New York: Pantheon Books, Inc.

RICHARDS, A. I. 1932. *Hunger and Work in a Savage Tribe.* London: G. Routledge & Sons.

——. 1936. "A Dietary Study in Northeastern Rhodesia," *Africa,* IX, No. 2, 166–96.

——. 1939. *Land, Labour and Diet in Northern Rhodesia.* Oxford: Oxford University Press, for the International Institute of African Languages and Cultures.

RICHARDSON, J., and KROEBER, A. L. 1940. "Three Centuries of Women's Dress Fashions: A Quantitative Analysis," *Anthropological Records,* V, No. 2, 111–54.

RUESCH, J., and BATESON, G. 1951. *Communication: The Social Matrix of Psychiatry.* New York: W. W. Norton & Co.

SHANNON, C. E., and WEAVER, W. 1950. *The Mathematical Theory of Communication.* Urbana: University of Illinois Press.

SPECK, F. G. 1915. *Family Hunting Territories and Social Life of Various Algonkian Bands of the Ottawa Valley.* (Canada Department of Mines, Geological Survey Mem. 70, "Anthropological Series," No. 8.) Ottawa: Government Printing Bureau.

SPOEHR, A. 1942. *Kinship System of the Seminole,* pp. 29–113. ("Anthropological Series, Field Museum of Natural History," Vol. XXXIII, No. 2.)

——. 1947. *Changing Kinship Systems,* pp. 153–235. ("Anthropological Series, Field Museum of Natural History," Vol. XXXIII, No. 4.)

——. 1950. "Observations on the Study of Kinship," *American Anthropologist,* LII, No. 1, 1–15.

STEWARD, J. H. 1938. *Basin-Plateau Aboriginal Sociopolitical Groups.* (Bureau of American Ethnology, Smithsonian Institution Bull. 120.) Washington, D.C.: Government Printing Office.

STEWART, J. Q. 1947. "Empirical Mathematical Rules Concerning the Distribution and Equilibrium of Population," *Geographical Review,* XXXVII, No. 3, 461–85.

SUTTER, J., and TABAH, L. 1951. "Les Notions d'isolat et de population minimum," *Population,* VI, No. 3, 481–89.

THOMPSON, L. 1950. *Culture in Crisis: A Study of the Hopi Indians.* New York: Harper & Bros.

WAGLEY, C. 1940. "The Effects of Depopulation upon Social Organization as Illustrated by the Tapirapé Indians," *Transactions of the New York Academy of Sciences,* Series 2, III, No. 1, 12–16.

WARNER, W. L. 1930–31. "Morphology and Functions of the Australian Murngin Type of Kinship System," *American Anthropologist,* XXXII, No. 2, 207–56; XXXIII, No. 2, 172–98.

——. 1937a. *A Black Civilization: A Social Study of an Australian Tribe.* New York: Harper & Bros.

——. 1937b. "The Family and Principles of Kinship Structure in Australia," *American Sociological Review,* II, 43–54.

White, L. A. 1949. *The Science of Culture.* New York: Farrar, Straus & Co.

Wiener, N. 1948. *Cybernetics.* Paris: Herman et Cie; New York: John Wiley & Sons, Inc.

WITTFOGEL, K. A., and GOLDFRANK, E. S. 1943. "Some Aspects of Pueblo Mythology and Society," *Journal of American Folklore,* LVI, 17–30.

ZIPF, G. K. 1949. *Human Behavior and the Principle of Least Effort.* Cambridge, Mass.: Addison-Wesley Press, Inc.

The Relation of Language to Culture

By HARRY HOIJER

CULTURAL ANTHROPOLOGISTS, during the last twenty-five years, have gradually moved from an atomistic definition of culture, describing it as a more or less haphazard collection of traits, to one which emphasizes pattern and configuration. Kluckhohn and Kelly perhaps best express this modern concept of culture when they define it as "all those historically created designs for living, explicit and implicit, rational, irrational, and non-rational, which exist at any given time as potential guides for the behavior of men" (1945, p. 97). Traits, elements, or, better, patterns of culture in this definition are organized or structured into a system or set of systems, which, because it is historically created, is therefore open and subject to constant change.

With this greater understanding of the nature of culture taken as a whole has come a new conception of the interrelationship of language and culture. Language may no longer be conceived as something entirely distinct from other cultural systems but must rather be viewed as part of the whole and functionally related to it. We have, then, a new set of problems, centering about this relationship, which are as yet only imperfectly envisaged and for the most part little examined. It is the purpose of this report to review these problems and to present them for your consideration and discussion.

It may be noted incidentally that this area of research has as yet no generally accepted designation. The terms "ethnolinguistics" and "metalinguistics," often employed, have still a wide variety of meanings, differing almost from one student to the next (see, e.g., Olmsted, 1950). "Ethnolinguistics" is perhaps the more diffuse in meaning: it has been applied to studies (like Sapir's "Time Perspective," 1916) which illustrate the role of linguistic research relative to the history of cultures; to the study of situations like the etiquette of receiving a guest (Voegelin and Harris, 1945, p. 457), where "talk and non-vocal behavior together constitute an ethnolinguistic situation"; to studies (like Mead's, 1939; also Lowie, 1940) of the usefulness of languages as tools of ethnological research; to the studies of Whorf (e.g., 1941c) and others on the relation of habitual behavior and thought to language; and probably to still other and diverse researches. "Metalinguistics," though more restricted (it has been applied, so far, mainly by Trager to the work of Whorf), has the disadvantage of a possible confusion with "metalanguage," a term much used by philosophers interested in semiotics, or the general theory of signs (Carroll et al., 1951, p. 4).

1. As a first step in the presentation that follows, it is necessary to examine the proposition (more or less generally accepted by anthropologists, at least since Tylor's time) that language does not stand separate from culture but is an essential part of it. Voegelin has

recently queried this proposition, finding it "debatable." He adds:

It is obvious that one does not find culture in limbo, since all human communities consist of human animals which talk; but culture can be, and as a matter of fact, is characteristically studied in considerable isolation; so also in even greater isolation, the human animal is studied in physical anthropology, and not *what* the human animal talks about, but rather the *structure* of his talk is studied in linguistics. *What* he talks about is called (by philosophers and semanticists) *meaning;* but for most anthropologists *what* he talks about is *culture* [1949*a*, p. 36].

Later, in answer to Opler's criticism, Voegelin attempts to justify this view:

If language were merely a part of culture, then linguists should be competent to discuss other parts of culture by virtue of their training in linguistics. We must admit that if a linguist can discuss problems in culture, it is by virtue of his being a student in culture, also, rather than by a transfer from linguistic training; and vice versa.

If language were merely a part of culture, primates should be able to learn parts of human language as they actually do learn parts of human culture when prodded by primatologists. No sub-human animal ever learns any part of human languages,—not even parrots. The fact that *Polly wants a cracker* is not taken by the parrot as part of a language is shown by the refusal of the bird to use part of the utterance as a frame (*Polly wants a ...*) with substitutions in the frame. . . . As George Herzog has phrased this, imitative utterances of sub-human animals are limited to one morpheme; to the parrot, then, *Polly wants a cracker* is an unchangeable unit. From this point of view, we can generalize: an inescapable factor of all natural languages is that they are capable of multi-morpheme utterances [1949*b*, p. 45].

Voegelin's first point, that a specialist in one aspect of culture should thereby be equally competent in all others, raises some interesting queries. Would he also insist that a political scientist (who most certainly is a specialist in an important aspect of culture) be equally competent as a sociologist, economist, or anthropologist? Is it true that cultural anthropologists are equally competent in social organization, technology, religion, and folklore? Can we not allow, in view of the wide range of the concept of culture (even omitting language), that a scholar be permitted to specialize? Linguistics, to be sure, requires a good many specialized methods and techniques, but so does folklore, and is that any reason for excluding the subject matter of either linguistics or folklore from culture?

The second point, that primates and other subhuman animals may learn something of culture (when "prodded") but nothing of language, opens the important question of the nature of culture. What do primates learn under the training of primatologists, and are these items truly a part of culture? It is, of course, firmly established that primates acquire techniques and learn to solve problems, though only very simple ones, much as men do. But the primate's learning is cumulative only in the sense that he adds new tricks to his repertory; there is no evidence that he abstracts from problems already learned certain general principles that might be combined to solve problems of increasing complexity. In brief, the primate learns only unchangeable units of human behavior by imitation or trial and error, just as the parrot learns single and unrelated (to him) morpheme utterances. The trick learned by the primate, like the utterances of the parrot, is not seen as a frame in which substitutions are possible but only as an act complete in itself and discrete from all others.

A human culture, on the other hand, is no mere repertory of discrete acts. Anthropologists, or at least most of them, have long since abandoned the notion that a culture is simply a collection of traits, of acts and artifacts. A culture is, rather, in the words of

Kluckhohn and Kelly, "a historically derived system of explicit and implicit designs for living, which tends to be shared by all or specially designated members of a group" (1945, p. 98). The emphasis in this definition lies on the phrase "designs for living"; a culture is only manifest in acts and artifacts, it does not consist of acts and artifacts. What the human learns, in the process of enculturation, is an organized (or structured) set of ways of behaving, which he abstracts from and applies to situations of his daily experience as these arise. In the course of time, and especially under the impact of many new situations (for example, during times of rapid acculturation), there emerge, in the human group, new ways of living and modifications of old ways, abstracted, consciously or unconsciously, from the situations and problems faced by members of the group. It is this feature of cumulating abstracted ways of living that so clearly distinguishes man's culture from the pseudo-culture of the primate, for the latter is but a random collection of discrete acts, possessed by individual animals and not shared, except by the accident of imitation, by others in the group and entirely without possibility of development except by the adding of new acts.

Language fits into this conception of culture without difficulty. Just as a culture consists of all ways of behaving that are historically derived, structured, and tending "to be shared by all or specially designated members of a group," so does a language include ways of speaking (a segment of behaving) with precisely the same attributes. A language, like the rest of culture, is acquired by learning, not discrete utterances (acts) of the *Polly wants a cracker* type, but frames in which all meaningful utterances may be fitted. Languages, like other aspects of cultures, are diverse, not alike; each society has its own language as it has its

own techniques, social and political forms, and patterns of economic and religious behavior. A language, like any other aspect of culture, is cumulative and ever changing, the "mountainous and anonymous work of unconscious generations" (Sapir, 1921, p. 235). Finally, it is quite impossible to conceive of either the origin or the development of culture apart from language, for language is that part of culture which, more than any other, enables men not only to make their own experiences and learning continuous but, as well, to participate vicariously in the experiences and learning of others, past and present, who are or have been members of the group. To the extent that a culture as a whole is made up of common understandings, its linguistic aspect is its most vital and necessary part.

2. The argument that language is an essential part of culture does not, of course, make its relationship with other aspects of culture apparent at first sight. It is, indeed, perfectly clear that language plays a unique role in the total network of cultural patterns, since, for one thing, it apparently functions together with most, if not all, other cultural behavior. Language, as Sapir has noted, "does not as a matter of fact stand apart from or run parallel to direct experience but completely interpenetrates with it" (1933, p. 11). It is an important question, therefore, to determine just what such interpenetration with experience signifies for the speakers of a language, and how it may relate to other aspects of their culture.

Most studies of the relation of language to culture, until recently, have emphasized an external and fairly obvious relation between vocabulary and the content of culture. It has been noted, over and over again, that the vocabulary of a people inventories their culture and reflects, with greater or less accuracy, the particular interests and emphases a people may have in such areas of their culture as technology, social organization, religion, and folklore. Peoples who, like the Chiricahua Apache, live by hunting and collecting are found to have detailed lists of animal and plant names and to name the topographic features of their environment with care and precision. Others, like the Australian aborigines, who emphasize kinship as a means of social control, have a large and complicated vocabulary of kin terms. Status systems, among such peoples as the Japanese and Koreans, are similarly reflected in vocabulary and even in certain partially grammatical features of language, such as the pronominal system.

The study of languages and their vocabularies may also be useful to the culture historian. This is evident, externally, simply in the geographical distribution of related languages, for such distribution often yields important clues as to the earlier location of a population and its later migrations. An illustration is found in the distribution of the Athapaskan-speaking Indians of today, where we find some eight or nine main linguistic subdivisions in western Canada and Alaska, while two others are found, respectively, along the Pacific Coast from Washington to northern California and among the Navaho and Apache tribes of the Southwest. The conclusion here is a clear one: there is little doubt, on linguistic grounds alone, that the original location of these peoples is the northern one and that, therefore, the Pacific Coast and southwestern Athapaskan-speaking societies have migrated southward to their present position.

Internal linguistic evidence may also be used, as Sapir has noted, to set cultural elements in chronologic relations with one another:

Language, like culture, is a composite of elements of very different age, some of its features reaching back into the mists of an impenetrable past, others being the product of a development of yesterday. If we now succeed in putting the changing face of culture into relation with the changing face of language, we shall have obtained a measure, vague or precise according to specific circumstances, of the relative ages of the culture elements. In this way language gives us a sort of stratified matrix to work in for the purposes of unraveling culture sequences [1916, p. 432].

Applications of this method are numerous; we need call attention, as illustration, to only two, Sapir's "Internal Linguistic Evidence of the Northern Origin of the Navaho" (1936) and Herzog's "Culture Change and Language: Shifts in the Pima Vocabulary" (1941).

Vocabulary, then, is quite clearly linked with many features of nonlinguistic culture, synchronically and diachronically, and the study of vocabulary is useful, if not essential, to a complete and well-rounded ethnographic account. But this use of linguistic data or even the clear association between vocabulary and the content of culture proves no more than the fact that language has a cultural setting. The same is true of the reverse situation, that is, that the linguist, if he is successfully to define vocabulary items, must know something of the rest of the culture. However, as Sapir remarked some years ago, "this superficial and extraneous kind of parallelism is of no real interest to the linguist except in so far as the growth or borrowing of new words throws light on the formal trends of the language. The linguistic student should never make the mistake of identifying a language with its dictionary" (1921, p. 234).

A language is, of course, far more than its dictionary, which may, indeed, be regarded more as a product of the language than as a part of it. To understand the true interrelationship of language and other cultural systems, we need to study, not the products of the language, but its patterns, lexical, morphological, and syntactic, and the relation of these, should such relations exist, to other patterns in the culture. It is this study that will be the concern of the sections that follow.

3. The central problem of this report is, then, a thesis suggested by Sapir in many of his writings and later developed in more detail by Whorf and others. In terms of this thesis, peoples speaking different languages may be said to live in different "worlds of reality," in the sense that the languages they speak affect, to a considerable degree, both their sensory perceptions and their habitual modes of thought. Sapir has stated this thesis in the following words:

Language is a guide to "social reality." Though language is not ordinarily thought of as of essential interest to the students of social science, it powerfully conditions all our thinking about social problems and processes. Human beings do not live in the objective world alone, nor alone in the world of social activity as ordinarily understood, but are very much at the mercy of the particular language which has become the medium of expression for their society. It is quite an illusion to imagine that one adjusts to reality essentially without the use of language and that language is merely an incidental means of solving specific problems of communication or reflection. The fact of the matter is that the "real world" is to a large extent unconsciously built up on the language habits of the group. No two languages are ever sufficiently similar to be considered as representing the same social reality. The worlds in which different societies live are distinct worlds, not merely the same world with different labels attached.

The understanding of a simple poem, for instance, involves not merely an understanding of the single words in their average significance, but a full comprehension of the whole life of the community as it is mirrored in the words, or as it is suggested by their overtones. Even comparatively simple acts of perception are very much more at the mercy of the social patterns called words than we might suppose. If one draws some dozen lines, for instance, of different shapes, one perceives them as divisible into such categories as "straight," "crooked," "curved," "zigzag" because of the classificatory suggestiveness of the linguistic terms themselves. We see and hear and otherwise experience very largely as we do because the language habits of our community predispose certain choices of interpretation [1929, p. 162].

Whorf, in a later study inspired by Sapir's example, analyzes "many hundreds of reports [to an insurance company] of circumstances surrounding the start of fires." He finds in these that "not only a physical situation *qua* physics, but the meaning of that situation to people, was sometimes a factor, through the behavior of the people, in the start of the fire" (1941*c*, p. 75). These instances, he says, "suffice to show how the cue to a certain line of behavior is often given by the analysis of the linguistic formula in which the situation is spoken of, and by which to some degree it is analyzed, classified, and allotted its place in that world which is 'to a large extent unconsciously built up on the language habits of the group'" (1941*c*, p. 77).

Comparison of widely divergent languages provides ample illustration of the fact that languages categorize reality in many different ways. Systems of kinship terminology, for example, obviously do not symbolize one system of biological relationships common to all mankind but denote, rather, socially and culturally determined relationships peculiar to a given society. English terms like "father," "mother," "brother," "sister," and "cousin" find no precise parallels in the vocabularies of peoples who do not share our system of kinship. Among the Chiricahua Apache, for instance, there are but two terms for relatives within one's own generation; these terms (*-k'is* and *-làh*) are used to all such relatives whether they are siblings, near cousins, or only remote cousins. *-k'is* is applied to all who are of the same sex as the speaker; *-làh*, to all who are of the opposite sex. Corresponding to these terms are contrasting patterns of behavior, to which, of course, the words themselves are cues. The Chiricahua Apache treats kin addressed as -*k'is* with great affection and familiarity; they are, in this society, the people with whom an individual feels most secure and at ease. In contrast, relatives addressed as -*làh* are treated with excessive formality and circumspection; one must even avoid being together with one's -*làh* except in the presence of others (Opler, 1941).

Similar examples may be given in respect to terms relating to the physical environment. Among the Navaho, for example, we find color terms corresponding roughly to our "white," "red," and "yellow," but none which are equivalent to our "black," "gray," "brown," "blue," and "green." Navaho has two terms corresponding to "black," one denoting the black of the darkness, the other the black of such objects as coal. Our "gray" and "brown" are, however, denoted by a single term in Navaho, and so also are our "blue" and "green." The Navaho, in brief, divide the color spectrum, in so far as their vocabulary is concerned, into segments different from our own.

Another fruitful source of examples is found in personal pronouns, especially those for the second and third persons. It is well known that many European languages have two second person pronouns (as French *tu, vous*) where only one is found in modern English. Navaho has no equivalents for English "he," "she," and "it"; this segmentation, a trace of an old gender system, does not exist in Navaho. But Navaho does divide third person pronouns into four categories: (1) that employed of persons or beings psychologically close to the speaker or of preferred interest, (2) that employed of persons or beings psychologically remote, such as non-Navaho (when contrasted with Navaho) or relatives treated with formality (as opposed to those treated with familiarity), (3) the indefinite third person, an "it" that refers only to an unspecified actor or goal, and (4) the third person that has reference to a place, condition, or time.

A final, and revealing, illustration may be added from the language of the Chiricahua Apache, the place name *tónòogàh*, for which the English equivalent (not the translation) is "Dripping Springs." Dripping Springs, a noun phrase, names a spot in New Mexico where the water from a spring flows over a rocky bluff and drips into a small pool below; the English name, it is evident, is descriptive of one part of this scene, the movement of the water. The Apache term is, in contrast, a verbal phrase and accentuates quite a different aspect of the scene. The element *tó*, which means "water," precedes the verb *nòogàh*, which means, roughly, "whiteness extends downward." *tónòogàh* as a whole, then, may be translated "water-whiteness extends downward," a reference to the fact that a broad streak of white limestone deposit, laid down by the running water, extends downward on the rock.

While these examples, and many other similar ones, seem clearly to indicate that language habits influence *sensory* perceptions and thought, we must not overestimate this influence. It is simply not true, for example, that the Chiricahua Apache, because he does not in speech distinguish between -*k'is*, is also unable to distinguish his siblings (of the same sex) from other relatives of that class in the same generation. He may, of course, distinguish them, much as we have been able to define in English terms like -*k'is* and -*làh*, that is, by circumlocutions of one sort or another. In the same way, it is perfectly evident that the Navaho, while they denote "brown" and "gray" by one term and "blue" and "green" by another, are quite able to discern the difference between brown and gray, blue and green. Again this may be done, should ambiguity otherwise result, by circumlocution, just as we can quite simply express in English the difference between the two Navaho words for our "black."

The fact of the matter, then, is not that linguistic patterns inescapably limit sensory perceptions and thought, but simply that, together with other cultural patterns, they direct perception and thinking into certain habitual channels. The Eskimo, who distinguishes in speech several varieties of snow surface (and who lacks a general term corresponding to our "snow"), is responding to a whole complex of cultural patterns, which require that he make these distinctions, so vital to his physical welfare and that of the group. It is as if the culture as a whole (including the language) selected from the landscape certain features more important than others and so gave to the landscape an organization or structure peculiar to the group. A language, then, as a cultural system, more or less faithfully reflects the structuring of reality which is peculiar to the group that speaks it. Sapir says:

> To pass from one language to another is psychologically parallel to passing from one geometrical system of reference to another. The environing world which is referred to is the same for either language; the world of points is the same in either frame of reference. But the formal approach to the same item of experience, as to the given point of space, is so different that the resulting feeling of orientation can be the same neither in the two languages nor in the two frames of reference. Entirely distinct, or at least measurably distinct, formal adjustments have to be made and these differences have their psychological correlates [1924, p. 153].

4. The most important of the studies that document the thesis outlined in section 3 is undoubtedly the work of Benjamin L. Whorf, specifically his paper on "The Relation of Habitual Behavior and Thought to Language" (1941c). Whorf's views are also summarized, in briefer and less technical form, in three other articles: "Science and Linguistics" (1940b), "Linguistics as an Exact Science" (1941a), and "Languages and Logic" (1941b). All four papers were reprinted in 1949, under the title *Four Articles on Metalinguistics*, by the Foreign Service Institute, Department of State, Washington, D.C. We shall summarize only the first of the papers listed above.

Whorf begins, as we have already noted, by an analysis of instances in which the meaning of a situation, as well as certain physical realities, appears to have influenced behavior. He notes, however, that such lexical meanings are limited in range and that "one cannot study the behavioral compulsiveness of such materials without suspecting a much more far-reaching compulsion from large-scale patterning of grammatical categories, such as plurality, gender and similar classifications (animate, inanimate, etc.), tenses, voices, and other verb forms, classifications of the type of 'parts of speech,' and the matter of whether a given experience is denoted by a unit morpheme, an inflected word, or a syntactical combination" (1941c, p. 77). These grammatical patterns tend in the same direction as the smaller and more limited lexical patterns. To be brief: the influence of language upon habitual thought and behavior does not "depend so much on *any one system* (e.g., tense, or nouns) within the grammar as upon the ways of analyzing and reporting experience which have become fixed in the language as integrated 'fashions of speaking' and which cut across the typical grammatical classifications, so that such a 'fashion' may include lexical, morphological, syntactic, and otherwise systemically diverse means coordinated in a certain frame of consistency"

(1941c, p. 92). Stemming from the fashions of speaking, or at least indicated by them, are features of the "habitual thought" or "thought world" of a people, by which Whorf means "more than simply language, i.e. than the linguistic patterns themselves." The thought world includes "all the analogical and suggestive value of the [linguistic] patterns . . . and all the give-and-take between language and the culture as a whole, wherein is a vast amount that is not linguistic yet shows the shaping influence of language. In brief, this 'thought world' is the microcosm that each man carries about within himself, by which he measures and understands what he can of the macrocosm" (1941c, p. 84).

The fashions of speaking peculiar to a people, like other aspects of their culture, are indicative of a view of life, a metaphysics of their culture, compounded of unquestioned, and mainly unstated, premises which define the nature of their universe and man's position within it. Kluckhohn and Leighton, in speaking of the Navaho, hold that "the lack of equivalences in Navaho and English is merely the outward expression of inward differences between two peoples in premises, in basic categories, in training in fundamental sensitivities, and in general view of the world" (1948, p. 215). It is this metaphysics, manifest to some degree in all the patterns of a culture, that channelizes the perceptions and thinking of those who participate in the culture and that predisposes them to certain modes of observation and interpretation. The metaphysics, as well, supplies the link between language as a cultural system and all other systems found in the same culture.

It does not follow, of course, that a cultural metaphysics is prohibitive of variation and change; it is not a closed logical system of beliefs and premises but rather a historically derived psychological system open to change. This may be shown by the history of our own culture. As Sapir puts it:

> As our scientific experience grows we must learn to fight the implications of language. "The grass waves in the wind" is shown by its linguistic form to be a member of the same relational class of experiences as "The man works in the house." As an interim solution of the problem of expressing the experience referred to in this sentence, it is clear that language has proved useful, for it has made significant use of certain symbols of conceptual relation, such as agency and location. If we feel the sentence to be poetic and metaphorical, it is largely because other more complex types of experience with their appropriate symbolisms of reference enable us to re-interpret the situation and to say, for instance, "The grass is waved by the wind" or "The wind causes the grass to wave." The point is that no matter how sophisticated our modes of interpretation become, we never really get beyond the projection and continuous transfer of relations suggested by the forms of our speech. After all, to say "Friction causes such and such a result" is not very different from saying "The grass waves in the wind." Language is at one and the same time helping and retarding us in our exploration of experience, and the details of these processes of help and hindrance are deposited in the subtler meanings of different cultures [1916, pp. 10–11].

5. To return to Whorf, he now proceeds to compare Hopi, an American Indian language, with the languages of western Europe. In the course of his study, it soon became evident that

> the grammar of Hopi bore a relation to Hopi culture, and the grammar of European tongues to our own "Western" or "European" culture. And it appeared that the interrelation brought in those large subsummations of experience by language, such as our own terms "time," "space," "substance," and "matter." Since with respect to the traits compared there is little difference between English, French, German, or other European languages with the *possible* (but doubtful) exception of Balto-Slavic and non-Indo-European, I have

lumped these languages into one group called SAE or "Standard Average European" [1941c, pp. 77–78].

Whorf reports, however, only a portion of the whole investigation, summed up in two questions: "(1) Are our own concepts of 'time,' 'space,' and 'matter' given in substantially the same form by experience to all men, or are they in part conditioned by the structure of particular languages? (2) Are there traceable affinities between (a) cultural and behavioral norms and (b) large-scale linguistic patterns?" (1941c, p. 78).

In the last question Whorf emphasizes that he is not seeking a correlation between language and the rest of culture, in the naïve sense that types of linguistic structure (e.g., "isolating," "synthetic," "inflectional," and the like) may be linked with broad cultural categories based, for example, on technology (e.g., "hunting" versus "agricultural," etc.). In this he follows general anthropological practice, summed up by Sapir in the following words: "All attempts to connect particular types of linguistic morphology with certain correlated stages of cultural development are vain. . . . Both simple and complex types of language of an indefinite number of varieties may be found at any desired level of cultural advance" (1921, p. 234). The relation of language to the rest of culture, as we have already indicated (see sec. 4), lies rather in the fact that all cultural systems (including language) refer back to the unformulated metaphysics that serve as the *raison d'être* of the culture as a whole. It is perhaps this relationship that Sapir envisaged when he said: "If it can be shown that culture has an innate form, a series of contours, quite apart from the subject-matter of any description whatsoever, we have something in culture that may serve as a term of comparison with and possibly as a means of relating it to language" (1921, pp. 233–34).

6. Hopi and SAE, it appears, contrast markedly in a number of large-scale linguistic patterns: (a) plurality and numeration, (b) nouns of physical quantity, (c) phases of cycles, (d) temporal forms of verbs, and (e) duration, intensity, and tendency. We may summarize these contrasts in the following paragraphs:

a) SAE applies the frame *cardinal number plus plural noun* to two objectively different situations: to aggregates, like "ten apples" or "ten men," which may be perceived as such, and to cycles, like "ten days," which may not be objectively perceived but form instead a metaphorical or imagined aggregate. In contrast, Hopi restricts cardinal numbers and plurals to entities that form or can form an objective group; it has no imaginary aggregates. For an expression like "ten days" Hopi uses ordinals with singulars, roughly as in the English expressions "until the eleventh day" or "after the tenth day." The significant contrast between SAE and Hopi lies, then, in that SAE may use the same frame for both aggregates and cycles (though cycles may also be differently expressed), whereas Hopi makes a clear linguistic difference between the two.

b) SAE distinguishes, by linguistic form, two kinds of noun: individual (bounded) nouns, which denote bodies with definite outlines (e.g., "dog," "man," "stick"), and mass (unbounded) nouns, which denote indefinite continua without boundaries or outlines (e.g., "air," "water," and "milk"). Not all the physical quantities denoted by mass nouns are, however, encountered as unbounded extents; we frequently have occasion to individuate them. We do this by means of a binomial frame composed of an individual noun, the relator "of," and the mass noun, as, for example, in "glass of water" or "piece of cheese." In many instances this frame may be interpreted as "container full of something," as in "cup of coffee," "bowl of milk," or "bag of flour," but in others the mass noun is individuated only as a body-type, as in "piece of wood," "lump of coal," or "pane of glass." The influence of the container-contents frame, according to Whorf, carries over to the body-type frame, so that in the latter, the body-type seems to contain something—a "stuff," "matter," or "substance"—that may therefore exist both as a formless item and as manifest in a body-type. This language pattern, then, often requires us "to name a physical thing by a binomial that splits the reference into a formless item plus a form" (1941c, p. 80).

Hopi nouns, in contrast, always have an individual sense, even though the boundaries of some items are vague or indefinite. There is no contrast between individual and mass nouns, hence no reference to container or body-type, and no "analogies on which to build the concept of existence as a duality of formless item and form" (Whorf, 1941c, p. 80).

c) Phases of cycles, the subjective consciousness of becoming later and later, are denoted in SAE by terms like "summer," "morning," "sunset," or "hour" that are linguistically little different from other nouns. They may be subjects ("summer has come"), objects ("he likes the summer"), singulars or plurals ("one summer" versus "many summers"), and numerated or counted as discrete "objects" ("forty summers"), much in the same way as with nouns denoting physical quantities. The experience of time and phasing thereby tends to be objectified in SAE as a sequence of separable units. More than this, the noun "time" itself may be treated as a mass noun, denoting an unbounded extent, and by its use in binomial frames like "moment of time" (linguistically parallel to "glass of water" or "piece of wood") "we are assisted to imagine that 'a summer' actually contains or consists of such-and-

such a quantity of 'time'" (Whorf, 1941c, p. 81).

In Hopi terms, denoted phases of cycles are linguistically distinct from nouns or other form classes; they are a separate form class called "temporals." "There is," says Whorf, "no objectification, as a region, an extent, a quantity, of the subjective duration-feeling. Nothing is suggested about time except the perpetual 'getting later' of it. And so there is no basis here for a formless item answering to our 'time'" (1941c, p. 81).

d) The temporal forms of SAE verbs, by which they are divided into a system of three major tenses—past, present, and future—is, to Whorf, another manifestation of the larger scheme of objectifying time that we have already found in other SAE linguistic patterns. Just as we set time units like hours, days, and years in a row, so do we arrange the past, present, and future on a linear scale, the past behind the present and the future before it. Though time, in reality, is a subjective experience of "getting later" or "changing certain relations in an irreversible manner," we can and do, by virtue of our general tendency to objectify time and our tense system, "construct and contemplate in thought a system of past, present, future, in the objectified configuration of points on a line" (1941c, p. 82). This often leads to certain inconsistencies, notable particularly in the diverse usages of the English present tense, as illustrated by equational statements (e.g., "Man is mortal"), inclusion in a sensuous field (e.g., "I see him"), and customarily valid statements (e.g., "We see with our eyes").

Hopi verbs have no tenses but only validity forms, aspects, and modal clause-linkage forms. There are three validity forms: (1) denoting simply that the speaker is reporting a past or present event, (2) that the speaker expects that an event will take place, and (3) that he makes a customarily valid statement. Aspect forms report differing degrees of duration in respect to the event; and the modal forms, employed only when an utterance includes two verbs or clauses, "denote relations between the clauses, including relations of later to earlier and of simultaneity." There is, therefore, no "more basis for an objectified time in Hopi verbs than in other Hopi patterns" (Whorf, 1941c, p. 82).

e) Duration, intensity, and tendency must, according to Whorf, find expression in all languages, but they need not be expressed in the same ways. In SAE it is characteristic to express them largely by metaphors of spatial extension, that is, by metaphors "of size, number (plurality), position, shape, and motion. We express duration by long, short, great, much, quick, slow, etc.; intensity by large, great, much, heavy, light, high, low, sharp, faint, etc.; tendency by more, increase, grow, turn, get, approach, go, come, rise, fall, stop, smooth, even, rapid, slow, and so on through an almost inexhaustible list of metaphors that we hardly recognize as such since they are virtually the only linguistic media available. The non-metaphorical terms in this field, like early, late, soon, lasting, intense, very, tending, are a mere handful, quite inadequate to the needs." This situation, it is clear, derives from our whole scheme of "imaginatively spatializing qualities and potentials that are quite non-spatial (so far as any spatially-perceptive senses can tell us)"; it rests on the patterns we have described in the preceding (1941c, p. 83).

Hopi, as might be expected, has no such metaphors. "The reason is clear when we know that Hopi has abundant conjugational and lexical means of expressing duration, intensity, and tendency directly as such, and that major grammatical patterns do not, as with us, provide analogies for an imaginary space." Hopi aspects "express duration

and tendency of manifestations, while some of the 'voices' express intensity, tendency, and duration of forces or causes producing manifestations. Then a special part of speech, the 'tensors,' a huge class of words, denotes only intensity, tendency, duration, and sequence. . . . A striking feature is their lack of resemblance to terms of real space and movement that to us 'mean the same.' There is not even more than a trace of apparent derivation from space terms" (Whorf, 1941c, pp. 83–84).

7. From the linguistic comparisons summarized in section 6, Whorf infers "certain dominant contrasts" in "habitual thought" in SAE and Hopi, that is, in the "microcosm that each man carries about within himself, by which he measures and understands what he can of the macrocosm."

The SAE microcosm has analyzed reality largely in terms of what it calls "things" (bodies and quasi-bodies) plus modes of extensional but formless existence that it calls "substances" or "matter." It tends to see existence through a binomial formula that expresses any existent as a spatial form plus a spatial formless continuum related to the form as contents is related to the outlines of its container. Non-spatial existents are imaginatively spatialized and charged with similar implications of form and continuum [1941c, p. 84].

The Hopi microcosm, on the other hand,

seems to have analyzed reality largely in terms of *events* (or better "eventing"), referred to in two ways, objective and subjective. Objectively, and only if perceptible physical experience, events are expressed mainly as outlines, colors, movements, and other perceptive reports. Subjectively, for both the physical and nonphysical, events are considered the expression of invisible intensity-factors, on which depend their stability and persistence, or their fugitiveness and proclivities. It implies that existents do not "become later and later" all in the same way; but some do so by growing, like plants, some by diffusing and vanishing, some by a process of metamorphoses, some by enduring in one shape till affected by violent forces. In the nature of each existent able to manifest as a definite whole is the power of its own mode of duration; its growth, decline, stability, cyclicity, or creativeness. Everything is thus already "prepared" for the way it now manifests by earlier phases, and what it will be later, partly has been, and partly is in act of being so "prepared." An emphasis and importance rests on this preparing or being prepared aspect of the world that may to the Hopi correspond to that "quality of reality" that "matter" or "stuff" has for us [Whorf, 1941c, p. 84].

The microcosm, here derived largely from an analysis of the linguistic system in a culture, is co-ordinated in many ways, says Whorf, to habitual behavior, that is, to the ways in which people act, rather than talk, about situations. He illustrates this point by describing and analyzing a characteristic feature of Hopi behavior, their emphasis on preparation: "This includes announcing and getting ready for events well beforehand, elaborate precautions to insure persistence of desired conditions, and stress on good will as the preparer of right results" (1941c, p. 85).

Hopi preparing behavior

may be roughly divided into announcing, outer preparing, inner preparing, covert participation, and persistence. Announcing ... is an important function in the hands of a special official, the Crier Chief. Outer preparing ... includes ordinary practising, rehearsing, getting ready, introductory formalities, preparing of special food, etc. (all of these to a degree that seems over-elaborate to us), intensive sustained muscular activity like running, racing, dancing which is thought to increase the intensity of development of events (such as growth of crops), mimetic and other magic, preparation based on esoteric theory involving perhaps occult instruments ... and finally the great cyclic ceremonies and dances, which have the significance of preparing rain and crops [Whorf, 1941c, p. 85].

"Inner preparing is the use of prayer and meditation, and at lesser intensity good wishes and good will, to further desired results" (Whorf, 1941c, p. 85). The Hopi, as fits with their microcosm, lay great stress on the powers of desire and thought, to them "the earliest, and therefore the most important, most critical and crucial, stage of preparing. Moreover, to the Hopi, one's desires and thoughts influence not only his own actions, but all nature" (1941c, pp. 85–86). Unlike ourselves, whose thinking is tied in with concepts of imaginary space, the Hopi supposes that his thinking, say of a corn plant, has actual contact or interaction with it. "The thought should then leave some trace of itself with the plant in the field. If it is a good thought, one about health and growth, it is good for the plant; if a bad thought, the reverse" (1941c, p. 86).

Covert preparation is mental collaboration from people who do not take part in the actual affair, be it a job of work, hunt, race, or ceremony, but direct their thought and good will toward the affair's success ... it is primarily the power of directed thought, and not merely sympathy or encouragement, that is expected of covert participants [Whorf, 1941c, pp. 86–87].

Finally, Hopi preparation, again in consonance with their microcosm, places great emphasis on

persistence and constant insistent repetition. ... To us, for whom time is a motion on a space, unvarying repetition seems to scatter its force along a row of units of that space, and be wasted. To the Hopi, for whom time is not a motion but a "getting later" of everything that has ever been done, unvarying repetition is not wasted but accumulated. It is storing up an invisible change that holds over into later events ... it is as if the return of the day were felt as the return of the same person, a little older but with all the impresses of yesterday, not as "another day," i.e. like an entirely different person. This principle joined with that of thought power and with traits of general Pueblo culture is ex-

pressed in the theory of the Hopi ceremonial dance for furthering rain and crops,
as well as in its short, piston-like tread,
repeated thousands of times, hour after
hour [Whorf, 1941c, p. 87].

8. In a similar vein, Whorf now attempts to summarize some of the linguistically conditioned features of our
own culture, "certain characteristics adjusted to our binomialism of form plus
formless item or 'substance,' to our
metaphoricalness, our imaginary space,
and our objectified time," all of which,
as we have seen, are linguistic (1941c,
p. 87). The form-substance dichotomy
supports, in Whorf's view, much of
Western philosophy, at least that which
holds a dualistic view of the universe,
and it similarly supports traditional
Newtonian physics. Other philosophies
(involving, for example, monistic, holistic, and relativistic views of reality)
and the physics of relativity, though
formulable in our culture, "are badly
handicapped for appealing to the 'common sense' of the Western average
man. This is not because nature herself
refutes them ... but because they must
be talked about in what amounts to a
new language." Newtonian conceptions
of space, time, and matter, on the other
hand, find a ready acceptance in our
"common sense," for: "They are recepts
from culture and language. That is
where Newton got them" (1941c, p.
88).

Our habit of objectifying time, since
it "puts before imagination something
like a ribbon or scroll marked off into
equal blank spaces, suggesting that
each be filled with an entry" (Whorf,
1941c, p. 88), fits well with our cultural
emphasis on historicity; the keeping of
records, diaries, and accounts, our habit
of producing, for the future, schedules,
programs, and budgets; and, as well,
the complicated mechanism of our
commercial structure, with its emphasis
on "time wages, rents, credit, interest,
depreciation charges, and insurance

premiums. No doubt this vast system
once built would continue to run under any sort of linguistic treatment of
time; but that it should have been built
at all, reaching the magnitude and particular form it has in the western
world, is a fact decidedly in consonance with the patterns of the SAE
languages" (1941c, p. 89).

9. Whorf adds further details on the
linguistically conditioned features of
western European culture, but we have
perhaps summarized enough to make
the contrast with the Hopi clear. Whorf
turns next to the historical implications
of his hypothesis, a brief attempt to answer the question: "How does such a
network of language, culture, and behavior [as the SAE and Hopi] come
about historically? Which was first,
the language patterns or the cultural
norms?" He summarizes the answer as
follows:

In the main they have grown up together, constantly influencing each other.
But in this partnership the nature of the
language is the factor that limits free plasticity and rigidifies channels of development in the more autocratic way. This is
because language is a system, not just an
assemblage of norms. Large systemic outlines can change to something really new
only very slowly, while many other cultural innovations are made with comparative quickness [1941c, p. 91].

It might be added, however, that the
dichotomy between linguistic systems
and other systems in the culture is by
no means so sharp as Whorf suggests.
Not all nonlinguistic aspects of a culture are mere "assemblages of norms";
there are some that are also structured,
perhaps as rigidly so as language and
possibly, therefore, as resistant to
change. The important point of difference, as between other cultural systems
and language, it seems to me, is not
that language is the more rigidly systemic but that the linguistic system so
clearly interpenetrates all other systems

within the culture. This alone might account for its larger role, if it has that, in the limiting of "free plasticity" and the rigidifying of "channels of development."

It is here, too, that we should raise the question, so often discussed: How does the hypothesis that language connects so intimately with other aspects of culture square with the fact, many times noted, that closely related languages (e.g., Hupa and Navaho) may be associated with cultures quite different in other respects and, vice versa, that cultures otherwise much alike (e.g., those of the Pueblo or Plains Indians) may be linked with languages that are very different? Does not this lack of coincidence between the boundaries of language groups and culture areas suggest that language and culture are distinct variables, not necessarily connected in any basic fashion?

If language and culture have been regarded by some as distinct variables (see, for example, Carroll *et al.*, 1951, p. 37), it is perhaps because (1) they define language too narrowly and (2) they limit culture (especially in establishing culture areas) to its more formal and explicit features, those which are most subject to borrowing and change.

It is quite possible that the features of a language (largely phonemic) by means of which we link it to others in a stock or family are among the least important when we seek to connect it to the rest of culture. The fashions of speaking that Whorf finds so important to habitual behavior and thought are, after all, derived from the lexical, morphological, and syntactic patterns of a language, and these, in turn, are arrangements of phonemic materials. Two or more languages, then, may well have their phonemic materials from the same historical source and yet develop, under the stimulus of diverse microcosms, quite different fashions of speech. In short, the fact that languages belong to a common stock does not prove that they have the same fashions of speaking; such proof, if it is forthcoming at all, must be demonstrated empirically.

The cultures included in the same culture area, on the other hand, tend to resemble one another only in discrete cultural features, those which are easily diffused, and not necessarily in the ways in which these features are combined into fashions of behaving or in the basic premises to which such fashions of behaving may point. The Navaho and Hopi, for example, both within the southwestern area, display many isolated points of similarity, in their common possession of clans, sand paintings, and other features of ritual and in certain weaving and horticultural techniques and products. But the patterning or arrangement of these traits in the two cultures is widely divergent; the patterning of Navaho ritual and family (or clan) organization, for example, is not at all like that of the Hopi. It is not surprising, therefore, that Whorf's (1941c) and my own (1951) accounts of the Hopi and Navaho languages, respectively, reveal wholly distinct linguistic microcosms, or that the Kluckhohn and Leighton description of the Navaho view of life (1948, pp. 216–38) is quite foreign to that given by Whorf for the Hopi.

10. To return to Whorf, he now sums up by providing answers to the questions posed in his paper. In response to the first of these ("Are our own concepts of 'time,' 'space,' and 'matter' given in substantially the same form by experience to all men, or are they in part conditioned by the structure of particular languages?" [1941c, p. 78]), he replies that concepts of "time" and "matter" appear, as between SAE and Hopi at least, to depend in large part on their separate linguistic structures.

Our own "time" differs markedly from Hopi "duration." It is conceived as like a space of strictly limited dimensions, or sometimes as like a motion upon such a space, and employed as an intellectual tool accordingly. Hopi "duration" seems to be inconceivable in terms of space or motion, being the mode in which life differs from form, and consciousness *in toto* from the spatial elements of consciousness. Certain ideas born of our own time-concept, such as that of absolute simultaneity, would be either very difficult to express or devoid of meaning under the Hopi conception, and would be replaced by operational concepts. Our "matter" is the physical sub-type of "substance" or "stuff," which is conceived as the formless extensional item that must be joined with form before there can be real existence. In Hopi there seems to be nothing corresponding to it; there are no formless extensional items; existence may or may not have form, but what it also has, with or without form, is intensity and duration, these being non-extensional and at bottom the same [1941c, p. 92].

The concept of space does not differ so strikingly, and Whorf suggests that

probably the apprehension of space is given in substantially the same form irrespective of language. . . . But the *concept of space* will vary somewhat with language, because as an intellectual tool [as, e.g., in Newtonian and Euclidean space, etc.] it is so closely linked with the concomitant employment of other intellectual tools, of the order of "time" and "matter," which are linguistically conditioned. We see things with our eyes in the same space forms as the Hopi, but our idea of space has also the property of acting as a surrogate of non-spatial relationships like time, intensity, tendency, and as a void to be filled with imagined formless items, one of which may even be called "space." Space as sensed by the Hopi would not be connected mentally with such surrogates, but would be comparatively "pure," unmixed with extraneous notions [1941c, pp. 92–93].

Whorf answers the second question of his paper ("Are there traceable affinities between [*a*] cultural and behavioral norms and [*b*] large-scale linguistic patterns?" [1941c, p. 78]) as follows:

There are connections but not correlations or diagnostic correspondences between cultural norms and linguistic patterns. Although it would be impossible to infer the existence of Crier Chiefs from the lack of tenses in Hopi, or vice versa, there is a relation between a language and the rest of the culture of the society which uses it. There are cases where the "fashions of speaking" are closely integrated with the whole general culture, whether or not this be universally true, and there are connections within this integration, between the kind of linguistic analyses employed and various behavioral reactions and also the shapes taken by various cultural developments. Thus the importance of Crier Chiefs does have a connection, not with tenselessness itself, but with a system of thought in which categories different from our tenses are natural. These connections are to be found not so much by focusing attention on the typical rubrics of linguistic, ethnographic, or sociological description as by examining the culture and the language (always and only when the two have been together historically for a considerable time) as a whole in which the concatenations that run across these departmental lines may be expected to exist, and if they do exist, eventually to be discoverable by study [1941c, p. 93].

11. Another attempt to show how a language may influence "the logical concepts of the people who speak it" is found in the work of Lee on the language of the Wintu Indians of California (see 1938, 1944a, b). We shall summarize two of these in detail: "Conceptual Implications of an Indian Language" and "Linguistic Reflection of Wintu Thought."

Lee begins the first of these papers as follows:

It has been said that a language will delineate and limit the logical concepts of the individual who speaks it. Conversely, a language is an organ for the expression of thought, of concepts and principles of classification. True enough, the thought of the individual must run along its grooves; but these grooves, themselves, are a heritage from individuals who laid them down in an unconscious effort to express their attitude toward the world. Grammar contains in crystallized form the accumulated and accumulating experience, the Weltanschauung of a people.

The study which I propose to present below is an attempt to understand, through a study of grammar, the unformulated philosophy of the Wintu tribe of California [1938, p. 89].

12. A Wintu verb, according to Lee, must employ one of two stems (here denominated as I and II), differentiated as ablaut forms (e.g., *wir-*, I, and *wer-*, II, "to come"). Stems of Type I denote states or events in which the grammatical subject of the verb participates as free agent and in which the speaker (whether or not identical with the grammatical subject) also participates "insofar as he has become cognizant of the activity or state described" (1938, p. 94).

A speaker "can use the stem [of Type I] alone, without suffix, thus stating generally known fact. But if he tries to particularize this, to delimit it as to time or subject, he is forced to quote, in the same breath, that particular experience of his which is the authority for his statement" (1938, p. 90). There are five suffixes for this purpose, as follows: denoting (1) that the speaker knows the state or event from hearsay; (2) that the speaker knows the state or event through having seen it or because there is unquestioned evidence; (3) that the speaker knows the state or event from sensory evidence other than visual (i.e., from the sense of smell, hearing, feeling, etc.); (4) that the speaker infers the state or event from circumstantial sensory evidence (e.g., Coyote, who sees Hummingbird's tracks end suddenly, and that the valley to the south is covered with gay flowers, says inferentially that Hummingbird must have gone south); and (5) that

the speaker infers the state or event from previous knowledge not obtained by hearsay or visual or other sensory evidence (e.g., a man who knows his father-in-law is bedridden and has been alone for a long time says, inferentially, "my father-in-law is hungry").

"The distinctions made by the suffixes so far given correspond to subjective differences in the speaker, not the grammatical subject. Other affixes, added to the stem and preceding any personal or temporal suffixes there may be, indicate differences of attitude on the part of the grammatical subject" (1938, p. 92). There are three of these: (1) indicating intent or purpose, (2) indicative of desire or effort, and (3) denoting "approximation, not quite related experience, whether past, present, or future" (1938, p. 93).

Type II stems denote states or events that exist or take place "irrespective of the agency of the subject" and which the speaker, "in speaking of it . . . asserts a truth which is beyond experience" (1938, p. 89). In statements belonging to this category, "attention is concentrated on the event and its ramifications, not on the actor. The verb is not particularized in terms of participation. There are rarely any personal suffixes, and the speaker never refers to himself. He is not an authority. He speaks of the unknown, and when he makes his assertion, he asserts truth which is subject neither to experience, doubt or proof" (1938, p. 95).

Stems of Type II are used to form the passive and medio-passive, to form the imperative, to "pose questions whose answers do not depend on knowledge on the part of speaker or hearer, and to make wishes of the daydream type. The suffix of ignorance, used variously to express negation, interrogation, or wonder, is attached to this stem" (1938, p. 94). In addition, Type II stems take a suffix which "is used to express, all in one, futurity.

causality, potentiality, probability, necessity; to refer to an inevitable future which might, can and must be, in the face of which the individual is helpless" (1938, p. 95).

These distinctions imply, according to Lee, that "the Wintu has a small sphere wherein he can choose and do, can feel and think and make decisions. Cutting through this and circumscribing it, is the world of natural necessity wherein all things that are potential and probable are also inevitable, wherein existence is unknowable and ineffable. This world the Wintu does not know, but he believes in it without question; such belief he does not tender even to the supernatural, which is within experience and can be referred to by means of *-nte* (I sense)" (1938, p. 102).

13. Lee's second paper, "Linguistic Reflection of Wintu Thought" (1944b), offers more evidence, from both language and other aspects of Wintu culture, to the same end. In language she notes that Wintu lacks a plural form of the noun; where plurality is expressed at all in the case of nouns, it is by means of a "root which is completely different from the singular word; *man* is wi• Da but *men* is q'i• s" (1944b, p. 181). But Wintu does emphasize a distinction between particular and generic, even though this is optional rather than compulsory, as is the case with our singular-plural distinction. Thus, from a primary form meaning "whiteness," a generic quality, the Wintu derive, by suffixation, a particular, meaning "the white one"; from a word meaning "deer" in the generic sense (e.g., "he hunted deer") a derivative referring to a particular deer (e.g., "he shot a deer"). In two versions of the same tale, told respectively by a man and a woman, "the man refers to a man's weapons and implements in the particular; the woman mentions them all as generic. The use

of the word sɛm ... is illuminating in this connection. As sɛm generic, it means *hand* or *both hands* of one person, the fingers merged in one mass; spread out the hands, and now you have delimited parts of the hand, sɛ-mum, *fingers*" (1944b, p. 182).

Lee sees the distinction between verb stems of Types I and II as parallel to this differentiation between the generic mass nouns (e.g., sɛm, "hand") and those which particularize (e.g., sɛ-mum, "fingers"). Verb stems of Type I are used in statements of experience which are particularizations of a given and undivided reality, particularizations in which the speaker's "consciousness, cognition, and sensation act as a limiting and formalizing element upon the formless reality," as appears to be demonstrated by the suffixes we have already illustrated (1944b, p. 183). The formless reality, given in the Wintu-conceived universe and accepted by them in faith, may only be expressed by verbs using Type II stems.

"Alone this stem forms a command ... the statement of an obligation imposed from the outside. With the aid of different suffixes, this stem may refer to a timeless state, as when setting given conditions for a certain activity; or to what we call the passive, when the individual does not participate as a free agent. In general, it refers to the not-experienced and not-known" (1944b, p. 183).

In brief (and Lee illustrates this point in many other regions of the language), these fashions of speaking suggest that

the Wintu assumes that reality is, irrespective of himself. Reality is unbounded content; in this he finds qualities which are not rigidly distinguished from each other. Toward reality he directs belief and respect. Upon it, as it impinges upon his consciousness, he imposes transitory shape. He individuates and particularizes, impressing himself only within careful limits, performing acts of will with diffidence and circumspection. He leaves the content essentially unaffected; only in respect to form does he pass judgement [1944b, p. 181].

This premise of "an original oneness," upon which the Wintu may impose "transitory shape" and from which he may individuate and particularize, underlies

not only linguistic categories, but his thought and behavior throughout. . . . It explains why kinship terms are classified, not with the substantives, but with the pronouns such as *this;* why the special possives [possessives?] used with them, such as the n D, in n DDa·n: *my father,* are really pronouns of participation, to be used also with aspects of one's identity as, for example, my act, my intention, my future death. To us, in the words of Ralph Linton, "society has as its foundation an aggregate of individuals." For the Wintu, the individual is a delimited part of society; it is society that is basic, not a plurality of individuals [1944b, p. 185].

Similar reflections of "the concept of the immutability of essence and the transiency of form, of the fleeting significance of delimitation," are found in Wintu mythology. The creator, "he who is above," came from matter that was already there; people did not "come into being," they "grow out of the ground," which always existed. "Dawn and daylight, fire and obsidian have always been in existence, hoarded; they are finally stolen, and given a new role." The names of myth characters, such as Coyote, Buzzard, Grizzly-Bear, Grosbeak, and Loon, probably "refer to something undelimited, as we, for example, distinguish between fire and a fire. These characters die and reappear in another myth without explanation. They become eventually the coyotes and grizzly-bears we know, but not through a process of generation. They represent a prototype, a genus, a quality which, however, is not rigidly differentiated from other qualities" (1944b, p. 186).

14. Lee's conclusions, it is evident, closely parallel those of Whorf and offer further illustration and testing of his hypothesis. There is only a little more data of this sort; some, which we lack the space to summarize, may be found in Astrov (1950) and Hoijer (1948, 1951) on the Navaho; Lee (1940) on the Trobriand language; and Whorf (1940a) on the language of the Shawnee. Other items in the bibliography relate mainly to theoretical discussion (see Kroeber, 1941; Nida, 1945; Voegelin and Harris, 1945; Greenberg, 1948; Hockett, 1949; Emeneau, 1950; Olmsted, 1950; Voegelin, 1950; Lévi-Strauss, 1951) either on points covered in this report or on others we have not treated in detail. The bibliography is not meant to be exhaustive; there is doubtless other material, especially in European sources, which has escaped my notice.

15. In conclusion, there is much in the thesis we have outlined that requires testing; the work of Whorf (on Hopi), Lee (on Wintu), and myself (on Navaho) serves only to rough out a hypothesis on the relation of language to culture, not conclusively to demonstrate it. We must, as Whorf has noted (1941c, p. 93), have many more contrastive studies of whole cultures, including linguistic as well as other patterns of culture, directed toward the discovery of diverse systems of thought and the connection of these to fashions of speaking and behaving generally. The reports on the Hopi, Wintu, and Navaho that we have, brief as they are, sufficiently point up the need for further research and suggest that such research may be fruitful.

The material reviewed also suggests that studies of this sort have a value, not only for the narrower disciplines of linguistics and anthropology, but as well for all of science. As Whorf has noted, the analysis and understanding of linguistic microcosms different from our own point "toward possible new types of logic and possible new cosmical pictures" (1941*b*, p. 16), of the greatest importance for an understanding of our own modes of thought and their evolution. "Western culture has made, through language, a provisional analysis of reality and, without correctives, holds resolutely to that analysis as final." But there are other cultures, "which by aeons of independent evolution have arrived at different, but equally logical, provisional analyses," and these may serve as correctives to our own (1941*b*, p. 18).

REFERENCES AND BIBLIOGRAPHY

ASTROV, MARGOT. 1950. "The Concept of Motion as the Psychological Leitmotif of Navaho Life and Literature," *Journal of American Folklore*, LXIII, 45–56.

CARROLL, JOHN B., *et al.* 1951. "Report and Recommendations of the Interdisciplinary Summer Session in Psychology and Linguistics, June 18–August 10, 1951." Ithaca, N.Y.: Cornell University. (Mimeographed.)

EMENEAU, M. B. 1950. "Language and Non-linguistic Patterns," *Language*, XXVI, 199–209.

GREENBERG, JOSEPH. 1948. "Linguistics and Ethnology," *Southwestern Journal of Anthropology*, IV, 140–47.

HERZOG, GEORGE. 1941. "Culture Change and Language: Shifts in the Pima Vocabulary." In SPIER, LESLIE (ed.), *Language, Culture, and Personality*, pp. 66–74. Menasha, Wis.

HOCKETT, CHARLES. 1949. "Biophysics, Linguistics, and the Unity of Science," *American Scientist*, XXXVI, 558–72.

HOIJER, HARRY. 1948. "Linguistic and Cultural Change," *Language*, XXIV, 335–45.

——. 1951. "Cultural Implications of Some Navaho Linguistic Categories," *ibid.*, XXVII, 111–20.

KLUCKHOHN, CLYDE, and KELLY, WILLIAM. 1945. "The Concept of Culture." In LINTON, RALPH (ed.), *The Science of Man in the World Crisis*, pp. 76–106. New York: Columbia University Press.

KLUCKHOHN, CLYDE, and LEIGHTON, DOROTHEA. 1948. *The Navaho*. Cambridge: Harvard University Press.

KROEBER, A. L. 1941. "Some Relations of Linguistics and Ethnology," *Language*, XVII, 287–91.

LEE, D. DEMETRACOPOULOU. 1938. "Conceptual Implications of an Indian Language," *Philosophy of Science*, V, 89–102.

——. 1940. "A Primitive System of Values," *ibid.*, VII, 355–79.

——. 1944*a*. "Categories of the Generic and Particular in Wintu," *American Anthropologist*, XLVI, 362–69.

——. 1944*b*. "Linguistic Reflection of Wintu Thought," *International Journal of American Linguistics*, X, 181–87.

LÉVI-STRAUSS, CLAUDE. 1951. "Language and the Analysis of Social Laws," *American Anthropologist*, LIII, 155–63.

LOWIE, ROBERT H. 1940. "Native Languages as Ethnographic Tools," *American Anthropologist*, XLII, 81–89.

MEAD, MARGARET. 1939. "Native Languages as Fieldwork Tools," *American Anthropologist*, XLI, 189–205.

NIDA, EUGENE A. 1945. "Linguistics and Ethnology in Translation Problems," *Word*, I, No. 2, 1–15.

OLMSTED, DAVID L. 1950. *Ethnolinguistics So Far*. ("Studies in Linguistics, Occasional Papers," No. 2.)

OPLER, MORRIS E. 1941. *An Apache Life-Way: The Economic, Social, and Religious Institutions of the Chiricahua Indians*. Chicago: University of Chicago Press.

SAPIR, EDWARD. 1916. "Time Perspective in Aboriginal American Culture: A Study in Method." In *Selected Writings of Edward Sapir*, pp. 389–462. Berkeley and Los Angeles: University of California Press, 1949.

——. 1921. *Language*. New York: Harcourt, Brace & Co.

——. 1924. "The Grammarian and His Language." In *Selected Writings of Edward Sapir*, pp. 150–59. Berkeley and Los Angeles: University of California Press, 1949.

——. 1929. "The Status of Linguistics as a Science," *ibid.,* pp. 160–66.

——. 1933. "Language," *ibid.,* pp. 7–32.

——. 1936. "Internal Linguistic Evidence Suggestive of the Northern Origin of the Navaho," *ibid.,* pp. 213–24.

VOEGELIN. C. F. 1949a. "Linguistics without Meaning and Culture without Words," *Word,* V, 36–42.

——. 1949b. "Relative Structurability," *ibid.,* pp. 44–45.

——. 1950. "A 'Testing Frame' for Language and Culture," *American Anthropologist,* LII, 432–35.

——. 1951. "Culture, Language, and the Human Organism," *Southwestern Journal of Anthropology,* VII, 357–73.

VOEGELIN, C. F., and HARRIS, ZELLIG. 1945. "Linguistics in Ethnology," *Southwestern Journal of Anthropology,* I, 455–65.

WHORF, BENJAMIN L. 1940a. "Gestalt Techniques of Stem Composition in Shawnee," *Prehistory Research Series, Indiana Historical Society,* I, No. 9, 393–406.

——. 1940b. "Science and Linguistics." In *Four Articles on Metalinguistics,* pp. 1–5. Washington, D.C.: Foreign Service Institute, Department of State, 1949.

——. 1941a. "Linguistics as an Exact Science," *ibid.,* pp. 7–12.

——. 1941b. "Languages and Logic," *ibid.,* pp. 13–18.

——. 1941c. "The Relation of Habitual Thought and Behavior to Language," *ibid.,* pp. 20–38.

Structural Linguistics

By ANDRÉ MARTINET

1.1. IT IS A difficult task to define "structural linguistics" and to show how it differs as a whole from pre- or non-structural linguistics. If we did not want to commit ourselves, we might decide to apply the term "structuralist" to any linguist who claims to be one and consider as representative of structuralism any school of linguistic thought which has inscribed the term on its banner. This would certainly not be fair to those who, in the silence of their studies, pursue research along lines that do not differ too much from the ones adopted and publicized by their more vocal fellow-scholars.[1] Applied and understood structuralism may, in the long run, prove more fruitful than spectacular theoretical discussions. Yet among theories and methods of comparable scholarly validity, the more widely and energetically promoted ones stand a better chance of shaping the linguistic research of tomorrow; this is our justification for allowing them, in the present survey, to stand so much in the foreground.

1.2. Proclaimed structuralism plays a central and brilliant role on the contemporary linguistic stage. Most of the outstanding linguistic theoreticians are convinced and active structuralists. In international gatherings their scientific opponents usually stand in the background, and outbursts of antistructuralism become rarer. But, in Europe at least, spontaneous reactions from the floor are a sign that large sections of the linguistic public respond unfavorably to what they would probably describe as the "excesses" of structuralism. This is confirmed by an examination of contemporary linguistic writings: few of the leading scholars in the field of historical and comparative linguistics have so far let modern structural methodology affect their research; as a matter of fact, it would be news to many professed structuralists that structuralism can usefully and successfully be applied to anything but synchronic description. The activities pursued under the rubric of "dialectology" bear little trace, to date, of structuralistic thinking,[2] and impressionistically recorded minutiae are still generally felt, by members of the dialectological schools, to be sacrosanct linguistic testimony and not raw material in need of structural integration.

1.3. It cannot be our aim here to discover and discuss all the causes of this widespread discrepancy between linguistic theoretical thinking and linguistic practice, which is, of course, far

1. Let us mention here, for instance, Gustave Guillaume and his structural treatments of a number of basic linguistic problems, e.g., in Le Problème de l'article et sa solution dans la langue française (Paris, 1919), and Temps et verbe ("Société Linguistique de Paris, Collection linguistique," No. 27 [Paris (1929)]).

2. Structuralism is conspicuously absent from Sever Pop's coverage of the field in La Dialectologie ("Université de Louvain, Récueil de travaux d'histoire et de philologie," B. Sér. 1, fasc. 38 [1950]).

more evident in those countries and fields of research where there existed powerful prestructural traditions. Even if there existed complete unity in the ranks of structuralists, we should still expect to find resistance in many quarters, and, as a convinced structuralist, this writer may be allowed to declare that this would be a healthy reaction against scientific totalitarianism. But, of course, such unity does not exist. Many linguists speak of structure, but few would agree on what "linguistic structure" actually means. Offhand, we could contrast those for whom structuralism is a leading principle, from which practical methods have to be derived, and those whose conception of language as a structure results in the main from the practice of linguistic description. It is the more interesting to notice that, in spite of profound theoretical divergences, there is a considerable amount of practical agreement among structuralists, at least in certain domains, so that, e.g., a phonemic description prepared by one adherent of a certain school of thought can often be readily utilized by scholars of another school with a minimum of reinterpretation, although the underlying principles would appear to be at such variance as to make co-operation impossible.

1.4. It would thus seem that, underlying all divergences, there must be, common to structuralists of all hues, some sort of general substratum which secures the basic unity of linguistic structuralism. It is suggested that this substratum is the conviction, or at least the more or less conscious assumption, that what characterizes a language and opposes it to all others is a *sui generis* type of organization[3] that transcends any random similarities between actual performances of isolated items. Were Persian *bad,* "bad," normally pronounced exactly as English "bad," it would still be Persian and not English, because it enters different combinations and paradigms, because it occupies a certain place in its semantic field, because every one of its phonemic constituents enters into specific combinations in the spoken chain and is distinguished in its own way from the other phonemes of the pattern. Substantial identity is not what counts. What counts is how the ultimate ends of language are achieved. A vocal product has no value unless it is placed in a given linguistic frame of reference. A bilingual is likely not to understand a word of language A if it appears in a language B context without such necessary warnings as vocal "quotes," namely, a pause before the A word or some extraordinarily distinct articulation of the whole or a part of that word, telling him that he has to shift from frame B to frame A.[4]

1.5. Even if we are right in assuming this common substratum, it cannot be expected that, at the present stage of structural research, when various types of procedure have been evolved, every worker will be conscious of its existence and most varied implications. For not a few excellent and productive scholars phonemics is, first and foremost, a technique for reducing languages to writing,[5] and structural morphology is mainly thought of as a means of improving grammatical teaching. For others, whose aims are not so avowedly practical, the ultimate goal of their research is obviously a refined analysis, without too

3. Cf. E. Sapir, *Language* (New York: Harcourt, Brace & Co., 1921), p. 127: "It must be obvious to any one . . . who has felt something of the spirit of a foreign language that there is such a thing as a basic plan, a certain cut to each language."

4. If the bilingual has clearly distinct sets of phonetic habits, phonetic nuances may be a sufficient warning.

5. Cf. the subtitle of Kenneth L. Pike's *Phonemics* ("University of Michigan Publications in Linguistics," Vol. III [Ann Arbor: University of Michigan Press, 1947]).

much thought being spent on an eventual synthesis of all the elements carefully isolated and labeled. For them, determining the structure actually means grouping linguistic units of like comportment without any attempt at discovering possible connections between the various classes thus isolated. For a large number of modern linguists, "structural linguistics" means, in practice, analysis and description, and hardly the investigation of the various ties which may bind all the units of a given linguistic system together or the study of what the phenomenon "language" actually is, i.e., what the universally valid principles are according to which all individual languages are organized into independent wholes.

1.6. What would seem to prevent, or at least retard, a wider consensus in matters of structural linguistics is certainly, above all, the wide variety of temperaments and interests and also, to a large degree, continental and national isolationism. Distance and, to some extent, political and language boundaries still count in today's scholarly world. Both temperamental differences and isolating factors have resulted in widely different terminological habits, which, at this stage, probably represent the highest barrier against universal co-operation. Terminological differences are of little or no importance if they result from the choice of different terms for the same concept, particularly if one term is nothing but the translation of another used in another language: Trubetzkoy, when writing in French, used *neutralisation* for what he called *Aufhebung* in the *Grundzüge;* Hjelmslev means exactly the same thing when he writes *udtryk* in Danish and *expression* in French and English. Conversely, terminological differences are extremely cumbersome when the same term is used for two or more totally different concepts, as is often the case with "form" or "expression," for instance. They are particularly dangerous when the two different concepts corresponding to a given term may seem often to coincide in practice but actually belong to different frames of reference, as is the case with, e.g., "morpheme" as used by Bloomfieldians, Trubetzkoyans, or glossematicians. Unfortunately, terminological divergences of this last category are most difficult to eliminate because they usually reflect different articulations of thought, every one of which is felt by its originator to be an essential part of his theoretical construction. Consequently, whoever wants to be acquainted with structural research in its entirety must get inured to different and often conflicting terminological practices. In the present survey it will often be found convenient to use glossematic terminology as a frame of reference. This should not be construed as a preferential treatment of that one aspect of structuralism, but only as a reflection of the fact that, of all the competing approaches, glossematics is the one whose theoretical foundations are the most elaborate and that few relevant problems have totally escaped Louis Hjelmslev's scrutiny.

1.7. It is usual, among scholars whose outlook is not limited to one specific approach, to distinguish between three main schools of structural linguistics, designated either by reference to some outstanding scholar who was or still is considered as the founder, the inspirer, or the leader of each one of them or by means of a geographical designation pointing to an original center of diffusion. Thus one speaks of a "Prague School," with Nikolai S. Trubetzkoy as a head figure; of a "Yale (or American) School," with Leonard Bloomfield as the leading mind; of a "Copenhagen School," with Louis Hjelmslev as the main promoter of "glossematics." A cruder dichotomy into Europeans and Americans can be propounded only by scholars unaware of the complexity of the European linguistic scene. Whether the three-cornered picture with Prague, Yale, and Copenhagen as its extremes is fully representative of the current situation might be doubted, but it probably still affords the best basis for a classification of the various existing trends, although the number of eclectics may seem to be on the rise.

1.8. There is no central figure among linguists of past generations to whom all professed structuralists would willingly pay homage. Yet it would seem that the teaching of Ferdinand de Saussure has, directly or indirectly, influenced most of linguistic structuralism. Although strict Bloomfieldians explicitly deny such an influence as far as they are concerned,[6] it cannot be doubted that a fair amount of cross-fertilization took place across the Atlantic in the thirties and before, so that no theoretical linguistic thinking can be assumed to be quite free from Saussurean "taint." It is a fact, however, that the Bloomfieldians' main concern with analysis contrasts with the constant emphasis placed by other schools on the structural nature of language; this may largely be ascribed to the deep and permanent influence of De Saussure's thinking on European scholars, so that it would not be a gross exaggeration to say that contemporary linguists stress the importance of structure in proportion to their indebtedness to the great Genevan.

1.9. Linguistic theoreticians of today, when they hail De Saussure as their master, are likely to forget that he was not only the scholar who first delineated the foundations of a structural theory but also the comparativist, who presented the first and so far most dazzling illustration of applied structuralism, when, on the basis of internal compara-

tive evidence, he postulated Indo-European laryngeals several decades before Kurylowicz identified some of them as Hittite *h*. If, to this day, Antoine Meillet's *Introduction à l'étude comparative des langues indo-européennes*, first published in 1902 and never basically affected by successive revisions, remains so largely satisfactory, it is undoubtedly because it embodies a masterly application of the structural principles of De Saussure to the field of Indo-European comparison. Accusations of inconsistency are frequently leveled at the *Cours de linguistique générale*, and it is true that, starting from and concentrating upon different statements of the *Cours*, various scholars have developed quite different structural theories. But it would be almost as unfair to take De Saussure to task for this as it would be to make him responsible for the current variety of laryngeal theories.

1.10. The influence exerted by Russian linguistic thinking around and after Baudoin de Courtenay on some of the structuralistic schools should not be underestimated. It intimately combined with that of De Saussure in the early days of the Prague movement. To the Russians we owe the term "phoneme" applied to something different from speech sound. No one today would accept the original definition of the "phoneme" as a *Lautabsicht*. Yet all the modern uses of the word derive from Baudoin's. All subsequent definitions have been devised and worded so as to obtain very much the same units as had first been evolved by reference to the "linguistic feeling" of native speakers. Daniel Jones received the term and the distinction from Shcherba[7] and managed to present the first practical formulation of the phonemic principle, which he found implicit in the teachings of Henry Sweet and Paul Passy.

6. Cf. Charles F. Hockett's review of *Travaux du Cercle linguistique de Copenhague*, Vol. V (1949) in *International Journal of American Linguistics*, XVIII (1952), 86–99.

7. See Daniel Jones, *The Phoneme* (Cambridge, England: W. Heffner & Sons, 1950).

This formulation, made with a view to solving practical, educational, and orthographic problems, is perfectly free from any structural implications. It is not improbable that Bloomfield originally borrowed his concept of the phoneme from the writings of Jones. To this day, the practice of Yale and that of London have many features in common,[8] and a Jonesian origin of the Bloomfieldian phoneme might account for the opinion entertained by some members of other schools that Bloomfieldian methods and practice would be more aptly labeled "descriptive" than "structural."

1.11. Among the other precursors of linguistic structuralism, one should mention Edward Sapir, whose structural-mindedness has, however, been far less instrumental in shaping current linguistic thinking in America than Bloomfield's more analytical approach.

1.12. Different philosophical backgrounds have, of course, largely contributed to giving to each movement its own initial slant, but, with the possible exception of behaviorism in the case of Bloomfield, it would be dangerous and misleading to identify each one of the structuralistic trends of this survey with any definite school of psychologists or logicians.

1.13. The type of linguistic experience of the pioneers and the material that was used as a test, at least in the initial stages of the research, must have been very decisive. The experience of the structural theoretician may be, in the main, limited to his native language and a few others, a sound knowledge of which he has acquired prior to his being involved in structuralistic pursuits. If, as is normally the case, these languages have already been submitted to previous analyses, either of the schol-

8. As pointed out by Fred W. Householder, Jr., in his review of Jones's book in *International Journal of American Linguistics*, XVIII (1952), 99–105.

arly type or practically and anonymously, having long since been reduced to writing, our man will no doubt have to check the validity of these previous analyses by applying the stricter methods he is propounding. But he will not be diverted by this task from what he considers his main duty, namely, giving an account of every language as a whole. He will refuse to conceive of a language as nothing but a body of actual utterances, because his internal conviction, based upon his experience as a user, tells him that the utterances are not "the language" but only the outward manifestation of it, the Saussurean *parole*. He may adopt the view that the only scientifically utilizable data will, for him, remain symptoms of the language, not its essence. Whether language as such is described in mentalistic terms or conceived of as a set of habits does not affect the fact that perceptible utterances are not the ultimate object of his study. He may at first be tempted to reach language proper directly, by introspection. But he will soon discover that, whatever the excellence of the results thus achieved, he will not be able to convince his fellow-scholars unless he devises a method that enables others to check the validity of the procedure at every step. His task will be to interpret observable symptoms and, through them, to accede to linguistic reality.

1.14. On the other hand, the theoretician may be mainly concerned with "exotic" languages hitherto not described, whose value as cultural media is so small that he does not feel the urge to master them and which only arouse his interest as linguistic samples. He will first record a body of utterances representing the sole contact he may establish with the new linguistic reality. This, the raw material he has to process, will be raw indeed, and not assumedly so, as would be the case if he were dealing with recordings of his own language. He will actually have to discover where morphemes begin and where they end, how some order can be brought into a jumble of strange sounds and noises. His task will be to discover identities and differences and not to find objective justifications for identities and differences which he intuitively knows to exist. He will not be conscious of any reality beyond that represented by his body of utterances. The order that he will finally manage to establish there he will call the "structure" of the language. Depending on his temperament and schooling, he will conceive of this structure as actually present in the utterances and revealed by his processing or as a principle of organization evolved by himself. But he will be tempted to dismiss as confusing and irrelevant the suggestion that the actual structure of the language is neither in the body of utterances nor in the product of his mental activity.

1.15. All the pioneers of linguistic structuralism have copiously drawn from their own native, usually Indo-European, languages. But, whereas some of them have been very active as language recorders, others have had practically no field-work experience. In the early days of the Prague School, Slavic languages and dialects were mainly resorted to. Yet many later theoretical developments resulted from the investigation of other European and "exotic" languages, and it should be remembered that Trubetzkoy was a Caucasian specialist. But it was generally understood that a good previous knowledge of the language was more than an asset for the would-be describer. In America, on the contrary, many linguists, in the wake of Franz Boas, had had to face the task of recording some native Indian language, and this type of experience certainly accounts for many features of the Bloomfieldian approach. One of the two founders of glossematics, J. Uldall, had

done some field work in America, but, as elaborated mainly by Hjelmslev, glossematics is, so far at least, less a descriptive method than a linguistic theory illustrated by reference to the best-known modern and ancient languages of the Old World.

1.16. It has been suggested that a convenient way of illustrating the methodological similarities and differences between the main structuralistic schools would be to present a few actual linguistic situations and the various descriptive solutions that every one of these would receive in the frame of the different theories. In order to be fully authoritative, such a treatment could result only from the co-operation of five or six scholars, or it would presuppose in a single author a versatility to which the present writer can make no claim. Moreover, it is not certain that bare practical illustrations would serve any useful purpose: pointing out, once more, that the final consonant of Russian *rot* is, from a Bloomfieldian standpoint, the phoneme /t/; according to traditional Prague practice, a realization of the apical archiphoneme; according to Hjelmslev, the result of a syncretism of *t* and *d*, will not make any clearer the theoretical justifications for the concepts of neutralization or syncretism. In what follows, we shall make an attempt at determining the amount of agreement on various theoretical planes in an effort to go beyond terminological differences, and, having discovered where agreement ceases, we shall try to sketch some of the implications of early theoretical divergences.

2.1. Common to all structuralists is the distinction between two levels of analysis, that of meaningful units, the "morphemes" of Prague and American usage; the "morphemes" and "pleremes" of Hjelmslev; and that of distinctive nonmeaningful ones, the "phonemes," "prosodemes," "chronemes," etc., of most schools; the "cenematemes" of the glossematicians. This agreement is, of course, imposed upon linguists of all schools by the very nature of the object of their science. The double linguistic articulation is precisely what opposes language proper to other types of semeiotic systems. This dichotomy is parallel to the classical distinction between phonetics, on the one hand, and morphology-syntax-lexicon, on the other. But structural research has shown that languages evince, on the level of distinctive units, an organization at least comparable to that which had long been recognized on the other level, and this is no mean merit of the phonemic research of the last two decades.

2.2. In most quarters, scholars concentrated at first almost exclusively upon the domain of distinctive units. Many reasons can be adduced for this initial preference. For the most structurally minded linguists, the first task was obviously to discover some sort of organization in the field of speech sounds, as it was felt that traditional grammar had long since achieved some sort of ordering, at least in morphological matters. Many scholars with a strong phonetic schooling were quite naturally tempted to concentrate on sounds rather than "grammar." It was widely felt to be methodologically correct to start with the smallest units of the spoken chain. The glossematicians are the only ones who have, from the start, posited an axiomatic parallelism between two planes, that of "content" (meaningful units) and that of "expression" (distinctive units), and pursued their research on both planes at the same time.[9]

2.3. This initial difference either accounts for or reflects one of the most serious methodological divergences among structuralists. Many of those who had at first concentrated on the analysis of utterances into phonemes would naturally be tempted to define larger units by reference to their phonematic aspect, whether they be non-

meaningful or meaningful units. But it is clear that phonematic identity cannot be made the sole criterion for the identification of meaningful units, since (1) obviously, different "morphemes" sound alike and (2) functionally identical "morphs" present different phonemic makeups. This identity has therefore to be eked out by other criteria, semantic or distributional, which will take care of homonymy and enable the analyst to group "morphs" according to their function. The concomitant or successive use of the phonemic and distributional criteria would seem to represent the normal Bloomfieldian practice. Against this practice it can be argued that the use of more than one criterion detracts from the neatness of the procedure and that, if one does not want to have recourse to meaning, one should endeavor to develop a technique of identification based either on the observation of the nonlinguistic response to speech or on an exclusive concentration upon concomitant changes observed in the behavior of speakers. Changing *now* to *yesterday* in *now I walk* will entail the change of *walk* to *walked*, just as the same change in *now I go* will determine the replacement of *go* by *went*, so that *went* is to *go* what *walked* is to *walk*; there is no need to analyze, first, *now, walk*, and so forth, into /naw/, /wɔk/, and the like; it should suffice to point out that *now* and *yesterday*, *walk* and *walked*, *go* and *went*, are functionally different because, e.g., *now* and *yesterday* frequently elicit different responses from the hearers. The theoretical advantage

9. References to glossematic theory are, in the main, based upon Louis Hjelmslev's *Omkring Sprogteoriens Grundlaeggelse* (Copenhagen, 1943); English equivalents of Hjelmslev's Danish terms are from an unpublished translation by Francis Whitfield. Zellig S. Harris' *Methods in Structural Linguistics* (Chicago: Univeristy of Chicago Press, 1951) has been considered as affording a handy and authoritative presentation of the main features of American structuralism.

achieved by such a procedure is that each level of analysis is thus kept fully distinct. By doing away with such proportions as phoneme : morpheme = phone : morph=allophones : allomorphs, one avoids conveying the impression that a "morpheme" is somehow "a family of morphs," an abstraction subsuming a number of actual speech data, each one nothing but a phonic sequence.

2.4. Glossematicians, with their constant emphasis on the distinctness and complete parallelism of the two planes of "expression" and "content," avoid what might be called the "phonemic bias" in the treatment of meaningful units. In practice, they do not seem to be too much concerned with problems of identification on either plane. Since they normally operate with well-known languages, they usually take meaningful units for granted, so that the phonemic discrepancy between the -*ae* of Latin *rosae* and the -*is* of *ciuis* is no problem. Their linguistic identity will be amply established when they are shown to "contract" exactly the same "functions." The fact that the Latin genitive is expressed (cf. the phrase "plane of expression" in reference to the domain of distinctive units) by means of different "formants" (approximately the Yale "allomorphs") has no bearing at all upon the study of its relational comportment. Notwithstanding the highly different theoretical backgrounds and terminological apparatuses, Hjelmslev's relational treatment of his units of content and the Bloomfieldians' setting-up of morpheme classes based on similarity of distribution lead, in practice, in very much the same direction.

2.5. Prague linguists have occasionally dealt with morphological problems, but there exists no authoritative treatment by any one of them of the domain as a whole. In very much the same way as the glossematicians, they seem to have taken "morphemes" for

granted; but, in contradistinction to the latter, they have concentrated upon the semantic contents of meaningful categories[10] and so far have left syntagmatic problems practically untouched.

3.1. The glossematicians have introduced the term "commutation" for the procedure whereby many structuralists identify structurally relevant features. Commutation is a consequence of the axiomatic statement that a distinction is relevant on one plane if it suffices to establish a distinction on the other plane: the distinction between [i] and [e] is relevant in English because it suffices to make *pin* another meaningful unit than *pen;* the nominative and the genitive are two different categories in Latin because [rosae] is distinct from [rosa].

3.2. Conscious commutation is practically universal in phonemic matters. In structural "morphology" it is usual to summarize it once and for all by stating that no meaningful category is to be recognized in a language unless it is, in some way, formally distinct: one has no right to speak of an "instrumental" case in Latin. A more detailed and really practical application of commutation to the determination of meaningful features is possible only if one is ready to recognize and operate with semantic differences in the same way as one recognizes and operates with phonetic ones: one must first have perceived the difference between [i] and [e] before one can submit it to the commutation test; one must have become aware of the semantic difference between nominative and genitive before one can check its structural existence by observation of the phonic differences involved in their expression. Thus commutation, as a fully valid procedure on both levels of analysis, can hardly be acceptable for those who recognize only vocal utterances, i.e.,

10. Cf. Roman Jakobson, "Beitrag zur allgemeinen Kasuslehre," *Travaux du Cercle linguistique de Prague,* VI (1936), 240–88.

phonic data, as a legitimate object of observation. It implies the recognition of the basic isomorphism and interdependence of two linguistic planes and their equal theoretical and practical importance. This, a basic tenet of glossematics ultimately derived from De Saussure's teachings, reflects preoccupations that are foreign to the Bloomfieldians' modes of thinking and diametrically opposed to their practice. Prague linguists are far more inclined to agree with the legitimacy of some amount of operational parallelism. But they would argue that the necessities of communication affect the two planes very differently, since they may be directly instrumental in increasing the number of meaningful units, whereas their influence on the number of distinctive units will be, at most, very devious. Besides, as long as one deals with those meaningful units whose denotative value is imprecise and whose relational value is high, namely, grammatical morphemes, the structural parallelism of the two planes can easily be maintained; but the lexicon proper seems far less easily reducible to structural patterning, once certain particularly favorable fields, such as kinship terms, numerals, and a few others, have been dealt with. Glossematics still has to prove its contention that all meaningful units can be reduced to a limited inventory of "figures" through an analysis similar to the one which has successfully been applied in the domain of distinctive units.

4.1. The respective positions of the different schools can be most clearly contrasted in their handling of what Hjelmslev calls "substance."

4.2. According to the glossematicians, language has recourse to two different types of substance for its two planes. On the plane of "expression" the substance may be phonic and therefore perceptible through the auditory organs; but it is also commonly graphic and therefore visually perceptible, and any other perceptible substance could be used, although maybe not quite so conveniently, for the same purposes. On the plane of "content," the substance is of a mental, semantic nature. It could no doubt be argued that the two substances could be conceived of as mental, because distinctive units can be thought of as auditory—more exhaustively, auditory-muscular images— or, if graphic substance is considered, as visual-muscular ones. But the distinction between the actual performance and its mental reflex may be disregarded, since actual production and reception are actually part of the linguistic communicative process. On the other hand, whatever external reality is connected with meaningful units does not appear anywhere in the course of this process, so that substance on the plane of content is necessarily mental.

4.3. The structural nature of language results from the fact that every language organizes these two substances according to its own patterns. It is not enough to point out that different languages make use of different substantial features, as when, e.g., Arabic makes use of pharyngeal articulations unknown in English or when some conceptual fields are extensively utilized in some languages and practically not represented in others. It must be stressed that such substantial features or stretches as are found in the most varied languages are submitted in each of them to a specific organization: the semantic substance corresponding to "I do not know" is organized differently in French "je ne sais pas" and German "ich weiss es nicht," although, of course, some languages may actually concur in particular instances, as when Danish "jeg ved det ikke" is found to coincide, syntagmatically at least, with German "ich weiss es nicht." On the plane of expression a substantial identical feature such as [ʔ] may be found to have a "phonematic" function in Arabic, a demarcative function in German, and probably a "prosodic" or "suprasegmental" one elsewhere, so that it occupies different places in the three patterns.

4.4. What Hjelmslev calls "form" is the type of organization to which the widely identical substance is submitted in every language. Form is expressed by him in terms of the various relations that every one of the units of a given plane entertains with the other units of the same plane. Form exists for expression and for content. It is felt by glossematicians that only form thus understood is properly linguistic and that substance, even when organized, deserves consideration only after the structure has been set up exclusively in formal terms.

4.5. The Prague point of view is clearly definable in the frame of the Hjelmslevian form versus substance opposition. The main object of Prague research is linguistically organized substance. As such, substance, on either plane, is amorphous. Substantial identity has no linguistic validity: German [k] and Cherkessian [k] may well be pronounced in the same way, but they cannot be said to be linguistically the same because both German /k/ and Cherkessian /k/ are what they are only by reference to the other phonemes of the respective patterns. German /k/ is the sum of every substantial feature that constantly distinguishes it from any other phoneme of the German pattern, and the same applies to Cherkessian /k/ in the frame of the Cherkessian pattern. Any actual substantial feature of the articulation of German /k/, such as the pulmonic action necessary for its production, that is not instrumental in keeping it distinct from another German phoneme is linguistically irrelevant. But any feature which

exerts a distinctive function is a part of the substance on which the attention of the linguist should be focused. Whatever in the substance is found to exert a communicative function, in the ordinary meaning of the term, is linguistically relevant. Units which are found to exert the same type of function are classified according to the substantial nature of their linguistically relevant features. Structure results from the various combinations of these features. Since it is largely dependent on the substance, it cannot be assumed that it would necessarily be the same if the substance changed. It is assumed that phonic substance is the normal primary substance of linguistic expression. It is not denied that other substances could be thought of which would play a similar role in communicative mediums. But a new substance would entail a new pattern.

4.6. The insistence on basing the paradigms of expression (the phonemic patterns) upon linguistically relevant substantial features does not imply a neglect of the study of the combinatory latitudes of the units in the spoken chain, but distributional criteria are decidedly less in the foreground here than with other schools.

4.7. When dealing with meaningful units, it becomes difficult not to operate with distributional criteria for classifying the units previously isolated. Had Prague linguists been more intent upon evolving a method for dealing exhaustively with the two planes, they might have been tempted to make larger use of these criteria on the plane of expression too. But, as a rule, when they have tackled problems connected with meaningful units, they have concentrated upon already described paradigms with a view to determining the linguistically relevant substantial features of the various units, so as to establish, on the plane of content as well, patterns based upon similarities and differences. The difficulties inherent in an objective appraisal of semantic reality have certainly contributed toward making such attempts relatively less convincing than when phonic substance was at stake.

4.8. The Yale approach is characterized by the set purpose of disregarding semantic substance entirely, as not lending itself to an objective scientific treatment. However, since the linguists of that school have never operated with the clean-cut Hjelmslevian distinction between form and substance, it cannot be said that what they evolve in structural morphology by the application of their distributional criteria is comparable to the relational "form of content" of the glossematicians. On the level of distinctive elements, there is no reluctance to operate with phonic substance, at least in the earlier stages of the research: the grouping of allophones into phonemes proceeds on the basis of their greater or lesser phonetic resemblances to one another. The real point here is not form versus substance, but directly observable phonic features versus nebulous semantic data. Research is concentrated exclusively upon the utterance as the only positively given aspect of language. Since, materially, an utterance is made up entirely of speech sounds, there will be at least a tendency to rely as long as possible upon speech elements and stretches. In the determination of distinctive units, one does not operate with meaning but with meaning identities and differences which may be conceived of as positive or negative nonlinguistic responses to speech. There is at least one theoretical attempt to do away entirely with anything but phonic data.[11] A well-nigh exclusive concentration on directly observable data has led, quite understandably, to the choice of distribution as the only principle of classification and a mistrust of paradigmatic reality. Since the only observable reality is the utterance, whatever is done with the units, once they have been extracted from it, cannot in itself become an object of study. An analysis of phonemes into their substantial components is admissible[12] in so far as these components are looked upon as concomitant elements in the utterance, but it should not lead to the establishment of paradigmatic patterns with which scholars could operate as with so many linguistic realities. On the whole, however, there is a tendency to discard phonic substance as soon as the structural level is reached. This similarity with the Hjelmslevian procedure is heightened by the fact that glossematicians actually operate with substance in their identification of distinctive units.

5. By stating that his theory bears in itself no existence postulate, Hjelmslev has, once and for all, eliminated the problem of the reality of the units with which structuralists operate. None but the most naïve beginner fails to perceive that such a unit as the phoneme is an abstraction, and even an abstraction of the second degree. But agreement ceases as soon as the question arises as to whether the word "phoneme" should be understood as designating one of the actual elements making up every utterance or as the name of a tool invented by the linguist in his effort to order linguistic data. The problem is not infrequently by-passed by practical-minded descriptivists as philosophical rather than scientific. Yet it has a direct bearing upon the legitimacy of certain techniques. If the phoneme is actually there, it is the duty of the linguist to discover it in any section

11. That of Bernard Bloch, "A Set of Postulates for Phonemic Analysis," *Language*, XXIV (1948), 3–46; cf. n. 8, p. 5.

12. See Charles F. Hockett, "Componential Analysis of Sierra Populaca," *International Journal of American Linguistics*, XIII (1947), 258–67.

of any utterance, and there can exist only one true answer to the question: How many phonemes make up this or that fraction of the utterance? If the phoneme is only an ordering principle, we shall make use of it as long as it offers a satisfactory solution to our problems of analysis; beyond that, we shall have to try other tools of the same operational nature. If we find that our definition of the phoneme does not enable us in a given case to reach a definite conclusion, we shall either reword our definition so as to make it cover that particular case too, or we shall register the situation as a marginal one from the point of view we have adopted. All this would not imply that a phonemic analysis does not, to a large extent, parallel the linguistic behavior of speakers: an analysis whose ultimate aim is to account for the functioning of a language is bound to result in a picture that will largely match some sort of mental organization corresponding to the language described. Once glossematicians have been set aside, it would be difficult to ascribe some of the two views contrasted here to one or the other of the remaining schools.

6. Not a few among the structuralists who are professedly concerned with organized substance, i.e., the ones grouped here under the Prague label, are bent upon discovering some general and permanent principle of organization which should characterize linguistic reality under all its aspects. The most favored principle is the principle of binarity, according to which the whole of language should be reducible to sets of binary oppositions. This principle should be valid not only along the syntagmatic axis (with possible exceptions in the case of co-ordinated complexes) but also in paradigmatic patterns, and on both the plane of meaningful units and that of phonol-

ogy.[13] Other convinced substantialists, without denying that there may exist more or less constant features in man's linguistic behavior, refuse to harden into "laws" conclusions derived from a necessarily limited body of data. They would further argue that, even on the basis of available information, the binarists' conclusions are not fully supported by facts.

7. It is also among Prague substantialists that there is to be found the largest number of scholars who are not satisfied with the practical or theoretical identification of structuralism with descriptive linguistics. This identification results, in some quarters (Yale), from a nearly exclusive concentration upon the setting-up of descriptive techniques, in others from a strict adherence to the Saussurean tenet that linguistic change proceeds at the expense of structure, a view highly reminiscent of neogrammarian theory and practice In the opinion of structural diachronicists, structural linguistics should afford not only a relevant principle for the classification of linguistic changes but also a total or partial explanation of many of these changes.[14]

8. The present conjunctures seem particularly favorable for a confrontation of the various structural theories and methods. Even among the most orthodox members of the various schools, international contacts have aroused a wholesome curiosity toward the opinions and practice of scholars in other quarters. It is true that the cur-

13. Roman Jakobson is the initiator and most active propagator of the application of the binary principle to phonology; see Jakobson, Fant, and Halle, *Preliminaries to Speech Analysis* (MIT Acoustics Laboratory, Technical Report No. 13, January, 1952).

14. Cf. André Martinet, "Function, Structure, and Sound Change," *Word*, VIII (1952), 1 ff.

rent theoretical divergences are too fundamental to allow for universal agreement, even on a few basic principles. But this does not exclude cross-fertilization, and contacts undoubtedly promote fruitful re-evaluations of one's own theoretical background and methodological practice. World-scale co-operation in the realm of linguistics cannot and should not result in total uniformization. It should give to everyone, whatever his place of residence and former schooling, the possibility of choosing a field of activity and a method best adapted to his temperament, abilities, and interests. Each one of the existing structuralistic approaches opens new vistas and brings new tools for a more fruitful treatment of some section of the vast domain of theoretical and applied linguistics, and all should be given credit for having contributed to the advancement of knowledge.

Advances in Folklore Studies

By STITH THOMPSON

FOLKLORE AND ethnology have always had so intimate and well-recognized a relationship that it is not possible to draw exact boundaries between them. The folklorist, especially in Europe and South America, is frequently concerned with traditional social organization and material culture; and the ethnologist, whether he is studying a group of people in central Africa or in central Europe, inevitably finds that he cannot properly perform his task if he does not know the songs and stories, the dances and games, the beliefs and magic practices, of those he studies.

In Europe this relationship is everywhere recognized in the organization of institutes, archives, university courses, and international congresses. In South America the folklore museums might well be called ethnological, since they deal with customs and material culture. In the United States, also, the ethnologists and other anthropologists for many years have given the most effective support to folklore studies and have continually collected and published tales, songs, and other oral literature. As a result of their interest and labors extending over three generations, the folklore of the North American Indians is now better recorded than that of any pre-literate group. And the American Folklore Society owes its very survival through many lean years to the loyal and continued efforts of American anthropologists.

Recently we have been hearing reports of a considerable withdrawal of American anthropologists from the American Folklore Society. There may, of course, be many reasons for this defection, but it would be a heavy blow for folklore as well as for ethnology if scholars in these fields should cease to support one another. The ethnologist can hardly hope to have an understanding of a people if he disregards so important a part of their lives as their tales and myths, their songs and dances, and their chants and ceremonies. Folklorists likewise frequently need the experience and skill of the trained ethnologist to set a model for their own work.

One reason for the lack of perfect harmony between ethnologist and folklorist is that folklore occupies a borderline position and has interests in addition to those of the ethnologist. Since, among other things, it deals with oral literature, the orientation of many folklorists toward the literature characterized by books and authors is natural and is needed, especially in the study of groups used to reading. This looking in both directions has made difficult not only the definition of folklore as a term but also the focusing of efforts of various folklorists. With those using folklore for propaganda or entertainment we are not here concerned; but even those who approach it in the spirit of real scholarship find that the field as a whole is too extensive for one man to cover. There is thus a tendency not only to specialize but often to feel that one's own peculiar interests are so important as to make all others negligible. It is the rare folklorist, as it is the rare anthropologist, who perceives his subject in the large, follows all its developments, and relates them to one another and to neighboring areas.

In spite of these and other obvious difficulties, great advance has occurred in the century and a half since the study of folklore began as a part of the romantic interest in primitivism. It has not seemed to make any great difference that there was no agreement as to exactly what field the study of folklore covered. The goal from the beginning has been the recovery of the lore of the folk, both in verbal expression and in traditional ways of thinking or behaving, and there has been no disagreement about a certain central core of material in which all folklorists are interested. Whether they are working in Scandinavia, Polynesia, or Kentucky, they concern themselves with traditional tales, myths, and legends; songs, chants, and verses; proverbs and sayings; and even such special forms as riddles. About so much there is general agreement. A considerable number of anthropologists think of other traditional aspects of the life of pre-literate peoples as belonging to ethnology but not to folklore; but, even allowing the anthropologists' claim to these parts of the field, the work of the folklorist does extend rather far over into the field of ethnology, especially as it concerns the Europeans and other peoples in Western civilization. Thus the study of all kinds of traditional beliefs and superstitions, of arts and crafts; of dances, games, and traditional instrumental music—all these occupy a middle ground and can be claimed as a legitimate subject for both the ethnologist and the folklorist. Most European folklorists also concern themselves with

customs based upon the calendar, with festivals, wedding ceremonies, old agricultural practices, cookery, the types of houses and buildings, implements, and all kinds of industrial processes. This is also true throughout South America and the Orient. It has seemed wise for the folklorist to use a rather wide interpretation of his field, and, although he may leave the ethnology of nonliterate peoples for special study, he very often has to concern himself with such matters.

Accepting, then, this wide interpretation of the subject, as it is actually found among working folklorists in various parts of the world today, what advances can we see, and in what directions do we seem to be moving? My remarks here are based upon a visit to practically all the folklorists of South America and to most of those in Europe, as well as upon an extensive correspondence with workers in other parts of the world (see Thompson, 1948).

It is obvious that, before any work with folk tradition can be undertaken, the traditions themselves must be collected. Afterward, they must be preserved and arranged properly, and finally it is hoped that they may all be studied. As for the collecting of folk material, the larger part is still done by amateurs. Some of these, because of their general ability and tact, are able to do first-class work. Certainly, most of the old collectors of folklore in the nineteenth century were untrained, but they often had remarkable success because of their understanding of what they were working with. The question of how to make amateur collecting more effective faces the leaders of folklore continually. Some countries have been helpful in the preparing of handbooks for these collectors. Unfortunately, we have nothing very good of this kind in the United States. Local societies and journals frequently give good leads to such amateur collectors, but, as archeologists and historians have long ago learned, the work of the amateur must be checked very carefully and must often be taken with a considerable grain of salt.

Perhaps the best use of amateur collecting in any broad systematic way has been developed by some of the European folklore archives, particularly those in Ireland and in Sweden.[1] Here the amateur is paid for his work and in every case must have a certain amount of preliminary training from the central folklore archive. The details of this preliminary training vary from country to country, but it seems to be necessary in order to avoid a great deal of lost motion and actual error in the work of the collector. Questionnaires of all kinds are sent out to suggest to the workers what they may expect to find. They are trained in the proper and sensible use of these questionnaires. In recent years they have also been trained in the use of recording machines of one kind or another, so that they collect more and more faithfully and become increasingly imbued with the ideal of authenticity. Collectors are also required, or at least encouraged, to keep an account of their actual experience with the people with whom they work. Later this may become very valuable to the student of folklore, who uses it in the archive or in published form.

In recent years some of the best of the folklore archives have regular staff members who go out into the field and collect traditional material. Some of them now have good sound trucks and excellent photographic apparatus. Joint field expeditions with ethnologists, linguists, students of tales and mythology, folk song and folk music specialists, and folk art scholars have been undertaken, and this development promises to be important in the future. Two kinds of collecting that have had only

indifferent success should be mentioned. One of these is the collecting of traditions through school children. The Irish have tried this on an extensive scale. They have found that the actual collections are not very good but that the greatest service that the work with school children has performed has been to bring to the attention of the Irish Folklore Commission a number of important informants. These informants are then visited by the trained collectors, and very valuable material has been found in this way. For school children there is always a tendency to change and embroider material in the way that they think their teacher would like, and some teachers are not slow to encourage such prettification. Another type of folklore collecting which has sometimes succeeded and sometimes not has been that made in response to an order from the government. We had our own experience during the 1930 depression, when the Federal Writers' Project of WPA attempted to collect folklore. In some states these inexperienced workers were merely told to go out and collect folklore. They were not properly informed as to what they should collect, and I think it is the opinion of most people who have examined these Federal Writers' Project records that, with notable exceptions, they are rather worthless. On the other hand, I am told that the valuable records in Sweden began with the order of Gustavus Adolphus in the early seventeenth century, which was sent out to all priests and officers to collect certain types of folk customs and traditions. I should suppose that success resulted because the task was made very definite and specific.

The most important work in folklore today is being done through the great folklore archives, most of them in Europe. The first of these, and in many ways still the greatest, is in Helsinki. This dates back to the 1830's and was

---

1. This information has been confirmed by a recent visit to the archives in both countries.

started in connection with the collecting of the folk songs that were worked over into the Finnish epic, the *Kalevala*. In spite of all the well-known vicissitudes of the Finnish people in the last century, collecting has gone on almost without interruption, and the material has always been carefully preserved and skilfully indexed and analyzed. They accept folklore in its very widest sense, and their archives are being daily added to by the very considerable local staff, some of whom are now making good use of their new sound truck.[2] Only slight variation in method is found in the similar archives at four places in Sweden, in Oslo, in Copenhagen, in Dublin, and in Paris. Specialized archives are established at several places in Germany and in southern Europe. The greatest archive of folktales is in Dublin. To give some idea of the scope of work of these Irish folklorists within the last twenty years, it may be mentioned that they have something over two million pages of manuscript, which is well bound and which is gradually being indexed. These European archives are supported by the state and are considered to be a serious and important part of the scholarly work which the state wishes to promote. Their goal is to make an actual record of the life of the people, especially that part which has become traditional, and also to study it in its historical setting.[3]

In some of the countries, notably Finland and the Scandinavian lands, folk museums have supplemented the work of the folklore archives. All the material culture is placed in special museums, some of them indoors and some outdoors. The museum movement in Sweden, for example, has gone on at a great rate, so that there are many hundreds of small folk museums, in addition to the great Northern Museum at Stockholm and the outdoor museum of Skansen.[4] The same picture is to be seen in Norway and, to an extent, in France.

On our continent the archiving and museum work has been much less important. In South America are several small folklore archives and a number of museums of folk-life. These are usually highly specialized and do not cover all aspects of the life of the people.[5] Of course, we have some museums of folk-life in the United States, but much of the material properly belonging there is kept in historical museums.[6] Our folklore section of the Library of Congress is our natural folklore archive, but it is only slowly developing and has not yet undertaken the extensive work of the European archives.

Before material can be properly archived and studied, it has to be classified. Long ago the Swedes and Finns worked out a practical classification for most of their folklore holdings. These classifications have been adapted to the situation in Ireland,[7] and, on the whole, they are valid for most of the rest of the world. The detailed classification of narrative materials, such as folktales, has been going on for some time. This was started by the Finns, and I have given a good part of my attention to

2. The results of the Finnish archive work may be followed in the *Mémoires* and the *Journal de la Société Finno-ougrienne* and "F. F. Communications," both published at Helsinki.

3. For these activities see files of *Folkliv*, which has been published since 1936 by Gustav Adolfs Akademi för Folklivsforskning.

4. See the works of Sigurd Erixon and Åke Campbell.

5. Examples are those at Tucumán and Córdoba in Argentina, Santiago de Chile, and São Paulo.

6. The only one which resembles the European folk-life museums is that at Cooperstown, New York.

7. Séan O'Súilleabháin (1942) has written the most accessible handling of the Swedish index system.

this problem throughout the last years.[8] The special problem of the classification of folk traditions, as distinct from fictional tales, is now being worked on in the archive at Oslo. It seems to me clear that the classification of riddles, which has recently been published by Professor Archer Taylor (1951), will solve the problem for that literary genre. The German folk song archives have been investigating the classification of folk songs, but the whole problem of where to place various kinds of folk songs remains to be worked out. An even more difficult problem is that of the classification of folk music. It is to be hoped that at some time all the archives in the world can have a uniform classification, just as they do now for folktales. It is at present possible to write any archive in the world and ask for all their versions of a particular tale numbered according to the Aarne-Thompson system.

Before leaving the subject of archives, some mention should be made of the problem of duplicating these archives. It has been at least the dream of many folklorists that microfilms should be made of all the great archives in the world and these brought to one or several depositories. Something is being done now by the Library of Congress, and it seems that negotiations are going on for still further work in this direction. It would be a very great thing if all the archives should appear in duplicate, for insurance against any accident to the present archives. Both the original records and the indexes should be microfilmed. The fact that few people in America can read Finnish should not deter us from making copies of the great Finnish depository.

The tremendous amount of material

that any folklorist must go through to assemble his information makes necessary not only indexes to archives but also adequate folklore bibliographies. This need is being taken care of rather well today. In Switzerland under the auspices of the International Commission of Folk Arts and Folklore is being published a large annual, the *Volkskundliche Bibliographie*. Recently there has also appeared a very extensive bibliography of American folklore, including American Indian. There are, in addition, several excellent annual bibliographies.

The various folklore archives are publishing a good deal of their collections, and little by little these materials are reaching scholars in other parts of the world. Much of the archive material, however, is still available only through indexes; but, thanks to the various systems of classification that have been evolved and to great labor on the part of the archivists, these indexes have been worked out with a great deal of skill. The field with which I am most familiar, the folktale, has now been rather well surveyed for fifteen or twenty countries,[9] and indexes are now being used to make available to the Western scholar the very extensive and hitherto little-known Japanese collections.

A result of the collecting done by the great folklore archives has been the development in the last twenty years of a very elaborate mapping of the folklore elements in various countries. Before the second World War the German folklore atlas was progressing,[10] and another good one has recently come out of Switzerland. At present, three large atlases are almost com-

---

8. Aarne (1910). This was revised and much expanded by Thompson in 1928 as *Types of the Folktale.*

9. These indexes are listed in Thompson, 1946, pp. 419–21.

10. *Atlas der deutschen Volkskunde* (Leipzig, 1937–38).

pleted for Sweden.[11] Here, in a series of maps, a very large amount of information is concentrated, and the whole is given a visual presentation. For any kind of study involving distribution, maps are invaluable, and it would seem that they must accompany nearly all comparative studies in the future. American folklorists have made relatively little use of cartography, though anthropologists have long used maps for their studies of American Indian culture elements. We should certainly undertake preliminary mapping, perhaps by states or small sections, of our large foreign population groups whose folklore has not yet been investigated.

Primarily, the work of folklorists has thus far been empirical. They have been interested in the *what* and to some extent in the *how*, but, because of many early unsafe speculations, they have latterly been slow to attempt to answer *why*. The descriptive and analytical work has, of course, frequently led to historical reconstructions, and these, in turn, have suggested many interesting theoretical questions which can be approached only after preliminary spadework has been carried through. But such questions are receiving attention. What, for example, is the relation of the individual to the tradition which he carries on—how compulsive is the tradition of his social group and how much freedom is there for the expression of individuality? What is the relation of the bearer of oral tradition to his group? How specialized is he, and what characteristics has he, artistic or personal, that cause approval or disapproval by his fellows? How is tradition, oral or material, modified by cultural patterns? These questions are being thought about by folklorists, and some of them are being clarified, as factual and historic investi-

11. I examined these in Uppsala and Stockholm in January, 1952.

gations furnish safe foundations for their study.

More general problems, not so directly dependent on prior explorations, are concerning folklorists everywhere, in archives and out. Aside from the broad general question of where folklore begins and other subjects end, we find much discussion, for example, of the various genres of folk-literature (see, e.g., Thompson, 1946, pp. 3–10). One can always argue about the relation of myths to tales, about whether a folk song is authentic or not, about the influence of commercialism on folk tradition in general, about the possibility of applying psychoanalysis to a social phenomenon like folklore. Some progress has certainly been made in recent years toward a successful methodology for the studying of folktales (summarized in Thompson, 1946, pp. 428–48), toward the study of style in folk narrative (Thompson, 1946, pp. 449–61) and folk song, toward a study of the relation of the performer to those for whom he performs (see Von Sydow, 1948, *passim*) and of the relation of folk tradition to such elements as language and cultural, religious, and political boundaries. Some students are investigating the relation between oral traditions and literature and are helping to clarify the effect which Western culture, in its path of conquest over the world, has exercised on less sophisticated groups of people. In common with the anthropologists, the folklorist must give much attention to acculturation, and, like the historian, he must know about the past of the group that he is working with. An examination of our books and journals will show progress in all these directions.

Both folklorists and ethnologists in America have failed to make adequate systematic studies of the material culture and customs of the dominant white groups, mostly of European origin.

Folk-life in the sense in which the Europeans use it has seldom seemed to be the business of either, but it must be hoped that some of the problems now so well worked on by Swedes, Finns, Irish, French, and others who will be assembling in the Ethnological Congress in Vienna this summer, may appeal to our own investigators.[12] It matters little whether they call themselves folklorists or ethnologists or anthropologists.

Folklore has not usually been a regular subject taught in the universities. Though there were professorships of folklore in northern Europe as early as the beginning of our century, in the rest of the world the study has ordinarily been a side issue. In American universities it made slow progress, but within the last fifteen or twenty years elementary courses in folklore have been offered in a large number of the colleges and universities. Only a very small number give graduate work and promote scholarly training of the new generation of folklorists.

The folklorists of the United States and South America need most of all to go to Europe and study the great folklore archives there. It would be possible to meet men there who make the serious study of folklore their life's work and to learn how folklore research is organized in an important way. With all our diversity of groups in America, we need a large number of trained collectors. We need, for example, to learn about the folklore of all our more recent immigrant groups, and this takes persons who are acquainted with the culture and language of those groups.[13] We have now a number of good folklore journals in America.[14] They will do their work better by ac-quaintance with folklorists over the world and by getting something of a world view, and they can especially profit by acquaintance with their fellows in other subjects closely related. It would do all our folklorists no end of good to see the serious work of Swedish or Finnish folklorists and ethnologists, as well as to acquire something of the earnestness and efficiency of their anthropological fellows here at home.

The activities of folklorists here and abroad have naturally been carried on without much regard to what interest their neighbors in the anthropological field might find in them. As one reviews their work, however, he is aware of certain problems that parallel those of anthropology. The developing of archives and training of collectors have in many countries been a joint enterprise, involving both groups of scholars.

Another considerable field in which the folklorist's work may be of even more interest to the anthropologist is that of the analysis and classification of tradition. Some of these classifications, like the Swedish and Irish, involve much material culture and social tradition and are parallel and often identical with similar classifications used by anthropologists. It is, however, especially in study of tales, traditions and legends, and music that the folklorist's work should be of direct importance to general ethnological study. Technical studies of the music of European peasants or American mountaineers involve the same general analytical processes as those used for central Africans or

12. An excellent symposium on these matters was held at the Congress for European and Western Ethnology at Stockholm in 1951. The report will soon appear in *Laos*, Vol. II.

13. For example, Dr. Jonas Balys, formerly in charge of the Lithuanian folklore archives, has had considerable success in collecting from Lithuanians in the United States.

14. Most important is the *Journal of American Folklore*, now more than sixty years old. Some regional journals are *New York Folklore Quarterly, Midwest Folklore*, and *Western Folklore*.

American Indians.[15] These techniques are highly specialized and are quite beyond my own competence, but their development and use are the common concern of folklorists and anthropologists.

Traditional narratives—tales, myths, and legends—are found over the whole earth and in every culture. Anthropologists need not be reminded of their presence in any group they may be studying, and the folklorist continues to collect and study them even among peoples dominated by written literature. Considered from a world-wide point of view, these narratives are a continuum, without a perceptible break between the simplest and the most complex cultures.

One of the important interests of the student of such material is to see how the tradition of a group resembles, and how it differs from, that of the rest of the world. In order to approach this problem, he must have adequate terms of reference. He should be able to identify a particular item as definitely and easily as a botanist identifies a plant and places it in its world-wide setting. He may find it unique or possibly identical with something known elsewhere.

One characteristic of narrative materials is that they consist of motifs which have enough significance or interest to the narrator to be remembered and carried on. Such motifs may be simple incidents with a single point of interest (fox persuades bear to fish through the ice with his tail). They may be persons, creatures, or objects (culture hero, gigantic bird, or magic rolling stone) or something memorable in the background of the action, whether place (the other world), social custom (mother-in-law avoidance), or an accepted taboo. These motifs are the stuff out of which narratives everywhere are constructed. It is therefore possible to analyze all stories, simple or complex, into constituent motifs and to make from these a world-wide classification. I am now busy with a revision of such a motif index (1932–36) which I believe will give a reasonably adequate coverage for every culture. Of course, if it is to be really useful, any such index must be continually expanded to meet changing conditions and needs.

By means of such an analysis one can see just what he is dealing with in the tales of any group—how much is unique and how much is shared with others. From workers in various parts of the world I am encouraged to believe that it has already shown its value.

Such study of the detailed motifs will not ordinarily be an end in itself, either for folklorist or for anthropologist. He may well interest himself in the complexes of motifs which form complete, self-sufficient tales. For simple stories with only a single narrative point, the tale-type will be equated with a motif; but for many stories it is a whole group of motifs which forms the constant tradition. The tale is handed on as a whole. The classification of such complex tales is not nearly so easy as the arrangement of motifs, for it is hard to determine just what point in the tale seems to be important enough to place it in a general scheme. But, in spite of these theoretical difficulties, the listing of the principal tale-types of Europe and western Asia by Aarne in 1910 has proved to be successful in practical use.

An index of tale-types, however, cannot be made useful for more than a field of actually continuous tradition. It is valid for Europe and western Asiatic peoples and for their areas of influence in other parts of the world. But for the tale-types of native Africa or North America, for example, special classifications will be necessary. That for the North American Indians is be-

15 See the researches of Hornbostle, carried on in America by George Herzog.

ing worked on but, so far as I know, not for other parts of the world.

The interrelation of motif and type classifications is particularly useful to folklorists for displaying what may be called the "anatomy" of folktales in any particular group. It shows how fluid the narrative material is or how completely it has crystallized into smaller or larger units. The tales of India, for example, show, upon a combined motif and type analysis (see, e.g., Emeneau, 1944–46), that for many groups in India the complete tales—often consisting of scores of motifs—are so formless as to be the despair of the man who tries to make a type index. On the other hand, a similar analysis of American Indian tales shows the existence of a considerable number of well-integrated tale complexes with wide distribution (Thompson, 1929). These results are interesting when one remembers that India was long spoken of as the primary homeland of the various European tales, and the fluidity rather than fixity of American Indian tales has frequently been emphasized.[16]

Motif and type analyses may well have their application to other aspects of culture than traditional narrative, though it is certain that they could not be adopted directly. In the field of beliefs and customs, basic units resembling motifs do exist, and they often form significant combinations which have for a long time engaged the attention of both folklorist and anthropologist.

Another activity of students of popular narrative during the past half-century has been the development of a methodology for the study of the life-history of a particular story (see Thompson, 1946, pp. 428–48). This historic-geographic method has no magic about it, but is a systematic application of principles used by all who interest themselves in dissemination studies. By

16. By Theodor Benfey for India and Franz Boas for the American Indian.

careful analysis of the tale into all its parts and an examination of the variations of each version, an approach is made toward a hypothetical archetype (always recognized as a purely theoretical construction), and from this archetype a study is made of the mutual relations of it and all the available versions. The goal is a reconstruction of the life-history of the narrative.

Because of unsafe generalizations made from time to time by those who have used the method, folktale students have continually sought to recognize its limitations and to improve it. It is a method of bringing before the investigator a whole assemblage of facts about the hundreds of versions of a tale in an unusually clear fashion. It does not absolve him from making use of every other aid he can muster—his knowledge of history, of language, of culture, of religious movements, and the like. Though anthropologists have not, on the whole, been hospitable to the folklorists' historic-geographic studies, it seems to me that the folklorists have by now put their house somewhat in order and can invite another inspection. For those anthropologists who are interested in the history of particular items—implements, beliefs, or customs—rather than in the complete study of a certain culture, at least a knowledge of how the best folktale students have employed the historic-geographic method should be suggestive and interesting and probably directly applicable to their own tasks.

In common with ethnologists, the folklorist is struggling with the problem of style, but his contributions have thus far been negligible. So far as it impinges on anthropological studies, then, the folklorists' most valuable work has probably been in the organizing of archives and systematic collecting, in the analysis of narrative material, and in a methodology for the investigation of folktales.

REFERENCES

AARNE, ANTTI. 1910. *Verzeichnis der Märchentypen.* ("F F Communications," No. 3.) Helsinki.

EMENEAU, MURRAY B. 1944–46. *Kota Tales.* 4 vols. Berkeley: University of California Press.

O'SÚILLEABHÁIN, SÉAN. 1942. *A Handbook of Irish Folklore.* Dublin: Educational Co. of Ireland.

SYDOW, C. W. VON. 1948. *Selected Papers on Folklore.* Copenhagen: Rosenkilde & Bagger.

TAYLOR, ARCHER. 1951. *English Riddles in Oral Tradition.* Berkeley: University of California Press.

THOMPSON, STITH. 1929. *Tales of the North American Indians.* Cambridge: Harvard University Press.

——. 1932–36. *Motif Index of Folk-Literature.* 6 vols. ("F F Communications," Nos. 106–9, 116, 117; also "Indiana University Studies," Nos. 96–97, 100, 101, 105–6, 108–10, 111–12.) Helsinki and Bloomington, Ind.

——. 1946. *The Folktale.* New York: Dryden Press.

——. 1948. "Folklore in South America," *Journal of American Folklore,* LXI, 256–60.

Culture, Personality, and Society

By A. IRVING HALLOWELL

HISTORICALLY VIEWED, specialized interest in and systematic investigation of problems in the area most familiarly labeled "personality and culture" are a twentieth-century development in anthropology.[1] Although it is chiefly

1. Since major sources in the form of books, contributions in periodicals, and two volumes of reprinted articles are easily accessible, this footnote is offered as a brief but direct guide to this literature. Furthermore, since it appeared impractical to review the full range of concrete contributions in a limited space and the symposium itself is concerned with an over-all and integrated view of anthropology, emphasis has been given to the wider rather than the narrower implications of personality and culture studies, their relation to the interests of general anthropology as well as to those of closely related disciplines.

For historical perspective see Lowie (1937, "Retrospect and Prospect"); Volkart (1951, for the "Outline of a Program for the Study of Personality and Culture" prepared by W. I. Thomas and submitted to the Social Science Research Council in 1933); Margaret Mead (1937, Introduction); Betty J. Meggers (1946, for a rather dim view of the newer trends); Clyde Kluckhohn (1944, on the influence of psychiatry on anthropology in America); Clyde Kluckhohn and Henry A. Murray (1948, Introduction).

Reprintings of two series of selected articles in the area of personality and culture studies, embodying a large amount of concrete data as well as theoretical discussion, are to be found in Kluckhohn and Murray (1948) and Haring (1949, rev. ed.). In this latter volume will be found an extensive and alphabetically arranged bibliography, which, together with the bibliographical references in Kluckhohn and Murray, lead directly to the source material. Since the writings of Bateson, Benedict, DuBois, Erikson, Fromm, Gillin, Gorer, Hallowell, Henry, Kardiner, Kluckhohn, LaBarre, Linton, Mead, Roheim, Sapir, Sullivan, etc., are listed in the Haring volume, it seems unnecessary to repeat them all in the bibliography of this article. Attention may be called to the fact, however, that a volume of the Selected Writings of Edward Sapir was edited by D. Mandelbaum and published in 1949. Since that time, a lengthy and extremely valuable review article by Z. S. Harris (1951), systematically expounding Sapir's views, has appeared. A bibliography of the writings of Margaret Mead is to be found in Psychiatry, X (1947), 117–20. Subsequently published books include Male and Female (1949), Soviet Attitudes toward Authority (1951), and Growth and Culture (Mead and Macgregor, 1951). Among the items not included in, or published subsequent to, Haring's bibliography, attention is particularly directed to the following: Proceedings of an Interdisciplinary Conference on Culture and Personality, ed. Sargent and Smith (1949), held under the auspices of The Viking Fund in 1947; the review of personality and culture studies from a psychoanalytic point of view by Roheim (1950), the annual series edited by him, "Psychoanalysis and the Social Sciences" (beginning 1947), and the Essays in his honor, ed. Wilbur and Muensterberger, under the title Psychoanalysis and Culture (1951); Erik H. Erikson's Childhood and Society (1950); the Proceedings of the American Psychopathological Association (1948), devoted to the general topic "Psychosexual Development in Health and Disease," ed. Hoch and Zubin (1949) and to which Ford, Hallowell, Henry, Mead, and Murdock contributed papers; and the general review of human sexual patterns of behavior by Ford and Beach (1951), and the monograph of the Berndts on the Australians (1951); studies of individual Navaho by Dyk (1947) and by the Leightons (1949), a Hopi by Aberle (1951), and an Indian of the Plains by Devereux (1951), L. K. Frank (1951), Honigmann (1949).

American anthropologists who have made this area their own, as early as 1923, in England, the topic of C. G. Seligman's presidential address to the Royal Anthropological Institute was the relations of anthropology and psychology,[2] and Lévi-Strauss, in the Introduc-

2. Seligman, 1924. Subsequent articles showing his continuing interest were published in 1928, 1929, and 1932. In 1936, Seligman wrote an Introduction to J. S. Lincoln's *The Dream in Primitive Cultures*, in which he said: "Today the Anthropologist must be aware of current psychological theory; he must make up his mind how far his researches should be directed by this, and on what class of material he should particularly focus his attention in order not only to test the theories of psychologists but also to further his own science. To put it briefly, how can a profitable give and take relationship between psychology and anthropology best be established at the present time?

"This is a problem to which the writer of this Introduction has given much thought of recent years. Brought up in the main in the Tylorian (comparative) School of Anthropology, having thereafter gained some knowledge of and made use of the Historical School of Rivers, and of late years watched the development of the functional method, the writer has become convinced that the most fruitful development—perhaps indeed the only process that can bring social anthropology to its rightful status as a branch of science and at the same time give it the full weight in human affairs to which it is entitled—is the increased elucidation in the field and integration into anthropology of psychological knowledge. That we have not progressed further than in fact we have is probably only in part due to the relatively scant amount of material available or to any inherent difficulty which Anthropologists should find in handling it. The writer hopes he is not being unfair to his colleagues, but cannot help considering that this failure is far more due to a lack of eclecticism, a determination of each exponent and adherent of a particular school to show little interest in the technique and conclusions of others."

Aside from the interest shown by S. F. Nadel, who acknowledges a debt to Gestalt psychologists (*Foundations* [1951], Vol. VI), the relations between psychology and anthropology envisioned by Seligman do not seem to have been realized, despite the fact that, on the psychological side, Sir F. C. Bartlett (1937, p. 419) suggested that "if the Anthropologist could tighten up his work and give it

tion to a posthumous reprinting of a volume of articles by Marcel Mauss (1950), has called attention to the manner in which the latter, at about the same time, seems to have anticipated certain later developments.

Despite the somewhat misleading nature of the dichotomy[3] implied by the label "personality *and* culture," a significant historical fact should not be overlooked. The differentiation in subject matter and point of view which, beginning in the Enlightenment, subsequently led to the crystallization of the separate disciplines and subdisciplines that we now know as the social and psychological sciences, while advancing knowledge in highly specialized areas, has by no means provided all the final answers to many perennial questions regarding the nature and behavior of man. Some of these questions inevitably remain of common concern to more than one discipline, so that cross-fertilization is not only inevitable but may be extremely fruitful. The Freudian conception of human nature, particularly the model of personality theory which has had an immense impact upon both psychological and social disciplines in this century, was developed independently not only of experimental psychology but likewise of the culture concept as developed in anthropology. The very conjunction, then, of the terms "personality" and "culture" provides an implicit clue to one of the major characteristics of the

a more definite direction by a judicious application of psychological methods, and if the psychologist could learn to humanize his experiments by a study of anthropological material, there would, I believe, be speedy and genuine advance on both sides."

3. Kluckhohn and Murray, for example, characterize "the bipolarity between 'personality and culture' as false or at least misleading in some important senses" (1948, p. xi); cf. Spiro. There have been other dichotomies (mind-matter, nature-man, body-mind, individual-society) which have had to be reordered with reference to some more inclusive unity.

studies pursued under this caption. What they have done is to refocus attention upon problems central to a deeper understanding of the nature of man, his behavior, and the primary significance of culture, at a more inclusive level of integration. In terms of the organization of knowledge today, this necessarily involves an interdisciplinary perspective.

Learning theory as developed in recent decades by psychologists, quite independently of the personality theories of psychoanalysis or psychiatry, may be cited as another example of specialized knowledge which is becoming more pertinent for anthropology at the same level of integration. Although culture, ever since the classical definition of Tylor, has been assumed to be a phenomenon that rests upon a learning process, without the intensive research of psychologists it is impossible to advance beyond the simplest kind of hypotheses in our own discipline. Only a few years ago Professor Kroeber, discussing "what culture is" and the use of such terms as "social heredity" and "social tradition," very pertinently remarked (1948, p. 253) that "perhaps *how it comes to be* is really more distinctive of culture than what it *is*." It is to *how* questions that much of personality and culture study is directed. Sophisticated knowledge of *how* a human being is groomed for the kind of adult life and social participation that prepares him for one kind of culture rather than for another, and likewise for passing it on, necessarily involves a learning theory as well as personality theory, in addition to any evaluation of the cultural determinants involved. A well-developed learning theory is relevant to promoting further knowledge of the whole process of cultural transmission as well as the processes involved in acculturation and culture change. Integrated knowledge of this order can hardly fail to be of interest

to all the social sciences. It should ultimately lead to formulations of greater predictive power than statements that "culture is always acquired by human individuals" or that culture is our "social inheritance" passed on from generation to generation by a process of conditioning, in contrast to our biological heritage transmitted through the "germ plasm." Today the latter term seems antiquated because we now know a great deal about the genes and how they operate. Relatively, we still know much less about the actual transmission of culture. One cannot fail to recall one of the central problems of anthropology as Boas conceived it. According to Benedict,[4] "he himself often said that this problem was the relation between the objective world and man's subjective world as it had taken form in different cultures." The actual processes and mechanisms of human adjustment which make this unique relationship possible in our species involve knowledge that transcends the descriptive facts of culture.

Today many reciprocal lines of interest have developed between anthropologists and those working in the psychological disciplines (psychoanalysts, psychiatrists, specialists in learning theory, perception, and social psychology, etc.), as well as with sociologists and other social scientists. Relations with those in the former group in particular have emerged mainly on the basis of the potentialities discerned in personality and culture studies rather than from any body of organized knowledge and theory now extant. It seems likely that these areas of reciprocal interest will be further developed and intensified. It is out of such an interchange that there may emerge a solid core of knowledge and theory that is directly relevant to all the disciplines that are now concerned with human be-

4. This is to Kroeber, Benedict, *et al.*, *Franz Boas* (1943).

havior, personality, and social relations.[5]

All the social and psychological disciplines must make some assumptions about the nature of man, society, culture, and personality,[6] no matter what areas of specialized research are undertaken. Among other things, some attitude must be adopted toward man's position in the natural universe and the necessary and sufficient conditions[7] or prerequisites, of a human existence as compared with a subhuman existence. It is the absence of such a core of generally accepted knowledge and theory which makes cross-disciplinary reference still difficult in many respects. Because anthropology has always maintained a perspective which has dealt with the evolutionary facts concerning

5. Cf. Murdock (1949), who "with tongue in cheek," has coined "lesocupethy" (from the two initial letters of learning, society, culture, personality, theory) points out that "there is as yet no general agreement as to an appropriate name for the emerging unified science. Such terms as 'human relations' and 'social relations' slight the psychological components and, to some, suggest application rather than theory. The 'science of human behavior' carries too strong a connotation of behaviorism and too weak an implication of important social and cultural factors. The general term 'social science' seems to exclude psychology." See also, Parsons and Shils (1951).

6. G. Gordon Brown in a recent article (1951) rejects the term "culture" "in the interests of clarity." He says: "I do not necessarily expect the concurrence of fellow anthropologists in thus slighting one of our most sacred terms but have personally found it expedient to think without it."

7. Cf. the remarks of J. H. Randall, Jr. (1944, pp. 355 ff.). Whitehead (1930, p. 99) has asserted: "It is a false dichotomy to think of Nature *and* Man. Mankind is that factor *in* Nature which exhibits in its most intense form the plasticity of Nature. Plasticity is the introduction of novel law. The doctrine of the Uniformity of Nature is to be ranked with the contrasted doctrine of Magic and Miracle, as an expression of partial truth, unguarded and uncoordinated with the immensities of the Universe. Our interpretations of experience determine the limits of what we can do with the world."

our species, on the one hand, and with the constancies and the widely varying aspects of cultural data, on the other, it should continue to be among the chief contributors to a developing science of man.

Society, culture, and personality may, of course, be conceptually differentiated for specialized types of analysis and study.[8] On the other hand, it is being more clearly recognized than heretofore that society, culture, and personality cannot be postulated as completely independent variables.[9] Man as an organic species, evolved from a primate ancestry, constitutes our basic frame of reference, and we find ourselves confronted, as observers, with the complexities of the human situation that have resulted from this process. Here I wish to consider man as the dynamic center of characteristic modes and processes of adjustment that are central to a human existence, in order to emphasize the integral reality of society, culture, and personality structure as human phenomena. It is this integral reality that constitutes the human situation as our unique subject matter. Our abstractions and constructs, which may be ordered in different ways and for different purposes and which may vary in their heuristic value, are derived from observations of the same integral

8. Nadel (1951, pp. 79 ff.) gives explicit references to the conceptual differences between "society" and "culture" that have been stressed by various anthropologists. "In recent anthropological literature," he observes, "the terms 'society' and 'culture' are accepted as referring to somewhat different things or, more precisely, to different ways of looking at the same thing."

9. Cf. Parsons and Shils (1951, p. 22): "Cultural patterns when internalized become constitutive elements of personalities and of social systems. *All concrete systems of action, at the same time, have a system of culture and are a set of personalities* (or sectors of them) and a social system or sub-system. Yet all three are conceptually independent organizations of the elements of action."

order of phenomena. And to it certain of our generalizations must eventually be directed. Instead of being primarily concerned, therefore, with definitions and with divergencies in point of view, I shall try to stress central issues and indicate the kind of basic assumptions and generalizations that seem reasonable to make if psychological data are considered integrally with sociocultural data.

Considered in purely material terms, man's constitution contains no chemical elements that are not found in other animals, rocks, and even distant nebulae.[10] Biologically, man is also continuous with other living things in nature. At the same time, he is morphologically distinct from his nearest animal kin. But a human mode of existence is dependent upon more than this. In evolutionary perspective, the level of functioning inherent in the human organism embodies novel possibilities of adaptation. Among these, and perhaps central, are inherent potentialities of a psychological order.[11] However, the

realization of these potentialities is contingent upon conditions outside the organism. One of the necessary conditions of psychological structuralization is association of the human individual with others of his species. Physical, social, or sensory isolation makes any full realization of these inherent potentialities impossible. That is, the development of a characteristically *human* psychological structure (mind or personality) is fundamentally dependent upon socially mediated experience in interaction with other persons. Inherent in the same condition is the concomitant development of a human social order and a cultural heritage. A human society, by minimal definition, requires organized relations, differentiated roles,[12] and patterns of social interaction, not simply an aggregation of people.[13] Since the

---

10. Cf. Shapley (1930), who essays a cosmic survey of the material universe known to us. "Our studies of the universe," he says, "show the uniformity of its chemical structure and generally of its physical laws. We are colloids. Our very bodies consist of the same chemical elements found in the most distant nebulae and our activities are guided by the same universal rules. The recent analyses of the chemical constitution of man, beast, rock and star have brought to light the remarkable uniformity of all chemical composition. Little as we human beings are, so temporary in time and space, yet the chemical elements of which we are composed are also the predominant elements in the crust of the earth and are prominent components in the structure of the fiery and gaseous stars. We are, chemically, made of nothing unusual or exotic."

11. Schneirla contrasts the "psycho-social" level of adaptation in human societies with the "bio-social" level of insect societies. "The individual learning capacity of insects, stereotyped and situation-limited as it is, plays a subordinate (facilitating) role in individual socialization and shows its greatest elaboration in

the foraging act (i.e., outside the nest). The various individuals make reproductive or nutritive contributions to colony welfare, and no individual learning that occurs can change the standard pattern of the species in lasting ways. The society is bio-social in the sense that it is a composite resultant of individual biological characteristics dominating group behavior.

"In contrast, human societies may be termed psycho-social, in that cultural processes dominate which are the cumulative and non-genetically transmitted resultants of experience and learning, under the influence of human needs and desires interacting variably with the procedures of labor or conflict, reasoning or routine."

12. Cf. Parsons and Shils (1951) on role as the unit of social systems. H. S. Jennings, discussing the differentia of social organization among infra-human animals, writes: "...only if the individuals play different functional roles is there social organization" (1942, p. 105).

13. Aberle, Cohen, *et al.* (1950, p. 101) define a society as "a group of human beings sharing a self-sufficient system of action which is capable of existing longer than the life-span of an individual, the group being recruited at least in part by the sexual reproduction of the members." As functional prerequisites to a society, i.e., *what* must get done, not *how* it is done, the authors list the following: (*a*) provision for adequate relationship to the envi-

structure represented by the organized relations of its component individuals is a function of their capacity for social adjustment through learning, even a superficial analysis indicates that a human society is dependent upon psychological processes. Since the persistence of any human social order over any considerable period of time involves the replacement of its personnel, the crucial importance of psychological processes is obvious. The maintenance of any particular form of human social organization not only requires provision for the addition of new individuals by reproduction but ways and means of structuralizing the psychological field of the individual in a manner that will induce him to act in certain predictable ways. From whatever angle we look at the situation, the psychological potentialities of man are integral to the maintenance of a social order. No natural boundary can be drawn between the individual and society when the latter is conceptualized as an identifiable unit with an observable structure that persists in time.

Viewed from the standpoint of the individual, a socialization process is the psychological concomitant of the process of physical maturation with which it is integrated in varying ways.[14] At

birth the human individual is prepared for only a very limited sphere of action because the neonate is undeveloped and dependent upon others. Psychological maturation is dependent upon the organization of inherent potentialities, in order that the individual may be prepared for autonomous action in the larger sphere that includes much more than the roles and patterns of social interaction that characterize his society. The socialization process *may* be viewed functionally as a necessary condition for the continuity of a social structure. But this structure is an abstraction from a larger reality. A human society requires the continuously motivated behavior of human beings in a culturally constituted behavioral environment that is cognitively structured with reference both to the nature of the cosmos as well as to the self, in which traditional meanings and values play a vital role in the organization of needs and goals, and in which the reorganization and redirection of experience, expressed in discovery, invention, and culture change, are potentially present. The psychological core of being human involves a level of integration that implies much more than a set of roles and habit patterns, important as these are.

Even though a chimpanzee may learn to ride a bicycle, all the motivations connected with such a performance and the needs and goals that may be connected with it are, for him, not of the same order as those of a human being. Even as an object it cannot be a bicycle to him. Although he may be-

---

ronment and for sexual recruitment, (*b*) role differentiation and role assignment, (*c*) communication, (*d*) shared cognitive orientation, (*e*) a shared, articulated set of goals, (*f*) the normative regulation of means, (*g*) the regulation of affective expression, (*h*) socialization, (*i*) the effective control of disruptive forms of behavior.

Although not directly concerned with explicit relations between society, culture, and personality structure, it is obvious, I think, that in answer to the question "*How* are these functional prerequisites mediated?" a necessary assumption is that the individual members of a society must become psychologically structured in a manner that will tend to maintain a *sociocultural* system and, at the same time, afford a satisfactory personal adjustment to life.

14. See Margaret Mead (1951) for a "study of the way in which human growth rhythms are patterned within human cultures." Three areas of research are defined: "(1) the nature of the human growth process, (2) the degree of individuality within the human growth process and (3) the way in which these growth processes, the generally human and the idiosyncratic, are interwoven in the process of learning to be a human being in a given culture" (p. 14).

come highly skilled in performance and respond adequately to the authoritative directions of a human being, the fact that he has learned to ride a bicycle does not qualify a chimp as a member of a human society. All he has learned are certain signs and skills. The level of psychological organization that is characteristic of the chimpanzee permits a great deal of learning, but under no conceivable conditions would it be possible for a chimp to invent a bicycle.[15] Men, given certain motivational conditions and technological knowledge, have been able to invent bicycles as well as ride them. One of the major conditions typical of, and a crucial implement in, the socialization process in man is a novel means of communication. Neither a human society nor a human personality can be conceived in functional terms apart from systems of symbolic communication.

At the level of human adjustment the *representation* of objects and events of all kinds plays as characteristic a role in man's total behavior as does the direct *presentation* of objects and events in perception. Thus skill in the manipulation of symbols is directly involved with the development of man's rational and creative capacities. But symbolization is likewise involved with all other psychic functions—attention, perception, interest, memory, dreams, imagination, etc. Representative processes are

15. The remarkably vivid account of Viki, adopted and brought up in the home of Dr. and Mrs. Hayes (see Hayes, 1951), dramatizes the inherent psychobiological limitations of the chimpanzee under optimum conditions of systematic motivation from infancy, designed to exploit the animal's full potentialities for comparison with children reared under comparable circumstances. The range of the imitative responses of the chimpanzee in all spheres *except* language has never been more sharply demonstrated. Within three years Viki *did* become "socialized" in the human sense; her responses did become appropriately conditioned to culturally defined situations; even her food habits were not "culture free"; she became a "carrier" of culture—but only up to a point.

at the root of man's capacity to deal with the abstract qualities of objects and events, his ability to deal with the possible or conceivable, the ideal as well as the actual, the intangible along with the tangible, the absent as well as the present object or event, with fantasy and with reality. Every culture as well as the personal adjustment of each individual gives evidence of this, both at the level of unconscious as well as conscious processes. Then, too, symbolic forms and processes color man's motivations, goals, and his affective life in a characteristic way. They are as relevant to an understanding of his psychopathological as to his normal behavior. [16]

Symbolic communication is the basis on which a common world of meanings and values is established and transmitted in human societies. Communication at this new level is a necessary condition for the operation of human societies in their characteristic form.

Since even a most highly evolved primate, like the chimpanzee, cannot master a human language and there is no evidence that at any subhuman level the graphic and plastic arts exist, extrinsic symbolic systems as media of communication are an exclusively human creation. They provide man with the central vehicle that has been used to build up culturally constituted modes of existence for himself. The transmission of culture, either generically or specifically conceived, is the over-all unifying factor in the temporal continuity of man from generation to generation. And, since man has been able to develop, live by, and transmit different images of the nature of the world and himself, rather than adapt himself to some given existential reality in an "objective" sense, distinct cultural traditions become the differential attributes of discrete human societies.

16. Hallowell (1950*a*, pp. 165–66). Cf. Cassirer (1944). Nissen (1951) discusses symbolization in phylogenetic perspective as a novel instrumentality of special significance in the human primate.

Consequently, there can be no natural cleavage, from the standpoint of
the dynamics of human adjustment, between the psychological organization of
the individual, culture, and society.
While a human mind has long been assumed to be a necessary psychological
substratum of a human existence and
implicitly, if not explicitly, of culture
and although Dewey pointed out many
years ago that a "social" existence was
a necessary condition for the development of a human mind in the individual,[17] it is no longer satisfactory to

17. Dewey (1917) drew attention to what
he considered to be a very fruitful conception
of Gabriel Tarde, far ahead of his time. This,
writes Dewey, was the idea that "all psychological phenomena can be divided into the
physiological and the social, and that when we
have relegated elementary sensation and appe-
tite to the former head, all that is left of our
mental life, our beliefs, ideas and desires fall
within the scope of social psychology." More
recent developments, continues Dewey, have
provided "an unexpected confirmation of the
insight of Tarde that what we call 'mind'
means essentially the working of certain beliefs and desires, and that these in the concrete—in the only sense in which mind may
be said to exist—are functions of associated
behavior, varying with the structure and operation of social groups." Thus, instead of being
viewed as "an antecedent and ready-made
thing, 'mind' represents a reorganization of
original activities through their operation in a
given environment. It is a formation, not a
datum, a product and a cause only after it
has been produced. Now, theoretically, it is
possible that the reorganization of native activities which constitute mind may occur
through their exercise within a purely physical medium. Empirically, however, this is
highly improbable. Consideration of the dependence in infancy of the organization of
the native activities into intelligence upon the
presence of others, upon sharing in joint activities and upon language, makes it obvious
that the sort of mind capable of development
through the operation of native endowment
in a non-social environment is of the moron
order, and is practically, if not theoretically,
negligible." The fact that Dewey makes use
of neither the term "culture" nor the term
"personality" makes the clarity of his statement all the more interesting and significant
in historical perspective.

speak of human societies as constituted
of individuals with human minds, and
let it go at that. We need to know what
the integral relations are between mind,
society, and culture. But we are still
handicapped in our thinking by these
familiar categorical terms; especially so
since, being traditionally associated
with disciplines approaching man from
different points of view, mind, society,
and culture have from time to time
been given substantive definition.

From the psychological point of view
the concept of "personality structure"
would appear to mark a conceptual
transition from an earlier period to now.
This concept and the theoretical constructs back of it force us to think in
terms of how the human individual is
specifically organized psychodynamical-
ly. It orients us toward the conditions
under which psychological structuralization takes place and the relations between differences in personality organization and behavioral differences. The
Freudian model of personality structure
and its derivative formulations has provided the most useful constructs so far
but not necessarily the final ones.[18]

Historically, there is some analogy
to the situation in physics at the end of
the nineteenth century. Up until that
time, physics had gotten along very well
on the assumption that the atom was
something very small, hard, possibly
spherical, and of more or less uniform
constitution throughout. The atom, in
short, was conceived essentially as an
ultimate particle of matter. It was not
supposed that it possessed a structure
and that a deeper knowledge of this
structure would revolutionize our conception of matter.

18. See Mullahy (1948) for an exposition
of psychoanalytic personality theories and the
relevant literature. Cf. Bronfenbrenner (1951)
and the "Symposium on Theoretical Models
and Personality Theory" in the *Journal of Personality*, Vol. XX, No. 1 (1951), to which
psychologists are the main contributors.

The generic concept of "mind" when applied to "individuals" as the "units" of "society" and as the "bearers" of "culture" may have been useful in relation to certain orders of abstraction in the past, but we can now see more clearly the limitations imposed by this kind of conceptualization.

Furthermore, structural concepts have already supplanted the older concept of "society" in many areas of sociological analysis. And the "pattern" concept is the most obvious cultural analogy (cf. Weakland, 1951, p. 59). The concept of personality structure belongs to the same conceptual trend. Unlike the concept "mind" of an older tradition, the concept of personality structure *assumes* a sociocultural matrix as an essential condition of ontogenetic development. It involves a systematic examination of the influence of the relevant factors that constitute this matrix, considered as independent variables with reference to the kind of personality structure that is produced and to which characteristic patterns of conduct, considered as dependent variables, are related. In terms of such a paradigm the structure of personality is conceived as being rooted in part in an organized system of intervening variables.[19]

To say that culture, viewed as an independent variable in relation to the human organism, "determines" or "conditions" *behavior* is to conceive the problem much too narrowly, if not inadequately. While it is quite true that the acquisition of motor skills and other habits of this order may be rather simply related to culture, what has impressed many psychologists as a more important contribution of anthropology is the demonstrable relations between

cultural variability and the motivational systems of human individuals, that is, the differential organization of drives, needs, emotions, attitudes, and so on, which lie at the core of relatively enduring *dispositions* to act in a predictable manner. As Else Frenkel-Brunswik has expressed it (Adorno, Frenkel, Brunswik, *et al.*, 1950, pp. 5 ff.):

Personality is a more or less enduring organization of forces within the individual. These persisting forces of personality help to determine response in various situations, and it is thus largely to them that consistency of behavior—whether verbal or physical—is attributable. But behavior, however consistent, is not the same thing as personality; personality lies *behind* behavior and *within* the individual. The forces of personality are not responses but *readiness* for response; whether or not a readiness will issue in overt expression depends not only upon the situation of the moment but upon what other readiness stands in opposition to it. Personality forces which are inhibited are on a deeper level than those which immediately and consistently express themselves in overt behavior. . . .

Although personality is a product of the social environment[20] of the past, it is not, once it has developed, a mere object of the contemporary environment. What has developed is a *structure* within the individual something which is capable of self-initiated action upon the social environment and of selection with respect to varied impinging stimuli; something which though always modifiable is frequently very resistant to fundamental change. This conception is necessary to explain consistency of behavior in widely varying situations, to explain the persistence of ideological trends in the face of contradictory facts and radically altered social conditions, to explain why people in the same sociological situation have different or even conflicting views on social issues, and why it is that people whose behavior has been changed through psychological manipulation lapse into their old ways as soon as the agencies of manipulation are removed.

19. For a simple diagram representing motives, attitudes, etc. as intervening variables see Newcomb (1950, p. 31). E. C. Tolman sets forth a model in which intervening variables constitute the crucial construct in Parsons and Shils (1951, Part 3).

20. "Cultural" may be substituted.

The conception of personality structure is the best safeguard against the inclination to attribute persistent trends in the individual to something "innate" or "basic" or "racial" within him.

The concept of personality structure has proved particularly useful because, in addition to providing an effective intellectual means for examining the factors underlying the psychodynamics of individual adjustment, it has been found possible to express the major central tendencies that are characteristic of a series of individuals who belong to a single society, tribal group, or nation, in more or less equivalent terms.[21] This does not mean, of course, that there are no idiosyncratic variations in the personality structure of such a series of individuals. On the contrary, this must be expected. What is assumed is that membership in a given sociocultural system, or subsystem, subjects human beings to a common set of conditions that are significant with reference to the personality organization of these individuals. As Kluckhohn and Murray phrase it (1948, p. 39):

The members of any organized enduring group tend to manifest certain personality traits more frequently than do members of other groups. How large or how small are the groupings one compares depends on the problem at hand. By and large, the motivational structures and action patterns of Western Europeans seem similar when contrasted to those of the Near East or to Eastern Asiatics. Most white citizens of the United States, in spite of regional,

21. Although the terminology employed has varied somewhat both with respect to semantic content as well as to linguistic expression, nevertheless similar phenomena have been brought to a focus in what has been characterized, e.g., as "basic personality structure" (Kardiner, 1939, 1945a); "modal personality structure" (DuBois, 1944); "communal aspects of personality" (Kluckhohn and Mowrer, 1944); "social character" (Fromm, 1941); and "national character" (see the survey of the literature by Klineberg, 1950). Cf. Honigmann's tabulation of "Some Concepts of Ethos" (1949, Appendix B, pp. 357–59).

ethnic, and class differences, have features of personality which distinguish them from Englishmen, Australians or New Zealanders. In distinguishing group-membership determinants, one must usually take account of a concentric order of social groups to which the individual belongs, ranging from large national or international groups down to small local units. One must also know the hierarchical class, political or social, to which he belongs within each of these groups. How inclusive a unit one considers in speaking of group-membership determinants is purely a function of the level of abstraction at which one is operating at a given time.

In this connection the question also arises: To what kind of cultural unit are personality data to be related? Can we assume that our cultural classifications, as, for example, well-established areal differences, necessarily have a one-to-one correspondence with differences in modal personality type? Devereux has argued (1951, p. 38) that

in many respects the segment or aspect of the basic personality which is determined by the areal ethos is, functionally at least, a far more important component of the total personality of a given Plains Indian, than is the segment determined by the culture pattern of his own particular tribe. In fact, it might even be argued that the *specific manner* in which, e.g., a Crow Indian differs from a Cheyenne Indian, is entirely different from the *specific manner* in which *either* of the two differs from a Pueblo Indian, and that these two distinctive types of intra-areal, respectively inter-areal, differences are also determined primarily by the influence which the respective areal ethoses exert upon the personality of the Plains Indian, and upon that of the Pueblo Indian.

On the basis of observations contained in seventeenth- and eighteenth-century documents the writer inferred a constellation of psychological characteristics which he generalized for the Indians of the Eastern Woodland area, despite the well-known linguistic and cultural difference between Algonkian peoples and the Iroquois (Hallowell, 1946). Later, Fenton (1948, pp. 505–10) expressed essential agreement that most of these traits seemed reasonably applicable to the modern Iroquois. Wallace (in press), on the basis of a sample of Rorschach protocols representing a highly acculturated Tuscarora community, demonstrated a core of personality characteristics common to these people and the Ojibwa, as well as differences which seemed congruent with cultural differences.

On the other hand, Rorschach data (unpublished) from the Hopi, Navaho, Zuni, and Papago suggest quite marked tribal differences, so far as psychological adjustment is concerned. No one has studied this material, however, with a view to determining both similarities and differences. At the same time, Kroeber (1947), reviewing autobiographical and dream material, was impressed with "the rather striking similarity of the untutored, unguided self-depiction of a particular Navaho and a particular Walapai," and he raises the question whether the likeness is a "coincidence," which, he says, he does not believe, "or mainly due to a regional though super tribal resemblance of culture; or whether perhaps it is generally expectable in folk cultures, as a recurrent type definable in socio-psychological terms, although varying somewhat in its outer cultural dress."

Perhaps it is not possible to give conclusive answers to such questions at the present time but only to view them as research problems still open for investigation. A closely related question would be whether or not there are definable psychological characteristics which, say in North America, may even transcend the cultural areas that have been defined and typify "Indians," as contrasted with Europeans or Melanesians (cf. Kroeber, 1948, p. 587).

Another question, of a different type, has been raised by Kroeber (1948, p.

597 n.; cf. p. 587), namely, "the possibility that cultures of unlike content can be alike psychologically; or their contents may be similar but their psychology dissimilar." In regard to the first possibility, a most suggestive psychological analogue has been drawn by Goldschmidt[22] between Yurok-Hupa, on the one hand, and emergent capitalistic Europe, on the other, i.e., two spatially distant and historically unconnected peoples. Goldschmidt's thesis is that, in both instances, "the structural character of the society is one which rewards certain personality configurations so that they dominate the social scene and set the patterns. It also creates a configuration of demands and tensions which are transmitted through child rearing to successive generations." Typical personality characteristics stressed are "a compulsive concern over asceticism and industriousness, patterns of personal guilt, as well as tendencies toward hostility, competition and loneliness."

What specific factors, or patterns of determinants, are the most crucial for the structuring of the personality, how and when and by what means they become psychologically effective in the socialization of the individual, have been objects of specific researches in the culture and personality area.

Ethnographic knowledge on a world-wide comparative scale, including observable differences in modes of child-training, value systems, and goals, together with the traditional emphasis upon the fact that culture is acquired by the individual, stimulated anthropologists to develop hypotheses concerning the relation of personality structure to cultural variables, once some of them became aware of the newer developments in personality theory. Be-

22. 1951, pp. 521–22; H. E. Erickson, approaching the Yurok material from the standpoint of child training, developed a somewhat different interpretation of their culture.

sides this, anthropologists, as contrasted with other social scientists and psychologists, were accustomed to doing field work in other cultures, so it was possible to test hypotheses in the field and to exploit the significant cross-cultural data as well. We may say, I think, that the general hypothesis underlying culture and personality studies has been confirmed. Moot points, such as how early personality structure is set, what reorganization is possible after the initial years of childhood, and what are the most crucial determining factors involved, concern personality theory itself rather than the fundamental hypothesis.[23] That human personality structure is a product of experience in a socialization process and that the resulting structure varies with the nature and conditions of such experience can scarcely be doubted.[24]

Reinforcement is now coming from psychologists through a renewed interest in the study of perception. Although long conceptualized as a basic function of the "mind" and chiefly investigated at the level of psychophysics, more recent studies have clearly shown the need of taking personality variables into account.[25] It is rapidly becoming a psychological commonplace that human beings groomed under different conditions may be expected to vary in perceptual experience, functionally related to needs, which, in turn, are in part defined by a culturally constituted order of reality. The properties of a universal objective order of reality, once reputed to be mediated to us directly through

cognitive processes, are now conceded to involve more complex determinants and intervening variables, related to noncognitive experiences of the human organism.[26]

The importance of this hypothesis for a deeper understanding of the nature of the integral relations that exist between personality, culture, and society is far-reaching. Since perception is fundamental to all human adjustment in the sense that it is made the basis of judgment, decision, and action, to experience the world in common perceptual terms must be considered a prime unifying factor in the integration of culture, society, and the functioning person. Indeed, through the operation of culturally derived constituents, perception in man may be said to have acquired an overlaid *social* function. Among other things, it becomes one of the chief psychological means whereby beliefs in reified images and concepts as integral parts of a culturally constituted reality may become substantiated in the experience of individuals.[27] Different world views as described in our ethnographic monographs take on a deeper significance when considered in relation to the functioning of perception in man. We are on our way to a better grasp of the significance of culture as *lived* rather than as described.[28]

26. This by no means implies an "absolute" relativism in perception. Recognition of this fact simply helps to define the real problem. A completely relativistic hypothesis would be as inadequate as a purely absolute one (see Gibson, 1950a).

27. See Hallowell (1951a); Dennis has a related chapter in Blake and Ramsey (1951).

28. Lewin (1948) has pointed out that "experiments dealing with memory and group pressure on the individual show that what exists as 'reality' for the individual is, to a high degree, determined by what is socially accepted as reality. This holds even in the field of physical fact: to the South Sea Islander the world may be flat; to the European it is round. 'Reality,' therefore, is not an abso-

23. See the critique by Orlansky (1949).

24. A highly representative example in which the conceptual frame of reference adopted and the hypotheses employed are clearly set forth in DuBois (1944).

25. See Blake and Ramsey (1951). Hilgard has a chapter on "The Role of Learning in Perception"; Bruner discusses "Personality Dynamics and the Process of Perceiving"; Miller, "Unconscious Processes and Perception"; etc.

As anthropologists, we may acquire a very detailed and thoroughgoing knowledge of the belief system, the social organization, as well as all the other aspects of a culture. We may learn to act with propriety, to sing a song or two, to dance, or to draw a bow. We may be bursting with empathy. We may even learn to speak the language. We may be aware of culture patterns and subtle relations that escape the people themselves. But the culture we study is not part of us. Our perceptions are not structured in the same mold. The very fact that our approach is objective, that we want to grasp it in its totality, is an index to the fact that we do not belong. We are not motivated to learn about another culture in order to live it but in order to talk or write about it, describe it, analyze it, seek out its history. The meaning of culture that emerges for us is a function of *our* background, interests, aims. In terms of this approach, substantive conceptualizations of culture rather than psychological or functional ones are almost inescapable. But culture may likewise be conceived as

---

lute. It differs with the group to which the individual belongs.

"This dependence of the individual on the group for a determination of what does and what does not constitute 'reality' is less surprising if we remember that the individual's own experience is necessarily limited. In other words, the probability that his judgment will be right is heightened if the individual places greater trust in the experience of the group, whether or not this group experience tallies with his own. This is one reason for the acceptance of the group's judgment, but there is still another reason. In any field of conduct and belief, the group exercises strong pressure for compliance on its individual members. We are subject to this pressure in all areas—political, religious, social—including our belief of what is true or false, good or bad, right or wrong, real or unreal. Under these circumstances it is not difficult to understand why the general acceptance of a fact or a belief might be the very cause preventing this belief or fact from even being questioned."

meaningful in terms of the psychological adjustment of the human being to his world of action and to concrete living, not as abstracted by an outsider. A psychological approach to culture, in the sense that what we wish to find out is the structural basis of the varying ways in which man has built up distinctive modes of life for himself, not only throws light upon the nature of man and the necessary conditions of a human existence but upon the substratum of particular cultures as descriptively generalized.

The psychological substratum of culture has been partially obscured until recently, because, in addition to the lack of effective theories of personality structure, development, and functioning, theories of learning adequate for handling this complicated process at the human level were not sufficiently developed. To some extent this is still true. Only a few years ago, Hilgard pointed out that sometimes psychologists have given the impression that "there are no differences, except quantitative ones, between the learning of lower animals and primates, including man." He goes on to say, however, that, "while this position is more often implied than asserted, it is strange that the opposite point of view is not more often made explicit—that at the human level there have emerged capacities for retaining, reorganizing, and foreseeing experiences which are not approached by the lower animals, including the other primates. No one has seriously proposed that animals can develop a set of ideals which regulate conduct around long-range plans, or that they can invent a mathematics to help them keep track of their experiences. Because a trained dog shows some manifestations of shame, or a chimpanzee some signs of cooperation, or a rat a dawning concept of triangularity, it does not follow that these lower organisms, clever as they are, have all the richness of human mental activity."[29]

The learning process when considered in relation to culture has often been conceptualized too simply in the past, among other reasons because it has not been considered in relation to the development of a personality structure and likewise to the potentialities for readjustment and creativity that this level of psychological organization in man permits, with appropriate motivation.

We now know that to say *merely* that the individual acquires culture through learning in a socialization process is only a confession of ignorance as to what this process actually involves. We know at least that culture as systematically described and topically organized by the ethnographer is not what is directly presented to and learned by the individual at any point in this process. We know that the socialization process from the very beginning is mediated by close personal relations of the child with adults and that there are important affective components involved. We know that mediation through symbolic modes of communication plays a role. We know that the individual beginning at a level of dependence must achieve the capacity for independent and autonomous action. We know that the individual must achieve some kind of patterned integration that we call "personality structure." We know that, while this structure may take different forms, there are likewise constant elements that are characteristic of a *human* personality structure in a generic sense. We know

29. Ernest R. Hilgard (1948, pp. 329–30). Cf. Miller and Dollard (1941) and Gibson's outline of what he considers to be desirable features of a theory of social learning in man (1950b). Whiting (1941), using the Hull model of learning theory, systematically analyzes the acquisition of Kwoma culture by the child. The chapter on "Inculcation of Supernatural Beliefs" is of special interest.

that, concretely viewed, culture becomes part of the individual. If this were not so, he could not live it nor could he hand it on.[30] Beliefs viewed abstractly as part of a culture objectively described become his beliefs; values are incorporated into his motivational system; his needs and goals, although culturally constituted, function as personal needs and goals. A culture as lived is not something apart from the individuals who live it or separable from the societal organization through which group living functions, any more than the characteristic features of an animal's morphology are something

30. Tolman (see Parsons and Shils, 1951, p. 359) has remarked that "psychology is in large part a study of the internalization of society and of culture within the individual human actor"; and Newcomb (1950, p. 6) speaks of the individual as having "somehow got society inside himself. Its ways of doing things become his own." Cf. Miller and Hutt (1949), who point out that "the interiorization of social values is only a relatively recent area of investigation."

Such statements, coming from psychologists in particular, are highly relevant for cultural anthropology. In so far as some anthropologists have given the impression, even if they have not always systematically defended the view, that, fundamentally, culture is to be considered as something apart from or outside the individual rather than as an integral part of him, some basic dichotomy between personality and culture is implied. An extreme statement of this position is embodied in the remark of White (1947) that, "as a matter of fact, the most effective way to study culture scientifically is to proceed as if the human race did not exist." Spiro has brought this problem to a focus in his 1951 article. "What cultural realists have failed to realize," he says, "is that once something is learned it is no longer external to the organism, but is 'inside' the organism; and once it is 'inside,' the organism becomes a biosocial organism, determining its own behavior as a consequence of the modifications it has undergone in the process of learning. But the individual-culture dichotomy accepted by the realists prevents them from acknowledging this most elementary point and, as a consequence, they think in terms of a superorganic culture determining the behavior of an organic adult."

apart from the gene system that is their substratum. A living, functioning culture is not, existentially, dependent upon a group of interacting human beings, abstractly considered, but upon the manner in which such individuals are psychologically structured. A culture may be said to be just as much the *expression* of their mode of human psychodynamic adjustment as it is a *condition* for the grooming of successive generations of individuals in this mode.

Fromm has pointed out (1949, pp. 5–6, 10):

Modern, industrial society, for instance, could not have attained its ends had it not harnessed the energy of free men for work in an unprecedented degree. He had to be moulded into a person who was eager to spend most of his energy for the purpose of work, who acquired discipline, particularly orderliness and punctuality, to a degree unknown in most other cultures. It would not have sufficed if each individual had to make up his mind consciously every day that he wanted to work, to be on time, etc., since any such conscious deliberation would have led to many more exceptions than the smooth functioning of society can afford. Threat and force would not have sufficed either as motive for work since the highly differentiated work in modern industrial society can only be the work of free men and not of forced labor. The *necessity* for work, for punctuality and orderliness had to be transformed into a *drive* for these qualities. This means that society had to produce such a social character in which these strivings were inherent.

Human beings, in other words, have to become psychologically structured in such a way that they "*want to act as they have to act* [author's italics] and at the same time find gratification in acting according to the requirements of the culture." According to Fromm, there must be some nuclear character structure "shared by most members of the same culture," i.e., "social character," the functioning of which is essen-

tial to the functioning of the culture as a going concern.[31] Child-training, viewed in the context of social structure, is "one of the key *mechanisms of transmission of social necessities into character traits* [author's italics]."

The behavioral manifestations upon which we depend for constructing our substantive pictures of cultures are always rooted in the personality structure of individuals. The only way in which a culture may be said to perpetuate itself is through the characteristic psychological structuralization of a group of individuals. It is only through organized personalities, not "individuals" or "minds," that human societies and culture attain living reality. In so far as a culture may in any sense be conceived abstractly, it is *our* abstraction, a convenience adapted to the kind of analysis we wish to make of the problems we wish to pursue. Culture can hardly be an abstraction for those to whom it is an intellectually unexamined mode of life. Human beings have died in defense of concrete beliefs, which, abstractly viewed, may be characterized as a part of their culture but which, psychologically considered, take on the kind of palpable reality that motivates actual behavior. I suspect that there still may linger in the minds of some a faint aura of an earlier day, when psychology meant psychophysics, or primarily a study of the mechanisms of behavior or the investigation of the properties of mind

31. Cf. the statement of Goldschmidt (*op. cit.*, p. 522): "The individualized pattern of social action, the internalized demands for personal success with its road theoretically open to all, the absence of fixity of social position and security in group solidarity, and the importance of property for social advancement and hence satisfaction of the *ego*—all these combine to support such traits of character as aggressiveness, hostility, competitiveness, loneliness and penuriousness. *Indeed, it is hard to see how a Hupa or Yurok could operate effectively in his society without these traits*" (italics ours).

in the most generic and abstract sense, and little else. In contrast, the rich and varied content of cultures appeared to be in another phenomenal dimension. Today, in some areas of social anthropology, abstract relations and patterns are given prime consideration. On the other hand, for an understanding of personality structure, its development, and relationship to a typically human mode of existence, cultural content in its full range and depth cannot be ignored.

Although the child requires socialization in order to achieve the psychological status that marks him as a human being, it is not necessary that he develop the particular personality structure that characterizes societies A, C, or N; B, D, or Z will provide the necessary conditions that are functionally equivalent. What we have to assume—and there is empirical evidence for this—is that there are generic attributes of human personality as well as provincial and variable kinds of organization. There is an obvious analogy with human speech. A necessary condition for socialization in man is the learning and use of a language. But different languages are functionally equivalent in this respect, and one language is comparable with another because human speech has certain common denominators.

While a human individual, therefore, on account of his inherent organic potentialities, can adjust himself to life under a variety of conditions, a particular culture, in so far as we assume it to be dependent upon a characteristic psychological organization of a group of individuals, cannot maintain its existence unless this condition is satisfied.[32] In terms of this hypothesis, man's

potentialities for readjustment and creativity are thrown into sharp relief as constant human phenomena. Particular cultures may rise, flourish, and disappear, but other modes of life take their place. While viewed in a provincial setting and in limited temporal perspective, it may seem adequate to speak of individuals as the "carriers" of a culture or the "creatures" of culture, this does not take into account *all* that we know about the nature of man. If we fail to give due weight to man's potentialities as creator and re-creator of the kind of life that is his most distinctive attribute, how are we to account for the emergence of a cultural mode of existence in the first place?[33] Surely, we must assume that it has been through the development of his own potentialities that man has made the

32. Newcomb (1950, p. 448) has generalized this point, emphasizing childhood experiences as the "essential link" in temporal continuity: "Childhood experiences provide the essential link in the chain by which the culture of any society and the common personality characteristics of its members are bound together and continue to be bound together over succeeding generations.... There would be neither common personality characteristics within a society nor a continuing culture were it not for common childhood experiences."

33. Bidney (1947, p. 395) postulates a "human nature" that "is logically and genetically prior to culture since we must postulate human agents with psychobiological powers and impulses capable of initiating the cultural process as a means of adjusting to their environment and as a form of symbolic expression. In other words, the determinate nature of man is manifested functionally through culture but is not reducible to culture." In another article (1949, p. 347) he points out: "In the development of modern cultural anthropology one may discern two major 'themes.' On the one hand there is the theme derived from the naturalistic, positivistic, evolutionary tradition of the Nineteenth Century that cultural reality represents an autonomous, superorganic, superpsychic level of reality subject to its own laws and stages of development or evolution. On the other hand, there is the recurring theme, which dates back to the humanistic tradition of the Renaissance and the rationalism of the Eighteenth Century philosophers of the Enlightenment, that human culture is the product of human discovery and creativity and is subject to human regulation."

world intelligible to himself in livable terms. Whatever form these images may have taken, they have emerged out of human experience, transmuted into symbolically articulated terms. Since creativity in the individual human being, in so far as we know anything about it, involves unconscious processes, we may assume that equivalent factors have been among those operative throughout man's history. If, therefore, we examine the relation between the individual and culture only with regard to the manner in which he becomes groomed as a participator in a static provincial and continuing mode of life, we may *avoid,* but never solve, the more perplexing problems that arise if we keep man as a whole constantly in view. When we do this, culture change, acculturation, and personal readjustment come into the foreground.

We know too little as yet about the psychological consequences of acculturation to make any broad generalizations. But we assume that changes in any established mode of life that eventuate in new or varied culture patterns imply readjustment in the habits, attitudes, and goals of the individuals concerned, that such processes of readjustment must be motivated, and that learning is involved.[34] The crucial question, however, turns upon the psychological depth of such readjustments. And this question, in turn, depends upon a number of situational variables: the time span covered, the rate of acculturation, the manner in which the relations between individuals of the interacting groups are structured, qualitative factors, etc. All the processes of social interaction involved are matched in complexity by those of a psychological nature.[35] We certainly cannot assume, even in an acculturation situation where

one group is dominant over the other and the pressures on the subordinate group are severe, that the latter can acquire a new personality structure by the same process or in terms of the same motivations which lead to the acquisition of new tools, house types, or a new language. In my own investigations of the Ojibwa, I believe I have secured sufficient evidence to demonstrate that considerable acculturation can occur without any profound effect upon the "modal" or "communal" aspects of personality. On the other hand, the same data indicate that, in one group at least, conditions exist that have greatly accelerated the breakdown of the aboriginal personality structure that has persisted in other groups despite a considerable degree of acculturation.[36]

If we wish to understand more about the potentialities of human beings for psychological reorganization and a reconstruction of their culture, a close examination of what happens under various conditions of acculturation will be fruitful. In one type of situation, it is

34. See Hallowell (1945) for a preliminary consideration of the problem.

35. See, in particular, Spindler and Goldschmidt (1952). Their research design is "oriented toward the understanding of the processes of change within a society [the Menomini Indians of Wisconsin] under the impact of modern American civilization, and is particularly concerned with the adoption of outward manifestations of cultural and social behavior in their relation to changes in the individual personality characteristics of its personnel, without for the present, treating either as the independent variable in the situation." The results of this particular investigation are being prepared for publication by George Spindler.

Adams (1951) discussed the hypothesis advanced by H. G. Barnett in "Personal Conflicts and Cultural Change" (1941) with reference to his own data.

36. The major summarization of data and conclusions may be found in Hallowell (1951b). Cf. Hallowell (1950b) and the brief presentation in *Acculturation in the Americas: Proceedings and Selected Papers of the XXIXth International Congress of Americanists,* ed. Sol Tax (1952).

true, a whole group of individuals may be forced back on their psychological heels, so to speak. But it would be interesting to know more about the conditions under which a positive psychological reorganization might take place. One would like to know which are the most important factors that might contribute to the latter outcome. I suspect that a crucial variable may be the kind of personality structure of the people undergoing acculturation.

Here I think we have one of the crucial points of human adjustment, considered from the standpoint of man's group living and the perpetuation of a particular cultural tradition. The type of personality structure that prepares the individual for group living in *one* set of cultural terms does not prepare him for a successful adjustment to life in *any* set of cultural terms. Nevertheless, the people of one society may have the kind of personality organization that, under given conditions, enables them to adjust more readily to a new mode of life than the people of some other society. Fully to understand the dynamics of acculturation, we need to take psychological, as well as cultural, facts into account.

Changes in the cultural patterning of existence are always possible to man so long as certain generic psychological conditions, prerequisite for the maintenance of *any* human society, are met. Evans-Pritchard (1951), for example, in discussing what is implied by the term "social structure," points out that "it is evident that there must be uniformities and regularities in social life, that a society must have some sort of order, or its members could not live together," and then goes on to say: "It is only because people know the kind of behavior expected of them, and what kind of behavior to expect from others, in the various conditions of social life, and coordinate their activities in sub-

mission to rules and under the guidance of values that each and all are able to go about their affairs. They can make predictions, anticipate events, and lead their lives in harmony with their fellows because every society has a form or pattern which allows us to speak of it as a system, or structure, within which, and in accordance with which, its members live their lives." It is evident in this passage that the writer is assuming that the human individual is capable of self-awareness, is aware of self-other relations, and consciously relates traditional values to his own conduct. What is assumed, without comment, is a level of psychological functioning that is characterized by self-awareness, one basic facet of human nature and the human personality (Hallowell, 1950a). Self and society may be considered as aspects of a single whole. This whole has been designated by Cottrell (1942) as the "self-other" system. Phrased in this way, explicit recognition is given to the self as a constant factor in the human personality structure, intrinsic to the operation of human societies and all situations of social interaction.

The attribute of self-awareness, which involves man's capacity to discriminate himself as an object in a world of objects other than himself, is as central to our understanding of the prerequisites of man's social and cultural mode of adjustment as it is for the psychodynamics of the individual. A human social order implies a mode of existence that has meaning for the individual at the level of self-awareness. A human social order, for example, is always a moral order. If the individual did not have the capacity for identifying the conduct that is his own and, through self-reflection, appraising it with reference to values and social sanctions, how would a moral order function in human terms? If I cannot assume moral responsibility for my conduct, how can guilt or shame arise? What conflict can there be between impulse and standards if I am unaware of values or sanctions? It is man's capacity for and development of self-awareness that makes such unconscious psychological mechanisms as repression, rationalization, and so on of adaptive importance for the individual. They would have no function otherwise. They allow the individual to function without full self-knowledge. They enable him to function in a moral order with something less than a perfect batting average.

Self-awareness, like gravity, was long taken for granted before it was subjected to analysis, genetically and functionally. We now know that it is one of the attributes of a generic personality structure that has to be built up in the individual in every human society during the socialization process. This has been one of the contributions of modern personality psychology. From the anthropological side we know that there are varying traditional concepts of the self in different societies that must contribute to the self-image of the individual. How far variables in self-concepts are related to differences in the needs and goals of the individual and consequently to behavioral differences needs further investigation.[37] However, both the generic and the specific aspects of the self with particular reference to variability in culturally derived content and the organization of the total personality are among the topics that need further clarification if social anthropology is to have a firm psychological foundation. Self-awareness is as inherent in the human situation as are social structure and culture.

37. Further elaboration of this topic will be found in my forthcoming paper, "The Self and Its Behavioral Environment," to be published in *Psychoanalysis and the Social Sciences,* Vol. IV.

Man, unlike his animal kin, acts in a universe that he has discovered and made intelligible to himself as an organism not only capable of consciousness but also of self-consciousness and reflective thought. But this has been possible only through the use of speech and other extrinsic symbolic means that have led to the articulation, communication, and transmission of culturally constituted worlds of meanings and values. An organized social life in man, since it transcends purely biological and geographic determinants, cannot function apart from communally recognized meanings and values, or apart from the psychological structuralization of individuals who make these their own. Learning a culture and the roles on which the persisting patterns of social structure depend is not equivalent to learning a set of habits or skills but involves a higher order of psychological integration. In order for this unique level of integration to be achieved in man, such unconscious mechanisms as conflict, repression, identification, etc., are intrinsic to the socialization process and consequently form a part of the psychodynamics of human adjustment. They are as inherent in the emergence and functioning of human societies as they are relevant to a full understanding of how the personality structure of the individuals exposed to a given cultural situation differs from, or is similar to, that of another set of individuals.

Personality, culture, and society form systems of relations that function as integral wholes in a wider universe of other-than-human reality. Considered from an integral point of view, they have no independent existence apart from the social adjustment of the individuals involved and the organization of human experience, in a manner that typifies the human situation.

REFERENCES

ABERLE, DAVID FRIEND. 1951. *The Psychosocial Analysis of a Hopi Life-History.* ("Comparative Psychological Monographs," Vol. XXI, No. 107.)

ABERLE, D. F.; COHEN, A. K.; DAVIS, A. K.; LEVY, M. J., JR.; and SUTTON, F. X. 1950. "The Functional Prerequisites of a Society," *Ethics*, LX, 100–111.

ADAMS, RICHARD N. 1951. "Personnel in Culture Change: A Test of a Hypothesis," *Social Forces*, XXX, 185–89.

ADORNO, T. W.; FRENKEL-BRUNSWIK, ELSE; LEVINSON, D. J.; and SANFORD, R. N. 1950. *The Authoritarian Personality.* New York: Harper & Bros.

BARNETT, HOMER G. 1941. "Personal Conflicts and Culture Change," *Social Forces*, XX, 160–71.

BARTLETT, F. C. 1937. "Psychological Methods and Anthropological Problems," *Africa*, X, No. 4, 401–19.

BATESON, GREGORY. 1942. "Social Planning and the Concept of 'Deutero-Learning.'" In BRYSON, L., and FINKELSTEIN, L. (eds.), *Science, Philosophy, and Religion: Second Symposium*, pp. 81–97. New York.

———. 1944. "Cultural Determinants of Personality." In HUNT, J. McV. (ed.), *Personality and the Behavior Disorders*, II, 714–35. New York: Ronald Press Co.

BERNDT, RONALD M. and CATHERINE H. 1951. *Sexual Behavior in Western Arnhem Land.* ("Viking Fund Publications in Anthropology," No. 16.) New York.

BIDNEY, DAVID. 1947. "Human Nature and the Cultural Process," *American Anthropologist*, XLIX, 375–99.

———. 1949. "The Concept of Meta-anthropology and Its Significance for Contemporary Anthropological Science." In NORTHROP, F. S. C. (ed.), *Ideological Differences and World Order*, pp. 323–55. New Haven: Yale University Press.

BLAKE, ROBERT R., and RAMSEY, GLENN W. (eds.). 1951. *Perception: An Approach to Personality.* New York: Ronald Press Co.

BRONFENBRENNER, URIE. 1951. "Toward an Integrated Theory of Personality." In BLAKE, ROBERT R., and RAMSEY, GLENN W. (eds.), *Perception: An Approach to Personality*, pp. 206–57. New York: Ronald Press Co.

BROWN, G. GORDON. 1951. "Culture, Society, and Personality: A Restatement," *American Journal of Psychiatry*, CVIII, 173–75.

CASSIRER, ERNST. 1944. *An Essay on Man.* New Haven: Yale University Press.

COTTRELL, LEONARD S., JR. 1942. "The Analysis of Situational Fields in Social Psychology," *American Sociological Review*, VII, 370–82.

DENNIS, WAYNE. 1951. "Cultural and Developmental Factors in Perception." In BLAKE, ROBERT R., and RAMSEY, GLENN W. (eds.), *Perception: An Approach to Personality*, pp. 148–69. New York: Ronald Press Co.

DEVEREUX, GEORGE. 1951. *Reality and Dream: Psychotherapy of a Plains Indian.* Prefaces by KARL A. MENNINGER and ROBERT H. LOWIE. Psychological tests edited and interpreted by ROBERT R. HOLT. New York: International Universities Press.

DEWEY, JOHN. 1917. "The Need for a Social Psychology," *Psychological Review*, XXIV, 266–77.

DOLLARD, J., and MILLER, N. 1950. *Personality and Psychotherapy: An Analysis in Terms of Learning, Thinking, and Culture.* New York: McGraw-Hill Book Co., Inc.

DUBOIS, CORA. 1944. *The People of Alor.* Minneapolis: University of Minnesota Press.

DYK, WALTER. 1947. *A Navaho Autobiography.* ("Viking Fund Publications in Anthropology," No. 8.) New York.

ERIKSON, ERIK H. 1950. *Childhood and Society.* New York: W. W. Norton & Co., Inc.

EVANS-PRITCHARD, E. E. 1951. *Social Anthropology.* London: Cohen & West, Ltd.

FENTON, WILLIAM N. 1948. "The Present Status of Anthropology in Northeastern North America: A Review Article," *American Anthropologist*, L, 494–515.

FORD, CLELLAN S., and BEACH, FRANK A. 1951. *Patterns of Sexual Behavior.* New York: Harper & Bros., and Paul B. Hoeber.

FROMM, ERICH. 1941. *Escape from Freedom.* New York: Farrar & Rinehart.

——. 1947. *Man for Himself: An Inquiry into the Psychology of Ethics.* New York: Rinehart & Co.

——. 1949. "Psychoanalytic Characterology and Its Application to the Understanding of Culture." In SARGENT, S. S., and SMITH, M. W. (eds.), *Culture and Personality,* pp. 1–12. New York: Viking Fund.

FRANK, L. K. 1949. *Society as the Patient.* New Brunswick, N.J.: Rutgers University Press.

——. 1951. *Nature and Human Nature.* New Brunswick, N.J.: Rutgers University Press.

GIBSON, J. J. 1950a. *The Perception of the Visual World.* Boston: Houghton Mifflin Co.

——. 1950b. "The Implications of Learning Theory for Social Psychology." In MILLER, JAMES GRIER (ed.), *Experiments in Social Process: A Symposium on Social Psychology.* New York: McGraw-Hill Book Co., Inc.

GOLDSCHMIDT, WALTER. 1951. "Ethics and the Structure of Society: An Ethnological Contribution to the Sociology of Knowledge," *American Anthropologist,* LIII, 506–24.

HALL, J. K.; ZILBOORG, G.; and BUNKER, H. A. (eds.). 1944. *One Hundred Years of American Psychiatry.* New York: Columbia University Press.

HALLOWELL, A. IRVING. 1945. "Sociopsychological Aspects of Acculturation." In LINTON, RALPH (ed.), *The Science of Man in the World Crisis,* pp. 171–200. New York: Columbia University Press.

——. 1946. "Some Psychological Characteristics of the Northeastern Indians." In JOHNSON, FREDERICK (ed.), *Man in Northeastern North America,* pp. 195–225. ("Papers of the R. S. Peabody Foundation for Archeology," Vol. III.) Andover, Mass.

——. 1950a. "Personality Structure and the Evolution of Man," *American Anthropologist,* LII, 159–73.

——. 1950b. "Values, Acculturation, and Mental Health," *American Journal of Orthopsychiatry,* XX, 732–43.

——. 1951a. "Cultural Factors in the Structuralization of Perception." In

ROHRER, J. H., and SHERIF, M. (eds.), *Social Psychology at the Crossroads,* pp. 164–95. New York: Harper & Bros.

——. 1951b. "The Use of Projective Techniques in the Study of Sociopsychological Aspects of Acculturation," *Journal of Projective Techniques,* XV, 26–44.

HARING, DOUGLAS G. (ed.). 1949. *Personal Character and Cultural Milieu: A Collection of Readings.* Rev. ed. Syracuse, N.Y.: Syracuse University Press.

HARRIS, ZELLIG S. 1951. "Review of Selected Writings of Edward Sapir," *Language,* XXVII, 288–333.

HAYES, CATHY. 1951. *The Ape in Our House.* New York: Harper & Bros.

HILGARD, ERNEST R. 1948. *Theories of Learning.* New York: Appleton-Century.

HOCH, PAUL H., and ZUBIN, JOSEPH. 1949. *Psychosexual Development in Health and Disease: Proceedings of the 38th Annual Meeting of the American Psychopathological Association, 1948.* New York: Grune & Stratton.

HONIGMANN, JOHN J. 1949. *Culture and Ethos of Kaska Society.* ("Yale University Publications in Anthropology," No. 40.) New Haven: Yale University Press.

HUNT, J. McV. (ed.). 1944. *Personality and the Behavior Disorders.* 2 vols. New York: Ronald Press Co.

JENNINGS, H. S. 1942. "The Transition from the Individual to the Social Level." In REDFIELD, ROBERT (ed.), *Levels of Integration in Biological and Social Systems,* pp. 105–19. ("Biological Symposia," Vol. VIII.) Lancaster, Pa.: Jacques Cattell Press.

KARDINER, ABRAM. 1939. *The Individual and His Society.* New York: Columbia University Press.

——. 1945a. *The Psychological Frontiers of Society.* (With the collaboration of RALPH LINTON, CORA DuBOIS, and JAMES WEST.) New York: Columbia University Press.

——. 1945b. "The Concept of Basic Personality Structure as an Operational Tool in the Social Sciences." In LINTON, RALPH (ed.), *The Science of Man in the World Crisis,* pp. 107–22. New York: Columbia University Press.

KARDINER, ABRAM, and OVERSEY, LIONEL. 1951. *The Mark of Oppression: A Psy-*

chological Study of the American Negro. New York: W. W. Norton & Co.

KLINEBERG, OTTO. 1950. *Tensions Affecting International Understanding: A Survey of Research.* (Social Science Research Council Bull. 62.) New York: Social Science Research Council.

KLUCKHOHN, CLYDE. 1944. "The Influence of Psychiatry on Anthropology in America during the Past One Hundred Years." In HALL, J. K., and OTHERS (eds.), *One Hundred Years of American Psychiatry,* pp. 489–618. New York: Columbia University Press.

———. 1949. *Mirror for Man.* New York: McGraw-Hill Book Co., Inc.

KLUCKHOHN, CLYDE, and MOWRER, O. H. 1944. "Culture and Personality: A Conceptual Scheme," *American Anthropologist,* XLVI, 1–29.

KLUCKHOHN, CLYDE, and MURRAY, H. A. (eds.). 1948. *Personality in Nature, Society, and Culture.* New York: Alfred A. Knopf.

KROEBER, A. L. 1947. "A Southwestern Personality Type," *Southwestern Journal of Anthropology,* III, 108–13.

———. 1948. *Anthropology.* New York: Harcourt, Brace & Co.

KROEBER, A. L.; BENEDICT, RUTH; EMENEAU, MURRAY B.; *et al.* 1943. *Franz Boas, 1858–1942.* (*American Anthropologist,* Vol. XLV, No. 3, Part II.)

LEIGHTON, ALEXANDER and DOROTHEA C. (With the assistance of CATHERINE OPLER.) 1949. *Gregorio, the Hand-Trembler: A Psychobiological Personality Study of a Navaho Indian.* ("Papers of the Peabody Museum of American Archeology and Ethnology, Harvard University," Vol. XL, No. 1.) Boston.

LEWIN, KURT. 1948. *Resolving Social Conflicts: Selected Papers on Group Dynamics.* Edited by GERTRUD WEISS LEWIN. New York: Harper & Bros.

LINTON, RALPH. 1945. *The Cultural Background of Personality.* New York: Appleton-Century-Crofts, Inc.

LOWIE, ROBERT H. 1937. *The History of Ethnological Theory.* New York: Farrar & Rinehart.

MANDELBAUM, DAVID G. (ed.). 1949. *Selected Writings of Edward Sapir in Language, Culture, and Personality.* Berke-

ley and Los Angeles: University of California Press.

MAUSS, MARCEL. 1950. *Sociologie et anthropologie.* Introduction à l'œuvre de Marcel Mauss par C. LÉVI-STRAUSS. Paris: Presses universitaires de France.

MEAD, MARGARET. 1937. *Cooperation and Competition among Primitive Peoples.* New York and London: McGraw-Hill Book Co., Inc.

———. 1949. *Male and Female.* New York: William Morrow & Co.

———. 1951. *Soviet Attitudes toward Authority.* New York: McGraw-Hill Book Co., Inc.

MEAD, MARGARET, and MACGREGOR, FRANCES COOKE. 1951. *Growth and Culture.* (A photographic study of Balinese childhood based upon photographs by GREGORY BATESON and analyzed in Gesell categories.) New York: G. P. Putnam's Sons.

MEGGERS, BETTY J. 1946. "Recent Trends in American Ethnology," *American Anthropologist,* XLVIII, 176–214.

MILLER, DANIEL K., and HUTT, MAX L. 1949. "Value Interiorization and Personality Development," *Journal of Social Issues,* V, 2–30.

MILLER, N., and DOLLARD, J. 1941. *Social Learning and Imitation.* New Haven: Yale University Press.

MOWRER, O. H., and KLUCKHOHN, CLYDE. 1944. "Dynamic Theory of Personality." In HUNT, J. McV. (ed.), *Personality and the Behavior Disorders,* pp. 69–135. New York: Ronald Press Co.

MULLAHY, PATRICK. 1948. *Oedipus: Myth and Complex: A Review of Psychoanalytic Theory.* Introduction by ERICH FROMM. New York: Heritage Press.

MURDOCK, GEORGE P. 1949. "The Science of Human Learning, Society, Culture, and Personality," *Scientific Monthly,* LXIX, 377–81.

MURPHY, G. 1947. *Personality: A Biosocial Approach to Origins and Structure.* New York: Harper & Bros.

MURRAY, H. A. 1938. *Exploration in Personality.* New York: Oxford University Press.

NADEL, S. F. 1937a. "The Typological Approach to Culture," *Character and Personality* (now *Journal of Personality*), V, 267–84.

——. 1937*b*. "Experiments on Culture Psychology," *Africa*, X, 421–35.

——. 1937*c*. "A Field Experiment in Racial Psychology," *British Journal of Psychology*, XXVIII, 195–211.

——. 1951. *The Foundations of Social Anthropology*. Glencoe, Ill.: Free Press.

NEWCOMB, THEODORE M. 1950. *Social Psychology*. New York: Dryden Press.

NEWCOMB, THEODORE M.; HARTLEY, E. L.; et al. (eds.). 1947. *Readings in Social Psychology*. New York: Henry Holt & Co.

NISSEN, HENRY W. 1951. "Phylogenetic Comparisons." In STEVENS, S. S. (ed.), *Handbook of Experimental Psychology*, chap. xi. New York: John Wiley & Sons.

ORLANSKY, H. 1949. "Infant Care and Personality," *Psychological Bulletin*, XLVI, 1–48.

PARSONS, TALCOTT, and SHILS, EDWARD A. (eds.). 1951. *Toward a General Theory of Action*. Cambridge: Harvard University Press.

RANDALL, JOHN HERMAN, JR. 1944. "Epilogue: The Nature of Naturalism." In KRIKORIAN, Y. H. (ed.), *Naturalism and the Human Spirit*, pp. 354–82. New York: Columbia University Press.

ROHEIM, GEZA. 1943. *The Origin and Function of Culture*. ("Nervous and Mental Disease Monograph Series," No. 63.) New York.

——. 1950. *Psychoanalysis and Anthropology: Culture, Personality, and the Unconscious*. New York: International Universities Press.

ROHRER, JOHN H., and SHERIF, MUZAFER (eds.). 1951. *Social Psychology at the Crossroads*. New York: Harper & Bros.

SAPIR, EDWARD. *See* MANDELBAUM and HARRIS.

SARGENT, S. STANSFELD, and SMITH, MARIAN W. (eds.). 1949. *Culture and Personality: Proceedings of an Interdisciplinary Conference Held under the Auspices of the Viking Fund, November 7 and 8, 1947*. New York: Viking Fund.

SCHNEIRLA, T. C. 1951. "The 'Levels' Concept in the Study of Social Organization in Animals." In ROHRER, J. H., and SHERIF, M. (eds.), *Social Psychology at the Crossroads*, pp. 83–120. New York: Harper & Bros.

SELIGMAN, C. G. 1924. "Anthropology and Psychology," *Journal of the Royal Anthropological Institute*, LIV, 13–46.

——. 1928. "The Unconscious in Relation to Anthropology," *British Journal of Psychology*, XVIII, 374–87.

——. 1929. "Temperament, Conflict and Psychosis in a Stone-Age Population," *British Journal of Medical Psychology*, IX, 187–202.

——. 1932. "Anthropological Perspective and Psychological Theory (Huxley Memorial Lecture for 1932)," *Journal of the Royal Anthropological Institute*, LXII, 193–228.

——. 1936. Introduction to LINCOLN, J. S, *The Dream in Primitive Cultures*. London: Cresset Press, n.d. Baltimore: Williams & Wilkins.

SHAPLEY, HARLOW. 1930. *Flights from Chaos*. New York: McGraw-Hill Book Co., Inc.

SLOTKIN, J. S. 1951. *Personality Development*. New York: Harper & Bros.

SPINDLER, GEORGE, and GOLDSCHMIDT, WALTER. 1952. "Experimental Design in the Study of Culture Change," *Southwestern Journal of Anthropology*, VIII, 68–83.

SPIRO, MELFORD E. 1951. "Culture and Personality: The Natural History of a False Dichotomy," *Psychiatry*, XIV, 19–46.

STEVENS, S. S. (ed.). 1951. *Handbook of Experimental Psychology*. New York: John Wiley & Sons, Inc.

SULLIVAN, H. S. 1947. *Conception of Modern Psychiatry*. Washington, D. C.: William Alanson White Psychiatric Foundation.

VOLKART, EDMUND H. (ed.). 1951. *Social Behavior and Personality*. ("Contributions of W. I. Thomas to Theory and Social Research.") New York: Social Science Research Council.

WALLACE, ANTHONY F. C. 1952. *The Modal Personality Structure of the Tuscarora Indians, as Revealed by the Rorschach Test*. (Bureau of American Ethnology Bull. 150.) In press.

WEAKLAND, JOHN HART. 1951. "Method in Cultural Anthropology," *Philosophy of Science*, XVIII, 55–69.

WHITE, LESLIE A. 1925. "Personality and Culture," *Open Court,* XXXIX, 145–49.

———. 1947. "The Locus of Mathematical Reality: An Anthropological Footnote," *Philosophy of Science,* XIV, 289–303.

WHITEHEAD, A. N. 1930. *Adventures of Ideas.* Cambridge: At the University Press.

WHITING, JOHN W. M. 1941. *Becoming a Kwoma: Teaching and Learning in a New Guinea Tribe.* New Haven: Yale University Press.

WILBUR, GEORGE B., and MUENSTERBERGER, WARNER (eds.). 1951. *Psychoanalysis and Culture: Essays in Honor of Geza Roheim.* New York: International Universities Press, Inc.

Acculturation

By RALPH BEALS

THIS SURVEY of acculturation is presented within the following restricted framework: (1) it is almost wholly confined to the work of anthropologists of the British Commonwealth, the United States, and Latin America; (2) in so far as it is possible to do so, problems of application are excluded from this paper, although this is difficult to do in British studies; and (3) especially in British writings the term "culture contact" is considered broadly synonymous with "acculturation."

I. HISTORICAL SURVEY

The recency and rapid proliferation of acculturation studies have resulted in the employment of widely differing definitions and methodologies. Theory and conceptualization likewise appear still to be in a formative stage. Some of these points seem best illustrated by a brief historical survey of the subject. The attempt to trace the origins and growth of a concept such as acculturation in the United States or the parallel usage of "culture contact" by British anthropologists is an instructive exercise for the student of culture change. Although early sporadic interest in the phenomena of contact situations may be found which resembles modern approaches rather than the traditional diffusionist discussions, one is driven to the employment of surmise and hypothetical reconstruction to account for the development of special terms and concepts.

The term "acculturation" is generally credited to American anthropologists. The occasional British student to refer to the word may concede its convenience but regards it with some horror. Paul Kirchhoff, however, has stated in conversation that the term was used in Germany by Walter Krickeberg in lectures somewhere in the mid-1920's to refer to the progress of development of a common basic culture among the tribes of diverse origin found on the upper Rio Xingu.[1] In a rather cursory examination of German literature I have found no appearance of the word in print, but it is of interest that Thurnwald was the earliest writer to use the word in the title of an article in English. This lends some support to a possible German origin for the term. Drawing upon an uncertain memory, it is clear that extended discussion and argument long preceded the first appearance of the term "acculturation" in the literature in the United States. My own memories place the appearance of the term at the level of graduate student

1. Since writing the above, R. H. Lowie has called my attention to the following passage by Krickeberg in the first (1910) edition of Buschan's *Illustrierte Völkerkunde* (pp. 97 f.): "Das beständige durcheinanderfluten ursprünglich heterogener Stamme brachte einen weitgehenden *kulturellen Ausgleich* (Akkulturation) zustande, durch den die Kultur in dem ganzen gewaltigen Dreieck zwischen Anden, Orinoko, Rio Negro und Madera ein sehr einheitliches Gepräge erhielt." This conforms to the ideas reported by Kirchhoff for a later date.

discussion somewhere about 1928 under circumstances which suggest it already had diffused widely from its point of origin. Who first used the term and attempted to conceptualize the field, and who were parties to the earliest discussions, would require reconstruction of a "memory" culture, the now partially vanished anthropological culture of the United States in the 1920's.[2]

Interest in acculturation studies in the United States probably originated in part as a reaction against these very reconstructions of "memory" cultures. The emphasis of the early part of the century upon studying or recovering the memory of "unmodified" cultures became increasingly difficult and of diminishing fruitfulness in the 1920's. At the same time, students became increasingly aware of the existence of contemporary cultures of no less interest for the elucidation of cultural principles.

Interest in contact phenomena in Great Britain and elsewhere may have had a similar origin, although it would appear that functionalism was the major reaction in Great Britain to the study of memory cultures. Rather I would tentatively suggest that the origin of interest in culture contact in Great Britain stemmed from two sources, namely, the increasing urgency of practical applications of anthropol-

2. A partial survey of United States textbooks in anthropology suggests the recency of the subject. No discussion appears in F. Boas and others, *General Anthropology* (1938); R. Lowie, *Introduction to Cultural Anthropology* (1st ed., 1934); E. Chapple and C. Coon, *Principles of Anthropology* (1942); or A. Goldenweiser, *Anthropology* (1937). In the second edition of Lowie (1940) there are five references in the Index to statements concerning cases of change through contact and a definition (p. 525) as "assimilation to an alien culture." J. Gillin, *The Ways of Men* (1948), and M. J. Herskovits, *Man and His Works* (1948), each contains a chapter on the subject.

ogy in colonial areas and in part as a reaction against certain limitations inherent in the more formal functionalist systems. This is not the place to argue the merits of formal functionalist systems; nevertheless, the more classical schemes seem to many to run into difficulties over the problem of culture change. Studies of culture contact offered the opportunity of applying the best of the functionalist approaches, as within a dynamic framework of change. Moreover, the rapidity of change in the colonial situation was such that classical functionalists like Malinowski could at least pretend that the time dimension did not exist, a pretense which extended only to their theoretical positions and not, as we shall see, to their methodological procedures.

The obvious utility of acculturation studies for the solution of practical problems was also a factor in their early popularity. The beginnings of interest in contact situations in Great Britain, France, and Holland coincided with the rise of a new sense of responsibility toward colonial peoples, while in the United States the great development of acculturation studies coincided with the depression era and its accompanying widespread concern with social problems. External cultural forces, then, may well have played an important part in the rise of acculturation studies.

Full acceptance of acculturation as a field of anthropological study is quite recent in the United States, if, indeed, it has yet been achieved. Thus at the annual meeting of the American Anthropological Association for 1936 the editor of the *American Anthropologist*, Leslie Spier, inquired in his annual report:

The question has also arisen how far we should go in printing material on the culture of natives who participate in civilized life. I refer here to the so-called acculturation studies. It is maintained on the one hand that studies of such hybrid cultures are best left to sociological or other journals concerned with aspects of modern life; on the other, that they belong in the *American Anthropologist*. Since your wishes should be followed, I would like an expression of your opinion of what we should include.

Following the editor's report, we find:

It was moved and seconded: It is the sense of the American Anthropological Association that papers in the field of acculturation lie within the interests of anthropology, and that, at the Editor's discretion, they be not discriminated against in the *American Anthropologist*. It was voted that the motion be tabled without prejudice [*Proceedings of the American Anthropological Association for 1936*, p. 322].

There is no record that this motion was ever removed from the table. Nevertheless, the editor apparently had no qualms, for acculturation is referred to six times in the volume index. Two articles by Herskovits (1937a, 1937b) in Volume XXXIX deal with acculturation, the word appearing in the title of one. Other references are to book reviews, one of which is Benedict's (1937) review of Redfield's *Chan Kom*. Another, Beals's (1939) review of Parson's *Mitla*, is the first review in this journal to discuss the problem of acculturation by name. Other references are to the merest mention of European contact. Gerhard Lindblom's (1937) review of Monica Hunter's *Reaction to Conquest* in the same volume remarks that the book "seems to me . . . first and foremost of sociological importance, but here I propose to regard it from an exclusively ethnological point of view." While recognizing the significance of this pioneering work, Lindblom evidently was reluctant to consider the new field to be anthropological. Apparently the editor interpreted the lack of action by the association as giving him a free hand. In the General Index for 1929–38, published under his direction,

seven additional items in Volume XXXIX are indexed under "acculturation," including every mention, however slight, to effects of European contact.

To trace the intellectual development which led to the earlier use of the term is difficult. Herskovits (1948, p. 523) notes a use by J. W. Powell in 1880 to refer to culture borrowing. W. J. McGee later speaks of "piratical acculturation," accounting for the only appearance of the word in the General Index of the *American Anthropologist* for 1888–1928. In the same period the term "culture contact" is indexed not at all. The term "acculturation" next appears in the program of the annual meeting for 1928 (p. 326), which lists a paper by M. J. Herskovits, "The Coto-Missies of Suriname: A Study in Acculturation." Presumably this paper used acculturation in the modern sense. Other papers may have been delivered at earlier annual meetings, but not all the programs were published. In the General Index for 1929–38 the earliest reference to acculturation is to Robert Redfield's (1929) "The Material Culture of Spanish-Indian Mexico." Although the problems are clearly acculturational, the word is not used in the article. Neither is the term "culture contact" employed. While the mixed character of the Spanish-Indian culture of Mexico is discussed, there is no emphasis on process.

The earliest article to be indexed under the term "culture contact" is Leslie Spier's (1929) "Problems Arising from the Cultural Position of the Havasupai." Emphasis in the article is on the dynamics of culture growth in relation to culture contacts on an aboriginal level. Significantly, while this and Redfield's article are indexed under "culture contact" and "acculturation," respectively, in the General Index, they are not so indexed in the Annual Index for the volume. Thus we may surmise a growing preoccupation with the problems of contact between 1929 and 1938 and, in the general handling of the 1929–38 General Index, an effort on the part of the editor, Leslie Spier, to apply "acculturation" solely to examples of European contacts and "culture contact" to those contacts occurring on an aboriginal level. The next reference in the General Index is to "Aboriginal Survivals in Mayo Culture," by Ralph L. Beals (1932). A considerable part of the article is devoted to discussion of contact problems, and it is the first article in the *American Anthropologist* to use the term "acculturation," except for McGee's much earlier usage. Later in the same year appears the first article with the word "acculturation" in the title: Richard Thurnwald's (1932) "The Psychology of Acculturation." This article is noteworthy for two things: it is the first to show interest in the psychological problems of acculturation and the first to attempt a systematic analysis of the concept and the processes involved.

In this same year Margaret Mead published her *Changing Culture of an Indian Tribe* (1932), the earliest major work in the United States devoted primarily to the effects of culture contact. The term "acculturation" is used only once in reference to degrees of acculturation. The following year, Elsie Clews Parsons (1933) used the term in "Some Aztec and Pueblo Parallels." While some subsequent articles discuss acculturational problems, notably Robert Redfield's (1934) "Cultural Changes in Yucatan," and, while even the most trivial references to European contact are indexed in the General Index, the next actual use of the term is in the "Memorandum for the Study of Acculturation" by Robert Redfield, Ralph Linton, and Melville J. Herskovits (1936).

A more hasty survey of British journals suggests that the appearance and use of the term "culture contact" roughly paralleled in time the United States use of the term "acculturation."

Malinowski wrote, on the need of studying the changing native as early as 1929: "A new branch of anthropology must sooner or later be started: the anthropology of the changing Native. Nowadays, when we are intensely interested, through some new anthropological theories, in problems of contact and diffusion, it seems incredible that hardly any exhaustive studies have been undertaken on the question of how European influence is being diffused into native communities" (p. 22). Malinowski clearly regarded this as a practical study and felt that the changing native was a result of European contact. The implication that no change existed before such contact is surprising, although he suggested the value of contemporary studies for understanding the process of diffusion.

The first systematic recognition of culture contact seems to have been in the "Five Year Plan of Research" in *Africa* (1932). This memorandum is clearly oriented toward practical administrative problems and the problems of culture change, although the term "culture contact" is not employed. Change as it is discussed is clearly concerned with the results of European contact. However, stemming from the work initiated under the "Five Year Plan," two years later L. P. Mair (1934) published "The Study of Culture Contact as a Practical Problem" in the same journal. This was the first of a series of articles by various authors which were later gathered together in *Memorandum XV* of the International Institute of African Languages and Cultures (1938). The year 1935 saw publication of the Redfield-Linton-Herskovits memorandum in *Man*, a year earlier than its publication in the United States.

Implicit in most of the British work both in the developmental period and later is a close relation between "practical" anthropology and culture contact studies and definition of culture contact as referring to European native contacts with special emphasis on administrative problems. Malinowski referred to French, Dutch, and German anthropologists as students of culture change and practical anthropology. Thus, after such a review, Malinowski (1945, p. 5) concludes:

Finally, in Great Britain and the United States, interest in culture change has of late become dominant. The names of W. H. R. Rivers and of Captain G. H. L. F. Pitt-Rivers head the list among early British scholars. The work of the Departments of Anthropology at Sydney and Capetown, under the initiative of A. R. Radcliffe-Brown; the teaching and research at Cambridge, London and Oxford; the special interest shown in culture change and applied anthropology by the Royal Anthropological Institute—all have started almost simultaneously with the American initiative associated with the names of Wissler, Redfield, Parsons, Herskovits, and Radin; as well as P. H. Buck (Te Rangi Hiroa) and Felix Keesing working at Honolulu. The International Institute of African Languages and Cultures has, since its foundation in 1926, made an attempt to take the question beyond national boundaries and, avoiding all political issues, has organized research on problems of contact in all African colonies, with the cooperation of science, missionary enterprise, and the administrative agencies of all the countries concerned.

This summary includes many names, both British and American, to say nothing of other national groups, which are not mentioned in my own historical summary. Reasons for this discrepancy are twofold. On the one hand, the directive for my memorandum recommended the omission of problems of application; on the other, I have endeavored to confine myself very largely to the authors who have been concerned with conceptualization and definition of the field and with the development of methodology. As an example one might cite B. Schrieke (ed.), *The Effect of Western Influence on Native Civilizations in the Malay Archipelago* (Batavia, 1929), an almost completely descriptive work except for some discussion of administrative policy.

In the subsequent sections of this survey I propose to discuss what seem to me major problems and issues raised by work in acculturation rather than to review the work of particular individuals or groups of individuals. The treatment will be concerned, first, with problems of conceptualization and definition and, second, with problems of methodology. In a final section I shall attempt some general appraisal of the present status of acculturation studies and point out some areas of needed investigation. In these succeeding sections I trust I will not be accused of cultural imperialism if for convenience I use the term "acculturation" as synonymous with "culture contact" as the latter is used in the British Commonwealth.

II. PROBLEMS OF DEFINITION AND USAGE

The earliest writers to employ the term "acculturation" apparently did not attempt a definition of the term; usage, nevertheless, is often clear. Parsons' Mitla study (1936) is described by the author as "concerned with acculturation, with what the Indian culture took from the Spanish." Acculturation to Parsons clearly meant only cases of syncretization and obvious cases of Spanish borrowing. Although pointing out that the product of Spanish-Indian contact in Mexico is a new and changing blend, she does not consider as acculturation those aspects of the blend which have no identifiable European component. Indian survivals or new organizations or relationships emerging as an indirect result of the blend are excluded. This same interpretation occurs earlier in Parsons (1933). A somewhat broader interpretation is suggested by Beals (1932), in which the entire set of processes involved in acceptance, rejection, and reorganization are considered to be acculturation.

The first systematic definition is that by Redfield, Linton, and Herskovits (1936): "Acculturation comprehends those phenomena which result when groups of individuals having different cultures come into continuous first-hand contact, with subsequent changes in the original cultural patterns of either or both groups." While widely criticized and modified by later writers, including the authors, this remains the most used definition, although full understanding of it requires consideration of the entire memorandum. Points in this definition which appear to have caused most difficulty are the following: (1) What is meant by "continuous first-hand contact"? (2) What is meant by "groups of individuals"? (3) The relation of acculturation to the concepts of culture change and diffusion. (4) What is the relation between acculturation and assimilation? (5) Is acculturation a process or a condition?

Among the striking problems raised is that of modifications of culture arising through intermittent contacts with missionaries or traders, who in some cases are bearers of a culture other than their own. Although there is little difficulty in considering acculturation as a special case of culture change, such cases as those referred to raise difficulty in distinguishing between acculturation and diffusion. Both represent culture change as the result of transmission of culture between groups. Herskovits (1948, pp. 523 ff.) solves this problem by considering diffusion to be "achieved cultural transmission," while acculturation is "cultural transmission in process." This viewpoint he modifies to include those instances in which documentation of transmission by ethnohistorical methods is possible, as opposed to cases in which diffusion must be inferred or its history reconstructed by inferential methods. In this position Herskovits is very close to that of Malinowski, who wrote as early as 1939 of "The Dynamics of Contemporary Diffusion." On the other hand, in the *Dynamics of Culture Change* (1945, p. 1) Malinowski remarks: "It [culture change] may be induced by factors and forces spontaneously arising within the community, or it may take place through the contact of different cultures. In the first instance it takes the form of *independent invention;* in the second it constitutes that process which in anthropology is usually called *diffusion.*" Clearly, however, Malinowski's whole interest is in what in the United States would today without hesitation be called acculturation; moreover, it is almost wholly with the study of acculturative processes as these arise in connection with practical problems related to colonial administration and with the impact of European culture upon native culture.

Although few discussions have reached print, some United States anthropologists have discussed the role of force, broadly conceived, as perhaps providing the proper distinction between diffusion and acculturation. In such discussions, force is broadly treated to include not only overt or naked force but pressures resulting from deprivations, introduction of compelling new goals, or psychological pressures arising from sentiments of inferiority and superiority. A corollary type of approach is the suggestion that acculturation be confined to situations in which one of the groups in contact, for whatever reason, loses complete freedom of choice or freedom to accept or reject new cultural elements. Such restrictions for the term "acculturation" would be rejected by others, who would, indeed, extend the term beyond its present usage. These divergent points of view will receive treatment below.

The fourth and fifth points above have received relatively little attention and have perhaps troubled sociologists more than they have anthropologists. In the main the literature of acculturation stresses dynamic aspects. Acculturation is seen by most writers as important because process is rapid and easily observable. Such rapidity of process is seen to afford abundant opportunities for comparison and an approach to laboratory conditions. Thurnwald (1932, p. 557) opens his article on the psychology of acculturation with the sentence, "Acculturation is a process, not an isolated event." By implication, rather than by direct statement, he is clearly dealing with the acquisition of cultural elements by one culture from another and says: "This process of adaptation to new conditions of life is what we call acculturation." Later (1938, pp. 179–80), he says: "For 'contact' is not a single event but implies the turning on of a switch which sets in motion an almost endless series of happenings; it is a process, but with different stages." Mair (1934) likewise recognizes the value of using contact studies to discover rules governing process of culture change, while Fortes (1936, p. 53) remarks: "Culture contact has to be regarded, not as a transference of elements from one culture to another, but as a continuous process of interaction between groups of different culture."

Without multiplying examples, one can assert confidently that acculturation studies are generally seen as dynamic in character and concerned with process. Such understandings are not, however, universal, nor, indeed, is recogni-

tion of the field of study itself. Thus, in a study many would consider at least partially acculturational, DuBois wrote: "Patterning and acculturation might be practically synonymous. However, acculturation seems to have been given special meaning. It is used most frequently to describe minimal cases of patterning; that is, cases in which dislocations accompanying the absorption of foreign features exceed integrations. More specifically, it seems to have been used to describe the manner in which a shattered aboriginal culture makes the best of a bad bargain. . . . The difference between patterning which represents integration and acculturation which represents at best only partial integration is not always obvious in cultural phenomena" (1939, p. 137). This might be ignored if the same author in 1951 in a useful short discussion of the dynamics of culture contact had not remarked: "Acculturation that was in vogue among anthropologists some fifteen or twenty years ago has since then been recognized as a dangerously fragmented phrasing of more inclusive inquiries into the nature of cultural and social dynamics" (1951, p. 32). Writers on acculturation will have some difficulty recognizing their subject in these terms.

Despite the general recognition of the dynamic aspect of acculturation studies, it is common, particularly in the United States, to speak of "degrees of acculturation" and of "partially or wholly acculturated individuals." In the case of a wholly acculturated individual, clearly the acculturative process has terminated and we are speaking of a condition. Moreover, it is difficult to see how this differs from sociological usages of the term "assimilation." The Redfield, Linton, and Herskovits definition, indeed, is modified by a note that "acculturation is to be distinguished from. . . *assimilation*, which is at times a phase of acculturation." Possibly what is generally meant is that assimilation is that form of acculturation which results in groups of individuals wholly replacing their original culture by another (as opposed to groups reformulating a "mixed" culture). Usage is far from consistent or clear, and the frequent reference to acculturated individuals (rather than groups) seems particularly ambiguous in terms of most of the formal definitions. In part these differences reflect emphasis upon institutional or sociocultural approaches, on the one hand, and upon individual and psychological approaches, on the other. Finally, field studies of acculturation frequently are essentially descriptive; we are given the results of acculturation rather than an attempt to discover its dynamics.

In terms of the Redfield, Linton, and Herskovits definition, acculturation should be viewed as a two-way process, affecting both groups in contact. Beyond an occasional suggestion that the culture of Europeans (mainly missionaries, traders, and administrators) undergoes some change as a result of contact or that Spanish culture in the New World was modified by Indian culture, only lip service has been paid to this aspect of acculturation. Fernando Ortiz (1940) has proposed the term "transculturation" to emphasize the reciprocal character of most contact situations. In his Preface to the work, Malinowski is enthusiastic about the new term, but one finds no serious consideration of the reciprocal aspects of culture contact in any of his own publications. "Transculturation" has had some use by Latin-American writers, and, were the term "acculturation" not so widely in use, it might profitably be adopted.

Most British discussions and definitions of culture contact are entirely concerned with the impact of European cultures upon native cultures. Fortes (1936, p. 54) is almost alone in raising the question of why African contact

agents, such as Hausa, Mosi, Dagomba, and Fulani, have been less influential than European contacts. Wagner (1936, p. 317) similarly points out the theoretical importance of Asian contacts with Africa. In the United States general discussions are usually carefully phrased to cover all types of culture contact. In actual practice, however, most United States and virtually all Latin-American studies of acculturation are, in fact, concerned with the impact of European upon non-European cultures. Scattered references could be found to pre-European acculturation situations, but specific studies or analyses are either of very minor scope or nonexistent. Perhaps the most notable examples of papers on acculturation in which European culture is not involved are Lindgren's (1938) "An Example of Culture Contact without Conflict: Reindeer Tungus and Cossacks of Northwestern Manchuria"; Ekvall's (1939) "Cultural Relations on the Kansu-Tibetan Border"; and Greenberg's (1941) "Some Aspects of Negro-Mohammedan Culture Contact among the Hausa."

A number of other studies, notably those of Robert Redfield, have centered about the problem of urban influence upon folk or rural cultures. Although Redfield is chary of applying the word "acculturation" to this situation, I believe most American scholars would so classify his studies.

Quite different in character are the studies of Herskovits on the Negro in the Americas. Avowedly considered acculturation studies by the author, in strict terms the situation does not represent "groups of individuals" in the same sense as do many of the British studies in Africa. Rather, uprooted individuals are moved out of their society and cultural setting and placed in a new culture. This usage is followed by many students in the American field, including such Latin-Americans as Arthur Ramos (1947). Of the same type are

Emilio Willems' studies of the acculturation of Germans and Japanese in Brazil. Sociologists also use the term increasingly in the same way to refer to the adaptations of immigrants. More recently Beals (1951) has suggested that not only can other immigrant groups in the United States be studied from the standpoint of acculturation but also the whole process of urbanization, whether dealing with the extension of urban influence to the rural populations or the migration of rural populations to the city, presents an acculturative situation. This point was made by Gregory Bateson (1935) with respect to contacts between groups within a culture, although he did not project it against a situation within a European-type culture.

This brief review clearly suggests that both definitions and usage of the term "acculturation" (or "culture contact") are varied and unsatisfactory. At the same time it must be recognized that a very large core of studies is easily and generally recognized today as being acculturational. The difficulties lie mainly at the fringes of the field and at least in part are logical rather than actual. While it may be asserted that acculturation studies should not be confined to situations involving European-type cultures, it is, in fact, extremely difficult to find situations where European-type cultures are not involved. Nevertheless, it seems clear that a re-examination of the subject is in order, particularly with respect to the reciprocal aspects of acculturation, its relation to the problem of assimilation, and the propriety of extending the term to studies of contact between groups within a culture and to studies of migrant groups.

III. PROBLEMS OF METHOD

Problems of method in the study of acculturation fall into two major categories: formal organized memoranda or schemes for study, and general discussions of specific problems, together with actual research studies. In the first category we find some six schemes presented: those of Thurnwald (1932), the Redfield, Linton, and Herskovits memorandum (1935, 1936), Bateson (1935), Linton (1940), Malinowski (1945), and Ramos (1947).

Despite its title and its emphasis upon the role of the individual, the Thurnwald article is primarily concerned with process. In this earliest memorandum we may note the following points, by now familiar to all students of acculturation: change of function; variable rates of acceptance for different traits; selection of traits, depending in part upon the conditions of contact; unforeseen consequences of adoption of new traits; attitudes and relationships between groups often determinant; group traditions important; circumstances of contact must be considered; occurrence of stages of reaction to contact which may include withdrawal from the strange or unknown, uncritical acceptance, complete assimilation, formation of new cultural entities, and rejection.

The Redfield, Linton, Herskovits memorandum merits somewhat more detailed treatment. The following discussion in outline form parallels the memorandum but is confined to the more critical issues:

1. Definition. This has been previously discussed.

2. Approach to the problem. Under subheading C, "Techniques Employed in the Studies Analyzed," we find "direct observation," "recent acculturation studied through interviews with members of acculturated groups," "use of documentary evidence," and "deductions from historical analyses and reconstructions." The authors thus clearly envisioned historical approaches as a proper part of the study of acculturation.

3. Analysis of acculturation. Under this heading the authors include de-

tailed subheadings concerning the types of contacts, the kinds of situations, and the processes involved. Such matters as contact only between selected or specialized groups from one or another culture, whether contacts are friendly or hostile, differences in size and complexity of groups, existence of force, and equality or inequality are among those included under the first two subheadings. Under "processes," the authors clearly consider significant such matters as order of selection of traits, manner of presentation of traits, resistances and the reasons therefore, and the way traits are integrated into the accepting culture, suggesting such factors as time, conflict arising out of new traits, and processes of adjustment.

4. Psychological mechanisms. The authors here consider the part played by the individual, and such problems as class, role, status, and personality differences.

5. The results of acculturation. These are defined as *Acceptance*, i.e., taking over the greater portion of another culture and assimilating both to behavior patterns and to inner values of the new culture; *Adaptation*, combining original and foreign traits either in a harmonious whole or with retention of conflicting attitudes which are reconciled in everyday behavior according to specific occasions; *Reaction*, where a variety of contra-acculturative movements arise, with emphasis on the psychological factors involved.

Bateson's paper is in part a critique of the memorandum, suggesting that it is premature to attempt to set up a system of categories before the basic problems have been clearly defined. He also suggests that the authors have been unduly influenced by the kinds of questions asked by administrative officers. As noted, he also suggests extension of the term "acculturation" to cover contacts between differentiated groups within a single culture and even for the acquisition of culture by the child (a common use by psychologists for which the term "enculturation" has more recently been used by a number of writers). Bateson then attempts to outline a series of problems, phrased in a combination of behavioral, psychiatric, and functional terms. Although points of considerable interest are made in this memorandum, apparently it has had little direct influence in actual acculturation studies.

Malinowski's "Method for the Study of Culture Contact" is essentially a rather mechanical organization of data for analytical purposes; his major headings are (A) white influences, interests, and intentions; (B) process of culture contact and change; (C) surviving forms of tradition; (D) reconstructed past; and (E) new forces of spontaneous African reintegration or reaction. The discussion and illustrations utilized adhere rigidly to Malinowski's classical functionalist approach, save for a slight and grudging bow to time elements in the category of the "reconstructed past." The "method" is also focused directly upon Africa and upon administrative or colonial problems, although the value of practical studies for the development of theory is stressed.

Both the Linton and the Ramos treatments essentially are refinements of the original Redfield, Linton, and Herskovits memorandum. The Ramos memorandum is much simpler, taking for granted many points spelled out in detail in the earlier document. Both writers, in different ways, lay greater stress upon psychological factors.

Aside from formal memoranda or outlines, there have been a considerable number of both explicit and implicit treatments of method centering around various phases of acculturation studies. In addition, a number of specialized emphases have made their appearance. In the following paragraphs I will attempt to summarize both discussions and field work with respect to the following points: (*a*) the use of historical data and approaches, (*b*) the comparative approach, (*c*) the "trait list" versus the holistic approach, (*d*) the role of the individual and psychological approaches, (*e*) linguistic acculturation studies, (*f*) the major cultural processes, and (*g*) quantification and indices.

a) THE USE OF HISTORICAL DATA AND APPROACHES

In the main, the use of historical data and approaches has been accepted, even by the majority of functionalist-trained scholars. Thus Richards writes (1935, p. 21):

But what, in concrete terms, does it mean to study a society as it "actually functions"? In most parts of Africa cultural changes are taking place so rapidly that the anthropologist cannot study what is, without studying what was. As Miss Hunter writes in a previous article in this series: "Any culture can only be fully understood in its historical context, and when the culture under consideration has undergone revolutionary changes within a generation the relative importance of the historical context is very much greater than when the culture has been comparatively static." Thus, paradoxically enough, it is just those anthropologists who have turned their backs most resolutely on "antiquarianism," to whom "history" of some kind or other is of greatest value.

L. P. Mair (1934, pp. 416–17) writes:

The central object of the inquiry [of the Baganda] seemed to be to find out how a working system of social cooperation had been affected by the various European influences to which it had been subjected for some years, and in particular to discover the respects in which there was more or less serious maladjustment. This required as its starting point a reconstruction of the system. . . .

It is obvious that such a reconstruction can never have the same factual value as the results of observation. . . . Nevertheless it seems essential for this type of inquiry. The functional theory of anthropology in general stresses the importance of studying native life as it is actually lived, and rejects the appeal to historical origins to explain peculiarities of social configuration. In a native society which has not recently suffered violent disturbance such explanations are unnecessary, and since they usually attempt to follow out a hypothetical course of evolution, they nearly always mislead. . . . Most native societies are now undergoing a process of rapid and forcible transformation, comparable only to the violent changes of revolution, and entirely distinct from the gradual, almost imperceptible, process of adaptation in which the normal evolution of human cultures consists. For this reason a straightforward description of such a society as the ethnologist finds it would not do justice to the crucial problems of the existing situation, which arose just where the traditional system has been forcibly wrenched away. . . . This does not mean that it is necessary to look for the "original" native culture.

Miss Mair later suggests that studies of historical sequences of change will be of little value and considers the crucial problem to be the study of the sum total of changes from the "zero point of what can be discovered of the independent native system." In interpreting Miss Mair's meaning it should be borne in mind that she is here emphasizing practical rather than theoretical significance.

Malinowski, on the whole, remained intransigent to the end concerning history, despite his inclusion of a column for the "Reconstructed Past" in his outline tables. This indeed he really viewed not as a "reconstructed past" but as the "past remembered" (1945, p. 29). The importance of the latter no one will quarrel with, but even his disciples today hardly will go as far as he does in criticizing Mair's suggestions. Thus he remarks (p. 30): "The ethnographer working on the reconstructed past would have to appear before the practical man with, at the best, 'damaged goods' in the line of practical advice and theoretical insight." In part, Malinowski's objections to history (and he had no objection to history in what he conceived to be its proper role and place) stem from a pervading feeling of its unscientific character, in part from his particular understanding of both science and history, and in part from his definition of culture change as resulting only from European contact. Thus in 1929 he manages clearly to convey the impression that change is only the result of European contact. Of course, Malinowski did not really believe this intellectually, for he has mentioned diffusion and change in other contexts frequently. Nevertheless, the aspect of European influence dominated his thinking and forms the basis for his objection to Mair's suggestion that one should seek a zero point for studies of culture change.

Fundamentally, Malinowski conceived of the zero point as a point at which culture change began. The implication clearly is that, before European contact, no change existed and the zero point must be at the first instant of European contact, a view that few other writers have sustained. Rather, if I understand Mair, she proposed establishing a zero point on the best and most convenient base line with respect to a specified series of changes permitted by the data and the situation. The most historical-minded would ask no more. And, indeed, the entire discussion may hinge primarily upon concepts of history and the occasional attempt to oppose history and science. Malinowski himself points out that this is futile and that the functional method "introduces the time element, at first on a smaller scale, but nonetheless in the real historical sense." If we accept time as a necessary dimension in a scientific approach (as it certainly is in modern physics), the old dichotomy largely disappears except for considerations of the proper employment of the time dimension.

Certainly, in a number of fields and more particularly in the work of American students of acculturation, historical data are used whenever possible. The approach of Herskovits and others with respect to the Negro in the New World makes the fullest possible use of historical materials. The same is true of most students in the Latin-American field. Thus in *Heritage of Conquest* by Sol Tax and others (1952), historical reference appears constantly in the discussions by a group of scholars of most diverse specific interests linked primarily by their concern with Middle America. It would seem, therefore, that the fundamental point of divergence is not in the use of history but in the type of problem and in the kind and extent of historical data used. There is more than a hint in the literature, especially in the writings of Malinowski, that historical interests are antiquarian rather than scientific, although clearly what is often meant is that historical interests are not "practical."

British writers likewise reveal what seems to many Americans either a curious unawareness of the nature of historical studies or a preoccupation with evolutionary approaches of a bygone century. Thus Miss Mair in the quotation above says that, since historical explanations "usually attempt to follow out a hypothetical course of evolution, they nearly always mislead." A similar attitude is expressed by Fortes (1936, p. 53):

I have indicated what I consider to be the limitations of a retrospective approach which treats the present state of affairs as an accomplished fact standing in contrast to a hypothetical "untouched" tribal culture. This is not rejecting history as a source of sociological data. Verifiable history, documenting the whole period of change, is indispensable to the student of social change. But history of the "before the deluge" kind does not, to my mind, illuminate the real problem, of which the problems raised by culture contact form but a part, namely, what are the causes of social change?

Earlier, though, he writes (1935, p. 6):

Ideally this method requires a temporal extension, continuous observation over a period of years, or repeated observations at intervals to yield definitive information on the causes of social change. But few anthropologists are likely to be in the position to satisfy this ideal; and this is where accurate history can step into the breach.

Wagner (1936, pp. 317–20) writes more concretely:

First it is necessary to obtain as concise a picture as possible of native culture prior to the contact. Secondly the nature of the various contact agencies must be determined. The third problem will be the functional analysis of the present stage of the cultural process that is resulting from the contact. A knowledge of this contact process as a whole ... can only be gained by following all three approaches. An analysis dealing merely with the phase of the process in evidence at the time of investigation, which disregarded the basis from which it started and the variety of causes that set it in motion and still keep it going, would be suspended in the air. It would miss the very essence of the problem which is to give an insight into the response of a culture to foreign influences. It is obvious that one cannot study the response alone without knowing in some detail what is responding and what it is that provokes the response. ...

To determine the basis from which the contact process started it is not always necessary or even desirable to go back to the beginning of the contact process as a whole ... but only to the situation before a particular set of contact influences became effective.

Schapera (1935, p. 316) is likewise specific in stating that analysis of culture contact calls for knowledge of the original culture and of the forces bearing upon it at various times. The first step he envisions is to reconstruct as far as possible a picture of the old culture before Europeans came upon the scene, utilizing the best methods possible. The second step is the study of the history and nature of contact, including not merely a chronology of events or institutions but also motives, interests, and personalities. A third step is to seek explanations of change either through tracing changes in specific elements of native culture, for example, religion, or through tracing the influence of specific elements or agencies.

Hunter (1934, pp. 336–37), after describing situations she could not understand, states:

I have given this very obvious example of the impossibility of understanding existing institutions without a knowledge of the past. It might be paralleled by examples from every aspect of the culture. Any culture can only be fully understood in its historical context, and when the culture under consideration has undergone revolutionary changes within a generation the relative importance of the historical context is very much greater than when the culture has been relatively static. (a) ... I decided ... the most possible method of gauging the changes resulting from the contact was to compare areas subject to different contact influences, and that the study would be simplified if I began in the most conservative areas, that is, the one least affected by contact influences.

Hunter both studied four areas and also made a reconstruction of the older culture. She then made a comparison, with the result that she was much better able both to understand present cultures and the significance of culture change and to predict crucial points when changes occurred. Urging use of journals and other documents, she also says (pp. 343–44):

I am not concerned with origins as such, or with tracing the spread of particular elements of culture whether material elements like tobacco, soap, or a complex of beliefs, but I am concerned to discover the reactions of Pondo culture to European culture, and to discover these reactions it is necessary as far as possible to distinguish elements borrowed from European culture from those which were a part of Pondo culture before the coming of the European.

b) THE COMPARATIVE APPROACH

Comparative approaches fall into two categories. The first consists of studies of groups with the same or similar original cultures which have been exposed to different degrees of the same contact situation, perhaps beginning at different times. The purpose here is to understand the steps by which the group with the most modified culture has arrived at its present situation.

The method is used by Hunter (1934), Richards (1935), and Culwick (1935), among British anthropologists, and also has been employed by American anthropologists, especially Hallowell (1949) and Redfield (1941). Essentially, the purpose is the reconstruction of past stages of acculturation, with the hope of gaining insight into processes. Few scholars, including users of the method, seem to have recognized that this is historical reconstruction by use of the basic age-area hypothesis; hence its employment has escaped the criticisms leveled at more avowedly historical approaches. Nevertheless, it must be grouped with other methods for reconstructing the past.

The second comparative approach is still almost unemployed in any systematic fashion: the comparison of various acculturative situations for the purpose of extracting generalizations about contact situations. It is true that a good many similar processes and end-results have been observed to occur in many different acculturative situations. An excellent summary is given by Herskovits (1948, p. 534). What is lacking still are detailed comparative analyses. As Fortes has said (1936, p. 26), a comparative sociology of culture contact is needed "without which we can never hope to perceive the causes of social change."

c) THE "TRAIT LIST" VERSUS THE HOLISTIC APPROACH

There is little discussion of the differences between the two approaches. British anthropologists, with their predominantly functionalist approach, tend to insist upon the importance of studying cultural wholes and occasionally have criticized efforts to study segments or parts of culture. In general, however, they dismiss the matter by essentially *ex cathedra* statements concerning the functional interrelatedness of cultures. In point of fact, however, no one has yet demonstrated a method by which cultures may be studied in their entirety. And, as Herskovits (1948) has pointed out, many significant studies have been accomplished by utilizing either an aspect of culture or through a frank dissection into traits as in the case of Parsons' *Mitla*. Indeed, the Malinowski method of study fundamentally involves listing elements of a culture. While he insists upon listing institutions, this is likewise a method involving temporary fragmentation of a culture, even though the fragments be somewhat larger than those of Parsons. The matter becomes more significant in connection with the discussion of quantification and indices.

d) THE ROLE OF THE INDIVIDUAL AND PSYCHOLOGICAL APPROACHES

Essentially, two different problems are involved here. The first emerges from studies concerned with the detailed mechanics of acculturation and centers about the role of specific individuals either in the donor or in the receiving culture. Thus Hunter (1934, pp. 347–49) discusses the importance of understanding the contact agents and their personalities (referring here to overt attitudes and behavioral patterns). Thurnwald (1935) likewise emphasizes the need to understand not only the agents of acculturation and their motivations but the changes which take place in the agents as a result of the contact situation. A great many studies in the United States likewise devote considerable attention to the role of specific individuals in contact situations. This is particularly marked in the numerous studies of revivalistic and nativistic cults.

Of a different order are investigations of personality structure and personality change in connection with acculturation situations. Perhaps the most active and consistent worker in this field has been A. Hallowell, whose writings range from broad analyses of general psychological processes (1945) to highly systematic investigations utilizing projective techniques. Based upon the general assumption of some relationship between a given culture and the personality of the individual culture bearers, most investigations have been devoted to exploring the problem of the amount and rapidity of personality change under conditions of culture contact and the relationships between personality and acceptance or rejection of culture change. The rather voluminous but scattered literature is closely related to the literature of the "culture-personality" approach in general. Also of considerable interest are studies employing personal documents, myth, and song to reveal psychological problems and characteristics (cf. Thurnwald, 1935; Barnouw, 1950).

Sociologists have also paid some attention to this problem, particularly in connection with structural-functional analysis. Both some sociologists (e.g., Merton, 1949, p. 53) and some anthropologists have tended to assign an independent causal status to the psychological or personality variables, a view sharply criticized by DuBois (1951). Others have merely considered sociocultural and psychological variables to be in dynamic relationship. An impor-

tant recent statement of the problem is Spindler and Goldschmidt's (1952) "Experimental Design in the Study of Culture Change," which attempts to isolate social and psychological variables and delineates a method for examining their interrelations.

e) LINGUISTIC ACCULTURATION

Although the similarity of linguistic and cultural change has been long recognized in general terms, few concrete studies dealing with the problem have emerged. George Herzog, Edward Spier, Jean Bassett Johnson, and Dorothy Lee all published articles in 1941 and 1943 dealing with specific examples of linguistic acculturation among North American Indian tribes. More recently George Barker (1947) has worked on the same problem with relation to Mexicans in the United States.

Studies thus far published are relatively preliminary and have included few theoretical statements. Generally, stress has been laid upon the interrelationship between sociocultural and linguistic factors in change. Despite some suggestion that linguistic studies could provide indices for acculturation, the field is little developed and is mentioned here merely because it appears to offer unexplored potentialities.

f) IDENTIFICATION OF MAJOR
CULTURAL PROCESSES

Although the identification of processes is perhaps the ultimate theoretical objective of acculturation studies, relatively little empirical investigation which permits of adequate generalization has taken place. Such work or speculation as has taken place has perhaps been primarily done by United States anthropologists, although there are notable exceptions, the most recent being Elkin (1951). But most British anthropologists seem to follow Miss Hunter (1934, p. 335) when she says:

"My interest in culture contact is primarily practical. ... The nature and extent of the changes taking place in the Bantu community are my first concern, the mechanism of change a secondary one."

In very broad terms there are agreements among students of culture contact as to some of the possible results. Virtually all discussions point out acceptance, syncretism, and reaction as being possible results of culture contact, with the recognition that in most cases all three effects may occur, with emphasis varying according to the conditions of contact as well as through time as the contact situation continues. Acceptance, without modification by other attitudes, ultimately leads to complete assimilation to the contact culture. Even if other responses intervene, assimilation may in some cases ultimately result. Syncretism is a frequent result of contact and has been well documented, especially in the studies of Latin-American Indian cultures and in the studies of the Negro in the New World. Less frequently mentioned in the various memoranda for study, but prominent in some of the actual studies both in the New World and in Africa, is the occurrence of spontaneous reformulations which often result in the modification of elements from either of the cultures in contact or produce entirely new structures. While the totality of the emergent culture may be regarded in some measure as a syncretism, large areas of the social structure may be essentially new. Perhaps the most thoroughly studied of the primary areas of phenomena is that of reaction. Clearly to be included in this category are the various revivalistic and nativistic movements. Not only has Linton (1943) given us a useful typology for organizing studies of such movements, but there are numerous analyses of special movements, such as the studies of the Peyote cult, the Ghost Dance, and related movements in North America; Williams' studies in New Guinea; and various others. Although often undertaken without being placed in an acculturational framework, they provide valuable materials for analysis.

Beyond these rather general terms, processual analysis does not seem adequately conceptualized. The majority of existing discussions of process are heavily psychological and essentially deal with the role of the individual in change or the impact of change upon the individual. Few explanations in sociological or cultural terms have been developed. Even those attempts made are often somewhat specialized in character, especially in studies with practical objectives. Thus Miss Hunter (1934, p. 350) says:

What administrator, missionary, and commercial man alike are really concerned to discover is what were the sanctions for social behavior under tribal conditions, and how these sanctions are being affected by contact with Europeans. The social sanctions, the bonds integrating the society, are only to be understood by studying the work and the interrelation of the institutions of the society, and it is the change in the working and interrelation of institutions resulting from European contact which we must discover.

One cannot quarrel with Miss Hunter's objectives and proposals, which are in line with her avowed preoccupation with practical problems, but one must suggest that they do not provide adequate conceptualizations for enlarging the theoretical framework, nor does she really suggest in any very profound way techniques for arriving at analysis of the processes of change. In this respect Redfield's studies offer considerably more in the way of theoretical formulation in his use of such concepts as secularization, individualization, and so on; but they are admittedly confined to those aspects of the contact situation which are related to the change from folk to urban. Fortes (1936) has pointed out that culture contact must be viewed as a continuous process of interaction. Despite his recognition of the importance of a comparative sociology of culture contact, he offers little in more concrete terms. Beyond very broad concepts, then, little progress has been made in accurate conceptualization of processes or their empirical identification, particularly in broad theoretical contexts. Perhaps the most important contribution in recent years is Elkin (1951), who has presented an analytical discussion of native reaction in Australia which deserves critical appraisal and testing in other areas and situations.

g) QUANTIFICATION AND INDICES

British anthropologists have been especially insistent upon the necessity of collecting quantified information. In situations of change, it becomes particularly important to know what proportions of a given population conform to various of the changing norms. Richards especially (1935) has emphasized the village census as a technique, but she is not unique in its use. Many problems of sampling and of reliability of data have not been adequately dealt with as yet. Wagner (1936) has pointed out the unreliability of data obtained by schedules and the impossibility of using them for house-to-house interviews or in any sort of random sampling, where problems of rapport are involved. He makes an ingenious suggestion for utilizing a genealogical method to get quantitative data which raises important sampling problems.

The use of quantitative approaches has also been suggested for developing indices of acculturation. Interesting proposals in this direction, as well as on the use of quantified data to meas-

ure relative rates of change as between different segments of a given culture and to make acculturation studies more directly comparable, were made by Leonard Broom in two short articles in 1939 and 1945, but this lead has never been followed up. Spindler (unpublished manuscript) and Spindler and Goldschmidt make use of quantified data to establish classes or strata representing (presumably) levels of acculturation within a group. Although there is considerable growth in quantification of data, there is little development of consistent methodologies or sophistication in statistical treatments which could contribute to growth in theoretical understanding.

IV. CONCLUSION

The survey and discussion here presented represent an inadequate coverage of the growing literature on acculturation. The work of anthropologists, both British and United States, in the Pacific area has been largely omitted from consideration for reasons of time. Moreover, there may appear to be an overemphasis on earlier literature. Nevertheless, there is some justification for such an emphasis.

Despite the fact that the interest in acculturation has reached a point where an entire volume on the subject may be organized from the papers presented at the Congress of Americanists or that a symposium on Middle American ethnology can be presented as a volume on acculturation (Tax *et al.*, 1951), recent literature has in the main been either descriptive in character, concerned with specialized problems, such as the psychological approaches, or has been frankly applied in nature. Most recent studies have followed lines laid down in the earlier literature and have made little theoretical contribution. One finds refinements of method and of field techniques, but one does not find great sharpening of concepts or the development of firm theoretical structures. Despite its bulk, the literature of acculturation does not seem to be cumulative in character.

Such a review as the present suggests strongly the need for serious stocktaking and reformulation of the field of acculturation. There is an urgent necessity to re-examine our conceptual apparatus and to reach agreement on objectives and methods which will produce more comparability in studies and which will develop a series of really significant hypotheses.

It would seem that such a re-examination could best take place within the framework of the broader problem of culture change. As Robert Nesbit has said (unpublished manuscript), the functionalists in sociology and anthropology have made a major contribution by emphasizing the *statics* of culture. Only recently has functionalist theory become interested again in change, an interest which clearly requires some modification of functionalist theory. Most particularly, it is necessary to introduce the time dimension if the dynamic situation is to receive adequate treatment.

If, as Julian Huxley (1952, p. 16) has said, "a study of the mechanism of cultural transmission and variation may be as important for anthropology as the study of genetics has been for biology," then there are few more important tasks in our field. Within the area of culture change, acculturation seems to offer the best possibilities for getting at an important part of the "genetics" of culture change. Nevertheless, to attempt to develop acculturation studies without reference to the total problem of cultural transmission and variation would seem to be undesirable.

This is not the place to attempt to define the directions which reformulations of acculturation should take. Nevertheless, a few comments may be in order. Apart from the basic task of sharpening our concepts and revising our theoretical structure, the following seem some of the needed steps:

1. It should be made clear that the study of acculturation is primarily concerned with the study of process. As process must in the main be inferred, we need clarification of the methods of inference.

2. Without in any way belittling the importance of psychological problems related to acculturational situations, a clear understanding of and division between sociocultural and psychological phenomena and explanations should be established.

3. Dynamic situations, as the physicists have long recognized, require the use of time as a dimension. New techniques and standards are called for.

4. Various specialized approaches need further exploration, especially the field of linguistics.

5. Quantification should be extensively developed. Quantification should not be developed for its own sake but to provide techniques for objectively determining relative rates of acculturation between various aspects of culture and between individuals in a given society, to establish types and classes, and to provide better comparative methods. Quantification should be developed in close relation to the advance of structural and functional types of analysis. Without this, quantification may result in unrealistic fragmentation of cultures without means of reintegrating the results.

6. Studies should aim increasingly at comparability. Emphasis must be given to the discovery of uniformities in culture processes and to research designs which will produce additive results.

7. It is of the utmost importance that both theoretical and empirical studies give adequate consideration to the reciprocal nature of acculturation and to instances of acculturation which do not involve European cultures.

8. There is need to explore the relation of acculturation to the broader problems of culture change and to such concepts as assimilation, syncretization, disorganization, and dysfunction. While in such theoretical exploration it is perhaps not too important that we define the limits of the field of acculturation with precision at this time, it is important that we explore the utility of typologies, the possible existence of continua, the usefulness of polar concepts, and the validity of using the acculturation approach in connection with migration phenomena and urbanism where contacts may be between individuals rather than organized social groups.

Because of the relatively greater number of anthropologists in the United States and the relatively less strong pressure upon them for applied studies, the development of theory and method is perhaps a particular responsibility of scholars in the United States. This statement is not an attempt to set up a "reserved area," upon which others should not poach, but rather a recognition of actualities and an assertion of special responsibilities. Finally, although further review perhaps should precede a decision, the time seems ripe for a new committee representing a variety of interests to re-examine the field and perhaps prepare a new research memorandum.

REFERENCES AND BIBLIOGRAPHY

The following does not pretend to be a complete bibliography of acculturation. Rather it represents only works cited in this paper plus a few others included either because of their historical significance or as representing important collections of papers.

AMERICAN ANTHROPOLOGICAL ASSOCIATION. 1937. "Proceedings of the Annual Meeting for 1936," *American Anthropologist*, XXXIX, 316–27.

BARKER, GEORGE. 1947. "Social Functions of Language in a Mexican-American Community," *Acta Americana*, V, 185–202.

BARNOUW, VICTOR. 1952. *Acculturation and Personality among the Wisconsin Chippewa*. ("American Anthropological Association Memoirs," No. 72.)

BATESON, GREGORY. 1935. "Culture Contact and Schimogenesis," *Man*, Art. 199.

BEALS, RALPH L. 1932. "Aboriginal Survivals in Mayo Culture," *American Anthropologist*, XXXIV, 28–39.

———. 1937. Review of PARSONS, E. C., *Mitla: Town of the Souls, ibid.*, XXXIX, 681–82.

———. 1951. "Urbanism, Urbanization and Acculturation," *ibid.*, LIII, 1–10.

BENEDICT, RUTH. 1937. Review of REDFIELD, R., and VILLA, A. R., *Chan Kom: A Maya Village*, *American Anthropologist*, XXXIX, 340–42.

BOAS, FRANZ, *et al.* 1938. *General Anthropology*. New York: D. C. Heath & Co.

BROOM, LEONARD. 1939. "The Cherokee Clan: A Study in Acculturation," *American Anthropologist*, XLI, 266–68.

———. 1945. "A Measure of Conservatism," *ibid.*, XLVII, 630–35.

BUSCHAN, G. 1910. *Illustrierte Völkerkunde*. 2 vols. Stuttgart: Strecker.

CHAPPLE, E., and COON, C. 1942. *Principles of Anthropology*. New York: Henry Holt & Co.

———. 1943. "Centenary of the American Ethnological Society," *American Anthropologist*, XLV, 181–243.

CULWICK, A. T. and G. M. 1935. "Culture Contact on the Fringe of Civilization," *Africa*, VIII, 163–70.

DuBOIS, CORA. 1939. *The 1870 Ghost Dance*. ("Anthropological Records," Vol. III, No. 1.)

———. 1951. "The Use of Social Science Concepts To Interpret Historical Materials: Comments on the Two Preceding Articles," *Far Eastern Quarterly*, XXI, 31–34.

EKVALL, ROBERT B. 1939. *Cultural Relations on the Kansu-Tibetan Border*. Chicago: University of Chicago Press.

ELKIN, A. P. 1932. "Five Year Plan of Research," *Africa*, V, 1–13.

ELKIN, A. P. 1951. "Reaction and Interaction: A Food Gathering People and European Settlement in Australia," *American Anthropologist*, LIII, 164–86.

FORTES, MEYER. 1936. "Culture Contact as a Dynamic Process," *Africa*, IX, 24–55.

GILLIN, JOHN. 1948. *The Ways of Men*. New York: D. Appleton–Century Co., Inc.

GOLDENWEISER, ALEXANDER. 1937. *Anthropology*. New York: F. S. Crofts & Co.

GREENBERG, JOSEPH H. 1941. "Some Aspects of Negro-Mohammedan Culture Contact among the Hausa," *American Anthropologist*, XLIII, 51–61.

HALLOWELL, A. I. 1945. "Sociopsychological Aspects of Acculturation." In LINTON, R. (ed.), *The Science of Man in the World Crisis*, pp. 171–200. New York: Columbia University Press.

———. 1949. "Ojibwa Personality and Acculturation." In TAX, SOL (ed.), *Acculturation in the Americas: Proceedings and Selected Papers of the XXIXth International Congress of Americanists*, pp. 105–14. Chicago: University of Chicago Press.

HERSKOVITS, MELVILLE. 1937a. "The Significance of the Study of Acculturation for Anthropology," *American Anthropologist*, XXXIX, 259–64.

———. 1937b. "African Gods and Catholic Saints in New World Negro Belief," *ibid.*, pp. 635–43.

———. 1938. *Acculturation: The Study of Culture Contact*. New York: J. J. Augustin.

———. 1948. *Man and His Works*. New York: A. A. Knopf.

HERZOG, GEORGE. 1941. "Culture Change and Language: Shifts in the Pima Vocabulary." In NEWMAN, STANLEY; SPIER, LESLIE; and HALLOWELL, A. I. (eds.), *Language, Culture, and Personality: Essays in Memory of Edward Sapir*, pp. 66–74. Menasha, Wis.: Sapir Memorial Publication Fund.

HUNTER, MONICA. *See* WILSON, MONICA HUNTER.

HUXLEY, JULIAN. 1952. "Biological Evolution and Human History," *American Anthropological Association News Bulletin*, VI, 16.

INTERNATIONAL CONGRESS OF AMERICANISTS. 1952. *Acculturation in the Americas: Proceedings and Selected Papers of the XXIXth International Congress of Americanists*. Chicago: University of Chicago Press.

INTERNATIONAL INSTITUTE OF AFRICAN LANGUAGES AND CULTURES. 1938. *Memorandum XV*. London.

JOHNSON, JEAN BASSETT. 1943. "A Clear Case of Linguistic Acculturation," *American Anthropologist*, XLV, 427–34.

LEE, DOROTHY. 1943. "The Linguistic Aspect of Wintu Acculturation," *American Anthropologist*, XLV, 435–40.

LINDBLOM, GERHARD. 1937. Review of HUNTER, MONICA, *Reaction to Conquest*, *American Anthropologist*, XXXIX, 688–90.

LINDGREN, ETHEL JOHN. 1938. "An Example of Culture Contact without Conflict: Reindeer Tungus and Cossacks of Northwestern Manchuria," *American Anthropologist*, XL, 605–21.

LINTON, RALPH (ed.). 1940. *Acculturation in Seven North American Indian Tribes*. New York: D. Appleton–Century Co.

———. 1943. "Nativistic Movements," *American Anthropologist*, XLV, 230–39.

LOWIE, ROBERT H. 1934. *Introduction to Cultural Anthropology*. 2d ed. New York: Farrar & Rinehart, Inc., 1940.

MAIR, L. P. 1934. "The Study of Culture Contact as a Practical Problem," *Africa*, VII, 415–22.

MALINOWSKI, B. 1929. "Practical Anthropology," *Africa*, II, 22–38.

———. 1939. "The Dynamics of Contemporary Diffusion." Summary in *Proceedings of the International Congress of Historical and Ethnological Sciences*. Copenhagen.

———. 1945. *The Dynamics of Culture Change: An Inquiry into Race Relations in Africa*. New Haven: Yale University Press.

MEAD, M. 1932. *The Changing Culture of an Indian Tribe*. New York: Columbia University Press.

MERTON, ROBERT. 1949. *Social Theory and Social Structure*. Glencoe, Ill.: Free Press.

ORTIZ, FERNANDO. 1940. *Contrapunteo del tobaco y el azucar.* Havana: J. Montero.

PARSONS, E. C. 1933. "Some Aztec and Pueblo Parallels," *American Anthropologist*, XXXV, 611–31.

——. 1936. *Mitla: Town of the Souls.* Chicago: University of Chicago Press.

RAMOS, ARTHUR. 1947. *Intradução à antropologia brasileira.* Vol. II. Rio de Janeiro.

REDFIELD, ROBERT. 1929. "The Material Culture of Spanish-Indian Mexico," *American Anthropologist*, XXXI, 602–18.

——. 1934. "Culture Changes in Yucatan," *ibid.*, pp. 57–69.

——. 1941. *The Folk Cultures of Yucatan.* Chicago: University of Chicago Press.

REDFIELD, R.; LINTON, R.; and HERSKOVITS, M. J. 1936. "Memorandum on the Study of Acculturation," *American Anthropologist*, XXXVIII, 149–52. (Also published in *Man, Africa,* and *Oceania.*)

RICHARDS, AUDREY I. 1935. "The Village Census in the Study of Culture Contact," *Africa*, VIII, 20–33.

SCHAPERA, I. 1935. "Field Methods in the Study of Modern Culture Contacts," *Africa*, VIII, 315–26.

SCHRIEKE, B. (ed.). 1929. *The Effect of Western Influence on Native Civilizations in the Malay Archipelago.* Batavia: G. Kolff & Co.

SPICER, EDWARD. 1943. "Linguistic Aspects of Yaqui Acculturation," *American Anthropologist*, XLV, 410–26.

SPIER, LESLIE. 1929. "Problems Arising from the Cultural Position of the Havasupai," *American Anthropologist*, XXXI, 213–22.

SPINDLER, GEORGE C., and GOLDSCHMIDT, WALTER. 1941. "Symposium on Acculturation," *American Anthropologist*, XLIII, 1–61.

——. 1952. "Experimental Design in the Study of Culture Change," *Southwestern Journal of Anthropology*, VIII, 68–83.

TAX, SOL, *et al.* 1951. *Heritage of Conquest: The Ethnology of Middle America.* Glencoe, Ill.: Free Press.

THURNWALD, RICHARD. 1932. "The Psychology of Acculturation," *American Anthropologist*, XXXIV, 557–69.

——. 1935. *Black and White in East Africa.* London: Humanities Press.

——. 1938. "The African in Transition: Some Comparisons with Melanesia," *Africa*, XI, 174–86.

WAGNER, GUNTER. 1936. "The Study of Culture Contact and the Determination of Policy," *Africa*, IX, 317–31.

WILSON, MONICA HUNTER. 1934. "Methods in the Study of Culture Contact," *Africa*, VII, 335–50.

——. 1936. *Reaction to Conquest.* London: H. Milford.

National Character*

By MARGARET MEAD

NATIONAL CHARACTER studies are a recent development in anthropological research on problems of personality and culture. They take both their form and methods from the exigencies of the post-1939 world political situation.[1] Although the national-character approach utilizes the premises and methods of the personality and culture field, historically it has had two distinguishing features: the group of persons with a shared social tradition whose culture is studied is selected because they are the citizens or subjects—the "nationals" —of a sovereign political state, and the society *may* be so inaccessible to direct field observation that less direct methods of research have to be used. These contemporary national character studies of culture at a distance resemble attempts to reconstruct the cultural character of societies of the past (Mead, 1951*b*) in which the study of documents and monuments has to be substituted for the direct study of individuals interacting in observable social situations. However, they differ from historical reconstruction in that, whether they are done at a distance or through field work in the given nation, they are based primarily on interviews with and observation of living human beings.

National character studies, like all culture and personality studies, are focused on the way human beings embody the culture they have been reared in or to which they have immigrated. These studies attempt to delineate how the innate properties of human beings, the idiosyncratic elements in each human being, and the general and individual patterns of human maturation are integrated within a shared social tradition in such a way that certain regularities appear in the behavior of all members of the culture which can be described as a *culturally* regular character. In this sense, "cultural character" is an abstraction which anthropologists use when their conceptual apparatus is devised to include assumptions about intra-psychic structure. A statement like "In culture X, married men must avoid their wives' mothers" is a cultural statement. "In culture X, the mother-in-law avoidance is enforced through a sense of shame" is an inexplicit culture and personality statement in which "sense of shame," a construct about intra-psychic behavior, is invoked without analysis or supporting psychological theory. But, "In culture X the mother-in-law avoidance is maintained through a sense of shame; the individual learns to associate exposure of certain parts of the body with social disapproval, so that he responds to the presence of his mother-in-law as he would to physical exposure" is a (still very simple) statement in which the words "learns to associate" involve a psychological theory of learning. A cul-

---

* In the preparation of this paper in its final form, I have been very much indebted to Professor David Mandelbaum's detailed criticism.

1. This development is summarized in Mead (1951c); also in French edition (see "Selective Bibliography").

ture and personality approach may use as one part of its conceptual apparatus a relatively simple tentative psychological scheme such as simple association-alism; the rounded-out system of Hullian learning theory (Hilgard and Marquis, 1940; Dollard and Miller, 1950), Gestalt perceptual theory (Kofka, 1935), and Freudian theories of character formation (see esp. Fromm, 1941; Kardiner, 1945; Erikson, 1950); the eclectic constructs of social psychology (Murphy, 1947); or others. Whether the type of psychological theory drawn upon is one that relies on detailed assumptions about the nature of innate drives and phylogenetically determined perceptual mechanisms or one that simply assumes that social behavior is learned and that the way it is learned is significant for the understanding of a culture, it is the *presence* of psychological theory, that is, the inclusion of intra-psychic processes in the descriptions of members of a society, that differentiates the culture and personality approach.

Once a theoretical scheme accepting intra-psychic behavior as investigable and relevant is used, some psychological theory is involved. This includes even such a scheme as Radcliffe-Brown used in his study of the Andaman Islands (1922), in which he utilized the psychological construct of "sentiments" as a signpost to indicate how far he meant to go in involving theories about intra-psychic behavior in his study of this culture, or Franz Boas' use of the explanatory phrase "automatic behavior." The tendency to characterize some anthropological works as involving "culture and personality" and others as not is really an attempt to draw an artificial dividing line at some point in the formulation of the problem. Actually, there is a continuum, at one end of which formal ethnographic work—like most social history—dodges the issue with statements like "Murder was much more frequent among the coastal tribes"

or "During the next century the times became much more unsettled, and robbery and murder were rife," without posing the problem of what correlates of the changed incidence of violence there were in the intra-psychic organization of individuals (Ware, 1940).

Practically speaking, it is possible to distinguish culture and personality studies from simple descriptive studies by determining the proportion of clusters of information on single individuals with which the anthropologist works. In a cultural study, it is theoretically possible to collect each item of information about the culture from a different individual, cross-checking only in order to guard against pathology or extreme idiosyncrasy of response. In a culture and personality study, actual studies of identified individuals must be undertaken by ongoing observation, retrospective life-histories (Dollard, 1935; Gottschalk, Kluckhohn, and Angell, 1945; Mead, 1949b, Introd.), or the use of projective tests (Henry, 1947; Abel, 1948); at the very least, the items of information about interpersonal behavior—especially that involved between young persons or immigrants and the older members of the society—must be organized *as if* these details of interpersonal interaction were occurring among individuals with specifiable characteristics of constitution, temperament, sex, degree of maturation, previous experience (Kardiner, 1939), and so forth. If, for example, having only the information that the vision experience required of young men in a certain culture is expressed in accounts of what is *seen* during the "vision" and that no "hearings" of any sort are allowed for, we consider this piece of information together with the possibility that some individuals in every culture may be primarily "auditory" in type and therefore will be handicapped when it comes to "seeing" visions, then we are proceeding *as if* it were possible to study identifiable individuals within that culture pattern. We have material on the cultural hope expressed by the Cheyenne that young men will be brave (Grinnell, 1923), and we have material on the assumption of a transvestite position by some Cheyenne, who refuse to assume the warrior role; if we attempt to explain these transvestites by assuming that they possess individual characteristics of timidity or negativism or have experienced a closer-than-usual tie with their mothers or unusual strictness from their fathers, these speculations (valuable, in the absence of field research, only for the construction of hypotheses and the identification of problems) are nevertheless within the culture and personality field. When it is possible to study the actual characteristics of individuals who are choosing or have chosen the transvestite role and the order of birth or the relative age and status of the actual children who show discrepant amounts of aggressiveness, our work becomes full culture and personality research.

Just as culture and personality research draws upon the developing conceptual schemes of psychology (principally upon learning theories, psychoanalytic psychology, and Gestalt psychology), so studies of national character draw upon the developing conceptual schemes of the culture and personality field (Sapir, 1934; Gorer, 1943b; Bateson, 1944; Mead, 1946b; Frank, 1948; Haring, 1948; Kluckhohn and Murray, 1948; Sargent and Smith, 1949). Conclusions drawn from detailed field work that has involved the use of psychological constructs on living, identified, observable groups of human beings are used as the conceptual background of national character studies (Gorer, 1938; Bateson and Mead, 1942; Kluckhohn and Leighton, 1946, 1947) of complex societies where no such complete field studies are possible. Fairly sharp distinctions can be drawn between the direct application of particular psychological schemes to the behavior of members of a society (which, without the "mediating variable" of "culture," results in oversimplified statements about a nation's members being "paranoid" [Brickner, 1943] or "regressed") and the explicit invoking of field studies to specify the kind of steps in cultural learning or unlearning which may lead to behavior that is characteristically paranoid or schizophrenic in many respects but that must be referred to cultural patterns rather than to any particular individual's idiosyncratic defect in "reality testing" (Mead, 1952). One of the difficulties encountered by students of national character is their dependence for this "mediating variable" upon a relatively new branch of anthropology that is not widely known to either anthropologists or psychologists.

The simplest meaning of the "mediating variable" can be discovered by examining the differences between the caricature statement, *Swaddling them as infants makes Russians incapable of freedom,* and the national-character statement, *The prolonged and very tight swaddling to which infants are subjected in Russian child-rearing practice is one of the means by which Russians communicate to their infants a feeling that a strong authority is necessary.*[2] The first statement assumes that swaddling, as an experience of certain human infants, somehow produces an attitude in adult Russians, independently of the entire history of Russia; the second insists that it is when Russians (who themselves embody their whole culture) handle their own children (who are in the process of learning to be Russians) in a particular way that this way of handling becomes a form of

2. For bibliography surrounding this controversy, see Endleman (1949); Gorer (1949); Orlansky (1949); Goldman (1950); Shub (1950); Mead (1951d, e); and Wolfe (1951).

communication between parent and child in which the child learns something the adult has already learned, not necessarily by the same means. The mediating variable used here is "culture." A second "mediating variable" is represented by the phrase "child-rearing practice," which invokes our entire systematic knowledge of infant growth and development and of the connections which clinical work has traced in individual cases between child-rearing practice and personality. Such a view of culture assumes, furthermore, that each member of a society is systematically representative of the cultural pattern of that society, so that the treatment accorded infant or immigrant, pupils or employees or rulers, is indicative of the culturally regular character-forming methods of that society (Bateson, 1942a; Mead, 1948; Joffe, 1949).

From the systematic invocation of this conceptual framework, we are able to say that a change in the pattern of interpersonal contact will be accompanied by a change in the response system of both parties—parent and child, native and stranger, employer and employee. Such changes may be merely temporary adjustments to a changed situation, but, if continued long enough, they may become part of the "character" of both members of the interacting pair. When such changes occur throughout a social system (as when, for example, equalitarian patterns of relationship are substituted for hierarchical patterns), an alteration in "cultural character" may be expected to occur as the intra-psychic correlate of what is usually called "social change" (Mead, 1940, 1947a, 1949c).

Professor Hallowell has outlined in an earlier paper, "Culture, Personality, and Society," some of the basic premises of the culture and personality approach. With Professor Hallowell's general approach to the field of personality and culture, particularly as exemplified in his field work and detailed papers on

aspects of the problem, I am very much in agreement, although I would not use the particular units or entities he used in presenting his analytical discussion. As the field of national character is derivative from the field of personality and culture, it will be necessary to rephrase very briefly some of the points that Professor Hallowell has discussed.

Culture and personality theory depends upon systematic studies of culture which have demonstrated that the culture of any people is learned and can be altered through such processes as borrowing, resistance, invention, and so forth; that cultural forms are not related in any demonstrable way to racial characteristics, except that, when certain cultural characteristics are attributed to certain physically identifiable members of a society, they may then learn them (Warner, Junker, and Adams, 1941); that the developing child shows patterns of regularity of maturation from fetal life through physical maturation (Gesell, 1945). It depends also upon systematic experimental studies of learning and perception (Hilgard and Marquis, 1940; Bateson, 1942b), systematic sociological studies of such correspondences as that between social status and differences in learning within a society (Davis and Havighurst, 1947), and clinical studies of individual children and individual adults (Fries, 1947; Adorno et al., 1950; Erikson, 1950).

Against the background of such systematic investigations, culture and personality studies on primitive peoples have been made, and the clarity of their psychocultural formulations has increased as the young disciplines of child development, learning psychology, Gestalt psychology, and psychoanalysis have been able to provide formulations more applicable cross-culturally, partly in response to the use which anthropologists have made of such formulations in the field. Systematic culture and personality field studies among primi-

tive peoples where the cultural and societal conditions were appropriate for
intensive work have, in turn, provided
the background for work in national
character—for the attempt to delineate
the regularities in character among the
members of a national group attributable to the factors of shared nationality
and the accompanying institutional correlates—nation-wide linguistic usages,
legal codes, economic activities, educational forms, and so forth.

Perhaps the most frequent misconception (Endleman, 1949; Orlansky,
1949; Goldman, 1950; Lindesmith and
Strauss, 1950; Little, 1950; Shub, 1950;
Wolfe, 1951) about work on national
character has been the belief that students of national character used the
same methods to study German or English or Japanese character that were
used for the study of the Alorese, the
Navaho, or the Pukapukans. In addition
to the objection that these methods of
observation would have been seriously
misapplied had they been used to study
societies not accessible to observation,
the legitimate objection has been made
that methods applicable to small primitive societies of relatively simple organization are not applicable to nation-
states of many millions, since the very
difference in size introduces qualitative
differences in the possible methods of
research. This misunderstanding was
fostered somewhat by those of us who
began the work in the field, because
we stressed the usefulness of the anthropological training which enabled us to
use the verbal reports and postural responses of living individuals (or their
written or artistic work treated as living
behavior) as our primary subject matter. Thus an anthropological skill learned
in field work among primitive peoples—
the skill of evaluating an individual informant's place in a social and cultural
whole and then recognizing the formal
patterns, explicit and implicit, of his
culture expressed in his spontaneous

verbal statements and his behavior—became identified as the single contribution the anthropologist could make to
the study of contemporary cultures.

It would be less misleading to say
that the study of national character is
a form of anthropology in which the
anthropologist draws upon experience
with and knowledge of the findings of
the body of pure research materials resulting from field work in culture and
personality, but uses new methods
(Mead, 1951a). Experience in the training of skilled members of the psychological disciplines to apply their psychological skills directly to cultural
materials, either primitive or complex
modern, indicates that the presence of
the cultural anthropologist who has a
command of personality and culture research methods and theory is essential
if studies of national character, as distinct from studies of projections or attitudes or descriptions of social perception patterns, are to result. Original
personality and culture studies of the
particular culture on which members
of the psychological disciplines are
working may, of course, be substituted
for the physical presence of an anthropologist on a working team.[3]

Studies of national character make
the following assumptions, based on the
types of research enumerated above:

1. There are no known differences
among races of men which either interfere with or facilitate the learning of
cultural forms (psychic unity of mankind).

2. There are wide individual differences among human beings which must
be taken into account; these may be
grouped with varying degrees of probable correctness as attributable to sex,
temperament, constitutional type, or
other repetitive genetic factors.

3. Cultures—the abstraction used by

3. See use of data from West's *Plainville*
(1945) in Kardiner's *The Psychological Frontiers of Society* (1945).

anthropologists to apply to historically developed, shared, learned behavior of members of a society—have systematic aspects which can be referred to the biologically given characteristics of their human characters, such as maturational sequences, hand-eye co-ordination, capacity for symbolic behavior, etc.

4. Cultures have other systematic aspects that can be referred to other regularities in nature; a cultural handling of the calendar, for example, can be referred to, and understood in terms of, our independently verified astronomical knowledge.

5. Human cultures may be seen as historically patterned systems of communication between individuals, within individuals, and between individuals and the nonhuman environment, which codify and give meaning to the child's, or the immigrant's, proprioceptive and exteroceptive experience (e.g., a lump in the throat comes to be experienced as sorrow, a tingling in the big toe as fear, the color red as a signal of danger, a circle as a sign of unity, the stars in the Great Bear as a constellation indicating the northern sky, and so forth).

6. Human cultures have certain holistic characteristics which may be referred to the comparable biologically given capacity of human beings to systemize experience and to the circumstance that a culture is shared by members of a *society*—itself organized as a whole in such a way that changes in one part have reverberations in other parts of the society.

7. The culture of each society has unique characteristics which may be referred in an infinite regression to antecedent conditions. No formulation on the basis of an analysis under points 3, 4, 5, and 6 should be expected to account for these unique characteristics without recourse to a known sequence of historical events.

8. Each culture may be expected to change concomitantly with impinging events which were hitherto outside the system—an invasion from a hitherto unknown people, an earthquake, an epidemic arising outside the society, and so on. Such changes should not contradict formulations made on the basis of points 3, 4, 5, and 6; but formulations based on these assumptions should not be expected to predict the occurrence of such changes but only to establish the limits within which such cultural change is likely to fall, if externally precipitated.

9. Cultures are carried by successive generations in such a way that each member of each generation, from infancy to old age, contributes to the perpetuation and reinterpretation of the cultural forms. Changes in the behavior of any member may be expected to set up repercussions within the society; changes in the behavior of a category of members may be expected to result in changes within the whole system.

10. Cultures, although individually unique, may be expected to show comparable features when cross-cultural categories (amount of capital goods, caste, class, size of primary groups, degree of segmentation, and so forth) are applied to them in such a way that the unique pattern of organization of each culture is also taken into account.

11. The version of the wider cultural pattern manifested by the members of any subgroup in a culture may be expected to be systematically related to the wider cultural pattern. But the reverse is not true; the wider pattern need not include any of the features which are *distinctive* of the particular pattern of the subgroup. In the United States, for example, wide patterns of common American behavior may be expected to recur in the behavior of Kentucky mountaineers, Texas ranchers, New England mill workers, second-generation Italian wine growers, and Pennsylvania farmers of German extraction;

and from an examination of several such groups it should be possible to delineate patterns which would be found, in different and distinctive form, among the others. But the nation-wide pattern so delineated would not provide a basis for predicting the version of the culture distinctive of Texas ranchers or New England mill workers without additional information on these particular groups.

12. Any member of a group, provided that his position within that group is properly specified, is a perfect sample of the group-wide pattern on which he is acting as an informant. So a twenty-one-year-old boy born of Chinese-American parents in a small upstate New York town who has just graduated *summa cum laude* from Harvard and a tenth-generation Boston-born deaf mute of United Kingdom stock are equally perfect examples of American national character, *provided that their individual position and individual characteristics are taken fully into account.*

13. Any cultural statement must be made in such a way that the addition of another class of informants previously unrepresented will not change the nature of the statement *in a way which has not been allowed for in the original statement.* So the representativeness of the informants used should be included in the statement, as, for example, "These statements are made about the culture prevailing in the rural south among people living in communities of less than twenty-five hundred people." Then further interviewing of a group of people in the rural South (women, for example) should not change the statement; if women were not properly represented, the anthropologist should have said "among men" instead of "among people" in the original statement of applicability.[4] (That is, the anthropologist samples in terms of structure of the group he is studying, and he is responsible for building a

sufficiently good model of that structure to enable him to place each informant within it and describe accurately the deficiencies of his material.)

We may now examine the present field of anthropological research defined as the application of the methods and findings of culture and personality research to the identification of culturally regular behavior in members of modern nation-states.

All citizens of modern nation-states are exposed to institutional patterns that have regularities attributable to the state of nationhood—national systems of government, taxation, money, criminal and civil law, transportation regulation, military service, systems of mass communication, and so forth. The degree of uniformity and central control differs from one nation to another, and statements about national character must take into account the degree of local government, regionalization, and so on, which will, in turn, be embodied in the national character of each member of the nation, in proportion to the distinctiveness of the participation of the particular subgroup to which they belong. For example, although gypsies may refuse to send their children to school, the devices they use to keep their children out of school in the United States or in the United Kingdom will be related to the state-administered standards of school attendance and may include crossing internal boundaries periodically to avoid state or local truant officers. Thus many patterns of the wider culture will be represented in institutionalized forms in the versions that subgroups display, in the very ways that members of subgroups avoid conformity or bend the institutions to local purposes. This is equally true of a pattern which may be stated as "the

4. For a careful statement of the limitations of the informant see Gorer and Rickman's *The People of Great Russia* (1949 and 1950), sec. 6, p. 116.

house in American culture is characterized by the presence of opaque walls,
a roof, hinged doors that can be closed,
and translucent windows." Houses may
be found that do not meet any of these
criteria, but they will be classified as
being to that degree special; an "open
doorway" between dining room and
living room is an open space where
otherwise a door would be—a version
of a door, not merely a version of an
entrance. People who have houses with
glass walls still reflect the cultural form,
as in a recent instance in the state of
Connecticut where the residents of a
glass house, in order to warn trespassers
off the grounds and away from the
transparent walls, put up a sign reading, "This house is now occupied. Please
respect the privacy of the occupants."

Statements applying to a whole nation cannot be made until the pattern
of differentiation is known, even though
the detail may not be. Thus in a study
of British culture it would be expected
that every type of informant capable of
expressing any political knowledge of
the sort would indicate somehow the
fact that Scotland is still in many respects a special administrative unit
within the United Kingdom. They may
speak of "getting married in Scotland"
or say that "the chart of meat cuts they
had for rationing during the war was
different in Scotland" or that "the ministry allowed them to build *brick* child-
welfare centers in Scotland," and so
forth. Such comments are enough to
indicate to the anthropologist the existence of some sort of special administrative treatment of Scotland. Such a clue
can then be followed up until its representation in the special versions of the
culture characteristic of subgroups can
be abstracted. This is not, however, a
method of studying the administrative
structure of the United Kingdom or of
any other literate society about which
it is possible to get both written documents and expert assistance. It is simply

a method of insuring the inclusion in
statements about the culture of the way
individuals who characterize themselves
as "British" will include in their self-
image some statement of the type of
relationship existing *between* Scotland
and England *within* Britain. Further
research would be necessary to establish whether the best commonwealth-
wide statement would be: to be "British" is to be also a member of a group
having a distinctive culture of its own
with which one is also identified (e.g.,
English, Welsh, Scottish), and the term
"British" will be preferred to the terms
"English," "Welsh," "Scottish," in those
contexts in which the entire British
political system is contrasted with
or distinguished from other national
groups. But, in order to make this statement, sufficient work would have to be
done to know, for instance, whether
Singhalese will use "British" in this
same way, and, if this is not known,
the anthropologist may have to limit his
statements to the United Kingdom or
to the British Commonwealth, exclusive
of those countries where the majority
of the population is not of United Kingdom derivation, and so forth.

So statements about the manifestations of national institutional patterns
may be limited to a series of subgroups.
One may speak of the New England
version of the American national culture by specifying the systematic responses of New Englanders to national
institutions and indicating by the retention of the qualifying regional adjective
"New England" that information on
those aspects of the regional pattern
that are assumed to be nation-wide is
limited to information collected from
New England informants and New
England materials. The assumption that
other regions will show manifestations
of "American national character" would
be based upon our knowledge of cultures. The New England study would
provide us with a *specific* set of ex-

pectations as to which measures of the United States government had a standardizing effect throughout the nation—e.g., income tax administration, pure food and drug acts, defense measures, federal communication regulations, currency controls—and which areas would demonstrate local differentiation, as, for example, marriage and divorce laws, public education, real estate taxes, and so on.

Additional types of selection may enter into a study of national culture, depending upon the accessibility of the society being studied and the particular political and class structure of the society at the moment of study. When a group now classified as a subgroup, a unit within the larger society that we are attempting to handle as a whole, has played or is playing a particularly decisive role in the definition of national policy (either inter- or intra-nationally), special attention may be given to the culturally regular character of this subgroup and to its version of the culture. For example, special studies might be made of the public school–educated Englishman in discussing British foreign policy; of Clydeside and the industrial areas of the north of England in discussing trade-unionism; of Polish culture in delineating the development of the Soviet secret police; of Texans in discussing the United States air force; of Cossacks in Russia and Sikhs in India in discussing military police; and so forth. Such emphases would be determined by the nature of the problem. Applied studies have to keep close to specific situations and be as contemporaneous as possible. If the stamp of Dsjerzhinsky, the Polish designer of the Soviet secret police, is still such that behavior within the contemporary MVD can best be understood after an investigation of the standards of asceticism and self-discipline expected from Polish saints, this will be included, especially if information on the functioning of the Soviet Union's political police is meager. But if we are making a study of the regular army in the United States, it may be most economical to utilize strictly contemporary material on the attitudes of today's army on the subjects of honor, patriotism, and so forth, in spite of the fact that the question might well be approached through a delineation of the special southern American regional variation on these themes because of the importance of the large number of regular army officers of southern regional origin. Or, if we wish to know something about the kind of political expectations that have developed out of an experience of the administrative system of the old Austro-Hungarian empire, we might start by making an intensive study of several representative Gallician communities which, except for having been on opposite sides of the old Austro-Hungarian border, shared a common or closely related local cultural tradition; or we might proceed by making an intensive study of the premises and practices of the Austro-Hungarian bureaucracy as revealed in documentary sources, including biographies and diaries. For the elucidation of some particular problem, it may be necessary to concentrate on exploring some small particular segment of a society and only a special aspect of its culture. In World War II, for example, some of the friction that arose between Americans and the British could be traced to the varying meanings they placed on their "partnership," and, in order to explain these particular disagreements, it was necessary to concentrate on British sports behavior and the sports ideals of the great public schools (from which the major coloring of the British handling of the word "partnership" was found to come) and on American business culture with a predominantly middle-class coloring (the source of American expectations about the "partnership" relation).

So far I have discussed studies of national *culture* and of aspects of national culture rather than studies of national *character*, a special form of the study of national culture which normally should follow, not precede, studies of a national culture. Although in emergency situations the direct study of national character by a highly trained anthropologist, who can take culture systematically into account while concentrating on certain culturally regular intra-psychic dynamics of a segment of the population, may be resorted to, it remains an emergency solution, as, for instance, in Geoffrey Gorer's initial work on the Japanese (1943*b*). The Columbia University Research in Contemporary Cultures study of the culture of the eastern European small towns is an example of the more ideal sequence in which culture is studied before character, and formulations about the intra-psychic dynamics follow. In certain instances, trained anthropologists are able to use their "native" knowledge of their own culture and/or long participant experience of another culture as a sufficient cultural background from which to proceed directly to a delineation of the character structure of the members of that society (Mead, 1942; C. and F. Kluckhohn, 1947; Gorer, 1948). A special elaboration of this technique of using knowledge of own culture as a background for material on national character studies is the method of using expert informants—psychiatrists, psychologists, political scientists —who can both provide primary observations and annotate them themselves, using some systematic theoretical approach.

Furthermore, certain types of research may be used both to provide a cultural description in which the intra-psychic dynamics are not spelled out and to describe character. Child-rearing practices, for example, may be used as a key to the values of a society, and

they may also be used as one essential part of a study of character formation. An analysis of the plots of films or popular novels may serve to document consciously recognized themes (such as *success* in the United States or *self-control* in Britain) along the lines originally developed by Madariaga in his *Englishmen, Frenchmen and Spaniards* (1928) or by Ruth Benedict in *The Chrysanthemum and the Sword* (1946*c*), in which differences in values are stated without any explicit psychological apparatus; an examination of plots (with the apparatus of Freudian psychology, for example) may also be used as a way of exploring covert themes assumed to be part of a national character, as Wolfenstein and Leites have done (1950). Even projective test protocols can be used to delineate elements of cultural content, although to do so would be extremely wasteful and clumsy. So if French Rorschach protocols are found to contain a large number of references to exotic and mythological figures, this may be analyzed from the point of view of French attitudes toward the exotic, or of the distinctively French way of handling certain types of threatening situations by distantiation (Abel, 1948).

National character studies attempt to trace the way in which the identified cultural behavior is represented in the intra-psychic structure of the individual members of the culture, combining cultural theory and psychological theory (principally learning theory, Gestalt psychology, Freudian psychology, and child-development studies) into a new psychocultural theory to explain how human beings embody the culture, learn it, and live it. For example, once the areas of approved and disapproved behavior have been descriptively outlined, the mechanisms which the individual uses in conforming may be analyzed in terms that show in detail how approved behavior is rewarded by praise, allotment of greater freedom, material gifts from parents, child nurses, servants, joking relations; how disapproved behavior is punished; and how in the course of experiencing these types of reward and punishment the individual not only learns to engage in or refrain from certain activities but also—over time and particularly during early developmental stages—establishes certain patterns of conformity involving identifiable emotions such as fear, shame, pride, guilt (Mead, 1950), etc., which will be systematically manifested by members of that society in the various situations where the questions of conforming to approved social behavior and avoiding disapproved behavior arise.

Explorations along such lines as these, undertaken in both primitive and contemporary societies, have provided material for the construction of interpretative schemes, such as Erikson's "tasks" (1950) or Riesman's types of orientation (1950, 1952). Thus material gathered within a contemporary society (in Erikson's case, clinical studies of American children; in Riesman's, masses of verbatim material from American adults carefully specified as to position in the society) can be used in combination with the theoretical schemes of personality and culture research to amplify the personality and culture conceptualizations by intensive elaboration of theory from other sources.

The anthropological approach to the study of contemporary culture makes the following definite contributions, in addition and complementary to traditional methods of studying contemporary complex societies:

1. It provides a way of analyzing the culture of a society as a whole. The study of cultural wholes was originally a historical development based upon the expectation that individual anthropologists would be the only students of a vanishing culture and upon the ac-companying requirement that as many categories of articulate scientific inquiry as possible be included within the observational scheme. With the new field methods developed during the last thirty years of research on living cultures, there has been added to this historical situation the intensive study of small primitive communities within which every individual could be known and the actual network of interrelationships mapped and studied. As soon as anthropological methods were applied to modern cultures, even in the form used in *Middletown* (R. S. and H. M. Lynd, 1929), it became clear that different methods of treating the culture would have to be devised. The methods so far developed have included various adaptations of sociological sampling methods suitable for the study of large communities, so large that their members cannot all be studied individually; positional studies in which small complex parts of the total structure are carefully localized and intensively studied, as when the organization of one of the several shops in a factory is studied (Chapple, 1949); and one specifically anthropological method of cross-checking on the precision with which findings on any segment of cultural material is actually representative of the whole culture (Bateson and Mead, 1942). This anthropological method consists of the intensive analysis of segments of the culture which are unsystematically related to each other and overlap in a variety of ways—the analysis of such segments, for example, as Soviet novels, the proceedings of party congresses, leadership in Soviet agriculture, controls in Soviet industry, the records of the Great Trials, a year's cartoons in *Krokodil*, and Komsomol organization (Mead, 1951d). These segments of material are chosen in such a way that the regularities found in the analysis of one segment can be checked against those found in another

segment; they must be congruent if the analysis is correct, because some of the same individuals are involved in different ways in a number of the segments —as officials, readers, workers, party members, and so forth. A variety of such segments providing comparable cross-checks but using organizational material and interviews were utilized in the "Yankee City" studies (Warner *et al.*, 1941–47).

2. The anthropological approach provides for the disciplined use of the primitive small society as a conceptual model. The anthropologist's small community model differs from the use of models—in engineering, for example— in which the model is constructed according to already known specifications, so that its use, while facilitating the process of conceptualization and permitting the use of developed analytical methods, is still limited to the state of knowledge of those who built it. The anthropologist, on the other hand, does not build his model—he finds it, in a living historical setting, and then analyzes it in such a way as to obtain types of information hitherto unobtainable. When studying complex societies, the historically given model, the biography of a single individual, the role played by a family in the industrial development of a region, the study of a single community or institution—all may function in this same way (see, e.g., Wiener, 1948; Lamb, 1950). The use of living models has the additional advantage that the unanalyzed and even unguessed-at complexities of human beings may be carried along within the model, increasing the probabilities that the derivations which are made will be "true to life."

3. The anthropological approach provides categories of analysis which have been developed comparatively and are thus freer from cultural bias. When the culture and personality approach is used and the concept of national char-

acter is added to the concept of national culture, it provides a way of incorporating into descriptions of contemporary behavior a specification of the way in which the individual organism embodies this culture. Such psychobiological specifications, whether based on studies of maturation, perception, or learning, fill in the gaps in the models used by historians, economists, and formal sociologists.

4. The culture and personality approach to the study of complex contemporary cultures has made and may be expected to continue to make one further contribution: it provides a particularly congenial atmosphere for interdisciplinary cross-stimulation and teamwork. This appears to be related to the circumstance that the whole culture and personality field is itself the product of interdisciplinary co-operation. We might use such scientific fields as optics or acoustics as examples. Thus the optical or acoustical engineer is dependent upon pure scientific work, which is a co-operative effort of physicists, physiologists, biochemists, and psychologists and which continues to be a field out of which cross-disciplinary insights arise. Formal linguistics can be integrated with the neurological study of brain lesions and processes of maturation and aging. Similarly, the anthropologically oriented study of modern cultures provides a flexible medium within which the methods of literary criticism (Armstrong, 1946; Spurgeon, 1935), architectural history (Garvan, 1951), equilibrium theory (Bateson, 1949; Lamb, 1951), content analysis (Lasswell, 1949*a*, *b*), biophysics, cybernetics,[5] sociometry, topological psychology, and so forth, can be integrated

5. H. von Foerster (ed.), *Cybernetics: Transactions of the Seventh Conference, March 23–24, 1950* (New York: Josiah Macy, Jr., Foundation, 1951), and *Transactions of the Eighth Conference, March 15–16, 1951* (New York: Josiah Macy, Jr., Foundation, 1952).

and used. It will be noted that most of these approaches were also the result of cross-stimulation between two or more disciplines rather than—as is the case with the core disciplines, which rigidly delimit their boundaries—of an attempt to establish a separate and valid "science." It may even be possible to suggest that this hospitality to other methods may be directly related to the persistent and stubborn attempt of anthropologists to keep together, despite extreme centrifugal pressures, the original cluster of anthropological sciences—ethnology, linguistics, physical anthropology, and archeology—as four ways of approaching the study of man.

I propose to discuss problems of criticism and methods of validation together, because they are at present inextricably linked. Criticism of the approach falls under the following main headings:

1. The methods that were suitable for the study of small, pre-literate societies are not suitable for the study of modern complex societies encompassing millions of people. With this statement the anthropologist working on modern cultures agrees and replies that neither are the methods suitable for studying fish in an aquarium suitable for studying fish in the environment of a large lake or sea—the ecologist does not take out of the laboratory his thermostatic controls but rather the *conceptual scheme* for observing the behavior of fish which observation within a small, controlled situation has given him. He may also take *categories of observation* and *habits of observation of fish behavior*. The criticism that the anthropologist uses the same *methods* for the study of both very small and very large societies is simply based on a misunderstanding. (There are other aspects of this criticism—the insistence that primitive man and modern man are different in kind, that large societies are qualitatively different from small ones in ways that make them incomparable, that noble Caucasians cannot be studied in the same terms as Africans and Mongolians—which are based on a difference in fundamental assumptions between anthropologists and many historians, economists, and members of other disciplines; these criticisms are of another order, and they necessitate going back to fundamental anthropological rejections of such matters as the fixity of evolutionary sequences, assumed racial inferiority, prelogical thought, and so forth.)

2. Anthropological methods are not appropriate to the study of large modern societies because of the sampling problem. In this criticism, the accuracy of studies of the Gallup Poll variety that use large statistically manageable groups of respondents specified only in respect to a few categories, such as age, sex, socio-economic status, and religious affiliation, is contrasted with the anthropological use of intensive work with individual informants. This criticism stems primarily from sociologists (Lindesmith and Strauss, 1950; Merton, 1951). A comparable criticism comes from social psychologists (Klineberg, 1944) concerned about distributions of attitudes and more interested in knowing *how many* middle-aged men will express dissatisfactions with their jobs than *how* job dissatisfaction and satisfaction are integrated within the cultural character. These criticisms have been stimulated further by the attempts of nonanthropologists to establish ideas like that of modal personality structure which imply a statistical model.

Part of this criticism can be met by a clarification of method, another part by the clarification of aims. Anthropological sampling is not a poor and inadequate version of sociological or socio-psychological sampling, a version where *n* equals too few cases. *It is simply a different kind of sampling*, in which the validity of the sample depends not so much upon the number of cases as upon the proper specification of the informant, so that he or she can be accurately placed, in terms of a very large number of variables—age, sex, order of birth, family background, life-experience, temperamental tendencies (such as optimism, habit of exaggeration, etc.), political and religious position, exact situational relationship to the investigator, configurational relationship to every other informant, and so forth. Within this very extensive degree of specification, each informant is studied as a perfect example, an organic representation of his complete cultural experience. This specification of the informant grew up historically as a way of dealing with the few survivors of broken and vanished cultures and is comparable to the elaboration with which the trained historian specifies the place of a crucial document among the few and valuable documents available for a particular period, or experiments in medicine in which a *large* number of measurements are made on a small number of cases.

The second misunderstanding centers around a differential interest in pattern. The sociologist or social psychologist who questions the anthropologist by saying, "But you don't know what the distribution of resistance to paternal authority is," is interested in *how much* of measurable quantities of an entity called "resistance to paternal authority" can be found to be distributed in the total population. But the anthropologist is interested in the *pattern* of resistances and respect, neutralities and intensities, in regard to parents and grandparents and siblings, and the way in which this pattern can be found in other sets of relationships between employer and employee, writer and reader, and so on. The difference in emphasis may be illustrated from linguistics: if one wants to know the grammatical structure of a language, it

is sufficient to use very few informants about whom the necessary specified information has been collected; if one wants to know how many people use a certain locution or a particular word in preference to another, then sampling of the wider type is necessary, although probably not sufficient. The statement that *to be* is an auxiliary verb in English will not be improved or altered by the collection of more and more samples of English speech, but the use of English-speaking informants from Ireland, the American West, and Tasmania may provide different dialect versions of its use. In dealing with culture, the anthropologist makes the same assumptions about the rest of a culture that the linguist makes about the language—that he is dealing with a system which can be delineated by analysis of a small number of very highly specified samples. The decision as to *how many* informants are needed is primarily a structural decision. In linguistic texts, if the customary way of telling folk tales includes *ratio recta*, charms, recipes, chants, and esoteric language, then a collection of folk-tale texts may be adequate for delineating the entire syntax of the language, with a full complement of forms. But if all folk tales in a particular culture are told in a stereotyped narrative style, with conversation in *ratio obliqua*, samples of these other kinds of material will have to be gathered separately. The question of adding informants is, in the same way, a matter of the way a society is structured, the degree of representativeness which is shared among members of both sexes, different ages, classes, generations, and so forth. Those social sciences that use the gas laws as their models, rather than the methods of structural biology, do not stress configuration. The transformation of the statement, "In American culture the dwelling house has opaque walls," into quantitative statements about how many Americans live in such houses—about how many members of a society act *directly* in terms of a cultural stereotype—actually makes it a statement of a different order. All the members of a society may recognize that the correct form of marriage is for a man to marry his mother's father's mother's father's sister's son's daughter's son's daughter, but actually no such marriage may exist at the moment of observation (Mead, 1935; Harris, 1951). The determination of the prevalence and incidence of any piece of behavior requires detailed observation of a large sample of individuals, in primitive societies by studying the entire community, in large complex societies by using elaborate sampling methods of the sociological sort.

3. A third criticism is that there is no way of *replicating* the observations; each anthropologist reports something different because individual informants cannot be treated like respondents on a questionnaire or test. This criticism, too, fails to take into account the element of pattern. No two texts of the same folk tale told by the same informant are absolutely identical; but, if a given method of linguistic analysis has been applied correctly to one set of texts, it is expected that a second set examined within the same framework will show the same pattern. The statement that "the people want children" is relatively meaningless, and the finding cannot be replicated; however, if answers to questions as to how many children there are per family, what is considered to be the ideal size for a family, how many adoptions there are, and how adoptions are phrased show that married couples say they have fewer children than they want and make an effort to persuade others to give children to them and that others give up their children reluctantly and as a great favor, then such findings, taken together, present a picture which

can be replicated. Similarly, the statement that "these are a very oral people" is interpretive if taken alone, but if it is supported with detailed descriptions of type of oral play, with photographs of such play, and with text and observational material, the descriptive term "oral," which refers to a definite theoretical framework, and the comparative word "very," which refers to the other peoples on which that particular anthropologist has experience or data, can be given explicit meaning. Any field record containing sufficiently detailed material is subject to this type of cross-check against comparable material collected either by another investigator or at a different date or by a split-halves handling of the single corpus. There have been instances in the personality and culture field in which all the detailed material has been thrown away, as in the presentation of interpretations of Rorschach records without the protocols. This, however, is a comment upon the procedure of particular field workers, not on the possibilities of studying culture in such a way that adequate replication is obtainable.

There is a variety of other criticisms which stem from various prejudices of the critics: that it is inappropriate for an anthropologist to study materials on which he is bound to have bias (which is equally applicable to his studies of primitive peoples); that the method ignores history (which is simply not true); that the stating of regularities in national character is a new kind of racism (which is also quite incorrect, as the whole approach is based on the premise that differences in national cultural behavior are learned).

It is, however, possible to deal with problems of method and validation from an anthropological standpoint, and this involves questions germane to the approach, not questions based on various sorts of cross-disciplinary failures in communication. The peculiar problems that face the student of national culture may be discussed under the following heads:

1. Against what comparative range of cultural behavior is the behavior identified for any national group to be placed? This involves the establishment of culture areas, the development of cross-cultural categories appropriate for cultures of complex societies which are comparable in level of abstraction with those which are used for pre-literate cultures, and ways of specifying the groups of cultures to which any statement of presence or absence, more or less, can be referred. The conventional anthropological base—*all recorded primitive cultures*—is much more difficult to use when making statements about historical cultures on which there is a great wealth of documentation. A precise insistence upon an enumerative background—"all cultures which have been studied by this method," "all folklores which have been recorded and analyzed," "the existing body of culturally differentiated projective test protocols"—seems the best present device for dealing with this difficulty.

2. What changes in the observer-observed ratio should be introduced in order to deal with the greater complexity and still preserve the essential anthropological method by which a cultural system which owes its regularities to the regularities of the human mind is analyzed by passing a large amount and variety of raw material through a single human mind? The complexity of material in a modern nation-state, the need to collect materials from both sexes, different classes, and occupations, and a variety of the cultural versions of regional subgroups obviously calls for a team; but the anthropological requirement of integration of all the material within a single analysis calls for teamwork of a special sort. It should be arranged that all data collected by any member of the team are shared, not merely in the sense of "made available," but actually read by, or looked at (in the case of visual records), or listened to (in the case of aural records), by each member of the team. This requirement obviously limits the amount of data that can be used, but the study of national culture does not involve documentary obligations of a historical, large statistical, or survey nature; the task is to delineate pattern. A smaller amount of material shared by the entire group assures an integration which is comparable but not identical with that obtained by the single field worker (see the discussion of method in Mead, 1951d).

The question of the composition of the team has many facets. The importance of having both sexes and different kinds of minds and experience represented is obvious. The desirability of interdisciplinary membership is primarily a function of the need to use special skills (such as projective testing or psychiatric interviews), or special areas of competence (as in providing historical depth or tapping bodies of existing economic or political analyses). These two kinds of diversity—diversity of age, sex, and temperament and diversity of disciplinary training—can cross-cut each other. Mixed national origin, including trained members of the culture being studied and representatives of at least two other national cultures, is practically a *sine qua non*. In the particular case of applied studies of cultures at a distance which have been undertaken since World War II to meet urgent practical needs, the team serves a different function, a real interacting group of human beings focused on small amounts of data becoming a model in reverse of the field situation, in which a single individual or a husband-and-wife pair respond to a whole community interacting before their observing eyes.

3. How are the anthropologists' methods of using the sought and guided spoken interview to be inte-

grated with the methods of historians who depend upon analysis of documents which were produced in some context other than that for which they are later used? Although a considerable amount of cross-disciplinary understanding can be provided by simply working together on records of the past —especially unpublished autobiographies and diaries—the most complete bridge is provided here when regularities of human psychology—such mechanisms as condensation, displacement, figure-and-ground relationships—are used systematically to analyze both the anthropological interview and the historical document.

4. What use can the anthropologists working on national character make of the findings of other disciplines to validate their findings?

a) Validation from other data.—Bodies of organized data which have been collected for a quite different purpose or within some other frame of reference (the materials in *The American Soldier*,[6] for example, or in *Fortune* surveys[7]) may be used as checks on the hypotheses which have been developed. Or some new collection of unorganized cultural materials, as, for instance, the collection of selections from *Yank* or the *American Song Bag*, the findings of a British Royal Commission, a collection of French political speeches, and so forth, may be used subsequently as a testing ground for hypotheses developed on the basis of other materials. Use of this method involves acceptance of the good faith of the anthropologist —as does any other validating experiment—but this is so much less often accorded to anthropological work that it seems necessary to give it special mention.

b) Validation from other bodies of

6. *Studies in Social Psychology in World War II* (4 vols.; Princeton: Princeton University Press, 1949–50).

7. As used by G. Gorer in *The American People* (1948).

theory.—If the anthropologist is working within a specific theoretical framework, his results can be tested in terms of that framework in two ways—for fit and for a nonfit which can be treated systematically. Whiting's *Kwoma* (1941) and DuBois's *Alor* (1944) are examples of testing for fit; Muensterberger's article on Chinese character (1951) is an example of emphasis on fit, the organization of field material in terms of a theory developed within a different culture, which demonstrates that the new material can be fitted into the old structure. Bateson's discussion of the frustration-aggression hypothesis is an example of looking at new material (Balinese) and using a culturally limited theoretical formulation as a way of systematizing the Balinese material (1941). Extension of the Gesell maturational framework originally based on the sequence observed in American middle-class children in New Haven— frogging, creeping, all fours, standing, then squatting—by analysis of the Balinese sequence—frogging, very little creeping, sitting, squatting, then standing (Mead and Macgregor, 1951)—is another example of expanding a theoretical framework, in its own terms, by the introduction of cross-cultural behavior. This procedure inevitably results in expanding the original theoretical framework, and the requirements of the method are that any discrepancy or incongruity between the analysis of the new material and the previous theoretical formulation should be such that this discrepancy can be handled by expanding the theoretical framework. Erikson's zonal-modal chart[8] has both served as a theoretical framework and been modified and expanded through this use, as was Kurt Lewin's theory of the relationship of success and failure to effort (Lewin, 1948).

Thus, to the extent that the student

8. For successive publications see Homburger (1937); Mead (1946a); Erikson (1950).

of national character relies on psycho-biological theoretical frameworks, the extra-anthropological aspects of such frameworks provide a way of validating the direction of his research. When the psychocultural theories which he uses can be definitely related to biological data which are ascertained by different methods and within a quite different framework (if, for example, a theory of the function of rhythmic mourning can be related to findings on epileptics,[9] or a theory of the way anger is organized in a given national character can be related to teething behavior), this is convincing cross-disciplinary validation and also tends to direct the national character theories involved into a more systematic framework—in contrast to cultural approaches resembling those of Ruth Benedict and Malinowski, in which the biological substratum was initially derived from a comparative study of cultures and then used as a point of reference in explaining them (Mead, 1946*b*).

c) However, the most convincing validation still remains one of pattern, of the testing of the hypothesis for intra-cultural and intra-psychic fit. Every piece of cultural behavior is so over-determined in its systematic relationship to every other piece that any discrepancy within the material should immediately demand a revision of the delineation hypothesis established so far. Just as the experienced field anthropologist works with congruencies and discrepancies, and each discrepancy or contradiction means that the whole pattern is still not understood, so any body of reliable observations which challenges the present formulations of national culture calls for their re-examination. If an attempt is made to delineate national character in addition to the national culture, then the criterion of internal consistency has to

9. H. von Foerster (ed.), *Cybernetics: Transactions of the Ninth Conference, March 20–21, 1952* (in preparation).

be invoked in relation to some psycho-cultural theory of personality. For example, the statements that in certain Moslem countries women respond with deep inferiority to the articulate lament present in the culture to the birth of a girl and that women do not rebel against their lot or appear to manifest any envy of the male role present a challenge to existing psychoanalytic personality theory which is sufficiently important to justify a demand for further explanation. When it is recognized that the male whose birth is so loudly celebrated carries a very strong load of fear and need for self-validation, so that the father's role as contrasted with the mother's is one of unenviable insecurity and vulnerability, the mechanism by which the daughter identifies contentedly with the more secure parent becomes clearer and less subject to challenge. While the student of national culture must primarily meet the challenge of internal congruity in terms of cultural materials, the student of national character must meet this double challenge of cultural and psychological consistency. This requirement should be read, of course, not as a demand for uniformities in culture or in character, but as a demand for the delineation of regularities which are systematically explicable in terms of our knowledge of the history of the culture and of the society and the biological nature of man.

d) One further form of validation is prediction, and this can be of two types: (1) a prediction of the form that events in the future will take, especially of the limits within which the predicted set of events will fall, and (2) the systematic relating of two completed series of events within the same society in terms of the description of the culture. Predictions can only be expected to state probabilities, and, like predictions from the laboratory to the real world, they cannot specify events belonging to a differently functioning system from that included in the studies of culture. For example, it should be easier to predict the possibilities of a dictatorship ending by assassination or by natural death than by accidental death, but it should not be expected that the actual assassination could be predicted any more than the date of natural death can be assigned. When an assassination occurs, however, the national pattern which has been delineated should be capable of explaining the patterns of an attack on a head of state, as, for example, the recent instance in which Puerto Rican malcontents launched attacks against buildings even when it was not certain that their intended victim was in them. A set of hypotheses about Japanese culture which could not explain the bombing of Manila after it had been declared an open city would have to be declared faulty; if the Japanese had continued isolated resistances in large numbers at the end of World War II in spite of the fact that the emperor was retained as the head of the state, then the hypotheses about Japanese culture on the basis of which it had been predicted that the decree of the emperor would be obeyed would have had to be re-examined.

For proof of the sort demanded in the experimental sciences, it is necessary to construct experiments in which the cultural membership of experimental groups is systematically varied and the hypotheses about their behavior systematically tested. Very few attempts of this sort have yet been made, and most of them have been partly accidental by-products of the Lewinian school of group-dynamics experimentation: French's (1944) findings on the behavior of his Italian-American group as compared with Harvard students (which could also be interpreted in terms of subgroup cultural difference), and the confirmation in the Bavelas (Lewin, 1943; Mead, 1943) test findings on Iowa children of the formula-

tions about the place of food in American character are examples of this sort of validations.

In attempting to evaluate cultural hypotheses made by individuals who, no matter how great their training in the use of cross-cultural categories, are never free from unrecognized cultural bias in all the areas of culture which have not yet been made articulate, blind interpretations by members of the same culture are not useful. Such methods as the use of blind Rorschachs (DuBois, 1944), in which Rorschach protocols are read blind and then tested against the judgment of the field workers on the same individuals and on the culture as a whole, are tests of *reliability*, but are not validations, as both the Rorschach specialist and the anthropologist share the same cultural approach and the same general theoretical frame of reference.

Methods of research developed in the study of national character may have important results in developing research bridges between anthropology and the other social sciences (particularly history). The study of national character has been, to date, in its references to contemporary political units primarily an applied science. We have studied national character not as the best setting within which to trace the correspondences between political forms and individual character formation—for very possibly a much smaller unit, such as the New England town or the Swiss canton, would be a far better locus for pure research—but because, in today's world, nation-states are of paramount political significance, and a great many activities of individuals and groups, both in domestic and in international settings, are conducted in terms of national values. For this reason, almost all the work in this field has been conducted in connection with national enterprises, either of problems of domestic morale or of the conduct of war or peace. The most extensive work has been done in the United States on Japan in wartime, with certain peacetime follow-ups on the spot;[10] on Germany, with special reference to postwar problems (Schaffner, 1945, 1948); on relationships between British and Americans during World War II (for bibliog., see Mead, 1949a, pp. 457–59; Métraux, 1951, pp. 210–13); on the Soviet Union (Gorer and Rickman, 1949; Mead, 1951d), with international participation in teams which have been financed in the United States. All these major researches have been initially conducted at a distance, and in the case of the Soviet Union no follow-up field work has been possible. Without field work, it is impossible to describe the society, and the proportions in which any given trait is manifested cannot be ascertained; in fact, all questions that depend upon statistical sampling or upon detailed mapping of interpersonal networks have to be begged. France,[11] Britain (Mead, 1947b; Gorer, 1950), Czechoslovakia,[12] and Poland[13] represent cases where work done at a distance has been followed or accompanied by field studies. China,[14] Syria,[15] Rumania (Benedict, 1946a), and to a very partial degree Italy have been studied only at a distance, using isolated individuals and enclaves. There has been an exploratory field study of Norway,[16] without any formulations in regard to the dynamics of Norwegian character. Field work is now going on in Holland,[17] preceded by unpublished preliminary work at a distance. The four UNESCO field studies in France, Australia, India, and Sweden,[18] with a primarily social-psychological focus, are now approaching publication. Burma (Gorer, 1943a; Hanks, 1949) and Thailand (Benedict, 1946b) and Greece were all tentatively analyzed during the war, and there have been follow-up field studies in Thailand and Burma. No work has been reported for any Latin-American country as a whole or on Denmark, Belgium, Ireland, Bulgaria, Hungary, Yugoslavia, Portugal, Spain, Indo-China, Pakistan, or on any of the Near Eastern countries except Syria, or on any of the countries of the British Commonwealth except the United Kingdom —as wholes, although there is a variety of valuable studies of particular communities or subgroups which have not been specifically oriented to problems of national culture and national character. In addition to these attempts to delineate whole cultures and the dynamics of the character, seen nationally, there has been a variety of studies of attitudes toward health, nutrition, military service, agriculture, visual and auditory mass communication, and so forth, in which partial attempts have been made to place problems of relief, technical assistance, psychological warfare, and others within a total national cultural setting.[19]

10. See series of articles on "The Problems Raised by *The Chrysanthemum and the Sword,*" *Japanese Journal of Ethnology* (published at 132, Shimohoya Hoya-machi, Tokyo), XIV, No. 4 (1949), 1–35.

11. M. Mead and R. Métraux, chapter in a volume on France, edited by Saul Padover and others (in preparation).

12. D. Rodnick and E. Rodnick, "Czechs, Slovaks, and Communism" (unpublished MS).

13. Unpublished field work by Dr. Sula Benet.

14. R. Bunzel, "Explorations in Chinese Culture" (unpublished report prepared for the Office of Naval Research); Weakland (1950); Abel and Hsu (1949).

15. Unpublished field work, Columbia University Research in Contemporary Cultures.

16. By David and Elizabeth Rodnick (1950–51).

17. By Dorothy Keur.

18. "UNESCO Community Studies" (in preparation).

19. *Culture Patterns and Technical Change: A Manual Prepared by the World Federation for Mental Health for UNESCO* (1951) (in press).

The status of the subject may be best dramatized by saying that, if a world organization were to be formed in which the constituent units were not the present nation-states but larger regional or smaller subnational units, the interest in "national character" would shift; reference to the old national units would become a matter of historical research, and they would be of only contemporary interest to the extent that individuals still bore the imprint of the national institutions within which they had been reared in some way which could be invoked to explain their contemporary behavior. So, in analyzing contemporary Polish national behavior, it is sometimes useful to refer in retrospect to the experience of groups of Poles still living who were once part of the nation-states of czarist Russia, imperial Germany, and the Austro-Hungarian Empire; and, from other points of view, the present position of Poles as part of the Soviet sphere of influence with its increasingly standardized political institutions may have to be invoked. In each case the problem and the context within which it is being discussed will determine which of these political units and their representations within the character of Poles should be invoked.

It is useful to divide the study of national character into a series of steps:

(1) developing initial hypotheses in which any material which is highly patterned can be used (Gorer, 1943*b*; Gorer and Rickman, 1949; Mead, 1951*d*); (2) subjecting these hypotheses to systematic scrutiny in the light of selected bodies of materials; (3) the determination by extensive sampling techniques of the prevalence and incidence of the behavior which have been identified; (4) validation of the findings through prediction and experiment. Where a society is inaccessible, step 3 is impossible, except in a very specialized form, such as extensive interviewing of either a skewed sample, like Soviet defectors, or of a disrupted society, like the scattered members of a single community. The very exigencies of the present world situation, which are responsible for directing research into this field, also often limit the conditions within which full-length field studies can be undertaken. Further development of this approach waits upon field studies within accessible complex modern states, involving systematic cooperation with historians and members of other disciplines who work on aspects of modern culture, on the one hand, and upon the further development of theory—from culture and personality research conducted within the more favorable settings of small primitive communities—on the other.

REFERENCES

ABEL, T. M. 1948. "The Rorschach Test in the Study of Culture," *Rorschach Exchange and Journal of Projective Techniques*, XII, No. 2, 79–93.

ABEL, T. M., and HSU, F. L. K. 1949. "Some Aspects of Personality of Chinese as Revealed by the Rorschach Test," *Rorschach Research Exchange and Journal of Projective Techniques*, XIII, No. 3, 285–301.

ADORNO, T. W.; FRENKEL-BRUNSWIK, E.; LEVINSON, J.; and SANFORD, R. N. 1950. *The Authoritarian Personality.* ("Studies in Prejudice Series.") New York: Harper & Bros.

ARMSTRONG, E. A. 1946. *Shakespeare's Imagination: A Study of the Psychology of Association and Inspiration.* London: Lindsay Drummond.

BATESON, G. 1941. "The Frustration-Aggression Hypothesis," *Psychological Review*, XLVIII, No. 4, 350–55. Reprinted in NEWCOMB, T. M.; HARTLEY, E. L.; *et al.* (eds.), *Readings in Social Psychology*, pp. 267–69. New York: Henry Holt & Co., 1947.

——. 1942a. "Morale and National Character." In WATSON, G. (ed.), *Civilian Morale*, pp. 71–91. Boston: Houghton Mifflin Co.

——. 1942b. "Social Planning and the Concept of Deutero Learning." In BRYSON, L., and FINKELSTEIN, L. (eds.), *Science, Philosophy, and Religion, Second Symposium*, pp. 81–97. New York: Conference on Science, Philosophy, and Religion. Also in NEWCOMB, T. M.; HARTLEY, E. L.; *et al.* (eds.), *Readings in Social Psychology*, pp. 121–38. New York: Henry Holt & Co., 1947.

——. 1944. "Cultural Determinants of Personality." In HUNT, M. (ed.), *Personality and the Behavior Disorders*, Vol. II. New York: Ronald Press Co.

——. 1949. "Bali: The Value System of a Steady State." In FORTES, M. (ed.), *Social Structure: Studies Presented to A. R. Radcliffe-Brown*, pp. 35–53. Oxford: Clarendon Press.

BATESON, G., and MEAD, M. 1942. *Balinese Character: A Photographic Analysis.* ("Special Publications of the New York Academy of Sciences," Vol. II.) New York.

BENEDICT, R. 1946a. "Rumanian Culture and Behavior." New York: Institute for Intercultural Studies. Mimeographed.

——. 1946b. "Thai Culture and Behavior." New York: Institute for Intercultural Studies. Mimeographed. Re-mimeographed as "Data Paper, South East Asia Program," Cornell University, 1951.

——. 1946c. *The Chrysanthemum and the Sword.* Boston: Houghton Mifflin Co.

BRICKNER, R. 1943. *Is Germany Incurable?* Philadelphia: J. B. Lippincott Co.

CHAPPLE, E. C. 1949. "The Interaction Chronograph: Its Evaluation and Present Application," *Personnel*, XXV, No. 4, 295–307.

DAVIS, W. A., and HAVIGHURST, R. J. 1947. *Father of the Man.* Boston: Houghton Mifflin Co.

DOLLARD, J. 1935. *Criteria for the Life History.* New Haven: Yale University Press. Reprinted, New York: Peter Smith, 1949.

DOLLARD, J., and MILLER, N. E. 1950. *Personality and Psychotherapy: An Analysis in Terms of Learning, Thinking, and Culture.* New York: McGraw-Hill Book Co., Inc.

DuBois, C. 1944. *The People of Alor: A Socio-psychological Study of an East Indian Island.* Minneapolis: University of Minnesota Press.

ENDLEMAN, R. 1949. "The New Anthropology and Its Ambitions," *Commentary*, VIII, No. 3, 284–91.

ERIKSON, E. 1950. *Childhood and Society.* New York: W. W. Norton & Co.

FRANK, L. K. 1948. *Society as the Patient.* New Brunswick, N.J.: Rutgers University Press.

FRENCH, J. R. P. 1944. *Organized and Unorganized Groups under Fear and Frustration*, pp. 231–308. ("Iowa University Series in Child Welfare," Vol. XX, Part V.)

FRIES, M. 1947. "Diagnosis of the Child's Adjustment through the Age Level Test," *Psychoanalytic Review*, XXXIV, 1–31.

FROMM, E. 1941. *Escape from Freedom.* New York: Farrar & Rinehart.

GARVAN, A. 1951. *Architecture and Town Planning in Colonial Connecticut.* New Haven: Yale University Press.

GESELL, A. 1945. *Embryology of Behavior.* New York: Harper & Bros.

GOLDMAN, I. 1950. "Psychiatric Interpretations of Russian History: A Reply to Geoffrey Gorer," *American Slavic and East European Review*, IX, No. 3, 151–61.

GORER, G. 1938. *Himalayan Village.* London: Michael Joseph.

——. 1943a. "Burmese Personality." New York: Institute for Intercultural Studies. Mimeographed.

——. 1943b. "Themes in Japanese Culture," *Transactions of the New York Academy of Sciences*, Series 2, V, No. 5, 106–24.

——. 1948. *The American People.* New York: W. W. Norton & Co.

——. 1949. "Some Aspects of the Psychology of the People of Great Russia," *American Slavic and East European Review*, VIII, No. 3, 155–66.

——. 1950. "Some Notes on the British Character," *Horizon*, XX, 369–79.

GORER, G., and RICKMAN, J. 1949. *The People of Great Russia.* London: Cresset

Press; New York: Chanticleer Press, 1950.

GOTTSCHALK, L.; KLUCKHOHN, C.; and ANGELL, R. 1945. *The Use of Personal Documents in History, Anthropology, and Sociology.* (Social Science Research Bull. 53.) New York.

GRINNELL, G. B. 1923. *The Cheyenne Indians.* New Haven: Yale University Press.

HANKS, L. M. 1949. "The Quest for Individual Autonomy in the Burmese Personality," *Psychiatry*, XII, No. 3, 285–300.

HARING, D. (ed.). 1948. *Personal Character and Cultural Milieu.* Syracuse: Syracuse University Press.

HARRIS, Z. S. 1951. *Methods in Structural Linguistics.* Chicago: University of Chicago Press.

HENRY, W. E. 1947. "The Thematic Apperception Technique in the Study of Culture-Personality Relations," *Genetic Psychology Monographs*, XXXV, No. 1, 3–135.

HILGARD, E. R., and MARQUIS, D. G. 1940. *Conditioning and Learning.* New York: Appleton-Century-Crofts.

HOMBURGER, E. 1937. "Configurations in Play—Clinical Notes," *Psychoanalytical Review*, XXII, 139–214.

JOFFE, N. 1949. "The Dynamics of Benefice among East European Jews," *Social Forces*, XXVII, No. 3, 238–47.

KARDINER, A. 1939. *The Individual and His Society.* New York: Columbia University Press.

———. 1945. *The Psychological Frontiers of Society.* New York: Columbia University Press.

KLINEBERG, O. 1944. *A Science of National Character.* (Society for the Psychological Study of Social Issues Bull. 19.)

KLUCKHOHN, C. and F. 1947. "American Culture: Generalized and Class Patterns." In *Conflicts of Power in Modern Culture: 1947 Symposium of the Conference on Science, Philosophy and Religion*, pp. 106–82. New York.

KLUCKHOHN, C., and LEIGHTON, D. 1946. *The Navaho.* Cambridge: Harvard University Press.

———. 1947. *Children of the People.* Cambridge: Harvard University Press.

KLUCKHOHN, C., and MURRAY, H. A. (eds.). 1948. *Personality in Nature, Society, and Culture.* New York: A. A. Knopf.

KOFKA, K. 1935. *Principles of Gestalt Psychology.* New York: Harcourt, Brace & Co.

LAMB, R. K. 1950. "Entrepreneurship in the Community," *Explorations in Entrepreneurial History*, II, No. 3, 114–27.

———. 1951. "Political Elites and the Process of Economic Development" (paper presented at the 27th annual Harris Institute, University of Chicago, June 20). In HOSELITZ, B. F. (ed.), *The Progress of Underdeveloped Areas*, pp. 30–53 ("Harris Foundation Lectures.") Chicago: University of Chicago Press, 1952.

LASSWELL, H. D. 1949a. "The Language of Power." In LASSWELL, H. D., and LEITES, N. (eds.), *Language and Politics*, pp. 3–19. New York: George Stewart.

———. 1949b. "Style and the Language of Politics." In LASSWELL, H. D., and LEITES, N. (eds.), *Language and Politics*, pp. 20–39. New York: George Stewart.

LEWIN, K. 1943. "Forces behind Food Habits and Methods of Change." In *The Problem of Changing Food Habits*, pp. 35–65. (National Research Council Bull. 108.)

———. 1948. *Resolving Social Conflicts: Selected Papers on Group Dynamics, 1935–1946.* Edited by G. W. LEWIN. New York: Harper & Bros.

LINDESMITH, A. R., and STRAUSS, A. L. 1950. "A Critique of Culture-Personality Writings," *American Sociological Review*, XV, No. 5, 587–600.

LITTLE, K. L. 1950. "Methodology in the Study of Adult Personality," *American Anthropologist*, LII, No. 2, 279–82.

LYND, R. S. and H. M. 1929. *Middletown.* New York: Harcourt, Brace & Co.

MADARIAGA, S. DE. 1928. *Englishmen, Frenchmen, Spaniards: An Essay in Comparative Psychology.* London: Oxford University Press.

MEAD, M. 1935. *Sex and Temperament in Three Primitive Societies*, Part II. New York: William Morrow & Co.

——. 1940. "Social Change and Cultural Surrogates," *Journal of Educational Sociology*, XIV, No. 2, 92–110.

——. 1942. *And Keep Your Powder Dry.* New York: William Morrow & Co.

—. 1943. "Anthropological Approach to Dietary Problems," *Transactions of the New York Academy of Sciences*, Series 2, V, No. 7, 177–82.

——. 1946a. "Research on Primitive Children." In CARMICHAEL, L. (ed.), *Manual of Child Psychology*, pp. 667–706. New York: John Wiley & Sons; London: Chapman & Hall, 1946.

——. 1946b. "Personality, The Cultural Approach to." In HARRIMAN, P. L. (ed.), *Encyclopedia of Psychology.* New York: Philosophical Library.

——. 1947a. "The Implications of Culture Change for Personality Development," *American Journal of Orthopsychiatry*, XVII, No. 4, 633–46.

——. 1947b. "The Application of Anthropological Techniques to Cross-national Communication," *Transactions of the New York Academy of Sciences*, Series 2, IX, No. 4, 133–52.

——. 1948. "A Case History in Cross-national Communication." In BRYSON, L. (ed.), *The Communication of Ideas*, pp. 209–29. New York: Institute for Religious and Social Studies.

——. 1949a. *Male and Female.* New York: William Morrow & Co.

——. 1949b. *The Mountain Arapesh.* V. *The Record of Unabelin with Rorschach Analyses.* ("Anthropological Papers of the American Museum of Natural History," Vol. XLI, Part III.) New York.

——. 1949c. "Character Formation and Diachronic Theory." In FORTES, M. (ed.), *Social Structure: Studies Presented to A. R. Radcliffe-Brown*, pp. 18–34. Oxford: Clarendon Press.

——. 1950. "Some Anthropological Considerations concerning Guilt." In REYMERT, M. L. (ed.), *Feelings and Emotions: The Mooseheart Symposium*, pp. 362–73. New York: McGraw-Hill Book Co., Inc.

——. 1951a. "Columbia University Research in Contemporary Cultures." In GUETZKOW, H. (ed.), *Groups, Leadership, and Men*, pp. 106–18. Pittsburgh, Pa.: Carnegie Press.

——. 1951b. "Anthropologist and Historian: Their Common Problems," *American Quarterly* (spring), pp. 3–13.

——. 1951c. "The Study of National Character." In LERNER, D., and LASSWELL, H. (eds.), *The Policy Sciences*, pp. 79–85. Stanford, Calif.: Stanford University Press.

——. 1951d. *Soviet Attitudes toward Authority.* New York: McGraw-Hill Book Co., Inc.

——. 1951e. "What Makes Soviet Character?" *Natural History*, LX, No. 7, 296–303, 336.

——. 1952. "Some Relationships between Social Anthropology and Psychiatry." In ALEXANDER, F., and ROSS, H. (eds.), *Dynamic Psychiatry*, pp. 401–48. Chicago: University of Chicago Press.

MEAD, M., and MACGREGOR, F. C. 1951. *Growth and Culture: A Photographic Analysis of Balinese Childhood.* New York: G. P. Putnam's Sons.

MERTON, R. K. 1951. "Selected Problems of Field Work in the Planned Community," *American Sociological Review*, XII, No. 3, 304–17.

MÉTRAUX, R. (ed.). 1951. "A Report on National Character." Prepared for the Working Group on Human Behavior under Conditions of Military Service, Research and Development Board. Unpublished.

MUENSTERBERGER, W. 1951. "Orality and Dependence: Characteristics of Southern Chinese." In ROHEIM, G., et. al. (eds.), *Psychoanalysis and the Social Sciences*, III, 95–108. New York: International Universities Press.

MURPHY, G. 1947. *Personality: A Biosocial Approach to Origins and Structure.* New York: Harper & Bros.

ORLANSKY, H. 1949. "Infant Care and Personality," *Psychological Bulletin*, XLVI, No. 1, 1–48.

RADCLIFFE-BROWN, A. R. 1922. *The Andaman Islanders.* Cambridge: At the University Press; new ed. Glencoe, Ill.: Free Press, 1948.

RIESMAN, D. 1950. *The Lonely Crowd.* New Haven: Yale University Press.

——. 1952. *Faces in the Crowd.* New Haven: Yale University Press.

SAPIR, E. 1934. "The Emergence of the Concept of Personality in a Study of Cultures," *Journal of Social Psychology*, V, 408–15.

SARGENT, S. S., and SMITH, M. W. (eds.). 1949. *Culture and Personality: Proceedings of an Interdisciplinary Conference.* New York: Viking Fund.

SCHAFFNER, B. 1945. "Round Table, 1945: Germany after the War," *American Journal of Orthopsychiatry*, Vol. XV, No. 3.

———. 1948. *Father Land.* New York: Columbia University Press.

SHUB, B. 1950. "Soviets Expose a Baby," *New Leader* (June 17), pp. 11–12.

SPURGEON, C. 1935. *Shakespeare's Imagery and What It Tells us.* Cambridge: At the University Press.

WARE, C. F. (ed.). 1940. *The Cultural Approach to History.* New York: Columbia University Press.

WARNER, W. L., *et al.* 1941–47. "Yankee City Series," Vols. I–IV. New Haven: Yale University Press.

WARNER, W. L.; JUNKER, B. H.; and ADAMS, W. A. 1941. *Color and Human Nature.* Washington, D.C.: American Council on Education.

WEAKLAND, J. 1950. "The Organization of Action in Chinese Culture," *Psychiatry*, XIII, No. 3, 361–70.

WEST, J. 1945. *Plainville, U.S.A.* New York: Columbia University Press.

WHITING, J. 1941. *Becoming a Kwoma.* New Haven: Yale University Press.

WIENER, N. 1948. *Cybernetics, or Control and Communication in the Animal and the Machine.* New York: John Wiley & Sons, Inc.

WOLFE, B. D. 1951. "The Swaddled Soul of the Great Russians," *New Leader* (January 29), pp. 15–18.

WOLFENSTEIN, M., and LEITES, N. 1950. *Movies: A Psychological Study.* Glencoe, Ill.: Free Press.

A SELECTIVE BIBLIOGRAPHY

BATESON, GREGORY. "Morale and National Character." In WATSON, GOODWIN (ed.), *Civilian Morale: Second Yearbook of the Society for the Psychological Study of Social Issues*, pp. 71–91. New York, 1942.

BENEDICT, RUTH. *The Chrysanthemum and the Sword: Patterns of Japanese Culture.* Boston: Houghton Mifflin Co., 1946.

ERIKSON, ERIK H. *Childhood and Society.* New York: W. W. Norton & Co., Inc., 1950.

GORER, GEOFFREY. *The American People.* New York: W. W. Norton & Co., Inc., 1948. English edition, *The Americans* (London, 1948).

———. "The Concept of National Character," *Science News*, No. 18. Hammondsworth, Middlesex, England: Penguin Books, 1950.

———. "Themes in Japanese Culture," *Transactions of the New York Academy of Sciences*, Series 2, V, No. 5, 106–24.

GORER, GEOFFREY, and RICKMAN, JOHN. *The People of Great Russia.* London: Cresset Press, 1949; New York: Chanticleer Press, 1949.

HARING, DOUGLAS. "Aspects of Personal Character in Japan," *Far Eastern Quarterly*, VI, 12–22. Reprinted in HARING, D. G. (ed.), *Personal Character and Cultural Milieu: A Collection of Readings*, pp. 355–65. Syracuse: Syracuse University Press, 1948.

KARDINER, ABRAM. *The Psychological Frontiers of Society.* New York: Columbia University Press, 1945.

KLINEBERG, OTTO. "A Science of National Character," *Journal of Social Psychology*, XIX (1944), 147–62.

KLUCKHOHN, CLYDE and FLORENCE. "American Culture: Generalized and Class Patterns." In *Conflicts of Power in Modern Society: 1947 Symposium of the Conference on Science, Philosophy, and Religion*, pp. 106–28. New York, 1948.

MEAD, MARGARET. *And Keep Your Powder Dry.* New York: William Morrow & Co., 1942. English edition, *The American Character* (London, 1944). Austrian edition, *Und halte dein Pulver trocken* (Vienna, 1947). German edition, *Und haltet euer Pulver trocken!* (Munich, 1946).

——. "Columbia University Research in Contemporary Cultures." In GUETZKOW, HAROLD (ed.), *Groups, Leadership and Men: Human Relations Research Sponsored by the United States Navy,* pp. 106–18. Pittsburgh, Pa.: Carnegie Press, 1951.

——. "The Study of National Character." In LERNER, D., and LASSWELL, H. D. (eds.), *The Policy Sciences: Recent Developments in Scope and Method,* pp. 70–85. Stanford, Calif., 1951. French edition, "L'Étude du caractère national." In *Les Sciences de la politique aux États-Unis.* ("Cahiers de la Fondation Nationale des Science Politiques," No. 19.) Paris, 1951.

MEAD, MARGARET, and MÉTRAUX, RHODA. *Research in Contemporary Cultures: A Manual on Theory and Practice in the Study of Culture at a Distance by Interdisciplinary Groups.* Prepared for the Human Relations Branch, Office of Naval Research. (To be published in 1953.)

ROHEIM, GEZA. *Psychoanalysis and Anthropology.* New York: International Universities Press, 1950.

SCHAFFNER, BERTRAM. *Father Land.* New York: Columbia University Press, 1948.

ZBOROWSKI, MARK, and HERZOG, ELIZABETH. *Life Is with People: The Jewish Little-Town of Eastern Europe.* New York: International Universities Press, 1952.

Cultural Values

By F. S. C. NORTHROP

CONTEMPORARY LEGAL science provides a convenient basis for giving an inventory of representative anthropological theories of cultural values. Law, like personal ethics, is concerned with norms. Since norms express the ethos of a culture, different theories of legal norms take one to the heart of the problem of cultural values.

Roughly contemporary legal theories of cultural norms fall into five groups: (1) legal positivism, (2) pragmatic legal realism, (3) neo-Kantian and Kelsenian ethical jurisprudence, (4) functional anthropological or sociological jurisprudence, and (5) naturalistic jurisprudence. Each group contains different subspecies and varieties.

LEGAL POSITIVISM

Legal positivism is the theory that cultural values are to be found and understood solely in terms of the positive legal constitutions, statutes, codes, and institutions themselves, perhaps supplemented by police power or force. The main representative of this theory of legal values is the British jurist, John Austin. The designation of this theory of cultural values as "positivism" is not an accident. It arises from the fact that this is the legal theory of traditional Anglo-American culture and that the philosophy of this culture is British empiricism, which is positivistic in its theory of scientific knowledge. Cultural values are positivistic in character when the meaning of the words "good" or "valuable" is given as a particular, inductively through the senses. This excessive emphasis on induction has the consequence also of making each science an independent science. Hence the restriction of legal education in any culture whose values are positivistic, such as modern England and pre-1932 United States, to nothing but the positive institutions, statutes, codes, and decisions contained in the books in the law-school libraries. No further study of the relation of law to society is required. Law, like ethics, on this positivistic theory of cultural values, is an autonomous science; knowledge of economics, sociology, or anthropology is quite unnecessary. To this Austin added the necessity of police power or force to give the law sanctions. The decisions and the constitutional norms were not law unless police power was added. Here again a factor derived from British empirical philosophy entered, namely, the materialistic power-politics philosophy of Hobbes.

Our designation of the first theory of cultural values in our inventory has revealed an additional fact. This theory is not merely culture-bound but also philosophy-bound. It holds only for that portion of Anglo-American culture which derives from British empirical philosophy.

PRAGMATIC LEGAL REALISM

The concepts selected to express the program of this conference, which place the inventory of cultural values under the category of "Problems of Process," is an anthropological illustration of the legal philosophy of pragmatic realism. According to this theory, cultural values are not given in the positive legal norms used to decide in a given dispute whether the conduct involved is to be permitted or prohibited; these norms of decision, the constitutional codes and statutes, are instead merely instruments for social change. Thereby positive legal norms and cultural values are transformed from ends into means. Furthermore, instead of the positive cultural norm, as expressed in a code, statute, or constitutional principle, being the measure of the conduct, the solution of the dispute is made the measure of the norm. If traditional norms prevent disputes from being resolved or merely generate new disputes when they are applied, then they are instrumentally demonstrated to be bad. "Problems of process" become the key to cultural values. At bottom, what this means is that cultural values center not in norms or propositions but, instead, in the problematic situation presented by men in society and in the process which brings the diverse competing and conflicting items in the social situation to a synthesis which produces equilibrium. The word "synthesis" is not a misnomer in this connection, since this legal and anthropological theory derives from the American philosopher, John Dewey. The last philosopher to influence Dewey before he created his instrumental pragmatism was Hegel.

It is not irrelevant to point out that the Yale Law School has been a center of this theory of law and that when students with law degrees coming from Asiatic and Continental European law schools are confronted with this legal philosophy for the first time, they are shocked. The shock arises not merely from the conflict with their European or Asian training but also because they

come from areas where dictators have been rampant, and they fear a theory of law which makes cultural values an instrument of the decision-maker rather than a constitutional control of him. In any event, we see that the problems of process theory of cultural values is both culture- and philosophy-bound. This theory is seriously considered largely in the United States and derives from its pragmatic instrumental philosophy.

At bottom, this theory of cultural values makes the solution of the problem in what Dewey calls "the problematic situation" the criterion of the good. Or, to put the matter more precisely, it makes the bringing to equilibrium of the diverse competing elements in the social situation the criterion of the good and of cultural value. But with a dictator in the social situation and with law made his instrument rather than a fixed norm to control him and with equilibrium made more easy by dictatorial than by democratic parliamentarian methods, what factor is there in this pragmatic instrumental theory of cultural values to insure that the cheap and easy way to equilibrium will not be taken?

The answer to this question as given by American pragmatists is that only that solution is a "true" solution which results from sensitivity to, rather than dictatorial blotting out of, all factors and interests in the problematic situation. This amounts, however, to the admission (*a*) that all values are not in process and (*b*) that there must be at least one constant noninstrumental norm even in an instrumental philosophy of cultural norms, the noninstrumental norm of objective sensitivity to every factor in the situation.

Even if this be granted, certain questions remain. To read the literature of the American proponents of this theory is to move in an aura of optimism.

Values in process and problem-solving become uncritically identified with progress. In Europe and Asia, to set norms and values in flux is all too often to create problems rather than to solve them and to produce demoralization and confusion rather than progress, whatever that vague word may mean. In short, outside the United States, this problem of process instrumental philosophy of cultural values has an aura of optimism which makes it seem culturally false and artificial.

The outstanding fact of our contemporary world is that its problematic international situation is shot through with conflicts between rival ideologies which are logically incompatible and hence not resolvable by the facile injunction to be sensitive to all the factors in the situation. Moreover, one major nation in the world has its explicit answer to the present problematic situation. Merely to counter with emphasis on problem-solving is not enough. The situation calls for a specification of what the answer is. But to specify an answer will be to specify the cultural norms according to which the decision-maker must operate. Again one has norms controlling the decision-maker rather than norms which are mere instruments of the decision-maker. Moreover, the question arises: What are these norms which solve the problem in the contemporary international problematic situation? To answer this question, it is necessary to go beyond instrumental pragmatism and legal realism.

Even so, this theory of cultural values has been necessary. We are living in a world in which the traditional norms are being reconstructed or giving place to new. Pragmatic legal realism is the necessary instrument for breaking from those values of one's part which are outmoded.

NEO-KANTIAN AND KELSENIAN ETHICAL JURISPRUDENCE

Kelsen and the neo-Kantians have one assumption in common concerning the nature of cultural values. This assumption is that values always involve an "ought" which cannot be derived from any "is." Put positively, this means that the basic norm of a culture cannot be found empirically but must be assumed a priori as the presupposition of any ethical or legal judgment whatever. Empiricism in culture or legal science merely gives the materials upon which the value judgment is based, but not the value norm itself, according to this theory.

In the United States Morris and Felix Cohen represent the neo-Kantian position. The difference between Kelsen and the neo-Kantians centers merely in the degree to which the a priori ethical norm of a society, which Kelsen calls "imputation," applies to the legal and social order as a whole. For Kelsen most of the law is given inductively in positive legal codes and statutes. To these codes and statutes of positive law, Kelsen adds but one *Grundnorm,* which is basically ethical and a priori in character. This *Grundnorm* is the a priori assumption that the positive laws given inductively ought to be. It is, according to Kelsen, only because of this ought, given as an ethical a priori by imputation, that the judge has the authority to use the inductively given positive law to send a violator of the law to the electric chair. Kelsen believes that the codes themselves do not give this ought. With the Kantian and neo-Kantians, not merely one solitary *Grundnorm* at the background and basis of the inductively given positive law but every proposition and statute in the entire positive law and in every instance of its application presuppose a continuous contribution of the presuppositions of the a priori ethical moral judgment.

That every culture is not merely the inductively given is of the behavior of the people in that culture but also the culture itself, through its leaders, passing normative judgment upon that behavior in the light of certain norms which express an ought rather than a mere is, cannot be denied. It is clear that man in society is not merely acting but also acting in the light of and under the control of both a personal and a social norm. There is, to be sure, the is of social action, but this is, if scientifically complete, includes the behavior of the murderer as well as the behavior of those who do not violate the ethos of the society. Clearly, therefore, the ought which defines the ethos is true only of a part of what is and requires something more than the is for its own definition. To this extent, therefore, the Kantians and the Kelsenian positivists are correct when they say that a scientific account of cultural values cannot be determined in any given society by the inductive description of the is of that society. Otherwise, any behavior whatever in that society would be good, and there would be no need whatever for norms, legal institutions, and the citizen's sense of having to reconcile what he can do inductively with what he ought to do. Upon this point everyone, including even the instrumental pragmatists when they resort to sensitivity to all the factors in the problematic situation, must agree. The cultural ought for any society is not to be identified with its inductively given is.

Kantian and Kelsenian ethical jurisprudence has one other characteristic: No conduct is ethical, embodying an ought, unless it is the kind of conduct which can be generalized for all men in the form of a determinate universal law. This is the point of Kant's categorical imperative.

Here modern a priori ethical jurisprudence holds a thesis in common with classical Greek and Roman Stoic natural-law jurisprudence. Both affirm that moral man and just man is universal man. By this they mean that to be moral and to stand for the ethos of one's culture means to stand for certain determinate commandments, codes, or principles which hold for all men. Any society which takes as its ethos the thesis that all men are equal under the law is one holding this Kantian, a priori, and ethical, or the classical Greek and Stoic Roman natural-law, theory of cultural values as values expressed in determinate universal laws.

This concept of cultural values has its basis in a particular conception of the method of scientific knowledge, namely, the method of deductively formulated scientific theory. The reason for this is that, in such a scientific method, no fact is ever supposed to be anything more than an enigma still to be scientifically accounted for, if it is to be given merely inductively. Before it can take on the status of a scientific fact, it must, according to this deductive theory of scientific method, be embodied in a deductively formulated theory. In other words, it must be shown to be an instance of a universal, determinate law. It is not an accident that Kelsen conceives of positive law as deductively formulated or that Kant, who is the author of the categorical imperative, was a physicist who had mastered the deductively formulated mathematical physics of Galileo and Newton before he wrote his moral philosophy. In fact, it is only in Kant's philosophy of mathematical physics, with its theory of any individual as an instance of a determinate universal law, that he can find the basis for his categorical imperative.

This theory of cultural values as things expressed in terms of determinate statutes and laws is also culture-bound. It characterizes the entire legal history of the Western world since the creation of Western law by the Roman Stoic philosophers. This concept of law, these lawyers tell us, derived straight through Greek philosophy from Greek physics. In fact, it was in ancient Greek physics that, for the first time, men on this earth arrived at the conception of man and nature in which every individual event and thing is thought of as scientifically known, only when it is imbedded in an abstractly constructed, deductively formulated theory.

To be sure, before this there had been codes expressing the cultural values of different societies in the world, but these codes were not technically formulated. They were expressed in concrete, inductively given language, and they were codes which restricted citizenship under the law to membership in a patriarchal joint family or to membership in a village community of elders or to membership in a blood-bound tribe.

Only following the discovery by the ancient Greek mathematical physicists of a new way of knowing man and nature as an instance of universal laws having nothing to do with inductively given family or tribal relations, did the concept of cultural values expressed in terms of abstractly constructed constitutions interpreted by means of a technical legal terminology arise. As the student of ancient law, Sir Henry S. Maine, has put the matter, the shift was made "from Status to Contract." The significance of his meaning becomes clear if we express it as the shift from inductively given family or tribe to theoretically constructed status under universal law in a deductively formulated, contractually written, constitution or theory. Upon this conception of cultural values as things expressed in universal, theoretically constructed, determinate laws, the Greek and Roman natural-law jurists and Kantian and Kelsenian ethical jurists are in agreement.

But this conception of cultural values is restricted largely to the cultures of the West and to Islam, in so far as it has drawn on Greek science and philosophy. In pre-Western Confucian Chinese culture, for example, there are, to be sure, codes, but they are of the inductive, natural-history, concrete type. Furthermore, they are used only as a last resort. Instead of being the good way to settle disputes, required by the ethos of their culture, they are used only when the good way prescribed by the ethos of a Confucian culture is not accepted by the disputants. The proper procedure for dispute-handling in a Confucian Chinese culture is not recourse to codes, after the manner of the Western concept of justice, but the softening of the insistence upon codified rights through the intervention of a mediator. Again we see the degree to which any theory of cultural values is bound both to a given culture and to the philosophy of that culture.

Notwithstanding the correctness of its thesis that the ought expressed in the ethos of any culture cannot be identified with the inductively given is of the total behavior of people in that culture, the Kantian ethics, with its absolute insistence upon the impossibility of deriving the ought from the is, has turned out to be incomplete and at bottom inadequate. This becomes evident the moment a judge in a Western court tries to use it. To tell him that he has to use an ought and that this ought must have the property of being expressible as a universal law is of little use to him in deciding a case; for the decision turns around whether this determinate, universal, propositionalized ought is to have one content rather than another. To be more precise, is it to be given the content of a laissez faire, a nationalized Socialistic, a Thomistic Roman Catholic, or a Communistic communal ethos? To such a crucial question Kelsenian and Kantian ethical legal and cultural science can give no answer. In practice, therefore, it leaves judicial decision completely relativistic and arbitrary. It also leaves anthropological legal and cultural science generally with nothing whatever to say with respect to the solution of the normative conflicts of the contemporary world.

FUNCTIONAL ANTHROPOLOGICAL OR SOCIOLOGICAL JURISPRUDENCE

The essence of functional anthropological or sociological jurisprudence is that a distinction must be drawn between the positive law and the living law. By "positive law" is meant the inductively given constitution, codes, and institutions and cases of Austin's and Kelsen's positivistic jurisprudence. By "living law" is meant the underlying inner order of the behavior of people in society, apart from the universal statutes, codes, and cases of the positive law. The thesis of sociological jurisprudence is that the good norm for the positive law to be used by the judge in making his decision is to be found by identifying it with the inner order of the anthropologically and sociologically given is of men in the society in question. Positive law is good if it corresponds to the underlying inner order of society as given by sociology or anthropology; it is bad if it does not so correspond. Since the inner order of society has content and varies often from one society to another, this theory of cultural values has the merit of giving to the judge who is operating his positive legal institutions a norm possessing content. He is not left with merely an abstract, vacuous, empty universal concept of justice, after the manner of the follower of the Kantian or Kelsenian autonomous ethical jurisprudence.

It is to be noted that this sociological jurisprudential theory completely rejects the thesis of Kant and Kelsen that the ought can never be identified with

any is. Sociological jurisprudence shows the sense in which the neo-Kantian doctrine is true and the sense in which it is false. The truth of the doctrine consists in the fact that the ought of the positive law cannot be derived from the is of positive law. The mere fact of the Constitution of the United States, with its particular norms and positive legal institutions, is no justification for the ought of that constitution and its institutions. The Kantian and Kelsenian jurisprudence is correct, therefore, in the thesis that the ought of a given subject cannot be derived from the is of that same subject. Thus an ought for positive law cannot be derived from the is of the positive law. But it does not follow from this that the ought of positive law cannot be derived from the is of something else.

It is at this point that the a priori Kelsenian and Kantian theory of cultural values committed the error which left it with nothing but an abstract, empty a priori. To get content, one must go to some subject matter. The pure abstract a priori notion of a universal norm can never give specific content. Specific content, by its very nature, has to be provided by an is. This means that the ought presupposes an is.

Nor does this present any difficulty. Clearly, it presents difficulty only for a person who insists upon restricting cultural values to an autonomous science of ethics or law. Then, clearly, the ought for the subject matter of that science cannot be identified with its is, and the Kantian-Kelsenian theory holds true. But why suppose that the ethical character of society lives in hothouse isolation from the rest of society and culture? Why assume that the positive law must be separated from the living law of the inner order of the society to which it refers?

To put the matter positively, let us assume that positive law can be constructed in terms of universal norms by any kind of positive hypothesis for society that the imaginations of men can construct. Clearly, the ought for any one of these hypotheses cannot be derived from the positive hypothesis itself. Thus, in this sense, the impossibility of deriving the ought of the positive law from the is of any inductively given positive law holds. But this does not prevent the criterion of the ought for the positive law from being derived from the inductively given is of the inner order of the behavior of people in society, quite apart from any given present or proposed positive law.

Prohibition legislation in the United States some few decades ago provides an instance. This legislation was legally passed. Hence, so far as positive law was concerned, it was an is. It happened, however, that it failed to correspond to the living-law habits of the people of the community. Hence it became a dead letter and was repudiated. Here the is of positive law was measured against the is of living law and found wanting. Thus sociological and anthropological jurisprudence teaches us that any adequate theory of cultural values must both distinguish the ought from the is and identify the ought with the is. This presents no contradiction or difficulty whatever, provided that one distinguishes between the different social manifestations of the is: one, the is of positive legal constitutions, codes, and institutions, and the other the is of the *de facto* inner order of the behavior of people in a specific society, independent of the positive law. To identify the is of the positive law with its ought is clearly a fallacy. But this in no way prevents the definition of the ought of the positive law in terms of the is of the living law. Put more concretely, this means that that positive law ought to be which corresponds to the living law of the society to which it refers; that positive law ought not to

be which does not so correspond. In contemporary anthropology one finds this theory of cultural values exhibited in the functional anthropology of Malinowski. It is also illustrated in the anthropology of cultural patterns of Kroeber and Benedict.

In practice, however, this sociological or anthropological jurisprudence and the anthropology and sociology of which it is the expression have turned out to be harder to put into practice than to write about in theory. This weakness is not discovered by the sociologists or anthropologists who hold the theory, since they never become the judges who have to apply it. In the Yale Law School, however, holders of this theory have been forced to bring it down to concrete application. One person who has done this is the late Professor Underhill Moore. In practice, he found no two sociological jurists to agree upon what the inner order or pattern of a given society was, which the judge is to use in judging the positive law. All too often, as Underhill Moore showed, they identified the inner order of the sociological is with their own particular, pet theory of political and social reform. One suspects also that the intuitive pattern which one anthropologist "finds" in Japanese culture might not be that found by another.

As a result, Underhill Moore found himself forced to determine the inner order of society of the sociological and anthropological is, which the jurist is to use to judge whether his positive-law universal norms are good or bad, by throwing away the intuitive, synoptic method of describing society of the traditional anthropologists and sociologists, who emphasized pattern, and by introducing an analytic, objective method grounded in the behavioristic psychology of Professor Clark Hull. He did this because he found, when he used the traditional method, that no two observers describing the same social pattern came out with the same description. To overcome this difficulty of the classical anthropological and sociological theory of cultural values, he introduced purely objective spatiotemporal descriptive concepts. When this was done, he found that different observers gave the same account of the inner order of the society which they investigated.

There is not time to go into the details of his system here. Suffice it to say that it consisted in defining the inner order of society as the high-frequency portion of the objectively observed spatiotemporal total behavior of society. This provided a truly objective criterion of the inner order of the sociological is, which is to be used by the lawyer to judge whether the positive law ought or ought not to be. That positive law which corresponds to the high-frequency behavior of the total behavior of people in society is, on this theory of cultural values of sociological and anthropological jurisprudence, the positive law that ought to be; the positive law that does not so correspond is the one that ought not to be. We have in this theory, therefore, the thesis that the ought of one kind of law, i.e., positive law, cannot be derived from the is of that law, but can be derived from the is of the underlying, empirically determinable, living law of an anthropological or sociological jurisprudence which uses an analytic objective method.

Underhill Moore saw, however, that even this is not enough to provide an adequate theory of cultural values. It is necessary, but it is not sufficient. In any society it is necessary to judge and to reform not merely the positive law but also the high-frequency behavior which is the inner order of the underlying living law. This is easy to see in the case of a foreign culture. The fact that the Germans, with an overwhelming, spontaneous enthusiasm, embraced

and followed Hitler in their living-law behavior will not be taken by most social scientists as a scientific justification for the thesis that such high-frequency behavior and the cultural norms which it embodied ought to be. In short, just as it is necessary to judge the is of the positive law against an ought beyond itself, so also it is necessary to judge the high-frequency behavior which is the is of the living law against an ought beyond itself.

Moreover, any society is not merely expressing its high-frequency living-law behavior but also reforming it. An adequate theory, therefore, of legal and cultural norms must provide meaning for judging the is of the living law to be bad or in need of reform. This calls for something beyond the living law itself. At this point, therefore, anthropological and sociological jurisprudence points beyond itself. The is which it provides cannot pass the judgment which must be passed upon itself. Beyond society and culture, only one thing remains, namely, nature.

NATURALISTIC JURISPRUDENCE

The thesis of naturalistic jurisprudence is that, just as the positive law cannot find the meaning for its ought in the is which is the positive law itself but must be judged as to its ought against the is of the living law of anthropological and sociological jurisprudence, so similarly the living law of anthropological and sociological jurisprudence cannot find the criterion for its ought in the is which is the living law or pattern of culture itself but can be judged only from the standpoint of the is of something beyond itself, namely, the inner order of nature as revealed by natural science. We have already found an illustration of this theory in the account of the concept of moral man as an instance of a universal law, as formulated by Roman Stoic lawyers and given to them through Greek philosophy by Greek natural science. Put more concretely, the theory is that, just as the ought for positive-law legal codes is the is of the inner order of society as specified by anthropological and sociological science, so the ought toward which this inner order of society is to be changed is the is of the inner order of natural man and nature as determined by the philosophically analyzed and articulated, empirically verified, knowledge of nature. It was, we have noted, the discovery by Greek mathematical physicists that true knowledge of any individual object or event involves understanding it as an instance of determinate universal laws in a deductively formulated theory that gave rise to the Western concept of moral and legal man as a citizen of nature rather than as a citizen of a patriarchal joint family or of a tribe, which, in turn, generated Western Roman legal universalism, with its thesis that all men, regardless of family, color, race, or religion, are equal under the law. This is something novel in the cultures of the world.

Asian cultures, to be sure, also achieve universalism, but it is of a different kind, relating all men to nature by intuitive immersion rather than by technically constructed constitutions in which all men are equal under the universal determinate codes. Because this Asian way of conceiving nature is verified empirically, it is as much a scientific theory as are the theories of the West. Whether the moral or legal classics of a given culture do or do not describe its sages as physicists has little, if anything, to do with the question as to whether its values are verified by appeal to nature. The Chinese classics make little or no reference to scientists. Nevertheless, as Needham and others have shown recently, the Chinese cultural values refer to nature for their source and verification.

A major consideration leading to this naturalistic theory of cultural values is the failure of recent attempts to find the ought for judging the high frequency of the living law of anthropological and sociological jurisprudence within the latter type of jurisprudence itself. Such attempts tried to identify the ought for judging today's scientifically determined inner order or pattern of culture with the is of tomorrow's inner order. To make such a theory succeed, it is necessary to be able today to determine what the inner order of tomorrow's society will be. For this, a historical social determinism is necessary. This is the reason, for example, why the Marxist theory of cultural values employs and requires a deterministic theory of social evolution. Underhill Moore also attempted such a theory. Both attempts, however, fail, as Underhill Moore in his case recognized.

The Communists' attempt consisted in using what they call the "dialectical deterministic theory of history." The necessity for this, if the evolution of Western civilization is to be explained, is obvious. The inner order of society as conceived by the ethos of the Holy Roman Empire, for example, is quite different from the inner order of society as conceived by the laissez faire ethos of nineteenth-century United States. The latter ethos is, in turn, different from that of the recent British Labour government or of the Marxist Soviet Russians. Such antitheses convinced Hegel and the Marxists following Hegel that historical evolution cannot proceed according to the traditional logic of identity. No logic of identity can deduce, from a given set of premises, the contradictory or antithesis of those premises. For example, from the thesis which designates the norms of the ethos of the Holy Roman Empire, one cannot, by the formal logic of identity, deduce the ethos of nineteenth-century laissez faire United States, nor can one from this ethos deduce that of the British Labour government, to say nothing about that of the Marxist Communists. The propositions which would describe these four inner orders of society are clearly, on certain basic points, mutually contradictory. Hegel and the Communists following him conclude, therefore, quite correctly, that, if there is a historical determinism in society, it must proceed by the logic of negation and not by the logic of identity. A process governed by negation is, by definition, dialectical. Hence, the Hegelian and Marxist dialectical determinism.

But calling dialectical evolution "deterministic" does not make it so. In fact, an evolution of culture which is dialectical clearly cannot be deterministic. To be dialectically deterministic, the negation of a thesis in time must generate one and only one antithesis. The negation of a given thesis, however, does not give rise to one and only one antithesis. One can negate the basic legal norms of the Holy Roman Empire in many different ways. It follows automatically, therefore, that a cultural evolution which is dialectical cannot be deterministic. Thus the Hegelian and Marxist attempt to find the ought for judging the inner order of today's society in the is, determinable today, of the inner order of tomorrow's society fails.

Underhill Moore's attempt rested on the logic of identity. He took physical science as his model at this point. Physical science does have a determinism in the sense that, given its postulates and a determination of the values of the present state of a physical system, T_1, one can at the present time, T_1, logically deduce the inner order of that same system at any later time, T_2—tomorrow, the day after tomorrow, or ten years from tomorrow. Underhill Moore, therefore, attempted, by the use of Clark Hull's behavioristic psychology, to set up a deductively formulated theory of anthropological and sociological jurisprudence, from which, given the high-frequency behavior of today's society, he could deduce that for tomorrow. He found that he was able to make the deduction only if he assumed the norms for tomorrow's order. In short, the deterministic method of connecting the inner order of the present state to the inner order of future states in cultural systems presupposes tomorrow's norms and hence cannot define them. Thus this method of finding a meaning within the cultural sciences alone for the ought to be used to judge the is of today's inner order or value pattern also fails.

It is to be noted in this connection that the most exact of the social sciences that we have today, namely, economics, has never been able to achieve a theoretical dynamics. In other words, it has not been able to deduce tomorrow's state of the economic system from today's. There are basic theoretical reasons why this must be the case. The attempt, therefore, to find the criterion for judging and reforming the inner order of today's society must be found in an is with content outside today's society. This is why the sociological and anthropological theory of cultural values leads inevitably into the naturalistic theory.

This does not mean that anthropology and sociology can be dispensed with. Quite the contrary. It means, instead, that there will be no adequate anthropological or sociological theory of cultural values and of the cultural methods for judging such values until anthropological and sociological science pays as much attention to the way in which members of any society know and conceptualize nature as it has given in the past to the inner order of social relations, which, as we shall see, is in major part the result of the conceptualization of nature.

Some sociological and anthropological scientists have recently come to this same conclusion. It will be fruitful to approach their work from that of the sociologist of law, Underhill Moore. His method of determining the inner order of society even at the present time, T_1, of the system, by observing the spatio-temporal total high-frequency behavior of people in society is unworkable for a total culture. He applied it to simple cultural phenomena, such as parking on a restricted block on a street in New Haven, Connecticut. To determine the inner order of the behavior of four hundred million Chinese in this manner is out of the question, and to do it for all the different cultures is even more impracticable. The same is roughly true of most of the other inductive methods of other schools of anthropological and sociological science, since they tend to be either so intuitive in their methods for determining the inner order of society that there is, as Underhill Moore noted, not sufficient agreement among them on what it is, or else their methods are so inductively piecemeal that the inner order of society is not exhibited.

At this point the cultural anthropology of Kluckhohn is exceedingly important. He found in his study of the Navaho Indians that no amount of inductive observation, however complete, gave him an understanding of their value system or their legal norms. It was not until he conceptualized the inductive facts which he saw in terms of the concepts which the Navahos themselves used to conceptualize these facts that their cultural values became evident and that the norms which they use for settling disputes followed logically and naturally. Furthermore, he found that, when their concepts were brought out into the open, he had a complete philosophy on his hands. Without this philosophy, the facts which he saw were not understood as the Navaho understood them, and the norms which

they use for settling disputes were not grasped, nor did they make sense.

Sorokin found the same thing earlier in sociology. He showed that the inner order which defines the *de facto* living law of any society is determined by the philosophy of the people in that society. This is the point of Sorokin's thesis —that causality in the cultural sciences is logico-meaningful rather than merely mechanical, as in natural science. The meanings which its people bring to the raw data of their experience are what determine the inner order or pattern of any particular culture. In fact, there are no objective bonds between people observable from an airplane which give their culture a pattern. The word "pattern" is merely a figure of speech. Only when many people conceptualize the raw data of their experience with the same basic, consistently related concepts, i.e., the same philosophy, does an "inner order" between them arise.

In other words, norms arise from knowledge, and knowledge involves conceptualizing and propositionalizing the experience that is known. Now philosophy is nothing but the name for the basic minimum and complete number of consistent concepts and propositions necessary to conceptualize the inductive data of experience. It appears, therefore, that the values of a culture are the fruits of living according to the basic philosophical assumptions used by a people in conceptualizing the raw data of their experience.

In short, the inner order of a given society is put upon an objectively determinable basis only when anthropological and sociological scientists not merely observe in the field as many facts as possible but also discover the philosophy used by the people in the culture in question to conceptualize those facts. If, moreover, at bottom, as in the Hindu and Moslem communities in a village of India, two different philosophies are used, then to that extent one is confronted with two cultures rather than with one.

It may be asked immediately: But how can one determine the philosophy of a culture in an objective way? To this the answer is twofold. First, the philosophy of the Navaho discovered and specified by Kluckhohn involves concepts quite foreign to those of the non-Navaho American culture from which he came. In this sense the philosophy of a culture other than one's own is surprisingly objective. Second, most cultures have their philosophy already present objectively in the basic treatises of the culture. Those of pre-Western Chinese philosophy are objectively present in the classics of Confucius and Mencius. Chiang Monlin has recently shown, through a description of his own childhood, the degree to which this Confucian philosophy infiltrated every nook and cranny of his early life. It appears, therefore, that an objective, workable, anthropological, and sociological science which can define the inner order or ethos of any culture must be not merely inductive with respect to the facts but also inductive with respect to the philosophical concepts used by the people in the society being studied for the conceptualization of those facts. In short, scientific anthropology and sociology must be an empirically verified, philosophical sociology and anthropology.

Kluckhohn and others demonstrate also that the inductive method must be that which supplements mere induction with deductively formulated theory. This is necessary because philosophical anthropology and sociology exhibit different cultures as different postulate sets for conceptualizing the raw data of experience.

But this philosophical sociological and anthropological science of cultural values leads straight over into natural-law jurisprudence and the philosophy of natural science as a criterion of cultural values. This comes out when Sorokin and Kluckhohn reveal that the concepts which the people in a given society use to define their legal and ethical norms and to generate their creatively constructed values arise from and are essentially connected with their inductive, empirically verified theories for conceptualizing nature.

If, for example, in the conceptualization of merely natural facts, quite apart from cultural and social phenomena, a people restrict themselves only to those meanings given through the senses, then the cultural values of that people tend to be those of what Sorokin calls "a sensate culture." If, on the other hand, in the conceptualization of natural phenomena they resort to what we today call "constructs" or to what Plato and Aristotle called "ideas" which are universals, that is, to concepts of individuals which have no meaning apart from universal scientific laws or postulates, then a people tend to free themselves from family- or tribally centered values of the more natural-history mode of knowing nature of a more sensate or of a more Asian intuitive culture. Similarly, Florence Kluckhohn, in her attempt to find a scientific principle for classifying the diverse cultural values of the many different cultures, finds herself forced to use the concepts of space and of time. Now these concepts are clearly concepts of natural science. More concrete examples can be given if one approaches nature by restricting one's self largely to what is given purely impressionistically, or by what Chiang Monlin, describing Chinese mentality, calls "naïve observation." Then what impresses one is the sequence from darkness of night through dawn to the brightness of day, through dusk to the blackness of night again, the sequence of the seasons and of the cycles of human existence. Thus one is led by one's empirically verified, and hence scientific, theory to a cyclical theory of time, in which time is regarded, not as something made quantitatively exact by astronomical measurements and calculations, but as something intuitively and impressionistically vague. Then appointments are rarely kept in social relations with the precision that occurs in the United States. Also this impressionistic cyclical theory of time in nature tends also to make the improvement of society pointless, since reform and improvement merely hasten the time when what is different from today becomes identical with what one has today.

This inevitable intrusion of the empirically verified concepts of nature used by a people into their values and norms for culture appears in our own time in another way. The Marxists and countless others have pointed out the manner in which the social and political and other values of society change with a change in technological instruments. But what is this but the effect of man's scientifically verified abstract theories of nature upon the norms and inner ordering relations of culture?

It appears, therefore, that an inventory of the major theories of cultural values as exhibited in contemporary legal, sociological, and anthropological science leads to the conclusion that each one of these theories has something to say for itself and that none alone is the whole truth. Unless cultural values are expressed in the positive law, the anthropological and sociological jurisprudential theory of cultural values can never be brought to bear in the concrete legal dispute or case. But, unless the positive law is referred to the living law of sociological jurisprudence, there is no criterion enabling the jurist to choose between one content of the positive law rather than another in his judging of any dispute. And unless sociological jurisprudence becomes philosophical and its philosophy in turn is tested against the concepts used by a people to know, integrate, and envisage themselves and nature, there is no criterion for judging or reforming the living law of anthropological and sociological jurisprudence. To inventory in a way that gives the meaning of what is inventoried is also to integrate.

BIBLIOGRAPHY

For the bibliography of the legal theories see the works indicated below. Since the corresponding anthropological theories of cultural values are well known to anthropologists, the bibliography of them is not included here.

POUND, ROSCOE. 1943. *Outlines of Lectures on Jurisprudence.* Cambridge: Harvard University Press.

FRIEDMANN, W. 1949. *Legal Theory.* 2d ed. London: Stevens & Sons, Ltd.

NORTHROP, F. S. C. (ed.). 1949. *Ideological Differences and World Order.* New Haven: Yale University Press.

———. 1952. "Contemporary Jurisprudence and International Law," *Yale Law Journal* (May), pp. 623–54.

NEEDHAM, JOSEPH. 1951. *Human Law and the Laws of Nature in China and the West.* London: Oxford University Press.

MAINE, SIR HENRY S. 1908. *Ancient Law.* London: John Murray.

KELSEN, HANS. 1946. *General Theory of Law and State.* Cambridge, Mass.: Harvard University Press.

EHRLICH, EUGEN. 1936. *Fundamental Principles of the Sociology of Law.* Cambridge, Mass.: Harvard University Press.

MOORE, UNDERHILL, and CALLAHAN, CHARLES C. 1943. *Law and Learning Theory: A Study in Legal Control.* New Haven: Yale Law Journal Co., Inc.

CHIANG MONLIN. 1947. *Tides from the West.* New Haven: Yale University Press.

COHEN, FELIX. 1935. *Ethical Systems and Legal Ideals: An Essay on the Foundation of Legal Criticism.* New York: Falcon Press.

——. 1937–38. "The Problems of a Functional Jurisprudence," *Modern Law Review,* I, 5.

COHEN, MORRIS R. 1931. *Reason and Nature,* pp. 333–457. New York: Harcourt, Brace & Co.

——. 1932. "Philosophy and Legal Science," *Colorado Law Review,* XXXII, 1103.

——. 1933. *Law and the Social Order* New York: Harcourt, Brace & Co.

The Concept of Value in Modern Anthropology

By DAVID BIDNEY

MODERN ANTHROPOLOGISTS have been so concerned with establishing the claim that their science is a natural, as well as a social, science that they have tended until recently to overlook the problem of values. As natural scientists, anthropologists were supposed to deal with facts and laws and to leave values to the philosophers and humanists. A historical survey of anthropological thought reveals that this attitude is a comparatively modern development and was not at all characteristic of the founders of anthropological science.

I. MODERN RATIONALISM AND THE IDEA OF PROGRESS

The concept of the continuity of culture history, involving progressive development from a lower to a higher degree of culture, was not original with Tylor and may be traced back to the rationalists of the age of Enlightenment. Their characteristic doctrine of the perfectibility of man in time implied that cultural progress was dependent upon man's rational efforts to perfect himself and his institutions. Culture or civilization was recognized as the instrument evolved by man, under divine providence, for the perfecting of humanity. Man was conceived as the creator of his cultural destiny, and there were thought to be no limits to his ability to transform the inherited, historical-cultural order in the light of newly emerging moral ideals. By living in harmony with the fixed laws of human nature and the order of cosmic nature, man could regulate his individual and social life in accordance with the dictates of reason so as to promote universal peace and the general happiness of mankind. Rousseau notwithstanding, the arts and sciences were appreciated as instruments for the progress of humanity rather than as impediments which corrupt and hinder human intelligence. In Germany, in particular, the concept of culture (*Cultur* or *Kultur*) was contrasted with Rousseau's deification of nature and the cult of sophisticated primitivism.

This humanistic conception of man as the creator and transformer of his culture implied a distinction between the fixed order of nature and the variable order of human culture. While nature herself was conceived as increasing in perfection through divine creativity in time, this meant only a gradual increment of forms of being, but no essential transformation in the order of nature as a whole. But in the sphere of human culture, which was manmade, there was continuous progress and transformation in the very organization of human life and society, as well as in the number and variety of human inventions and discoveries.

Once it became apparent that culture was a natural process and that man was, by nature, a self-perfecting, culture-producing animal, then philosophers and historians attempted to describe the "natural history" of man from "rudeness" to civilization. The concept of natural history, as originally utilized by Vico, Herder, Rousseau, and Ferguson, involved the assumption of the continuity of cultural development from savagery to civilization. Culture history was progressive precisely because it was continuous and did not involve any radical breaks with the past. This meant also that time was an essential factor in the evolution of human culture and that time made for progress.

The idea of progress which the eighteenth-century of philosophers generally accepted was also combined with an antithetical theory of history which assumed the essential discontinuity of history and the comparatively stationary character of time. As rationalists, they glorified their own age of Enlightenment and prophesied an even greater era of human progress in the future, while deploring the vice, ignorance, and superstition of the past, such as the Middle Ages. Man was indeed perfectible, but progress was not inevitable and required eternal vigilance and constantly renewed effort, lest the opposing forces of darkness and deception gain the ascendancy once more. Gibbon had demonstrated in his *Decline and Fall* how civilization had declined from the high point it had reached in the second century and how long and difficult had been the task of recovering from the triumph of barbarism and superstition. The constant factor in history was human nature, and it was conceived to be the task of the historian to demonstrate the universal principles of human nature as they manifest themselves in the course of historical experience.

In agreement with their rationalistic, Aristotelian, and Stoic interpretation of the state of man's nature as being an ideal rational state conforming to the dictates of common sense and morality, the eighteenth-century philosophers could reinterpret the concept of natural history. Following the Stoic maxim that to live in conformity with nature is to live in accord with the dictates of reason, one may argue that natural history is rational history. Natural history, morality, and reason coincide, so that the historian may differentiate those historical processes and institutions which are "natural," in the sense of being in accord with the requirements of human nature and reason, from those which he designates as "unnatural," because he evaluates them as being contrary to human nature and reason. In this way the philosopher-historian can moralize about "progress" and "retrogression" in culture history and can appeal to history for justification of his moral principles. Thus, in place of the old dichotomy of the "state of nature" versus the state of civilization, there is introduced the duality of natural cultural history and "natural laws," on the one hand, and arbitrary, "unnatural" cultural conventions which interfere with, or contravene, natural law and natural history, on the other.

This mode of thought may be exemplified by Adam Smith's discussion of "the natural progress of opulence" in his *Wealth of Nations*. Smith was prepared to generalize that the natural course of things invariably led to similar stages of economic development from agriculture, through manufacturing, to foreign trade in every society. Natural necessity and the natural inclinations of man combined to produce this rational economic sequence, but governments tend to interfere with this natural order and to produce an unnatural, retrograde order which gives precedence to manufactures and foreign

trade. Thus we have the beginning of
what Dugald Stewart called "theoretical or conjectural history" which de-
duces the probable stages of culture
history from a psychological analysis of
the normal lines of development for
rational men. This comparative-histori-
cal method of historical reconstruction
was developed systematically by the
nineteenth-century cultural anthropologists. The thesis that natural history is
also rational history was taken over by
the cultural evolutionists, and this accounts for their preoccupation with the
fixed and necessary stages of cultural
development from the simple and irrational to the complex and rational.

On the whole, the predominant tendency of eighteenth-century anthropological thought was to emphasize the discontinuities of culture history and to
abstract historical experiences in order
to demonstrate their various theoretical
analyses. The chronological order of
events and actual historical origins
were not essential, and hypothetical
history would do where actual records
were not available. The ultimate objective was a normative, moral, cultural
science of man, based upon inductive
generalizations concerning the nature
of man, which would prescribe the
ideal conditions of human virtue and
happiness suitable to the "proper state
of man's nature."

II. POSITIVISM AND THE ORIGIN
OF THE SOCIAL SCIENCES

With the advent of the Darwinian
theory of biological evolution and with
the introduction of new archeological
evidence bearing upon the antiquity of
man, the quest for human origins was
revived. Unlike the seventeenth- and
eighteenth-century thinkers, the nineteenth-century culture historians and
ethnologists were interested in the natural history of cultural development
as an end in itself. Ethnology, as Tylor,
Lubbock, Maine, and Morgan under-

stood it, was essentially a historical discipline and was that part of culture
history especially concerned with the
culture of pre-literate peoples.

Under the influence of the positivistic philosophy of science deriving
from Comte, evolutionary ethnologists
professed an interest in discovering the
psychological laws underlying the culture history of mankind. That is, the
nineteenth-century ethnologists, unlike
the eighteenth-century social philosophers, did not appeal directly to the
empirical and introspective evidence
of individual psychological phenomena
or to selected records of history for inductive generalizations of human nature. Like Comte, their approach was
primarily historical and social, and they
hoped to arrive at a knowledge of
man's nature through a comparative
study of culture history. Psychological
laws were to be discovered as the final
product of the study of comparative
culture history, and they were not to
be regarded as the presuppositions of
historical study. Man was to be known
through a study of culture history, not
culture history through a study of man.

Furthermore, the evolutionary ethnologists sought to evaluate the natural
history of culture and the stages of cultural progress. They were interested
not only in the mental and spiritual
development of mankind but also in
the comparative development of the
arts, customs, and social institutions in
historical societies. While Tylor still
spoke of ethnology as essentially a reformer's science, just as the eighteenth-
century philosophers had thought, his
proximate interest was in theory rather
than in practice. The first objective of
the ethnologist was to describe and
evaluate the stages of cultural evolution and the historical sequence of
modes of thought and action in the various types of culture. In the course of
his historical researches, Tylor came
upon cultural phenomena which he

termed "survivals" of a previous age in which they had ethno-functional significance. This meant that the ethnologist could, after all, exercise an indirect, practical function by indicating the ethno-historical origins of extant folkloristic myths, superstitions, and obsolete customs. By making people conscious of the anachronistic character of these cultural survivals, the way would be prepared for eventual cultural reform. But the cultural anthropologist considered himself primarily a natural scientist interested in the cultural evolution of man and in the mental laws underlying cultural development.

Modern ethnological thought has been built largely upon the foundations of Comtean positivism. Tylor was much influenced by Comte's conception of a natural history of mankind, subject to laws of growth comparable to those of physics. Tylor felt, however, that in the present state of knowledge the data were insufficient for the construction of a general philosophy of history, although he admitted in principle the possibility of a natural science of human culture history. If law was anywhere, it was everywhere.

Thus the laws of nature as manifested in culture history replaced the wisdom of man and the providence of God as the conditions of human evolution and progress. Like the Stoics of old, the social scientists urged man to conform to nature, but the nature they asked man to conform to was a historical nature, not one fixed and eternal. By conforming to the laws of history and to the rational, scientific ideals indicated therein, man would be certain of achieving the ultimate goal of civilization as a self-conscious agent of nature. Their guiding principle was that of a progressive development in history, in contrast to any theory of degeneration from a more advanced to a less advanced stage.

III. EVOLUTIONARY POSITIVISM AND THE EVALUATION OF PROGRESS

As was mentioned previously, modern ethnological thought has been greatly influenced by the positivistic philosophy of science of Comte. It remains to indicate how positivism affected the evaluation of the idea of progress itself.

While the eighteenth-century philosophers did indeed speak of progress and of the perfectibility of man, progress was, for them, measured by the growth of rationalism in all phases of culture. Hence they were opposed to the authority of tradition, especially that of the Christian church, and all forms of supernaturalism and myth. Everything had to be within the limits of reason. They were not opposed to theology and metaphysics as such, provided that they were in accord with the evidence of the senses and the arguments of natural reason.

According to positivism, the concept of progress had to be sharply redefined and re-evaluated. Intellectual progress was measured by the Comtean law of the three stages, namely, from theology, through metaphysics, to positive science. This meant that progress was evaluated as a linear process from a primitive to a final stage of civilization, in the course of which man evolved out of theology and metaphysics. The stage of positive science was thought to be incompatible with theological and metaphysical thought. Culture history was interpreted as essentially a rational process, involving development from prescientific to scientific thought. The institutions of a culture were held to correspond to the mental stage achieved by a given society.

Thus, in taking over the positivistic philosophy of science and philosophy of culture history, the evolutionary ethnologists also assumed the value theory which positivism presupposed. This may be illustrated by Frazer's thesis that the development of primitive thought was from magic, through religion, to science. Frazer differed from Comte only in his suggestion that science was not necessarily the final stage of mental development and that some new, and as yet unknown, mental stage was possible and conceivable.

IV. TYLOR AND THE EVALUATION OF RELIGION

The positivistic value theory presupposed in evolutionary ethnology is perhaps best exemplified in Tylor's analysis of the origin and evolution of religion. In his *Primitive Culture* Tylor maintained that animism, the belief in spiritual beings, was the primary form of religion. He assumed that primitive man arrived at this dualistic philosophy of religion through observing the difference between the living organism and the corpse and inferring that there must be some vital entity in the former which was lacking in the latter. Furthermore, the savage's experience of dreams might provide another source from which he could derive the notion of souls as being ethereal images of bodies. Tylor suggested that primitive man combined, or associated, the two types of experience into the idea of a ghost-soul common to man, animals, and some objects.

The significant point in Tylor's interpretation of religion in primitive culture is that he bases religious belief upon a psychological delusion and mistaken logical inference. Primitive man is said to confuse subjective and objective reality, ideal and real objects. The evolution of religious thought from pluralistic animism, or even from pre-animism as Marett suggested, to the monotheism of civilized peoples is therefore based on an initial delusion concerning the objective reality of souls independent of bodies. On this premise,

religion is incompatible with a genuinely realistic, scientific mentality. While there is progressive evolution within religion itself from the primitive amoral spirits, demons, and nature-powers up to the moral deity of civilized peoples, the rational course of cultural development indicates, as Frazer so clearly realized, that religion is a passing phase of human culture destined to be superseded by the scientific antimetaphysical mentality of the future. Man evolves out of religion and into science, or whatever the stage which may supersede science.

It is of interest to note in this connection that the evolutionary ethnologists differentiated rather sharply between religious belief and moral values. In accordance with their positivistic thesis, they assumed that religion was essentially a delusion, though having pragmatic value in enabling primitive and prescientific man to face the crises of life; but moral values were held to be objective and to provide a valid criterion for measuring and evaluating progress in culture. Thus Tylor speaks of progress and degeneration in civilization and of the partial deterioration of moral virtues in urban life. The positive science of man in society called for a science of moral laws and for the moral evaluation of culture history.

When Andrew Lang (1909) and, later, Father Schmidt (1931) objected to Tylor's thesis of the unilinear development of religion from animism and pointed out that the concept of a high god was to be found in the most primitive cultures, Tylor replied that such notions must have been derived through acculturation and as a result of contact between natives and civilized individuals, such as missionaries, since his evolutionary theory precluded such beliefs at the primitive level. For Tylor, the more coherent and nobler ideals had to develop out of the less coherent and morally deficient beliefs. Lang and

Schmidt, on the other hand, were prepared to grant that the concept of a supreme deity or high god may have originated as a direct result of primitive man's reflections upon the order of nature and that the evolution of religion may have been subject in many instances to a process of degeneration rather than of progress. The methodological significance of Lang's theory is that he derived faith in a high god from metaphysical, intellectual contemplation of nature and held this faith to be independent of the belief in spirits and ghosts which he, in agreement with Tylor, derived from animistic psychological experiences. This meant that for Lang and Schmidt the validity of faith in a supreme deity did not depend upon the psychological delusions of animistic thought, since the origin of the former was independent of the latter.

On the whole, I find that contemporary cultural anthropologists have been inclined to accept the Marett-Tylor-Frazer evolutionary interpretation of religion and to explain the origin and development of religion from a stage of pre-animism, through pluralistic animism, to monotheistic thought. Religion and mythology are, therefore, closely linked, since myths are but traditional rationalizations used to validate religious ritual—a thesis developed by Robertson-Smith in *The Religion of the Semites* and made current in modern ethnology by Boas and Malinowski. It is little wonder that contemporary cultural anthropologists find that religion is largely a lost cause and that its adherents in contemporary life are fighting a losing battle against the advance of science. In all fairness it may be said that modern cultural anthropology has contributed in large measure to this negative evaluation of religion. Religion is usually treated in the textbooks of anthropology as a branch of culture which is very significant for the study of primitive cultures and in the folklore

of all peoples but of little importance for the scientific anthropologists themselves, who have no need of such hypotheses. How to find substitutes for traditional religion, which will promote the feeling of solidarity and peace of mind which religion formerly produced, remains an unresolved ethnological problem.

V. CULTURAL PLURALISM AND THE AESTHETIC EVALUATION OF CULTURE PATTERNS

With the advent of the twentieth century, the thesis of the cultural evolutionist, that cultural development was always from the simple to the complex and from the amoral to the moral and that there were definite, fixed stages of cultural evolution making for cultural progress, was subjected to devastating criticism, especially by British and American ethnologists, such as Rivers and Boas. Boas, in particular, reacted rather sharply to the tendency of the evolutionists to set up scales of cultural progress applicable to all mankind and was, therefore, inclined to limit himself in practice to the study of particular cultures and to the diffusion of culture traits over given areas. Anthropology was understood as the study of particular cultures conceived as functional, integrated wholes rather than as the study of the evolution of the culture of mankind as a whole. In contrast to the monistic theory of cultural evolution involving mankind as a whole, Boas and his followers in America preferred a pluralistic theory of the history of cultures. The notion, accepted by Tylor, that our western European civilization represents the highest point of cultural development seemed to him obviously ethnocentric, and he therefore preferred the alternative of cultural pluralism and cultural relativity.

So far as the concept of progress was concerned, Boas admitted that there had been progress in technological achievements, as well as refinement and clarification in conceptual thought, but he denied that there had been any linear progress in the sphere of the arts, religion, and morality. In contrast to the certainty of the eighteenth-century rationalists and the nineteenth-century evolutionists that there was a rational norm of cultural progress, Boas and his followers were not all certain that there was any such rational and empirical criterion. According to *The Mind of Primitive Man*: "The evaluation of intellectual coordination of experience, of ethical concepts, artistic form, religious feeling is so subjective in character that an increment of cultural values cannot readily be defined." Progress was said to be relative to a special ideal, and absolute progress was denied. Boas was afraid that the tendency to value our own form of civilization as higher than that of the rest of mankind —a tendency which he equated with the ethnocentric actions of primitive man— would lead to nationalistic arrogance. Instead of laying down categorically a fixed scale of cultural values, he concluded that "the general theory of valuation of human activities, as developed by anthropological research, teaches us a higher tolerance than the one we now profess." In this respect, the attitude of American anthropologists coincided strikingly with the liberal and democratic climate of opinion of their culture.

While American anthropologists were critical of the theory of cultural progress, they continued, nevertheless, to think in terms of a positivistic, inductive philosophy of science and had little sympathy with philosophical systematization of culture history and with metaphysical concepts and norms. In practice, they carried on their field investigations and applied their cultural knowledge on the romantic assumption of an irreducible plurality of types of culture, each of which had an intrinsic value of its own, and therefore made no attempt, on principle, at a comparative evaluation of cultures.

Ruth Benedict's *Patterns of Culture* gave articulate expression to the accepted ethnological mode of thinking. Given historic cultures, whether literate or pre-literate, were regarded as aesthetic patterns or configurations, each of which is a legitimate expression of the potentialities of human nature. There is, it was held, no absolute normality or abnormality of social behavior; the abnormal is only that which is divergent from the cultural pattern of the community. For Benedict, as for Boas, a frank recognition of cultural equality and tolerance for the coexisting patterns of culture provide the only scientific basis for intercultural harmony. Her basic assumption is that there is a kind of Leibnitzian pre-established harmony of cultures which makes it possible for all to coexist together. This was essentially a pluralistic cultural world rather than the "one world" of which we hear so much nowadays. Although each culture was thought to be an integrated whole, revealing distinct patterns, such as the Apollonian and Dionysian patterns which she discerned in some native cultures, she did not think of the culture of humanity as constituting a possible integrated whole.

In retrospect, it appears that American anthropologists continued to reflect the prevailing attitude of their democratic society. As liberals and democrats, they merely accentuated tendencies inherent in their culture but professed to have derived their "higher tolerance" from a comparative study of primitive cultures. They uncritically assumed the value of cultural differences and their mutual compatibility. The idea of an "ethics of violence" (Sorel, 1925 and 1941) and of perpetual crises brought about through the conflict of social classes and national interests, which Marx and Sorel taught, did not enter into their peaceful scientific perspective at all. Had they thought in terms of the possible incompatibility and conflict of ideologies and of the doctrine of social revolution rather than of social evolution, they would not have labored under the naïve optimism of cultural laissez faire. It has taken the impact of the second World War to shake this romantic cultural optimism and to awaken anthropologists to the reality of cultural crises and to the need for cultural integration on a world scale.

VI. CULTURAL RELATIVISM AND THE TRANSVALUATION OF VALUES

In time, this aesthetic, romantic, and liberal attitude toward the variety of culture systems led to explicit avowal of a doctrine of cultural relativism. The sociologist Sumner gave classic expression to this thesis in his *Folkways* (1940, p. 79), when he stated that "the goodness or badness of mores consists entirely in their adjustment to the life conditions and the interests of the time and place." Among contemporary cultural anthropologists, Herskovits in particular has articulated the thesis of cultural relativism most explicitly. In *Man and His Works* he devotes an entire chapter to "The Problem of Cultural Relativism" and attempts to meet current criticism of this position. I shall, therefore, summarize briefly his main arguments in behalf of cultural relativism, with a view to indicating his basic presuppositions.

Ethnocentrism is defined as "the point of view that one's own way of life is to be preferred to all others" (Herskovits, 1948, p. 68). In so far as ethnocentrism is associated with a liberal, tolerant perspective which respects the rights of others to their own cultural values, it is apparently highly commendable; it becomes reprehensible when it is associated with intolerance of other culture systems.

From a philosophical perspective, it is extremely interesting to note that Herskovits, in common with "metalinguists" such as Whorf, adopts the thesis of historical idealism and quotes Cassirer with approval to corroborate his view that "experience is culturally defined" (Herskovits, 1948, p. 27). Reality as known is a function of culture. "Even the facts of the physical world are discerned through the enculturative screen so that the perception of time, distance, weight, size and other 'realities' is mediated by the conventions of any given group" (1948, p. 63). It is because Herskovits explicitly adopts the epistemological thesis of historical idealism that he is so uncompromising in his advocacy of cultural relativism. For him there is literally no other reality than cultural reality, and hence he maintains quite logically that the perspective of an individual is culturally conditioned by his cultural environment and that the only values which are acceptable to the individual are those which are relatively valid for his society at a given time. His basic thesis is that "evaluations are relative to the cultural background out of which they arise" (1948, p. 63).

Thus Herskovits maintains that the term "primitive" is not to be taken in the sense in which the evolutionary anthropologists understood it, namely, as an evaluative term implying the judgment that the culture of native peoples is inferior in quality to that of historic civilizations. If used at all, the term "primitive" should be employed descriptively as a synonym for nonliterate (1948, p. 75).

Herskovits distinguishes between cultural absolutes and cultural universals. There are cultural universals in the formal sense that there are universal types of institutions, such as the family and systems of morality—a thesis which Wissler and Malinowski had previously discussed. But the content of any given system of morality is conditioned by the historical-cultural experience of a society and hence is to be explained as a function of a given culture system. As Herskovits puts it: "Morality is a universal, and so is enjoyment of beauty, and some standard of truth. The many forms these concepts take are but products of the particular historical experience of the societies that manifest them" (1948, p. 76). That is why there can be no absolutes in the sense of fixed standards which admit of no variations. There are, for Herskovits, no concrete universal norms or values because there are no objective absolute values. There are only abstract, formal, cultural universals whose content varies historically with cultural experience and social change.

As a liberal and a democrat, Herskovits, like Boas, asks us to show a high degree of tolerance and respect for cultural differences in the name of cultural relativism. While each individual is to abide by the social code of his society and time—since otherwise there would be no social discipline—he must respect the right of others to conform to their social codes also. The difficulty which some find in accepting the doctrine of cultural relativism is attributed to "an enculturative experience wherein absolutes are stressed" (1948, p. 77). It is only in a puritanical culture such as ours, wherein cultural absolutes are presupposed, that cultural relativism is difficult to comprehend. Once we learn to discount our ethnocentric biases, we will emerge from "the ethnocentric morass in which our thinking about ultimate values has for so long bogged down" (1948, p. 78).

Thus we are told to transcend our ethnocentrism in the name of cultural relativism. "Cultural relativism" is used as a value-charged term denoting a positive, praiseworthy attitude, while "ethnocentrism" denotes a negative value incompatible with an unbiased,

objective approach. Herskovits does not explain how it is theoretically possible to have cultural relativism without ethnocentrism, in view of the fact that cultural conditioning necessarily leads the members of any given society to prefer their own value system above all others. What he apparently has in mind is a culture system which inculcates the relative validity of its own values for its own adherents, together with recognition of the equal value of other value systems. He implies, therefore, an ideal cultural relativism totally different from the real cultural relativism of historic cultures, which recognize the absolute validity of their values and deny equal recognition to other value systems. A major source of confusion in Herskovits' thesis is that he fails to differentiate clearly between this implicit ideal cultural relativism which he advocates and the real, historic-cultural relativism which he posits to account for the variety of actual value systems. As an idealist and romanticist, Herskovits respects cultural differences as an absolute good, notwithstanding his disavowal of any absolute standards in the name of cultural relativism.

There are, apparently, two kinds of ethnocentrism—a vicious and a benign kind. The vicious kind of ethnocentrism involves belief in objective absolute values and hence intolerance of other codes. The benign kind involves preference for one's own value system, as well as mutual respect for those of other societies. How it is possible to transcend ethnocentrism of the intolerant variety, if there is no objective standard of comparison, is not explained. Furthermore, it is not at all clear why one should prefer his own system of cultural values rather than some other system, provided that the cultural blinkers which have been imposed on him do not prevent him from envisaging some other system. It may be expedient to adhere to a given social code at a given time and place, but it is difficult to see why one should adhere to it exclusively or exercise moral restraint in the presence of other culture systems. The fact of cultural relativism in historic cultures does not logically imply the absolute value of cultural differences and the obligation to respect them. The "is" of cultural relativism does not imply the "ought." To derive the ought from the is of culture is to commit what I have elsewhere termed "the positivistic fallacy" (Bidney, 1944).

As an axiological position, the doctrine of cultural relativism involves what Nietzsche has termed "the transvaluation of values." The absolute values of truth, goodness, and beauty which men profess are thought to have only a limited, relative, historical validity for a given society and culture. All so-called "absolute" values are really "relative absolutes," whose validity is recognized only within the context of a given culture. We must distinguish, however, sociological relativism from cultural relativism. According to sociological relativism, cultural values are a function of social organization and vary with its modes. That is, the sociological relativist explains the origin of particular values by reference to the society and the class interests which it fosters. Thus Nietzsche evaluated moral values by reference to two social classes, the masters and the slaves, engaged in a conflict of wills to power, and Marx evaluated moral values as reflecting the economic interests of classes, such as capitalists and workers. By contrast, the cultural relativist does not explain the origin of social values but accepts them as given. Philosophically, some contemporary ethnologists apparently find historical-cultural idealism most congenial and postulate cultural reality as a reality *sui generis* which renders all the phenomena of experience intelligible. At most, we are informed that cultural relativism is a fact of ethnographic ex-perience and is a necessary product of cultural conditioning. Values are said to be conditioned by culture, but culture itself must be taken as given and as self-explanatory. This is what is meant by the statement that culture is a closed system.

This relativistic transvaluation of values is incompatible with the idea of absolute progress. Cultural relativism was partly a direct consequence of the opposition of contemporary anthropologists to the doctrine of linear evolution and cultural progress. Evolutionary cultural progress has been hastily dismissed as a reflection of narrow ethnocentrism and nationalistic bias in favor of Western culture.

I find it difficult, therefore, to follow Kroeber when he states in his revised *Anthropology* (1948, p. 265) that the idea of progress as advocated by nineteenth-century anthropologists was "favorable to attitudes of relativity, instead of fixity or a perfection already achieved." The cultural evolutionists were, indeed, opposed to fixity and static perfection, but this did not imply a doctrine of cultural relativity, since the latter negated the idea of absolute progress. In so far as ethnologists recognized the relativity of morals, they did so in spite of the theory of evolutionary progress, not because of it. The cultural evolutionists were convinced that, with the advance of scientific intelligence and moral experience, the relativity of epistemic and moral evaluation which springs from prescientific mythological thought would tend to be superseded by rational, scientific norms of universal validity. That was why the evolutionary ethnologists looked upon ethnology as a reformer's science, intolerant of the "survivals" of superstition in their own culture. They looked for rational social laws and moral norms of universal validity as the final product of a science of man in society and were far from content with a romantic interest in cultural pluralism and cultural relativism. The latter sophistic attitude was characteristic of Sumner and of the romantic, sentimental followers of Boas, who no longer took the idea of cultural progress seriously.

The issue as interpreted by the cultural relativists apparently turns on two alternatives: either one accepts a doctrine of fixed absolute values, or else one denies objective norms in favor of historic relativity and relative validity of values. I do not think, however, that we are necessarily limited to these two alternatives. In the sphere of natural science there is a cumulative advance in man's knowledge of nature, notwithstanding the continuous re-evaluation of beliefs and postulates. The scientist does not argue that, because some former truth values are rejected as a result of new, objective evidence, there is therefore no objective criterion of truth in the sense of verified knowledge. On the contrary, it is because of his faith in an objective order of nature amenable to gradual human discovery that he is prepared constantly to question his assumptions and generalizations and to alter them in accordance with his empirical evidence. The natural scientist does not use objective evidence to discredit objective truth values. Similarly, in the sphere of moral truth values, it is not logical to reject objective moral norms simply because some alleged objective moral norms are seen to have a purely subjective validity within a given cultural context. Subjectivity and objectivity are correlatives in all spheres of value, and both aspects are required for an adequate evaluation of the cultural situation. There is no reason why there may not be a cumulative increment in our knowledge and achievement of moral ideals comparable to our advance in the attainment of truth values in the natural sciences. Murder and theft are examples of negative moral values which are, even now, con-

crete ethnological universals, even though there is considerable disparity as regards the area of their application in different cultures.

The cultural relativists perceive that social culture determines the ideological perspective of its adherents and hence can see no common measure in cultural values. There are, for them, only historic "relative absolutes," since each culture system claims to be absolutely valid. Relativity is then regarded as identical with subjectivity. What is overlooked by the relativists is the important consideration to which Kant drew attention in his essay "Idea for a Universal History with Cosmopolitan Intent," namely, that "in man those mature faculties which aim at the use of reason shall be fully developed in the species, not in the individual" (1949, p. 118). That is, man has a capacity for reason which is historically developed in the history of human society but not in the experience of the individual, since the life of the individual is far too short to achieve complete rationality. Mankind has the potentiality for developing rationality to its fullest extent, and rationality is therefore a universally valid ideal. In the meantime, a beginning may be made by visualizing such potentially universal rational ideals as are suggested by the available accumulation of knowledge and experience and by attempting to realize them in practice. Thus, if society through its culture is responsible for warping the perspective of the individual through its relative absolutes, it is also the only means for achieving in time whatever degree of objectivity and universality man is capable of attaining. Similarly, if it is true that the perspective of the individual is a product of his culture, it is also true that individuals may, in turn, affect the cultural perspective of their society in the direction of greater rationality and objectivity.

VII. CULTURAL RELATIVISM AND THE "STATEMENT ON HUMAN RIGHTS"

The doctrine of cultural relativism is apparently regarded as one of the major achievements of contemporary ethnology by many American anthropologists, although there have been some notable exceptions, such as Cooper, Hallowell (1952), Kluckhohn (1949), and Mead (1950), and there have been indications of a growing appreciation of humanistic values. It appears to be an essential element in that "Copernican revolution" which anthropologists attribute to their science. This impression is strengthened by the "Statement on Human Rights" which Herskovits (1947) drafted on behalf of the executive board of the American Anthropological Association in 1947 and submitted to the United Nations Commission on Human Rights. In this statement the author submits three basic propositions: (1) The individual realizes his personality through his culture; hence respect for individual differences entails a respect for cultural differences. (2) Respect for differences between cultures is validated by the scientific fact that no technique of qualitatively evaluating cultures has been discovered. (3) Standards and values are relative to the culture from which they derive, so that any attempt to formulate postulates that grow out of the beliefs or moral codes of one culture must to that extent detract from the applicability of any Declaration of Human Rights to mankind as a whole.

Here again Herskovits reiterates his distinction between universals and absolutes in human culture and reaffirms his thesis of the relative, historical validity of so-called "absolutes" on the ground that every people regards its own values as "eternal verities" because they have been taught to regard them as such. There is, he maintains, no means of evaluating cultural values

comparatively, since any attempt at comparative evaluation presupposes an ethnocentric perspective. To avoid ethnocentric judgments, one must, therefore, suspend judgment altogether and try to act and regard other culture systems as if they were of equal validity with one's own, even though it may be difficult to believe that they really are equal but different.

The only absolute right which the cultural relativist recognizes is the negative right to be different and to adhere to one's own culture. There can be no absolute, positive rights, since "what is held to be a human right in one society may be regarded as anti-social by another people" (Herskovits, 1947, p. 542). For example, standards of freedom and justice are to be regarded as cultural universals whose actual content will vary with different cultures. Hence, in practice, one must not interfere or intervene in the affairs of another society, no matter how their behavior affects one's sensibilities, since to do so would be to infringe on their right to be different. The cultural relativist is so afraid of ethnocentrism and possible intolerance that he is prepared, in theory at least, to tolerate any violation of his cultural standards by members of another society, on the assumption that, no matter what the consequences may be for others, they would still be in accord with the principle of the relativity of values.

Nevertheless, Herskovits does concede that in instances where political systems deny citizens the right of participation in their government or seek to conquer weaker peoples, "underlying cultural values may be called on to bring the peoples of such states to a realization of the consequences of the acts of their governments, and thus enforce a brake upon discrimination and conquest" (Herskovits, 1947, p. 543). In effect, he is urging citizens to oppose their governments when they embark upon discrimination and conquest, assured that there will probably be found universal, latent values which might serve as a justification for such opposition. He is assuming that "the people" of a given state are bound to oppose discrimination and conquest, once they understand the true consequences of such policies. That is, discrimination and conquest are assumed to be objective, universal, negative values and not merely relative, ethnocentric "absolutes" of a given culture.

In practice, extreme liberalism and extreme conservativism tend to converge upon a common policy. Extreme cultural relativists are opposed to a declaration of objective universal rights of man for fear of infringing upon the freedom and cultural values of given societies. Extreme conservatives, together with nondemocrats who would safeguard the interests of the "elite," are opposed to a declaration of universal rights because they are against any policies which tend to equalize effective social standards at the expense of special interests. Both parties prefer the status quo.

My general impression is that cultural relativists are so concerned to safeguard cultural differences that they fail to appreciate the polar requirement of a common core of objective cultural values. There can be no mutual respect for differences where there is no community of values also. I suspect that, on the whole, there are more concrete similarities and identities in the cultural values of different societies than the cultural relativist has so far explicitly recognized. Otherwise, even the degree of co-operation in world affairs which mankind has so far attained would not have been possible.

Finally, the cultural relativists fail to see that cultural ideologies are effective precisely because they are believed and acknowledged to have absolute value by their adherents, and not only for their adherents. If a given value system were not accepted as objectively valid, it would soon lose its effectiveness as a motivation for conduct. That is why pragmatic sociologists, such as Sorel (1941, pp. 142–45) and Pareto (1935, p. 1300; Degre, 1943, pp. 45–50), regard social myths as indispensable for social action, regardless of their truth value. What is important is that the myth should be believed and serve as an inspiration for heroic action.

The practical alternatives are not cultural absolutism versus cultural relativism, as contemporary anthropologists are inclined to hold, but rather rational norms with a potentiality for universal acceptance and realization versus mythological absolutes destined to lead to perpetual crises and conflicting political policies. Far from resolving our international problems, cultural relativism leads to conflicting political and social mythologies. The only effective alternative to a mythical relative absolute is a better, more rational, and more objective ideal of conduct and belief, capable of overcoming the limitations of the former.

VIII. FUNCTIONALISM AND THE BIOLOGICAL EVALUATION OF VALUES

The distinction between cultural universals and cultural absolutes is one which received its most explicit expression through the work of Malinowski. Approaching culture from a biogenetic perspective, Malinowski was concerned to demonstrate the function of cultural institutions in satisfying primary and derived human impulses, needs, and requirements. There are, he pointed out, basic human needs and universal cultural responses, organized into institutions designed to satisfy these needs. Hence arise universal "instrumental imperatives of culture" (1944*a*), leading to economic institutions, social control through morality and law, education, and political organization.

There are cultural universals because

there are universal human needs, biological, derived, and integrative. But the actual empirical content of a culture varies with the social context in relation to a given geographical environment. To explain a given cultural institution is to indicate its social function in promoting the existence and welfare of a given society; beyond that one cannot go. No one has insisted more emphatically than Malinowski upon the necessity for evaluating cultural traits with reference to the sociocultural context and upon the falsification which results when traits are abstracted from their context. This approach he carried to the extreme of denying the validity of comparative and historical analysis of culture forms apart from functions. In effect, this meant an insistence upon the relativity of all cultural traits and symbols to their sociocultural context and the instrumental, utilitarian nature of all cultural values. The only absolute value implicit in Malinowski's theory is survival value, all other cultural values being understood as means to this end.

Malinowski's functionalistic approach led him to re-evaluate primitive mythology and religion (1948, pp. 72–124). As against previous scholarly attempts to interpret myths intellectualistically as primitive man's philosophy of nature, he maintained that myths were to be understood as motivated by a practical concern to face the crises of life. The function of myth was to validate the cultural institutions, customs, and rites of a culture, not to explain them intellectually, and to provide a common bond of social solidarity through a common faith. Thus myth was evaluated positively as having a functional, pragmatic value for a given society in facing the crises of life. So understood, myth was not merely primitive man's superstitions and delusions but his constructive response to overcome his natural fears and perplexities in adjusting to his environment. The function exer-

cised by myth in primitive societies continues to be exercised by religion in contemporary civilized societies. Unlike the positivists, Malinowski does not regard religion as something to be evolved out of and superseded in the course of scientific progress, but rather as something which continues to fulfil a necessary function in contemporary life which scientific knowledge to date has failed to achieve. Contemporary ethnologists, under the influence of psychoanalytical throught, are now beginning to adopt a similar functionalistic approach to the evaluation of religion.

In his posthumous work, *Freedom and Civilization,* Malinowski (1944b) revealed himself as a democrat and a liberal passionately concerned with individual liberty and with transcultural, international ideals. He was outspoken in his denunciation of totalitarian tyranny, notwithstanding his professed position that human freedom is a relative function of culture and is to be understood by reference to some cultural context. He finally distinguished between "intrinsic constraints" and "arbitrary constraints" which involve an abuse of power, thereby postulating transcultural values having objective validity by which to evaluate social systems. I know of no better example in contemporary anthropology of the disparity of ethnological theory and practice under critical conditions. In the end, Malinowski, too, was prepared to justify the very ideals of a democratic society for which his scientific theory of cultural relativism failed to account.

IX. FUNCTIONALISM AND THE SOCIOLOGICAL EVALUATION OF CULTURE

The functionalism of Radcliffe-Brown differs from that of Malinowski, inasmuch as the former tends to adopt a comparative sociological approach in interpreting the data of primitive culture. Social anthropology is for Radcliffe-Brown, as it is for his followers among British anthropologists, concerned with the comparative study of the relation of cultural phenomena to social structure and is said to differ from ethnology, which is devoted to the historical study of cultural processes and events (1952). According to this sociological approach, moral and religious values are products of social life and are to be understood in terms of their functions in promoting the solidarity and welfare of a given society. Cultures are viewed as functioning wholes, all the parts of which are closely interrelated. To evaluate any given institution, one must indicate its place in the culture as a whole and the special function it performs in promoting the existence of the society in which it is found. The ultimate, absolute value for Radcliffe-Brown is the survival value of the society, all other cultural values being subservient as means or instruments to this end.

As an indication of the transvaluation of values implicit in this type of sociocultural theory, it is of interest to bear in mind that in *The Elementary Forms of the Religious Life* Durkheim identifies the object of religious worship with society. If society is the ultimate reality *sui generis*, then indeed society is what the classical philosophers and theologians have meant by God, even though they were not aware of it. Religion is said to be, not a system of ideas and beliefs corresponding to some determinate object, such as nature or the infinite, but a system of actions and sentiments whose objective cause is society itself. Religion is simply the concentrated expression of the whole collective life. "The idea of society is the soul of religion" (1926, p. 419). For Durkheim, religion is not a delusion, and to this extent he finds himself in agreement with William James. He differs from James in that he assigns the objective cause, as distinct from the subjective belief of the believers, to society rather than to some metaphysical entity. In religion, man worships himself and his ideals collectively. All the traditional formulas of religion are now transferred to this god of the sociologist, whom mankind apparently have always worshiped and called by a variety of names, without understanding his true nature. The problem of the social scientist in our times is, as Durkheim sees it, to create new symbols of religion capable of evoking a new faith for all mankind. What form these symbols would take was, for him, "something which surpasses the human faculty of foresight" (1926, p. 428). That mankind would continue to worship and be inspired by the mythological constructs of their own imaginations is something which Durkheim assumes as a matter of course, just as cultural relativists, in general, tend to assume that men would continue to adhere to, and respect, their cultural values, even after they were convinced by the ethnologists that their so-called "absolute" and "universal" values were but subjective delusions.

X. APPLIED ANTHROPOLOGY AND THE PROBLEM OF CULTURAL UNIVERSALS

Cultural anthropology, like the older discipline of sociology, has now become an applied science, as well as a "pure" science devoted to empirical knowledge gained by field investigations. A significant reason for the popularity of the functional, dynamic approach to the study of cultural processes has been the insight it has provided into the evaluation of primitive institutions. Malinowski in particular was conscious of the need for applied anthropology devoted to the study of the acculturated native as he exists rather than the "uncontaminated" native as he was before contact with

Western man (1945). The task of the anthropologist has now been interpreted as being, in part, that of advising governments, missionaries, and commercial interests concerning native needs and the means to be employed in obtaining native co-operation in alien enterprises.

The evils of ethnocentrism become most apparent in the contacts between races and cultures. To impose by force of arms customs and institutions which are alien to a native society and to punish natives for failing to conform to these impositions are now recognized as an uncivilized procedure which is detrimental to the true interests of both parties. As a result, many anthropologists have come to the conclusion that the primary message of their discipline is that of the higher tolerance of cultural relativism, the recognition that all so-called "absolutes" have only a relative, historical validity, and that there is no justification for imposing our own ethnocentric absolutes upon other peoples with different cultural traditions and customs.

An older generation of anthropologists, who thought in terms of a theory of progressive cultural evolution, recommended a policy of humane tolerance of native cultures on other grounds. It was thought to be the white man's responsibility to assist natives in achieving the goal of civilization. The native was not to be despised for the primitiveness of his culture but counseled and guided in overcoming his deficiences. Evolutionary applied anthropology saw cultural evolution as a necessary but slow process which might be accelerated through acculturation and indoctrination.

By contrast, the modern cultural relativist adopts a romantic attitude toward native cultures, insisting upon the intrinsic value of the variety of native cultures and questioning the wisdom of interference, no matter how well intentioned. The natives, they advise, should be assisted to develop the potentialities of their own cultures and to lead lives of their own, rather than to acquire our Western culture, which they cannot understand or appreciate adequately. Laura Thompson's *Culture in Crisis* (1950) is an eloquent exposition of this point of view. The case is made even stronger by pointing out, as many have done, that to impose our own mode of living upon natives without the corresponding rights and privileges has resulted in detribalized, demoralized natives who have lost their self-respect and will to live.

The problem is undoubtedly a difficult one, and there is no easy solution. But I do think it is important that we clarify further the principles on which we may act and the goals we may set before us. I would like to stress the point once more that it is a falsification of the issue to contrast cultural absolutism with cultural relativism and to attribute all the virtues to the latter and all the vices to the former.

All absolutes are not necessarily ethnocentric, and all cultural ideologies are not of equal value. Belief in transcultural absolutes, in rational norms and ideals which men may approximate in time but never quite realize perfectly, is quite compatible with a humane policy of tolerance of cultural differences. If cultural progress is a valid and objective ideal, it is the duty of the anthropologist as a student of culture history and of comparative cultural dynamics to co-operate in the common task by indicating some of the conditions for its realization in our own and other cultures. To urge cultural laissez faire because of the ethnocentric follies and crimes of the past is a counsel of despair which fails to face the real issues which confront mankind. If there is danger of nondemocratic procedures in imposing ethnocentric ideals and institutions upon the adherents of alien cultures, there is equally the danger that the liberal advocates of cultural laissez faire may fail to correct gross injustices committed by those who recognize no common human rights and values. In practice, it is frequently necessary to choose between the greater good and the lesser evil rather than between an absolute good and an absolute evil. And there are times when the evil and injustice which require correction are far more obvious than the possible harm which may result from some ethnocentric predilections. The second World War and the crimes of genocide have provided a superabundance of instances which may illustrate this point.

XI. MODERN ANTHROPOLOGY AND THE COMPARATIVE STUDY OF VALUES

As I see it, the most important and difficult task which confronts the cultural anthropologist is that of making a critical and comparative study of values. The choice is no longer between a romantic cultural pluralism and a fixed evolutionary absolutism but rather between a world in perpetual crisis and a world order based on rational principles capable of winning the adherence of the nations of the world.

In their anxiety to avoid and obviate the evils of national ethnocentrism, especially when allied with the quest for power and domination over weaker peoples, modern and contemporary anthropologists have unwittingly tended to substitute serial ethnocentrism for the static ethnocentrism and absolutism which they abhor. By "serial ethnocentrism" I mean the attitude of viewing each culture from its own perspective only, as if that were the primary and sole virtue of the objective anthropologist. So timid and wary has the modern anthropologist become, lest he commit the fallacies of the comparative

evolutionary ethnologist of the nineteenth century, that the very thought of comparative analysis, of "the comparative method," strikes him with terror. We are reminded repeatedly, by functionalists and nonfunctionalists alike, that each culture must be viewed as an integrated whole and that no culture traits or institutions may be understood apart from a given cultural context. Thus comparative studies are viewed as unscientific adventures reminiscent of an outmoded era in cultural anthropology.

As against this extreme attitude, I maintain that comparative studies of cultures and their values are indispensable if anthropology is to approximate its objectives as a science of man. So long as anthropology remains at the descriptive stage, which is the first stage of empirical science, anthropologists may rest content with cultural pluralism, on the ground that they do not wish to overstep the bounds of scientific fact. But if anthropology is to attain the stage of making significant generalizations concerning the conditions of the cultural process and the values of civilization, then comparative studies of cultures and their values must be made with a view to demonstrating universal principles of cultural dynamics and concrete rational norms capable of universal realization. Hitherto the task of suggesting and prescribing normative ideals and goals has been left, for the most part, to utopian philosophers and to cynical sociologists who equated social ideals with myths. I suggest that it is high time that anthropology came of age and that anthropologists show their respect for human reason and science by co-operating with other social scientists and scholars with a view to envisaging practical, progressive, rational ideals worthy of winning a measure of universal recognition in the future.

REFERENCES

BIDNEY, DAVID. 1944. "On the Concept of Culture and Some Cultural Fallacies," *American Anthropologist*, XLVI, 30–44.

DEGRE, GERARD L. 1943. "Society and Ideology." Ph.D. thesis, Columbia University, New York.

DURKHEIM, ÉMILE. 1926. *The Elementary Forms of the Religious Life*. New York: Macmillan Co.

HALLOWELL, A. I. 1952. "The Self and Its Behavioral Environment." In ROHEIM, GEZA (ed.), *Psychoanalysis and the Social Sciences*, Vol. IV.

HERSKOVITS, MELVILLE. 1947. "Statement on Human Rights," *American Anthropologist*, XLIX, 539–43.

——. 1948. *Man and His Works*. New York: A. A. Knopf.

KANT, IMMANUEL. 1949. *The Philosophy of Kant*. Edited by FRIEDRICH. ("Modern Library.") New York: Random House.

KLUCKHOHN, C. 1949. *Mirror for Man*. New York: Whittlesey House, McGraw-Hill Book Co., Inc.

KROEBER, ALFRED L. 1948. *Anthropology*. New York: Harcourt, Brace & Co.

LANG, ANDREW. 1909. *The Making of Religion*. 3d ed. London: Longmans, Green & Co.

MALINOWSKI, B. 1944a. *A Scientific Theory of Culture and Other Essays*. Chapel Hill: University of North Carolina Press.

——. 1944b. *Freedom and Civilization*. New York: Roy Publishers.

——. 1945. *The Dynamics of Culture Change*. New Haven: Yale University Press.

——. 1948. *Magic, Science, and Religion and Other Essays*. Glencoe, Ill.: Free Press.

MEAD, MARGARET. 1950. "The Comparative Study of Cultures and the Purposive Cultivation of Democratic Values, 1941–1949." (Paper submitted to Tenth Conference on Science, Philosophy, and Religion, held in New York City in 1950.)

PARETO, VILFREDO. 1935. *The Mind and Society*. New York: Harcourt, Brace & Co.

RADCLIFFE-BROWN, A. R. 1952. "Historical Note on British Social Anthropology," *American Anthropologist*, LIV, 275–77.

SCHMIDT, WILHELM. 1931. *The Origin and Growth of Religion*. London: Methuen & Co.

SOREL, GEORGE. 1941. *Reflections on Violence*. New York: P. Smith. 1st ed., London: Allen & Unwin, 1925.

SUMNER, WILLIAM GRAHAM. 1940. *Folkways*. Boston: Ginn & Co. (Also 1907, 1911.)

THOMPSON, LAURA. 1950. *Culture in Crisis*. New York: Harper & Bros.

Human Ecology

By MARSTON BATES

THE WORD "oecology" was coined by Ernst Haeckel (1870) in the course of an effort to formulate a logical scheme of zoölogical sciences. His primary division was into the sciences concerned with structure (morphology) and those concerned with function (physiology). His scheme still seems logical, and his definition of ecology agrees closely with what many of us today think ecology ought to be. He wrote that

just as morphology falls into two main divisions of anatomy and development, so physiology may be divided into a study of inner and outer phenomena, or of "Relations-Physiologie" and "Conservations-Physiologie." The first is concerned with the functioning of the organism in itself, the second with its relationships with the outer world. These two disciplines thus have their points of origin in entirely different and widely separated regions of science.

The outer physiology, the study of the relations of animals with the outside world, may in turn be divided into two parts, the ecology and the chorology, of animals. By *ecology*, we understand the study of the economy, of the household, of animal organisms. This includes the relationships of animals with both the inorganic and the organic environments, above all the beneficial and inimical relations with other animals and plants, whether direct or indirect; in a word, all of the intricate interrelations that Darwin referred to as the conditions of the struggle for existence. This ecology (often also called "biology" in the narrowest sense) comprises the largest part of so-called "natural history" in the usual sense of the word.

Haeckel's word "chorology" did not catch on; the concept was too closely similar to that of zoögeography. Ecology, however, has gradually become established as a word and as a science, though there is no universal agreement about its usage or its meaning. This is particularly true in the case of "human ecology." Yet any appraisal of the development of human ecology requires a reasonably explicit statement of what is meant by the term.

A casual survey of usage in recent literature and in university organization shows at least five rather divergent ways in which ecology is being applied as a label for human studies.

1. Human ecology stemming from medicine, stressing the environmental relations of disease and growing from this into related fields of thought. The medical science of epidemiology is very readily transposed into the "ecology of disease"; and the word "ecology" also fits readily into the vocabulary of public health workers, since they are always concerned with the environmental relations of man (Corwin, 1949). Cambridge University, in England, has established a Department of Human Ecology, dedicated to the study of public health and epidemiological problems, and the philosophy of this has been described in the inaugural lecture of the professor (Banks, 1950).

2. Human ecology stemming from geography. "Geography" is as protean a word as "ecology," and the two are sometimes used as though they were synonyms. Thus a textbook of geography may have the subtitle "an ecological study of society" (White and Renner, 1948), and definitions of "human geography" and "human ecology" frequently appear to be interchangeable. The question "What is geography?" has been debated at length (e.g., Parkins, 1934), as has the problem of distinguishing between ecology and geography (Barrows, 1923; Thornthwaite, 1940). The special hazards of "environmentalism" in geography have been discussed by Platt (1948).

This geographical usage of "ecology" has a specialized subsidiary, in which "environment" is equated with "climate," so that study of men and environment comes to mean man and climate. This usage is illustrated by the *Journal of Human Ecology* published by the Weather Science Foundation of Crystal Lake, Illinois.

3. Human ecology stemming from sociology. The American sociologists have attempted to give ecology a specific meaning as the study of community structure. This is illustrated in the books by Hawley (1950) and Quinn (1950).

4. Human ecology as a tag to indicate that a particular study has broad relevance to problems of human conduct. This sort of usage is nicely shown by the title of a book by Zipf (1949): *Human Behavior and the Principle of Least Effort: An Introduction to Human Ecology.* The book is largely devoted to language analysis, and, as far as I can discover, the word "ecology" does not occur in the text.

5. Human ecology stemming from anthropology. Here I would classify attempts to use the word in the original sense of Haeckel, only with "man" instead of "animal" as the central focus

of interest. The book by Bews (1935) exemplifies this usage.

Clearly, the term "human ecology" has not yet come to be generally applied to a specific and well-defined field of inquiry, and it seems likely that attempts like those of the sociologists so to limit it will fail because their usage is at variance with the usual interpretation of the word in biology. It seems to me better that the word be left with a general and rather vague meaning. The tendency in both the biological and the social sciences to develop numerous special subsciences with "-ology" labels has many unfortunate consequences. It tends to foster the development of special technical vocabularies for each of the segregated fields and thus to hamper the development of general concepts and the study of broad interrelationships. Specialization is necessary, but it does not seem so necessary to freeze our patterns of specialization into a congeries of formal disciplines with labels like "ecology," "demography," "climatology," and so forth. The extreme result of such splitting can be seen in the medical sciences; but the tendency, I think, has handicapped the biological sciences as compared with the physicochemical sciences, where specialization has less often had formal, Greek-root labeling.

It might be useful to regard ecology as a pervasive point of view rather than as a special subject matter. The ecological point of view—whereby the organism is regarded as a whole unit functioning in its environmental context—would carry over from the biological to the social sciences and might thus be especially helpful in relating the concepts of the one field to those of the other. The establishment of such relations is not easy, and most attempts to transfer concepts have possibly been misleading.

Biologists are likely to be impressed by the fact that man is an animal and to reason that his behavior must thus be explicable in biological terms. But any animal is also an aggregation of chemical elements. Biologists do not argue that, because of this, animal behavior must be completely explicable in known physicochemical terms. They recognize that the factor of life influences the whole nature of scientific study, so that physicochemical propositions must be examined anew in the living context. With the shift from animal to man, an analogous shift has been made because of the complicating factor of culture, and biological propositions must be examined anew in the cultural context.

An important and difficult problem in the scientific study of man is the problem of sorting out the cultural from the biological elements or of finding the biological elements by dissecting away the cultural overlay. The ecological approach might be particularly suitable for this, because, in attempting to analyze the environmental relationships of man, the necessity of finding some method of sorting out and handling the physical, biological, and cultural factors becomes obvious at once. The peculiarity and pervasiveness of the cultural factors are even more emphasized if this study is approached from a background of animal ecology.

Biochemistry is a protean sort of science that has served to bridge the apparent gap between the physical and the biological sciences. Perhaps in a comparable way, ecological anthropology—or human ecology—may furnish the conceptual interconnections between the biological and the social sciences. Human ecology, then, would be the natural history of man, or, in its narrowest sense, the biology of man. This, returning to Haeckel's original definition, means his "outer physiology."

The little book by Elton (1927) provides the easiest introduction to animal ecology. A group of Chicago authors (Allee *et al.*, 1949) have written a comprehensive review of the subject. They found it convenient, in organizing their material, to use four main topical divisions: "The Analysis of the Environment," "Populations," "The Community," and "Ecology and Evolution." These topics may also serve conveniently for summarizing some of the material in which the ecological point of view seems pertinent in human studies.

ANALYSIS OF THE ENVIRONMENT

The concept of "environment" is certainly difficult and may even be misleading; but we have no handy substitute. It seems simple enough to distinguish between the organism and the surrounding environment and to separate forces acting on an organism into those that are internal and inherent and those that are external and environmental. But in actual practice this system breaks down in many ways, because the organism and the environment are constantly interacting so that the environment is modified by the organism and vice versa. I have attempted elsewhere (Bates, 1950) a slight and superficial analysis of this situation from the biological point of view.

In the case of man, the difficulties with the environmental concept are compounded because we have to deal with man as an animal and with man as a bearer of culture. If we look at man as an animal and try to analyze the environmental forces that are acting on the organism, we find that we have to deal with things like climate, soil, vegetation, and such-like factors common to all biological situations; but we also find, always, very important environmental influences that we can only class as "cultural," which modify the physical and biological factors. But man, as we know him, is always a bearer of culture; and, if we study human culture, we find that it, in turn, is modified by the environmental factors of climate and geography. We thus easily get into great difficulties from the necessity of viewing culture, at one moment, as a part of the man and, at another moment, as a part of the environment.

This perhaps helps to explain the difference in materials, emphasis, and conclusions that one is likely to find between textbooks of human geography and textbooks of cultural anthropology. The geographer tends to regard culture as a part of the man and is thus preoccupied in describing and explaining the environmental relationships of the man-culture system. The anthropologist, on the other hand, is likely to be preoccupied with culture as a thing-in-itself, and he thus tends to describe and explain human behavior directly in cultural terms. It may be that the chief virtue in stressing an ecological point of view lies in the consequent necessity of reconciling these apparent differences: of treating culture in one context as a part of the man and in another as a part of the environment.

The difficulties introduced by cultural factors are apparent in the studies of the effect of climate on man. The biologist can study the temperature conditions of the normal habitats of his organisms in nature and can check the effect on them of other temperature conditions in laboratory experiments, thus arriving at a description of the optimum and limiting temperatures for various species or for particular kinds of activity. But with man the variable of culture is always interposed between the climate and the organism—clothing, housing, and custom must always be taken into account.

Human geographers, in their study of climate, have relied largely on measurements of climate derived from standard meteorological stations. Such measurements, because of their standardiza-

tion, are essential for the comparison of conditions in different geographical regions; they serve as a sort of index to differences or similarities. But biologists have come to recognize that very few organisms live under the environmental conditions measured in a Stevenson screen and that, for purposes of ecological study, other sorts of environmental conditions must be measured. In addition to the geographical climate, we must take into consideration the "ecoclimate" (the climate of the habitat) and the "microclimate" (the climate surrounding the individual organism). These concepts have as yet been little used in human studies, but they would surely be useful. The ecoclimate for man would be the climate of the cities, villages, clearings, or forests in which he lives, perhaps extending to the climate of the interior of his houses. The microclimate would be the climate that affected him directly as an organism—the conditions directly surrounding his skin, under his clothes, or inside his bedding.

Studies of this sort are becoming of increasing interest, particularly to the physiologists, and they are often carried out under some such rubric as "environmental physiology." Investigation at this level was greatly stimulated during the second World War by the necessity of determining suitable clothing design for arctic, tropical, and desert conditions. These studies have been summarized in books edited by Adolph (1947) and Newburgh (1949), which, in turn, contain extensive bibliographies. The introductory chapter by Frederick Wulsin in the Newburgh book forms a sort of synthesis of the geographical, physiological, and anthropological points of view toward these problems of climate-culture-man, thus outlining what could well be called the "ecological approach."

We have, on the one hand, the problem of the climatic relations of man as a species and, on the other hand, the problem of possible differences among human races in climatic adaptation. It is easy to assume that, since the races show a pattern of geographical distribution, they represent adaptations to different geographical environments; and, with a certain amount of ingenuity, all sorts of adaptive traits can be described. These, however, often break down under close analysis. The problem is one aspect of the general biological problem of adaptive differences among closely related populations. There is an extensive literature on this subject. The discussion, as long as it stayed at the descriptive stage, was, in general, unrewarding, and we are only beginning to understand adaptative differences in populations as we make progress with laboratory analysis of physiological characters. The diagnostic, structural characters of populations often turn out to be nonadaptive but to be correlated with differences in physiology or behavior that clearly are adaptive.

With man, of course, we again have the complicating factor of culture, since the different human races are often the bearers of different types of culture. We may, indeed, get involved in very parallel sorts of arguments in discussing racial adaptations to climate and cultural adaptations to climate. We have also to distinguish between the inherent adaptive traits of the population and the acclimatization of the individual growing up in a particular environment. Coon, Garn, and Birdsell (1950), for instance, have described races largely in adaptive terms. As an example, they point out that "a Yahgan Indian can go fishing in his canoe in chilly Antarctic waters for hours at a time with no clothing but a single sealskin on his back, and no other heat than a smoldering fire in the clay hearth amidships. An urban New Yorker would probably catch pneumonia were

he to try to follow the Fuegian's example." Sure; but what if the New Yorker had been raised from infancy in the Yahgan environment? The experimental approach to such questions with man is very difficult; but otherwise how are we to distinguish between inherent differences in racial physiology, differences in individual acclimatization, and differences in cultural conditioning?

The experiments are arranged for us in places where different races live in the same climatic environment, with similar or different cultures, and here surely is a rewarding field for ecological or physiological study. A beginning has been made in studies like those by Robinson and others (1941) on Negroes and Whites in the southern United States; such studies have generally failed to show clear physiological differences between the races in things like adaptation to work under heat stress. For literature references I might cite, in addition to Coon, Garn, and Birdsell (1950), Price (1939), and Bates (1952).

The analysis of the human environment should go beyond climate, to include factors like physiography, resources, food supply, and disease. The study of physiography and resources has fallen largely to the geographers, but the ecologist would have to consider them, too. The ecological point of view, with its center of interest on man as a functioning organism, may again give a different perspective on cultural problems. The geographer perhaps tends to stress the ways in which physiography and resources have shaped cultural patterns, while the ecological approach would bring out more strongly the ways in which the meaning of these environmental factors change under different cultural circumstances. The sea that is a barrier to a man of one culture may be a highway for a man of another. We are likely to think of resources in terms of our Western industrial culture; but the term has equal validity, though with different meanings, for peoples of other cultures.

This is nicely brought out in the study of the Nuer by Evans-Pritchard (1940)—a study that might easily be called ecological—in which he develops concepts of "ecologic time" and "ecologic distance." It is also brought out in the studies like those by Kroeber (1939) and Steward (1938) on American Indian cultures.

Food supply (nutrition) and disease have in common the fact that they have generally been studied by physiologists and physicians. Foods have got surprisingly little attention from anthropologists, and physiologists and nutritionists have tended to confine their interest to the food materials of contemporary Western culture. The result is a wide gap in our knowledge of human ecology, which is only gradually being filled by extension from both the anthropological and the nutritional sides. The work of Richards (1932) should be cited in connection with the anthropological side of this problem, and a paper by Laura Thompson (1949) may serve as an example of an ecological approach to a nutritional study. Analytical studies of the food values of the materials used by different peoples are slowly increasing in frequency; a paper by Anderson *et al.* (1946) is a good example of this recent work.

The neglect of the study of disease as an environmental factor influencing human development is understandable, though nonetheless regrettable. It reflects the rarity with which medical and anthropological interests have been combined in a single investigator or in a working team. The disease picture of the world has, of course, altered radically in the last few hundred years through the spread of pathogens in the course of Western expansion and trade.

It will probably always be impossible to form an accurate picture of disease distribution in the pre-Columbian world; yet this disease pattern was surely an important element in determining the pace and direction of human evolution and cultural development. It is worth while, then, to try to garner and evaluate all the clues that we can find.

We can get an idea of the environmental importance of disease from its relation to recorded history. Zinsser (1935) has brought this out in his classic study of typhus and history. Hackett (1937) has reviewed the evidence with regard to the relation between malaria and historical developments in Greece and Italy. It seems to me probable that malaria was brought to America by the Spaniards—and what a different environment tropical America would present for man without malaria! The whole history of European-American cultural contact is understandable only when disease is taken into account—smallpox, malaria, yellow fever, and the rest of the list of contagions that Western man brought suddenly to new areas.

But the chief interest of disease for the ecologist perhaps lies in its effect on the equations of population dynamics, since the behavior of populations is one of his chief study interests.

POPULATIONS

Biology has become more and more preoccupied with the study of populations. This stems in part from the realization, which became general about the turn of the century, that "species" was definable only in population terms—that a "species" was a population with certain characteristics more or less isolated from similar populations by reproductive behavior. The individual organism studied by the biologist was significant largely in so far as it represented a sample from a population.

Evolution, then, became a history not so much of changes in individuals as of changes in populations. Population genetics, population behavior, and the community relations of mixed populations thus became matters of great interest.

The ecologist studying the environmental relations of organisms would have to be concerned as much with populations and with communities of populations as with individuals. The study of the behavior of populations and communities has, in fact, come to be the chief function of ecology, since individual reactions are still most often studied under the rubric "physiology." There has been an attempt in America to split ecology into two sciences: an "autecology," concerned with individual reactions, and a "synecology," concerned with populations and communities. This seems to me an extreme of the deplorable separatist tendency in labeling biological sciences.

The study of human populations has, for the most part, had little relation with this biological interest. Such studies are generally carried out under the label "demography" and are primarily concerned with the collection and analysis of statistical material. Since statistical material is, for the most part, available only for regions under Western domination, demography has largely been concerned with the study of population conditions within Western culture. This, from the point of view of anthropology and human evolution, represents a rather special case. As statistical services are developed in non-Western areas, demographic studies of great interest and significance become possible, like the recent study of India by Kingsley Davis (1951). For the most part, however, the fragmentary records available for non-Western cultures can hardly be dealt with by standard methods. The inadequacy of the material presently available is nicely shown by the scholarly compilation of African materials made by Kuczynski (1948).

For the ecologist, the situation in the modern world is the end-point of a series of historical processes, and he would like to understand not only the factors governing this present situation but also the changes that occurred in the past. Carr-Saunders (1922) has written a review of population history from this evolutionary point of view, and Gordon Childe (1951) has summarized our archeological knowledge in terms of possible population dynamics. Childe has provided a conceptual framework for the study of population history by relating it to three cultural "revolutions"—the Neolithic, which turned on the domestication of plants and animals; the Urban, which involved the organization of cities and the specialization of working functions; and the Industrial, based on the exploitation of power sources, such as steam and electricity.

We can appreciate the effect of the Industrial Revolution on human population growth because it is recent and well-documented. It is analyzed in every textbook of population study. Childe argues, and documents from archeological materials, the existence of similar great changes in population relations with each of the previous revolutions. He is saying, in other words, that we must examine human population dynamics in four quite different environmental contexts: that of food-gathering economy, that of Neolithic economy, that of urban economy, and that of industrial economy.

Most of human evolution, through the million years of the Pleistocene, must have taken place in the context of a food-gathering economy. Our understanding of this evolutionary process, then, is going to depend on our understanding of the social, biological, and environmental relationships that prevailed under such an economy. The factors governing natality, mortality, and population density would be quite different from those operating in a post-Neolithic economy and should be a matter of keen concern to every student of human evolution. But our relevant information seems to be very scanty. Krzywicki (1934) has attempted to summarize what is known about the vital statistics of "primitive" peoples, but he found little that is clear or definite. The anthropologists who have studied contemporary food-gathering people have generally been little interested in these problems of quantitative relationships.

Children, in such an economy, are a handicap longer than they are in an agricultural economy. Lactation is prolonged, and a mother cannot handle more than one infant at a time. There seems to be considerable evidence that infanticide has been general among food-gathering peoples available for study, so that children are spaced several years apart. Taboos on intercourse may also have existed, though these seem more characteristic of agricultural peoples. One wonders how far back in time infanticide extends; and whether possibly in Pleistocene man the spacing of infants may have been governed by the suppression of ovulation during lactation—a matter that has been insufficiently studied in contemporary man. Factors governing death must also have had special characteristics during the Pleistocene. I cannot see how, with sparse populations organized into small bands wandering over limited territories, contagious diseases can have had the importance that they have assumed under other population conditions. Disease may well have been caused chiefly by pathogens with life-histories insuring maintenance and dispersal—as in the case of malaria, yellow fever, and the various helminths. Perhaps the contagions developed with the closer man-to-man association of post-Neolithic economies.

Such questions are the sort that arise when one takes an ecological view of human populations. They are difficult questions but not hopeless ones, and many students have undertaken imaginative attacks on the problems they pose. The studies of Weidenreich (1939) suggest that possibly the chief cause of death for Pleistocene man was man. Vallois (1937) has shown how one can get clues to the average life-span of fossil man. Such studies, always difficult, become somewhat easier as one moves forward in time, and all sorts of studies become possible with archeological materials. It is perhaps unjust to cite random examples without carefully surveying the literature, but I might cite the studies of Angel (1947) on Greek skeletons and of Cook (1949) on the population of central Mexico. The study by Russell (1948) of British medieval populations shows what can be accomplished by careful detective work among the records of more recent times.

THE COMMUNITY

No organism lives in isolation, nor is the behavior of any organism understandable without reference to other organisms. The oak tree, the cricket, the nitrifying bacterium, the mushroom of the fairy ring—all are involved with one another in complicated patterns of food and energy relations, of protection and support, of competition and co-operation. But these relationships are not diffused at random through the biosphere. Closely associated organisms tend to form systems of relationships among themselves, forming patterns that are relatively complete and independent of other similar aggregations. Such associations, which go to make up a particular kind of forest, a pond, a bog, a coral reef, or tidal flat, are called "biotic communities."

The study of such communities is a major preoccupation of biological ecology. I cannot see, however, how this study can carry over directly to the human field. The human community is a very different thing from the biotic community and must be studied by very special methods. It is an accident of language convenience that we use the same word for both concepts. A biotic community is perhaps more properly called a "biocenosis" or "biome," and with such labeling the semantic confusion disappears. We may be able to call both Miami and the sawgrass swamps of the Everglades "communities," but we cannot call them both "biocenoses."

Post-Neolithic man has come to form a biological community system of his own, with his domesticated plants and animals, his parasites and hangers-on, like weeds and rats and cockroaches; and the relationships among these organisms make an interesting and important field for study. But it is biological ecology as much as human ecology. When we move on into the field of social relations within the human community, to the study of Miami or of a Seminole village, we have moved into a field where biological factors are so completely swamped by cultural factors that we had better frankly admit that we have moved into a whole new area of science, where even analogies may be dangerous. Yet man as a bearer of culture has developed from man as an animal, and his biological inheritance is still with him. The ecological point of view may be useful in trying to understand this biological basis of human nature.

Man is definitely a social animal—that is, he customarily lives as a part of aggregations that are larger than the family (parents and immediate offspring). The most simple known human economies are based on groups of several families, and it seems probable that man has been a social animal for a very long time. The fossil record gives some evidence of this, though necessarily indirect. It seems to me probable that man was a social animal before he became a bearer of culture, since I cannot imagine how the primordial elements of culture could have arisen in a nonsocial animal.

For the biological roots of human social behavior, then, we must look to the social mammals, and particularly the social primates. I think our psychologists have been too much preoccupied with the behavior of caged animals, and especially of the great apes. It is true that the apes are man's closest living relatives, but this does not mean that man must necessarily, at some time, have passed through a period of apelike behavior. The fossil record increasingly indicates a long evolutionary separation of the human and ape lines, with man perhaps developing from the extinct Australopithecines. The Pongid apes do not seem to be particularly strongly social—though we know extraordinarily little about their behavior in nature, since in the ape's natural habitat he is able to keep out of the way of observing man. The most careful field study of an ape, that by Carpenter (1940) on the gibbon, shows that the animal lives in family, rather than clan or tribal, groups; and there is evidence that the groupings in the other apes are small. Now it may perfectly well be that the Australopithecines were much more strongly social than the present Pongids and thus that man and his immediate ancestors have been social for several million years, while the Pongid line was going about the business of family living.

Whatever the case, since the Pongids present insurmountable difficulties for field study, we are driven to use more amenable primates for studies of field behavior. The finest field study of a social primate yet to be made is that of Carpenter (1934) on the howler monkeys of Panama. It is ironic that this splendid field study covers an animal that is unknown in the laboratory, while the best-known laboratory animals, the Indian rhesus and the American Cebus, have not been studied in their native habitats. It would seem particularly easy, and surely rewarding, to carry out detailed field studies of the rhesus monkeys in India.

There is not space here to consider the relevance to human problems of the various elements of studies of behavior in social mammals: social organization and leadership, the peck-order, sexual relations, co-operative behavior in food-gathering, communications, in-group and out-group relations, and so forth. It may be well, however, to consider one important topic—territory.

The contemporary realization of the importance of territory in vertebrate behavior dates from the publication of a book by Eliot Howard (1920) called *Territory in Bird Life*. A variety of kinds of territory are now recognized, but territorial, or "home-range," behavior of some sort appears to be universal in birds and mammals. General discussion of territorial phenomena can be found in papers by Nice (1941), Errington (1946), and Davis (1949). In the social mammals, such as deer, wolves, and monkeys, the herd or clan has a definite territory over which it ranges and which it defends from intrusion by solitary individuals or members of other herds or clans. Carpenter's howler study contains a particularly good analysis of territorial behavior in those animals.

Since territorialism seems to be a universal phenomenon among mammals, it must have characterized man's mammalian ancestors. It seems, in fact, to project in a recognizable form in contemporary food-gathering cultures (e.g., with the Semang of Malaya, as described by Forde [1934]). Man's "in-

stinctive" (precultural) equipment, then, would include elements leading to group cohesion and territorial restriction. This has considerable implications. For one thing, Errington (1946) has shown how territory availability may be the immediate factor governing limitation of mammalian population—the excess individuals unable to find and occupy territories being those most subject to predation and to the hazards of the physical environment. The population of Pleistocene man may, similarly, have been governed by the territorial requirements of the small tribal groups. The frequency with which the cause of death in Pleistocene man was his fellow-man (Weidenreich, 1939) may well indicate that territorial arrangements were maintained aggressively by these early men.

Sir Arthur Keith (1949) has carried the implications of territory in human evolution to an extreme. He is so impressed with the fixity of tribe-territorial arrangements that he would allow early man no mobility at all. I do not see that his deductions necessarily follow. All mammals, as far as they have been studied, show strong territorial habits; yet populations have spread over the globe, fused, separated, replaced one another, in the most complex fashions. Territory serves as a brake on population movements in normal times, but it by no means precludes such movements. At most, the tribe-territory arrangements of early man would mean that "migrations" would not be the vast movements that we sometimes imagine, like the sweeping of the hordes of Huns across Asia. Migration with food-gathering man would rather be a sort of infiltration process, an accumulation of small territorial readjustments and perhaps, under environmental stress, the complete displacement of the small tribal groups. But such displacements can, in the frame of geologic time, cover the whole planet.

The Neolithic discovery of agriculture and pastoralism would mark the end of the simple pattern of clan and territory. Cultural adaptations enabled men to live in larger aggregations, so that the village, the city, and finally the nation could be built up. With this history one can hope that eventually mankind as a whole will be the social unit, and the planetary surface the tribal territory. But these processes are governed by cultural evolution, and I often suspect that many of our troubles are caused by biological hangovers from our long Pleistocene submission to clan loyalties and territorial defense.

ECOLOGY AND EVOLUTION

Haeckel, in his original definition of ecology, pointed out that it would be concerned with "alle diejenigen verwickelten Wechsel, welche Darwin als die Bedingungen des Kampfes um's Dasein bezeichnet." The phrase "struggle for existence" is rather out of fashion because it clearly carries implications that may be dangerously misleading. We might better say now that ecology is concerned with the external factors that control the survival and abundance of individuals and populations, whether or not this involves "struggling."

This is perhaps half of evolution, the other half (genetics) being concerned with the internal factors of the organism itself, with the mechanisms that lead to the development of new potentialities in the organism (mutation or the origin of variation), and with the mechanisms that govern the inheritance of these potentialities. Neither half makes sense by itself, because the organism is meaningless except in some environmental context; and the environment is meaningless (to the biologist) except in terms of organic processes. The "nature versus nurture" controversy, in other words, turns on meaningless terms.

Yet the internal and external factors, which together result in the living systems that we can observe, require different methods of study, so that the distinction between the ecological and the genetic points of view is fruitful, at least at our present level of understanding—a fruitfulness that depends on the geneticist's having a considerable knowledge of ecological work and vice versa. This condition is coming generally to prevail among biologists, but its development among students of man is hampered by the special difficulties of both human genetics and human ecology. The realization of the need, however, is certainly growing.

The 1950 *Cold Spring Harbor Symposium of Quantitative Biology* (Vol. XV of the series) was devoted to the "Origin and Evolution of Man." This provides an excellent summary of the background knowledge and current interests of physical anthropologists and human geneticists. But in reading the volume, one is impressed by the general lack of emphasis on the ecological aspects of the problem under review. There is only rather incidental discussion of the forces governing survival in human populations and of possible changes in such forces in different geological and geographical circumstances, of human environmental adaptations, and of human population dynamics.

Partly this situation reflects the interests of the particular people writing the chapters of this symposium. A truly balanced and complete coverage of the topics directly pertinent to human evolution would hardly be manageable, and the symposium was quite sensibly directed at the more specific objective of furthering understanding between the geneticists and the physical anthropologists. But it also reflects a relative scarcity of students preoccupied with the ecological aspects of human evolution. Structure is more easily handled than function, and perhaps the structural problems—the fossil lineages, the racial traits, and the genetic mechanisms—must be clarified before we can even define the functional questions. Surely now, however, we have reached the point where the functional, ecological relations can be fruitfully emphasized.

Both the biological and the social sciences are in a stage of development where students are preoccupied with facts and wary of speculation. This, in the present connection, may be something of a handicap. We have a modicum of facts about Pleistocene man and the Pleistocene environment, and more abundant information about contemporary man and his environment. It seems to me that now we need a certain amount of bold speculation, aimed at relating these, to furnish us with hypotheses that will help us in organizing our facts and in guiding our search for new facts. Our hypotheses, however carefully we frame them, are bound to be wrong, but we are, I think, overly afraid of being wrong. The process of science seems to consist in setting up and demolishing conceptual schemes. As Conant (1951) has said: "Science is an interconnected series of concepts and conceptual schemes that have developed as a result of experimentation and observation and are fruitful of further experimentation and observation." Our information about man's relations with his environment seems, at every point, to be meager indeed; but it also seems to be scattered and unrelated. Perhaps more than new information, we need a consolidation and relation of these facts that have been so diversely garnered; and the questions of origins, of evolution, provide a convenient focus for this consolidation process.

I have tried, in this paper, to outline some of the topics that seem particularly appropriate for study from the ecological point of view. But, in closing, I should like to emphasize again that I do not think "ecology" can profitably be developed as a special subject matter, a special discipline within the complex of the social sciences. The subject, man, is divisible only as a matter of arbitrary convenience. We have to specialize in order to be able to handle the materials that we must study; but I think the arbitrary basis of our specialization is more easily kept in mind if we use vernacular labels for our topics—environmental analysis or adaptation, population, community structure, evolution, or what-have-you. Some topics will be more readily studied from an ecological point of view, others from a physiological, morphological, geographical, or some other point of view. But the subject—man, his origins, his present circumstances, and his destiny—forms a single pattern that cannot be broken into pieces that are separately understandable.

REFERENCES

ADOLPH, E. F., and ASSOCIATES. 1947. *Physiology of Man in the Desert.* New York: Interscience Publishers.

ALLEE, W. C.; EMERSON, A. E.; PARK, O.; PARK, T.; and SCHMIDT, K. P. 1949. *Principles of Animal Ecology.* Philadelphia: W. B. Saunders Co.

ANDERSON, R. K.; CALVO, JOSÉ; SERRANO, GLORIA; and PAYNE, G. C. 1946. "A Study of the Nutritional Status and Food Habits of Otomi Indians in the Mezquital Valley of Mexico," *American Journal of Public Health,* XXXVI, 883–903.

ANGEL, J. L. 1947. "The Length of Life in Ancient Greece," *Journal of Gerontology,* II, 18–24.

BANKS, A. L. 1950. *Man and His Environment.* Cambridge: At the University Press.

BARROWS, H. H. 1923. "Geography as Human Ecology," *Annals of the Association of American Geographers,* XIII, 1–14.

BATES, MARSTON. 1950. *The Nature of Natural History.* New York: Charles Scribner's Sons.

——. 1952. *Where Winter Never Comes: A Study of Man and Nature in the Tropics.* New York: Charles Scribner's Sons.

BEWS, J. W. 1935. *Human Ecology.* London: H. Milford.

CARPENTER, C. R. 1934. *A Field Study of the Behavior and Social Relations of Howling Monkeys (Alouatta palliata).* ("Comparative Psychology Monographs," Vol. X, No. 2.) Baltimore, Md.: Johns Hopkins Press.

——. 1940. *A Field Study in Siam of the Behavior and Social Relations of the Gibbon (Hylobates lar).* ("Comparative Psychology Monographs," Vol. XVI, No. 5.) Baltimore, Md.: Johns Hopkins Press.

CARR-SAUNDERS, A. M. 1922. *The Population Problem: A Study in Human Evolution.* Oxford: Clarendon Press.

CHILDE, V. G. 1951. *Man Makes Himself.* ("Mentor Books.") New York: New American Library. First published in England in 1936.

CONANT, J. B. 1951. *Science and Common Sense.* New Haven: Yale University Press.

COOK, S. F. 1949. *Soil Erosion and Population in Central Mexico.* ("Ibero-americana," No. 34.) Berkeley: University of California Press.

COON, C. S.; GARN, S. M.; and BIRDSELL, J. B. 1950. *Races: A Study of the Problems of Race Formation in Man.* Springfield, Ill.: Charles C. Thomas.

CORWIN, E. H. L. (ed.). 1949. *Ecology of Health.* (New York Academy of Medicine Centennial, Institute on Public Health, 1947.) New York: Commonwealth Fund.

DAVIS, DAVID. 1949. "An Animal's Home Is Its Castle," *Scientific Monthly,* LXIX, 249–53.

DAVIS, KINGSLEY. 1951. *The Population of India and Pakistan.* Princeton, N.J.: Princeton University Press.

ELTON, CHARLES. 1927. *Animal Ecology.* New York: Macmillan Co.

ERRINGTON, P. L. 1946. "Predation and Vertebrate Populations," *Quarterly Review of Biology,* XXI, 144–77, 221–45.

EVANS-PRITCHARD, E. E. 1940. *The Nuer: A Description of the Modes of Livelihood and Political Institutions of a Nilotic People.* London: Oxford University Press.

FORDE, C. D. 1934. *Habitat, Economy, and Society: A Geographical Introduction to Ethnology.* New York: E. P. Dutton Co.

HACKETT, L. W. 1937. *Malaria in Europe: An Ecological Study.* London: H. Milford.

HAECKEL, ERNST. 1870. "Ueber Entwickelungsgang und Aufgabe der Zoologie," *Jenäische Zeitschrift für Medicin und Naturwissenschaft,* V, 353–70.

HAWLEY, A. H. 1950. *Human Ecology: A Theory of Community Structure.* New York: Ronald Press Co.

HOWARD, H. E. 1920. *Territory in Bird Life.* London: John Murray.

KEITH, SIR ARTHUR. 1949. *A New Theory of Human Evolution.* New York: Philosophical Library.

KROEBER, A. L. 1939. *Cultural and Natural Areas of Native North America.* Berkeley: University of California Press.

KRZYWICKI, LUDWIK. 1934. *Primitive Society and Its Vital Statistics.* London: Macmillan & Co., Ltd.

KUCZYNSKI, R. R. 1948. *Demographic Survey of the British Colonial Empire,* Vol. I: *West Africa.* London and New York: Oxford University Press.

NEWBURGH, L. H. (ed.). 1949. *Physiology of Heat Regulation and the Science of Clothing.* Philadelphia: W. B. Saunders Co.

NICE, MARGARET. 1941. "The Role of Territory in Bird Life," *American Midland Naturalist,* XXVI, 441–87.

PARKINS, A. E. 1934. "The Geography of American Geographers," *Journal of Geography,* XXXIII, 221–30.

PLATT, R. S. 1948. "Environmentalism versus Geography," *American Journal of Sociology,* LIII, 351–58.

PRICE, A. G. 1939. *White Settlers in the Tropics.* ("Special Publications," No. 23.) New York: American Geographical Society.

QUINN, J. A. 1950. *Human Ecology.* New York: Prentice-Hall Book Co., Inc.

RICHARDS, AUDREY I. 1932. *Hunger and Work in a Savage Tribe: A Functional*

Study of Nutrition among the Southern Bantu. London: George Routledge & Sons.

ROBINSON, S.; DILL, D. B.; WILSON, J. W.; and NIELSEN, M. 1941. "Adaptations of White Men and Negroes to Prolonged Work in Humid Heat," *American Journal of Tropical Medicine*, XXI, 261–87.

RUSSELL, J. C. 1948. *British Medieval Population*. Albuquerque: University of New Mexico Press.

STEWARD, J. H. 1938. *Basin-Plateau Aboriginal Sociopolitical Groups*. (Bureau of American Ethnology Bull. 137.) Washington: Government Printing Office.

THOMPSON, LAURA. 1949. "The Relations of Men, Animals, and Plants in an Island Community (Fiji)," *American Anthropologist*, LI, 253–67.

THORNTHWAITE, C. W. 1940. "The Relation of Geography to Human Ecology," *Ecological Monographs*, X, 343–48.

VALLOIS, H. V. 1937. "La Durée de la vie chez l'homme fossile," *Anthropologie*, XLVII, 499–532.

WEIDENREICH, FRANZ. 1939. "The Duration of Life of Fossil Man in China and the Pathological Lesions Found in His Skeleton," *Chinese Medical Journal*, LV, 34–44.

WHITE, C. L., and RENNER, G. T. 1948. *Human Geography: An Ecological Study of Society*. New York: Appleton-Century-Crofts.

ZINSSER, HANS. 1935. *Rats, Lice, and History*. Boston: Little, Brown & Co.

ZIPF, G. K. 1949. *Human Behavior and the Principle of Least Effort: An Introduction to Human Ecology*. Cambridge, Mass.: Addison-Wesley Press.

The Strategy of Physical Anthropology

By S. L. WASHBURN

THE STRATEGY of a science is that body of theory and techniques with which it attacks its problems. All sciences have their traditional ways of marshaling and analyzing data, and the effectiveness of a science may be judged by the way its strategy actually solves problems and points the way to new research. For many years physical anthropology changed little and was easy to define. Physical anthropologists were those scientists, interested in human evolution and variation, who used measurements as their primary technique. The main training of a physical anthropologist consisted in learning to make a small number of measurements accurately, and one of the great concerns of the profession has been to get agreement on how these measurements should be taken. The assumption seems to have been that description (whether morphological or metrical), if accurate enough and in sufficient quantity, could solve problems of process, pattern, and interpretation.

It was essential to get a general appreciation of the varieties of primates, including man, before the problems of evolution could be understood. As knowledge of the primates increased, the kinds of problems to be solved became more and more defined. Is man's closest living relative an arboreal ape or a tiny tarsier? By what methods could such a problem be attacked? Should as many characters as possible be compared, or would a few critical ones settle the matter? Should adaptive characters be stressed, or does the solution of the problems of phylogeny lie in nonadaptive features? Does the body evolve as a unified whole, or may different parts change at different times?

The general understanding of the primates and of human races proceeded rapidly and productively in the nineteenth century. The classifications of Flower and Lydekker (1891) and Deniker (1900) are remarkably close to those of today. The principal progress since that time has been in the discovery of fossils, and the quantity and quality of descriptive materials has increased greatly. Many small problems have been clarified, but the main outlines of the classification of the primates were clear more than fifty years ago.

During the last fifty years, although excellent descriptive data were added, techniques improved, and problems clarified and defined, little progress was made in understanding the process and pattern of human evolution. The strategy of physical anthropology yielded diminishing returns, and, finally, application of the traditional method *by experts* gave contradictory results. After more than a century of intensive factfinding, there is less agreement among

714

informed scientists on the relation of man to other primates than there was in the latter part of the nineteenth century. (Schultz, 1936, 1950*a*, *b*; Simpson, 1945; and Straus, 1949, have recently summarized many of these conflicting views and the evidence for them.) With regard to race, agreement is no greater, for some recognize a few races based on populations, while others describe a great number, many of which are types and refer to no populations at all.

Difficulties of this sort are by no means confined to physical anthropology but are common in many parts of descriptive zoölogy. The dilemma arises from continuing the strategy which was appropriate in the first descriptive phase of a science into the following analytic phase. Measurements will tell us which heads are long, but they will not tell us whether longheaded people should be put into one biological category. A photograph may show that a person is fat, but it gives no clue to the cause of the fat, and a grouping of fat people may be as arbitrary as one of longheads.

It is necessary to have a knowledge of the varieties of head form, pigmentation, body build, growth pattern, etc., before the problems of evolution, race, and constitution can be clearly stated. But all that can be done with the initial descriptive information is to gain a first understanding, a sense of problem, and a preliminary classification. To go further requires an elaboration of theory and method along different lines. Having passed through its initial descriptive phase, physical anthropology is now entering into its analytic stage. Change is forced on physical anthropology partially by the fact that its own strategy has ceased to yield useful results but, far more, by the rise of modern evolutionary theory (treated elsewhere in this symposium by Carter). The meeting of genetics, paleontology, and evolutionary zoölogy created the new sys-

tematics (neozoölogy), just as the impact of the new evolutionary theory is creating a new physical anthropology. Anthropologists are fortunate that their problems are logically and methodologically similar to those which have been debated and largely solved in zoölogy. Therefore, their task is far simpler than that which confronted taxonomists fifteen years ago. The anthropologist may simply adopt the new evolutionary point of view, and his task is primarily one of adapting to this intellectual environment and devising techniques suitable to his particular needs. The nature and implication of the changes will be made clearer by considering the contrast between the old and the new systematically, under the headings of purpose, theory, technique, and interpretation. These comparisons will be made briefly in Table 1, and then each will be considered in some detail. It should be remembered in making the comparisons that the differences are in degree only and that brief contrasts, especially in a table, make them appear unduly sharp. As Stewart (1951) has rightly pointed out, the new physical anthropology has evolved from the old, and there is a real continuity. However, a great change is taking place in a short time. If this is called "evolution," it is evolution of a quantum type. It is a burst of acceleration on the part of a species which had been quiescent for a long period of time. Actually, the physical anthropology of 1950 will seem much more like that of 1900 than it will like that of 1960. Since the transition described in this paper is still taking place, it would be very difficult to discern its magnitude from the anthropological literature. The remarks in this paper are based heavily on the discussions which have been held at the Wenner-Gren summer seminars for physical anthropologists, and those reading only current American physical anthropology would get little idea of the size or importance of these changes. Since the transition in zoölogy is now general and international, that in anthropology soon will be, and it is hoped that the extent and nature of the changes now taking place in other countries may be discussed at length at this conference.

This point can be made clear by examples. It has long been known that browridges vary in size and form. Cunningham (1909) gave a classification into which the majority of browridges can be fitted. The classification of browridges by this or similar schemes is a standard part of traditional physical

TABLE 1

OLD	NEW
Purpose	
Primarily classification	Understanding process
Problems solved by classification and correlation	Classification a minor part, and the *cause* of differences critical
Description of difference enough	
Theory	
Relatively little and unimportant; facts speak for themselves	Theory is critical, and the development of consistent, experimentally verified hypotheses a major objective
Technique	
Anthropometry 80 per cent, aided by morphological comparison	Measurement perhaps 20 per cent, supplemented by a wide variety of techniques adapted to the solution of particular problems
Interpretation	
Speculation	The primary objective of the research is to prove which hypotheses are correct; the major task begins where the old left off

PURPOSE

In commenting on the contrasts between the new and the old physical anthropology outlined in Table 1, it should be stressed that the area of interest or ultimate purposes of the field are the same. The understanding and interpretation of human evolution remains the objective. However, the immediate purpose of most scientific investigations will be but a small step toward the final goal. The investigator will be concerned with race, constitution, fossil man, or some similar problem. In the past the primary purpose of the majority of investigations of this sort was classification rather than the interpretation of any part of the phenomenon being investigated.

anthropology. But what do the differences mean, and to what are they related? The classification gives no answers to these problems. To say that one fossil has browridges of Type II and another of Type III does not give any information on the significance of the difference, nor does it allow any inference to be made concerning relationship. In general, big browridges are correlated with big faces, but the appearance of size is also dependent on the size and form of the braincase. Microcephals appear to have large ridges, but this is due solely to the small size of the brain. In such an extreme case everyone would interpret the difference as being due to the change in size of the brain, but how much of the difference between the browridge of Java man and modern man is due to the difference in the face, and how much to a difference in the brain? In the literature a phylogeny of browridges is presented (Weidenreich, 1947). This can be interpreted only if the ridges are sufficiently independent in size and form that tentative conclusions may be drawn from the classification and historical sequence. No one doubts the validity of the descriptive statements, but there is very real doubt that any conclusions can be drawn from this sort of table. This is because the ridge is anatomically complex and because the same general form of ridge may be due to a diversity of different conditions. For example, the central part of the divided type of ridge may be due to a large frontal sinus, acromegaly, a deposit of mechanically unoriented bone, or highly oriented bone. The general prominence of the region may be due to a large face or a small brain; but probably, with faces of equal mass, those associated with long cranial bases and large temporal muscles have larger browridges than those which are associated with shorter bases and larger masseter muscles. The description of the differences between an Australian Aboriginal and a Mongoloid can be done by the traditional methods, but it can be interpreted only if the anatomical causes lying behind the differences are analyzed. The description offers no technical difficulty, but analysis is possible only by the use of a variety of methods which have not been part of the equipment of anthropology (see paper by Rowe in this symposium).

This example shows the way in which classification was the aim and tool of physical anthropology. As viewed traditionally, if one was interested in browridges, the procedure was to classify the structures and then to draw conclusions on the interrelations of races or fossil men. That is, the classification

gave a tool to be used in the analysis of evolution and variation. It was, in this sense, final knowledge. But in a different sense the classification merely outlined the problems to be investigated. No description of the types of browridges gives understanding of the reasons for any of them. The classifications show what kinds exist, under what circumstances they are found, and so pose a series of problems which need investigation. To traditional physical anthropology, classification was an end, something to be used. To the new physical anthropology, classifications merely pose problems, and methods must be devised to solve them.

The traditional reliance on classification as a method of analysis produced two of the characteristics of traditional zoölogical taxonomy and physical anthropology. (1) If classification is the primary aim and tool, then agreement on method is all-important. Therefore, the efforts of physical anthropologists have been to get agreements on how to take measurements and observations. Introductions to physical anthropology are largely instructions on how to take measurements, with little or no indication of what it is that the measurements are supposed to mean. International congresses have ended with pleas for uniformity, so that classification might continue. One may hope that this congress will break with the traditions of the past and urge that undue emphasis on uniformity is undesirable and will stress the need for new techniques for the solution of particular problems. (2) The second result of the emphasis on classification is that, when difficulties arise, they are met by making the classifications more complicated. This may be illustrated in the study of race. By the early part of the nineteenth century, several simple classifications of races existed, and causal explanations had been offered. Races were due to climate, isolation, etc. In the meantime, classifications of races have become vastly more numerous, and many are extremely complex, but explanations of cause and process have remained much as they were. Dobzhansky (1950) points out that the principal task of the anthropologist now should be to try to understand the causes and process of race formation. Dobzhansky's clear and eloquent plea should be read by all anthropologists, and I have only one qualification, or rather explanation. Traditional anthropologists thought that they were dealing with cause and process much more than Dobzhansky thinks they were. The difference really lies in the attitude toward classification. The traditional physical anthropologist thought that classification, if done in sufficient detail, would give the clues to problems of cause and process. Classifications were accompanied by remarks on how they were explained by hybridization, environment, etc. If one believes that classifications alone give understanding, then one will make the classifications more and more complicated, just as anthropologists have been doing. However, if one thinks that classification can do no more than map the results of process, then one will be content with a very rough mapping until the processes have been analyzed. The new physical anthropology is separated from the old, not by any difference in the desire to know causes, but by a very real difference in belief as to the extent to which classification can reveal causes.

Some classification is a necessary first stage in ordering the data in an area of knowledge, but its meaning depends on understanding the processes which produce the variety of form. After the first stage of preliminary description, scientists must turn to problems of process or face an era of futile elaboration of classifications which cannot be interpreted for lack of adequate techniques and theories.

THEORY

It is a characteristic of the first stage of a science that theory is not considered important. If classification can solve problems and if it can be reached by marshaling enough facts, then theory need be of little concern. However, as knowledge increases and problems are more precisely formulated, theory becomes of great importance. For a considerable time after the idea of organic evolution had been accepted, comparisons were made without any general theoretical concern, other than that the parts compared should be homologous. Later, anthropology was particularly disturbed by the controversy as to whether deductions concerning relationship should be made on the basis of adaptive or nonadaptive characters. This, in turn, raised the question of whether it was better to compare many features, or whether the comparison of a few critical ones might not give more reliable results. Parallel evolution became recognized as a complicating feature, but, on the whole, physical anthropology continued to operate without any great concern for its theoretical foundations. It should be stressed that this general point of view was characteristic of much of historical zoölogy, ethnology, and archeology. Theoretical issues were not absent, but they were not deemed very important, and the major effort went into collecting specimens and data and describing facts. The realization has been growing for some years that facts alone will not settle the problems and that even the collection of the "facts" was guided by a complex body of unstated assumptions.

The necessary guiding theories have been recently set forth by numerous zoölogists, and the new zoölogy states simply that evolution is the history of genetic systems. Changes in isolated populations are due to mutation, selection, and accidents of genetic sampling (drift). The major cause of change is selection, which is a simple word covering a vast number of mechanisms (Dobzhansky, 1951). The implications of this theory for physical anthropology are numerous and complicated. The basic issue may be stated as follows: If evolution is governed primarily by adaptation, the demonstration of the nature and kind of adaptation is the principal task of the anthropologist. Evolution is a sequence of more effective behavior systems. To understand behavior, live animals must be studied first, and then, when fossils are found, the attempt can be made to interpret the differences by a knowledge of the living forms. It is necessary to remember that fossils were alive when they were important. They were the living, adapted forms of their day, and they must be understood in that setting. In so far as the record is fragmentary, the task is full of uncertainty; but this is a difficulty inherent in the kind of material and does not alter the logical problem.

Traditional physical anthropology was based on the study of skulls. Measurements were devised to describe certain features of the bones, and, when the technique was extended to the living, the measurements were kept as close to those taken on the skeleton as possible. From a comparative and classificatory point of view this was reasonable, and for a while it yielded useful results, but it brought the limitations of death to the study of the living. Whereas the new physical anthropology aims to enrich the study of the past by study of the present, to understand bone in terms of function and life, the old tried to reduce the living to a series of measurements designed to describe bones. Similarity in measurements or combinations of measurements was believed to show genetic affinity. Although it is true that humans of similar genotype are metrically similar, it is not true that similar measurements necessarily mean genetic similarity. Boyd (1950) has discussed this in detail. However, the point is so important that one example will be given here. Straus (1927) has shown that the ilium is approximately the same length in males and females, but the upper part is longer in males, and the lower longer in females. It is only an accident that the two different parts happen to give approximately the same total length. The descriptive statement that the ilium length is the same in male and female is correct and could be proved beyond doubt with elaborate statistics. However, the conclusion that the bones are anatomically or genetically similar would be wrong. The basis for dividing the ilium into upper and lower parts is that these have different functions. The upper is concerned primarily with muscle origin and sacral articulation. The lower ilium is an important segment of the pelvic inlet, which grows rapidly at puberty (Greulich and Thoms, 1944), making the large female inlet suitable for childbirth. The understanding of the ilium which leads to the division into upper and lower segments is based on an appreciation of its function in the living, on the different adaptive nature of the two parts. It is in this sense that the understanding of the living enriches and brings life to the study of the bones. The metrical discrimination is based on anatomical understanding which can be partially expressed metrically and given deeper meaning by statistics. But the original discrimination is based on an appreciation of an adaptive complex. After the choice to measure upper and lower ilium has been made, measurements help by showing the degree of difference, the variability and the correlation of parts, and prove that the anatomical judgment was justified. *But no statistical manipulation will make a discrimination which is not inherent in the original measurements.* Statistics may bring out relations which are there but which are not obvious to the investigator, as shown by Howells (1951).

If a measurement is regarded as genetically determined, nonadaptive, and not correlated with others, it might then be used in the comparison of races without further question. This seems to have been the approximate working hypothesis of traditional physical anthropology. However, if traits are anatomically complex, adaptive, and correlated, they will be useful for description, but comparisons will not automatically yield solutions to problems of affinity. Present genetic and evolutionary theory suggests that characters are, for the most part, complex and adaptive, but this does not give information about any particular situation. The theory that the measurements were nonadaptive allowed one to work blindly and with confidence. The traditional measurements, accurately taken and treated with proper statistics, *gave certain answers.* The belief that traits are complex and adaptive means that the metrical comparisons *pose problems,* which must then be investigated by other methods. Measurements tell us that roundheads have become more common (Weidenreich, 1945), but they do not tell us that roundheads are genetically similar or why roundheads have become more common. From an anatomical point of view, is brachycephalization due to changes in the brain, dura, sutures, or base of the skull? From an evolutionary point of view, is the change due to adaptation or genetic drift? It should be stressed that, although all seem agreed that selection is the most important factor in evolution, there is no agreement on the importance of genetic drift (Carter, 1951; Dobzhansky, 1951) or the extent to which traits of little or no adaptive importance exist or spread.

In the past, investigators have assumed that characters were adaptive or nonadaptive, but this is the very question which needs investigation (as discussed by Dobzhansky, 1950). Further, it should be stressed that it is not a question of one or the other, but of selective pressures varying from very little to very great. Some characteristic features of a race may be due to drift, others to strong selection, others to mild selection, still others to mixture due entirely to cultural factors. Whether a particular trait or gene frequency is highly adaptive or of little importance can be settled only by research, and the answer will surely differ at different times and places.

Closely related to the idea of nonadaptation is the concept of orthogenesis. If evolution is *not* caused by selection, then the long-term changes must be due to some other cause, and change may be accounted for by some inner irreversible force. This general concept has been very common in anthropology. For example, it has been maintained that, since man's arms are shorter than apes', man could not be descended from an ape, as this would reverse the course of evolution. According to the theory that evolution is adaptive, there is no reason why man's ancestors may not have had much longer arms. When selection changed, arms may have become shorter. (Actually, the difference is small; Schultz, 1950a.) According to the irreversible orthogenetic-force theory, man could not be descended from an ape, and a few measurements settle the matter. According to the theory of natural selection, man could be descended from an ape, but the theory does not prove that he was. All it does is indicate the kind of adaptive problem which must be understood before the data of comparative anatomy and the fossil record can be interpreted. Certainly, one of the reasons why the theory of orthogenesis, irreversibility, and the importance of nonadaptive characters was popular is that it allowed conclusions to be drawn by a few rules based on little evidence. The theory of selection offers no simple answers but merely points the direction in which answers must be sought. The successive adaptive radiations of the primates must be understood in terms of the evolution of more efficient behavior. The elucidation of the adaptive mechanisms will require all the help which paleontology, anatomy, archeology, and experiment can give. Far more work will be done to reach less definitive conclusions, but an understanding of the pattern and process of primate evolution will be gained. The belief that selection is the major cause of evolution alters the way evolution should be studied. In so far as anthropological conclusions have been based on the concepts of orthogenesis, irreversibility, and the use of nonadaptive traits, the conclusions need re-examination. Parallelism needs to be interpreted as the result of similar selection on related animals rather than be used as a way of discounting resemblances.

Aside from the concept of selection, there are two other aspects of evolutionary theory which are of the utmost importance for anthropology. These are, first, that descriptions should be based on populations and, second, that genes, or traits, may vary independently. Taken together, these two facts mean that the anthropological concept of type is untenable, and refusal to accept this fact is the main reason why some anthropologists have been reluctant to adopt genetic concepts. Both these points have been elaborated by numerous authors and are discussed in this symposium by Boyd and Carter. The implications for anthropology of the concept of population and independence of genes are best understood

by the history of the concept of race (Count, 1950). In the earlier racial classifications a race was a group of people living in one part of the world who were obviously different from other people in physical characters. Thus the peoples of Europe, Africa south of the Sahara, eastern Asia, Australia, and the Americas were early recognized as races. How the peoples of India should be treated was always a problem, for a variety of reasons which lie beyond the scope of this essay. In the main, this classification is the same as that which Boyd (1950) gives on the basis of gene frequencies. Even the difficulty with regard to India is present in Boyd's classification. As knowledge increased, the larger areas were subdivided, and groups such as the Bushmen or Polynesians were recognized. The division of the world into areas occupied by more or less physically distinct groups was completed before 1900. The genetic study of race seems to be substantiating a large part of this general classification of mankind, although parts will surely be changed.

After 1900, to an increasing extent, a fundamentally different kind of "race" came to be used. In this race the group described was not a breeding population but a segment of such a population sorted out by various criteria. This second kind is called "type." Originally the Australoid race meant the populations of aboriginal Australia. By extension, the Australoid type was any skull, whether found in South Africa or America, which had certain morphological features common in the population of Australia. Similarly, the Mongoloid, or Negroid, race applies to groups of populations which have already been found to have genetic individuality. But there is no suggestion that the Mongoloid or Negroid types can be substantiated genetically.

The difficulty with the typological

approach has been recognized by many (especially Huxley and Haddon, 1936; Benedict, 1940; Dahlberg, 1942), who pointed out that the more unrelated characters are used for sorting, the more races (types) there will be. Weidenreich (1946) objected to adding the blood groups to the traditional anthropological characters, on the ground that this would make the theoretical total of races 92,780! With the typological approach, the more that is known, the more types there will be; but, no matter how much is known, the number of populations remains unchanged. However much is ultimately known about the genetics and anatomy of the Australian aborigines, there are still the same tribes living on the same continent. Populations are reproductive groups which are defined by the ethnologist or archeologist, or deduced from the way skeletons are found. The intensity of anatomical and genetical investigation does not increase the number of populations.

A "race" is a group of genetically similar populations, and races intergrade because there are always intermediate populations. A "type" is a group of individuals who are identical in those characters (genetic or phenotypic) by which the type was sorted (but *not* in other features!). The race concept and the type concept are fundamentally different, and modern zoölogical theory is compatible only with the race concept.

If anthropologists should adopt current zoölogical practice, several of the classifications of human races would be discarded, and the strategy of some schools of thought would be entirely abandoned. However, the change may be less than it appears at first sight. The reason for this is that most physical anthropologists simply were not interested in theory. In the majority of classifications, exemplified by that of Hooton (1946), some of the races refer to populations and others to types. Even the type descriptions usually contain data on the whole series, prior to the type analysis. At present *there is no anthropological theory of race,* but two old, incompatible concepts carried along side by side. One of the primary tasks in developing a new physical anthropology is systematically to apply the modern zoölogical concept of race, to discard the types, and to put the traditional information into the form in which it will be most useful for the understanding of race formation.

In summarizing the contrast between the old and the new physical anthropology with regard to theory, the main point to emphasize is that the application of a consistent, experimentally verified, evolutionary theory is the first task of the physical anthropologist. Since investigators were not interested in theory and since there is great diversity in actual practice, no useful purpose would be served by trying to discuss the implications of the new evolutionary theory in more detail. In the past, all the useful ideas were present in traditional physical anthropology, but so were the useless ones.

Boyd (1950) has stressed the break with the past, and Stewart (1951) the continuity with the past. Actually, physical anthropology is in a period of rapid transition in which both continuity and great change are important. At such a time disagreements are to be tolerated and major changes of personal opinion expected. For example, in 1940 Boyd criticized anthropologists for using adaptive characters when he maintained that they should use only nonadaptive ones. In 1950 he was equally vehement in his criticism of anthropologists for not seeking to use adaptive traits. At neither time were anthropologists as a profession doing either consistently, and at both times the real issue was to try to demonstrate which traits were adaptive, an issue which can be settled only by research.

Agreement is needed on the following points: (1) physical anthropology needs a consistent, proved, theoretical framework; (2) the necessary evolutionary and genetic theories are available and should be applied to the problems of human evolution; (3) untenable concepts should be abandoned; (4) a time of transition should be *welcomed* in which great differences in personal opinion are to be expected. These differences should be settled by research and not allowed to become personal or national issues.

TECHNIQUE

A successful scientific strategy depends on theories and techniques adequate to solve problems. As theories change, techniques must alter also, as they exist only to solve problems and not as ends in themselves. Traditional physical anthropology was committed to the view that description alone would solve its problems, and, in practice, description of a very limited kind. The same measurements were applied to the solution of problems of the classification of the primates, relations of fossil men, description of race, human growth, and constitution. The technical training of a physical anthropologist was primarily indoctrination in the measurements of a particular school. In spite of the vast progress in biology, the practices of the physical anthropologist remained essentially the same for over one hundred years, although modified in detail and refined. As pointed out earlier, these techniques were an efficient part of the strategy of a descriptive science. They helped to outline the classification of the primates, fossil men, and races. The problems of interpreting human evolution and variation were clarified, but the traditional techniques failed to solve the problems of process. There are more different theories of man's origin and differentia-

tion now than there were fifty years ago, and in this sense the strategy of physical anthropology failed. This was due partly to the theoretical dilemmas outlined before and partly to inadequacy of the techniques.

The reasons why the traditional anthropometric measurements are inadequate to do more than they already have done, that is, outline a rough classification and indicate problems, can be made clear by an example. A variety of measurements and observations are traditionally taken on the nose (length, breadth, shape of profile, form of lower margin). Then these data are compared, on the basic assumption that *nose* is an independent entity which has been described and whose attributes may be compared. But the concept of adaptation suggests that the middle part of the face should be viewed in a very different way. Benninghoff (1925) and recently Seipel (1948) have shown by the use of the split-line technique that the face is highly organized in response to the stresses of mastication. The margins of the piriform aperture are thick in stressed, and thin in unstressed, forms. Further, the breadth of the aperture corresponds approximately to the intercanine distance, or breadth, of the incisor teeth. In man the incisors develop in the subnasal area, and, as Baker (1941) has shown, developing teeth exert a positive force increasing the size of the surrounding bone. Gans and Sarnat (1951) have shown that the growth in the region of the maxillary-premaxillary suture is accelerated at the time of eruption of the permanent canine tooth. This supplements the observations of Seipel (1948) on the way the erupting canine causes the reorganization of a large area of the face in the chimpanzee. Far from being an independent structure which can be described by itself, the nose is an integrated part of the face, and variations in its form can be interpreted only as a part of the functioning face. The form of the nose is the result of a variety of factors. Just how many and how they are interrelated can be discovered only by research, but it seems clear that the most important ones, as far as gross form is concerned, are the teeth and forces of mastication. But these are not included in the traditional descriptions of the nose, nor will looking at skulls or measuring them give this kind of information.

Since the problem of interpreting the form of the nose is part of the problem of understanding the functioning pattern of the face, the methods needed to interpret this form must describe the pattern. The traditional measurements will not do this, and they must be supplemented by techniques which are appropriate to this particular problem. Such methods are the split-line technique of Benninghoff, alizarin vital stain, experimental removal of teeth, marking sutures, etc. Some of these techniques can be applied directly to man. Others require experimental animals, but at least this much is necessary to understand what is done when a simple measurement is taken across the nasal aperture. There is no way of telling in advance what methods, in addition to measurement, will be needed, as these depend on the particular problem to be solved. What is needed in research and in education is an elastic approach, showing the problems which have arisen from the traditional classifications and techniques and encouraging every attempt to develop new and more efficient methods.

INTERPRETATION

The traditional method of interpretation in physical anthropology primarily was speculation. Races, for example, have been attributed to endless mixtures, hormones, minerals, climate, adaptation, isolation, and chance, but little effort has been devoted to proving any of the theories. Similarly, measurements have been claimed to be adaptive or nonadaptive, but detailed proof substantiating either point of view is lacking. Actually, all dimensions of the human body serve functions, and the practical issue is to show what, in an anatomical sense, is being measured and what genetic or environmental factors may modify it. The face as a whole may be highly adaptive, and its main course in human evolution determined by selection, but small differences between races may be due to genetic drift. What is needed is *proof* of adaptation or drift in particular cases.

The point may be made clearer by returning to the example of the nose. It has often been suggested that big noses appear when faces become small. But this theory has many exceptions and gives no idea of the factors actually involved. Since the split-line technique shows that the nasal bones are actually stressed by the forces of mastication, would it be reasonable to suppose that these bones would be bigger if the forces were reduced? If one nasal bone of a rat is removed on the first day of life, the other nasal bone grows to approximately one and a half times normal size. Further comparable removal of interparietal and parietal bones shows that these also grow large if free to do so. It seems to be a general rule that cranial roofing bones will grow bigger if forces normally stopping growth are removed. Schaeffer (1920) pictures skulls in which the nasal bones are entirely absent and the roof of the nose is formed by the maxillae. Piecing these lines of evidence together, it appears that the answer is again a question of pattern. Other things being equal, less pressure may result in more growth of nasal bone, but the actual proportions will depend on the interrelations of the size of the nasals, frontal processes of the maxillae, and the pressures.

Instead of relating nose form to selection or climate, it is necessary to insert an intermediate step, the analysis of the nose. Rather than saying that the pigmy's broad nose is an adaptation to the tropics, it may be that the nose is the result of a short face with large incisor teeth. The short face may be correlated with small total size (stature?), and the big teeth need explanation. Not enough is known about the form of the face to be sure that the racial differences of the nose should be correlated with climate at all.

Perhaps the relation of speculation, proof, and the importance of new methods can be best illustrated by theories concerning race mixture. It has become customary in physical anthropology to account for most of the races of the world by mixture. Of the four interrelated causes of difference recognized by zoölogists (mutation, selection, drift, and migration), only one has been regarded as the principal source of new varieties of man. The absence of evidence for three primary races has been pointed to by Boyd (1950) and numerous others, and it is probably only rarely that mixture has been a major cause of race formation. The differentiation of races, for whatever reasons, must be accounted for on other grounds, as mixture can only make gene frequencies more alike.

If the Indians are a result of Mongoloid and Australian mixture, then they should have high blood group N, and considerable B. Actually they have the least N in the world, and B only among the Eskimo. In other words, the postulated mixture does not explain the facts known about the Indians. The more complicated hypotheses work no better. If Negroids are an important element in the mixture, then Rh° should appear in the Indian, and it does not. If European elements are there, A2 and Rh negative should be present. It is clear that mixture alone will not explain the American Indian blood groups. Drift and/or selection must have operated also to change the gene frequencies, because what is found in the American Indian is something new, not found in the Old World or derivable from Old World frequencies by any mixtures. In spite of all the work that was done by traditional methods, it was possible for competent investigators to hold a number of divergent views as to the origin of the American Indian. The advent of a technique which made it possible to deal with the theories in objective, quantitative terms clearly shows that much of the speculation was unfounded and the role of mixture, as opposed to differentiation, exaggerated. The blood groups provide precise techniques for measuring mixture, provided that the mixture is relatively recent, as Carbon 14 suggests in the case of the American Indian (Johnson, 1951).

In summary, the traditional physical anthropologist thought that his task was finished when he had classified and speculated. This era is past, and there are enough classifications and speculations. Now methods must be developed which will prove which speculations were on the right track. The best of the past should be combined with new techniques to bring proof in the place of speculation.

CONCLUSION

The attempt has been made to consider under the headings of purpose, theory, technique, and interpretation the changes now taking place in physical anthropology. The strategy of the traditional descriptive investigations has been contrasted with the developing analytic strategy, with its emphasis on theory, process, and experiment. The whole change is precisely parallel to that which has taken place in systematics.

The new strategy does not solve problems, but it suggests a different way of approaching them. The change from the old to the new affects the various parts of physical anthropology very differently. In studies of growth and applied anthropology, where the knowledge of dimensions is directly useful, changing theories make little difference. In evolutionary investigations the theoretical changes are of the greatest importance, and much of the anthropological work on race and constitution is eliminated by the rejection of the concept of type. However, one of the main implications of the new point of view is that there is a far more detailed interrelationship between the different parts of anthropology than under the old strategy. A dynamic analysis of the form of the jaw will illuminate problems of evolution, fossil man, race, growth, constitution, and medical application. The unraveling of the process of human evolution and variation will enrich the understanding of other mammalian groups, whereas the detailed description of a fossil has a much more limited utility. By its very nature,

the investigation of process and behavior has a generality which is lacking in purely descriptive studies. The problems of human evolution are but special cases of the problems of mammalian evolution, and their solution will enrich paleontology, genetics, and parts of clinical medicine.

But some of the problems of human evolution are unique to man. In so far as man has adapted by his way of life, the study of human evolution is inseparably bound to the study of archeology and ethnology. It is because of the importance of the cultural factor that a separate study of human evolution is necessary. Human migrations, adaptations, mating systems, population density, diseases, and ecology—all these critical biological factors become increasingly influenced by the way of life. If we would understand the process of human evolution, we need a modern dynamic biology and a deep appreciation of the history and functioning of culture. It is this necessity which gives all anthropology unity as a science.

LITERATURE CITED

BAKER, L. W. 1941. "The Influence of the Formative Dental Organs on the Growth of the Bones of the Face," *American Journal of Orthodontics*, XXVII, 489–506.

BENEDICT, R. 1940. *Race: Science and Politics.* ("Modern Age Books.") New York: Viking Press.

BENNINGHOFF, A. 1925. "Spaltlinien am Knochen, eine Methode zur Ermittlung der Architektur platter Knochen," *Anatomischer Anzeiger*, LX, 189–205.

BOYD, W. C. 1950. *Genetics and the Races of Man.* Boston: Little, Brown & Co.

CARTER, G. S. 1951. *Animal Evolution.* London: Sidgwick & Jackson.

COUNT, E. W. 1950. *This Is Race.* New York: Henry Schuman.

CUNNINGHAM, D. J. 1909. "The Evolution of the Eyebrow Region of the Forehead, with Special Reference to the Excessive

Supraorbital Development of the Neanderthal Race," *Transcriptions of the Royal Society, Edinburgh*, XLVI, 283–311.

DAHLBERG, G. 1942. *Race, Reason, and Rubbish.* New York: Columbia University Press.

DENIKER, J. 1900. *The Races of Man.* New York: Charles Scribner's Sons.

DOBZHANSKY, T. 1950. "Human Diversity and Adaptation," *Cold Spring Harbor Symposia on Quantitative Biology*, Vol. XV: *Origin and Evolution of Man*, pp. 385–400. Cold Spring Harbor, Long Island, N.Y.: Biological Laboratory.

———. 1951. *Genetics and the Origin of Species.* 3d ed. New York: Columbia University Press.

FLOWER, W. H., and LYDEKKER, R. 1891. *Mammals Living and Extinct.* London: Adam & Charles Black.

GANS, B. J., and SARNAT, B. G. 1951. "Sutural Facial Growth of the *Macaca rhesus* Monkey," *American Journal of Orthodontics*, XXXVII, 827–41.

GREULICH, W. W., and THOMS, H. 1944. "The Growth and Development of the Pelvis of Individual Girls before, during, and after Puberty," *Yale Journal of Biology and Medicine*, XVII, 91–97.

HOOTON, E. A. 1946. *Up from the Ape.* Rev. ed. New York: Macmillan Co.

HOWELLS, W. W. 1951. "Factors of Human Physique," *American Journal of Physical Anthropology*, n.s., IX, 159–91.

HUXLEY, J. S., and HADDON, A. C. 1936. *We Europeans.* New York: Harper & Bros.

JOHNSON, F. 1951. *Radiocarbon Dating.* ("Memoirs of the Society for American Archaeology," No. 8.)

SCHAEFFER, J. P. 1920. *The Nose, Paranasal Sinuses, Nasolacrimal Passageways, and Olfactory Organ in Man.* Philadelphia: Blakiston's Son & Co.

SCHULTZ, A. H. 1936. "Characters Common to Higher Primates and Characters Specific for Man," *Quarterly Review of Biology*, XI, 259–83, 425–55.

———. 1950a. "The Physical Distinctions of Man," *Proceedings of the American Philosophical Society*, XCIV, 428–49.

———. 1950b. "The Specializations of Man and His Place among the Catarrhine Primates," *Cold Spring Harbor Symposia on Quantitative Biology*, Vol. XV: *Origin and Evolution of Man*, pp. 37–52. Cold Spring Harbor, Long Island, N.Y.: Biological Laboratory.

SEIPEL, C. M. 1948. "Trajectories of the Jaws," *Acta odontologica Scandinavica*, VIII, 81–191.

SIMPSON, G. G. 1945. *The Principles of Classification and a Classification of Mammals.* (American Museum of Natural History Bull. 85.) New York.

STEWART, T. D. 1951. "Three in One: Physical Anthropology, Genetics, Statistics," *Journal of Heredity*, XLII, 255–56, 260.

STRAUS, W. L. 1927. "The Human Ilium: Sex and Stock," *American Journal of Physical Anthropology*, XI, 1–28.

———. 1949. "The Riddle of Man's Ancestry," *Quarterly Review of Biology*, XXIV, 200–223.

WEIDENREICH, F. 1945. "The Brachycephalization of Recent Mankind," *Southwestern Journal of Anthropology*, I, 1–54.

———. 1946. *Apes, Giants, and Man.* Chicago: University of Chicago Press.

———. 1947. "The Trend of Human Evolution," *Evolution*, I, 221–36.

Relations of Anthropology to the Social Sciences and to the Humanities

By ROBERT REDFIELD

INTRODUCTION

As a "background" or "inventory" paper, this contribution is written for the eye rather than the ear and so without summaries or graces of rhetoric. For convenience in discussion, each section bears a title and each paragraph a number. The topic is treated from the viewpoint of an American anthropologist. British anthropology is in view, to lesser degree; other anthropology very little. The treatment derives from understanding of the subject that has been provided by Kroeber in a long series of his publications; indeed, there is no fundamental idea that I can find to add to his.

THE SOCIAL AND THE METHODO-LOGICAL RELATIONS BETWEEN DISCIPLINES

1. An academic discipline is at once a group of men in persisting social relations and a method of investigation. "Anthropology" is both the professors and other practitioners of that discipline and the problems characteristic of it, with the ways of going to work upon them. The relations between anthropology and any other discipline are, accordingly, of two sorts: social (societal and personal), on the one hand, and logical or methodological, on the other. The societal relations appear in such institutions as professional organizations and departmental arrangements; the personal relations appear in the attitude and sentiments characteristic of anthropologists with regard to the representatives of other disciplines, and vice versa. The methodological relations exist in the resemblances and differences between anthropology and another discipline as to assumptions made, as to choice of subject matter and questions asked, as to concepts employed, and as to operations followed, from the abstractions achieved by the mind to the concrete and particular devices of field or laboratory.

2. The two kinds of relations, social and methodological, are mutually influential, but neither determines the other. Where a methodological relationship is discovered, as recently between some anthropologists and some practitioners of "depth psychology," closer social relations also develop. Nevertheless, as societies, the disciplines are within the general society and are influenced by attitudes characterizing the general society; for this reason the social relations between anthropology and another discipline do not correspond precisely to

728

the methodological relations between them. As a way of work, anthropology at Columbia is substantially the same as anthropology at Chicago, and sociology in the one institution is very similar to sociology in the other; the difference in social relations between the two disciplines as seen at the two universities is to be explained by events in social, not methodological, relations. Viewing the whole United States, one sees that the social relations between sociology and anthropology are closer than those between anthropology and political science; this is partly due to greater similarity in ways of work. On the whole, again, sociology has taken a lead in introducing anthropology into academic respectability; yet the rapid success of anthropology here tends now to color the attitudes directed toward anthropology by sociology or other social sciences with those directed in society generally to the *arriviste*. These commonplaces illustrate the influence of societal attitudes upon the relations between our disciplines. Methodological relations are accordingly helped or hindered.

3. Considering the relations of anthropology to the natural sciences, on the one hand, and to the humanities, on the other, one may recognize the effects of both methodological and societal influences. The social relations of anthropology to the natural sciences are closer than they are to the humanities, and closer than are the relations of other social sciences to the natural sciences. In universities anthropology is rarely grouped with literature and the arts, and the professional connections which anthropology enjoys in the Social Science Research Council, the National Research Council, and the American Association for the Advancement of Science are valued, by anthropologists, more highly and are more energetically exploited than are the relations with the humanities that are

provided by the American Council of Learned Societies. With psychology, anthropology is admitted by natural scientists to special grouping in the NRC and the AAAS, and chapters of Sigma Xi admit anthropologists where other social scientists may be refused. Both the degree of welcome given anthropology by the natural sciences and the relative weakness of anthropological connections with the humanities are undoubtedly in large part expressions of the fundamental conception which anthropology long ago formed of itself and still realizes in important degree: as a discipline interested in the phenomena and the forces of nature as they are, and how they have come to be, "without preconceptions and without primary ulterior motives of existing philosophy, theology, politics, or philanthropy" (Kroeber, 1948, p. 841). At the same time, the orientation of anthropology toward the sciences rather than toward the humanities may be seen as an aspect of a general societal phenomenon: the arrangement of the disciplines in a hierarchy of status wherein the "harder" natural sciences occupy the uppermost positions and the humanist is the man farthest down. The point that will now be developed is that, while anthropology is pulled toward realization of a methodology like that of the natural sciences by both the attractiveness of superior status and its own fundamental conception of its nature, there is, nevertheless, in the very way of work which anthropology has developed, a strong check upon this pull, so that anthropology is held back from science toward a substantial, if not wholly recognized, connection with the humanities.

THE POLARITIES OF THE ANTHROPOLOGICAL FIELD

4. The existence, within anthropology, of two major centers of interest is

simply apparent in the opposition of physical anthropology to cultural anthropology. Other separations made within the discipline are secondary to this one: the attempted emphasis on generalizing, "synchronic" method as against "diachronic" history already assumes a cultural anthropology separated from physical anthropology, and both archeology and linguistics reach toward connections with other ways of understanding man as a human being rather than as an animal. The deep-lying and persisting determination of anthropologists to see all man, animal and human, as a whole keeps together the several subdisciplines or ways of work in spite of their differences; yet it is physical anthropology alone that is truly biological and so most separable.

5. Kroeber has identified the two polar fields as "first, man viewed as any other animal; and second, man's culture as an extraordinary product, that powerful exudate, influential above all on himself, which is peculiar to man and sets him off from all other animals" (1948, p. 840). Several circumstances suggest a restatement of this pair of foci. First, there is the continuing uncertainty as to whether the central substantive concept of the one subfield is to be culture or society or social relations, and even whether it is necessary to choose. Second, there is the recently developed interest among anthropologists in personality, which is not culture but another aspect of that aspect of mankind which culture also expresses. And, third, there is a return in our times of a conscious concern, as yet unprovided with dependable methods of work, with human nature. This term, replacing a misconceived "psychic unity," may be understood to refer to the characteristics of all human beings as acquired in whatever society. The conception of universal human qualities has reappeared, among other places, in the recognition recently given

by such men as Firth and Kluckhohn to the existence of moral values universal in all cultures because necessary conditions for these values are present in all societies.

6. The alternative statement of the two polarities of anthropology is, then, that anthropology is organized around an interest in man seen as something with the characteristics of all life, and around an interest in man seen as something human—a quality not shared, or very little shared, with other forms of life. The quality that induces the second polarity—humanity—is manifest in three basic forms: as it appears in individuals (personality), in persisting social groups or societies (culture), and in all socialized members of our species (human nature). It is this humanity, subject matter of that part of the anthropological field organized around the second polarity, that links anthropology, in spite of the powerful pulls toward natural science, with the disciplines which bear the name of that subject matter: "the humanities."

THE AMBIGUITY OF THE ANTHROPOLOGICAL METHOD

7. By "method" may here be meant the logical character of the problems set and of the arrangements of propositions in the more ultimate written product: "a science" is a different kind of book from "a history." For long it has been recognized that a second methodological polarity provides tensions within the anthropological effort: that which seeks the writing of histories and that which seeks the writing of sciences, or possibly a science. Following Kroeber (1936), Rickert, and Windelband, one identifies the effort toward the making of histories with that toward "descriptive integration," the reconstructive effort to preserve reality within its contexts of unique positions in time, space, and quality, and the

test of validity by the degree of the fit of the phenomena reported within the totality of conceptual findings. The history which arranges its descriptive integration in chronological order is, by this view, but one form of history. One identifies "science" with the transmutation of phenomena into abstract concepts that provide understanding away from the particular phenomena, with the explication of process, and with the building of competent general precise propositions (theories).

8. Anthropologists must then "do history" in presenting to a reader a culture or a personality, especially where it is presented in discharge of a felt responsibility to present "all of it." They may or may not "do history" or "do science" in the comparisons and other arrangements of more widely drawn facts. It is possible, as in much of the work of Boas or Nordenskiöld, to preserve a spirit more scientific than historical without writing either much science or much history, and the work of G. Elliott Smith suggests that it is possible to write a good deal of history without maintaining a spirit essentially historical. The prevailing orientation of anthropology since its beginning has probably been more strongly directed toward science than toward history, but the proposition will be challenged. In the nineteenth century, at least in England, the choice of orientations was not forced, for the logical character of the major propositions—generalizations as to the way in which things always or usually develop through time— seemed to serve both history and science. The influences of developing natural science and of positivism in respect to human society helped to push anthropologists toward the making of a conscious decision as to their method, and some (W. D. Strong, very recently Evans-Pritchard, and others) pronounced anthropology a history; others, notably Radcliffe-Brown, declared it a generalizing science; while others found it unnecessary to say. The sense of tension as to the goal set persists and is one of the disturbing and stimulating aspects of anthropology.

9. Again, as in the case of any other society, the conceptions which the members hold of themselves and their ideals influence, but do not determine, the conduct of anthropologists with respect to history and science. The scientific bent of Radcliffe-Brown is more apparent in his statements as to what anthropology should be and in his limited use of generalizing concepts as guides for research than in any more nearly ultimate part-science that he has written for us. In his Marett lecture Evans-Pritchard rejects the scientific models, "natural systems," "general principles or laws," and adopts explicitly models provided by history and even art. Nevertheless, as Forde and others have remarked, the details of his program—and probably his practice— provide for comparisons in separated societies for the discovery of "general patterns" and for the advancing of new hypotheses that can be broken down as field-work problems. The approach is surely far less explicitly scientific than is that of Radcliffe-Brown, but the outcome is not likely to be so different as to deserve another nomenclature for the discipline.

THE PARTIAL CORRELATION BETWEEN FIELD AND METHOD

10. In the old concepts of *Geisteswissenschaften* and *Naturwissenschaften* the two polarities of subject matter and of method were consistently aligned: history was seen as concerned with human events and values in an individualizing way, and science with subhuman phenomena in a generalizing way. The whole later (and characteristically American) development of social science in the image of the natural

sciences denies the necessity of the alignment, and few would attempt to hold it now. Nevertheless, in Kroeber's words, "the history of the sciences as a whole shows some sort of objective or partial correlation to exist between material and objective" (1936, p. 317). As Kroeber arranged subject matter into four levels of phenomena and four "approaches" (of which scientific and historical concern us now), he found that there "is something . . . which invites the historical approach in the uppermost level . . . and the scientific in the lowest" (1936, p. 328). It is somehow easier to be scientific in treating matter or life-forms and harder to do this as one goes toward humanity. Kroeber could not find very much to fill in the pigeonhole in his scheme representing the scientific treatment of the superorganic. There is, in some degree, an inherent consistency between the method of descriptive integration and humanity, on the one hand, and the method of generalizing science and the nonhuman, on the other.

THE "HOLISTIC" NATURE OF HUMANITY

11. The subject matter, humanity, provides one of the two polarities of the anthropological field. The nature of this subject matter exerts the influence that brings it about that the human is more easily treated by the method of descriptive integration than by that of generalizing science. And this nature also, correspondingly, checks the effort of anthropology, otherwise directed strongly in the direction set by examples from the natural sciences, and helps maintain a connection with the humanities thus inherent in our discipline.

12. What is this relevant nature of the subject matter, humanity? It is the fact that it is the nature of humanity, in its three forms, to cease to be itself in so far as it is decomposed into parts or elements. What is in this respect true of

stone or oyster is yet more true of culture, personality, and human nature. The effort of the scientific mind to reduce the reality to elements amenable to analysis, comparison, and even mensuration early results in a distortion or in the disappearance of the subject matter as common sense knows it. A culture or a personality is "known" in the first place and convincingly by an effort of comprehension which is not analytic, which insists on a view of the whole as a whole. When more is known of human nature, the same is likely to be said of that. The attempts of anthropological and other science to represent a culture by a list, a formula of structural relationships, or a single underlying pattern are resisted and corrected by the insistence of the reality itself which is so much more than any of these. This "more" is the whole apprehended without resolution into elements. The same assertion may be made of a personality.

EFFECTS OF THE HUMAN REALITY UPON ANTHROPOLOGY

13. Of all scientifically oriented students of man in society, the anthropologist is most accustomed to viewing the human reality "holistically." The small community of which he has characteristically been the sole responsible investigator has been seen by him in its entirety and as a whole. A complex community viewed in the same way is commonly identified as viewed "from the anthropological approach" (*Middletown*). So with respect to the more specialized social sciences the influence of the anthropologist is to correct and enlarge the understanding achieved by more segmental and analytical approaches through consideration of the entirety. This entirety, seen as social structure, a system of social relations, or more commonly as culture, is again offered by the anthropologist in correction and amplification of the analytic,

experimentally conceived science of psychology. And the more integrated view of the human personality taken by psychoanalysis is congenial to the anthropologist, while yet it, too, requires from him the context of culture which he supplies to these students of the human individual also. To that recent restatement of the more scientifically oriented study of man which now appears under the name of "the behavioral sciences," the anthropologist makes his contribution, but characteristically so as to demand that account be taken of culture and of personality seen as a whole. The very simplicity of the anthropologist's concepts, especially with regard to culture and particularly with regard to personality, leaves him free to return easily to the immediately apprehended real whole.

14. The complete identification of anthropology with "the behavioral sciences" is also checked by the necessity that the anthropologist, in understanding a culture or a personality, be guided by projection of his own human qualities into the situation to be understood. The anthropologist's own human nature is an instrument of work. In this respect the position of the anthropologist is like, on the one hand, that of the psychoanalyst; on the other, it is like that of the humanists of the Western tradition, at least since the Renaissance. A psychoanalyst, examining his science or his healing, has recently written: "We first give free rein to the imagination, in order to sense how the situation looks to the patient, and then we examine the situation carefully, to test the intuitive impressions thus gained" (French, p. 29). The psychoanalyst's intuitions and the anthropologist's also are provided with content by what each apprehends about his own and his neighbor's human qualities. And when Ruth Benedict wrote in her presidential address that the great tradition of the humanities "is distinguished by command of vast detail about men's thinking and acting in different periods and places, and in the sensitivities it has consequently fostered to the qualities of men's minds and emotions" (1948, p. 588), her words applied as well to anthropological students of culture, society, and personality.

THE VARIETY OF MODELS IN ANTHROPOLOGICAL THINKING[1]

15. These ideas may be reviewed in terms of the conception of alternative models for achieving knowledge or for organizing knowledge so as to communicate understanding and to provide foresight. The models of overwhelming influence in our times are those provided by the natural sciences. As a pattern to follow in achieving new knowledge, the natural science model conceives of a number of necessarily related steps: activities that begin with a problem seen and conclude with a theory tested. Such a model for work has been described recently by Donald G. Marquis (1948), who regards the social sciences as each separately developing one or a few of the steps necessary to make up a science; anthropology, by this view, already achieves careful observation and description but requires more effort in the direction of testable theory. Among models for the organization of achieved knowledge, the causal model is prominent in the natural sciences: in this model, classes of phenomena are arranged in the form of general causal laws which would make it possible for an ideal observer to predict all future states of a system from conditions at a given time. It is represented in the field of human society by the Marxian theory of history and by Pareto's general equilibrium theory. A recent example of thinking that approximates this model is provided by Kardiner's theory of

1. The assistance of Milton Singer in connection with this section is acknowledged.

basic personality, in which general causal relations are said to connect the "primary" institutions of a culture with the personalities of its carriers and the "secondary" institutions. The causal model may be developed by conceiving a system of universal relationships out of the observation of one or a few cases, as in the instance just given, or it may, in a somewhat weaker form, be developed more inductively from statistical intercorrelations of traits and trait complexes, as in Murdock's *Social Structure* and in other studies from the cross-cultural files at Yale University. A moderate statement of the causal model, contenting itself with "tendencies rather than universal principles," more characteristic of many anthropologists, is made by Firth (1944).

16. The other model, also in part derived from examples in the natural sciences, which influences anthropology is the functional model. In this a culture or a society is seen as an organization of means designed to achieve certain ends. "The ends may be attributed to individuals, to associations of individuals, or, in some sense to the culture as a whole" (personal communication from Singer). These ends may be found in needs or impulses more or less biologically rooted or (as in art and religion as viewed by Malinowski) as acquired ends to some extent defined by culture. The means may be found in almost anything interior or exterior to the culture society. The functional model, familiar in physiology, in anthropology is characteristically associated with Malinowski but may be illustrated by work done by Kluckhohn, among others; and a functional model strongly associated with conceptions of structure is apparent in the work of more than one British anthropologist and, in sociology, in the work of Talcott Parsons and his associates.

17. While these models that receive support from their success in the natural sciences are paramount in anthropology as in much other social science, having recently exerted influence upon the developing conception of "the behavioral sciences," they have not been unchallenged. Evans-Pritchard is one who has recently denounced the adoption of those models as an error of anthropology and called for models drawn from history—albeit a history more comparative than some (1950). There hover about anthropological thinking other models than the causal and the functional. In the studies of Whorf and others as to the relationships of linguistic categories to modes of thought, there may be detected a logical model wherein the major premises of a culture might be discovered and from them be deduced much of the rest of the culture. The relations between the elements of an integrated culture are then seen as those of logical consistency. Sorokin's characterizations of cultural types probably represent this model. And from the point of view of the immediate interest in relations of anthropology to the humanities it is well to recognize the influence of an aesthetic model. It is possible to read many an anthropological account of a culture, and perhaps more particularly some of those provided by M. Mead, as a constructed work of art. According to this model, a culture might be conceived in terms also appropriate to works of art: theme, plot, phrasing, style, classic, or romantic. In Benedict's *Patterns of Culture* the emphasis on rites and ceremonials gives some plausibility to a dramatic interpretation of the cultures she there compares: in this view each culture is a play written by the past for the present, each individual an actor of a role. And Benedict herself told us of the influence upon her of Santayana's study of three great Western poets as "contrasting studies

of the genius of three great civilizations" (1948, p. 591). By this road one may arrive at attempts to distinguish national or tribal character by conceptions more familiar to the history of humanistic learning than to those of the behavioral sciences. Indeed, it may be possible to identify among models for the organization of conceptions of culture a fifth model still farther away from the models of natural science and also identifiable with the arts: the symbolic model. In such a model a culture is conceived as represented in its characteristic properties as a whole by certain symbolic representations—epic, dance form, allegory, etc. The symbols may be transformations of the reality represented and of the impulses projected of perhaps quite fantastic nature: assumed is the capacity of symbol-creating and imaginative beings to frame meanings for themselves. Cassirer has told us about the relations of symbolic representations to culture. The symbolic model may be illustrated by Warner's concept of symbol system; in this case the reality conceived to be represented is emphatically the social structure. Other symbolic models, emphasizing religious conceptions or ideal behavior as that which is symbolized, may also be seen in recent studies of the mythology of primitive and other peoples.

18. The dominance in anthropology of models associated with the natural sciences is not matched by corresponding success in executing studies based on these models. Anthropological formulations of knowledge do not serve as bases of prediction comparable with those provided for prediction in the natural sciences. The literature does not show competent general propositions applicable to all cases within precisely defined classes and allowing of exact predictive application. Though exceptions may be recognized (as in the predic-

tion of linguistic change according to phonemic pattern), the success of anthropology in prediction takes place chiefly as a consequence of understanding gained of particular cases—the anthropologist studies the Indian tribe in transition, the social movement among Japanese-Americans in confinement, the discontents of colonialized peoples—and foresees, more clearly than do most who lack his special knowledge, what will occur. Even where anthropological knowledge about the behavior of people and the expected consequences upon them of courses of action is framed in the form of general propositions, as in Leighton's *The Governing of Men*, the usefulness of the propositions suggests comparison rather with the formulated wisdom of a humane man than with the tables and formulas of the electrical engineer. Moreover, the validity of a characterization of a culture by any of the models employed, but especially those which approximate the aesthetic, logical, or symbolic models, is not today established (whatever may develop in the future) by experimental or any other precise proof such as is demanded in many fields of the natural sciences. Rather it may be said that the reader of an account of a culture or system of social institutions is satisfied as to the truth of what he reads only in part by the correspondences between the more comprehensive propositions and the documentation offered. In part the proof, if proof it be, seems to issue from the conviction brought upon the reader as to the congruence of the parts within a whole conceived. It is as if, in the establishment of "truth" about a culture or a personality, a part is played by an act of apprehension of the totality on the part of him who accepts the presentation as true. And such an act of apprehension is characteristic of the understanding of a work of art and plays a part also in humanistic activity.

ANTHROPOLOGY AS "FREEDOM IN TENSION"

19. One might speak of anthropology as enjoying and also as suffering from the consequences of the polarities and ambiguities of its subject matter and its method. The coherence of the discipline is threatened by the variety of attachments which anthropologists make to problems and fields of inquiry that, though linked to anthropology, are far apart from one another. But the very tensions within anthropology, the disposition to become concerned with questions marginal to any sector of the immense and variegated study of man, make anthropology the freest and most explorative of the sciences.

20. Anthropology is thus provocatively undecided as to whether its subject matter is mankind *in toto* or man as a cultural being: "social anthropology" is taught in some places as a discipline by itself. It is unclear as to whether it moves toward the writing of a science (or perhaps separable sciences of social relations and of culture) or toward the writing of histories. Its views as to such histories as it does write vary from the more humanistic impressions of aboriginal history and of Indian personalities, as in the work of Radin, toward histories compared and reduced to generalizations about developments, cycles, transformations. It finds common cause with students of the behavior of rats in mazes, of human neuroses, of economic history, geography, geology, or the half-life of radioactive elements; and it also finds that it shares interests with Burckhardt, James Henry Breasted, Santayana, and the great works of Shakespearean criticism.

21. Experiencing such pulls toward disintegration, anthropology remains integrated by a number of centripetal forces. There is, first, the deeply es-

tablished commitment toward viewing mankind, this creature both unique and yet one among all other creatures, objectively, completely, as all nature is looked at by all naturalists. This commitment holds together the two polarities of subject matter. It is helped to this end by the conception of the societal, for society, in the wide sense, may be and perhaps must be studied in all life-forms in which individuals maintain relations with one another from the *Paramecia* onward. It is helped also by the establishment of all societies on the land or on the sea; ecological problems are unifying. Both as history and as science, mankind may be viewed as one of many life-forms. And now anthropology, the years having established its university chairs, its associations, and its founding fathers, is helped to maintain its unity through the fact that it is itself a society, one of the societies of the greater society of scholars and scientists.

22. On the other hand, in so far as mankind is viewed as a unique realm of nature made up of persons and traditions, of moral life, self-consciousness, and creative activity directed by ideals, anthropology is not one thing but two: a science and history of that animal which is man; and a history and perhaps also a science or two of that special subject matter, humanity. In this direction anthropology becomes an influence upon the other social sciences to recognize, in their work, the holistic reality of humanity. And in this direction it is drawn toward interests shared with the humanities.

THE DEVELOPING RELATIONS OF ANTHROPOLOGY

23. Current trends suggest that anthropology will, at least in the near future, continue to extend and to deepen its connections with other disciplines without losing its character as a distinct discipline in itself. It will par-

ticipate in the renewed effort to realize the causal model in the study of man that appears in "the behavioral sciences." This will affect anthropology by stimulating more formal and precise designs of research, while the essential commitment of anthropology to the humane reality will hold back the behavioral sciences from becoming mechanical and meaningless. And the experience of anthropology in examining the general propositions of the other social sciences in the light of knowledge of widely different societies and cultures will continue to exert another kind of corrective and expansive influence on social science. From other social or biological sciences anthropology receives frequent and varied stimulus. The recent influence on anthropology, in the United States especially, of "depth psychology" is undeniable and far-reaching; the influence of learning theory on anthropology is claimed but is not fully demonstrated; the influence of sociological theory has become great in the work of many recent anthropologists. Anthropology is a creature and a creator of many frontiers.

24. In the future the interests which anthropology shares with humanistic learning are likely to deepen and to become more fully recognized. At least four developments taking place in anthropology move it in this direction. One is the attempt to characterize "as wholes" the ways of life of both national and tribal peoples: the studies of national character, of fundamental value systems, of themes and basic culture patterns. As suggested above (par. 17), such characterizations have long been made by historians, philosophers of history, and students of literature and the other arts, and the holistic apprehension is itself perhaps an aesthetic mode of thought. At any rate, the help that Benedict found she got from humanists is likely to be drawn upon more fully by anthropologists as they explore the literature and the methodology of studying American, French, or Siamese character.

25. The very extension of the field of anthropology to include civilized peoples, and especially those civilized peoples whose civilization is an outgrowth of an indigenous tribal and peasant culture, tends to bring the anthropologist together with the humanist in such a study. "Regional studies" may have one development into a study not so much of a region as of a culture: a single localized long-standing way of life composed of a Little Tradition of the nonliterate and illiterate and a Great Tradition of the literate and philosophic few. These two aspects of the one reality are to be found, respectively, in the community study of the anthropologist and in the study of the art and literature by the humanist. The two traditions have made each other—in the Far East and the Near East—and anthropologists are likely to join with Sinologists and other specialists of literature and history in the complete study of these culture-civilizations.

26. A third tendency in anthropology draws anthropologists into new connections, on the one hand, with science, and, on the other, with humanistic studies—the developing interest in personalities. Conceived as a "modal personality" or as a problem in the causation of a human type by reason of customs of child-training or of some other sort, this field of study is scientific. Yet here again it is the anthropologist who characteristically holds back (as exemplified in M. Mead's recent statements on the relations among child-training, social institutions, and personality as wholes of interdependent parts) from strictly deterministic forms of explanation of personality formation or of the relations of attitudes to type of personality. And as anthropologists have come to look more intensively at particular personalities, they have come

to produce discussions of the interrelations of individual and society, personality and culture, which parallel the works of literary people. Biographies of Indians or of Africans, presented in relation to ethnographic accounts, evoke comparison with the biographies of the historians and, indeed, with the work of novelists. The division of labor in developing understanding of Newburyport between W. Lloyd Warner and J. P. Marquand is not altogether clear. Furthermore, an interest appears in some anthropologists (as in the work of Radin on the creative individual in the formation of mythology and that of Bunzel on Pueblo potters) in the human individual as modifier and creator of his culture; at this point anthropology has moved over into a field more often identified with the humanities: the study of the producers and the creative products of humanity.

27. Finally, the developing explicit concern with values moves anthropology into developing relationship with the humanities. In the first place, there is the current anthropological interest in exploration of the concept of "value," as value is represented in those human beings who are the objects of anthropological study. Anthropologists have always studied values, for the attitudes of preference that are connected with acts and material objects are centrally characteristic of culture and personality; but now the conception is examined, its sources investigated, its varieties looked into, and its validations developed. This links the anthropologist with the philosopher. And also the anthropologist is drawn to value in another aspect: to value as it appears in the anthropologist himself. How do the anthropologist's own values affect his work? The earlier assumption that his own values are entirely removable as factors of consequence in anthropological research now comes to be questioned. The conception of anthropology as a purely theoretical part of natural history is now qualified by the recognition of applied anthropology, of "action anthropology," and of the responsibility of anthropologists in Point 4 and related programs. These engagements seem to make difficult or perhaps even impossible anthropology as a pure science alone. In advising men of action, in participating in social change—indeed, in being themselves agents of social change in acculturated societies—anthropologists come to entertain the question: What, then, is the good life?

REFERENCES

BENEDICT, RUTH. 1948. "Anthropology and the Humanities," *American Anthropologist*, n.s., L, No. 4, Part I, 585–93.

EVANS-PRITCHARD, E. E. 1950. "Social Anthropology, Past and Present," *Man*, L, No. 198, 118–24.

FIRTH, RAYMOND. 1944. "The Future of Social Anthropology," *Man*, XLIV, No. 8, 19–22.

FRENCH, THOMAS M. 1952. *The Integration of Behavior*, Vol. I. Chicago: University of Chicago Press.

KROEBER, A. L. 1936. "So-called Social Science," *Journal of Social Philosophy*, I, No. 4, 317–40.

———. 1948. *Anthropology*. New York: Harcourt, Brace & Co.

MARQUIS, DONALD G. 1948. "Scientific Methodology in Human Relations," *Proceedings of the American Philosophical Society*, XCII, No. 6, 411–16.

Problems of Application

Applied Anthropometry

By RUSSELL W. NEWMAN

INTRODUCTION

BECAUSE OF limitations of space and the particular interest of the author, this paper does not attempt to cover the vast range of material implied in the program title, "Applied Human Biology." The field, accordingly, is narrowed to one branch of anthropology, i.e., physical anthropology, and within that branch to the application of essentially anthropometric techniques. It is intended that overlap with the papers on growth and constitution and on medicine be minimal.

It is to be noted that the preceding general sections of this symposium, the historical approach and problems of process, were divided into three phases: methods, results, and theory; this section on problems of application has been allotted but one phase, results. It is true that the final test of an applied science is in the results obtained, but applied physical anthropology has its methodology and theory as well as results. They are not necessarily unique or divorced from "theoretical" anthropology, but the contributions of "applied" physical anthropology are frequently made in the forms of methodology and theory.

As the first paper of the section, it is appropriate briefly to define the term "applied." Webster's definition of "using and adapting abstract principles and theory in connection with concrete problems, especially with a utilitarian

aim," is sufficiently succinct to encompass all the present lines of approach; but, for our purpose, to this must be added *using abstract methods*, since many of the methods, e.g., measurements, of applied physical anthropology are borrowed or inherited from its parent-discipline. It does not seem profitable to insist on a strict interpretation of what may constitute "a utilitarian aim" in anthropometry; Krogman (1951) has expressed an inclusive definition when he says: "The individual is the ultimate unit."

BACKGROUND

The probably best method of illustrating the present scope of applied anthropometry is to give some examples that are representative of past and future problems. An anthropometric study of American boys and girls carried on between 1937 and 1939 is representative of one class of investigation. An exceedingly large number of individuals, over 147,000, from age four through age seventeen were measured. The data were collected under the aegis of the United States Department of Agriculture, and the dimensions for measurement were selected to give a basis for the sizing of young people's garments. After the collection phase, these data were subjected to rather intensive statistical analyses. The data collected in the 1930's are gradually being incorporated into children's and

741

junior-size garments by means of what are called "Commercial Standards." It seems reasonable to assume that use of the data will eventually result in better-fitting and uniform garments to the satisfaction of wearer, retailer, and manufacturer.

There are certain focal points in this survey that need emphasis. One point was the need of a better sizing system. The pressure for this study came mainly from the retailers, especially mail-order houses, where trial fittings were impossible and garment returns were correspondingly high. Garment sizes, as expressed in the label sizes, were based on chronological age, but manufacturers did not agree on what constituted a given size, and competitive practices tended to reduce the size of the garments.

The initial problem, then, was to provide data for an adequate sizing system for growing children. Since few of the traditional growth studies recorded measurements that can be directly translated into clothing patterns, the existing literature did not provide a solution. The method used was that of an extensive anthropometric survey. It might be argued that 147,000 children seems to be an excessively large group, but sex differences approximately halved this number at once, and the range of ages sampled further reduced the number in any working unit. The essence of the statistical analyses carried out on these data was that measurements rather than chronological age form the basis for the sizing system. This was contrary to established clothing trade practices and has met with a certain amount of resistance on the part of manufacturers.

Another innovation, almost as novel, involved the theoretical approach to these measurements. It is obvious that the anthropometric data gathered in the survey described individuals and not clothing. The anthropometrist thinks in terms of so-called "skin measurements"; but the clothing designer thinks in terms of pattern or garment dimensions. This presented a mental hurdle that had to be removed before a standardized sizing system could be adopted throughout the industry. A further complication was that different styles of the same garment and even differing quality in the same garment meant that a given dimension on the child could not be covered by a uniform clothing dimension. Since the anthropometric data pertained solely to human measurements, the standard was based on the concept of a boy or girl with given dimensions, and no attempt was made to say how the manufacturer must cut his garments to fit this child. The solution seems obvious now, but it was a clever compromise at the time.

Just what is a "Commercial Standard," and of what does it consist? First, it defines a group of garments which have similar characteristics, e.g., sweaters, pajamas, etc. Second, it examines the range of dimensions found in a given segment of the population, e.g., boys from age six to age twelve. Certain crucial dimensions, usually length and girth, are selected and divided into a reasonable number of intervals. The number of intervals depends on how close the garment must fit, qualities of stretch or adjustability, etc. Third, these intervals in the critical or principal dimensions form the basis for sizes. All other pertinent dimensions are related to, and defined in terms of, these sizes. Fourth, those manufacturers of the clothing industry concerned with the particular garments must agree to accept these sizes, if they wish to include in the garment label the fact that their garments conform to the standard. The size specifies who is going to be fitted, not how he or she is to be fitted; the distinction is very important. Assume that boys' pajama makers have traditionally made six sizes to handle the so-called boys' line, ages six to twelve, but they have tried to cut the pajamas so that a seven-year-old would wear a size 7 and an eight-year-old would wear a size 8, etc. Under the Commercial Standard system six sizes might still be required, if the dimensional range so indicated; but the manufacturer is told to make his smallest size fit a boy with this stature and this hip circumference and these other dimensions associated with this stature and this hip, his next larger size to fit a boy with these dimensions, etc. The label size can remain the same, but all manufacturers will be starting out to fit similar boys. The customer then selects the proper size on the basis of the principal dimensions, regardless of chronological age.

The problem of children's garments has been emphasized at length because it contains many of the important features of applied anthropometry: (1) Data which are pertinent to the problem must be available or be gathered. In this case the data required were dimensions for translation into clothing patterns. (2) The data must be organized and presented in a manner that is not too divergent from existing practices. Industry, government, and even other sciences are not amenable to a complete scrapping of previous practices without regard to the violence engendered by such a move. (3) The new concept or system must have demonstrable advantages over the old. In this example the advantages were a reduction in returned goods and in the accompanying economic loss. (4) The results of the applied anthropometry must be skilfully and patiently sold to the manufacturers, retailers, and consumers. Unless the results are spectacular, the world will not beat a path to the anthropometrist's door. He must either be somewhat of a salesman himself or be represented by someone who is. In the case of the children's clothing sizes it was handled on an industry-wide basis, and acceptance of the Commercial Standards is purely voluntary. This was necessary because the government had underwritten the work and could not favor one concern over another. Also, a sizing system becomes most useful when all or almost all of the manufacturers adhere to it.

PRESENT STATUS

Having expounded the principles of applied anthropometry, we may ask what are some of the current and future problems and the individual complexities that may plague the investigator? An excellent field for applied anthropometry lies in space-requirement work. Space requirements are frequently one of the many facets of human engineering, and anthropometry is the logical field to investigate and define the morphological aspects of this problem.

Space-requirement studies have this much in common: no two are really alike! The pertinent dimensions change with the specific type of equipment to be used, the position and movements of the operator, and the amount of adjustability or number of sizes that are economically feasible. Thus every problem is unique, and the anthropometrist must make a careful analysis of his problem before he sets about gathering data. Generally, new data are usually required, since the number of possible measurements is almost infinite. The population which is to be served must be identified and sampled. Conventional anthropometric measurements are seldom useful, and new techniques and even new apparatus must be devised. The anthropometrist must either be a gadgeteer himself or secure the services of a sympathetic engineer.

The selection and collection of the dimensional data are the easiest parts of the investigation. A competent anthropometrist will have an adequate background in this type of work and should encounter no great difficulties. The resulting analyses and applications of these data block a simple and straightforward solution. This is due partly to the originality of each investigation and the lack of theoretical knowledge on which to draw, but principally to the basic limitations under which the investigator works. The object to be fitted, whether it is a chair, desk, automobile cab, airplane cockpit, or complex industrial machine, has a limited or nonexistent range of adjustability. The anthropometrist must somehow reconcile the variability found in his sample to the design of the object and provide for use by as many individuals as possible. Where adjustability is possible, the problem is simplified, it being necessary only to establish the limits of adjustability to fit the population. This presupposes that adjustment in one dimension does not throw another critical dimension out of alignment; e.g., seat adjustment can be based on leg-reach to foot pedals only if hand controls remain at the proper distance. The anthropometrist will meet situations where adjustability is not possible, e.g., in cases where it may introduce a structural weakness, as in airplane seats. If no adjustments or different sizes are available, it will be difficult to find a proper criterion for establishing the proper distance from the user. In a situation where reach, either arm or leg, is critical, what should be the optimum distance? The mean, mode, or median dimension of the series is never satisfactory, since many individuals would then be unable to attain the required reach. Similarly, the shortest reach found in the sample, or the tenth percentile, or some other statistic weighted toward the small end of the dimension may prove totally unsatisfactory for individuals with a long reach. There have not been sufficient precedents established to guide the anthropometrist effectively in many

such situations. Most spatial-requirement studies are complicated with many variables. Although it may be axiomatic that a man cannot perform properly when his controls, etc., are at uncomfortable distances, the resolution of this discrepancy alone may not provide the answer to increased or maximum efficiency. Other factors, such as the types of movements, sequence of operations, and perceptual demands on the operator, must be investigated simultaneously. This phase of human engineering has been handled principally by applied experimental psychologists. The techniques used are not beyond the scope of an anthropologist, but they require a considerable background not usually found in our profession. Unfortunately, the scarcity of physical anthropologists or their reluctance to participate in such studies has resulted in many experiments completed without technical anthropometric aid or advice.

After this brief review of just two different types of applied anthropometry—clothing sizes and space requirements—an over-all estimate of the field is appropriate. What at the present time are the particular advantages which anthropometry has to offer and the disadvantages under which it labors? Selected examples of *strengths* and *weaknesses* are given below.

STRENGTHS

First, *anthropometry brings a fresh approach to many problems, especially industrial applications.* The basic sizing concept of the manufacturer in the ready-to-wear clothing industry might be stated as something like this: if we provide a reasonable number of traditional sizes, the consumer population somehow will be able to fit into them. The opposite approach, that of applied anthropometry, is this: if we first define in terms of dimensions the population which is to be fitted, we can then determine how many sizes and what garment dimensions are necessary adequately to fit it. The change of emphasis or fresh approach is possible only through anthropometry. Its ramifications on children's garment sizes have already been pointed out. The technique has been carried one step further on garments for women's clothing in the United States Army. In this instance a sizable number of Wacs and nurses were measured, the data analyzed, and a complete and somewhat radical sizing system actually innovated. It is still too early to see how this new system will work out in practice, but, if successful, it may prove contagious.

Second, *anthropometry has a tradition of experience with and regard for biological variability.* Our field does not have a monopoly on variability, but it is an important part of every anthropometric investigation. The anthropometrist, because of his background, is equipped not only to assess but also to handle variability in his analyses and thus to help solve problems that plague certain industries. The following statement has been attributed to the shoe industry as being the philosophy on variability of that trade: if the shoe does not fit accurately in every detail or does not feel perfectly comfortable, it is not the responsibility of the shoe industry, since no two pairs of feet are alike. It is quite probable that no two pairs of feet are actually alike in every minute detail, but such a concept of variability can be carried to a ridiculous end. Variability is no excuse for poor fitting (in shoes or anything else) until it has been proved that a workable system, allowing for a reasonable variation, cannot be found.

Third, *there are few biological disciplines with a greater appreciation of the concept of "population" and of techniques appropriate to the gathering of adequate samples.* The concept of the population to be handled or fitted by a particular machine or garment is an important consideration not always entirely appreciated by industry. The entire clothing industry, for example, including both footwear and handwear manufacturers, has long operated on the "standard-size" principle. This so-called "standard size" is all too often a statistical monstrosity consisting of the average of all known biological dimensions. One item, e.g., a shoe size, is modeled from this group of mean values, and larger and smaller sizes are graded evenly up and down in all dimensions. The first fallacy in this system is the idea that there is a large group of potential consumers who are average in all dimensions. There will *not* be a large group if dimensions whose distribution in the population is skewed (i.e., weight and practically all girth measurements) are used in conjunction with length measurements. The second misconception is that these dimensions can be graded evenly up and down from the average as a unit. If curvilinear relationships occur (as they do in weight and girths), a given change in length will not be associated with an even change in other dimensions. It is necessary to use somewhat sophisticated statistical techniques on a large number of subjects to uncover the proper relationships, and, above all, it is necessary to think in terms of the total population to be fitted.

Fourth, *anthropometrists have training in and a regard for precise measuring techniques.* Precise measuring techniques are readily definable in terms of easily located reference points and, therefore, are reproducible by other workers. It is a normal procedure in anthropometric work either to define the measurements taken or to refer to some standard wherein the reader can obtain an adequate definition. One of the most common complaints that an anthropometrist working with industry receives is that his anatomical definitions are too esoteric for the laymen; however, the precise use of anatomical landmarks is one of the techniques that makes anthropometric investigations really valuable. The clothing trade has never settled on a body of definitions and landmarks to be used by all workers, and, therefore, no one can be sure just what is meant by the measurements already collected by this industry.

WEAKNESSES

First, *there is, unfortunately, a preoccupation in the profession with conventional and classical measurements that are often totally unsuited for applied studies.* One of the most frustrating queries made to the applied anthropometrist by professional and nonprofessional people alike is: Why is it necessary to go on measuring all the time; why can't you find the answers in all the measurements that have been collected throughout the world? The answer is very simple. It is almost impossible to find answers to any *specific* problem in the literature because the measurements taken are not appropriate, and, even if they were, the data are not supplied in a usable form. An applied anthropometrist seldom can be satisfied with means and standard deviations; he generally is interested in relationships, and the common statistical measures do not provide the answers. Similarly, too many anthropologists have collected and published series without regard to age distribution, nutritional status, and other factors which may bias the data.

Second, *no one can accuse physical anthropology of being a brash and bustling science, and lack of salesmanship, including self-salesmanship, is a disadvantage in this work.* There is an axiom that cannot be repeated too often in applied anthropometry: collecting the measurements and analyzing the data are only the first stages of the problem;

selling the results is the crucial and difficult portion. This usually requires patience, diplomacy, tact, and a willingness to compromise. In general, the anthropometrist will be hopelessly handicapped unless he is consulted before the other scientists and design engineers have finished their work. Once an item is in production or even almost ready for production, any recommended changes will have to overcome objections and inertia on the part of engineers, production men, executives, and a host of other individuals. There are very few cases where anthropometry has occupied its proper role in collecting and analyzing the necessary data *prior to* fabrication. This is primarily because of the lack of dissemination of information on the potential usefulness of the field. The need for an anthropometrist in the planning stage will not be recognized until skilful publicity has made industry and government dimensional-engineering conscious. It is not known exactly who publicized Hooton's study on reclining seats, but there is a strong suspicion that the furniture manufacturer and the railroad company rather than the anthropologists were largely instrumental in letting the public, and therefore potential customers, hear about the advantages of scientific seating through anthropometric analyses.

Third, *there is an unfortunate lack of knowledge as to what the measurements already devised really mean in terms of function.* The measurements traditional to physical anthropology seem to have been chosen primarily because they were definable in terms of skeletal landmarks. This situation may be convenient for academic comparisons between racial populations, but it greatly handicaps the applied anthropometrist in studies involving any sort of movement. Except for a gradually accumulating body of data on the lower limbs during walking, we know remarkably little about landmarks and body measurements which have important functional significance in human movements. Thus it is quite possible to measure the wrong dimensions and come up with results that look fine when the subject is in a static position but which fail as soon as the subject moves. This type of problem requires the combined skills of several disciplines, but few physical anthropologists have initiated or even participated in such studies to date.

Fourth, *there is a distinct shortage of theory to which the worker can turn for advice and guidance*. The paucity of theoretical concepts can be attributed to three causes: (1) the uniqueness of each investigation; (2) the small number of studies that have been accomplished to date; and (3) the past history of physical anthropology, in which the emphasis has been on groups rather than on individuals. An example of this difference in perspective is the problem of predictability. For almost a century anthropologists have had techniques available for the estimate of stature from long bones. The original data were published in the form of tables in which no measure of reliability was included. Even the regression formulas published by Pearson in 1899 have been reproduced without such a statistical measure. The appropriate standard or probable error of estimate may be of little use to the investigator publishing mean statures on a skeletal series, but it is absolutely necessary in a medicolegal problem where an individual with a known stature is being checked against putative remains. Statistical predictability is an essential part of applied anthropometry, and physical anthropologists must utilize and apply the most recent advances in this field to their applied problems.

The exact status of applied anthropometry in the United States is difficult to ascertain. Part of this difficulty lies in determining which activities and workers should be counted. Should we count the continuing activity of the clothing industry to apply anthropometric measurements to sizing, even though no professional physical anthropologist is assisting or employed? Should we count the locomotion research carried out at Columbia, California, and elsewhere by anatomists, engineers, and others? If only professional physical anthropologists are counted, the number of workers is relatively small, and almost all are engaged in activities sponsored by the government. As might be expected, the bulk of applied anthropometry in government work is directed toward military problems. At present, there are not more than twelve individuals engaged in applied anthropometry for the Department of Defense, and only half of these have permanent civilian positions. The others are either military personnel temporarily assigned to such duty or anthropologists working on a contract basis. Conservatively, at least twice this number could be profitably employed by the armed forces. The British Ministry of Defense has only one full-time applied physical anthropologist whose work has come to our attention. There are no professional physical anthropologists doing either full-time or part-time research for the Navy or in such technical services of the Army as Ordnance, Engineers, Signal Corps. There are no physical anthropologists doing full-time industrial anthropometry and very few who have even done much consulting work. Thus the present status of applied anthropometry is still that of an infant science, slowly and painfully working its way into prominence. The small demand for services today can be attributed primarily to the lack of information on the potentialities of the field by those who are in a position to make use of it; this can be corrected only by proper advertisement or salesmanship. On the other hand, any demand engendered by such action must be met by competent workers, and this is best insured by proper training. We might well ask if such preparation will be available to students through formal education. It is perfectly possible for a modern physical anthropologist to spend a useful lifetime on fruitful research without ever once working in paleoanthropology, skeletal analysis, or primatology; but each and every student must, under the present conditions, be grounded in these studies. To take the other extreme, there is just one course offered in applied anthropometry at a major American university (that on "Applications of Physical Anthropology" at Harvard). It is admittedly a difficult task to assemble and teach a coherent course in this field, where references and source materials are often obscure because of security regulations and limited editions, but the future of applied anthropometry, if it is to have one, depends on the availability and competence of today's and tomorrow's students. Without attempting to dictate to our schools and colleges, but only as a suggestion, perhaps it is not necessary or practical to expose all embryonic physical anthropologists to a course in applied anthropometry. It may be sufficient merely to have available an adequate survey of the field to date; one that would cover the problems, methods of measurements and analyses, and results. Such a compendium need not and cannot provide actual data for many future problems, but it may stimulate and serve as a guide to the budding research workers. Inasmuch as applied anthropometry is a field in which bibliographies are almost nonexistent because of the practical nonavailability for various reasons of many of the military reports, a source book seems the only answer.

Applied physical anthropology is a field which gained its principal momentum under wartime stress. Its activity at the present time is symptomatic of our national effort to strengthen our technology by recourse to sciences formerly considered largely academic. The principal selling points at present—increased comfort and efficiency—are given a high rating by our culture. Furthermore, the sense of urgency and crisis so characteristic of the last decade has permitted and encouraged innovations in technology, if not in philosophy. Now established, this acceptance of scientific tinkering should persist for some time. There is a good future for applied physical anthropology if it can withstand the competition of other sciences also expanding into applied fields. The future depends on the availability and competence of physical anthropologists. Every opportunity missed through reluctance of anthropologists to participate or through lack of trained workers will result in fewer demands in the future or the adoption of anthropometric techniques by other sciences.

GENERAL BIBLIOGRAPHY

KROGMAN, WILTON M. 1951. "The Role of Physical Anthropology in Dental and Medical Research," *American Journal of Physical Anthropology,* n.s., IX, No. 2, 211–18. A brief outline of areas of research, including applied anthropometry; absence of bibliographic references limits the usefulness of this article.

O'BRIEN, RUTH, and GIRSHICK, M. A. 1939. *Children's Body Measurements for Siz-* *ing Garments and Patterns: A Proposed Standard System Based on Height and Girth of Hips.* ("U.S. Department of Agriculture Miscellaneous Publications," No. 365.)

O'BRIEN, RUTH, and SHELTON, W. C. 1941. *Women's Measurements for Garment and Pattern Construction.* ("U.S. Department of Agriculture Miscellaneous Publications," No. 454.)

O'BRIEN, RUTH; GIRSHICK, M. A.; and HUNT, E. P. 1941. *Body Measurements of American Boys and Girls for Garment and Pattern Construction: A Comprehensive Report of Measuring Procedures and Statistical Analysis of Data on 147,000 American Children.* ("U.S. Department of Agriculture Miscellaneous Publications," No. 366.)

RANDALL, FRANCIS E. 1948. *Applications of Anthropometry to the Determination of Size in Clothing.* ("Environmental Protection Series," Report No. 133, Quartermaster Climatic Research Laboratory.) Unclassified. A presentation of anthropometric sizing theory with pertinent examples.

RANDALL, F. E.; DAMON; BENTON; BRUES; and PATT. 1946. *Human Body Size in Military Aircraft and Personal Equipment.* (Army Air Forces Technical Report No. 5501, Air Materiel Command, Wright AFB.) Unclassified. A summary of many projects carried out during World War II by the Army Air Corps; the diversity of problems make it the most useful single work in the field to date.

"Symposium on Applied Physical Anthropology," *American Journal of Physical Anthropology,* n.s., VI, No. 3 (1948), 315–73. Seven excellent papers cover most of the field of applied anthropometry; the individual bibliographies are especially useful.

Growth and Constitution

By J. M. TANNER

THE CHIEF problems in the field of human growth and constitution, unlike the principal answers, can be simply stated. In what ways do men consistently differ from one another, and how do these differences come to exist? These questions embrace morphology, physiology, and psychology; the historical trisection has no theoretical place in constitutional study, though in the techniques of investigation it necessarily serves as the present-day framework. "Consistently" is used in its ordinary and somewhat loose sense: constitutionalists are not concerned with aspects of physiology or behavior, which change a great deal in a single individual from day to day or even from year to year; but neither are they solely interested in structures or functions which remain entirely unchanged throughout adult life. In any group of people studied, one can divide up the total variability observed in a character over a period of time into the between-individual variability and the within-individual variability, by which latter is meant the changes which occur with time in a single individual. It is with the between-individual variability that the constitutionalist is concerned, and it is perhaps fair to say that his interest in a character increases according to the ratio of its between-individual variability to its within-individual. "Differential anthropology" the subject has sometimes been called. Giacinto Viola,

the greatest constitutionalist of the first half of this century, defined his subject as "the science of individual variations and nothing else," and constitution as "the total of all the morphological and functional characters by virtue of which an individual differs from other individuals" (Viola, 1937).

No explicit distinction between heredity and environment enters into these statements, but obviously the genetic background looms very large in constitutional work. The relation of constitution and genetics is given nicely by comparing Viola's definition of the one with J. B. S. Haldane's definition of the other: "Genetics is the branch of biology which is concerned with innate differences between similar organisms" (Haldane, 1942). The only difference between the statements lies in the word "innate"; the majority of constitutionalists do not wish to be restricted absolutely to the study of innate differences, but this is very largely because in the human the contributions of heredity and environment are so difficult to disentangle; it is the genetic that holds the major interest. The study of constitution preceded the science of genetics and contained the germ from which genetics developed; genetics, grown mightily, is now gradually absorbing its parent, and the distinction between human genetics and the study of constitution grows yearly less. Neel, a medical geneticist, has recently remarked that "the distinction between the anthropologist wo appreciates the significance of recent genetic developments and is applying them, and the geneticist interested in gene frequencies and their phenotypic counterpart in human populations, is one which is increasingly difficult to maintain" (Neel, 1949). Since, however, many of the characters which the constitutionalist is mainly concerned with have a very complex genetical background, the two sciences will not fuse for a long time. And even when the genetics of constitutional characters is fully understood, it may be that some persistent differences in adult temperament, for example, will be found to be due more to early learning experiences than to strict genetical influence, and, if these differences are relatively ineradicable, they will still remain in the province of constitutional study.

The constitutionalist has two aims in pursuing his subject. He wishes, first of all, to add to our knowledge about ourselves, so that eventually we shall have a picture not only of how men in general evolved and behave relative to other animals and the world around them but also of how different people come into being and how they behave relative to one another. From this comes his second aim, that of application. It is perhaps best stated by the first scientific anthropometrist of the modern period, Beneke, who lived at a time when the disappointments, the perplexities, and the complications of human biology were less obtrusive than nowadays. "The different constitutions and the different resistances conditioned by them form only the soil in which certain diseases develop when the individual is subjected to certain stresses. The importance of this point of view for general hygiene and therapy goes without saying. It is in our power to lead the different constitutions happily through the dangers of life if we

recognise them correctly and if we understand rightly their physiological differences" (Beneke, 1881).

The difficulty still is "to recognise them correctly" and to "understand rightly their physiological differences." The first of these two problems must necessarily precede the second, and a great deal of constitutional research has been aimed at its solution. Stated at the simplest level and following now the traditional division into morphology, physiology, and psychology, the solution implies, first, a workable and accurate classification of physical differences.

PHYSIQUE

PROBLEMS AND PROGRESS IN THE CLASSIFICATION OF PHYSIQUE

The problems that beset the classifier of physique are mainly problems of logical and scientific procedure and are very similar to the difficulties met with in zoölogical taxonomy. They can be epitomized in three problems, though the three, being really parts of a whole, interlock and cannot be answered separately. They are (a) choice of variables, (b) measurement versus appearance, and (c) types versus components.

The human body varies, even in externals alone, in a thousand ways, and it seems impossible to catalogue every facet. Each classification must needs be based on the selection of some characters and the ignoring of many others. It is perfectly possible to construct classifications based on the shape of the head, the conformation of the ear, or the presence of agglutinogens in the red blood corpuscles. Such classifications exist or have existed. Two of them at least tell us something about the prehistory of man, and one of these may eventually tell us something about the mechanism of his evolution. Both of them have practical application, one in the sizing of hats, the other in the distinction of fathers. But none has any relevance at present to the problems of the constitutionalist, because none as yet links up with other data on the physiology or behavior of man. One day, certainly, these links will be forged and fitted, for the final coat will have all its chain in place. But classifications depend for their usefulness on the degree to which they shed light on the relations between one set of facts and another. For the solution of the problem that Beneke posed, the choice of relevant variables is crucial and, so far as one can see, can be guided only by evidence after the event. If a classification by ear lobes proves unilluminating of social and medical relationships, it must be discarded, and due record made that it has been tried and found wanting.

It is in more complicated bodily characteristics that significance in relation to medical and psychological problems seems at present to lie. All five contemporary classifications of physique emphasize the shape or conformation of the entire body rather than any particular feature. Bodily shape, however, unlike the breadth of the nose or the presence of agglutinogen B, is a hard thing to measure, though in many ways it is simple enough to see. This brings us to the next aspect of our problem, measurement versus appearance, or anthroposcopy versus anthropometry. There have been traditions of measurement and of visual discrimination, each stretching back several hundred years; though they have never been blankly opposed, it has always been difficult to get them working together equably. Some investigators, becoming exasperated at the inability of their calipers to define what their eyes so obviously saw, have closed their instrument cases in disgust; others, fearful of the free play of their imagination, have carefully blinded themselves before daring to approach their subject. The problem to some extent remains,

but a better understanding of modern biometrical procedures should do much to clarify both the logical and the practical issues involved. There is also another way in which the two approaches have been brought closer. Anthropometry starts with a battery of measurements being taken on the man; anthroposcopy with either the man himself or photographs of him for examination. Recently the technique of photogrammetry, or measurement by means of photography, has been adapted to the human, so that measurements can be accurately and expeditiously taken from standardized photographs. Though not all the bodily measurements usually required can be secured in this way, a great number can, and the technique known as "photogrammetric anthropometry" (Tanner, 1951c, 1953a) brings together at source, so to speak, the visual and metric approaches and enables both to proceed simultaneously from similar initial data.

The five classifications of physique which are still in current use are those of Sigaud, Kretschmer (1948), Viola (1932), Sheldon *et al.* (1940), and factor analysis (see Burt and Banks, 1947; Tanner, 1947). An excellent presentation of the first three of these, with a description of earlier classifications, will be found in Schreider (1937). Sigaud used a fourfold typology, wherein the majority of mankind is divided into "Digestives," "Respiratories," "Musculars," and "Cerebrals." A few unfortunates fall between these discrete categories and are called "Undefined Types." Sigaud had an exceedingly low opinion of these and bent his therapeutic and educational energies to diminishing their number. His is a pure typology, with no hint of the later doctrine of continuously variable components. This classification is practically obsolete, but there still exists a small group in France who use it.

Kretschmer's classification is very well

known and was devised against a background of psychiatry. It is also a typology, but with three rather than four categories, the "Pyknic," the "Athletic," and the "Leptosome." The pyknic is short, stocky, and moderately rotund; the athletic, large-muscled, broad-shouldered, and powerful; the leptosomic, linear and narrow. The types were defined anthroposcopically and have never been either very clearly illustrated by photographs or satisfactorily objectified by measurement. The classification, however, was used by a considerable number of workers between 1920 and 1940 and is still in common use in Germany. Elsewhere it has been almost entirely dropped in favor of a continuous-component system of one sort or another.

Viola's massive work is much less well known in the English-speaking countries, because of the lack of translations and the paucity of Italian literature to be found in English and American medical libraries. The amount of published work embodying this classification is greater than that of any other; it numbers some seven or eight hundred papers (for bibliography, see Benedetti, 1936–37). The Italian school is fundamentally a metric one and, unlike the previous two discussed, is much concerned with niceties of technique and accuracies of procedure; Viola was the first to give a comprehensive scheme for the external measurement of the entire body.

Viola's classification does everything necessary to turn from a typology to a component system except take the final step. Subjects are placed along a linearity-nonlinearity continuum on the basis of a rather complicated combination of ten body measurements, but the final assessment is into longitype, brachitype, normotype, or mixed type. The difference between the last two is chiefly that of dysplasia, the mixed being more dysplastic than the normotype.

While, as it stands, this system is basically a twofold typology, it would be extremely simple to turn it almost unaltered into a single continuously variable component of build. This component would not be the same as Sheldon's "ectomorphy," discussed below, but an axis which has at one end extreme ectomorphy and at the other extreme endomorphy. As the majority of physiological relations with physique so far described involve a relation with ectomorphy coupled with the inverse relation with endomorphy, the Viola component might well prove worth while defining and using. Constitutional work seems to have greatly declined in Italy since the time of Viola's death in 1943, and there is not much information on physiological relations available from that source.

Besides the chief dichotomy, Viola used extensively a measure of general body size and a measure of dysplasia between different parts of the body. His school collected large volumes of standardizing data for people of all ages and regions, since the initial step in calculating the type was to work out the amount that each of the subject's ten measurements deviated from the mean for his age, sex, and region. This procedure led in practice to the type changing with age, although this does not seem necessarily to follow from the method of approach; probably Viola, if he had so wished, could have avoided it, had he arranged his way of combining the measurements somewhat differently. This problem is a recurrent one in the classification of physique.

Sheldon was not the first to realize that typologies violated the facts and drew hard-and-fast lines arbitrarily through continua; Raymond Pearl, in particular, had pointed this out. But Sheldon was the first to devise a classification which took the tenet of components instead of typologies as its fundamental. "The concept of types," he wrote, "has been useful in the study of personality, but, like the poles supporting a clothes-line, it provides only end suspension for distributive classifications. As the line becomes filled, the notion of types recedes and finally vanishes altogether, perhaps submerged under a smooth distribution. The path of progress is from the notion of dichotomies to the concept of variation along dimensional axes" (Sheldon *et al.*, 1940).

Sheldon's choice of variables sprang from his initial observational technique. He started by sorting nude standardized photographs, showing front, side, and back views of some four thousand male college students. Disregarding the attribute of largeness or general size, which his classification almost entirely ignores, he sorted for extremes of body shape, and found three. Since each extreme represented the end of the distribution of a component, the sorting gave three as the number of fundamental components. Each individual was then assigned a place in the distribution of each component, since everyone, by hypothesis, had some of each component in his makeup. This was done anthroposcopically, using a rating scale of 1 to 7 with equal-appearing intervals between the numerals (i.e., the man rated 3 appears to be as much more than one rated 2 as the 2 is more than the 1). Thus the first extreme example was rated 7-1-1, the second extreme 1-7-1, and the third extreme 1-1-7. The components were named "endomorphy," "mesomorphy," and "ectomorphy" on a theory, not generally accepted, of their genesis from embryonic germ layers. They are best described by reference to their extreme manifestations. The extreme in endomorphy approaches the spherical as nearly as is humanly possible; he has a round head, a large fat abdomen predominating over his thorax, and weak, floppy, penguin-like arms and legs, with a great deal of fat in the upper arm and thigh but slender wrists and ankles. He has, relative to his general size, a large liver and spleen and gut, large lungs, and a heart shaped differently from the other extremes. He has a great deal of subcutaneous fat and, in lay parlance, would be simply called a fat man; but there is more to it than that, because fatness is only one of his characteristics. His whole body, including his thoracic and pelvic skeleton, is much greater in the anteroposterior direction than are those of the other extremes. It seems that fatness is related to this build more or less inevitably, and it is thought that the amount of weight put on as a person gets older is fairly directly related to his rating in endomorphy. The man high in endomorphy can, of course, delay the tide by dieting and exercise, but only to a point; the "endopene," as the individual low in endomorphy is called, can meanwhile eat as he wills and sit as long as he pleases without suffering any change of contour.

The extreme in mesomorphy is the classical Hercules, Sigaud's "Muscular," Kretschmer's "Athletic." In him bone and muscle predominate. He has a cubical massive head, broad shoulders and chest, and heavily muscled legs and arms, with the distal segments strong in relation to the proximal. Relative to his size, his heart muscle seems also to be large. He has a minimal amount of subcutaneous fat, and the anteroposterior diameters of his body are small.

The extreme in ectomorphy is the linear man; he has a thin, peaked face with a receding chin and high forehead, a thin narrow chest and abdomen, a narrow heart, and spindly arms and legs. He has neither much muscle nor much subcutaneous fat, but, relative to his size, he has a large skin area and a large nervous system.

The majority of people have a moderate amount of each component and so have, as their "somatotype," as the set of three ratings is called, such numbers as 433, 344, or 352. The number of possible combinations of seven things taken three at a time is three hundred and forty-three, but the three components are not independent. They are negatively intercorrelated, so that a high rating in one precludes to some extent high ratings in the others. Thus there are 235's, 335's, and 435's, but no 135's or 535's, 635's or 735's. Also there are 641's and 444's, but no 771's, 555's, 333's, or 111's. Sheldon has described, in all, eighty-eigth somatotypes, seventy-six of them being in his original group of students. Only about fifty are at all common. It will be realized that, despite the numbering system and the verbal convenience of referring to a 711 as an endomorph, the somatotype is not like the conception of the old discrete typologies; it is a pigeonhole in which is placed everybody, who, on the continuous scales, is nearer that pigeonhole than any other. Workers in this field now use halves in their rating scales, converting them to thirteen-point scales, with a correspondingly larger number of smaller pigeonholes.

Sheldon originally tried to put his somatotypes onto an anthropometric basis and published tables which purported to give the somatotypes of men aged sixteen to twenty-one from a series of measurements of their pictures coupled with the height/ $\sqrt[3]{}$ weight ratio. These have been found open to considerable objection, however, and at present all somatotyping is done anthroposcopically from a picture, in which the pose must be highly standardized, aided by reference to tables of height/ $\sqrt[3]{}$ weight ratios, which are now available from age sixteen to age sixty-five. The difficulty in this situation is being sure that all workers are rating the same and, in particular, that an investigator is not gradually altering his sights so that all his 4's in mesomorphy, for example, are really 4½'s, his 3½'s really 4's, and so on. Properly trained

somatotypers have an allowable error of ½ in their ratings, but no more; that is to say, a rater will change some of his ratings by this amount when he rerates a series of pictures, and two different raters may differ by this amount. Differences of a whole rating, however, should be comparatively rare. One of the pressing technical problems in somatotyping is a proper biometrical appraisal of the relations of ratings to anthropometric measurements, both of the pictures and of the subject himself. The former would give standards by which workers could all be sure they were judging their somatotypes correctly, and it would also enable ratings finer than ½ to be made for each component, which might be desirable in some correlational work. The prediction of somatotype from a series of measurements of the living subject is highly important, as it is not always possible to secure photographs, yet very desirable to translate results into terms of somatotypes, now that so many studies using somatotypes have been carried out. The height/ $\sqrt[3]{}$ weight ratio correlates highly with ectomorphy, but the best measurements for discriminating the other two components have not yet been worked out.

The accurate prediction of endomorphy, mesomorphy, and ectomorphy by multiple regressions from at any rate photogrammetric diameters should be a simple enough matter, but it brings up immediately the fundamental question of changes of measurements with age or malnutrition. The somatotype, by definition, changes neither with age nor with nutritional state or state of athletic training. Sheldon talks of the "morphogenotype," meaning the build that the gene complex would have produced in optimal environmental conditions, and the "morphophenotype," the build actually appearing. In much of America and western Europe and very likely in many other parts of the world also, the two approximate fairly closely. The somatotype is defined by Sheldon as the best effort a skilled observer can make at gauging the morphogenotype. Departing very slightly from this, we may say that the somatotype is the appearance of the individual when growth ceases, that is, at about twenty, given adequate nutrition at that time. If during the growing period the genes' expression has been limited by environmental inclemency, then the somatotype will be some way off from the morphogenotype; if not, it will represent the morphogenotype exactly. In either case further vicissitudes do not alter it, however much they may alter the manifest appearance or morphophenotype. When an investigator somatotypes a starved subject, he ignores the height/ $\sqrt[3]{}$ weight ratio, which is only appropriate for properly nourished people, and he guesses what the man would look like were he not starved. Since the skeletal shape gives considerable information as to the somatotype, this is not so difficult as it may sound, and, after guessing the somatotype, a very accurate estimate of the weight loss can often be made. (Another urgent problem in this field is the defining of normal weight-for-height standards for each somatotype at each age; Sheldon now has this information for men for the majority of somatotypes over most of the age span. A more accurate definition of obesity should proceed from this work.) In malnutrition, measurements of the pictures will be, of course, quite powerless to predict the somatotype, at least in the regressions appropriate for the well-nourished. Possibly regressions could be devised by means of skeletal dimensions alone or in combination with some muscular dimensions taken by roentgenography, which would overcome this difficulty. If purely skeletal regressions are possible, they would open up the whole field of temporal change in body build

in past populations. Age changes in measurements do not raise the same difficulty, since age can be incorporated into the equations; the biometry, though tedious, is straightforward enough.

There are many imperfections in the somatotype classification; nevertheless, on the purely physical side somatotyping is the most sustained and successful attack on the problem of classification yet made. Whatever its theoretical background, it is intensely practical and communicates information very readily. To know that a man is a large 325 with light hair and blue eyes is to recognize him.

CONSTITUTIONAL PSYCHOLOGY

This, however, is not ultimately enough. A classification must ultimately stand or fall by the way it links up with facts and classifications in other fields. Sheldon himself has always proceeded on this assumption, and soon after publication of his classification of physique he produced a second volume of the "Constitutional Research Project Series" describing a classification of temperament and relating this to physique (Sheldon and Stevens, 1942). Later there came a third volume, incorporating information on the usefulness of somatotyping in the study of delinquency (Sheldon et al., 1949), and further works are planned on somatotypes in psychiatry and general medicine. The whole body of work is assuming massive proportions.

Practically all those who have concerned themselves with human physique have been interested also in the relation between body build and behavior. The older authors took such a relation for granted and felt no need for justifying statistics. More recently, research has been concentrated on finding out what elements of behavior remain more or less consistent and unaltered throughout life, whether these are related to physical differences, and, if so, to what differences and how closely. Intellectual capacity in the sense of ability to score highly on I.Q. tests remains relatively constant, but is very slightly, if at all, related to build. The relationship with build is greater for temperament, by which is meant the deepest layer of personality, wherein lie habits of behavior ranging from such traits as "indiscriminate amiability" right down into obviously physique-conditioned aptitudes, such as love of

of behavior as obtained from a 50-hour clinical history. The traits fell into three clusters, and from this start, by adding other traits gradually, Sheldon produced three components of temperament, each defined by twenty traits. Each trait is rated on a seven-point scale, and the average of the twenty ratings gives the score in each component. A selection of traits is given in Table 1. The temperamental components are called "viscerotonia," "somatotonia," and "cerebrotonia," and, when

TABLE 1

A SELECTION OF TRAITS FROM SHELDON'S SCALE OF TEMPERAMENT

Trait No.	Viscerotonia	Somatotonia	Cerebrotonia
1	Relaxation in posture and movement	Assertiveness of posture and movement	Restraint in posture and movement, tightness
2	Love of physical comfort	Love of physical adventure	Inhibited social address
3	Greed for affection and approval	Psychological callousness	Secretiveness of feeling, emotional restraint
4	Smooth, easy communication of feeling; extraversion of viscerotonia	Horizontal mental cleavage; extraversion of somatotonia	Vertical mental cleavage; introversion
5	Relaxation and sociophilia under alcohol	Assertiveness and aggression under alcohol	Resistance to alcohol and to other depressant drugs
6	Need of people when troubled	Need of action when troubled	Need of solitude when troubled
7	Orientation toward childhood and family relationships	Orientation toward goals and activities of youth	Orientation toward later periods of life

physical adventure and relaxation in posture. Kretschmer described originally two types of temperament, the "cyclothyme" and the "schizothyme," which corresponded more or less to Jung's "extravert" and "introvert"; he related these closely to the types of build, the cyclothyme being pyknic, the schizothyme leptosomic. Later he also ascribed a particular temperament to the athletic.

Sheldon carried the same work much farther and used, for his description of temperament, components rather than types, in precisely the same way as he had for physique. He began by rating some thirty subjects on fifty traits chosen to define the persistent aspects

the scores in these of two hundred subjects were related to their somatotype components, Sheldon found correlations of the order of 0.8 between viscerotonia and endomorphy, somatotonia and mesomorphy, and cerebrotonia and ectomorphy.

This is a somewhat closer, or at any rate more precise, relation than has previously been described, and the study has been criticized, though more on the grounds of incredulity than of conflicting evidence. The chief problems calling for attention seem to be two. First is that of the extent to which different raters of Sheldon's temperamental traits agree when each has acquired the necessary prolonged life-history of the subject, and the extent to which the ratings of a subject differ at different times in his life. The genetical background of the temperamental components also needs to be examined. Scales constructed on traits of this sort are always liable to petrify what is really plastic. Second, the work needs confirmation, with particular efforts to avoid any possible "halo" effect, that is, with the somatotyper and the psychologist separate, and the psychologist working either from another man's notes or from a recording of another man's interviews, so that he never sees the subject's physique at all. One such study has been done, and, though it covered only a portion of the field, relating dominant cerebrotonia to dominant ectomorphy, in this portion it confirmed Sheldon's findings (Seltzer, Wells, and McTernan, 1948). Other objective, but possibly less illuminating, studies are those that relate somatotype to choice of job (Garn and Gertler, 1950) or to the likelihood of becoming delinquent (Sheldon *et al.*, 1949; Glueck and Glueck, 1950).

There are two theories as to how the relationships between physique and temperament come about. One ascribes them to the actions of pleiotropic or linked genes, the other to early conditioning. The first maintains that genes concerned in body shape also have effects on the brain and endocrine structure and that these dictate temperament: alternatively, it maintains that there exist separate but closely linked genes for each. Sheldon appears to subscribe to this view, since he talks about viscerotonia being a "component of temperament measured at the least-conditioned level of dynamic expression" (Sheldon *et al.*, 1949, p. 25). This theory is supported by work on rats, which have been shown to possess genes which alter, at the same time, behavior and coat color and size (Keeler, 1942). The other view is, for

example, that the highly mesomorphic child, on mixing with other children, finds by chance that he can knock down the others and continues thereafter to do so because of his success and because it comes to be expected of him. The two theories are not, of course, mutually exclusive; probably conditioning supports and reinforces an originally genetic tendency.

CONSTITUTIONAL PHYSIOLOGY

One gap, and a very important one, is visible in the constitutional field. Very little has yet appeared on the relation between body build and physiological function. That this study bridges the gap between morphological differences and psychological ones is generally realized, and a considerable number of speculative tracts have been written concerning the relation between physiological function and behavior in man. Most of them deal with supposed endocrinological differences and can scarcely be regarded as serious scientific literature, whatever their source. Only very recently have advances in endocrinology made progress in this field possible, and, owing to the arduous and expensive techniques involved, rapid advances can scarcely be expected even now. The sort of problems being pursued are whether those high in ectomorphy habitually have more thyroxine secretion than other people; whether those high in endomorphy habitually have more corticosterone secretion; and so forth. It has already been shown that the cholesterol in the blood serum, the level of which stays very constant in any particular individual, is correlated positively with endomorphy (Gertler, Garn, and Sprague, 1950; Tanner, 1951a), as is also the level of blood uric acid (Gertler, Garn, and Levine, 1951). Studies of blood pressure and cardiac output have also been made, but the results are at present somewhat uncertain. Kretschmer's school has recently entered the physiological field also and reports differences among their three types in blood sugar reactions following drugs and in various other items. Serum albumen and serum antitrypsin are said to be higher in leptosomes than in pyknics (Kretschmer, 1948, pp. 88–102). The chronaxie of various muscles is said to be lower in the leptosome than in the athletic, a finding which amplifies the report of a negative relation between ectomorphy and reaction time.

It seems likely that studies of this sort, coupled with information about changes in physiological function during the growth of the child, will do more than anything else to bring together classical human genetics and constitutional work, to the mutual benefit of both. Eventually, we may hope to see the endocrinological differences between people thoroughly clarified, and their complement—differences in brain structure and function—adequately delineated also. Very little work has yet been done on these latter differences; the Vogts alone have seriously endeavored to come to grips with the problem. It is a basic one and part of the general question of the relation between external body shape and tissue composition. Much useful information could be secured by detailed histological study of cases of sudden death, coupled with their external anthropometry. We do not know, for instance, whether somebody high in mesomorphy has more muscle fibers or bigger muscle fibers than somebody low in this component. Probably he has more fibers, but this statement is based merely on inference. Similarly, with those high in endomorphy; presumably they have more fat cells than those low in it and, in addition, perhaps a greater tendency for the fat cells to fill up with fat. Quantitative histological differences in endocrine glands are probable, and are virtually certain in the brain nuclei. But nothing is known for sure about these things.

Recently it has become possible to measure the total amount of fat and of water in the body. The former is directly related to the specific gravity, which can be calculated by measuring the body volume either by underwater weighing or by stereoscopic photogrammetry. The total body water can be calculated by chemical means. It has been found that the two are inversely proportional to each other: i.e., the more fat, the less total water. This is so, since the nonfat part of the body (the "lean body mass") varies little in water content from one person to another. Somewhat surprisingly, these studies, at least so far, have led to the conclusion that the relative amounts of bone and muscle must be fairly closely the same in everybody. Body fat, however, varies from about 1 to 40 per cent of total body weight in adult men. Similar findings have been reported for guinea pigs and cattle (see Kraybill, Bitter, and Hankins, 1952). This technique has made possible the measurement of how closely the rating of endomorphy relates to the total body fat, and in 81 healthy well-nourished men aged eighteen to forty-six, the correlation was found to be as high as −0.85 (Dupertuis, Pitts, Osserman, Welham, and Behnke, 1951*a, b*). More methods of this sort seem likely soon to be developed, and, indeed, some, involving isotope dilution technique, are already to hand but are cumbersome and expensive, since at present only stable isotopes are certainly safe to give healthy people.

These methods have the disadvantage that they give information only about the amount of chemical in the entire body. For localization, at least in the simple case of bone, muscle, and fat, roentgenometric techniques have been used, particularly in growth studies and in the calf area (see Tanner, 1953*a*). They can be easily applied to all parts of the body and have perhaps not been used in constitutional work to the degree they merit.

Lastly, in discussing constitutional physiology, it must be remembered that traits which do not link up with external body build but are nevertheless characteristic of persons are equally the concern of. the anthropologist. Resting heart rate is one of these; though not linked to physique, it is strongly related to body temperature, another constitutional characteristic, and very probably reflects structural and biochemical differences in certain parts of the brain (Tanner, 1951*b*).

ANDROGYNY AND DYSPLASIA

Two aspects of physique not yet discussed are androgyny and dysplasia. By the former is meant the degree of femininity of body form in the male and of masculinity in the female. Considerable attention has been paid to the measurement of androgyny, and in current use there are scales based on ratings or general appearance (Sheldon *et al.*, 1940; Seltzer, 1945; Bayley and Bayer, 1946) and scales dependent solely on bodily measurements constructed by the use of discriminant functions between males and females (Tanner, 1951*c*). Androgyny is not independent of somatotype, since those high in mesomorphy tend to be more masculine than those high in endomorphy; the physiological relations between the two sets of components are not yet clear. The degree of androgyny, unlike the somatotype, seems to be established by events taking place at adolescence (see Tanner, 1953*a*) and probably bears a fairly close relation to hormone secretion at that time, and possibly later. Several studies have been made relating masculinity of physique to physiological and psychological data, such as choice of career (Seltzer, 1945).

Dysplasia is the name given to the degree to which one part of the body fails to harmonize with another. Viola measured dysplasia by adding up the percentage deviations of particular measurements from the average of them all; Kretschmer estimated it by anthroposcopy alone. Sheldon assigns somatotypes to five different regions separately and computes dysplasia as the sum of all the differences in ratings; but very few somatotypes, if any, can be trusted to obtain mutual agreement on quantitative differences between regions—this is asking too much of critical anthroposcopy except in fairly gross instances. There is at present no metrical technique available, and one is badly needed. Dysplasia reflects either mutually incompatible genes or environmental stresses at particular times during growth and is suspected of being of medical and sociological importance, though little definite is known about this.

FACTOR ANALYSIS AND CONSTITUTIONAL STUDY

The technique of factor analysis, though originally developed somewhat outside the strictly biometrical fold, is now an integral part of multivariate analysis and should really be discussed only in connection with analysis of variance, generalized distance, canonical components and correlations, discriminant functions, and similar biometrical tools. The application of biometrical method in physical anthropology has been somewhat tardy because the biometry, being that of multivariate distributions, is generally complex and makes very considerable demands on the investigator's time. Nevertheless, these methods are being more and more used, and it seems a safe guess that the coming generation of anthropologists must be familiar with them or lose their hold on this field of science.

Only factor analysis will be discussed here, since it has led to a method for classifying both physique and temperament. (The next step would be to use canonical correlation technique on the results so obtained, to see how closely temperament and physique are related, and by what factors; but this has not yet been done.) Factor analysis is essentially a technique for reducing a large number of measurements, all of which are intercorrelated, to a smaller number of factors, which account for most of the variability defined by the original measurements. The factors may be themselves intercorrelated, in which case they are called "oblique," or they may all be independent of one another, when they are called "orthogonal." The starting point is a table of correlation coefficients for a group of, say, a dozen measurements, and the finishing line a series of, say, three orthogonal factors A, B, and C, which together account for perhaps 80 per cent of the variability defined by the dozen measurements. Factor analysis enables one to escape completely from the otherwise well-deserved charge of measuring the same thing over and over again. The factor scores for any individual can be estimated by an equation of the type Factor $A = a$ (chest breadth) $+ b$ (stature) $+ c$ (hip width); and, conversely, the correlations of each measurement with each factor can be examined to shed light on the way in which various measurements hang together and on the choice of measurements required to define most parsimoniously the shape of the whole body or whatever part of it is required.

There are several alternative techniques of factor analysis in use, their main difference lying in whether oblique or orthogonal factors are obtained and whether or not a general factor is first extracted. All physical measurements are positively intercorrelated, and this gives rise, under most factorial techniques, to a *general factor* of gross size, with which all the measurements are correlated. After this there remain, in the technique most widely applied and tested in anthropology, several *group factors*, which can themselves each be subdivided into smaller groups. The most comprehensive discussions, replete with anthropological illustration, will be found in Burt's recent papers (Burt, 1947, 1949, 1950; Burt and Banks, 1947), and a comparison with the somatotype classification is given in Tanner (1947). Thurstone (1947) and Howells (1951) may be read for a somewhat different approach.

The results of analyzing various tables of correlations are highly consistent and provide quite a satisfactory series of factors according to which one can classify people. Any individual can be placed by finding his score in each factor, or in as many factors as the purpose in hand warrants. In Table 2 is given a summary of results to date, set forth as subdivided group factors. The true situation is probably not so simple as this and should include some factors for head and hand size and shape which do not altogether fit the simple subdivision plan. Also the division at 3A and 3B into limb and trunk prior to transverse-sagittal direction is somewhat arbitrary because of lack of data and may be reversed. Burt's latest analysis (1949) of measurements taken following Viola's system gives evidence that broadness of body is divisible into breadth chiefly transversely and in the skeleton and breadth chiefly sagittally and in fat. It would seem that these factors are orthogonalized forms of Sheldon's mesomorphy and endomorphy. Linearity of body is almost identical with ectomorphy, and its subdivision into limb and trunk linearity, which is ignored in the Sheldon system, is a valuable and constant feature of the factor-analysis classification.

Factors are essentially statistics, just like standard deviations; they cannot be equated a priori with any genetical or physiological mechanisms. Not enough work using them has been done to know whether or not they will prove useful in the practical sense in relating physique to physiological function or

THE GENETICS OF BUILD AND THE IMPORTANCE OF ANIMAL STUDIES

There is no doubt that physique is very largely genetically determined. Yet no sustained effort at defining the hereditary factors concerned has yet been made in man. Such studies as there are will be found reviewed in a recent text of clinical genetics (Tanner,

TABLE 2

SUMMARY OF FACTOR-ANALYSIS CLASSIFICATION OF PHYSIQUE, IN TERMS
OF ORTHOGONAL SUBDIVIDED GROUP FACTORS

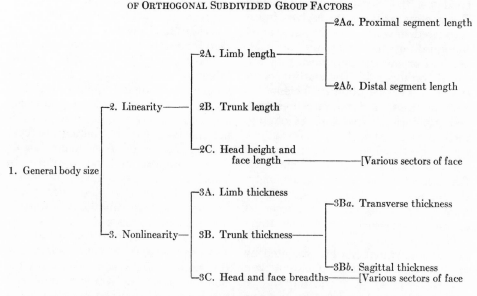

behavior. In the analysis of shape they will probably be useful only if it turns out that they do represent fairly directly physiological mechanisms, and it seems not unlikely that at any rate one of the systems of factors will be successful in doing so. The relationship of factors to the events during growth has been tentatively explored, with some positive results, by Tanner (1947).

Factor analysis has also been used extensively in the classification of temperamental traits, but a discussion of this falls outside the scope of the present essay. A description will be found in Cattell (1946).

1953*b*). A great deal of light can be thrown on this subject by working with inbred lines of laboratory animals, and collaboration between zoölogists and anthropologists along these lines seems to be shyly starting. Many of the variations of physique found in man are seen in other mammals. There are linear and nonlinear strains of horses, rabbits, dogs, and probably monkeys, and the factor-analysis technique has been applied to the measurement of cattle, with results not too dissimilar from those in man (Tanner and Burt, in press). It is known that in rats and mice genes exist which alter coat color and body size concomitantly, and this sort of study should provide a beginning for the genetic analysis of shape, growth rate, and physiological function.

BIBLIOGRAPHIC SOURCES FOR PHYSIQUE STUDIES

Lastly a word as to bibliographic sources. The journals largely devoted to constitutional matters are:

1. *Zeitschrift für Konstitutionslehre* (*Zeitschrift für die gesamte Anatomie, Teil 2*), published in Vienna beginning as the *Zeitschrift für angewandte Anatomie und Konstitutionslehre* in 1914, changing its name to *Zeitschrift für Konstitutionslehre* in 1922 and again to *Zeitschrift für menschliche Vererbungs- und Konstitutionslehre* in 1936. It carried yearly bibliographies of the relevant literature from 1919 up to 1931.

2. *Endocrinologia e patologia costituzionale*, published in Bologna from 1922 to 1941, when it changed its name to *Endocrinologia e scienza della costituzione*. Each number carries abstracts of current literature.

3. *Biotypologie*, published in Paris since 1932. This also carries abstracts, but on a much smaller scale.

In addition to these, a considerable number of papers bearing on constitution are to be found in *Human Biology*, the *American Journal of Physical Anthropology*, *Scritti biologici*, *Rivista di antropologia*, *Anthropologie*, and the *Zeitschrift für Morphologie und Anthropologie*.

Good bibliographies are to be found in Brugsch and Lewy (1926–31), Martin (1928), Schreider (1937), Tucker and Lessa (1940), and Krogman (1941a).

GROWTH

The study of growth is a natural complement to the study of physique. "Here and elsewhere," said Aristotle, "we shall not obtain the best insight into things until we actually see them growing from the beginning." The problem in the field of growth that the constitutionalist is interested in is not difficult to formulate. One man differs from another in physique and function; how did the two come to differ? At what stage after the fertilization of the ova did the differences first appear? What caused them—genes, maternal environment, events during postnatal growth? What is the physiological mechanism by which they came about? To none of the questions is there at present anything but the vaguest answer. The differences are predominantly genetic, most are traceable back to the prenatal period and probably begin very early in it; and as to the mechanism of their production, nothing useful can be said.

Growth is a large subject, and anthropologists have traditionally been concerned almost exclusively with a small part of it, the physical growth of the child. Even there it is mainly with the postnatal period that they have been occupied. But the solution of our questions demands research in much more of the field than this and brings us into contact with very fundamental problems. Growth covers a multitude of phenomena, from the enlargement and division of single cells to the use of mass standard weight curves in judging whether a child is sick or not. The central problem of form and organization is but one aspect of the study of growth, and the tracing of evolutionary origins by comparing morphological differences is but another. Darwin used to say that a knowledge of mathematics added an extra sense to the scholar's mind; it is no less true that a knowledge of growth adds an extra dimension to the biologist's insight.

The field being so vast, it is exceedingly difficult for any one individual to be well acquainted with all parts of it. Certainly there has been little liaison between zoölogists and anthropologists; each has been busy plowing his separate furrow. Anthropologists, and particularly those with a pediatric background, have been too often quite ignorant of work done on species other than the human and ignorant indeed of the fundamental methods and theory of their subject. Zoölogists, on the other hand, have often ignored the enormous mass of precise data on man, an archive which exceeds by far anything available on other species and which would have served admirably to exemplify some of their generalizations and to temper others. The gap is largely due to the historical curiosities of the medical curriculum and seems now to be narrowing.

BIBLIOGRAPHIC SOURCES

The discussion of growth in the context of this essay is somewhat easier than that of constitution, in that a considerable number of reviews covering various aspects exist, by reference to which the reader can obtain further information and a fuller bibliography. Nevertheless, one of the prime difficulties has been, and still is, the lack of any English textbook on the subject. There is a small Italian text (Castaldi, 1928), now somewhat out of date; but otherwise we must do the best we can with portions of D'Arcy Thompson's classic *On Growth and Form* (1942), Scammon's brilliant chapter in the *Measurement of Man* (Harris *et al.*, 1930), the compilation of Brody (1945), and Huxley's *Problems of Relative Growth* (1932). Thanks to Krogman, the human sector of the field boasts excellent bibliographies. The most useful to the zoölogist or to the advanced medical or anthropological student is one giving a basic syllabus of some 250 papers, annotated and classified by subject matter (Krogman, 1950). A very comprehensive one for the years 1926–39 was given in *Tabulae biologicae* (Krogman, 1941*a*), and additional material is to be found in the *Bibliogra-*

phy of Human Morphology (Krogman, 1941*b*), and in the White House Conference volumes (1932). The earlier literature is listed in Martin and Bach (1926) and in Baldwin (1921). In addition, abstracts of current papers are given in *Child Development Abstracts*. Growth of animals is, on the contrary, very badly served, and the pediatrician who wishes to explore this field must at present do so without map or compass. Perhaps the best introduction is by way of the series of articles in the D'Arcy Thompson *Festschrift* (Le Gros Clark and Medawar, 1945), Brody (1945), a recent *Symposium of the Society for Experimental Biology* (Vol. II, 1948), another at Princeton (Parpart, 1949), and the contents of the journal *Growth*. In a more specialized portion of the field Needham's *Chemical Embryology* (1931) and *Biochemistry and Morphogenesis* (1942) are invaluable and exceedingly well documented.

It is convenient to discuss the present situation in growth studies under two headings, "General and Theoretical Problems" and "Problems in Human Growth." The former may be subdivided into two sections, the first concerned with methodology, the second with chemical and cellular studies.

GENERAL AND THEORETICAL PROBLEMS

The *methodology* of the investigation of growth processes is badly in need of clarification. Growth data as a rule consist of a series of measurements spread out in time, and, in order to use these measurements for testing some hypothesis, suitable statistical techniques are necessary. These techniques are by no means all worked out; nor are those that have been published readily available to biologists; nor are they at all simple. Multivariate time series are about the most complicated things that biometry has to offer; yet that is what a very great deal of growth work involves. A monograph, preferably by a biometrically minded biologist with a mathematical statistician at his elbow, is badly needed here. A start in this direction has been made in an article by Tanner (1951d), but this covers only portions of the field.

There are two possible approaches to the study of growth; either a single organism can be measured at different times as it grows, or many organisms, each of a different age, can be measured. Growth studies of the former type have come to be called "longitudinal," those of the latter "cross-sectional." The mathematical techniques for dealing with the two differ considerably, and this has not always been realized: very many papers have confused the between-individual and the within-individual, between-time, sources of variability and thus thrown away a large part of their information. In general, the longitudinal technique is favored where possible, since in the study of the growth process it is the changes with time common to individuals that are initially of greatest interest. In many circumstances involving experiment, however, it is impossible to preserve the organism after the measurement is taken, but here homozygous stocks of animals may be expected to be of great and increasing value. Provided that pre- and postnatal nutritional and climatic circumstances are kept as constant as possible, a homozygous stock is practically a single individual, blessed for the experimenter's benefit with many times nine lives. Between-strain differences take the place of between-individual ones. There are as yet few papers exploiting the possibilities of this approach: one is that by Gregory and Castle (1931), relating general body-size differences between strains of rabbits to speed of cell division as far back as the thirtieth hour after fertilization. The field of comparative mammalian growth is largely untouched; even the basic data, of lin-

ear dimension increases in various strains and species during the period of growth, are quite unavailable (see Tanner, 1953a).

Much more ingenuity has been shown in fitting curves to growth data than in obtaining data which warrant such ingenious fits. Exponentials, logistics, and Gompertz curves have been the ones most frequently used, and, as it was only very recently that practicable and efficient fitting methods became available, the fits are mostly open to mathematical objection. It has not always been realized that closeness of fit is not, in general, any evidence that the equation used represents some fundamental biological property of the data; the fit depends on the number of parameters, and its usefulness on the adequacy with which the data distinguish between two or more possible hypothetical curves. This point has been most clearly discussed by Sholl (1948). It seems likely that progress here will follow, first, the devising of an equation which adequately represents (in the biological as well as in the mathematical sense) the growth of a single organism followed from intrauterine life to maturity and, second, the identification of the parameters of such a curve with definite physiological, genetic, and nutritional effects. A curve with parameters which do not reify in this way will probably not be very useful. One approach to this would be through comparison of growth curves between homozygous stocks differing in only a single gene affecting size or shape.

The form in which the relation between two dimensions of an organism, both growing, should be represented has also been much discussed (see Tanner, 1951d). Some have advocated using the ratios of their simple velocities, others the ratio of their multiplicative velocities, that is, of the velocities of each divided by absolute size;

this latter is the technique of growth allometry. Richards and Kavanagh (1945) have given a most valuable discussion of present views on this. These authors also describe most penetratingly the extension and mathematical formulation of D'Arcy Thompson's method of transformations in the study of growing form, a subject followed up and exemplified in the work of Medawar (1945) and Needham (1950).

The subject of cellular growth in tissue culture has recently been discussed by Willmer (1945). Morphogenesis and organization are very adequately covered in Needham's *Biochemistry and Morphogenesis* (1942).

PROBLEMS IN HUMAN GROWTH

In the last twenty-five years very great progress has been made in documenting the physical growth of children from birth to maturity. Considerable numbers of children have been followed over this whole span, and many more over substantial parts of it. Besides physical measurements, roentgenograms and photographs have been taken on a good number of children and physiological and psychological data on some. The greater part of this mass of information remains, however, quite undigested. A large amount is unpublished, and most of the rest has appeared quite simply as pure information, not as data associated with the testing of any hypothesis. It is indeed hard to discern in the literature of human growth any sense of outstanding critical problems such as are usually found in other branches of science. There is need for an individual or, better than that, a group statement as to precisely what it is hoped to achieve by this collecting of data, apart simply from normal standards. One view of the major problem has been given at the beginning of this section— the defining of the times and mecha-

nisms of individual differentiation. Very little headway has been made with this, partly because of the lack of suitable biometrical techniques, partly because of insufficient physiological knowledge; and partly because of inadequate genetical material.

For cataloguing purposes we may split up growth into four periods: prenatal, birth to adolescence, adolescence, and the adult period. The information on the prenatal period leaves a good deal to be desired; it is, of course, purely cross-sectional. The best-known work is that of Scammon and Calkins (1929), which has an excellent bibliography. There is some literature on the relation of parent size to dimensions of the fetus at birth, but none relating dimensions of the newborn baby to the shape of the adult man. Large babies as a rule grow to be large adults, though the strength of the correlation remains in doubt, and there seems to be some maternal restraining mechanism preventing the fetus of a large man growing too big *in utero* for his small wife to handle, though this is not absolutely certain. A certain amount has been written on the relation of maternal nutrition to newborn size, but the evidence is at present contradictory. About the physiological side of this period we know very little, and the whole question of whether or not primate fetal endocrine glands secrete and how they react to maternal trophins is quite unsettled.

For the next period, birth to adolescence, there are few published longitudinal studies. Not very much attention has been paid to this period, perhaps partly because it is a time of technical difficulty alike physically, physiologically, and psychologically. It is thought that there is an acceleration of growth known as the "juvenile" or "midgrowth spurt" at about five to seven years, and it has been suggested that this occurs only in breadths and not in lengths (Tanner, 1947). If true, this would be important for the analysis of field or gradients of growth in man, but the whole existence of the spurt remains in doubt until pure longitudinal data are examined and adequate statistical procedures applied to them. There is no review specifically of this period, and there is a very definite need for one.

On adolescence, however, an immense amount of work has been concentrated. Little discussion is required here, as two recent reviews (Stuart, 1946; Tanner, 1953a) cover the subject fairly completely. The latter deals at length with the endocrinological control of pubescence and with human adolescence in relation to that of other animals.

The growth, or the change, of the adult is quite another story. We have very little longitudinal data available and not a great deal of cross-sectional information. Such problems as who puts on weight, when, how, and with what medical results urgently call for solution, and there is the strongest need for an adult longitudinal growth study. Man seems to differ from some other mammals in stopping growth except in fat quite soon after puberty, and it is said that only in the human female is there a recognizable menopause. The comparison of man's adult growth processes with those of other animals is obviously full of interest.

The genetics of growth remains the central citadel, with scarcely a shot fired at it. The time of menarche is to a considerable extent genetically determined, and Reynolds (1943) has shown that the order in which various ossification centers appear also depends on heredity, but the genetic mechanisms have not been investigated. The nearest approach to this is perhaps Sawin's extensive work on rabbits (see Tanner and Sawin, 1953, for bibliography).

There is a large literature, however, on the effect of environment, mostly in the nutrition sense, on growth. Sanders (1934) covers the literature up to 1933. It seems that short periods of starvation in man or animals cause slowing of growth at the time but are followed by a compensatory acceleration, which soon brings the animal back to its constitutional growth curve, apparently none the worse. More prolonged malnutrition can cause lasting change in animals, but there is no really critical evidence as to just how severe the malnutrition must be before such a thing happens in man. There are size differences between children and adults of social classes, but it is by no means clear whether these are partly or wholly due to feeding. If genetic isolation mechanisms, on the other hand, are involved, we know next to nothing about them. Again, it is clear that children now reach puberty considerably earlier than they did a generation ago; but whether this is wholly nutritional or due in part to breaking up of genetic isolates is not known. Malnutrition certainly does delay puberty in man and other animals.

In connection with environmental effects, the medical use of growth records should be mentioned. The rate at which a child is growing has been extensively used as an index of his health, the idea in its crudest form being that a malnourished child is smaller than a well-nourished one. There is no general agreement, however, as to exactly how standards of growth should be used so as best to detect minor malnutrition or disease. The possibilities and the various methods at present in use have been reviewed by Tanner (1952); the last word seems still to remain with Stuart, whose opinion it is that the only test for suboptimal nutrition in the child is to give him for several weeks a known optimal diet under conditions of known psychological stabilization and to see if he then gains weight.

REFERENCES

BALDWIN, B. T. 1921. *The Physical Growth of Children from Birth to Maturity.* ("University of Iowa Studies in Child Welfare," Vol. I, No. 1.)

BAYLEY, N., and BAYER, L. M. 1946. "The Assessment of Somatic Androgyny," *American Journal of Physical Anthropology,* n.s., IV, 433–61.

BENEDETTI, P. 1936–37. "La Situazione odierna del movimento scientifico sulla costituzione individuale," *Endocrinologia e patalogia costituzionale,* n.s., XII, No. 2, 109–81.

BENEKE, F. W. 1881. *Constitution und constitutionelles Kranksein des Menschen.* Marburg: Elwert.

BRODY, S. 1945. *Bioenergetics and Growth.* New York: Reinhold Publishing Corp.

BRUGSCH, T., and LEWY, F. H. (eds.). 1926–31. *Die Biologie der Person.* 4 vols. Berlin and Vienna: Urban & Schwarzenberg.

BURT, C. 1947. "Factor Analysis and Physical Types," *Psychometrika,* XII, 171–88.

———. 1949. "Subdivided Factors," *British Journal of Psychology* (Stat. Sec.), II, 41.

———. 1950. "Group Factor Analysis," *ibid.,* III, 40.

BURT, C., and BANKS, C. 1947. "A Factor Analysis of Body Measurements for British Adult Males," *Annals of Eugenics,* XIII, 238–56.

CASTALDI, L. 1928. *Accrescimento corporeo e costituzione dell'uomo.* Firenze: Niccolai.

CATTELL, R. B. 1946. *Description and Measurement of Personality.* Yonkers: World Book Co.

DUPERTUIS, C. W.; PITTS, G. C.; OSSERMAN, E. F.; WELHAM, W. C.; and BEHNKE, A. R. 1951*a.* "Relation of Specific Gravity to Body Build in a Group of Healthy Men," *Journal of Applied Physiology,* III, 676.

———. 1951*b.* "Relation of Body Water Content to Body Build in a Group of Healthy Men," *ibid.,* IV, 364–67.

GARN, S. M., and GERTLER, M. M. 1950. "An Association between Type of Work and Physique in an Industrial Group," *American Journal of Physical Anthropology,* n.s., VIII, 387–98.

GERTLER, M. M.; GARN, S. M.; and LEVINE, S. A. 1951. "Serum Uric Acid in Relation to Age and Physique in Health and in Coronary Heart Disease," *Annals of Internal Medicine,* XXXIV, 1421–31.

GERTLER, M. M.; GARN, S. M.; and SPRAGUE, H. B. 1950. "Cholesterol, Cholesterol Esters, and Phospholipids in Health and in Coronary Artery Disease. II. Morphology and Serum Lipids in Man," *Circulation,* II, 380–91.

GLUECK, S. and E. 1950. *Unravelling Juvenile Delinquency.* New York: Commonwealth Fund.

GREGORY, P. W., and CASTLE, W. E. 1931. "Further Studies on the Embryological Basis of Size Inheritance in the Rabbit," *Journal of Experimental Zoölogy,* LIX, 199–211.

HALDANE, J. B. S. 1942. *New Paths in Genetics.* New York and London: Harper & Bros.

HARRIS, J. A.; JACKSON, C. M.; PATERSON, D. G.; and SCAMMON, R. E. 1930. *The Measurement of Man.* Minneapolis: University of Minnesota Press.

HOWELLS, W. W. 1951. "Factors of Human Physique," *American Journal of Physical Anthropology,* n.s., IX, 159–91.

HUXLEY, J. S. 1932. *Problems of Relative Growth.* London: Methuen.

KEELER, C. 1942. "The Association of the Black (Non-agouti) Gene with Behaviour in the Norway Rat," *Journal of Heredity,* XXXIII, 371–84.

KRAYBILL, H. F.; BITTER, H. L.; and HANKINS, O. G. 1952. "Body Composition of Cattle. II. Determination of Fat and Water Content," *Journal of Applied Physiology,* IV, 575–83.

KRETSCHMER, E. 1948. *Körperbau und Charakter.* 19th ed. Berlin: Springer. English trans.: *Physique and Character.* 2d ed. London: Kegan Paul, Trench, Trubner, 1925.

KROGMAN, W. M. 1941*a.* "Growth of Man," *Tabulae biologicae Amsterdam,* XX, 1–936.

———. 1941*b*. *A Bibliography of Human Morphology*. Chicago: University of Chicago Press.

———. 1950. "The Physical Growth of the Child: Syllabus," *Yearbook of Physical Anthropology 1949*, V, 280–90.

LE GROS CLARK, W. E., and MEDAWAR, P. B. (eds.). 1945. *Essays on Growth and Form Presented to D'Arcy Wentworth Thompson*. Oxford: Clarendon Press.

MARTIN, R. 1928. *Lehrbuch der Anthropologie*. 3 vols. Jena: Fischer.

MARTIN, R., and BACH, J. 1926. "Grössen- und Massen-Verhältnisse beim Menschen," *Tabulae biologicae Amsterdam*, III, 617–720.

MEDAWAR, P. B. 1945. "Size, Shape and Age." In LE GROS CLARK, W. E., and MEDAWAR, P. B. (eds.), *Essays on Growth and Form Presented to D'Arcy Wentworth Thompson*, pp. 157–87. Oxford: Clarendon Press.

NEEDHAM, A. E. 1950. "The Form Transformation of the Abdomen of the Female Pea-Crab, *Pinnotheres pisum* Leach," *Proceedings of the Royal Society, B.*, CXXXVII, 115–36.

NEEDHAM, J. 1931. *Chemical Embryology*. 3 vols. Cambridge: At the University Press.

———. 1942. *Biochemistry and Morphogenesis*. Cambridge: At the University Press.

NEEL, J. V. 1949. "The Detection of the Genetic Carriers of Hereditary Disease," *American Journal of Human Genetics*, I, 19–36.

PARPART, A. K. (ed.). 1949. *The Chemistry and Physiology of Growth*. Princeton: Princeton University Press.

REYNOLDS, E. L. 1943. "Degree of Kinship and Pattern of Ossification," *American Journal of Physical Anthropology*, n.s., I, 405–16.

RICHARDS, O. W., and KAVANAGH, A. J. 1945. "The Analysis of Growing Form." In LE GROS CLARK, W. E., and MEDAWAR, P. B. (eds.), *Essays on Growth and Form Presented to D'Arcy Wentworth Thompson*, pp. 188–230. Oxford: Clarendon Press.

SANDERS, B. S. 1934. *Environment and Growth*. Baltimore: Warwick & York.

SCAMMON, R. E., and CALKINS, L. A. 1929. *The Development and Growth of the External Dimensions of the Human Body in the Fetal Period*. Minneapolis: University of Minnesota Press.

SCHREIDER, E. 1937. *Les Types humain*. Paris: Hermann.

SELTZER, C. C. 1945. "The Relationship between the Masculine Component and Personality," *American Journal of Physical Anthropology*, n.s., III, 33–47.

SELTZER, C. C.; WELLS, F. L.; and McTERNAN, E. B. 1948. "A Relationship between Sheldonian Somatotype and Psychotype," *Journal of Personality*, XVI, 431–36.

SHELDON, W. H.; HARTL, E. M.; and McDERMOTT, E. 1949. *The Varieties of Delinquent Youth*. New York: Harper & Bros.

SHELDON, W. H., and STEVENS, S. S. 1942. *The Varieties of Temperament*. New York: Harper & Bros.

SHELDON, W. H.; STEVENS, S. S.; and TUCKER, W. B. 1940. *The Varieties of Human Physique*. New York: Harper & Bros.

SHOLL, D. 1948. "The Quantitative Investigation of the Vertebrate Brain and the Applicability of Allometric Formulae to Its Study," *Proceedings of the Royal Society, B*, CXXXV, 243–58.

STUART, H. C. 1946. "Normal Growth and Development during Adolescence," *New England Journal of Medicine*, CCXXXIV, 666–72, 693–700, 732–38.

TANNER, J. M. 1947. "The Morphological Level of Personality," *Proceedings of the Royal Society of Medicine*, XL, 301.

———. 1951*a*. "The Relation between Serum Cholesterol and Physique in Healthy Young Men," *Journal of Physiology*, CXV, 371–90.

———. 1951*b*. "The Relationships between the Frequency of the Heart, Oral Temperature and Rectal Temperature in Man at Rest," *ibid.*, pp. 391–409.

———. 1951*c*. "Current Advances in the Study of Physique: Photogrammetric Anthropometry and an Androgyny Scale," *Lancet*, I, 574–79.

———. 1951*d*. "Some Notes on the Reporting of Growth Data," *Human Biology*, XXIII, 93–159.

TANNER, J. M. 1952. "The Assessment of Growth and Development in Children," *Archives of Disease in Childhood,* XXVII, No. 131, 10–33.

———. 1953a. "Growth of the Human at the Time of Adolescence." In FRAZER, F. (ed.), *Lectures on the Scientific Basis of Medicine.* London: Athlone Press.

———. 1953b. "The Inheritance of Morphological and Physiological Traits." In SORSBY, A. (ed.), *Clinical Genetics.* London: Butterworth.

TANNER, J. M., and BURT, A. W. A. *Factor Analysis of Cattle.* In press.

TANNER, J. M., and SAWIN, P. B. 1953. *Morphogenetic Studies of the Rabbit.* Vol. XI: *Genetic Differences in the Growth of the Vertebral Column and Their Relation to Growth and Development in Man.*

THOMPSON, D'A. W. 1942. *On Growth and Form.* New ed. Cambridge: At the University Press.

THURSTONE, L. L. 1947. "Factorial Analysis of Body Measurements," *American Journal of Physical Anthropology,* n.s., V, 15–28.

TUCKER, W. B., and LESSA, W. A. 1940. "Man: A Constitutional Investigation," *Quarterly Review of Biology,* XV, 265–89.

VIOLA, G. 1932. *La Costituzione individuale.* Bologna: Cappelli.

———. 1937. "Il mio metodo di valutazione della costituzione individuale," *Endocrinologia e patologia costituzionale,* XII, 387–480.

WHITE HOUSE CONFERENCE ON CHILD HEALTH AND PROTECTION. SECTION I, MEDICAL SERVICE, COMMITTEE A, GROWTH AND DEVELOPMENT. 1932. *Growth and Development of the Child.* 4 vols. New York: Century Co.

WILLMER, E. N. 1945. "Growth and Form in Tissue Cultures." In LE GROS CLARK, W. E., and MEDAWAR, P. B. (eds.), *Essays on Growth and Form Presented to D'Arcy Wentworth Thompson,* pp. 264–94. Oxford: Clarendon Press.

Applied Anthropology in Medicine

By WILLIAM CAUDILL

SOCIAL ANTHROPOLOGISTS and other social scientists have recently been doing some unusual things: participating with physicians in conferences on social medicine, teaching in medical schools, working with public health services in Peru, studying the social structure of hospitals and the flow of life on the wards, interviewing patients about to undergo plastic surgery, and doing psychotherapy with Plains Indians. While much of this work is still unpublished, Ackerknecht (1942–47) has continued to write his excellent papers on primitive medicine; Mead and Henry (1949) have discussed the general relationship of anthropology to psychosomatic medicine; Hall (1951) has outlined the progress of sociological research in the field of medicine; and Clausen (1950) has reviewed social science research in the national mental health program. Governmental agencies and private foundations[1] have become increasingly active in the study of the social aspects of health and illness, and sections devoted to this area of interest are beginning to appear on the programs of the

annual meetings of anthropological and sociological societies.

All this activity is indicative of a tentative liaison between social science and medicine, but, as yet, there has been little real intercommunication. One of the purposes of this paper is to bring into juxtaposition references to theories and research projects which are widely separated today, in the hope that this may stimulate thinking about infrequently related topics and lead to the formulation of new problems. To this end, work done within a wide range of social-scientific thought will be reviewed under the following headings: "Primitive Medicine in Nonliterate Societies"; "The Organization and Practice of Medicine in Contemporary Western Society"; "Psychosomatic Medicine, Social Medicine, and Multiple Stress in Disease"; and "Types of Disorders."

In view of the scope of such a discussion, the field of medicine will be given broad definition, and the focus will be on research in which the concepts and methods of social science have played an important part, whether the investigators happened to be anthropologists, sociologists, physicians, or members of an interdisciplinary team. Equally, attention will be given to theoretical as well as applied studies, because application inevitably includes theory and cannot go forward without being grounded in more general knowledge. The areas of culture

1. One need only mention the names of the Russell Sage Foundation, the Commonwealth Fund, the Milbank Memorial Fund, and the Josiah H. Macy, Jr., Foundation. A new organization in New York City, the Health Information Foundation, is preparing for publication an inventory of the use of social science in health research throughout the United States as a means of assessing the problem areas in which research grants would be most helpful.

and personality and physical anthropology in medicine will not, however, be touched upon, as these are dealt with in other inventory papers for this symposium. Emphasis will be placed on recently published and still unpublished[2] work, in order to give a clearer picture of the present achievements and future trends of social science in medicine. It is impossible to cover all the relevant literature or current research in so vast a field that itself exists more in the writer's imaginative hopes than in present reality; therefore, only examples or type cases will be cited.

PRIMITIVE MEDICINE IN NON-LITERATE SOCIETIES

Disease in some form is one of the fundamental vital problems facing every society, and every known society has developed methods for coping with disease and thus created a medicine. Although almost every anthropologist since the end of the nineteenth century has included, too often in passing, some reference to medicine or disease in his monographs, Ackerknecht (1945*a*) recently could point to the "deplorable state of affairs in ethnography," despite the fact that "the recording of medical data from primitive societies has improved somewhat during the last twenty-five years." The ethnographic material that is available is relatively good concerning concepts of disease and therapeutic practices, but studies of disease itself are almost totally lacking.

Outstanding over the years is the classic statement by Rivers (1924) of the relations between *Medicine, Magic, and Religion,* and the work of Clements

2. I have been in correspondence with well over a hundred social scientists and physicians from several branches of medicine concerning their current, and frequently unpublished, work. Since it is impossible here to thank each by name, I should at least like to take this opportunity to express my gratitude.

(1932) in tracing the world-wide distribution of five basic concepts of disease as attributable to sorcery, breach of taboo, object intrusion, spirit intrusion, and soul loss. Since 1935, a few really good studies have been published: for example, the work of Field (1937) on the religion and medicine of the Ga people; Spencer (1941) on disease, religion, and society in the Fiji Islands; and Harley (1941) on the Mano of Liberia, which includes an analysis of African medicine in general. In broader terms, Sigerist (1951) has most recently reviewed primitive and archaic medicine in the first volume of his projected *History of Medicine*.

The modern anthropological and medical viewpoint on primitive medicine is perhaps best summed up in the series of scholarly papers written by Ackerknecht (1942–47) over the past ten years. He emphasizes that primitive medicine is not a queer collection of errors and superstitions, nor is it to be explained by simply stating that, in the medical field, primitives use spells, prayers, blood-letting, human fat, and spittle. "What counts are not the forms but the place medicine occupies in the life of a tribe or people, the spirit which pervades its practice, the way in which it merges with other traits from different fields of experience" (Ackerknecht, 1942*b*). In discussing primitive medicine and culture pattern, Ackerknecht stresses three points: (1) there is not one "primitive medicine" but numerous different primitive medicines; (2) the differences between primitive medicines are much less differences in "elements" (they share many common elements) than differences in the medical pattern which they build up and which is conditioned fundamentally by their cultural pattern; (3) the degree of integration of the different elements of medicine into a whole, and of the whole medicine into a culture pattern, varies considerably. He illustrates these points by a comparison of the systems of medicine in Cheyenne, Dobu, and Thonga cultures (1942*b*). This is one of the very few cross-cultural analyses of primitive medicine in terms of culture patterns. Such work might well be done for other groups on which there is good material in both medicine and general ethnography: for example, the Ga (Field, 1937), Azande (Evans-Pritchard, 1937), and Mano (Harley, 1941), in Africa; Murngin (Warner, 1937), in Australia; Apache (Opler, 1936, 1941), Ojibwa (Hallowell, 1934, 1942, 1950), Navaho (Kluckhohn and Spencer, 1940; Kluckhohn, 1944*a*, Leighton and Leighton, 1941, 1944, 1949), and Maya (Redfield and Redfield, 1940; Gillin, 1948; Adams, 1951) in North America.

In summarizing why he feels primitive medicine is often successful, Ackerknecht first notes the large number of objectively effective factors found in primitive medicines: baths, cauterization, surgery from fracture treatment to trephining, inoculation against smallpox and snake bite, and an enormous pharmacopoeia, including opium, quinine, digitalis, and many other useful drugs. It must be remembered, however, that such treatment "is not done in a rational sense, but in an entirely magical sense accompanied by spells or prayers or manual rites or dances" (Ackerknecht, 1942*a*). A further reason for the success of primitive medicine lies in its psychotherapeutic qualities. These may be used to heal, as in Opler's (1936) comparison of the treatment of functional disorders by Apache shamans and modern psychiatrists, and to destroy, as in Cannon's (1942) discussion of voodoo death. The primitive psychotherapist's strength comes not only from the interpersonal ties between doctor and patient but also from the reinforcing effect of the frequent participation of the entire community in his treatment. Beyond this, there are the phenomena of broad restitutive movements, such as the Ghost Dance (Mooney, 1896) and Peyote Cult (La Barre, 1938), in nonliterate societies which might profitably be compared with Dianetics, Alcoholics Anonymous, Christian Science, and other healing cults (Reed, 1932) in modern society.

In general, as Ackerknecht (1942*b*) says: "We think that already a large comparative study of primitive medicine would be a great value for medical history and medicine as a whole. We even sincerely believe that general anthropology would profit from such studies." The remainder of this section will give a more detailed review of a few of the more recent anthropological projects related to medicine in non-Western societies.

In a manuscript soon to be published, John Whiting and Irvin Child (1952) have used cross-cultural material from seventy-five societies to test the hypothesis that child socialization practices are related to adult conceptions of the cause of disease. They take a clue from Kardiner in thinking of the customs related to illness as part of the projective systems of a culture, and they believe that the magical medical theories and practices of primitive societies seem likely to be retained more because of their compatibility with personality variables than because of their practical physiological utility. They are thus proposing to use the customs relating to illness as a sort of projective test for a culture as a whole.

In working with the data, Whiting and Child separated the process of child socialization into five systems of behavior—oral, anal, sexual, dependence, and aggression. Each of these five systems was analyzed in terms of initial indulgence, age of socialization, and severity of socialization. The analysis of explanations of illness was based on

(1) the agency causing the illness; (2) the degree of patient responsibility for the illness; (3) the act, or failure to act, of the patient; (4) the materials which have to do with the production of illness; and (5) the means by which such materials have an effect—whether they are ingested, brought into external contact with the body, used in ritual, etc. The data on socialization were rated by a team of three independent judges, while another similar team rated the data on explanations of illness.

The authors take the psychoanalytic concept of fixation and explore it by using the customary therapeutic practices found in a society as indices of positive fixation, and the customary explanations of illness as indices of negative fixation. One of their major hypotheses is: "In any society the greater the custom potential of socialization anxiety for a system of behavior, the greater will be the custom potential of explanations of illness which attribute illness to events associated with that system." Testing the seventy-five societies in terms of this hypothesis, a strong association is shown between high oral socialization anxiety and oral explanations of illness. Equally, societies which do not have high oral socialization anxiety do not tend to have oral explanations for illness. Whiting and Child, for reasons they discuss at length, do not find, however, any very striking correlation between positive fixation in child socialization and customary adult therapeutic practices.

Although the authors do not make the point, one of the implications for applied anthropology in their material is that the introduction to another society of new therapeutic techniques is more likely to meet with success than attempts to change underlying ideas concerning the causation of disease. Hence the planning of a program of Western medicine for a non-Western

society should take into account the separation of these two aspects of the problem more than has heretofore been the case. As will be noted later, this is borne out by the practical observations of the Leightons (1944) on the Navaho and of Foster (1951) on health services in Latin America.

Such a problem also has theoretical implications, as Ackerknecht (1942a) notes when he says that to understand primitive medicine we have to go far from our standards and concepts, but "these apparently very remote studies are by no means unrelated to our time ...they lead us back to some of our own problems and thus appear as a legitimate branch of real social sciences." The discussion of just this topic forms the basis of a forthcoming book by Francis L. K. Hsu (1952), in which the effects of a cholera epidemic on a village in western Yunnan are analyzed under the title *Religion, Science, and Human Crisis: A Study on China in Transition and Its Implications for the West* (see also Hsu, 1943).

Hsu questions the usual anthropological distinctions made between religion and magic and between magic and real knowledge. He says: "If we follow the thought and ways of a culture as expressed through the bearers of the culture, magic and real knowledge are not only intertwined, but may even be undistinguished, so that, for reaching one and the same end, the individual oscillates between one and the other, or resorts to both simultaneously, with the greatest facility and ease of mind." Thus, during the epidemic in West Town, prayer meetings were held at the same time as volunteer prescriptions and moral advice spread; modern anticholeric injections were taken along with traditional medicines. Among Hsu's informants, the thirty-one individuals who took some form of modern precaution also contributed to, or had active roles in, the prayer meetings. The injection or any other device, new or old, was a measure to be taken together with the other means of cure and prevention. To rely on any one thing alone was thought thoroughly unwise.

In the light of the causes and behavior of cholera known to modern science, some of the traditional measures had definite scientific bearing on the epidemic, while others were purely magico-religious in nature. For example, the taboos on meat and fish, while considered part of the effort to please the gods, might actually prevent the spread of cholera, as the bacillus grows best in alkaline media at a temperature between 30° and 40° C. On the other hand, the prayers, rituals, and moral injunctions could hardly be conceived of in a scientific sense to prevent physical spread of the epidemic. Furthermore, some measures might be opposed to scientific knowledge, i.e., opening the fingertips to let out blood might lead to serious infection and render futile any later treatment by serum.

While the distinction between the phenomena (magic and science) was visible in the anthropologist's analysis, such a distinction had little reality in the minds of West Towners. The fact that the people represented by the schools, the refugee college, and the hospital were free from cholera should have provided adequate proof of the effectiveness of scientific measures as against the ineffectiveness of the traditional pattern. Yet most West Towners not only failed to show much enthusiasm for the former, but even those who took injections also supported the prayer meetings and other age-old safeguards. It seems likely that, as the years go by and an increasing proportion of the local population turns to the modern injections, they will not necessarily withdraw their support from the measures of ancestral custom. As Hsu says, "The modern injection will then, in the

minds of the local peoples, be ranked side by side with the prayer meetings, the many local prescriptions, and food taboos." This is a good illustration of the implicit conclusion in the Whiting and Child study that new methods of treatment will probably meet with more success than attempts to influence ideas concerning the cause of disease.

Are these ideas, then, true for non-Western societies but untrue for Western? The honored place in West Town is reserved for the spirits and priests. The culture of America is, on the other hand, one in which the spirits and gods of non-Christian beliefs have no established position and scientific technicians, pseudo or genuine, are believed to provide answers about the unknown. The similarity in the two cultures lies in the fact that both peoples react to new stimuli by reinterpreting them to conform with the old. The difference comes from what constitutes the old. As Hsu remarks, "It is not fantastic to say that, to achieve popular acceptance, magic has to be dressed like science in America, while science has to be cloaked by magic in West Town."

The undisputed technological achievement of America often leads to the uncritical belief that the more efficient means will automatically replace the less efficient and that the "real knowledge" of science will triumph over "magic and superstition." This is not necessarily the case in West Town, nor, for that matter, in America. Whenever a new element is accepted by a culture —whether it be a deity, a style of dress, or a method of treating a disease—its place will be determined by the framework of what Boas has called the "traditional material" of a culture and by the social processes of "reinterpretation and syncretism" discussed by Herskovits. Thus the problems of a cholera epidemic in western Yunnan must be seen as one instance of the fundamental problem of culture change in the face of Western contact, to which there is no categorical answer. Yet changes, when they occur, are selective: matters which do not concern life or death, such as the more efficient transportation provided by trains and buses, are more readily accepted on a trial basis than are innovations touching the basic existence of a people, such as new agricultural techniques for the farmer, whose livelihood depends on any given crop, or new and strange therapeutic measures to meet the always intensely personal threat of disease. Such generalizations could well be extended to include Florence Kluckhohn's (1950) recent emphasis on dominant and variant value orientations and could have tremendous importance for the introduction of public health programs in other cultures.

As Hsu's work has shown that Western ways will not be accepted simply because they are "better," so the Leightons (1941, 1944) have done a brilliant job of indicating, in a practical sense, how Navaho and Western medicine might harmoniously exist side by side. The Leightons stress that it is oversimplification to say that Navaho religion is directed at the curing of sickness; yet it is hard to find another way to express the facts briefly. There are thirty-five principal Navaho ceremonials, and the majority are concerned with disease but are aimed at what the Navahos consider first causes rather than at symptoms. The Navaho theory of illness is not that it is caused by germs, bad food, or improper bodily function, as we believe, but rather that the patient fell out of harmony with the forces of nature, and such discord makes him susceptible to catching a sickness, breaking his leg, or developing other symptoms. The consequence of this belief is that the most important thing is to restore through ritual the harmony which has been disrupted, so that the body can heal itself. As will

be seen later, this is not far from Galdston's (1951) position on social medicine or the broader conceptualizations of psychosomatic medicine.

As Navaho ideas of health are part of their religious faith, they do not readily accept the much-needed advantages of Western medicine. The question is, what can be done about it? In their book *The Navaho Door,* the Leightons (1944) give many directly practical guides (in terms of specific illnesses, such as pneumonia, tuberculosis, and syphilis) for the doctor, nurse, and public health worker as to how Navahos might be treated in the hospital, in out-patient care, and in general health education.

For example, with reference to hospitalization, the Leightons emphasize that it is hard to picture the extent of personal adjustment a Navaho must make when he becomes a bed-patient. It seems as if the doctors and nurses could not be very much interested in him because they come to see him only at long intervals instead of staying with him constantly, as the family would. When he has been sick at home before and has had a ceremonial, the medicine man has given him his undivided attention for as much as nine days and nights. There were many other people there, too, all laboring to get him well. In the hospital it seems as if no one cares whether he gets well or not, and all he can do is lie there and feel homesick for his hogan and mutton.

Along these same lines, Joseph (1942) has published on interpersonal relations between white physicians and Indian patients, and Loomis (1945) has discussed the Taos County Cooperative Health Association, which is a spontaneous collaborative creation of the local Spanish-speaking people and the doctors. Also, Foster (1951) has edited a mimeographed report of a program of applied anthropology carried out in Latin America by Charles Erasmus, Isabel Kelly, Kalervo Oberg, and Ozzie Simmons, of the Smithsonian Institution of Social Anthropology, in cooperation with the Institute of Inter-American Affairs.

In the work summarized by Foster, interviewing and participant observation were carried out in eight health centers in Mexico, Colombia, Peru, and Brazil. The data reported include (1) a discussion of folk medicine and local illnesses, such as *ojo* ("evil eye") and *susto* ("magical fright"), as well as the concepts of "hot" and "cold" which are applied to diseases, food, etc.; (2) attitudes of the local population toward services offered by the centers; and (3) the unformalized cultural premises of operating personnel which seemed to bear on the success or failure of the centers.

The failure of centers to keep a higher percentage of patients who had been enrolled is explained by Foster as due to three very common criticisms voiced by the local people: frequent lack of tact on the part of doctors, nurses, and other personnel; time lost in going to the center; and failure to treat sick children if appointments for routine examinations had not been kept. The latter was the most bitter criticism and stemmed, in part, from the failure of the people to understand the distinction between preventive medicine, which was the basic goal of the centers, and clinical treatment of the sick. The tendency of doctors and nurses to ignore, if not to ridicule, folk concepts of illness probably strengthened the popular belief that certain categories of disease were not understood and could not be treated by medical men. *Curanderos* did a brisk business in all places studied. A few instances came to the attention of the investigators in which nurses or doctors knew certain folk concepts, did not discredit them, and on very rare occasions even made use of them. The success of such individuals in gaining popular confidence was in striking contrast to other center personnel.

In a concluding section, Foster points up the types of cultural knowledge that a technical aid administrator should have in order to plan the work of a health center effectively. These include a knowledge of folk medicine, local costs of living, local political organization, the extent of literacy, family social organization, and value systems. Apropos of the latter, Foster says that a Mexican doctor made the observation that the American public insists on optimism in its health advertising, whereas the Mexican is more receptive to the *doloroso*, the heartrending, the painful, and sad.[3]

Work similar to that outlined by Foster has recently been done by a number of other social scientists. In a hectographed report published in Spanish by the Instituto de Nutrición de Centro América y Panamá, Adams (1951) has discussed the local theories of disease and its treatment in several Guatemalan villages and the relationship of the villagers to Western-trained doctors working in the area. Hydrick's (1942) work some years ago on rural hygiene in the Netherlands East Indies should also be cited as an important study in applied anthropology. In 1947, F. W. Clements was a

3. One is reminded of the story by Saki. The breakfast food, Pipenta, had not been selling well, and the young man who wished to marry his employer's daughter attempted a new advertising campaign, renaming the product Filboid Studge. "Spayley put forth no pictures of massive babies springing with fungus-like rapidity under its forcing influence. . . . One huge somber poster depicting the Damned in Hell suffering a new torment from their inability to get at the Filboid Studge which elegant young friends held in transparent bowls just beyond their reach. . . . The poster bore no fulsome allusions to the merits of the new breakfast food, but a single grim statement ran in bold letters along its base: 'They cannot buy it now'" (Munro, 1942, pp. 176–79).

member of a field party investigating
food production and consumption as
part of a survey of nutrition and dentition in five New Guinea villages.[4]
Benjamin D. Paul, now anthropologist
on the staff of the School of Public
Health, Harvard University, is compiling a series of cross-cultural cases
for the use of public health specialists.
This work has begun with the study
of American medicine on the island of
Yap. Lyle Saunders, a sociologist in the
department of medicine, University of
Colorado, is completing a manuscript
on the problems of medical care among
Spanish-speaking people of the Southwest. In addition, he is working with
an anthropologist, Gordon Hewes, on a
study of the folk medicine of these
people. Also, a manual prepared for
UNESCO by Margaret Mead under the
title of *Culture Patterns and Technical
Change* has chapters on medicine and
the treatment of health and disease.

Lastly, the earlier work of S. C.
Dodd and the current work of Edward
Wellin deserve mention because they
involve the problem of controlled culture change. In order to measure hygienic progress, Dodd (1934) attempted "a controlled experiment on rural
hygiene in Syria." A survey was made
in 1931 to measure the hygienic status
of a number of villages, and the villages were then divided into an experimental and a control sample. The experimental sample was educated in hygiene for two years by an itinerant
clinic, and a resurvey was made in
1933 to measure the change.

For the past year Wellin has been
studying several villages in the valley

4. In a personal communication Dr. Clements informs me that this work has now been
published under the title of *Nutrition Survey
of New Guinea and Papua* (Canberra: Government Printer). Further information can
be obtained through Dr. F. W. Clements at
the Institute of Child Health, Royal Alex-
andra Hospital for Children, Camperdown,
New South Wales, Australia.

of Ica, Peru, prior to the introduction
of health services. He is now working
with the local public health service to
determine what type of program might
be put into effect. He will then be able
to assess the on-going social processes
and results of such a program in the
villages he has previously studied. In a
personal communication, Wellin sounds
a warning against what an anthropologist might decide to study as opposed
to what might be most useful for a
health service. He says: "My experience with public health organizations
has not been very extensive as yet, but
in the light of my work so far I'd say
that anthropologists sometimes tend to
misunderstand where their contribution
to public health lies. I had preconceived the area of native ideas as to
causation and cure of disease to be a
primary research focus. Actually, the
far more prosaic business of household
culture and family structure is more
useful. Public health is less interested
in local curative medicine than in preventive medicine, preventive care, hygiene, and communicable diseases. The
analogy may not be so hot, but it is
like paying so much heed to where
they bury the afterbirth that one hasn't
noticed who lugged it out; and to strain
the analogy, it may be more vital to a
health action program to know who
lugged it out than to know where the
darn thing is buried."

MEDICINE IN CONTEMPORARY WESTERN SOCIETY

The place of medicine in the social
structure of Western society has long
occupied medical historians (Shyrock,
1947; Sigerist, 1951) and increasingly
has become a conscious problem for
medicine in general (New York Academy of Medicine, 1947). Stimulated by
this interest, social scientists have come
to examine (1) medicine as part of the
social system; (2) community attitudes
toward health, illness, and medical

practice; (3) the professional roles associated with medicine; (4) the social structure of hospitals; and (5) the interaction of patients on various kinds of wards and its effect on their progress in treatment. A few of the more recent studies under these headings are discussed below.

MEDICINE IN THE SOCIAL SYSTEM

Parsons (1951a, 1951b) has had an enduring interest in the position of medicine in our society and the social context of the doctor-patient relationship.[5] His thesis is that illness, particularly psychosomatic or emotional illness, may be thought of as a special type of "deviant" behavior—one of a set of alternatives which are open to the individual. The role of the sick person in our society is a sanctioned and institutionalized one, whereas the alternatives to illness may be participation in nonsanctioned deviant groups (the delinquent gang, and exotic religious sect) or in a life of social isolation (the solitary hobo, eccentric, and criminal).

Parsons feels there are four main aspects of illness not merely as a "condition" but also as a social role. The sick person is (1) exempted from the performance of certain of his normal social obligations; (2) not held morally responsible for being ill; (3) defined as being in need of help; and (4) obligated, by the contingent legitimation of the sick role, to try to get well as quickly as possible. Conversely, the social role of the physician demands that he (1) place the welfare of the patient foremost and grant his essentially unconditional support; (2) assume explicit or implicit control of the sanc-

5. In Parsons' (1951b) recent book, see especially chap. x, "Social Structure and Dynamic Process: The Case of Modern Medical Practice." Prior to Parsons a very astute analysis of this topic was made by Henderson (1935).

tions in many areas of the patient's life; (3) have access to physical and mental intimacies of the patient not ordinarily revealed in normal relationships; and (4) be barred from taking advantage of, or reciprocally participating in, such intimacies. It should be emphasized that, while these aspects are part of the role of the psychotherapist, they are also part of the role of the physician in general. Modern psychotherapy has but refined and extended the physician's role as this was already established in the social structure of Western society.

Parsons suggests that the apparent increase in chronic and mental illness in our society may constitute a diversion of tendencies to deviance from other channels of expression into the role of illness, with consequences less dangerous to the stability of society than other alternatives might be. In any case, the physician stands at a strategic point in the balance of forces in our society. This means not only that all medical care, and particularly psychotherapy, is a process which helps individual patients in treatment but that it may also, in a wider sense, be thought of as a form of social control. This wider aspect of the physician's role would be a rewarding area of exploration for future research.

Schneider (1947) has provided a specific example of illness as a form of deviance by analyzing the social dynamics of physical disability in army basic training. The kinds of disabilities which still permitted the soldier to remain part of the group most frequently were rheumatic, asthenic, and gastrointestinal complaints. Hardly anyone went to the dispensary to say he was emotionally frightened and upset; instead, he said he had low back pains, stomach trouble, or a "trick knee." Physical disability was defined as external to the person—something that happened to him through no fault of his own. It was a weakness, but a kind of weakness that did not usually arouse blame or condemnation. This does not mean that these were the only disabilities which occurred, rather it reflected the high social valuation given the heightened demands on masculinity and physical capacity.

The sick role was sanctioned at first by the men in the training group because it focused resentment against the army. When the majority of men had made their adjustment, they no longer supported the sick in their role. The group did not, however, attempt to punish the sick but only maintained the social distance now between them. As Schneider says: "The existence and perpetuation of this neurotic response —the sick role—cannot be ascribed only to the peculiar or accidental psychic history of the person but must be considered also as a function of the cultural situation in which that psychiatric history takes place." Major functions of the sick role were, first, the support of the major goal of the army culture by draining off deviance and allowing the group to become more homogeneous and, second, by providing the individual soldier with a relatively nonpunishing escape from a situation which was psychologically intolerable for him.

Both Parsons and Schneider are saying that psychologically grounded physical disability must not be thought of solely as an individual "flight into illness." The flight itself occurs within a socially limited set of alternatives which perform a positive function by providing a sanctioned, but nonvalued, role for deviant behavior. Thus some types of deviant behavior should not be thought of as being against the society but rather as conforming to alternative and less valued patterns of action that are built into the structure of the society itself.[6]

These ideas are in line with those of Ackerknecht (1947*b*), who says: "Disease and its treatment are only in the abstract purely biological processes. Actually such facts as whether a person gets sick at all, what kind of disease he acquires, and what kind of treatment he receives, depend largely upon social factors. . . . I have been particularly impressed in the course of my anthropological and historical studies by the degree to which even the notion of disease itself depends rather on the decisions of society than on objective facts." As an example, Ackerknecht cites *pinto* (dyschromic spirochetosis), a skin disease so common among many South American tribes that the few healthy men are regarded as pathological to the point of being excluded from marriage. Or again, "When malaria, called also ague at the time, was at its peak in the Mississippi Valley . . . around the middle of the last century, people used to say: 'He is not sick, he's only got the ague' and as Timothy Flint puts it, 'the patient was not allowed to claim the immunities of sickness'" (Ackerknecht, 1947*b*). It is then quite possible at a certain point in a society's history to die of a disease without ever being sanctioned as sick by the society itself.

The social science approach to the cultural context of the doctor-patient relationship has its applied side in at least one instance. Early in 1950 the California Medical Association approved a suggestion of its committee on medical economics that it direct a social-psychological research study of doctor-patient relationships in Alameda County. This material has been written up by Dr. Rollen Waterson in some very attractive public relations litera-

6. Once again reference must be made to the important work of Florence Kluckhohn (1950) on dominant and *variant* value orientations in a culture. Dr. Kluckhohn's recent thinking along these lines, some of which is available in dittoed form, has far outstripped publication.

ture and is also available in a more formal report by Ernest Dichter, the psychologist who did the study. It is encouraging to find Waterson saying, "The relationship of the doctor and patient does not exist in a vacuum ... we have not yet given sufficient attention to the sciences that deal with human relations."[7]

COMMUNITY ATTITUDES TOWARD HEALTH, ILLNESS, AND MEDICAL PRACTICE

While community surveys of health facilities are legion, there have been very few studies of community attitudes toward health, illness, and medical practice. Social scientists are, however, beginning to do work on this problem. George Lyman Koos, of the department of sociology, University of Rochester, has recently completed a study of a rural town in upper New York State. A random one-in-five sample of 514 households was chosen for repeated interviewing from an estimated 2,700 households. Each interview was designed to cover not only the health experience of the household, but the cultural and economic factors which motivated the course of action. Out of the accumulated 2,000 interviews has come much valuable data on why people think and behave as they do about health and illness. This study will be published late in 1952 under the title *Regionville: A Study of Health Attitudes and Behavior*. In addition, a similar study of 1,000 families in the urban population of Rochester is under way.

Suggestive work on where people take their troubles has been done by Steiner (1945); Ramsey and Seipp (1948) and Redlich (1950) have written on popular knowledge about psychiatry; and Woodward (1951) has re-

cently completed an extensive study of changing ideas about mental illness and its treatment. Woodward's study was one of a series carried out by the firm of Elmo Roper at the request of the Louisville city administration and designed to make citizens articulate with respect to problems facing the municipality. A cross-section of 3,971 Louisville residents was interviewed at home; and age, sex, education, occupation, and other variables were controlled in analyzing the data. Some of the conclusions were: (1) the public has given up many old beliefs and superstitions about mental illness; (2) there is still a gross failure in ability to recognize serious mental symptoms; (3) there is considerable loss of faith in repressive and punitive forms of treatment; (4) the psychiatrist is coming to be regarded as the logical person to handle clearly identifiable cases of mental disorder; and (5) among the professions the lawyers represent a minor stronghold of reaction against psychiatry and modern ideas in the treatment of juvenile delinquency.

More toward the action side, the Health Information Foundation is aiding in the financing of a series of "community self-surveys" on health problems. The philosophy behind this work is that cultural changes occur with least conflict and confusion along lines of established community patterns. The research in each community will follow the same design, and work has been begun by Sol Kimball, at the University of Alabama, John Gillin, at the University of North Carolina, and John Useem, at Michigan State College. The general design of the studies centers around the investigation of the social processes which occur when a community (1) defines its own health problems; (2) discovers facts in relation to these problems; (3) makes decisions for action; and (4) carries out the proposed action.

7. This material can be obtained from Dr. Rollen W. Waterson, Alameda–Contra Costa Medical Association, 354 Twenty-first Street, Oakland 12, California.

PROFESSIONAL ROLES

Sociologists have, in part, come to study medicine out of their long-standing interest in the professions in the social structure of Western society. Sponsored by the Russell Sage Foundation, Robert K. Merton at Columbia University is directing a detailed analysis of medicine, nursing, social work, and other professions in modern society. Also stemming from the Russell Sage Foundation is the current work of Harvey Smith on the development of psychiatry as a social institution, including the problems of certification and sanctioning; competing psychotherapies; the changing social organization of the profession and its relationships within medicine and to the social and psychological sciences; the function of associations and societies; and public relations. Smith emphasizes that the role of the beginning psychiatrist is a peculiarly difficult one, as, unlike his colleagues in some other specialties who have more opportunity for gradual development, he appears full-blown upon the scene—his very first referral is likely to present as complex a treatment problem as any he will ever have to face.

Hall (1946, 1948, 1949) has written a stimulating series of papers on the informal organization of the medical profession, the stages in a medical career, and types of medical careers. He discusses the implications of the fact that medicine is "not only a professional but a social group" in which work is "carried on within the framework of an elaborate social machinery rather than within a freely competitive milieu" (1946). In line with this, Hall analyzes the cultural and social aspects of gaining admittance to medical schools, getting an internship and residency, acquiring a practice, and developing informal relations with colleagues. Others who have done work in this area are: A. M. Lee (1944) on the social dynamics of the physician's status; Williams (1946, 1950) on lay attitudes and the woman physician's dilemma; and Rosen (1944) on the specialization of medicine. Of interest here are the studies of Everett C. Hughes and his students at the University of Chicago: Lortie (1949) on the anaesthesiologist as a doctor without patients, and McDowell (1950) on the osteopath and the recruitment of his clientele. The problems of the marginal practitioner are also beginning to be studied, as in Wardwell's (1952) work on the chiropractor.

Not only doctors but other members of the medical team have come in for role analysis by social scientists. Devereux and Weiner (1950), writing on the occupational status of nurses, note that the nurse is caught between progress notes, ward rounds, and the alternate swabbing of floors and throats and usually has neither the time nor the opportunity to dispense emotional gratification to the patient. Moreover, such emotional support as she is able to give is all too often viewed both by the nurse herself and by the hospital system as ancillary to her role and almost unprofessional. Devereux and Weiner point to "the rigid hospital tradition in which a nurse cannot as a rule have any prerogatives of initiative" as one factor in such a state of affairs. Wyatt (1947), in discussing guidance problems of student nurses, also speaks of the authoritarianism in nursing schools and the touch of asceticism and of the convent from which nursing has come.

Devereux and Weiner go on to say that one of the basic conditions of the ability to give human warmth is the security of the person called upon to dispense it and that the professional status of nurses is today vague and indefinite. This is particularly true for psychiatric nurses, as has been noted by Caudill *et al.* (1952) in the study of social structure on mental hospital wards. Many nurses said they preferred to work on the locked wards, as there was more "real" nursing; they were unsure of themselves on the open wards, where they defined their role largely as a domestic and policing one. Such a situation is not helped when the patients sense the vagueness of the nurse's position and her ambivalence in it and act out more toward her than toward the physician.

Much of the dissatisfaction expressed by nurses may stem from the lack of an opportunity to replenish and satisfy their own emotional needs. As Devereux and Weiner observe, nurses are among the few cloistered professional groups remaining on the contemporary scene—many are cut off in nurses' residences from the warmth of a home of their own and sometimes from the simplest affect gratification to be found in everyday living. Also, due to the long hours demanded on hospital shifts, they are thrown out of step with the common work and leisure schedule of the world outside the hospital.

Many of the theoretical problems in the nurse's status and role which are approached from sociological and psychodynamic points of view by Devereux and Weiner and by Wyatt are discussed in terms of their practical applied-anthropological implications by Wilson (1950), of the Tavistock Institute of Human Relations in Great Britain. Much thought is, of course, also being given these problems by the nursing profession (Petry, Arnstein, and McIver, 1952).

THE SOCIAL STRUCTURE OF HOSPITALS

The anthropologist and sociologist have always been interested in various types of organization for work in different societies. In our society, industries and labor unions have received considerable attention, and recently the hospital has become a focus of research. Excellent studies have been done by Harvey Smith (1949), Albert Wessen (1951), and Edith Lentz (1950) on general hospitals, and by H. Warren Dunham (1947) and Paul Barrabee (1951) on mental hospitals. Almost all this work is unpublished to date and hence not readily available.

Harvey Smith was asked by the American Hospital Association to study the social organization of three hospitals (two general hospitals of 500 and 100 beds, respectively, and a 268-bed Veterans Administration hospital) and to help with the establishment of supervisory training programs. During the course of his work, Smith found that the hospitals showed, to a far greater degree than industrial concerns, high interpersonal tensions, bitter conflicts between departments, and an amorphous structure (in contrast to what might appear on paper in the formal organization chart) which lacked defined roles and areas of authority and responsibility. As clues in the understanding of such a situation, Smith discusses the implications of three very important facts about the social structure of hospitals.

First, all the basic substructures of the hospital (medical staff, nurses, patients, special services, such as X-ray, pharmacy, etc.) are subject to a system of dual controls—one is the acknowledged formal administrative line of authority, the other is the more informal but very potent power of the doctor. No administrative procedure can withstand the demands of the doctor in the name of "emergency"; and the tensions existing between members of these two authority systems are often chronic and extreme. For example, the medical director of one hospital said: "I am in charge of professional services, although that's a bad joke; I don't know how I can be in charge of them when I have no control over pay, budget, personnel, or anything else." On the other hand, the pathologist complains: "My girls in the laboratory have one trouble, every doctor in the hospital is their boss." On a different level, Edith Lentz (1950) has documented similar problems of morale in a hospital business office and suggested some solutions out of her detailed comparative study of a Catholic hospital and a nonsectarian hospital located in a small city in upper New York State.[8]

Second, Smith points out another significant difference between the structure of industry and that of the hospital: in industry the actual production work is done by workers at the bottom of the authority hierarchy; in hospitals the productive workers (the doctors) have high prestige.[9]

Third, Smith emphasizes that a hospital is a system of discrete and mobility-blocked levels within which the consciousness of status is at a maximum. Unlike almost any other organization for work in our society, a hospital permits of little upward movement—no service worker can become a technician, no technician can become a nurse, and no nurse can become a doctor. If an individual wishes to change his occupational class, he must leave the system for a long period of outside training before returning at a higher level. Such a social structure makes for the development of quite different value systems on the various levels, and interpersonal relationships between levels

8. Dr. Lentz is working in collaboration with Dr. Temple Burling and Dr. Robert N. Wilson, and can be reached at the New York State School of Industrial and Labor Relations, Cornell University. Their next study will be of a large municipal hospital.

9. An analogy to a large university is appropriate. Like the hospital, the university has a system of dual control, and the productive workers (the faculty) have high prestige. How many readers of this paper, after making an academic joke, have allowed students to smoke in classrooms in the face of furiously red "No Smoking" signs, despairingly put up each year by the administration?

are highly formalized. All this has important effects on the nature and flow of communication through the system.

This problem in communication is of particular importance in mental hospitals, where the illnesses of most patients are rooted in the pathology of interpersonal relations. In its historical development, the mental hospital has taken over much of the formal structure of the general hospital, more or less as a matter of course; yet it seems likely that such a rigid hierarchical structure is neither administratively the most efficient nor therapeutically the most effective setting for patients suffering from difficulties in getting along with their fellow-men. The need for collaborative research between medicine and social science on other types of environmental settings more conducive to the successful treatment of physical and mental illnesses can better be seen after a review of some of the work that has been done concerning interaction on various types of wards.

WARD INTERACTION AND
THERAPEUTIC SETTING

It is only recently that the medical profession has come to seek for a conscious and systematic awareness of something they have intuitively sensed and acted upon for a long time: this is the fact that patients on a ward are not an aggregate of individuals but a social group, and hence their therapeutic progress may be directly influenced by the nature and extent of their interpersonal relations with other patients and with staff members; moreover, their observable behavior, which is a datum of significance for any illness in any hospital, is related not only to factors in their illness but also to the influence of the situation upon their actions. As is the case with the material on the over-all hospital social organization, much of the work done on ward interaction has not yet reached publication.

Leo W. Simmons (1950), with the co-operation of the Russell Sage Foundation, has been doing a series of studies on interpersonal relations at the New York Hospital, the immediate objective of which is to promote research in the application of social science principles in medical and nursing practice. Studies under way include: (1) training of the student nurse; (2) role and function of the head nurse; (3) a comparison of day and night nursing; (4) recurring problems of human relations in ward care within the therapeutic triangle of physicians, nurses, and patients; (5) problems in the medical care of unwed mothers; (6) familial conflicts in so-called "clinic prone patients"; and (7) problems of medical, familial, and community adaptation of patients with permanent colostomies.

An extremely interesting research project is being carried out on a male metabolic ward at Peter Bent Brigham Hospital in Boston by Renée Fox (1952), who is the sociologist on a primarily medical research team headed by Dr. George W. Thorn. The patients on this ward are all suffering from chronic progressively debilitating kidney and metabolic diseases, such as Cushing's disease, Addison's disease, chronic glomerular nephritis, and malignant hypertension. These patients are dying, and death is very near and real on the ward. It is a world of the artificial kidney machine, the "Adrenalectomy Club," cortisone, and "No Death This Month" parties. The research physician working on this ward can learn much from such patients, but as yet can do little to help them. The study, then, is one of the social context of stress: patients must develop ways of coming to terms with being experimented upon and with the probability of death; physicians must somehow come to terms

with the emotional conflict aroused by the drastic cleavage in their role when they cannot as yet cure and must all the more, therefore, learn from their dying patients.

Turning to the study of interaction in mental hospitals, outstanding recent work has been done by the team of Alfred Stanton, a psychiatrist, and Morris Schwartz, a sociologist, who made observations over a period of three years on a disturbed women's ward of a private mental hospital specializing in the treatment of psychoses by psychoanalytic psychotherapy. Stanton and Schwartz have developed their ideas around three central conceptions: (1) a mental hospital ward is an interacting system in which the type of activity engaged in by any one person is to some extent determined by other persons on the ward; (2) following Sullivan, psychiatry is viewed as a study of interpersonal relations, and the phenomenon of mental illness is regarded as a type of participation in the social process rather than as an entity residing within a person; and (3) the activities of the group form a describable pattern, the understanding of which is necessary for any complete understanding of particular members.

In the first two articles to be cited, Stanton and Schwartz (1949a, b) discuss the social processes involved when two staff members with power over a patient disagree on how the patient's case should be handled. They note that the patient participates in this disagreement by increased agitation and dissociative behavior, which, given the situation, is the only manner of expression open to him. They conclude: "If our hypothesis is correct that the patient's dissociation is a reflection of, and a mode of participation in, a social field which itself is seriously split, it accounts for the sudden cessation of excitement following any resolution of this split in the social field. . . . In other words, the phenomena are not completely 'autistic' in the sense that they are not derived entirely from the patient's past history or from an unconscious which is isolated from reality" (Stanton and Schwartz, 1949*b*). A third, and more general, article analyzes the great situational differences between psychotherapy conducted within the hospital, where "the administrative psychiatrist is invested with awe inspiring power over the lives of his patients," and psychotherapy carried on in the outer world, where "the patient may accept, reject, or revise the opinion" of the psychiatrist (Stanton and Schwartz, 1949*c*).

Further articles report on incontinence (Schwartz and Stanton, 1950) and the question of need fulfilment (Schwartz, Schwartz, and Stanton, 1951). It was found that incontinence—ordinarily considered a highly individual regressive type of behavior—was significantly related to the social process, in that incontinence increased in conflict, abandoning, isolating, devaluing, and unconstructive situations on the ward between one patient and another or between patients and staff members. On the question of need fulfilment, the staff operated on the principle that a patient should get what he asked for unless there was a clear reason why he should not, and this reason should be given the patient if his request was refused. The staff believed that their behavior was such as to make this situation obtain on the ward. Yet this was not the case: active and demanding patients had, in fact, their requests much more frequently granted than did withdrawn patients, whose requests often were not even recognized, let alone acted upon. Lacking any real recognition of this state of affairs, the staff continually told the patients either implicitly or directly that a demanding attitude was harmful, when such an in-

terpretation was, at best, a distortion and, at worst, a flat misstatement. Such a situation made for a significant barrier to the patient's improvement, as there was some basis in reality for withdrawn patients feeling discriminated against.

The general work of Stanton and Schwartz will be summarized in a joint monograph to be published in the latter part of 1952. Schwartz is going on to do a further study to determine by "action clinical research" the types of intervention and change in the social structure of the ward which will maximally facilitate the recovery of patients.

Other important work in this area has been done by Szurek (1947), Fromm-Reichmann (1947), Rowland (1938, 1939), Devereux (1944, 1949), and Dembo and Haufmann (1935). Still unpublished is the research of Grey (1949) and Brody (1949) on the relationships between social class and ethnic factors and the behavior and treatment of psychiatric patients in mental hospitals. For example, when information obtained from psychiatrists on matched groups of patients was later independently correlated with social-class position: 65 per cent of the middle-class and 25 per cent of the lower-class patients were given individual psychotherapy; 100 per cent of the middle-class and 40 per cent of the lower-class patients had more than six sessions; and 75 per cent of the middle-class patients and 22 per cent of the lower-class patients were regarded as improved.

The studies described so far have dealt with the interaction of patients and staff or with the effect on patient behavior of the over-all social structure of the hospital. Information on a third social influence—the interpersonal relationships of patients with one another—is almost totally lacking, beyond what is available in patients' autobiographical accounts. In order to learn what questions to ask, and to obtain some real feeling for this important area of life in a mental hospital, the research team of Caudill, Redlich, Gilmore, and Brody had one of its members undergo the experience of being a patient on a less-disturbed ward of a small private mental hospital connected with a psychiatric training center (Caudill *et al.*, 1952). Results of this work strongly emphasize that patients, especially those in relatively long-term therapy, should be thought of as a structured group which tries to meet many of its problems by developing a shared set of values and beliefs translated into action through a system of social roles and cliques. Patients exerted very strong pressures, often at considerable variance with stated hospital policy, on one another for attitudes toward the self, other patients, therapy and the therapist, and nurses and other hospital personnel.

Many of the problems of the patient group arose because the staff, while exercising control over the patients, did not give recognition to the patient world as a social group but, rather, interpreted the behavior of the patients almost solely in individual dynamic-historical terms. The patient group, lacking an adequate channel of communication to the staff, protected itself by turning inward and developing a social structure insulated as much as possible from friction with hospital routine. Nevertheless, such friction did occur, and the subsequent frustration led to behavior on the part of the patients which, although it overtly resembled neurotic behavior arising from personal emotional conflicts, was, in fact, to a considerable extent due to factors in the immediate situation.

At the same time, much of what would be thought of as primitive instinctual "antisocial" behavior in the outer world became "social" behavior in the hospital, owing to the wider range of tolerance and suspension of judgment among the patients. Seen in this way, a mental hospital ward is not only, in the traditional sense, a place where the patient should be free, if need be, to regress with some degree of comfort but is also a place where primitive instinctual forces are themselves enmeshed and utilized in the subculture and role system of the patient group. Thus psychotherapy carried out in the hospital must contend not only with such forces due to regression but also such forces supported by a social system.

Further work is now being carried out on (1) the value systems of patient groups and the roles by which these values are implemented; (2) the social structure and values of the mobility-blocked levels of the hospital staff hierarchy; (3) the interaction processes between levels of the staff in the light of the differences in values which may be found to exist; and (4) a study of the flow of reports on patient behavior in terms of omissions, additions, and distortions, as these reports are channeled upward through the hospital hierarchy to the point where decisions are made, and then back down again.

Other workers in this area include Kegeles, Hyde, and Greenblatt (1952), who have been studying spontaneous group structure by means of sociometric and observational techniques on the female acute wards of Boston Psychopathic Hospital; and Jules Henry, who is planning a study of patient interaction at McMillan Hospital in St. Louis. In a more applied sense, the Russell Sage Foundation has recently authorized a two-year study of ward-patient care, focused on the role and function of the attendant, in mental hospitals throughout the United States. Richard Hobson is now at work on a comparative study of this problem in four mental hospitals in the Boston area. The general problem of the manipulation of the hospital environment has received considerable attention since Sullivan's (1931) treatment of schizophrenics at Sheppard twenty years ago, but the research implications of his work still need emphasizing. He eliminated the nurses, substituted attendants trained by himself, and was able to achieve some remarkable "social" recoveries with hebephrenic patients. The implications of Sullivan's work have been carried out most recently by Jerome D. Frank (1952) in connection with chronic hospitalized schizophrenics. Favorable results have also been reported when the environment was changed so as to allow the patients a measure of self-government, as at Boston Psychopathic in the work of Hyde and Solomon (1950). And the Menninger Clinic has given much attention to the problem of providing patients with opportunities to achieve short-run obtainable goals that will develop self-esteem and a sense of accomplishment (Menninger, 1937).

In addition, Caudill *et al.* (1952) have suggested that a review would seem to be indicated of the important question of whether mental patients who are still able to function in some areas of life should be admitted to a hospital at all beyond the need for diagnostic study. It is quite possible that many patients would fare better in ambulatory treatment. At the same time, patients must frequently be removed from the anxiety-provoking setting of the home. This dilemma raises many theoretical and practical problems and would seem to call for collaborative research between social science and psychiatry on other types of environmental settings. A team of anthropologists and psychiatrists, headed by John Gillin, Frank LeBar, and Gordon Blackwell, is now working on a problem of this nature at a large veterans' mental hospital in Roanoke, Virginia. They note that furloughed or discharged psychiatric patients who seem to have made a good adjustment to conditions inside the hospital frequently find themselves in difficulty when they return to their home town or take up residence in other communities. One hypothesis being used to explain some of this failure is that the sociocultural conditions of the hospital and consequently the problem-solving techniques which the patient has learned in the hospital are not sufficiently similar to a noninstitutional environment to provide the patient with useful newly learned solutions to some of his problems in the outer world. Since Gillin has already directed a three-year study of representative samples of southeastern culture and social organization, this work will provide an empirical base for analyzing the everyday problems of discharged psychiatric patients in this region. The aim of the present project is, then, to point up disconformities, and to suggest solutions for them, between the learning provided in the sociocultural setting of the hospital and what is expected in the life of the local communities.

Finally, all types of work mentioned in this section need somehow to be related to problems of the state hospital system and the belated, but growing, interest in this country in family and colony care for mental patients. Some two hundred years ago in the Belgian town of Gheel, psychotic patients came from their own communities to live in the homes of villagers without restraint, and this system still obtains today (Kilgour, 1936). In the United States, the most active workers for family care have been Crutcher (1944) and Pollock (1945). Pollock stresses that such a system needs (1) a small central hospital to receive patients, (2) a group of trained families easily accessible to the central hospital, and (3) a well-organized plan of operation. He says: "In this way one-fourth of the mentally ill and one-third of the mentally defective patients could readily be placed in family care" (1945). There will never, and perhaps should not, be enough psychiatrists to give individual therapy to the tremendous numbers in our culture who are in need of help. As we are not likely to see any fundamental culture change in the near future, we can, at least, try to divert some of the millions of dollars being spent on bigger buildings to house more and more mentally ill people to research on a clearer understanding of how we might abet the spontaneous forces working for health that can be found in community life and on the wards of mental hospitals themselves. The interested anthropologist can both gain in theoretical knowledge and practically contribute to such work.

PSYCHOSOMATIC MEDICINE, SOCIAL MEDICINE, AND MULTIPLE STRESS IN DISEASE

The recent interest shown by physicians in the psychological and social concomitants of disease seems to be the resultant of two broad trends—the apparent great increase in the incidence of chronic physical and mental illness in the Western world and the reawakened interest in the multiple stress and multicausal aspects of all types of disease. Anthropologists have concerned themselves little with such problems; yet, if the collaboration between anthropology and medicine is to prove truly fruitful, it will probably be in this rich unworked area. As Perrott (1945) has pointed out, about twenty-five million people in this country have some chronic disease, and nearly one million deaths and one billion days of disability a year can be ascribed to chronic illness. Rheumatism, heart disease, diseases of the circulatory system, and allergic diseases lead in incidence. Just why there should be this tremendous upsurge (if, indeed, it is so and not, in part, a statistical artifact of more accurate diagnosis and coverage) is a complex matter. Certainly, the control of

communicable disease, the reduction of infant mortality, and the increase in life-expectancy have brought about a shift in the distribution of age and illness within the population. Much time previously spent in the short-term treatment of acute illness has been replaced by medical care of chronic sickness and we seem to have exchanged mortality for morbidity. In addition, as we have already seen in Parsons' suggestions, increased chronic and mental illness may constitute a diversion of tendencies to deviance from other channels of expression into the role of illness. Moreover, the heightened interest shown by physicians in such diseases, plus the recognition given them through the payment of sick benefits, may easily stimulate a rising incidence, as in the case of miner's nystagmus (Halliday, 1943).

The confusion in this general area of medical interest is still great. Physicians working in this area seem to fall into four groups, forming two large categories. All workers in these four groups are concerned with the interrelationship of emotional and organic factors, and all are sophisticated beyond the old mind-body problem, yet there is little intercommunication or integration in the total field.

The first large category of workers comes, on the one hand, from epidemiology, preventive medicine, and public health and, on the other, from those whose ideas are associated with the many conflicting definitions of social medicine (Galdston, 1949). Both groups take a broad view of whole populations and incidence rates of disease. They have, however, their own quarrels with one another, as when Galdston (1951) says:

> It should now be clear wherein Social Medicine differs from preventive and from government medicine and why it can not be equated to them either by extension or by addition. They are separated by the

insurmountable difference in the conceptualization of *etiology* which as common to both preventive medicine and government medicine is seen to be rather direct, simple, and also naïve, while in Social Medicine it is conceived as being co-extensive with, and indeed a function of . . . the nature, structure, and operation of the total milieu into which the individual is born, in which he grows and lives, and wherein he reproduces his kind.

Such quarrels have their historical roots. Public Health arose out of the practical urgency to control epidemic communicable disease. Its main concepts are, therefore, the pragmatic ones of sanitation and environment (meaning cold climate, swampy ground, and poor housing rather than an awareness of culture). The deficiency of a sole reliance on these concepts, along with bacteriological epidemiology, was dramatically shown by the decimating fury with which the 1918–19 influenza epidemic swept through most of the world. Social Medicine came out of a more scholarly European tradition including the work of Virchow, Meynne, Von Pettenkofer, Grotjahn, and Ryle—all of which has been summarized in an excellent article by Rosen (1947). Though the ideas of these men are barely finding their way into American medicine today, the anthropologist cannot fail to be intrigued by the somewhat rhetorical statement of Virchow in 1848 that "medicine is a social science, and politics nothing but medicine on a grand scale"; or by the words of Grotjahn in 1904 before the German Society of Public Health: "Between man and nature there is culture, which is linked to the social structures within which alone, man can be truly man. . . . Hygiene must, therefore, also study intensively the effects of the social conditions in which men are born, live, work, enjoy themselves, procreate and die" (Rosen, 1947). Beyond the blinding light shed by laboratory medicine, some of the

reasons why these ideas did not become a part of American preventive medicine are indicated by Kramer (1947), who traces the difficulty with which even elementary sanitary measures concerning sewage and water supply were introduced in the latter nineteenth century because they conflicted with the sacredness of private property. The early success of public health in America was more in the area of *personal* hygiene.

The second large category of workers comes either from internal medicine, seeking emotional correlates of organic disease, or from psychiatry, seeking organic correlates of emotional disease. There is also much quarreling within these groups, frequently over the problem of specificity, as in a recent article by Alexander and Szasz (1952), where they disagree with the formulations of Dunbar: "The specific correlation is not between overt personality features and vegetative response but between the latter and certain, mostly unconscious, emotional constellations which may be present in very different types of personalities and which may appear and disappear during the life of the same person." Workers in these groups are interested in the intensive investigation of small series of individual patients— one might almost say they are learning so much in their study of the trees that they are not aware they are living in a forest. There is little factual or theoretical interchange with workers in public health or social medicine. While this may come with time, it is just at this point that the interest of the anthropologist lies: in attempts to relate the insights gained in intensive study to a better understanding of the larger group phenomena implied in epidemiological statistics. One may search almost in vain for titles indicative of such material among the 2,400 items in Dunbar's (1946) Herculean bibliography, in the 260 references cited by Alexander in his recent book on psychosomatic medicine, and in 545 epitomes given by Turner (1951) in a digest of selected references on chronic illness. Halliday's (1948) book seems to be the lone major attempt to date to bridge this gap. He begins: "This study in psychosocial medicine is based on the application of the concepts of psychosomatic medicine to the illnesses of communities and social groups." Because it occupies this spanning position between two bodies of still largely unrelated material, Halliday's book is an important landmark, although his facts seem better than his social theory in the eyes of a social scientist. While it is reasonably certain that culture has a part to play in the understanding of the multicausality of chronic illness, few workers coming from the afore-mentioned groups have yet grasped what the anthropologist means by "culture." This is evident in their several approaches to the problem of multiple stress.

The approach of the internist to the problems of psychosomatic medicine is well brought out in an excellent symposium on life-stress and bodily disease edited by Wolff, Wolf, and Hare (1950). In Wolff's formulation of the nature of stress in man at the conclusion of this volume, he points to the dangers of parasites, meteorological and climatic crises, and other forces in the physical environment. He goes on to say that man "is a tribal or group creature with a long period of development and dependent for his very existence upon the aid, support and encouragement of other men. He lives his life so much in contact with men, and in such concern about their expectations of him, that perhaps the greatest threat of all is his doubt in his ability to live the life of a man. He is threatened by those very forces in society upon which he is dependent for nourishment and life." While an anthropologist would certainly not deny these statements, he

would take exception to the overemphasis on man *against* nature, society, and culture.

Alexander is perhaps the best known of the workers who have approached psychosomatic medicine from a background in psychoanalysis. He says: "The psychosomatic approach in medical research and therapy consists in the co-ordinated application of somatic (i.e., anatomical, physiological, pharmacological and surgical) methods and concepts, on the one hand, and psychological methods and concepts, on the other" (Alexander and Szasz, 1952). Alexander also advances the concept of a multicausal explanation for all diseases, and, among the many factors of possible etiological importance, he feels that "the psychosomatic point of view added the factors [of the] . . . nature of infant care (weaning habits, toilet training, sleeping arrangements, etc.) . . . accidental emotional traumatic experiences of infancy and childhood . . . emotional climate of family and specific personality traits of parents and siblings . . . later emotional experiences in intimate personal and occupational relations" (1950, pp. 51–52). Again the anthropologist would agree with these statements but would hasten to point out that at least three of the four cited factors are manifestly of a cultural nature and that real theoretical (more than practical therapeutic) problems will go unrecognized unless this is taken into account.

Much of the confusion is concerned with the locus of culture. One has the impression from writers in psychosomatic medicine that it is as if culture were an outer layer to be peeled off and anything below this is noncultural.[10]

10. It would seem to me to be a more complex and more rewarding problem to think of culture, beginning with the most intimate emotional perceptions at birth as in how and when the child experiences (the culturally patterned availability of) its mother's breast,

Alexander contrasts what he calls "personality types" with deep-seated emotional conflicts, and, although it is never explicitly stated, one feels the former are equated with culture and the latter thought of as noncultural. The recent writings of Ackerman (1951), Henry (1951a), and Parsons (1952) would, however, suggest that there are intimate connections between social role and deeper psychodynamics. Since much of the structure of the ego and superego (derived initially through contact with people and objects in the outer world) is unconscious and repression brings highly personalized, but still culturally influenced, material into the unconscious, a locus for culture can be found in the unconscious. The implications of this problem might well be an area of further study for anthropologists and psychiatrists. In any case, it is certainly true, as Mead (1947) so well puts it, that the cultural process can be conceived not only "in terms of a generalized raising or lowering of thresholds so that few or many individuals will succumb to a disease condition to which their specific idiosyncratic circumstances make them liable, but as the *pattern* of interaction between the psychosomatic functioning organism and the cultural system. This pattern will then be found to be as specific as the sort of pattern which is found in the study of the individual psychodynamics of particular pathological conditions."

Perhaps the point can be made clearer by a brief return to Alexander's material. He says:

Under given cultural conditions certain defenses against emotional conflicts appear more frequently than others. Our culture, for example, puts great emphasis on independence and personal accomplishment; hence the frequency among peptic-ulcer patients of the hyper-active go-getter type.

This surface picture is but a defense (overcompensation) against deep-seated dependent longings and has no direct correlation with the ulcer formation. The true psychosomatic correlations are between emotional constellations and vegetative responses [1950, p. 75].

Certainly, the anthropologist would agree that defenses are culturally patterned, but he would feel that "deep-seated dependent longings" might also be so. At least this problem would be worth investigating in the urban American middle-class family whose structure has been pruned to include a bare minimum of mother, father, and several children. Such a family usually moves frequently from one neighborhood to another during a child's early years, ties to community playmates are broken, and the father is removed by work from the home during most of the child's waking hours. Under these conditions, the emotional attachment to the mother is intense and culturally patterned. It is true that our culture emphasizes independence and personal accomplishment, and the child's intense emotional attachment to the mother must be resolved in order to achieve these goals. This is a difficult task, it is more than likely to activate deep-seated dependent longings, and the whole process is not a chance, but a culturally patterned, occurrence. Such an extension of Alexander's ideas is *not* meant to imply the ridiculous supposition that all people with such underlying conflicts will develop peptic ulcers, because there are probably other crucial etiological factors in such a multicausal disease. What is suggested, however, is that not only defenses[11] but unconscious

as built into the whole conscious and unconscious structure of the personality.

11. Although Alexander does not admit defenses to the emotional etiology of peptic ulcer, he does do so for hypertension in the American Negro when he says: "It would appear that the difficulties inherent in the social adjustment which the American Negro must make induced the need for an extraordinary

conflicts as well may be culturally patterned.

Further thinking by psychiatrists and anthropologists along the lines sketched above might help to explain the phenomena noted by workers in social medicine. Ryle (1948), in his *Changing Disciplines*, speaks of "our modern endemics" and says: "In the midst of great social changes we have not succeeded in registering and explaining the accompanying changes in the quantity and quality of many of our main diseases." As examples, he cites gastric and duodenal ulcer: "We have watched these diseases—which were at one time, judging by earlier records of the clinic and the dead-house, relatively rare—becoming in the course of two generations two of the most common of all. . . . Every endeavor, orthodox and unorthodox, medical and surgical, has been made to discover a cure, but with no very outstanding or encouraging results. . . . And yet the causes (for ulcer will probably find its place among the 'multiple-stress' diseases) must have been developing contemporaneously with rising incidence." Furthermore, as Galdston (1951) points out, it is not the poor or those in the lowest social strata that are always and most subject to the modern endemic disorders. The pattern of socio-economic incidence of diabetes, coronary disease, hypertensive disorders, and gastric and peptic ulcer does not conform to the socio-economic pattern of tuberculosis or infant mortality.

Finally, while the developments in social medicine should prove stimulating to the anthropologist, there is need for a word of caution, as the work of precise definition and theory and the

degree of self control, which then becomes the crucial etiological factor" (1950, p. 152). While it may indeed be true that defenses are crucial in one disease and not in another, such problems might be further illuminated by the use of more systematic cultural theory and analysis.

gathering of real data has scarcely begun. Physicians from many branches of medicine are starting to think along these lines, and, if anthropologists are willing to do likewise, there is a large task ahead for the combined efforts of medicine and social science.

TYPES OF DISORDERS

In spite of the much promising thought outlined in preceding sections, the amount of work done on actual illnesses combining the approaches of social science and medicine is, as yet, pitifully small; this is even more the case for nonliterate than for Western societies. Nevertheless, certain types of work concerning chronic illnesses, other disorders such as facial deformity, and mental illnesses need briefly to be reviewed.

CHRONIC ILLNESSES AND OTHER DISORDERS

Chronic illnesses occurring in specific occupations provide an intriguing field for research. Halliday (1943, 1948) has studied miner's nystagmus—a disease usually involving oscillation of the eyeballs when the eyes are moved downward. In 1921 a government investigating committee unanimously agreed that the essential cause of this disease was deficient illumination, and steps were taken to improve lighting in the pits. Yet, between 1922 and 1930, the incidence of miner's nystagmus in Scotland increased fivefold. Halliday feels that this increase becomes more understandable in terms of the psychological effects of unemployment, falling wages, increased mechanization of the pits, and the advertising provided by the *Nystagmus Report* of 1922 (see also Trist and Bamforth, 1951). Similarly, King (1948) has worked on the problem of the high incidence of eyestrain among hosiery linkers, whose job has been considered for the last twenty years, by popular opinion and government sanction, to be damaging to the eyes. A careful analysis of the job, however, points up the fact that linking is primarily a kinesthetic task and operators use their sense of touch almost to the exclusion of their eyes.

Both in Great Britain and in the United States, attention is being given to the family as the unit of treatment. Pearse and Crocker (1943) have reported on the work of the Peckham experiment in which a family health center offering recreation and enjoyment as well as a periodic health overhaul for all family members was established in a section of London. They say: "It is families in their natural habitat or everyday settings . . . that have to be sought for study. Nor is it families in isolation, one taken from here and another picked from there, that can form the selected group, for they must be so aggregated that they may act in mutual synthesis with each other. . . . Health does not demand education of the individual, nor education of the populace— the accepted and popular methods—but education of the family as a live functioning organism." A similar study made by the Cornell University College of Medicine and the Community Service Society has been described by Richardson (1945) in his book, *Patients Have Families*. As did the Peckham experiment, this study had its roots in the biological concept of homeostasis: the physiological system of the body is seen as seeking to maintain a dynamic equilibrium between internal and external environment; disease is considered a disturbance in the equilibrium, while the symptoms of disease are regarded as evidences of the body's attempt to regain an optimum state. This concept may be extended to include the family, which must also maintain a dynamic balance by means of an adequate system of interpersonal relationships within itself and in relation to the commu-

nity. Family life is thus seen, through disturbances in these relationships, as a compelling influence in the origin and perpetuation of chronic or recurring illness. Precise knowledge of the structure and situation of the family is, then, essential to an understanding of the illness, and the family should be considered as the unit of treatment.

Jurgen Ruesch's (1946) work on chronic disease and psychological invalidism at the Langley Porter Clinic has been done in collaboration with an anthropologist, Martin B. Loeb. One hundred and twenty-three convalescent patients were seen in an extensive outpatient study, while sixty-four in-patients were studied intensively. Complete medical, psychiatric, and sociological workups were done on all patients. Ruesch says in conclusion:

Seventy-five per cent of our patients with delayed recovery derived from the lower class, as opposed to only twenty-eight per cent lower middle class people in the general population. . . . This conclusion is supported by a previous study of ours on head injury. In a series of acute head injuries, accident-prone people and those with speedy recovery derived primarily from the lower class, but those with prolonged symptoms were primarily from the middle class. . . . These facts might support the theory that delayed recovery and psychosomatic diseases are conditions affecting middle class people and climbers, as contrasted with the conduct disorders affecting primarily the lower class and decliners.

Further studies along these lines have been made by Ruesch on thyroidectomized patients and patients with duodenal ulcer (Ruesch *et al.*, 1946; Ruesch, 1948; Ruesch, Jacobson, and Loeb, 1948).

The work of Ruesch and Loeb needs further testing, but it stands to date as almost the only example of this type of research. There are, however, some indications that other investigations will be forthcoming. Eric D. Wittkower writes from the Allan Memorial Institute of Psychiatry in Montreal that a team composed of a psychiatrist, four social workers, and a sociologist will be studying the social pathology of rheumatoid arthritis in two contrasting populations located in an agricultural and an industrial community.

Detailed studies of the incidence and cultural context of chronic or other illnesses in nonliterate societies are practically impossible to find. While this is primarily so because physicians and anthropologists have not made such studies, it may also in some part be due, as noted by Ackerknecht (1945*b*) and Murdock (1952), to the probable rarity of communicable, degenerative, and mental (at least in our forms of psychosis) diseases in semi-isolated precontact populations which had a low average life-expectancy. Nevertheless, any nonliterate society undoubtedly suffers a host of functional disorders, together with infections, digestive ailments, respiratory diseases, gynecological troubles, etc. Henry (1940) has done some suggestive work on speech disturbances among the Pilaga. Roberts and Solomon at Harvard are in the process of finishing a study of the innate and acquired determinants of nausea and vomiting among the Navaho, Zuni, and Texans in the Rimrock area. From time to time interesting medical statistics are published on nonliterate groups, but these have seldom been further explored in cultural terms by anthropologists. For example, Eagle and Gillman (1938) surveyed the post mortem statistics on 2,778 cases in the Johannesburg Hospital between 1928 and 1935. The combined figures showed that "Europeans had seven times as many, and Eurafricans two times as many peptic ulcers as the Bantu."

There are many further areas of interest in which, from the anthropological point of view, work has scarcely begun. The role and function of alcohol has been discussed by Bunzel (1940) in two Central American cultures; by Devereux (1948) for the Mohave; and by Horton (1943) in his exhaustive cross-cultural study. Bales (1942) has written on types of social structure as a factor in "cures" for alcohol addiction. Most recently, Snyder and Landman (1951) have published on drinking patterns and rates of alcohol pathology in Irish and Jewish cultures. There has been little anthropological work on suicide since Steinmetz' article in 1894 (Steinmetz, 1894; Zilboorg, 1936; Devereux, 1940); sociologists, on the other hand, have done a good deal more to follow up Durkheim's (1951) classic statement of the problem (Lunden, 1947; Simpson, 1950; Porterfield, 1952). As longevity has increased, the medical profession has devoted itself more and more to the problems of old age. Cross-cultural studies would add insight and perspective on these problems; yet there is only Simmons' pioneer work and outline for further field research (Simmons, 1945*a*, 1945*b*). Again there has been somewhat more activity on the sociological side: for example, Belknap and Friedsam (1949) have taken some of the general propositions stated by Linton and Parsons and have done a very neat methodological study of age and sex categories as sociological variables in the mental disorders of later maturity. By analysis of the life-cycles of the two sexes in the culture of the United States, they show that old age, like other age divisions, is not to be understood solely as the expression of biological processes (see also Cavan *et al.*, 1949; Shock, 1951). In another area an anthropologist, Mark Zborowski, is working on a study of the cultural components in attitudes toward pain at the Kingsbridge Veterans Hospital.

In recent years an increasing number of psychosocial studies of the physically handicapped have been made (Barker et al., 1946). Particularly important here is the work of Frances Macgregor (1950, 1951), a sociologist, who for the last six years has been engaged in a research study of plastic surgery patients at the Manhattan Eye, Ear, and Throat Hospital and New York University College of Medicine. At the latter institution an interdisciplinary project, including a psychiatrist, sociologist, cultural anthropologist, psychologist, and social worker, has just been completed. Some of the areas of investigation were (1) the personality difficulties which plastic surgery may help to correct or create; (2) the relationship between the age at which the deformity is acquired and the type of adjustment which may be expected; (3) the relationship between kinds of adjustment and socio-economic status, sex, religion, and nationality; (4) the patterns of interaction between a disfigured person and his family, friends, and other members of society; and (5) the problems involved in the desire to change one's physical traits to avoid national or racial stereotyping. Since the social scientists are working in direct co-operation with the surgeon, the study has many applied aspects, such as devising more adequate techniques for preparing the patient for surgery and clarifying his expectations for him and for the surgeon.

A final area of interest might well be a further anthropological exploration of the social context of those epidemic and communicable diseases which have been brought under control by preventive medicine. The work of Hsu (1952) on cholera and of Ackerknecht (1947b) on malaria are cases in point. The problem is highlighted by Sigerist (1943) when he observes that leprosy is defined as morally bad in Western society, tuberculosis less so. Hence we ostracize the one, but do not insist on such drastic isolation for the other,

when, in point of fact, leprosy is the less communicable.

MENTAL ILLNESS

The cross-cultural study of mental illness is part of the broader problem of the relationship between anthropology and psychiatry (Kluckhohn, 1944b; Mead, 1952). The focus of concern here, however, is on the narrower area of studies specifically done on mental illness. The literature and problems in this area have been reviewed in three articles, all with good bibliographies, by Ackerknecht (1943), Yap (1951), and Demerath (1942). The major conclusion of these three authors is that knowledge of comparative psychopathology is woefully inadequate. There has been a great deal of speculation and many papers written on data gathered incidental to the main problem of the field worker, but almost no good incidence or intensive studies. Ackerknecht feels that, "while there is no doubt concerning the existence of mental diseases in primitive society, its frequency, especially in its Western forms has become extremely questionable." Yap, however, offers a caution against too great cultural relativity and notes that "there are basic pathological processes to be found in insanity everywhere," although "detailed symptomatology . . . may vary from one culture to another." Demerath formulates a number of research questions, such as: What mental disorders are found in various cultures? How do symptoms differ cross-culturally? In what ways may the incidence of mental disorder be associated with acculturation or advancing civilization? He believes that definitive answers cannot be given now and that satisfactory understanding must be predicated "on reliable diagnoses (and derived statistics of incidence) made by psychiatrists who are willing honestly to entertain sociological hypotheses." Two of the very few reasonably convincing incidence studies to date are by Carothers (1947) and an earlier paper by Skliar and Starikowa (1929). When psychiatrists have gone into the field, as did the Leightons (1942), Moloney (1945), and Erikson (1950), it has not been with the intensive study of mental illness in mind. Recently, however, Edward Stainbrook, of the department of psychiatry at Yale, has worked with Charles Wagley in Brazil on a comparative study of schizophrenia in Bahia and the United States. One other problem, which might well be developed in its applied or clinical aspects, is the use of formal linguistic analysis as a tool in the study of psychopathology. Such work has been begun by Newman (1938, 1941) on the spoken language of patients with affective disorders and more recently by Grewel (1951) in the study of aphasia. A somewhat broader frame of reference is suggested by Lee (1950), in that the structure of a language may give one a key to the codifications of reality in a culture.

There is a good deal more work going on in our society on the social and cultural components of mental illness. Research in epidemiology has been summarized by Lemkau, Tietze, and Cooper (1943), Felix and Bowers (1948), Felix and Kramer (1952), and in a monograph published by the Milbank Memorial Fund which includes an excellent bibliography of 362 items compiled by Ernest M. Gruenberg (Milbank Memorial Fund, 1950). By and large, socio-environmental factors, such as age, sex, occupation, residence, marital status, race, and nationality, have been correlated with various types of mental illness—this involves the standardization of diagnostic classification, a problem still far from solved. Most studies of prevalence or incidence have been confined to hospitalized psychotics, although there have been attempts to go beyond this: notably, nationally conducted censuses, the draft

and armed forces data from two world wars, and occasional studies of sample populations. On the whole, as Lemkau *et al.* (1943) say: "Such attempts have been generally unsuccessful because of a widespread failure on the part of informants and enumerators to recognize or report any but the most obvious cases." At present an important study is being carried out by F. C. Redlich and A. B. Hollingshead, as principal investigators, at Yale on the relationship between social status and psychiatric disorder. Also, Paul Barrabee at the Boston Psychopathic Hospital is studying the stresses of ethnic membership in Irish, Jewish, and Italian mental patients.

Ecological research in mental disorder has been reviewed by Faris (1944) and by Dunham (1947). The major agreements seem to be: (1) all types of mental disorder within the city tend to show a similar pattern of residence concentration in and around the central business district, with rates declining toward the periphery; (2) the schizophrenic rates characteristically show this pattern, with the concentration of the high rates in areas of low economic status, while manic-depressive rates show much more scatter; (3) persons residing in areas not primarily populated by their own ethnic or racial groups show much higher illness rates than do the numerically dominant group. All such studies suffer though from the limitation of being done on hospitalized populations, and Burgess (in Tietze, Lemkau, and Cooper, 1941) has pointed out the theoretical problem of whether schizophrenics migrated to the bottom of the social scale or were produced there, while Stycos (1949) has considered further methodological problems.

A number of extremely promising projects, usually referred to as "community studies of mental health," have been begun in recent years. Quite a few anthropologists are participating as members of interdisciplinary teams in these studies, which have both theoretical and applied aspects. Under the direction of Alexander Leighton a large group of workers headed by Robert Rapoport (anthropologist), Jay S. Tyhurst (psychiatrist), and Allister MacMillan (psychologist) have been studying for several years a county in one of the provinces of Canada comprising 20,000 people equally divided into English- and French-speaking segments and occupationally separated into fishing, lumbering, farming, and town groups. It is hoped that the results will have bearing on (1) clarification as to what constitutes mental health aside from the mere absence of pathology; (2) illumination concerning the relationship between personality formation and social environment; (3) indications as to which types of stress in the social environment are most important in the production of psychiatric disorders; and (4) the uncovering of leads for further research, particularly opportunities for programs in preventive psychiatry in which public service can be combined with testing hypotheses.

A second study concerns cultural and psychiatric factors in the mental health of the Hutterites. Joseph W. Eaton, Department of Sociology and Anthropology, Wayne University, is the principal investigator, with Robert J. Weil and Bert Kaplan as psychiatric and psychological consultants (Eaton, 1951*a*, *b;* Eaton and Weil, 1951; Eaton, Weil, and Kaplan, 1951). The Hutterites were chosen because they are an ethnically Swiss sect of Anabaptist Christians who live in ninety-three separate farming colonies in North and South Dakota, Montana, Manitoba, and Alberta. They have for centuries lived in a slowly changing social system, including a religious communal system of property ownership, and a family system stripped of nearly all but the pro-

creative and affection-giving functions. They represent an extreme in resistance to the disorganizing effects of acculturation. Nearly all members of this rapidly increasing sect are direct biological descendants of about fifty original Hutterite families and, as such, provide an excellent opportunity for research in human population and genetics. An epidemiological survey of mental illness, severe neurosis, mental deficiency, and antisocial behavior was made in the entire group of 8,700 Hutterites. The incidence of most mental illnesses was found to be lower than that of other epidemiological surveys but higher than had been expected on the basis of cases known to hospitals, doctors, and previous students of the sect. There were four times as many cases of manic-depression as of schizophrenia. The field work for this study has been completed, and full publication should be forthcoming shortly.

Other projects of a less cross-cultural nature and with more emphasis on psychiatric service to the community are being carried out in Phoenix (Clausen, 1950) and, headed by Erich Lindemann, in a residential suburb of Boston. David Aberle (1950), as anthropologist, and Kaspar Naegele (1951), as sociologist, have reported on some aspects of the latter project, in which Fred Richardson has also been doing applied anthropological work. Out of such studies anthropologists should be able to gain knowledge of methods and techniques for a systematic cross-cultural study of mental disorder in nonliterate communities.

On a less broad scale, Jules Henry (1951*b;* Henry and Warson, 1951) recently has done some very stimulating analysis of psychiatric cases in which the family is seen as a field of forces made up of a complex of interactional systems; and out of such work may come the ability to speak precisely of types of family as well as individual pathology. In addition, cultural problems in the doctor-patient psychotherapeutic relationship have been reported on by Devereux (1951) in a study of psychotherapy with a Plains Indian, and by Ruesch and Bateson (1951) in an analysis of the social matrix of psychiatry in terms of communication theory.

CONCLUSION

From the foregoing review it is obvious that much work needs to be done in all areas but that there have been some promising beginnings. There are urgent practical reasons for fostering the application of social science in medicine in the increasing incidence of chronic and mental disease in Western society and in the governmental commitment to the Point 4 program, which means that our medical techniques and ideas must be interpreted to the people of other cultures. On a more academic level there would seem to be much to be gained by the formulation of new problems interrelating previously discrete areas of knowledge: theoretical, and even practical, insights might come from a comparison of such widely divergent phenomena as the social processes at work in a Navaho curing ceremonial and those spontaneous processes (too often unrecognized) occurring between patients on a mental hospital ward, or in the relationship between the individual inner experience of culture and the increase of gastric ulcer in certain social classes of the United States and Great Britain. Equally, one might paraphrase the title of Lawrence K. Frank's (1948) well-known book and say that we need to investigate society as the doctor. As Ackerknecht

(1945a) has pointed out, the modern ethnographer is perfectly well qualified to report on a host of data in the field of primitive medicine, but he is often blinded by his own professional training. As Jules Henry (1949) says: "Almost twenty years ago when I was a graduate student of anthropology, the Apache Indians of New Mexico mentioned to me twitchings they experienced in various parts of the body. Since these twitchings were discussed not as symptoms of illness but as events enabling the Apache to predict future happenings, it did not occur to me at the time to relate those twitchings to any kind of malfunction."

Just where anthropology might fit into the scheme of things is a complex problem. Medicine today is itself in a state of flux: old definitions of disease and health are being called into question; there are many competing concepts of comprehensive medicine, environmental medicine, social medicine, psychosomatic medicine, preventive medicine, etc.; and fields of medicine have become so specialized that it is only with difficulty that they can achieve integration even in a hospital (Lidz and Fleck, 1950). There is much discussion of how the social sciences are to find their place in an already overcrowded medical curriculum (Sigerist, 1946). It is not, then, a simple matter to determine where applied anthropology fits into the maze that now constitutes the field of social science in medicine. If anthropologists and physicians are successfully to achieve a much-to-be-desired collaboration, both groups need to be aware of the many hidden pitfalls in interdisciplinary research (Caudill and Roberts, 1951).

REFERENCES

ABERLE, DAVID F. 1950. "Introducing Preventive Psychiatry into a Community," *Human Organization*, IX, 5–9.

ACKERKNECHT, ERWIN H. 1942a. "Problems of Primitive Medicine," *Bulletin of the History of Medicine*, XI, 503–21.

———. 1942b. "Primitive Medicine and Culture Pattern," *ibid.*, XII, 545–74.

ACKERKNECHT, ERWIN H. 1943. "Psychopathology, Primitive Medicine, and Primitive Culture," *ibid.*, XIV, 30–67.

——. 1945*a*. "On the Collecting of Data concerning Primitive Medicine," *American Anthropologist*, XLVII, 427–32.

——. 1945*b*. "Primitive Medicine," *Transactions of the New York Academy of Sciences*, Ser. 2, VIII, 26–37.

——. 1946. "Natural Diseases and Rational Treatment in Primitive Medicine," *Bulletin of the History of Medicine*, XIX, 467–97.

——. 1947*a*. "Primitive Surgery," *American Anthropologist*, XLIX, 25–45.

——. 1947*b*. "The Role of Medical History in Medical Education," *Bulletin of the History of Medicine*, XXI, 135–45.

ACKERMAN, NATHAN W. 1951. " 'Social Role' and Total Personality," *American Journal of Orthopsychiatry*, XXI, 1–17.

ADAMS, RICHARD N. 1951. "Un Analisis de las enfermedades y sus curaciones en una población indígena de Guatemala (con sugerencias relacionadas con la práctica de medicina en el area Maya)," *Instituto de Nutrición de Centro America y Panama*. Guatemala. (Dittoed and paper-bound.)

ALEXANDER, FRANZ. 1950. *Psychosomatic Medicine*. New York: W. W. Norton & Co.

ALEXANDER, FRANZ, and SZASZ, THOMAS S. 1952. "The Psychosomatic Approach in Medicine." In ALEXANDER, FRANZ, and ROSS, HELEN (eds.), *Dynamic Psychiatry*, pp. 369–400. Chicago: University of Chicago Press.

BALES, FREED. 1942. "Types of Social Structure as Factors in 'Cures' for Alcohol Addiction," *Applied Anthropology*, I, 1–13.

BARKER, R. G.; WRIGHT, B. A.; and GONICK, M. R. 1946. *Adjustment to Physical Handicap and Illness: A Survey of the Social Psychology of Physique and Disability*. (Social Science Research Council Bull. 55.) New York.

BARRABEE, PAUL. 1951. "A Study of a Mental Hospital: The Effect of Its Social Structure on Its Functions." Unpublished Ph.D. dissertation, Department of Social Relations, Harvard University.

BELKNAP, I., and FRIEDSAM, H. J. 1949. "Age and Sex Categories as Sociological Variables in the Mental Disorders of Later Maturity," *American Sociological Review*, XIV, 367–76.

BRODY, BENJAMIN. 1949. "Ethnicity and Psychological Characteristics of Forty Psychiatric Patients." Unpublished Ph.D. dissertation, Committee on Human Development, University of Chicago.

BUNZEL, RUTH. 1940. "The Role of Alcoholism in Two Central American Cultures," *Psychiatry*, III, 361–87.

CANNON, WALTER B. 1942. "Voodoo Death," *American Anthropologist*, XLIV, 169–81.

CAROTHERS, J. C. 1947. "A Study of Mental Derangement in Africans, and an Attempt To Explain Its Peculiarities in Relation to the African Attitude to Life," *Journal of Mental Science*, XCIII, 548–97. Reprinted in *Psychiatry*, XI (1948), 47–86.

CAUDILL, W.; REDLICH, F. C.; GILMORE, H. R.; and BRODY, E. B. 1952. "Social Structure and Interaction Processes on a Psychiatric Ward," *American Journal of Orthopsychiatry*, XXII, 314–34.

CAUDILL, W., and ROBERTS, B. 1951. "Pitfalls in the Organization of Interdisciplinary Research," *Human Organization*, X, 12–15.

CAVAN, R. S.; BURGESS, E. W.; HAVIGHURST, R. J.; and GOLDHAMMER, H. 1949. *Personal Adjustment in Old Age*. Chicago: Science Research Associates.

CLAUSEN, JOHN A. 1950. "Social Science Research in the National Mental Health Program," *American Sociological Review*, XV, 402–9.

CLEMENTS, FORREST E. 1932. "Primitive Concepts of Disease," *University of California Publications in American Archaeology and Ethnology*, XXXII, 185–252.

CRUTCHER, HESTER B. 1944. *Foster Home Care for Mental Patients*. New York: Commonwealth Fund.

DEMBO, T., and HAUFMANN, E. 1935. "The Patient's Psychological Situation upon Admission to a Mental Hospital," *American Journal of Psychology*, XLVII, 381–408.

DEMERATH, N. S. 1942. "Schizophrenia among Primitives," *American Journal of Psychiatry*, XCVIII, 703–7.

DEVEREUX, GEORGE. 1940. "Primitive Psychiatry," *Bulletin of the History of Medicine*, VIII, 1194–1213; XI (1942), 522–42.

———. 1944. "The Social Structure of a Schizophrenic Ward and Its Therapeutic Fitness," *Journal of Clinical Psychopathology*, VI, 231–65.

———. 1948. "The Function of Alcohol in Mohave Society," *Quarterly Journal of Studies on Alcohol*, IX, 207–51.

———. 1949. "The Social Structure of the Hospital as a Factor in Total Therapy," *American Journal of Orthopsychiatry*, XIX, 492–500.

———. *Reality and Dream: Psychotherapy of a Plains Indian.* New York: International Universities Press.

DEVEREUX, GEORGE, and WEINER, F. R. 1950. "The Occupational Status of Nurses," *American Sociological Review*, XV, 628–34.

DODD, S. C. 1934. *A Controlled Experiment on Rural Hygiene in Syria.* ("Publications of the American University of Beirut, Social Science Series," No. 7.)

DUNBAR, FLANDERS. 1946. *Emotions and Bodily Changes.* 3d ed. New York: Columbia University Press.

DUNHAM, H. WARREN. 1947. "The Current Status of Ecological Research in Mental Disorder," *Social Forces*, XXV, 321–26.

DUNHAM, H. WARREN, and WEINBERG, KIRSON. 1947. "Social Psychological Study of a Mental Hospital." Unpublished manuscript.

DURKHEIM, ÉMILE. 1951. *Suicide.* Glencoe, Ill.: Free Press.

EAGLE, P. C., and GILLMAN, J. 1938. "The Incidence of Peptic Ulcers in the South African Bantu," *South African Journal of Medical Sciences*, III, 1–6.

EATON, J. W. 1951a. "The Assessment of Mental Health," *American Journal of Psychiatry*, CVIII, 81–90.

———. 1951b. "Social Processes of Professional Teamwork," *American Sociological Review*, XV, 707–13.

EATON, J. W., and WEIL, R. J. 1951. "Psychotherapeutic Principles in Social Research," *Psychiatry*, XIV, 439–54.

EATON, J. W.; WEIL, R. J.; and KAPLAN, B. 1951. "The Hutterite Mental Health Study," *Mennonite Quarterly Review*, XXV, 3–19.

ERIKSON, E. H. 1950. *Childhood and Society.* New York: W. W. Norton & Co.

EVANS-PRITCHARD, E. E. 1937. *Witchcraft, Oracles, and Magic among the Azande.* Oxford: Clarendon Press.

FARIS, R. E. L. 1944. "Ecological Factors in Human Behavior." In HUNT, J. McV. (ed.), *Personality and the Behavior Disorders*, II, 736–57. New York: Ronald Press Co.

FELIX, R. H., and BOWERS, R. V. 1948. "Mental Hygiene and Socio-environmental Factors," *Milbank Memorial Fund Quarterly*, XXVI, 125–47.

FELIX, R. H., and KRAMER, M. 1952. "Research in Epidemiology of Mental Illness," *Public Health Reports*, LXVII, 152–60.

FIELD, M. J. 1937. *Religion and Medicine of the Ga People.* London: Oxford University Press.

FRANK, JEROME D. 1952. "Group Psychotherapy with Chronic Hospitalized Schizophrenics." In BRODY, E. B., and REDLICH, F. C. (eds.), *Psychotherapy with Schizophrenics*, pp. 216–30. New York: International Universities Press.

FROMM-REICHMANN, F. 1947. "Problems of Therapeutic Management in a Psychoanalytic Hospital," *Psychoanalytic Quarterly*, XVI, 325–56.

FOSTER, GEORGE (ed.). 1951. "A Cross-cultural Anthropological Analysis of a Technical Aid Program." Washington: Smithsonian Institution. (Mimeographed.)

FOX, RENÉE CLAIRE. 1952. "Ward F-Second and the Research Physician: A Study in Stress and Ways of Coming to Terms with Stress." Unpublished manuscript, Department of Social Relations, Harvard University.

FRANK, LAWRENCE K. 1948. *Society as the Patient.* New Brunswick: Rutgers University Press.

GALDSTON, IAGO (ed.). 1949. *Social Medicine: Its Derivations and Objectives.* New York: Commonwealth Fund.

GALDSTON, IAGO (ed.). 1951. "Social Medicine and the Epidemic Constitution," *Bulletin of the History of Medicine*, XXV, 8–21.

GILLIN, JOHN. 1948. "Magical Fright," *Psychiatry*, XI, 387–400.

GREWEL, F. 1951. "Aphasia and Linguistics," *Folia phoniatrica*, III, 100–105.

GREY, ALAN. 1949. "Relationships between Social Status and Psychological Characteristics of Psychiatric Patients." Unpublished Ph.D. dissertation, Committee on Human Development, University of Chicago.

HALL, OSWALD. 1946. "The Informal Organization of the Medical Profession," *Canadian Journal of Economics and Political Science*, XII, 30–44.

———. 1948. "The Stages in a Medical Career," *American Journal of Sociology*, LIII, 327–37.

———. 1949. "Types of Medical Careers," *ibid.*, LV, 243–53.

———. 1951. "Sociological Research in the Field of Medicine: Progress and Prospects," *American Sociological Review*, XVI, 639–44.

HALLIDAY, JAMES L. 1943. "Dangerous Occupation, Psychosomatic Illness, and Morale," *Psychosomatic Medicine*, V, 71–84.

———. 1948. *Psychosocial Medicine*. New York: W. W. Norton & Co.

HALLOWELL, IRVING A. 1934. "Sin, Sex, and Sickness in Saulteaux Belief," *British Journal of Medical Psychology*, XVIII, 191–99.

———. 1942. *The Role of Conjuring in Saulteaux Society*. Philadelphia: University of Pennsylvania Press.

———. 1950. "Values, Acculturation, and Mental Health," *American Journal of Orthopsychiatry*, XX, 732–43.

HARLEY, GEORGE W. 1941. *Native African Medicine*. Cambridge: Harvard University Press.

HENDERSON, L. J. 1935. "The Patient and Physician as a Social System," *New England Journal of Medicine*, CCXII, 819–23.

HENRY, JULES. 1940. "Speech Disturbances in Pilaga Indian Children," *American Journal of Orthopsychiatru*, X, 362–69.

———. 1949. "Anthropology and Psychosomatics," *Psychosomatic Medicine*, XI, 216–22.

———. 1951a. "The Inner Experience of Culture," *Psychiatry*, XIV, 87–103.

———. 1951b. "Family Structure and the Transmission of Neurotic Behavior," *American Journal of Orthopsychiatry*, XXI, 800–818.

HENRY, JULES, and WARSON, S. 1951. "Family Structure and Psychic Development," *American Journal of Orthopsychiatry*, XXI, 59–73.

HORTON, DONALD. 1943. "The Function of Alcohol in Primitive Societies: A Cross-cultural Study," *Quarterly Journal of Studies on Alcohol*, IV, 199–320.

HSU, FRANCIS L. K. 1943. *Magic and Science in Western Yunnan*. New York: International Secretariat of the Institute of Pacific Relations.

———. 1952. *Religion, Science, and Human Crises: A Study on China in Transition and Its Implications for the West*. London: Routledge & Kegan Paul. (In press.)

HYDE, R. W., and SOLOMON, H. C. 1950. "Patient Government: A New Form of Group Therapy," *Digest of Neurology and Psychiatry*, XVIII, 207–18.

HYDRICK, J. L. 1942. *Intensive Rural Hygiene Work in the Netherlands East Indies*. New York: Netherlands Information Bureau.

JOSEPH, ALICE. 1942. "Physician and Patient: Some Aspects of Interpersonal Relations between Physicians and Patients, with Special Regard to the Relationship between White Physicians and Indian Patients," *Applied Anthropology*, I, 1–6.

KEGELES, S. S.; HYDE, R. W.; and GREENBLATT, M. 1952. "Social Network on an Acute Psychiatric Ward." Boston: Boston Psychopathic Hospital. (Mimeographed.)

KILGOUR, A. J. 1936. "Colony Gheel," *American Journal of Psychiatry*, XCII, 959–65.

KING, PEARL H. M. 1948. "Task Perception and Inter-personal Relations in Industrial Training, Part II," *Human Relations*, I, 373–412.

KLUCKHOHN, CLYDE. 1944a. *Navaho Witchcraft.* ("Papers of the Peabody Museum of Harvard University," Vol. XXII, No. 2.) Cambridge, Mass.

——. 1944b. "The Influence of Psychiatry on Anthropology in America during the Past One Hundred Years." In HALL, J. K.; ZILBOORG, G.; and BUNKER, H. A. (eds.), *One Hundred Years of American Psychiatry,* pp. 489–518. New York: Columbia University Press.

KLUCKHOHN, CLYDE, and SPENCER, K. 1940. *A Bibliography of the Navaho Indians.* New York: J. J. Augustin.

KLUCKHOHN, FLORENCE. 1950. "Dominant and Substitute Profiles of Cultural Orientations: Their Significance for the Analysis of Social Stratification," *Social Forces,* XXVIII, 376–93.

KRAMER, HOWARD D. 1947. "The Beginnings of the Public Health Movement in the United States," *Bulletin of the History of Medicine,* XXI, 352–76.

LA BARRE, WESTON. 1938. *The Peyote Cult.* ("Yale University Publications in Anthropology," No. 19.) New Haven.

LEE, A. M. 1944. "The Social Dynamics of the Physician's Status," *Psychiatry,* VII, 371–77.

LEE, DOROTHY. 1950. "Lineal and Nonlineal Codifications of Reality," *Psychosomatic Medicine,* XII, 89–97.

LEIGHTON, A. H. and D. C. 1941. "Elements of Psychotherapy in Navaho Religion," *Psychiatry,* IV, 515–23.

——. 1942. "Some Types of Uneasiness and Fear in a Navaho Indian Community," *American Anthropologist,* XLIV, 194–209.

——. 1944. *The Navaho Door.* Cambridge: Harvard University Press.

——. 1949. *Gregorio the Hand-Trembler: A Psychobiological Personality Study of a Navaho Indian.* ("Papers of the Peabody Museum of Harvard University," Vol. XL, No. 1.) Cambridge, Mass.

LEMKAU, P.; TIETZE, C.; and COOPER, M. 1943. "A Survey of Statistical Studies in the Prevalence and Incidence of Mental Disorders in Sample Populations," *Public Health Reports,* LVIII, 1909–27.

LENTZ, EDITH. 1950. "Morale in a Hospital Business Office," *Human Organization,* IX, 17–21.

LIDZ, THEODORE, and FLECK, STEPHEN. 1950. "Integration of Medical and Psychiatric Methods and Objectives on a Medical Service," *Psychosomatic Medicine,* XII, 103–7.

LOOMIS, CHARLES P. 1945. "A Cooperative Health Association in Spanish Speaking Villages," *American Sociological Review,* X, 149–60.

LORTIE, DAN C. 1949. "Doctors without Patients: The Anaesthesiologists." Unpublished M.A. thesis, Department of Sociology, University of Chicago.

LUNDEN, W. A. 1947. "Suicides in France, 1910–1943," *American Journal of Sociology,* LII, 321–34.

MACGREGOR, FRANCES C. 1950. "Screening Patients for Nasal Plastic Operations," *Psychosomatic Medicine,* XII, 277–91.

——. 1951. "Some Psycho-social Problems Associated with Facial Deformities," *American Sociological Review,* XVI, 629–38.

McDOWELL, HAROLD D. 1950. "Osteopathy: A Study of a Semi-orthodox Healing Agency and the Recruitment of Its Clientele." Unpublished M.A. thesis, Department of Sociology, University of Chicago.

MEAD, MARGARET. 1947. "The Concept of Culture and the Psychosomatic Approach," *Psychiatry,* X, 57–76. Reprinted in HARING, DOUGLAS (ed.), *Personal Character and Cultural Milieu.* Syracuse: Syracuse University Press, 1949.

——. 1952. "Some Relationships between Social Anthropology and Psychiatry." In ALEXANDER, F., and ROSS, H. (eds.), *Dynamic Psychiatry,* pp. 401–48. Chicago: University of Chicago Press,

MENNINGER, W. C. 1937. "Psychoanalytic Principles Applied to the Treatment of Hospitalized Patients," *Bulletin of the Menninger Clinic,* I, 35–43.

MILBANK MEMORIAL FUND. 1950. *Epidemiology of Mental Disorder.* New York: Milbank Memorial Fund.

MOLONEY, J. C. 1945. "Psychiatric Observations in Okinawa Shima," *Psychiatry,* XIII, 391–401.

MOONEY, JAMES. 1896. "The Ghost Dance and the Sioux Outbreak of 1890," *14th Annual Report of the Bureau of American Ethnology*, Part II. Washington: Smithsonian Institution.

MONRO, H. H. 1942. *The Short Stories of Saki*. New York: Viking Press.

MURDOCK, GEORGE P. 1952. "Anthropology and Its Contribution to Public Health," *American Journal of Public Health*, XLII, 7–11.

NAEGELE, K. D. 1951. "Some Problems in the Study of Hostility and Aggression in Middle-Class American Families," *Canadian Journal of Economics and Political Science*, XVII, 65–75.

NEWMAN, S. 1941. "Behavior Patterns in Linguistic Structure: A Case Study." In SPIER, L.; HALLOWELL, A. I.; and NEWMAN, S. S. (eds.), *Language, Culture, and Personality*, pp. 94–106. Menasha, Wis.: Sapir Memorial Publication Fund.

NEWMAN, S., and MATHER, V. G. 1938. "Analysis of Spoken Language of Patients with Affective Disorders," *American Journal of Psychiatry*, XCIV, 913–42.

NEW YORK ACADEMY OF MEDICINE. 1947. *Medicine in the Changing Order*. New York: Commonwealth Fund.

OPLER, MORRIS E. 1936. "Some Points of Comparison and Contrast between the Treatment of Functional Disorders by Apache Shamans and Modern Psychiatric Practice," *American Journal of Psychiatry*, XCII, 1371–87.

———. 1941. *An Apache Life-Way*. Chicago: University of Chicago Press.

PARSONS, TALCOTT. 1951a. "Illness and the Role of the Physician: A Sociological Perspective," *American Journal of Orthopsychiatry*, XXI, 452–60.

———. 1951b. *The Social System*. Glencoe, Ill.: Free Press.

———. 1952. "The Superego and the Theory of Social Systems," *Psychiatry*, XV, 15–25.

PEARSE, INNES H., and CROCKER, LUCY H. 1943. *The Peckham Experiment*. London: George Allen & Unwin.

PERROTT, GEORGE. 1945. "The Problem of Chronic Disease," *Psychosomatic Medicine*, VII, 21–27.

PETRY, L.; ARNSTEIN, M.; and McIVER, P. 1952. "Research for Improved Nursing Practices," *Public Health Reports*, LXVII, 183–88.

POLLOCK, HORATIO M. 1945. "A Brief History of Family Care of Mental Patients in America," *American Journal of Psychiatry*, CII, 351–61.

PORTERFIELD, A. L. 1952. "Suicide and Crime in Folk and Secular Society," *American Journal of Sociology*, LVII, 331–38.

RAMSEY, G. V., and SEIPP, M. 1948. "Attitudes and Opinions concerning Mental Illness," *Psychiatric Quarterly*, XXII, 428–44.

REDFIELD, R. and M. P. 1940. *Disease and Its Treatment in Dzitas, Yucatan*. ("Carnegie Institution of Washington Publications," No. 523, Vol. VI, No. 32.) Washington.

REDLICH, F. C. 1950. "What the Citizen Knows about Psychiatry," *Mental Hygiene*, XXXIV, 64–79.

REED, L. S. 1932. *The Healing Cults*. Chicago: University of Chicago Press.

RICHARDSON, HENRY B. 1945. *Patients Have Families*. New York: Commonwealth Fund.

RIVERS, W. H. R. 1924. *Medicine, Magic, and Religion*. New York: Harcourt, Brace & Co.

ROSEN, GEORGE. 1944. *The Specialization of Medicine*. New York: Froben Press.

———. 1947. "What Is Social Medicine?" *Bulletin of the History of Medicine*, XXI, 674–733.

ROWLAND, H. 1938. "Interaction Processes in a State Mental Hospital," *Psychiatry*, I, 323–37.

———. 1939. "Friendship Patterns in a State Mental Hospital," *ibid.*, II, 363–73.

RUESCH, JURGEN. 1948. "Social Technique, Social Status, and Social Change in Illness." In KLUCKHOHN, CLYDE, and MURRAY, HENRY A. (eds.), *Personality in Nature, Society, and Culture*, pp. 117–30. New York: A. A. Knopf.

RUESCH, JURGEN, and BATESON, GREGORY. 1951. *Communication: The Social Matrix of Psychiatry*. New York: W. W. Norton & Co.

RUESCH, JURGEN; JACOBSON, A.; and LOEB, M. B. 1948. "Acculturation and Illness," *Psychological Monographs: General and Applied*, LXII, 1–40.

RUESCH, JURGEN, et al. 1946. *Chronic Disease and Psychological Invalidism*. Berkeley: University of California Press.

RYLE, JOHN. 1948. *Changing Disciplines*. London: Oxford University Press.

SCHNEIDER, DAVID M. 1947. "The Social Dynamics of Physical Disability in Army Basic Training," *Psychiatry*, X, 323–33.

SCHWARTZ, CHARLOTTE G.; SCHWARTZ, MORRIS S.; and STANTON, ALFRED H. 1951. "A Study of Need-Fulfillment on a Mental Hospital Ward," *Psychiatry*, XIV, 223–42.

SCHWARTZ, MORRIS S., and STANTON, ALFRED H. 1950. "A Social Psychological Study of Incontinence," *Psychiatry*, XIII, 399–416.

SHOCK, NATHAN W. 1951. *A Classified Bibliography of Gerontology and Geriatrics*. Stanford: Stanford University Press.

SHYROCK, R. H. 1947. *The Development of Modern Medicine: An Interpretation of the Social and Scientific Factors Involved*. New York: A. A. Knopf.

SIGERIST, HENRY E. 1943. *Civilization and Disease*. Ithaca, N.Y.: Cornell University Press.

———. 1946. "The Social Sciences in the Medical School." In SIGERIST, HENRY E., *The University at the Crossroads*, pp. 127–42. New York: Henry Schuman.

———. 1951. *A History of Medicine*, Vol. I: *Primitive and Archaic Medicine*. New York: Oxford University Press.

SIMMONS, LEO. 1945a. *The Role of the Aged in Primitive Society*. New Haven: Yale University Press.

———. 1945b. "A Prospectus for Field-Research in the Position and Treatment of the Aged in Primitive and Other Societies," *American Anthropologist*, XLVII, 433–38.

———. 1950. "Studies in the Application of Social Science in Medicine and Nursing at the New York Hospital–Cornell Medical Center." New York: Russell Sage Foundation. (Mimeographed.)

SIMPSON, G. 1950. "Methodological Problems in Determining the Aetiology of Suicide," *American Sociological Review*, XV, 658–63.

SKLIAR, N., and STARIKOWA, K. 1929. "Zur vergleichenden Psychiatrie," *Archiv für Psychiatrie und Nervenkrankheiten*, LXXXVIII, 554–85.

SMITH, HARVEY. 1949. "Sociological Study of Hospitals." Unpublished Ph.D. dissertation, Department of Sociology, University of Chicago.

SNYDER, CHARLES R., and LANDMAN, RUTH H. 1951. "Studies of Drinking in Jewish Culture," *Quarterly Journal of Studies on Alcohol*, XII, 451–74.

SPENCER, DOROTHY M. 1941. *Disease, Religion, and Society in the Fiji Islands*. ("Monographs of the American Ethnological Society.") New York: J. J. Augustin.

STANTON, ALFRED H., and SCHWARTZ, MORRIS S. 1949a. "The Management of a Type of Institutional Participation in Mental Illness," *Psychiatry*, XII, 13–25.

———. 1949b. "Observations on Dissociation as Social Participation," *ibid.*, pp. 339–54.

———. 1949c. "Medical Opinion and the Social Context in the Mental Hospital," *ibid.*, pp. 243–49.

STEINER, JESSE. 1945. *Where People Take Their Troubles*. Boston: Houghton Mifflin Co.

STEINMETZ, S. R. 1894. "Suicide among Primitive Peoples," *American Anthropologist*, VII, 53–60.

STYCOS, J. M. 1949. "A Consideration of Methodology in Research on Mental Disorder," *Psychiatry*, XII, 301–11.

SULLIVAN, H. S. 1931. "Socio-psychiatric Research: Its Implications for the Schizophrenia Problem and for Mental Hygiene," *American Journal of Psychiatry*, X, 977–91.

SZUREK, S. A. 1947. "Dynamics of Staff Interaction in Hospital Psychiatric Treatment of Children," *American Journal of Orthopsychiatry*, XVII, 652–64.

TIETZE, C.; LEMKAU, P.; and COOPER, M. 1941. "Schizophrenia, Manic Depressive Phychosis, and Social-economic

Status," *American Journal of Sociology*, XLVIII, 167–75.

TRIST, E. L., and BAMFORTH, K. W. 1951. "Some Social and Psychological Consequences of the Longwall Method of Coal-getting," *Human Relations*, IV, 3–38.

TURNER, VIOLET B. 1951. *Chronic Illness*. ("Federal Security Agency, Public Health Bibliography Series," No. 1.) Washington: Government Printing Office.

WARDWELL, WALTER I. 1952. "A Marginal Role: The Chiropractor," *Social Forces*, XXX, 339–48.

WARNER, W. LLOYD. 1937. *A Black Civilization*. New York: Harper & Bros.

WESSEN, ALBERT F. 1951. "The Social Structure of a Modern Hospital." Unpublished Ph.D. dissertation, Department of Sociology, Yale University.

WHITING, JOHN, and CHILD, IRVIN. 1952. *Child Training and Personality Development: A Cross-cultural Survey*. New Haven: Yale University Press. (In press.)

WILLIAMS, J. J. 1946. "Patients and Prejudice: Lay Attitudes toward Women Physicians," *American Journal of Sociology*, LI, 283–87.

———. 1950. "The Woman Physician's Dilemma," *Journal of Social Issues*, VI, 38–44.

WILSON, A. T. M. 1950. *Hospital Nursing Auxiliaries: Notes on a Background Survey and Job Analysis*. London: Tavistock Publications, Ltd.

WOLFF, HAROLD G.; WOLF, STEWART G.; and HARE, CLARENCE C. (eds.). 1950. *Life Stress and Bodily Disease: Proceedings of the Association for Research in Nervous and Mental Diseases, December 2 and 3, 1949*. Baltimore: Williams & Wilkins.

WOODWARD, J. L. 1951. "Changing Ideas on Mental Illness and Its Treatment," *American Sociological Review*, XVI, 443–54.

WYATT, FREDERICK. 1947. "Guidance Problems among Student Nurses," *American Journal of Orthopsychiatry*, XVII, 416–25.

YAP, M. A. 1951. "Mental Diseases Peculiar to Certain Cultures: A Survey of Comparative Psychiatry," *Journal of Mental Science*, XCVII, 313–27.

ZILBOORG, G. 1936. "Suicide among Civilized and Primitive Races," *American Journal of Psychiatry*, XCII, 1347–69.

The Application of Linguistics to Language Teaching

By MARY R. HAAS

IN ORDER to clarify the contribution made by linguistics to the problem of language teaching,[1] particularly in the last decade, it is important to make a distinction at the outset among the following: (1) language learning, (2) language description (= descriptive linguistics), and (3) language teaching.

The distinction between language learning and language teaching may at first appear somewhat arbitrary, since we are accustomed to think that the former is the result of the latter. But that is only one of the meanings. By the use of the term "language learning" we wish also to imply the acquisition of knowledge of a foreign language by a special methodological procedure which is quite distinct from the acquisition of such knowledge as the result of what is traditionally called "language teaching." In particular, we wish to stress that this special kind of language learning originally had as its primary purpose scientific language description. The fact that it also often resulted in a facility in the use of the foreign language which was in no way different from the facility acquired from the best of language teaching remained for a long time a definitely secondary con-

sideration for the majority of those who were adept in the use of the method. But when linguists were finally called upon to make a contribution toward the improvement of methods of language teaching, their previous good record in the fields of language learning and language description inevitably caused the problem to pose itself in the following terms: In what way can the methods and techniques that linguists have successfully applied to language learning and language description be transferred to the field of language teaching?

When Franz Boas first turned his attention to linguistic matters, his interest was focused on two essential problems of the greatest importance to him as an anthropologist: (1) the necessity of learning totally new and strange unwritten languages for the purpose of direct communication with the speakers thereof or, more specifically, for the purpose of directly eliciting ethnological information otherwise unobtainable and (2) the function of making accurate and full records of such languages for analytical and documentary purposes (1911, pp. 59–63).

The successful implementation of these two goals led directly to the use of what later came to be known as the "informant method" of learning languages. In using this method the inves-

---

1. In this paper the problem is discussed from the point of view of developments in the United States during the first half of the twentieth century.

tigator set about to record and learn a previously unwritten language by making a phonetic recording of words, phrases, sentences, and, as soon as possible, texts from the dictation of a native speaker of that language. Translations into English or into the usual contact language of the region were also obtained. Interlinear translations, as literal as possible, were provided for texts.

The most efficient and accurate way of achieving a knowledge of a language directly from an informant required that the linguist operate by working on the following problems common to all languages: (1) phonology (referred to by Boas [1911, pp. 15–24] as "phonetics"), (2) morphology (referred to by Boas [1911, pp. 24–43] as "grammatical categories"), and (3) syntax. Of these, problems of syntax received less explicit attention from Boas and his contemporaries and immediate followers than did problems of phonology and morphology; but recognition of the threefold nature of linguistic problems was never completely lacking, and later linguists, though able greatly to refine many of their techniques of analysis, did not add anything new to this general over-all picture of language.

In the field of phonetics Boas stressed two points, both of which were later to turn out to be of great importance in the application of theoretical linguistic knowledge to the practical problems of teaching languages. These were: (1) the total number of sounds that may be found as one proceeds from language to language is unlimited (1911, p. 15) but (2) "every single language has a definite and limited group of sounds" and "the number of those used in any particular dialect is never excessively large" (1911, p. 16).

Boas learned a number of diverse and difficult languages by means of his special approach to the problem. He did not, however, "teach" any of these languages in any of the traditional senses of that term. What he taught was the method. His way of teaching the method appears to have been highly successful; certainly, it made a deep impression on his many students. Kroeber (1943, p. 14) has described the method well: "In the teaching of linguistics, Boas' approach was wholly inductive and empirical. He set before students an interlinear text and proceeded to analyze it, developing the structure of the language as he proceeded. This was a thoroughly novel method and exceedingly stimulating to students."

One other feature of Boas' unique approach to language study must be stressed: Each language was treated as a separate and complete system of communication within the culture or society making use of that language. Its structure, moreover, was to be studied in terms of its own internal patterning without reference to the structure of any other language or to any preconceived notion about language in general.

Edward Sapir, whose initiation into the study of American Indian languages was under the tutelage of Boas, made important advances in the science of linguistics on all fronts. In particular, he advanced the study of phonology by his conceptualization of the phoneme (also conceptualized by other linguists at about the same time). His brilliant analyses of a number of previously unstudied American Indian languages are a monumental achievement. In his stimulating book *Language* (1921) and also in various articles, he stresses again and again the essential structural differences between languages, the amazing variety of structures found, and the necessity of studying the structure of each language in and for itself without reference to the structure of any other language.

Another point of primary importance,

in view of later developments, is that, while Sapir did not ever actually write a descriptive grammar of a literary language, he was fully convinced not only of the feasibility but of the necessity of using the scientific linguist's approach to the problem, and he passed this conviction on to his students. As one instance of this conviction may be cited the fact that, among several important projects he did not live to finish, was one devoted to the descriptive analysis of English.

But perhaps the most important achievement of all—and this can be said without in any way diminishing the importance of his scholarly researches and publications—was the stimulating effect Sapir had on his students, the unique ability to impart to them his own supreme enthusiasm for the study of language in all its facets.

Leonard Bloomfield, while not actually a student of Boas, was influenced by him in many ways. A specialist in Germanic linguistics and a teacher of modern languages, Bloomfield also made notable contributions to our knowledge of unwritten, including American Indian, languages. His approach to field work, like his approach to modern languages in general, was based on the premise that languages are meant to be spoken. Hence he acquired a speaking knowledge of a language before undertaking to make a detailed analysis. And, instead of eliciting paradigmatic and other grammatical constructions by direct questioning of the informant, he preferred to garner such material entirely from the extensive oral texts which he transcribed.

But Bloomfield's most important contribution by far was his book *Language* (1933). In this he articulated all the essential features of descriptive linguistic methodology and laid the foundations for most of the important theoretical discussions of the past two decades, as well as for the important analy-

ses of specific linguistic structures which were produced in the same period. He provides not only a statement of the methodology employed in phonemicization but also chapters on the techniques of analyzing morphology and syntax, as well as others on all other problems pertinent to the discipline of linguistic science. His final chapter is devoted to practical applications, and some of the opinions expressed there are pertinent to the present discussion. However, the most important of these opinions, in so far as they apply to teaching methods, are more fully elaborated in his earlier *An Introduction to the Study of Language* (1914), and these are accordingly taken up in greater detail in the following paragraphs.

Viewing the work of Boas, Sapir, and Bloomfield in its totality, it seems fair to say that, of the three, only Bloomfield was deeply concerned with the problem of the application of linguistics to language teaching. This is due in large part to the circumstances surrounding their respective careers. Boas and Sapir were anthropologists, and their teaching duties were directed toward the teaching of anthropology and the training of professional anthropologists.[2] Bloomfield, on the other hand, while fully appreciative of the contributions made by anthropologists to the

2. Boas, in particular, was not interested in making a distinction between the anthropologist and the linguist. Any well-trained student of Boas took linguistics in his stride, just as he took ethnology, physical anthropology, and archeology in his stride. Sapir, though himself a product of Boas' view of his discipline, veered away from the strictness of this view, particularly in his later years. Thus his earlier students, even those who are primarily interested in linguistics, are best described as anthropologists rather than as linguists. Among his later students, on the other hand, there are a few who are best described as linguists rather than as anthropologists. Among these are some who, at Sapir's express wish, did not take their doctorates in anthropology but in linguistics.

field of linguistics, was not, strictly speaking, an anthropologist. He was, indeed, primarily a language teacher and early became interested in applying the important principles developed in linguistic science to the more practical problems of language teaching. As early as 1914, he worked out most of the basic principles that were to play a very important role in some of the sweeping reforms that were later instituted in the teaching of languages at many universities. In *An Introduction to the Study of Language* (1914, pp. 294–95), his most important criticisms of the traditional methods of teaching modern languages are as follows: (1) the relatively small number of class hours, (2) undue reliance on written homework, (3) the learning of grammatical rules and other "facts" about the language instead of learning the language itself, (4) the reliance on translation as a means of determining understanding and competence, and (5) the inability of large numbers of teachers to speak the languages they are engaged in teaching. He also constantly deplores the fact that language teachers in general have so little fundamental knowledge of the nature of language, i.e., of scientific linguistics. The result of this misguided view of the proper nature of language teaching is, in Bloomfield's words (1914, p. 293), as follows: "Of the students who take up the study of foreign languages in our schools and colleges, not one in a hundred attains even a fair reading knowledge, and not one in a thousand ever learns to carry on a conversation in the foreign language."

Specific recommendations made by Bloomfield at the same time toward the improvement of language teaching are also worthy of note. The prerequisites of the teacher are: (1) that he should know the language he is teaching—in other words, he should have "a knowledge comparable to that of an educated native speaker" (1914, p. 297) —and (2) that he should also know how to teach the language; being simply an educated native or the equivalent thereof is not enough. Recommendations for improving procedure in instruction include: (1) drill in correct pronunciation (accompanied by instruction in the phonetics of the language contrasted with the phonetics of the students' own language) should be instituted at the very beginning of the study of the language and continued until mastery is achieved (1914, p. 299); (2) "the first phonetic examples should be characteristic words and phrases" of useful and usable content (1914, p. 300); (3) material chosen for concentrated work should be drilled into the student "until every phrase of it has been thoroughly assimilated" (1914, p. 302); and (4) since the constant supervision of the teacher is necessary for such thoroughgoing assimilation, "the work must be done almost entirely in the classroom" and "eight hours a week of class-work are not too much in the first year or two" (1914, p. 302).

Bloomfield's criticisms and recommendations, as outlined above, went largely unheeded for almost three decades. Linguists—what few of them there were—were devoting themselves largely to the study of unwritten American Indian languages (or, now and again, to other so-called "primitive" languages) and occasionally giving regular university courses or seminars in the study of such languages. Such courses were not designed for the purpose of teaching students to speak the languages being studied but had the more strictly scientific purpose of teaching them the techniques of linguistic analysis so that they could go out into the field and apply what they had learned to the recording and analysis of other unstudied and unwritten languages. Language teachers, on the other hand, went right on teaching their specialties according to traditional methods (with the focus on grammar, reading, and translation); not one in a hundred language students ever learned to speak the language he was studying; and language teachers and language students alike remained largely in total ignorance even of the existence of such a science as linguistics.

Then, shortly before the United States was drawn into World War II, a new demand arose which served to precipitate a number of changes in traditional attitudes toward language teaching. Under the threat of the possibility of war, a few people, particularly some of the officials and consultants connected with the American Council of Learned Societies. became deeply concerned over the fact that the linguistic competences and resources of this country were totally inadequate for war on a global basis. Only a handful of modern languages was being taught in our colleges and universities, and these mostly the more "usual" languages of Europe, such as French, German, Spanish, Italian, and, more rarely, Russian. Languages of the Orient, except for Chinese and Japanese, were totally unknown. Not only were there no teachers available for such languages as Thai, Annamese, Burmese, Hindustani, and Pashtu, there were not even any respectable teaching aids available for any of them.

The realization of this deplorable state of affairs had such a sobering effect that the American Council of Learned Societies organized a special committee, the Committee on the National School of Modern Oriental Languages and Civilizations, for the purpose of tackling various problems, but particularly the problem of implementation. It was decided at the outset to employ for the purpose students who had been trained in the latest techniques of linguistic analysis. As a re-

sult, linguists who had studied under Sapir or Bloomfield or their students (many of whom had previously worked only on American Indian languages) were soon engaged in analyzing the structures of various Far Eastern, Near Eastern, and African languages. Their instructions were explicit: they were to use the methods which they had previously used with success in their study of American Indian or other "primitive" languages. In other words, even though they might be working on a language having a literary history of several centuries, they were directed to obtain the services of native speakers of the languages as informants and to let the living speech of these informants serve as the basis for their analysis of the phonemics, morphology, and syntax of the language. Whether or not they actually learned to speak the language themselves and whether or not they concerned themselves with the traditional writing system employed for the language in question were left to the discretion of the individual investigator. Some did one, some did the other, some did neither, and a few did both; but all concerned themselves primarily with linguistic analysis.

Their work of analysis had barely gotten off to a good start, however, before many of them were required to begin teaching the languages on which they had been working. It was at this point that Bloomfield's strictures on teaching methods were quite suddenly and completely vindicated. There was no time for discussion or debate as to how these languages were to be taught. The teaching was going to be done by trained linguists, and it was inevitable that they should endeavor to utilize to the fullest their knowledge of linguistic analysis and to bring their knowledge directly to bear on the practical problems of teaching.

There were two ways open to the

linguist, largely depending on the amount of time he had been allowed to spend on the analysis of the language before the problem of teaching became imminent. The two methods, both of which required the services of informants or native speakers of the language, may be briefly described as follows:

1. If the linguist had spent little or no time in previous analysis of the language, his students could participate with him in the task of analyzing the language. The linguist would show the students how to elicit the necessary linguistic material from the informant, how to work out the grammatical structure from the examples collected, and how to analyze and classify what they had recorded. Each student would also make his own alphabetical file of grammatical forms and lexical items collected. In addition, he would be expected to memorize as many of the examples as possible and to practice them faithfully until he could rattle them off without a moment's hesitation. Except for the work of memorization, this method of learning a language was almost exactly like the procedures employed for many years in teaching courses in "Field Methods in Linguistics" at the Linguistic Institute of the Linguistic Society of America in special summer courses and at a few universities as a part of their regular curriculum. There was, however, one interesting difference. Courses in field methods had previously employed the services of informants who spoke unwritten languages, usually American Indian, occasionally African or some other. The method was now being applied with equal success to languages of the Orient whose literary traditions extended back many centuries.

2. The second way in which linguists used linguistics as an aid in teaching a language could be applied only if the linguist had been given a little time in advance for making at least a start on its analysis. He would, by this method, spend many hours with the informant alone, analyze the linguistic material in advance, and then organize the basic grammatical material in a systematic manner for presentation to his students. He would also prepare in advance exercises for drill in pronunciation and grammar and well-conceived conversational material for memorization. Imitation and memorization were the keynotes of the method. And, since the emphasis was on learning to speak the language, any type of material that could be used to increase the student's speaking and comprehensive competence was promptly put to use in this manner. Even by this method, then, the informant remained a necessary part of the classroom situation. He served as the living model for the students to imitate, and later, as their skills developed, he carried on conversations with the students in a fashion that was based as nearly as possible on real life-situations—situations which might arise, for instance, if the student actually were to find himself in the country where the language being studied was spoken.

The application of linguistic techniques to the problems of language learning and language teaching, as briefly described above, was largely initiated and sponsored by the Intensive Language Program of the American Council of Learned Societies from 1942 to 1945. The program consistently emphasized the following points, most of which were a development of the recommendations urged by Bloomfield almost three decades previously: (1) the actual teaching must be done by a trained linguist, (2) informants were to serve as drillmasters for small sections of students (not more than ten per section), (3) the number of class hours per week should be around fifteen to eighteen, (4) the ultimate goal of the student was to acquire accurate pronunciation, a good speaking knowledge, and good auditory comprehension of the language. The success of the program was so marked (good results normally being obvious in a few weeks) that when the Army instituted its now famous Army Specialized Training Program in 1943–44 for language and area studies in various universities throughout the United States, the instructional procedures worked out under the Intensive Language Program were adopted and recommended for the teaching of all languages coming under the Army Program. The prime objective of the Army was to have the trainee acquire a good command of the spoken language, and the experiments conducted by the Intensive Language Program indicated that their methods were successful in achieving this objective in a relatively short period of time (six to nine months).

The fact that the Army recommended the procedures adopted by the Intensive Language Program meant that the new methods were to be applied to all languages coming under the program, in other words, to the more "usual" languages like German, French, and Spanish, as well as to the so-called "exotic" languages. More than this, since there were not enough trained linguists available to take charge of all the courses being offered, it meant that many professional language teachers found themselves under the necessity of acquiring at least some knowledge of linguistic science in order properly to fulfil their duties. To meet this need, the Linguistic Society of America issued two booklets, (1) *Outline Guide for the Practical Study of Foreign Languages,* by Leonard Bloomfield, and (2) *Outline of Linguistic Analysis,* by Bernard Bloch and George L. Trager. It was recommended that the two booklets be used together.

Bloomfield's booklet is especially devoted to the description of the way in which a linguist works with an informant and elicits the information he needs. The Bloch and Trager booklet, on the other hand, explains in considerable technical detail how to analyze a language, once the necessary information has been elicited from the informant. Excellent as they are, however, neither of the booklets totally succeeded in taking care of the immediate goals, namely, to show large numbers of language teachers and language students how to become linguists, or at least how best to profit from the linguist's approach to language study. The Bloch and Trager booklet, in particular, is too difficult and too severely technical for the layman who lacks previous training in linguistic science. At the present time the Bloomfield booklet is not referred to as often as it should be. The Bloch and Trager booklet, on the other hand, immediately filled a somewhat different but perhaps even more important need: It is now very widely used as an ancillary textbook in various types of linguistics courses ranging all the way from general introductory courses to courses in phonetics and phonemics, linguistic analysis, and field methods in linguistics.

The setting-up of the Army Specialized Training Program also immediately created another primary need. Since the emphasis was on the oral approach to language study, a need for well-planned conversational textbooks was at once apparent. This was true not only of the exotic languages, for which no textbooks worthy of the name were in existence, but also even of the "usual" languages, since the existing textbooks for these languages almost universally emphasized the reading and translation approach. In most cases the only way to fill the need for teaching materials was for each instructor in charge of a language to prepare his textbook materials as he went along from day to day. Although much of this material was never actually published (except for some of it which was worked into the *Basic Courses* described in the following paragraph), it represented a truly tremendous burst of activity, in view of the fact that a total of twenty-eight languages was being implemented in this way. These languages were as follows: Arabic, Annamese, Bengali, Bulgarian, Burmese, Chinese, Czech, Dutch, Finnish, French, German, Greek, Hindustani, Hungarian, Italian, Japanese, Korean, Malay, Norwegian, Persian, Polish, Portuguese, Russian, Serbo-Croatian, Spanish, Swedish, Thai, and Turkish. Even though much of the material was not published, it was reproduced by mimeograph or ditto process, and copies of many things found their way into a few university libraries. Hence there is a large reservoir of material available for reference or consultation, even if not for wide distribution. This is particularly important in the case of the lesser-known languages.

In the meantime the Armed Forces Institute was beginning to supply *Basic Courses* in a number of languages. Each *Basic Course* contained a series of conversational texts sufficiently well conceived to be worthy of extensive drill and memorization on the part of students using the texts. The planning of these courses was done by a group of linguists, and the basic outline for each course is the same, including the type of material presented and the order in which it is presented. Unlike previous textbooks, these are definitely geared to the intensive method. Each *Basic Course* contains thirty units, twenty-four of which are conversational texts and six of which are review units. The first twelve units are also accompanied by phonograph recordings of the materials in the conversational texts, as recorded by a native speaker

of the language. These phonograph recordings can be used by students working individually or in groups who do not have access to an informant. They can also be profitably used as material for additional drill outside regular class hours by students who do have the opportunity of working with an informant.

Armed Forces Institute textbooks were eventually made available in twenty languages. After the war they were reissued as civilian textbooks. The following languages are treated: Burmese, Chinese, Danish, Dutch, French, German, Greek, Hindustani, Hungarian, Italian, Japanese, Korean, Malay, Portuguese, Russian, Serbo-Croatian, Spanish, Thai, and Turkish.[3] All these textbooks were written by linguists, and the total amount of research that formed the background for their preparation is impressive. This is particularly true of the half-dozen or so languages which previously lacked even the most rudimentary type of implementation. While some of the texts are no doubt better or more useful than others—as is bound to happen in the case of any large-scale project such as this—the total contribution to language-teaching implementation made by these twenty books is sufficient to demonstrate in a very forcible manner the value that can accrue when the principles of linguistic science are applied to problems of language teaching.

So much for some of the principal researches and contributions made by linguists in the way of large-scale experimentation toward the improvement of language-teaching methods and by way of production of implementation during World War II and immediately there-

3. The work of preparing textbooks along these lines has by no means come to a standstill. The American Council of Learned Societies is sponsoring further work of this type, and textbooks for additional languages appear from time to time.

after. The question now arises: Have any of the results spilled over into the postwar period?

Perhaps the most obvious and beneficial immediate result was a great burst of discussion about the relative merits and demerits of the so-called "Army" method and traditional methods. It had been a long, long time since language teachers in general had done any real soul-searching about the values, benefits, and results of their teaching methods. As has already been pointed out, Bloomfield's earlier strictures had gone unheeded for nearly three decades. Therefore, if the large-scale wartime experimentation had done nothing else besides shaking a large number of teachers loose from their complacency, this in itself could be considered a gain. That it actually did much more than this, however, is a fact which has been widely, if not universally, conceded.

Some language teachers were delighted with the results achieved by the new methods; others (particularly those who had little firsthand contact with them) hated the very thought of the innovations. As a consequence, during the past decade the pages of professional language-teaching journals[4] have been filled with literally scores of articles devoted to the debate, sometimes extremely heated, of both sides of the issue. In addition, two books have appeared which attempt to assess the contributions made by the Intensive Language Program and the Army Specialized Training Program to postwar civilian language-teaching methods up

4. For example, the *Modern Language Journal*, the *French Review*, the *German Quarterly*, and *Hispania*. Bibliographies citing articles which appeared up to 1947 are to be found in Angiolillo (1947, pp. 423–40) and Matthew (1947, pp. 188–211). Articles discussing the problems raised are still continuing to appear in the journals mentioned, but they are somewhat less numerous than in the period 1943–47.

to the year 1947. These are *Armed Forces' Foreign Language Teaching*, by Paul F. Angiolillo, and *Language and Area Studies in the Armed Services*, by Robert J. Matthew.

Having sifted through the numerous articles which appeared up to 1947, Angiolillo makes the cautious statement (1947, p. 337) that "the consensus is nearly unanimous that the ASTP can not be disregarded as of little value by anyone concerned with peacetime teaching of foreign languages." Specific influences attributed to the ASTP include the following: (1) "Foreign-language instruction will henceforth ... be required to be useful in a thoroughly practical sense" (1947, p. 339), which means that it will more and more be directed to "an aural-oral proficiency in language learning" (1947, p. 340); (2) more class hours per week will be devoted to language study (1947, p. 342), the most usual recommendation being not less than eight to ten hours per week (1947, p. 345); (3) "speaking fluency will precede reading" (1947, p. 345); and (4) new textbooks will be prepared "in conformity with some of the principles and procedures of language teaching originating in the armed forces or the Intensive Language Program" (1947, p. 355).

Other ways in which the ASTP has influenced present-day thinking about language teaching include the following, again quoting from Angiolillo (1947, p. 349): "(1) all explanations pertaining to the mechanics of the language should follow the illustrative examples; (2) reading need not wait upon the completion of the formal study of grammar; (3) verbs should be learned through normal and natural oral use, not through paradigms; (4) writing in the foreign language should be determined by what the student can say; (5) translations from or to the foreign language should be held to a minimum." While it is true that these suggestions do not enjoy "the unanimous endorsement of language teachers" (1947, p. 349), it remains a fact that, whereas prior to World War II there were almost no language teachers to be found who were thinking along these lines, today there is a large and constantly growing number of them.

Another point of considerable importance is one which somehow usually escapes notice as one of the assets attributable to the ASTP. Because of the wide publicity given to the ASTP, it was inevitable that publicity should be given to linguistic science and to the leaders in this field. As a consequence, the more important works of Boas, Sapir, and Bloomfield have come to be known, at least by name and quite often by perusal, to scores of language teachers who had never previously been exposed to any knowledge of the important results of linguistic science as it has been developing in the past few decades. This is a decided improvement along one of the lines so urgently desired by Bloomfield, namely, that language teachers should know more about linguistics. As language teachers in general learn more and more about this discipline, the wider and wider application of the principles of linguistics to language teaching is bound to result.

The stimulus provided by the ASTP toward the improvement in teaching languages to civilians along lines recommended by linguists has been given considerable attention because the results of this experiment became very widely known and can be said to have had extremely far-reaching effects. However, this example is not the only one deserving to be cited as showing the results of the application of linguistics to problems of language teaching.

In the late 1930's the English Language Institute was founded at the University of Michigan under the direction of Professor Charles C. Fries. The principal aims of this institute are (1) to make thorough scientific analyses of the English language, with a view to improving methods of teaching English to those of foreign speech; (2) to prepare textbooks for this purpose; and (3) to teach the English language to foreigners and check and improve their textbooks against this classroom experience. The over-all ideal, according to Fries (1945b, p. v), is "to interpret, in a practical way for teaching, the principles of modern linguistic science and to use the results of scientific linguistic research."

Perhaps the most important principle back of the research being conducted at the English Language Institute is that which maintains that no single textbook can be prepared which has as its purpose the teaching of English to all foreigners. In other words, it is necessary to make a scientific study not only of the English language but also of the specific native language used by the particular group of foreigners who are expected to benefit from the use of the text. Or, to quote Fries again (1949, p. 97):

The more we deal with English as a foreign language the more we are impressed with the need of special materials for each linguistic background. "Foreign" language teaching is always a matter of teaching a specific "foreign" language to students who have a specific "native" language background. The problems of the Chinese student are very different from those of a Spanish speaker. . . . There should be provision for the developing of satisfactory new [text] materials for a variety of linguistic groups that we are not now equipped to serve.

Important published results of the research being conducted at the English Language Institute include: *Teaching and Learning English as a Foreign*

Language (1945*b*), by C. C. Fries, the first chapter of which, "On Learning a Foreign Language as an Adult," should be read by anyone attempting to acquire a knowledge of a foreign language in college or university as well as later; *The Intonation of American English* (1946), by Kenneth L. Pike, the best detailed analysis of American English intonation now available; and a series of volumes entitled *An Intensive Course in English for Latin American Students* (1945*a*), by the Research Staff of the English Language Institute, C. C. Fries, director. Another important textbook, *An Intensive Course in English for Chinese Students,* is in process of preparation, and a preliminary volume or two have already appeared. Other important books written by University of Michigan linguists are: *Phonemics* (1947), by Kenneth L. Pike, and *Morphology: The Descriptive Analysis of Words* (1949), by Eugene A. Nida. In addition, Nida's *Learning a Foreign Language: A Handbook for Missionaries* (1950), an outgrowth of his work at the Summer Institute of Linguistics for missionaries at the University of Oklahoma, is one of the most detailed books describing the method of working directly with an informant that have yet appeared.

The linguists associated with the English Language Institute have also made another important contribution to the field of applied linguistics by founding, in 1948, a journal entitled *Language Learning: A Quarterly Journal of Applied Linguistics,* in which articles devoted to the exchange of ideas, discussion of problems, and new classroom techniques are particularly prominent.

Important work is also going on at various other centers. There is, for example, the excellent program for teaching modern languages by the intensive method in the Division of Modern Languages at Cornell University. George L. Trager and Henry Lee Smith are conducting important researches on the English language at the Foreign Service Institute of the State Department and are also directing other researches on more exotic languages for the purpose of making better teaching materials available. The Annual Round Table Meetings on Linguistics and Language Teaching held at Georgetown University, though started only in 1949, have already become an institution and provide an excellent opportunity for discussion of all phases of the problems inherent in the application of linguistics to language teaching (DeFrancis, 1951).

The development of the ideas which form the background for the application of linguistics to the problems of language teaching has taken place gradually during the last half-century. The basic premise is that each language requires thorough scientific analysis and description and that the latter includes the preparation of a descriptive grammar, texts, and a descriptive dictionary. At first, such scientific descriptions were made of previously unstudied and unwritten languages, and the works of Boas, Sapir, Bloomfield, and their students provide many outstanding examples of this type of research. Later it became obvious that such descriptions could and should be made of literary languages as well, and a few outstanding language teachers with linguistic training took it upon themselves to emphasize that teaching aids, including conversation manuals, readers, and student dictionaries, should properly be based only upon sound scientific descriptions of this type.

Other ideas for the improvement of language teaching were borrowed from linguistics, especially the "informant" method coupled with emphasis on oral-aural proficiency. But the principal contribution that linguistics has to make is the preparation of complete scientific descriptions of English and of each and every foreign language to be taught. With such scientific descriptions as the backdrop, better and better teaching materials can be produced. Furthermore, in order to profit to the fullest extent from these new ideas, language teachers and language students alike need to receive some basic training in linguistics. Many universities are now equipped to provide this training, and more and more prospective language teachers are beginning to avail themselves of this opportunity.

We are still a long way from having achieved all these goals, but tremendous strides in the right direction have been made during the past decade.

REFERENCES

ANGIOLILLO, PAUL F. 1947. *Armed Forces' Foreign Language Teaching.* New York: S. F. Vanni. (Bibliography, pp. 423–40.)

BLOCH, BERNARD, and TRAGER, GEORGE L. 1942. *Outline of Linguistic Analysis.* Baltimore: Linguistic Society of America.

BLOOMFIELD, LEONARD. 1914. *An Introduction to the Study of Language.* New York: Henry Holt & Co.

———. 1933. *Language.* New York: Henry Holt & Co.

———. 1942. *Outline Guide for the Practical Study of Foreign Languages.* Baltimore: Linguistic Society of America.

BOAS, FRANZ. 1911. *Introduction to Handbook of American Indian Languages.* (Bureau of American Ethnology Bull. 40, Part I.) Washington, D.C.

DEFRANCIS, JOHN (ed.). 1951. *Report on the Second Annual Round Table Meeting on Linguistics and Language Teaching, Georgetown University, Washington, D.C.*

FRIES, CHARLES C. (ed.). 1945a. *An Intensive Course in English for Latin American Students.* Vols. I–IV. By the Research Staff of the English Language Institute, Charles C. Fries, director. ("University of Michigan Publications, English Language Institute," No. 2.) Ann Arbor.

———. 1945b. *Teaching and Learning English as a Foreign Language.* ("University of Michigan Publications, English Language Institute," No. 1.) Ann Arbor.

———. 1949. "An Investigation of Second Language Teaching," *Language Learning,* II, 89–99.

HAAS, MARY R. 1943. "The Linguist as a Teacher of Languages," *Language,* XIX, 203–8.

KROEBER, A. L. 1943. *Franz Boas, the Man,* pp. 5–26. ("Memoirs of the American Anthropological Association," No. 61.) Menasha, Wis.

Language Learning: A Quarterly Journal of Applied Linguistics. 1948–52. Vols. I–IV.

MATTHEW, ROBERT J. 1947. *Language and Area Studies in the Armed Services.* Washington, D.C.: American Council of Education. (Bibliography, pp. 188–211.)

———. 1949. *Morphology: The Descriptive Analysis of Words.* ("University of Michigan Publications in Linguistics," Vol. II.) Rev. ed. Ann Arbor.

NIDA, EUGENE A. 1950. *Learning a Foreign Language: A Handbook for Missionaries.* New York: Committee on Missionary Personnel of the Foreign Missions Conference of North America.

PIKE, KENNETH L. 1946. *The Intonation of American English.* ("University of Michigan Publications in Linguistics," Vol. I.) Ann Arbor.

———. 1947. *Phonemics.* ("University of Michigan Publications in Linguistics," Vol. III.) Ann Arbor.

SAPIR, EDWARD. 1921. *Language.* New York: Harcourt, Brace & Co.

Applied Anthropology in Industry

By ELIOT D. CHAPPLE

THE TOPIC "Applied Anthropology in Industry" is somewhat of a misnomer if "applied anthropology" is taken to mean the deliberate introduction of change into an industrial situation. By far the greatest amount of research work done in this field is not "applied" in this sense; it has been primarily concerned with understanding the processes of change in one particular type of social institution. For the purposes of this paper, applied anthropology is regarded as that aspect of anthropology which deals with the description of changes in human relations and in the isolation of the principles that control them. Perhaps it should also be emphasized that such a definition, by necessity, includes an examination of those factors which restrict the possibility of change in human organization.

As here defined, therefore, applied anthropology requires the explicit introduction of time as the major dimension in studies of interpersonal relations. It is systematically diachronic rather than synchronic. It can even be called "historical" if we remember that it is quite unlike any of the "historical" schools of anthropology, whose effects were assumed to occur through a kind of action at a distance, within the vague limits of periods of time of almost geological magnitude. It is history—but of the sequence of actual events involving individual people, recorded on a day-to-day and even hour-to-hour basis.

The beginning of the use of anthropological concepts and methods in industry can probably best be fixed in the researches conducted under the direction of Professor Elton Mayo at the Hawthorne Works of the Western Electric Company just outside Chicago. Actually, anthropological ideas had been reflected previously in the so-called "scientific management school," particularly in the later work of Mary Parker Follett (1942), who was familiar with, and to some extent influenced by, the work of B. Malinowski. However, the Hawthorne studies, for practical purposes, mark the first important and generative introduction of anthropology into the study of modern industrial and political institutions, and with their results we must concern ourselves briefly.

When the Committee on Industrial Physiology was set up at Harvard University through grants from the Rockefeller Foundation, as a committee of the several schools—business, medicine, public health, law, and arts and sciences—its initial interest was in the study of fatigue among industrial workers. Elton Mayo, one of its principal members, was an Australian psychiatrist and a friend of Malinowski and Radcliffe-Brown. As a psychiatrist, Mayo was primarily a follower of Janet rather than of Freud. His interest was in the influence (which, with Tawney, he considered to be deleterious in contrast to that of peasant or primitive cultures) of modern industrial society on the production of psychiatric disorders. He was convinced that much of what was classified under the heading of "fatigue" or "feelings of fatigue" among workers in modern industry was not physiological in origin but was the result of what he called "obsessive thinking." He had performed some successful experiments in a textile mill in Philadelphia, where there had been very high labor turnover, and he had treated "fatigue" by allowing workers to talk freely to a nurse (Mayo, 1933). The establishment by the Western Electric Company of the Relay Assembly Test Room at the Hawthorne Works, in collaboration with the Harvard group, was intended to test on an experimental basis the effects of various physical changes on fatigue—intensity of illumination, humidity, temperature, as well as rest periods during the day, food intake, and so forth. As is well known, the results of the experiment were completely contrary to engineering, medical, and economic expectation. Whether changes were, in terms of management logics, for "better" or for "worse," productivity in this group of six girls consistently increased. Detailed examination of the evidence clearly indicated that human relations factors were primarily responsible for this sustained increase in output (Whitehead, 1938; Roethlisberger and Dickson, 1939).

The analysis of these relationships further indicated that the interaction patterns of the individuals in this group, both within and outside the plant, had resulted in the formation of a tightly knit group. Its output increased as the members spent more and more time with one another in free give-and-take while they were working, a situation made possible by the unusual relationships which they had to supervisory authority. Because of the country-wide as well as company-wide interest in the study, the girls were afforded frequent opportunities to take the initiative in going to their supervisor and to control the interpersonal conditions of their work.

This discovery of the overriding importance of human relations factors marked a turning point in the history of the Western Electric studies. Mayo brought in, as a consultant, W. Lloyd Warner, who had recently come to the department of anthropology at Harvard. Warner, a student of Radcliffe-Brown, Malinowski, and Robert Lowie, had recently returned from a field trip in northern Australia among the Murngin. As a result of his influence and Mayo's own interest in anthropology, a marked change took place in the research. In what was called the "Bank Wiring Observation Room," a segment of a working department in a "natural" industrial situation was physically set off from the rest of the department and the relationships of the workers described and analyzed in terms of the concepts of the "functional" school of anthropology.

An observer, seated in the back of the room, made daily records of what he heard and saw, and an interviewer worked with each man on a regular basis. For the first time, a systematic description of the social organization of an industrial working group was obtained. It clearly demonstrated the significance of cultural processes and techniques in determining what the investigators referred to as the "informal" organization of the group. These clique and teamwork patterns among individuals were opposed to the "formal" organization—the hierarchical departmental groupings on the organization chart.

This artificial distinction between "formal" and "informal"—in industry and government symbolized by the organization chart; in the family by the kinship terminology—tended to obscure the significance of this part of the Western Electric investigation. So much was made of the fact that workers have "informal" relations (as fundamental in determining their attitudes) that the overriding importance of the culture of the Bank Wiring Observation Room in determining these relations, and rendering absurd the semantic dichotomy, was neglected. These cultural factors included specific techniques performed by the workers; the interdependence of one operation and one operator upon another through the ordering of the flow of the work; the influence of the spatial differentiation of the room; and how these factors, operating upon individuals with different personalities, produced an effective and working system of relations with well-defined equilibrium characteristics—represented both in the limitation of output and in the behavior of the individuals toward one another.

Many of the incidents reported in the room clearly show how changes in personality or in cultural process or technique directly affect (disturb) the system of relations. Much of the work in the field of applied anthropology in industry which has been done since then has merely restated for different types of industrial situations, and usually much more unsystematically, the principles which can be derived from this fundamental study.

It is most interesting to find that, from the anthropological point of view, the significance of the Hawthorne experiments was little realized even by the investigators themselves. To a considerable extent, this derives from what might be called the "interview bias" of the researchers and their inability to describe the behavior of people objectively. In the texts and also in the observations and interviews themselves, we repeatedly find shorthand sociological and psychiatric concepts substituted for actual first-order abstractions

—the who does what to whom, when, and where, of anthropological field method. Terms such as "antagonism," "social distance," "interests," "sentiments," and "obsessions" interfere with the descriptive account.

The bias referred to above, however, was far more important in its effects on the future direction of industrial research. In part it resulted from the heavy psychiatric preoccupations of the principal investigators. At the time that the Bank Wiring Observation Room was set up, a plant-wide interviewing program was also under way to ascertain the attitudes of the workers toward their work situations. The findings of this program indicated that such interviewing had a marked cathartic effect, and the interviewing in the Bank Wire Observation Room seemed to substantiate this. As a result, both Mayo and the Western Electric Company concluded that the installation of an interviewing program on a permanent basis would be of major therapeutic value and would have the palliative effects on personnel relations which they hoped to obtain.

The efforts of the group then became directed toward the institution of a counseling program, using a nondirective type interview (comparable to, but apparently developed independently of, the technique associated with Carl Rogers [1942]). At the beginning, the counseling was intended to provide both an organized system of plant psychotherapy and a means of communication up the line through which information relating to emotional and working problems would be funneled to top management through a staff personnel unit. Counselors were assigned to the floor, their interviews analyzed, and reports and general recommendations made to management without violating personal anonymity.

Gradually this communication function became less and less important, and, for reasons connected with the organizational stresses within the company as the program went on, greater and greater stress was laid on the counselor-client relationship itself. It therefore set out upon a course exactly parallel to that of Rogers, with the basic emphasis on the client-oriented interview and with the assumption that it was sufficient for industrial purposes to help the individual reorganize his concepts and attitudes to adapt him better to the external environment.

The results of this change in the emphasis of the Western Electric work from the anthropological to the psychiatric or clinical-psychological approach in industrial relations had considerable influence in retarding the development of applied anthropology in industry. Counseling programs—both within the American Telephone & Telegraph Company, of which the Western Electric Company is a branch, and in industry generally—became widespread. Except for a few anthropologists who continued along the line suggested by the Bank Wiring Observation Room, most of the effort in industry was devoted to trying out counseling systems and finding, after a shorter or longer period, that they were of only minor benefit in the over-all personnel picture. The significance and the potentialities of a new attack on organization problems was only dimly perceived in management circles. As for counseling, the rise of industrial unionism provided a far more powerful and direct method by which communication could be conducted up the line.

Except for his influence on the later stages of the Western Electric Company study, Warner's own work was primarily devoted to community research. Through the support of the Committee on Industrial Physiology, community research programs were conducted in Newburyport, Massachusetts; County Clare, Ireland; and Nat-

chez, Mississippi. Only in the first of these was there any continued emphasis on industrial problems. This work, published as a volume in the "Yankee City Series" by Warner and J. O. Low (1947), was more concerned with the implications for community social stratification of the increasing mechanization of the shoe industry than in trying to accomplish, on a factory-wide basis, an organizational study comparable to that done on a small scale in the Bank Wiring Observation Room.

Warner's own interests then and since have been consistently in the phenomena of social stratification. His conceptual influence in the field of applied anthropology in industry has been limited to the use by a number of his students of his taxonomic system of classification of individuals into "status" positions. Essentially the method is intended to provide a bridge from the cultural objects and symbols associated with an individual to the patterns of interaction in which the individual takes part. This means that the relationship—different symbols, different patterns of interaction—is assumed to be the case. Without discussing the adequacy of the methods by which this relationship of symbol and referent is established or the utility of the assumption, it is sufficient to point out here that Warner's influence has been felt in showing the variety of ways that systems of relations in a community in which a member of an industrial organization participates affect his behavior and the behavior of others toward him within the industrial setting. A great deal of energy has been expended by his students in demonstrating that family allegiance, early upbringing, clubs and associational membership, religious affiliation, as well as more generalized cultural patterns, need to be taken into consideration.

The work of this group was facilitated in 1943 through the formation at the University of Chicago of the Committee on Human Relations in Industry, of which Warner was chairman and Burleigh B. Gardner was executive secretary. After completing his research work in Natchez, Mississippi, Gardner went to the Hawthorne Works of the Western Electric Company to be in charge of employee relations research in connection with the personnel counseling program previously referred to. With the background of five years' work at Hawthorne, Gardner and his associates began an extensive program in a number of companies, including such well-known firms as Sears, Roebuck and Company, Container Corporation of America, and Libby, Mac-Neill and Libby. Gardner's own point of view is well represented in his book, *Human Relations in Industry* (1945), which is based primarily upon his Western Electric Company experience and which combines a discussion of the kinds of organizational problems which are found in a large enterprise with a relatively detailed account of the various factors external to industry which affect the attitudes of individuals in the various organizational positions in a company.

The conceptual approach of the members of the committee was broadened to some extent by the early addition to its membership of William F. Whyte, a student of E. D. Chapple and C. M. Arensberg, who had been investigating boys' gangs and the way in which they fitted into the social structure of the city in the North End of Boston (Whyte, 1943). Whyte brought to the group some of the operational procedures developed by Chapple, the most important of which, for his purposes, was the method of determining which person in a contact originated or initiated action for another individual or for a group of individuals. He also employed descriptively quantitative categorizations of these relationships in

terms of the frequency and duration with which they occurred. These methods were reinforced by more explicit awareness of the application of semantics to the analysis of interview material based again upon Chapple's conceptual scheme. The combination of these two approaches resulted in an extremely fertile period of research investigation, in later years primarily carried out by Whyte and his group.

Gardner devoted a great deal of his time to work with Sears, Roebuck and Company in association with James C. Worthy of the Sears personnel department. After several years' work with the committee, Gardner left the University of Chicago to be a full-time private consultant in applied anthropology; and William F. Whyte became the new executive secretary. With Whyte's later departure to join the staff of the New York State School of Industrial Relations, Cornell University, the research activity of the Committee on Human Relations in Industry was markedly reduced. Whyte, however, has continued to apply his methods to other industries at Cornell, with the exception that his work is increasingly oriented toward problems of collective bargaining and industrial relations generally.

It is difficult to summarize the work of much of this group because of the number of different situations which they have described. Yet it must be realized that primarily they are publishers of case material, with a twofold emphasis—on reporting the case and on emphasizing the importance to its solution of an understanding of human relations principles and techniques.

Among the more important reports published by this group were: "The Man in the Middle: Positions and Problems of the Foreman," by Gardner and Whyte (1945); "From Conflict to Cooperation: A Study in Union-Management Relations" (the so-called "Buchs-

baum case"), which was written by
Whiteford, Whyte, and Gardner and
incorporated statements by Mr. Buchsbaum, president of S. Buchsbaum and
Company, Samuel Laderman, president
and manager, and Sidney Garfield,
business agent and financial secretary
of the International Chemical Workers
Union, Local 241, AF of L (Buchsbaum *et al.*, 1946); Whyte's *Human
Relations in the Restaurant Industry*
(1948*a*); and such representative articles as "Incentive for Productivity: The
Case of the Bundy Tubing Company,"
by W. F. Whyte (1948*b*); "The Industrial Rate Buster: A Characterization,"
by Melville Dalton (1948); "Restriction of Output and Social Cleavage in
Industry," by Collins, Dalton, and Roy
(1946); and recently "The Collective
Bargaining Process: A Human Relations Analysis," by Sidney Garfield and
W. F. Whyte (1951); and "Pattern for
Industrial Peace," by W. F. Whyte
(1951).

This list is by no means a complete
bibliography. It is given, however, to
provide the text for a brief summary in
terms of applied anthropology of the
principal conclusions which the group
has achieved.

Their findings fall into two categories: First, those which contribute to
our increased understanding of the
problems affecting individuals in given
positions within the organizational
structure, such as the monograph on
the position of the foreman; or which
show the predisposing influence of participation in other organizational structures on the individual's behavior in
the industrial situation. Dalton's study
of the rate buster is a good example of
the latter. He shows how conformity
with group-imposed patterns of restriction of output were characteristic of
individuals of urban, ethnic, and, in
this specific study, Catholic background, while those who were noncon-
formist had Protestant, frequently rural,

backgrounds with a somewhat higher
socioeconomic status, and their interaction outside the job was limited almost entirely to the immediate family.
These studies and the many incidents
described in the writings of the group
re-emphasize the importance of examining the total interaction pattern of an
individual if we are to understand his
behavior within any single institution.
Their interest, therefore, in these researches is upon isolating and describing the various factors in the social
situation which tend to differentiate the
individual's reaction pattern; and from
this analysis—and only incidentally—do
they proceed to an examination of how
changes might be brought about in a
described situation.

The second category of the group's
studies has to do with the changes
which have taken place in a company,
either as the result of the pressure of circumstances or in some instances as the result of deliberately
imposed change—usually, however,
change which is not the result of recommendations of the applied anthropologists. Of these, one of the best known
is the Buchsbaum case, in which the
owner of the company, who had fought
unionization bitterly, was converted to
the acceptance of a union during the
process of negotiations to settle a strike.
Upon his conversion, he changed his
behavior and that of his supervisors,
working out a highly effective pattern
of co-operation with the union. With
the acceptance of the union by Mr.
Buchsbaum, marked changes took place
in the organizational structure of the
plant and the union, which brought
about much higher production and a
high degree of morale.

This case epitomizes to a considerable extent the approach to the management of change which is characteristic of the Gardner-Whyte group. They
follow quite closely the prescriptions of
F. J. Roethlisberger (1941), the princi-

pal follower of Elton Mayo in this country, who believes that only by the process of conversion—or as he would call it "understanding"—can improvements in industrial relations or in organizational effectiveness be achieved. Gardner and Whyte have developed techniques for securing this kind of change in an individual, which they have used with considerable success in a number of reported situations. Essentially, these are adaptations of the historical events in which Mr. Buchsbaum took part: namely, a period of intensive interviewing (in his case, by the union leaders) both of the supervisor and of those whom he supervises, with the primary emphasis upon developing in the supervisor sufficient emotional stability through his adjustment to the investigators (who are the interviewers) that he can meet with his workers and allow them to act upon him—to tell him to his face their grievances and the problems that they attribute to him. By stage-managing this group situation, the investigators have found that in many instances they have been able to get the supervisor to accept intellectually and adapt emotionally to the group's "letting its hair down," and the situation is said to have a marked cathartic effect on all concerned. Because of the emotional quality of the interaction at such a meeting, the process of understanding the kinds of problems in which the individuals find themselves is accelerated; the authors state that, temporarily at least, they obtain an improvement in the relationships of the supervisor to his workers.

In effect, this procedure is an extension to group practice of the counseling technique worked out at the Western Electric Company. Preparatory to this group meeting, at which a kind of confession and absolution are obtained, the counseling process is going on both for the supervisor and, to a lesser extent, for his workers, and the Gardner-Whyte

group has many sage comments on differential treatment from their experience with this procedure. They have consequently been interested in experimenting with various techniques by which changes in behavior can be achieved through the use of group activities. Argyris and Taylor have described one investigation of this sort (1951), conducted under the direction of Whyte, which they call the "member-centered conference," at which people from various levels and various departments within the organization meet together regularly to discuss such material as they wish, with the function of the leader being merely to make sure that a "permissive" atmosphere exists and that the individuals are free to talk and formulate their problems and attitudes toward one another explicitly. This work is akin to much of that being done in the field of so-called "group dynamics" in social psychology and may well prove to be useful for some kinds of situations.

From an anthropological point of view, however, these researches, although extremely suggestive, are self-limiting as they are presently carried out. Since the aim of science is to predict, the question as yet unanswered is: Under what *specific* organizational conditions is a given social technique—like the member-centered conference—indicated? In their work on the collective bargaining process, Garfield and Whyte describe a number of instances in which a certain sequence of behaviors by given individuals produces results, i.e., in facilitating the successful accomplishment of the collective bargaining process. They also show, in other cases quoted in this work, instances in which a given sequence does not produce success. The problem this group has not yet set itself is the precise description of the conditions which can lead us to predict that organizational situation A requires a sequence of interactions by given individuals of type X. In other words, we need to advance from the intuitive formulations of the skilled clinician to the objective and abstract method of the scientist or engineer.

This lack of systematic examination of organizational structure seems to be produced by two factors; first, in a very real sense these investigators have been unwilling to follow out analytically the implications of the tight controls imposed by cultural process and technique on individuals of given personalities. Although intuitively they seem to be well aware of the importance of cultural factors, by failing to describe them systematically and abstractly, they have not grasped the potentialities of producing change by altering them. Second, as in the case of the Mayo group, they have in effect placed their bets on the conversion process; and, by so doing, have accentuated their unwillingness to define and to utilize to the maximum the analysis of interaction patterns within their cultural context. They thus ignore the very troublesome fact that susceptibility to conversion is relatively rare in the general population and that in any case it requires for success a kind of human relations skill in the practitioner which is also very infrequently found. There is no question that some people achieve a better adjustment to those with whom they have to work, whether as supervisors or as members of a working team, by intensive "therapy." On the other hand, if applied anthropology is to depend upon this as its primary weapon, it is faced with failure both as a science and as a discipline of social utility. Conversion, or the achievement of "insight" or "understanding," by itself is not enough; it may merely make possible a more sophisticated state of frustration for the individual. The fact is that, unless the structure changes, the change in attitude has little lasting impact, and structural changes involve systematic

alteration of the human organization through its controlling cultural techniques and routines. Applied anthropology, if it is to be truly scientific, must be able to secure its successes without reliance on the intellectual and emotional sophistication of the members of any given institution.

Somewhat to one side of the investigators mentioned, yet developing out of the same sources, is the work of E. D. Chapple and his associates. The separation is twofold; first, because Chapple has developed a general theory of anthropology of which his industrial work represents only one aspect, and, second, because his theory is built upon, and restricted to the use of, a thoroughgoing operational method (Chapple and Arensberg, 1940; Chapple and Coon, 1942).

Initially, Chapple made the assumption that the phenomena of human relations could be reduced to the interaction of individuals; and by limiting himself to the observation of what could be observed—namely, the manifestation of response activity and its cessation—he was able to measure with accuracy the time durations of such periods of action and inaction which make up the interaction of a given individual. Not only could the durations of action and inaction, response and lack of response, be measured with a stop watch or any other time-recording device, but also one could classify these alternating actions and inactions by their sequence positions in relation to the action-inaction pattern of another person. This means that one can determine which of two persons initiates an action by observing that one of them acts after both have been inactive. Similarly, when both are acting at the same time, one can determine which of the two dominates the other by outacting him: that is, by persisting in action until the other person has stopped his overt behavior.

This is not the place to discuss the general findings obtained by the measurement of interaction. It is sufficient to state that in the industrial field two types of investigation have been conducted, the first being limited to what might be called "macroscopic" measurements of interaction, namely, the durations of interaction sequences between two or more persons, the duration of the period of time during which they do not interact, from which one can then compute the frequency, and the classification of such events in terms of which of two or more persons takes the initiative in beginning it. The other type of study, which might be called "microscopic," involves the detailed measurement of the interaction of two or more persons within any single contact or event. These measurements are obtained by the use of a computing machine developed for the purpose, called the Interaction Chronograph, which measures—most commonly in the interview, but actually in any type of contact—the quantitative aspect of the adjustment of two or more persons: their activity relative to inactivity, their pace or tempo, the degree and quantitative characteristics of their adjustment to one another, the relative degree of initiative they show with regard to one another, as well as the relative degree of dominance, and, finally, a series of derived factors such as flexibility, capacity to listen, and so on.

The point to be stressed in regard to Chapple's work is that all these measurements and classifications of sequence are strictly operational in character. There is no concern with intent or other intuitive judgments on the part of the observer. The recording is done on the basis of observations of overt activity, reflected through sound and/or the action of skeletal muscles. Those other investigators who have used some of these operations have done so more on an intuitive basis than in strictly

operational terms, notably W. F. Whyte, whose work thereby can be regarded more as clinical in nature than as quantitative in the usual meaning of the word.

The work of Chapple and his associates can be divided, as stated above, into two types, although, conceptually, the two are part of a single system, since the quantitative characteristics of interaction of two people *within* a contact provide measurable indicators of what, for lack of a better word, might be called the "intensity" or "quality" of the relationship. He therefore introduces other dimensions with which to differentiate relationships besides those afforded from measures of the duration of interaction or its frequency. Because of the practical problems involved in exploring each line of investigation to the full, and particularly in developing a comprehensive understanding in quantitative terms of the subtleties of the adjustments of two persons during any contact, these two types of researches have to a large extent been pursued independently.

In dealing with the quantitative aspects of relationships on the macroscopic level, the group lays great stress upon the controlling effect of cultural tendencies and processes. This means that the first task of an investigator in the industrial field is to secure a complete description of the order of actions as they occur spatially within the physical layout of the factory, in flow-chart form, as they involve the physical processing either of materials or of pieces of paper or whatever requires an action of one person before another person can be in a position to act. Although much of this material is unpublished, F. L. W. Richardson, Jr., has illustrated the use of these flow charts in several factory studies, not always to the level of specificity with which they are actually recorded (*Southern New England Telephone Company;* Richardson and

Walker, 1948). The first step, therefore, in the analysis is to determine the flow from person to person, without, however, including a detailed analysis of what a person does in substeps while the piece of paper or the material is at his particular work station, except to record the time aspects involved. The resulting flow charts are, therefore, unlike those found in industrial engineering, since the steps are limited to those which involve contacts between people or sequences between people. On the basis of this analysis, quantitative information is obtained about the contacts themselves, either by direct observation, as illustrated in the article by Horsfall and Arensberg called "Teamwork and Productivity in a Shoe Factory" (1949), or through the administration of contact questionnaires or other methods of obtaining records of the time spent between people in the organization (Chapple, 1949a).

On this structural foundation, the rates of occurrence of events are analyzed to determine whether they fall within defined statistical limits, i.e., what other investigators like to call "established routines," or whether they show wide fluctuation and thus exhibit an erratic occurrence on whose frequency or duration an individual cannot depend with any regularity. By applying quantitative procedures in terms of the theory of equilibrium, the significantly erratic points in the organization are located and the causes of this erratic occurrence isolated (Chapple, 1941). Most frequently this is due to the inadequate working-out of the routine techniques and processes which make up the cultural environment of the factory, and the process of achieving emotional and interactional stability of the individuals is achieved by reorganizing the cultural sequences involved. This may involve changes in the organizational responsibility of supervisors, since the tradition in indus-

try is to set up supervisory units in terms of supposed similarities in function or nature of the cultural object or process. They fail to organize them in terms of the human relations flow and the rates of contact or lack of them which derive from the cultural necessities themselves. Secondarily, problems arise from the personalities of the individuals as they are brought together in interaction due to the requirements of the cultural process. Persons whose interaction patterns (personalities) are incompatible commonly need to be separated by some cultural means or other.

The basic assumption in this approach to human relations in industry is that attitudes and emotional reactions, as well as productivity, are functions of the interactional situation and that this interactional situation represents the interplay of personality and cultural process and technique. Consequently, unlike the members of the Gardner-Whyte school, the facilitation of change by members of the Chapple group is primarily brought about by changing the interactional system through changing the cultural patterns and, secondarily, by the transfer of personalities to situations within which their interactional pattern makes it possible for them to adjust. The general theory of culture employed is described by Chapple and Coon in *Principles of Anthropology*, in which book, because of their belief that the term "culture" had become for the anthropologist a portmanteau, and thereby almost meaningless, word, they developed at length the specific ways in which techniques and processes directly affect the interactions of persons, without ever mentioning the word "culture." This tour de force led some reviewers to object to the title of the book: "It couldn't be anthropology since culture is nowhere treated."

In spite of the ambivalences of authorship of this background paper and of a conceptual scheme, it is worth emphasizing to an anthropological audience the remarkable resources which one has in bringing about social change if one changes the cultural patterns. Much of the work in the field of applied anthropology illustrates the subtle dependence of human relations systems on environmental and technological patterns and the way in which whole social organizations change as a consequence of changes in one of these patterns. In industry, by determining the areas of stress and the cultural processes and techniques which control the relationships undergoing stress, it is possible to bring about substantial and significant changes in the relationships of people in the organization. This can be done, moreover, without requiring the individual to be converted to the investigator's own understanding of human relations and very often without the individual's being any the wiser. By changing layout, changing material handling, changing methods of keeping records—changing a hundred and one things which make up the culture of an industrial organization—a reorganization and re-formation of relationships can be achieved naturally and inevitably (Chapple and Wright, 1946). Needless to say, to make such cultural changes stick, one has to develop techniques to see that the old patterns do not re-emerge through the natural tendency of systems of human relations to return to a previous state of equilibrium. But this merely means regarding the methods of management as cultural processes and building such techniques into the supervisory system.

The work of Chapple and his associates on the microscopic level in dealing with the adjustment of individuals to one another by measuring their interaction with the Interaction Chronograph cannot be described in detail here (Chapple, 1949*b*). It is sufficient

to point out that the method of measuring the interaction of an individual with another under standardized interactional condition—that is, using a standardized interview in terms of both what is said and the quantitative aspects of when and how long—provides an extremely useful description of the personality and, from a practical point of view, has proved to be very successful in the field of the selection and placement of individuals in all types of positions from those of clericals or sales girls or factory operators to people in the higher realms of management.

The utility of the procedure becomes maximal when it is part of an organizational study. Since it becomes possible not merely to place people in the organizational position for which their personality fits them but also to define the organizational position in the same quantitative terms as the personality, one can then define and prescribe a given type of personality for a particular organizational position. This means that the organizational structure can be reinforced with an individual who is capable of carrying out the interactions needed to make it operate effectively. By appraising the individuals one comes in contact with in these terms, one can use this instrument as a diagnostic tool in association with the analysis of the organizational structure and, through statistical techniques, determine whether a given situation is created by cultural and organizational stresses or by the personality limitations of a given individual.

This paper does not pretend to provide a complete analysis and summary of all the work done in the field of industry by applied anthropologists. There are investigators following traditional anthropological lines who have not been mentioned; rather, I have attempted to describe briefly the main currents and directions taken by the research work in this field. In summing up the progress to date, it is perhaps worth while to stress the potentialities for research by anthropologists in industry. This is particularly true for those persons who are interested in the specific impact of culture through its techniques, processes, and the like on human relations. The individual investigator has available a wide variety of cultural factors and a multiplicity of industrial and business organizations built upon them within the continental limits of the United States. More important, he can conduct experiments as he wishes, particularly if, after some apprenticeship, he enters the industrial field as a consultant, since experiments, planned or unplanned, in the adaptation to change are a necessary condition of business existence.

A further advantage of industrial research is the fact that the anthropologist can study his subjects with the greatest of ease. They are usually fixed in one work place from seven to eight hours each day, and, as a result, one can rely upon direct observation of human relations rather than trying to reconstruct what one would like to observe by reliance on the semantically booby-trapped and time-consuming analysis of interviews.

Moreover, in business or industry or government, for that matter, on the job in any case, the anthropologist is dealing with a central activity of people, not merely because such a great proportion of the day is devoted to interaction within it, but also because the job provides within it the major sources of stress in our society. And, pleasantly enough, it is susceptible to the traditional skills of the anthropologist as well as his traditional interests—a hardboiled and hardheaded description of the culture of a group in the broadest sense, or, if you prefer, of the social organization of an ongoing group. Once the anthropologist gets over his nostalgia for the vanishing primitive, he will find that the industrial situation affords him a magnificent opportunity to improve his understanding of changes in human relations, not merely through observation over a long period of time, but also through the use of deliberate and controlled experiment.

REFERENCES

ARGYRIS, CHRIS, and TAYLOR, GRAHAM. 1951. "The Member-centered Conference as a Research Method. II," *Human Organization*, X, No. 1, 22–27.

BUCHSBAUM, HERBERT J.; LADERMAN, SAMUEL; GARFIELD, SIDNEY; WHITEFORD, ANDREW H.; WHYTE, W. F.; and GARDNER, BURLEIGH B. 1946. "From Conflict to Cooperation: A Study in Union-Management Relations," *Applied Anthropology*, Vol. V, No. 4 (entire issue).

CHAPPLE, E. D. 1941. "Organization Problems in Industry," *Applied Anthropology*, I, No. 1, 2–9.

——. 1949a. "Field Methods and Techniques," *Human Organization*, VIII, No. 2, 22–28.

——. 1949b. "The Interaction Chronograph: Its Evolution and Present Application," *Personnel*, XXV, No. 4, 295–307.

CHAPPLE, E. D., and ARENSBERG, C. M. 1940. "Measuring Human Relations: An Introduction to the Study of the Interaction of Individuals," *Genetic Psychology Monographs*, XXII, 3–147.

CHAPPLE, E. D., and COON, C. S. 1942. *Principles of Anthropology*. New York: Henry Holt & Co.

CHAPPLE, E. D., and WRIGHT, E. F. 1946. *How To Supervise People in Industry*. Chicago and New York: National Foremen's Institute.

COLLINS, ORVIS; DALTON, MELVILLE; and ROY, DONALD. 1946. "Restriction of

Output and Social Cleavage in Industry," *Applied Anthropology*, V, No. 3, 1–14.

DALTON, MELVILLE. 1948. "The Industrial Rate-Buster: A Characterization," *Applied Anthropology*, VII, No. 1, 1–16.

FOLLETT, MARY PARKER. 1942. *Dynamic Administration: The Collected Papers of Mary Parker Follett*. Edited by HENRY C. METCALF and L. URWICK. New York and London: Harper & Bros.

GARDNER, BURLEIGH B. 1945. *Human Relations in Industry*. Chicago: Richard D. Irwin, Inc.

GARDNER, BURLEIGH B., and WHYTE, WILLIAM F. 1945. "The Man in the Middle: Position and Problems of the Foreman," *Applied Anthropology*, Vol. IV, No. 2 (entire issue).

GARFIELD, SIDNEY, and WHYTE, WILLIAM F. 1951. "The Collective Bargaining Process: A Human Relations Analysis. IV," *Human Organization*, X, No. 1, 28–32.

HORSFALL, ALEXANDER B., and ARENSBERG, CONRAD M. 1949. "Teamwork and Productivity in a Shoe Factory," *Human Organization*, VIII, No. 1, 13–25.

MAYO, ELTON. 1933. *The Human Problems of an Industrial Civilization*. New York: Macmillan Co.

RICHARDSON, F. L. W., JR., and WALKER, CHARLES. 1948. *Human Relations in an Expanding Company*. New Haven: Yale University, Labor and Management Center.

ROETHLISBERGER, F. J. 1941. *Management and Morale*. Cambridge: Harvard University Press.

ROETHLISBERGER, F. J., and DICKSON, W. J. 1939. *Management and the Worker: An Account of a Research Program Conducted by the Western Electric Company, Hawthorne Works, Chicago*. Cambridge: Harvard University Press.

ROGERS, C. R. 1942. *Counseling and Psychotherapy*. Boston: Houghton Mifflin Co.

WARNER, W. L., and LOW, J. O. 1947. *The Social System of the Modern Factory*. New Haven: Yale University Press.

WHITEHEAD, T. N. 1938. *The Industrial Worker: A Statistical Study of Human Relations in a Group of Manual Workers*. Cambridge: Harvard University Press.

WHYTE, WILLIAM FOOTE. 1943. *Street Corner Society*. Chicago: University of Chicago Press.

———. 1948a. *Human Relations in the Restaurant Industry*. New York: McGraw-Hill Book Co., Inc.

———. 1948b. "Incentives for Productivity: The Bundy Tubing Company Case," *Applied Anthropology*, VII, No. 2, 1–16.

———. 1951. *Pattern for Industrial Peace*. New York: Harper & Bros.

Applied Anthropology in Government: United States

By EDWARD A. KENNARD and GORDON MACGREGOR

THE INTENSIVE application of the concepts and approach of the discipline of anthropology has been undertaken in the administrative work of the federal government within the last twenty years. The first intensive anthropological studies for administrative planning and its effects were initiated in 1934 by the Bureau of Indian Affairs of the United States Department of Interior and the Soil Conservation Service of the Department of Agriculture. However, there had been an early attempt by the federal government to apply anthropology to gain an understanding of the American Indians for the better management of their affairs nearly seventy years ago, through the foresight of J. Wesley Powell. This early explorer of the West foresaw the basic cross-cultural conflict between the ways of life of the incoming American pioneer and those of the Indian tribesmen on the plains. When he was selected to organize and become the first chief of the Bureau of American Ethnology of the Smithsonian Institution, he initiated ethnological studies of Indian cultures for the use of the Bureau of Indian Affairs. The Bureau of American Ethnology, following the pattern of interest of anthropology of the time, subsequently devoted itself more and more exclusively to studies of reconstruction of the earlier ways of life of the Indians.

Little use of this work was made by the administration serving the Indians.

One other early attempt to utilize anthropology in connection with federal administration was made in the Philippines. From 1906 to 1910 ethnographic studies were carried on under the direction of Dr. Albert Jenks, for the Department of Interior, to apprise the government of the peoples, conditions, and cultures of this complex archipelago. The survey was terminated under local pressure from persons overly sensitive to the possible effect of comparisons that would be drawn between the population of the Philippine Islands and other more uniformly civilized peoples.

The first intensive application of modern cultural anthropological concepts and techniques to administrative problems of the federal government was introduced by Mr. John Collier, commissioner of the Bureau of Indian Affairs. After counsel with leading anthropologists of the country, he requested two ethnologists of the Bureau of American Ethnology to serve as consultants. Subsequently, the late Scudder McKeel and four other anthropologists were appointed by the Indian Bureau to form an Applied Anthropology Unit. The special responsibility of this unit was the investigation of the nature of the existing leadership and informal government patterns of American Indian groups on their reservations. On the basis of these studies (Applied Anthropology Unit, 1936–38), recommendations were made on the patterns for the new Indian councils for local self-government, authorized by the Indian Reorganization Act of 1934. However, while the research was in progress, organization agents of the Indian Service were discussing model plans based on English common law for tribal constitutions and councils with Indian leaders. Constitutions were drafted, subjected to tribal vote, councils elected, charters approved for tribal incorporation, and tribal business ventures entered into before research on the existing social structure and evaluation of the degree of each tribe's acculturation could be completed. As a result, anthropologists did little of the total planning that went into the formation of constitutions and councils.

In retrospect it is clear that the anthropologists who did undertake research before organization took place were more interested in the still functioning Indian patterns of leadership and social structure than in the new patterns and trends of social groupings and the new social values that were developing under reservation conditions. The personal disorganization stemming from reservation life and the tribal cleavages that resulted from differential degrees of acculturation undergone by the so-called "full-blood" and "mixed-blood" groups as a consequence of varying experiences with the dominant American way of life were not fully appreciated. More important, the Indian administration was envisaged as an agency of American culture directly involved in a clash with Indian cultures, rather than as an integral part of the social universe of the Indian on the reservation. The whole pattern of reciprocal relationships between Indians and Indian Service was lost sight of in facing the glaring conflicts that existed.

In the same period of the mid-thirties, a larger number of anthropologists were also employed with other social scientists, economists, and natural resources specialists in the planning of economic development programs for Indian reservations. In a unit known as Technical Cooperation—Bureau of Indian Affairs of the Soil Conservation Service, United States Department of Agriculture, assigned to the study of Indian lands, teams of scientists analyzed the resources, their contemporary utilization, the history of resource development, Indian economic development in the fields of agriculture and cattle-raising (which on an intensive, commercial scale were new to their cultures), traditional and social organization in relation to economic activity, education and administrative relationships and policy (Technical Cooperation, 1937–40). Out of this came a picture of the irrational, vacillating policies of land use and ownership which have marked American Indian policy, the relatively small degree of Indian utilization of their resources, and the almost total lack of real understanding by Indians of the techniques of an agricultural economy or of the principles or motivations underlying successful agricultural enterprise in the American economic system. Indians working in industry and living in urban centers were also studied for their economic and social adjustment. Most significant was the Indian pattern of achieving either a higher or a lower performance compared with the norm of white workers and the instability of Indian social adaptation under urban conditions. Indians moved off reservations for economic reasons but usually returned for social reasons, i.e., rejection in the urban environment and attraction of the familiar reservation environment.

In general, the anthropological studies in the research and planning of the Technical Cooperation unit revealed on broad economic and social levels a situation observed by anthropologists interested in political leadership and groupings, namely, that the significant pattern of social relationships, the social groupings, and the attitudes and values prevailing in Indian social motivation and behavior continued, after nearly one hundred years of contact with Indian Service administration, to stem from Indian ways of life. Anthropologists insisted in their reports, therefore, that Indian administration would have to recognize the still functioning ways of Indian life and Indian thought if any real success were to be achieved in promoting change, particularly economic change, toward greater adaptation to the dominant cultural environment surrounding them. It was clearly evident that, as administration and other forces of white life insisted upon complete conformity to American life-patterns which opposed Indian values and cherished Indian institutions, the Indians built resistances by removing themselves from co-operative effort and assuming an inviolate position of indifference or by creating social fronts behind which Indian life continued.

From the anthropologists' insistence that functioning Indian life be recognized as a real force to be reckoned with, there arose a curious opposition on the part of administrators to anthropologists themselves. The administrators, failing to understand the significance of expressions of traditional ways of behavior by Indian groups, assumed that anthropologists, in insisting on recognizing these, were arguing for preservation of aboriginal Indian life. Many administrators and missionaries have believed for years that customs and symbols of Indian life that were in opposition to assimilation should at least be ignored, if not actively suppressed by education, regulation, and sometimes force. This stems from one of the major tenets of the American people

which underlies the idea of the American "melting pot," namely, that distinct behavioral differences cannot be tolerated. Every effort has been brought to bear upon every group coming into this country to conform to the theoretical American pattern. The value of conformity was bound to produce in American administrators a strong emphasis upon assimilation of the American Indian. The failure of the anthropologists in not fully appreciating the role of conformity in the American value system, which most administrators shared, and the lack of basic indoctrination of administrators in the pertinent concepts of the discipline of anthropology have led to a long and continuing misunderstanding between the two groups.

The Education Division of the Bureau of Indian Affairs has made continuous and effective use for the last seventeen years of a few anthropologists on its staff in relating its program to contemporary Indian cultures, languages, art, history, and acculturation. Stimulated by the belief that young Indians should know the history and traditional background of their own tribes as well as that of other tribes and cultural groups, Willard W. Beatty, director of education, assigned Underhill and others (Beatty, n.d.–1946) to write simple histories and ethnographic descriptions for Indian school use. These authentic texts, based on anthropological studies, immediately became popular in schools throughout the nation. Kennard and Young developed practical orthographies of the Navaho, Hopi, and Siouan languages for use in bilingual school texts. The Navaho orthography was also used in a Navaho newspaper. These were used for developing a greater facility in reading.

Sterner and Macgregor (1938–40) undertook studies of high-school graduates of Indian boarding schools to ascertain the cultural and social determinants of their postschool adjustments and the utilization of their vocational training. The desire to re-establish social relationships and the availability of natural resources in their Indian communities were found to be stronger determinants in influencing their decisions in postschool life than specific industrial training. Studies by anthropologists were also made for other divisions of the bureau on systems of land tenure and distribution, on the relation of social groupings and of Indian land-use practices to proposed irrigation systems, and on traditional tribal and subtribal boundaries. J. and R. Useem and Macgregor (1943) conducted a study of cultural determinants of Sioux Indians employed as industrial and sugarbeet field workers in wartime and as residents in small cities at the beginning of World War II.

The most profound work of anthropologists in the Indian Service was undertaken in the Research on Indian Education. This was a co-operative project between the Bureau of Indian Affairs and the Committee on Human Development of the University of Chicago. This project undertook interdiscipline studies of 1,000 children in twelve reservation communities representing five Indian tribes. The research, utilizing primarily the disciplines of anthropology, medicine, psychology, and psychiatry, was set up as a scientific analysis and an aid for the improvement of Indian Service policy, administration, and educational programs. Professional scientists were aided by administrators, teachers, agriculturists, nurses, and others in gaining the field data. Analysis of the history, cultural background, and contemporary social organization and interpersonal relationships of twelve communities and investigation of the personalities of children by means of a battery of cross-cultural and projective tests, interviews, and observation were carried out. Re-

ports were made of the basic findings in four volumes. Anthropologists collaborating with psychiatrists co-ordinated the total project, directed the field studies, and prepared the reports. A second phase of the research was jointly undertaken by the Bureau of Indian Affairs and the Society of Applied Anthropology. This phase was concerned with the interpretation of findings at the administrative level and with the formulation of recommendations. The major part of this work was carried on by Dr. Laura Thompson, who has written a report of the entire project (1951).

The Bureau of Indian Affairs has also employed an anthropologist in the Missouri River Basin Unit. This was one of several investigation units of bureaus of the Department of the Interior established to determine and evaluate the effects of constructing new dams and reservoirs, in the program for the control of floods, irrigation, and development of power of the Missouri River watershed. In the Indian Service Investigation Unit this anthropologist analyzed social patterns, attitudes toward resettlement and future occupations, new administrative patterns, and acculturation of Indians forced to remove to new lands beyond the construction areas. Attitude studies revealed the degree of dependency built up over the years by the Indians on the Bureau of Indian Affairs and the strength of ties of Indians to one another and to the residue of tribal lands still in their possession. However, the trend toward assimilation in the larger local white society was also definitely clear.

The application of anthropology by the United States Department of Agriculture to the problems of rural people began in 1934 under the Soil Conservation Service, with socio-economic surveys of the Navaho, Spanish-American, and Anglo-American people in the middle Rio Grande Valley of New Mexico and Arizona. These surveys were undertaken by economists, rural sociologists, and cultural anthropologists to analyze the nature of the dependency of these peoples of separate racial and cultural antecedents upon their land resources. The three groups had come into the area in succession, dispossessing predecessors and, later, except for the Anglo-Americans, accommodating themselves to those who followed. The anthropologists in this research, which was reported to the Department of Agriculture in the Tewa Basin studies, revealed the predominant cultural factors which operated in land-use practices and resource exploitation among these groups living in a common geographic area. Anthropologists also contributed to these studies an approach to land and people as an organic whole. This revelation of the role of culture led to the use of anthropologists by the Department of Agriculture in other studies of rural communities, where they shed much light on the agricultural heritage of many ethnic groups. American regional groups were also shown to be carrying agricultural practices from one area to another. John Provinse (1942) and Solon Kimball, of the Soil Conservation Service, did important work on the Navaho Reservation in showing the relation of traditional social groups to delineated land areas, which led to redistricting of the reservation for land-management purposes.

The pioneering work of anthropologists for the Department of Agriculture in the Southwest soon led to their use on a national basis. When the Bureau of Agricultural Economics became the research and planning unit of the department, M. L. Wilson, then undersecretary, and Dr. Carl Taylor, an eminent rural sociologist in charge of the Division of Farm Population and Rural Welfare, gave strong support to the utilization of cultural anthropologists in the research. Multi-discipline studies, which also utilized the discipline of social psychology, were made of six selected rural communities to evaluate factors of stability and instability in rural areas. The anthropological approach again led to the study of the total community rather than of segmented social groups or areas of social problems.

Anthropologists were also sent by the Bureau of Agricultural Economics to the Columbia River Basin to participate in interdepartmental economic and social investigations. Lloyd Fisher made a notable study of levels of living and culturally patterned use of income, reported as one of the twenty-eight publications of the Columbia River Basin Investigations. Anthropologists, with others, made comparative studies of settlement types in concentrated, dispersed, and linear villages of America. Analysis of Farm Security Projects of the Department of Agriculture were also examined in California, Arizona, and Montana for their success in terms of permanent settlement and in terms of supervision by guidance or by management of the settlers' activities. These studies have not yet been brought together or published, owing to interruption by World War II.

The outbreak of the war brought many anthropologists into the service of the government, where, usually in collaboration with other social scientists, they were called upon to contribute either special knowledge of the cultures or areas that had long been one of the primary fields of anthropological investigation or the theoretical basis for handling problems dealing with people of other cultures.

One of the first wartime agencies that utilized anthropologists in handling its problems was the War Relocation Authority, charged with the management of the camps to which the Pacific Coast Japanese were removed after the declaration of martial law. Arensberg (1942), Embree (1943), Leighton (1945), and Spicer (1946) all participated at different periods. Spicer has given a full account of the problems and the work of anthropologists as community analysts in his final War Relocation Authority Report on the life and feelings of the Japanese toward the centers in *Impounded People*. Leighton, in his study, *The Governing of Men*, which describes the research at Camp Poston, makes explicit an important point that was largely ignored in the early experience of anthropologists in the Bureau of Indian Affairs, namely, that it is equally important to study the assumptions, social organization, and behavior patterns of the administrative group, as well as of those administered, since the two groups constitute an interacting continuum. This point was further reinforced by the experience of anthropologists in military government in the Navy, as reported by Useem (1946), Whiting (1946), and others.

In any government agency it is also important to define the role of the anthropologist in relation to those who have the authority and responsibility for decisions and actions. Leighton's account of the "Bureau of Sociological Research" at Poston, its relationship to the administration and the administered, and the problem of having its role clearly defined and understood by both groups is almost a typical case, the difficulties increased by the pressures of a nation at war. But the problem is always present, and, even in instances where the anthropologist's role is clearly defined in relation to an administrative organization, it will not necessarily stay so defined with changes in personnel and changing policy orientations. Keeping the role defined is a continuous task.

During the war anthropologists also participated with other social scientists in Civil Affairs Training Schools to prepare officers for duty in occupied areas. In this work these scientists drew on theoretical formulations and descriptive materials and also improvised techniques utilizing immigrant communities to demonstrate cultural differences in concrete social (Kluckhohn, 1949) situations. The training of administrators and the systematic gathering of information about the cultures of the contemporary Micronesians continued after the war when these islands of the Pacific Ocean became the responsibility of the United States. The School of Naval Administration at Stanford, in preparing administrators for their assignments in Micronesia, placed heavy reliance upon anthropologists as advisers (Spoehr, 1951). That the transfer of administrative responsibility for the Trust Territory of the Pacific to the Department of the Interior will not mean the abandonment of this approach is indicated by the appointment of H. G. Barnett to take charge of the programs in applied anthropology.

The Office of War Information utilized the services of anthropologists in conjunction with other social scientists in understanding the cultural background of people in Europe and the Far East, the function of given symbols and themes in their national lives, and the kinds of behavior that might be expected of military and home-front groups under the conditions of combat and increasing disruption. The account of the functions and activities of the Foreign Morale Analysis Division in the prosecution of the war against Japan, its relations with the administrative structure, and the problems of communication within the organization have been described by Leighton in *Human Problems in a Changing World* (1949).

Anthropologists also contributed to the analysis of patterned relations that were structured differently in the United States and England, which was designed to reduce friction between allies with common goals (Mead, 1947).

Through the combined efforts of the American Council of Learned Societies and the Linguistic Society of America, the techniques of descriptive linguistics, developed largely by anthropologists working with languages outside the Indo-European family, were applied to the analysis of some thirty-five languages considered essential to the conduct of military operations. As a result, a series of manuals based upon an analysis both of English (the language of the learner) and also of the language to be learned were produced, and the technique of utilizing informant and linguist in the teaching situation became standardized. Much of this work was done within the War Department as well as by contract with the council.

One of the major concerns of anthropological theory has been cultural and social change. Most of our knowledge of the processes involved is historical, derived from archeological or distribution data, with some studies based upon ethnographic description combined with a series of observations recorded at earlier dates. However, there are relatively few studies based upon continuous observation and reporting. Yet this seems one of the most crucial problems that need to be systematically attacked, especially by anthropologists working within the context of the government.

Leighton speculated upon the possibility of developing a systematic approach to the collection, analysis, and reporting of material, gathered by teams of social scientists in various countries geared to trend reporting, that would seek to detect situations of increasing tension and conflict before they were manifested in national or international violence. At the present time, there is a great deal of reporting upon events and developments abroad, through the medium of the Foreign Service and the various intelligence services. However, since most of this material is classified, there is at present no way to verify it. It is possible that this is being done, but, if so, there is no way for the social scientist outside these organizations to know the assumptions, criteria of validity, or interpretations that are placed upon the data.

One of the efforts of the Foreign Service Institute, Department of State (the training division), is to equip members of the Foreign Service and others who go abroad under government auspices with as much social science theory and background information on the peoples and cultures, economies, and political structures as is possible. Anthropologists and linguists are members of the staff as well as those trained in other social science disciplines and the field of administration.

Perhaps one of the most promising developments is the training of a small corps of area specialists. These officers expect to devote the major portion of their careers to serving in one of the major world areas. China, Japan, Southeast Asia, India, Pakistan, the Arabic Near East, and the U.S.S.R. are the areas in which some have already been trained. The prerequisites for becoming an area specialist are a knowledge of the language and a systematic understanding of the civilizations of the area. This training is designed to give the officer control of the major communication system and some awareness of the problems of the peoples and the governments of the area as they define them. The aim is not to make an anthropologist, an economist, or a political scientist of this officer but to equip him to perform his reporting and negotiating functions with as little bias and projection of his own American experience upon the foreign scene as possible (Bennett, 1951).

Similarly, in the training of the technician going abroad under the Point 4 program, the greatest emphasis is placed upon formulations derived largely from anthropology. Since it is impossible to present even a schematic picture of many of the cultures and peoples with whom he will be working, the focus is upon cross-cultural processes. The effort is made to create awareness of this dimension of the problem, so that the technician will learn in the field and will seek the significance of those behaviors that tend to puzzle him or else lead to his rejection of the people he is dealing with. A significant aspect is the effort to make explicit some of the most pervasive of the implicit assumptions and values of American culture that he shares with his group.

Anthropologists are now being employed in the agencies which are responsible for the American Point 4 program. David Rodnick is serving as a consultant to the Mutual Security Agency in regard to the cultural problems involved in the relations of Americans with Europeans. John Embree, before his death, was a consultant to the same agency (then known as Economic Cooperation Administration) in regard to their programs of technical and economic assistance to Southeast Asia. This agency plans to employ a few anthropologists to serve in the field with their local administrative organization in assisting teams of technicians. Similarly, the Technical Cooperation Administration of the Department of State has an anthropologist as an adviser on its program planning staff. It is appointing anthropologists as advisers and research officers to Point 4 country staffs in Latin American, Near Eastern, independent African, and South Asian countries.

Under the United States Scientific and Cultural Cooperation Program the Smithsonian Institution established an Institute of Social Anthropology. This institute has been working in collaboration with the Institute of Inter-American Affairs in its Point 4 program for Latin America. Anthropologists have been sent to Latin-American universities to train local students in becoming social scientists. American anthropologists in these parts have also undertaken research related to the technical assistance programs. Recently, a cross-cultural anthropological analysis (Foster, 1951) of eight co-operative health centers was undertaken in collaboration with the United States Public Health Service. This analysis stressed the culture and attitudes of the peoples toward these programs which were directed by North American and South American medical officers. It demonstrated clearly the necessity for all technicians in any intercultural technical assistance program to understand the basic cultural core and customs (in this case folk medicine and curing practices) before a program involving new concepts can be adapted and carried to the people concerned.

The great problem for the anthropologist is defining his role. Frequently, busy administrators seek a "magic" solution to complex problems that may be badly defined or look to the social scientist as a man who must come up with an "answer" out of a supposed fund of knowledge. It seems to us, particularly in areas where there is less published research than there is on Oceania or the North American Indians, that his value lies primarily in his capacity to learn and to discover patterned relationships that a more specialized approach might overlook.

The great opportunity for the anthropologist lies in the problem of the extent to which purposive change can be introduced, how rapidly, and with what consequences to different segments of the society. This problem provides the opportunity for continuous observation over a period of time, the conscious awareness of the fact that there are certain to be unintended consequences from introduced changes, and the need to discover situations of tension and potential conflict before they become disruptive.

Inevitably, in this kind of situation there will be not only the opportunity but also the necessity of taking into account those characteristics of American behavior that tend to be thrown into bold relief in daily contact and relationship with foreigners in their countries. Since there will be less opportunity for the Americans to live as an encysted group while conducting this kind of program, it would seem to present a series of type cases of cross-cultural processes.

REFERENCES

APPLIED ANTHROPOLOGY UNIT. 1936–38. *Reports Series.* Office of Indian Affairs, U.S. Department of the Interior, Washington, D.C.

ARENSBERG, CONRAD M. 1942. "Report on a Developing Community, Poston, Arizona," *Applied Anthropology,* II, No. 1, 2–21.

BEATTY, W. W. (ed.) n.d.–1946. *Indian Life and Customs.* ("Pamphlets of the Education Division, U.S. Office of Indian Affairs," Nos. 1–6.) Lawrence, Kan.: Haskell Institute.

BENNETT, WENDELL C. 1951. *Area Studies in American Universities.* New York: Social Science Research Council.

EMBREE, JOHN. 1943. "Dealing with Japanese," *Applied Anthropology,* II, No. 2, 37–41.

FOSTER, GEORGE (ed.) 1951. *A Cross-cultural Anthropological Analysis of a Technical Aid Program.* Washington, D.C.: Smithsonian Institution.

KLUCKHOHN, CLYDE. 1949. *Mirror for Man.* New York: Whittlesey House; McGraw-Hill Book Co., Inc.

LEIGHTON, ALEXANDER. 1945. *The Governing of Men.* Princeton: Princeton University Press.

———. 1949. *Human Problems in a Changing World.* New York: E. P. Dutton Co.

MEAD, MARGARET. 1947. "Application of Anthropological Techniques to Cross-national Communication," *Transactions of the New York Academy of Sciences,* Ser. 2, IX, No. 4, 133–52.

PROVINSE, JOHN H. 1942. "Cultural Factors in Land Use Planning" in LA FARGE, O. (ed.), *The Changing Indian,* pp. 55–71. Norman, Okla.: University of Oklahoma Press.

SPICER, EDWARD H. 1946. *Impounded People: Japanese Americans in Relocation Centers.* (W.R.A. Report.) Washington, D.C.: Government Printing Office.

SPOEHR, ALEXANDER. 1951. "Anthropology and the Trust Territory," *Clearinghouse Bulletin,* I, No. 2, 1–3.

STERNER, ARMIN H., and MACGREGOR, GORDON. 1938–40. *Pine Ridge.* (Sherman and Phoenix School Surveys in Indian Education.)

TECHNICAL COOPERATION—BUREAU OF INDIAN AFFAIRS. 1937–40. *Reports Series.* (U.S. Department of Agriculture, Soil Conservation Service.)

THOMPSON, LAURA. 1951. *Personality and Government.* Mexico: Inter-American Institute.

USEEM, JOHN. 1946. "Americans as Governors of Natives in the Pacific," *Journal of Social Issues,* II, No. 3, 39–49.

USEEM, JOHN; MACGREGOR, GORDON; and USEEM, RUTH. 1943. "Wartime Employment and Cultural Adjustments of the Rosebud Sioux," *Applied Anthropology,* II, No. 2, 1–9.

WHITING, JOHN M. 1946. Address at American Anthropological Association Meeting, Chicago.

Applied Anthropology in Government: British Africa

By DARYLL FORDE

INTRODUCTION

In ANY strict sense the phrase "applied anthropology in government" must refer to the actual application of anthropological knowledge by those administratively responsible in the formulation and execution of government policy. There is, as will be seen, considerable direct and indirect evidence that such application has been significant in the administration of British territories in Africa throughout the present century and even before. Such application implies, however, prior investigations and reports involving field and library studies. And it is in connection with the extent to which and the means whereby colonial governments could or should secure anthropological information that could assist and improve public administration that most of the questions concerning applied anthropology arise.

The phrase "applied anthropology" is also sometimes more loosely applied to the introduction of anthropological principles and data by anthropologists themselves, by students of colonial administration, and by politicians and laymen in the public discussion of social issues concerning the administration and development of the peoples of colonial territories. Such an appraisal of issues of colonial policy in anthropological terms must be recognized as normative, in so far as it is concerned with values and approaches which, it is held, ought or ought not to inform colonial policy. Since, however, such public discussion—through political and other pressures and by helping to form the climate of opinion among at least the better-informed section of the British people—affects the outlook and the range of considerations entertained by colonial administrations, this application of anthropological findings in the analysis of colonial development must also be borne in mind. An excellent recent account of the significance of anthropological findings for such discussions is to be found in Dr. Mair's paper on "The Role of the Anthropologist in Non-autonomous Territories" (Mair, 1950).

THE SCOPE OF APPLIED ANTHROPOLOGY IN DEPENDENT TERRITORIES

The scope of applied anthropology must necessarily be vague when the field of anthropological study itself contains a diversity of approaches and objectives and when, in view of the variety of social conditions and administrative forms in different territories, the levels of application of anthropological knowledge must be so varied. In this paper attention will be confined to the application of findings in social anthropology, and, since we are here concerned only with British Africa, consideration of the scope of applied anthropology will be restricted to its role in the government of dependent territories. In such territories, where private and voluntary organizations to encourage and pioneer major developments in welfare, economic, and even political organization are so little developed, governments—however primitive or limited their administrative apparatus—have in some respects a wider field of immediate social responsibility than have the independent governments of more advanced societies, and their need for the sociological information which anthropologists secure from nonliterate peoples is correspondingly greater. It is also important to recognize that governments in colonial territories are inevitably concerned in some degree with the guidance of a general process of Westernization, that is, with the direction and control of a deliberate modification and even transformation of the traditional way of life of the peoples for whose affairs they are responsible. Such modification not only relates, moreover, to specific economic and political developments but involves responsibility for meeting multifarious social repercussions in family and community life and new cultural demands that arise in these and other fields. Examples are the sponsoring and guidance of co-operative and trade-union organizations; the provision of literature bureaus for the production and publication of books and pamphlets, both literary and practical, in vernacular and European languages; the development of broadcasting; and the creation of a public opinion favorable to necessary measures of public health under conditions of increasing urbanization and rapid transport. All these fall, at least initially, to the lot of colonial governments.

Anthropological knowledge, in the sense of information concerning both general principles and particular cultural and social conditions derived from the scientific and independent study of societies, is significant in a special sense for governments of dependent territories. This is so because the basic knowledge of habits of thought and patterns of behavior among the people, which political leaders and administrative officials in autonomous responsible governments presume themselves to have acquired in the course of their general education and life as citizens, has, in the case of colonial government, to be acquired, if at all, by deliberate inquiry in the course of duty. Such knowledge may be obtained by providing government officials and those responsible for framing policy with time and opportunities for direct observation and reflection on native institutions; or it may be derived from the studies of specialist investigators. The inquiries of the latter may range all the way from studies pursued from intrinsic interest in the character of a particular society and culture or in scientific problems concerning cultural and social process with no thought for assistance to administration to *ad hoc* reports on specific conditions concerning which a government needs information in order to frame or revise policy in a particular field. The practical value of a study in a particular governmental situation need not, however, be dependent on the original motives and terms of reference of the investigator who is in a position to supply crucial information. Independent self-justifying field study of the culture and social institutions of nonliterate peoples has been traditionally a field of inquiry of anthropologists, and the aid of anthropologists has also been available where information of a more specific character or organized directly in relation to particular administrative questions has been required by colonial governments.

ANTHROPOLOGY IN ADMINISTRATION IN BRITISH AFRICA BEFORE THE SECOND WORLD WAR

The application of social anthropology in actual administration involves, as indicated above, both a grasp of general principles developed in the study of small-scale non-European societies and also the assembling of the ethnographic data relevant to particular administrative problems. Its importance and effectiveness depend, therefore, on the degree to which both these interdependent aspects of anthropological study—the formulation of general principles concerning cultural and social processes in nonliterate societies based on comparative studies and the systematic collection of ethnographic information by reliable field methods in the light of these principles and theoretical problems—have been appreciated and used by colonial administrations.

Needless to say, no comprehensive and systematic information is available concerning the detailed procedures of the various British African administrations over the long period which goes back in many cases well beyond the beginning of the century. It is, however, possible to indicate the extent to which the British colonial administrations have, on the one hand, given their staffs anthropological training and/or opportunities to pursue anthropological inquiries in connection with administrative duties and have, on the other, encouraged academic anthropological studies likely to be useful to them and sought anthropological advice from specialists, in order to obtain studies and reports which would be of service in framing or implementing policy.

In the political or administrative services of the British colonies in Africa and elsewhere, a tradition of at least informal association and consultation with academic anthropologists was early established. From early in the century a large proportion of administrative officers serving in Africa came from the universities of Oxford and Cambridge, where such pioneers as Sir James Frazer, Dr. A. C. Haddon, and Dr. R. R. Marrett were able, through their lectures and their accessibility to inquirers, to encourage both an interest in the objective study of primitive peoples and a recognition of the administrative importance of an intimate understanding of native institutions. Successive generations of young administrators, many of whom returned for discussion and advice during their leave periods, were in this way brought into touch with current anthropological thought.

Although the resources in men and funds devoted to anthropological study and teaching at this period were exiguous in the extreme and such studies did not receive any significant support from colonial administrations, the influence of academic anthropology did to some extent filter throughout the administrative services through contacts with the universities and with the Royal Anthropological Institute, of which many of the more scholarly administrators became Fellows. In this way the work of a number of distinguished anthropologist-administrators, such as Johnston, Hobley, Bullock, Dundas, Palmer, Talbot, Rattray, and Meek, was encouraged and developed.

Officers who showed special interest in and aptitude for anthropological studies were sometimes given special facilities to pursue investigations. Thus several administrators in British West Africa, P. A. Talbot (1915, 1923, 1926, 1932), R. Rattray (1923, 1927, 1929, 1932), and C. K. Meek (1925, 1931, 1937) were seconded for various periods as government anthropologists and devoted a considerable part of their period of service to investigations and the preparation of publications which not only contributed greatly to ethnographic knowledge but appear to have been valued by their administrations as providing anthropological data useful in connection with both routine administration and the formulation of policy.

In East Africa, too, there early appeared administrators with anthropological interests and experience who applied their knowledge in administration, beginning with the pioneers Sir Harry Johnston (1897, 1902–4, 1907, 1919), who was already publishing studies in the eighties of the last century when he was His Majesty's consul in the Oil Rivers Protectorate at Beira and later as special commissioner to Uganda, and Sir Claude Hobley (1910, 1922, and numerous papers), who, entering the service of the British East Africa Company in 1890 as a geologist, served for over twenty years as an administrator. They have been followed by others like Sir Charles Dundas, A. C. Hollis, Orde Browne, H. E. Lambert, G. W. B. Huntingford, and A. T. Culwick.

In the Rhodesias early administrators who themselves carried out and published systematic anthropological inquiries included Bullock (e.g., 1928), Dale (Dale and Smith, 1920), Gouldsbury and Sheane (1911), and Coxhead (1914); and this tradition has been continued by the more recent studies of Brelsford (e.g., 1943, 1944*a, b*, 1946, 1951; Brelsford and Allan, 1947), White (e.g., 1948, 1949, 1950), and others.

Political officers of the Anglo-Egyptian Sudan, from Sir Harold Mac-Michael (e.g., 1912, and papers in *Sudan Notes and Records,* 1918–27, and in the *Journal of the Royal African Society*), whose studies of the Arab Sudan are well known, to P. Howell (e.g., 1941; Howell and Thomson, 1946; and later papers), a recognized authority on the Nilotes, have made notable contributions to the study of the cultural history and social organization of the peoples.

Administrative officers in all territories were, from an early period, encouraged and sometimes required to contribute records and reports on ethnographic and social matters arising from local or territory-wide inquiries. In this way, the District or Divisional Offices and the Provincial, Regional, or Central Secretariats built up a considerable body of anthropological information to which reference could be made in connection with any local issue or wider question of development. The character and quality and, indeed, the actual preservation and accessibility of this documentation have naturally varied greatly, since each colonial territory was free to decide from time to time on the emphasis and care to be given to it. With periodic shortages of staff, changes in personal interests, and the absence of trained personnel and facilities for handling archives, it is not surprising that notable differences are found in the range and standard of such anthropological material and the degree to which it actually served to guide local or territory-wide policy. In most territories official "District Notebooks" were early instituted, and these, where well maintained, have afforded a continuous record of *ad hoc* ethnographic information on such matters as tribal boundaries, social organization, and economy concerning the peoples of the area. There have, however, as was pointed out in *An African Survey* (Hailey, 1938, pp. 49, 1615), which made recommendations for their improvement, been considerable differences in the systems used for keeping these records and in the value of the material they contain. Alternatively or in addition, regular files have been kept and reviews undertaken from time to time on particular aspects of the social life and the political and economic problems of an ethnic group, a district, or a region. The latter have occasionally been printed for publication or wide official circulation (e.g., Ward-Price, 1933).

In Nigeria from the late twenties, following unforeseen disturbances in the eastern provinces connected with the introduction of taxation, systematic inquiries into ethnic groupings, social organization, and economic life were undertaken. Existing records were collated and supplemented by field investigations by administrative officers and the results incorporated in a series of detailed Intelligence Reports covering practically the whole of Southern Nigeria. For the preparation of these reports a number of administrative officers, selected as far as possible for their knowledge and aptitude in these matters, were freed from other duties for considerable periods. The peoples of large parts of Northern Nigeria were similarly studied over the same period in connection with reassessment for taxation, and the results were embodied in a series of "Reassessment Reports." Both Intelligence and Reassessment Reports have remained on file in Divisional, Provincial, and Central Offices and have been continually consulted and sometimes revised or amplified by subsequent inquiries as need arose.[1]

In East Africa the Kenya central secretariat maintains archives of papers and reports bearing on native tribes and their customs. The Kenya Land Commission, whose report and volumes of evidence were published from 1933 on, made extensive use of the findings

of anthropologically experienced administrators and of independent scholars who had worked in relevant areas.[2] In Tanganyika Territory, which has been under British Mandate since the first World War, an early experiment in direct collaboration between an administrative officer and a professional anthropologist was made in the twenties (see Brown and Hutt, 1935); and the recording and analysis of customary law was assigned to an anthropologist attached to the administration (see Cory, 1952; Cory and Hartnoll, 1945).

Some British colonial governments in Africa also quite early sought the assistance of professional anthropologists, to provide themselves with knowledge of the social organization and customs of particular peoples or areas as a background for their administration. Thus the services of Northcote Thomas were obtained by the West African colonies before and during the first World War. As a government anthropologist, he carried out studies among the Ibo- and Edo-speaking peoples of Nigeria and in Sierra Leone (1910, 1913–14, 1916).

The Anglo-Egyptian Sudan has also over a long period provided facilities and funds for field study and publication by anthropologists. Suggesting peoples and problems which were likely to be of both administrative and scholarly interest, it early provided facilities for the Seligmans (e.g., 1918, 1932) and later E. E. Evans-Pritchard (1933–35, 1937, 1937–38, 1940a, b) and S. F. Nadel (1942a, 1947) to carry out studies among both Islamic and pagan peoples. These studies have been encouraged and assisted, apparently, on the principle that scholarly work of this

1. Unfortunately, it was not found possible to publish these reports, but they have been made accessible to visiting scholars, both anthropologists and students of colonial administration, and they have more recently been made available as source material for the relevant sections of the *Ethnographic Survey of Africa* being prepared and published by the International African Institute (see below).

2. *Report of the Kenya Land Commission, September, 1933* (Cmd. 4556); *Evidence and Memoranda* (3 vols.; Col. No., No. 91); and *Summary of Conclusions Reached by H.M. Govt.* (Cmd. 4580; London: H.M. Stationery Office, 1934).

kind was of general educative value for all concerned with the area, as well as in the hope that the findings would be of direct utility.

In the early thirties the administration of the Bechuanaland Protectorate invited Schapera, who had already undertaken independent researches among the Tswana group of tribes, to make comprehensive studies of native law, land tenure, and related matters and to prepare the results for publication and use by the administration (1938, 1943).

Systematic study of the native peoples of what later became the Union of South Africa began with the independent work of W. H. I. Bleek in the third quarter of the last century. But the Natal and Cape governments also made official inquiries into native laws and customs relevant to administration. Thus the Natal government set up a Commission on Native Affairs which reported in 1852, while a compendium of Kaffir laws and customs, which was to serve as a guide to magistrates in native affairs, was prepared for the Cape government in 1858 (MacLean, 1858). The Cape government set up commissions in 1873 and 1880 which reported on the laws and customs of peoples in further territories annexed to the Cape, suggesting legislation and measures for introducing some degree of local government in native territories.[3]

After the South African War, a commission of inquiry to consider native affairs reported in 1905 on the administrative bearing of a wide range of native institutions. Following consequent suggestions for the establishment of teaching and research appointments in the university colleges of South Africa for the study of native life, the Union government set up the Coleman Com-

3. *Cape of Good Hope: Report and Proceedings of the Government Commission on Native Laws and Customs* (1883).

mission to consider the need for scientific investigations of native life, which recommended the establishment of central institutions for the scientific study of native language and customs to promote research and instruct persons intending to work among the natives. Owing to conflicting local claims, however, a series of separate university departments concerned with Bantu linguistics and anthropology were established in Cape Town, Johannesburg, Pretoria, Stellenbosch, and Fort Hare, and the government in the later twenties made a small annual grant for the conduct of researches into native life and languages. But a plan for the special training in anthropology of government officials and others concerned with native life never materialized, anthropological instruction being confined to voluntary attendance at vacation courses at the universities and visits of university teachers to administrative conferences.

Professor Schapera, in a report published in the thirties on "The Present State and Future Development of Ethnographical Research in South Africa" (1934), stressed that

it is not merely for the sake of science that the missionary, the administrative officer and the teacher should acquire a working knowledge of anthropological principles... without a thorough knowledge and understanding of the native culture few of them can hope to carry out with success the mission they have to fulfil. . . . None of the South African universities is yet specifically engaged in this, perhaps the most important function for which they were originally instituted . . . contact with the professional anthropologist . . . is maintained by the occasional vacation courses that are held at different centres. . . . The Union government has hitherto steadfastly refrained from actively supporting its officers to receive the special training which would equip them so much more efficiently for the work they have to do. It has refused to entertain suggestions of vocational training from the universities, and has also given no facilities to its officers to attend Vacation Courses.

On the other hand, the government had in the late twenties established a post of government anthropologist in the Department of Native Affairs,[4] and it would appear that the policy of the government of South Africa has been to conduct its own investigations and to receive inquiries from and give advice to government officials through that department. The office of the government anthropologist was reported in 1948/49[5] as having a staff of five Europeans and six natives, of whom four of the former are trained anthropologists. The department has also, since the second World War, extended its activities to Southwest Africa.

From the end of the first World War, the desirability of providing some formal anthropological training for colonial administrators in British colonial territories appears to have been accepted in principle, even if it did not have high priority in training schemes. In the twenties arrangements were made whereby periods of extended leave were provided for officers interested in pursuing anthropological courses at British universities. Anthropology was included in the curriculum of the one-year training course later organized at the universities of Oxford and Cambridge for intending members of the Colonial Administrative Service. This course was reorganized after the second World War, and probationers now pursue a full-time course of studies over one session, which includes the general principles of social anthropology and also a more intensive study of the ethnography and social insti-

4. See series of official publications of the Department of Native Affairs by the government anthropologist, starting in 1930. The series has now reached No. 26.

5. *Official Year Book of the Union of South Africa, 1948–49.*

tutions of the peoples of the region within which they are expected to work. They also have intensive teaching in an African language important to that territory.

INDEPENDENT CONTRIBUTIONS TO APPLIED ANTHROPOLOGY BEFORE THE SECOND WORLD WAR

Probably the most important among the independent developments for the long-term application of anthropological study to governmental problems in Africa was the establishment of the International African Institute shortly after the first World War (see Forde, 1945). From the work of the British Colonial Office Advisory Committee on Native Education in Tropical Africa, which had been appointed by the colonial secretary in 1923, grew a movement, largely inspired by its secretary, Sir Hanns Vischer, to create a center of research and information on the cultures and languages of the peoples of Africa, which should contribute, in particular, to the harmonious solution of problems of economic and political development. It was realized from the outset in Britain that these objects could be satisfactorily achieved only if studies and information were related to conditions in all African territories and that the investigation of problems should not be limited by national frontiers. With the support of the European and colonial governments concerned and of interested missionary and scientific organizations in Europe and the United States, the Institute was inaugurated in 1926, under the first chairmanship of Lord Lugard, with the express aim of achieving a closer association between scientific knowledge and research and the interests of African peoples, colonial governments, and other European agencies in African territories. While French, German, and other Continental scholars participated fully in framing and supervising the Institute's program of field research and publication, which had received the generous support of the Rockefeller Foundation,[6] the greater part of the field investigations, including those carried out by its research fellows from other countries, was, in fact, undertaken in British territories, where facilities were more readily obtained. The research program was related to practical problems of the effects of culture contact, but it was made clear both to governments and to research workers that, especially at that stage, fundamental contributions to knowledge of African cultures and social systems were of primary importance and likely to be of the greatest long-term value. The field research fellows of the Institute undertook studies in Nigeria, the Gold Coast, Sierre Leone, the Anglo-Egyptian Sudan, Uganda, Kenya, Tanganyika, northern Rhodesia, Nyasaland, and South Africa, during the period 1932–39. Although these, when measured against the multiplicity of problems and the variety of social change in Africa under conditions of increasing economic contact with the outside world, provided specific and detailed information on only a few peoples, most of them had a wide bearing on governmental problems as examples both of the results, in terms of concrete findings, that could be obtained by intensive field work and of the sociological complexity underlying administrative problems.

In its quarterly journal *Africa* and in its "Memoranda" the Institute was able to publish not only the preliminary results of its field workers but a growing body of shorter studies and discussions by other anthropologists, by administrative officers and colonial educationists, concerning both the broader aspects and particular instances of social change in relation to governmental action.[7]

The series of longer monographs on particular peoples published by the Institute usually analyzed in detail not only the indigenous background but also the character and effects of new political and economic developments with regard to the changing structure of African societies and the administrative systems which sought to control and guide them (e.g., Orde-Browne, 1933; Westermann, 1934; Brown and Hutt, 1935; Hunter, 1936 [Pondo]; Schapera, 1938; East, 1939 [Tiv]; Richards, 1939; Nadel, 1942b [Nupe]; Krige and Krige, 1943 [Lovedu]). The extent and rapidity with which the indigenous cultures were being fundamentally affected by the impact of European civilization emerged in these studies with regard to such diverse fields as the changing role of the chief in centralized societies, the modifications of land tenure, and the rapidly increasing ratio of production for exchange among communities which a generation before had depended almost entirely on local production for their subsistence.

The decision to concentrate in its own research projects on the deeper understanding of the processes of culture contact, on the evaluation of those features of African societies making for social cohesion, and on the precise manner in which Western ideas and commercial and governmental activities were affecting various institutions contributed to the creation of a climate of opinion concerning the need

6. *A Five Year Plan of Research* ("International African Institute Memoranda," No. 9 [1932]).

7. Among the many papers that might be cited are the following: In *Africa*: Driberg (1928); Schapera (1928); Malinowski (1930); Mitchell (1930); Mair (1931); Orchardson (1931); Tagart (1931); Clifton Roberts (1935); Orde-Browne (1935); Fortes (1936); Mair (1936); Wagner (1936); Hall (1938); Forde (1939); Wilson (1940). In the "Memoranda": Fortes (1938); Malinowski (1938); Read (1938); Wagner (1939); Mair (1940).

to give greater responsibility to Africans in the development of the new social structures that must inevitably follow from increasing participation in the world economy. The governments of African territories recognized in many particular instances that the analyses provided by the Institute's research workers in articles and monographs illuminated and suggested new lines of approach for many of their practical problems and showed themselves anxious to obtain the further services of field workers who had proved themselves in these studies.[8]

The orientation of intensive studies of African cultures toward the present and future functioning of social institutions, both traditional and nascent, in culture-contact conditions resulted from a happy conjunction of both a functional or dynamic approach to ethnographic analysis on the part of anthropologists themselves (as led in British circles by Radcliffe-Brown and Malinowski) and the realization, re-

8. Several of the research fellows contributed studies or reports on particular questions of moment to the governments of the territories in which they worked. Thus Dr. Fortes was invited by the Gold Coast government to provide a study of Tallensi marriage law for use in reviewing native court cases, and to give advice in connection with the development of native administration in the Northern Territories; an investigation of the effects of migratory labor on the development of village life in Nyasaland was carried out by Dr. M. Read; Dr. Nadel provided material relevant to the question of setting up pagan as well as Mohammedan courts in the Nupe area of Nigeria and provided economic data needed in connection with reassessment for taxation; he was later appointed government anthropologist in the Anglo-Egyptian Sudan to undertake investigations in the Nuba Hills in connection with the need to develop native authorities. Professor Schapera, at the request of the high commissioner, prepared a handbook on Tswana law and custom for the use of administrative officers of the Bechuanaland Protectorate. See also *Methods of Study of Culture Contact in Africa* ("International African Institute Memoranda," No. 15 [1938]).

ferred to above, on the part of those with experience of colonial administration during and immediately after the first World War that colonial development must depend less on a priori principles of efficiency and economy in administration and more and more on an intimate grasp of the social systems and cultural values with which the administrator has to deal in implementing desired programs of development. The anthropologists, for their part, became students of the colonial administrations, in that they included in their field of inquiry the effects on African societies of actions initiated and sustained by European agencies and personnel, whether governmental, commercial, or missionary. They studied the views and behavior of Europeans as actors in the situation as well as those of the Africans.

Independent of the International African Institute's program and financed from various private sources, but influenced by the same trend toward a dynamic analysis of the observed field situation, a number of other studies of value to the administrations concerned were carried out during this period by professional anthropologists. Thus Professor Evans-Pritchard presented an analysis of Nuer political organization, first published in *Sudan Notes and Records* (1933–35; see also 1940*b*). Studies by Dr. A. I. Richards contributed to the understanding of economic and political problems among the Bemba of Rhodesia (e.g., 1939, 1940, 1941). Dr. J. S. Harris, an American anthropologist, engaged in field studies among the Southern Ibo, extended his investigation with the assistance of the administration, and provided it with a report on agriculture and landholding among the Ozuitem Ibo (1943–44*a*, *b*). Mrs. Leith Ross (1939) and Miss Green (1941) studied the role of women and the economy of other Ibo communities. Mr. Godfrey

Wilson carried out studies among the Nyakyusa and Ngonde in southern Tanganyika Territory (1936, 1937, 1938, 1939). Dr. L. Mair investigated economic and political change among the Ganda (1933, 1934, 1940, etc.) and Daryll Forde published similar studies concerning the Yakö of southeastern Nigeria (1937*a, b*, 1939).

Lord Hailey and his collaborators, which included a number of anthropologists, some of them also associated with the International African Institute, were meanwhile compiling and analyzing the material for his monumental *African Survey*, published in 1938. In connection with political, economic, and the broader social aspects of African affairs, this stressed the importance of harnessing trained research personnel for the investigation and solution of the problems arising from widespread cultural change. "The task," Lord Hailey wrote (1938, p. 1662), "of guiding the social and material development of Africa gives rise to problems which cannot be solved by the application of routine knowledge; they require a special knowledge, which can only be gained by an intensive study of the unusual conditions. This study must be pursued in the field of the social as well as in that of the physical sciences."

These developments and the anthropological approach and results they embodied did much to dispel one administrative view of the academic anthropologist which Dr. Richards has phrased as a person who was either "burying his head in the sands of antiquity ... afraid to look at the rapidly changing scene around him" or "anxious to keep the African peoples in a series of ethnographic Mappin Terraces[9] for his own observation." It has

9. Part of the London Zoölogical Gardens where animals are allowed to continue a "natural" existence (Richards, 1944).

to be recognized, however, that, with the important exception of the founding of the Rhodes-Livingstone Institute before the war, which is referred to later, they did not lead to any systematic provision on the part of colonial governments for the direct use of the services of professional anthropologists. Although many administrative factors, including economic conditions in the colonial territories, may have contributed to inertia, it must also be admitted that very often anthropological findings which should have been of considerable value in framing and implementing policy were not appreciated by administrators, since they were embodied in lengthy studies or specialist papers. While from a scientific point of view these represented a great advance in the functional analysis of native institutions, they often assumed a knowledge of, and primary interest in, theoretical problems, and the relevance of their results to the immediate and even long-term problems of administration was not always brought home. Thus the administrative utility and the possibilities of providing professionally competent ethnographic surveys and special studies of particular institutions of administrative importance were not generally appreciated on either side.

Sir Phillip Mitchell, the present governor of Kenya, is perhaps exceptional in the poor view that he now takes of the contribution of the academic anthropologists during the interwar years, whom he accuses of "asserting that they only were gifted with understanding, busied themselves with enthusiasm about all the minutiae of obscure tribal and personal practices [from which] resulted a large number of painstaking and often accurate records ... of such length that no one had time to read them and often, in any case, irrelevant, by the time they became available, to the day to day business of government."[10] But he recognizes that "the study of social and economic circumstances are (*inter alia*) essential for the legislator, the governor and the administrator," more especially as "it has always been a matter of particular difficulty in colonial Africa to ensure that those who are responsible ... (and in African circles a heavy responsibility may rest on very young shoulders) should be adequately informed not only of past events and old customs, but of current social, political and economic conditions." He himself has initiated in Uganda and in Kenya the creation of posts of judicial advisers "to be filled by an officer ... enjoying the confidence of the High Court, and as expert as circumstances permitted in the native law, lore and practice, and language." Lord Hailey's recent survey of native administration in Africa (1951, p. 190) also records the Kenya view that anthropologists are likely to produce information with little practical relevance and so should be employed "on terms which will secure their collaboration in enquiries the scope of which has been detailed in advance."

Professor Schapera (1951) and Dr. L. Mair (1951, p. 336) have, in reply, recently restated the position as it appears to the professional anthropologist, attempting to remove administrative misconceptions as to both the conditions under which a field anthropologist can obtain data for analysis in connection with practical problems and also the assumed mutual irrelevance of "academic" and "practical" information (see also the final section of this paper).

10. *Journal of African Administration*, 1951, pp. 56–59. See, however, his more appreciative views in "The Anthropologist and the Practical Man" (1930) and his Preface to Orde-Browne (1933).

DURING AND AFTER THE SECOND WORLD WAR

The impact of the second World War on Africa greatly accelerated previous trends in both economic and political fields and gave a remarkable impetus to research in social anthropology in connection with administrative needs. Not only were campaigns fought in eastern Africa, but African forces were raised in large numbers for service overseas, while production for export of scarce materials, both mineral and agricultural, had to be rapidly speeded up at a time when the supply of the basic trade goods—cottons and hardware—was severely curtailed. Concern for African participation in the war effort combined with the reinforcement of liberal and egalitarian sentiments, also generated by the war, to encourage in administrative circles, as well as among laymen concerned with colonial affairs, a widespread expectation of a "new deal" for Africa when once the energies liberated in war were available for peacetime development.

During the war itself the services of specialists on various aspects of the cultures and institutions of African peoples were seconded for investigations arising from the considerable social problems involved in the recruiting and training of Africans and the need to increase production especially of African crops.

In West Africa an Institute of Arts, Industries, and Social Science was established in 1943. Based on Achimota, near Accra, under the direction of Mr. H. V. Meyerowitz, it developed pilot production units for the adaption of West African crafts to larger-scale production and new uses.[11] The services

11. Experiments were made in such fields as the production of roofing tiles and wooden shingles for building purposes, and the installation of more efficient imported looms for hand

of a sociologist, Dr. M. Fortes, were secured and preparation made for intensive social surveys in the Gold Coast. Pressures and difficulties arising from the war situation impeded the development of the Institute, but the Ashanti Social Survey was carried out after the war under Dr. Fortes, with the assistance of a human geographer and a specially attached economist. The preliminary results of this intensive comparative survey in a series of Ashanti communities of social change and related problems of economic and political development have been published (Fortes, 1948, 1949; Fortes, Steel, and Ady, 1947). Unfortunately, the detailed studies have not yet been completed for publication.

The Colonial Office, following proposals by the Nigerian government, made a grant to the International African Institute to arrange and supervise an intensive study of the peoples of Bamenda in the British Cameroons, where difficulties had been encountered in framing acceptable plans for educational development and economic difficulties were appearing in connection with migrant labor and Fulani immigration. The services of an experienced anthropologist, Dr. P. Kaberry, were secured to carry out and report on this investigation (1946, 1950, 1952), which was to be specially concerned with the economic role and social status of women.

With the establishment toward the end of the war of the British Colonial Development and Welfare Fund, considerable sums were made available to finance social research in colonial territories and a Colonial Social Science Research Council, of which an anthropologist, Professor R. Firth, was the first secretary, was established to formulate and supervise a program of

weaving, under the supervision of a European hand-textile specialist.

studies in which anthropological investigations were given an important place. A panel of anthropologists was invited to present its views on the scope of work which could most usefully be undertaken, and considerable attention was directed toward African territories, the governments of which were consulted in detail in deciding on the field and scope of the studies. Professor R. Firth, while still serving as secretary of the council, visited British West Africa to consult the colonial governments on their views and their needs (1947), and Professor Schapera, of Cape Town, was later invited to review anthropological problems in Kenya Colony and to advise on priority among those found to require investigation (1949). A special sociological committee of the council, on which the leading university departments of anthropology are represented, was subsequently set up to consider in detail and to arrange for the supervision of research in anthropological and cognate fields.

Under this scheme and apart from longer-term appointments to social research institutes that were established (see below), some twenty-five anthropologists have been appointed by the Colonial Office for *ad hoc* assignments in British African territories over periods of two to four years to undertake investigations requested or approved by the colonial government in question. The recruitment of research workers has not been confined to the British. A number of American, Canadian, Dutch, and South African anthropologists have been given Colonial Office grants for this purpose.[12] The resulting studies are in course of publi-

12. See Annual Reports of the Colonial Social Science Research Council from 1944 to 1945, in Command Paper entitled *Colonial Research*, issued annually by H.M. Stationery Office, London.

cation (e.g., Mayer, 1949; Peristiany, 1951; Southall, 1952).[13]

The Colonial Office has also financed the preparation by the International African Institute of an ethnographic survey of Africa. Under the editorship of the institute's director (Professor Daryll Forde), this survey, which is being published in self-contained parts, each devoted to a particular group of related peoples, seeks to collate and make more generally available the wealth of unco-ordinated material on the ethnic groupings and social conditions of African peoples for the benefit of scholars, administrators, and others concerned with African affairs. Ten parts have appeared or are in the press, and others will appear early in 1953.[14]

It was appreciated from the outset both by the Colonial Office, the council, and the colonial governments that for the most part basic ethnographic field investigation and fundamental studies of social structure were indispensable to provide the anthropological knowledge required for tackling the manifold practical problems involved in the development plans formulated by the colonial governments after the war. Thus it was realized that difficulties facing projects for the improvement of cattle-rearing in East Africa, involving the related problems of overstocking and soil erosion, in many areas could best be helped from an anthropological point of view by undertaking detailed analyses of the economies and authority systems of the Nilo-Hamitic and Bantu peoples concerned. Similarly, in West Africa, economic problems,

13. Studies are also being published for the Colonial Office by H.M. Stationery Office in a new series of "Colonial Research Studies"; see No. 3, P. Mayer, *Two Studies in Applied Anthropology in Kenya* (1951), and No. 4, G. W. B. Huntingford, *Nandi Work and Culture* (1950).

14. See periodical announcements in *Africa*, quarterly.

such as those arising from soil exhaustion in areas of very dense population among the Southern Ibo of Nigeria and related proposals for the establishment of oil presses and for transfers of population, or from difficulties encountered in the Gambia in attempting to expand food cultivation to overcome severe seasonal food shortages, were recognized as demanding a much clearer comprehension of the social systems, the customary rules of landholding, and the economic values of the peoples concerned. At the same time the services of more senior anthropological investigators have been sought for problems of greater political urgency. Thus Mr. G. I. Jones, of the University of Cambridge, was asked to investigate and report on the social and cultural background of a series of "ritual murders" in Basutoland (1951).

The familiar difficulty whereby the administrative and technical departments of colonial governments, working on comparatively short-term plans, are likely to underestimate the long-term value of basic ethnographic research has been less acute than might have been expected. The number of unfruitful efforts before the war to achieve rapid modification in a desired direction of the economic activities and social life of African peoples, such as the unsuccessful attempts to introduce green manuring in the Forest Belt agriculture of southern Nigeria or the obstinacy of the problems of adjusting East African cattle economies to modern conditions of disease control and external markets, had given some appreciation of the need for basic knowledge of both principles and data in the social field and for a more tentative approach to social planning in the light of this fuller ethnographic understanding. The Nigerian government itself during this period seconded a number of its officers to prepare reports on land tenure in various areas, and the need to consider land tenure in the context of the general social structure is stressed in the reports, which make extensive use of anthropological data (Chubb, 1948; Rowling, 1948*a*, *b*, 1949; Cole, 1949).

"The Report on Native Tribunals of Kenya Colony," in 1945, giving the results of an investigation undertaken by Mr. A. Phillips, a government crown counsel, toward the end of the war, not only made considerable use of anthropological evidence in appraising and making proposals for reform of native courts in Kenya but recommended the systematic study and recording of customary law and of the functions of the still vigorous judicial institutions as prerequisite to effective reform and development of native tribunals.

Professor Schapera's recent review (1949) of anthropological research needs in Kenya, commissioned by the Colonial Office and the administration, listed a series of practical problems in connection with which anthropological investigations had been proposed by officers of the Kenya administration, including studies of the nomadic pastoral peoples of the Turkana and northern frontier districts of Kenya (the Turkana, Boran, Galla, etc.) "in order to provide the background necessary for understanding administrative problems." Arrangements for implementing several of these recommendations have since been made.

URBAN POPULATIONS AND MIGRANT LABOR

While studies and reports on the cultural factors and social patterns operative among "tribal" populations among whom subsistence production has continued to predominate have naturally attracted the first attention of anthropologists and those concerned to use their knowledge, there has also been a growing recognition of the need for study of new cultural patterns and so-

cial structures emerging among the urban and commercial farming populations of tropical Africa that have emerged in connection with the growth of overseas trade, ports, internal communication centers and markets, mines, and secondary industries. In this connection anthropologists and others applying in some measure anthropological field techniques have, under governmental auspices, studied the social conditions in the West African port of Takoradi-Sekondi and the East African ports of Mombasa and Dar-es-Salaam (Batson, 1948; Busia, 1950; Silberman, 1950). The postwar program of the Rhodes-Livingstone Institute, following the allocation of substantial grants from the Colonial Development and Welfare Fund, proposed to focus its anthropological research on the effects of industrialization and labor migration as dominant forces in the social development of central Africa (Gluckman, 1945).

Problems of method and organization of field inquiry concerning the combination of techniques of firsthand study through participant observation, prolonged informal interview, and long residence developed by field anthropologists, on the one hand, and the presentation of a schedule or questionnaire to a sample of a population for subsequent statistical analysis as developed in urban sociology, on the other, have become a major concern for field research in the larger aggregates of population in Africa, more especially where an unknown degree of heterogeneity and an indeterminate social structure are involved. Anthropologists have had little difficulty in pointing out that a brief investigation by sampling with a fixed schedule or questionnaire, followed by a statistical analysis of replies, has very limited value for scientific understanding or the formulation of long-term policy for social development in areas where the culture is alien and little known to the investigators or to those who will use their conclusions. Some advance has, as will be seen from references given, been made by individual anthropologists and by research institutes mainly concerned with anthropological research in attempting to combine the two techniques. It is also being recognized that, where circumstances permit, great advantage can be derived from a readiness to depart from the tradition of the lone investigator, solitarily immersed in the culture of the people studied, in favor of the formation of teams, including locally trained native personnel, so that the concentration of research manpower necessary for speedy execution of comprehensive quantitative studies may be carried out.

AFRICAN RESEARCH INSTITUTES AND COLLEGES

Anthropological research financed by colonial and metropolitan governments with the aim of direct or ultimate assistance to the administrators and peoples of the areas concerned developed from the earlier interests of individual scholars and the support of independent university and other research institutions in the United Kingdom. With increasing governmental concern to obtain the desired studies, the question of establishing in Africa itself research organizations to pursue social studies inevitably arose. There was at an early stage considerable discussion on the desirability of constituting an official anthropological service for the colonial territories. A Colonial Research Service was, in fact, subsequently set up to cover several branches of applied science, but anthropology was not included. It was, however, decided to establish and finance institutes of social and economic research which would undertake anthropological and cognate researches for groups of British territories in the main regions.

Already before the war, in 1938, the Rhodes-Livingstone Institute had been founded on the initiative of the Northern Rhodesian government, which contributed half the initial funds, and with the financial support of the Beit Trust, the British South Africa Company, and the mining companies. The object of the Institute was to promote social research, primarily by anthropologists, in the Rhodesias and Nyasaland, and its early program included field studies, monographic and comparative, on the social institutions of little-known peoples in the area and also an investigation of the effects of modern industry on the social life of peoples providing the labor force for mines and industry.[15] The work of the first director, Mr. G. Wilson, on the economics of detribalization was a pioneer study, by a social anthropologist, of urban labor conditions and their social repercussions.[16]

The postwar program of the Rhodes-Livingstone Institute (assisted considerably by grants from the Colonial Development and Welfare Fund to finance field studies by four field research officers, in addition to the director, Dr. Max Gluckman) was, as indicated above, based on the view that industrialization with labor migration dominates the whole trend of social development in central Africa and that other problems should be studied within this framework (Gluckman, 1945; Anon., 1946, p. 116). Field work was accordingly directed mainly toward both urban areas (mining and nonmining) and to rural areas of different types from which labor migrates but which are in many diverse stages of social change, sample studies being planned to cover

15. See *Director's Report to Trustees of Rhodes-Livingstone Institute on the Work of the First Three Years, 1938–40* (Livingstone, 1940).

16. *An Essay on the Economics of Detribalisation in N. Rhodesia*, Parts I and II (Livingstone, 1941, 1942).

such subjects as changes in kinship organization and political values, religious and magical beliefs, and especially witchcraft. Special attention was also given, at the suggestion of the Northern Rhodesian government, to land tenure in close co-operation with the Agriculture Department and its field officers. Preliminary results, at least, of these sample studies, which were carried out among the Lala, Lamba, Cewa, Ngoni, Tonga, and other peoples, have been published by the Institute and elsewhere.[17] An intensive urban study is in progress in the Copper Belt.[18]

An East African Institute of Social Research, attached to Makerere College, Uganda, and financed from the British Colonial Development and Welfare Fund, was established in 1950 under the direction of Dr. Audrey Richards, following lengthy consideration of its potential services to education, administration, and economic advance in East Africa. Reporting annually to the Council of Makerere College and to the Colonial Social Science Research Council of the British Colonial Office, it has its own staff and an independent program of research, which is, however, framed in consultation with both the Colonial Office and the colonial governments concerned. The initial program of the Institute[19] envisaged work to be carried out in Uganda, Kenya, Tanganyika, and Zanzibar in the fields of social anthropology, economics, law, psychology, and linguistics. The Institute

has been planned as a comprehensive center of East African studies for the extension of knowledge of the cultures and languages of its peoples and their present-day reactions to modern political, economic, and educational policies. It is building up archives of documents and conducting field studies of both an ethnographic and a specialist character. Stress is laid on the pooling of data obtained in different tribal areas, so as to throw light on wide problems of both theoretical and practical interest. Immediate attention is being given by a small research team, whose members are working in different areas, to the comparative study of East African political systems, with reference to their adaptation to modern conceptions of local government and the needs of present-day activity. Other current or projected investigations are concerned with (1) effects of differing education policies on social and personal life; (2) effects on character and personality of indigenous methods of upbringing; (3) incentives to labor in areas or peoples of different social character, patterns of migratory labor, and participation of Africans and Indians in recent economic developments; and (4) differential race attitudes among East African peoples.

The director has stressed the importance of experimentation in social research methods at the present time in such areas as Africa and also of co-operation with the governments and their research departments, for which the Institute is prepared to organize and execute studies of administrative importance and to supply information on particular questions with reference to areas or peoples where it already has

17. See, e.g., *Rhodes-Livingstone Journal*, No. 1 (1944 and ff.); "Rhodes-Livingstone Papers," No. 14 (1948) and later ones; "Communications from the Rhodes-Livingstone Institute" (mimeog.), No. 1 (1943) and others; also Gluckman, Mitchell, and Barnes (1949) and Colson and Gluckman (1951).

18. See "7th Annual Report C.S.S.R.," Appen. IV: "Report of Work of Rhodes-Livingstone Institute," in *Colonial Research* (1950–51) (Cmd. 8303; London: H.M. Stationery Office).

19. See "7th Annual Report C.S.S.R.," Appen. III: "Report on Work of East African Institute of Social Research," in *Colonial Research* (1950–51) (Cmd. 8303; London: H.M. Stationery Office), pp. 86 ff.; and *Africa*, XXI (1951), 62, 63, and 147, 148.

a research officer working. It has also from the beginning offered facilities to accredited but independently financed anthropologists and other social scientists desiring to collaborate in its program. Its own initial scientific staffing has been planned to include, besides the anthropologist-director, five other social anthropologists, two urban sociologists, a linguist, an economist, and a legal expert. Research has begun on intensive social study by a combination of both anthropological field methods and social survey of Jinja, a center of rapid industrial development near the site of a hydroelectric installation under construction; on a Buganda immigrant labor survey for which a series of specialist studies have actually been made; on a series of studies of political organization among the Lacustrine Bantu (Baganda, Busoga, Banyankole, etc.); on studies of Kikuyu family life and child rearing; and on the ethnography and social structure among peoples in the Lake Province of Tanganyika and in West and East Kenya. These studies are being carried out by members of the Institute's staff and by some six other anthropologists, mostly financed by the British Colonial Office grants, who are working in collaboration with the Institute.

In West Africa, where the activities of the wartime Institute of Arts, Industries, and Social Science had been suspended, the greater part of government-sponsored anthropological field researches have so far been directed by the Colonial Social Sciences Research Council and its field studies committee, which has obtained the co-operation of the departments of anthropology in Britain in selecting and supervising the work of field investigators engaged in a series of studies in North, West, and East Nigeria, in the Gold Coast, Sierra Leone, and the Gambia. But a West African Institute of Social and Economic Research was established in 1950, with its headquarters at Ibadan in association with the University College, under the direction of an economist. Although the initial program places more emphasis on economic research, on a statistical basis, into national income, entrepreneurial, banking, and allied problems, some investigations of an anthropological character are planned, including an intensive study of Yoruba political institutions.[20]

Anthropological approaches are also included in the program of the Economic Survey of the Cocoa Producing Areas of Nigeria which has been independently organized and financed by the Nigerian Cocoa Marketing Board operating under the authority of an *ad hoc* committee.[21] This survey, which includes on its staff an anthropologist with earlier experience on the Gold Coast, Mr. K. Baldwin, is making sample studies in a number of cocoa-growing Yoruba communities and is issuing interim confidential reports analyzing occupation distribution, family sizes, indebtedness, organization of farm work, levels of consumption and property holdings, the structure and function of co-operative marketing, etc.

The University College of the Gold Coast, one of the two university colleges established since the war in West Africa, includes a department of social studies, of which Dr. K. Busia, the well-known African anthropologist, is the head. One of his first tasks was to undertake a social survey of Takoradi-Sekondi, in order to provide essential information toward meeting acute problems of overcrowding, unemployment, juvenile delinquency, and other malaises arising from the rapid and uneven expansion of this port area.

20. See "7th Annual Report C.S.S.R.," in *Colonial Research* (1950–51) (Cmd. 8303; London: H.M. Stationery Office), p. 83.

21. Under the chairmanship of A. W. Ashby, director of the Institute for Research in Agricultural Economics, Oxford.

ATTITUDES OF ANTHROPOLOGISTS TO APPLIED ANTHROPOLOGY

Mr. G. Wilson, shortly after his appointment as the first director of the Rhodes-Livingstone Institute, analyzed the role of anthropology in the public service in a paper which commanded the general assent of his colleagues (1940). Stressing that the proper virtue of applied anthropology was to be both useful and true, to combine practical relevance with scientific accuracy, he was concerned for a thoroughgoing realization of the limits of the scientific method in its application to human affairs and their wholehearted acceptance on both sides:

The social anthropologist cannot, as a scientist, judge of good and evil, but only of objective social fact and its implications. ... There is no scientific ideal of human welfare; there can be no scientifically authoritative direction of events; the social anthropologist is entitled, as a man, to his own moral and political views—they are no more and no less worthy of respect than those of any other well informed citizen—but he is not entitled to pass them off as "scientific."

Hence, he points out, the social anthropologist as a scientist can have no answer to such questions as "What ought we to do about African marriage, chieftainship, beer-drinking in town?" but he can usefully answer related questions as to the nature of the situation with which administrators have to deal. The conception of "technical information" is for him the key to the correct relationship between social scientists, on the one hand, and men of affairs, on the other:

Human societies, like the earth on which they live, have a hard material reality which cannot be mastered without patient and objective study. It is the scientists' business to undertake that patient and objective study, it is the business of government and industry to make use of their results in fashioning out of the present

whatever future they desire. The scientists must make it their boast that both governments and oppositions can trust them equally because they say nothing that they cannot prove, because they are always pedestrian and never leave the facts. The men of affairs must make it their boast that they allow the scientists perfect freedom in their researches and pay to their results when published the attention which proven fact deserves. ...

Experienced missionaries, compound managers and administrators all too rarely commit to paper that understanding of African institutions which they have acquired ... further it is now widely recognized that systematic and detailed knowledge cannot in any case be easily picked up in his spare time by a busy man who has no special training in research; even when he is stationed for years in one spot it is only an exceptionally gifted man who can attain it under such conditions. We do not expect technical veterinary or medical knowledge in a District Commissioner, and we are now realising that it is just as unreasonable to expect trained sociological knowledge either. The services of trained social anthropologists are essential to the effective development of Africa.

Wilson goes on to show that, while even the barest information, such as simple and accurate accounts of marriage, chieftainship, economic life, legal procedure, and so on, from a hundred changing tribes and compounds is badly needed for administrative purposes, the social anthropologist can provide more than this:

He claims to be able to explain the facts which he describes. ... The social facts which he finds do not, he maintains, just occur at random; each is necessarily connected with other facts in the same area ... they are inescapably linked together; if one of them changes then all the others must change too ... and this means that every social fact can, at any given moment, be explained as the necessary correlate of other social facts. ... Thus social anthropologists, if they are successful, do not only add to the detailed knowledge of fact at the disposal of responsible public men, they alter the nature of that knowledge and so make it more useful.

On the one hand,

the social scientists confine their gaze to the abstract field of matter-of-fact social necessity, but they do not imagine that this field of theirs is all the world there is. ... The scientist, once he has mastered the mutual implication of the facts of some social situation, is in a position to give technical, but not political, advice and criticisms to the men who have to deal with it.... [But] the complement of this limitation is the undoubted fact that many a wise policy has proved abortive in the past because obstructed by social conditions whose relevance to it was hidden from its authors [or has] had untoward effects which were in no way foreseen at the moment of its inception; but time and patient research can foresee in detail the probable effects of any given policy.

When we turn to the status of the advisory anthropologist vis-à-vis the government using his services, it is necessary, in the first place, to appreciate clearly the distinction between the direct participation in government of anthropologists, i.e., of professionally trained government servants with theoretical and factual knowledge concerning social processes in nonindustrial society who participate regularly in discussion of policy, and the services which may be rendered to colonial governments by independent investigators whose function is to report as consultant anthropologists on a given ethnographic situation. Both these functions may be useful, and they are not mutually exclusive, but discussion of the role of the anthropologist in government has been somewhat confused by a failure to maintain the distinction both on the part of anthropologists in general discussions on this topic and in colonial administrations desirous of securing their services.

As mentioned above, there was some discussion after the war in official and advisory circles concerning the desirability of establishing a regular service of government anthropologists who would be available for investigations in colonial territories. The establishment of such a cadre of government anthropologists did not materialize, and at the present moment Tanganyika is the only African territory under British administration which has appointed government anthropologists. Other anthropologists engaged in investigations under government auspices have been appointed *ad hoc* by the Colonial Office, with the agreement of the territory concerned, to carry out specific inquiries on short-term contract, or are attached to one of the autonomous social science research institutes. In both cases, however, the official functions of the anthropologists appear to be of the second category, namely, to present fact-finding reports and analyses likely to be of long-term value to the administration.

It is not possible to speak of a definite view held by professional anthropologists with regard to the question of the contractual terms and specific obligations of the anthropologist whose investigations are financed by government. All would probably agree with Evans-Pritchard's (1946) recognition that "a body of knowledge about human societies, like all knowledge, can be used in a common sense way to solve social problems and there is surely no one who holds that it should not be so used"; but there are those who, like him, fear that research effort of importance in tackling theoretical problems may be diverted by the linking of ethnographic investigations to practical inquiries on the part of professional anthropologists who have not entered government service. Evans-Pritchard would, for this reason, himself prefer the appointment of anthropological advisers as members of the regular colonial government service. He further suggests that, while "only a man with anthropological training and field work experience is fully capable of interpreting and applying anthropological knowledge . . . an essential point is that such an adviser should be in the administrative service and have knowledge of bureaucratic machinery from the inside." By implication he would hold that, although governments should support anthropological field research financially in their own long-term interests, this should be undertaken by independent scholars with no specific obligation to the administration. Stressing that "an anthropologist within his own scientific field will use the knowledge he acquires by research to solve anthropological problems, and these may have no practical significance whatever," and, while conceding that it may possibly be laudable on ethical grounds for one with anthropological training to investigate practical problems, he suggests that, "if he does so, he must realise that he is no longer acting in the anthropological field but in the non-scientific field of administration."

It is doubtful whether this extreme view of the incompatibility between scientific research aims and the provision of anthropological knowledge considered useful by an administration is generally accepted. Schapera (1949), while agreeing that problems that may be important for practical purposes may be of minor significance for theory and vice versa, also reminds us, on the one hand, that some theoretical problems, such as the nature and functioning of political authorities, are as relevant to the administration as to the anthropologist and, on the other, that the recording, for government purposes, of tribal law and custom and their social contexts also provides the anthropologist with data for theoretical analysis. As regards the relations between governments and anthropologists, he is more concerned about the excessive expectations which administrators may entertain and the corresponding temp-tation for anthropologists to overreach themselves in their desire to satisfy those who are financing the research; he concludes that "it is as dangerous for the government to regard an anthropologist as one who 'knows all about native life' as it is for the anthropologist to imagine that he can in fact discuss with equal authority kinship systems, rotation of crops, overstocking and household budgets." He voices a general trend of opinion among British anthropologists in considering that the role of the anthropologist, whether as an *ad hoc* consultant or in regular government service, should be limited to an advisory capacity, where

he can show from his knowledge of the people what would be the probable effect of certain measures, or if certain results are desired, what would be the most suitable methods of achieving them. But this does not mean that his advice need necessarily be accepted, since conditions of policy may demand that a certain line should be followed, whatever the result. Nevertheless, by seeking the advice of the anthropologist, the authorities concerned will at least be able to visualise more clearly what the consequences of their action are likely to be.

Like Evans-Pritchard, and voicing what is probably the general academic opinion, he urges (referring to Kenya) the appointment of permanent anthropological advisers; his point being that, for the best use to be made of anthropological knowledge from whatever source, it is desirable that the results of such investigations should be collated and that the colonial administrations should be in a position to formulate in terms of specific anthropological inquiries the special problems on which *ad hoc* investigation is needed. The main function of such an adviser would then be to keep abreast of relevant anthropological research and, in relation to the needs of district or departmental officers, to supply in suitable form, when available, such information as they may require or to arrange investigations, by himself or others specially engaged, which will yield the desired information. While Evans-Pritchard considers such posts should be filled by professional anthropologists of some standing and seniority from outside the administrative service, Schapera, writing of Kenya, considered that "a retired district officer with some knowledge of anthropology would be a suitable person for the post."

There is probably some divergence of view among academic anthropologists as to the range of social situations and problems which social anthropologists should tackle. The majority view, to judge from the programs framed by professional anthropologists who have directed research institutes in Africa or formulated programs at the invitation of governments, would appear to be that field research by anthropological methods of direct observation and inquiry could and should, without detriment to continued study of "tribal" societies, be extended to urbanized wage-earning communities and to the problems of social structure and cultural values which they present. This is based on the view that both the techniques and the theoretical interests of the social anthropologist are needed for the effective analysis of underlying social processes which are accompanying industrialism and Westernization in Africa.

It must be recognized, however, that there are those who would hold that the diversion of the slender resources of professional anthropology to such studies cannot be undertaken without detriment to the study of tribal groups and that the latter is the more urgent because their traditional social systems and cultural patterns are likely to be completely disrupted and no longer available for study in the near future. This issue, into which a considerable element of personal inclination must

enter, is important only because the total financial resources available for anthropological training and research are still so limited.

Whatever the bias in these directions, it is common ground that the quality of the service which social anthropology can render to colonial administrations is dependent on its own theoretical achievements, since all attempts to understand and to handle wisely a given practical social problem depend on the extent to which the facts can be established and analyzed in relation to a more general body of sociological knowledge. This being so, any wholesale diversion of funds for field inquiries and publication to narrowly prescribed short-term investigations would not only retard the scientific development of social anthropology but would be against the long-term interests of colonial administrations.

Thus, while academic anthropologists in general support the increased participation of anthropologists in the service of colonial governments, there is some anxiety lest the increasing recruitment of anthropologists for such services may be at the expense of funds and facilities for fundamental research. On the other hand, as the subjects, terms of appointment, and arrangements for supervision confirm,[22] the academic anthropologists in receipt of government grants or appointed to institutes have in practice been given great freedom in the planning, supervision, and execution of their field investigations, and in the great majority of cases theoretical as well as practical interests have been well served. While our knowledge of many African societies remains inadequate, almost any anthropological assignment of reasonable scope affords opportunities for the study of new data and the consideration of theoretical problems.

22. For details see Colonial Office reports and other reports cited earlier.

REFERENCES

ANON. 1946. "A Seven-Year Plan of Research," *Africa*, XVI, No. 2, 116–17.

BATSON, E. 1948. *Report on Proposals for a Social Survey of Zanzibar, 1946.* Zanzibar: Government Printer. (Final report not yet published.)

BRELSFORD, WM. VERNON. 1943. "Shimwalule: A Study of a Bemba Chief and Priest," *African Studies*, I, 207–23.

———. 1944a. "Aspects of Bemba Chieftainship." ("Communications from the Rhodes-Livingstone Institute," No. 2.) (Mimeographed.)

———. 1944b. *The Succession of Bemba Chiefs: A Guide for District Officers.* Lusaka, Northern Rhodesia: Government Printer.

———. 1946. *Fishermen of the Bangweulu Swamps: A Study of the Fishing Activities of the Unga Tribe.* ("Rhodes-Livingstone Institute Papers," No. 12.)

———. 1951. "Northern Rhodesia: Urban Councils on the Copperbelt," *Corona*, III, No. 11, 430–32.

BRELSFORD, WM. VERNON, and ALLAN, W. 1947. *Copperbelt Markets: A Social and Economic Study.* Lusaka, Northern Rhodesia: Government Printer.

BROWN, C. G., and HUTT, A. M. 1935. *Anthropology in Action.* London: Oxford University Press.

BULLOCK, CHARLES. 1928. *The Mashona.* Cape Town and Johannesburg: Juta & Co., Ltd. Rev. ed., 1950.

BUSIA, K. A. 1950. *Report on a Social Survey of Sekondi-Takoradi.* London: Crown Agents.

CHUBB, L. T. 1948. *Report on Ibo Land Tenure.* Zaria, Northern Nigeria: Gaskiya Corporation.

CLIFTON ROBERTS, C. 1935. "Witchcraft and Colonial Legislation," *Africa*, VIII, 488–94.

COLE, C. W. 1949. *Reports on Land Tenure in Nigeria—Niger Province, Zaria Province.* Kaduna: Government Printer.

COLSON, E., and GLUCKMAN, M. (eds.). 1951. *Seven Tribes of British Central Africa.* London: Oxford University Press.

CORY, H. 1952. *Sukuma Law and Custom.* London: International African Institute (in press).

CORY, H., and HARTNOLL, M. M. 1945. *Haya Customary Law, Tanganyika Territory.* London: P. Lund, Humphries & Co., Ltd., for the International African Institute.

COXHEAD, J. C. C. 1914. *The Native Tribes of N.E. Rhodesia, Their Laws and Customs.* ("Rhodes-Livingstone Institute Occasional Papers," No. 5.)

DALE, .ANDREW MURRAY, and SMITH, E. W. 1920. *The Ila-speaking Peoples of Northern Rhodesia.* London: Macmillan & Co., Ltd.

DRIBERG, J. H. 1928. "Primitive Law in Eastern Africa," *Africa*, I, 63–72.

EAST, R. M. 1939. *Akiga's Story: The Tribe as Seen by One of Its Members.* London: Oxford University Press.

EVANS-PRITCHARD, E. E. 1933–35. "The Nuer: Tribe and Clan," *Sudan Notes and Records*, XVI (1933), 1–53; XVII (1934), 1–57; XVIII (1935), 37–87.

———. 1937. *Witchcraft, Oracles and Magic among the Azande.* Oxford: Clarendon Press.

———. 1937–38. "Economic Life of the Nuer: Cattle," *Sudan Notes and Records*, XX (1937), 209–45; XXI (1938), 31–77.

———. 1940a. *The Political System of the Anuak of the Anglo-Egyptian Sudan.* ("London School of Economics and Political Science, Monographs on Social Anthropology," No. 4.)

———. 1940b. *The Nuer.* Oxford: Clarendon Press.

———. 1946. "Applied Anthropology," *Africa*, XVI, 92–98.

FIRTH, R. 1947. "Social Problems and Research in British West Africa," *Africa*, XVII, 77–91, 170–79.

FORDE, DARYLL. 1937a. "Social Change in a West African Village Community," *Man*, XXXVII, Art. 5, 10–12.

———. 1937b. "Land and Labour in a Cross River Village, Southern Nigeria," *Geographical Journal*, XC, No. 1, 24–51.

———. 1939. "Government in Umor: A Study of Social Change and Problems of indirect rule in a Nigerian Village Community," *Africa*, XII, 129–62.

———. 1945. "Social Development in Africa and the Work of the International African Institute," *Journal of the Royal Society of Arts*, XCIII, No. 4682, 71–83.

FORTES, M. 1936. "Culture Contact as a Dynamic Process (an Investigation in the Northern Territories of the Gold Coast)," *Africa*, IX, 24–55.

———. 1938. *Social and Psychological Aspects of Education in Taleland (Northern Gold Coast)*. ("Memoranda of the International African Institute," No. 17.) London.

———. 1948. "The Ashanti Social Survey: A Preliminary Report," *Journal of the Rhodes-Livingstone Institute*, Vol. VI.

———. 1949. "Time and Social Structure: An Ashanti Case Study." In FORTES, M. (ed.), *Social Structure: Studies Presented to A. R. Radcliffe-Brown*, pp. 54–84. Oxford: Clarendon Press.

FORTES, M.; STEEL, R. W.; and ADY, P. 1947. "Ashanti Survey, 1945–46: An Experiment in Social Research," *Geographical Journal*, CX, 149–79.

GLUCKMAN, MAX. 1945. "7 Year Research Plan of the Rhodes-Livingstone Institute of Social Studies in British Central Africa," *Journal of the Rhodes-Livingstone Institute*, Vol. IV.

GLUCKMAN, M.; MITCHELL, C.; and BARNES, J. 1949. "The Village Headman in British Central Africa," *Africa*, XIX, 89–106.

GOULDSBURY, CULLEN, and SHEANE, HUBERT. 1911. *The Great Plateau of Northern Rhodesia*. London: Edward Arnold.

GREEN, M. M. 1941. *Land Tenure in an Ibo Village in S.E. Nigeria*. ("London School of Economics and Political Science, Monographs on Social Anthropology," No. 6.)

HAILEY, LORD. 1938. *An African Survey*. London: Oxford University Press.

———. 1951. *Native Administration in British African Territories*, Part I. London: H. M. Stationery Office.

HALL, R. DE Z. 1938. "Study of Native Court Records as a Method of Ethnological Enquiry," *Africa*, XI, 412–27.

HARRIS, J. S. 1943–44a. "Papers on the Economic Aspect of Life among the Ozuitem Ibo," *Africa*, XIV, No. 1, 12–23.

———. 1943–44b. "Some Aspects of the Economics of Sixteen Ibo Individuals," *ibid.*, No. 6, pp. 302–35.

HOBLEY, CHARLES WILLIAM. 1910. *Ethnology of the Akamba and Other East African Tribes*. Cambridge: At the University Press.

———. 1922. *Bantu Beliefs and Magic*. London: H. F. & G. Witherby.

HOWELL, P. 1941. "The Shilluk Settlement," *Sudan Notes and Records*, Vol. XXIV.

HOWELL, P., and THOMSON, W. G. P. 1946. "The Death of a Reth of the Shilluk and the Installation of His Successor," *Sudan Notes and Records*, Vol. XXVII.

HUNTER, M. 1936. *Reaction to Conquest*. London: Oxford University Press.

JOHNSTON, SIR HARRY. 1897. *British Central Africa*. London: Methuen & Co.

———. 1902–4. *The Uganda Protectorate*. 2 vols. London: Hutchinson & Co.

———. 1907. "The Basis for a Comparative Grammar of the Bantu Languages," *Journal of the African Society*, VII, 13–19, 25–27.

———. 1919. *A Comparative Study of the Bantu and Semi-Bantu Languages*. 2 vols. Oxford: Clarendon Press.

JONES, G. I. 1951. *Basutoland Medicine Murder: A Report on the Recent Outbreak of "diretlo" Murders in Basutoland*. London: H. M. Stationery Office.

KABERRY, P. 1946. "Preliminary Report on Fieldwork in Bamenda, British Cameroons." London: International African Institute. (Mimeographed.)

———. 1950. "Land Tenure among the Nsaw of the British Cameroons," *Africa*, XX, 307–23.

———. 1952. *Women of the Grassfields: A Study of the Economic Position of Women in Bamenda, British Cameroons*. London: H. M. Stationery Office, for the Colonial Office (in press).

KRIGE, J. D. and E. J. 1943. *A Realm of a Rain Queen: A Study of Lovedu Society*. New York.

LEITH ROSS, SYLVIA. 1939. *African Women: A Study of the Ibo of Nigeria*. London: Faber & Faber, Ltd.

MACLEAN, JOHN. 1858. *Compendium of Kafir Laws and Customs*. Mount Coke: Wesleyan Mission Press.

MacMichael, Sir Harold Alfred. 1912. *Tribes of Northern and Central Kordofan.* Cambridge: At the University Press.

Mair, L. P. 1931. "Native Land Tenure in East Africa," *Africa,* IV, 314–49.

——. 1933. "Buganda Land Tenure," *ibid.,* VI, 187–205.

——. 1934. *An African People in the 20th Century.* London: G. Routledge & Sons.

——. 1936. "Chieftainship in Modern Africa," *Africa,* IX, 305–16.

——. 1940. *Native Marriage in Buganda.* ("Memoranda of the International African Institute," No. 19.) London.

——. 1950. "The Role of the Anthropologist in Non-autonomous Territories." In MacInnes, C. M. (ed.), *Principles and Methods of Colonial Administration.* London: Parthenon Press.

——. 1951. Review of Lord Hailey's *Native Administration in the British Territories of Africa, Africa,* XXI, 336–39.

Malinowski, B. 1930. "The Rationalization of Anthropology in Administration," *Africa,* III, 45–430.

——. 1938. *Methods of Study of Culture Contact in Africa.* ("Memoranda of the International African Institute," No. 15.) London.

Mayer, P. 1949. *The Lineage Principle in Gusii Society.* ("Memoranda of the International African Institute," No. 24.) London.

Meek, Charles Kingsley. 1925. *The Northern Tribes of Nigeria.* 2 vols. London: Oxford University Press.

——. 1931. *A Sudanese Kingdom.* London: K. Paul, Trench, Trubner & Co.

——. 1937. *Law and Authority in a Nigerian Tribe.* London: Oxford University Press.

Mitchell, Sir Phillip. 1930. "The Anthropologist and the Practical Man," *Africa,* III, 217–23.

Nadel, S. F. 1942a. "The Hill Tribes of Kadero," *Sudan Notes and Records,* Vol. XXV.

——. 1942b. *A Black Byzantium.* London: Oxford University Press.

——. 1947. *The Nuba.* London: Oxford University Press.

Orchardson, I. Q. 1931. "Some Traits of the Kipsigis in Relation to Their Contact with Europeans," *Africa,* IV, 466–74.

Orde-Browne, G. St. J. 1933. *The African Labourer.* London: Oxford University Press.

——. 1935. "Witchcraft and British Colonial Law," *Africa,* VIII, 481–87.

Peristiany, J. 1951. "The Age Set System of the Pastoral Pokot," *Africa,* XXI, 279–302.

Rattray, Robert Sutherland. 1923. *Ashanti.* Oxford: Clarendon Press.

——. 1927. *Religion and Art in Ashanti.* Oxford: Clarendon Press.

——. 1929. *Ashanti Law and Constitution.* Oxford: Clarendon Press.

——. 1932. *Tribes of the Ashanti Hinterland.* 2 vols. Oxford: Clarendon Press.

Read, M. 1938. *Native Standards of Living and African Culture Change (Ngoni, Nyasaland).* ("Memoranda of the International African Institute," No. 16.) London.

Richards, A. I. 1939. *Land, Labour, and Diet in Northern Rhodesia.* London: Oxford University Press.

——. 1940. *Bemba Marriage and Present Economic Conditions.* ("Rhodes-Livingstone Institute Papers," No. 4.)

——. 1941. *African Chieftainship in Transition.* Supplement to *Journal of the Royal African Society.*

——. 1944. "Practical Anthropology in the Lifetime of the International African Institute," *Africa,* XIV, 289–301.

Rowling, C. W. 1948a. *Notes on Land Tenure in the Benin, Kukuruku, Ishan, and Asaba Divisions of Benin Province.* Lagos: Government Printer.

——. 1948b. *A Study of Land Tenure in the Cameroons Province.* London: Colonial Office Land Tenure Panel. (Duplicated.)

——. 1949. *Reports on Land Tenure in Nigeria—Kano Province, Plateau Province.* Kaduna: Government Printer.

Schapera, I. 1928. "Economic Changes in South African Native Life," *Africa,* I, 170–88.

——. (ed.). 1934. *The Present State and Future Development of Ethnographical Research in South Africa* ("Bantu Studies," Vol. VIII, No. 3.)

——. 1938. *A Handbook of Tswana Law*

and Custom. London: Oxford University Press.

———. 1943. *Native Land Tenure in the Bechuanaland Protectorate.* Lovedale, South Africa: Lovedale Press.

———. 1949. *Some Problems of Anthropological Research in Kenya Colony.* ("Memoranda of the International African Institute," No. 23.) London.

———. 1951. "Anthropology and the Administrator," *Journal of African Administration,* Vol III.

SELIGMAN, C. G. 1918. *The Kababish: A Sudan Arab Tribe.* ("Harvard African Studies," Vol. II.) Cambridge, Mass.

SELIGMAN, C. G. and B. Z. 1932. *Pagan Tribes of the Nilotic Sudan.* London: G. Routledge & Sons.

SILBERMAN, S. 1950. "Social Survey of Old Town, Mombasa," *Journal of African Administration,* Vol. II. (Final report not yet published.)

SOUTHALL, A. 1952. *Lineage Formation among the Luo.* ("Memoranda of the International African Institute," No. 26.) London.

TAGART, E. S. B. 1931. "The African Chief under European Rule," *Africa,* IV, 63–76.

TALBOT, PERCY A. 1915. *Woman's Mysteries of a Primitive People* (Ibibio). London.

———. 1923. *Life in Southern Nigeria.* London: Macmillan & Co., Ltd.

———.1926. *Peoples of Southern Nigeria.* 4 vols. London: H. Milford.

———. 1932. *Tribes of the Niger Delta.* London: Sheldon Press.

THOMAS, NORTHCOTE W. 1910. *Anthropological Report on the Edo-speaking Peoples of Nigeria.* 2 vols. London: Harrison & Sons.

———. 1913–14. *Anthropological Report on the Ibo-speaking Peoples of Nigeria.* 6 vols. London: Harrison & Sons.

———. 1916. *Anthropological Report on Sierra Leone.* 3 vols. London: Harrison & Sons.

WAGNER, G. 1936. "The Study of Culture Contact and the Determination of Policy," *Africa,* IX, 317–31.

———. 1939. *The Changing Family among the Bantu Kavirondo.* ("Memoranda of the International African Institute, No. 18.) London.

WARD-PRICE, HENRY LEWIS. 1933. *Land Tenure in the Yoruba Provinces.* Lagos, Nigeria: Government Printer.

WESTERMANN, DIEDRICH. 1934. *The African Today and Tomorrow.* London: Oxford University Press. Rev. ed., 1949.

WHITE, C. M. N. 1948. "Witchcraft, Divination, and Magic among the Balovale Tribes," *Africa,* XVIII, 81–104.

———. 1949. "Stratification and Modern Changes in an Ancestral Cult," *ibid.,* XIX, 324–31.

———. 1950. "Notes on the Political Organisation of the Kabompo District and Its Inhabitants," *African Studies,* IX, 185–93.

WILSON, GODFREY. 1936. "An Introduction to Nyakyusa Society," pp. 253–91. ("Bantu Studies," Vol. X.)

———. 1937. "Introduction to Nyakyusa Law," *Africa,* X, 16–36.

———. 1938. *The Land Rights of Individuals among the Nyakyusa.* ("Rhodes-Livingstone Institute Papers," No. 1.)

———. 1939. *The Constitution of Ngonde* ("Rhodes-Livingstone Institute Papers," No. 3.)

———. 1940. "Anthropology as a Public Service," *Africa,* XIII, 43–61.

Applied Anthropology in Government: The Netherlands

By G. JAN HELD

DIFFICULT AS it is to frame a satisfactory exposition on applied anthropology in English-speaking countries, the task is infinitely harder for Holland. In the strictest Dutch sense there is no applied anthropology, even though Dutch scientists and scholars have long addressed themselves to problems which elsewhere are classified under this label. Clarification of this paradoxical state of affairs demands closer understanding of the functional and historical interrelationships among ethnology, in its narrow, historical Dutch sense, government policy and action, and the other so-called "Indological sciences."

In Holland, ethnological study commenced at an early date and from the beginning has been utilized by the other Indological sciences—philology, history, Islamology, Indonesian law, etc. As early as 1864 ethnology was included in the training course followed by prospective civil servants.

Malinowski (1945, p. 4), in recalling the forerunners of today's practical anthropology, says: "Historically, perhaps, the palm of priority belongs to Holland, where it is sufficient to name such pioneers as C. Snouck Hurgronje, who was able both to preach and to practice the value of anthropology in the fair and rational treatment of Natives; C. van Vollenhoven, whose interest in customary law was as theoretical-ly revealing as it has become practically influential; the ethnographic work of missionaries and administrators, as well as the more recent influence of such experienced administrators as van Eerde and Schrieke."

Although one may be of the opinion that Holland deserves praise for the treatment of the Indonesian peoples, it remains to consider the extent to which this praise can be credited to Dutch ethnology. Without laboring the vexing problem of universally acceptable definitions, we have, I believe, to state that anthropology had to be developed to a certain degree before one could reasonably speak of its "application." Now, in Holland, ethnology as a science developed so slowly that for a long time it could have but little practical influence.

Modern anthropology recently turned to the study of a number of problems long familiar to the Indological sciences. In England and America anthropology has developed rapidly and has had a growing voice in the practical solutions of these problems. In Holland, however, ethnology has contributed little to the analysis of them. In contrast to the other Indological sciences generally, ethnology in Holland had virtually no interest in practical affairs either at home or overseas.

If we are to judge Dutch ethnology on its own merits and not in the reflected light of the performances of ethnology in other countries, we certainly are not justified in claiming for anthropology the achievements of other sciences. Not until the latter part of the interwar period did anthropology in Holland gain sufficient strength and assurance that application of its theoretical insights was seriously considered.

If, for instance, the modern anthropologist wants to study government policy with respect to native land problems in Indonesia, he will find that it is Indonesian law, not ethnology, which can offer him the desired information. This discipline of Indonesian law never was, nor is it to be, confused with anthropology; nor is it so considered by Dutch scholars.[1] Unless one is aware

1. Kennedy's article on the same subject (1944) praises highly the five-year training which the Dutch civil servants received in Leiden and Utrecht universities. With reference to its high standards and its extensive emphasis on Indonesian culture and languages, he says: "Thus, every official in the East Indian civil service was a trained anthropologist" (p. 158). Consequently, he considers the Netherlands East Indies as "probably the best test case of anthropology applied to the administration of a colonial possession" (p. 157).

First, Kennedy expresses warm admiration for the effects in actual colonial practice of their training. He is of the opinion that the past success of the colonial policy of the Dutch was largely due to their having gained "a deep and sympathetic understanding of native attitudes and native ways" (p. 158). He pays high tribute to the accomplishments of sciences, such as that of customary law, the creation of the noble spirit and fine intellect of C. van Vollenhoven.

One thing, however, does not escape Kennedy's attention, namely, the curious fact that "Dutch anthropologist-administrators . . . cherished the native cultures to such an extent that they were blind to the need for adjustive change in these cultures to suit changing world conditions. This," he goes on to say, "to my mind, is the one great danger in having anthropologists as administrators" (p. 161).

We must, I believe, agree with Kennedy when he speaks of such "an 'anti-acculturation' attitude" (p. 162). It is another question, however, how far this attitude was favored by sciences such as that of customary law; and,

of such distinctions, it will prove difficult to understand the views concerning Indonesian culture expressed in Dutch literature, and to see where Dutch anthropology now stands among the humanistic sciences or why this is so.

That ethnology in Holland continued to follow its own line of thought, at a time when in other countries this science had already progressed in other directions, is partly the result of certain historical circumstances. Indonesia, the field wherein Dutch ethnology was born and developed, is culturally so complicated that it was, from the start, parceled out among various disciplines. This made it very difficult for any science to study that society as a whole. Without a sound knowledge of Arabic and Moslem culture, for instance, it will appear to be difficult to understand Indonesian Islam. Such a study, a full-time job in itself, does not provide a scholar sufficient opportunity to keep abreast of rapid and unexpected developments in other fields of science.

---

further, how far general anthropology may be held responsible for certain views advocated in the name of the earlier Dutch ethnology.

In the case of the Dutch civil servant there is indeed a knowledge—in later years increasingly sound—of anthropology. Considering the general nature of their training, I would, however, prefer to follow the normal Dutch custom and call the civil servants "Indologists" rather than "anthropologists." I believe that the actual influence of "anthropology" on Dutch colonial policy has always been relatively slight because Dutch "ethnology," as opposed to the other Indological sciences, cannot be considered very influential. Repeated reference to Dutch ethnology in arguments against acculturation involves no implications for anthropology in general, nor does it prove that those who argue on this basis are anthropologists.

This is, of course, not meant in any way as a criticism of the Dutch civil servant or of the standards of his training. I disagree with Kennedy only when he points to the Netherlands East Indies as a test case for the application of anthropology.

The situation in Holland with respect to ethnology was originally no different from that in other countries, where the subject was also long considered a "science of leftovers." The offerings of other sciences, such as the study of law, language, politics, etc., were so rich, varied, and mature that very few scholars were interested in what was still left over. And the problem of creating a science of "bits and pieces" was considerably more difficult here than in many other countries which were lacking in such a profusion of related studies.

The great Dutch scholar G. A. Wilken (1847–91), the second to hold the chair of ethnology in Leiden University, looked upon his field as practically unlimited, and perhaps even illimitable, comprehensible only to a man who knew all the other sciences together. In all earnestness he took up the studies he supposed ethnology had to deal with —Arabic, Sanskrit, and even Roman law. The tragedy of this outstanding scholar was that, when he died at the early age of forty-four, he felt his failure in performing a task which it was actually impossible to complete.

That this was indeed a utopian goal was gradually discovered by ethnologists in other countries, who applied the same comparative method used by Wilken, albeit on a more modest scale and in less complicated fields. Eventually, however, the attempts to describe primitive cultures in their totality resulted in a useful classification into geographically and culturally defined complexes of the enormous amount of material collected. This was not the product of Dutch ethnology, however, for that science found itself confronted with so many other well-disciplined branches of cultural science that the idea of a holistic approach must have appeared simply preposterous.

That legal, economic, religious, and other Indonesian cultural systems each functions as a system in this culture was indeed discovered by the specialists in the various fields. Adat Law or customary law lays sufficient stress on the fact that it does not want to be confused with, for instance, Roman law or any other historical legal complex but that it really is an Indonesian legal system, functioning in a living reality of Indonesian society. It is for this reason that these specialties are important also for the modern anthropologist.

All these social part-systems, however, were studied by specialists, who made use of the special techniques and methods appropriate to their own fields. Legal systems were studied in connection with the science of law; market and subsistence systems in connection with the study of economics; and so forth. Nobody studied society as a whole. Since this is the main contribution that anthropology has made to the understanding of human society, the conclusion must be that in Holland anthropology, and consequently applied anthropology also, were not early, but rather late, developments.

After Wilken's death, ethnology in Holland continued to exist mainly through the force of an established tradition, but it had little to contribute and was satisfied largely with repeating what had already been said by others. The Indological sciences, on the other hand, flourished under the able guidance of distinguished scholars.

That ethnology could do better than this was proved by the Amsterdam Professor S. R. Steinmetz (1862–1940), a disciple of Wilken. As early as 1899 he advocated a functional approach to anthropology and pointed to the need for a typological description after the rules of a method which he called "deductive-sociological." He introduced the official distinctions between sociography and sociology, on the one hand, and ethnography and ethnology, on the other. Although he fostered a dangerous distinction when restricting the first pair to the analysis of the "cultural" and "semicultural" peoples and the second to the "natural" peoples, he considered these as the sciences which should describe the total culture of all peoples.

Later, however, Steinmetz felt compelled to give up this approach because a description of Western society in its totality appeared methodologically an impossible task to complete. At the same time he did insist that this would be practicable for primitive societies. It is easily understood that sociography drifted more and more in the direction of modern sociology, although it never became completely separated from ethnological thinking. Especially after World War II has this development been considerably accelerated. This ethnologically oriented type of sociology has resulted in a good number of descriptive accounts of (mainly) Dutch communities and social phenomena. Steinmetz and his followers expressed their views in the journal *Mens en Maatschappij* ("Man and Society"), published since 1926. They pleaded, with increasing success, for the application of social science to practical problems.

In its analysis of Indonesian problems, ethnology might have profited considerably from the work done by Steinmetz, had he found better opportunities to influence the Indological sciences. In Dutch universities, however, the various disciplines are grouped together in fixed, coherent complexes within different departments. In the case of Steinmetz this was the department of geography, the students of which were mostly trained for teaching careers in Holland and not for professions in Indonesia. And, of course, it was exactly in Indonesia that ethnology first found its most appropriate field of investigation. Moreover, normally cultural field research is not explicitly in-

cluded in academic training in Holland, so that Steinmetz' disciples had little opportunity to obtain practical experience in the field of ethnology.

Whereas ethnology, in the study of Indonesian problems, found itself at a disadvantage over against general Indology, it experienced in Holland a similar situation with respect to sociology. Consequently, the conception of society as a whole developed only slowly and little by little. That all social phenomena are interrelated was generally accepted, but this interrelatedness was conceived as a consecutive agglutination rather than as a tendency to synchronic consistency.

Once the interrelatedness of social phenomena, of customs and mores, was observed and before the idea of social structure was conceived, it was only natural that scholars should look for some kind of binding force to keep them all together. This binding force was seen as a kind of ethos, a particularly Eastern type of thought, functioning as a general background for the whole of Indonesian culture. In comparison with the classic, all-embracing comparative method, this seemed to mark such an advance that it was seen as the birth of a new ethnology which at last had found its proper field of interest in the study of this Eastern mental background.

In a foreign culture it is more obvious that social phenomena are often interrelated in unexpected and apparently illogical ways. Consequently, it was the emotional arational element in Eastern mentality which mainly caught the attention of ethnology.

Undoubtedly, the study of Eastern mentality could have led to important results, and it really did so in a number of cases. When in 1903 F. D. E. van Ossenbruggen first elucidated the principle of four- and fivefold division in Javanese culture, he convincingly proved that this was a distinct pattern of classification which could be called confused and abstruse only by those who did not want to see it with the eyes of the Javanese himself.

At the same time, however, new problems were created, many of which were insoluble in the light of social psychology and the extent of knowledge about social organization of those days. That mentality is also a response to cultural patterns could not become sufficiently clear until anthropology began to analyze such patterns. It was practically inevitable that Dutch ethnology should fall into the trap of the psychological fallacy, so that no further serious attempts were made to explain social facts in terms of other social facts. That the part-systems studied by the Indological sciences were all structurally interrelated was a truth which became increasingly obscure. Ethnology confined itself to the offering of general comment, phrased in terms of magical thinking, on the facts, especially facts in the field of religion.

The specialists proceeded with their studies after their own methods and techniques. When they reached the limits of their fields, they referred to ethnology for further general comment. The science of Indonesian law, for instance, after having described the legal system as such, called on ethnology to confirm the view that the background of this system resides in what has been termed a "feeling for cosmic equilibrium."

Under such circumstances ethnological theory could obviously develop only slowly, since it was geographically restricted in its outlook and activity and methodologically consisted mainly of conceptions derived from classic ethnology and more recent, but rather sketchy, ideas of primitive mentality. Even Van Vollenhoven, though certainly not lacking in an interest in ethnology, makes little use of its theoretical conceptions. Snouck Hurgronje, himself one of the best ethnographers in the field, apparently owed very little to ethnology as a science.

In this period, which roughly covered the first quarter of our century, a great mass of ethnographic materials on Indonesia was assembled. This collection, for the most part, was not made to find answers to theoretical questions—very few such questions had even been posed. Not that there were no able and intelligent observers to make valuable contributions to our knowledge of Indonesian culture, but an insufficiency of theoretical tough-mindedness certainly produced much uncritical and even dilettantish work which had unfavorable effects upon ethnological theory. A vivid and shrewd evaluation of all this is offered by C. van Vollenhoven in his study *La découverte du droit indonésien* (1933).

It is, of course, difficult to state precisely when ethnology in Holland awoke to its relative impotence. Most Dutch ethnologists will, I believe, agree in crediting Professor J. P. B. de Josselin de Jong and Dr. W. H. Rassers, both of Leiden University, for the work of reconstruction.

This work of reconstruction could have been done by first pulling down part of what had been built up so far. This would have meant that such conceptions as diffusion, participation in culture, social organization, and so forth would have had to be rediscussed and reinterpreted in scientific disputation with the other Indological sciences. Rather than this, Dutch anthropology has preferred to follow a course aimed at a quiet recovery of its own strength. Self-evidently this situation makes it more difficult for the outsider to see where Dutch anthropology stands.

The program was one of slow but steady advance, the results of which became manifest in new research into such problems as secret societies, religious systems, political and social organization, and so forth. To this work, mostly done as library research for academic theses, was added the processing of field materials collected by civil servants and missionaries during their stays in Indonesia.

In the years shortly before World War II, the situation changed considerably. Growing acceptance of the holistic approach caused the Indological sciences gradually to recognize the importance of a structural analysis. Moreover, a number of young anthropologists in various positions in Indonesia were active in research. The organization of an anthropological service was under consideration. Owing to the war, however, this development came to a dead stop. After the war things were taken up again, but much still remains undone; although a few results could be considered achieved.

I hope that what has been said so far will demonstrate some of the difficulties in explaining the meaning of applied anthropology in Holland. In Holland applied or practical anthropology, in the sense in which this is understood in England, America, and Australia, is probably one of the youngest branches of our social science. Arising from a historically different type of ethnology, having little to say about its achievements and experiences, it may have a future but it has little of a past.

Nevertheless, many problems of interest to the modern applied anthropologist have already been studied by Dutch cultural sciences deliberately with a view to practical application. And on this work Dutch ethnological theory, or rather the lack of such theory, has exerted a marked, though not in every respect fortunate, influence.

It is perhaps both odd and unfortunate that anthropology, the social science which paid so much attention to the process of change, developed so much later in Holland than in other countries. By means of constant reiter-

ation, Dutch ethnology almost convinced itself that Eastern society differed so intrinsically from Western, owing to its "Eastern mentality," that change seemed hardly feasible. That Eastern society was static as compared with dynamic Western society was repeated time and again. Changing a society, which so clearly was the product of a typical mentality, needs must seem to be nothing but an infringement on this mentality itself and on freedom of thought in general, an idea frankly repulsive to Dutch liberal feelings.

Therefore, it was often in the name of ethnology itself that change was frowned upon. Especially regretted as a sheer loss of culture was the disappearance of folkloristically interesting and picturesque elements. Out of this miasma of value judgments a rather unprofitable discussion arose, couched in terms of the antithesis between East and West and the possibilities for "the twain to meet." What was condemned as already too Western by one was still too Eastern in the eyes of another. Preservation of unimportant culture elements was sometimes advocated with great fervor, while important changes were brought about without much insight into possible consequences. This situation was, of course, not peculiar to Holland alone, but its effects were more serious, since the problems of change were more pressing in her dependencies than in many other parts of the world.

Obviously, this has had its good side also, because introduction of change, in the cases where this was inevitable, was usually brought about only after much deliberation. There was little of the rash reform which results in evil rather than good effects. Peaceful and quiet preservation, however, is a dynamic force in itself, since the tendency to change is inherent in cultural structure. The tendency to synchronic consistency, which is indeed noteworthy in many Indonesian culture complexes, was viewed too much as a state of static equilibrium, and the dangers rather than the benefits of acculturation were too one-sidedly stressed.

At this very time an Indonesian professor of sociology, T. S. G. Mulia, criticizes ethnology as a science mainly occupied with the dislocation which supposedly would be the effect of Western influence on closed Eastern societies. "On the basis of the data collected so far," Professor Mulia says, "ethnology wants to investigate whether these developments result in cultural impoverishment and destruction of culture or in the uprising of new culture" (1950, p. 30). It is easily understood that Professor Mulia applies to sociology rather than to this ethnology for an analysis of the modern processes of change.

Indeed, ethnology understood in this way has provided little help in solving practical problems. When, for instance, such an excellent observer as the well-known missionary, Dr. A. C. Kruyt—who brought together an enormous mass of material—tries to describe the change in Toraja society "From Heathen to Christian" (*Van Heiden to Christen*), the conception of change itself dwindles down to nothing. However, owing to his sympathetic understanding of native life, he was able to harmonize practical missionary work to a remarkably high degree with the needs of the population.

Down to 1949 government activities in Indonesia increased steadily in extent and in depth. Besides the normal governmental functions of administration, legislation, jurisdiction, and police, an increasingly complicated and comprehensive welfare service was organized under the influence of changing colonial ideals, dealing with such things as control of usury, popular credit, pawnshops, narcotics, education, health, agricultural information, and so forth.

All this has been excellently described by A. D. A. de Kat Angelino in his *Colonial Policy* (1931).

The services were under the management of thoroughly, usually academically, trained specialists, each of them working in the field of his specialty. During their work they collected as much practical knowledge of the Indonesian culture as was necessary for its proper execution. In the case of highly technical services this was sometimes very little. In other cases, however, so much knowledge was gained that, for handling it, specific scientific methods were necessary. This is the case, for instance, in the study of Adat Law, which analyzed such a great body of material, brought together during the administration of justice or by deliberate research, that often one learns more about Indonesian culture in this science than in ethnography itself.

In general, the government tried to limit its activities to the schema of needs and to remain neutral in the schema of values accepted by the Indonesian peoples. It will be obvious that practical knowledge about governmental operations was not in all cases sufficient. At a rather early date the government recognized that social engineering could be more effectively undertaken if a broader insight into Indonesian culture, especially into its value system, could be gained.

Therefore, in 1891 C. Snouck Hurgronje was appointed adviser for native (and later, temporarily, also Arabic) affairs. In this capacity he played an important role in ending the unhappy and long-drawn-out Acheh war. Guided by his special knowledge of Moslem things and by his extraordinary personal talents, he cleared away many misunderstandings concerning the diffusion and the influence of Islam.

In the complicated government apparatus every organ had its own strictly defined field of activity, outside interference with which was often strongly resented. The tendency to traditionalize a given situation appears, for instance, in the fact that the same connection between Moslem and native affairs was maintained when Snouck Hurgronje left in 1906 to become a professor in Leiden, even to the inclusion of political affairs and Indonesian political parties in which Snouck Hurgronje had taken an interest.

The investigators commissioned to carry on cultural research and to give advice if requested were therefore government officials and had, in this capacity, to respect the division of labor and authority in government. This also meant, of course, that no others interfered with the specific work of the cultural researchers and that they were relatively free to do as they saw fit. As a result, quite a lot of work could be done in the fields of archeology, philology, and history. Investigations into human behavior, however, often had to be handled with care, since interference in what was considered the competency of other government instances might cause unpleasantness.

Outside the framework of government organization, relatively little cultural research work has been done. The Dutch universities do not normally explicitly include field research in their training programs, and, moreover, the costs for research in Indonesia were prohibitive. There are, indeed, private institutions in Holland for the promotion of such research, but their funds usually do not permit large-scale operations.

Such institutions are, for instance, the Royal Institute for the Tropics (Koninklijk Instituut voor de Tropen) in Amsterdam; the Royal Linguistic, Geographic, and Ethnological Institute (Koninklijk Instituut Voor Taal-, Land- en Volkenkunde) in The Hague; the Utrecht Society for the Arts and Sciences (Utrechts Genootschap van Kun-

sten en Wetenschappen); the Royal Netherlands Geographic Society (Koninklijk Nederlands Aardrijkskundig Genootschap); and the Netherlands Bible Society (Nederlands Bijbel Genootschap) in Amsterdam.

A remarkable contribution to scientific field work has been made by the Netherlands Bible Society, the more remarkable perhaps because missionary bodies do not everywhere find a way to make use of ethnology in their activities. In Holland the Bible Society was the first to realize the value of deliberate scientific investigations, and it was for its delegates that a program of Indonesian languages was first organized in the Dutch universities. The main object was, and is, of course, the translation of the Bible and the preparation for this; but it is understandable that in many cases the Bible Society delegates came to fulfil a position comparable to that of the applied anthropologist in our times. For many decades Indology and ethnology have been considered customary subject matter in training courses for missionaries, often given at a university level.

The training of the "Officials for the Study of the Indonesian Languages" (Ambtenaren voor de Beoefening der Indonesische Talen—short: Taalambtenaren) or government linguists, includes, after six years of classical high school (Gymnasium), a six- or seven-year course in Arabic, Sanskrit, Indonesian languages, and cultures.

A permanent problem since the beginning of their work in 1879 has been the regulation of their activity and usefulness, varying with the appreciation of the importance of detached cultural research. In some cases they were charged with the care of some specialized task of government activity. The Service for Popular Literature (Dienst voor Volkslectuur), for instance, was first set up as a committee to fulfil the need for suitable literature created by school education. Under able management, this service developed in a few decades into an important publishing and information agency in which the government found itself in the role not only of printer, publisher, bookseller, and librarian but also of journalist, propagandist, and critic. The Archeological Service (Oudheidkundige Dienst) followed a comparable course, because it came to include in its program not only archeological research but also rebuilding and reconstruction, further preservation of monuments, and to a degree the protection of Indonesian art in general. In other cases, however, only such research could be completed as seemed acceptable within the limits of the narrow administrative regulations. An example is found in the case of paleontologic work done by officials of the Geological Service or physical anthropology done by Public Health servants.

The problem of defining the administrative position of the purely scientific investigator was always highly complicated. Various solutions have been offered, none of them too satisfactory. In some cases the investigator was placed at the disposal of an administrator with high authority. This position was profitable for the investigator, in that he could rely on the higher authority for the technical equipment needed in his field work. Moreover, if scientific advice was wanted in a practical case, the higher authority had the power to see that the advice was acted on.

The obvious disadvantage, on the other hand, is that the investigator often had to direct his attention to problems he was not interested in or familiar with. Being an official himself, the investigator had, of course, to oblige his superior, at the cost not only of his personal feelings but sometimes of science as well. If the investigator was not a very strong personality, he ran the risk of being employed as a jack-of-all-trades, especially if other

personnel were scarce. A versatile and active person in such a situation is likely to give the impression that science knows how to handle every possible practical difficulty. Enthusiastic champions of anthropology sometimes put him in an awkward position by recommending anthropology as a universal remedy for all colonial troubles.

Occasionally, the government seconded a civil servant's studying a particular situation. It was sometimes felt that such a practical man of affairs would do just as well as, or perhaps better than, a professional scientist, who might be biased by theoretical considerations and not acquainted with the details of the practical problem. To these part-time investigators we owe indeed some outstanding studies. In other cases, however, their work was not entirely satisfactory, since it contained misleading and sometimes even dangerous generalizations, supposedly justified by theoretical science. If science makes unjustified claims for its ability to solve practical problems, one may expect, of course, that, on the other hand, science will be used in practical matters for dubious aims.

There are also investigators in charge of local institutions, founded or underwritten partly with private funds, as, for instance, the Kirtya Liefrinck-van der Tuuk in Den Pasar (Bali); the Matthes Foundation in Makasar (Celebes); and the Malinckrodt Foundation in Bandjermasin (Borneo). This form of organization provides more freedom for scientific research, although the management of a well-run and prospering foundation and the care of a museum which usually goes with it demand more than scientific abilities alone. After World War II the activities of such institutions were drastically curtailed in Indonesia.

The most important institution, the Royal Batavian Society for the Arts and Sciences (Lembaga Kebudajaan Indo-

nesia "Koninklijk Bataviaasch Genootschap van Kunsten en Wetenschappen") in Djakarta possesses a very good
library and a beautiful museum. Although in some cases this society gave,
and still gives, advice to the government, its staff is fully occupied with the
internal work of the society and its
publishing activities.

Besides the investigators placed at
the disposal of high administrators and
those in charge of local institutions, a
few were placed directly under the director of the Department of Education,
who usually confined himself to indicating a field for research work, for the
rest permitting the investigator to study
what and how he liked. With a view to
scientific freedom, this was nearly the
best solution thinkable under the circumstances. The drawback, however,
was that it left the official to his own
devices—usually for a period of years
under primitive conditions—so that he
ran a heavy risk of becoming isolated.
The influence he had in the treatment
of any practical problem depended on
his personal qualities. Having a more
intimate knowledge of the district and
a greater freedom of movement, he
was sometimes able to criticize government actions and was therefore considered a public nuisance. In other cases,
owing to his superior knowledge, he
was looked upon as a local oracle.

In my opinion, on the basis of my
reading of the Dutch experience, it is
not advisable for the cultural scientist
to take the place of the social engineer.
If the social engineer is not present, the
anthropologist is perhaps best qualified
to act as his substitute, since his interests lead him into many fields. This is
possibly the reason why so much of the
extensive social engineering done in Indonesia is considered the equivalent of
applied anthropology in other countries.

Actually, however, the anthropologist
cannot take the place of the expert or
the man of practical affairs. Important,
for instance, though land problems may
be for society as a whole, the anthropologist had better be careful in expressing his opinions on the intricacies
of agrarian law, unless he is well versed
in the detailed knowledge of the subject amassed by Indological disciplines.

Moreover, if the anthropologist
wants to offer practical help, he has, of
course, to accept the regulations laid
down for the specialist by the higher
authorities. And it is exactly the regulation itself which the cultural scientist
often has to criticize. Consequently, the
cultural scientist, being an official himself, had to be placed in an administrative position such that high officials
would be willing to learn from his criticism. Before 1949 the government linguist held practically the same rank
during his whole term of office. If he
wanted to advance, he usually had to
secure a position in university teaching or in the higher ranks of the Department of Education. As a consequence, he would be lost to practical
work at a time when he had gathered
the kind of experience most requisite
for practical application.

If the anthropologist becomes too
engrossed in social engineering, he gets
so entangled in practical policy that
he will have to compromise with science. He cannot start from a given political situation, because the acceptance
of a given situation needs must have
its moral implications. Only very exceptionally gifted persons will be able
under such circumstances to maintain
the spiritual freedom which is the privilege and the duty of the practitioner
of science.

Only through exhibiting determined
tenacity toward the canons of scientific
freedom can the anthropologist be prevented from considering himself all-
knowing. That he is sometimes considered as such by others is a nearly
inevitable consequence of the holistic

anthropological approach. It is a living necessity for the anthropologist to remain in contact with science. He needs a good library and continuous contact with fellow-workers. It is, in my opinion, not advisable for an investigator to concentrate on one restricted geographical area, as was often done under the former government.

In the years before World War II the importance of anthropology was more and more widely recognized. This would have led in Indonesia to the organization of an anthropological service if the war and its aftermath had not intervened. That this service would not have shied away from practical problems is evident from the character of some assignments which were in preparation or already being carried out before the war. They included investigations into such problems as the difference in cultural participation between ethnic groups on the island of Lombok; the remarkable pugnacity of the people of Adonara; the increased bride-price in southern Sumatra; and the percentage of unmarried women in Nias. The number of investigators active in different capacities, either temporarily or permanently, was about fifteen, not including those with specific assignments (Archeological Service, Popular Literature, Museum, etc.).

As one of the few happy results of the war, the insight into the necessity of better-organized teamwork increased. It was felt that the university would be most appropriate as a new center of activity. However, since the Indonesian university is set up after the Dutch model, it appeared necessary to propose an amendment to the Law on University Education, cultural research not being mentioned therein explicitly as a university task. The former government hesitated to accept this amendment because this would have led to an unprecedented increase in the influence and the independence of the university.

Notwithstanding this, the funds for a university institute were voted, and consequently the investigators, considerably decreased in number owing to the war, were included on the university staff. The difficulties are far from being cleared away, partly because the situation up to the present has not been definitively legalized and partly because the university has no experience of active research work. In principle the university staff consists only of teachers of the rank of professor, helped by their technical assistants. Consequently, the members of the new Institute for Cultural and Linguistic Research (Lembaga Penjelidikan Bahasa dan Kebudajaan) of the University of Indonesia in Djakarta are too easily considered teachers for general affairs.

Our discussion has brought us up to the contemporary period, and I presume that I would be excused if I ended here. An attempt to forecast the future of anthropology would require that I assume the mantle of the prophets. However, without claiming such distinction, it might be helpful if I try to make a tentative, and personal, prognosis.

The political separation between Holland and Indonesia makes itself felt also in the field of anthropology. Anthropology in Holland is still connected with that in Indonesia, but by a rather thin thread. The young Republic has made it clear that it still wants the help of specialists in various professions, primarily technicians and medical men. Until now, however, very few cultural scientists or anthropologists have been invited.

This is not due to the fact that Indonesians fail to appreciate the potential help of the social sciences in general. There are a number of practical problems, such as education, industrialization, etc., to which these sciences are expected to contribute. Anthropology, however, is to a degree suspect for its presumed advocacy of the cultural status quo and is even considered as "colonialistic" in its type of thought. The interest in *primitive* societies, as exhibited even by the most modern and progressive anthropology, can hardly be expected to harmonize with the interests of a young and fervent nationalism.

It is true that anthropology has not restricted its attention entirely to primitive societies but has taken up the study of modern Western communities. It is also true that anthropology sees modern civilization in broader perspective for being set against a background of primitive societies. Notwithstanding all this, it is understandable that Indonesian nationalism shies away from anthropology and prefers to place its trust in sociology, as indicated by the criticism of Professor Mulia, mentioned above.

There is a current tendency to identify *Ilmu Kebudajaan* (the Indonesian term meaning "culturology" for the older *Volkenkunde* or "ethnology") with sociology. If a professional sociologist is invited to teach this subject matter, it is hardly to be expected that too much space will be left over for anthropology proper.

The maintenance and preservation of existing culture has often been advocated in the name of ethnology. The modern temper in Indonesia, however, asks whether it is worth while to maintain what exists. From discussions during recent congresses held in Djakarta and Bandung, one gets the impression that change is still visualized as a pendulum swing between East and West.

It is regrettable that anthropology can do so little to help shed light upon such problems. It would be extremely useful if more Indonesians could be induced to take up the study of anthropology, as was advocated in a resolution adopted by the VII Pacific Science Congress in New Zealand in 1949. The Indonesian government did offer about ten scholarships for the study of anthropology, but there was a marked hesitation on the part of officialdom to comply with planning along these lines.

So long as there are so few Indonesian anthropologists, I believe there will be little likelihood of developments toward applied anthropology from this, its original source. Whatever comes will have to be mainly in the hands of non-Indonesians, at least for the time being. Such a situation would hurt national feelings and probably would be interpreted as a new form of colonialism. Foreign anthropologists who want to analyze the present conflict situation might well remember that, so far, existing problems seldom have been studied in their total cultural context. It would perhaps be advisable to maintain and establish closer relations between anthropology and the humanistic disciplines, such as philology, linguistics, history, and also psychology.

It is still an open question whether Holland will be in a position to give Indonesian anthropology further guidance and assistance. Until 1949 relations between anthropology in Holland and in Indonesia were so close that our discussion has time and again led us from one area into the other. We are faced with an odd, and in a sense unfortunate, situation. Holland now has a number of young anthropologists but lacks the funds to give them a start in practical research. Indonesia needs anthropologists but lacks the experience which could make it conscious of this need. Other countries have the anthropologists and the funds, but they lack the scientific equipment built up by generations of Dutch science. A bright spot, in this discipline's development at least, is the recent organization of an anthropological service in western New Guinea, with a staff of six qualified anthropologists.

Another bright spot, perhaps, is the establishment this year of the Institute of Social Studies in The Hague. Of its purposes it is said: "It was considered that the contribution of Dutch scholarship to the understanding of the history and problems of the eastern world and of international society should be enabled to continue and further to develop. The need existing in many countries for scientific training as a preparation for administration and other social activities was another consideration leading to the establishment of the Institute."

However, although the names of at least four anthropologists appear in the teaching staff of this institute, its main program—a course in public administration—has a sociological, not an anthropological, background and orientation. As at present set up, it is there-fore not very likely that it will be an important vehicle for the study and dissemination of anthropology or applied anthropology. The fact that sociology takes precedence over anthropology is perhaps to be explained partly as a consequence of earlier inadequacies for which anthropology is blamed.

I believe that anthropology in Holland will further develop into a general science of man. In so far as the solution of practical problems is concerned, there is more to be expected of help offered by sociography and sociology.

In Indonesia anthropology will have to use every effort to retain its foothold. If anthropology gets no encouragement, there is reason to fear that a break may develop in traditional scholarship. Consequently, it is unlikely that it will become practically important. This is regrettable for a science which can help, as Kluckhohn (1949, p. 1) says, to "provide a scientific basis for the crucial dilemma of the world today: How can peoples of different languages, and dissimilar ways of life get along peaceably together?"

REFERENCES

BAAL, J. VAN. 1939. "De Vevolking van Zuid-Nieuw-Guinea onder Nederlandsch Bestuur: 36 Jaren," *Tijdschrift v.d. Indische Taal-, Land- en Volkenkunde*, LXXIX, 309–414.

BERTLING, C. T. 1949–50. "Wereldbeschouwing en sociale Ordening in Indonesië," *Indonesië*, III, 270.

BURGER, D. H. 1948–50. "Structuurveranderingen in de Javaanse Samenleving," *Indonesië*, II, 381, 486; III, 1, 101, 225, 347, 381, 512.

DUYVENDAK, J. PH. 1938. *Ethnologische Belangstelling*. Batavia.

———. 1946. *Inleiding tot de Ethnologie van de Indische Archipel*. 2d ed. Groningen.

EERDE, J. C. VAN. 1923. *A Review of the Ethnological Investigations in the Dutch Indian Archipelago*. Amsterdam.

Encyclopaedie van Nederlandsch-indië. 1917–21. 2d ed. The Hague and Leiden.

FISCHER, H. TH. 1948. *Inleiding tot de Volkenkunde van Nederlands-Indië*. 2d ed. Haarlem.

HAAR, B. TER. 1948. *Adat Law in Indonesia*. Edited by E. ADAMSON HOEBEL and A. ARTHUR SCHILLER. New York.

HEINE-GELDERN, R. VON. 1945. "Prehistoric Research in the Netherlands Indies." In HONIG, PIETER, and VERDOORN, FRANS (eds.), *Science and Scientists in the Netherlands Indies*, pp. 129–67. New York.

———. 1946. "Research on Southeast Asia: Problems and Suggestions," *American Anthropologist*, n.s., XLVIII, 149–76.

HIDDING, K. A. H. 1937–38. "The Bureau for Popular Literature," *Bulletin of the Colonial Institute*, I, 185–94.

JOSSELIN DE JONG, J. P. B. DE. 1948. *Customary Law, a Confusing Fiction.* ("Mededelingen van de Koninklijke Vereniging Indisch Instituut," No. 80.) Amsterdam.

KAT ANGELINO, A. D. A. DE. 1931. *Colonial Policy.* 2 vols. The Hague.

KENNEDY, RAYMOND. 1944. "Applied Anthropology in the Dutch East Indies," *Transactions of the New York Academy of Sciences,* Ser. 2, VI, No. 5, 157–62.

KLUCKHOHN, CLYDE. 1949. *Mirror for Man.* New York: Whittlesey House, McGraw-Hill Book Co.

LOCHER, G. W. 1948–49. "Inleidende Beschouwingen over de Ontmoeting van Oost en West in Indonesië," *Indonesië,* II, 411, 538.

MALINOWSKI, BRONISLAW. 1945. *The Dynamics of Culture Change.* New Haven.

MULIA, T. S. G. 1950. "Indonesische Sociologie," *Indonesia* (Dec.). Also in *Cultureel Nieuws,* No. 11 (August, 1951), pp. 28–32.

NAERSEN, F. H. VAN. 1946. *Cultuurcontacten en sociale Conflicten in Indonesië.* Wageningen and Amsterdam.

NEYS, R. 1945. *Westerse Acculturisatie en Oosters Volksonderwijs.* Utrecht.

NOOTEBOOM, C. 1934–35. "Adonare, het Moordenaarseiland, Volkenkunde en Bestuur," *De Locomotief,* December 1 and 5, 1934, and January 19, 1935.

––––. 1940. "Volkenkunde en koloniale Practijk," *Koloniaal Tijdschrift* (July).

––––. 1947–48. "Het Belang van socioethnologisch Onderzoek in het Nieuwe Indonesië," *Indonesië,* I, 43.

VERMOOTEN, W. H. 1941. *De Mens in de Geographie.* Assen.

VERSLUYS, J. D. 1947–48. "Sociale Structuur en Adatrechtspraak op Soemba," *Indonesië,* I, 253.

––––. 1949–50. "Maatschappelijke Verandering op Timor," *ibid.,* III, 130, 201.

VOLLENHOVEN, C. VAN. 1933. *La Découverte du droit indonésien.* Paris.

Applied Anthropology in Government: United Nations

By ALFRED MÉTRAUX

IT SHOULD be plainly stated, at once, that anthropology has so far played a very slight part in the work of the United Nations and the specialized agencies, and there is no reason to suppose that this situation will change in the years to come. It is true that several anthropologists have served, or are now serving, on the staff of these international organizations, but they have seldom been employed in their capacity as anthropologists; while, therefore, their specialized knowledge may have proved useful to them, it has not been indispensable. It is chiefly under the general heading of "social scientists" that anthropologists have been enrolled in the Department of Social Affairs and the Trusteeship Department of the United Nations, or in the United Nations Educational, Scientific, and Cultural Organization (UNESCO) or the World Health Organization (WHO).

The United Nations turn to anthropologists, first and foremost, on account of their familiarity with a given geographical area. It is for this reason, rather than because of the methods and views that they uphold, that they are asked to help in the work of the United Nations. Their very existence might be overlooked, were it not pointed out by English-speaking officials, who seem to be almost alone in real-izing that there is a practical value in anthropology. The services rendered by anthropologists to British colonial administration have considerably influenced the status of anthropology in international administration.

The following queries included in the questionnaire sent by the Trusteeship Council to trust territories constitute, so to speak, an official recognition of the importance of anthropology in colonial administration: "Does the territory maintain a Department of Anthropology or a government anthropologist? If so, describe the organisation, duties and result of the work. If not, what provisions are being made for continuous, systematic research by trained social scientists into both the traditional and the changing social, political, religious and economic life of the indigenous inhabitants?"

Any international program applied to an underdeveloped country—the natural preserve of anthropologists—ought to afford opportunities for enlisting their co-operation. It is reasonable, for instance, that anthropologists should have accompanied visiting missions to trust territories or been put in charge of fundamental education projects; but they have rarely been given a chance to apply their science in practice or even to add to its theory. With few exceptions, anthropologists in the United

880

Nations have had to abandon the pursuit of their science to devote themselves to their administrative duties.

UNESCO is the best placed of all the specialized agencies, so far as anthropology is concerned. It has a Department of Social Sciences, and its program lies partly in the domain of science; for these reasons it has been able to draw upon the services of anthropologists to carry out projects falling clearly within the competence of their science.

The establishment of an expanded program of technical assistance for the economic development of underdeveloped countries through the United Nations and the specialized agencies, coinciding as it has with the development of fundamental education, should open up new and extensive prospects for anthropology. The hopes raised in anthropologists by administrators and the representatives of member-states have not all been fulfilled; but it should be borne in mind that this program has only just been set on foot and that certain administrative regulations put difficulties in the way of the recruitment of anthropologists.

TECHNICAL ASSISTANCE AND ANTHROPOLOGY

Technical assistance, the field in which anthropology will have a noteworthy part to play in the United Nations, may be broadly defined as a United Nations scheme to bring to the economically backward countries the technical knowledge and methods that will enable them to raise their standard of living and to have their share in the progress of the highly industrialized countries. This form of assistance was suggested to guard against possible accusations of imperialism and to enable the areas in need of assistance to apply for it without any loss of dignity or any fear of thereby forfeiting their sovereignty. The chief aim of technical

assistance is to narrow the present gap between the living standards of the industrialized and the underdeveloped countries. The inequality in this respect to be seen in all parts of the world is a threat to peace. Not only does the contrast encourage an inclination to rebel, but the poverty prevalent in large areas of the world is a handicap to the more fortunate countries, in that their level of production is directly affected by the economic weakness of potential customers.

The United Nations regard this disparity as a growing source of danger. For any technical progress tends to act as a stimulus for further discoveries, in that it creates new demands and gives rise to fresh solutions for certain technical problems. "The under-developed areas thus tend to fall farther and farther behind and they are likely to continue to do so unless deliberate and effective measures are taken to bring to them the benefits of modern science and technology."

The development that technical assistance seeks to achieve in the underdeveloped countries has been defined as "a cumulative process where agricultural improvements, health, education, social measures and industrialization are introduced in a gradual interplay." The promoters of technical assistance are fully aware that economic development is bound to affect all aspects of a people's life to varying degrees. Food, health, social welfare, and education are the main fields in which they wish to introduce changes, and they are persuaded that, "given a wide and equitable distribution of its benefits, it is likely to result in a substantial increase in the security of the individual and in social stability."

There is a most important principle that must not be overlooked when the implications of technical assistance projects are being considered. Help may be given only on requests from governments, and it must not overstep the limits laid down in such requests. Above all, technical assistance is designed to equip the peoples with the tools of their future prosperity and to give them the opportunity of self-development in accordance with their own material and spiritual interests. Its aim is to encourage them to shape their future with their own hands.

Fundamental education, one of UNESCO's most important activities, has become a prominent feature of technical assistance, although the administrative services dealing with it were set up long before the technical assistance services. Indeed, from the very beginning, fundamental education has been regarded as one of UNESCO's primary functions.

What is meant by "fundamental education"? It has been defined in many different ways and has become the nucleus of a whole philosophy. In brief, fundamental education may be described as a form of instruction for communities in the underdeveloped areas of the world, comprising entire zones or isolated localities in the more highly developed territories. It aims not only at teaching the three "R's" but also at "improving the life of the nation, influencing the natural and social environment and imparting knowledge of the world."

Its aims, which we do not intend to list in full, include some of direct concern to anthropologists: (1) knowledge and understanding of the human environment (economic and social, organization, law, and government); (2) the development of qualities to fit men to live in the modern world, such as personal judgment and initiative, freedom from fear and superstition, sympathy and understanding for different points of view; (3) spiritual and moral development, belief in ethical ideals, and the habit af acting upon them, with the duty to examine traditional standards of behavior and to modify them to suit new conditions.

Fundamental education and technical assistance are closely linked not only administratively but, above all, by the similarity of their aims and the essential relationship between their activities. Technical assistance can succeed only if the peoples for whom it is intended are able to listen to and act upon the advice of the technicians. In other words, no program of economic rehabilitation can be drawn up save hand in hand with a fundamental education campaign. So strongly has this need been felt that in the first year of technical assistance twenty-seven countries appealed to UNESCO for educational assistance.

One of the main principles of fundamental education and of economic development alike is that they must be based upon the social, human, and economic environment which they have to transform and must bring about a "successful synthesis between traditional forces and ideas and the modern progressive movement through schools."

The increasingly frequent allusions made in various documents to the need for taking the social factor into consideration surely testify to the indirect and doubtless unconscious influence of the warnings uttered by social scientists. In the resolution adopted by the Economic and Social Council on March 4, 1949, it is expressly stated that "due attention shall be paid to national sovereignty and national legislation of the under-developed countries and to the *social conditions* which directly affect their economic development" (our emphasis).

An official document lays down that the forms of economic development in advanced countries cannot be applied indiscriminately to backward countries and states that "in every country, development must be brought about mainly through the efforts of the local population and by means of appropriate changes in economic and social structure."

But the clearest definition of the place that should be given, in every project, to the cultural and social considerations comes from the Food and Agriculture Organization, which, in one of its reports, expresses the view that "the successful implementation of any programme of assistance to underdeveloped countries depends more upon the method of approach than upon any other single factor." In the same document we find the following statements, which cannot but meet with the full support of anthropologists: "Past traditions must be respected and the expert must be ready to work through existing patterns, utilizing to the fullest the inherent potentialities. . . . It will often be well to present new ideas as an improvement on an older method, not only because this is psychologically sound but also because such improvements may be better than an entirely new method." Need for a global approach is stressed: "Sometimes the problem which appears paramount may itself be caused by other and more fundamental situations which need first attention."

In UNESCO's report prepared at the request of the Economic and Social Council we find the following paragraphs, which are worth quoting in full:

Such examples make it obviously necessary to associate with projects of economic development specialists with experience in anthropology and sociology. Their advice will help to ensure that the economic development scheme conforms to the way of life valued by the people themselves. The assistance of social scientists is obviously not enough in itself to enable a scheme to avoid all the risks inherent in major social changes, but at least it gives some hope that these risks will be considerably reduced. Their help will be particularly effective if it is understood that their services do not dispense with the necessity for the closest possible contact with those persons in the local population who are best able to interpret the national culture. One of the main functions of the social scientist, indeed, will be to make sure that the opinions of such people are given the fullest consideration.

When a mission is sent to survey the technical needs and problems of a given country, in response to its request for technical assistance, an expert should be included in the team to conduct on the spot a survey of the sociological implications of the projected assistance programme. The primary function of this expert should be to advise in protecting the native cultures as the protection of national cultures is one of UNESCO's duties.

The experts concerned must obviously have a thorough knowledge of the culture within which the technical assistance program is operating and must also be able to describe it objectively, so as to foresee the effect that the changes introduced will have on that culture as a whole. Anthropologists are the scientists best fitted by their training to meet these requirements.

CONSEQUENCES OF SOCIAL CHANGES WARRANTING THE PARTICIPATION OF ANTHROPOLOGISTS

The task which the technical assistance and fundamental education services propose to allot to anthropologists is an extremely delicate one; it amounts to guiding the transition from one form of culture to another in order to avert the disastrous consequences that many countries of the world have suffered from such changes in the past.

Progress, in the form in which the United Nations seeks to propagate it throughout the world, must inevitably destroy the many forms of local culture still surviving on several continents. These cultures have their defects, no doubt, but they are nonetheless the outcome of a long adaptation to local conditions, and their followers find in them a satisfaction for which even the most advanced technology cannot always compensate. The members of a village community often enjoy a measure of protection that they will lose when swamped in the proletariat of a new type of society. The leisurely well-ordered rhythm of country life has all too often been replaced by joyless, soul-deadening toil. We have learned by now that no culture has succeeded in bringing into play all the potentialities of human nature and that some of the humblest forms of culture have solved problems that baffled the more highly developed. Higher standards of living—industrialization—will inevitably destroy such values and thus tend toward the impoverishment of the human race. The choice lies not between guns and butter but between butter and certain forms of art, certain religious or philosophical traditions. The danger of standardization is largely theoretical, for it must be remembered that requests for technical assistance and fundamental education are being received from countries where development is in full swing and which have to a great extent broken with their past traditions. It is the materially and spiritually impoverished countries which are calling most urgently for help in overcoming their present difficulties.

No reasonable person could suppose that it would be possible to turn vast areas of the world into preserves for the protection of native cultures. Even if, for sentimental reasons, we might wish to do so, the representatives of the cultures concerned would undoubtedly be the first to wish to escape from their traditional way of life and to denounce our efforts as unjust and discriminatory. It must be remembered that the initial impetus toward change and development has to come from the governments and peoples of the underdeveloped countries. And they are traveling along the path of progress faster than their advisers had expected. They are trying to go ahead too quickly—at a dangerous rate. If any attempt is made to check them, they raise the cry of "reaction" or assert that they are being made the victims of a sinister imperialism. Heads of missions often find that one of their most difficult problems is to restrain ill-timed enthusiasm and curb the impulse toward premature innovation. Nowadays it is the most highly cultivated representatives of the colored races who protest most vehemently when white men advise them to maintain their traditional customs. They even tend to regard anthropologists as the agents of an insidious imperialism which, under the cloak of respect and affection, is striving to perpetuate its supremacy and to debar the colored races from all access to power and happiness.

A good example of the impatience shown in this respect by representatives of former "colonial" peoples is to be found in a United Nations report on the *Non-self-governing Territories* (1951, p. 94). During a committee debate on vernacular languages, Mr. Lopez, delegate from the Philippines, said among other things that he "did not understand the somewhat romantic attachment evidenced in some quarters for indigenous culture as such, however little developed it might be." He himself felt that the indigenous inhabitants must be given access to a broader and more highly developed culture in order to free them from primitive superstition. Sentimental considerations must not be allowed to become an obstacle in the path of progress of indigenous peoples, although that progress must be achieved gradually.

It cannot be denied, however, that too high a price is often paid for the introduction of industrialism, and this might perhaps be avoided. The impact of mechanization is appalling in its leveling-down effect. Anyone who has ever visited a mining camp or a sugar-cane plantation can bear witness to the degradation brought about by the transfer from the tribal way of life to that of the hired laborer. Our own society has passed through a similar crisis, and, the wiser for our experience, we might perhaps be able to save other cultures from making the same mistakes and enduring the same sufferings as ourselves. When the transformation is on a vast scale, the original culture may be shaken to its foundations or even destroyed. As Dr. Gordon Bowles so aptly remarks: "The tragedy lies, not in the disappearance of a culture, it lies in the replacement of a functioning society with a mass of disunited individuals who, as victims of circumstance, can fall easy prey to exploitation of one sort or another."

It all too frequently happens that the plans made for assisting economically backward peoples make no allowance for the tastes and feelings of those who are to benefit from the so-called "improvements." Economists and technicians, because they deal in statistics and handle practical problems, become imbued with an alarming self-confidence. They seldom have any inkling of the relationship that exists between the various institutions of a group and fail to realize that its culture cannot be altered piecemeal. It requires the experience and acquired instinct of the anthropologist to foresee what repercussions any slight change may have on a society as a whole. It is the far-reaching consequences of an apparently desirable reform which, when perceived by the members of a particular society, give rise to opposition for which the technicians and economists can find no explanation. Hygiene and literacy are not in themselves a source of happiness and prosperity. On the contrary, they may even, in certain cases, have a disintegrating effect. Any educational system which is not suited to a particular form of culture will tend to undermine its intellectual and moral foundations, replacing them by standards which are not its own. As a result, we find these groups of uprooted, maladjusted individuals, who are a dead weight and a danger to peoples at the transitional stage of culture. There is nothing more pathetic than the fate of the colored student who, having taken his degree at some great Western university, refuses to return to his own country or, returning there, tries to get himself accepted by the representatives of Western civilization. If he succeeds, he becomes the enemy of his own group; and if, as more often happens, he fails, he sinks into discouragement or turns to politics as an outlet for his resentment.

All changes imposed from without, even when supported by a central government, inevitably meet with opposition, varying in intensity from one country, background, and social class to another. The apathy for which foreign experts so often blame native workers is due in many instances to a latent antagonism which remains hidden until, suddenly intensified, it breaks out in open revolt. Indifference may also result from a lack of incentives. Customs and institutions which to us seem harmful and incompatible with our conception of human happiness may nevertheless represent, to the members of certain groups, a source of satisfaction for which they are given no substitute. This applies particularly to improvements that require a period of years in which to make themselves felt.

It is worth mentioning that economic development programs seldom take into account the gap between the traditional standards of life and the unbridled consumption which often follows the rapid expansion of a new type of economy. Anthropologists have called the attention of economists to the demoralization which frequently accompanies a sudden increase in purchasing power and in supplies of consumer's goods whenever new wants are not simultaneously being created. A tie-up must be established between the interests of a culture and those resulting from the economic development or exploitation of a given region. Many troubles arising within communities which are in process of change come precisely from the difficulty of harmonizing traditional needs with the fresh opportunities opened up by technological transformation.

No change will be accepted or produce a lasting effect unless it is based on a system of values. The chief task of the anthropologist in technical assistance programs will be to discover the psychological motives underlying customary behavior. If a culture is to be transformed, the innovations introduced, while meeting the wishes of individuals, must not clash with attitudes deeply rooted in that culture. It is not enough, therefore, for the anthropologist to be acquainted with the social, economic, and religious structure of a group; he must also analyze the traditional usages, ideas, and system of values which together make up what is called the *ethos* of any human group.

The United Nations official publications outvie one another in declaring that all development in the economic and educational spheres must be carried out with and by the people to whom technical assistance is given. This principle imposes a further obligation upon the anthropologist: that of seeking out, in the community concerned, those men who not only have real authority but who also serve as models and examples to the rest of the population. It is they who must be won over and induced to co-oper-

ate in the necessary changes. As Margaret Mead has so aptly remarked, an innovation may produce widely differing results, according to the category or group of men who accept it.

In short, what the United Nations and the specialized agencies require are the services of a number of good anthropologists whom they could employ in their economic development programs as well as in their technical assistance and fundamental education projects. The main function of these experts would consist of explaining to foreign technicians the nature of the culture amid which they are working and in acting as spokesmen and interpreters of scientific and industrial civilization to the members of that culture. In this connection it should be pointed out that an anthropologist not only must be familiar with exotic cultures but must also be able to take an objective and scientific view of the one to which he himself belongs by birth and upbringing.

WAYS IN WHICH ANTHROPOLOGISTS PARTICIPATE IN TECHNICAL ASSISTANCE AND FUNDAMENTAL EDUCATION PROGRAMS

It may be necessary for an anthropologist to take part in each of the three phases of a technical assistance project. While it is desirable that anthropologists should be included in any team of technicians and education experts, so as to help them in their task and to guide their relations with the local population, their presence is almost a necessity at the preliminary stage. The Department of Social Sciences of UNESCO attaches special importance to the exploratory missions which pave the way for any technical assistance project and specifies that a social scientist must be included among the five specialists stipulated.

Preliminary surveys are even more needed for fundamental education projects than for technical assistance. As regards their nature and the kind of data they are designed to assemble, they are exactly similar to traditional ethnographical inquiries. They merely concentrate on the institutions and the customs with which the educators will have to deal in the country where they are to work.

UNESCO proposes to intrust these investigations to a team headed by a social anthropologist but including such other specialists as agronomists, medical practitioners, nutritionists, experts in soil conservation, etc. Anthropologists cannot fail to be grateful for this support. No anthropologist, however able, can bring to the study of a culture all the technical knowledge that is needed in order to understand it properly. Thus, when I was carrying out research in Marbial, I was glad to have the assistance of an agronomist, who, though knowing nothing of ethnography, was able to tell me about peculiarities in the local agriculture that I would have entirely overlooked. By studying in the light of modern agronomy the agricultural methods used by the peasants, he was able to show me their merits or faults as the case might be. The same applies to all aspects of the culture in question covered by other branches of science.

UNESCO is of the opinion that an inquiry may be undertaken at the very outset of a project and that the data assembled should be translated forthwith into action, for the inquiry ought to give the education expert or technician an insight into the problems he will have to solve and show him their relative importance.

Technical assistance and fundamental education are attaching increasing importance to evaluations. After several years, an anthropologist will be asked to assess the nature and extent of the changes that have been brought about by the execution of a technical assistance or fundamental education program. In this assessment, both the methods applied and the resultant changes should be taken into account. If a technical assistance or fundamental education project is to be fairly judged as a whole, a series of operations is necessary, roughly as follows: (1) preliminary survey; (2) definite statement of aims in relation to methods; (3) keeping of systematic records; (4) surveys of progress achieved and effectiveness of methods used; and (5) follow-up survey to check on persistency of effects, a certain number of years after end of project.

This schedule is, of course, applicable to every one of the activities included in technical assistance programs, but the social sciences and anthropology may well take it as their guide when assessing the general cultural and social consequences.

The joint field working party which will be sent in 1952 under technical assistance to the Andean regions of South America to develop action programs in countries with large indigenous populations has been instructed to adopt an approach "guided by a scientific and therefore objective evaluation of all the complex social and economic variables involved in the life and work of selected indigenous groups." The official document adds: "Only by a rigorous application of scientific methods including careful experimental design and comparative checking of results achieved can practical lessons be learned that will be applicable on a regional scale." Therefore, it has been decided that the party will be headed by an anthropologist.

As UNESCO is preparing a pamphlet on the methods applied in social surveys, it is hoped that it will be possible to make specific recommendations "on procedures and techniques for an objective evaluation of progress achieved."

The specialized agencies are contemplating joint action to facilitate these evaluations. The World Health Organization has already adopted an instrument for such measurements and has a standard pattern for reporting. The methods adopted by WHO require that "the staff member in charge of a project define his objective and measure his success in achieving as an integral part of his work." It should, however, be added that WHO is not yet concerning itself with the socio-economic implications of its missions.

ESTABLISHMENT OF A BRIEFING CENTER FOR EXPERTS IN THE FIELDS OF FUNDAMENTAL EDUCATION AND TECHNICAL ASSISTANCE

The problems and difficulties that may be encountered by technical assistance experts when unfamiliar with or utterly ignorant of the cultural background of the country in which they are working have not been overlooked by the techncial assistance services. At a meeting of the technical assistance board in Paris, UNESCO suggested the establishment of a center for training and orientation of European technical assistance experts, on the understanding that a similar center would be set up in the United States of America.

One of the chief aims of such a center would be to arrange for anthropologists to give instruction to experts to enable them to "perform their assignments with a minimum of friction and a maximum of understanding and adjustment to the cultural environment of under-developed countries."

UNESCO has also engaged in the training of experts, so that, quite apart from their technical knowledge, they may be acquainted with fundamental education methods "to assist the assimilation of skills and ideas, in other words to enable these specialists to interpret their technology in digestible and prac-tical form to the mass of the people who must apply it to the business of living." This training will be focused mainly on the social sciences, with special reference to anthropology, psychology, and ecology.

It is intended to inculcate

the techniques of community studies; the use of social science methods, of statistical and census techniques, of cartography, of technical (health and agricultural) surveys, the use of community studies as a basis for educational and economic plans; the necessity for striking a balance between planning and the spontaneous development of a project by popular activity in response to local needs as they are felt and expressed; the impossibility of imposing progress upon a people; the need for periodic assessment of progress, the technique of evaluation against the bench mark of basic survey, language problems and the codification and use of vernacular languages.

Instruction in educational methods will also be largely based on the experience of anthropologists and their recommendations, so that the experts may gain a clear idea of the approach necessary for illiterate and so-called "primitive" peoples (the avoidance of paternalism, the treatment of superstition and taboos, the use of appropriate symbolisms, etc.).

LIMITATIONS AND DUTIES
OF ANTHROPOLOGISTS

Having thus defined the functions of the anthropologist, we shall now turn our attention to what has actually been accomplished. It must be admitted that, in practice, the hopes of anthropologists have been disappointed. In a year only one anthropologist has been employed in a UNESCO technical assistance project. This failure to give practical effect to clearly expressed intentions is attributable to the machinery employed for the granting of assistance. As we have seen, requests must come from the countries themselves, which have to state both the nature of the assistance and the type of technicians required. No country has felt the need for anthropologists or asked for their inclusion in a mission, with the exception of Liberia, which requested, at the suggestion of the late Dr. John Embree, an anthropologist as head of the group of educators it needed. The choice of a competent anthropologist for such a responsible position appeared indispensable in view of the cultural diversity of the region and the impossibility of applying an educational scheme regardless of the cultural backgrounds of the various ethnic groups living within the borders of this Negro republic. Otherwise, even when technical assistance deems the participation of anthropologists in a project to be desirable, it refrains from making any such suggestion out of consideration for the wishes of the country concerned.

As there is no prospect of any change in this situation, anthropologists will be able to perform the useful services expected of them only if they are assigned to a mission not in their capacity as anthropologists but as experts who can take an active part in any given project. Apart from their general scientific training, they will be required to have a practical knowledge of one of the fields in which most applications for technical assistance are received: fundamental education, agricultural propaganda, health drives, etc. It is possible—and this is borne out by facts—to combine a broad training in anthropology with practical skill. It is in this technical guise, then, that anthropologists may be assigned to field work for technical assistance. And this will be no disadvantage to the anthropologists. The need to take part in the "spadework" will give them a clearer realization of the difficulties encountered by technicians. And—still more

important—by making an active contribution to the mission, they will dispel a prejudice entertained by various administrative circles with regard to anthropologists. The latter are often accused of antiquarianism, of being engrossed in all the traditional forms of the cultures with which they are concerned. It is feared that they unconsciously take the side of the most conservative elements in the cultures in process of transformation. By playing a direct part in an economic development project, the anthropologist will allay these misgivings and no longer be styled "reactionary."

Although anthropologists can, in a pinch, be experts on education or agriculture, there is one role they must never undertake—that of administrator. Control of a project and ethnographic research are utterly incompatible. One and the same person cannot be asked to distribute work, appoint or dismiss a staff, take decisions regarding buildings or the adoption of new methods, and, at the same time, go from hut to hut collecting information on the beliefs and the customs of the people. The ethnographer is obliged to show a certain humility and familiarity which are inconsistent with the authoritative attitude that must be assumed by the administrator. How could he refuse his main informers the positions and advantages they ask of him? It would be difficult for him to recommend the introduction of health measures and modern hygiene if he spends his time questioning medicine men and coaxing them to give information on their practices. The ethnographer acting as a member of a technical assistance or fundamental education mission should have the standing and the functions of adviser, together with absolute freedom.

The monograph *Fundamental Education*, in which UNESCO has summed up its concept of the methods and aims of fundamental education, contains a paragraph which might well be pondered by anthropologists. Among those things experts should ask themselves when evaluating the results of a fundamental education project, we find the following criteria, in the form of questions:

Is there evidence that the people are taking increasing interest in studying their traditions, customs and institutions with a view to developing better standards and to adjusting them to the requirements of modern living? Are they keeping up their traditional practices and attitudes of family solidarity without developing in the youth undue hostility towards or dependence upon paternalism? Do they examine their beliefs and practices so as to rid them of superstitious elements? Is their friendliness increased rather than diminished as a result of their contacts with "civilization" and the ways of "civilized peoples"?

These questions presuppose that educators know what are the best elements in any culture. The anthropologist may reasonably wonder whether this is so, and he is entitled to ask fundamental education services to define the ethical principles which guide them in deciding whether an institution is good or bad.

Educators could, of course, hand over this responsibility to anthropologists. The latter would, however, doubtless find it perplexing, wedded as they are to their ethnocentric view of culture. Furthermore, they would have to ask themselves the following questions: Are cultures so precious that they are worth preserving at the expense of their representatives? Is culture of greater value than the people in whom it is vested? Do not the members of any given culture have the right to reject it outright if they think fit? And are not the essential features of a culture better preserved in many cases by the acceptance than by the rejection of changes?

The time has surely come to arrange for specialists to discuss these weighty problems. The question was raised at a meeting of the Committee on International Relations in Anthropology; and the American Anthropological Association, on the recommendation of this committee, adopted the following proposal:

That the Executive Board of the American Anthropological Association recommend to the Director-General of UNESCO the establishment of a representative International Commission of UNESCO to define the meaning of culture in terms of the positive right of peoples of the world to their ways of life.

This commission would be instructed to define the concept of culture and to specify its practical implications in the revolutionary period through which we are passing, for, as Professor Herskovits so rightly remarks:

The time has come, it would seem, for wider dissemination of its [culture] implications, so that it can be used by all whose concern is to make most effective the adjustment, especially of native, primitive peoples, to an expanding world scene.

This proposal was sympathetically received, and action is being taken with a view to the convening of the conference contemplated in the resolution.

HUMAN RIGHTS AND ANTHROPOLOGY

Under UNESCO's auspices, the support of physical and cultural anthropology has been enlisted for the campaign against racial prejudice and discrimination. UNESCO has assumed responsibility for propagating and winning public support throughout the world for the Universal Declaration of Human Rights issued by the United Nations. This responsibility fell to it by reason of its structure and functions. In the campaign to combat racial prejudice, which has become almost a religion, it was necessary to secure the co-operation of anthropologists, who have long demonstrated the absurdity of the so-called "scientific" bases of racial prejudice.

The Economic and Social Council, at its sixth session, voted a resolution by which the director-general of UNESCO was requested "to consider the desirability of initiating and recommending the general adoption of a programme of disseminating scientific facts designed to remove what is generally known as racial prejudice." As a result, the general conference of UNESCO, at its fourth session, adopted the following resolutions for the 1950 program: "To study and collect scientific materials concerning questions of race, to give wide diffusion to the scientific information collected, and to prepare an educational campaign based on this information."

Such a program could not be carried out unless UNESCO had at its disposal the "scientific facts" mentioned in the resolution of the Economic and Social Council. In view of the confusion existing with regard to the concept of race and the diversity of opinions on the implications of that concept, it was found necessary to convene a group of experts and seek their opinion. In December, 1949, ten anthropologists and sociologists met in Paris to draw up a statement in which they endeavored to summarize the present attitude of scientists toward the question of race. This document received widespread publicity and met with the approval of the general public. However, it was sharply criticized by physical anthropologists and biologists, especially in England, and a second conference was convened, confined this time to representatives of the biological sciences. A second statement was drafted, the conclusions of which, though no different from those of the first, were free of the faults which had been censured. This new text was submitted to the majority of well-known geneticists and physical anthropologists, so as to receive their approval or criticism before its final publication.

We may question the expediency of statements drawn up by a group for subsequent presentation to the public as the Voice of Science. Scientifically, such declarations serve some useful purpose, in that they compel scientists to take general stock of their field of knowledge so as to ascertain where full agreement may be reached and where it is still remote. UNESCO, by encouraging such meetings, breaks down the isolation of certain scientists and brings them into contact with the representatives of related disciplines. Lastly, it is desirable for the public to know that common sense and science do not find the same answers to certain questions and that it is rash to pass judgment on problems that have not yet been solved by patient research.

The Department of Social Sciences was instructed to carry out a number of surveys into the sociological aspects of the racial question. In its choice of subjects, it was guided by the principle that surveys should be planned from the international standpoint and should produce practical results that hold good for the whole community of nations. We possess a considerable body of information on the nature of racial prejudice, its effects and dangers. The time has come to turn our attention to definite matters: first and foremost, the study of societies where the existence of different races has not led to conflict but to a *modus vivendi* which can be described as successful or tolerable. Such is the case in Brazil. Accordingly, in 1951, UNESCO undertook a large-scale survey of the main aspects of relations between the black and white peoples in five typical areas of that country: Pernambuco, Bahia, Rio de Janeiro, São Paulo, and the inland areas of the northeast. These surveys, which were conducted by Brazilian scientists with the co-operation of a few foreign scientists, have shed much light on the real nature of interracial relations and the causes of friction that are beginning to emerge under the pressure of economic factors.

UNESCO's present program provides for a general critical study of the positive measures that have been or are being taken in various countries to enable racial minorities fully to enjoy their rights. The practical value of such research therefore depends on whether the effectiveness of the methods so far employed to prevent racial or other discrimination can be scientifically assessed. The Subcommission on Prevention of Discrimination and Protection of Minorities has already listed the constitutional and legislative provisions which all the member-states of the United Nations have enacted to insure civic equality for all. In many cases the letter of the law is far from being observed in actual practice. The tremendous advantage of anthropological methods is that they enable us to come to closer grips with reality and to dispel illusions based on appearances and official statements.

Accordingly, the Department of Social Sciences would like to make a study of the real effects of the assimilation policies pursued in various colonial countries and to assess the nature and scope of the changes which the efforts of the colonizers have brought about in the customs and mentality of the native peoples. The educated native is one of the burning problems of the world today, and one that a better knowledge of his cultural background and the changes it has undergone may help us to understand. This is a complex and important task on which UNESCO may have, sooner or later, to embark.

CONCLUSIONS

The place that may be taken by anthropology in the work of the United Nations and the influence it may exert depend entirely upon the future of the social sciences. It may be doubted whether the world is yet ready to submit its conflicts and tensions to scientific analysis. UNESCO's Department of Social Sciences was intrusted by the general conference, at which sixty states were represented, with the task of investigating the origin of tensions likely to lead to war. This investigation was skilfully conducted by qualified specialists, but it cannot be said to have had the slightest practical effect.

Are we to resign ourselves to the disappointment of the hopes that many people had placed in social science? I do not think so. The results achieved by patient investigation will sooner or later become part of the common heritage of our civilization and will influence the outlook of those responsible for the conduct of international affairs. Natural science will no longer be alone in setting up trends of thought which give a new turn to the course of history.

The concept of culture and environment is certainly the most valuable contribution that anthropology has made to contemporary thought. When this concept has penetrated the public as a whole, it will no doubt breed a spirit of tolerance between the various nations and cultures which is far from existing at present. The idea of biological predestination will give way to the idea that change is unending and that man is master of his fate. Nothing is more valuable to the politician and the administrator than a sense of the interrelationship of cultures. That alone can provide the adaptability which is needed in dealing with men of so many different ethnic groups.

Until this sense of cultural interrelationship has been implanted, the only service that anthropology can render to the United Nations will be the provision of advisers to work with the technical assistance and fundamental education missions. The scope of their functions must, however, be strictly limited. They will be merely the interpreters or, so to speak, the advocates of two cultures between which contact is established. It is not for them to decide what changes shall be introduced or to act as dictators, for, whether they will or no, they belong to a particular culture and share its ideals and its prejudices. They must rest content with indicating those underlying influences by which the men of a given culture are impelled—remembering that cultures evolve and that they are far from being identical, even within one homogeneous society. They must be conscientious enough to restrain their sympathy for any particular group and give fair treatment to recalcitrants and opponents. If in a given society the elders seem to them to possess a charm and wisdom lacking in the younger generation, they must refrain from taking sides with the former. Anthropological method does not, in itself alone, suffice to qualify anthropologists as interpreters of alien cultures; a long familiarity with such cultures is indispensable, as are qualities of mind and heart that science cannot confer. Anthropology makes it possible to obtain a clear and rapid insight into a complex body of institutions, but it does not always bring with it a feeling for the shades of thought and emotion that are inseparable from the values of any culture. That is why the task of the anthropologist is so difficult and why the results he achieves are sometimes equaled by people who lack his scientific training.

By proclaiming the importance of culture, by pointing out the danger of preaching science and industrialization with injudicious zeal, anthropologists have indirectly rendered a signal service to the United Nations and to such governments as have been willing to listen to them.

BIBLIOGRAPHY

BOWLES, GORDON T. 1950. "Point Four and Improved Standards of Living," *Annals of the American Academy of Political and Social Sciences* (March), pp. 144–47.

Expanded Programme of Technical Assistance. 1951. Third report of the Technical Assistance Board to the Technical Assistance Committee, United Nations, Economic and Social Council, E/2054.

Experience with Human Factors in Agricultural Areas of the World. 1949. U.S. Department of Agriculture: Extension Service and Office of Foreign Agricultural Relations.

Fundamental Education: Common Ground for All Peoples. 1947. Report of a Special Committee to the Preparatory Commission of the United Nations Educational, Scientific, and Cultural Organization. Paris: UNESCO.

Fundamental Education: Description and Programme. 1949. "Monographs on Fundamental Education." Paris: UNESCO.

The Haiti Pilot Project. Phase One, 1947–1949. 1951. Paris: UNESCO.

HOYT, ELISABETH E. 1951. "Want Development in Underdeveloped Areas," *Journal of Political Economy*, LIX, No. 3 (June), 194–202.

KENNARD, EDWARD A. 1948. "Cultural Anthropology and the Foreign Service." Reprinted from *American Foreign Service Journal* (November), pp. 18–19, 42, 44.

LINTON, RALPH. 1950. "An Anthropologist Views Point Four," *American Perspective*, IV, No. 2 (spring), 113–21.

MEAD, MARGARET. 1946. "Professional Problems of Education in Dependent Countries," *Journal of Negro Education*, XV, No. 3 (summer), 346–57.

MÉTRAUX, ALFRED. 1949. "Anthropology and the UNESCO Pilot-Project of Marbial (Haiti)," *America indigena,* IX, No. 3 (July), 183–94.

——. 1951*a.* "Technical Assistance and Anthropology," *American Anthropologist,* .LIII, No. 3 (July–September), 419–20.

——. 1951*b.* "UNESCO and Anthropology," *ibid.,* No. 2 (April–June), pp. 294–300.

MOORE, WILBERT E. 1948. "Theoretical Aspects of Industrialization," *Social Research,* XV, No. 3 (September), 277–303.

Non-self-governing Territories: Summaries and Analyses of Information Transmitted to the Secretary-General during 1950, Vol. III. 1951. New York: United Nations.

Provisional Questionnaire as Approved by the Trusteeship Council, 25 April, 1947. 1947. New York: United Nations, Trusteeship Council.

Technical Assistance for Economic Development: A Human Approach. 1951. ("UNESCO and Its Programme," No. 5.) Paris: UNESCO.

Technical Assistance for Economic Development: Plan for an Expanded Cooperative Programme through the United Nations and the Specialized Agencies. 1949. Lake Success, N.Y.: United Nations.

Technical Assistance for Economic Development: Program of the United Nations and the Specialized Agencies. 1950. ("International Conciliation," No. 457.) New York: Carnegie Endowment for International Peace.

Technical Aids in Anthropology:
A Historical Survey

By JOHN HOWLAND ROWE

INTRODUCTION

THIS PAPER deals with the application of technological knowledge and laboratory methods to the problems of anthropological research and teaching. One important part of this field, the subject of age determination, is omitted because it is being covered in other papers by Robert F. Heizer and Kenneth Oakley. Even with this omission, the subject is a vast one, with an abundant and widely scattered literature, and time has not permitted me to cover it with any degree of thoroughness.

We owe to Paul Fejos the first organized treatment of the field of technical aids in anthropology, offered as a course in Columbia University in 1951–52. It was this course which inspired the planning committee to include the subject in the program of the International Symposium on Anthropology. Fejos generously placed his wide experience at my disposal, and this paper owes much to his guidance and counsel. My appreciation is due also to numerous other colleagues who have been most generous with bibliographical references and information about unpublished new developments. I am especially grateful to A. L. Kroeber, Junius B. Bird, Lita S. Binns, Margaret T. J. Rowe, Robert F. Heizer, Theodore D. McCown, S. L. Washburn, John Collier,

Jr., Barbara R. Honeyman, Lucile E. Hoyme, Clement W. Meighan, Sol Tax, Robert H. Lowie, C. W. Asling, and Bernard G. Hoffman. Only lack of time prevented me from approaching many other colleagues with long lists of questions.

In taking stock of the situation of anthropology in 1952, the reader will probably want to ask how much use has been made of technical aids in anthropological research. The material in this paper will help to answer this question, but it has certain limitations which must be kept in mind:

1. I have used a broad definition of anthropology in selecting the studies to be surveyed, including any project which has some relevance to subjects that anthropologists are interested in. Many of these studies are not by anthropologists and were not published in an anthropological context.

2. In spite of a deliberate effort to include studies made in other countries in this survey, I have not succeeded in covering developments abroad in the same detail as those in the United States.

3. The fact that some technological method has been used successfully once or twice in solving a problem of anthropological interest does not by any means indicate that it is common

knowledge even to the specialists in that part of anthropology to which it is relevant. It is even possible that there are one or two successful uses of technological aids turned up in the course of this survey which I am the first anthropologist to notice. I hope there are not many, but I have been much impressed with the amount of interesting and relevant information buried in technical journals which anthropologists would not normally handle unless they got an assignment like this.

Some historical background data are included in most of the sections, in order to show how long after the development of a particular technique it was first applied in anthropology. There is little or no time lag for certain devices (phonograph, X-ray, sound spectrograph) and a lag of many years for others (microfilm and tabulating machines, for example). The historical survey indicates a steady inertia; time and again technical devices have come into general use only after years of desultory experimentation by the few anthropologists who happened to get interested in them first.

A case could have been made for including sections on the typewriter and the automobile, both technical aids which are about as widely used as photography. Their uses and limitations are, however, somewhat more generally known than those of most of the procedures included for discussion. On the same debatable grounds I am omitting discussion of the use of power sources in the field, a subject suggested for inclusion by the planning committee.

PHOTOGRAPHY

The first practicable photographic processes were made public in 1839 by Daguerre in France and Talbot in England. The two processes were quite different; Daguerre's yielded a positive on a metal plate, while Talbot's produced a negative on paper from which prints could be made. The two types are usually called the "daguerreotype" and the "calotype," respectively. Both processes were improved almost immediately and had attained wide popularity by 1841; both were replaced in the middle 1850's by the so-called "wet collodion process," involving a transparent negative which had to be prepared, exposed, and developed immediately. "Dry plates," the glass-plate negatives still used occasionally for special work, were perfected by 1879 and rapidly replaced the wet process because they freed the photographer from the necessity of carrying his laboratory around with him. Roll film was introduced by Eastman: paper film in 1888 and nitrocellulose film in 1889 (see Taft, 1938; Stenger, 1939; Lécuyer, 1945; and Newhall, 1949).

The photographic methods available naturally limited the application of the process to anthropological or other research. Until the introduction of the dry plate, photography was a difficult business, requiring cumbersome equipment and a lot of time and trouble, and it was most extensively used for posed portraits and local landscapes. In spite of all difficulties, however, a few travelers to out-of-the-way places did take their cameras along, and we owe them some precious records as much as a century old. Another drawback of early photography was that it was slow. Daguerreotypes of street scenes usually show the streets deserted because pedestrians and riders moved out of the picture before they could be caught by the camera. The earliest pictures showing moving figures which I have seen date from 1859. It was not possible to record rapid motion until nearly the end of the century. The necessity for posing the subjects in early ethnographic photography started a tradition which has lingered on long after the introduction of fast lenses and fast film made the practice ridiculous.

The first public description of Daguerre's method was made in the French Academy of Sciences on August 19, 1839, by one of the most distinguished scientists of the day, Dominique-François Arago (1786–1853). Arago took advantage of the opportunity to point out some of the potential uses to which photography might be put, and among others he suggested that it should prove especially valuable in archeology. Recalling the arduous labors of the French scholars who went to Egypt with Napoleon in 1798 to copy hieroglyphic inscriptions on the ancient monuments, he pointed out the much greater exactness and saving of time that would have been possible if the daguerreotype had been available then (Arago, 1839, pp. 257–59).

Following this suggestion, it is highly probable that the first photographs of archeological monuments were taken in the middle 1840's, and the subjects probably were Roman ruins in France and Italy. Egypt had to wait ten years but then provided part of the subject of one of the first travel books published with photographic illustrations, *Égypte, Nubie, Palestine et Syrie* (1852), by the romantic traveler and amateur archeologist, Maxime du Camp (1822–94). Du Camp traveled in the Near East between 1849 and 1851 for the express purpose of studying and photographing the ruins of the area. Two of his magnificent calotypes are reproduced by Lécuyer (1945, pp. 61 and 64).

In the 1850's, archeological photographs became relatively abundant, though few were published because of the expense. The standard engravings, however, came to be based increasingly on photographs, resulting in an impressive improvement in their accuracy. Sometime it would be most interesting to check the archeological illustrations of this period for traces of the influence of photography.

One of the earliest photographic expeditions in the New World was that of Désiré Charnay (1828–1915), who studied the ancient cities of Mexico and Yucatan for the French Ministry of State in 1857–59 (Charnay, 1863). E. George Squier's archeological work in Peru during the American Civil War was also documented by photography (Squier, 1877).

At the time of the invention of photography, no distinction was made between ethnology and physical anthropology, as becomes apparent from a perusal of the earliest manuals of ethnological method for travelers. It is thus not surprising to find that the first anthropological photographs of living persons have both ethnological and physical interest. They were daguerreotypes of a Botocudo man and woman, taken by a Paris photographer named Thiesson in 1844. No expedition to Brazil was involved: the Botocudos had been brought to Paris for a visit. The pictures were displayed to the French Academy of Sciences by the anatomist Antoine-Étienne-Renaud-Augustin Serres (1786–1868), with the comment that a collection of daguerreotypes of different human races would be of immense interest for the natural history of man (Serres, 1844). Serres made some studies on the two Botocudos and on some Ioways who happened to be in Paris at the same time. The next year, he sent Thiesson to Portugal, Spain, and Italy to take more pictures for a "Musée photographique des races humaines" which he planned to organize; the first results of this expedition were twenty-two pictures of Negroes taken in Lisbon and Cadiz. Serres pointed out to the academy that "comparative anthropology" was a retarded branch of natural history because it was so difficult to secure comparative materials, and he expressed the hope that photography would help to improve the situation (Serres, 1845). It would be most interesting to know what became of the "Musée photographique" project and whether any of Thiesson's original daguerreotypes are still in existence. Ultimately, of course, Serres's hopes were realized by others; there can be no doubt that photography has been of immense aid in forming the comparative perspective of anthropology and making its results convincing to a wider public.

In the United States, daguerreotypes of Indians were taken at least as early as 1847 (Taft, 1938, p. 249). Many daguerreotypists joined the California gold rush. Vance's collection of California views sold in New York in 1851 included a large number of pictures of California Indians. None of them have been preserved (Taft, 1938, pp. 251–55). After the gold rush, photographers accompanied many of the expeditions to the west, especially when the close of the Civil War released a number of adventurous camera men who had become accustomed to wet-plate photography under difficulties while they attempted to record the camps and battlefields of the great struggle. Taft reproduces pictures of Pawnees taken in 1866 and of Shoshones of 1870 (Taft, 1938, pp. 281–82 and 299). Many of these early ethnographic photographs have been published in later studies of western Indians. They are as good as most modern ethnographic photographs and better than some.

It would be most interesting to review a series of anthropological reports which have made extensive use of photographs and comment critically on the skill with which the technique was utilized. In many cases it would perhaps be unfair to judge the author's photographic ability from the small and often indecipherable halftones which illustrate his report, but one can hardly avoid the feeling that if the profession attached any real importance to photographic illustrations as a means of presenting evidence, it could and would insist on a higher standard of reproduction, regardless of the extra cost. It can be cogently argued that a proper use of illustration will save many pages of text and give a clearer impression of the materials presented (cf. Joos's remarks at the beginning of a report published in a series which rarely uses illustrations of any kind: Joos, 1948).

The general review suggested would demand more time and space than the present project allows, and in any case it would be presumptuous on the part of one who has some pretty black photographic sins on his own conscience. I prefer to discuss instead one particular recent development in ethnographic photography which has some special interest.

It has long been fashionable in Europe for travelers interested in photography to publish an album of their best pictures upon their return home; these albums usually contain a brief text and the pictures are not elaborately captioned; the photographs are large and clear, and the reader is expected to "read" them rather than the author's words. A sensitive traveler who has spent some time with the natives in the area he has visited will sometimes turn out an album which manages to give an extraordinary amount of ethnographic information without pretending to be a monograph. One of these albums, and not a particularly well-presented one at that, is Gregor Krause's two-volume work on the people and ceremonies of Bali, which appeared in 1920. The photographs were selected from a collection of some 4,000 made while Krause was a physician in the Dutch service from 1912 to 1914. Krause's album fell into the hands of Mr. and Mrs. Miguel Covarrubias in the 1920's and inspired them to make two trips to Bali (1930 and 1933) for the purpose of studying Balinese life and illustrating it with drawings, paintings, and photographs. Rose Covarrubias was the photographer, and the book which resulted from this work in 1937 included a selection of her pictures grouped together at the end. The Covarrubias book quickly became an anthropological classic of its type and had an important effect in stimulating American ethnographers to do more with photographs than had been their custom.

The next step was taken by John Collier, Jr., and Aníbal Buitrón. They collaborated in the summer of 1946 on a study of the valley of Otavalo in northern Ecuador and published their results in 1949 in the form of an essay, in which the whole story of life in Otavalo is carried in the pictures and the text serves merely as a running commentary. The result is magnificent. It is not, of course, a satisfactory substitute for an elaborate monograph from the technical ethnological point of view, but it is not supposed to be. It does suggest the potential value of photography as an aid in gathering and presenting ethnographic data.

For the last year and a half, Collier has been working on the further development of photography as a tool of direct research in social science in connection with the Cornell Stirling County Project directed by Alexander Leighton. This project is a study of environment in psychiatric disorders, based on field work with the white population of a county in the Maritime Provinces of Canada. In the first six months, Collier built up a file of 3,000 negatives illustrating technological change and social life; this file is used to orient seminar students who come to work on the project and as a source for illustrations for their studies. Further experimentation with photography as a research tool has involved showing photographs to the informants and using them as a basis for questioning. This use has improved the interview relationship by helping to concentrate the informant's attention and giving him the feeling that he is talking about the picture instead of himself; it has also brought out numerous points that the interviewers would not have thought to ask about if the informant had not mentioned them. Collier is planning to try out the results of this work on the Navajo reservation in the summer of 1952, to see how they work in the face of a language barrier (Collier, letter to the writer of March 4, 1952).

There have also been some interesting developments in archeological photography, chiefly as a result of the growing acquaintance of archeologists with high-quality photography in the field of art. It was demonstrated long ago on Greek and Roman specimens that the same object could be shown either as a piece of junk or as a work of art, depending on how it was displayed or photographed; and there is every reason to give one's specimens all the interest possible so that the reader will be tempted to study the picture.

To conclude this section I append brief notes on various special applications of photography which have come to my attention. The length of the list is limited only by the time I have been able to devote to thumbing through anthropological and technical journals. It is exclusive of aerial photography, photographic surveying, X-ray photography, photography by infrared and ultraviolet light, microfilming, moving pictures, and photomicrography, each of which is treated separately in this paper.

a) The best treatment of photography in the context of illustration in general is Ridgway, 1938, an indispensable manual for every author.

b) Stereoscopic photography, done on a commercial scale since 1850 and very popular in the second half of the nineteenth century, has begun to come back into favor, new equipment having been designed to make possible the viewing and projection of stereoscopic color transparencies. There has been some experimenting with stereoscopic transparencies in the field of somatotyping. Curtet (1942) points out that stereoscopic photographs have been used successfully in deciphering worn ancient coins and suggests that they might be useful in studying prehistoric engravings.

c) Stroboscopic light is another new development in photography. It is superior to floodlighting, in that it is not hot and causes no discomfort to a human subject, and to flash bulbs because it gives shadowless pictures and greater surface detail. It is now being used in somatotype photography (see Sheldon, 1952, Appendix 3). A short description of it will be found in Kaplan, 1951, p. 24.

d) High-speed photography is not often called for in anthropological research, but Mary Ellen Goodman and Harold E. Edgerton used it in an effort to find out how flint fractures when it is flaked. The procedure devised was very ingenious, but it proved impossible to catch the fracture in progress because the breaking was completed in less than 1/540 of a second (Goodman, 1944).

e) The utility of film-strip sequences in describing technical operations in archeology (and, by inference, in ethnography as well) is discussed by Pittioni, 1936.

f) The first color film of general utility was Kodachrome, appearing in 1935. In 1938 Agde called attention to the value of color photography in archeology. It has since been widely used in anthropological research, chiefly in the preparation of lecture illustrations. Recently several different institutions have undertaken the marketing of pre-

pared units of color slides of anthropological subjects; of special interest is the Wisconsin Anthropological Color Slide Project (Hailer and Baerreis, 1951).

g) Nearly every manual of field or laboratory method in anthropology contains a section on photography and photographic problems (cf., e.g., the 6th ed. of *Notes and Queries on Anthropology*, ed. Seligman [1951], pp. 353–59). A very valuable article on the problems of archeological photography is Frantz, 1950.

Bibliography: Agde, 1938; Arago, 1839; Charnay, 1863; Collier and Buitrón, 1949; Covarrubias, 1937; Curtet, 1942; Du Camp, 1852; Frantz, 1950; Goodman, 1944; Hailer and Baerreis, 1951; Joos, 1948; Kaplan, 1951; Krause, 1920; Lécuyer, 1945; Newhall, 1949; Pittioni, 1936; Ridgway, 1938; B. Z. Seligman (ed.), 1951; Serres, 1844, 1845; Sheldon, 1952; Squier, 1877; Stenger, 1939; Taft, 1938.

MOTION PICTURES

Motion-picture photography, or cinematography as it was originally called, was first presented to the public in 1895. Hornbostel, in 1904, suggested that the technique was used first in anthropology by A. C. Haddon on the Torres Straits Expedition of 1898. A perusal of the reports of this expedition brought to light no mention of cinematography, but it is possible that Hornbostel was referring to some preliminary report which I have not consulted. Certainly, the Torres Straits Expedition was the sort of carefully planned project with technical interests that would have been likely to experiment with a new method of this sort.

Since the 1890's, great quantities of anthropological movies have been made, mostly in ethnography. Such movies are rarely discussed in the field reports of their producers, and it is exceedingly difficult to find out anything about the techniques used, except by lengthy correspondence with individual anthropologists. Time has not permitted me to cover the field with anything like the thoroughness that would be desirable.

An idea of the number and variety of films of anthropological interest that are available for exhibition can be obtained by examining the H. W. Wilson Company's annual *Educational Film Guide* (see Krahn, 1951) and the mimeographed supplement circulated to Fellows of the American Anthropological Association in 1949. The supplement listed 96 films not found in the Wilson *Guide*, including ones taken or directed by M. J. Herskovits, J. Alden Mason, Paul Fejos, Harry Tschopik, Jr., and F. G. Rainey. Of course, only a few of the anthropological films that have been taken are listed in such guides, and films available in Europe are not covered.

A vast footage of film of anthropological interest has been taken by commercial companies in connection with the production of entertainment films and travel pictures. Little of this ever sees the light in any form that would be helpful to the profession. In fact, most anthropologists become so conditioned to the conventions of commercial films that they try to imitate all the worst features of entertainment movies when they make their own pictures. Paul Fejos, who knows this subject as I do not, commented to me on the consistency with which anthropological photographers concentrate on obvious aspects of behavior, like dances, public gatherings, and manufacturing processes, while they ignore magnificent chances to record social relationships, parental authority, minor daily activities, and stresses in the community. A sensitive producer can show such matters in pictures without recourse to extensive commentary. Animation can be used to tie the sequences together and

has been effectively so used by Weckler in *Land of Mokil.*

From a technical viewpoint, one of the best anthropological films is a production called *Nomads of the Jungle,* showing one day in the life of the Sakai of Malaya. The production staff which made this film had the advantage of six weeks' briefing from Fejos before it left for the field.

Ethnographers are likely to think of motion pictures as an ideal method for describing such elaborate cultural features as dances, but here some caution is necessary. Philippa Pollenz has discussed the use of movies for this purpose and points out that it is rarely possible to film dances, as they are normally performed, in such a way that the dance can be described or reproduced from study of the film alone. Film can be used for this purpose only if the routines are rearranged for the camera (Pollenz, 1949, p. 435).

Motion pictures have been used in psychological studies of behavior. Florence Goodenough has called attention to a study of children at the Yale Psycho-clinic in which motion pictures were used (Goodenough, 1936).

In physical anthropology, films have been used to show the locomotion and behavior of primates. C. R. Carpenter made three 16-mm. films on the behavior of rhesus monkeys and gibbons in Indonesia in 1940. Movies have also been used in Sheldon's constitutional studies.

In archeology, films have no direct research use, but many archeologists have turned to motion pictures to provide an entertaining popular account of their excavations or to present the results for educational purposes.

The use of motion pictures in phonetic studies is discussed in the section on experimental phonetics.

The new edition of *Notes and Queries on Anthropology* contains a short section on cinematography (Seligman [ed.], 1951, pp. 359–61).

Bibliography: Goodenough, 1936; Krahn, 1951; Pollenz, 1949; B. Z. Seligman (ed.), 1951.

PHOTOGRAMMETRIC ANTHRO-POMETRY AND STANDARD-IZED PHOTOGRAPHY

Attempts have been made ever since 1904 to take anthropometric measurements directly from photographs instead of on the subject. The chief problems involved are (1) achieving a standard scale for all pictures taken; (2) accurate location of the landmarks for measuring; and (3) avoiding distortion in the photographic process. It is only recently that solutions to all these problems have been proposed.

James Gavan made a preliminary report to the Viking Fund Seminar in Physical Anthropology of 1949 of a technique of standardized photography designed to make accurate measurements from photographs possible, and an abstract of it appeared in Kaplan, 1951 (pp. 25–26). Gavan, Phillip Lewis, and S. L. Washburn have since completed a manuscript on this subject, which they have submitted to the *American Journal of Physical Anthropology*. The method involves posing the subject 21 feet from the camera against a marked grid, indicating the anthropometric landmarks by pasting gummed loose-leaf reinforcements on the subject's skin, using a 12-inch focal length lens, and printing the pictures on a nonshrinkable paper. An interesting discussion of the problems involved followed the 1949 demonstration, and Gavan amplified his account with remarks on additional precautions taken to insure the accuracy of the measurements. This type of standardized photography is not proposed as a substitute for direct measurement but rather to supplement it and serve as a check. Errors are constantly being made in

direct measurement, and in case of doubt a check on a standardized photograph makes it possible to tell immediately whether the recorded measurement is reasonable or not.

A somewhat different system of standardized photographs is used by W. H. Sheldon and his staff in somatotyping. It was first described by Sheldon in 1940 (pp. 30–31). Since then, a number of improvements have been made in the method. The form currently used is described in Appendix 3 to Sheldon's forthcoming book, *The Adult Male* (to be published in the fall of 1952). I was permitted to consult the manuscript through the courtesy of Barbara R. Honeyman. Somatotyping photography uses a 9½-inch lens and poses the subject at a distance of 14 feet 9 inches. For very tall people the distance is somewhat greater, in order to get the whole body on the film. The users of this method believe that these conditions, together with the use of stroboscopic lighting, result in pictures "with all visible parts of the body free from detectable photographic distortion." These photographs are used to read proportion rather than absolute dimensions, so that the precision demanded in photoanthropometry is not considered necessary.

Bibliography: Bertillon and Chervin, 1909, pp. 65–110; Gavan in Kaplan, 1951; Sheldon, 1940, 1952; Tanner and Weiner, 1949.

ULTRAVIOLET LIGHT

Ultraviolet light is invisible light beyond the violet end of the spectrum. When an object is examined under ultraviolet light in a darkened room, it will fluoresce, or become visible, giving off a new radiation which is longer in wave length than the invisible ultraviolet light which illuminates it. This fluorescence can be photographed with the aid of a filter. Examination and photography under ultraviolet light have been used for many years in museum laboratories for the detection of restoration and forgery in antiquities; the value of the method lies in the fact that two surfaces which appear identical in ordinary light may fluoresce quite differently under ultraviolet. A restorer may imitate the surface appearance of a piece of pottery or stone sculpture so cleverly that the patch looks exactly like the original, but it will usually show up in a different color under ultraviolet light. Forgeries are detected by comparing the appearance of the suspected object with that of a group of similar genuine ones under ultraviolet radiation. The method is discussed in detail with interesting photographs by Rorimer (1931), and instructions for ultraviolet photography will be found in Eastman Kodak Company, 1951, pp. 28–37. Both these works contain extensive bibliographies. The first use of ultraviolet examination in anthropology probably occurred in 1931 at the National Museum of Canada (Collins, 1932, p. 8).

Differences in fluorescence may be produced by differences in age as well as by differences of material, and this principle is also used in detecting forgeries. It might theoretically be possible to sort a mixed lot of genuine ancient specimens into age categories by ultraviolet examination, provided that the specimens were of the same material and had been preserved under comparable conditions; the method is worth testing, although it might be very difficult to demonstrate that a difference found in the examination was due to age differences and not to a difference of preservation conditions. Junius B. Bird has been experimenting with this possibility on Peruvian pottery and textiles. He has gotten no results on pottery, but he got systematic and suggestive differences on the textiles. The method is a simple one and could be tried by anyone.

Two further applications of ultraviolet light were made in Haury's Ventana Cave study. A tubular pipe with a cake in the bottom was found near the surface of the lower case, and R. E. Heineman suggested examining the pipe under ultraviolet light in the hope of determining whether or not it had been used for smoking tobacco. A stained bit of the rim of this pipe reacted in exactly the same way as did the stained mouthpiece of a modern briar pipe, suggesting, but not proving, that tobacco was the substance smoked. In the course of this examination, a simple painted design was revealed on the outside of the pipe; this design had apparently been painted on with organic pigment which had been absorbed by the porous base to the point of being invisible in normal light. Haury remarks: "This chance discovery of an unseen character on the pipe led to the examination of nearly all of the Ventana collection under ultra-violet light but without producing any significant results" (Haury, 1950, p. 332; see also p. 331 and Pl. 23a).

Bibliography: Eastman Kodak Company, 1951; Haury, 1950; Rorimer, 1931.

INFRARED RADIATION

Infrared is invisible radiation from beyond the red end of the spectrum. It can be photographed readily on special films but produces nothing comparable to the visible fluorescence of ultraviolet, so cannot be used for direct examination. Infrared photographs show quite different contrasts from those of photographs in ordinary light and hence call attention to certain details that might otherwise be overlooked; they produce very spectacular landscape pictures, for example, vegetation appears white and the sky black. An infrared photograph will penetrate atmospheric haze to give a clear view of distant objects, but it will not penetrate fog. By the use of special flash bulbs or screened flood lamps, infrared photographs may be taken in total darkness, the only thing showing being a dull red glow from the lamp. On some charred or bleached documents, the original writing may be made visible by infrared photography. Human skin is relatively transparent to infrared rays, and hence structures immediately below the skin, like superficial veins, can be studied in infrared photographs. This is not a complete catalogue of the applications of the technique, but it is suggestive of its possibilities. For further information the reader should consult Clark, 1946, and Eastman Kodak Company, 1951.

Relatively little experimentation with infrared photography has been attempted in anthropology. James N. Spuhler has used infrared pictures for studying the superficial veins of the anterior thorax, borrowing the technique from medicine (Spuhler in Kaplan, 1951, p. 25). William Madsen, of the University of California, Berkeley, has plans to try infrared flash photography as a means of recording night ceremonies without disturbing the participants, during a field trip to Mexico this year.

Bibliography: Clark, 1946; Eastman Kodak Company, 1951; Kaplan, 1951; C. G. Seligman, 1934.

X-RAY

The X-rays were discovered by Wilhelm Konrad Roentgen, professor of physics at the University of Würzburg, Bavaria, toward the end of 1895. Soon after the discovery was announced, Stewart Culin, of the University of Pennsylvania, began looking for archeological applications of the new technique. He started experimenting with it early in 1897, as soon as the university has installed X-ray apparatus. In May of that year, Culin and Dr. Charles Lester Leonard made a successful radiograph of a Peruvian mummy from Pachacamac, collected by Max Uhle. In 1898 Culin published an X-ray photograph of a spear-thrower from Colorado, showing beads under the wrapping.

The examination of unopened mummy bundles by X-ray was such an obvious application of the technique that it probably occurred independently to a number of different investigators in the years following. Altogether, a large number of mummies, mainly Egyptian and Peruvian, have been examined in this way; a bibliography of the earlier literature on the subject will be found in Moodie, 1931, pp. 16–17.

Paul F. Titterington has used X-rays to reveal methods of drilling in stone pipes and to study the size and concentration of temper grains in pottery (Titterington, 1933; Titterington in Griffin [ed.], 1951, pp. 94–96). X-rays have also been used successfully in the laboratory study of archeological copper and bronze objects (cf. Gettens, 1933; Collins, 1934). Drier used X-ray diffraction patterns in potsherd classification (Drier, 1939). X-rays have often been used to detect forgeries, e.g., by Titterington. Rowe used them to read an inscription on a colonial Inca portrait where the writing had been painted over (Rowe, 1951). This application of X-rays was, of course, borrowed from the field of the fine arts, in which the method is often used to detect overpainting and reveal the original work.

Another important use of X-rays is in experimental phonetics, where X-ray photography has yielded valuable information regarding the positions of the vocal organs during articulation. A fuller discussion of this use will be found in the section on experimental phonetics.

The use of X-rays in physical anthropology is so extensive that it is impossible to cover it adequately in a paper of this length. Some of the types of uses may be mentioned, however. X-rays have been widely used in the study of pathology in bone; chapter x of Hooton's *Indians of Pecos Pueblo* (Hooton, 1930) will serve as an example. Another important use has been in studies of growth. Krogman's syllabus, *The Physical Growth of the Child* (1951), gives numerous references on this subject, and attention may also be called to Greulich and Pyle's *Radiographic Atlas of Skeletal Development of the Hand and Wrist* (1950). Other new developments in this field are discussed by Goff, Hall, Reynolds, and Krogman in Kaplan, 1951, pp. 27–28. Soft X-rays, showing the soft parts as well as bone, can be used to study the relationship between skull and tissue on the living head, thus providing a check on suggested methods of reconstructing the appearance of a living individual from his bones.

An ingenious use of X-rays in studying cranial deformation has been suggested by Sergio Quevedo, of the University of Cuzco; he takes standardized X-ray photographs of deformed skulls and describes the deformation in terms of a quadrilateral inscribed between fixed points in the brain case (Quevedo, 1946).

Bibliography: Collins, 1934; Culin, 1898; Drier, 1939; Gettens, 1933; Greulich and Pyle, 1950; Griffin (ed.), 1951; Hooton, 1930; Kaplan, 1951; Krogman, 1951; Moodie, 1931; Quevedo Aragón, 1946; Rowe, 1951; Titterington, 1933.

MICROFILM AND REFLEX COPYING

Microfilm is 35-mm. slow film on which manuscripts or printed materials are photographed in successive exposures. Present costs (around four cents an exposure in the United States) make it one of the cheapest of copying processes; usually two facing pages can be photographed in one exposure. Any camera taking 35-mm. film can be used for making microfilm. The finished film cannot ordinarily be read with the naked eye, but reading machines are available for public use in most libraries. The film can also be shown in most projectors equipped for film strips. The original exposures are negative, but positive copies can be made at a cost less than half that of the original negative.

Microfilming is one of the most important research tools developed in the last generation. It makes it possible and economical for the scholar who does not live near a first-class research library to secure copies of any written materials which he needs in his work. Major libraries all over the world maintain photographic laboratories which will furnish, at a few days' notice, microfilms of any materials not protected by copyright.

General use of the microfilm process began about 1935 in the United States. Libraries were quick to adopt it; the Bibliothèque Nationale in Paris has had a microfilm service since 1937. University Microfilms, at the University of Michigan, began "publication" of doctoral dissertations on microfilm in 1938. An obvious use of the process is in copying historical documents, and a large and growing number of historians are making their own microfilms of the materials they find in those archives which do not have a commercial microfilm service attached.

Anthropologists have been very slow to take advantage of the facilities which microfilm offers for research; perhaps our traditional emphasis on direct work with informants or with original specimens is one of the reasons. I began buying microfilms of rare works on Peru in 1943, and in the same year George Kubler showed me his portable equipment used for making microfilms in Mexico; I do not know of any earlier use of the method in anthropology. In addition to its utility as a direct research tool, microfilm has proved very useful for making copies of anthropological field notes and museum catalogues as a safeguard against loss.

The type of program instituted by University Microfilms has been of particular importance to scholarship because of the constantly increasing cost of regular publication. University Microfilms began offering microfilm copies of doctoral dissertations in 1938, as noted above; in 1945 its coverage was extended to include other monographs for which immediate publication could not be arranged. It publishes a series called "Microfilm Abstracts" which contains summaries of the works recorded and price information for those who wish to purchase positive microfilm copies of the whole work. The author is charged a small sum to cover the cost of making the original negative, and the cost of copies is usually less than the cost of a printed book of comparable size. The fact that a monograph is available on microfilm does not prevent the author from copyrighting it or publishing it in printed form later if he desires. Anthropology was one of the last disciplines to take advantage of this service; the first anthropology dissertation was listed in "Microfilm Abstracts" only in 1950. A scattering of papers in related fields, such as classical archeology, will be found as far back as 1944. Within the last three years, nearly twenty titles in anthropology have been added.

A somewhat similar project is the Microfilm Collection of Manuscripts on Middle American Cultural Anthropology, directed by Sol Tax and issued by the Department of Photographic Reproduction of the University of Chicago Library. This project was started in 1946 with the backing of The Viking Fund, and its purpose is to make available edited field notes and drafts of manuscripts not yet ready for final publication. Many libraries have subscribed for the complete set, and copies are thus generally available to interested researchers throughout the United States and abroad. The only serious difficulty encountered in this project has been a scarcity of manuscripts available to be reproduced!

One of the most notable contributions of the Chicago project is its inclusion of typed field notes in the materials microfilmed. Publication of field notes in microfilm, of course, provides valuable documentation for a published monograph at minimal expense. Most of us, at one time or another, have wished that we could have a look at a colleague's field notes because his monograph does not happen to present the information gathered in precisely the terms in which we want to use it.

Another copying process of great potential value to scholarship is the use of contact or reflex copying papers, such as Kodagraph. These are very slow papers which can be laid, emulsion side down, on the material to be copied, pressed flat, and exposed by shining a light through the back. The copy is a mirror negative, when developed, and any number of positive copies can be made from it. For some work, the cost per page is about the same as that in microfilming for the negative alone; for large pages it is somewhat more. It is, of course, possible to read the negative directly by holding it up to a mirror. The advantage of the process is that it involves no expensive lenses or elaborate lighting.

The chief problem involved in its use is achieving perfect contact between the page being copied and the reflex paper. There is no problem with loose, flat sheets, but if the pages to be copied have been folded or are bound in a book, the problem may be serious. F.

G. Ludwig Associates, Pease Road, Woodbridge, Connecticut, have developed a plastic cushion which takes care of the difficulty and which they market under the name "Contoura."

Reflex copying has been tested for anthropological use by Bernard G. Hoffman at the University of California, Berkeley, and he is well satisfied with the results achieved.

Bibliography: De Sola, 1944; Hoffman, MS; Lécuyer, 1945; McCrum, 1950.

AERIAL RECONNAISSANCE AND PHOTOGRAPHY

The first aerial photograph was taken in France in 1856; four years later, a successful one was made in the United States. These early pictures were, of course, made from balloons and under very difficult conditions, for it was not easy to manipulate the wet plates of the day in an aeronaut's basket, and the hydrogen gas used in the balloons fogged the film on contact. Balloons were used for aerial reconnaissance in the American Civil War, and photographs were made from them. Thereafter, observation from the air became a fairly common military procedure. There is no record that anyone put it to anthropological uses, however.

Air observation in anthropology had to wait until long after the invention of the airplane—indeed, until flying became common during the first World War. In the war years, French, English, and German fliers, working in the Near East, began to notice the clarity with which many large-sized archeological sites showed up from the air, even when they were nearly invisible from the ground. There were men with archeological interests serving with all three armies, and several were inspired to collect and study the pictures brought back by the reconnaissance planes. No one has succeeded in discovering who was the first to notice the archeological importance of air observation; the discovery was probably made independently by several different people in that bare country where there was little else to attract the attention beyond the ruins of ancient cities and the long straight lines of Roman roads.

After the war, air observation in archeology was developed separately by the English and the French. The outstanding English pioneer in this work was O. G. S. Crawford, who worked throughout the 1920's, observing and photographing archeological sites in England from the air. This work culminated in a magnificent monograph, *Wessex from the Air* (Crawford and Keiller, 1928), which illustrated the value of air observation in distinguishing minute changes in vegetation which marked out the lines of ancient walls and ditches and its importance as a means of visualizing the relations even of well-known sites to the country in which they stand. *Wessex from the Air* includes a bibliography of the pioneer English and German work in air archeology. On the French side, the outstanding works are those of Léon Rey in Macedonia (1921) and Antoine Poidebard in Syria (1934). Poidebard combed the Syrian desert by air and on the ground between 1925 and 1932 for traces of the Roman frontier defenses in this area, and his report throws a flood of light on Roman military planning. Poidebard went on to combine aerial reconnaissance with underwater exploration in a study of the ancient harbor works at Tyre; this project is discussed under "Diving Equipment."

The first aerial photographs of an American site were taken by Wells and McKinley in 1921–22 (Smithsonian Institution, 1922, pp. 92–105). The subject was the Cahokia mound group in Illinois. The pictures show little that is not equally visible from the ground, and no one was inspired to follow up the technique. In 1930 Neil M. Judd made a successful aerial survey of prehistoric irrigation canals in Arizona, the sort of project to which aerial reconnaissance is ideally suited (Judd, 1931). Lindbergh's flights over Yucatan in 1929 probably constituted the first use of aerial observation in Mesoamerican archeology.

Peru is another area like the Near East, where the country is dry and open and covered with the remains of ancient cities and engineering works. The value of aerial photography for Peruvian archeology was demonstrated by the Shippee-Johnson Peruvian Expedition of 1931 (Shippee, 1932*a*, *b*). One of their most spectacular discoveries was a fortified line along the Santa River Valley ("The Great Wall of Peru"). More recently, large-scale markings on the desert near Nazca have been discovered and mapped from the air. These markings are so large and so peculiar that I suspect I would be inclined to disbelieve them if I had not seen them several times myself (Reiche, 1949).

One of the most instructive of all reports on aerial observation in archeology is Erich Schmidt's *Flights over Ancient Cities of Iran* (1940). The flights were made in 1935–37 as part of the Iranian program of the Oriental Institute of the University of Chicago. The sites are spectacular and the photographs beautiful, but more important is the care that Schmidt takes to explain the particular advantages of aerial observation in desert country. In a number of cases he contrasts a plan of an unexcavated site made on the ground with enormous labor to an aerial photograph on the same scale; in each case the photograph shows more archeological detail in a more recognizable fashion than does the plan. It is often possible to sketch restorations of fortification walls and streets

directly on the aerial photograph from indications which do not appear in the plan at all.

Almost every year brings wider use of aerial observation in archeology. Since shortly before the last war, Hans-Georg Bandi has been applying the technique in Switzerland (Sauter, 1947). It has been used for surveying earthworks in Siam (Williams-Hunt, 1950) and for locating shore-line sites in Australia and Malaya (Williams-Hunt, 1948). Recent works on the archeology of central Mexico have been illustrated by aerial photographs (e.g., Armillas, 1950).

It should be pointed out that aerial photography makes possible the study of types of ancient remains which our earth-bound predecessors would not even have considered "sites." Much of the work of Curwen and others on prehistoric agriculture in England depends on the traces of ancient cultivation that can be observed from the air under favorable circumstances (see Payne, 1948, for references), and Bradford has elucidated a Roman system of land survey from air views (Bradford, 1947).

Especially in very flat country, aerial photographs can be used as the basis for excellent maps, rapidly constructed. Only a few ground measurements are needed to control the photographs. This technique has proved especially useful in mapping large and complex sites in Peru. The maps of the Viru Valley Project of 1946 were based on an air mosaic furnished by the Servicio Aereofotográfico Nacional, and more recently Richard P. Schaedel and his assistants at the University of Trujillo have used air photographs for mapping a whole series of complex ceremonial centers on the north coast of Peru (Ford and Willey, 1949; Schaedel, 1951*a*, *b*).

There is a number of general articles about the history and methods of air archeology. The best is Riley, 1946.

Others worth consulting are Reeves, 1936; St. Joseph, 1951, and Vaufrey, 1946 (in part a review of an important German publication, *Luftbild und Vorgeschichte*, which I have not seen). The two recent publications by Paul Chombart de Lauwe (1948 and 1951) cover ethnographic air observation as well as archeology and will be discussed below.

It is rather surprising to anyone familiar with the great contributions of air reconnaissance to archeology to note how little use has been made of this technique in ethnographic studies. This subject has so far been developed almost exclusively by the French. French interest in it seems to have grown out of the French tradition of cultural geography, which is sufficiently interested in man as well as in the land that certain sections of a French geographical report would not be at all out of place in an ethnographic monograph. The influential studies seem to have been those of Charles Robequain (1929) and Pierre Gourou (1936a, b) on the cultural geography of Annam. Both writers made extensive use of official air photographs to illustrate land-use and settlement patterns in the areas studied. Geographers in other areas were, of course, making a similar use of aerial photographs; these particular ones are mentioned because they seem to have provided the direct inspiration for the use of aerial photographs in French ethnography.

There has, of course, been some casual use of aerial photographs in ethnographic monographs, primarily to give an impression of the landscape. One appears, for example, in John Gillin's *Moche* (1947). What I am interested in discussing, however, is the recognition of aerial observation as a tool of ethnographic research, and this dates from 1948 and the publication of Paul Chombart de Lauwe's *La Découverte aérienne du monde*. This work contains a chapter on air observation in ethnography by Marcel Griaule, using primarily African examples. The only earlier work of a remotely similar sort cited is the work of the geographers in Annam. Griaule's paper is not on a highly technical level, but it does make a good case for the potential importance of aerial observation to ethnography. The subject is further developed by Chombart de Lauwe in a more recent work (1951).

On the basis of these publications and of some slight experience of my own in utilizing aerial photographs for ethnographic purposes in Colombia in 1948, it can be stated that the air view is an incomparable and perhaps indispensable tool in studying the patterns of settlement and land use in a modern community, because it shows in a very vivid fashion transient human activities that would not find a place on a topographic map. The condition of house roofs, sanitary arrangements, the state of crop cultivation at a particular date, irrigation or drainage arrangements, and land tenure are all commonly revealed in a clear aerial view. Incidentally, my informants were enormously interested in the photographs we secured, and it was easy to base questions on items observed in the pictures. A series of views taken at different times of the year would be especially revealing in any area where there is seasonal change. Mapping can, of course, be done from ethnographic aerial photographs as well as from archeological ones; I tried this with the Colombian pictures in a very amateurish fashion.

In aerial reconnaissance it is very desirable for the anthropologist to go on the flight and see the terrain with his own eyes. If possible, he should also plan and take the photographs, as Schmidt did; often the details wanted will not be obvious to a photographer who is not also an anthropologist, nor will he know which view will be most effective from a research point of view. Another good arrangement is to have the reconnaissance done co-operatively by an anthropologist and a trained aerial cameraman. The chief purpose of the photographs is to enable some of the interpretation of the air view to be done on the ground at leisure; the pictures will not reveal anything that is not more clearly visible to the eye. The simplest introduction to the art of aerial photography is a Kodak pamphlet (Eastman Kodak Company, 1947). See also Smith, 1943, and American Society of Photogrammetry, 1936. Sisam, 1947, gives an interesting series of air photographs, showing land-use patterns all over the world. Steer, 1947, gives a discussion of the use of stereoscopic air photographs in archeology.

For photographing small areas from the air, there has been some experimental use of kites (Bascom, 1941) and captive balloons (Guy, 1932). Guy also describes the use of a 9.3-meter extension ladder for this purpose. All three methods are tricky to handle but might be useful in certain situations.

Bibliography: American Society of Photogrammetry, 1936; Bascom, 1941; Bradford, 1947; Chombart de Lauwe (ed.), 1948; Chombart de Lauwe, 1951; Crawford, 1928; Crawford and Keiller, 1928; Eastman Kodak Company, 1947; Ford and Willey, 1949; Gourou, 1936a, b; Guy, 1932; Judd, 1931; Payne, 1948; Poidebard, 1934; Reeves, 1936; Reiche, 1949; Rey, 1921; Riley, 1946; Robequain, 1929; St. Joseph, 1951; Sauter, 1947; Schaedel, 1951a, b; Schmidt, 1940; Shippee, 1932a, b; Sisam, 1947; Smith, 1943; Smithsonian Institution, 1922; Steer, 1947; Vaufrey, 1946; Williams-Hunt, 1948, 1950.

DIVING EQUIPMENT

While it cannot be said that archeologists are commonly required to work underwater, a number of very important archeological studies have involved submarine investigation, and it should at least be recognized that there is a body of experience on the record the next time the problem arises.

The earliest underwater archeological work to come to my attention is that undertaken by Edward Herbert Thompson in the Cenote of Sacrifice at Chichen Itza in 1909. Thompson became intrigued by the possibility of recovering some of the offerings which had been thrown into the cenote in ancient times and installed an orange-peel scoop to dredge the cenote bottom. Having found large quantities of valuable specimens by dredging, he then brought in diving equipment, complete with submarine telephones, and made a series of descents which yielded even more spectacular discoveries than the dredging. The divers worked in complete darkness, and no attempt at underwater photography was made. T. A. Willard has published Thompson's own graphic account of this work (Willard, 1926).

Another occasion for underwater research appeared during aerial reconnaissance carried out in Syria by Antoine Poidebard in 1934. There had been considerable controversy in the archeological literature regarding the arrangement of the port works of the southern harbor of ancient Tyre, and the air views suggested that substantial traces of the foundations of the breakwaters might be found *in situ* in the sea offshore. Poidebard got together a diving crew and worked on this project for three seasons (1934–36), with excellent results. Local sponge divers guided the French professionals, and the key sections of the ancient breakwaters were mapped in some detail. A number of underwater photographs were taken, some from the surface and some by the divers, using an underwater camera. The divers also brought up for petrographic analysis specimens of the building blocks found. Poidebard's report on this work appeared in 1939 and is well worth reading.

Bibliography: Poidebard, 1939; Willard, 1926.

SURVEYING

The making of maps and plans is an important part of both archeological and ethnographic field work. There is an enormous literature on the subject, and courses are taught in it at every university which has engineering instruction. It is thus rather depressing to find that most archeologists know only one mapping method (usually an unnecessarily cumbersome one), and few ethnographers know any at all.

A recent paper by Spaulding (1951) summarizes the use of surveying techniques in archeology and thus makes it possible for us to abbreviate our discussion here. The following remarks are intended as a supplement to Spaulding's paper.

The problem in archeological surveying is that archeologists wish to map smaller areas than professional surveyors usually concern themselves with, and they demand a lower order of accuracy. These requirements are met most efficiently by simple methods, like the compass traverse, plane-tabling with a peep-sight alidade, and the use of reference lines of string to simplify measurements with the tape. However, if the inquiring archeologist reads an ordinary book on surveying or enrols in an engineering course on the subject, he soon finds himself enmeshed in theodolites, logarithms, verniers, and similar matters which are quite irrelevant to his needs and only serve to confuse him. The obvious solution would be for someone to write a simple book on anthropological surveying, but no one has done it yet. Until we have such a special manual, the clearest and simplest work on the subject is Debenham's *Map Making* (1940). I have had

excellent results using this book with students. It is written for people interested in making maps as a hobby, and the methods described are well adapted to most anthropological problems.

Photographic surveying (photogrammetry), discussed by Spaulding, is a new technique with considerable promise. One variety of it is the construction of maps from aerial photographs, and some references to this subject will be found in the section on aerial reconnaissance.

The problems of surveying in ethnography are very similar to those in archeology, and similar methods are applicable to both subjects. Ethnographic monographs frequently include plans of villages or house clearings of about the same size and degree of complexity as those of archeological sites, although the ethnographic plan is likely to reflect less measurement and more use of the imagination. One interesting, though somewhat rare, use of surveying is to make plans of houses showing the location of all furnishings at the time the plan was made. Even though the arrangement may be changed from one day to the next in the house measured, such a plan gives an almost photographic glimpse of domestic arrangements which can be obtained in no other way. Examples of the technique will be found in Cordry and Cordry, 1941, Figures 2–3. I utilized it with good results in 1947.

Bibliography: Bertillon and Chervin, 1909, pp. 65–110; Cordry and Cordry, 1941; Debenham, 1940; Merrill, 1941; Spaulding, 1951.

GEOPHYSICAL EXPLORATION

At the suggestion of Paul Fejos and with the backing of The Viking Fund, Helmut de Terra experimented with the application of geophysical methods to archeological survey work during the studies preceding the discovery of Tepexpan man in February, 1947. The geophysical work was conducted by Dr. Hans Lundberg, of Toronto. The method used was the one called the "linear electrode method," known to geophysicists since 1916. De Terra describes it as follows:

It consists in sending an alternating current of low frequency into two conductor cables which are staked to the ground at a specified distance parallel to each other. In the electrical field thus established, lines of equal potentiality are traced by means of metal sounding rods through which the current enters the amplifier causing a buzzing sound in the earphones. The "no sound effect" locates the points of equipotentiality which are marked on the ground by wooden stakes that eventually form lines which are plotted on the map. . . . Homogeneity of the ground will cause these lines to run parallel to the electrodes, whereas lesser or greater conductivity of certain earth substances will result in deflections with convergent lines at places of greater electrical resistance and divergent patterns marking localities of greater conductivity [De Terra, Romero, and Stewart, 1949, p. 34].

Investigation of the anomalies found indicated that they were associated with geological and soil conditions. The Tepexpan skeleton was discovered in one of the pits dug to investigate the electrical anomalies found in the survey, but no one has suggested that its presence was reflected in any way in the equipotential lines of the survey map. It happened to coincide with a jog in the formations marking the edge of an ancient lake, and the jog was reflected in the equipotential lines. De Terra's statement that "without the geophysical survey the Tepexpan Man would not have been discovered" should not be taken to mean that the presence of human remains could be deduced from anything in the geophysical survey. De Terra was just lucky.

This one experiment is scarcely enough on which to base an evaluation of the utility of geophysical survey methods in archeology. It is not impossible that such methods might yield direct and valuable results in another type of site.

Bibliography: De Terra, 1947; De Terra, Romero, and Stewart, 1949.

MINE DETECTORS

Mine detectors are electronic exploration devices developed during the recent war for locating buried land mines. The military models were made available as surplus after the war and have been tested by a number of archeologists for their possible value in locating important features of a site before excavation. I have not come across any published accounts of these tests and will have to confine myself to discussing the ones made at the University of California in Berkeley.

The earlier type of mine detector used by the United States Army can be recognized by the fact that its pickup unit is a round, flat plate. It was designed to locate metallic mines and gives a buzz when the pickup head approaches any metal object, even a single nail. Military experience was that it would pick up metal objects to a maximum depth of around 18 inches. The metal does not have to be iron; brass and aluminum were widely used for land mines as well. This type of mine detector has been tested for archeological work by Clement W. Meighan, of the University of California Archaeological Survey, during exploration of a series of sixteenth-century California Indian sites on Drake's Bay. The field work was done in September, 1949. The mine detector was procured when it was discovered that some of the sites contained a number of iron spikes, probably salvaged from early shipwrecks. It was desirable to recover as much of this old iron as possible for study, but the sites were extensive, thin, and not otherwise especially productive. The mine detector worked very well and permitted the recovery of a large number of spikes in a short time. In the case of one cache of badly rusted spikes, Meighan reports that the mine detector reacted strongly to the rust flakes even after the spikes themselves had been removed. He is confident that the metallic mine detector will prove valuable in locating coins and other small metal objects in sites of the contact period.

As the war went on, nonmetallic mines were developed as an answer to the metallic mine detector, and it became necessary to design a new detector which would pick up nonmetallic as well as metallic mines. The United States Army's solution was the Detector Set AN/PRS-1, recognizable by its cylindrical pickup unit. This device reacts to variations in radiation resistance set up by dielectric characteristics of the earth below the pickup head. It will react to any anomaly in the ground: a rock, an air pocket, a pool of water, a root, etc. This characteristic effectively limits its use to relatively homogeneous sites in which the only structural anomalies are artifacts; otherwise, it would pick up so much irrelevant material as to make it no more advantageous than test-pitting. Another drawback is that it registers only objects 5 inches deep or less. This depth is sufficient for military purposes, for mines have to be laid very near the surface in order to be effective, but it is inadequate for most archeological needs. This type of mine detector would give useful results only in a very carefully selected situation. The University of California Archaeological Survey has also tested this detector but has not yet found a site where it has proved useful.

Bibliography: Meighan, 1950.

EARTH-MOVING MACHINERY

In certain types of archeological sites, the removal of large quantities of sterile earth poses a problem which is most satisfactorily met by the use of earth-moving machinery. American archeology, with its tradition of meticulous small-scale excavation, avoided the problem until the exigencies of salvage work in river basins threatened by flooding forced it to turn to machinery in an effort to increase the speed of the work. In the Near East, where large-scale excavation with relatively unskilled labor has long been practiced, machinery has been used for years wherever it was not too costly to operate. The most widely used piece of earth-moving equipment is the Decauville Railway, invented by the French engineer Paul Decauville in the nineteenth century. This device, also called "contractor's railway" in English, consists of easily movable sections of very narrow-gauge track and small dump cars, often pushed by hand. It can be shifted around almost as easily as a toy railroad to fit the changing needs of the excavation. A full discussion of its use in archeological excavation will be found in Du Mesnil du Buisson, 1934. The same author illustrates small scoop-and-bucket excavators and recommends their use when feasible, but he does not mention any specific excavation in which they have been used.

Use of power equipment by the River Basin Surveys in the United States started in March, 1948. The road patrol, small bulldozer, and carry-all were all tested, with good results for certain types of sites. This work is described in detail by Wedel (in Griffin, 1951, pp. 17–33).

A few months later, Ashley Montagu used a mechanical excavator and a bulldozer to remove the overburden at the Swanscombe site in England, with a substantial saving of time and effort (Montagu, MS and 1949).

Use of earth-moving machinery in archeology would doubtless be more widespread than it is, except for the expense of the equipment and operators and the fact that much archeological field work is carried on in areas where the machinery is simply not available. In a site where there is a lot of sterile earth to be moved, its advantages are obvious, and no appreciable damage is caused to the underlying specimens.

Bibliography: Du Mesnil du Buisson, 1934; Griffin, 1951; Montagu, 1949a, b.

SOUND RECORDING

Thomas A. Edison patented his first phonograph in 1877, but it was not perfected to a point at which it could be produced and distributed until 1888. The very next year, Jesse Walter Fewkes, who was planning field work in the Southwest with the Hemenway Expedition, undertook to experiment with the new device to see whether or not it was worth his while to include one in the expedition's equipment. He got hold of a phonograph and took it to the Passamaquoddy Indian reservation in Maine, where he recorded some forty cylinders of pronunciation samples, vocabularies, folklore texts, conversations, and music. Few anthropologists since have made such thorough and judicious use of sound-recording equipment (Fewkes, 1890). The only type of use with which Fewkes did not experiment was the recording of interviews, and that was not very practicable with Edison cylinders having a playing time of from 2 to 4 minutes each.

The early phonographs reproduced with a horn for an amplifier and had a lot of surface noise, but the reproduction was recognizable and usable, and Fewkes was very much impressed with his results. He published six different articles in 1890 calling attention to the possibilities of the phonograph in ethnographic field work. While these articles were appearing, Fewkes himself

was off on his southwestern field trip, in the course of which he packed in a treadle-operated phonograph to Zuni to record ritual songs. These recordings, and later ones of Hopi music, were turned over to Benjamin Ives Gilman for analysis and publication (Gilman, 1891 and 1908). Gilman's work marks the beginning of comparative musicology in the United States.

Franz Boas, who had been interested in Indian music since he attempted to record some Bella Coola songs in musical notation in 1885, took a phonograph to the Northwest Coast in the 1890's and recorded a large number of Kwakiutl songs. In 1898, Charles S. Myers used a phonograph to record the music of the Torres Straits islanders on A. C. Haddon's great expedition for Cambridge University.

The father of comparative musicology in Germany was Carl Stumpf, and he recognized the importance of the phonograph for musical analysis as soon as he read Gilman's paper of 1891. It was not until 1900 that he had a chance to do some recording himself, the occasion being the German tour of a troupe of Siamese musicians. With his first records, Stumpf organized the Berlin Phonogramm Archive in the Psychological Institute, and this archive, under the able direction of Erich Moritz von Hornbostel, became a repository for records of anthropological interest from all over the world and a center of instruction in the field use of the phonograph for anthropologists and scientifically minded travelers. A similar archive was founded at Vienna in 1901, and, by 1909, there were record collections at Paris, St. Petersburg, Washington, Chicago, Berkeley, Cambridge, and other anthropological centers (Stumpf, 1911; Hornbostel, 1933; Gilman, 1909; Hajek, 1933).

The acceptance of the phonograph by German anthropologists can be dated to 1903, when the Berlin Anthropological Society held a meeting especially devoted to its evaluation. Felix von Luschan reported his successful use of a small phonograph to record text and music on a field trip to Turkey in 1901, and Abraham and Hornbostel presented an analysis of the music. Hornbostel kept the interest alive by contributing instructions for field recording to various German manuals of field method and by publishing analyses of recordings sent into the Archive.

American field workers also made extensive use of the phonograph for recording Indian songs and tales. A. L. Kroeber started the record collection at Berkeley in 1902 with some Yuki recordings, and in 1907 he made the first use of the phonograph for recording interview material, filling a long series of cylinders with information on Yurok lands and hunting and fishing rights.

Cylinder records remained in use for field work well into the 1930's; the last ones in the Berkeley collection are dated 1938. Meanwhile, of course, disk recording had been developed to a point where it was markedly and obviously superior to the cylinders, both in quality and in length of playing time. The cylinder machines remained in favor for field work because they were cheap and portable and did not get out of order easily; there was a demand for secondhand ones among anthropologists for years after they ceased to be manufactured. In 1931 a secondhand Edison could be bought for from $15 to $35 (Roberts, 1931; Herzog, 1936).

In the early 1930's some aluminum-disk recording phonographs were developed, which, though more expensive and bulkier than the cylinder ones, were still not too impractical as field equipment. George Herzog, Helen Roberts, and Lincoln Thompson designed one such machine, which was built by the Sound Specialties Company of Waterbury, Connecticut. At about the same time, Robert Lachmann had a similar machine built for him in Germany for the use of the Archive of Oriental Music at the Hebrew University in Jerusalem (Roberts and Thompson, 1935). The use of this type of equipment was largely restricted to expeditions the primary purpose of which was recording music, however, and the tradition of sound recording as a normal part of ethnographic field work died out with the obsolescence of the cylinder method. When it was revived, after the second World War, it was on the basis of the new magnetic recording method.

The first practicable magnetic recorder, using steel wire, was patented in Denmark in 1898 by Valdemar Poulsen. An improved Poulsen wire recorder was marketed in the United States by the American Telegraphone Company, beginning in 1903; the Telegraphone was sold chiefly as a dictation machine. It was compact, worked well, and produced a recording far superior to anything possible on the phonograph cylinders of the time; its chief disadvantage was that it had a very low playback level, and earphones were needed in order to listen to it. Unfortunately, the promotion was badly handled, and the Telegraphone never got established as an important rival of phonograph-type dictating machines. As far as I know, the Telegraphone was never used in anthropological field work, though Hornbostel, at least, was familiar with Poulsen's invention (Hornbostel, 1923, p. 421). Several dictating machines using the magnetic principle were marketed in Germany and England in the 1920's and 1930's; but, just as the magnetic recorder was developed to a point where it could be used for field work, the war came along and civilian production was out of the question (Begun, 1949).

The postwar revival of interest in sound recording as a part of anthropological field work is due very largely to the efforts of The Viking Fund, through the interest of Paul Fejos. The Fund got the first unreleased St. George wire recorder during the war and then spent some $7,000 for wire recorders in the first year that commercial sets were available. The wire recorder was demonstrated at Viking Fund meetings in the spring of 1946. In 1947, the Fund began to loan out wire recorders for field work, a service to the profession which is only now being terminated. Most anthropology departments in the United States now own or have access to magnetic recording equipment, and its use is now nearly as normal as that of the phonograph was fifty years ago.

The Wenner-Gren Foundation recommends the wire recorder as the most satisfactory field-work instrument because the stainless-steel wire used withstands the effects of extreme temperatures and dampness better than the cellulose tape used on tape recorders and because the tape has a tendency to deteriorate in time. The fidelity of wire is sufficient for all ordinary field work. Some students of comparative music, however, prefer to use tape because it gives a slightly higher fidelity, due in part to the capstan drive used on tape recorders which insures a constant recording speed.

Some use is still being made of disk recording, but chiefly when it is possible to bring the informants into the studio instead of taking the equipment into the field. Recordings made by other methods are often reproduced on disks for convenience of reproduction; the process is somewhat expensive but can be justified, especially in the case of linguistic text, because it is much easier to pick out a short phrase or a single word for repetition on a disk than on a wire or tape.

Moving-picture sound track has had a relatively restricted use for anthropological field recording because it is a bulky and expensive proposition. It has a number of advantages, however, in that the accompanying pictures give a valuable commentary on the sound. Paul Fejos recorded Yagua, Bora, and Witoto vocabularies on sound track in Peru in 1941, with pictures showing the informants pronouncing the words as they are spoken. Stanley Newman succeeded in making a partial phonemic analysis of the Yagua language on the basis of this material (Fejos, 1943).

C. F. Voegelin's survey, "Magnetic Recording of American Indian Languages and the Relationship of This to Other Kinds of Memory" (1950), gives much valuable information about the uses that American linguists have made of both disk and magnetic records, and the reader is referred to it for information on this subject.

On the whole, ethnographers have not shown any remarkable ingenuity at exploiting recording equipment for other purposes than the study of music and language. Kroeber's experiments in using the Edison phonograph to record interview data have inspired few imitators. Attention may be called, however, to an interesting series of experiments made by a psychologist who checked the accuracy of reports on counseling interviews by making disk recordings (Covner, 1942a, b; 1944a, b). He concluded that less than one-third of the material appearing in the interviews was included in the counselor's report and that from a tenth to a quarter of the information included was not accurate.

Bibliography: Abraham and Hornbostel, 1904; Begun, 1949; Covner, 1942a, b, 1944a, b; Fejos, 1943; Fewkes, 1890; Gilman, 1891, 1908, 1909; Gilman and Stone, 1908; Hajek, 1933;

Herzog, 1936; Hornbostel, 1923, 1933; Myers, 1907; Roberts, 1931; Roberts and Thompson, 1935; Stumpf, 1911; Voegelin, 1950.

EXPERIMENTAL PHONETICS

Although only a few anthropologists (e.g., Pliny Earle Goddard, A. L. Kroeber, and Floyd G. Lounsbury) have personally carried on research in experimental phonetics, every ethnographer and linguist who takes down native words in phonetic transcription is applying the results of such research, whether he knows it or not. The phonetic symbols of the transcription are shorthand abbreviations for descriptions of the position of the vocal organs in the articulation of particular sounds, and these descriptions were arrived at by ingenious laboratory means. Anyone who will take the trouble to compare the phonetic transcriptions used before the development of this experimental work (for present purposes, say before about 1891) with those made even in the first two decades of the present century will quickly convince himself of the important role played by experimental work in the history of anthropological linguistics. This work was an indispensable prerequisite to the development of present-day descriptive methods. Nineteenth-century linguists, working only by inspection and introspection, were unable to break away from the preconceptions about the nature of speech which they had inherited from classical philology.

Most ethnographers—and many linguists, for that matter—are simply taught the results of a half-century of laboratory work and urged to go on from there without inquiring as to how these results were arrived at or how reliable they may be. As a matter of fact, no general book on descriptive linguistics which I have examined takes adequate cognizance of the results of

X-ray studies of vowel production published in the 1930's, with the result that the instructions they give for vowel discrimination are both unrealistic and unnecessarily cumbersome. Other important modifications of phonetic theory are suggested by even more recent acoustic studies made with the Sound Spectrograph, and it is a serious mistake to assume that all the important problems in this field were solved a generation ago.

Two main lines of investigation have been followed in experimental phonetics: articulation and acoustics. For a number of reasons, better headway was made with the former subject than with the latter; articulation could be observed more directly and described to laymen in nonmathematical terms. Problems of acoustics were not entirely neglected, but it is less than ten years since suitable equipment was devised for acoustic analysis.

Laboratory study of articulation can be said to have begun with the introduction of the artificial palate in 1871. This device, still used in the form in which it was introduced, consists of a thin plate of black vulcanite especially molded to fit the roof of the subject's mouth. It is covered with a thin coating of powdered chalk and inserted; the subject pronounces a single sound and the palate is immediately removed. The subject's tongue removes the chalk from the areas where it touches the palate during the articulation, revealing the black color of the plate in these areas. The record so formed is called a "palatogram"; it is then recorded on a cast of the roof of the mouth or in a drawing or photograph, and the artificial palate reused for another sound (see Kingsley, 1887; Scripture, 1902). Goddard and Kroeber made extensive use of the artificial palate in describing the sounds of California Indian languages (Goddard, 1905, 1907). The sort of problem that needs to be kept in mind in using any laboratory device of this sort is illustrated by a recent study indicating that palatograms change with rates of articulation (Stetson, Hudgins, and Moses, 1940).

Another device widely used in the earlier years of experimental phonetics was the kymograph. Strictly speaking, the kymograph is nothing but a smoked cylinder which revolves at a constant speed while a stylus driven by a long screw moves along its face. The stylus produces a continuous line spiraling around the cylinder. Any slight impulse transmitted to the stylus will cause it to draw a wavy line instead of a straight one. Phoneticians usually used the kymograph with the Marey tambours (introduced in 1885), a pair of delicate diaphragms connected by a flexible tube. The tambours were used for recording the muscular movements involved in articulation and for securing a curve of the combination of breath and sound energy emerging from the mouth during speech. The term "kymograph" is often used loosely in phonetic literature to include the tambours as well as the recording cylinder. The whole apparatus was improved and put to new uses between 1885 and 1891 by the Abbé Jean-Pierre Rousselot (1846–1924), the founder of experimental phonetics as a discipline and the man who named it in 1889. Rousselot used not only the kymograph but every other device available in his time, and his laboratory was the model for others in Germany, England, and the United States. The University of California, for example, possesses a kymograph built for Goddard under Rousselot's direction.

Much experimentation was undertaken in the 1890's with flexible wires for studying tongue position, mirrors for photographing the larynx, and other miscellaneous devices. The reader interested in these methods will find discussions of them in Rousselot, 1897–1908 and Scripture, 1902.

One of the most useful methods of studying articulation has been X-ray photography. The X-ray was used in Germany as early as 1897 for studying articulation; a bibliography of the early work on the subject will be found in Parmenter, Treviño, and Bevans, 1931, a work which describes the technique used at the University of Chicago. Slightly more recent is the work of Holbrook and Carmody at Berkeley, using a modification of the Chicago technique (see Holbrook, 1933; Carmody, 1936 and 1937). An example of the use of drawings from X-rays in teaching phonetics will be found in Forchhammer, 1941. The X-ray method has proved particularly useful in studying tongue position during the production of those sounds for which the palatogram gives an inadequate record. It has also revealed movements of the jaw, pharynx, and larynx that had not previously been taken into account.

Some use has been made of moving pictures in the study of phonetics, particularly since the introduction of sound movies. I have not attempted to collect a bibliography on this subject and will merely call attention to Lenk, 1932, and Hegedüs, 1933, as examples of the use of this technique.

Acoustic phonetics goes back to the phonautograph devised by Léon Scott in 1857. This was a kymograph cylinder with a horn attached to the stylus instead of a tambour. The horn had a thin membrane at the small end, and the stylus was a stiff bristle attached to the membrane. This device gave a tracing of the sound waves produced by speech, and it was used almost immediately in phonetic studies. Koenig, in 1882, suggested the use of sensitive flames (manometric flames) as a means of seeing sound. Sound from a horn is led into a small chamber divided by a diaphragm; illuminating gas, flowing behind the diaphragm, varies its pressure according to the pressure of sound on the diaphragm, and the varying gas pressure causes a small flame on the gas jet to waver. A curve of the variations in the flame can be made with revolving mirrors. This method had a limited application because the flame curves are harder to analyze than the tracings of the phonautograph (see Scripture, 1902, pp. 17–31). In more recent years, recordings of sound waves have been more generally made with the oscillograph, first devised in 1891 but not applied immediately to experimental phonetics. The cathode-ray oscillograph is the one usually used today (Curry, 1935). The oscillograph makes a tracing comparable to the phonautograph one, a curve that can be analyzed mathematically.

The phonograph trace provides a record of sound, which can be made visible if sufficiently enlarged. In the early days of the phonograph, much ingenuity was devoted to making enlarged drawings and photographs of phonograph traces, but very little valuable information resulted from such studies (see Marichelle, 1897).

The trouble with even the best of the acoustic records described so far, such as the oscillograph tracings, was that they represented the sound waves too accurately. The waves of speech are complex sound waves which can be analyzed mathematically into a series of simple sinusoidal waves of different frequencies. These simple waves are combined in a particular relationship which is called their "phase." Two complex waves having the same components but in different phases will look entirely different. Now it happens that phase is quite irrelevant in acoustical phonetics because the human ear does not hear phase differences. Our two hypothetical waves having the same components with different phases will sound exactly alike. All that the ear picks up is the different frequencies present and the distribution of power among them. The presence of phase distinctions in the oscillograph tracings thus presented serious difficulties in the interpretation of the curves in terms of the distinctions made by the ear.

These difficulties are avoided in a new device, the Sound Spectrograph, developed by the Bell Laboratories during the last war and disclosed to the public in 1945. It produces a visible representation of speech, making the same distinctions that the ear makes, and it promises to hold the answer to a whole series of acoustic problems that have been bothering phoneticians for two generations. The first linguistic study based on it is Joos, 1948, to which I am indebted for the information summarized above. See also Potter, Kopp, and Green, 1947; Meyer-Eppler, 1950. Joos's study is an excellent general introduction to the whole subject of acoustic phonetics and makes a number of important contributions to phonetic theory on the basis of Sound Spectrograph studies.

Mention should also be made of two other devices which have proved useful in phonetic analysis. The Repeater is an endless loop with a small unit of speech on it to be played on a wire or tape recorder to give mechanical repetition of an utterance, so that it can be studied in detail. Paul Fejos and The Viking Fund staff built what was probably the first Repeater in 1948; a number of linguists, notably Floyd Lounsbury, have experimented with it since. The Speech Stretcher is a device designed by Martin Joos; it plays a recorded utterance at half-speed but at the normal frequency and is exceedingly useful for phonetic demonstration, as well as in analysis of difficult cases (see Joos, 1948, pp. 127–29).

Bibliography: Carmody, 1936, 1937; Curry, 1935; Forchhammer, 1941; Goddard, 1905, 1907; Hegedüs, 1933; Holbrook, 1933; Joos, 1948; Kingsley, 1887; Lenk, 1932; Marichelle, 1897; Meyer-Eppler, 1950; Parmenter, Treviño, and Bevans, 1931; Potter, Kopp, and Green, 1947; Rousselot, 1897–1908; Scripture, 1902; Stetson, Hudgins, and Moses, 1940.

INDEXING AND CALCULATING MACHINES

The most versatile and accessible equipment for statistical work at present is that manufactured by the International Business Machines Corporation and hence usually referred to as "IBM machines." The data to be tabulated must first be coded, so that they can be punched on standard cards. The cards are then fed into a machine, which sorts and tabulates any desired combination of facts by brushes which make electrical contact through the holes in the cards. An excellent account of the machines in current use and what they will do will be found in Frederick P. Thieme's article, "The Use of IBM Machines in Analyzing Anthropological Data" (Griffin [ed.], 1951, pp. 128–32).

Punch-card tabulating machines were developed between 1880 and 1890 by Dr. Herman Hollerith. Hollerith worked on the United States Census of 1880 as a special agent and became seriously concerned about the amount of work that went into hand calculation of the census statistics. He saw that the rate of population increase was such that the problem would be entirely out of hand by 1890 if nothing was done. His machine was used successfully in the 1890 Census and attracted wide attention. It was improved considerably in the next ten years and by 1900 was widely adopted.

As far as I have been able to dis-cover, the Hollerith method was not used in anthropology until the late 1920's, when E. A. Hooton installed tabulating machines at the physical anthropology laboratory at Harvard to handle the masses of data which he was accumulating on his American criminal project (described in Hooton, 1939). Hooton's project involved taking 125 measurements and observations on each of 17,000 individuals in an attempt to get an adequate sample, and he wanted to look for correlations between various physical features and between physical features and "sociological" ones in this great mass of data. The task would have been quite impractical without the help of tabulating machines. Hooton makes this point clear in discussing his new sampling standard:

> The anthropologist must measure hundreds and even thousands of individuals in order that he may be sure that his data properly represent the populations which he is investigating. This means an appalling mass of statistics which must be mathematically reduced if any conclusions are to be drawn from them.
>
> In the old days of hand tabulation and computation no sensible anthropologist was likely to study more than a few hundred subjects of any group, simply because he knew that the arithmetical labor of reducing his statistics would have to be counted in years [Hooton, in Baehne (ed.), 1935, p. 383].

IBM machines are most useful in projects in which it is proposed to study a moderate number of factors on a large number of subjects (say over 500). The limiting factor is the time required to set up the machine for intricate calculations; Dr. L. M. Thomas, of the International Business Machines Corporation, is quoted as saying that the use of the machines is not economical if it takes more than half of the investigator's time to set up the machine (Kaplan, 1951, p. 29). This limitation still leaves the IBM machine with a vast field of utility in physical anthropology in problems in which a relatively small number of variables is handled in a single operation. Hooton's example has been widely followed, and the IBM machine is now a standard tool in physical anthropology.

IBM machines have been used in sociology at least since the early 1930's, but I do not know of any ethnological application of them. There are two obvious reasons for this situation: in the first place, ethnologists commonly work with smaller communities than sociologists and talk to a smaller number of people. They try to get more data out of fewer informants. In the second place, their approach is qualitative rather than quantitative, and their data are rarely susceptible of statistical analysis. When the IBM machines are used in ethnology, it will probably be because of the application of sociological survey methods to the anthropological data.

Archeological data are more often subjected to statistical analysis, but usually to analysis of such a simple sort that it can be done with the aid of a hand calculator or slide rule. George W. Brainerd and Anna O. Shepard have been using peripheral punch cards for tabulating distributions. These cards are simpler to use than IBM cards, but the punching indicates only presence or absence instead of a numerical value (see Brainerd in Griffin [ed.], 1951, pp. 125–27; Thieme in Kaplan, 1951, p. 29).

Bibliography: Baehne (ed.), 1935 (articles by Arkin, pp. 1–20; Hooton, pp. 383–88; Johnson, pp. 409–14); Griffin (ed.), 1951 (articles by Brainerd, pp. 117–27; Thieme, pp. 128–32); Hooton, 1939; Kaplan, 1951 (abstract of remarks by Thieme and Thomas, pp. 29–30).

COLOR DESCRIPTION

Several branches of anthropology have an interest in the precise description of color. Physical anthropology is concerned with skin pigmentation and hair and eye color; archeology with designating colors of pigments on specimens for description and reproduction; and ethnography with differences of color classification in different cultures, as well as the description of specimens. A variety of methods has been used.

The first approach to precise color description in physical anthropology involved the use of specially designed standard sample series; these were printed on paper or made in a variety of materials to simulate the texture of skin, hair, or eyeballs. All these scales proved unsatisfactory in practice. One of the best, a series of 30 samples for classifying hair color, the "Haarfarbentafel nach Fischer-Saller," still does not have enough samples in each range to give anything like a close description.

Physical anthropologists next turned to the color top, a method involving the spinning of disks to mix a color matching the one to be described. Because of observer fatigue, however, the top method is very difficult to use; repeated observations on the same color often do not match.

In 1939 Edwards and Duntley used the new Hardy photoelectric recording sprectrophotometer at the Massachusetts Institute of Technology for studying skin pigmentation, with highly satisfactory results; the difficulty was that the M.I.T. machine was the only one of its kind. In 1951, however, Weiner called attention to a new photoelectric spectrophotometer which is portable but gives results comparable to the Hardy device. It is manufactured in England. Weiner feels that it at last provides the answer to the color-description problem in physical anthropology.

For describing archeological or ethnographic specimens, the use of color dictionaries has long been standard practice. There is a large number of different dictionaries available; the two most widely used are probably Ridgway, 1912, and Maerz and Paul, 1930. Anna O. Shepard, who tried both, prefers Ridgway for describing pottery colors; she discusses the whole problem of color description in her study of the technology of Pecos pottery (Shepard, 1936*b*, p. 432). On the other hand, Watson Smith and his staff used Maerz and Paul with good results in describing and reproducing the mural paintings from Awatovi (1936–39). Both these dictionaries contain large series of classified color samples, each numbered and many of them named as well. The user matches samples against his specimen color and identifies the latter by the number of the dictionary sample or samples which resemble it most closely.

A somewhat different color-description system is the Munsell Color System (Munsell Color Company, Inc., 1929–42). This involves some trained judgment on the part of the user, for he must rate the color he wishes to describe in terms of scales for three different characteristics, and many specimen colors will fall between the samples. Lila M. O'Neale preferred this system to either of the color dictionaries, however, and used it in her textile analysis studies.

Michael Kasha, studying archeological textiles from Chihuahua, at Miss O'Neale's suggestion analyzed the dyes with a Beckman photoelectric spectrophotometer and managed to identify all the dyestuffs used, even the organic ones (Kasha, 1948). Identification of organic dyes had previously been considered impossible, so this is an impressive example of the important results that may be expected from the precise description of color. It suggests that the photoelectric spectrophotometer will prove as useful in archeology and ethnography as it has in physical anthropology.

An interesting theoretical discussion of the problems of color classification will be found in Bradley, 1938.

Bibliography: Bradley, 1938; Edwards and Duntley, 1939; Kasha, 1948; Maerz and Paul, 1930; Munsell Color Company, Inc., 1929–42; Ridgway, 1912; Shepard, 1936*b*; Weiner, 1951.

CHEMISTRY AND SPECTRO-GRAPHIC ANALYSIS

The great anthropological importance of chemistry lies in the field of archeology, where chemical testing methods can be used to study the changes undergone by antiquities in the earth and in the air, the nature of archeological deposits, the substances used in ancient technological processes, and sometimes the processes themselves. Chemical methods are also useful in the preservation of antiquities and in their cleaning and restoration for study or exhibition purposes.

Although archeologists interested in chemistry are not numerous, there is a group of chemists who are interested in archeology, and they are sufficiently numerous to have presented a Symposium on Archaeological Chemistry at the 117th meeting of the American Chemical Society in 1950 (Caley [ed.], 1951). Earle R. Caley, who edited the proceedings of this symposum, presented a valuable paper on the "Early History and Literature of Archaeological Chemistry" (pp. 64–66), which covers the period from the publication of the first paper on the subject (in England in 1796) to the beginnings of the excavations at Olympia in 1875, an event which he takes as marking the beginning of excavation on modern scientific principles. He notes, among other interesting facts, that Layard's *Discov-*

eries in the Ruins of Nineveh and Babylon (1853) was the first archeological report to contain an appendix describing the results of chemical examination of the objects recovered. In the 156 years since the subject was invented, archeological chemistry has accumulated a very extensive bibliography, of which I have been able to review only a fraction.

In spite of the great theoretical interest of the subject, I have been able to find very few studies on the changes undergone by antiquities in the earth and in the air, except as such matters are taken up with reference to problems of cleaning and restoration. The best general work is that of Rathgen (1905, pp. 1–56). Rosenberg (1917) discusses what happens to iron and bronze in earth containing carbonic acid and chlorides. Rutherford J. Gettens contributed an article on bronze corrosion to the 1950 symposium, and it includes a short bibliography on the subject (Caley [ed.], 1951, pp. 67–71). Metals have received relatively more attention than any other material. As Paul Fejos pointed out to me, however, nothing, not even the most "perishable" organic matter, is entirely annihilated in the ground; even though it becomes so altered as to be invisible to the naked eye, its former state may be detected by suitable chemical tests. The present survey indicates that this field remains almost entirely unexplored.

Even more rare than studies of change in materials are analyses of the earth that makes up the bulk of any archeological site. A recent example of this technique is the appendix written by T. H. Buehrer for Emil Haury's Ventana Cave report (Haury, 1950, pp. 549–63). Chemical analysis of site constituents has also been a part of the study of total site content carried out at the University of California (see the section on "Site Analysis," below).

Studies involving the chemical identification of substances found in archeological specimens are very numerous, and I have not tried to make an exhaustive review. Perhaps because of the abundance of Egyptian specimens in most of the older museums, a notable number of analyses have been run on pieces from Egypt; the standard work on this subject is Lucas, 1934. The type of contribution that chemists can make to archeology is well illustrated in an article by Newell (1933), which gives chemical evidence that lime was not used for any purpose in Egypt until Roman times, contrary to the generally received opinion among archeologists. Analyses of Greek, Roman, and Maya specimens are discussed by Foster (1933, 1934, 1935). In the field of textiles, much ingenuity has been concentrated on the problem of identifying ancient dyes and mordants; one of the best studies of this sort, using chemical reagents to define the properties of the substances considered and with due consideration of the available literary evidence, is Pfister's monograph on Hellenistic dyeing methods in Syria (Pfister, 1935). Pottery pigments have been identified chemically in a number of cases; Hawley's 1929 study of prehistoric pottery pigments in the American Southwest is a good example, because the author based an elaborate historical reconstruction on the results of the laboratory tests.

It is important for the anthropologist not to surrender his critical faculty in the face of an authoritative-looking laboratory report. Mistakes are made in other disciplines besides anthropology. An interesting example is the case of Colin G. Fink's claim that the ancient Egyptians possessed a chemical method of plating antimony on copper, a claim resulting from Fink's observations on an ewer and basin of Old Kingdom date which had been sent to him for cleaning (Fink, 1934, p. 236). Forbes points out that subsequent investigation revealed that the "antimony plating" was due to the electrolytic reduction of the copper objects carried out by Fink; "the antimony is simply an impurity of the copper and the so-called plating due to the method of restoration and not a process applied to the original object" (Forbes, 1950, p. 264).

Preservation of antiquities is another subject on which there is an extensive literature, mostly written by museum technicians, although occasional contributions have been made by archeologists. In addition to Rathgen (1905, 1915–24), Leechman, 1931, and Plenderleith, 1934, are the standard references. Some very ingenious techniques have been developed in this field, like Laudermilk's method of preserving textile ash with rosin and acetone, worked out originally for criminological use (Laudermilk, 1937).

Cleaning and restoration of archeological specimens is usually not done under the direction of archeologists but for purposes of museum display; nevertheless, it has some interest to research workers as well, for proper cleaning often reveals important characteristics of the object that would not otherwise have been noted. The works on preservation techniques also treat this subject, and we may add British Museum, Department of Scientific and Industrial Research, 1926, to the list. Fink, who has done much experimental work in cleaning and restoration, devised, among other techniques, one for using electro-osmosis to remove salts entangled with the grains of pigment on pottery and return the disturbed pigment to its original position (Fink, 1933).

A special problem, involving both chemical and microscopic procedures, is the identification of wood and wood charcoal fragments. Maby (1932) describes the method used.

Spectrographic analysis is an alternative method of determining the chemical elements present in a specimen. The elements are identified without difficulty from the characteristic patterns of lines which appear in a spectrum produced with a minute quantity of the specimen to be tested. The method is especially valuable for qualitative analysis because of the small size of the sample needed and the accuracy with which minute traces of elements that would be missed in a chemical analysis can be detected. It is often such traces that enable the chemist to identify the precise origin of the specimen being studied. Quantitative analysis is usually done by chemical methods, because quantities cannot be calculated accurately from the spectrum lines. Spectrographic analysis has been used most frequently for the study of metal, glass, and pottery. General references on the subject are Hülle, 1933, and Winkler, 1933, dealing primarily with metal tests. Haury has a report on spectrographic analysis of a copper bell from the American Southwest (Haury, 1947).

Spectrographic analysis was used for glass by Ritchie (1937) and Farnsworth and Ritchie (1938). The earlier of these papers is particularly important, for the laboratory work furnished evidence that true glass had been manufactured in China over five hundred years earlier than anyone had previously believed. Shepard has done spectrographic analysis of pottery (Shepard, 1936b).

Bibliography: British Museum, Department of Scientific and Industrial Research, 1926; Caley (ed.), 1951; Farnsworth and Ritchie, 1938; Fink, 1933, 1934; Foster, 1933, 1934, 1935; Haury, 1947, 1950; Hawley, 1929; Hülle, 1933; Laudermilk, 1937; Leechman, 1931; Lucas, 1934; Maby, 1932; Newell, 1933; Pfister, 1935; Plenderleith, 1934; Rathgen, 1905, 1915–24; Ritchie, 1937; Rosenberg, 1917; A. Schmidt, 1934; Shepard, 1936*b;* Winkler, 1933.

MICROSCOPY, POTTERY TECH-NOLOGY, METALLOGRAPHY, AND PETROGRAPHY

The microscope is used extensively in laboratory studies of archeological textiles, pottery, metal, and stone, usually in combination with photography. The combined technique is called "photomicrography" and is widely used in the natural sciences and in commercial testing laboratories (see Allen, 1941; Shillaber, 1944).

In the study of textiles, the microscope is indispensable for identifying fibers and analyzing weaves. For the analysis of complex weaves, it is very important to be able to see the threads in three dimensions, and students of textiles consequently prefer to use a stereoscopic microscope. Margaret Rowe, at the Yale University Art Gallery, uses a Bausch and Lomb model mounted on a long arm so that it is not necessary to set the microscope down on the textile, even when examining a large piece. Students of textiles also use simple pocket microscopes, not much bigger than a fountain pen, which give 20× magnification or more. Photomicrographs are commonly used to illustrate textile studies.

The technological study of ancient pottery involves using the microscope for examining thin sections and identifying minerals present, together with other laboratory methods, such as chemical or spectrographic analysis, measures of hardness and porosity, and firing tests. A good general discussion of the procedures followed and their significance is given by Frederick R. Matson, Jr., in Griffin, 1951, pp. 102–16;

more elaborate accounts will be found in Shepard, 1936*b* and 1942.

The father of pottery technology studies is probably Louis Franchet, who published a series of articles and a book on the subject around 1910 (see especially Franchet, 1911). Although Franchet's work on Neolithic pottery leaves much to be desired from a modern point of view, it represents a considerable improvement over the uninformed speculations of many of the prehistorians of the time. Gisela M. A. Richter's valuable archeological studies of Greek pottery rest on a basis of technological knowledge discussed in her 1923 book, *The Craft of Athenian Pottery.* A number of southwesternists then became interested in the subject, and we have papers by Hawley (1929, 1930), Shepard (1936*b,* 1942), and Colton (1939) applying laboratory methods to southwestern problems. Anna Shepard's work has been particularly important in raising the standards of archeological pottery studies. Matson has studied Indian pottery from Michigan (Matson in Greenman, 1937, pp. 99–124) and Hellenistic pottery from Iraq (Matson, m1945). The subject may be said to have come of age in archeology with the Conference on Archeological Technology in Ceramics, which met at the University of Michigan in 1938 under the sponsorship of the National Research Council (Shepard and Horton, 1939).

The laboratory study of metals involves chemical or spectrographic analysis, tests for hardness, heating tests, and metallographic examination. It is the last of these processes which yields the most information about the processes of manufacture used in making the specimen studied, especially if it is of copper or iron or an alloy of one of these metals. Metallography consists in polishing a surface on the specimen to be examined, etching this surface with acid, and examining the crystalline structure of the metal revealed by this process. The method is a standard one in industrial and engineering practice (see Kehl, 1943). The best bibliography on its application to archeological specimens (92 titles) appears in Fink and Polushkin, 1936.

In examining ancient metal objects by the metallographic technique, it is often possible to decide whether the object has been hammered, whether it has been annealed (treated by heat), and even, in some cases, the approximate temperature to which it was heated. The clearest account of what this technique will do, together with a discussion of its theoretical basis, will be found in Mathewson, 1915. Wilson and Sayre (1935) also give some explanation of this sort, but, as Shepard was quick to point out (1936a), they do not make it entirely clear how the evidence is interpreted.

The earliest metallographic study in archeology that I have come across is Foote and Buell's work on three Peruvian bronze axes collected by the Bingham expedition (1912). Since that date, the method has come into general use, as interest in the history of metallurgy has developed. There is a particularly active group interested in the subject in England, and in 1945 the Royal Anthropological Institute appointed an Ancient Mining and Metallurgy Committee. The results of its work have been appearing in *Man* since 1948. The standard general work on Old World metallurgy is Forbes, 1950, which contains extensive bibliographies. The recent work of Herbert Maryon on hammering and soldering techniques also deserves mention (Maryon, 1936, 1949).

For New World metallurgy, the standard general reference is Rivet and Arsandaux, 1946, with a bibliography of 341 items. Some of the finest technological studies in this field are those

of Paul Bergsøe on ancient Ecuadorean gold, platinum, copper, and lead (Bergsøe, 1937, 1938). Leonard Frank has an excellent recent article on some copper implements from Wisconsin and Minnesota, which takes up the question of knowledge of annealing in this area and concludes that there is no proof of it (Frank, 1951). Some other references to studies of metal objects will be found in the section on chemistry.

Two Swiss scholars, Marcel Grosjean and Albert Périer, have made the ingenious suggestion that the metallographic method might be applied to the study of human teeth and bone. Their note on the subject (1939) describes the results of some tests made on teeth.

Petrographic examination is another distinct laboratory technique which is used, together with spectrographic analysis and other procedures, in the study of stone specimens and pottery. It involves grinding a thin section of the material to be examined, mounting it on a glass slide, passing light through it, and examining it in a petrographic microscope to identify minerals and observe the crystalline structure. The use of this technique in European prehistory is discussed by Obenauer, 1933, and Schmitt, 1939. A good example of its use in the New World field is David H. Howell's study of pipestone and red-shale artifacts in the United States (1940). Howell concludes that it would be theoretically possible to identify the particular outcrop from which the material used in these specimens comes.

Bibliography: Allen, 1941; Bergsoe, 1937, 1938; Colton, 1939; Fink and Polushkin, 1936; Foote and Buell, 1912; Forbes, 1950; Franchet, 1911; Frank, 1951; Greenman, 1937; Griffin, 1951; Grosjean and Périer, 1939; Hawley, 1929, 1930; Howell, 1940; Kehl, 1943; Maryon, 1936, 1949; Mathewson, 1915; Matson, m1945; Obenauer, 1933; Richter, 1923; Rivet and Arsandaux, 1946;

Schmitt, 1939; Shepard, 1936*a, b,* 1942; Shepard and Horton, 1939; Shillaber, 1944; Wilson and Sayre, 1935.

BACTERIOLOGY AND DIATETICS

This section is concerned with the laboratory study of arrow poisons and the analysis of foodstuffs to determine their dietary value. These subjects are treated together because they both have ethnological rather than archeological interest; there is no other logical reason for grouping them.

Arrow poisons are studied to determine their active ingredients and the physiological effects they produce. The usual methods involved are chemical analysis and tests on laboratory animals of the drugs found. The earliest work on this subject which has come to my attention is that by Louis Lewin (1894 and 1923). I have not been able to consult either edition of this work to see whether the author cites any earlier studies. More recently, a series of studies on arrow poisons has been published by the Swedish chemist, C. G. Santesson (e.g., Santesson, 1931, 1936), and a number of other writers have contributed to the subject. An interesting result of this work on arrow poisons has been the adoption of one of them, curare, for medical use in our own culture.

It has often been suggested that some arrow poisons depend for their effect on the presence of infection-producing bacteria. The first laboratory work on this problem was done by Hall (Hall, 1928; Hall and Whitehead, 1927). Hall found no seriously pathogenic bacteria on two Malayan blowgun darts submitted to him by E. W. Gifford; tests on Bushman arrows verified the presence of some pathogenic bacteria, but probably none that could not be accounted for by the unsanitary conditions in which the arrows were prepared and used.

Fish poisons have also been analyzed and tested; Heizer, 1949, gives a bibliography on this subject. There is a vast literature, including discussions of laboratory tests, on the subject of stimulants and narcotics; some references will be found in Cooper, 1949.

As far as I know, the only study of the dietary value of the foodstuffs used in another culture which has been made is Rivera's analysis of certain staples in the Coast Salish diet (Rivera, 1949). The contribution of this project was to furnish data on the food value of salmon and saskatoon berries in the dried form in which the Indians usually ate them, instead of in the fresh form, in which they have been analyzed by students of White dietary habits. The results are most interesting and make one wonder why this subject has not received more attention.

Bibliography: Cooper, 1949; Hall, 1928; Hall and Whitehead, 1927; Heizer, 1949; Lewin, 1894, 1923; Rivera, 1949; Santesson, 1931, 1936.

MOULAGE AND CASTING

Molds and casts are used in archeology and physical anthropology for greater convenience in studying certain features and for demonstration and teaching purposes. The types of casts made in physical anthropology (dental casts, life-masks, etc.) are similar to those used in medicine, and the methods for making them are discussed systematically by Clarke (1940). A number of new casting techniques were described at the Viking Fund Seminar in Physical Anthropology in 1949 (see the abstracts in Kaplan, 1951, pp. 20–21).

Casting is often of great importance in archeology. Its most spectacular use is perhaps in the case of objects of perishable material which have decayed in such circumstances that the earth in which they are buried does not fall in to fill up the resulting cavity. Leonard Woolley's experience with the harp at Ur is a well-known example. As he tells it, "a simple hole in the ground was found, and then a second; something unusual about their shape seemed to call for special treatment, and accordingly plaster-of-paris was poured in to fill up the void which decaying wood had left: the result was a complete plaster cast of a harp whose substance had long since vanished . . . and thus the first hint that we had of a grave's presence also enabled us to preserve the best object in it before we knew what it was" (Woolley, 1937, pp. 85–86). In similar fashion, casts of some of the bodies of people killed in the destruction of Pompeii were recovered many years ago.

Casting makes it possible to bring home an accurate facsimile of a large-sized monument in cases where the original cannot or should not be removed. The practice is commonly used by archeologists in dealing with sculpture, but discussions of methods and problems involved are seldom included in the reports. Neil M. Judd, however, did publish an account of his experiences in making casts of the Maya sculptures of Quiriguá (Judd, 1915).

For recording inscriptions and sculpture in low relief, the standard method is to make a paper squeeze mold of the surface. The technique is described briefly in B. Z. Seligman ([ed.], 1951, pp. 365–68). More recently, a latex solution has been used for this purpose; its value for field use was demonstrated by George G. Cameron in 1948, when he used it to reproduce Darius' inscriptions at Bisitun (Cameron, 1950).

Casts are widely used for duplicating museum specimens for teaching purposes, and for sale to the public, but the practice is commoner in Europe than in the United States. The University Museum in Philadelphia has used the sale of casts as an effective method of encouraging public interest in its archeological work.

Bibliography: Cameron, 1950; Clarke 1940; Judd, 1915; Kaplan, 1951; B. Z. Seligman (ed.), 1951; Woolley, 1937.

SITE ANALYSIS

In 1913, at the suggestion of A. L. Kroeber, E. W. Gifford undertook the analysis of all the constituent materials of a California shell-mound site, to see whether laboratory methods might throw some new light on archeological problems. He sifted the shell-mound materials through three screens, sorted the larger materials by eye, and had the finest ones analyzed chemically, to determine the proportion of ash and shell which they contained (Gifford, 1916).

Recently, Sherburne F. Cook has elaborated the method, in collaboration with A. E. Treganza and Robert F. Heizer (Cook, 1946; Cook and Treganza, 1947; Treganza and Cook, 1948; Cook and Treganza, 1950; and Cook and Heizer, 1951). The original purpose of these studies was to arrive at an estimate of the length of occupation of the site analyzed, by a calculation based on the estimated population and an inference as to its rate of food consumption. Too many variables were involved in this calculation to give its results much weight, so the method was developed rather toward the reconstruction of cultural data. By sorting the constituent materials of a site, determining their weight and volume, and identifying the chemical constituents, it has been possible to make convincing estimates of the aboriginal population and bring out evidence for reconstructing its living habits which would not otherwise have been available. The California work indicates that the technique of physical analysis gives best results in dry sites, and its applicability to dry areas like the Southwest and Peru is obvious.

Bibliography: Cook, 1946; Cook and Heizer, 1951; Cook and Treganza, 1947, 1950; Gifford, 1916; Treganza and Cook, 1948.

SPECIAL TECHNIQUES IN PHYSICAL ANTHROPOLOGY

It is probable that more special equipment and laboratory processes are used in physical anthropology than in any other type of anthropological research. A number of them have been discussed in previous sections of this paper, but no exhaustive treatment will be attempted. The standard methods of physical anthropology are described by Martin (1928), and Volume III of his work contains an immense bibliography of the subject. The references on techniques will be found on pages 1215–32. Lucile E. Hoyme has undertaken a historical survey of anthropometric instruments, which should provide a valuable historical perspective; a preliminary version of her paper was presented at the 20th annual meeting of the American Association of Physical Anthropologists in 1951, and an abstract of it has been published (Hoyme, 1951). The author is now extending her coverage, and she plans to rewrite the paper for publication.

Many new techniques in physical anthropology were described at the Viking Fund meeting in 1949 and are reported by Kaplan (1951). Only two of the least widely known ones will be noticed here—the split-line technique and alizarine staining.

The split-line technique was discussed by Neil Tappan at the Viking Fund meeting (see Kaplan, p. 22). It is a method of studying the stress patterns in bone. The bone has to be partly decalcified first; then an awl is inserted into its surface, and the line of split that is produced is marked with ink. It is assumed that the lines of split reflect internal structural features of the bones. The method has been used to study growth in the jaws by Seipel (1948).

Alizarine red "S" (sodium sulphalizarate) has the property of staining red all calcifying tissues which are present and growing at the time it is injected, except enamel. It can therefore be used to measure growth in bone: bone laid down prior to or after the dye is injected remains white. For obvious reasons, this technique cannot be used on human subjects, who might not appreciate growing up with partially reddened skeletons, but much valuable comparative information can be secured on animals. This technique was described by Schour in 1936, and a number of studies using it have been published, the most important being Massler and Schour, 1951. Noback and Baer discussed the use of alizarine red at the 1949 Viking Fund Seminar in Physical Anthropology, and their communications are abstracted in Kaplan, 1951, pp. 21–22.

Bibliography: Baer, 1951; Hoyme, 1951; Kaplan, 1951; Martin, 1928; Massler and Schour, 1951; Schour, 1936; Seipel, 1948.

BIBLIOGRAPHY

An asterisk indicates that the item was not consulted at first hand. An "m" before the date (e.g., m1945) indicates that the work in question was published on microfilm.

ABRAHAM, O., and HORNBOSTEL, E. M. VON. 1904. "Ueber die Bedeutung des Phonographen für vergleichende Musikwissenschaft." *Zeitschrift für Ethnologie,* 36. Jahrgang, Heft 2, pp. 222–233. Berlin.

AGDE, H. 1938. "Farbenphotographie bei Grabungen." *Nachrichtenblatt für Deut-*

sche Vorzeit, 14. Jahrgang, Heft 7, pp. 194–195. Leipzig.

ALLEN, ROY MORRIS. 1941. *Photo-micrography.* D. Van Nostrand Company, Inc., New York.

AMERICAN SOCIETY OF PHOTOGRAMMETRY. 1936. "Bibliography of Photogrammetry." *Photogrammetric Engineering,* vol. II, no. 4, October–December, pp. i–iv, 1–117. Washington.

ARAGO, DOMINIQUE-FRANÇOIS. 1839. "Le daguerréotype." *Comptes rendus hebdomadaires des séances de l'Académie des Sciences,* tome IX, 2e semestre, no. 8, séance du lundi, 19 août, pp. 250–267. Paris.

ARMILLAS, PEDRO. 1950. "Teotihuacán, Tula y los Toltecas. Las culturas postarcaicas y pre-aztecas del centro de México. Excavaciones y estudios, 1922–1950." *Runa,* vol. III, partes 1–2, pp. 37–70. Buenos Aires.

BAEHNE, GEORGE WALTER (ed.). 1935. *Practical Applications of the Punched Card Method in Colleges and Universities.* Columbia University Press, New York.

BAER, MELVYN J. 1951. "Growth of the face as shown by intra-vital staining with alizarin red 'S'" (abstract). *American Journal of Physical Anthropology,* n.s., vol. 9, no. 2, June, p. 235. Philadelphia.

BASCOM, WILLIAM R. 1941. "Possible applications of kite photography to archaeology and ethnology." *Transactions of the Illinois Academy of Sciences,* vol. 34, no. 2, December, pp. 62–63. Springfield.

BEGUN, SEMI JOSEPH. 1949. *Magnetic Recording.* Murray Hill Books, Inc., New York, Toronto.

BERGSOE, PAUL. 1937. *The Metallurgy of Gold and Platinum among the Pre-Columbian Indians.* Danmarks Naturvidenskabelige Samfund, Ingeniorvidenskabelige Skrifter, Nr. A 44. Kobenhavn.

———. 1938. *The Gilding Process and the Metallurgy of Copper and Lead among the Pre-Columbian Indians.* Danmarks Naturvidenskabelige Samfund, Ingeniørvidenskabelige Skrifter, Nr. A 46. København.

BERTILLON, ALPHONSE, and CHERVIN, ARTHUR. 1909. *Anthropologie métrique.* *Conseils pratiques aux missionaires scientifiques sur la maniére de mesurer, de photographier et de décrire des sujets vivants et des pièces anatomiques. Anthropométrie, photographie métrique, portrait descriptif, craniométrie.* (Extrait des publications de la Mission G. de Créqui Montfort et E. Sénéchal de la Grange relatives á l'anthropologie bolivienne.) Imprimerie Nationale, Paris.

BRADFORD, JOHN. 1947. "A Technique for the Study of Centuriation." *Antiquity,* vol. XXI, no. 84, December, pp. 197–204. Gloucester.

BRADLEY, MORTON C., JR. 1938. "Systems of Color Classification." *Technical Studies in the Field of the Fine Arts,* vol. VI, no. 4, April, pp. 240–275. Lancaster, Pa.

BRITISH MUSEUM, DEPARTMENT OF SCIENTIFIC AND INDUSTRIAL RESEARCH. 1926. *The Cleaning and Restoration of Museum Exhibits. Third Report upon Investigations Conducted at the British Museum.* Published under the authority of His Majesty's Stationery Office. London.

CALEY, EARLE R. (ed.). 1951. "Symposium on Archaeological Chemistry." *Journal of Chemical Education,* vol. 28, no. 2, February, pp. 63–96. Easton, Pa.

CAMERON, GEORGE G. 1950. "Darius Carved History on Ageless Rock." *National Geographic Magazine,* vol. XCVIII, no. 6, December, pp. 825–844. Washington.

CARMODY, FRANCIS J. 1936. "Radiographs of Thirteen German Vowels." *Archives Néerlandaises de Phonétique Expérimentale,* tome XII, pp. 27–33. Amsterdam.

———. 1937. *X-Ray Studies of Speech Articulations. Notes and X-Ray Films of the Late Richard T. Holbrook, Arranged and Explained.* University of California Publications in Modern Philology, vol. 20, no. 4, pp. i–viii, 187–238. Berkeley.

CHARNAY, DÉSIRÉ. 1863. *Cités et ruines américaines; Mitla, Palenqué, Izamal, Chichen-Itza, Uxmal, recueillies et photographiées par Désiré Charnay, avec un texte par M. Viollet-le-Duc, architecte du gouvernement, suivi du voyage et des documents de l'auteur.* Gide, Editeur; A. Morel et Cie., Paris.

CHOMBART DE LAUWE, PAUL HENRY. *1951. Photographies aériennes: methode, procédés, interprétation; l'étude de l'homme sur la terre.* Librairie Armand Colin, Paris.

——. (ed.). 1948. *La découverte aérienne du monde.* Préface de E. de Martonne, Membre de l'Institut. Horizons de France, Paris.

CLARK, WALTER. 1946. *Photography by Infrared, Its Principles and Applications.* Second edition. John Wiley & Sons, Inc., New York; Chapman and Hall, Ltd., London.

CLARKE, CARL DAME. 1940. *Molding and Casting; Its Technique and Application. For Moulage Workers, Sculptors, Artists, Physicians, Dentists, Criminologists, Craftsmen, Pattern Makers and Architectural Modelers.* The John D. Lucas Company, Publishers, Baltimore.

COLLIER, JOHN, JR., and BUITRÓN, ANÍBAL. 1949. *The Awakening Valley.* University of Chicago Press, Chicago.

COLLINS, WILLIAM F. 1934. "The Mirror-Black and 'Quicksilver' Patinas of Certain Chinese Bronzes." *Journal of the Royal Anthropological Institute of Great Britain and Ireland,* vol. LXIV, January–June, pp. 69–79. London.

COLLINS, W. H. 1932. "General activities of the National Museum of Canada." Canada, Department of Mines, National Museum of Canada, Bulletin no. 70, *Annual Report for 1931,* pp. 1–24. Ottawa.

COLTON, HAROLD S. 1939. "The Reducing Atmosphere and Oxidizing Atmosphere in Prehistoric Southwestern Ceramics." *American Antiquity,* vol. IV, no. 3, January, pp. 224–231. Menasha.

COOK, SHERBURNE F. 1946. "A Reconsideration of Shellmounds with Respect to Population and Nutrition." *American Antiquity,* vol. XII, no. 1, July, pp. 50–53. Menasha.

COOK, SHERBURNE F., and HEIZER, ROBERT F. 1951. *The Physical Analysis of Nine Indian Mounds of the Lower Sacramento Valley.* University of California Publications in American Archaeology and Ethnology, vol. 40, no. 7, pp. i–iv, 281–312. Berkeley and Los Angeles.

COOK, SHERBURNE F., and TREGANZA, ADAN E. 1947. "The Quantitative Investigation of Aboriginal Sites: Comparative Physical and Chemical Analysis of Two California Indian Mounds." *American Antiquity,* vol. XIII, no. 2, October, pp. 135–141. Menasha.

——. 1950. *The Quantitative Investigation of Indian Mounds, with Special Reference to the Relation of the Physical Components to the Probable Material Culture.* University of California Publications in American Archaeology and Ethnology, vol. 40, no. 5, pp. i–iv, 223–261. Berkeley and Los Angeles.

COOPER, JOHN M. 1949. "Stimulants and Narcotics." *Handbook of South American Indians,* Bureau of American Ethnology, Bulletin 143, vol. 5, pp. 525–558. Washington.

CORDRY, DONALD BUSH, and CORDRY, DOROTHY M. 1941. *Costumes and Weaving of the Zoque Indians of Chiapas, Mexico.* Southwest Museum Papers, no. 15. Los Angeles.

COVARRUBIAS, MIGUEL. 1937. *Island of Bali.* With an album of photographs by Rose Covarrubias. Alfred A. Knopf, New York.

COVNER, BERNARD J. 1942a. "Studies in Phonographic Recordings of Verbal Material: I. The Use of Phonographic Recordings in Counseling Practice and Research." *Journal of Consulting Psychology,* vol. VI, no. 2, March–April, pp. 105–113. Colorado Springs.

——. 1942b. "Studies in Phonographic Recordings of Verbal Material: II. A Device for Transcribing Phonographic Recordings of Verbal Material." *Journal of Consulting Psychology,* vol. VI, no. 3, May–June, pp. 149–151. Colorado Springs.

——. 1944a. "Studies in Phonographic Recordings of Verbal Material: III. The Completeness and Accuracy of Counseling Interview Reports." *The Journal of General Psychology,* vol. 30, second half, April, pp. 181–203. Provincetown.

——. 1944b. "Studies in Phonographic Recordings of Verbal Materials: IV. Written Reports of Interviews." *Journal* of Applied Psychology, vol. 28, no. 2, April, pp. 89–98. Lancaster, Pa.

CRAWFORD, OSBERT GUY STANHOPE. 1928. *Air Survey and Archaeology*. Ordnance Survey Professional Papers, n.s., no. 7 (second edition). London.

CRAWFORD, O. G. S., and KEILLER, ALEXANDER. 1928. *Wessex from the Air*. With contributions by R. C. C. Clay and Eric Gardner. Clarendon Press, Oxford.

CULIN, STEWART. 1898. "An Archaeological Application of the Röntgen Rays." *Bulletin of the Free Museum of Science and Art of the University of Pennsylvania*, vol. 1, no. 4, June, pp. 182–83. Philadelphia.

CURRY, ROBERT. 1935. "Speech Recording and Analysis with the Cathode Ray Oscillograph." *Archives Néerlandaises de Phonétique Expérimentale*, tome XI, pp. 107–118. Amsterdam.

CURTET, ALBERT. 1942. "Observation sur un procédé propre à faciliter le déchiffrage de gravures sur pierres préhistoriques." *Bulletin de la Société Préhistorique Française*, vol. XXXIX, nos. 3–4, mars–avril, p. 102. Paris.

DEBENHAM, FRANK. 1940. *Map Making*. Second edition. Blackie & Son Limited, London and Glasgow.

DE SOLA, RALPH. 1944. *Microfilming*. Essential Books, New York.

DE TERRA, HELMUT. 1947. "Preliminary Note on the Discovery of Fossil Man at Tepexpan in the Valley of Mexico." *American Antiquity*, vol. XIII, no. 1, July, pp. 40–44. Menasha.

DE TERRA, HELMUT; ROMERO, JAVIER; and STEWART, T. DALE. 1949. *Tepexpan Man*. Viking Fund Publications in Anthropology, no. 11. New York.

DRIER, ROY WARD. 1939. "A New Method of Sherd Classification." *American Antiquity*, vol. V, no. 1, July, pp. 31–35. Menasha.

DU CAMP, MAXIME. °1852. *Egypte, Nubie, Palestine et Syrie, dessins photographiques recueillis pendant les années 1849, 1850 et 1851, accompagnés d'un texte explicatif et précédés d'une introduction*. Gide et J. Baudry, Paris.

DU MESNIL DU BUISSON, ROBERT, COMTE. 1934. *La technique des fouilles archéologiques. Les principes généraux*. Librairie Orientaliste Paul Geuthner, Paris.

EASTMAN KODAK COMPANY. 1947. *Pictures from the Air with Your Camera*. Eastman Kodak Company, Rochester.

——. 1951. *Infrared and Ultraviolet Photography. A Kodak Data Book*. Fourth edition. Eastman Kodak Company, Rochester.

EDWARDS, EDWARD A., and DUNTLEY, S. QUIMBY. 1939. "The Pigments and Color of Living Human Skin." *American Journal of Anatomy*, vol. 65, no. 1, July 15, pp. 1–33. Philadelphia.

FARNSWORTH, MARIE, and RITCHIE, PATRICK D. 1938. "Spectrographic Studies in Ancient Glass: Egyptian Glass, Mainly of the Eighteenth Dynasty, with Special Reference to Its Cobalt Content." *Technical Studies in the Field of the Fine Arts*, vol. VI, no. 3, January, pp. 154–173. Lancaster, Pa.

FEJOS, PAUL. 1943. *Ethnography of the Yagua*. Viking Fund Publications in Anthropology, no. 1. New York.

FEWKES, JESSE WALTER. 1890. "A Contribution to Passamaquoddy Folklore." *Journal of American Folklore*, vol. III, no. 11, October–December, pp. 257–280. Boston and New York.

FINK, COLIN GARFIELD. 1933. "Incrustations on Porous Pottery: A New Method of Cleaning without Loss of Pigment." *Technical Studies in the Field of the Fine Arts*, vol. II, no. 2, October, pp. 58–61. Lancaster, Pa.

——. 1934. "Chemistry and Art." *Industrial and Engineering Chemistry*, vol. 26, no. 2, February, pp. 234–238. Easton, Pa.

FINK, COLIN GARFIELD, and POLUSHKIN, EUGENE PAUL. 1936. *Microscopic Study of Ancient Bronze and Copper*. American Institute of Mining and Metallurgical Engineers, Technical Publication no. 693 (Class E, Institute of Metals Division, no. 209). Metals Technology, vol. 3, no. 2, February, art. 5. York, Pa.

FOOTE, H. W., and BUELL, W. H. 1912. "The Composition, Structure and Hardness of Some Peruvian Bronze Axes." *American Journal of Science*, Fourth Series, vol. XXXIV (whole no. CLXXX-

IV), no. 200, August, art. XII, pp. 128–132. New Haven.

FORBES, ROBERT JAMES. 1950. *Metallurgy in Antiquity. A Notebook for Archaeologists and Technologists.* E. J. Brill, Leiden.

FORCHHAMMER, JÖRGEN. 1941. "Die Sprachlaute in Wort und Bild." *Wörter und Sachen,* Band 22, Neue Folge, Band IV, 1941–42, Heft 1, pp. 18–44. Heidelberg.

FORD, JAMES ALFRED, and WILLEY, GORDON R. 1949. *Surface Survey of the Virú Valley, Peru.* Anthropological Papers of the American Museum of Natural History, vol. 43, part 1. New York.

FOSTER, WILLIAM. 1933. "Chemistry and Grecian Archaeology." *Journal of Chemical Education,* vol. 10, no. 5, May, pp. 270–277. Easton, Pa.

———. 1934. "Grecian and Roman Stucco, Mortar, and Glass." *Journal of Chemical Education,* vol. 11, no. 4, April, pp. 223–225. Easton, Pa.

———. 1935. "Further Applications of Chemistry to Archaeology." *Journal of Chemical Education,* vol. 12, no. 12, December, pp. 577–579. Easton, Pa.

FRANCHET, LOUIS. 1911. *Céramique primitive. Introduction à l'étude de la technologie. Leçons professés à l'École d'Anthropologie en 1911.* Librairie Paul Geuthner, Paris.

FRANK, LEONARD. 1951. "A Metallographic Study of Certain Pre-Columbian American Implements." *American Antiquity,* vol. XVII, no. 1, July, pp. 57–60. Salt Lake City.

FRANTZ, ALISON. 1950. "Truth before Beauty, or, the Incompleat Photographer." *Archaeology,* vol. 3, no. 4, Winter, pp. 202–214. Cambridge.

GETTENS, RUTHERFORD J. 1933. "Mineralization, Electrolytic Treatment, and Radiographic Examination of Copper and Bronze Objects from Nuzi." *Technical Studies in the Field of the Fine Arts,* vol. 1, no. 3, January, pp. 118–142. Lancaster, Pa.

GIFFORD, EDWARD WINSLOW. 1916. *Composition of California Shellmounds.* University of California Publications in American Archaeology and Ethnology, vol. 12, no. 1, pp. 1–29. Berkeley.

GILLIN, JOHN. 1947. *Moche: A Peruvian Coastal Community.* Smithsonian Institution Publications in Social Anthropology, no. 3.

GILMAN, BENJAMIN IVES. 1891. "Zuñi Melodies." *Hemenway Southwestern Archaeological Expedition: A Journal of American Ethnology and Archaeology,* vol. 1, art. 2, pp. 63–91. Boston and New York.

———. 1908. "Hopi Songs." *Hemenway Southwestern Expedition: A Journal of American Ethnology and Archaeology,* fifth and concluding volume, pp. i–xiv, 1–226. Boston and New York.

———. 1909. "The Science of Exotic Music." *Science,* n.s., vol. XXX, no. 772, October 15, pp. 532–535. New York.

GILMAN, BENJAMIN IVES, and STONE, KATHARINE H. 1908. "The Hemenway Southwestern Expedition." *Hemenway Southwestern Expedition: A Journal of American Ethnology and Archaeology,* fifth and concluding volume, pp. 227–235. Boston and New York.

GODDARD, PLINY EARLE. 1905. "Mechanical Aids to the Study and Recording of Language." *American Anthropologist,* n.s., vol. 7, no. 4, October–December, pp. 613–619. Lancaster, Pa.

———. 1907. *The Phonology of the Hupa Language.* Part I: *The Individual Sounds.* University of California Publications, American Archaeology and Ethnology, vol. 5, no. 1, Berkeley.

GOODENOUGH, FLORENCE L. 1936. "The Measurement of Mental Functions in Primitive Groups." *American Anthropologist,* n.s., vol. 38. no. 1. January–March, pp. 1–11. Menasha.

GOODMAN, MARY ELLEN. 1944. "The Physical Properties of Stone Tool Materials." *American Antiquity,* vol. IX, no. 4, April, pp. 415–433. Menasha.

GOUROU, PIERRE. 1936a. *Esquisse d'une étude de l'habitation annamite dans l'Annam septentrional et central du Thanh Hoá au Bình-Dinh.* Publications de l'École Française d'Extrême-Orient, vol. XXVIII. Les Éditions d'Art et d'Histoire, Paris.

GOUROU, PIERRE. 1936b. *Les paysans du delta Tonkinois; étude de géographie humaine.* Publications de l'École Française d'Extrême-Orient, vol. XXVII. Les Éditions d'Art et d'Histoire, Paris.

GREENMAN, EMERSON F. 1937. *The Younge Site: An Archaeological Record from Michigan, with Appendices by Frederick R. Matson, Jr., and Byron O. Hughes.* Occasional Contributions from The Museum of Anthropology of the University of Michigan, no. 6. Ann Arbor.

GREULICH, WILLIAM WALTER, and PYLE, S. IDELL. 1950. *Radiographic Atlas of Skeletal Development of the Hand and Wrist, Based on the Brush Foundation Study of Human Growth and Development Initiated by T. Wingate Todd.* Stanford University Press, Stanford; Oxford University Press, London.

GRIFFIN, JAMES B. (ed.). 1951. *Essays on Archaeological Methods. Proceedings of a Conference Held under Auspices of the Viking Fund.* Anthropological Papers, Museum of Anthropology, University of Michigan, no. 8. Ann Arbor.

GROSJEAN, MARCEL, and PÉRIER, ALBERT. 1939. "Application des procédés optiques métallographiques à l'étude microscopique des tissus durs (dents et os)." *Compte rendu des séances de la Société de Physique et d'Histoire Naturelle de Genève* (supplément aux *Archives des Sciences Physiques et Naturelles*), vol. 56, no. 2, avril–juillet, pp. 88–89. Genève.

GUY, P. L. O. 1932. "Balloon Photography and Archaeological Excavation." *Antiquity*, vol. VI, no. 22, June, pp. 148–155. Gloucester.

HADDON, ALFRED CORT, and OTHERS. 1901–35. *Reports of the Cambridge Anthropological Expedition to Torres Straits.* University Press, Cambridge. 6 vols.

HAILER, HAROLD H., and BAERREIS, DAVID A. 1951. "The Wisconsin Anthropological Color Slide Project." *American Antiquity*, vol. XVII, no. 1, July, p. 88. Salt Lake City.

HAJEK, LEO. 1933. "Das Phonogramm-Archiv der Akademie der Wissenschaften in Wien." *Zeitschrift für vergleichende Musikwissenschaft*, Jahrgang 1, Heft 1, pp. 15–16. Berlin.

HALL, IVAN C. 1928. "A Pharmaco-bacteriologic Study of Two Malayan Blow-Gun Poisoned Darts." *American Anthropologist*, n.s., vol. 30, no. 1, January–March, pp. 47–59. Menasha.

HALL, IVAN C., and WHITEHEAD, RICHARD W. 1927. "A Pharmaco-bacteriologic Study of Africa Poisoned Arrows." *Journal of Infectious Diseases*, vol. 41, no. 1, July, pp. 51–69. Chicago.

HAURY, EMIL W. 1947. "A Large Pre-Columbian Copper Bell from the Southwest." *American Antiquity*, vol. XIII, no. 1, July, pp. 80–82. Menasha.

———. 1950. *The Stratigraphy and Archaeology of Ventana Cave.* University of Arizona Press, Tucson; University of New Mexico Press, Albuquerque.

HAWLEY, FLORENCE M. 1929. "Prehistoric Pottery Pigments in the Southwest." *American Anthropologist*, n.s., vol. 31, no. 4, October–December, pp. 731–749. Menasha.

———. 1930. "Chemical Examination of Prehistoric Smudged Wares." *American Anthropologist*, n.s., vol. 32, no. 3, July–September, pp. 500–502. Menasha.

HEGEDÜS, LUDWIG. 1933. "Kinematographie der Mundlippen während der Artikulation." *Archives Néerlandaises de Phonétique Expérimentale*, tome VIII–IX, pp. 82–85. La Haye.

HEIZER, ROBERT F. 1949. "Fish Poisons." *Handbook of South American Indians*, Bureau of American Ethnology, Bulletin 143, vol. 5, pp. 277–281. Washington.

HERZOG, GEORGE. 1936. *Research in Primitive and Folk Music in the United States. A Survey.* American Council of Learned Societies, Bulletin no. 24. Washington.

HOFFMAN, BERNARD G. MS. "The Use of Contact or Reflex Copying Papers in Anthropology." 1952. 12 pp. The author, University of California, Berkeley.

HOLBROOK, RICHARD T. 1933. "The Application of X-Rays to Speech-Analysis." *Mélanges de philologie offerts à Jean-Jacques Salverda de Grave*, pp. 175–185. Société Anonyme d'Éditions

J.-B. Wolters, Groningue–La Haye–Batavia.

HOOTON, EARNEST ALBERT. 1930. *The Indians of Pecos Pueblo: A Study of Their Skeletal Remains.* Department of Archaeology, Phillips Academy, Andover, Papers of the Southwestern Expedition, no. 4. New Haven.

——. 1939. *The American Criminal: An Anthropological Study. With the Collaboration of the Statistical Laboratory of the Division of Anthropology, Harvard University.* Vol. 1: *The Native White Criminal of Native Parentage.* Harvard University Press, Cambridge.

HORNBOSTEL, ERICH MORITZ VON. 1923. "Phonographische Methoden." In AB-DERHALDEN, EMIL (ed.), *Handbuch der biologischen Arbeitsmethoden,* Abt. V: "Methoden zum Studium der Funktioner der einzelnen Organe des tierischen Organismus," Teil 7, Heft 3, "Untersuchung der Sinnesorgane," pp. 419–438. Urban & Schwarzenberg, Berlin and Wien.

——. 1933. "Das Berliner Phonogramm-archiv." *Zeitschrift für vergleichende Musikwissenschaft,* Jahrgang 1, Heft 2, pp. 40–45. Berlin.

HOWELL, DAVID H. 1940. "Pipestone and Red Shale Artifacts." *American Antiquity,* vol. VI, no. 1, July, pp. 45–62. Menasha.

HOYME, LUCILE E. 1951. "A Historical Survey of Anthropometric Instruments" (abstract). *American Journal of Physical Anthropology,* n.s., vol. 9, no. 2, June, pp. 246. Philadelphia.

HÜLLE, WERNER. 1933. "Die Spektranalyse im Dienste der Vorgeschichtsforschung." *Nachrichtenblatt für Deutsche Vorzeit,* 9. Jahrgang, Heft 6. pp. 84–86. Leipzig.

JOOS, MARTIN. 1948. *Acoustic Phonetics.* Linguistic Society of America, Language Monograph no. 23 (supplement to *Language,* vol. 24, no. 2, April–June). Baltimore.

JUDD, NEIL M. 1915. "The Use of Glue Molds in Reproducing Aboriginal Monuments at Quirigua, Guatemala." *American Anthropologist,* n.s., vol. 17, no. 1, January–March, pp. 128–138. Lancaster, Pa.

——. 1931. "Arizona's prehistoric canals, from the air." *Explorations and Field-Work of the Smithsonian Institution in 1930* (Publication 3111), pp. 157–166. Washington.

KAPLAN, BERNICE A. 1951. "New Techniques in Physical Anthropology. A Report of the Fifth Summer Seminar in Physical Anthropology." *Yearbook of Physical Anthropology, 1949,* pp. 14–33. New York.

KASHA, MICHAEL. 1948. *Chemical Notes on the Coloring Matter of Chihuahua Textiles of Pre-Columbian Mexico.* Carnegie Institution of Washington, Publication 574, Contributions to American Anthropology and History, no. 45, appendix, pp. 151–157. Washington.

KEHL, GEORGE L. 1943. *The Principles of Metallographic Laboratory Practice.* Second edition, fifth impression. Metallurgy and Metallurgical Engineering Series. McGraw-Hill Book Company, Inc., New York and London.

KINGSLEY, NORMAN W. 1887. "Illustrations of the Articulations of the Tongue." *Internationale Zeitschrift für allgemeine Sprachwissenschaft,* III. Band, pp. 225–248. Leipzig.

KRAHN, FREDERIC A. 1951. *Educational Film Guide, 1951 Edition. An Index to 8,251 16 Mm Motion Pictures.* The H. W. Wilson Company, New York.

KRAUSE, GREGOR. 1920. *Bali.* Erster Teil: *Land und Volk.* Zweiter Teil: *Tänze, Tempel, Feste.* Schriften-Serie: Geist, Kunst und Leben Asiens, Band II u. III, Insel Bali. Folkwang-Verlag G.m.b.H., Hagen i. W. 2 vols.

KROGMAN, WILTON MARION. 1951. "The Physical Growth of the Child. Syllabus." *Yearbook of Physical Anthropology, 1949,* pp. 280–299. New York.

LAUDERMILK, J. D. 1937. "The Preservation of Textile Remains." *American Antiquity,* vol. II, no. 4, April, pp. 277–281. Menasha.

LAYARD, AUSTEN H. 1853. *Discoveries in the Ruins of Ninevah and Babylon.* G. P. Putnam & Company, New York.

LÉCUYER, RAYMOND. 1945. *Histoire de la photographie.* Baschet et Cie., Paris.

LEECHMAN, DOUGLAS. 1931. "Technical Methods in the Preservation of Anthropological Museum Specimens." National Museum of Canada, *Annual Report for 1929*, pp. 127–158. Ottawa.

LENK, W. 1932. "Die Sprechfilm im Dienste der Experimentalphonetik." *Zeitschrift für Experimental-Phonetik*, Band 1, Heft 3 und 4, 24. März, pp. 95–100. Leipzig.

LEWIN, LOUIS. °1894. *Die Pfeilgifte. Historische und experimentelle Untersuchungen*. G. Reimer, Berlin.

——. °1923. *Die Pfeilgifte; nach eigenen toxikologischen und ethnologischen Untersuchungen*. J. A. Barth, Leipzig.

LUCAS, A. 1934. *Ancient Egyptian Materials and Industries*. Second edition, revised. Edward Arnold & Co., London.

MABY, J. CECIL. 1932. "The Identification of Wood and Wood Charcoal Fragments." *The Analyst*, vol. LVII, no. 670, January, pp. 2–8. Cambridge, England.

McCRUM, BLANCHE PRICHARD. 1950. *Microfilms and Microcards: Their Use in Research. A Selected List of References*. Library of Congress, Reference Department. General Reference and Bibliography Division. Washington. (Sold by the Card Division, Library of Congress, Washington 25, D.C.)

MAERZ, ALOYS JOHN, and PAUL, M. REA. 1930. *A Dictionary of Color*. First edition. McGraw-Hill Book Co., Inc., New York.

MARICHELLE, H. 1897. *La parole d'après le tracé du phonograph*. Préface de M. E.-J. Marey. Librairie Ch. Delagrave, Paris.

MARTIN, RUDOLF. 1928. *Lehrbuch der Anthropologie in systematischer Darstellung, mit besonderer Berücksichtigung der anthropologischen Methoden, für Studierende, Aerzte und Forschungsreisende*. Zweite, vermehrte Auflage. Verlag von Gustav Fischer, Jena. 3 vols.

MARYON, HERBERT. 1936. "Soldering and Welding in the Bronze and Early Iron Ages." *Technical Studies in the Field of the Fine Arts*, vol. V, no. 2, October, pp. 74–108. Lancaster, Pa.

——. 1949. "Metal Working in the Ancient World." *American Journal of Archaeology*, vol. 53, no. 2, pp. 93–125. Menasha.

MASSLER, MAURY, and SCHOUR, ISAAC. 1951. "The Growth Pattern of the Cranial Vault in the Albino Rat as Measured by Vital Staining with Alizarine Red 'S.'" *The Anatomical Record*, vol. 110, no. 1, May, pp. 83–101. Philadelphia.

MATHEWSON, C. H. 1915. "A Metallographic Description of Some Ancient Peruvian Bronzes from Machu Picchu." *American Journal of Science*, fourth series, vol. XL (whole no. CLXL), no. 240, December, art. XLI, pp. 525–616. New Haven.

MATSON, FREDERICK ROGNALD, JR. °m1945. "A Technological Study of the Unglazed Pottery and Figurines from Seleucia on the Tigris." Ph.D. dissertation, University of Michigan, 1939. University Microfilms, Publication no. 660. Ann Arbor (abstract in *Microfilm Abstracts*, vol. 6. no. 1. 1945, pp. 7–8, Ann Arbor).

MEIGHAN, CLEMENT W. MS. "Report on the 1949 excavation of 16th century Indian shellmounds at Drake's Bay." 1950. University of California Archaeological Survey, MS. no. 79. Department of Anthropology, Berkeley.

MERRILL, ROBERT H. 1941. "Photographic Surveying." *American Antiquity*, Vol. VI, no. 4, April, pp. 343–346. Menasha.

MEYER-EPPLER, W. 1950. "Die Spektranalyse der Sprache." *Zeitschrift für Phonetik und allgemeine Sprachwissenschaft*, 4. Jahrgang, Heft 3–4. Mai-August, pp. 240–252; Heft 5–6, September-Dezember, pp. 327–364. Berlin.

MONTAGU, M. F. ASHLEY. 1949. "A Report of Archaeological Work at Swanscombe and Galley Hill, Kent, England: June to September, 1948." *Bulletin of the Philadelphia Anthropological Society*, vol. 2, no. 6, May–June, pp. 2–3. Philadelphia.

——. MS. "Report on Expedition to Swanscombe, Kent, England, 26 May to 13 September 1948. 31 January, 1949." In the files of the Wenner-Gren Foundation for Anthropological Research, New York.

MOODIE, ROY L. 1931. *Roentgenologic studies of Egyptian and Peruvian Mummies*. Field Museum of Natural History,

Anthropology, Memoirs, vol. III. Chicago.

MUNSELL COLOR COMPANY, INC. 1929–42. *Munsell Book of Color.* Pocket edition. Munsell Color Company, Inc., Baltimore.

MYERS, CHARLES S. 1907. "The Ethnological Study of Music." *Anthropological Essays Presented to Edward Burnett Tylor in Honour of His 75th Birthday Oct. 2, 1907,* pp. 235–253. Clarendon Press, Oxford.

NEWELL, LYMAN C. 1933. "Chemistry in the Service of Egyptology." *Journal of Chemical Education,* vol. 10, no. 5, May, pp. 259–266. Easton, Pa.

NEWHALL, BEAUMONT. 1949. *The History of Photography, from 1839 to the Present Day.* The Museum of Modern Art, New York.

OBENAUER, K. 1933. "Die Verwendung petrographischer Methoden in der Vorgeschichte." *Nachrichtenblatt für Deutsche Vorzeit,* 9. Jahrgang, Heft 10, pp. 188–190. Leipzig.

PARMENTER, C. E.; TREVIÑO, S. N.; and BEVANS, C. A. 1931. "A Technique for Radiographing the Organs of Speech during Articulation." *Zeitschrift für Experimental-Phonetik,* Band 1, Heft 2, 1. Juli, pp. 63–84. Leipzig.

PAYNE, F. G. 1948. "The Plough in Ancient Britain." *The Archaeological Journal,* vol. CIV for 1947, pp. 82–111. London.

PFISTER, R. 1935. "Teinture et alchimie dans l'Orient hellénistique." *Institut Kondakov, Seminarium Kondakovianum,* vol. VII, pp. 1–59. Praha.

PITTIONI, RICHARD. 1936. "Die Reihenphotographie in der Urgeschichte." *Nachrichtenblatt für Deutsche Vorzeit,* 12. Jahrgang, Heft 1, pp. 3–4. Leipzig.

PLENDERLEITH, H. J. 1934. *The Preservation of Antiquities.* The Museums Association, London.

POIDEBARD, ANTOINE. 1934. *La trace de Rome dans le désert de Syrie. Le limes de Trajan à la coquête arabe. Recherches aériennes (1925–1932).* Introduction de Franz Cumont. Haut-Commissariat de la République Française en Syrie et au Liban, Service des Antiquités et des Beaux-Arts, Bibliothèque Archéologique et Historique, tome XVIII. Librairie Orientaliste Paul Geuthner, Paris. 2 vols.

————. 1939. *Un grand port disparu: Tyr. Recherches aériennes et sous-marines, 1934–1936.* Conclusion par L. Cayeux de l'Académie des Sciences. Haut-Commissariat de la République Française en Syrie et au Liban, Service des Antiquités et des Beaux-Arts, Bibliothéque Archéologique et Historique, tome XXIX. Librairie Orientaliste Paul Geuthner, Paris. 2 vols.

POLLENZ, PHILIPPA. 1949. "Methods for the Comparative Study of the Dance." *American Anthropologist,* n.s., vol. 51, no. 3, July–September, pp. 428–435. Menasha.

POTTER, RALPH K.; KOPP, GEORGE A.; and GREEN, HARRIET C. 1947. *Visible Speech.* D. Van Nostrand Company, Inc., New York.

QUEVEDO ARAGÓN, SERGIO A. 1946. *La teleradiografía en el estudio de las deformaciones craneanas.* Edición conmemorativa del CCL aniversario de la Universidad Nacional del Cuzco [no. 1]. Cuzco.

RATHGEN, FRIEDRICH. 1905. *The Preservation of Antiquities. A Handbook for Curators.* Translated, by permission of the authorities of the Royal Museums, from the German, by GEORGE A. AUDEN and HAROLD A. AUDEN. University Press, Cambridge.

————. *1915–24. Die Konservierung von Altertumsfunden, mit Berücksichtigung ethnographischer und kunstgewerblicher Sammlungsgegenstände.* Handbücher der Königlichen Museen zu Berlin, (VII). Berlin & Leipzig. 2 vols.

REEVES, DACHE M. 1936. "Aerial Photography and Archaeology." *American Antiquity,* vol. II, no. 2, October, pp. 102–107. Menasha.

REICHE, MARIA. 1949. *Mystery on the Desert. A Study of the Ancient Figures and Strange Delineated Surfaces Seen from the Air near Nazca, Peru.* Editora Médica Peruana, S.A., Lima.

REY, LÉON. 1921. *Observations sur les premiers habitats de la Macédoine, recueillies par le Service Archéologique de l'Armée d'Orient, 1916–1919 (région de Salonique)*. E. de Boccard, Éditeur, Paris.

RICHTER, GISELA MARIE AUGUSTA. 1923. *The Craft of Athenian Pottery: An Investigation of the Technique of Black-figured and Red-figured Athenian Vases*. Publication of the Committee on Education, The Metropolitan Museum of Art. Yale University Press, New Haven.

RIDGWAY, JOHN LIVESY. 1938. *Scientific Illustration*. Stanford University Press, Stanford; Humphrey Milford, Oxford University Press, London.

RIDGWAY, ROBERT. 1912. *Color Standards and Color Nomenclature*. Published by the author. Washington.

RILEY, D. N. 1946. "The Technique of Air-Archaeology." *The Archaeological Journal*, vol. CI for 1944, pp. 1–16. London.

RITCHIE, PATRICK D. 1937. "Spectrographic Studies on Ancient Glass: Chinese Glass, from pre-Han to T'ang Times." *Technical Studies in the Field of the Fine Arts*, vol. V, no. 4, April, pp. 209–220. Lancaster, Pa.

RIVERA, TRINITA. 1949. "Diet of a Food-gathering People, with Chemical Analysis of Salmon and Saskatoons." In SMITH, MARIAN W. (ed.), *Indians of the Urban Northwest*, Columbia University Contributions to Anthropology, no. 36, pp. 19–36. New York.

RIVET, PAUL, and ARSANDAUX, H. 1946. *La métallurgie en Amérique précolombienne*. Université de Paris, Travaux et Mémoires de l'Institut d'Ethnologie, no. XXXIX. Paris.

ROBEQUAIN, CHARLES. 1929. *Le Thanh hoá. Étude géographique d'une province annamite*. Publications de l'École Française d'Extrême-Orient, vols. XXIII–XXIV. Les Éditions G. Van Oest, Paris et Bruxelles.

ROBERTS, HELEN H. 1931. "Suggestions to Field-Workers in Collecting Folk Music and Data about Instruments." *Journal of the Polynesian Society*, vol. 40, no. 3 (no. 159), September, pp. 103–128. New Plymouth.

ROBERTS, HELEN H., and THOMPSON, LINCOLN. 1935. "The Re-recording of Wax Cylinders." *Zeitschrift für vergleichende*

Musikwissenschaft, Jahrgang 3, Heft 2, pp. 75–83. Berlin.

RORIMER, JAMES J. 1931. *Ultra-violet Rays and Their Use in the Examination of Works of Art*. The Metropolitan Museum of Art, New York.

ROSENBERG, GUSTAV ADOLF THEODOR. 1917. *Antiquités en fer et en bronze, leur transformation dans la terre contenant de l'acide carbonique et des chlorures et leur conservation*. Ouvrage publié par la Fondation Carlsberg. Gyldendalske Boghandels Sortiment, København.

ROUSSELOT, JEAN-PIERRE. 1897–1908. *Principes de phonétique expérimentale*. H. Welter, Paris. 2 vols.

ROWE, JOHN HOWLAND. 1951. "Colonial Portraits of Inca Nobles." *The Civilizations of Ancient America, Selected Papers of the XXIXth International Congress of Americanists*, pp. 258–268. Chicago.

ST. JOSEPH, J. K. 1951. "A Survey of Pioneering in Air-Photography." *Aspects of Archaeology in Britain and Beyond, Essays Presented to O. G. S. Crawford*, pp. 303–315. H. W. Edwards, London.

SANTESSON, C. G. 1931. "An Arrow Poison with Cardiac Effect from the New World." *Comparative Ethnographical Studies*, no. 9, pp. 155–187. Göteborg.

——. 1936. "Pfeil- und Fischgift aus Kolumbien und Ekuador." *Etnologiska Studier*, no. 2, pp. 15–29. Göteborg.

SAUTER, M. R. 1947. "L'exploration archéologique aérienne en Suisse." *l'Anthropologie*, tome 51, nos. 3–4, pp. 362–363. Paris.

SCHAEDEL, RICHARD P. 1951a. "The Lost Cities of Peru." *Scientific American*, vol. 185, no. 2, August, pp. 18–23. New York.

——. 1951b. "Mochica Murals at Pañamarca." *Archaeology*, vol. 4, no. 3, Autumn, pp. 145–154. Cambridge.

SCHMIDT, ALFRED. 1934. "Chemische und physikalische Untersuchungsmethoden im Dienste der Vorgeschichtswissenschaft." *Nachrichtenblatt für Deutsche Vorzeit*, 10. Jahrgang, Heft 7, pp. 149–154. Leipzig.

SCHMIDT, ERICH FRIEDRICH. 1940. *Flights over Ancient Cities of Iran*. Special Publication of the Oriental Institute of the University of Chicago. University of Chicago Press, Chicago.

SCHMITT, FRITZ R. 1939. "Möglichkeiten und Grenzen des Einsatzes der Petrographie bei der Untersuchung von Vorzeitfunden." *Nachrichtenblatt für Deutsche Vorzeit*, 15. Jahrgang, Heft 2, pp. 47–51. Leipzig.

SCHOUR, ISAAC. 1936. "Measurements of Bone Growth by Alizarine Injections." *Proceedings of the Society for Experimental Biology and Medicine*, vol. 34, no. 2, March, pp. 140–141. Utica.

SCRIPTURE, EDWARD WHEELER. 1902. *The Elements of Experimental Phonetics.* Charles Scribner's Sons, New York; Edward Arnold, London.

SEIPEL, CARL MICHAEL. 1948. "Trajectories of the Jaws." *Acta Odontologica Scandinavica*, vol. VII, no. 2, June, pp. 81–191. Stockholm.

SELIGMAN, BRENDA Z. (ed.). 1951. *Notes and Queries on Anthropology.* Sixth edition, revised and rewritten by a committee of the Royal Anthropological Institute of Great Britain and Ireland. Routledge and Kegan Paul Ltd., London.

SELIGMAN, C. G. 1934. "Infra-red Photographs of Racial Types." *Nature,* vol. 133, no. 3356, Saturday, February 24, pp. 279–280. London.

SERRES, ANTOINE-ÉTIENNE-RENAUD-AUGUSTIN. 1844. "[Présentation de cinq portraits représentant deux naturels de l'Amérique du Sud (Botocudes), et pris au daguerréotype par le procédé de M. Thiesson.]" *Comptes rendus hebdomadaires des séances de l'Académie des Sciences,* tome XIX, 2me semestre, no. 10, séance du lundi 2 septembre, p. 490. Paris.

——. 1845. "Observations sur l'application de la photographie a l'étude des races humaines." *Comptes rendus hebdomadaires des séances de l'Académie des Sciences,* tome XXI, no. 3, séance du lundi 21 juillet, pp. 242–246. Paris.

SHELDON, WILLIAM HERBERT. 1940. *The Varieties of Human Physique: An Introduction to Constitutional Psychology.* With the collaboration of S. S. STEVENS and W. B. TUCKER. Harper & Brothers Publishers, New York and London.

——. MS. "The Adult Male" (to be published Fall, 1952).

SHEPARD, ANNA OSLER. 1936a. "Metallographic Study of Copper Artifacts." *American Antiquity,* vol. II, no. 2, October, pp. 139–140. Menasha.

——. 1936b. *The Technology of Pecos Pottery.* Department of Archaeology, Phillips Academy, Andover; Papers of the Southwestern Expedition, no. 7, pp. 389–587. New Haven.

——. 1942. *Rio Grande Glaze Paint Ware, a Study Illustrating the Place of Ceramic Technological Analysis in Archaeological Research.* Carnegie Institution of Washington, Publication 528, Contributions to American Anthropology and History, vol. VII, no. 39, pp. 129–262. Washington.

SHEPARD, ANNA OSLER, and HORTON, DONALD. 1939. "Conference on Archaeological Technology in Ceramics." *American Antiquity,* vol. IV, no. 4, April, pp. 358–359. Menasha.

SHILLABER, CHARLES PATTEN. 1944. *Photomicrography in Theory and Practice.* John Wiley & Sons, Inc., New York; Chapman and Hall, Ltd., London.

SHIPPEE, ROBERT. 1932a. "The 'Great Wall of Peru' and Other Aerial Photographic Studies by the Shippee-Johnson Peruvian Expedition." *The Geographical Review,* vol. XXII, no. 1, January, pp. 1–29. New York.

——. 1932b. "Lost Valleys of Peru. Results of the Shippee-Johnson Peruvian Expedition." *The Geographical Review,* vol. XXII, no. 4, October, pp. 562–581. New York.

SISAM, J. W. B. 1947. *The Use of Aerial Survey in Forestry and Agriculture.* Imperial Agricultural Bureaux, Joint Publications no. 9. Published by the Imperial Forestry Bureau, Oxford; Imperial Bureau of Pastures and Field Crops, Aberystwyth.

SMITH, HAROLD THEODORE UHR. 1943. *Aerial Photographs and Their Applications.* D. Appleton–Century Company Incorporated, New York, London.

SMITHSONIAN INSTITUTION. 1922. *Explorations and Field-Work of the Smithsonian*

Institution in 1921. Smithsonian Miscellaneous Collections, vol. 72, no. 15 (Publication 2669). Washington.

SPAULDING, ALBERT C. 1951. "Recent Advances in Surveying Techniques and Their Application to Archaeology." In GRIFFIN, J. B. (ed.), 1951, pp. 2–16. Ann Arbor.

SQUIER, EPHRAIM GEORGE. 1877. *Peru. Incidents of Travel and Exploration in the Land of the Incas.* Harper and Brothers, New York.

STEER, KENNETH. 1947. "Archaeology and the National Air-Photograph Survey." *Antiquity,* vol. XXI, no. 81, March, pp. 50–53. Gloucester.

STENGER, ERICH. 1939. *The History of Photography: Its Relation to Civilization and Practice.* Translation and footnotes by EDWARD EPSTEAN. Mack Printing Company, Easton, Pa.

STETSON, R. H.; HUDGINS, C. V.; and MOSES, E. R., JR. 1940. "Palatograms Change with Rates of Articulation. A Study of Synchronous Kymographic and Palatographic Recording." *Archives Néerlandaises de Phonétique Expérimentale,* tome XVI, pp. 52–61. Amsterdam.

STUMPF, CARL. 1911. *Die Anfänge der Musik.* Verlag von Johann Ambrosius Barth, Leipzig.

TAFT, ROBERT. 1938. *Photography and the American Scene: A Social History, 1839–1889.* The Macmillan Company, New York.

TANNER, J. M., and WEINER, J. S. 1949. "The Reliability of the Photogrammetric Method of Anthropometry, with a Description of a Miniature Camera Technique." *American Journal of Physical Anthropology,* n.s., vol. 7, no. 2, June, pp. 145–186. Philadelphia.

TITTERINGTON, P. F. 1933. "Has the X-Ray a Place in the Archaeological Laboratory?" *American Anthropologist,* n.s., vol. 35, no. 2, April–June, pp. 297–300. Menasha.

TREGANZA, ADAN E., and COOK, SHERBURNE F. 1948. "The Quantitative Investigation of Aboriginal Sites: Complete Excavation with Physical and Archaeological Analysis of a Single Mound." *American Antiquity,* vol. XIII, no. 4, April, pp. 287–297. Menasha.

VAUFREY, R. 1946. "La Photographie aérienne et la préhistoire." *l'Anthropologie,* tome 50, nos. 1–2, pp. 291–293. Paris.

VOEGELIN, C. F. 1950. "Magnetic Recording of American Indian Languages and the Relation of This to Other Kinds of Memory." *Proceedings of the American Philosophical Society,* vol. 94, no. 3, June 20, pp. 295–300. Philadelphia.

WEINER, J. S. 1951. "A Spectrophotometer for Measurement of Skin Colour." *Man,* vol. LI, article 253, pp. 152–153 (November). London.

WILLARD, T. A. 1926. *The City of the Sacred Well, Being a Narrative of the Discoveries and Excavations of Edward Herbert Thompson in the Ancient City of Chi-chen Itza with Some Discourse on the Culture and Development of the Mayan Civilization as Revealed by Their Art and Architecture, Here Set Down and Illustrated from Photographs.* Grosset and Dunlap, Publishers, New York.

WILLIAMS-HUNT, P. D. R. 1948. "Archaeology and Topographical Interpretation of Air-Photographs." *Antiquity,* vol. XXII, no. 86, June, pp. 103–105. Gloucester.

——. 1950. "Irregular Earthworks in Eastern Siam: An Air Survey." *Antiquity,* vol. XXIV, no. 93, March, pp. 30–36. Newbury, Berks.

WILSON, CURTIS L., and SAYRE, MELVILLE. 1935. "A Brief Metallographic Study of Primitive Copper Work." *American Antiquity,* vol. 1, no. 2, October, pp. 109–112. Menasha.

WINKLER, I. 1933. "Die qualitative und quantitative Spektranalyse vorgeschichtlicher Legierungen." *Nachrichtenblatt für Deutsche Vorzeit,* 9. Jahrgang, Heft 6, pp. 86–88. Leipzig.

WOOLLEY, CHARLES LEONARD. 1937. *Digging Up the Past.* Pelican Books, A 4. Penguin Books Limited, London.

Index

Index*

* Prepared by Sol Tax with the assistance of Lois Ablin.